HALSBURY'S
Laws of England

FIFTH EDITION
2018

Volume 6

This is volume 6 of the Fifth Edition of Halsbury's Laws of England, containing the titles BUILDING and BUILDING CONTRACTS.

These replace the titles BUILDING and BUILDING CONTRACTS contained in volume 6 (2011). Upon receipt of volume 6 (2018), the old volume 6 (2011) may be archived.

For a full list of volumes comprised in a current set of Halsbury's Laws of England please see overleaf.

Fifth Edition volumes:

1 (2017), 1A (2017), 2 (2017), 3 (2011), 4 (2011), 5 (2013), 6 (2018), 7 (2015), 8 (2015), 9 (2017), 10 (2017), 11 (2015), 12 (2015), 12A (2015), 13 (2017), 14 (2016), 15 (2016), 15A (2016), 16 (2017), 17 (2017), 18 (2009), 19 (2011), 20 (2014), 21 (2016), 22 (2012), 23 (2016), 24 (2010), 25 (2016), 26 (2016), 27 (2015), 28 (2015), 29 (2014), 30 (2012), 31 (2012), 32 (2012), 33 (2017), 34 (2011), 35 (2015), 36 (2015), 37 (2013), 38 (2013), 38A (2013), 39 (2014), 40 (2014), 41 (2014), 41A (2014), 42 (2011), 43 (2011), 44 (2011), 45 (2010), 46 (2010), 47 (2014), 47A (2014), 48 (2015), 49 (2015), 50 (2016), 50A (2016), 51 (2013), 52 (2014), 53 (2014), 54 (2017), 54A (2017), 55 (2012), 56 (2017), 57 (2018), 58 (2014), 58A (2014), 59 (2014), 59A (2014), 60 (2011), 61 (2010), 62 (2016), 63 (2016), 64 (2016), 65 (2015), 66 (2015), 67 (2016), 68 (2016), 69 (2018), 70 (2018), 71 (2013), 72 (2015), 73 (2015), 74 (2011), 75 (2013), 76 (2013), 77 (2016), 78 (2018), 79 (2014), 80 (2013), 81 (2018), 82 (2018), 83 (2018), 84 (2013), 84A (2013), 85 (2012), 86 (2017), 87 (2017), 88 (2012), 88A (2018), 89 (2011), 90 (2011), 91 (2012), 92 (2015), 93 (2017), 94 (2017), 95 (2017), 96 (2012), 97 (2015), 97A (2014), 98 (2013), 99 (2012), 100 (2018), 101 (2018), 102 (2016), 103 (2016), 104 (2014)

Consolidated Index and Tables:

2018 Consolidated Index (A–E), 2018 Consolidated Index (F–O), 2018 Consolidated Index (P–Z), 2018 Consolidated Table of Statutes, 2018 Consolidated Table of Statutory Instruments, 2018 Consolidated Table of Cases (A–G), 2018 Consolidated Table of Cases (H–Q), 2018 Consolidated Table of Cases (R–Z, ECJ Cases)

Updating and ancillary materials:

2018 annual Cumulative Supplement; monthly Noter-up; annual Abridgments 1974–2017

June 2018

HALSBURY'S
Laws of England

Volume 6

2018

Members of the LexisNexis Group worldwide

United Kingdom	RELX (UK) Ltd, trading as LexisNexis, 1–3 Strand, London WC2N 5JR and 9–10 St Andrew Square, Edinburgh EH2 2AF
Australia	Reed International Books Australia Pty Ltd trading as LexisNexis, Chatswood, New South Wales
Austria	LexisNexis Verlag ARD Orac GmbH & Co KG, Vienna
Benelux	LexisNexis Benelux, Amsterdam
Canada	LexisNexis Canada, Markham, Ontario
China	LexisNexis China, Beijing and Shanghai
France	LexisNexis SA, Paris
Germany	LexisNexis GmbH, Dusseldorf
Hong Kong	LexisNexis Hong Kong, Hong Kong
India	LexisNexis India, New Delhi
Italy	Giuffrè Editore, Milan
Japan	LexisNexis Japan, Tokyo
Malaysia	Malayan Law Journal Sdn Bhd, Kuala Lumpur
New Zealand	LexisNexis New Zealand Ltd, Wellington
Singapore	LexisNexis Singapore, Singapore
South Africa	LexisNexis, Durban
USA	LexisNexis, Dayton, Ohio

FIRST EDITION	*Published in 31 volumes between 1907 and 1917*
SECOND EDITION	*Published in 37 volumes between 1931 and 1942*
THIRD EDITION	*Published in 43 volumes between 1952 and 1964*
FOURTH EDITION	*Published in 56 volumes between 1973 and 1987, with reissues between 1988 and 2008*
FIFTH EDITION	*Published between 2008 and 2014, with reissues from 2014*

© 2018 RELX (UK) Ltd

A CIP Catalogue record for this book is available from the British Library.

ISBN 978-1-4743-0953-0

9 781474 309530

ISBN for the set: 9781405734394
ISBN for this volume: 9781474309530
Typeset by LexisNexis
Printed and bound by CPI Group (UK) Ltd, Croydon, CR0 4YY

Visit LexisNexis at www.lexisnexis.co.uk

BUILDING

Consultant Editor

GIDEON SCOTT HOLLAND, MA,

of Lincoln's Inn;
Barrister

BUILDING CONTRACTS

Consultant Editor

ANNA RABIN, LLB,

Solicitor of the Senior Courts of England and Wales;
Director, Construction Law Consultant Ltd

The law stated in this volume is in general that in force on 1 May 2018, although subsequent changes have been included wherever possible.

Any future updating material will be found in the Noter-up and annual Cumulative Supplement to Halsbury's Laws of England.

TABLE OF CONTENTS

HOW TO USE HALSBURY'S LAWS OF ENGLAND

Volumes

Each text volume of Halsbury's Laws of England contains the law on the titles contained in it as at a date stated at the front of the volume (the operative date).

Information contained in Halsbury's Laws of England may be accessed in several ways.

First, by using the tables of contents.

Each volume contains both a general Table of Contents, and a specific Table of Contents for each title contained in it. From these tables you will be directed to the relevant part of the work.

Readers should note that the current arrangement of titles can be found in the Noter-up.

Secondly, by using tables of statutes, statutory instruments, cases or other materials.

If you know the name of the Act, statutory instrument or case with which your research is concerned, you should consult the Consolidated Tables of statutes, cases and so on (published as separate volumes) which will direct you to the relevant volume and paragraph.

(Each individual text volume also includes tables of those materials used as authority in that volume.)

Thirdly, by using the indexes.

If you are uncertain of the general subject area of your research, you should go to the Consolidated Index (published as separate volumes) for reference to the relevant volume(s) and paragraph(s).

(Each individual text volume also includes an index to the material contained therein.)

Updating publications

The text volumes of Halsbury's Laws should be used in conjunction with the annual Cumulative Supplement and the monthly Noter-up.

The annual Cumulative Supplement

The Supplement gives details of all changes between the operative date of the text volume and the operative date of the Supplement. It is arranged in the same volume, title and paragraph order as the text volumes. Developments affecting particular points of law are noted to the relevant paragraph(s) of the text volumes.

For narrative treatment of material noted in the Cumulative Supplement, go to the annual Abridgment volume for the relevant year.

Destination Tables

In certain titles in the annual *Cumulative Supplement*, reference is made to Destination Tables showing the destination of consolidated legislation. Those Destination Tables are to be found either at the end of the titles within the annual *Cumulative Supplement*, or in a separate *Destination Tables* booklet provided from time to time with the *Cumulative Supplement*.

The Noter-up

The Noter-up is issued monthly and notes changes since the publication of the annual Cumulative Supplement. Also arranged in the same volume, title and paragraph order as the text volumes, the Noter-up follows the style of the Cumulative Supplement.

For narrative treatment of material noted in the Noter-up, go to the annual Abridgment volume for the relevant year.

REFERENCES AND ABBREVIATIONS

ACT .... Australian Capital Territory
A-G .... Attorney General
Admin .... Administrative Court
Admlty .... Admiralty Court
Adv-Gen .... Advocate General
affd .... affirmed
affg .... affirming
Alta .... Alberta
App .... Appendix
art........................... article
Aust......................... Australia
B .... Baron
BC .... British Columbia
C .... Command Paper (of a series published before 1900)
c.............................. chapter number of an Act
CA .... Court of Appeal
CAC.......................... Central Arbitration Committee
CA in Ch .... Court of Appeal in Chancery
CB .... Chief Baron
CCA.......................... Court of Criminal Appeal
CCR.......................... County Court Rules 1981 (as subsequently amended)
CCR.......................... Court for Crown Cases Reserved
CJEU .... Court of Justice of the European Union
C-MAC .... Courts-Martial Appeal Court
CO............................ Crown Office
COD.......................... Crown Office Digest
CPR.......................... Civil Procedure Rules
Can .... Canada
Cd............................ Command Paper (of the series published 1900–18)
Cf .... compare
Ch............................ Chancery Division
ch .... chapter
cl .... clause
Cm........................... Command Paper (of the series published 1986 to date)
Cmd .... Command Paper (of the series published 1919–56)
Cmnd........................ Command Paper (of the series published 1956–86)
Comm....................... Commercial Court

Comr	Commissioner
Court Forms (2nd Edn)	Atkin's Encyclopaedia of Court Forms in Civil Proceedings, 2nd Edn. See note 2 post.
CrimPR	Criminal Procedure Rules
DC	Divisional Court
DPP	Director of Public Prosecutions
EAT	Employment Appeal Tribunal
EC	European Community
ECJ	Court of Justice of the European Community (before the Treaty of Lisbon (OJ C306, 17.12.2007, p 1) came into force on 1 December 2009); European Court of Justice (after the Treaty of Lisbon (OJ C306, 17.12.2007, p 1) came into force on 1 December 2009)
EComHR	European Commission of Human Rights
ECSC	European Coal and Steel Community
ECtHR Rules of Court	Rules of Court of the European Court of Human Rights
EEC	European Economic Community
EFTA	European Free Trade Association
EGC	European General Court
EWCA Civ	Official neutral citation for judgments of the Court of Appeal (Civil Division)
EWCA Crim	Official neutral citation for judgments of the Court of Appeal (Criminal Division)
EWHC	Official neutral citation for judgments of the High Court
Edn	Edition
Euratom	European Atomic Energy Community
EU	European Union
Ex Ch	Court of Exchequer Chamber
ex p	ex parte
Fam	Family Division
Fed	Federal
Forms & Precedents (5th Edn)	Encyclopaedia of Forms and Precedents other than Court Forms, 5th Edn. See note 2 post
GLC	Greater London Council
HC	High Court
HC	House of Commons
HK	Hong Kong
HL	House of Lords
HMRC	Her Majesty's Revenue and Customs
IAT	Immigration Appeal Tribunal
ILM	International Legal Materials

INLR	Immigration and Nationality Law Reports
IRC	Inland Revenue Commissioners
Ind	India
Int Rels	International Relations
Ir	Ireland
J	Justice
JA	Judge of Appeal
Kan	Kansas
LA	Lord Advocate
LC	Lord Chancellor
LCC	London County Council
LCJ	Lord Chief Justice
LJ	Lord Justice of Appeal
MR	Master of the Rolls
Man	Manitoba
n.	note
NB	New Brunswick
NI	Northern Ireland
NS	Nova Scotia
NSW	New South Wales
NY	New York
NZ	New Zealand
OHIM	Office for Harmonisation in the Internal Market
OJ	The Official Journal of the European Union published by the Publications Office of the European Union
Ont	Ontario
P.	President
PC	Judicial Committee of the Privy Council
PEI	Prince Edward Island
Pat	Patents Court
q.	question
QB	Queen's Bench Division
QBD	Queen's Bench Division of the High Court
Qld	Queensland
Que	Quebec
r	rule
RDC	Rural District Council
RPC	Restrictive Practices Court
RSC	Rules of the Supreme Court 1965 (as subsequently amended)
reg	regulation
Res	Resolution
revsd	reversed

Rly	Railway
s	section
SA	South Africa
S Aust	South Australia
SC	Supreme Court
SI	Statutory Instruments published by authority
SR & O	Statutory Rules and Orders published by authority
SR & O Rev 1904	Revised Edition comprising all Public and General Statutory Rules and Orders in force on 31 December 1903
SR & O Rev 1948	Revised Edition comprising all Public and General Statutory Rules and Orders and Statutory Instruments in force on 31 December 1948
STI	Simon's Tax Intelligence (1973–1995); Simon's Weekly Tax Intelligence (1996-current)
Sask	Saskatchewan
Sch	Schedule
Sess	Session
Sing	Singapore
TCC	Technology and Construction Court
TS	Treaty Series
Tanz	Tanzania
Tas	Tasmania
UDC	Urban District Council
UKHL	Official neutral citation for judgments of the House of Lords
UKPC	Official neutral citation for judgments of the Privy Council
UN	United Nations
V-C	Vice-Chancellor
Vict	Victoria
W Aust	Western Australia
Zimb	Zimbabwe

NOTE 1. A general list of the abbreviations of law reports and other sources used in this work can be found at the beginning of the Consolidated Table of Cases.

NOTE 2. Where references are made to other publications, the volume number precedes and the page number follows the name of the publication; eg the reference '12 Forms & Precedents (5th Edn) 44' refers to volume 12 of the Encyclopaedia of Forms and Precedents, page 44.

NOTE 3. An English statute is cited by short title or, where there is no short title, by regnal year and chapter number together with the name by which it is commonly known or a description of its subject matter and date. In the case of a foreign statute, the mode of citation generally follows the style of citation in use in the country concerned with the addition, where necessary, of the name of the country in parentheses.

NOTE 4. A statutory instrument is cited by short title, if any, followed by the year and number, or, if unnumbered, the date.

TABLE OF STATUTES

TABLE OF STATUTORY INSTRUMENTS

TABLE OF PROCEDURE

CIVIL PROCEDURE

Civil Procedure Rules 1998, SI 1998/3132 (CPR)

Practice Directions supplementing CPR

TABLE OF CASES

PARA

E

J

PARA

Decisions of the European Court of Justice are listed below numerically. These decisions are also included in the preceding alphabetical list.

BUILDING

1. LEGISLATIVE FRAMEWORK

1. Outline of the legislative framework.

The principal enactment relating to the control of building throughout England and Wales is the Building Act 1984[1], which consolidated various earlier enactments concerning building and buildings and related matters[2]. The Act gives the appropriate national authority[3] power to make regulations (known as 'building regulations') for any of the purposes of securing the health, safety, welfare and convenience of persons in or about buildings and of others who may be affected by buildings or matters connected with buildings, furthering the conservation of fuel and power, and preventing waste, undue consumption, misuse or contamination of water[4]. In addition to making provision relating to building regulations[5], the Act provides for the supervision of plans and work by approved inspectors and public bodies[6]. It also contains provisions relating to buildings, including requirements in relation to drainage, the provision of sanitary conveniences, defective premises, demolition and yards and passages[7].

Building control in London was previously governed by the London Building Acts and byelaws[8]. Although many of these provisions have been repealed and the Building Act 1984 largely applies to inner London[9], certain aspects of inner London building control are still governed by the London Building Acts, and byelaws may still be made[10]. In relation to an area outside inner London, for which there is in force a local Act[11] containing provisions that impose an obligation or restriction as to the construction, nature or situation of buildings, the local authority[12] must keep a copy of those provisions at its offices for inspection by the public at all reasonable times free of charge[13].

Several aspects of building control are outside the scope of the Building Act 1984[14]. In particular, separate provision is made for safety at sports grounds, and for the safety of stands at sports grounds[15]. Further powers in respect of houses which are unfit for human habitation or which are insanitary are conferred by housing legislation[16]. Building operations, or the making of any material change in the use of a building, will generally require planning permission[17] in addition to any consent that may be required under regulations[18]. The construction of buildings over highways maintainable at the public expense is restricted by the Highways Act 1980[19]. The Party Wall etc Act 1996 makes provision in respect of party walls and excavation and construction in proximity to certain buildings or structures[20].

1   The Building Act 1984 does not extend to Scotland or to Northern Ireland: s 135(1), (2).
2   The construction of buildings outside inner London, together with the health, safety, welfare and convenience of their inhabitants, was, until the consolidation in 1984, largely governed by the Public Health Act 1936 Pt II (ss 14–90), the Public Health Act 1961 Pt II (ss 4–37) and the Health and Safety at Work etc Act 1974 Pt III (ss 61–76), and by regulations made under them. The building regulation legislation in the Public Health Act 1936 was founded upon local authority byelaws. This method of control was altered by the Public Health Act 1961 to a system of national regulations administered by local authorities (see the Public Health Act 1961 ss 4–11, Sch 1 (now repealed)) and, in relation to building regulations, local authorities were given all such functions under the Public Health Act 1936 ss 64, 65 (now both repealed) (which conferred power to pass plans and to enforce building byelaws), as they had in relation to building byelaws (see the Public Health Act 1961 s 4(4) (now repealed)). However, the need to meet the conditions of modern building methods and new and fast-changing types of materials and services resulted in the Health and Safety at Work etc Act 1974 Pt III which substantially revised the main provisions of the legislation of 1936 and 1961, with the addition of various matters of building control and methods of building regulation. The Building Act 1984, which is operative throughout England and Wales, largely consolidated the Public Health Act 1936 Pt II, the Public Health Act 1961 Pt II and the Health and Safety at Work etc Act 1974 Pt III, as well as certain other enactments concerning

building and buildings and related matters: see the Building Act 1984 s 133(2), Sch 7. All powers and duties conferred or imposed by the Building Act 1984 are in addition to, and not in derogation of, any other powers and duties conferred or imposed by Act, law or custom, and, subject to any express provision of the Building Act 1984, all such other powers and duties may be exercised and must be performed in the same manner as if that Act had not been passed: s 130. For transitional provisions see s 132, Sch 5 (Sch 5 amended by the Clean Air Act 1993 s 67(3), Sch 6). As to the application of the Building Act 1984 to inner London see PARA 3.

3 Ie the Secretary of State or, where statutory functions have been transferred in relation to Wales, the Welsh Ministers: see PARA 5.

4 See the Building Act 1984 s 1; and PARA 7. As to the power to make building regulations see PARAS 7, 12.

5 See the Building Act 1984 Pt I (ss 1–46); and PARA 7 et seq.

6 See the Building Act 1984 Pt II (ss 47–58); and PARA 74 et seq.

7 See the Building Act 1984 Pt III (ss 59–90); and PARA 100 et seq. As to sewers and drains generally see ENVIRONMENTAL QUALITY AND PUBLIC HEALTH vol 46 (2010) PARAS 998–1081. As to sanitary conveniences generally see ENVIRONMENTAL QUALITY AND PUBLIC HEALTH vol 46 (2010) PARAS 987–997.

8 As to the London Building Acts and building control legislation in inner London see PARA 2.

9 See PARA 2. As to the application of the Building Act 1984 to inner London see PARA 3. As to the meaning of 'inner London' see PARA 2 note 2.

10 See eg the London Building Acts (Amendment) Act 1939 s 97; and the Building Act 1984 ss 1(3), 88, Sch 1 para 10; and PARA 4.

11 As to the meaning of 'local Act' see PARA 6 note 2.

12 'Local authority' means the council of a district or London borough, the Common Council of the City of London, the Sub-Treasurer of the Inner Temple, the Under Treasurer of the Middle Temple or, for the purposes of the Building Act 1984 Pt I (see PARA 7 et seq) and Pt II (see PARA 74 et seq) and Pt IV (ss 91–131) (see PARA 70 et seq) so far as it relates to them, the Council of the Isles of Scilly but, in relation to Wales, means the council of a county or county borough: s 126 (definition substituted by the Local Government Act 1985 ss 16, 102(2), Sch 8 para 14(4)(a), Sch 17; and amended by the Local Government (Wales) Act 1994 s 22(3), Sch 9 para 15(3)). As to areas and authorities in England and Wales see LOCAL GOVERNMENT vol 69 (2018) PARA 36 et seq.

13 See the Building Act 1984 ss 88(1), 90(1), Sch 3 para 5. Any question as to what provisions of a local Act are provisions of which a copy is to be so kept must, on the application of the local authority, be determined by the Secretary of State: s 90(2).

14 Eg in relation to London: see PARAS 2–4.

15 This material is covered elsewhere in this work. As to the safety of sports grounds see the Safety of Sports Grounds Act 1975; PARA 146; and SPORTS LAW vol 96 (2012) PARA 135 et seq. As to the safety of stands at sports grounds see the Fire Safety and Safety of Places of Sport Act 1987 Pt III (ss 26–41); PARA 146; and SPORTS LAW vol 96 (2012) PARA 147.

16 See HOUSING vol 56 (2017) PARA 562 et seq. As to the obligations of lessors of small houses see LANDLORD AND TENANT vol 62 (2016) PARAS 311–312.

17 See the Town and Country Planning Act 1990; and PLANNING.

18 Regulations made under the Town and Country Planning Act 1990 may provide for the combination in a single document, made in such form and transmitted to such authority as may be prescribed, of an application for planning permission in respect of any development and an application required, under any enactment specified in the regulations, to be made to a local authority in respect of that development: see s 332(1); and PLANNING vol 82 (2018) PARA 425. Applications for planning permission are regulated by the Town and Country Planning (General Permitted Development) Order 1995, SI 1995/418: see PLANNING vol 81 (2018) PARA 354 et seq.

19 See the Highways Act 1980 s 177; and HIGHWAYS, STREETS AND BRIDGES vol 55 (2012) PARA 362.

20 See BOUNDARIES vol 4 (2011) PARA 384.

2. The London Building Acts legislation.

Building works and the construction of buildings in inner London has historically been largely governed in accordance with the London Building Acts[1] and byelaws made under them. This continued to be the case even after the introduction of the Building Act 1984 (which consolidated earlier building legislation), since many provisions of the Act did not originally apply to inner London[2]. However, regulations made under the Building Act 1984[3] later applied various provisions of the Act[4], and other regulations made under it[5], to inner London. At the same time, any provisions of the London Building Acts or principal byelaws which conflicted or overlapped with the Building Act 1984 or with regulations made under it were repealed or modified[6].

Most of the Building Act 1984, and the regulations made under it, now apply to inner London[7], and it is only certain provisions of the London Building Acts legislation which remain in force in relation to inner London[8].

1   The principal Acts are the London Building Act 1930, the London Building Act (Amendment) Act 1935 and the London Building Acts (Amendment) Act 1939, which may be cited together as the London Building Acts 1930 to 1939: see the London Building Acts (Amendment) Act 1939 s 1, which further provides for those Acts to be construed as one. At 1 April 1965 there were also operative, as building control measures in the London County Council area, the London County Council (General Powers) Act 1954 s 7; the London County Council (General Powers) Act 1955 ss 5–13; and the London County Council (General Powers) Act 1958 ss 15–17. The London Government Act 1963 s 43 applied (subject to certain modifications) the relevant provisions of all the Acts mentioned above to the respective local authorities in Greater London; and certain additional provisions were enacted in the Greater London Council (General Powers) Act 1965 s 6, the Greater London Council (General Powers) Act 1966 s 22, the Greater London Council (General Powers) (No 2) Act 1978 s 7, and the Greater London Council (General Powers) Act 1982 s 3. All these Acts may be cited together as the London Building Acts 1930 to 1982. The London Building Acts, being local Acts, are not reproduced in detail in this work. For further coverage of the law in relation to London see LONDON GOVERNMENT vol 71 (2013) PARAS 199, 335, 336.

2   The provisions of the Building Act 1984 which did not apply to inner London when the Building Act 1984 was introduced were listed in ss 46, 88, 91(2), Sch 3 (as originally enacted). 'Inner London' means the area comprising the inner London boroughs, the City of London, the Inner Temple and the Middle Temple: Building Act 1984 s 126.

3   Ie the Building (Inner London) Regulations 1985, SI 1985/1936; and the Building (Inner London) Regulations 1987, SI 1987/798.

4   As to the application of the Building Act 1984 to inner London see PARA 3.

5   See the Building (Inner London) Regulations 1985, SI 1985/1936; and the Building (Inner London) Regulations 1987, SI 1987/798.

6   See the Building (Inner London) Regulations 1985, SI 1985/1936; and the Building (Inner London) Regulations 1987, SI 1987/798. As to the power of building regulations to repeal or modify certain Acts in relation to inner London see also the Building Act 1984 Sch 3 para 3; and PARA 3.

7   See PARA 3.

8   These include provisions relating to (1) dangerous and noxious businesses (see the London Building Act 1930 Pt XI (ss 143–145)); (2) dwelling houses on low-lying land (see Pt XII (ss 146–148)); (3) the naming and numbering of streets (see the London Building Acts (Amendment) Act 1939 Pt II (ss 5–15)); (4) the construction of buildings (see the London Building Act (Amendment) Act 1935 s 3); (5) special and temporary buildings and structures (see Pt IV (ss 29–31)); (6) means of escape in a fire (see Pt V (ss 33–43); and the Greater London Council (General Powers) Act 1966 s 22); (7) dangerous and neglected structures (see the London Building Acts (Amendment) Act 1939 Pt VII (ss 60–70); the London County Council (General Powers) Act 1955 ss 5–9; the London County Council (General Powers) Act 1958 ss 3(1), 13(2), 15–16); (8) superintending architects (see the London Building Acts (Amendment) Act 1939 ss 73–74); (9) byelaws (see the London Building Act (Amendment) Act 1935 s 8; and the London Building Acts (Amendment) Act 1939 Pt X (s 97)); (10) fees and expenses (see the London Building Act (Amendment) Act 1935 s 14; the London Building Acts (Amendment) Act 1939 ss 91, 94, 95, 96); (11) legal proceedings (see the London Building Acts (Amendment) Act 1939 Pt XI (ss 101–126)); (12) charges as to London Building Act consents etc (see the Greater London Council (General Powers) Act 1982 s 3); and (13) miscellaneous matters (see the London Building Acts (Amendment) Act 1939 Pt XII (ss 132–157)).

3. Application of the Building Act 1984 to inner London.

Certain provisions of the Building Act 1984 relating to:

(1)   the provision of exits[1];

(2) the provision of water supply[2];

(3) means of escape from fire[3];

(4) the raising of chimneys[4];

(5) cellars and rooms under subsoil water level[5];

(6) dangerous buildings[6];

(7) the maintenance of entrances to courtyards[7]; and

(8) facilities for inspecting local Acts[8],

do not apply to inner London[9]. In addition, the provisions relating to the drainage of buildings, the use and ventilation of soil pipes and the repair of drains[10] do not apply to the Inner Temple or the Middle Temple[11]. Further, the provisions of Part IV of the Building Act 1984[12] do not apply in relation to the power[13] of the council of an inner London borough to make byelaws in relation to the demolition of buildings in the borough[14].

Where[15] local authorities[16], or a prescribed[17] person or class of persons other than local authorities, are made responsible for enforcing, or performing prescribed functions[18] under or in connection with, building regulations in force in inner London, then[19] building regulations may in that connection provide for any relevant provision[20] of the Building Act 1984 to apply[21] in relation to any such authority, person or class of persons as that provision applies in relation to a local authority outside inner London[22].

Building regulations may[23] repeal or modify any provision of:

(a) the London Building Acts 1930 to 1939[24];

(b) an Act passed before 20 September 1974, in so far as that provision applies to or to any part of inner London, and relates to, or to the making of, byelaws for or for any part of inner London with respect to any matter for or in connection with which provision can be made by building regulations[25]; or

(c) byelaws made or having effect under the said Acts or of any such byelaws as are mentioned in head (b) above[26],

if it appears to the appropriate national authority[27] that the repeal or, as the case may be, the modification of that provision is expedient:

(i) in consequence of the application[28] of certain provisions of the Public Health Act 1936[29], the Public Health Act 1961[30] and the Health and Safety at Work etc Act 1974[31] to inner London[32];

(ii) in consequence of certain provisions[33] of the Building Act 1984[34]; or

(iii) in connection with any provision contained in building regulations that apply to or to any part of inner London[35].

Before making any building regulations that provide for the repeal or modification of any such provision the appropriate national authority must[36] consult any local authority which appears to be concerned[37].

1 Ie the Building Act 1984 s 24(1), (2), (4): see PARA 39.

2 Ie the Building Act 1984 s 25: see PARA 40.

3 Ie the Building Act 1984 s 72(1)–(4), (6), (7): see PARA 57.

4 Ie the Building Act 1984 s 73: see PARA 112.

5 Ie the Building Act 1984 ss 74, 75: see PARA 113.

6 Ie the Building Act 1984 ss 77–83: see PARAS 115–118.

7 Ie the Building Act 1984 s 85: see PARA 120.

8 Ie the Building Act 1984 s 90: see PARA 1.

9 Building Act 1984 ss 46, 88, Sch 3 para 1 (amended by SI 1985/1936; SI 1987/798), Building Act 1984 Sch 3 para 5 (amended by SI 1987/798).

10 Ie the Building Act 1984 ss 59–61: see PARAS 100–102.

11 Building Act 1984 Sch 3 para 6.

12 Ie the Building Act 1984 Pt IV (ss 91–131).

13 Ie the power under the Building Act 1984 Sch 3 Pt IV: see PARA 4.

14 See the Building Act 1984 s 131, Sch 3 para 13 (amended by SI 1987/798).

15 Ie by the Building Act 1984 s 91(2) (see PARA 70) or by building regulations made under s 1(3), Sch 1 para 6 (see PARA 9), or Sch 3 para 14(1) (repealed): see Sch 3 para 2(1). As to the meaning of 'building regulations' see PARA 7.

16 As to the meaning of 'local authority' see PARA 1 note 12.

17 Ie prescribed by building regulations: see the Building Act 1984 s 126.

18 'Functions' includes powers and duties: Building Act 1984 s 126.

19 Ie without prejudice to the Building Act 1984 Sch 1 para 6 (see PARA 9) and Sch 3 para 14(1) (repealed).

20 For these purposes, 'relevant provision' means any of the following provisions of the Building Act 1984 that may be prescribed for the purposes of Sch 3 para 2(1): s 4 (see PARA 16), ss 8–10 (see PARAS 18–21), s 16 (see PARA 33), s 18(1), (4), (5) (s 18 repealed), ss 21–23 (see PARAS 36–38), s 24(1), (2), (4) (see PARA 39), ss 26–29 (repealed with savings), s 32 (see PARA 42), s 36 (see PARA 62), s 37 (see PARA 63), s 39 (see PARA 65), and s 40 (see PARA 66): Sch 3 para 2(2).

21 Ie with any prescribed modifications, and notwithstanding the Building Act 1984 Sch 3 para 1 (see the text and notes 1–9): see Sch 3 para 2(1). 'Modifications' includes additions, omissions and amendments, and related expressions must be construed accordingly: s 126.

22 Building Act 1984 Sch 3 para 2(1).

23 Ie without prejudice to the generality of the Building Act 1984 Sch 1 para 11(1) (see PARA 9): see Sch 3 para 3.

24 Building Act 1984 Sch 3 para 3(a). The text refers to the London Building Act 1930, the London Building Act (Amendment) Act 1935, and the London Building Acts (Amendment) Act 1939. See further PARA 2.

25 Building Act 1984 Sch 3 para 3(b).

26 Building Act 1984 Sch 3 para 3(c).

27 Ie the Secretary of State or, where statutory functions have been transferred in relation to Wales, the Welsh Ministers: see PARA 5.

28 Ie by virtue of the Health and Safety at Work Act 1974 s 70(1) (which section is repealed by and incorporated in the Building Act 1984: see now Sch 5 para 5).

29 Ie any of the Public Health Act 1936 ss 61, 62, 67 (all repealed).

30 Ie any of the Public Health Act 1961 ss 4(2), (5), (6), (7), 5, 9 (all repealed).

31 Ie any of the Health and Safety at Work Act 1974 ss 61–74, 76 (all repealed).

32 Building Act 1984 Sch 3 para 3(i).

33 Ie the Building Act 1984 Sch 3 para 2 (see the text and notes 15–23) or Sch 3 para 14 (repealed).

34 Building Act 1984 Sch 3 para 3(ii).

35 Building Act 1984 Sch 3 para 3(iii).

36 Ie without prejudice to the requirements as to consultation in the Building Act 1984 s 14(3): see PARA 14.

37 Building Act 1984 Sch 3 para 4 (amended by the Local Government Act 1985 s 16, Sch 8 para 14(4)(b)(i)).

4.   Byelaws for the demolition of buildings in inner London.

Provision is made by the Building Act 1984[1] with respect to the making of byelaws for the inner London[2] boroughs, with respect to certain matters, and for the inner London boroughs, the Inner Temple and the Middle Temple, with respect to certain other matters[3]. The council of an inner London borough may make byelaws in relation to the demolition of buildings in the borough[4]:

> (1)   requiring the fixing of fans at the level of each floor of a building undergoing demolition[5];

> (2)   requiring the hoarding up of windows in a building from which sashes and glass have been removed[6];

> (3)   regulating the demolition of internal parts of buildings before any external walls are taken down[7];

> (4)   requiring the placing of screens or mats, the use of water or the taking of other precautions to prevent nuisances arising from dust[8];

(5) regulating the hours during which ceilings may be broken down and mortar may be shot, or be allowed to fall, into any lower floor[9];

(6) requiring any person proposing to demolish a building to give to the borough council such notice of his intention to do so as may be specified in the byelaws[10].

Such byelaws may make different provision for different cases, and in particular may provide that, in their application to an area specified in the byelaws, the byelaws have effect subject to such modifications[11] or exceptions as may be so specified[12]. No such byelaws may apply to a building (not being a dwelling house) belonging to a board carrying on a railway undertaking and used by that board as a part of, or in connection with, that undertaking[13].

1 Ie by the Building Act 1984 s 88(3), Sch 3 Pt IV (paras 10–13): see the text and notes 2–13. The provisions of Pt IV (ss 91–131) (general matters: see PARA 70 et seq) do not apply in relation to Sch 3 Pt IV: see Sch 3 para 13 (amended by SI 1987/798).
2 As to the meaning of 'inner London' see PARA 2 note 2.
3 Building Act 1984 s 88(3) (amended by the Local Government Act 1985 s 102(2), Sch 17).
4 Building Act 1984 Sch 3 para 10(1) (amended by the Local Government Act 1985 s 16, Sch 8 para 14(4)(b)(ii)). As to the making of building regulations to modify or repeal the provisions of the Building Act 1984 Sch 3 Pt IV (byelaws) on the ground of inconsistency with other provisions see s 1(3), Sch 1 para 11(1); and PARA 9.
5 Building Act 1984 Sch 3 para 10(1)(a).
6 Building Act 1984 Sch 3 para 10(1)(b).
7 Building Act 1984 Sch 3 para 10(1)(c).
8 Building Act 1984 Sch 3 para 10(1)(d).
9 Building Act 1984 Sch 3 para 10(1)(e).
10 Building Act 1984 Sch 3 para 10(1)(f).
11 As to the meaning of 'modifications' see PARA 3 note 21.
12 Building Act 1984 Sch 3 para 10(2).
13 Building Act 1984 Sch 3 para 10(3).

5. The Secretary of State and the Welsh Ministers.

Many statutory functions relating to building law which were previously vested in Ministers of the Crown are now exercisable by the Secretary of State[1] (in relation to England) and by the Welsh Ministers (in relation to Wales)[2]. The functions currently exercisable by the Welsh Ministers are those functions under the Building Act 1984 which were transferred to the National Assembly for Wales[3] by Order in Council and subsequently transferred to the Welsh Ministers[4]. Further functions under the Building Act 1984[5], along with certain functions under the Sustainable and Secure Buildings Act 2004[6] and the Climate Change and Sustainable Energy Act 2006[7], are transferred to the Welsh Ministers by Order in Council[8].

Legislation enacted following the establishment of the Welsh Assembly Government (now the Welsh Government)[9] which confers functions on the Secretary of State and the Welsh Ministers often refers to those bodies collectively as 'the appropriate national authority'[10], and that expression is used throughout this title to cover any situation where the function in question is exercised in relation to England by the Secretary of State and in relation to Wales by the Welsh Ministers, and also where functions may be carried out jointly.

1 In any enactment, 'Secretary of State' means one of Her Majesty's principal secretaries of state: see the Interpretation Act 1978 s 5, Sch 1. The office of Secretary of State is a unified office, and in law each Secretary of State is capable of performing the functions of all or any of them. As to the office of Secretary of State see CONSTITUTIONAL AND ADMINISTRATIVE LAW vol 20 (2014) PARA 153.
2 As to the functions transferred see note 3. As to the establishment of the Welsh Assembly Government (now the Welsh Government) under the Government of Wales Act 2006 see

CONSTITUTIONAL AND ADMINISTRATIVE LAW vol 20 (2014) PARA 373 et seq.

3   Ie by Order in Council under the Government of Wales Act 1998 s 22 (now repealed): see CONSTITUTIONAL AND ADMINISTRATIVE LAW vol 20 (2014) PARA 380 et seq). All functions under the Building Act 1984 were so transferred, with the exception of functions under the following provisions: s 1 (see PARA 7), s 2 (see PARA 12), s 3(1) (see PARA 16), s 5(1) (see PARA 17), s 6 (see PARA 23), s 8(2), (3), (6) (see PARA 18), s 9(1) (see PARA 19), s 11 (see PARA 22), s 12 (see PARA 24), s 13 (see PARA 24), s 14 (see PARA 14), s 16(9) (see PARA 33), s 16(10) (so far as it relates to the function of prescribing fees) (see PARA 33), s 17 (see PARA 33) and s 19(7) (see PARA 34), s 20(5) (so far as it relates to the function of prescribing the time and manner of appeals) (see PARA 35), s 20(10) (see PARA 35), s 35 (see PARA 61), s 38(1) (see PARA 64), s 43(3) (see PARA 69), s 44 (see PARA 15), s 47 (see PARA 74), s 48 (see PARA 75), s 49 (see PARA 72), s 50 (except s 50(2)) (see PARA 83), ss 51–58 (see PARA 84 et seq), s 92 (see PARA 135), s 120, Sch 1 (see PARA 9) and Sch 4 (see PARA 89 et seq), and the Treasury function under s 87(4) (see PARA 122): see the National Assembly for Wales (Transfer of Functions) Order 1999, SI 1999/672, Sch 1 (item substituted by SI 2000/253). The Treasury approval requirement under the Building Act 1984 s 87(3) continues in effect: see the National Assembly for Wales (Transfer of Functions) Order 1999, SI 1999/672, Sch 1 (item as so substituted).

As to the exercise of transferred functions see the Government of Wales Act 2006 Sch 3, Sch 11 paras 33–35; and CONSTITUTIONAL AND ADMINISTRATIVE LAW vol 20 (2014) PARA 380 et seq.

4   Ie by the operation of the Government of Wales Act 2006 Sch 11 paras 26, 30 (see CONSTITUTIONAL AND ADMINISTRATIVE LAW vol 20 (2014) PARA 380), which provide that instruments transferring functions to the National Assembly for Wales under the Government of Wales Act 1998 s 22 (repealed) (see note 3) continue to have effect following the transfer of the Assembly's executive functions to the Welsh Ministers as conferring those functions on those Ministers.

5   The functions conferred or imposed on the Secretary of State by or under the Building Act 1984 were, so far as exercisable in relation to Wales, transferred to the Welsh Ministers (subject to the Welsh Ministers (Transfer of Functions) (No 2) Order 2009, SI 2009/3019, arts 3, 4 (see below): art 1, 2(a).

Such functions so far as exercisable in relation to excepted energy buildings in Wales which were previously excluded from being transferred by art 3(a) are now transferred to the Welsh Ministers: see the Wales Act 2017 s 54(1). Section 54(1) does not operate to transfer any functions that are reserved by the Welsh Ministers (Transfer of Functions) (No 2) Order 2009, SI 2009/3019, arts 3(b), (c), 4 (see below): Wales Act 2017 s 54(2).

The Welsh Ministers (Transfer of Functions) (No 2) Order 2009, SI 2009/3019, art 2(a) does not transfer:

(1)   functions under the Building Act 1984 s 44(5) (functions exercisable by the Secretary of State as a Crown authority; see PARA 15) (Welsh Ministers (Transfer of Functions) (No 2) Order 2009, SI 2009/3019, art 3(b)); or

(2)   functions under the Building Act 1984 s 42(7) (see PARA 68) or s 134(1) (power of the Secretary of State to appoint a day for a modification to cease to have effect or for a provision to come into force) (Welsh Ministers (Transfer of Functions) (No 2) Order 2009, SI 2009/3019, art 3(c)).

An 'excepted energy building' is a building that satisfies the following two conditions: Schedule para 1. The first condition is that the building falls within one of the following descriptions:

(a)   a generating station whose construction, extension or operation requires or required the consent of the Secretary of State under the Electricity Act 1989 s 36 or any ancillary development (Welsh Ministers (Transfer of Functions) (No 2) Order 2009, SI 2009/3019, Schedule para 2(a));

(b)   a generating station whose construction or extension requires or required development consent under the Planning Act 2008 (Welsh Ministers (Transfer of Functions) (No 2) Order 2009, SI 2009/3019, Schedule para 2(b));

(c)   an electric line whose installation, or continued installation, above ground requires the consent of the Secretary of State under the Electricity Act 1989 s 37 or any ancillary development (Welsh Ministers (Transfer of Functions) (No 2) Order 2009, SI 2009/3019, Schedule para 2(c));

(d)   an electric line whose installation above ground requires or required development consent (Schedule para 2(d));

(e) a pipe-line whose construction requires or required authorisation under the Pipe-lines Act 1962 s 1(1) or development consent (Welsh Ministers (Transfer of Functions) (No 2) Order 2009, SI 2009/3019, Schedule para 2(e)); or

(f) a facility for the storage of gas underground in natural porous strata by a gas transporter or surface works or pipes associated with such a facility (Schedule para 2(f)).

The second condition is that the building is not used, or not to be used, entirely as one or more of the following: (i) a residence; (ii) a shop; (iii) an office; (iv) a showroom; (v) a canteen; or (vi) an outbuilding ancillary to a building used, or to be used, entirely for one or more of the purposes set out in heads (i) to (v): Schedule para 3 (not yet in force). 'Outbuilding' means a shed, greenhouse, summerhouse, garage or similar building that is not attached to any other building other than another outbuilding: Schedule para 4 (not yet in force). 'Residence' includes a dwelling house, a flat and any common parts, and a room used for residential purposes and any common parts: Schedule para 4. 'Room used for residential purposes' means a room or a suite of rooms which is not a dwelling house or a flat and which is used by one or more persons to live and sleep: Schedule para 4 (not yet in force).

The transfer by art 2(a) of functions under the Building Regulations 2000, SI 2000/2531, Pt 5A (see now the Building Regulations 2010, SI 2010/2214, Pt 6; and PARA 44 et seq) (energy performance of buildings) is subject to the following provisions (see the Welsh Ministers (Transfer of Functions) (No 2) Order 2009, SI 2009/3019, art 4(1)). Functions under the Building Regulations 2000, SI 2000/2531, reg 17A (revoked; see now the Building Regulations 2010, SI 2010/2214, reg 24; and PARA 46) (methodology of calculation and expression of energy performance) are transferred only so far as they are exercisable for the purposes of (A) the Building Regulations 2000, SI 2000/2531, reg 17B (revoked; see now the Building Regulations 2010, SI 2010/2214, reg 25; and PARA 46) (minimum energy performance requirements for buildings); and (B) the construction EPC provisions: Welsh Ministers (Transfer of Functions) (No 2) Order 2009, SI 2009/3019, art 4(2).

Functions under the Building Regulations 2000, SI 2000/2531, reg 17F (revoked; see now the Building Regulations 2010, SI 2010/2214, reg 30; and PARA 51) (energy assessors) are transferred only so far as they are exercisable in relation to the functions of energy assessors under, or in relation to, the construction EPC provisions: Welsh Ministers (Transfer of Functions) (No 2) Order 2009, SI 2009/3019, art 4(3).

6   The functions of the Secretary of State under the Sustainable and Secure Buildings Act 2004 s 6 (Secretary of State to report on building stock; see PARA 8) are, so far as exercisable in relation to Wales, transferred to the Welsh Ministers: Welsh Ministers (Transfer of Functions) (No 2) Order 2009, SI 2009/3019, art 2(b)(i).

7   The functions of the Secretary of State under the Climate Change and Sustainable Energy Act 2006 s 14 are, so far as exercisable in relation to Wales, transferred to the Welsh Ministers: Welsh Ministers (Transfer of Functions) (No 2) Order 2009, SI 2009/3019, art 2(b)(ii).

8   Ie by the Welsh Ministers (Transfer of Functions) (No 2) Order 2009, SI 2009/3019 (an Order in Council made under the Government of Wales Act 2006 s 58: see CONSTITUTIONAL AND ADMINISTRATIVE LAW vol 20 (2014) PARA 380). Any pre-commencement power to confer or impose a relevant function on the Secretary of State has effect as a power to confer or impose the function on the Welsh Ministers, the First Minister or the Counsel General: Welsh Ministers (Transfer of Functions) (No 2) Order 2009, SI 2009/3019, art 5(1) (not yet in force). For these purposes: (1) a pre-commencement power is a power which was exercisable immediately before 31 December 2011; and (2) a relevant function is a function which, had it been a function of the Secretary of State immediately before 31 December 2011, would have been transferred to the Welsh Ministers by art 2: see art 5(2).

9   The Welsh Assembly Government was renamed the 'Welsh Government' by the Wales Act 2014 s 4(1): see CONSTITUTIONAL AND ADMINISTRATIVE LAW vol 20 (2014) PARA 380.

10 See eg the Commons Act 2006 s 61(1).

6. Meaning of 'building'.

For the purposes of Part I of the Building Act 1984[1] and any other enactment[2], whether or not contained in that Act, that relates to building regulations[3], or that mentions 'buildings' or 'a building' in a context from which it appears that those expressions are there intended to have the same meaning as in Part I of the Building Act 1984, means any permanent or temporary building, and, unless the context otherwise requires, it includes any other structure or erection[4] of whatever kind or nature, whether permanent or temporary[5]. For these purposes, unless the context otherwise requires:

(1) a reference to a building includes a reference to part of a building[6]; and

(2) a reference to the provision of services, fittings and equipment in or in connection with buildings, or to services, fittings and equipment so provided, includes a reference to the affixing of things to buildings or, as the case may be, to things so affixed[7].

1 Ie the Building Act 1984 Pt I (ss 1–46): see PARA 7 et seq.

2 'Enactment' includes an enactment contained in a local Act: Building Act 1984 s 126. 'Local Act' includes a provisional order confirmed by Parliament, and the confirming Act so far as it relates to that order: s 126. 'Act' includes an enactment contained in a local Act: s 126.

3 As to the meaning of 'building regulations' see PARA 7.

4 For these purposes, 'structure or erection' includes a vehicle, vessel, hovercraft, aircraft or other movable object of any kind in such circumstances as may be prescribed, being circumstances that in the opinion of the appropriate national authority justify treating it for those purposes as a building: Building Act 1984 s 121(2). 'Prescribed' means prescribed by building regulations: see s 126. As to the appropriate national authority (ie the Secretary of State, or where the statutory functions have been transferred in relation to Wales, the Welsh Ministers) see PARA 5.

5 Building Act 1984 s 121(1). As to the classification of buildings for the purposes of building regulations see PARA 7. The building regulations apply only to 'buildings'; walls and bridges that are not part of a building are not 'a building' for purposes of the regulations. Each structure in a development must be looked at separately in order to see whether the building regulations apply to it: *Seabrink Residents Association Ltd v Robert Walpole Campion & Partners (a firm)* (1988) 14 Con LR 62. As to whether a bus and a lorry constitute 'temporary' buildings see *Gumbrell v Swale RDC* [1936] 3 All ER 935.

6 Building Act 1984 s 121(3)(a). Under previous legislation, a neon installation was held to be not part of a building but is something on a building and, accordingly, the regulations did not apply: *Price v Claudgen Ltd* [1967] 1 All ER 695, [1967] 1 WLR 575, HL.

7 Building Act 1984 s 121(3)(b).

2. BUILDING REGULATIONS

(1) Building Regulations; In General

7. Power to make building regulations.

The appropriate national authority[1] may, for any of the purposes of:

(1)   securing the health, safety, welfare and convenience of persons in or about buildings[2] and of others who may be affected by buildings or matters connected with buildings[3];

(2)   furthering the conservation of fuel and power[4];

(3)   preventing waste, undue consumption, misuse or contamination of water[5];

(4)   furthering the protection or enhancement of the environment[6];

(5)   facilitating sustainable development[7]; or

(6)   furthering the prevention or detection of crime[8].

make regulations[9] with respect to: (a) the design and construction of buildings; (b) the demolition of buildings; (c) services, fittings and equipment provided in or in connection with buildings; and (d) as from a day to be appointed, the action to be taken as a result of a building's contribution to or effect on emissions of carbon dioxide (whether or not from the building itself)[10]. Such regulations are known as building regulations[11].

In making building regulations the appropriate national authority must have regard, in particular, to the desirability of preserving the character of protected buildings that are of special historical or architectural interest[12].

For the purposes of building regulations and of a direction given or instrument made with reference to building regulations, buildings may be classified by reference to size, description, design, purpose, location or any other characteristic whatsoever[13].

1   Ie the Secretary of State or, where statutory functions have been transferred in relation to Wales, the Welsh Ministers: see PARA 5.

2   As to the meaning of 'building' see PARA 6.

3   Building Act 1984 s 1(1)(a).

4   Building Act 1984 s 1(1)(b) (substituted by the Sustainable and Secure Buildings Act 2004 s 1(1)).

5   Building Act 1984 s 1(1)(c) (as substituted: see note 4).

6   Building Act 1984 s 1(1)(d) (as substituted: see note 4).

7   Building Act 1984 s 1(1)(e) (as substituted: see note 4).

8   Building Act 1984 s 1(1)(f) (as substituted: see note 4).

9   See the Building Act 1984 s 1(4). In exercise of this power the following regulations have been made: the Building (Inner London) Regulations 1985, SI 1985/1936; the Building (Inner London) Regulations 1987, SI 1987/798; the Building (Repeal of Provisions of Local Acts) Regulations 2003, SI 2003/3030; the Building (Local Authority Charges) Regulations 2010, SI 2010/404; the Building Regulations 2010, SI 2010/2214; the Building (Approved Inspectors etc) Regulations 2010/2215 the Energy Performance of Buildings (England and Wales) Regulations 2012, SI 2012/3118 (see PARA 48 et seq)' and the Building (Repeal of Provisions of Local Acts) Regulations 2012, SI 2012/3124.

It is appropriate to draw a distinction between the regulations the purpose of which is to prevent damage to the health, safety or welfare of persons and regulations the purpose of which is to prevent damage to property. The statutory regime of the Building Act 1984 and the Building Regulations 1985, SI 1985/1065 (now repealed) was concerned with the health, safety and welfare of persons, but had no purpose referable to the protection of property or chattels. It has been held that even where the purpose of the statutory regime under the Building Act 1984 is concerned with avoiding damage to property, it was not fair, just or reasonable to impose a duty of care at common law on the council: *Tesco Stores Ltd v Wards Construction (Investment) Ltd* (1995) 76

BLR 94. 'The Building Act 1984 replaced the previous system of local byelaws with nationally applicable regulations made by the Secretary of State': *Southwark London Borough Council v Tanner* [2001] 1 AC 1 at 9, sub nom *Southwark London Borough Council v Mills* [1999] 4 All ER 449 at 454, HL, per Lord Hoffmann.

10 Building Act 1984 s 1(1), (1A) (s 1(1) amended by the Sustainable and Secure Buildings Act 2004 s 1, Building Act 1984 s 1(1A) added by the Sustainable and Secure Buildings Act 2004 s 1; and prospectively amended, as from a day to be appointed, by the Infrastructure Act 2015 s 37). As to consultation before building regulations are made see PARA 14.

11 Building Act 1984 ss 1(2), 122(a). A reference to building regulations, in a particular case in relation to which a requirement of building regulations is for the time being dispensed with, waived, relaxed or modified by virtue of s 8 (see PARA 18) or s 11 (see PARA 22) or any other enactment, is a reference to building regulations as they apply in that case, unless the context otherwise requires: s 122(b). As to the application of building regulations to the Crown see PARA 15.

For any reference to building byelaws as defined in the Public Health Act 1936 s 343, or byelaws made under Pt II with respect to buildings, works and fittings, that occurs in an Act, or in an instrument having effect under an Act, there is substituted a reference to building regulations: Building Act 1984 s 89(1). References to byelaws include 'exemptions and savings' under earlier building legislation: see eg *Tanner v Oldman* [1896] 1 QB 60, DC.

12 Building Act 1984 s 1A(1) (s 1A added by the Sustainable and Secure Buildings Act 2004 s 2). For these purposes, 'protected buildings' means: (1) listed buildings within the meaning of the Planning (Listed Buildings and Conservation Areas) Act 1990 s 1(5); and (2) buildings situated in areas designated as conservation areas under s 69: Building Act 1984 s 1A(2) (as so added). See *R (on the application of Actis Sa) v Secretary of State for Communities and Local Government* [2007] EWHC 2417 (Admin), [2007] All ER (D) 30 (Nov); and PLANNING vol 83 (2018) PARAS 1181, 1255.

13 Building Act 1984 s 34.

8. Report on building stock.

The appropriate national authority[1] must, for the period of two years beginning from 16 November 2004[2], and for each succeeding period of two years, prepare a report on progress during the period in connection with the following purposes[3] in the context of the building stock in England and Wales: (1) furthering the conservation of fuel and power; (2) preventing waste, undue consumption, misuse or contamination of water; (3) furthering the protection or enhancement of the environment; and (4) facilitating sustainable development[4]. Such a report must (in particular) deal with:

(a) building regulations made during the period for any of those purposes[5];

(b) proposals current at the end of the period to make building regulations for any of those purposes[6];

(c) effects or likely effects of regulations or proposals dealt with in the report under heads (a) and (b) above[7];

(d) proposals considered by the appropriate national authority during the period for the setting of targets for any of those purposes in relation to:
(i) buildings in England and Wales; or
(ii) services, fittings or equipment provided in or in connection with such buildings[8];

(e) overall changes during the period in:
(i) the efficiency with which energy is used in buildings in England and Wales;
(ii) levels of emissions from such buildings that are emissions considered by the Secretary of State to contribute to climate change;
(iii) the extent to which such buildings have their own facilities for generating energy;

(iv) the extent to which materials used in constructing, or carrying out works in relation to, such buildings are recycled or re-used materials[9].

The report must contain an estimate, as at the end of the period, of the number of dwellings in England and Wales[10].

1 Ie the Secretary of State or, where statutory functions have been transferred in relation to Wales, the Welsh Ministers: see PARA 5.
2 Ie the date on which the Sustainable and Secure Buildings Act 2004 s 6 came into force: see s 11(4).
3 Ie in connection with the purposes mentioned in the Building Act 1984 s 1(1)(b)–(e): see PARA 7.
4 Sustainable and Secure Buildings Act 2004 s 6(1), (4); Building Act 1984 s 1(1)(b)–(e) (substituted by the Sustainable and Secure Buildings Act 2004 s 1).
5 Sustainable and Secure Buildings Act 2004 s 6(2)(a).
6 Sustainable and Secure Buildings Act 2004 s 6(2)(b).
7 Sustainable and Secure Buildings Act 2004 s 6(2)(c).
8 Sustainable and Secure Buildings Act 2004 s 6(2)(d).
9 Sustainable and Secure Buildings Act 2004 s 6(2)(e).
10 Sustainable and Secure Buildings Act 2004 s 6(3).

9. Subject matter of building regulations.

Building regulations[1] may provide for particular requirements of the regulations to be deemed to be complied with where prescribed[2] methods of construction[3], prescribed types of materials or other prescribed means are used in or in connection with buildings[4]. Building regulations may be framed to any extent by reference to a document published by or on behalf of the appropriate national authority[5] or another person or a body, or by reference to the approval or satisfaction of a prescribed person or body[6].

Building regulations may include provision as to the giving of notices[7], the deposit of plans[8] of proposed work or work already executed (including provision as to the number of copies to be deposited)[9], the retention by local authorities[10] of copies of plans deposited with them in accordance with the regulations[11], the inspection and testing of work[12], and the taking of samples[13]. Building regulations may provide for requiring local authorities and approved inspectors[14] in prescribed circumstances to consult a prescribed person before taking a prescribed step in connection with any work or other matter to which building regulations are applicable[15]. Building regulations may:

(1) authorise local authorities to accept, as evidence that the requirements of building regulations as to matters of a prescribed description are or would be satisfied, certificates[16] to that effect by persons of a class or description prescribed in relation to those matters or by a person nominated in writing by the appropriate national authority in a particular case[17];

(2) provide for the issue by local authorities of certificates to the effect that, so far as the authority concerned has been able to ascertain after taking all reasonable steps in that behalf, the requirements of building regulations as to matters of a prescribed description are satisfied in a particular case, and for such certificates to be evidence (but not conclusive evidence) of compliance with the regulations[18];

(3) make provision:
(a) for prohibiting, in prescribed circumstances, the carrying out of proposed work of a prescribed class involving matters of a prescribed description unless there has been deposited with the prescribed authority as regards those matters a certificate such as is mentioned in head (1) above[19];

(b)   for enabling, in the cases where such a certificate is required by virtue of head (a) above, a dispute as to whether a certificate ought to be issued to be referred to the appropriate national authority[20];

(c)   for enabling the appropriate national authority, on such a reference, to give such directions as it thinks fit[21].

Building regulations may provide for requiring that, in prescribed circumstances, a person of a prescribed class or description is to give to a local authority or an approved inspector a certificate to the effect that the requirements of building regulations as to matters of a prescribed description are satisfied[22]. They may also provide for requiring that such certificates be given within such periods or at such times and in such forms as may be prescribed[23], and that a local authority or an approved inspector is not to exercise or perform a prescribed power or duty unless such a certificate has been given to them or him, or unless such a certificate has been given to them or him and the certificate has been accepted by them or him[24]. Such regulations may make provision as to the acceptance of such certificates by local authorities and approved inspectors; and other steps to be taken by local authorities or approved inspectors in connection with such certificates[25]. Building regulations may provide for such certificates to be treated as evidence (but not conclusive evidence) of the matters certified[26].

Building regulations may provide that in relation to any work of any type that is being, or that is proposed to be, carried out in prescribed circumstances, there is to be an appointed person[27] who is of a prescribed class or description who is appointed by a person determined in accordance with building regulations; and such regulations may make provision for a person to appoint himself[28]. Building regulations may provide that the appointed person in relation to any work is to have such duties in relation to the planning and management of the carrying out of that work as may be prescribed for purposes connected with facilitating compliance with the requirements of building regulations in relation to that work[29]. They may also impose duties (in relation to the appointed person, or anything that he does, or proposes to do, in connection with his duties) on persons who are participating, or who are to participate, in the carrying out of that work[30]. These include duties to comply with directions given to them by the appointed person and duties that are framed by reference to determinations made by that person[31].

Building regulations may authorise local authorities to charge prescribed fees for or in connection with the performance of prescribed functions[32] of theirs relating to building regulations[33]. Building regulations may make a prescribed person or class of persons responsible (instead of local authorities) for performing prescribed functions of local authorities under or in connection with building regulations, and for that purpose may provide for a prescribed enactment relating to building regulations and a prescribed provision of such regulations to apply (with any prescribed modifications[34]) in relation to a prescribed person or a person of a prescribed class as that enactment or provision applies in relation to a local authority[35].

Building regulations may[36], for any of the purposes for which building regulations may be made[37], make provision with respect to any of the following matters:

(i)   preparation of sites[38];

(ii)   suitability, durability, use and re-use of materials and components, including surface finishes[39];

(iii)   structural strength and stability, including precautions against overloading, impact and explosion[40], measures to safeguard adjacent buildings and services[41], and underpinning[42];

(iv)   fire precautions, including structural measures to resist the outbreak and spread of fire and to mitigate its effects[43], services, fittings and equipment designed to mitigate the effects of fire or to facilitate fire-fighting[44], means of escape in case of fire and means for securing that such means of escape can be safely and effectively used at all material times[45];

(v)   resistance to moisture and decay[46];

(vi)   measures affecting the transmission of heat[47];

(vii)   measures affecting the transmission of sound[48];

(viii)   measures to prevent infestation[49];

(ix)   measures affecting the emission of smoke, gases, vapours, fumes, grit or dust or other noxious or offensive substances[50];

(x)   drainage, including waste disposal units[51];

(xi)   cesspools[52] and other means for the reception, treatment or disposal of foul matter[53];

(xii)   storage, treatment and removal of waste[54];

(xiii)   installations utilising solid fuel, oil, gas, electricity or any other fuel or power (including appliances, storage tanks, heat exchangers, ducts, fans and other equipment[55]);

(xiv)   water services (including wells and bore-holes for the supply of water) and associated fittings and fixed equipment (including equipment for monitoring and measuring supplies of water[56]);

(xv)   telecommunications services (including telephones and radio and television wiring installations[57]);

(xvi)   lifts, escalators, hoists, conveyors and moving footways[58];

(xvii)   plant providing air under pressure[59];

(xviii)   standards of heating, artificial lighting, mechanical ventilation and air-conditioning and provision of power outlets[60];

(xix)   open space about buildings and the natural lighting and ventilation of buildings[61];

(xx)   accommodation for specific purposes in or in connection with buildings, and the dimensions of rooms and other spaces within buildings[62];

(xxi)   means of access to and egress from buildings and parts of buildings[63];

(xxii)   prevention of danger and obstruction to persons in and about buildings (including passers-by[64]);

(xxiii)   measures relating to the security of buildings[65];

(xxiv)   measures affecting the use of fuel or power[66];

(xxv)   equipment for monitoring and measuring supplies of fuel, power or heat[67];

(xxvi)   recycling facilities (including facilities for composting)[68];

(xxvii)   the production of heat or the generation of electricity by microgeneration (as defined for these purposes by building regulations)[69];

(xxviii)   matters connected with or ancillary to any of the matters mentioned above[70].

Building regulations may require things to be provided or done in connection with buildings, as well as regulating the provision or doing of things in or in connection with buildings[71]; and they may prescribe the manner in which work is to be carried out[72].

The following may be regulated by building regulations:

(A) alterations and extensions of buildings and of services, fittings and equipment in or in connection with buildings[73];

(B) new services, fittings or equipment provided in or in connection with buildings[74];

(C) buildings and services, fittings and equipment in or in connection with buildings, so far as affected by alterations or extensions of buildings[75], or new, altered or extended services, fittings or equipment in or in connection with buildings[76];

(D) the whole of a building, together with any services, fittings or equipment provided in or in connection with it, in respect of which there are or are proposed to be carried out any operations that[77] constitute the construction of a building for these purposes[78];

(E) buildings or parts of buildings, together with any services, fittings or equipment provided in or in connection with them, in cases where the purposes for which or the manner or circumstances in which a building or part of a building is used change or changes in a way that constitutes a material change of use[79] of the building or part within the meaning of the expression 'material change of use' as defined for these purposes by building regulations[80];

(F) buildings or parts of buildings, together with any services, fittings or equipment provided in or in connection with them, in cases where the persons in occupation of a building or part of a building change in prescribed circumstances[81].

Subject to certain exceptions[82], building regulations do not apply to or in connection with buildings erected before the date on which the regulations come into force[83]The following building regulations may, however, be made to apply to or in connection with buildings erected before the date on which the regulations come into force:

(I) regulations falling within heads (A) to (E) above[84];

(II) regulations made with respect to the demolition of buildings[85];

(III) regulations made with respect to the use of materials or components (including surface finishes) that (in whole or in part) have been produced from, or incorporate, recycled items[86];

(IV) regulations made with respect to the re-use of materials or components (including surface finishes)[87];

(V) regulations which are framed by reference to a change in the occupants of a building (or part)[88], and either made for the purpose of furthering the conservation of fuel and power[89] or made (otherwise than for that purpose) with respect to measures calculated to secure, or to contribute to, the prevention or reduction of emissions (whether or not from the building in question) of smoke, gases, vapours or fumes[90].

The provision that may be made by building regulations includes provision imposing on a person carrying out work of any type in relation to a building (whenever erected), or in relation to any service, fitting or equipment provided in or in connection with a building (whenever erected) a requirement to do things for the purpose of furthering the conservation of fuel and power or a requirement to do things (otherwise than for that purpose) with respect to measures calculated to secure, or to contribute to, the prevention or reduction of emissions (whether or not from the building in question) of smoke, gases, vapours or fumes[91]. The provision that may be made by building regulations also includes provision imposing on a person carrying out work of any type in relation to a building (whenever erected), or in relation to any service, fitting or equipment provided in or in connection with a building (whenever erected), a requirement to do things for the purpose of securing the health, safety, welfare and convenience of persons in or about buildings and of others who may be affected by buildings or matters connected with buildings, in so far as it relates to the resistance or resilience of buildings in respect of flooding[92]. In both these cases[93], the things which may be required to be done are things to be done in relation to the work in question (as well as other things if they are to be done in relation to the building in question or to any service, fitting or equipment provided in or in connection with that building)[94].

Building regulations may authorise local authorities to fix by means of schemes and to recover such charges for or in connection with the performance of functions of theirs relating to building regulations as they may determine in accordance with principles prescribed by the regulations[95]. Building regulations may provide for a provision of them to apply generally, or in a particular area, make different provision for different areas and generally different provision for different circumstances or cases, and include such supplemental and incidental provisions as appear to the appropriate national authority expedient[96].

As from a day to be appointed[97], if building regulations impose a requirement in relation to a building as respects its contribution to or effect on emissions of carbon dioxide (whether or not the requirement relates to emissions from the building itself), the regulations may make provision for a person to whom the requirement applies to meet it (in whole or in part) by taking action[98] otherwise than in relation to the building. by taking action otherwise than in relation to the building[99].

Provision made[100]for the use of certificates as evidence of compliance with building regulations[101]may include provision:

(AA)   for the creation and maintenance of a register for keeping track of the use of certificates for that purpose[102];

(BB)   about the administration of the register[103];

(CC)   for charges to be imposed in connection with the registration of any matter in the register or for the disclosure of information held in the register[104].

If building regulations make provision for the creation and maintenance of a register, building regulations must make provision for the register to be administered by, or by a person acting on behalf of, the Secretary of State or the Welsh Ministers[105].

Building regulations made by the Welsh Ministers may make provision for the use, in relation to action taken in respect of a building in Wales, of a register administered by, or by a person acting on behalf of, the Secretary of State[106].

Building regulations made by the Secretary of State may make provision about the use of such a register for that purpose[107].

Building regulations may make provision for the creation and maintenance of a fund[108] including provision about:

(AA)   the administration of such a fund[109];

(BB)   the purposes for which proceeds from such a fund may be used[110].

Building regulations may make provision about the calculation of payments to be made into a fund[111]:

(AA) the calculation of payments to be made into a fund[111];

(BB) the maximum payment which may be required to be made into such a fund in respect of a building[112].

Building regulations made by the Welsh Ministers may make provision for a payment or payments in respect of a building in Wales to be made to a fund administered by, or by a person acting on behalf of, the Secretary of State[113].

Building regulations made by the Secretary of State may make provision about the use of such a fund for that purpose[114].

1   As to the meaning of 'building regulations' see PARA 7. In exercise of this statutory power the Building Regulations 2010, SI 2010/2214, and the Building (Approved Inspectors etc) Regulations 2010, SI 2010/2215, have been made. The Building Regulations 2010, SI 2010/2214, revoke and replace the Building Regulations 2000, SI 2000/2531: see the Building Regulations 2010, SI 2010/2214, Sch 5 (which lists all the regulations revoked and the extent of revocation). The Building (Approved Inspectors etc) Regulations 2010, SI 2010/2215, revoke and replace the Building (Approved Inspectors etc) Regulations 2000, SI 2010/2532: see the Building (Approved Inspectors etc) Regulations 2010, SI 2010/2215, Sch 8 (which lists all the regulations revoked and the extent of revocation).

2   Ie prescribed by building regulations: see the Building Act 1984 s 126.

3   For the purposes of the Building Act 1984 Pt I (ss 1–46) and any other enactment (whether or not contained in the Building Act 1984) that relates to building regulations, or that mentions 'buildings' or 'a building' in a context from which it appears that those expressions are intended to have the same meaning there as in Pt I, references to the construction or erection of a building include references to:

(1)   the carrying out of such operations (whether for the construction of a building, the roofing over of an open space between walls or buildings, or otherwise) as may be designated in building regulations as operations falling to be treated for those purposes as the construction or erection of a building (s 123(1)(i)); and

(2)   the conversion of a movable object into what is by virtue of s 121(1), (2) (see PARA 6) a building (s 123(1)(ii)).

'Construct' and 'erect' are to be construed accordingly: s 123(1). As to the meaning of 'enactment' see PARA 6 note 2.

4   Building Act 1984 s 1(3), Sch 1 para 1(a).

5   Ie the Secretary of State or, where statutory functions have been transferred in relation to Wales, the Welsh Ministers: see PARA 5.

6   Building Act 1984 Sch 1 para 1(b).

7   Building Act 1984 Sch 1 para 2(a). As to the form of notices and certificates see PARA 135. For the authentication and service of notices and certificates see PARAS 136–137.

8   See *Cynat Products Ltd v Landbuild (Investment and Property) Ltd* [1984] 3 All ER 513. 'Plans' includes drawings of any other description, and also specifications or other information in any form: Building Act 1984 s 126.

9   Building Act 1984 Sch 1 para 2(b).

10 As to the meaning of 'local authority' see PARA 1 note 12.

11 Building Act 1984 Sch 1 para 2(c).

12 Building Act 1984 Sch 1 para 2(d).

13 Building Act 1984 Sch 1 para 2(e).

14 As to the meaning of 'approved inspector' see PARA 72.

15 Building Act 1984 Sch 1 para 3. The requirement of consultation is expressly saved where a Crown authority exercises its power to dispense with or relax requirements of building regulations: see s 44(5); and PARA 15.

16 See note 7.

17 Building Act 1984 Sch 1 para 4(a).

18 Building Act 1984 Sch 1 para 4(b).

19 Building Act 1984 Sch 1 para 4(c)(i).

20 Building Act 1984 Sch 1 para 4(c)(ii).

21 Building Act 1984 Sch 1 para 4(c)(iii).

22 Building Act 1984 Sch 1 para 4A(1)(a) (Sch 1 para 4A added by the Sustainable and Secure Buildings Act 2004 s 8).

23 Building Act 1984 Sch 1 para 4A(1)(b) (as added: see note 22).

24 Building Act 1984 Sch 1 para 4A(1)(c) (as added: see note 22).

25 Building Act 1984 Sch 1 para 4A(1)(d) (as added: see note 22).

26 Building Act 1984 Sch 1 para 4A(2) (as added: see note 22).

27 Building Act 1984 Sch 1 para 4B(1) (Sch 1 para 4B added by the Sustainable and Secure Buildings Act 2004 s 9).

28 Building Act 1984 Sch 1 para 4B(2) (as added: see note 27). Building regulations may require appointments to be made within such periods or at such times as may be prescribed (Sch 1 para 4B(3)(a) (as so added)) and may make provision in relation to the termination of a person's appointment and the replacement of an appointed person (Sch 1 para 4B(3)(b) (as so added)).

29 Building Act 1984 Sch 1 para 4B(4)(a) (as added: see note 27).

30 Building Act 1984 Sch 1 para 4B(4)(b) (as added: see note 27).

31 Building Act 1984 Sch 1 para 4B(5) (as added: see note 27).

32 As to the meaning of 'functions' see PARA 3 note 19.

33 Building Act 1984 Sch 1 para 5(1). The wording of what is now Sch 1 para 5(1) is in the form of a power, as distinct from a duty, to charge the prescribed fees, but in exercising the discretion whether to levy such charges an authority must act responsibly and on relevant considerations: see *Ayr Harbour Trustees v Oswald* (1883) 8 App Cas 623, HL; *Dutton v Bognor Regis UDC* [1972] 1 QB 373, sub nom *Dutton v Bognor Regis United Building Co Ltd* [1972] 1 All ER 462, CA; *Anns v Merton London Borough Council* [1978] AC 728 at 754, 755, [1977] 2 All ER 492 at 501, HL, per Lord Wilberforce (*Dutton v Bognor Regis UDC* above; and *Anns v Merton London Borough Council* overruled on another point by *Murphy v Brentwood District Council* [1991] 1 AC 398, [1990] 2 All ER 908, HL).

The appropriate national authority may by order repeal the Building Act 1984 Sch 1 para 5: see s 120(1), Sch 1 para 5(2).

34 As to the meaning of 'modifications' see PARA 3 note 21.

35 Building Act 1984 Sch 1 para 6. Powers exercisable under Sch 1 para 6 otherwise than by a local authority are expressly excluded from the power of a Crown authority to dispense with or relax requirements of building regulations: see s 44(5); and PARA 15.

36 Ie without prejudice to the generality of the Building Act 1984 s 1(1): see PARA 7.

37 Ie for any of the purposes mentioned in the Building Act 1984 s 1(1): see PARA 7.

38 Building Act 1984 Sch 1 para 7(a)(i).

39 Building Act 1984 Sch 1 para 7(a)(ii) (amended by the Sustainable and Secure Buildings Act 2004 s 3).

40 Building Act 1984 Sch 1 para 7(a)(iii)(a).

41 Building Act 1984 Sch 1 para 7(a)(iii)(b).

42 Building Act 1984 Sch 1 para 7(a)(iii)(c).

43 Building Act 1984 Sch 1 para 7(a)(iv)(a).

44 Building Act 1984 Sch 1 para 7(a)(iv)(b).

45 Building Act 1984 Sch 1 para 7(a)(iv)(c).

46 Building Act 1984 Sch 1 para 7(a)(v).

47 Building Act 1984 Sch 1 para 7(a)(vi).

48 Building Act 1984 Sch 1 para 7(a)(vii).

49 Building Act 1984 Sch 1 para 7(a)(viii).

50 Building Act 1984 Sch 1 para 7(a)(ix) (amended by the Sustainable and Secure Buildings Act 2004 s 3).

51 Building Act 1984 Sch 1 para 7(a)(x).

52 'Cesspool' includes a settlement tank or other tank for the reception or disposal of foul matter from buildings: Building Act 1984 s 126.

53 Building Act 1984 Sch 1 para 7(a)(xi).

54 Building Act 1984 Sch 1 para 7(a)(xii).

55 Building Act 1984 Sch 1 para 7(a)(xiii).

56 Building Act 1984 Sch 1 para 7(a)(xiv) (amended by the Sustainable and Secure Buildings Act 2004 s 3).

57 Building Act 1984 Sch 1 para 7(a)(xv).

58 Building Act 1984 Sch 1 para 7(a)(xvi).

59 Building Act 1984 Sch 1 para 7(a)(xvii).

60 Building Act 1984 Sch 1 para 7(a)(xviii).

61 Building Act 1984 Sch 1 para 7(a)(xix).

62 Building Act 1984 Sch 1 para 7(a)(xx).

63 Building Act 1984 Sch 1 para 7(a)(xxi).

64 Building Act 1984 Sch 1 para 7(a)(xxii).

65 Building Act 1984 Sch 1 para 7(a)(xxiia) (Sch 1 para 7(a)(xxiia)–(xiid) added by the Sustainable and Secure Buildings Act 2004 s 3).

66 Building Act 1984 Sch 1 para 7(a)(xxiib) (as added: see note 65).
67 Building Act 1984 Sch 1 para 7(a)(xxiic) (as added: see note 65).
68 Building Act 1984 Sch 1 para 7(a)(xxiid) (as added: see note 65).
69 Building Act 1984 Sch 1 para 7(a)(xxiie) (added by the Climate Change and Sustainable Energy Act 2006 s 11).
70 Building Act 1984 Sch 1 para 7(a)(xxiii).
71 Building Act 1984 Sch 1 para 7(b).
72 Building Act 1984 Sch 1 para 7(c).
73 Building Act 1984 Sch 1 para 8(1)(a).
74 Building Act 1984 Sch 1 para 8(1)(b).
75 Building Act 1984 Sch 1 para 8(1)(c)(i).
76 Building Act 1984 Sch 1 para 8(1)(c)(ii).
77 Ie by virtue of the Building Act 1984 s 123(1): see note 3.
78 Building Act 1984 Sch 1 para 8(1)(d).
79 As to the meaning of 'material change of use' see PARA 11.
80 Building Act 1984 Sch 1 para 8(1)(e).
81 Building Act 1984 Sch 1 para 8(1)(f) (added by the Sustainable and Secure Buildings Act 2004 s 3).
82 Ie subject to the Building Act 1984 Sch 1 para 8(3)–(6) (see the text and notes 84–94), to ss 2(2), 2A (see PARA 12) and as from a day to be appointed, Sch 1 para 7A(12) (see note 98): Sch 1 para 8(2) (prospectively amended by the Infrastructure Act 2015 s 37). At the date at which this volume states the law no such day had been appointed. So much of Sch 1 para 8 as restricts the application of building regulations does not apply to building regulations made under s 2(2): see s 2(2); and PARA 12. Schedule 1 para 8(2) does not impose any restriction on the building regulations that may be made by virtue of s 2A: see s 2A(5); and PARA 12.
83 Building Act 1984 Sch 1 para 8(2) (substituted by the Sustainable and Secure Buildings Act 2004 s 3).
84 Building Act 1984 Sch 1 para 8(3)(a) (Sch 1 para 8(3)–(5), (6) added by the Sustainable and Secure Buildings Act 2004 s 3).
85 Building Act 1984 Sch 1 para 8(3)(b) (as added: see note 84).
86 Building Act 1984 Sch 1 para 8(3)(c) (as added: see note 84).
87 Building Act 1984 Sch 1 para 8(3)(d) (as added: see note 84).
88 Ie in accordance with the Building Act 1984 Sch 1 para 8(1)(f): see the text and note 81.
89 Ie for the purpose mentioned in the Building Act 1984 s 1(1)(b): see PARA 7.
90 Building Act 1984 Sch 1 para 8(3)(e), (4) (as added: see note 84).
91 Building Act 1984 Sch 1 para 8(5) (as added: see note 84).
92 Building Act 1984 Sch 1 para 8(5A) (added by the Flood and Water Management Act 2010 s 40(1)).
93 Ie the things whose doing may be required by virtue of the Building Act 1984 Sch 1 para 8(5) or Sch 1 para 8(5A): see the text and notes 91–92.
94 Building Act 1984 Sch 1 para 8(6) (as added (see note 84); and amended by the Flood and Water Management Act 2010 s 40(2)).
95 Building Act 1984 Sch 1 para 9.
96 Building Act 1984 Sch 1 para 10. Building regulations may repeal or modify:
    (1)   any of the following provisions of the Building Act 1984: s 15 (see PARA 55), s 19 (see PARA 34), ss 21–29 (see PARAS 36–40), ss 41, 59–87 (see PARA 100 et seq), ss 91–119 (see PARA 70 et seq), s 123(2) (see PARA 109) and s 126 (except as to the definitions of 'contravention', 'local authority' (as it applies for the purposes of Pt I and Pt II, 'modifications', 'plans', 'prescribed' and 'substantive requirements'), and Sch 3 paras 1, 5–14 (see PARA 3); or
    (2)   any provision of an Act passed before 20 September 1974; or
    (3)   any provision of a local Act passed before the day on which the Deregulation and Contracting Out Act 1994 was passed (ie 3 November 1994),
if it appears to the appropriate national authority that it is inconsistent with, or is unnecessary or requires alteration in consequence of, any provision contained in or made under any enactment relating to building regulations: Building Act 1984 Sch 1 para 11(1) (amended by the Deregulation and Contracting Out Act 1994 s 32(1); and SI 1986/452). Building regulations may repeal or alter the Local Government (Miscellaneous Provisions) Act 1976 s 12(1) (byelaws as to supply of heat) or any provision of byelaws in force by virtue of it, and make any modification of s 12(2) that the appropriate national authority considers is appropriate in consequence of the repeal or alteration: Building Act 1984 Sch 1 para 11(2).

In the exercise of the power under Sch 1 paras 10, 11, the Building Repeal of Provisions of Local Acts) Regulations 2012, SI 2012/3124 was made.

97   As from a day to be appointed, the Building Act 1984 Sch 1 para 7A is added by the Infrastructure Act 2015 s 37. At the date at which this volume states the law no such day had been appointed.

98   Such action may include:

   (1)   doing things which consist of, or cause or contribute, directly or indirectly to reductions in emissions of carbon dioxide or the removal of carbon dioxide from the atmosphere (Building Act 1984 Sch 1 para 7A(3)(a) (as prospectively added: see note 97));

   (2)   agreeing with another person that the person will do things within head (1) (Building Act 1984 Sch 1 para 7A(3)(b) (as so prospectively added));

   (3)   making a payment or payments to a fund which is administered by, or by a person acting on behalf of, the Secretary of State or the Welsh Ministers and the proceeds of which are used to pay (directly or indirectly) for activities within head (1) (Sch 1 para 7A(3)(c) (as so prospectively added)).

Schedule 1 para 8(2) (see text and notes 82, 83), does not prevent building regulations from providing for action within Sch 1 para 7A(3) to be taken in relation to a building erected before the date on which the regulations come into force: Sch 1 para 7A(12) (as so prospectively added).

99   Building Act 1984 Sch 1 para 7A(1), (2) (as prospectively added: see note 97).

100   Ie under the Building Act 1984 Sch 1 para 4A (see text and notes 22–26).

101   Ie by virtue of action within the Building Act 1984 Sch 1 para 7A(3) (see note 98).

102   Building Act 1984 Sch 1 para 7A(4)(a) (as prospectively added: see note 97).

103   Building Act 1984 Sch 1 para 7A(4)(b) (as prospectively added: see note 97).

104   Building Act 1984 Sch 1 para 7A(4)(c) (as prospectively added: see note 97).

105   Building Act 1984 Sch 1 para 7A(5) (as prospectively added: see note 97).

106   Building Act 1984 Sch 1 para 7A(6) (as prospectively added: see note 97).

107   Building Act 1984 Sch 1 para 7A(7) (as prospectively added: see note 97).

108   Ie of a kind referred to in the Building Act 1984 Sch 1 para 7A(3)(c): see note 98.

109   Building Act 1984 Sch 1 para 7A(8)(a) (as prospectively added: see note 97).

110   Building Act 1984 Sch 1 para 7A(8)(b) (as prospectively added: see note 97).

111   Building Act 1984 Sch 1 para 7A(9)(a) (as prospectively added: see note 97). The text refers to a fund of a kind referred to in the Building Act 1984 Sch 1 para 7A(3)(c): see note 98.

111   Building Act 1984 Sch 1 para 7A(9)(a) (as prospectively added: see note 97). The text refers to a fund of a kind referred to in the Building Act 1984 Sch 1 para 7A(3)(c): see note 98.

112   Building Act 1984 Sch 1 para 7A(9)(b) (as prospectively added: see note 97).

113   Building Act 1984 Sch 1 para 7A(10) (as prospectively added: see note 97).

114   Building Act 1984 Sch 1 para 7A(11) (as prospectively added: see note 97).

10.   Requirements relating to building work.

The current building regulations[1] impose less detailed control than earlier regulations. Detail is now to be found in the documents containing practical guidance which are approved by the appropriate national authority[2].

'Building work' means:

   (1)   the erection or extension of a building[3];

   (2)   the provision or extension of a controlled service or fitting[4] in connection with a building[5];

   (3)   the material alteration[6] of a building, or a controlled service or fitting[7];

   (4)   work required[8] in relation to a material change of use[9];

   (5)   the insertion of insulating material into the cavity wall of a building[10];

   (6)   work involving the underpinning of a building[11];

   (7)   work required[12] to ensure that the building complies with requirements relating to a change of energy status[13];

   (8)   work required[14] to ensure that the thermal element complies with relevant requirements[15];

   (9)   work required[16] to ensure that the building complies with the requirements relating to energy performance[17].

Building work must be carried out so that it complies with the applicable requirements[18] mentioned in heads (a) to (n) below, and so that the method of complying with any such requirement does not result in the failure of any part of the building work to comply with another such requirement[19]. The applicable requirements are those relating to:

(a)   structure (that is loading, ground movement and disproportionate collapse)[20];

(b)   fire safety (that is means of warning and escape, internal fire spread (linings and structure), external fire spread and access and facilities for the fire service)[21];

(c)   site preparation and resistance to contaminants and moisture[22];

(d)   toxic substances (that is cavity insulation)[23];

(e)   resistance to the passage of sound[24];

(f)   ventilation[25];

(g)   sanitation, hot water safety and water efficiency (that is cold water supply, water efficiency, hot water supply and systems, sanitary conveniences and washing facilities, bathrooms and kitchen and food preparation areas)[26];

(h)   drainage and waste disposal (that is foul water drainage, wastewater treatment systems and cesspools, rainwater drainage, building over sewers, separate systems of drainage and solid waste storage)[27];

(i)   combustion appliances and fuel storage systems (that is air supply, the discharge of products of combustion, warning of the release of carbon monoxide, the protection of buildings, the provision of information, the protection of liquid fuel storage systems and protection against pollution)[28];

(j)   protection from falling, collision and impact (that is stairs, ladders and ramps, protection from falling, vehicle barriers and loading bays, protection from collision with open windows, etc, manifestation of glazing, safe opening and closing of windows etc, safe access for cleaning windows etc and protection against impact from and trapping by doors)[29];

(k)   conservation of fuel and power[30];

(l)   access to and use of buildings (including access to and use of buildings other than dwellings[31], access to extensions to buildings other than dwellings, sanitary conveniences in dwellings and in extensions to buildings other than dwellings, access to and use of dwellings)[32];

(m)   glazing (that is protection against impact, the manifestation of glazing, the safe opening and closing of windows, etc and safe access for cleaning windows, etc)[33];

(n)   electrical safety (that is design and installation)[34];

(o)   security (that is unauthorised access)[35]; and

(p)   physical infrastructure for high speed electronic communications network[36] (that is in-building physical infrastructure)[37]

However, the requirements mentioned in heads (a) to (d)[38], and (f) to (j)[39], and heads (m)[40] and (n)[41] above (except for the requirements relating to water efficiency[42], wastewater treatment systems and cesspools[43], and protection against pollution[44]) do not require anything to be done except for the purpose of securing reasonable standards of health and safety for persons in or about buildings and others who may be affected by buildings, or matters connected with buildings[45].

Where building work is of a kind described in head (7), (8) or (9) above[46] and the carrying out of that work does not constitute a material alteration, that work need only comply with the applicable requirements relating to the conservation of fuel and power in head (k) above[47].

Building work must be carried out with adequate and proper materials which are appropriate for the circumstances in which they are used, are adequately mixed and prepared, and are applied, used or fixed so as adequately to perform the functions for which they are designed, and in a workmanlike manner[48]. The local authority may take such samples of the material to be used in the carrying out of building work as may be necessary to enable it to ascertain whether such materials comply with the provisions of the Building Regulations 2010[49].

The requirements of building regulations are subject to exemptions in respect of certain buildings, public bodies and work[50].

1 See the Building Regulations 2010, SI 2010/2214. As to the power to make building regulations see PARA 7.
2 Ie the Secretary of State or, where statutory functions have been transferred in relation to Wales, the Welsh Ministers: see PARA 5. As to approval documents see PARA 23.
3 Building Regulations 2010, SI 2010/2214, reg 3(1)(a). For these purposes, 'building' means any permanent or temporary building but not any other kind of structure or erection, and a reference to a building includes a reference to part of a building: reg 2(1).
4 For these purposes, 'controlled service or fitting' means a service or fitting in relation to which the Building Regulations 2010, SI 2010/2214, Sch 1 Pts G, H, J, L or P imposes a requirement: reg 2(1).
5 Building Regulations 2010, SI 2010/2214, reg 3(1)(b).
6 An alteration is material if the work, or any part of it, would at any stage result in: (1) a building or controlled service or fitting not complying with a relevant requirement where previously it did; or (2) a building or controlled service or fitting which before the work commenced did not comply with a relevant requirement, being more unsatisfactory in relation to such a requirement: Building Regulations 2010, SI 2010/2214, reg 3(2). For the purposes of reg 3(2), 'relevant requirement' means any of the following requirements of Sch 1: Sch 1 Pt A (structure), Sch 1 Pt B para B1 (means of warning and escape), Sch 1 Pt B para B3 (internal fire spread; structure), Sch 1 Pt B para B4 (external fire spread), Sch 1 Pt B para B5 (access and facilities for the fire service), Sch 1 Pt M (access and facilities for disabled people): reg 3(3).
7 Building Regulations 2010, SI 2010/2214, reg 3(1)(c).
8 Ie by the Building Regulations 2010, SI 2010/2214, reg 6: see PARA 11.
9 Building Regulations 2010, SI 2010/2214, reg 3(1)(d).
10 Building Regulations 2010, SI 2010/2214, reg 3(1)(e).
11 Building Regulations 2010, SI 2010/2214, reg 3(1)(f).
12 Ie required by the Building Regulations 2010, SI 2010/2214, reg 22: see PARA 45.
13 Building Regulations 2010, SI 2010/2214, reg 3(1)(g).
14 Ie required by the Building Regulations 2010, SI 2010/2214, reg 23: see PARA 45.
15 Building Regulations 2010, SI 2010/2214, reg 3(1)(h). 'Thermal element' means a wall, floor or roof (but does not include windows, doors, roof windows or roof-lights) which separates a thermally conditioned part of the building (the 'conditioned space') from: (1) the external environment (including the ground); or (2) in the case of floors and walls, another part of the building which is (a) unconditioned; (b) an extension falling within Sch 2 Class 7 (see PARA 16); or (c) conditioned to a different temperature (but only in the case of a building which is not a dwelling, where the other part of the building is used for a purpose which is not similar or identical to the purpose for which the conditioned space is used), and includes all parts of the element between the surface bounding the conditioned space and the external environment or other part of the building as the case may be: reg 2(3), (4).
16 Ie required by the Building Regulations 2010, SI 2010/2214, reg 28: see PARA 45.
17 Building Regulations 2010, SI 2010/2214, reg 3(1)(i).
18 Ie the applicable requirements contained in the Building Regulations 2010, SI 2010/2214, Sch 1: see the text and notes 20–34. The following provisions apply to any building in England and to an excepted energy building in Wales (see PARA 5): Building Regulations &c (Amendment) Regulations 2015, SI 2015/767, reg 1. The applicable requirements contained in the Building Regulations 2010, SI 2010/2214, Sch 1 are:
    (1)   the applicable requirements contained in Sch 1 that apply in all cases, subject to reg 4(1C) (reg 4(1A)(a) (reg 4(1A)–(1D) added by SI 2015/767)); and

(2)   any applicable requirement contained in the Building Regulations 2010, SI 2010/2214, Sch 1, and described in the first column of Sch 1 as an optional requirement, that applies in relation to the building work in question by virtue of reg 4(1B), (1C), (1D) (reg 4(1A)(b) (as so added)).

An optional requirement as described in head (2) applies to building work in any case where the planning permission under which the building work is carried out specifies that optional requirement by reference to the Building Regulations 2010, SI 2010/2214 and makes it a condition that the requirement must be complied with: reg 4(1B) (as so added). An optional requirement applies in substitution for a requirement of Sch 1 to the extent that the terms of the optional requirement in the second column of Sch 1 so provide: reg 4(1C) (as so added). An optional requirement applies, and another optional requirement will not apply, to the extent that the terms of the first-mentioned optional requirement in the second column of Sch 1 so provide: reg 4(1D) (as so added).

The local authority may make such tests of any building work as may be necessary to establish whether it complies with any of the applicable requirements contained in Sch 1: see reg 45. The Building Regulations 2010, SI 2010/2214, reg 45 does not apply in respect of any work specified in an initial notice, an amendment notice or a public body's notice, which is in force: reg 19(1). Regulation 45 does not apply in respect of any work in relation to which a final certificate or a public body's final certificate has been accepted by the local authority: reg 19(2). As to initial notices, amendment notices, public bodies' notices, final certificates and public bodies' final certificates see PARA 72 et seq.

19 Ie except as may be provided for in the Building Regulations 2010, SI 2010/2214, reg 4(1C), (1D) (see note 18): reg 4(1) (amended by SI 2015/767; and SI 2018/558).

Where certain building work is carried out by a specified person (as to the types of work and the specified persons see the Building Regulations 2010, SI 2010/2214, Sch 3; and PARA 25), the local authority is authorised to accept, as evidence that the requirements of regs 4, 7 (see the text to note 45) have been satisfied, a certificate to that effect by the person carrying out the building work: regs 20(1), (2). The person carrying out the building work must, not more than 30 days after completion of the work (1) give to the occupier a copy of the certificate; and (2) give to the local authority notice to that effect, or the certificate: reg 20(3). However, reg 20(3) does not apply where a person carries out any building work described in Sch 4 (see PARA 25): reg 20(4). A local authority must store in a retrievable form copies of the notices and certificates given to it in accordance with head (2): reg 20(3A) (reg 20(3A) (reg 20(3A)–(3D), (5), (6) added in relation to England by SI 2012/3119; and in relation to Wales by SI 2013/747). If the whole or part of the work was paid for using a green deal plan, the person carrying out the work must, include in the certificate referred to in the Building Regulations 2010, SI 2010/2214, reg 20(2) and in the notice given to the local authority referred to in head (1), a statement to that effect: reg 20(3B) (as so added). Such a statement that relates to a part of the work must specify which part was paid for using the green deal plan: reg 20(3C) (as so added; and repealed in relation to England by SI 2014/579). As to the meaning of 'green deal plan' see the Energy Act 2011 s 1; and HOUSING vol 56 (2017) PARA 889. A certificate given in accordance with the Building Regulations 2010, SI 2010/2214, reg 20 is evidence (but not conclusive evidence) that the requirements specified in the certificate have been complied with, and in relation to a building in Wales, the certificate must contain this wording: reg 20(5) (as so added; and amended by SI 2018/558). The certificate must include a statement describing its evidentiary effect, in terms substantially the same as reg 20(5): reg 20(6) (as so added).

Where certain building work is inspected by a third party certifier (as to the types of work and the third party certifier see the Building Regulations 2010, SI 2010/2214, Sch 3A; and PARA 25), the local authority is authorised to accept, as evidence that the requirements of regs 4, 7 (see the text to note 45) have been satisfied, a certificate to that effect by the third party certifier: regs 20A(1), (2) (reg 20A added by SI 2014/579; and SI 2018/558). The person carrying out the building work must, not more than 7 days after the completion of the work, notify the third party certifier that the work has been completed: Building Regulations 2010, SI 2010/2214, reg 20A(3) (as so added). Where the third party certifier, having taken all reasonable steps to ascertain that it is the case, is satisfied within the limits of professional skill and care that the requirements of regs 4, 7 have been complied with, the third party certifier must, not more than 30 days after receiving notification of completion of the work under reg 20A(3) (a) give the occupier a copy of the certificate; (b) give to the local authority notice to that effect, or the certificate: reg 20A(4) (as so added). If the third party certifier is unable to certify that the requirements of regs 4, 7 have been complied with and therefore cannot provide the certificate, the third party certifier must notify the local authority to that effect: reg 20A(5) (as so added). A certificate given in accordance with reg 20A is evidence (but not conclusive evidence) that the requirements specified in the certificate have been complied with: reg 20A(6) (as so added). The certificate must include a statement describing its evidentiary effect, in terms substantially the same as reg 20A(6): reg 20A(7) (as so added).

The Building Regulations 2010, SI 2010/2214, reg 20 does not apply in respect of any work specified in an initial notice, an amendment notice or a public body's notice, which is in force: reg 19(1). However, in relation to building work which is the subject of an initial notice (as to which see PARA 74 et seq), regs 20, 20A apply as if references to the local authority were references to the approved inspector: see the Building (Approved Inspectors etc) Regulations 2010, SI 2010/2215, reg 20(1); and PARA 87.

20 See the Building Regulations 2010, SI 2010/2214, Sch 1 Pt A.

21 See the Building Regulations 2010, SI 2010/2214, Sch 1 Pt B.

22 See the Building Regulations 2010, SI 2010/2214, Sch 1 Pt C.

23 See the Building Regulations 2010, SI 2010/2214, Sch 1 Pt D.

24 See the Building Regulations 2010, SI 2010/2214, Sch 1 Pt E. Where a person carries out building work in relation to which Sch 1 para El (protection against sound from other parts of the building and adjoining buildings) imposes a requirement, or carries out work which is required to be carried out to a building to ensure that it complies with Sch 1 para E1 by virtue of reg 6(1)(f) or 6(2)(b) (see PARA 11), the person must: (1) ensure that appropriate sound insulation testing is carried out in accordance with a procedure approved by the appropriate national authority; and (2) give a copy of the results of that testing to the local authority: see reg 41; and PARA 31. Regulation 41 does not apply in respect of any work specified in an initial notice, an amendment notice or a public body's notice, which is in force: reg 19(1).

25 See the Building Regulations 2010, SI 2010/2214, Sch 1 Pt F. Where a person carries out building work to which Sch 1 para F1(1) (means of ventilation) applies, the person carrying out the work must, for the purpose of ensuring compliance with Sch 1 para F1(1): (1) ensure that testing of the mechanical ventilation air flow rate is carried out in accordance with a procedure approved by the appropriate national authority; and (2) give notice of the results of the testing to the local authority not later than five days after the final test is carried out: see reg 42. Regulation 42 does not apply in respect of any work specified in an initial notice, an amendment notice or a public body's notice, which is in force: reg 19(1).

Where Sch 1 para F1(1) imposes a requirement in relation to building work, the person carrying out the work must not later than five days after the work has been completed give sufficient information to the owner about the building's ventilation system and its maintenance requirements so that the ventilation system can be operated in such a manner as to provide adequate means of ventilation: reg 39.

Where Sch 1 para F1(2) (ventilation testing) imposes a requirement on building work (not including the provision or extension of any fixed system for mechanical ventilation or any associated controls where testing and adjustment is not possible), the person carrying out the work must, for the purpose of ensuring compliance with Sch 1 para F1(2), give to the local authority a notice confirming that the fixed building services have been commissioned in accordance with a procedure approved by the appropriate national authority: see reg 44. The notice must be given to the local authority not later than the date on which the notice required by reg 16(4) is required to be given (see PARA 28), or where that regulation does not apply, not more than 30 days after completion of the work: see reg 44. Regulation 44 does not apply in respect of any work specified in an initial notice, an amendment notice or a public body's notice, which is in force: reg 19(1). 'Fixed building services' means any part of, or any controls associated with: (1) fixed internal or external lighting systems, but does not include emergency escape lighting or specialist process lighting; or (2) fixed systems for heating, hot water, air conditioning or mechanical ventilation: reg 2.

Regulation 44 is designated as a provision to which the Building Act 1984 s 35 (penalty for contravening building regulations) (see PARA 61) does not apply: Building Regulations 2010, SI 2010/2214, reg 47 (substituted by SI 2012/3119; SI 2018/552; and SI 2018/558; amended by SI 2013/747; SI 2014/110; and SI 2014/579). Regulation 44 does not apply in respect of any work specified in an initial notice, an amendment notice or a public body's notice, which is in force: reg 19(1) (amended by SI 2012/3119; SI 2013/747; SI 2016/285; and SI 2016/611).

26 See the Building Regulations 2010, SI 2010/2214, Sch 1 Pt G (prospectively amended in relation to Wales by SI 2018/552).

27 See the Building Regulations 2010, SI 2010/2214, Sch 1 Pt H (amended by SI 2015/767; and further amended by SI 2018/558).

28 See the Building Regulations 2010, SI 2010/2214, Sch 1 Pt J.

29 See the Building Regulations 2010, SI 2010/2214, Sch 1 Pt K (substituted by SI 2012/3119; and SI 2018/558).

30 See the Building Regulations 2010, SI 2010/2214, Sch 1 Pt L. Where a person carries out building work to which Sch 1 para L1(a)(i) (limiting heat gains and losses through thermal elements and other parts of the building fabric) imposes a requirement, that person must, for the purpose of ensuring compliance with regs 26, 26A (see PARA 46), and Sch 1 para L1(a)(i): (1) ensure that pressure testing is carried out in such circumstances and in accordance with such procedures as are approved by the appropriate national authority; and (2) give notice of the results of the testing to the local authority no later than seven days after the final test is carried out: see reg 43 (amended SI 2012/3119; SI 2013/747; SI 2014/579; SI 2015/767; SI 2015/1486; and SI 2018/558). The Building Regulations 2010, SI 2010/2214, reg 43 does not apply in respect of any work specified in an initial notice, an amendment notice or a public body's notice, which is in force: reg 19(1).

Where Sch 1 para L1 imposes a requirement in relation to building work, the person carrying out the work must not later than five days after the work has been completed provide to the owner sufficient information about the building, the fixed building services and their maintenance requirements so that the building can be operated in such a manner as to use no more fuel and power than is reasonable in the circumstances: reg 40.

Where Sch 1 para F1(2) (ventilation testing) imposes a requirement on building work (not including the provision or extension of any fixed system for mechanical ventilation or any associated controls where testing and adjustment is not possible or would not affect the energy efficiency of that fixed building service), the person carrying out the work must, for the purpose of ensuring compliance with Sch 1 para L1(b) (providing energy efficient fixed building services etc), give to the local authority a notice confirming that the fixed building services have been commissioned in accordance with a procedure approved by the appropriate national authority: see reg 44. The notice must be given to the local authority not later than the date on which the notice required by reg 16(4) is required to be given (see PARA 28), or where that regulation does not apply, not more than 30 days after completion of the work: see reg 44. Regulation 44 does not apply in respect of any work specified in an initial notice, an amendment notice or a public body's notice, which is in force: reg 19(1).

31 'Dwelling' includes a dwelling house and a flat: Building Regulations 2010, SI 2010/2214, reg 2. 'Dwelling house' does not include a flat or a building containing a flat; and 'flat' means separate and self-contained premises constructed or adapted for use for residential purposes and forming part of a building from some other part of which it is divided horizontally: reg 2.

32 Building Regulations 2010, SI 2010/2214, Sch 1 Pt M (substituted by SI 2015/767; and SI 2018/558).

33 Building Regulations 2010, SI 2010/2214, Sch 1 Pt N (revoked in relation to England by SI 2015/767). As to applicable provisions for other buildings in Wales see the Building Regulations 2010, SI 2010/2214, Sch 1 Pt N (added by SI 2018/558).

34 Building Regulations 2010, SI 2010/2214, Sch 1 Pt P.

35 Building Regulations 2010, SI 2010/2214, Sch 1 Pt Q (added in relation to England by SI 2015/767; and prospectively added in relation to Wales by SI 2018/552))

36 For these purposes, 'high-speed electronic communications network' means an electronic communications network which is capable of delivering broadband access services at speeds of at least 30 Mbps: Building Regulations 2010, SI 2010/2214, reg 44C (reg 44A–44C added by SI 2016/361; SI 2016/490; and SI 2018/558).

37 Building Regulations 2010, SI 2010/2214, Sch 1 Pt R (added by SI 2016/361; and SI 2016/490). 'In-building physical infrastructure' means physical infrastructure or installations at the end-user's location, including elements under joint ownership, intended to host wired or wireless access networks, where such access networks are capable of delivering electronic communications services and connecting the building access point with the network termination point: reg 44C (as added: see note 36). 'Access point' means a physical point, located inside or outside the building, accessible to undertakings providing or authorised to provide public communications networks, where connection to the high-speed ready in-building physical infrastructure is made available; 'high-speed ready in-building physical infrastructure' means in-building physical infrastructure intended to host elements, or enable delivery, of high-speed electronic communications networks; 'network termination point' means a physical point at which an occupier is provided with access to high-speed electronic communications networks: reg 44C (as so added).

The requirements of Sch 1 para R1 apply (insofar as applicable to other buildings) also to: (1) educational buildings and buildings of statutory undertakers (notwithstanding the Building Act 1984 s 4(1)); (2) Crown buildings; and (3) building work carried out or proposed to be carried out by Crown authorities: Building Regulations 2010, SI 2010/2214, reg 44A(1) (as added: see note 36). As to the meaning of 'educational buildings and buildings of statutory undertakers' see PARA 47 note 2; definition applied by reg 44A(2) (as so added).

The requirements of Sch 1 para R1 do not apply to the following types of building or building work:

(a) buildings which are listed in accordance with the Planning (Listed Buildings and Conservation Areas) Act 1990 s 1 (see PLANNING vol 83 (2018) PARA 1181) or in a conservation area designated in accordance with s 69 (see PLANNING vol 83 (2018) PARA 1255), where compliance with Sch 1 para R1 would unacceptably alter their character or appearance (Building Regulations 2010, SI 2010/2214, reg 44B(a) (as so added));

(b) buildings occupied by the Ministry of Defence or the armed forces of the Crown or otherwise occupied for purposes connected to national security (reg 44B(b) (as so added));

(c) buildings situated in isolated areas where the prospect of high-speed connection is considered too remote to justify equipping the building with high-speed ready in-building physical infrastructure or an access point (reg 44B(c) (as so added));

(d) major renovation works in cases in which the cost of compliance with Sch 1 para R1 would be disproportionate to the benefit gained (reg 44B(d) (as so added)).

38 Ie the Building Regulations 2010, SI 2010/2214, Sch 1 Pts A–D.
39 Ie the Building Regulations 2010, SI 2010/2214, Sch 1 Pts F–K.
40 Ie the Building Regulations 2010, SI 2010/2214, Sch 1 Pt N (only applies in relation to a building in Wales: see note 33).
41 Ie the Building Regulations 2010, SI 2010/2214, Sch 1 Pt P.
42 Ie the Building Regulations 2010, SI 2010/2214, Sch 1 para G2.
43 Ie the Building Regulations 2010, SI 2010/2214, Sch 1 para H2.
44 Ie the Building Regulations 2010, SI 2010/2214, Sch 1 para J7.
45 Building Regulations 2010, SI 2010/2214, reg 8(amended by SI 2012/3119; and SI 2018/558).
46 Ie in the Building Regulations 2010, SI 2010/2214, reg 3(1)(g), (h) or (i).
47 Ie the requirements of the Building Regulations 2010, SI 2010/2214, Pt L: reg 4(2).
48 Building Regulations 2010, SI 2010/2214, reg 7. The local authority may make such tests of any building work as may be necessary to establish whether it complies with reg 7: see reg 45. The Building Regulations 2010, SI 2010/2214, reg 45 does not apply in respect of any work specified in an initial notice, an amendment notice or a public body's notice, which is in force: reg 19(1). Regulation 45 does not apply in respect of any work in relation to which a final certificate or a public body's final certificate has been accepted by the local authority: reg 19(2).
49 Building Regulations 2010, SI 2010/2214, reg 46. The text refers to the Building Regulations 2010, SI 2010/2214.
50 As to exempt buildings, public bodies and work see PARAS 16–17.

11. Requirements relating to a material change of use.

There is a material change of use where there is a change in the purposes for which or the circumstances in which a building[1] is used, so that after that change:

(1) the building is used as a dwelling[2], where previously it was not[3];

(2) the building contains a flat[4], where previously it did not[5];

(3) the building is used as an hotel or a boarding house, where previously it was not[6];

(4) the building is used as an institution[7], where previously it was not[8];

(5) the building is used as a public building[9], where previously it was not[10];

(6) the building is not exempt from building regulations by reason of it being controlled under other legislation, not frequented by people, a greenhouse or agricultural building, a temporary building, an ancillary building or a small detached building[11], where previously it was[12];

(7) the building, which contains at least one dwelling, contains a greater or lesser number of dwellings than it did previously[13];

(8) the building contains a room for residential purposes, where previously it did not[14];

(9) the building, which contains at least one room for residential purposes, contains a greater or lesser number of such rooms than it did previously[15]; or

(10) the building is used as a shop, where previously it was not[16].

Where there is a material change of use of the whole of a building, such work, if any, must be carried out as is necessary to ensure that the building complies with the applicable requirements[17]. The applicable requirements are those relating to:

(a)   in all cases, means of warning and escape, internal fire spread (linings and structure), external fire spread (roofs), access and facilities for the fire service, interstitial and surface condensation, ventilation, cold water supply, hot water supply and systems, sanitary conveniences and washing facilities, bathrooms, kitchens and food preparation areas, foul water drainage, solid waste storage, combustion appliances, conservation of fuel and power and electrical safety[18];

(b)   in the case of a material change of use described in heads (3) to (5) or head (6) above, structure[19];

(c)   in the case of a building exceeding 15 metres in height[20], external fire spread (walls)[21];

(d)   in the case of a material change of use described in head (1), (2), (3), (4), (7), (8) or (9) above[22] or, where the material change provides new residential accommodation, head (6) above[23], resistance to contaminants[24];

(e)   in the case of a material change of use described in head (1) above, resistance to moisture[25];

(f)   in the case of a material change of use described in head (1), (2), (3), (7), (8) or (9) above[26], resistance to the passage of sound[27];

(g)   in the case of a material change of use described in head (5) above[28], where the public building consists of or contains a school, acoustic conditions in schools[29];

(h)   in the case of a material change of use described in head (1) or (2) above[30], water efficiency and hot water supply and systems[31];

(i)   in the case of a material change of use described in head (3), (4), (5) or (10) above[32], access to and use of buildings other than dwellings[33].

(j)   in the case of a material change of use described in head (1), (2) or (7) above[34], security[35].

Where there is a material change of use of part only of a building, such work, if any, must be carried out as is necessary to ensure that:

(i)   that part complies in all cases with any applicable requirements referred to in head (a) above[36];

(ii)   in a case in which heads (b), (e), (f), (g) or (h) above apply, that part complies with the requirements referred to in the relevant head[37];

(iii)   in a case to which head (c) above applies, the whole building complies with the requirement referred to in that head[38];

(iv)   in a case to which head (i) above applies, that part and any sanitary conveniences provided in or in connection with that part comply with the requirements referred to in that head[39] and that the building complies with the requirement relating to access to the building[40] to the extent that reasonable provision is made to provide either suitable independent access to that part or suitable access through the building to that part[41]; and

(v)   in a case to which head (j) applies in respect of a material change of use described in heads (2) or (7), that part complies with the requirement referred to in head (j)[42].

1   As to the meaning of 'building' see PARA 10 note 3.
2   As to the meaning of 'dwelling' see PARA 10 note 31.

3 Building Regulations 2010, SI 2010/2214, reg 5(a).

4 As to the meaning of 'flat' see PARA 10 note 31.

5 Building Regulations 2010, SI 2010/2214, reg 5(b).

6 Building Regulations 2010, SI 2010/2214, reg 5(c).

7 For these purposes, 'institution' means an institution (whether described as a hospital, home, school or other similar establishment) which is used as living accommodation for, or for the treatment, care or maintenance of persons: (1) suffering from disabilities due to illness or old age or other physical or mental incapacity; or (2) under the age of five years, where such persons sleep on the premises: Building Regulations 2010, SI 2010/2214, reg 2(1).

8 Building Regulations 2010, SI 2010/2214, reg 5(d).

9 For these purposes, 'public building' means a building consisting of or containing: (1) a theatre, public library, hall or other place of public resort; (2) a school or other educational establishment not exempted from the operation of building regulations by virtue of the Building Act 1984 s 4(1)(a) (see PARA 16); or (3) a place of public worship: Building Regulations 2010, SI 2010/2214, reg 2(2). However, a building is not to be treated as a place of public resort because it is, or it contains, a shop, storehouse or warehouse, or is a dwelling to which members of the public are occasionally admitted: reg 2(2). 'Shop' includes premises: (a) used for the sale to members of the public of food or drink for consumption on or off the premises; (b) used for retail sales by auction to members of the public; (c) used by members of the public as a barber or hairdresser, or for the hiring of any item; and (d) where members of the public may take goods for repair or other treatment: reg 2(1).

10 Building Regulations 2010, SI 2010/2214, reg 5(e).

11 Ie the building is not a building described in the Building Regulations 2010, SI 2010/2214, Sch 2 Classes 1–6: see PARA 16.

12 Building Regulations 2010, SI 2010/2214, reg 5(f).

13 Building Regulations 2010, SI 2010/2214, reg 5(g).

14 Building Regulations 2010, SI 2010/2214, reg 5(h). 'Room for residential purposes' means a room, or a suite of rooms, which is not a dwelling house or a flat and which is used by one or more persons to live and sleep and includes a room in a hostel, an hotel, a boarding house, a hall of residence or a residential home, but does not include a room in a hospital, or other similar establishment, used for patient accommodation: reg 2(1). As to the meanings of 'dwelling house' and 'flat' see PARA 10 note 31.

15 Building Regulations 2010, SI 2010/2214, reg 5(i).

16 Building Regulations 2010, SI 2010/2214, reg 5(j).

17 Building Regulations 2010, SI 2010/2214, reg 6(1).

18 Building Regulations 2010, SI 2010/2214, reg 6(1)(a). The text refers to the requirements of the Building Regulations 2010, SI 2010/2214, Sch 1 paras B1–B3, B4(2), B5, C2(c), F1, G1, G3(1)–(3), G4–G6, H1, H6, J1–J4, L1, P1: see PARA 10.

19 Building Regulations 2010, SI 2010/2214, reg 6(1)(b). The text refers to the requirements of Sch 1 paras A1–A3: see PARA 10.

20 For these purposes, 'height' means the height of the building measured from the mean level of the ground adjoining the outside of the external walls of the building to the level of half the vertical height of the roof of the building, or to the top of the walls or of the parapet, if any, whichever is the higher: Building Regulations 2010, SI 2010/2214, reg 2(1).

21 Building Regulations 2010, SI 2010/2214, reg 6(1)(c). The text refers to the requirements of Sch 1 para B4(1): see PARA 10.

22 Ie as described in the Building Regulations 2010, SI 2010/2214, reg 5(a), (b), (c), (d), (g), (h), (i).

23 Ie as described in the Building Regulations 2010, SI 2010/2214, reg 5(f).

24 Building Regulations 2010, SI 2010/2214, reg 6(1)(d). The text refers to the requirements of Sch 1 para C1(2): see PARA 10.

25 Building Regulations 2010, SI 2010/2214, reg 6(1)(e). The text refers to the requirements of Sch 1 para C2: see PARA 10.

26 Ie as described in the Building Regulations 2010, SI 2010/2214, reg 5(a), (b), (c), (g), (h), (i).

27 Building Regulations 2010, SI 2010/2214, reg 6(1)(f). The text refers to the requirements of Sch 1 paras E1–E3: see PARA 10.

28 Ie as described in the Building Regulations 2010, SI 2010/2214, reg 5(e).

29 Building Regulations 2010, SI 2010/2214, reg 6(1)(g). The text refers to the requirements of Sch 1 para E4: see PARA 10.

30 Ie as described in the Building Regulations 2010, SI 2010/2214, reg 5(a) or 5(b).

31 Building Regulations 2010, SI 2010/2214, reg 6(1)(h). The text refers to the requirements of Sch 1 paras G2 and G3(4): see PARA 10.

32 Ie as described in the Building Regulations 2010, SI 2010/2214, reg 5(c), (d), (e) or (j).
33 Building Regulations 2010, SI 2010/2214, reg 6(1)(i) (substituted by SI 2015/767; and SI 2018/558). The text refers to the requirements of Sch 1 para M1.
34 Ie as described in the Building Regulations 2010, SI 2010/2214, reg 5(a), (b) or (g).
35 Building Regulations 2010, SI 2010/2214, reg 6(1)(j) (substituted by SI 2015/767; and amended by SI 2018/558). The text refers to the requirements of Sch 1 para Q1.
36 Building Regulations 2010, SI 2010/2214, reg 6(2)(a). The text refers to the requirements listed in note 18.
37 Building Regulations 2010, SI 2010/2214, reg 6(2)(b).
38 Building Regulations 2010, SI 2010/2214, reg 6(2)(c).
39 Building Regulations 2010, SI 2010/2214, reg 6(2)(d)(i).
40 Ie the requirement of the Building Regulations 2010, SI 2010/2214, Sch 1 para M1(a): see PARA 10.
41 Building Regulations 2010, SI 2010/2214, reg 6(2)(d)(ii).
42 Building Regulations 2010, SI 2010/2214, reg 6(2)(e) (added by SI 2015/767).

12. Continuing requirements.

Building regulations[1] may impose on owners[2] and occupiers of buildings to which building regulations are applicable such continuing requirements as the appropriate national authority[3] considers appropriate for securing, with respect to any designated provision of building regulations[4], that the purposes of that provision are not frustrated; but a continuing requirement so imposed does not apply in relation to a building unless a provision of building regulations so designated as one to which the requirement relates applies to that building[5]. Building regulations may impose on owners and occupiers of buildings of a prescribed[6] class (whenever erected, and whether or not any building regulations were applicable to them at the time of their erection) continuing requirements with respect to all or any of the following matters:

(1)   the conditions subject to which any services, fittings or equipment provided in or in connection with a building of that class may be used[7];

(2)   the inspection and maintenance of any services, fittings or equipment so provided[8];

(3)   the making of reports to a prescribed authority on the condition of any services, fittings or equipment so provided[9].

If a person contravenes[10] a continuing requirement so imposed, the local authority[11], without prejudice to its right to take proceedings for a fine in respect of the contravention, may execute any work or take any other action required to remedy the contravention[12], and recover from that person the expenses reasonably incurred by it in so doing[13]. Where a local authority has such power to execute any work or take any other action, it may, instead of exercising that power, by notice require the owner or the occupier of the building to which the contravention relates to execute that work or take that action[14].

Building regulations may impose, on owners and occupiers of buildings, continuing requirements which:

(a)   require the inspection and testing of a building: (i) as respects the use of fuel and power in or in connection with the building; or (ii) as respects its contribution to or effect on emissions (whether or not from the building) of smoke, gases, vapours or fumes[15];

(b)   require the inspection and testing of any service, fitting or equipment provided in or in connection with a building: (i) as respects the use of fuel and power in or in connection with the service, fitting or equipment; or (ii) as respects its contribution to or effect on emissions (whether or not from it or the building) of smoke, gases, vapours or fumes[16];

(c)   require the implementation, in relation to a building, or any service, fitting or equipment provided in or in connection with a building, of: (i) measures for the purpose of furthering the conservation of fuel and power[17]; or (ii) measures (otherwise than for that purpose) that are calculated to secure, or to contribute to, the prevention or reduction of emissions (whether or not from the building in question or a thing provided in or in connection with it) of smoke, gases, vapours or fumes[18];

(d)   require the keeping of records in relation to matters within head (a), (b) or (c) above[19]; or

(e)   require the making of reports in relation to any of those matters to a prescribed authority[20].

Those requirements may be imposed in the case of buildings, or in the case of services, fittings and equipment provided in or in connection with buildings, irrespective of both when the buildings were erected, and whether building regulations were applicable to them at the time of their erection[21].

1   As to the meaning of 'building regulations' see PARA 7.
2   'Owner' means the person for the time being receiving the rackrent of the premises in connection with which the word is used, whether on his own account or as agent or trustee for another person, or who would so receive it if those premises were let at a rackrent: Building Act 1984 s 126. 'Rackrent', in relation to property, means a rent that is not less than two-thirds of the rent at which the property might reasonably be expected to let from year to year, free from all usual tenant's rates and taxes, and deducting from it the probable average annual cost of the repairs, insurance and other expenses, if any, necessary to maintain the property in a state to command such rent: s 126. 'Premises' includes buildings, land, easements and hereditaments of any tenure: s 126. As to the meaning of 'building' see PARA 6.
3   Ie the Secretary of State or, where statutory functions have been transferred in relation to Wales, the Welsh Ministers: see PARA 5.
4   Ie any provision of building regulations designated in the regulations as a provision to which those requirements relate: Building Act 1984 s 2(1).
5   Building Act 1984 s 2(1).
6   Ie prescribed by building regulations: see the Building Act 1984 s 126. At the date at which this volume states the law no such class of persons had been prescribed.
7   Building Act 1984 s 2(2)(a). So much of Sch 1 para 8 (see PARA 9) as restricts the application of building regulations does not apply to regulations made by virtue of s 2(2): s 2(2).
8   Building Act 1984 s 2(2)(b). See note 7.
9   Building Act 1984 s 2(2)(c). See note 7.
10 'Contravention' includes failure to comply, and 'contravene' has a corresponding meaning: Building Act 1984 s 126.
11 As to the meaning of 'local authority' see PARA 1 note 12.
12 Building Act 1984 s 2(3)(a).
13 Building Act 1984 s 2(3)(b).
14 Building Act 1984 s 2(4). Section 99 (content and enforcement of notice requiring works) (see PARA 126) and s 102 (appeal against notice requiring works) (see PARA 138) apply in relation to a notice given under s 2(4), subject to the modification that references in ss 99, 102 to the execution of works are references to the execution of works or the taking of other action, and references to works must be construed accordingly: s 2(5). As to the meaning of 'modifications' see PARA 3 note 21. Section 8 (relaxation of building regulations) (see PARA 18), s 9 (application for relaxation) (see PARA 19), s 10 (advertisement for relaxation of building regulations) (see PARA 21), and s 39 (appeal against refusal to relax building regulations) (see PARA 65) have effect in relation to continuing requirements imposed by virtue of s 2 subject to the modification that a direction under ss 8, 9 must, if it so provides, cease to have effect at the end of such period as may be specified in the direction: s 2(6).
15 Building Act 1984 s 2A(1), (2)(a) (s 2A added by the Sustainable and Secure Buildings Act 2004 s 4). The Building Act 1984 s 2(3)–(6) (see the text and notes 12–14) applies in relation to continuing requirements imposed by virtue of s 2A as it applies in relation to continuing requirements imposed by virtue of s 2: s 2A(4) (as so added).
16 Building Act 1984 s 2A(1), (2)(b) (as added: see note 15).

17 Ie the purpose mentioned in the Building Act 1984 s 1(1)(b): see PARA 7.
18 Building Act 1984 s 2A(1), (2)(c) (as added: see note 15).
19 Building Act 1984 s 2A(1), (2)(d) (as added: see note 15).
20 Building Act 1984 s 2A(1), (2)(e) (as added: see note 15).
21 Building Act 1984 s 2A(3) (as added: see note 15). Schedule 1 para 8(2) (see PARA 9) does not impose any restriction on the building regulations that may be made by virtue of s 2A: s 2A(5) (as so added).

13. Optional building requirements.

Building regulations[1] made by the Secretary of State[2] in relation to England may include a requirement that applies only where a planning authority[3] makes compliance with the requirement a condition of a grant of planning permission ('optional requirement')[4].

Building regulations may specify:

(1)   that an optional requirement is capable of applying only in respect of development[5] of a kind described in the regulations[6];

(2)   conditions that must be satisfied before a planning authority may make compliance with an optional requirement a condition of the grant of planning permission[7];

(3)   the steps that a planning authority must take to inform a person subject to an optional requirement of the requirement[8].

Where building regulations include an optional requirement that would (to any extent) be inconsistent with another requirement imposed by the regulations, the building regulations must provide that the other requirement does not apply in any case where the optional requirement applies or that the other requirement applies in any such case with modifications specified in the regulations[9].

1 As to the meaning of 'building regulations' see PARA 7.
2 As to the Secretary of State see PARA 5.
3 'Planning authority' means: (1) a local planning authority within the meaning of the Town and Country Planning Act 1990 (see s 336(1); and PLANNING vol 81 (2018) PARA 160); (2) the Secretary of State (in the exercise of functions of granting planning permission):Building Act 1984 s 2B(7) (added by the Deregulation Act 2015 s 42).
4 Building Act 1984 s 2B(1), (2) (as added: see note 3). As to the meaning of 'planning permission' see the Town and Country Planning Act 1990 s 336(1); and PLANNING vol 81 (2010) PARA 162; definition applied by the Building Act 1984 s 2B(7) (as so added).
5 As to the meaning of 'development' see the Town and Country Planning Act 1990 s 55; and PLANNING vol 81 (2018) PARA 333; definition applied by the Building Act 1984 s 2B(7) (as added: see note 3).
6 Building Act 1984 s 2B(3) (as added: see note 3).
7 Building Act 1984 s 2B(4) (as added: see note 3).
8 Building Act 1984 s 2B(5) (as added: see note 3)
9 Building Act 1984 s 2B(6) (as added: see note 3).

14. Consultation with Building Regulations Advisory Committee and other bodies.

The Building Regulations Advisory Committee for England and the Building Regulations Advisory Committee for Wales currently advise the Secretary of State or as the case may be, the Welsh Ministers[1] on the exercise of its power to make building regulations[2], and on other subjects connected with building regulations[3]. Before making any building regulations containing substantive requirements[4], the Secretary of State or the Welsh Ministers must consult the Building Regulations Advisory Committee for England or as the case may be, the Building Regulations Advisory Committee for Wales and such other bodies as appear to be representative of the interests concerned[5]. Before making any building regulations containing provision as to the repeal or modification of any provision of a local

Act[6] passed before 3 November 1994[7], the Secretary of State or the Welsh Ministers must consult: (1) the Building Regulations Advisory Committee for England or as the case may be, the Building Regulations Advisory Committee for Wales[8]; (2) such persons or bodies as appear to be representative of local authorities in England or as the case may be, Wales[9]; and (3) such other bodies as appear to be representative of the interests concerned[10].

1 As to the Secretary of State and the Welsh Ministers see PARA 5.
2 As to the power to make building regulations see PARA 7. As to the meaning of 'building regulations' see PARA 7.
3 See the Building Act 1984 s 14(1) (s 14(1) substituted by, s 14(5) added by SI 2009/3019). Provision is made for the payment of expenses incurred by members of both Committees by s 14(2), (6) (s 14(2) amended, s 14(6) added by SI 2009/3019).
4 'Substantive requirements', in relation to building regulations, means the requirements of building regulations with respect to the matters mentioned in the Building Act 1984 s 1(1A) (including requirements imposed by virtue of s 2(1) or s 2(2)(a) or (b) (see PARA 12) and requirements that are of a kind mentioned in s 2A(2)(a), (b) or (c) and are imposed by virtue of s 2A(1) (see PARA 12)), as distinct from procedural requirements: s 126.
5 Building Act 1984 s 14(3), (7) (s 14(3) amended by, s 14(7) added by SI 2009/3019).
6 As to the meaning of 'local Act' see PARA 6 note 2.
7 Ie containing provision of the kind authorised by the Building Act 1984 Sch 1 para 11(1)(c) (see PARA 9). The text refers to 3 November 1994, being the date on which the Deregulation and Contracting Out Act 1994 came into force.
8 Building Act 1984 s 14(4)(a), (8)(a) (s 14(4) added by the Deregulation and Contracting Out Act 1994 s 32(2); Building Act 1984 s 14(4)(a), (b) amended by, s 14(8) added by SI 2009/3019).
9 Building Act 1984 s 14(4)(b), (8)(b) (as added and amended: see note 8). As to the meaning of 'local authority' see PARA 1 note 12.
10 Building Act 1984 s 14(4)(c), (8)(c) (as added: see note 8).

15. Application to the Crown.

As from a day to be appointed, the following provisions have effect[1]. Except in so far as building regulations[2] provide otherwise, the substantive requirements[3] of building regulations:

(1)   apply in relation to work carried out[4] or proposed to be carried out by or on behalf of a Crown authority[5] (whether or not in relation to a Crown building[6]) as they would apply if the person by or on behalf of whom the work was or is to be carried out were not a Crown authority[7]; and

(2)   so far as they consist of continuing requirements[8], apply to Crown authorities (whether or not in relation to Crown buildings) as they apply to persons who are not Crown authorities[9].

In so far as building regulations so provide as regards any of the substantive requirements of building regulations, those requirements:

(a)   apply in relation to work carried out or proposed to be carried out as mentioned in head (1) above in inner London[10]; and

(b)   so far as they consist of continuing requirements, apply to Crown authorities there as mentioned in head (2) above[11],

even if those requirements do not apply there in the case of work carried out or proposed to be carried out otherwise than by or on behalf of a Crown authority or, in the case of continuing requirements, do not apply there to persons other than Crown authorities[12].

Except in so far as building regulations provide otherwise, building regulations and the enactments[13] relating to building regulations:

(i)　　　apply in relation to work carried out or proposed to be carried out in relation to a Crown building otherwise than by or on behalf of a Crown authority, and, in the case of the provision relating to continuing requirements[14] and building regulations made by virtue of it, apply in relation to a Crown building to persons other than Crown authorities, as they would apply if the building were not a Crown building[15]; and

(ii)　　apply in relation to work carried out or proposed to be carried out by or on behalf of a government department acting for a person other than a Crown authority as they would apply if the work had been or were to be carried out by that person[16].

Where work is carried out or proposed to be carried out by or on behalf of a Crown authority[17], or a Crown authority is or, apart from any dispensation or relaxation, will be subject to continuing requirements[18], that authority may exercise the like powers[19] of dispensing with or relaxing the substantive requirements of building regulations or, as the case may be, the continuing requirements in question as are conferred on the Secretary of State[20] and local authorities[21], subject to the like requirements[22] as to consultation, if any, as apply[23] in the case of a local authority[24], and the like requirements as in the case of the Secretary of State[25], and no application is necessary for the exercise[26] of any such powers[27].

1　The Building Act 1984 s 44 is to be brought into force by order under s 134(1) as from a day to be appointed. At the date at which this volume states the law no such day had been appointed.

2　As to the meaning of 'building regulations' see PARA 7.

3　As to the meaning of 'substantive requirements' see PARA 14 note 4.

4　The provisions of the Building Act 1984 s 44 (not yet in force), with any necessary modifications, apply in relation to the making of a material change in the use of a building within the meaning of building regulations made for the purposes of Sch 1 para 8(1)(e) (see PARA 9) as they apply in relation to the carrying out of work: s 44(10) (not yet in force: see note 1). See note 7.

　　For the purposes of building regulations which, in accordance with Sch 1 para 8(1)(f) (see PARA 9), are framed by reference to a change in the occupants of a building (or part), s 44 applies, with any necessary modifications, in relation to the making of a change of occupants as it applies in relation to the carrying out of work: s 44(11) (prospectively added by the Sustainable and Secure Buildings Act 2004 s 3(1), (8)). As to the meaning of 'modifications' see PARA 3 note 21.

5　For these purposes, 'Crown authority' means the Crown Estate Commissioners, a Minister of the Crown, a government department, any other person or body whose functions are performed on behalf of the Crown (not being a person or body whose functions are performed on behalf of Her Majesty in her private capacity), or a person acting in right of the Duchy of Lancaster or the Duchy of Cornwall: Building Act 1984 s 44(8) (not yet in force: see note 1). As to the meaning of 'functions' see PARA 3 note 19. As to the Crown Estate Commissioners see CROWN AND CROWN PROCEEDINGS vol 29 (2014) PARA 194 et seq. As from 4 May 2007, the National Assembly for Wales Commission is to be treated as a government department and any reference in the Building Act 1984 s 44 to the Crown is to be construed accordingly: National Assembly for Wales Commission (Crown Status) Order 2007, SI 2007/1118, art 3; Government of Wales Act 2006 s 161(1).

6　'Crown building' means a building in which there is a Crown interest or Duchy interest: Building Act 1984 s 44(8) (not yet in force: see note 1). 'Crown interest' means an interest belonging to Her Majesty in right of the Crown, or belonging to a government department, or held in trust for Her Majesty for the purposes of a government department: s 44(8) (not yet in force: see note 1). 'Duchy interest' means an interest belonging to Her Majesty in right of the Duchy of Lancaster, or belonging to the Duchy of Cornwall: s 44(8) (not yet in force: see note 1). As to the meaning of 'building' see PARA 6.

7　Building Act 1984 s 44(1)(a) (not yet in force: see note 1). Section 38 (civil liability for breach of duties imposed by building regulations) (see PARA 64) and any building regulations made by virtue of s 38(1) apply in relation to duties imposed by building regulations in their application in accordance with s 44(1)–(3): s 44(4) (not yet in force: see note 1).

The provisions of s 44(1), (4)–(10) (not yet in force) apply in relation to the United Kingdom Atomic Energy Authority as if the Authority were a Crown authority, a building belonging to or occupied by the Authority were a Crown building, and the references in s 44(1) (not yet in force) to not being a Crown authority were references to being neither a Crown authority nor the Authority, but the said provisions do not by virtue of s 45(1) apply in relation to dwelling houses or offices belonging to or occupied by the Authority: s 45(1) (not yet in force). The provisions of s 45 are to be brought into force by order made under s 134(1) as from a day to be appointed. At the date at which this volume states the law no such day had been appointed. As from a day to be appointed, s 44(11) also applies to the United Kingdom Atomic Energy Authority: see s 45(1) (prospectively substituted by the Sustainable and Secure Buildings Act 2004 s 3(9)). At the date at which this volume states the law no such day had been appointed. Subject to the said provisions as applied by the Building Act 1984 s 45(1), building regulations and the enactments relating to building regulations do not apply in relation to buildings belonging to or occupied by the Authority, except dwelling houses and offices: s 45(2) (not yet in force). As to the United Kingdom Atomic Energy Authority see ENERGY AND CLIMATE CHANGE vol 44 (2011) PARA 787 et seq.

8 For these purposes, 'continuing requirement' means a continuing requirement of building regulations imposed by virtue of the Building Act 1984 s 2(1) or s 2(2)(a) or s 2(2)(b) (see PARA 12): s 44(8) (not yet in force: see note 1). As from a day to be appointed, the definition of 'continuing requirement' is replaced as follows: 'continuing requirement' means a continuing requirement of building regulations: (1) imposed by virtue of s 2(1) or s 2(2)(a) or s 2(2)(b); or (2) of a kind mentioned in s 2A(2)(a), (b) or (c) and imposed by virtue of s 2A(1): s 44(8) (definition prospectively substituted by the Sustainable and Secure Buildings Act 2004 s 4(4)(b)). At the date at which this volume states the law no such day had been appointed.

9 Building Act 1984 s 44(1)(b) (not yet in force: see note 1).

10 Building Act 1984 s 44(2)(a) (not yet in force: see note 1). As to the meaning of 'inner London' see PARA 2 note 2.

11 Building Act 1984 s 44(2)(b) (not yet in force: see note 1).

12 Building Act 1984 s 44(2) (not yet in force: see note 1).

13 As to the meaning of 'enactment' see PARA 6 note 2.

14 Ie in the case of the Building Act 1984 s 2: see PARA 12. As from a day to be appointed, s 44(3)(a) will also apply in the case of s 2A (see PARA 12): see s 44(3)(a) (prospectively amended by the Sustainable and Secure Buildings Act 2004 s 4(4)(a)). At the date at which this volume states the law no such day had been appointed.

15 Building Act 1984 s 44(3)(a) (not yet in force: see note 1). See note 14.

16 Building Act 1984 s 44(3)(b) (not yet in force: see note 1).

17 Building Act 1984 s 44(5)(a) (not yet in force: see note 1). For the purposes of s 44(5), work carried out or proposed to be carried out by or on behalf of a government department acting for another Crown authority must be treated as carried out or proposed to be carried out by or on behalf of that department (and not by or on behalf of the other Crown authority): s 44(7) (not yet in force: see note 1). See note 7.

18 Building Act 1984 s 44(5)(b) (not yet in force: see note 1). See note 7.

19 If any question arises under the Building Act 1984 s 44 as to which Crown authority is entitled to exercise any such powers as are mentioned in s 44(5), that question must be referred to the Treasury, whose decision is final: s 44(9) (not yet in force: see note 1). As to the Treasury see CONSTITUTIONAL AND ADMINISTRATIVE LAW vol 20 (2014) PARA 262 et seq. See note 7.

20 The Secretary of State's functions under the Building Act 1984 s 44(5) have not been transferred to the Welsh Ministers in relation to Wales: see PARA 5.

21 Ie by virtue of the Building Act 1984 s 8 (see PARA 18) (other than a power that by virtue of s 1(3), Sch 1 para 6 (see PARA 9) is exercisable otherwise than by a local authority): see s 44(5) (not yet in force: see note 1). As to the meaning of 'local authority' see PARA 1 note 12.

In relation to continuing requirements, references in s 44(5) to s 8 are references to s 8 as modified by s 2(6) (see PARA 12): s 44(6) (not yet in force: see note 1). See note 7.

22 But not the requirements of the Building Act 1984 s 8 (see PARA 18) as to consultation with the local authority: see s 44(5)(i) (not yet in force: see note 1).

23 Ie by virtue of the Building Act 1984 Sch 1 para 3: see PARA 9.

24 Building Act 1984 s 44(5)(i) (not yet in force: see note 1). See note 7.

25 Building Act 1984 s 44(5)(ii) (not yet in force: see note 1). See note 7. The text refers to the requirements which apply by virtue of s 10 (see PARA 21).

26 Ie by virtue of the Building Act 1984 s 44(5) (not yet in force).

27 Building Act 1984 s 44(5) (not yet in force: see note 1). See note 7.

(2) Exemption From, and Relaxation Of, Building Regulations

(i) Exemption from Building Regulations

16. Exemption from building regulations.

Building regulations[1] may exempt a prescribed[2] class of buildings[3], services, fittings or equipment from all or any of the provisions of building regulations[4]. The appropriate national authority[5] may by direction exempt from all or any of the provisions of building regulations a particular building, or buildings of a particular class at a particular location, either unconditionally or subject to compliance with any conditions specified in the direction[6]. A person who contravenes a condition specified in such a direction, or permits such a condition to be contravened, is liable on summary conviction to a fine[7], and also to a further fine for each day on which the offence continues after he is convicted[8].

The Building Act 1984 states that nothing in Part I of the Act[9] with respect to building regulations, and nothing in any building regulations themselves applies in relation to certain specified educational buildings and buildings of statutory undertakers[10]. However, certain regulations relating to CO_2 emission rates and the conservation of fuel and power are specifically applied to such buildings by the Building Regulations 2010[11].

Subject to certain exceptions[12], the building regulations do not apply to:

(1)   the erection of any building or extension of:
        (a)   buildings controlled under other legislation[13];
        (b)   buildings not frequented by people[14];
        (c)   greenhouses and agricultural buildings[15];
        (d)   temporary buildings[16];
        (e)   ancillary buildings[17];
        (f)   small detached buildings[18];
        (g)   extensions[19]; or

(2)   the carrying out of any work to or in connection with such a building or extension, if after the carrying out of that work it is still a building or extension of a kind described in heads (a) to (g) above[20].

However, greenhouses, small detached buildings and extensions are not completely exempt from building regulations. Certain requirements relating to cold water supply[21] and hot water systems[22] still apply to:

(i)   any greenhouse which receives a cold or hot water supply from a source shared with or located inside a dwelling[23]; and

(ii)   any qualifying small detached building[24] and any qualifying extension of a building[25], which in either case receives a cold or hot water supply from a source shared with or located inside any building (other than an exempt[26] building or extension)[27].

The requirements relating to electrical safety[28] apply to any greenhouse used for domestic purposes, and any qualifying small detached building and extension[29] which in any case receives its electricity from a source shared with or located inside a dwelling[30].

The requirements relating to physical infrastructure for high speed electronic communications networks[31] apply to certain buildings controlled under other legislation[32].

1   As to the meaning of 'building regulations' see PARA 7.
2   Ie prescribed by building regulations: see the Building Act 1984 s 126. The Building Regulations 2010, SI 2010/2214, Sch 2 prescribes the buildings so exempted: see the text and notes 13–19.

3   As to the meaning of 'building' see PARA 6.
4   Building Act 1984 s 3(1).
5   Ie the Secretary of State or, where statutory functions have been transferred in relation to Wales, the Welsh Ministers: see PARA 5.
6   Building Act 1984 s 3(2). As to whether a bus and a lorry constitute 'temporary' buildings see *Gumbrell v Swale RDC* [1936] 3 All ER 935.
7   The fine imposed is one not exceeding level 5 on the standard scale: see the Building Act 1984 s 3(3). As to the powers of magistrates' courts to issue fines on summary conviction see SENTENCING vol 92 (2015) PARA 176. Civil sanctions may be imposed in respect of offences under the Building Act 1984 by virtue of the powers under the Regulatory Enforcement and Sanctions Act 2008 Pt 3 (ss 36–71): see ss 36, 38(2), Sch 6; and CONSTITUTIONAL AND ADMINISTRATIVE LAW vol 20 (2014) PARA 331 et seq.
8   Building Act 1984 s 3(3). The fine imposed must not exceed £50 for each day on which the default continues after conviction: see s 3(3). As to continuing offences see PARA 144.
9   Ie the Building Act 1984 Pt I (ss 1–46).
10   See the Building Act 1984 s 4(1). Note that as from a day to be appointed, s 4 is repealed by the Sustainable and Secure Buildings Act 2004 ss 5(a), 11(2), Schedule. At the date at which this volume states the law no such day had been appointed.

The Building Act 1984 Pt I and the building regulations do not apply to:

(1)   a building required for the purposes of a school or other educational establishment erected or to be erected according to: (a) plans that have been approved by the appropriate national authority (Building Act 1984 s 4(1)(a)(i) (substituted by the Education Act 1996 s 582(1), Sch 37 para 59) (prospectively repealed)); (b) particulars submitted and approved under regulations made under the Education Act 1996 s 544 (see EDUCATION vol 36 (2015) PARA 1346) (Building Act 1984 s 4(1)(a)(ii) (substituted by the Education Act 2002 s 215(1), Sch 21 para 6) (prospectively repealed));

(2)   a building belonging to statutory undertakers, the United Kingdom Atomic Energy Authority or the Civil Aviation Authority and held or used by them for the purposes of their undertaking, unless it is: (a) a house; or (b) a building used as offices or showrooms, and not forming part of a railway station or in the case of the Civil Aviation Authority not being on an aerodrome owned by the Authority (Building Act 1984 s 4(1)(b) (amended by the Airports Act 1986 s 83(5), Sch 6 Pt I) (prospectively repealed));

(3)   a building belonging to a person who holds a licence under the Transport Act 2000 Pt I Ch I (air traffic services) and held or used by the person for the purpose of carrying out activities authorised by the licence, unless it is: (a) a house; or (b) a building used as offices or showrooms (Building Act 1984 s 4(1)(c) (added by SI 2001/4050) (prospectively repealed)).

Offices and showrooms that form part of a railway station are covered by the exemption under the Building Act 1984 s 4(1)(b) (see head (2) above): *Manchester City Council v Railtrack plc* [2002] EWHC 2719 (Admin), [2003] 01 EG 66 (CS), [2002] All ER (D) 137 (Dec).

The words 'the United Kingdom Atomic Energy Authority', in head (2) (together with the Building Act 1984 Sch 6 para 4), cease to have effect upon the coming into force of the repeal of the Atomic Energy Authority Act 1954 s 5(5) (see ENERGY AND CLIMATE CHANGE vol 44 (2011) PARA 794) contained in the Building Act 1984 s 133(2), Sch 7: s 4(2) (prospectively repealed). At the date at which this volume states the law no order bringing into force the repeal of the Atomic Energy Authority Act 1954 s 5(5) had been made. As to the United Kingdom Atomic Energy Authority see ENERGY AND CLIMATE CHANGE vol 44 (2011) PARA 787 et seq.

'Statutory undertakers' means persons authorised by an enactment or statutory order to construct, work or carry on a railway, canal, inland navigation, dock harbour, tramway or other public undertaking; but does not include a universal service provider (within the meaning of the Postal Services Act 2011 Pt 3 (ss 27–67): see POSTAL SERVICES vol 85 (2012) PARA 201 et seq) or a relevant company (within the meaning of the Postal Services Act 2000 Pt IV: see POSTAL SERVICES vol 85 (2012) PARA 201): Building Act 1984 s 126 (definition amended by the Gas Act 1986 s 67(4), Sch 9 Pt I; the Electricity Act 1989 s 112(4), Sch 18; the Water Act 1989 s 190(1), (3), Sch 25 para 70(4), Sch 27 Pt I; the Postal Services Act 2011, s 91(1), (2), Sch 12, Pt 3, para 122; SI 2001/1149; and SI 2009/1941). As to the meaning of 'enactment' see PARA 6 note 2. As to the meaning of 'construct' see PARA 9 note 3. 'House' means a dwelling house, whether a private dwelling house or not: Building Act 1984 s 126. 'School' includes a Sunday school or a Sabbath school: s 126. As to the meaning of 'erect' see PARA 9 note 3. As to the meaning of 'plans' see PARA 9 note 8.

11 Notwithstanding the Building Act 1984 s 4(1), the requirements in the Building Regulations 2010, SI 2010/2214, relating to CO_2 emission rates and certain requirements relating to conservation of fuel and power apply to educational buildings and buildings of statutory undertakers in certain circumstances: see reg 34; and PARA 47.

12 Ie subject to the Building Regulations 2010, SI 2010/2214, reg 9(2)–(4) (see the text and notes 21–32) and reg 21(1) (see PARA 44).

13 Building Regulations 2010, SI 2010/2214, reg 9(1)(a), Sch 2 Class 1 (reg 9(1) amended by SI 2016/361; and SI 2016/490). The exempt buildings for these purposes are:

   (1)   any building in which explosives are manufactured or stored under a licence granted under the Explosives Regulations 2014, SI 2014/1638 where:

      (a)   the whole building is used for that manufacture or storage (Building Regulations 2010, SI 2010/2214, Sch 2 Class 1 para 1(1)(a) (Sch 2 Class 1 para 1 substituted by SI 2014/1638)); and either

      (b)   a minimum separation distance of greater than 0 metres is prescribed by virtue of the Explosives Regulations 2014, SI 2014/1638, reg 27(1), Sch 5 (Building Regulations 2010, SI 2010/2214, Sch 2 Class 1 para 1(1)(b) (as so substituted)); or

      (c)   a minimum separation distance of 0 metres is prescribed by virtue of the provisions referred to in head (1)(b) and the assent of the local authority was required by reg 13(3) or would have been so required but for reg 13(4)(b), (c), (d), (e), (f) or (g) (Building Regulations 2010, SI 2010/2214, Sch 2 Class 1 para 1(1)(c) (as so substituted)).

   (2)   where only a part of a building is used for the manufacture or storage of explosives under a licence granted under the Explosives Regulations 2014, SI 2014/1638:

      (a)   a minimum separation distance of greater than 0 metres is prescribed by virtue of reg 27(1), Sch 5 (Building Regulations 2010, SI 2010/2214, Sch 2 Class 1 para 1(2)(a) (as so substituted));

      (b)   a minimum separation distance of 0 metres is prescribed by virtue of the provisions referred to in head (2)(a) and the assent of the local authority was required by reg 13(3) or would have been so required but for the Explosives Regulations 2014, SI 2014/1638, reg 13(4)(b), (c), (d), (e), (f) or (g) (Building Regulations 2010, SI 2010/2214, Sch 2 Class 1 para 1(2)(b) (as so substituted)), that part of the building where the licence specifies that manufacture or storage may take place (Sch 2 Class 1 para 1(2) (as so substituted));

   (3)   any building (other than a building containing a dwelling or a building used for office or canteen accommodation) erected on a site in respect of which a licence under the Nuclear Installations Act 1965 (see ENERGY AND CLIMATE CHANGE vol 44 (2011) PARA 884 et seq) is for the time being in force (Building Regulations 2010, SI 2010/2214, Sch 2 Class 1 para 2); and

   (4)   a building included in the schedule of monuments maintained under the Ancient Monuments and Archaeological Areas Act 1979 s 1 (see NATIONAL CULTURAL HERITAGE vol 77 (2016) PARAS 1014–1015) (Building Regulations 2010, SI 2010/2214, Sch 2 Class 1 para 3).

14 Building Regulations 2010, SI 2010/2214, reg 9(1)(a), Sch 2 Class 2. The type of building exempt for these purposes is a detached building into which people do not normally go, or into which people go only intermittently and then only for the purpose of inspecting or maintaining fixed plant or machinery, unless any point of such a building is less than one and a half times its height from any point of a building into which people can or do normally go, or the nearest point of the boundary of the curtilage of that building, whichever is the nearer: Sch 2 Class 2.

15 Building Regulations 2010, SI 2010/2214, reg 9(1)(a), Sch 2 Class 3. The buildings exempt for these purposes are: (1) greenhouses (Sch 2 Class 3 para 1); and (2) buildings used for agriculture, or buildings principally for the keeping of animals, provided in each case that: (a) no part of the building is used as a dwelling; (b) no point of the building is less than one-and-a-half times its height from any point of a building which contains sleeping accommodation; and (c) the building is provided with a fire exit which is not more than 30 metres from any point in the building (Sch 2 Class 3 para 2). The descriptions of buildings in Sch 2 Class 3 paras 1, 2 do not include a greenhouse or a building used for agriculture if the principal purpose for which they are used is retailing, packing or exhibiting: Sch 2 Class 3 para 3. For the purposes of Sch 2 Class 3 para 2, 'agriculture' includes horticulture, fruit growing, the growing of plants for seed and fish farming: Sch 2 Class 3 para 4.

16 Building Regulations 2010, SI 2010/2214, reg 9(1)(a), Sch 2 Class 4. The text refers a building which is not intended to remain where it is erected for more than 28 days: Sch 2 Class 4. For these purposes, 'day' means any period of 24 hours commencing at midnight and excludes any Saturday, Sunday, Bank holiday or public holiday: reg 2(1).

17 Building Regulations 2010, SI 2010/2214, reg 9(1)(a), Sch 2 Class 5. The buildings exempt for these purposes are: (1) a building on a site, being a building which is intended to be used only in connection with the disposal of buildings or building plots on that site (Sch 2 Class 5 para 1); (2) a building on the site of construction or civil engineering works, which is intended to be used only during the course of those works and contains no sleeping accommodation (Sch 2 Class 5 para 2); (3) a building, other than a building containing a dwelling or used as an office or showroom, erected for use on the site of and in connection with a mine or quarry (Sch 2 Class 5 para 3).

18 Building Regulations 2010, SI 2010/2214, reg 9(1)(a), Sch 2 Class 6. The buildings exempt for these purposes are: (1) a detached single storey building, having a floor area which does not exceed 30m², which contains no sleeping accommodation and is a building no point of which is less than one metre from the boundary of its curtilage, or which is constructed substantially of non-combustible material (Sch 2 Class 6 para 1); (2) a detached building designed and intended to shelter people from the effects of nuclear, chemical or conventional weapons, and not used for any other purpose, if its floor area does not exceed 30m², and the excavation for the building is no closer to any exposed part of another building or structure than a distance equal to the depth of the excavation plus one metre (Sch 2 Class 6 para 2); (3) a detached building, having a floor area which does not exceed 15m², which contains no sleeping accommodation (Sch 2 Class 6 para 3). For these purposes, 'floor area' means the aggregate area of every floor in a building or extension, calculated by reference to the finished internal faces of the walls enclosing the area, or if at any point there is no such wall, by reference to the outermost edge of the floor: reg 2(1).

19 Building Regulations 2010, SI 2010/2214, reg 9(1)(a), Sch 2 Class 7. The text refers to the extension of a building by the addition at ground level of a conservatory, porch, covered yard or covered way, or a carport open on at least two sides, where the floor area of that extension does not exceed 30m2, provided that in the case of a conservatory or porch which is wholly or partly glazed, the glazing satisfies the requirements of Sch 1 Pt K4, K5.1, K5.2, K5.3, and K5.4 (see PARA 10): Sch 2 Class 7 (amended by SI 2012/3119; and SI 2018/558).

20 Building Regulations 2010, SI 2010/2214, reg 9(1)(b).

21 Ie the requirements of the Building Regulations 2010, SI 2010/2214, Sch 1 para G1: see PARA 10.

22 Ie the requirements of the Building Regulations 2010, SI 2010/2214, Sch 1 para G3(2), (3): see PARA 10.

23 Building Regulations 2010, SI 2010/2214, reg 9(2)(a).

24 Ie a small detached building falling within the Building Regulations 2010, SI 2010/2214, Sch 2 Class 6: see note 18.

25 Ie an extension of a building falling within the Building Regulations 2010, SI 2010/2214, Sch 2 Class 7: see note 19.

26 Ie a building or an extension of a kind described in the Building Regulations 2010, SI 2010/2214, Sch 2.

27 Building Regulations 2010, SI 2010/2214, reg 9(2)(b).

28 Ie the requirements of the Building Regulations 2010, SI 2010/2214, Sch 1 Pt P: see PARA 10.

29 Ie any green house and any small detached building falling within the Building Regulations 2010, SI 2010/2214, Sch 2 Class 6 and any extension of a building falling within Sch 2 Class 7.

30 Building Regulations 2010, SI 2010/2214, reg 9(3) (amended by SI 2012/3119; and SI 2018/558).

31 Ie the requirements of the Building Regulations 2010, SI 2010/2214, Sch 1 para R1: see PARA 10.

32 Ie buildings falling within Sch 2 Class 1 paras 1, 2.

17. Exemption of public bodies from procedural requirements of building regulations.

Building regulations[1] may exempt a local authority[2], a county council, or any other body that acts under an enactment[3] for public purposes and not for its own profit and is prescribed[4] for these purposes, from compliance with any requirements of those regulations that are not substantive requirements[5]. A local authority, county council or other body that is so exempted is referred to as an 'exempt body'[6]. Without prejudice to the obligation of an exempt body to comply with substantive requirements of building regulations, the function of enforcing building regulations that is conferred on local authorities[7] is not exercisable in relation to work carried out[8] by an exempt body, and accordingly nothing in the provision relating to the removal or alteration of offending work[9] applies in relation to work so carried out[10], and a local authority may not institute proceedings[11] for a contravention[12] of building regulations by an exempt body[13].

1 As to the meaning of 'building regulations' see PARA 7.
2 As to the meaning of 'local authority' see PARA 1 note 12.
3 As to the meaning of 'enactment' see PARA 6 note 2.
4 Ie prescribed by building regulations: see the Building Act 1984 s 126. The Mayor's Office for Policing and Crime has been so prescribed and is exempt from compliance with the building regulations in so far as the requirements in the regulations are not substantive requirements: see Building Regulations 2010, SI 2010/2214, reg 10(1), (2) (reg 10(1) amended by SI 2011/3058, SI 2010/2214 reg 10(2) amended by SI 2011/3058, SI 2016/285, SI 2016/611).
5 Building Act 1984 s 5(1). As to the meaning of 'substantive requirements' see PARA 14 note 4.
6 Building Act 1984 s 5(2).
7 Ie by the Building Act 1984 s 91(2): see PARA 70.
8 The reference to the carrying out of work includes a reference to the making of a material change of use: Building Act 1984 s 5(4). As to material change of use see PARA 11.
9 Ie the Building Act 1984 s 36(1)–(5): see PARA 62.
10 Building Act 1984 s 5(3)(a).
11 Ie under the Building Act 1984 s 35: see PARA 61.
12 As to the meaning of 'contravention' see PARA 12 note 10.
13 Building Act 1984 s 5(3)(b).

(ii) Relaxation of Building Regulations

18. Relaxation of building regulations.

If on an application for a direction[1] the appropriate national authority[2] considers that the operation of a requirement in building regulations[3] would be unreasonable in relation to the particular case to which the application relates, it may, after consultation with the local authority[4], give a direction dispensing with or relaxing that requirement[5]. If building regulations so provide as regards a requirement contained in the regulations, the power to dispense with or relax that requirement is exercisable by the local authority (instead of by the appropriate national authority after consultation with the local authority)[6]. If building regulations so provide as regards any requirement contained in the regulations, and a public body[7] considers that the operation of any such requirement would be unreasonable in relation to any particular work carried out or proposed to be carried out by or on behalf of the public body, the public body may give a direction dispensing with or relaxing that requirement[8].

However, the provisions relating to the relaxation of building regulations described above[9] do not apply to the renovation of an individual thermal element that constitutes a major renovation[10] do not apply to the consideration of high-efficiency alternative systems for new buildings[11] do not apply to nearly zero-energy requirements for new buildings[12] do not apply do not apply to carbon dioxide emission rates for new buildings[13] and to in-building physical infrastructure[14].

1 Ie a direction under the Building Act 1984 s 8: see the text and notes 2–8.
2 Ie the Secretary of State or, where statutory functions have been transferred in relation to Wales, the Welsh Ministers: see PARA 5.
3 As to the meaning of 'building regulations' see PARA 7. Building regulations may provide as regards a requirement contained in the regulations that the Building Act 1984 s 8(1)–(5) (see the text and notes 4–8) does not apply: see s 8(6); the Building Regulations 2010, SI 2010/2214, reg 11(3); and the text and note 12.
4 As to the meaning of 'local authority' see PARA 1 note 12.
5 Building Act 1984 s 8(1). Such a direction may be made in relation to continuing requirements, but

it ceases to have effect at the end of a period specified in the direction: see s 2(6); and PARA 12.

6   Building Act 1984 s 8(2). Building regulations made by virtue of s 8(2) may except applications of
    any description: s 8(3). The power under s 8(1) to dispense with or relax any requirement is
    exercisable by the local authority: Building Regulations 2010, SI 2010/2214, reg 11(1). Any
    notification by the local authority to an applicant that it has refused his application to dispense
    with or relax any requirement of the building regulations must inform the applicant of the effect
    of the Building Act 1984 s 39(1), (3) (appeal against refusal etc to relax building regulations):
    Building Regulations 2010, SI 2010/2214, reg 11(2).
7   For these purposes, 'public body' means a local authority, a county council, or any other body that
    is prescribed for the purposes of the Building Act 1984 s 5 (see PARA 17): s 8(5). 'Prescribed' means
    prescribed by building regulations: see s 126.
8   Building Act 1984 s 8(4).
9   Ie the Building Act 1984 s 8(1)–(5): see the text and notes 1–8.
10 Ie the Building Regulations 2010, SI 2010/2214, reg 23(1)(a): see PARA 46.
11 Ie the Building Regulations 2010, SI 2010/2214, reg 25A: see PARA 46.
12 Ie the Building Regulations 2010, SI 2010/2214, reg 25B: see PARA 46
13 Ie the Building Regulations 2010, SI 2010/2214, reg 26: see PARA 46.
14 Building Regulations 2010, SI 2010/2214, reg 11(3) (substituted in relation to England by
    SI 2013/1105 and in relation to Wales by SI 2013/747; amended by SI 2016/361; SI 2016/490; and
    SI 2018/558). The text refers to the Building Regulations 2010, SI 2010/2214, Sch 1 para R1: see
    PARA 48.

19. Application for relaxation of building regulations.

An application for relaxation of building regulations[1] must be in such form and
must contain such particulars as may be prescribed[2]. The application must be
made to the local authority[3], and, except where the power of giving the direction
is exercisable by the local authority, the local authority must at once transmit the
application to the appropriate national authority[4] and give notice to the applicant
that it has been so transmitted[5]. An application by a local authority in connection
with a building[6] or proposed building in the area of that authority must be made
to the appropriate national authority, except where the power of giving the
direction is exercisable by that authority[7].

1   Ie under the Building Act 1984 s 8(1) or s 8(2): see PARA 18.
2   Building Act 1984 s 9(1). 'Prescribed' means prescribed by building regulations: see s 126. As to
    the meaning of 'building regulations' see PARA 7.
3   As to the meaning of 'local authority' see PARA 1 note 12.
4   Ie the Secretary of State or, where statutory functions have been transferred in relation to Wales,
    the Welsh Ministers: see PARA 5.
5   Building Act 1984 s 9(2).
6   As to the meaning of 'building' see PARA 6.
7   Building Act 1984 s 9(3).

20. Relaxation of building regulations for existing work.

Neither the appropriate national authority[1] nor a local authority[2] may give a
direction[3] for relaxation of building regulations[4] that will affect the application of
building regulations to work that has been carried out before the giving of the
direction[5] if the local authority has, before the making of the application for the
direction, become entitled[6] to pull down, remove or alter the work to which the
application relates[7], or if, when the application is made, there is in force an
injunction or other direction given by a court that requires the work to be pulled
down, removed or altered[8]. After the making of such an application for a direction
in relation to existing work, and until the application is withdrawn or finally
disposed of, no notice to pull down, remove or alter the work[9] can be given as
regards the work to which the application relates on the ground that it
contravenes[10] the requirement to which the application relates[11].

If an application for such a direction in relation to existing work is made after any person has in consequence of the carrying out of the work to which the application relates in contravention of building regulations, become liable to a penalty continuing from day to day, the daily penalty is not recoverable in respect of any day after the making of the application and before it is withdrawn or finally disposed of[12]. In a case where an application is withdrawn or is finally disposed of without any direction being given, the appropriate national authority or, as the case may be, the local authority may order that the daily penalty is not recoverable in respect of any day during such further period not exceeding 28 days as may be specified in the order[13]. The giving of such a direction in relation to existing work does not affect the liability of a person for an offence committed before the giving of the direction, except so far as that liability depends on the continuation of the offence after the giving of the direction[14].

1 Ie the Secretary of State or, where statutory functions have been transferred in relation to Wales, the Welsh Ministers: see PARA 5.
2 As to the meaning of 'local authority' see PARA 1 note 12.
3 Ie a direction under the Building Act 1984 s 8: see PARA 18.
4 As to the meaning of 'building regulations' see PARA 7.
5 Building Act 1984 s 9(4), Sch 2 para 1.
6 Ie under the Building Act 1984 s 36(3): see PARA 62.
7 Building Act 1984 Sch 2 para 2(a).
8 Building Act 1984 Sch 2 para 2(b).
9 Ie a notice under the Building Act 1984 s 36(1), (2): see PARA 62.
10 As to the meaning of 'contravention' see PARA 12 note 10.
11 Building Act 1984 Sch 2 para 3(1). If an application for such a direction is made less than 12 months after the completion of the work to which the application relates, s 36(4) (see PARA 62) does not prevent the giving of such a notice as regards that work at any time within a period of three months from the date on which the application is withdrawn or finally disposed of: Sch 2 para 3(2). If an application for such a direction is made after a notice to pull down, remove or alter the work under s 36 (see PARA 62) has been given on the ground that the work to which the application relates contravenes the requirement to which the application relates (not being an application prohibited by Sch 2 para 2 (see the text to notes 6–8)), if a person to whom a notice has been given under s 36(1), (2) fails to comply with the notice within a period expiring 28 days after the application is withdrawn or finally disposed of, or such longer period as a magistrates' court may allow, the local authority may pull down or remove the work in question, or effect such alterations in it as they deem necessary, and may recover from him the expenses reasonably incurred by them in doing so: s 36(3), Sch 2 para 3(3). If, before the giving of such a direction, such a notice has been given, and the contravention of building regulations by virtue of which the notice was given comes to an end when the direction is given, the local authority is not, after the giving of the direction, entitled to proceed under s 36(3) by virtue of that notice: Sch 2 para 6.
      The provisions of Sch 2 para 3(1), (3), (4) do not apply to an application that is a repetition, or substantially a repetition, of a previous application under s 8 (see PARA 18): Sch 2 para 4. As to continuing offences see PARA 144.
12 Building Act 1984 Sch 2 para 3(4).
13 Building Act 1984 Sch 2 para 3(5).
14 Building Act 1984 Sch 2 para 5.

21. Advertisement of proposal for relaxation.

Not less than 21 days before giving a direction[1] for the relaxation of building regulations[2] in respect of any particular work, the appropriate national authority[3], the local authority[4] or the public body[5], as the case may be, must publish in a local newspaper circulating in the area where the site of the work is situated a notice[6]:

(1)   indicating the situation and nature of the work and the requirement to be dispensed with or relaxed[7]; and

(2)   stating that representations with regard to the effect that the direction
        may have on public health or safety may be made by a date specified in
        the notice, being a date not less than 21 days from the date of the
        notice[8].

Where the direction is proposed to be made on an application, the appropriate
national authority or the local authority may, as a condition of entertaining the
application, require the applicant to pay or undertake to pay the cost of
publication[9]. No such notice need be published where it appears to the
appropriate national authority, the local authority or the public body, as the case
may be, that any effect that the direction may have on public health or safety will
be limited to premises[10] adjoining the site of the work, but in that case he or it
must give such a notice to the owner[11] and occupier of those premises[12].

No such notices[13] need be so published or given where the work affects only an
internal part of a building[14]. The appropriate national authority may, instead of
publishing or giving such notices, require the local authority to so give or publish
the notices[15]. Before giving the direction, the appropriate national authority, the
local authority or the public body must consider any representations duly made in
pursuance of such notices so published or given[16]. If, after a local authority has
received such representations, it refuses the application to which the
representations relate and an appeal is brought against its refusal, the local
authority must transmit to the appropriate national authority copies of those
representations[17].

1   Ie under the Building Act 1984 s 8(1), (2) or s 8(4): see PARA 18.
2   As to the meaning of 'building regulations' see PARA 7.
3   Ie the Secretary of State or, where statutory functions have been transferred in relation to Wales,
    the Welsh Ministers: see PARA 5.
4   As to the meaning of 'local authority' see PARA 1 note 12.
5   This term is not expressly defined for the purposes of the Building Act 1984 s 10; but see s 8(5);
    and PARA 18.
6   As to the form, authorisation and service of notices see PARAS 135–137.
7   Building Act 1984 s 10(1)(a).
8   Building Act 1984 s 10(1)(b).
9   Building Act 1984 s 10(1).
10 As to the meaning of 'premises' see PARA 12 note 2.
11 As to the meaning of 'owner' see PARA 12 note 2.
12 Building Act 1984 s 10(2).
13 Ie under the Building Act 1984 s 10(1), (2): see the text and notes 1–12.
14 Building Act 1984 s 10(3). As to the meaning of 'building' see PARA 6.
15 Building Act 1984 s 10(4).
16 Building Act 1984 s 10(5).
17 Building Act 1984 s 10(6).

22. Relaxation in relation to certain types of building matter.

If the appropriate national authority[1] considers that the operation of a
requirement of building regulations[2] would be unreasonable in relation to a
particular type of building matter[3], it may, either on an application made to it or
of its own accord, give a direction dispensing with or relaxing that requirement
generally in relation to that type of building matter, either unconditionally[4], or
subject to compliance with any conditions specified in the direction, being
conditions with respect to matters directly connected with the dispensation or
relaxation[5]. Such a direction, if it so provides, ceases to have effect at the end of
such period as may be specified in the direction[6] and it may be varied or revoked
by a subsequent direction of the appropriate national authority[7]. Building
regulations may[8] require a person making such an application to pay the

appropriate national authority the prescribed[9] fee, and such regulations may prescribe different fees for different cases[10], and the appropriate national authority may in a particular case remit the whole or part of a fee so payable[11]. Before giving such a direction, the appropriate national authority must consult such bodies as appear to be representative of the interests concerned[12]. Where the appropriate national authority gives such a direction, it must publish notice of that fact in such manner as it thinks fit[13]. A person who contravenes a condition specified in a direction so given, or permits such a condition to be contravened[14], is liable on summary conviction to a fine[15] and is also subject to a further fine for each day on which the offence continues after he is convicted[16].

If at any time such a direction dispensing with or relaxing a requirement of building regulations ceases to have effect by virtue of its period of operation expiring, or is varied or revoked by direction of the appropriate national authority, that fact does not affect the continued operation of the direction, with any conditions specified in it, in a case in which before that time plans[17] of the proposed work were, in accordance with building regulations, deposited[18] with a local authority[19].

1 Ie the Secretary of State or, where statutory functions have been transferred in relation to Wales, the Welsh Ministers: see PARA 5.
2 As to the meaning of 'building regulations' see PARA 7.
3 For these purposes, 'building matter' means any building or other matter whatsoever to which building regulations are in any circumstances applicable: Building Act 1984 s 11(8). As to the meaning of 'building' see PARA 6.
4 Building Act 1984 s 11(1)(a).
5 Building Act 1984 s 11(1)(b).
6 Building Act 1984 s 11(2)(a).
7 Building Act 1984 s 11(2)(b).
8 Ie without prejudice to the Building Act 1984 s 1(3), Sch 1 para 10: see PARA 9.
9 Ie prescribed by building regulations: see the Building Act 1984 s 126.
10 Building Act 1984 s 11(3)(a).
11 Building Act 1984 s 11(3)(b).
12 Building Act 1984 s 11(4).
13 Building Act 1984 s 11(5).
14 As to the meaning of 'contravene' see PARA 12 note 10.
15 The fine imposed is one not exceeding level 5 on the standard scale: see the Building Act 1984 s 11(6). As to the powers of magistrates' courts to issue fines on summary conviction see SENTENCING vol 92 (2015) PARA 176. Civil sanctions may be imposed in respect of offences under the Building Act 1984 by virtue of the powers under the Regulatory Enforcement and Sanctions Act 2008 Pt 3 (ss 36–71): see ss 36, 38(2), Sch 6; and CONSTITUTIONAL AND ADMINISTRATIVE LAW vol 20 (2014) PARA 331 et seq.
16 Building Act 1984 s 11(6). The fine imposed must not exceed £50 for each day on which the default continues after conviction: see s 11(6). As to continuing offences see PARA 144.
17 As to the meaning of 'plans' see PARA 9 note 8.
18 In the Building Act 1984, a reference to the deposit of plans in accordance with building regulations is a reference to the deposit of plans in accordance with building regulations for the purposes of s 16 (see PARA 33), unless the context otherwise requires: s 124.
19 Building Act 1984 s 11(7)(a) (amended by the Statute Law Repeals Act 2004). As to the meaning of 'local authority' see PARA 1 note 12.

(3) Approved Documents

23. Approval of documents for purposes of building regulations.

For the purpose of providing practical guidance with respect to the requirements of any provision of building regulations[1] the appropriate national authority[2] or a body designated[3] by the appropriate national authority for these purposes may approve and issue any document[4] (whether or not prepared by the appropriate national authority or by the body concerned), or approve any document issued or proposed to be issued otherwise than by the appropriate national authority or by the body concerned, if in the opinion of the appropriate national authority or, as the case may be, the body concerned the document is suitable for that purpose[5]. Such an approval takes effect in accordance with a notice[6] that is issued by the appropriate national authority or, as the case may be, the body giving the approval and that identifies the approved document in question, states the date on which the approval of it is to take effect, and specifies the provisions of building regulations for the purposes of which the document is approved[7]. The appropriate national authority or, as the case may be, the body that gave the approval may from time to time approve and issue a revision of the whole or any part of an approved document[8] issued for these purposes[9], and approve any revision or proposed revision of the whole or any part of an approved document[10]. The appropriate national authority or, as the case may be, the body that gave the approval may withdraw its approval of a document, and such a withdrawal of approval takes effect in accordance with a notice that is issued by the appropriate national authority or body concerned and that identifies the approved document in question[11], and which states the date on which the approval of it is to cease to have effect[12].

A failure on the part of a person to comply with an approved document does not of itself render him liable to any civil or criminal proceedings[13]. However, if, in any proceedings whether civil or criminal, it is alleged that a person has at any time contravened[14] a provision of building regulations a failure to comply with a document that at that time was approved for the purposes of that provision may be relied upon as tending to establish liability[15], and proof of compliance with such a document may be relied on as tending to negative liability[16].

1 As to the meaning of 'building regulations' see PARA 7.
2 Ie the Secretary of State or, where statutory functions have been transferred in relation to Wales, the Welsh Ministers: see PARA 5.
3 See the Building Act 1984 s 6(8). At the date at which this volume states the law no such body had been designated.
4 References in the Building Act 1984 ss 6, 7 (compliance or non-compliance with approved documents) (see the text and notes 5–16) to a document include references to a part of a document; and accordingly, in relation to a document of which part only is approved, a reference in s 6(2)–(8) or in s 7 to the approved document is a reference only to the part of it that is approved: s 6(2).
5 Building Act 1984 s 6(1).
6 In any proceedings, whether civil or criminal a document purporting to be a notice so issued as mentioned in the Building Act 1984 s 6(3) must be taken to be such a notice unless the contrary is proved (s 7(2)(a)), and a document that appears to the court to be the approved document to which such a notice refers must be taken to be that approved document unless the contrary is proved (s 7(2)(b)).
7 Building Act 1984 s 6(3).
8 References in the Building Act 1984 s 6(4), (5) and in s 7 to an approved document are references to that document as it has effect for the time being, regard being had to any revision of the whole or any part of it that has been approved under s 6(4): s 6(6).
9 Building Act 1984 s 6(4)(a). Where a body ceases to be a body designated for the purposes of s 6, the provisions of s 6(4), (5) (see the text and notes 10–12) have effect as if any approval given by that body had been given by the appropriate national authority: s 6(7).
10 Building Act 1984 s 6(4)(b). Section 6(3), with the necessary modifications, applies in relation to an approval that is given under s 6(4) to a revision as it applies in relation to an approval that is given under s 6(1) to a document: s 6(4). As to the meaning of 'modifications' see PARA 3 note 21. See note 9.
11 Building Act 1984 s 6(5)(a). See note 9.
12 Building Act 1984 s 6(5)(b). See note 9.

13 Building Act 1984 s 7(1). The burden of showing non-compliance with an approved document falls on the local authority, but once it has shown such non-compliance, the burden is on the builder to show that the works do nonetheless comply with the building regulations: *Rickards and Rickards v Kerrier District Council* (1987) 151 JP 625.

14 As to the meaning of 'contravention' see PARA 12 note 10.

15 Building Act 1984 s 7(1)(a). See also note 13.

16 Building Act 1984 s 7(1)(b).

(4) Type Approval

24. Power to approve type of building matter.

As from a day to be appointed, the following provisions have effect[1] with a view to enabling the appropriate national authority[2], either on an application[3] made to it or of its own accord, to approve a particular type of building matter[4] as complying, either generally or in a class of case, with particular requirements of building regulations[5]. Such an application for the approval of a type of building matter must comply with any requirements of building regulations as to the form of such applications and the particulars to be included in them[6]. Where the appropriate national authority so approves a type of building matter as complying with particular requirements of building regulations either generally or in a class of case[7], it may issue a certificate to that effect specifying:

(1)   the type of building matter to which the certificate relates[8];

(2)   the requirements of building regulations to which the certificate relates[9]; and

(3)   where applicable, the class or classes of case to which the certificate applies[10].

Such a certificate, if it so provides, ceases to have effect at the end of such period as may be specified in the certificate[11]. If, while such a certificate is in force, it is found, in a particular case involving building matter of the type to which the certificate relates, that the building matter in question is of that type, and the case is one to which the certificate applies, that building matter is in that particular case deemed to comply with the requirements of building regulations to which the certificate relates[12].

The appropriate national authority may vary such a certificate, either on an application[13] made to it or of its own accord[14]. However, in the case of a certificate issued on an application made by a person[15], the appropriate national authority, except where it varies the certificate on the application of that person, must before varying it give that person reasonable notice that it proposes to do so[16]. The appropriate national authority may revoke a certificate so issued[17], but, before doing so in the case of a certificate issued on an application made by a person[18], must give the person on whose application the certificate was issued reasonable notice that it proposes to do so[19]. Where the appropriate national authority issues such a certificate or varies or revokes a certificate so issued, it must publish notice of that fact in such manner as it thinks fit[20].

The appropriate national authority may by building regulations delegate to a person or body, to such extent and subject to such conditions as it may think fit, the powers of approval conferred on it by the provisions described above[21].

1   In so far as the Building Act 1984 ss 12, 13 enable regulations to be made, they came into force on 1 December 1984 by virtue of s 134(2). At the date at which this volume states the law no order had been made bringing s 12 or s 13 into force for remaining purposes.

2   Ie the Secretary of State or, where statutory functions have been transferred in relation to Wales, the Welsh Ministers: see PARA 5.

3   Building regulations may require a person making an application under the Building Act 1984 s 12(1) to pay the appropriate national authority the prescribed fee, and, without prejudice to Sch 1 para 10 (see PARA 9), regulations so made may prescribe different fees for different cases, and the appropriate national authority may in a particular case remit the whole or part of a fee so payable: s 12(7) (not yet in force). As to the meaning of 'building regulations' see PARA 7. 'Prescribed means prescribed by building regulations: see s 126.

4   As to the meaning of 'building matter' see PARA 22 note 3; definition applied by virtue of the Building Act 1984 s 12(12) (not yet in force).

5   Building Act 1984 s 12(1) (not yet in force).

6   Building Act 1984 s 12(2) (not yet in force).

7   For the purposes of the Building Act 1984 s 12(3) (see the text and notes 8–10), a class of case may be framed in any way that the appropriate national authority thinks fit: s 12(11) (not yet in force).

8   Building Act 1984 s 12(3)(a) (not yet in force). See note 12.

9   Building Act 1984 s 12(3)(b) (not yet in force). See note 12.

10 Building Act 1984 s 12(3)(c) (not yet in force). See note 12.

11 Building Act 1984 s 12(4) (not yet in force). See note 12.

12 Building Act 1984 s 12(5) (not yet in force). If at any time a certificate under s 12(3) (see the text to notes 7–10) ceases to have effect by virtue of s 12(4) (see the text to note 11), or is varied or revoked under s 12(6) (see the text to notes 13–14) or s 12(8) (see the text to notes 17–19), that fact does not affect the continued operation of s 12(5) by virtue of that certificate in a case in which before that time plans of the proposed work were, in accordance with building regulations, deposited with a local authority: s 12(10)(a) (not yet in force) (amended by the Statute Law (Repeals) Act 2004). As to the meaning of 'plans' see PARA 9 note 8. As to references to the deposit of plans in accordance with building regulations see PARA 22 note 18.

13 Building regulations may require a person making an application under the Building Act 1984 s 12(6) to pay the appropriate national authority the prescribed fee, and, without prejudice to Sch 1 para 10 (see PARA 9), regulations so made may prescribe different fees for different cases, and the appropriate national authority may in a particular case remit the whole or part of a fee so payable: s 12(7).

14 Building Act 1984 s 12(6) (not yet in force). See note 12.

15 Ie under the Building Act 1984 s 12(1): see the text to notes 1–5.

16 Building Act 1984 s 12(6) (not yet in force). See note 12. For the purposes of any variation of a certificate under s 12(6), a class of case may be framed in any way that the appropriate national authority thinks fit: s 12(11) (not yet in force).

17 Ie under the Building Act 1984 s 12(3): see the text to notes 7–10.

18 Ie under the Building Act 1984 s 12(1): see the text to notes 1–5.

19 Building Act 1984 s 12(8) (not yet in force). See note 12.

20 Building Act 1984 s 12(9) (not yet in force).

21 Building Act 1984 s 13(1) (not yet in force). So far as those powers are for the time being so delegated to a person or body, s 12, except s 12(7) (see note 13) as far as the end of s 12(7)(a), and any building regulations made by virtue of s 12(7) (subject to any prescribed conditions) have effect in relation to that person or body with the substitution of references to that person or body for references to the appropriate national authority: s 13(2) (not yet in force).

(5) Plans and Notices

(i) Giving of Notices, Plans and Certificates

25. Giving of a building notice or deposit of plans.
A person who intends to:

(1)   carry out building work[1];

(2)   replace or renovate a thermal element in a building to which the energy efficiency requirements apply[2];

(3)   make a change to a building's energy status[3]; or

(4)   make a material change of use[4],

must give[5] to the local authority a building notice[6], or deposit full plans[7] with the local authority[8]. A person must deposit full plans where he intends to carry out:

(a)   building work in relation to a building to which the Regulatory Reform (Fire Safety) Order 2005[9] applies, or will apply after the completion of the building work[10];

(b)   work which includes the erection of a building fronting on to a private street[11]; and

(c)   building work in relation to which a requirement[12] as to building over sewers is imposed[13].

A person is not required to give a building notice or deposit full plans where he intends to carry out work consisting only of certain types of work[14].

A person intending to carry out building work to which electricity safety requirements is imposed[14] is required to give a building notice or deposit full plans where the work consists of:

(i)   the installation of a new circuit[15];

(ii)   the replacement of a consumer unit[16]; or

(iii)   any addition or alteration to existing circuits in a special location[17].

Where the statutory provision relating to local authority powers in relation to partly completed work[18] applies, the owner must comply with the requirements of that provision instead of with the provisions described above[19]. Where a person proposes to carry out building work which consists of emergency repairs, and it is not practicable to give a building notice to the local authority[20] or deposit full plans[21] before commencing the work, and the work is not specifically excepted work[22], the person must give a building notice to the local authority as soon as reasonably practicable after commencement of the work[23].

1   Building Regulations 2010, SI 2010/2214, reg 12(1)(a). As to the meaning of 'building work' see PARA 10.

2   Building Regulations 2010, SI 2010/2214, reg 12(1)(b). As to the meaning of 'thermal element' see PARA 10 note 15. As to the meaning of 'building' see PARA 10 note 3.

3   Building Regulations 2010, SI 2010/2214, reg 12(1)(c).

4   Building Regulations 2010, SI 2010/2214, reg 12(1)(d). As to the meaning of 'material change of use' see PARA 11.

5   Ie in accordance with the Building Regulations 2010, SI 2010/2214, reg 13: see PARA 26.

6   Building Regulations 2010, SI 2010/2214, reg 12(2)(a). Regulation 12 does not apply in respect of any work specified in an initial notice, an amendment notice or a public body's notice, which is in force: reg 19(1). As to an initial notice, an amendment notice and a public body's notice see PARA 72 et seq. 'Building notice' means a notice given in accordance with reg 12(2)(a) and reg 13 (see PARA 26): reg 2(1).

7   Ie in accordance with the Building Regulations 2010, SI 2010/2214, reg 14 (see PARA 27). 'Full plans' means plans deposited with a local authority for the purposes of the Building Act 1984 s 16 (see PARA 33) in accordance with the Building Regulations 2010, SI 2010/2214, reg 12(2)(b) and reg 14 (see PARA 27): reg 2(1).

8   Building Regulations 2010, SI 2010/2214, reg 12(2)(b). As to notice given for a proposal to carry out building work to which the Domestic Fire Safety (Wales) Measure 2011 applies (see PARA 58).

9   Ie the Regulatory Reform (Fire Safety) Order 2005, SI 2005/1541: see FIRE AND RESCUE SERVICES vol 51 (2013) PARA 70.

10   Building Regulations 2010, SI 2010/2214, reg 12(3).

11   Building Regulations 2010, SI 2010/2214, reg 12(4). 'Fronting' has the meaning given in the Highways Act 1980 s 203(3) (see HIGHWAYS, STREETS AND BRIDGES vol 55 (2012) PARA 157); and 'private street' has the meaning given in s 203(2) (see HIGHWAYS, STREETS AND BRIDGES vol 55 (2012) PARA 10): Building Regulations 2010, SI 2010/2214, reg 12(9).

12   Ie in relation to which the Building Regulations 2010, SI 2010/2214, Sch 1 para H4 imposes a requirement: see PARA 10.

13   Building Regulations 2010, SI 2010/2214, reg 12(5).

14 Building Regulations 2010, SI 2010/2214, reg 12(6) (amended by SI 2014/579; and SI 2018/588). A person intending to carry out building work is not required to give a building notice or deposit full plans where the work consists only of:

(1)   the installation of: heat producing gas appliances; heating or hot water systems; combustion appliances; mechanical ventilation or air conditioning systems; lighting systems; fixed low or extra-low voltage electrical installations; replacement doors or windows; sanitary conveniences etc; cold water supply; systems to produce electricity, heat or cooling; cavity wall insulation; replacement roof coverings; or any building work which is necessary to ensure that any such appliance, service or fitting which is installed complies with Sch 1 (as more specifically described in column 1 of the Table in Sch 3) if the work is to be carried out by a person described in the corresponding entry in column 2 of Sch 3 (see Sch 3 (substituted by SI 2014/57; amended by SI 2015/1486; SI 2016/285; SI 2017/856; and SI 2017/1274));

(2)   work consisting of:

(a)   replacing any fixed electrical equipment which does not include the provision of:

(i)   any new fixed cabling (Building Regulations 2010, SI 2010/2214, Sch 4 para 1(a)(i) (Sch 4 para 1(a)–(e) revoked in relation to England; substituted in relation to Wales by SI 2018/558)); or

(ii)   a consumer unit (Building Regulations 2010, SI 2010/2214, Sch 4 para 1(a)(ii) (as so revoked and substituted));

(b)   replacing a damaged cable for a single circuit only (Building Regulations 2010, SI 2010/2214, Sch 4 para 1(b) (as so revoked and substituted));

(c)   re-fixing or replacing enclosures of existing installation components, where the circuit protective measures are unaffected (Sch 4 para 1(c) (as so revoked and substituted));

(d)   providing mechanical protection to an existing fixed installation, where the circuit protective measures and current carrying capacity of conductors are unaffected by the increased thermal insulation (Sch 4 para 1(d) (as so revoked and substituted));

(e)   installing or upgrading main or supplementary equipotential bonding (Sch 4 para 1(e) (as so revoked and substituted));

(f)   in relation to an existing fixed building service, which is not a fixed internal or external lighting system:

(i)   replacing any part which is not a combustion appliance (Sch 4 para 1(f)(i));

(ii)   adding an output device (Sch 4 para 1(f)(ii)); or

(iii)   adding a control device (Sch 4 para 1(f)(iii)),

where testing and adjustment of the work is not possible or would not affect the use by the fixed building service of no more fuel and power than is reasonable in the circumstances (Sch 4 para 1(f) (amended by SI 2011/1515));

(g)   providing a self-contained fixed building service, which is not a fixed internal or external lighting system, where:

(i)   it is not a combustion appliance (in relation to England, other than a fixed flueless gas cooker) (Sch 4 para 1(g)(i) (amended by SI 2014/579; and SI 2018/558));

(ii)   any electrical work associated with its provision is exempt from the requirement to give a building notice or to deposit full plans by virtue of the Building Regulations 2010, SI 2010/2214, reg 9 (see PARA 16) or in relation to England , reg 12(6A) (reg 12(6)(b) in relation to Wales) (see PARA 25) (Sch 4 para 1(g)(ii) (as so amended));

(iii)   testing and adjustment is not possible or would not affect its energy efficiency (Sch 4 para 1(g)(iii)); and

(iv)   in the case of a mechanical ventilation appliance, the appliance is not installed in a room containing an open-flued combustion appliance whose combustion products are discharged through a natural draught flue (Sch 4 para 1(g)(iv));

(h)   replacing an external door (where the door together with its frame has not more than 50% of its internal face area glazed) (Building Regulations 2010, SI 2010/2214, Sch 4 para 1(h));

(i)   in existing buildings other than dwellings, providing fixed internal lighting where no more than 100m^2 of the floor area of the building is to be served by the lighting (Sch 4 para 1(i));

(j)   replacing:
        (i)   a sanitary convenience with one that uses no more water than the one it replaces (Sch 4 para 1(j)(i));
        (ii)   a washbasin, sink or bidet (Sch 4 para 1(j)(ii));
        (iii)   a fixed bath(Sch 4 para 1(j)(iii));
        (iv)   a shower (Sch 4 para 1(j)(iv));
        (v)   a rainwater gutter (Sch 4 para 1(j)(v); or
        (vi)   a rainwater downpipe (Sch 4 para 1(j)(vi)),
        where the work does not include any work to underground drainage, and includes no work to the hot or cold water system or above ground drainage, which may prejudice the health or safety of any person on completion of the work (Sch 4 para 1(j));

(k)   in relation to an existing cold water supply:
        (i)   replacing any part (Sch 4 para 1(k)(i));
        (ii)   adding an output device (Sch 4 para 1(k)(ii)); or
        (iii)   adding a control device (Sch 4 para 1(k)(iii));

(l)   providing a hot water storage system that has a storage vessel with a capacity not exceeding 15 litres, where any electrical work associated with its provision is exempt from the requirement to give a building notice or to deposit full plans by virtue of reg 9 or reg 12(6)(b) (Sch 4 para 1(l));

(m)   installation of thermal insulation in a roof space or loft space where:
        (i)   the work consists solely of the installation of such insulation (Sch 4 para 1(m)(i)); and
        (ii)   the work is not carried out in order to comply with any requirement of the Building Regulations 2010, SI 2010/2214 (Sch 4 para 1(m));

(3)   work which:
    (a)   is not in a kitchen, or a special location (as to the meaning of which see below) (Sch 4 para 2(a) (Sch 4 paras 2, 3 (revoked in relation to England by SI 2012/3119; added in relation to Wales by SI 2018/558));
    (b)   does not involve work on a special installation (as to the meaning of which see below) (Building Regulations 2010, SI 2010/2214, Sch 4 para 2(b) (as so revoked and added)); and
    (c)   consists of adding light fittings and switches to an existing circuit, or adding socket outlets and fused spurs to an existing ring or radial circuit (Sch 4 para 2(c) (as so revoked and added));

(4)   work on:
    (a)   telephone wiring or extra-low voltage wiring for the purposes of communications, information technology, signalling, control and similar purposes, where the wiring is not in a special location (Sch 4 para 3(a) (as so revoked and added));
    (b)   equipment associated with such wiring (Sch 4 para 3(b) (as so revoked; and added));
    (c)   pre-fabricated equipment sets and associated flexible leads with integral plug and socket connections (Sch 4 para 3(c) (as so revoked; and added)).

(5)   installation of thermal insulation to suspended timber floors where the work:
    (a)   consists of the installation of such insulation only (Sch 4 para 3A(a) (Sch 4 para 3A added in relation to England by SI 2012/3119 and in relation to Wales by SI 2013/747)); and
    (b)   the work is not carried out in order to comply with any requirements of the Building Regulations 2010, SI 2010/2214 (Sch 4 para 3A(b) (as so added));

(6)   electrical installations in dwellings if the work is to be inspected by a person registered in respect of the electrical installations by NAPIT Registration Limited or Stroma Certification Ltd (a 'third party certifier') who has been appointed by the person intending to carry out the building work before the commencement of that work (see Sch 3A Table (added in relation to England by SI 2014/579; and amended by SI 2014/2362).

For these purposes, 'kitchen' means a room or part of a room which contains a sink and food preparation facilities: Building Regulations 2010, SI 2010/2214, Sch 4 para 4 (definition revoked in relation to England by SI 2012/3119; added in relation to Wales by SI 2018/558). 'Self-contained' in relation to a fixed building service means consisting of a single appliance and any associated controls which is neither connected to, nor forms part of, any other fixed building service: Building Regulations 2010, SI 2010/2214, Sch 4 para 4. 'Special installation' means an electric floor or ceiling heating system, an outdoor lighting or electric power installation, an electricity generator, or an extra-low voltage lighting system which is not a pre-assembled lighting set bearing the CE marking referred to in the Electrical Equipment (Safety) Regulations 2016, SI 2016/1101, reg 39: Building Regulations 2010, SI 2010/2214, Sch 4 para 4 (definition revoked in relation to England by SI 2012/3119; added in relation to Wales by SI 2018/558). 'Special location' means a location within the limits of the relevant zones specified for a bath, a shower, a swimming or paddling pool or a hot air sauna in the Wiring Regulations as published by the Institution of Electrical Engineers and the British Standards Institution: Building Regulations 2010, SI 2010/2214, Sch 4 para 4 (definition revoked in relation to England; added in relation to Wales by SI 2018/558).

14 Ie by the Building Regulations 2010, SI 2010/2214, Sch 1 Pt P: see PARA 10.

15 Building Regulations 2010, SI 2010/2214, reg 12(6A)(a) (added by SI 2012/3119; and SI 2018/558).

16 Building Regulations 2010, SI 2010/2214, reg 12(6A)(b) (as so added).

17 Building Regulations 2010, SI 2010/2214, reg 12(6A)(c) (as so added). 'Special location' means:
   (1)   within a room containing a bath or shower, the space surrounding a bath tap or shower head, where the space extends:
          (a)   vertically from the finished floor level a height of 2.25 metres or the position of the shower head where it is attached to a wall or ceiling at a point higher than 2.25 metres from that level (reg 12(9) amended by SI 2012/3119; and SI 2018/558); and
          (b)   horizontally where there is a bath tub or shower tray, from the edge of the bath tub or shower tray to a distance of 0.6 metres or where there is no bath tub or shower tray, from the centre point of the shower head where it is attached to the wall or ceiling to a distance of 1.2 metres (Building Regulations 2010, SI 2010/2214, reg 12(9)(a)(ii) (definition as so added);
   (2)   a room containing a swimming pool or sauna heater (reg 12(9)(b) (definition as so added)).

18 Ie the Building (Approved Inspectors etc) Regulations 2010, SI 2010/2215, reg 19: see PARA 82.

19 Building Regulations 2010, SI 2010/2214, reg 12(7).

20 Ie in accordance with the Building Regulations 2010, SI 2010/2214, reg 13.

21 Ie in accordance with the Building Regulations 2010, SI 2010/2214, reg 14.

22 Ie the Building Regulations 2010, SI 2010/2214, reg 12(6) does not apply: see note 14.

23 Building Regulations 2010, SI 2010/2214, reg 12(8).

26. Particulars and plans where a building notice is given.

A building notice[1] must state the name and address of the person intending to carry out the work[2] and must be signed by him or on his behalf, and must contain or be accompanied by a statement that it is given for the statutory purposes[3], a description of the proposed building work[4], renovation or replacement of a thermal element, change to the building's energy status or material change of use[5], particulars of the location of the building[6] to which the proposal relates and the use or intended use of that building[7]. In the case of a new dwelling, such a notice must contain or be accompanied by:

   (1)   a statement whether or not any optional requirement applies to the building work, and if so which[8]; or

   (2)   a statement that planning permission has not yet been granted for the work, and that the information required by head (1) will be supplied before the end of a period of twenty eight days beginning on the day after that permission is granted[9].

In the case of the erection or extension of a building, a building notice must be accompanied by:

   (a)   a plan[8] showing:
          (i)   the size and position of the building, or the building as extended, and its relationship to adjoining boundaries[9];
          (ii)   the boundaries of the curtilage of the building, or the building as extended, and the size, position and use of every other building or proposed building within that curtilage[10];

       (iii)   the width and position of any street on or within the boundaries of the curtilage of the building or the building as extended[11];

(b)   a statement specifying the number of storeys (each basement level being counted as one storey) in the building to which the proposal relates[12]; and

(c)   particulars of the provision to be made for the drainage of the building or extension[13], and the steps to be taken to comply with any local enactment which applies[14].

Where a building notice has been given, a person carrying out building work, renovation or replacement of a thermal element, change to the building's energy status or making a material change of use must give the local authority, within such time as they specify, such plans as are, in the particular case, necessary for the discharge of their functions in relation to building regulations and are specified by them in writing[15].

A building notice ceases to have effect on the expiry of three years from the date on which that notice was given to the local authority, unless before the expiry of that period the building work to which the notice related was commenced, or the change to the building's energy status or the material change of use described in the notice was made[16].

1 As to the meaning of 'building notice' see PARA 25 note 6.
2 The owner of a building who authorises a contractor to carry out building works on his behalf is a 'person carrying out building works' for the purposes of the building regulations; the meaning of that term is not restricted to the person who physically performs the work: *Blaenau Gwent Borough Council v Khan* (1993) 35 Con LR 65, (1993) Times, 4 May, DC.
3 Building Regulations 2010, SI 2010/2214, reg 13(1)(a). The statutory purposes referred to in the text are specifically the purposes of reg 12(2)(a): see PARA 25.
4 As to the meaning of 'building work' see PARA 10.
5 Building Regulations 2010, SI 2010/2214, reg 13(1)(b). As to the meaning of 'thermal element' see PARA 10 note 15. As to the meaning of 'material change of use' see PARA 11.
6 As to the meaning of 'building' see PARA 10 note 3.
7 Building Regulations 2010, SI 2010/2214, reg 13(1)(c).
8 Building Regulations 2010, SI 2010/2214, reg 13(1)(d)(i) (reg 13(1)(d), (1A) added by SI 2015/767; and amended by SI 2018/558).
9 Building Regulations 2010, SI 2010/2214, reg 13(1)(d)(ii) (as added: see note 8). In the case of a new dwelling, where a statement under head (2) has accompanied the building notice, a statement in the terms required by head (1) must be provided to the local authority before the end of a period of twenty eight days beginning on the day after planning permission is granted for the building work, and the statement must state that it is supplementary to the information given in respect of the work pursuant to heads (1) and (2): reg 13(1A) (as so added).
8 Ie a plan to a scale of not less than 1:1250: see the Building Regulations 2010, SI 2010/2214, reg 13(2)(a).
9 Building Regulations 2010, SI 2010/2214, reg 13(2)(a)(i).
10 Building Regulations 2010, SI 2010/2214, reg 13(2)(a)(ii).
11 Building Regulations 2010, SI 2010/2214, reg 13(2)(a)(iii).
12 Building Regulations 2010, SI 2010/2214, reg 13(2)(b).
13 Building Regulations 2010, SI 2010/2214, reg 13(2)(c)(i).
14 Building Regulations 2010, SI 2010/2214, reg 13(2)(c)(iii).
15 Building Regulations 2010, SI 2010/2214, reg 13(3). Neither a building notice nor plans which accompany it or are given under reg 13(3) are to be treated for the purposes of the Building Act 1984 s 16 (see PARA 33) as having been deposited in accordance with building regulations: Building Regulations 2010, SI 2010/2214, reg 13(4).
16 Building Regulations 2010, SI 2010/2214, reg 13(5).

27. Full plans.

Full plans[1] must be accompanied by a statement that they are being deposited for statutory purposes[2]. Full plans must be deposited in duplicate and the local authority may retain one copy[3]. Where a requirement as to fire safety is imposed[4] in relation to proposed building work[5], an additional two copies of any such plans as demonstrate compliance with that requirement must be deposited, both of which may be retained by the local authority[6]. Full plans must consist of:

(1) a description of the proposed building work, renovation or replacement of a thermal element[7], change to the building's energy status or material change of use[8], and the required[9] plans, particulars and statements[10];

(2) where requirements are imposed as to building over sewers[11], particulars of the precautions to be taken in building over a drain, sewer or disposal main to comply with those requirements[12]; and

(3) any other plans which are necessary to show that the work would comply with the Building Regulations 2010[13].

Full plans must be accompanied by a statement as to whether the building is a building in relation to which the Regulatory Reform (Fire Safety) Order 2005[14] applies, or will apply after the completion of the building work[15].

1 As to the meaning of 'full plans' see PARA 25 note 7.
2 Building Regulations 2010, SI 2010/2214, reg 14(1). The statement must indicate that the full plan is being deposited for the purpose of reg 12(2)(b): see PARA 25.
3 Building Regulations 2010, SI 2010/2214, reg 14(2)(a).
   Where full plans are deposited by means of an electronic communication in accordance with the Building Act 1984 s 94A (see PARA 137), there is no need to deposit the full plans in duplicate, and the Building Regulations 2010, SI 2010/2214, reg 14 applies as if reg 14(2)(a) were omitted: see reg 48(2)(a).
4 Ie by the Building Regulations 2010, SI 2010/2214, Sch 1 Pt B: see PARA 10.
5 As to the meaning of 'building work' see PARA 10.
6 Building Regulations 2010, SI 2010/2214, reg 14(2)(b). Where full plans are deposited by means of an electronic communication in accordance with the Building Act 1984 s 94A (see PARA 137), only one copy need be deposited which may be retained by the local authority: see reg 48(2)(b).
   Regulation 14(2)(b) does not require the deposit of additional copies of plans where the proposed building work relates to the erection, extension or material alteration of a dwelling house or flat: regs 14(6), 48(2)(c). As to the meaning of 'material alteration' see PARA 10 note 6. As to the meaning of 'dwelling house' see PARA 10 note 31. As to the meaning of 'flat' see PARA 10 note 31.
7 As to the meaning of 'thermal element' see PARA 10 note 15.
8 As to the meaning of 'material change of use' see PARA 11.
9 Ie required by the Building Regulations 2010, SI 2010/2214, reg 13(1), (1A), (2): see PARA 26.
10 Building Regulations 2010, SI 2010/2214, reg 14(3)(a) (amended by SI 2015/767; and SI 2018/558).
11 Ie by the Building Regulations 2010, SI 2010/2214, Sch 1 para H4: see PARA 10. See also PARA 43.
12 Building Regulations 2010, SI 2010/2214, reg 14(3)(b).
13 Building Regulations 2010, SI 2010/2214, reg 14(3)(c).
14 Ie the Regulatory Reform (Fire Safety) Order 2005, SI 2005/1541: see FIRE AND RESCUE SERVICES vol 51 (2013) PARA 70.
15 Building Regulations 2010, SI 2010/2214, reg 14(4).

28. Notice of commencement and completion of certain stages of work.
A person who proposes to carry out building work[1] must not commence that work unless he has given the local authority notice that he intends to commence work[2], and at least two days[3] have elapsed since the end of the day on which he gave the notice[4]. A person carrying out building work[5] must notify the local authority as required by the authority in accordance with statutory provisions[6]. Where a person fails to comply with these requirements[7], he must comply within a reasonable time with any notice given by the local authority requiring him to cut

into, lay open or pull down so much of the work as prevents it from ascertaining whether the Building Regulations 2010 have been complied with[8].

A person carrying out building work must, not more than five days after that work has been completed, give the local authority notice to that effect[9]. Where a building[10] is being erected to which the Regulatory Reform (Fire Safety) Order 2005[11] applies, or will apply after the completion of the work, and that building, or any part of it, is to be occupied before completion, the person carrying out that work must give the local authority at least five days' notice before the building or any part of it is occupied[12].

If the local authority has given notice specifying the manner in which any work contravenes the requirements in the Building Regulations 2010, a person who has carried out any further work to secure compliance with the regulations must within a reasonable time after the completion of such further work give notice to the local authority of its completion[13].

1   As to the meaning of 'building work' see PARA 10.
2   Building Regulations 2010, SI 2010/2214, reg 16(1)(a). Regulation 16 does not apply in respect of any work specified in an initial notice, an amendment notice or a public body's notice, which is in force: reg 19(1). As to an initial notice, an amendment notice and a public body's notice see PARA 72 et seq. The provisions of reg 16(1)–(4) apply only to a person who is required by reg 12 (see PARA 25) to give a building notice or deposit full plans: reg 16(8). However, reg 16(1) does not apply where reg 12(8) applies (ie where (1) a person proposes to carry out building work which consists of emergency repairs; (2) it is not practicable to give the local authority a building notice or deposit full plans before commencing the work; and (3) the building work is not work specified in Sch 3, 3A or Sch 4: see PARA 25): reg 16(9). As to the meaning of 'building notice' see PARA 25 note 6. As to the meaning of 'full plans' see PARA 25 note 7.
3   As to the meaning of 'day' see PARA 16 note 16.
4   Building Regulations 2010, SI 2010/2214, reg 16(1)(b). See note 2.
5   The owner of a building who authorises a contractor to carry out building works on his behalf is a 'person carrying out building works' for the purposes of the building regulations; the meaning of that term is not restricted to the person who physically performs the work: *Blaenau Gwent Borough Council v Khan* (1993) 35 Con LR 65, DC.
6   Building Regulations 2010, SI 2010/2214, reg 16(2) (reg 16(2), (3) substituted, reg 16(3A), (3B) added by SI 2015/767); and amended by SI 2018/558). The statutory provisions referred to in the text is the Building Regulations 2010, SI 2010/2214, reg 16(3): reg 16(2). Subject to the conditions in the Building Regulations 2010, SI 2010/2214, reg 16(3A), (3B), where a local authority receives notice of intention to commence building work under reg 16(1) they may give the person carrying out the work a notice in writing which requires that person to notify the authority that a specified stage of the work (other than a stage specified in reg 16(4), (5) has been reached (reg 16(3)(a) (as so substituted)) and may specify one or more periods of time, applying to each such required notification, which may be either or both of the following:
    (1)   a period before or after the work has been carried out within which the notification must be made (reg 16(3)(b)(i) (as so substituted)); and
    (2)   a period during which the work concerned must not be covered up (reg 16(3)(b)(as so substituted)).
    A local authority may only specify a stage of the building work in accordance with reg 16(3)(a) if at the time they do so they intend to carry out an inspection of that stage: reg 16(3A) (as so added). For these purposes, the local authority's intention to carry out an inspection of a stage of building work must be based on their assessment of the risk of breach of the Building Regulations 2010, SI 2010/2214 if they do not inspect the work: reg 16(3B) (as so added). See note 2.
7   Ie the Building Regulations 2010, SI 2010/2214, reg 16(1), (2): see the text and notes 1–10.
8   Building Regulations 2010, SI 2010/2214, reg 16(6) (amended by SI 2012/3119; and SI 2018/558).
9   Building Regulations 2010, SI 2010/2214, reg 16(4). See note 2.
10 As to the meaning of 'building' see PARA 10 note 3.
11 Ie the Regulatory Reform (Fire Safety) Order 2005, SI 2005/1541.
12 Building Regulations 2010, SI 2010/2214, reg 16(5) (amended by SI 2012/3119; and SI 2013/747).
13 Building Regulations 2010, SI 2010/2214, reg 16(7).

29.   Completion certificates.
A local authority must within the specified period[1] give a completion certificate in all cases (including a case where a certificate has already been given for a building occupied before the work is completed[2] where they are satisfied, after taking all reasonable steps, that, following completion of building work carried out on it, a building complies with the relevant statutory provisions[3].

A local authority must within the specified period[4] give a completion certificate in respect of part or all of a building where building work is being carried out and where all of the following circumstances apply:

(1)   part or all of the building is to be occupied before the work is completed[5];

(2)   the building is subject to the Regulatory Reform (Fire Safety) Order 2005[6];

(3)   the authority is satisfied, after taking all reasonable steps, that, regardless of completion of the current building work, those parts of the building which are to be occupied before completion of the work currently comply with the requirements relating to fire safety[7].

A completion certificate[8] is evidence, but not conclusive evidence, that the requirements specified in the certificate have been complied with[9], and in a case where a certificate has already been given for a building occupied before the work is completed, the certificate must contain this wording[10].

1   Ie eight weeks starting from the date on which the person carrying out the building work notifies the local authority that the work has been completed: Building Regulations 2010, SI 2010/2214, reg 17(2) (reg 17(1), (2) substituted and reg 17(2A) added in relation to England by SI 2012/3119; and in relation to Wales by SI 2013/747).
2   Ie under the Building Regulations 2010, SI 2010/2214, reg 17A (see text and notes 4–10): reg 17(1) (as substituted: see note 2).
3   Building Regulations 2010, SI 2010/2214, reg 17(1) (as substituted: see note 1). The relevant provisions referred to in reg 17(1) are any applicable requirements of the following provisions:
    (1)   reg 25A (high energy alternative systems for new buildings) (see PARA 46 (reg 17(2A)(a) (as added: see note 1));
    (2)   reg 26 (target CO_2 emission rates for new buildings) (see PARA 46 (reg 17(2A)(b) (as so added));
    (3)   reg 26A (target fabric energy efficiency requirements for new dwellings) (see PARA 46) (reg 17(2A)(c) (as so added); and amended by SI 2016/285; SI 2016/611; and SI 2018/558);
    (4)   Building Regulations 2010, SI 2010/2214, reg 36 (water efficiency of new dwellings) (see PARA 53) (reg 17(2A)(d));
    (5)   reg 38 (fire safety information) (see PARA 56) (reg 17(2A)(e));
    (6)   Sch 1 (see PARA 10) (reg 17(2A)(f));
    (7)   Energy Performance of Buildings (England and Wales) Regulations 2012, SI 2012/3118, reg 7A (see PARA 52) (Building Regulations 2010, SI 2010/2214, reg 17(2A)(g) (added in relation to England by SI 2016/285; and in relation to Wales by SI 2016/611; and SI 2016/285)
    The Building Regulations 2010, SI 2010/2214, reg 17 is designated as a provision to which the Building Act 1984 s 35 (penalty for contravening building regulations) (see PARA 61) does not apply: Building Regulations 2010, SI 2010/2214, reg 47 (substituted by SI 2012/3119; SI 2018/552; and SI 2018/558; amended by SI 2013/747; SI 2014/110; and SI 2014/579) . Regulation 17 does not apply in respect of any work specified in an initial notice, an amendment notice or a public body's notice, which is in force: reg 19(1) (amended by SI 2012/3119; SI 2013/747; SI 2016/285; and SI 2016/611).
4   Ie four weeks starting from the date that notice is received by the local authority in accordance with the Building Regulations 2010, SI 2010/2214, reg 16(5) (see PARA 28: reg 17A(2) (as so added).
5   Building Regulations 2010, SI 2010/2214, reg 17A(1)(a) (added in relation to England by SI 2012/3119; and in relation to Wales by SI 2013/747). The Building Regulations 2010, SI 2010/2214, reg 17A is designated as a provision to which the Building Act 1984 s 35 (penalty

for contravening building regulations) (see PARA 61) does not apply: Building Regulations 2010, SI 2010/2214, reg 47 (substituted by SI 2012/3119; SI 2018/552; and SI 2018/558; amended by SI 2013/747; SI 2014/110; and SI 2014/579). The Building Regulations 2010, SI 2010/2214, reg 17A does not apply in respect of any work specified in an initial notice, an amendment notice or a public body's notice, which is in force: reg 19(1) (amended by SI 2012/3119; SI 2013/747; SI 2016/285; and SI 2016/611).

6   Building Regulations 2010, SI 2010/2214, reg 17A(1)(b) (as so added). The text refers to the Regulatory Reform (Fire Safety) Order 2005, SI 2005/1541: Building Regulations 2010, SI 2010/2214, reg 17A(1)(b) (as so added).
7   Building Regulations 2010, SI 2010/2214, reg 17A(1)(c) (as so added). The text refers to the Building Regulations 2010, SI 2010/2214, reg 38, Sch 1 Pt B.
8   Ie given in accordance with the Building Regulations 2010, SI 2010/2214, reg 17 (see notes 1–3) or reg 17A.
9   Building Regulations 2010, SI 2010/2214, reg 17(4). The certificate must include a statement describing its evidentiary effect, in terms substantially the same as reg 17(5) (added in relation to England by SI 2012/3119; and in relation to Wales by SI 2013/747).
10 Building Regulations 2010, SI 2010/2214, reg 17A(3). The certificate must include a statement describing its evidentiary effect, in terms substantially the same as reg 17A(3) (added in relation to England by SI 2012/3119; and in relation to Wales by SI 2013/747).

30. Energy performance certificates.

Where a building[1] is erected or a building is modified so that it has a greater or lesser number of parts designed or altered for separate use than it previously had, where the modification includes the provision or extension of any of the fixed services for heating, hot water, air conditioning or mechanical ventilation, then the person carrying out the work must:

(1)   give an energy performance certificate for the building to the owner of the building[2];
(2)   give to the local authority notice to that effect[2]; and
(3)   include in that notice the reference number under which the energy performance certificate has been registered[3].

The law relating to the energy performance of buildings and the requirements in relation to energy performance certificates are covered in more detail elsewhere in the title[3].

1   As to the meaning of 'building' see PARA 44 note 2.
2   Energy Performance of Buildings (England and Wales) Regulations 2012, SI 2012/3118, reg 7A(1), (2)(a).
2   See the Energy Performance of Buildings (England and Wales) Regulations 2012, SI 2012/3118, reg 7A(2)(b); and PARA 48.
3   Energy Performance of Buildings (England and Wales) Regulations 2012, SI 2012/3118, reg 7A(2)(c). The text refers to energy performance certificate registered in accordance with the Energy Performance of Buildings (England and Wales) Regulations 2012, SI 2012/3118, reg 27(4) (see PARA 49), except in the case of an energy performance certificate issued under reg 9A (energy performance certificates in respect of excluded buildings) (see PARA 48).
3   See the Energy Performance of Buildings (England and Wales) Regulations 2012, SI 2012/3118; and PARA 44 et seq.

31. Notice of testing and commissioning.

Where a person carries out building work[1] in relation to which the Building Regulations 2010[2] impose a requirement relating to the resistance to the passage of sound[3], the person carrying out the work must ensure that appropriate sound insulation testing is carried out and must give a copy of the results of the testing to the local authority[4].

Where a new dwelling is created by building work[5] and the Building Regulations 2010[6] impose a requirement that there must be adequate means of ventilation provided for people in the building[7], the person carrying out the work must ensure that testing of the mechanical ventilation air flow rate is carried out and must give notice of the results of the testing to the local authority[8].

Where, in relation to the erection of a building the Building Regulations 2010 impose a requirement that reasonable provision must be made for conservation of fuel and power in the building by limiting heat gains and losses through thermal elements and other parts of the building fabric[9], the person carrying out the work must[10] ensure that pressure testing is carried out[10] and must give notice of the results of the testing to the local authority[11].

Where the Building Regulations 2010 impose a requirement that fixed systems for mechanical ventilation must be commissioned by testing and adjusting as necessary to secure that there is adequate means of ventilation provided for people in the building[12], and where they impose a requirement that fixed building services are to be commissioned by testing and adjusting as necessary to ensure that they use no more fuel and power than is reasonable in the circumstances[13], then the person carrying out the building work must give to the local authority a notice confirming that the fixed building services have been commissioned in accordance with a procedure approved by the appropriate national authority[14].

The provisions described above[15] do not apply in respect of any work specified in an initial notice, an amendment notice or a public body's notice, which is in force[16].

1   As to the meaning of 'building work' see PARA 10.
2   Ie the Building Regulations 2010, SI 2010/2214.
3   Ie work in relation to which the Building Regulations 2010, SI 2010/2214, Sch 1 para E1 (see PARA 10) imposes a requirement, and work which is required to be carried out to a building to ensure that it complies with Sch 1 para E1 by virtue of reg 6(1)(f) or 6(2)(b) (see PARA 11).
4   Building Regulations 2010, SI 2010/2214, reg 41(1), (2). The results of the testing must be recorded in a manner approved by the appropriate national authority, and be given to the local authority not later than the date on which the notice required by reg 16(4) (see PARA 28) is given: reg 41(3). Regulation 41 is designated as a provision to which the Building Act 1984 s 35 (penalty for contravening building regulations) (see PARA 61) does not apply: Building Regulations 2010, SI 2010/2214, reg 47 (substituted by SI 2012/3119; SI 2018/552; and SI 2018/558; amended by SI 2013/747; SI 2014/110; and SI 2014/579). The Building Regulations 2010, SI 2010/2214, reg 41 does not apply in respect of any work specified in an initial notice, an amendment notice or a public body's notice, which is in force: reg 19(1) (amended by SI 2012/3119; SI 2013/747; SI 2016/285; and SI 2016/611). As to the appropriate national authority (ie the Secretary of State or, where statutory functions have been transferred in relation to Wales, the Welsh Ministers) see PARA 5. As to the meaning of 'local authority' see PARA 1 note 12.
        Note that in relation to building work which is the subject of an initial notice (as to which see PARA 74 et seq), the Building Regulations 2010, SI 2010/2214, reg 41 applies as if references to the local authority were references to the approved inspector: see the Building (Approved Inspectors etc) Regulations 2010, SI 2010/2215, reg 20(1); and PARA 87. In such cases the results of the testing must be given to the approved inspector not later than five days after completion of the work to which the initial notice relates: see reg 20(5)(a); and PARA 87.
        Where building work consists of the erection of a dwelling house or a building containing flats, the Building Regulations 2010, SI 2010/2214, reg 41 does not apply to any part of the building in relation to which the person carrying out the building work notifies the local authority, not later than the date on which notice of commencement of the work is given under reg 16(1), that, for the purpose of achieving compliance of the work with Sch 1 para E1, the person is using one or more approved design details, provided that (1) the notification specifies (a) the part or parts of the building in respect of which the person is using the design detail; (b) the design detail concerned; and (c) the unique number issued in respect of the specified use of that design detail; and (2) the building work carried out in respect of the part or parts of the building identified in the notification is in accordance with the design detail specified in the notification: see reg 41(4).
        In relation to building work which is the subject of an initial notice, reg 41(4) applies as if for the words 'not later than the date on which notice of commencement of the work is given under the Building Regulations 2010, SI 2010/2214, reg 16(1)' there were substituted the words 'prior to commencement of the building work on site': see the Building (Approved Inspectors etc)

Regulations 2010, SI 2010/2215, reg 20(5)(b); and PARA 87.

    As to the meanings of 'dwelling house' and 'flat' see PARA 10 note 31.

5 Building Regulations 2010, SI 2010/2214, reg 42(1). As to the meaning of 'dwelling' see PARA 10 note 31.

    Regulation 42 is designated as a provision to which the Building Act 1984 s 35 (penalty for contravening building regulations) (see PARA 61) does not apply: Building Regulations 2010, SI 2010/2214, reg 47 (substituted by SI 2012/3119; SI 2018/552; and SI 2018/558; amended by SI 2013/747; SI 2014/110; SI 2014/579). Regulation 42 does not apply in respect of any work specified in an initial notice, an amendment notice or a public body's notice, which is in force: reg 19(1) (amended by SI 2012/3119; SI 2013/747; SI 2016/285; and SI 2016/611).

6 See note 2.

7 See the Building Regulations 2010, SI 2010/2214, Sch 1 para F1(1); and PARA 10.

8 Building Regulations 2010, SI 2010/2214, reg 42(2). The notice must record the results and the data upon which they are based in a manner approved by the appropriate national authority, and must be given to the local authority not later than five days after the final test is carried out: reg 42(3). Note that in relation to building work which is the subject of an initial notice (as to which see PARA 74 et seq), reg 42 applies as if references to the local authority were references to the approved inspector: see the Building (Approved Inspectors etc) Regulations 2010, SI 2010/2215, reg 20(1); and PARA 87.

9 Building Regulations 2010, SI 2010/2214, reg 43(1). As to this requirement see Sch 1 para L1(a)(i); and PARA 10. As to the meaning of 'thermal element' see PARA 10 note 15.

    Regulation 43 is designated as a provision to which the Building Act 1984 s 35 (penalty for contravening building regulations) (see PARA 61) does not apply: Building Regulations 2010, SI 2010/2214, reg 47 (substituted by SI 2012/3119; SI 2017/552; and SI 2018/558; amended by SI 2013/747; SI 2014/110; and SI 2014/579). The Building Regulations 2010, SI 2010/2214, reg 43 does not apply in respect of any work specified in an initial notice, an amendment notice or a public body's notice, which is in force: reg 19(1) (amended by SI 2012/3119; SI 2013/747; SI 2016/285; and SI 2016/611).

10 Ie for the purpose of ensuring compliance with Building Regulations 2010, SI 2010/2214, regs 26, 26A (see PARA 46 and Sch 1 para L1(a)(i) PARA 10: reg 43(2) (amended by SI 2014/579; and SI 2018/558).

10 Ie that such testing is carried out in such circumstances as are approved by the appropriate national authority (Building Regulations 2010, SI 2010/2214, reg 43(2)(a)(i)) and that it is carried out in accordance with a procedure approved by the appropriate national authority (reg 43(2)(a)(ii)).

11 Building Regulations 2010, SI 2010/2214, reg 43(2)(b). The notice must record the results and the data upon which they are based in a manner approved by the appropriate national authority (reg 43(3)(a)) and must be given to the local authority not later than seven days after the final test is carried out (reg 43(3)(b)).

    Note that in relation to building work which is the subject of an initial notice (as to which see PARA 74 et seq), reg 43 applies as if references to the local authority were references to the approved inspector: see the Building (Approved Inspectors etc) Regulations 2010, SI 2010/2215, reg 20(1); and PARA 87.

    A local authority is authorised to accept, as evidence that the requirements of the Building Regulations 2010, SI 2010/2214, reg 43(2)(a)(ii) (see note 10) have been satisfied, a certificate to that effect by a person who is registered by the Independent Air Tightness Testing Scheme Limited or the Air Tightness and Testing and Measurement Association in respect of pressure testing for the air tightness of buildings: reg 43(4) (amended by SI 2012/3119; SI 2013/747; SI 2015/767 and SI 2015/1486). Where such a certificate records the results and the data upon which they are based in a manner approved by the appropriate national authority (ie where the certificate contains the information required by reg 43(3)(a)) then reg 43(2)(b) does not apply: reg 43(5).

12 The Building Regulations 2010, SI 2010/2214, reg 44 applies to building work in relation to which Sch 1 para F1(2) (see PARA 10) imposes a requirement, but does not apply to the provision or extension of any fixed system for mechanical ventilation or any associated controls where testing and adjustment is not possible: reg 44(1).

13 The Building Regulations 2010, SI 2010/2214, reg 44 applies to building work in relation to which Sch 1 para L1(b) (see PARA 10) imposes a requirement, but does not apply to the provision or extension of any fixed building service where testing and adjustment is not possible or would not affect the energy efficiency of that fixed building service: reg 44(2).

14 Building Regulations 2010, SI 2010/2214, reg 44(3). The notice must be given to the local authority (1) not later than the date on which the notice required by reg 16(4) is required to be given; or (2) where that regulation does not apply, not more than 30 days after completion of the work: reg 44(4). Note that in relation to building work which is the subject of an initial notice (as to which see PARA 74 et seq), reg 44 applies as if references to the local authority were references to the approved inspector: see the Building (Approved Inspectors etc) Regulations 2010, SI 2010/2215, reg 20(1); and PARA 87. In such cases, the notice must be given to the approved inspector not later than five days after completion of the work to which the initial notice relates: see reg 20(6). However, where reg 17 applies (see PARA 80), the notice must be given to the approved inspector not later than the date on which the initial notice ceases to be in force or, if earlier, the end of the five-day period referred to above: see reg 20(6). Where the Building Regulations 2010, SI 2010/2214, reg 20 applies by virtue of the Building (Approved Inspectors etc) Regulations 2010, SI 2010/2215, reg 20, the notice must be given not later than the date on which the notice or certificate required by that regulation must be given: see reg 20(6).

15 Ie the Building Regulations 2010, SI 2010/2214, regs 41–44.

16 Building Regulations 2010, SI 2010/2214, reg 19(1). As to initial notices see PARA 74 et seq. As to amendment notices see PARA 76. As to a public body's notice see PARA 89 et seq.

32. Notice of potential consumption of wholesome water.

Where the requirements relating to water efficiency in new dwellings[1] apply[2], the person carrying out the work must give the local authority[3] a notice which specifies which of the requirements[4]applies to the dwelling and the potential consumption of wholesome water per person per day in relation to the completed dwelling[5]. The notice shall be given to the local authority not later than five days after the work has been completed[6].

1 As to the meaning of 'dwelling' see PARA 10 note 31.

2 Ie the Building Regulations 2010, SI 2010/2214, reg 36 (see PARA 53): reg 37(1) (as substituted: see note 5).

3 As to the meaning of 'local authority' see PARA 1 note 12. Note that in relation to building work which is the subject of an initial notice (as to which see PARA 74 et seq), the Building Regulations 2010, SI 2010/2214, reg 37 applies as if references to the local authority were references to the approved inspector: see the Building (Approved Inspectors etc) Regulations 2010, SI 2010/2215, reg 20(1); and PARA 87.

4 Ie in the Building Regulations 2010, SI 2010/2214, reg 36(2)(a) or (b) (see PARA 53): reg 37(1) (as substituted: see note 5).

5 Building Regulations 2010, SI 2010/2214, reg 37(1) (reg 37(1) substituted by SI 2015/767; and amended by SI 2018/558). As from 1 November 2018, the Building Regulations 2010, SI 2010/2214, reg 37 is amended in relation to Wales so that the notice only has to specify the potential consumption of wholesome water per person per day in relation to completed dwelling: reg 37 (prospectively amended by SI 2018/552). Regulation 37 is designated as a provision to which the Building Act 1984 s 35 (penalty for contravening building regulations) (see PARA 61) does not apply: Building Regulations 2010, SI 2010/2214, reg 47 (substituted by SI 2012/3119; SI 2018/552; and SI 2018/558; amended by SI 2013/747; SI 2014/110; and; SI 2014/579). Regulation 37 does not apply in respect of any work specified in an initial notice, an amendment notice or a public body's notice, which is in force: reg 19(1) (amended by SI 2012/3119; SI 2013/747; SI 2016/285; and SI 2016/611).

6 Building Regulations 2010, SI 2010/2214, reg 37(2).

(ii) Passing or Rejection of Plans and Imposition of Conditions

33. Passing or rejection of plans.

Where plans[1] of any proposed work are, in accordance with building regulations[2], deposited with a local authority[3], it is the duty of the local authority, subject to any other provision of the Building Act 1984 that expressly requires or authorises it in certain cases to reject plans, to pass the plans unless they are defective[4], or they show that the proposed work would contravene[5] any of the building regulations[6]. If the plans are defective, or show that the proposed work would contravene any of the building regulations, the local authority may reject the plans, or pass them[7] subject to either or both of the following conditions[8]. The conditions are that such modifications as the local authority may specify must be made in the deposited plans[9], and that such further plans as it may specify must be deposited[10]. A local authority may only pass plans subject to such a condition if the person by whom or on whose behalf they were deposited has requested it to do so[11], or has consented to its doing so[12]. Such a request or consent must be in writing[13].

The authority must within the relevant period[14] from the deposit of the plans give notice[15] to the person by whom or on whose behalf they were deposited whether they have been passed or rejected[16]. A notice that plans have been rejected must specify the defects on account of which, or the regulation or provision of the Building Act 1984 for non-conformity with which, or under the authority of which, they have been rejected[17]. A notice that plans have been passed must specify any condition subject to which they have been passed[18], and state that the passing of the plans operates as an approval of them only for the purposes of the requirements of the building regulations, and any provision of the Building Act 1984[19] that expressly requires or authorises the local authority in certain cases to reject plans[20].

Where the deposited plans are accompanied by:

(1)   a certificate[21] given by a person approved for these purposes[22] to the effect that the proposed work, if carried out in accordance with the deposited plans, will comply with such provisions of the regulations prescribed[23] for these purposes as may be specified in the certificate[24]; and

(2)   such evidence as may be prescribed that an approved scheme applies, or the prescribed insurance cover has been or will be provided, in relation to the certificate[25],

the local authority may not, except in prescribed circumstances[26], reject the plans on the ground that:

(a)   they are defective with respect to any provisions of the building regulations that are so specified[27]; or

(b)   they show that the proposed work would contravene any of those provisions[28].

In any case where a question arises[29] between a local authority and a person who proposes to carry out any work whether plans of the proposed work are in conformity with building regulations, or whether the local authority is prohibited from rejecting plans of the proposed work[30], that person may refer the question to the appropriate national authority for its determination, and an application for such a reference must be accompanied by such fee as may be prescribed[31]. Where deposited plans accompanied by a certificate and evidence[32] are passed by the local authority, or notice of the rejection of deposited plans accompanied by a certificate and evidence is not given within the relevant period from the deposit of the plans, the authority may not institute proceedings[33] for a contravention of building regulations that arises out of the carrying out of the proposed work in accordance with the plans, and is a contravention of any of the provisions of the regulations specified in the certificate[34].

1   As to the meaning of 'plans' see PARA 9 note 8.
2   As to the meaning of 'building regulations' see PARA 7.
3   As to the meaning of 'local authority' see PARA 1 note 12.
4   Building Act 1984 s 16(1)(a).

5 As to the meaning of 'contravene' see PARA 12 note 10.
6 Building Act 1984 s 16(1)(b). A local authority which wrongly approves faulty design plans owes no duty of care to a building owner who is consequently in breach of building regulations: *Investors in Industry Commercial Properties Ltd v South Bedfordshire District Council (Ellison & Partners (a firm), third parties)* [1986] QB 1034, [1986] 1 All ER 787, CA.
7 Ie subject to the Building Act 1984 s 16(4): see the text to notes 11–12.
8 Building Act 1984 s 16(2).
9 Building Act 1984 s 16(3)(a).
10 Building Act 1984 s 16(3)(b).
11 Building Act 1984 s 16(4)(a).
12 Building Act 1984 s 16(4)(b).
13 Building Act 1984 s 16(5).
14 For the purposes of the Building Act 1984 Pt I (ss 1–46), the 'relevant period', in relation to the passing or rejection of plans, means five weeks or such extended period (expiring not later than two months from the deposit of the plans) as may before the expiration of the five weeks be agreed in writing between the person depositing the plans and the local authority: s 16(12).
15 As to the form, authentication and service of notices see PARAS 135–137.
16 Building Act 1984 s 16(6).
17 Building Act 1984 s 16(7).
18 Building Act 1984 s 16(8)(a).
19 Ie other than the Building Act 1984 s 16.
20 Building Act 1984 s 16(8)(b).
21 Every local authority must keep, in such manner as may be prescribed, a register containing such information as may be prescribed with respect to certificates given to them under the Building Act 1984 s 16(9), including information (where applicable) as to whether such notices or certificates have been accepted or rejected: ss 11(2), 56(1), (3), Schedule (s 56(1)–(4) prospectively repealed by the Sustainable and Secure Buildings Act 2004)). Every register kept under the Building Act 1984 s 56 must be available for inspection by the public at all reasonable hours: s 56(4) (prospectively repealed).
   It has been so prescribed that the register which local authorities must keep under s 56 with respect to certificates given under s 16(9) which have been accepted or are presumed to have been accepted must contain information as to: (1) the description of the work to which the certificate relates and of the location of the work; (2) the name and address of any person who signed the certificate; and (3) the date on which the certificate was accepted or was presumed to have been accepted: Building (Approved Inspectors etc) Regulations 2010, SI 2010/2215, reg 30(1)(b), (2), (3) (reg 30(2) amended by SI 2012/3119 and SI 2014/58). The information prescribed in heads (1)–(4) above must be entered in the register as soon as practicable and in any event within 14 days of the occurrence to which it relates: reg 30(5). A register must include an index for enabling a person to trace any entry in the register by reference to the address of the land to which the notice or certificate relates: reg 30(4).
22 Building regulations may make provision for the approval of persons for the purposes of the Building Act 1984 s 16(9) by the appropriate national authority, or by a body (corporate or unincorporated) that, in accordance with the regulations, is designated for the purpose, and any such approval may limit the description of work, or the provisions of the regulations, in relation to which the person concerned is so approved: see s 17. In exercise of this power, it is provided that the provisions of the Building (Approved Inspectors etc) Regulations 2010, SI 2010/2215, regs 3–7 (see PARA 72) apply in relation to the approval and the termination of approval of persons to certify plans in accordance with the Building Act 1984 s 16(9), and the designation and the termination of designation of bodies to approve such persons, as they do in relation to the approval of inspectors and the designation of bodies to approve inspectors respectively: Building (Approved Inspectors etc) Regulations 2010, SI 2010/2215, reg 29(1).
23 Ie prescribed by building regulations: see Building Act 1984 s 126. The Building Regulations 2010, SI 2010/2214, regs 4, 6 (see PARAS 10–11) are prescribed provisions for the purposes of the Building Act 1984 s 16(9) in so far as either requires compliance with the Building Regulations 2010, SI 2010/2214, Sch 1 Pt A (structure) (see PARA 10) and Sch 1 Pt L (conservation of fuel and power) (see PARA 10): Building (Approved Inspectors etc) Regulations 2010, SI 2010/2215, reg 29(2).
24 Building Act 1984 s 16(9)(a). If a person: (1) gives a notice or certificate that purports to comply with the requirements of s 16(9) and that contains a statement that he knows to be false or misleading in a material particular; or (2) recklessly gives a notice or certificate that purports to comply with those requirements, and that contains a statement that is false or misleading in a

material particular, he is guilty of an offence: see s 57(1); and PARA 99. A person guilty of such an offence is liable on summary conviction to a fine not exceeding the statutory maximum or imprisonment for a term not exceeding six months or both, and on conviction on indictment to a fine or imprisonment for a term not exceeding two years or both: s 57(2). Where a person approved for the purposes of s 16(9) convicted of such an offence, the court by or before whom he is convicted must, within one month of the date of conviction, forward a certificate of the conviction to the person by whom the approval was given: s 57(3). As to the powers of magistrates' courts to issue fines on summary conviction see SENTENCING vol 92 (2015) PARA 176. Civil sanctions may be imposed in respect of offences under the Building Act 1984 by virtue of the powers under the Regulatory Enforcement and Sanctions Act 2008 Pt 3 (ss 36–71): see ss 36, 38(2), Sch 6; and CONSTITUTIONAL AND ADMINISTRATIVE LAW vol 20 (2014) PARA 331 et seq.

25 Building Act 1984 s 16(9)(b). Where deposited plans are accompanied by a certificate as mentioned in s 16(9), the evidence of insurance required is a declaration signed by the insurer that a named scheme of insurance approved by the appropriate national authority applies in relation to the certificate which accompanies the plans: Building (Approved Inspectors etc) Regulations 2010, SI 2010/2215, reg 29(3). As to the appropriate national authority (ie the Secretary of State or, where statutory functions have been transferred in relation to Wales, the Welsh Ministers) see PARA 5.

26 The prescribed circumstances are where:
    (1)   the certificate states that the work shown in the plans complies with the requirements of the Building Regulations 2010, SI 2010/2214, Sch 1 Pt A (structure) (see PARA 10) (Building (Approved Inspectors etc) Regulations 2010, SI 2010/2215, reg 29(4)(a));
    (2)   the Building Regulations 2010, SI 2010/2214, Sch 1 para A3 (see PARA 10) applies to the work shown in the plans (Building (Approved Inspectors etc) Regulations 2010, SI 2010/2215, reg 29(4)(b)); and
    (3)   the certificate does not contain a declaration that the person giving the certificate does not, and will not until the work is complete, have a professional or financial interest in the work (reg 29(4)(c)).
    A person approved under the Building Act 1984 s 16(9) must have no professional or financial interest in the work he supervises unless it is minor work: Building (Approved Inspectors etc) Regulations 2010, SI 2010/2215, regs 9(1), 29(5). Such a person will be regarded as having a professional or financial interest in the work described in such a certificate if: (a) he is or has been responsible for the design or construction of any of the work in any capacity; or (b) he or any nominee of his is a member, officer or employee of a company or other body which has a professional or financial interest in the work; or (c) he is a partner or is in the employment of a person who has a professional or financial interest in the work: regs 9(2), 29(5). For these purposes, a person will be treated as having a professional or financial interest in the work even if he has that interest only as trustee for the benefit of some other person, and in the case of married people or civil partners living together, the interest of one spouse or partner, if known to the other, is deemed to be also an interest of the other: regs 9(3), 29(5). For these purposes, (i) involvement in the work as an approved inspector; (ii) entitlement to any fee paid for his function as an approved inspector; and (iii) potential liability to pay any sum if a claim is made under the insurance cover provided for the purposes of the Building Act 1984, are not to be regarded as constituting a professional or financial interest: Building (Approved Inspectors etc) Regulations 2010, SI 2010/2215, regs 9(4), 29(5).

27 Building Act 1984 s 16(9)(i).

28 Building Act 1984 s 16(9)(ii).

29 Ie under the Building Act 1984 s 16.

30 Ie by virtue of the Building Act 1984 s 16(9): see the text and notes 21–28.

31 Building Act 1984 s 16(10). The fee which must accompany an application for a reference under s 16(10) is:
    (1)   where the question is whether plans of proposed work are in conformity with building regulations, an amount equal to half the plan charge fixed by the charging scheme made and published by the local authority concerned, subject to a minimum of £100 and a maximum of £1,000 (Building (Local Authority Charges) Regulations 2010, SI 2010/404, reg 14(1)(a));
    (2)   where the question is whether the local authority is prohibited from rejecting plans of proposed work by virtue of the Building Act 1984 s 16(9), £100 (Building (Local Authority Charges) Regulations 2010, SI 2010/404, reg 14(1)(b)).

32 See heads (1), (2) in the text.

33 Ie under the Building Act 1984 s 35: see PARA 61.
34 Building Act 1984 s 16(11).

34. Use of short-lived materials.

Until a day to be appointed, the provisions described below have effect[1]. Building regulations[2] may provide that these provisions apply to any materials specified in the regulations as being materials that are, in the absence of special care, liable to rapid deterioration, or are otherwise unsuitable for use in the construction of permanent buildings[3].

Where plans[4] of a building are, in accordance with building regulations, deposited[5] with a local authority[6], and the plans show that it is proposed to construct[7] a building of such materials, or to place or assemble on the site a building constructed of such materials, the authority may, notwithstanding that the plans conform with the regulations reject the plans, or in passing the plans fix a period on the expiration of which the building must be removed, and impose with respect to the use of the building such reasonable conditions, if any, as having regard to the nature of the materials used in its construction it deems appropriate[8]. However, no condition may be imposed that conflicts with any condition imposed on the grant of planning permission for that building under Part III of the Town and Country Planning Act 1990[9]. If a building, in respect of which plans ought under the building regulations to have been deposited, but have not been deposited, appears to the authority to be constructed of such materials, the authority, without prejudice to its right to take proceedings in respect of any contravention[10] of the regulations, may fix a period on the expiration of which the building must be removed, and if it thinks fit, impose such conditions with respect to the use of the building as might have been imposed[11] upon the passing of plans for the building, and where it fixes such a period it must forthwith give notice of it, and of any conditions imposed, to the owner[12] of the building[13]. A local authority may from time to time extend any period so fixed, or vary any conditions so imposed[14]. However, unless an application in that behalf is made to it by the owner of the building in question, it must not exercise its power of varying conditions except when granting an extension, or further extension, of the period fixed with respect to the building[15]. A person aggrieved[16] by such an action of a local authority in rejecting plans, or in fixing or refusing to extend any period, or in imposing or refusing to vary any conditions, may appeal to a magistrates' court[17].

The owner of a building in respect of which a period has been fixed must, on the expiration of that period, or, as the case may be, of that period as extended, remove the building, and, if he fails to do so the local authority must remove it and may recover from him the expenses reasonably incurred by it in so doing[18] and without prejudice to the right of the authority to exercise that power, he is liable on summary conviction to a fine[19] and also to a further fine for each day during which the building is allowed to remain after he is convicted[20]. In addition, a person who uses a building in contravention of a condition imposed in this way, or who permits a building to be so used, is liable on summary conviction to a fine[21] and also to a further fine for each day on which the offence continues after he is convicted[22].

1 The Building Act 1984 s 19 ceases to have effect upon the coming into force of s 20, which supersedes it: s 19(9) (prospectively repealed). At the date at which this volume states the law no order under s 134(1) bringing s 20 into force had been made. As to the provision to be made by s 20 when it is eventually brought into force see PARA 35, .
2 As to the meaning of 'building regulations' see PARA 7.

3   Building Act 1984 s 19(7) (prospectively repealed: see note 1). Section 19 applies in relation to an
     extension of an existing building as it applies in relation to a new building: s 19(8) (prospectively
     repealed: see note 1). As to the meaning of 'building' see PARA 6.
4   As to the meaning of 'plans' see PARA 9 note 8.
5   As to references to the deposit of plans in accordance with building regulations see PARA 22 note
     18.
6   As to the meaning of 'local authority' see PARA 1 note 12.
7   As to the meaning of 'construct' see PARA 9 note 3.
8   Building Act 1984 s 19(1) (prospectively repealed: see note 1). As to the supply and marketing of
     construction products see the Construction Products Regulations 2013, SI 2013/1387; and
     CONSUMER PROTECTION.
9   Building Act 1984 s 19(1) (amended by the Planning (Consequential Provisions) Act 1990 s 4,
     Sch 2 para 67(1)). As to the prospective repeal of the Building Act 1984 s 19 see note 1. The text
     refers to the Town and Country Planning Act 1990 Pt III (ss 55–106C): see PLANNING vol 81
     (2018) PARA 333 et seq.
10 As to the meaning of 'contravention' see PARA 12 note 10.
11 Ie under the Building Act 1984 s 19(1): see the text to notes 1–9.
12 As to the meaning of 'owner' see PARA 12 note 2.
13 Building Act 1984 s 19(2) (prospectively repealed: see note 1).
14 Building Act 1984 s 19(3) (prospectively repealed: see note 1).
15 Building Act 1984 s 19(3) (prospectively repealed: see note 1).
16 As to persons aggrieved see JUDICIAL REVIEW vol 61 (2010) PARA 656.
17 Building Act 1984 s 19(4) (prospectively repealed: see note 1). As to appeals generally see PARAS
     139–140.
18 Building Act 1984 s 19(5)(a) (prospectively repealed: see note 1).
19 The fine imposed is one not exceeding level 1 on the standard scale: see Building Act 1984 s
     19(5)(b) (prospectively repealed: see note 1). As to the powers of magistrates' courts to issue fines
     on summary conviction see SENTENCING vol 92 (2015) PARA 176. Civil sanctions may be
     imposed in respect of offences under the Building Act 1984 by virtue of the powers under the
     Regulatory Enforcement and Sanctions Act 2008 Pt 3 (ss 36–71): see ss 36, 38(2), Sch 6; and
     CONSTITUTIONAL AND ADMINISTRATIVE LAW vol 20 (2014) PARA 331 et seq.
20 Building Act 1984 s 19(5)(b) (prospectively repealed: see note 1). The fine imposed must not
     exceed £5 for each day on which the default continues after conviction: see s 19(5)(b)
     (prospectively repealed: see note 1). As to continuing offences see PARA 144.
21 The fine imposed is one not exceeding level 1 on the standard scale: see Building Act 1984 s 19(6)
     (prospectively repealed: see note 1).
22 Building Act 1984 s 19(6) (prospectively repealed: see note 1). The fine imposed must not exceed
     £5 for each day on which the default continues after conviction: see s 19(6) (prospectively repealed:
     see note 1).

35. Use of materials unsuitable for permanent building.
As from a day to be appointed, the provisions described below have effect[1].
Where plans[2] of any proposed work[3] are, in accordance with building regulations,
deposited[4] with a local authority[5], and the plans show that the proposed work
would include or consist of such work, the authority may, notwithstanding that
the plans conform with the regulations reject the plans[6], or in passing the plans:
   (1)   fix a period on the expiration of which such work or the relevant
           building[7] (as the authority may in passing the plans direct) must be
           removed[8]; and
   (2)   if it thinks fit, impose with respect to the use of the relevant building or
           with respect to the work such reasonable conditions, if any, as it
           considers appropriate[9].
However, no condition as to the use of the relevant building may be imposed
that conflicts with any condition imposed or having effect as if imposed under Part
III[10] or Part VIII[11] of the Town and Country Planning Act 1990, or under the
Planning (Listed Buildings and Conservation Areas) Act 1990[12] or the Planning
(Hazardous Substances) Act 1990[13].

If, in the case of any work in respect of which plans ought by virtue of building regulations to have been deposited with a local authority but have not been so deposited, the work appears to the authority to include or consist of such work, the authority, without prejudice to its right to take proceedings in respect of any contravention[14] of the regulations, may fix a period on the expiration of which the work or the relevant building (as the authority may in fixing the period direct) must be removed, and if it thinks fit, impose any conditions that might have been imposed in passing plans for the first-mentioned work, and where it fixes such a period it must forthwith give notice of it, and of any conditions imposed, to the owner[15] of the relevant building[16].

If, in the case of any work appearing to the local authority to be work provided in or in connection with a building, being work consisting of a service, fitting or item of equipment of a type which has been prescribed by the appropriate national authority as likely to be unsuitable[17], and plans of the work were not required by building regulations to be deposited with the authority, and were not so deposited, the authority may at any time within 12 months from the date of completion of the work fix a period on the expiration of which the work must be removed, and if it thinks fit, impose any conditions that, if plans of the work had been required to be, and had been, so deposited, might have been imposed[18] in passing the plans, and where it fixes such a period it must forthwith give notice of it, and of any conditions imposed, to the owner of the relevant building[19].

A local authority may from time to time extend any period fixed, or vary any conditions imposed, but, unless an application in that behalf is made to it by the owner of the relevant building, it must not exercise its power of varying conditions except when granting an extension or further extension of the period fixed with respect to the work or building, as the case may be[20].

A person aggrieved[21] by the action of a local authority in rejecting plans, in fixing or refusing to extend any period, or in imposing or refusing to vary any conditions, may appeal to the appropriate national authority within the prescribed time and in the prescribed manner[22].

Where a period has been fixed with respect to any such work or with respect to the relevant building the owner of that building must on the expiration of that period, or, as the case may be, of that period as extended, remove the work or building with respect to which the period was fixed[23], and if he fails to do so, the local authority may remove that work or building, as the case may be, and may recover from him the expenses reasonably incurred by it in doing so[24].

A person who contravenes a condition so imposed or permits such a condition to be contravened or who fails to remove the work or building with respect to which the period was so fixed[25] is liable on summary conviction to a fine[26], and also to a further fine for each day on which the offence continues or, as the case may be, on which the work or building is allowed to remain after he is convicted[27].

1 The Building Act 1984 s 20 (see the text and notes 2–27) is to be brought into force by order made under s 134(1)(b) as from a day to be appointed. At the date at which this volume states the law no such order had been made. Upon s 20 being brought into force, s 19 ceases to have effect: see s 19(9) (prospectively repealed). As to the provision currently made by s 19 see PARA 34. Upon s 19 ceasing to have effect: (1) any building regulations made, period fixed, condition imposed or other thing done by virtue of s 19 will be deemed to have been made, fixed, imposed or done by virtue of s 20 (s 20(11)(a) (not yet in force)); and (2) anything begun under s 19 may be continued under the Building Act 1984 as if begun under s 20, but any appeal under s 19(4) that is pending at the time when s 19 ceases to have effect, and any proceedings arising out of such an appeal, must proceed as if s 19 were still in force (s 20(11)(b) (not yet in force)). As to the meaning of 'building regulations' see PARA 7.

2 As to the meaning of 'plans' see PARA 9 note 8.

3   The Building Act 1984 s 20 applies to any work:
   (1)   consisting of a part of a building, being a part in the construction of which there is used any material or component of a type that, in relation to a part of that description, is prescribed for these purposes under s 20(10) (s 20(9)(a) (not yet in force: see note 1)); and
   (2)   provided in or in connection with a building, being work consisting of a service, fitting or item of equipment of a type so prescribed for these purposes (s 20(9)(b) (not yet in force: see note 1)).

     The appropriate national authority may by building regulations prescribe a type of material or component for the purposes of head (1) above if in its opinion materials or components of that type are likely to be unsuitable for use in the construction of a particular part of a permanent building in the absence of conditions with respect to the use of the building or with respect to any material or component of that type used in the construction of a part of that description: s 20(10)(a) (not yet in force: see note 1). The appropriate national authority may by building regulations prescribe a type of service, fitting or equipment for the purposes of head (2) above if in its opinion services, fittings or equipment of that type are likely to be unsuitable for provision in or in connection with a permanent building in the absence of conditions with respect to the use of the building or with respect to a service, fitting or equipment of that type so provided: s 20(10)(b) (not yet in force: see note 1). As to the meaning of 'building' see PARA 6. 'Prescribed' means prescribed by building regulations: see s 126. As to the appropriate national authority (ie the Secretary of State or, where statutory functions have been transferred in relation to Wales, the Welsh Ministers) see PARA 5. Building Act 1984 s 19(1) (prospectively repealed: see note 1). As to the supply and marketing of construction products see the Construction Products Regulations 2013, SI 2013/1387; and CONSUMER PROTECTION.

4   As to references to the deposit of plans in accordance with building regulations see PARA 22 note 18.
5   As to the meaning of 'local authority' see PARA 1 note 12.
6   Building Act 1984 s 20(1)(a) (not yet in force: see note 1). As to notification that plans have been rejected or passed see PARA 33.
7   For these purposes, the 'relevant building' means, in any particular case, the building mentioned in the Building Act 1984 s 20(9)(a) or, as the case may be, s 20(9)(b) (see note 3): s 20(8) (not yet in force: see note 1).
8   Building Act 1984 s 20(1)(b)(i) (not yet in force: see note 1).
9   Building Act 1984 s 20(1)(b)(ii) (not yet in force: see note 1).
10   Ie the Town and Country Planning Act 1990 Pt III (ss 55–106C) (control over development): see PLANNING vol 81 (2018) PARA 333 et seq.
11   Ie the Town and Country Planning Act 1990 Pt VIII (ss 197–225K) (special controls): see PLANNING vol 83 (2018) PARA 797 et seq.
12   See PLANNING vol 83 (2010) PARA 1181 et seq.
13   Building Act 1984 s 20(1) (amended by the Planning (Consequential Provisions) Act 1990 s 4, Sch 2 para 67(2)) (not yet in force). As to the bringing into force of the Building Act 1984 s 20 see note 1.
14   As to the meaning of 'contravention' see PARA 12 note 10.
15   As to the meaning of 'owner' see PARA 12 note 2.
16   Building Act 1984 s 20(2) (not yet in force: see note 1).
17   Ie work which appears to the local authority to fall within the Building Act 1984 s 20(9)(b): see note 3.
18   Ie under the Building Act 1984 s 20(1) (not yet in force): see the text and notes 2–13.
19   Building Act 1984 s 20(3) (not yet in force: see note 1).
20   Building Act 1984 s 20(4) (not yet in force: see note 1).
21   As to persons aggrieved see JUDICIAL REVIEW vol 61 (2010) PARA 656.
22   Building Act 1984 s 20(5) (not yet in force: see note 1).
23   Building Act 1984 s 20(6)(a) (not yet in force: see note 1).
24   Building Act 1984 s 20(6)(b) (not yet in force: see note 1).
25   Ie a person who contravenes the Building Act 1984 s 20(6): see the text and notes 23–24.
26   The fine imposed is one not exceeding level 5 on the standard scale: see the Building Act 1984 s 20(7) (not yet in force: see note 1). As to the powers of magistrates' courts to issue fines on summary conviction see SENTENCING vol 92 (2015) PARA 176. Civil sanctions may be imposed in respect of offences under the Building Act 1984 by virtue of the powers under the Regulatory Enforcement and Sanctions Act 2008 Pt 3 (ss 36–71): see ss 36, 38(2), Sch 6; and CONSTITUTIONAL AND ADMINISTRATIVE LAW vol 20 (2014) PARA 331 et seq.

27 Building Act 1984 s 20(7) (not yet in force: see note 1). The fine imposed must not exceed £50 for each day on which the default continues after conviction: see s 20(7) (not yet in force: see note 1). However, s 20(7) does not prejudice a local authority's rights under s 20(6) (see the text and notes 23–24): s 20(7) (not yet in force: see note 1). As to continuing offences see PARA 144.

36. Provision of drainage.

Where plans[1] of a building[2] or of an extension of a building are, in accordance with building regulations[3], deposited with a local authority[4], the local authority, or on appeal a magistrates' court[5], may require a proposed drain[6] to connect with a sewer[7] where[8]:

(1)   that sewer is within 100 feet of the site of the building or, in the case of an extension, the site either of the extension or of the original building, and is at a level that makes it reasonably practicable to construct[9] a drain to communicate with it, and, if it is not a public sewer[10], is a sewer that the person constructing the drain is entitled to use[11]; and

(2)   the intervening land is land through which that person is entitled to construct a drain[12].

Any question arising[13] between a local authority and the person by whom, or on whose behalf, plans are deposited as to whether a proposed drain is to be connected with a sewer may on the application of that person be determined by a magistrates' court[14].

Notwithstanding head (1) above, a drain may be required to be made to connect with a sewer that is not within the distance specified there, but is otherwise such a sewer, if the authority undertakes to bear so much of the expenses reasonably incurred in constructing, and in maintaining and repairing, the drain as may be attributable to the fact that the distance of the sewer exceeds the distance mentioned in head (1) above[15]. If any question arises as to the amount of a payment to be so made to a person, that question may on his application be determined by a magistrates' court, or he may require it to be referred to arbitration[16].

As from a day to be appointed, the provisions described above will not apply to works in connection with which approval is required in accordance with the provisions of the Flood and Water Management Act 2010[17] relating to sustainable drainage[18].

1 As to the meaning of 'plans' see PARA 9 note 8.
2 As to the meaning of 'building' see PARA 6.
3 As to the meaning of 'building regulations' see PARA 7.
4 As to the meaning of 'local authority' see PARA 1 note 12. As to references to the deposit of plans in accordance with building regulations see PARA 22 note 18.
5 See CRIMINAL PROCEDURE vol 27 (2015) PARA 142; MAGISTRATES vol 71 (2013) PARA 436.
6 'Drain' means a drain used for the drainage of one building or of buildings or yards appurtenant to buildings within the same curtilage, and manholes, ventilating shafts, pumps or other accessories belonging to the drain: Building Act 1984 s 126.
7 'Sewer' does not include a drain, but otherwise it includes all sewers and drains used for the drainage of buildings and yards appurtenant to buildings, and any manholes, ventilating shafts, pumps or other accessories belonging to the sewer: Building Act 1984 s 126.
8 Building Act 1984 s 21(4) (amended by SI 2001/3335).
9 As to the meaning of 'construct' see PARA 9 note 3.
10 For these purposes, 'public sewer' has the same meaning as in the Water Industry Act 1991 s 219(1) (see WATER AND WATERWAYS vol 100 (2018) PARA 506): Building Act 1984 s 126 (definition substituted by the Water Act 1989 s 190(1), (3), Sch 25 para 70(4), Sch 27 Pt I; and amended by the Water Consolidation (Consequential Provisions) Act 1991 s 2(1), Sch 1 para 39(1), (6)).

11 Building Act 1984 s 21(4)(a). The site of the building may in some cases extend to include a detached outbuilding within the curtilage of the main building: *Meyrick v Pembroke Corpn* (1912) 76 JP 365, DC; cf *Wright v Wallasey Local Board* (1887) 18 QBD 783.

12 Building Act 1984 s 21(4)(b).

13 Ie under the Building Act 1984 s 21(4): see the text and notes 1–12.

14 Building Act 1984 s 21(3) (amended by SI 2001/3335). As to the procedure on applications to a magistrates' court see the Building Act 1984 s 103(1); and PARA 139.

15 Building Act 1984 s 21(5). The words 'require' and 'undertake' were construed as requiring a resolution of the authority in *Princes Investments Ltd v Firmley and Camberley UDC* [1962] 1 QB 681, [1962] 2 All ER 104, DC. See also *Provident Mutual Life Assurance Association v Derby City Council* [1981] 1 WLR 173, 79 LGR 297, HL, where it was held that no resolution was required for a council to hold an 'opinion' or to 'think fit'.

16 Building Act 1984 s 21(6). In an arbitration under the Building Act 1984, the reference is to a single arbitrator appointed by agreement between the parties, or in default of agreement by the appropriate national authority: s 111. As to the appropriate national authority (ie the Secretary of State or, where statutory functions have been transferred in relation to Wales, the Welsh Ministers) see PARA 5. The provisions of the Arbitration Act 1996, subject to certain exceptions and adaptations, apply to an arbitration under the Building Act 1984 s 111: see the Arbitration Act 1996 s 94; and ARBITRATION vol 2 (2017) PARA 509. As to the making of building regulations to modify or repeal the provisions of the Building Act 1984 s 111 on the grounds of inconsistency with other provisions, etc see s 1(3), Sch 1 para 11(1); and PARA 9.

17 Ie the Flood and Water Management Act 2010 Sch 3 (not yet in force): see WATER AND WATERWAYS.

18 Building Act 1984 s 21(7) (prospectively added by the Flood and Water Management Act 2010 Sch 3 para 26(1)). At the date at which this volume states the law no day had been appointed for the Building Act 1984 s 21(7) to be brought into force.

37. Drainage of buildings in combination.

Where a local authority[1] might[2] require each of two or more buildings[3] to be drained separately into an existing sewer[4], but it appears to the authority that those buildings may be drained more economically or advantageously in combination, the authority may, when the drains[5] of the buildings are first laid, require that the buildings be drained in combination into the existing sewer by means of a private sewer[6] to be constructed[7] either by the owners[8] of the buildings in such manner as the authority may direct or, if the authority so elects, by the authority on behalf of the owners[9]. A local authority must not, except by agreement with the owners concerned, exercise this power in respect of any building for which drainage plans[10] have been previously passed by it[11].

A local authority which makes such a requirement must fix the proportions in which the expenses of constructing, and of maintaining and repairing, the private sewer are to be borne by the owners concerned[12], or in a case in which the distance of the existing sewer from the site of any of the buildings in question is or exceeds 100 feet, it must fix the proportions in which those expenses are to be borne by the owners concerned and the local authority, and must forthwith give notice[13] of its decision to each owner affected[14]. An owner aggrieved[15] by the decision[16] of a local authority concerning the fixing of such proportions may appeal to a magistrates' court[17]. Subject to any such appeal, any expenses reasonably incurred in constructing, or in maintaining or repairing, the private sewer must be borne in the proportions so fixed[18], and those expenses, or, as the case may be, contributions to them, may be recovered accordingly by the persons, whether the local authority or the owners, by whom they were incurred in the first instance[19].

A sewer so constructed by a local authority is not deemed to be a public sewer by reason of the fact that the expenses of its construction are in the first instance defrayed by the authority, or that some part of those expenses are borne by it[20].

1 As to the meaning of 'local authority' see PARA 1 note 12.

2   Ie under the Building Act 1984 s 21: see PARA 36.
3   As to the meaning of 'building' see PARA 6.
4   As to the meaning of 'sewer' see PARA 36 note 7.
5   As to the meaning of 'drain' see PARA 36 note 6.
6   'Private sewer' means a sewer that is not a public sewer: Building Act 1984 s 126. For these purposes, 'public sewer' has the same meaning as in the Water Industry Act 1991 s 219(1) (see WATER AND WATERWAYS vol 100 (2018) PARA 506): Building Act 1984 s 126 (definition substituted by the Water Act 1989 s 190(1), (3), Sch 25 para 70(4), Sch 27 Pt I; and amended by the Water Consolidation (Consequential Provisions) Act 1991 s 2(1), Sch 1 para 39(1), (6)).
7   A reference in the Building Act 1984 Pt I (ss 1–46) to the construction of a sewer includes a reference to the extension of an existing sewer: s 125(1).
8   As to the meaning of 'owner' see PARA 12 note 2.
9   Building Act 1984 s 22(1). As to the making of building regulations to modify or repeal the provisions of s 22 on the grounds of inconsistency with other provisions, etc see s 1(3), Sch 1 para 11(1); and PARA 9.
10 As to the meaning of 'plans' see PARA 9 note 8.
11 Building Act 1984 s 22(2).
12 Building Act 1984 s 22(3)(a).
13 For the form of notices see PARA 135. As to the authentication of notices and their service see PARAS 136–137.
14 Building Act 1984 s 22(3)(b).
15 As to persons aggrieved see JUDICIAL REVIEW vol 61 (2010) PARA 656.
16 Ie under the Building Act 1984 s 22(3): see the text to notes 12–14.
17 Building Act 1984 s 22(4). See CRIMINAL PROCEDURE vol 27 (2015) PARA 142; MAGISTRATES vol 71 (2013) PARA 436. As to appeals generally see PARAS 139–140.
18 Building Act 1984 s 22(5)(a).
19 Building Act 1984 s 22(5)(b).
20 Building Act 1984 s 22(6).

38.   Provision of facilities for refuse.

It is unlawful for any person except with the consent[1] of the local authority[2] to close or obstruct the means of access by which refuse or faecal matter is removed from a building[3], and the local authority in giving its consent may impose such conditions as it thinks fit with respect to the improvement of an alternative means of access or the substitution of other means of access[4]. A person who contravenes[5] this provision is liable on summary conviction to a fine[6].

1   Such consent must be given in writing: see the Building Act 1984 s 92(1); and PARA 135.
2   As to the meaning of 'local authority' see PARA 1 note 12.
3   As to the meaning of 'building' see PARA 6.
4   Building Act 1984 s 23(3). As to the making of building regulations to modify or repeal the provisions of s 23 on the grounds of inconsistency with other provisions, etc see s 1(3), Sch 1 para 11(1); and PARA 9.
5   As to the meaning of 'contravene' see PARA 12 note 10.
6   Building Act 1984 s 23(4). The fine imposed must not exceed level 4 on the standard scale: s 23(4). As to the powers of magistrates' courts to issue fines on summary conviction see SENTENCING vol 92 (2015) PARA 176. Civil sanctions may be imposed in respect of offences under the Building Act 1984 by virtue of the powers under the Regulatory Enforcement and Sanctions Act 2008 Pt 3 (ss 36–71): see ss 36, 38(2), Sch 6; and CONSTITUTIONAL AND ADMINISTRATIVE LAW vol 20 (2014) PARA 331 et seq.

39.   Provision of exits etc.

Where:

(1)   plans[1] of a building[2] or of an extension of a building are, in accordance with building regulations[3], deposited[4] with a local authority[5]; and

(2)   the building or, as the case may be, the building as extended will be a building to which the following provisions apply[6],

the authority must reject the plans[7] unless they show that the building, or, as the case may be, the building as extended, will be provided with such means of ingress and egress and passages or gangways[8] as the authority, after consultation with the fire and rescue authority[9], deems satisfactory, regard being had to the purposes for which the building is intended to be, or is, used and the number of persons likely to resort to it at any one time[10]. Any question arising[11] between a local authority and the person by whom, or on whose behalf, plans are deposited as to whether the means of ingress or egress or passages or gangways already existing, or proposed to be provided, ought to be accepted by the authority as satisfactory may on the application of that person be determined by a magistrates' court[12].

Where building regulations imposing requirements as to the provision of means of escape in case of fire are applicable to a proposed building or proposed extension of a building, or would be so applicable but for a direction[13] dispensing with such requirements the provisions described above, and any provision of a local Act that has effect in their place, does not apply in relation to the proposed building or extension[14].

1   As to the meaning of 'plans' see PARA 9 note 8.
2   As to the meaning of 'building' see PARA 6.
3   As to the meaning of 'building regulations' see PARA 306.
4   As to references to the deposit of plans in accordance with building regulations see PARA 22 note 18.
5   As to the meaning of 'local authority' see PARA 1 note 12.
6   Subject to the Building Act 1984 s 24(3), s 24 applies to:
    (1)   a theatre, and a hall or other building that is used as a place of public resort (s 24(4)(a));
    (2)   a restaurant, shop, store or warehouse to which members of the public are admitted and in which more than 20 persons are employed (s 24(4)(b));
    (3)   premises in respect of which a club premises certificate has effect under the Licensing Act 2003) (Building Act 1984 s 24(4)(c) (substituted by the Licensing Act 2003 s 198(1), Sch 6 paras 90, 91));
    (4)   a school not exempted from the operation of building regulations (Building Act 1984 s 24(4)(d)); and
    (5)   a church, chapel or other place of public worship (s 24(4)(e)),
    but not:
    (a)   a private house to which members of the public are admitted occasionally or exceptionally (s 24(4)(i));
    (b)   a building that was used as a church, chapel or other place of public worship immediately before the date on which the Public Health Acts Amendment Act 1890 s 36 (repealed), or a corresponding provision in a local Act, came into operation in the district or rating district (Building Act 1984 s 24(4)(ii)); or
    (c)   a building that was so used immediately before 1 October 1937 (ie the commencement date of the Public Health Act 1936 (see ENVIRONMENTAL QUALITY AND PUBLIC HEALTH)) in a district or rating district where neither the Public Health Acts Amendment Act 1890 s 36 (repealed) nor such a corresponding provision ever came into operation (Building Act 1984 s 24(4)(iii)).
    As to the meaning of 'school' see PARA 16 note 10. As to the meaning of 'house' see PARA 16 note 10. As to the meaning of 'local Act' see PARA 6 note 2.
    The provisions of s 24(1), (2), (4) do not apply to inner London: see Sch 3 para 1; and PARA 2 note 2.
7   As to the notice of rejection see the Building Act 1984 s 16(6), (7); and PARA 33.
8   A passageway is not a gangway: *Jennings v Norman Collison (Contractors) Ltd* [1970] 1 All ER 1121, CA.
9   As to the meaning of 'fire and rescue authority' see PARA 55 note 11.
10 Building Act 1984 s 24(1) (amended by the Fire and Rescue Services Act 2004 s 53(1), Sch 1 para 57). See note 6. The local authority is not entitled to reject the plans on account of the narrowness of, and congestion of traffic in, adjoining streets: *R v Cambridge Corpn, ex p Cambridge Picture Playhouse Ltd* [1922] 1 KB 250, DC.

As to the making of building regulations to modify or repeal the provisions of the Building Act 1984 s 24 on the grounds of inconsistency with other provisions, etc see s 1(3), Sch 1 para 11(1); and PARA 9.

11 Ie under the Building Act 1984 s 24(1): see the text and notes 1–10.

12 Building Act 1984 s 24(2). See note 6. As to the procedure on applications to a magistrates' court see s 103(1); PARA 139. See further CRIMINAL PROCEDURE vol 27 (2015) PARA 142; MAGISTRATES vol 71 (2013) PARA 436.

13 Ie under the Building Act 1984 s 8: see PARA 18.

14 Building Act 1984 s 24(3).

40. Provision of water supply.

Where plans[1] of a house[2] are, in accordance with building regulations[3], deposited[4] with a local authority[5], the authority must reject the plans[6] unless a proposal is put before it that appears to it to be satisfactory for providing the occupants of the house with a supply of wholesome water sufficient for their domestic purposes:

(1)   by connecting the house to a supply of water in pipes provided by water undertakers[7];

(2)   if in all the circumstances it is not reasonable to require the house to be connected, by otherwise taking water into the house by means of a pipe[8]; or

(3)   if in all the circumstances neither of the preceding alternatives can reasonably be required, by providing a supply of water within a reasonable distance of the house[9],

and the authority is satisfied that the proposal can and will be carried into effect[10].

Any question arising[11] between a local authority and the person by whom, or on whose behalf, plans are deposited as to whether the local authority ought to pass the plans may on the application of that person be determined by a magistrates' court[12]. If, after any such plans have been passed, it appears to the local authority that the proposal for providing a supply of water has not been carried into effect, or has not resulted in a supply of wholesome water sufficient for the domestic purposes of the occupants, the authority must give notice to the owner[13] of the house prohibiting him from occupying it, or permitting it to be occupied, until the authority, being satisfied that such a supply has been provided, has granted him a certificate to that effect[14]. Until a certificate is so granted, the owner must not occupy the house or permit it to be occupied[15]. A person aggrieved[16] by the refusal of the authority to grant such a certificate may apply to a magistrates' court for an order authorising the occupation of the house, and, if the court is of opinion that a certificate ought to have been granted, the court may make an order authorising the occupation of the house, and such an order has the like effect as a certificate of the local authority[17].

1   As to the meaning of 'plans' see PARA 9 note 8.

2   As to the meaning of 'house' see PARA 16 note 10.

3   As to the meaning of 'building regulations' see PARA 7.

4   As to references to the deposit of plans in accordance with building regulations see PARA 22 note 18.

5   As to the meaning of 'local authority' see PARA 1 note 12.

6   As to the notice of rejection see the Building Act 1984 s 16(6), (7); and PARA 33.

7   Building Act 1984 s 25(1)(a) (amended by the Water Act 1989 s 190, Sch 27 Pt I). The provisions of the Building Act 1984 s 25 do not apply to inner London: see Sch 3 para 1; and PARA 3. As to the making of building regulations to modify or repeal the provisions of s 25 on the grounds of inconsistency with other provisions, etc see s 1(3), Sch 1 para 11(1); and PARA 9.

The Water Industry Act 1991 s 67 (standards of wholesomeness of water) (see WATER AND WATERWAYS vol 101 (2009) PARA 634) and any regulations made under s 67 apply for the purposes of the Building Act 1984 s 25(1) as they apply for the purposes of the Water Industry Act 1991 Pt III Ch III (ss 67–86A) (see WATER AND WATERWAYS): Building Act 1984 s 25(7) (added by the Water Act 1989 s 190, Sch 25 para 70; and amended by the Water Consolidation (Consequential Provisions) Act 1991 s 2, Sch 1 para 39(1), (3)).

8 Building Act 1984 s 25(1)(b).
9 Building Act 1984 s 25(1)(c).
10 Building Act 1984 s 25(1).
11 Ie under the Building Act 1984 s 25(1): see the text and notes 1–10.
12 Building Act 1984 s 25(2). As to the procedure on applications to a magistrates' court see s 103(1); and PARA 139. See further CRIMINAL PROCEDURE vol 27 (2015) PARA 142; MAGISTRATES vol 71 (2013) PARA 436.
13 As to the meaning of 'owner' see PARA 12 note 2.
14 Building Act 1984 s 25(3).
15 Building Act 1984 s 25(4). A person who contravenes s 25(4) is liable on summary conviction to a fine not exceeding level 1 on the standard scale and to a further fine not exceeding £2 for each day on which the offence continues after he is convicted: s 25(6). As to the powers of magistrates' courts to issue fines on summary conviction see SENTENCING vol 92 (2015) PARA 176. As to the meaning of 'contravene' see PARA 12 note 10. As to continuing offences see PARA 144. Civil sanctions may be imposed in respect of offences under the Building Act 1984 by virtue of the powers under the Regulatory Enforcement and Sanctions Act 2008 Pt 3 (ss 36–71): see ss 36, 38(2), Sch 6; and CONSTITUTIONAL AND ADMINISTRATIVE LAW vol 20 (2014) PARA 331 et seq.
16 As to persons aggrieved see JUDICIAL REVIEW vol 61 (2010) PARA 656.
17 Building Act 1984 s 25(5).

(iii) Proposed Departure from Plans

41. Proposed departure from plans.

As from a day to be appointed the following provisions have effect[1]. Where plans[2] of any proposed work have been passed[3] by a local authority[4], the person by or on whose behalf the plans were in accordance with building regulations[5] deposited[6] with the authority may (and in such cases as may be prescribed[7] must) for the purpose of obtaining the approval of the authority to any proposed departure or deviation from the plans as passed, deposit plans of the departure or deviation[8].

1 In so far as the Building Act 1984 s 31 enables regulations to be made, it came into force on 1 December 1984 by virtue of s 134(2). At the date at which this volume states the law no order bringing s 31 into force for remaining purposes had been made.
2 As to the meaning of 'plans' see PARA 9 note 8.
3 Ie under the Building Act 1984 s 16: see PARA 33.
4 As to the meaning of 'local authority' see PARA 1 note 12.
5 As to the meaning of 'building regulations' see PARA 7.
6 As to references to the deposit of plans in accordance with building regulations see PARA 22 note 18.
7 Ie prescribed by building regulations: see the Building Act 1984 s 126.
8 Building Act 1984 s 31(1) (not yet in force: see note 1). Section 16 (passing or rejection of plans: see PARA 33) applies in relation to plans deposited under s 31(1) as it applies in relation to the plans originally deposited: s 31(2) (not yet in force: see note 1).

(iv) Lapse of Deposit of Plans

42. Lapse of deposit of plans.

Where plans[1] of any proposed work have, in accordance with building regulations[2], been deposited[3] with a local authority[4], and the plans have been passed[5] by the authority, or notice of rejection[6] of the plans has not been given within the relevant period[7] from their deposit, and the work to which the plans relate has not been commenced within three years from the deposit of the plans, the local authority may, at any time before the work is commenced, by notice to the person by whom or on whose behalf the plans were deposited, or to the owner[8] for the time being of the land to which the plans relate, declare that the deposit of the plans is of no effect[9].

Where such a notice has been given, the Building Act 1984 and the building regulations[10], as respects the proposed work, have effect as if no plans had been deposited[11].

1   As to the meaning of 'plans' see PARA 9 note 8.
2   As to the meaning of 'building regulations' see PARA 7.
3   As to references to the deposit of plans in accordance with building regulations see PARA 22 note 18.
4   As to the meaning of 'local authority' see PARA 1 note 12.
5   As to notice that plans have been passed see the Building Act 1984 s 16(6), (8); and PARA 33. As to the form, authorisation and service of notices see PARAS 135–137.
6   As to the requirement to give notice that plans have been rejected see the Building Act 1984 s 16(6), (7); and PARA 33.
7   As to the meaning of the 'relevant period' see PARA 33 note 14.
8   As to the meaning of 'owner' see PARA 12 note 2.
9   Building Act 1984 s 32(1). A plan showing several houses, some of which were built within the period, can be declared void as regards houses not commenced within the period: see *Harrogate Corpn v Dickinson* [1904] 1 KB 468, CA. See also *White v Sunderland Corpn* (1903) 88 LT 592, DC.
10   Ie the Building Regulations 2010, SI 2010/2214.
11   Building Act 1984 s 32(2).

(v) Consultation with Sewerage Undertaker

43. Consultation with sewerage undertaker.
Where full plans[1] have been deposited with the local authority and requirements in relation to building over sewers are imposed[2] in relation to the building work[3] which is the subject of those plans[4], the local authority must consult the sewerage undertaker as soon as practicable after the plans have been deposited[5], and before issuing[6] any completion certificate in relation to the building work[7]. Where a local authority is so required to consult the sewerage undertaker it must:

(1)   give to the sewerage undertaker, in a case where it is consulting it following the deposit of full plans, sufficient plans to show whether the work would, if carried out in accordance with those plans, comply with the applicable requirements[8] relating to building over sewers[9];

(2)   have regard to any views expressed by the sewerage undertaker[10]; and

(3)   not pass plans or issue a completion certificate until 15 days have elapsed from the date on which it consulted the sewerage undertaker, unless the sewerage undertaker has expressed its views to the local authority before the expiry of that period[11].

1   As to the meaning of 'full plans' see PARA 25 note 7.
2   Ie by the Building Regulations 2010, SI 2010/2214, Sch 1 para H4: see PARA 10.
3   As to the meaning of 'building work' see PARA 10.
4   Building Regulations 2010, SI 2010/2214, reg 15(1).
5   Building Regulations 2010, SI 2010/2214, reg 15(2)(a).
6   Ie in accordance with the Building Regulations 2010, SI 2010/2214, reg 17 (see PARA 29) or reg

17A (see PARA 29).
7 Building Regulations 2010, SI 2010/2214, reg 15(2)(b) (amended by SI 2012/3119; and SI 2013/747).
8 Ie the requirements of the Building Regulations 2010, SI 2010/2214, Sch 1 para H4: see PARA 10.
9 Building Regulations 2010, SI 2010/2214, reg 15(3)(a).
10 Building Regulations 2010, SI 2010/2214, reg 15(3)(b).
11 Building Regulations 2010, SI 2010/2214, reg 15(3)(c).

(6) Energy Performance of Buildings

(i) Energy Efficiency Requirements

44. Application of energy efficiency requirements.
Building regulations contain energy efficiency requirements[1] which apply to the erection of any building[2] which:

(1)　is a roofed construction having walls[3];
(2)　uses energy to condition the indoor climate[4]; and
(3)　does not fall within one or more of the following categories[5]:
　　(a)　buildings which are:
　　　　(i)　listed buildings[6];
　　　　(ii)　buildings in a conservation area[7]; or
　　　　(iii)　buildings included in the schedule of monuments[8], where compliance with the energy efficiency requirements would unacceptably alter their character or appearance[9];
　　(b)　buildings which are used primarily or solely as places of worship[10];
　　(c)　temporary buildings with a planned time of use of two years or less, industrial sites, workshops and non-residential agricultural buildings with low energy demand[11];
　　(d)　stand-alone buildings other than dwellings with a total useful floor area of less than 50 square metres[12].

The energy efficiency requirements also apply to the extensions of any such building (with the exception of certain extensions[13]) and the carrying out of any work to or in connection with any such building or extension[14].

1 'Energy efficiency requirements' means the requirements of the Building Regulations 2010, SI 2010/2214, reg 23 (see PARA 45), reg 25A (see PARA 46), reg 25B (see PARA 45), reg 26 (see PARA 46), reg 26A (see PARA 46), reg 28 (see PARA 45), reg 40, Sch 1 Pt L (conservation of fuel and power: see PARA 10); in relation to England reg 43 46; and in relation to excepted energy buildings in Wales, reg 26B 46: reg 2(1) (amended by SI 2011/1515; SI 2012/3119; SI 2013/747; SI 2013/1959; SI 2014/110; SI 2014/579; SI 2016/285; SI 2016/611; and SI 2018/558).
2 For the purposes of the Building Regulations 2010, SI 2010/2214, Pt 6 (regs 21–35) (energy efficiency requirements), 'building' means the building as a whole or parts of it that have been designed or altered to be used separately: reg 35(1).
3 Building Regulations 2010, SI 2010/2214, reg 21(1)(a), (2)(a).
4 Building Regulations 2010, SI 2010/2214, reg 21(1)(a), (2)(b).
5 Building Regulations 2010, SI 2010/2214, reg 21(1)(a), (2)(c).
6 Building Regulations 2010, SI 2010/2214, reg 21(3)(a)(i). The text refers to buildings listed in accordance with the Planning (Listed Buildings and Conservation Areas) Act 1990 s 1: see PLANNING vol 83 (2018) PARA 1181 et seq.
7 Building Regulations 2010, SI 2010/2214, reg 21(3)(a)(ii). The text refers to areas designated in accordance with the Planning (Listed Buildings and Conservation Areas) Act 1990 s 69: see PLANNING vol 83 (2010) PARA 1255.

8   Building Regulations 2010, SI 2010/2214, reg 21(3)(a)(iii). The text refers to the schedule of
    monuments maintained under the Ancient Monuments and Archaeological Areas Act 1979 s 1: see
    NATIONAL CULTURAL HERITAGE.
9   Building Regulations 2010, SI 2010/2214, reg 21(3)(a).
10 Building Regulations 2010, SI 2010/2214, reg 21(3)(b).
11 Building Regulations 2010, SI 2010/2214, reg 21(3)(c), (5). See also the European Parliament and
    Council Directive (EC) 2010/31 (OJ L153, 18.6.2010, p 13).
12 Building Regulations 2010, SI 2010/2214, reg 21(3)(d).
13 The energy efficiency requirements apply to the extension of any building as described in heads
    (1)–(3) in the text other than an extension to which the Building Regulations 2010, SI 2010/2214,
    reg 21(4) applies: see reg 21(1)(b). Regulation 21(4) applies to any extension of a building falling
    within Sch 2 Class 7 (see PARA 16) except a conservatory or porch:
    (1)   where any wall, door or window separating the conservatory or porch from that
          building has been removed and not replaced with a wall, door or window (reg 21(4)(a))
          or;
    (2)   into which the building's heating system has been extended (reg 21(4)(b)).
          In Wales, the reference to the building's heating system referred to in head (2) is to a
          building's heating system that has been extended to heat the conservatory or porch or a
          conservatory or porch in which a fixed heating appliance has been provided to heat the
          conservatory or porch: see reg 21(4)(b), (c) (reg 21(4)(b) amended, reg 21(4)(c) added by
          SI 2014/110 in relation to Wales).
14 Building Regulations 2010, SI 2010/2214, reg 21(1)(c).

45. Conservation of fuel and power.

Where there is a change to a building's energy status[1], such work, if any, must
be carried out as is necessary to ensure that the building complies with the
applicable requirements of the building regulations which relate to the
conservation of fuel and power[2].

Where the renovation of an individual thermal element[3] constitutes a major
renovation or amounts to the renovation of more than 50% of the element's
surface area, such work must be carried out as is necessary to ensure that the
whole thermal element complies with the requirement to limit heat gains and
losses in so far as that is technically, functionally and economically feasible[4].
Where the whole or any part of an individual thermal element is proposed to be
replaced and the replacement constitutes a major renovation or (in the case of part
replacement) amounts to the replacement of more than 50% of the thermal
element's surface area, the whole of the thermal element must be replaced so as to
ensure it similarly complies with those requirements[5].

In relation to England, where building work[6] is proposed in relation to an
existing building with a total useful floor area over 1,000 square metres, and that
work consists of or includes:

(1)   an extension[7];
(2)   the initial provision of any fixed building services[8]; or
(3)   an increase to the installed capacity of any fixed building services[9],

then such work, if any, must be carried out as is necessary to ensure that the
building complies with the requirements relating to the conservation of fuel and
power[10].

In relation to Wales, where building work is proposed in relation to an existing
building:

(a)   with a total useful floor area over 1,000 square metres and the work
      consists of or includes the works mentioned in head (2) or head (3)[11];
(b)   consists of or includes an extension or the extension of the building's
      heating system or the provision of a fixed heating appliance, to heat a
      previously unheated space[12]

then such work, if any, must be carried out as is necessary to ensure that the building complies with the requirements relating to the conservation of fuel and power[13].

However, no such work is required to be carried out if it is not technically, functionally and economically feasible[14].

Where building work is of a kind described above[15] and the carrying out of that work does not constitute a material alteration[16], that work need only comply with the applicable requirements of the building regulations relating to the conservation of fuel and power[17].

1 'Change to a building's energy status' means any change which results in a building becoming a building to which the energy efficiency requirements of the Building Regulations 2010, SI 2010/2214, where previously it was not: reg 2. As to the meaning of 'energy efficiency requirements' see PARA 44 note 1. As to the meaning of 'building' for these purposes see PARA 44 note 2.
2 Building Regulations 2010, SI 2010/2214, reg 22. As to the requirements relating to the conservation of fuel and power see Sch 1 Pt L; and PARA 10. See also ENERGY AND CLIMATE CHANGE vol 42 (2011) PARA 193. As to energy efficiency and conservation in residential accommodation see ENERGY AND CLIMATE CHANGE vol 42 (2011) PARA 196.
3 As to the meaning of 'thermal element' see PARA 10 note 15.
4 Building Regulations 2010, SI 2010/2214, reg 23(1) (reg 23 substituted in relation to England by SI 2012/3119 and in relation to Wales by SI 2013/747). The text refers to the requirements of the Building Regulations 2010, SI 2010/2214, Sch 1 para L1(a)(i) which requires that reasonable provision must be made for the conservation of fuel and power in buildings by limiting heat gains and losses through thermal elements and other parts of the building fabric.
   Regulation 23, in so far as it applies to Crown buildings or to building work carried out or proposed to be carried out by the Crown authorities, is designated as a provision to which the Building Act 1984 s 35 (penalty for contravening building regulations) (see PARA 61) does not apply: Building Regulations 2010, SI 2010/2214, reg 47 (substituted by SI 2012/3119; SI 2018/552; and SI 2018/558; amended by SI 2013/747; SI 2014/110; and SI 2014/579).
5 Building Regulations 2010, SI 2010/2214, reg 23(2) (as substituted: see note 4).
6 As to the meaning of 'building work' see PARA 10.
7 Building Regulations 2010, SI 2010/2214, reg 28(1)(a). Regulation 28 has been substituted in relation to Wales: see reg 28 (substituted by SI 2014/110; and SI 2018/558); and text and notes 11–14.
8 Building Regulations 2010, SI 2010/2214, reg 28(1)(b). As to the meaning of 'fixed building services' see PARA 10 note 25.
9 Building Regulations 2010, SI 2010/2214, reg 28(1)(c).
10 Building Regulations 2010, SI 2010/2214, reg 28(2). See note 2.
11 Building Regulations 2010, SI 2010/2214, reg 28(1) (reg 28 substituted in relation to Wales by SI 2014/110; and SI 2018/558).
12 Building Regulations 2010, SI 2010/2214, reg 28(2) (as substituted: see note 11).
13 Building Regulations 2010, SI 2010/2214, reg 28(3) (as substituted: see note 11). See note 2.
14 Building Regulations 2010, SI 2010/2214, reg 28(3) in relation to England ; reg 28(4) in relation to Wales (as substituted (see note 11)).
15 Ie work required by the Building Regulations 2010, SI 2010/2214, reg 22 (see the text and notes 1–2), work required by reg 23 (see the text and notes 3–5), and work required by reg 28 (see the text and notes 6–14): see regs 3(1)(g), (h), (i), 4(2).
16 As to the meaning of 'material alteration' see PARA 10 note 6.
17 Building Regulations 2010, SI 2010/2214, reg 4(2). The text refers to the conservation of fuel and power requirements of Sch 1 Pt L (see PARA 10).

46. Minimum energy performance requirements.

The appropriate national authority[1] must approve minimum energy performance requirements for new buildings[2] which includes new dwellings[3], in the form of target CO_2 emission rates and new dwellings, in the form of target fabric energy efficiency[4] rates, which must be calculated and expressed in accordance with the approved methodology[5].

In relation to Wales, minimum energy performance requirements must be approved by the Welsh Ministers, calculated and expressed in accordance with the approved methodology approved[6] for new buildings (other than new dwellings), in the form of target primary energy consumption rates and new dwellings, in the form of target fabric performance values[7].

Where a building is erected, it must be a nearly zero-energy building[8].

Where a building[9] is erected, it must not exceed the target CO_2 emission rate for the building that has been so approved[10]. Not later than the day before the work starts, the person carrying out the work must give the local authority[11] a notice which specifies:

(1)   the target CO_2 emission rate for the building, calculated and expressed in accordance with the approved methodology[12];

(2)   the CO_2 emission rate for the building as designed, calculated and expressed in accordance with the approved methodology[13]; and

(3)   a list of specifications to which the building is to be constructed[14].

Not later than five days after the work has been completed[15], the person carrying out the work must give the local authority:

(a)   a notice which specifies the target CO_2 emission rate for the building, calculated and expressed in accordance with the approved methodology[16], the CO_2 emission rate for the building as constructed, calculated and expressed in accordance with the approved methodology and whether the building has been constructed in accordance with the list of specifications[17], and if not a list of any changes to those specifications[18]; or

(b)   a certificate by an energy assessor[19] (who is accredited to produce such certificates for that category of building) accompanied by the information referred to in head (a)[20].

Where a dwelling is erected, it must not exceed the target fabric energy efficiency rate for the dwelling that has been approved[21] , applying the approved methodology of calculation and expression of the energy performance of buildings[22].

Not later than the day before the work starts, the person carrying out the work must give the local authority[23] a notice which specifies:

(i)   the target fabric energy efficiency rate for the dwelling, calculated and expressed in accordance with the approved methodology[24];

(ii)   the fabric energy efficiency rate for the dwelling as designed, calculated and expressed in accordance with the approved methodology[25]; and

(iii) a list of specifications to which the dwelling is to be constructed[26].

Not later than five days after the work has been completed[27], the person carrying out the work must give the local authority:

(A)   a notice which specifies the target fabric energy efficiency rate for the dwelling, calculated and expressed in accordance with the approved methodology[28], the fabric energy efficiency rate for the dwelling as constructed, calculated and expressed in accordance with the approved methodology and whether the dwelling has been constructed in accordance with the list of specifications[29], and if not a list of any changes to those specifications[30]; or

(B)   a certificate by an energy assessor[31] (who is accredited to produce such certificates for that category of building) accompanied by the information referred to in head (A)[32].

In relation to Wales, where a dwelling is erected, it must not exceed the target fabric performance values for the dwelling which have been approved[33]), applying the approved methodology of calculation and expression of the energy performance of buildings[34].

In relation to Wales, not later than the day before the work starts, the person carrying out the work must give the local authority a notice which specifies:

(I)   the target fabric performance values for the dwelling, calculated and expressed in accordance with the approved methodology[35];

(II)   the fabric performance values for the dwelling as designed, calculated and expressed in accordance with the approved methodology[36]; and

(III)   a list of specifications to which the dwelling is to be constructed[37].

Not later than five days after the work has been completed, the person carrying out the work must give the local authority:

(AA)   the target fabric performance values for the dwelling, calculated and expressed in accordance with the approved methodology[38], the fabric performance values for the dwelling as constructed, calculated and expressed in accordance with the approved methodology and whether the dwelling has been constructed in accordance with the list of specifications[39], and if not a list of any changes to those specifications[40]; or

(BB)   a certificate by an energy assessor[41] (who is accredited to produce such certificates for that category of building) accompanied by the information referred to in head (A)[42].

1   Ie the Secretary of State or, where statutory functions have been transferred in relation to Wales, the Welsh Ministers: see PARA 5.

2   Before construction of a new building starts, the person who is to carry out the work must analyse and take into account the technical, environmental and economic feasibility of using high-efficiency alternative systems (such as the following systems) in the construction, if available decentralised energy supply systems based on energy from renewable sources, cogeneration, district or block heating or cooling, particularly where it is based entirely or partially on energy from renewable sources and heat pumps: Building Regulations 2010, SI 2010/2214, reg 25A(1) (reg 25A added in relation to England by SI 2012/3119 and in relation to Wales by SI 2013/747). The person carrying out the work must not later than the beginning of the day before the day on which the work starts, give the local authority a notice which states that the analysis referred to in Building Regulations 2010, SI 2010/2214, reg 25A(1) has been undertaken, is documented and the documentation is available to the authority for verification purposes and ensure that a copy of the analysis is available for inspection at all reasonable times upon request by an officer of the local authority: reg 25A(2) (as so added). Such analysis may be carried out for individual buildings or for groups of similar buildings or for common typologies of buildings in the same area and in so far as it relates to collective heating and cooling systems, may be carried out for all buildings connected to the system in the same area: reg 25A(4) (as so added). An authorised officer of the local authority may require production of the documentation in order to verify that this regulation has been complied with: reg 25A(3) (as so added). 'Cogeneration' means simultaneous generation in one process of thermal energy and one or both of the following: (1) electrical energy; (2) mechanical energy; 'district or block heating or cooling' means the distribution of thermal energy in the form of steam, hot water or chilled liquids, from a central source of production through a network of multiple buildings or sites, for the use of space or process heating or cooling; 'energy from renewable sources' means energy from renewable non-fossil sources, namely wind, solar, aerothermal, geothermal, hydrothermal and ocean energy, hydropower, biomass, landfill gas, sewage treatment plant gas and biogases; 'heat pump' means a machine, a device or installation that transfers heat from natural surroundings such as air, water or ground to buildings or industrial applications by reversing the natural flow of heat such that it flows from a lower to a higher temperature. (for reversible heat pumps, it may also move heat from the building to the natural surroundings): reg 25A(5) (as so added). Regulation 25A is designated as a provision to which the Building Act 1984 s 35 (penalty for contravening building regulations) (see PARA 61) does not apply: Building Regulations 2010, SI 2010/2214, reg 47 (substituted by SI 2012/3119; SI 2018/552; and SI 2018/558; amended by SI 2013/747; SI 2014/110; SI 2014/579; and

SI 2018/552). As to the meaning of 'local authority' see PARA 1 note 12. Note that in relation to building work which is the subject of an initial notice (as to which see PARA 74 et seq), the Building Regulations 2010, SI 2010/2214, reg 25A applies as if references to the local authority were references to the approved inspector: see the Building (Approved Inspectors etc) Regulations 2010, SI 2010/2215, reg 20(1); and PARA 87.

3 'New dwelling' does not include a dwelling that is formed by a material change of use of a building: Building Regulations 2010, SI 2010/2214, reg 35(1) (definition added by SI 2015/767; and amended by SI 2018/558).

4 'Fabric energy efficiency' means the space heating and cooling requirements per square metre of floor area of a new dwelling: Building Regulations 2010, SI 2010/2214, reg 35(1) (definition added by SI 2013/1959).

5 Building Regulations 2010, SI 2010/2214, reg 25 (substituted by SI 2013/1959; and SI 2018/558; amended by SI 2013/1959; SI 2014/110; SI 2016/285; and SI 2016/611). The appropriate national authority must approve:
   (1) a methodology of calculation of the energy performance of buildings, including methods for calculating asset ratings and operational ratings of buildings (Building Regulations 2010, SI 2010/2214, reg 24(1)(a)); and
   (2) ways in which the energy performance of buildings, as calculated in accordance with the methodology, is to be expressed (reg 24(1)(b)).
   'Asset rating' means an energy performance indicator determined from the amount of energy estimated to meet the different needs associated with a standardised use of the building; 'operational rating' means an energy performance indicator determined from the amount of energy consumed during the occupation of a building over a period of time and the energy demand associated with a typical use of the building over that period: reg 24(2) (amended by SI 2016/285; and SI 2016/611).
   The Secretary of State must carry out a review of any minimum energy performance requirements approved by the Secretary of State under building regulations in relation to dwellings in England: Building Act 1984 s 2C (added by the Housing and Planning Act 2016 s 165).

6 Ie pursuant to the Building Regulations 2010, SI 2010/2214, reg 24: see note 5.

7 Building Regulations 2010, SI 2010/2214, reg 25C (added by SI 2014/110; amended by SI 2016/611; and SI 2018/558).

8 Building Regulations 2010, SI 2010/2214, reg 25B (added by SI 2012/3119; and SI 2018/558). The Building Regulations 2010, SI 2010/2214, reg 25B comes into force in relation to England in respect of new buildings owned and occupied by public authorities and in relation to Wales in respect of new buildings occupied by public authorities on 1 January 2019; reg 25B comes into force in respect of all other new buildings on 31 December 2020: see the Buildings Regulations &c (Amendment) Regulations 2012, SI 2012/3119, Sch 1 (amended by SI 2013/181); and the Buildings Regulations &c (Amendment) (Wales) Regulations 2013, SI 2013/747, Schedule. 'Nearly zero-energy building' means a building that has a very high energy performance, as determined in accordance with a methodology approved under the Building Regulations 2010, SI 2010/2214, reg 24 (see note 5), where the nearly zero or very low amount of energy required should be covered to a very significant extent by energy from renewable sources, including energy from renewable sources produced on-site or nearby: reg 35(1) (amended by SI 2015/767).
   Regulation 23, in so far as it applies to Crown buildings or to building work carried out or proposed to be carried out by the Crown authorities, is designated as a provision to which the Building Act 1984 s 35 (penalty for contravening building regulations) (see PARA 61) does not apply: Building Regulations 2010, SI 2010/2214, reg 47 (substituted by SI 2012/3119; SI 2018/552; and SI 2018/558; amended by SI 2013/747; SI 2014/110; and SI 2014/579).
   Regulation 25B, in so far as it applies to Crown buildings or to building work carried out or proposed to be carried out by the Crown authorities, is designated as a provision to which the Building Act 1984 s 35 (penalty for contravening building regulations) (see PARA 61) does not apply: Building Regulations 2010, SI 2010/2214, reg 47 (substituted by SI 2012/3119; SI 2018/552; and SI 2018/558; amended by SI 2013/747; SI 2014/110; and SI 2014/579).

9 As to the meaning of 'building' see PARA 44 note 2.

10 See the Building Regulations 2010, SI 2010/2214, reg 26. The text refers to the building that has been approved pursuant to reg 25 (see text and notes 1–5), applying the methodology of calculation and expression of the energy performance of buildings approved pursuant to reg 24 (see note 5): reg 26 (amended by SI 2016/285; and SI 2016/611). Regulation 26, in so far as it applies to Crown buildings or to building work carried out or proposed to be carried out by the Crown authorities, is designated as a provision to which the Building Act 1984 s 35 (penalty for

contravening building regulations) (see PARA 61) does not apply: Building Regulations 2010, SI 2010/2214, reg 47 (substituted by SI 2012/3119; SI 2018/552; and SI 2018/558; amended by SI 2013/747; SI 2014/110; and SI 2014/579).

11 As to the meaning of 'local authority' see PARA 1 note 12. Note that in relation to building work which is the subject of an initial notice (as to which see PARA 74 et seq), the Building Regulations 2010, SI 2010/2214, reg 27 applies as if references to the local authority were references to the approved inspector: see the Building (Approved Inspectors etc) Regulations 2010, SI 2010/2215, reg 20(1); and PARA 87.

12 Building Regulations 2010, SI 2010/2214, reg 27(1), (2)(a) (reg 27(2)(a), (b), (3)(a)(i), (ii), (4) amended by SI 2016/285; and SI 2016/611). The text refers to the methodology approved pursuant to reg 24 (see note 5): reg 27(2)(a) (as so amended). Regulation 27 is designated as a provision to which the Building Act 1984 s 35 (penalty for contravening building regulations) (see PARA 61) does not apply: Building Regulations 2010, SI 2010/2214, reg 47 (substituted by SI 2012/3119; SI 2018/552; and SI 2018/558; amended by SI 2013/747; SI 2014/110; and SI 2014/579). Regulation 27 does not apply in respect of any work specified in an initial notice, an amendment notice or a public body's notice, which is in force: reg 19(1) (amended by SI 2012/3119; SI 2013/747; SI 2016/285; and SI 2016/611).

13 Building Regulations 2010, SI 2010/2214, reg 27(1), (2)(b) (as amended: see note 12). See note 6.

14 Building Regulations 2010, SI 2010/2214, reg 27(1), (2)(c). For these purposes, 'specifications' means specifications used for the calculation of the CO_2 emission rate: reg 27(5).

15 In relation to building work which is the subject of an initial notice the Building Regulations 2010, SI 2010/2214, reg 27(3) applies as if after the words 'work has been completed' there were inserted 'or, if earlier, the date on which in accordance with the Building (Approved Inspectors etc) Regulations 2010, SI 2010/2215, reg 17 the initial notice ceases to be in force': see reg 20(2); and PARA 87.

16 The text refers to the methodology approved pursuant to reg 24 (see note 5).

17 Ie the list of specifications referred to in head (3) in the text: Building Regulations 2010, SI 2010/2214, reg 27(3)(a) (as amended: see note 12).

18 Building Regulations 2010, SI 2010/2214, reg 27(3)(a) (as amended: see note 12).

19 As to energy assessors see PARA 51.

20 Building Regulations 2010, SI 2010/2214, reg 27(3)(b), (4). A local authority is authorised to accept, as evidence that the requirements of reg 26 have been satisfied, a certificate to that effect by an energy assessor who is accredited to produce energy performance certificates for that category of building: reg 27(4) (as amended: see note 12).

21 Ie pursuant to the Building Regulations 2010, SI 2010/2214, reg 25 (see text and notes 1–5)

22 Building Regulations 2010, SI 2010/2214, reg 26A (added by SI 2013/1959; amended by SI 2014/110; SI 2016/285; SI 2016/611; and SI 2018/558). The text refers to the methodology approved pursuant to the Building Regulations 2010, SI 2010/2214, reg 24 (see note 5): reg 26A (as so added and amended).

23 Note that in relation to building work which is the subject of an initial notice (as to which see PARA 74 et seq), the Building Regulations 2010, SI 2010/2214, reg 27A applies as if references to the local authority were references to the approved inspector: see the Building (Approved Inspectors etc) Regulations 2010, SI 2010/2215, reg 20(1); and PARA 87

24 Building Regulations 2010, SI 2010/2214, reg 27A(1), (2)(a) (reg 27A added in relation to England by SI 2013/1959; added and amended in relation to Wales by SI 2013/1959; and SI 2014/110; Building Regulations 2010, SI 2010/2214, reg 27A(2), (3), (4) amended by SI 2016/285; and SI 2016/611). The text refers to the methodology approved pursuant to the Building Regulations 2010, SI 2010/2214, reg 24 (see note 5): reg 27A(2)(a) (as so added and amended). Regulation 27A is designated as a provision to which the Building Act 1984 s 35 (penalty for contravening building regulations) (see PARA 61) does not apply: Building Regulations 2010, SI 2010/2214, reg 47 (substituted by SI 2012/3119; SI 2018/552; and SI 2018/558; amended by SI 2013/747; SI 2014/110; and SI 2014/579).

25 Building Regulations 2010, SI 2010/2214, reg 27A(1), (2)(b) (as so added and amended: see note 24). See note 24.

26 Building Regulations 2010, SI 2010/2214, reg 27A(1), (2)(c) (as so added and amended: see note 24). For these purposes, 'specifications' means specifications used for the calculation of the fabric energy efficiency rate: reg 27A(5) (as so added).

27 In relation to building work which is the subject of an initial notice the Building Regulations 2010, SI 2010/2214, reg 27A(3) applies as if after the words 'work has been completed' there were inserted 'or, if earlier, the date on which in accordance with the Building (Approved Inspectors etc) Regulations 2010, SI 2010/2215, reg 17 the initial notice ceases to be in force': see reg 20(2A); and

PARA 87.

28 The text refers to the methodology approved pursuant to reg 24 (see note 5).
29 Ie the list of specifications referred to in head (iii) in the text: Building Regulations 2010, SI 2010/2214, reg 27A(3)(a) (as added and amended: see note 24).
30 Building Regulations 2010, SI 2010/2214, reg 27A(3)(a) (as added and amended: see note 24).
31 See note 19.
32 Building Regulations 2010, SI 2010/2214, reg 27A(3)(b), (4) (as added and amended: see note 24). A local authority is authorised to accept, as evidence that the requirements of reg 26A (see text and notes 21, 22) have been satisfied, a certificate to that effect by an energy assessor who is accredited to produce energy performance certificates for that category of building: reg 27A(4) (as so added and amended).
33 Ie pursuant to the Building Regulations 2010, SI 2010/2214, reg 25C(b) (see text and notes 6, 7): reg 26B.
34 Building Regulations 2010, SI 2010/2214, reg 26B (added by SI 2014/110; amended by SI 2016/611; and SI 2018/558). The text refers to the methodology approved pursuant to the Building Regulations 2010, SI 2010/2214, reg 24 (see note 5): reg 26B (as so added and amended).
35 Building Regulations 2010, SI 2010/2214, reg 27B(1), (2)(a) (reg 27B added in relation to Wales by SI 2014/110; reg 27B(2), (3), (4) amended by SI 2016/611). The text refers to the methodology approved pursuant to the Building Regulations 2010, SI 2010/2214, reg 24 (see note 5): reg 27B(2)(a) (as so added and amended).
36 Building Regulations 2010, SI 2010/2214, reg 27B(1), (2)(b) (as so added and amended: see note 35). See note 35.
37 Building Regulations 2010, SI 2010/2214, reg 27B(1), (2)(c) (as so added). For these purposes, 'specifications' means specifications used for the calculation of the fabric performance values: reg 27B(5) (as so added). See note 35.
38 The text refers to the methodology approved pursuant to reg 24 (see note 5).
39 Ie the list of specifications referred to in head (III) in the text: Building Regulations 2010, SI 2010/2214, reg 27B(3)(a) (as added and amended: see note 35).
40 Building Regulations 2010, SI 2010/2214, reg 27B(3)(a) (as added and amended: see note 35).
41 See note 19.
42 Building Regulations 2010, SI 2010/2214, reg 27B(3)(b), (4) (as added and amended: see note 35). A local authority is authorised to accept, as evidence that the requirements of reg 26B have been satisfied, a certificate to that effect by an energy assessor who is accredited to produce energy performance certificates for that category of building: reg 27B(4) (as so added and amended).

47. Educational buildings, buildings of statutory undertakers and Crown buildings.

Notwithstanding the fact that the Building Act 1984 exempts certain educational buildings and buildings of statutory undertakers[1] from building regulations[2], the following provisions are specifically applied to such buildings, Crown buildings and building work carried out or proposed to be carried out by Crown authorities by the Building Regulations 2010.

The provisions referred to above are those that relate to[3]:

(1)   the power to dispense with or relax building regulations which do not apply to provisions relating to energy efficiency requirements[4];
(2)   the application of energy efficiency requirements[5];
(3)   requirements for major renovation of thermal elements[6]
(4)   minimum energy performance requirements for new buildings in the form of target CO_2 emission rates[7];
(5)   consideration of high-efficiency alternative systems for new buildings[8];
(6)   nearly zero-energy requirements for new buildings[9];
(7) CO_2 emission rates for new buildings[10];
(8)   interpretation of the provisions relating to energy efficiency requirements[11].

1 For these purposes, 'education buildings and buildings of statutory undertakers' means buildings which fall within the Building Act 1984 s 4(1)(a), (b) or (c) (see PARA 16) (Building Regulations 2010, SI 2010/2214, reg 34(2) (reg 34 substituted by SI 2013/181).
2 See the Building Act 1984 s 4(1) (prospectively repealed); and PARA 16.

3 Ie in so far as applicable by virtue of the Building Regulations 2010, SI 2010/2214, reg 21 (see PARA 44): reg 34(1) (as substituted and amended: see note 4).

4 Building Regulations 2010, SI 2010/2214, reg 34(1) (reg 34 as substituted (see note 1); reg 34(1) amended by SI 2013/1105, SI 2013/1959; SI 2016/285; and SI 2018/558). The text refers to the Building Regulations 2010, SI 2010/2214, reg 11(3) (see PARA 18): reg 34(1) (as so substituted and amended).

5 Building Regulations 2010, SI 2010/2214, reg 34(1) (as substituted and amended: see note 4). The text refers to the Building Regulations 2010, SI 2010/2214, reg 21 (see PARA 44): reg 34(1) (as so amended).

6 Building Regulations 2010, SI 2010/2214, reg 34(1) (as substituted and amended: see note 4). The text refers to the Building Regulations 2010, SI 2010/2214, reg 23(1)(a) (see PARA 45): reg 34(1) (as so substituted and amended).

7 Building Regulations 2010, SI 2010/2214, reg 34(1) (as substituted and amended: see note 4). The text refers to the requirements of reg 25(a) (see PARA 46): reg 34(1) (as so substituted and amended). For the purposes of buildings in Wales the text refers to the requirements of reg 25 (as originally exacted).

8 Building Regulations 2010, SI 2010/2214, reg 34(1) (as substituted and amended: see note 4). The text refers to the requirements of reg 25A (see PARA 46): reg 34(1) (as so substituted and amended).

9 Building Regulations 2010, SI 2010/2214, reg 34(1) (as substituted and amended: see note 4). The text refers to the requirements of reg 25B (see PARA 46): reg 34(1) (as so substituted and amended).

10 Building Regulations 2010, SI 2010/2214, reg 34(1) (as so substituted and amended: see note 4). The text refers to the requirements of reg 26 (see PARA 46): reg 34(1) (as so substituted and amended).

11 Building Regulations 2010, SI 2010/2214, reg 34(1) (as substituted and amended: see note 4). The text refers to the interpretation of Pt 6 (regs 21–35) which is in reg 35 (see PARA 46): reg 34(1) (as so amended).

(ii) Energy Performance Certificates

48. Energy performance certificates.

Where a building[1] is to be sold or rented out, the relevant person[2] must make available[3] free of charge a valid energy performance certificate[4] to any prospective buyer or tenant[5]:

(1) at the earliest opportunity[6]; and

(2) in any event no later than whichever is the earlier of:

  (a) in the case of a person who requests information about the building, the time at which the relevant person first makes available any information in writing about the building to the person[7]; or

  (b) in the case of a person who makes a request to view the building, the time at which the person views the building[8].

The relevant person must ensure that a valid energy performance certificate has been given free of charge to the person who ultimately becomes the buyer or tenant[9].

Where a building is to be sold or rented out and no valid energy performance certificate is available for that building, the relevant person must secure that an energy performance certificate is commissioned for the building before the building is put on the market[10]. Before marketing the building, a person acting on behalf of the relevant person must be satisfied that an energy performance certificate has been commissioned[11] for the building[12]. The relevant person and a person acting on behalf of the relevant person must use all reasonable efforts to secure that a valid energy performance certificate is obtained for the building before the end of a period of seven days starting with the day on which the building was first put on the market[13]. Where any person subject to such a duty[14] is unable, despite using all reasonable efforts, to secure that a valid energy performance certificate is obtained for the building before the end of the seven day period so specified, the person must secure that the certificate is obtained before the end of the period of 21 days immediately following the seven day period[15].

Where a building is erected or a building is modified so that it has a greater or lesser number of parts designed or altered for separate use than it previously had, where the modification includes the provision or extension of any of the fixed services for heating, hot water, air conditioning or mechanical ventilation, the person carrying out the building work must:

(i)   give an energy performance certificate for the building to the owner of the building[16];

(ii)   give to the local authority notice to that effect[17]; and

(iii)   include in that notice the reference number under which the energy performance certificate has been registered[18](except in the case of an energy performance certificate[19] issued in respect of excluded buildings)[20].

The energy performance certificate and notice must be given not later than five days after the building work has been completed[21].

The duties relating to energy performance certificates where a building is to be sold or rented out[22] or on marketing[23] do not apply in relation to a dwelling which is to be sold or rented out where the relevant person can demonstrate that:

(A)   the dwelling is suitable for demolition[24];

(B)   the resulting site is suitable for redevelopment[25];

(C)   all the relevant planning permissions, listed building consents and conservation area consents exist in relation to the demolition[26]; and

(D)   in relation to the redevelopment:

    (I)   either outline planning permission or planning permission exists, or both[27]; and

    (II)   where relevant, listed building consent exists[28].

The duty relating to energy performance certificates where a building is to be sold or rented out[29] does not apply in relation to any prospective buyer or tenant of a building other than a dwelling which is to be sold or rented out where:

(AA)   the relevant person can demonstrate that the building is to be sold or rented out with vacant possession, the building is suitable for demolition and the resulting site is suitable for redevelopment[30]; and

(BB)   the relevant person believes on reasonable grounds that the prospective buyer or tenant intends to demolish the building[31].

The duty relating to energy performance certificates on marketing[32] does not apply in relation to a building other than a dwelling which is to be sold or rented out where the relevant person can demonstrate that:

(aa)   the building is to be sold or rented out with vacant possession[33];

(bb)   the building is suitable for demolition[34];

(cc)   the resulting site is suitable for redevelopment[35];

(dd)   all the relevant planning permissions, listed building consents and conservation area consents exist in relation to the demolition[36]; and

(ee)   in relation to the development either outline planning permission or planning permission exists, or both and where relevant, listed building consent exists[37].

An energy performance certificate must contain specified information, include a recommendation report[38] and be issued by an accredited energy assessor[39].

The energy performance certificate must be valid, and must be displayed in a prominent place clearly visible to members of the public who visit the building[40].

Where a building has a valid energy performance certificate, a building unit is in such a building or has a valid energy performance certificate and is offered for sale or rent on or after 9 January 2013, the relevant person, or, where applicable, a person acting on behalf of the relevant person, must ensure that the energy performance rating[41] of the building expressed in the energy performance certificate is stated in any advertisement of the sale or rental in commercial media[42].

1   'Building' means a roofed construction having walls, for which energy is used to condition the indoor climate, and (other than in the Energy Performance of Buildings (England and Wales) Regulations 2012, SI 2012/3118, reg 9(4) (see note 39) and reg 11 (see text and notes 41, 42) reference to a building includes reference to a building unit in that building: reg 2(1) (definition amended by SI 2013/181).
      Subject to the Energy Performance of Buildings (England and Wales) Regulations 2012, SI 2012/3118, reg 5 and any other exemptions in the Energy Performance of Buildings (England and Wales) Regulations 2012, SI 2012/3118, and notwithstanding the Building Act 1984 s 4 (see PARA 16, these Regulations apply to all buildings including buildings which are exempt from building regulations by virtue of that section.
      Energy Performance of Buildings (England and Wales) Regulations 2012, SI 2012/3118, Pt 2 (regs 5–13) does not apply to:
      (1)   buildings officially protected as part of a designated environment or because of their special architectural or historical merit, in so far as compliance with certain minimum energy performance requirements would unacceptably alter their character or appearance (reg 5(1)(a));
      (2)   buildings used as places of worship and for religious activities (reg 5(1)(b));
      (3)   temporary buildings with a time of use of two years or less (reg 5(1)(c));
      (4)   industrial sites, workshops and non-residential agricultural buildings with low energy demand (reg 5(1)(d));
      (5)   non-residential agricultural buildings which are in use by a sector covered by a national sectoral agreement on energy performance (reg 5(1)(e));
      (6)   residential buildings which are used or intended to be used for less than four months of the year or for a limited annual time of use and with an expected energy consumption of less than 25% of what would be the result of all-year use (reg 5(1)(f));
      (7)   stand-alone buildings with a total useful floor area of less than 50m2 (reg 5(1)(g)).
      Nothing in Pt 2 requires an energy performance certificate to be given or made available to a prospective buyer or tenant at any time before the construction of the building has been completed: reg 5(2).
      As to a duty to cooperate where a duty is imposed by the Energy Performance of Buildings (England and Wales) Regulations 2012, SI 2012/3118, see reg 45. As to the application of the Energy Performance of Buildings (England and Wales) Regulations 2012, SI 2012/3118 to the Crown see reg 44. As to the duty to review the Energy Performance of Buildings (England and Wales) Regulations 2012, SI 2012/3118 see reg 47.

2   'Relevant person' (other than in the phrase 'green deal relevant person') means:
      (1)   in relation to a building which is to be sold, the seller;
      (2)   in relation to a building which is to be rented out, the prospective landlord;
      (3)   in relation to an air-conditioning system, the person who has control of the operation of the system; and
      (4)   in relation to a building which is constructed, the person who carries out the construction: Energy Performance of Buildings (England and Wales) Regulations 2012, SI 2012/3118, reg 2(1).

3   Where Pt 2 requires a relevant person to give or make available a valid energy performance certificate to any person, it is sufficient for the relevant person to give or make available a copy of a valid certificate: Energy Performance of Buildings (England and Wales) Regulations 2012, SI 2012/3118, reg 12. An energy performance certificate made available in accordance with reg 6(2), an energy performance certificate given in accordance with reg 6(5), an energy performance certificate given in accordance with reg 7A(2)(a), (b) may be made available or given electronically if the intended recipient consents to receiving it electronically: see reg 13.

4   'Energy performance certificate' means a certificate which:

(1) in the case of a certificate entered on the register before 9 January 2013 complied with the requirements of the Energy Performance of Buildings (Certificates and Inspections) (England and Wales) Regulations 2007, SI 2007/991, reg 11(1);

(2) in the case of a certificate entered on the register on or after 9 January 2013 complies with the requirements of the Energy Performance of Buildings (England and Wales) Regulations 2012, SI 2012/3118, reg 9(1);

(3) in the case of a certificate issued in respect of an excluded building under reg 9A, complies with the requirements of reg 9A(2); or

(4) in the case of a certificate entered on the register before 6 April 2016 complies with the requirements of the Building Regulations 2010, SI 2010/2214, reg 29: Energy Performance of Buildings (England and Wales) Regulations 2012, SI 2012/3118, reg 2(1) (definition amended by SI 2016/284).

As to the registration of energy performance certificates and disclosure of data relating to energy performance certificates see the Energy Performance of Buildings (England and Wales) Regulations 2012, SI 2012/3118, regs 27–32, Sch B1 (regs 28,32, Sch B1 amended by SI 2018/362).

5   Energy Performance of Buildings (England and Wales) Regulations 2012, SI 2012/3118, reg 6(1), (2). Regulation 6(2) does not apply if the relevant person believes on reasonable grounds that the prospective buyer or tenant:

(1) is unlikely to have sufficient means to buy or rent the building (reg 6(3)(a));

(2) is not genuinely interested in buying or renting a building of a general description which applies to the building (reg 6(3)(b)); or

(3) is not a person to whom the relevant person is likely to be prepared to sell or rent out the building (reg 6(3)(c)).

Nothing in reg 6(3) authorises the doing of anything which constitutes an unlawful act of discrimination: reg 6(4).

A person becomes a prospective buyer or tenant in relation to a building when he or she:

(a) requests any information about the building from the relevant person or the relevant person's agent for the purpose of deciding whether to buy or rent the building (reg 3(a));

(b) makes a request to view the building for the purpose of deciding whether to buy or rent the building (reg 3(b));

(c) makes an offer, whether oral or written, to buy or rent the building (reg 3(c)).

6   Energy Performance of Buildings (England and Wales) Regulations 2012, SI 2012/3118, reg 6(2)(a).

7   Energy Performance of Buildings (England and Wales) Regulations 2012, SI 2012/3118, reg 6(2)(b)(i).

8   Energy Performance of Buildings (England and Wales) Regulations 2012, SI 2012/3118, reg 6(2)(b)(ii).

9   Energy Performance of Buildings (England and Wales) Regulations 2012, SI 2012/3118, reg 6(5).

10 Energy Performance of Buildings (England and Wales) Regulations 2012, SI 2012/3118, reg 7(1), (2).

11 An energy performance certificate is commissioned when a request is made which is properly addressed to an energy assessor who is accredited to produce energy performance certificates for the category of building in question and which is in such form, contains all such information and is accompanied by such payment or undertaking to make such payment as is usually necessary to obtain a certificate: Energy Performance of Buildings (England and Wales) Regulations 2012, SI 2012/3118, reg 7(6)(d).

12 Energy Performance of Buildings (England and Wales) Regulations 2012, SI 2012/3118, reg 7(3).

13 Energy Performance of Buildings (England and Wales) Regulations 2012, SI 2012/3118, reg 7(4). 'The market' means the property market in England and Wales; a building is put on the market when the fact that it is or may become available for sale or rent is, with the intention of marketing the building, first made public in England and Wales by or on behalf of the relevant person; a fact is made public when it is advertised or otherwise communicated (in whatever form and by whatever means) to the public or to a section of the public: reg 7(6)(a)–(c);

14 Ie duty in the Energy Performance of Buildings (England and Wales) Regulations 2012, SI 2012/3118, reg 7(4).

15 Energy Performance of Buildings (England and Wales) Regulations 2012, SI 2012/3118, reg 7(5).

16 Energy Performance of Buildings (England and Wales) Regulations 2012, SI 2012/3118, reg 7A(1), (2)(a) (reg 7A added by SI 2016/284).

17 Energy Performance of Buildings (England and Wales) Regulations 2012, SI 2012/3118, reg 7A(2) (as added: see note 16)

18 Ie in accordance with the Energy Performance of Buildings (England and Wales) Regulations 2012, SI 2012/3118, reg 27(4) PARA 51: reg 7A(2)(c) (as added: see note 16)

19 Ie issued under the Energy Performance of Buildings (England and Wales) Regulations 2012, SI 2012/3118, reg 9A: reg 7A(2)(c) (as added: see note 16)

20 Energy Performance of Buildings (England and Wales) Regulations 2012, SI 2012/3118, reg 7A(2)(c) (as added: see note 16). 'Excluded building' means a building owned, occupied or used by or for the purposes of the Security Service, the Secret Intelligence Service or the Government Communications Headquarters, any of the armed forces, the Royal Family, a prison; a contracted out prison within the meaning of the Criminal Justice Act 1991 (see PRISONS AND PRISONERS vol 85 (2012) PARA 521 or a young offender institution: Energy Performance of Buildings (England and Wales) Regulations 2012, SI 2012/3118, reg 2(1).

21 Energy Performance of Buildings (England and Wales) Regulations 2012, SI 2012/3118, reg 7A(3) (as added: see note 16).

22 Ie under the Energy Performance of Buildings (England and Wales) Regulations 2012, SI 2012/3118, reg 6 (see text and notes 5–9): see reg 8(1).

23 Ie under the Energy Performance of Buildings (England and Wales) Regulations 2012, SI 2012/3118, reg 7 (see text and notes 10–15): see reg 8(1).

24 Energy Performance of Buildings (England and Wales) Regulations 2012, SI 2012/3118, reg 8(1)(a). 'Dwelling' means a building or part of a building occupied or intended to be occupied as a separate dwelling: reg 2(1).

25 Energy Performance of Buildings (England and Wales) Regulations 2012, SI 2012/3118, reg 8(1)(b).

26 Energy Performance of Buildings (England and Wales) Regulations 2012, SI 2012/3118, reg 8(1)(c).

27 Energy Performance of Buildings (England and Wales) Regulations 2012, SI 2012/3118, reg 8(1)(d)(i).

28 Energy Performance of Buildings (England and Wales) Regulations 2012, SI 2012/3118, reg 8(1)(d)(ii).

29 Ie under the Energy Performance of Buildings (England and Wales) Regulations 2012, SI 2012/3118, reg 6 (see text and notes 5–9): see reg 8(2).

30 Energy Performance of Buildings (England and Wales) Regulations 2012, SI 2012/3118, reg 8(2)(a).

31 Energy Performance of Buildings (England and Wales) Regulations 2012, SI 2012/3118, reg 8(2)(b).

32 Ie under the Energy Performance of Buildings (England and Wales) Regulations 2012, SI 2012/3118, reg 7 (see text and notes 10–15): see reg 8(3).

33 Energy Performance of Buildings (England and Wales) Regulations 2012, SI 2012/3118, reg 8(3)(a).

34 Energy Performance of Buildings (England and Wales) Regulations 2012, SI 2012/3118, reg 8(3)(b).

35 Energy Performance of Buildings (England and Wales) Regulations 2012, SI 2012/3118, reg 8(3)(c).

36 Energy Performance of Buildings (England and Wales) Regulations 2012, SI 2012/3118, reg 8(3)(d).

37 Energy Performance of Buildings (England and Wales) Regulations 2012, SI 2012/3118, reg 8(3)(e).

38 As to recommendation reports see PARA 49.

39 An energy performance certificate entered on the register on or after 9 January 2013 must:
    (1) show the asset rating of the building, calculated and expressed in accordance with the methodology approved by the Secretary of State under the Building Regulations 2010, SI 2010/2214, reg 24 (see PARA 46) (reg 9(1)(a) (substituted by SI 2016/284));
    (2) include a reference value in order to make it possible to compare and assess the energy performance of the building (Energy Performance of Buildings (England and Wales) Regulations 2012, SI 2012/3118, reg 9(1)(b) (amended by SI 2016/284));
    (3) be issued by an energy assessor who is accredited to produce energy performance certificates for the category of building to which the certificate relates (Energy Performance of Buildings (England and Wales) Regulations 2012, SI 2012/3118, reg 9(1)(c));
    (4) include a recommendation report unless there is no reasonable potential for energy performance improvements compared to the energy performance requirements in force (reg 9(1)(d));
    (5) include the reference number under which the set of data from which the certificate may be produced has been entered onto the register in accordance with reg 27, the address

of the building, an estimate of the total useful floor area of the building and the date on which it was issued (reg 9(1)(e) (amended by SI 2013/10));

(6)   where it relates to a building or a building unit which is a green deal property, include the information specified in Sch A1 in connection with each green deal plan that has been entered into in respect of that green deal property and for which payments are still to be made under that plan (Energy Performance of Buildings (England and Wales) Regulations 2012, SI 2012/3118, reg 9(1)(ea), Sch A1 (added by SI 2013/10));

(7)   be valid for the purposes of the Energy Performance of Buildings (England and Wales) Regulations 2012, SI 2012/3118, Pt 2 (regs 5–13)in accordance with reg 9(2) (reg 9(1)(f) (amended by SI 2013/10)).

'Energy performance' in relation to a building means the calculated or measured amount of energy needed to meet the energy demand associated with ,a typical use of the building, which includes, inter alia, energy used for heating, cooling, ventilation, hot water and lighting: Energy Performance of Buildings (England and Wales) Regulations 2012, SI 2012/3118, reg 2(1) (definition added by SI 2016/284). 'Building unit' means a section, floor or apartment within a building which is designed or altered to be used separately: Energy Performance of Buildings (England and Wales) Regulations 2012, SI 2012/3118, reg 2(1). 'Total useful floor area' means the gross floor area as measured in accordance with the guidance issued from time to time by the Royal Institution of Chartered Surveyors or by any body replacing that Institution: reg 2(1).'Green deal plan' means an energy plan which is a green deal plan in accordance with the Energy Act 2011 s 1(3) (see ENERGY AND CLIMATE CHANGE): Energy Performance of Buildings (England and Wales) Regulations 2012, SI 2012/3118, reg 2(1) (definition added by SI 2013/10). 'Green deal property' has the meaning given by the Energy Act 2011 s 12(5)(b); and ENERGY AND CLIMATE CHANGE: Energy Performance of Buildings (England and Wales) Regulations 2012, SI 2012/3118, reg 2(1) (definition added by SI 2013/10). As to the meaning of 'energy assessor' see PARA 51 note 1.

The Energy Performance of Buildings (England and Wales) Regulations 2012, SI 2012/3118, reg 9(1) is subject to reg 9(6) which states reg 9 does not apply to an energy performance certificate to which reg 9A applies: reg 9(1), (6) (reg 9(1) amended, reg 9(6) added by SI 2016/284). An energy performance certificate is only valid for the purposes of the Energy Performance of Buildings (England and Wales) Regulations 2012, SI 2012/3118, Pt 2 if it was entered on the register no more than 10 years before the date on which it is made available and no other energy performance certificate for the building has since been entered on the register: reg 9(2). An energy performance certificate is only valid for the purposes of complying with the green deal disclosure obligations if it was issued by an energy assessor or produced under reg 30 pursuant to a request for the disclosure of general access data relating to a green deal property, no more than twelve months before the date on which the energy performance certificate is provided in connection with those obligations: reg 9(2A) (added by SI 2013/10). An energy performance certificate must not contain any information or data (except for the address of the building) from which a living individual (other than the energy assessor or his employer) can be identified, nor must it contain any information relating to a green deal plan for which the payment period has finished: Energy Performance of Buildings (England and Wales) Regulations 2012, SI 2012/3118, reg 9(3), (3A) (reg 9(3A) added by SI 2013/10). Certification for building units on or after 9 January 2013 may be based for a non-residential building, on a common certification of the whole building for blocks with a common heating system or on the assessment of another representative building unit in the same block: Energy Performance of Buildings (England and Wales) Regulations 2012, SI 2012/3118, reg 9(4) (amended by SI 2014/880). Certification on or after 9 January 2013 for a building which consists of a single dwelling may be based on the assessment of another representative building of similar design and size with a similar actual energy performance quality if such correspondence is guaranteed by the energy assessor issuing the energy performance certificate: reg 9(5). 'Green deal disclosure obligations' means the obligations to provide an energy performance certificate in the Energy Act 2011 s 12 and the Green Deal Framework (Disclosure, Acknowledgment, Regulations 2012, SI 2012/2079, Pt 7 (regs 41–50) (see LANDLORD AND TENANT vol 62 (2016) PARA 315: Energy Performance of Buildings (England and Wales) Regulations 2012, SI 2012/3118, reg 2(1) (definition added by SI 2013/10). 'General access data' means information that is required by the Energy Performance of Buildings (England and Wales) Regulations 2012, SI 2012/3118, to be included in an energy performance certificate, a display energy certificate, an inspection report, or a recommendation report: reg 2(1). 'Payment period' has the meaning given in the Green Deal Framework (Disclosure, Acknowledgment, Regulations 2012, SI 2012/2079, reg 2(1): Energy Performance of Buildings (England and Wales) Regulations 2012, SI 2012/3118, reg 2(1) (definition added by SI 2013/10).

Where a building in relation to which an energy performance certificate is requested to be issued is an excluded building and the person who requests the energy performance certificate notifies the energy assessor (whether in writing or otherwise) that the building is an excluded building and he requests (whether in writing or otherwise) that the energy performance certificate is issued under the Energy Performance of Buildings (England and Wales) Regulations 2012, SI 2012/3118, reg 9A, an energy performance certificate issued under reg 9A must:

(a)   comply with the requirements set out in heads (a)-(e) of regulation 9(1), other than the requirement as to the reference number under which data entered onto register (reg 9A(1), (2)(a) (reg 9A added by SI 2016/284); and

(b)   be valid for the purposes of the Energy Performance of Buildings (England and Wales) Regulations 2012, SI 2012/3118, Pt 2 in accordance with reg 9(4) (reg 9A(1), (2)(b) (as so added)).

An energy performance certificate issued under reg 9A is only valid for the purposes of Pt 2 if it was issued no more than 10 years before the date on which it is made available and no other energy performance certificate for the building has since been issued under reg 9A or entered onto the register: reg 9A(4) (as so added). An energy performance certificate must not contain any information or data (except the address of the building) from which a living individual (other than the energy assessor or energy assessor's employer) can be identified: reg 9A(3) (as so added). Where reg 9A applies, the energy assessor must not enter any data relating to the building onto the register: reg 9A(5) (as so added). This provision is referred to in the Queen's printer copy as reg 9A(4). It is submitted this is in error and should be reg 9A(5). Certification for building units may be based for a non-residential building, on a common certification of the whole building for blocks with a common heating system or on the assessment of another representative building unit in the same block: reg 9A(6) (as so added). This provision is referred to in the Queen's printer copy as reg 9A(5). It is submitted this is in error and should be reg 9A(6). Certification for a building which consists of a single dwelling may be based on the assessment of another representative building of similar design and size with a similar actual energy performance quality if such correspondence is guaranteed by the energy assessor issuing the energy performance certificate: reg 9A(7) (as so added). This provision is referred to in the Queen's printer copy as reg 9A(6). It is submitted this is in error and should be reg 9A(7). As to energy assessors see PARA 51.

40   Energy Performance of Buildings (England and Wales) Regulations 2012, SI 2012/3118, reg 10(2). This applies to a building, other than a dwelling, which satisfies all the following requirements:

(1)   it has a total useful floor area of more than $500m^2$(reg 10(1)(a));

(2)   it is frequently visited by the public (reg 10(1)(b)); and

(3)   an energy performance certificate has been made available in accordance with reg 6 or 7A or in the case of certificate entered on the register before 6 April 2016, the Building Regulations 2010, SI 2010/2214, reg 29(2) (Energy Performance of Buildings (England and Wales) Regulations 2012, SI 2012/3118, reg 10(1)(c) (amended by SI 2016/284)).

41   'Energy performance rating' means an indication of the energy efficiency of a building or building unit, calculated using the methodology approved by the Secretary of State under the Building Regulations 2010, SI 2010/2214, reg 24 (see PARA 46) and expressed on a scale of A+ to G, (or A to G in the case of a building that is a dwelling), with G representing the least energy efficient rating: Energy Performance of Buildings (England and Wales) Regulations 2012, SI 2012/3118, reg 11(3) (amended by SI 2014/880; and SI 2016/284).

42   Energy Performance of Buildings (England and Wales) Regulations 2012, SI 2012/3118, reg 11(1), (2) (reg 11(2) amended by SI 2014/880, SI 2015/609; and SI 2016/284).

(iii) Display Energy Certificates and Recommendation Reports

49.   Display Energy Certificates and Recommendation Reports.

The following provisions apply on and after the 9 January 2013 to buildings[1] occupied by public authorities and frequently visited by the public with a total useful floor area of over $500m^2$, and 9 July 2015 to buildings occupied by public authorities and frequently visited by the public with a total useful floor area of between $250m^2$ and $500m^2$. Every occupier of a building referred to in these provisions must have in its possession or control at all times a valid recommendation report[2] relating to the building unless there is no reasonable potential for energy performance improvements compared to the energy performance requirements in force and display at all times a valid display energy certificate[3] in a prominent place clearly visible to members of the public who visit the building[4].

1   As to the meaning of 'building' see PARA 48 note 1.
2   'Recommendation report' means recommendations made by an energy assessor for the cost-effective improvement of the energy performance of a building: Energy Performance of Buildings (England and Wales) Regulations 2012, SI 2012/3118, reg 4(1) (amended by SI 2013/181). A recommendation report made on or after 9 January 2013 must include:

(1)   recommended cost-effective measures that could be carried out in connection with a major renovation of the building envelope or technical building systems (Energy Performance of Buildings (England and Wales) Regulations 2012, SI 2012/3118, reg 4(2)(a));

(2)   recommended cost-effective measures for individual building elements that could be carried out without the necessity for a major renovation of the building envelope or technical building systems (reg 4(2)(b));

(3)   an indication as to how the owner or tenant can obtain more detailed information about improving the energy efficiency of the building, including more detailed information about the cost-effectiveness of the recommendations (reg 4(2)(c)); and

(4)   information on the steps to be taken to implement the recommendations (reg 4(2)(d)).

Any cost-effective measure which the energy assessor recommends must be technically feasible for the building to which the recommendation report relates: reg 4(3). A recommendation report made on or after 9 January 2013 ceases to be valid at the end of the following periods:

(a)   for a report which is included in an energy performance certificate, ten years from the date of that certificate (reg 4(4)(a));

(b)   for a report which is required to be held in respect of the building under reg 14(3)(a) (see text and note 3) where the total useful floor area of the building is over 1,000m², seven years from the nominated date applying to the report and in the case of any other building, ten years from the nominated date applying to the report (reg 4(4)(b) (amended by SI 2014/880).

'Building element' means a controlled service or fitting or a thermal element within the meaning of those expressions in the Building Regulations 2010, SI 2010/2214, reg 2(1) and (3) (see PARA 10 notes 4, 15); 'major renovation' means the renovation of a building where more than 25% of the surface area of the building envelope undergoes renovation; 'technical building systems' means technical equipment for the heating, cooling, ventilation, hot water, lighting (or for any combination thereof) of a building: Energy Performance of Buildings (England and Wales) Regulations 2012, SI 2012/3118, reg 4(5) (amended by SI 2013/181; and SI 2016/284). 'Building envelope' means the integrated elements of a building which separate its interior from the outdoor environment: Energy Performance of Buildings (England and Wales) Regulations 2012, SI 2012/3118, reg 2(1). As to the registration of recommendation reports and disclosure of data relating to recommendation reports see the Energy Performance of Buildings (England and Wales) Regulations 2012, SI 2012/3118, regs 27–32, Sch B1.

As to a duty to cooperate where a duty is imposed by the Energy Performance of Buildings (England and Wales) Regulations 2012, SI 2012/3118, see reg 45. As to the application of the Energy Performance of Buildings (England and Wales) Regulations 2012, SI 2012/3118 to the Crown see reg 44. As to the duty to review the Energy Performance of Buildings (England and Wales) Regulations 2012, SI 2012/3118 see reg 47.

3   'Display energy certificate' means a certificate which complies with the Energy Performance of Buildings (England and Wales) Regulations 2012, SI 2012/3118, reg 15 or in the case of a certificate issued in respect of an excluded building under reg 15A, complies with reg 15A(2): reg 2(1) (definition substituted by SI 2016/284).]

A display energy certificate issued under the Energy Performance of Buildings (England and Wales) Regulations 2012, SI 2012/3118, reg 15 must:

(1)   show the operational rating of the building, calculated and expressed in accordance with the methodology approved by the Secretary of State under the Building Regulations 2010, SI 2010/2214, reg 24 (see PARA 46) relating to the period of 12 months ending no earlier than three months before the nominated date (Energy Performance of Buildings (England and Wales) Regulations 2012, SI 2012/3118, reg 15(1)(a) (reg 15(1) renumbered and amended, reg 15(1)(a) substituted by SI 2016/284));

(2)   show the operational ratings for the building which were shown in any certificates displayed by the occupier during the two years before the nominated date (Energy

Performance of Buildings (England and Wales) Regulations 2012, SI 2012/3118, reg 15(1)(b) (as so renumbered and amended));

(3) include a reference value in order to make it possible to compare and assess the energy performance of the building (reg 15(1)(c) (as so renumbered and amended));

(4) be issued by an energy assessor who is accredited to produce display energy certificates for that category of building (reg 15(1)(d) (as so renumbered and amended));

(5) include the following information:

    (a) the reference number under which the set of data from which the certificate may be produced has been entered onto the register in accordance with reg 27 (see PARA 51) (reg 15(1)(e)(i) (as so renumbered and amended));

    (b) the address of the building; (reg 15(1)(e)(ii) (as so renumbered and amended));

    (c) the total useful floor area of the building (reg 15(1)(e)(iii) (as so renumbered and amended));

    (d) the name of the energy assessor who issued it (reg 15(1)(e)(iv) (as so renumbered and amended));

    (e) the name and address of the energy assessor's employer, or, if he is self-employed, the name under which he trades and his address (reg 15(1)(e)(v) (as so renumbered and amended));

    (f) the date on which it was issued (reg 15(1)(e)(vi) (as so renumbered and amended));

    (g) the nominated date (reg 15(1)(e)(vii) (as so renumbered and amended)); and

    (h) the name of the approved accreditation scheme of which the energy assessor is a member (reg 15(1)(e)(viii) (as so renumbered and amended)).

Head (a) does not apply in relation to a display energy certificate which is displayed by an occupier of a building at any time before that occupier has been in occupation of the building for 15 months: reg 16. Regulation 15 does not apply to a display energy certificate issued under reg 15A: reg 15(2) (added by SI 2016/284). 'Nominated date', in relation to a display energy certificate, means a date no later than three months after the end of the period over which the operational rating is calculated, which is nominated by the energy assessor who issued the certificate: Energy Performance of Buildings (England and Wales) Regulations 2012, SI 2012/3118, reg 2(1). 'Operational rating' means an energy performance indicator determined from the amount of energy consumed during the occupation of a building over a period of time and the energy demand associated with a typical use of the building over that period: reg 2(1) (definition substituted by SI 2016/284). As to the meaning of 'energy assessor' see PARA 51 note 1.

Where a building in relation to which a display energy certificate is requested to be issued is an excluded building and the person who requests the display energy certificate notifies the energy assessor (whether in writing or otherwise) that the building is an excluded building and requests (whether in writing or otherwise) that the display energy certificate is issued under the Energy Performance of Buildings (England and Wales) Regulations 2012, SI 2012/3118, reg 15A, a display energy certificate issued under reg 15A must comply with the requirements of heads (1) to (5), other than the requirement to provide the reference number under which data entered onto register in head (a): reg 15A(1), (2) (added by SI 2016/284). Where the Energy Performance of Buildings (England and Wales) Regulations 2012, SI 2012/3118, reg 15A applies, the energy assessor must not enter any data relating to the building onto the register: reg 15A(3) (as so added).

A display energy certificate for a building referred to in reg 14(1)–(3) is valid for 12 months beginning with the nominated date where the total useful floor area of the building is over 1,000m² or 10 years beginning with the nominated date in the case of any other building: Energy Performance of Buildings (England and Wales) Regulations 2012, SI 2012/3118, reg 14(4). As to the registration of display energy certificates and disclosure of data relating to display energy certificates see the Energy Performance of Buildings (England and Wales) Regulations 2012, SI 2012/3118, regs 27–32, Sch B1.

4 Energy Performance of Buildings (England and Wales) Regulations 2012, SI 2012/3118, reg 14(1)–(3) (reg 14(2) amended by SI 2014/880).

(iv) Inspection of air conditioning systems

50. Inspection of Air-conditioning Systems.

The following provisions apply to air-conditioning systems[1] with an effective rated output[2] of more than 12kW[3]. Where the relevant person[4] has the power to control the temperature of more than one individual air-conditioning unit in a building, each unit is considered to be a component of a single air-conditioning system for these purposes[5].

It is the duty of the relevant person in relation to an air-conditioning system referred to in the above provisions applies to ensure that accessible parts of the system are inspected by an energy assessor at regular intervals not exceeding five years and the first inspection of the accessible parts of the system must take place before:

(1)   where the system is first put into service on or after 1 January 2008, the last day of the period of five years beginning with the date on which the system is first put into service[6]; and

(2)   where head (1) does not apply, in the case of a system with an effective rated output of more than 250kW 4 January 2009 or in the case of a system with an effective rated output of more than 12kW, 4 January 2011[7].

Where an energy assessor undertakes an inspection of the system[8] he must make a written report of the inspection and give it to the relevant person as soon as practicable after completing the inspection[9].

1   'Air-conditioning system' means a combination of all the components required to provide a form of air treatment in which the temperature is controlled or can be lowered, and includes systems which combine such air treatment with the control of ventilation, humidity and air cleanliness: Energy Performance of Buildings (England and Wales) Regulations 2012, SI 2012/3118, reg 2(1).

2   'Effective rated output' means the maximum calorific output specified and guaranteed by the manufacturer of the system as being deliverable during continuous operation while complying with the useful efficiency indicated by the manufacturer Energy Performance of Buildings (England and Wales) Regulations 2012, SI 2012/3118, reg 17(3).

3   Energy Performance of Buildings (England and Wales) Regulations 2012, SI 2012/3118, reg 17(1).

4   As to the meaning of 'relevant person' see PARA 48.

5   Energy Performance of Buildings (England and Wales) Regulations 2012, SI 2012/3118, reg 17(2).

6   Energy Performance of Buildings (England and Wales) Regulations 2012, SI 2012/3118, reg 18(1), (2), (3)(a) (reg 18(1), (2) amended by SI 2015/609).

    As to a duty to cooperate where a duty is imposed by the Energy Performance of Buildings (England and Wales) Regulations 2012, SI 2012/3118, see reg 45. As to the application of the Energy Performance of Buildings (England and Wales) Regulations 2012, SI 2012/3118 to the Crown see reg 44. As to the duty to review the Energy Performance of Buildings (England and Wales) Regulations 2012, SI 2012/3118 see reg 47.

7   Energy Performance of Buildings (England and Wales) Regulations 2012, SI 2012/3118, reg 18(1), (2), (3)(b) (as amended: see note 6).

8   Ie under the Energy Performance of Buildings (England and Wales) Regulations 2012, SI 2012/3118, reg 18: reg 19(1) (amended by SI 2015/609; and SI 2016/284). As to the meaning of 'energy assessor' see PARA 51 note 1.

9   Energy Performance of Buildings (England and Wales) Regulations 2012, SI 2012/3118, reg 19(1) (as amended: see note 8). 'Inspection report' means a report issued by an energy assessor in accordance with reg 19(1) or in the case of a report issued in respect of an excluded building, issued by an energy assessor in accordance with reg 19A(2): reg 2(1) (definition substituted by SI 2016/284). The inspection report must include an assessment of the air-conditioning efficiency and the sizing of the system compared to the cooling requirements of the building, and contain appropriate advice on cost-effective improvement to the energy performance of the system, replacement of the system and alternative solutions: reg 19(2). The inspection report must be in a form including the following information:

    (1)   the reference number under which the set of data from which the report may be produced has been entered onto the register in accordance with reg 27 (see PARA 51) (reg 19(3)(a));

    (2)   the address of the building in which the system is located (reg 19(3)(b));

    (3)   the name of the energy assessor (reg 19(3)(c));

    (4)   the name and address of the energy assessor's employer, or, if such a person is self-employed, the name under which that person trades and their address (reg 19(3)(d));

    (5)   the date on which the inspection occurred (reg 19(3)(e));

(6)   the name of the approved accreditation scheme of which the energy assessor is a member (reg 19(3)(f)).

Regulation 19 does not apply to inspection reports issued under reg 19A: reg 19(4) (added by SI 2016/284). The relevant person must keep the most recent inspection report made by an energy assessor pursuant to the Energy Performance of Buildings (England and Wales) Regulations 2012, SI 2012/3118, reg 19 and where the relevant person changes, the previous relevant person must give to the new relevant person any inspection report kept by him under reg 20: reg 20. Where the relevant person changes and the new relevant person is not given any inspection report, the new relevant person must ensure that the system is inspected within three months of the day on which he becomes the relevant person: reg 21.

Where a building in relation to which an inspection report is requested to be issued is an excluded building and the person who requests the inspection report notifies the energy assessor (whether in writing or otherwise) that the building is an excluded building and requests (whether in writing or otherwise) that the inspection report is issued under reg 19A, an energy assessor undertakes an inspection of the system under reg 18 must make a written report of the inspection and give it to the relevant person as soon as practicable after completing the inspection: reg 19A(1), (2) (reg 19A added by SI 2016/284). An inspection report issued under reg 19A must comply with the requirements of the Energy Performance of Buildings (England and Wales) Regulations 2012, SI 2012/3118, reg 19(2) and heads (2)–(6): reg 19A(3) (as so added). Where reg 19A applies, the energy assessor must not enter any data relating to the building onto the register: reg 19A(4) (as so added). As to the registration of inspection reports and disclosure of data relating to inspection reports see the Energy Performance of Buildings (England and Wales) Regulations 2012, SI 2012/3118, regs 27–32, Sch B1.

(v) Energy Assessors

51.   Energy assessors.

An energy assessor[1] must be a member of an accreditation scheme[2] approved by the appropriate national authority[3].

An energy assessor must include in an energy performance certificate or inspection report a declaration of any personal or business relationship (other than in relation to producing the certificate or inspection report) that he has with:

(1)   the person who commissioned the certificate or inspection report[4];

(2)   any person on whose behalf the certificate or inspection report was commissioned[5]; and

(3)   any person who the energy assessor believes has or may have a personal or business relationship with a person referred to in head (1) or (2) or has or may have an interest in the building[6].

Energy assessors must carry out energy assessments[7] with reasonable care and skill[8]. This duty of care is enforceable by

(a)   the relevant person[9];

(b)   in the case of an energy performance certificate, any prospective or actual buyer or tenant during the period of validity of the certificate[10]; and

(c)   in the case of a display energy certificate, the occupier of the building[11].

Any person may[12], copy or issue a copy of any document produced by an energy assessor[13].

1   'Energy assessor' means an individual who is a member of an accreditation scheme: Energy Performance of Buildings (England and Wales) Regulations 2012, SI 2012/3118, reg 2(1).
2   'Accreditation scheme' means a scheme approved by the appropriate national authority in accordance with the Energy Performance of Buildings (England and Wales) Regulations 2012, SI 2012/3118, reg 22: reg 2(1).
3   Energy Performance of Buildings (England and Wales) Regulations 2012, SI 2012/3118, reg 22(1). As to the appropriate national authority (ie the Secretary of State or, where statutory functions have been transferred in relation to Wales, the Welsh Ministers) see PARA 5.

Before approving an accreditation scheme the appropriate national authority must be satisfied that the scheme contains adequate provision:

(1) for ensuring that members of the scheme carry out consistent and accurate energy assessments in an independent manner (Energy Performance of Buildings (England and Wales) Regulations 2012, SI 2012/3118, reg 22(3)(a));

(2) for ensuring that members of the scheme are fit and proper persons who are qualified (by their education, training and experience) to carry out energy assessments Energy Performance of Buildings (England and Wales) Regulations 2012, SI 2012/3118, reg 22(3)(b));

(3) for requiring members of the scheme to prepare energy performance certificates, display energy certificates, recommendation reports and inspection reports using a standard form for each type of document (reg 22(3)(c));

(4) for ensuring that a code is produced and published as regards the conduct required of its members (reg 22(3)(d));

(5) for indemnity arrangements in relation to relevant person and prospective or actual buyers or tenants (reg 22(3)(e));

(6) for facilitating the resolution of complaints against members of the scheme; (reg 22(3)(f));

(7) for requiring the sets of data from which there may be produced energy performance certificates (other than data relating to a certificate issued under reg 9A (see PARA 48)), display energy certificates (other than data relating to a certificate issued under reg 15A (see PARA 49)), recommendation reports (other than one that is included in an energy performance certificate issued under reg 9A (energy performance certificates in respect of excluded buildings) or issued in relation to a building together with a display energy certificate issued in relation to that building under reg 15A (display energy certificates in respect of excluded buildings)) and inspection reports (other than data relating to a certificate issued under reg 19A (see PARA 49)) prepared by members of the scheme to be entered onto the relevant register maintained by the Secretary of State pursuant to reg 27 (Energy Performance of Buildings (England and Wales) Regulations 2012, SI 2012/3118, reg 22(3)(g) (substituted by SI 2016/284)); and

(8) for the keeping of a register of the members of the scheme (Energy Performance of Buildings (England and Wales) Regulations 2012, SI 2012/3118, reg 22(3)(h)).

As to the meaning of 'excluded building' see PARA 48 note 20. As to a duty to cooperate where a duty is imposed by the Energy Performance of Buildings (England and Wales) Regulations 2012, SI 2012/3118, see reg 45. As to the application of the Energy Performance of Buildings (England and Wales) Regulations 2012, SI 2012/3118 to the Crown see reg 44. As to the duty to review the Energy Performance of Buildings (England and Wales) Regulations 2012, SI 2012/3118 see reg 47.

4 Energy Performance of Buildings (England and Wales) Regulations 2012, SI 2012/3118, reg 23(a).

5 Energy Performance of Buildings (England and Wales) Regulations 2012, SI 2012/3118, reg 23(b).

6 Energy Performance of Buildings (England and Wales) Regulations 2012, SI 2012/3118, reg 23(c).

7 'Energy assessment' includes a reference to:

(1) the preparation and issuing of energy performance certificates (Energy Performance of Buildings (England and Wales) Regulations 2012, SI 2012/3118, reg 26(a));

(2) the preparation and issuing of display energy certificates (reg 26(b));

(3) the preparation and issuing of recommendation reports (reg 26(c));

(4) the preparation and issuing of inspection reports (reg 26(d));

(5) the carrying out of any inspections undertaken for the purposes of preparing any of the documents referred to in heads (1)–(4) (reg 26(e)).

8 Energy Performance of Buildings (England and Wales) Regulations 2012, SI 2012/3118, reg 24(1). Any cause of action arising in relation to the duty imposed by reg 24(1) is deemed not to be an action founded on tort for the purposes of the Limitation Act 1980 (see LIMITATION PERIODS): reg 24(3).

9 Energy Performance of Buildings (England and Wales) Regulations 2012, SI 2012/3118, reg 24(2)(a).

10 Energy Performance of Buildings (England and Wales) Regulations 2012, SI 2012/3118, reg 24(2)(b).

11 Energy Performance of Buildings (England and Wales) Regulations 2012, SI 2012/3118, reg 24(2)(c).

12 Ie for the for the purpose of complying with any duty imposed by the Energy Performance of Buildings (England and Wales) Regulations 2012, SI 2012/3118: reg 25.

13 Energy Performance of Buildings (England and Wales) Regulations 2012, SI 2012/3118, reg 25.

(vi) Enforcement

52. Energy performance of buildings: enforcement.

Local weights and measures authorities are responsible for enforcing the duties relating to certificates and air-conditioning inspections[1]. An authorised officer of an enforcement authority may require the production of a valid energy performance certificate, a recommendation report or an inspection report[2]. If such an authorised officer believes that a person has committed a breach of any duty under any of the specified provisions, he may give a penalty charge notice to that person[3]. The recipient of a penalty charge notice may require the enforcement authority to review the notice[4] and, if the enforcement authority confirms the notice, may appeal to the county court[5]. Obstruction of an enforcement authority and imitation of an authorised officer of an enforcement authority are offences[6].

1   See the Energy Performance of Buildings (England and Wales) Regulations 2012, SI 2012/3118, reg 34(1). Every local weights and measures authority is an enforcement authority and is charged with the duty of enforcing within its area regs 6(2), 6(5), 7(2), 7(3), 7(4), 7(5), 7A(2), 7A(3), 10(2), 11(2), 14(3), 18(1), 20, 21 and 35(5) (see PARA 48 et seq; ENERGY AND CLIMATE CHANGE vol 42 (2011) PARA 195): reg 34(2) (amended by SI 2014/880; and SI 2016/284). As to the enforcement of duties in relation to local authority buildings see the Energy Performance of Buildings (England and Wales) Regulations 2012, SI 2012/3118, reg 34A (added by SI 2015/1681; and amended by SI 2016/284). As to enforcement plans see reg 34B (added by SI 2015/1681). As to requirement for enforcement authorities to make annual reports as to actions taken see reg 34C (added by SI 2015/1681). As to local weights and measures authorities see WEIGHTS AND MEASURES vol 101 (2018) PARA 1019.

    As to a duty to cooperate where a duty is imposed by the Energy Performance of Buildings (England and Wales) Regulations 2012, SI 2012/3118, see reg 45. As to the application of the Energy Performance of Buildings (England and Wales) Regulations 2012, SI 2012/3118 to the Crown see reg 44. As to the duty to review the Energy Performance of Buildings (England and Wales) Regulations 2012, SI 2012/3118 see reg 47.

2   See the Energy Performance of Buildings (England and Wales) Regulations 2012, SI 2012/3118, reg 35 (amended by SI 2016/284).

3   Enforcement of the regulations is by way of civil penalties which are specified in penalty charge notices: see Energy Performance of Buildings (England and Wales) Regulations 2012, SI 2012/3118, regs 2(1), 36, 37 (reg 36 amended by SI 2016/284). As to the amount penalty charge see the Energy Performance of Buildings (England and Wales) Regulations 2012, SI 2012/3118, reg 38. The amount of the penalty charge is recoverable from the recipient of the penalty charge notice as a debt: see reg 41.

4   See the Energy Performance of Buildings (England and Wales) Regulations 2012, SI 2012/3118, reg 39.

5   See the Energy Performance of Buildings (England and Wales) Regulations 2012, SI 2012/3118, reg 40. As to service of documents see reg 42.

6   See the Energy Performance of Buildings (England and Wales) Regulations 2012, SI 2012/3118, reg 43(1), (2). A person guilty of such an offence is liable on summary conviction to a fine not exceeding level 5 on the standard scale: reg 43(3). As to the powers of magistrates' courts to issue fines on summary conviction see SENTENCING vol 92 (2015) PARA 176.

(7) Water Efficiency

53. Water efficiency of new dwellings.

The potential consumption of wholesome water by persons occupying a new dwelling[1] must not exceed either:

(1)   125 litres per person per day[2]; or

(2)   where the planning permission under which the building work[3] is carried out specifies the optional requirement of 110 litres per person per day and makes it a condition that requirement must be complied with,[4]

as measured in either case in accordance with a methodology approved by the Secretary of State[5].

1   In the Building Regulations 2010, SI 2010/2214, Pt 7 (regs 36, 37) 'new dwelling' does not include a dwelling that is formed by a material change of use of a building such that the building, which contains at least one dwelling, contains a greater or lesser number of dwellings than it did previously (see reg 5(g) PARA 11: see reg 36(4) (reg 36(1), (2) substituted and reg 36(3), (4) added by SI 2015/767; and amended by SI 2018/558). As from 1 November 2018, the requirements relating to water efficiency in relation to Wales is amended to provide that the potential consumption of wholesome water by persons occupying a dwelling must not exceed:
    (1)   110 litres per person per day where the dwelling is erected (reg 36(1)(a), (2), (3)(a) (prospectively amended by SI 2018/552);
    (2)   125 litres per person per day where there is a material change of use of a building such that the building is used as a dwelling or contains a flat, where previously it was not; (see reg 5(a), (b) (see PARA 11) (reg 36(1)(b), (2) (3)(b) (as so prospectively amended).
2   Building Regulations 2010, SI 2010/2214, reg 36(1), (2)(a) (as so added).
3   As to the meaning of 'building work' see PARA 10).
4   Building Regulations 2010, SI 2010/2214, reg 36(1), (2)(b), (3)(as so added).
5   Building Regulations 2010, SI 2010/2214, reg 36(1)–(3) (as so added).

(8) Fire Safety

54. Building regulations relating to fire safety.

Building regulations may make provision for fire precautions including structural measures to resist the spread of fire, services to mitigate effects of fire or facilitate fire-fighting and means of escape in case of fire[1]. Building work must be carried out so that it complies with fire safety requirements[2]. Where there is a material change of use, work must be carried out to ensure that the building complies with requirements relating to means of warning and escape, internal and external fire spread[3].

1   See the Building Act 1984 Sch 1 para 7(a)(iv); and PARA 9.
2   See the Building Regulations 2010, SI 2010/2214, reg 4, Sch 1 Pt B; and PARA 10. In September 2017, the Department for Communities and Local Government published guidance on interim mitigation measures, which relate to buildings that do not meet the requirements of the Building Regulations guidance, due to the fire-hazardous core filler within aluminium composite material (ACM) of the cladding. A building safety programme was established with the aim of ensuring that high rise residential buildings are safe and that residents feel safe in them. Following an independent review of building regulations and fire safety and an interim report published in December which concluded that the regulatory system to ensure fire safety in high-rise and complex buildings was not fit for purpose, an independent report was published in May 2018. The report recommended a new regulatory framework for building safety and changes to enforcement powers and penalties: see 'Building a Safer Future Independent Review of Building Regulations and Fire Safety: Final Report' on the Government website. In response to the report, the Ministry of Housing, Communities and Local Government government has committed to launch a consultation on banning the use of combustible materials in cladding systems on high-rise residential buildings.
3   See the Building Regulations 2010, SI 2010/2214, reg 6; and PARA 11.

55. Consultation with fire and rescue authority.

Where, in the case of a requirement as to:
(1)   structural fire precautions[1];
(2)   the provision of means of escape from buildings[2] in case of fire[3]; or

(3)   the provision of means for securing that such means of escape can be safely and effectively used at all material times[4],

contained in building regulations[5], the power to dispense with or relax that requirement[6] is exercisable[7] by a local authority[8], or a public body[9] proposes to exercise the power conferred on it[10] to dispense with or relax that requirement, the local authority or public body, if they are not the fire and rescue authority[11], must before exercising the power in relation to any premises[12] or proposed premises consult the fire and rescue authority[13].

1 Building Act 1984 s 15(1)(a).
2 As to the meaning of 'building' see PARA 6.
3 Building Act 1984 s 15(1)(b).
4 Building Act 1984 s 15(1)(c).
5 As to the meaning of 'building regulations' see PARA 7.
6 Ie conferred by the Building Act 1984 s 8(1): see PARA 18.
7 Ie by virtue of Building Act 1984 s 8(2): see PARA 18.
8 As to the meaning of 'local authority' see PARA 1 note 12.
9 As to the meaning of 'public body' see PARA 18 note 7; definition applied by the Building Act 1984 s 15(2).
10 Ie by Building Act 1984 s 8(4): see PARA 18.
11 'Fire and rescue authority' in relation to any premises or proposed premises, means: (1) where the Regulatory Reform (Fire Safety) Order 2005, SI 2005/1541, applies to the premises or proposed premises, the enforcing authority within the meaning given by art 25 (see FIRE AND RESCUE SERVICES vol 51 (2013) PARA 99); and (2) in any other case, the fire and rescue authority under the Fire and Rescue Services Act 2004 for the area in which the premises are or are to be situated: Building Act 1984 s 126 (definition added by SI 2005/1541).
12 As to the meaning of 'premises' see PARA 12 note 2.
13 Building Act 1984 s 15(1) (amended by the Fire and Rescue Services Act 2004 s 53(1), Sch 1 para 57). As to the making of building regulations to modify or repeal the provisions of the Building Act 1984 s 15, on the ground of inconsistency with other provisions see s 1(3), Sch 1 para 11(1); and PARA 9.

56. Fire safety information.

Where building work[1]:

(1)   consists of or includes the erection or extension of a relevant building[2]; or

(2)   is carried out in connection with a relevant change of use of a building[3],

and there are requirements relating to fire safety[4] imposed in relation to the work[5], the person carrying out the work must give fire safety information[6] to the responsible person[7] not later than the date of completion of the work, or the date of occupation of the building or extension, whichever is the earlier[8].

1 As to the meaning of 'building work' see PARA 10.
2 Building Regulations 2010, SI 2010/2214, reg 38(1)(a). A 'relevant building' is a building to which the Regulatory Reform (Fire Safety) Order 2005, SI 2005/1541 (see FIRE AND RESCUE SERVICES vol 51 (2013) PARA 70) applies, or will apply after the completion of building work: Building Regulations 2010, SI 2010/2214, reg 38(3)(b).
3 Building Regulations 2010, SI 2010/2214, reg 38(1)(b). A 'relevant change of use' is a material change of use where, after the change of use takes place, the Regulatory Reform (Fire Safety) Order 2005, SI 2005/1541 (see FIRE AND RESCUE SERVICES) will apply, or continue to apply, to the building: Building Regulations 2010, SI 2010/2214, reg 38(3)(c).
4 Ie the Building Regulations 2010, SI 2010/2214, Sch 1 Pt B imposes a requirement: see PARA 10.
5 Building Regulations 2010, SI 2010/2214, reg 38(1).
6 'Fire safety information' means information relating to the design and construction of the building or extension, and the services, fittings and equipment provided in or in connection with the building or extension which will assist the responsible person to operate and maintain the building or extension with reasonable safety: Building Regulations 2010, SI 2010/2214, reg 38(3)(a).

'Responsible person', in relation to a workplace, means the employer, if the workplace is to any extent under his control; and in relation to any other premises, means (1) the person who has control of the premises (as occupier or otherwise) in connection with the carrying on by him of a trade, business or other undertaking (for profit or not); or (2) the owner, where the person in control of the premises does not have control in connection with the carrying on by that person of a trade, business or other undertaking: Regulatory Reform (Fire Safety) Order 2005, SI 2005/1541, art 3 (definition applied by the Building Regulations 2010, SI 2010/2214, reg 38(3)(d)).

7 See note 6.

8 Building Regulations 2010, SI 2010/2214, reg 38(2).

57. Means of escape from fire.

If it appears to a local authority[1], after consultation with the fire and rescue authority[2], that[3] a building meeting the statutory description[4] is not provided with[5], or a proposed building of that description will not be provided with[6] such means of escape in case of fire as the local authority, after such consultation, deems necessary from each storey whose floor is more than 20 feet above the surface of the street or ground on any side of the building, the authority must by notice[7] require the owner[8] of the building, or, as the case may be, the person proposing to erect[9] the building, to execute such work or make such other provision as may be necessary[10]. In so far as such a notice requires a person to make provision otherwise than by the execution of works, he is, if he fails to comply with the notice, liable on summary conviction to a fine[11] and to a further fine for each day on which the offence continues after he is convicted[12]. In such proceedings, it is open to the defendant to question the reasonableness of the authority's requirements[13].

Where building regulations[14] imposing requirements as to the provision of means of escape in case of fire are applicable to a proposed building or proposed extension of a building, or would be so applicable but for a direction[15] dispensing with such requirements, the provisions described above[16], and any provision of a local Act[17] that has effect in place of those provisions, do not apply in relation to the proposed building or extension[18].

The law relating to fire safety generally and, in particular, the fire precautions required to be taken in respect of non-domestic premises, are covered elsewhere in this work[19].

1 As to the meaning of 'local authority' see PARA 1 note 12.

2 As to the meaning of 'fire and rescue authority' see PARA 55 note 11.

3 Building Act 1984 s 72(1) (amended by the Fire and Rescue Services Act 2004 Sch 1 para 57). The provisions of s 72(1)–(4), (6) do not apply to inner London: see s 88(1), Sch 3 para 5; and PARA 3. As to the making of building regulations to modify or repeal the provisions of s 72 on the ground of inconsistency with other provisions see s 1(3), Sch 1 para 11(1); and PARA 9.

4 Ie a building that exceeds two storeys in height and in which the floor of any upper storey is more than 20 feet above the surface of the street or ground on any side of the building: see the Building Act 1984 s 72(6) (amended by the Housing Act 2004 s 53(3), 266, Sch 16; and SI 2005/1541). As to the meaning of 'street' see PARA 103 note 15.

5 Building Act 1984 s 72(1)(a). See note 3.

6 Building Act 1984 s 72(1)(b). See note 3.

7 The provisions of the Building Act 1984 s 99 (content and enforcement of notice requiring works) (see PARA 126), and s 102 (appeal against notice requiring works) (see PARA 138) apply in relation to a notice given under s 72(1) in so far as it requires a person to execute works: s 72(2). As to the form, authentication and service of such notices see PARAS 135–137. See note 3.

8 As to the meaning of 'owner' see PARA 12 note 2.

9 As to the meaning of 'erect' see PARA 109 note 1.

10 Building Act 1984 s 72(1). See note 3.

11 Ie a fine not exceeding level 4 on the standard scale: Building Act 1984 s 72(3). As to the powers

of magistrates' courts to issue fines on summary conviction see SENTENCING vol 92 (2015) PARA 176. Civil sanctions may be imposed in respect of offences under the Building Act 1984 by virtue of the powers under the Regulatory Enforcement and Sanctions Act 2008 Pt 3 (ss 36–71): see ss 36, 38(2), Sch 6; and CONSTITUTIONAL AND ADMINISTRATIVE LAW vol 20 (2014) PARA 331 et seq.

12 Building Act 1984 s 72(3). The fine imposed must not exceed £2 for each day on which the offence continues after conviction: see s 72(3). As to continuing offences see PARA 144. See note 3.

13 Building Act 1984 s 72(4). See note 3.

14 As to the meaning of 'building regulations' see PARA 7.

15 Ie under the Building Act 1984 s 8: see PARA 18.

16 Ie the Building Act 1984 s 72: see the text and notes 1–15, 17–19.

17 As to the meaning of 'local Act' see PARA 6 note 2.

18 Building Act 1984 s 72(5).

19 See FIRE AND RESCUE SERVICES. As to the fire precautions to be taken in respect of non-domestic premises see the Regulatory Reform (Fire Safety) Order 2005, SI 2005/1541. As to fire safety at sports grounds see the Fire Safety and Safety of Places of Sport Act 1987; and SPORTS LAW vol 96 (2012) PARA 135 et seq.

58. Provision of automatic fire suppression systems.

Building work[1] in Wales which comprises or includes:

(1)   constructing a building for use as a residence[2], or a number of residences[3];

(2)   converting a building, or part of a building, to use as a residence, or a number of residences[4];

(3)   subdividing one or more existing residences so as to create one or more new residences[5];

(4)   amalgamating existing residences so as to create a new residence or new residences[6]

must, in respect of each residence, when that work is completed or the residence is occupied as a residence, whichever is the earliest[7], comply with the following requirements:

(a)   each residence must be provided with an automatic fire suppression system[8];

(b)   the system is operating effectively[9]; and

(c)   the system complies with such requirements as may be prescribed[10].

As from a day to be appointed, it is the duty of a local authority[11] to enforce these provisions in relation to its area[12].

In Wales, where building work [13] consists of the erection or material change of use[14] of a building in relation to:

(i)   care homes[15];

(ii)   rooms for residential purposes other than rooms in a hostel providing temporary accommodation to those who are ordinarily resident elsewhere, an hotel, a prison or young offender institution and a hospital[16];

(iii)   dwelling-houses and flats[17],

the building must be provided with an automatic fire suppression system which is installed and operates in accordance with specified requirements[18].

1 'Building work' means the erection, extension or alteration of a building: Domestic Fire Safety (Wales) Measure 2011 s 6(1). The Domestic Fire Safety (Wales) Measure 2011 does not apply to building work carried out for the purpose of discharging any function of a Minister of the Crown or if building regulations imposing requirements as to the provision of automatic fire suppression systems apply to that work, or would apply but for a direction under the Building Act 1984 s 8: Domestic Fire Safety (Wales) Measure 2011 s 1(3).

2 'Residence' means any:

(1)   dwelling-house (see PARA 10 note 31);

(2)   flat (see PARA 10 note 31);

(3)   care home (see SOCIAL SERVICES vol 95 (2017) PARA 3);

(4)   hall of residence;

(5)   a room or suite of rooms, which is not a dwelling-house or a flat and which is used by one or more persons to live and sleep and includes a room in a hostel or a boarding house, but does not include:

    (a)   a room in an hotel;

    (b)   a room in a hostel provided for temporary accommodation to those who are ordinarily resident elsewhere;

    (c)   a room in a hospital or other similar establishment used for patient accommodation;

    (d)   rooms in a prison or young offender institution;

    (e)   premises for the accommodation of persons remanded on bail;

    (f)   premises for the accommodation of persons who may be required to reside there by a probation order; or

(6)   children's home, where 'children's home" has the meaning given in the Care Standards Act 2000 s 1 of but which does not include:

    (i)   an institution within the further education sector as defined by the Further and Higher Education Act 1992 s 91(3);

    (ii)   an establishment used to accommodate children only for the purposes of any one or more of the following:

        (A)   a holiday;

        (B)   a leisure, sporting, cultural or educational activity; so long as no one child is accommodated there for more than 28 days in any twelve month period;

    (iii)   a young offender institution, and

where a building contains one or more residences, includes any part of that building intended to be used by those occupying that residence or those residences for purposes ancillary to that occupation in common with one another or with other users of the building: Domestic Fire Safety (Wales) Measure 2011 s 6(1). The Welsh Ministers may, by order, amend the definition of 'residence': see s 6(2), (3).

3   Domestic Fire Safety (Wales) Measure 2011 s 1(2)(a).

4   Domestic Fire Safety (Wales) Measure 2011 s 1(2)(b).

5   Domestic Fire Safety (Wales) Measure 2011 s 1(2)(c).

6   Domestic Fire Safety (Wales) Measure 2011 s 1(2)(d).

7   Domestic Fire Safety (Wales) Measure 2011 s 1(1).

8   Domestic Fire Safety (Wales) Measure 2011 s 1(4)(a). References in s 1(4) to an automatic fire suppression system also include any supply of energy, water, or other substance, necessary for the effective functioning of the system: s 1(5).

9   Domestic Fire Safety (Wales) Measure 2011 s 1(4)(b).

10   Domestic Fire Safety (Wales) Measure 2011 s 1(4)(c). In exercise of the power under s 1(4), the Building Regulations (Amendment No 3) and Domestic Fire Safety (Wales) Regulations 2013, SI 2013/2730 has been made. As to the provision of information for the purpose of demonstrating that the work is capable, when completed, of complying with the requirements of the Domestic Fire Safety (Wales) Measure 2011 s 1(4) see s 3. As to the authentication and service of documents see s 4 (not yet in force); and PARAS 129–130.

11   'Local authority' means a county council or county borough council in Wales: Domestic Fire Safety (Wales) Measure 2011 s 6(1).

12   See the Domestic Fire Safety (Wales) Measure 2011 s 2, Sch 1, Sch 2 (not yet in force). Proceedings in respect of an offence created by or under the Domestic Fire Safety (Wales) Measure 2011 may only be instituted by the local authority or the Welsh Ministers: s 5 (not yet in force). The Domestic Fire Safety (Wales) Measure 2011 ss 2, 5, Sch 1, Sch 2 comes into force as from a day to be appointed under s 9(3). However, at the date at which this volume states the law, no such day had been appointed.

13   As to the meaning of 'building work' see PARA 10.

14   For these purposes a material change of use comprises or includes a change of use within the Building Regulations 2010, SI 2010/2214, reg 5 (a), (b), (c), (d), (g), (h) or (i) (see PARA 11): reg 37A(2) (regs 37A, 37B added in relation to Wales by SI 2013/2730; and SI 2018/558).

15   Ie as defined in the Care Standards Act 2000 s 3 (see SOCIAL SERVICES vol 95 (2017) PARA 3): Building Regulations 2010, SI 2010/2214, reg 37A(1)(a) (as so added). Regulation 37A(1) is subject to reg 37A(4), (5): reg 37A(1) (as so added). Regulation 37A does not apply to buildings which are:

(1)   listed in accordance with the Planning (Listed Buildings and Conservation Areas) Act 1990 s 1 (see PLANNING vol 83 (2018) PARA 1181 et seq)Building Regulations 2010, SI 2010/2214, reg 37A(4)(a) (as added: see note 1));

(2)   in a conservation area designated in accordance with the Planning (Listed Buildings and Conservation Areas) Act 1990 s 69 (see PLANNING vol 83 (2018) PARA 1255 (Building Regulations 2010, SI 2010/2214 (reg 37A(4)(b) (as added: see note 1);

(3)   included in the schedule of monuments maintained under the Ancient Monuments and Archaeological Areas Act 1979 s 1 (see NATIONAL CULTURAL HERITAGE, PARA 1014) (Building Regulations 2010, SI 2010/2214 (reg 37A(4)(b) (as added: see note 1)

where installation of a fire suppression system would unacceptably alter their character or appearance: reg 37A(4) (as so added). Regulation 37A does not apply to temporary buildings with a planned time of use of two years or less: reg 37A(4) (as so added)

16 Building Regulations 2010, SI 2010/2214, reg 37A(1)(b) (as added (see note 1) and amended by SI 2017/1274). See note 3.

17 Building Regulations 2010, SI 2010/2214, reg 37A(1)(c) (as added: see note 1). See note 3.

18 Building Regulations 2010, SI 2010/2214, reg 37A(3) (as added: see note 1). The requirements of an automatic fire suppression system are the requirements set out in any document approved and issued under the Building Act 1984 s 6 (see PARA 23) for the purpose of providing practical guidance as to the requirements of reg 37A: reg 37B (as added: see note 1).

(9) Local Authority Charges

59. Local authority charges.

Local authorities are authorised to fix by means of a scheme and to recover such charges from time to time as they may determine for or in connection with the performance of their functions relating to building regulations[1]. They are authorised, by means of a charging scheme, to make a charge for or in connection with:

(1)   the passing or rejection of plans of proposed building work which have been deposited with the local authority (referred to as 'a plan charge')[2];

(2)   the inspection of building work for which plans have been deposited with the local authority (referred to as an 'inspection charge')[3];

(3)   the consideration of a building notice which has been given to the local authority in accordance with building regulations (referred to as a 'building notice charge')[4];

(4)   the consideration of building work reverting to local authority control (referred to as a 'reversion charge')[5]; and

(5)   the consideration of an application in respect of unauthorised building work[6] and the inspection of any building work to which that application relates (referred to as a 'regularisation charge')[7].

In determining the amount of the charges to be made within a charging scheme, a local authority must have regard to the overriding objective that the authority must ensure that, taking one financial year with another, the chargeable income (that is income derived by the authority from performing chargeable functions and providing chargeable advice[8]) as nearly as possible equates to the chargeable costs (that is costs incurred by the authority in performing chargeable functions and providing chargeable advice)[9]. At the end of each financial year, the authority must conduct a review of the level of charges set under its charging scheme for the purpose of achieving the overriding objective[10]. A local authority must determine the charges referred to in their charging scheme by reference to the costs of providing services in relation to particular building work or building work of particular descriptions, having regard in doing so to the overriding objective[11]. A local authority is authorised to make provision in its charging scheme for information to be supplied where it is required for the purpose of determining any charge[12]. A local authority must make provision in its charging scheme about the handling and consideration of complaints relating to the determination of any charge[13].

Where a local authority does not give notice of passing or rejection of plans within the required statutory period[14], it must refund any plan charge paid[15]. However, no refund is payable where the reason for the delay is the failure by the person by whom or on whose behalf the plans were deposited to supply the authority with information requested of the person by the authority a reasonable time before the date on which it reasonably required the information in order to comply with its duties in relation to the passing or rejection of plans[16].

Where, in relation to the determination of a charge the amount of work required of an officer of a local authority is less than that which was estimated, and payment has been made of the charge as determined under the charging scheme, the authority must make a refund of an amount equal to the charge attributable to work that was not required[17]. Conversely, where, in relation to a determination of a charge the amount of work required of an officer of a local authority is more than that which was estimated, and payment has been made only of the charge determined under the charging scheme, the authority may raise a supplementary charge in respect of the additional work[18]. In respect of plans which are deposited with a local authority[19], the plan charge and inspection charge may be aggregated for the purpose of calculating any refund or supplementary charge[20]. Any payment of a refund or request for a supplementary charge must be accompanied by a statement setting out the basis for the refund or supplementary charge and, in the case of the latter, a calculation of that charge[21].

A local authority must, not less than seven days before the date on which a charging scheme (including any replacement scheme) is to come into effect, publish in its area, in such manner as it considers appropriate, the fact that it has made the charging scheme, the date on which it comes into effect and the address where it may be inspected[22]. Amendments to charging schemes must be similarly publicised[23].

Although individual local authorities are authorised to set their own fees under their charging schemes, the fee which must accompany an application for a reference to the appropriate national authority[24] is subject to specified maximum and minimum amounts[25]. No fee is payable in respect of the determination of any question relating to building work solely required for disabled persons[26].

1 Building (Local Authority Charges) Regulations 2010, SI 2010/404, reg 3(1). However, in relation to an existing dwelling which is, or is to be, occupied by a disabled person as a permanent residence, a local authority may not fix or recover any charges where the whole of the building work in question is solely: (1) for the purpose of providing means of access for the disabled person by way of entrance or exit to or from the dwelling or any part of it; or (2) for the purpose of providing accommodation or facilities designed to secure the greater health, safety, welfare or convenience of the disabled person: see regs 3(2), 4 (reg 4 amended by SI 2015/643).

The provisions of the Building (Local Authority Charges) Regulations 2010, SI 2010/404, are designated as provisions to which the Building Act 1984 s 35 (penalty for contravening building regulations) (see PARA 61) does not apply: Building (Local Authority Charges) Regulations 2010, SI 2010/404, reg 13.
2 Building (Local Authority Charges) Regulations 2010, SI 2010/404, reg 5(1)(a). The plans referred to are those deposited in accordance with the Building Act 1984 s 16 (see PARA 33). As to the passing or rejection of plans see PARA 33 et seq. As to the meaning of 'building work' see PARA 10; definition applied by the Building (Local Authority Charges) Regulations 2010, SI 2010/404, reg 2.
3 Building (Local Authority Charges) Regulations 2010, SI 2010/404, reg 5(1)(b).

4 Building (Local Authority Charges) Regulations 2010, SI 2010/404, reg 5(1)(c). As to the meaning of 'building notice' (ie a notice given in accordance with the Building Regulations 2010, SI 2010/2214, reg 12(2)(a) or reg 13) see PARA 25 note 6.

5 Building (Local Authority Charges) Regulations 2010, SI 2010/404, reg 5(1)(d).

6 Ie under the Building Regulations 2010, SI 2010/2214, reg 18: see PARA 71.

7 Building (Local Authority Charges) Regulations 2010, SI 2010/404, reg 5(1)(e) (amended by SI 2010/2214).

8 A local authority is authorised by means of a charging scheme, to make a charge in relation to a request for advice as regards any particular case (referred to as 'chargeable advice') where such a charge is made in anticipation of the future exercise of their chargeable functions in relation to that case; but no charge may be made for the first hour of time spent by an officer of the authority in providing chargeable advice: Building (Local Authority Charges) Regulations 2010, SI 2010/404, reg 5(2).

9 See the Building (Local Authority Charges) Regulations 2010, SI 2010/404, reg 6.

10 See the Building (Local Authority Charges) Regulations 2010, SI 2010/404, reg 6.

11 See the Building (Local Authority Charges) Regulations 2010, SI 2010/404, reg 7. As to the principles of a charging scheme as to payment see reg 8.

12 Building (Local Authority Charges) Regulations 2010, SI 2010/404, reg 9.

13 Building (Local Authority Charges) Regulations 2010, SI 2010/404, reg 10.

14 Ie the period required by the Building Act 1984 s 16 (see PARA 33).

15 Building (Local Authority Charges) Regulations 2010, SI 2010/404, reg 11(1).

16 Building (Local Authority Charges) Regulations 2010, SI 2010/404, reg 11(2).

17 Building (Local Authority Charges) Regulations 2010, SI 2010/404, reg 11(3). However, this is subject to the rule that a local authority may disregard one hour of an officer's time in calculating the amount of the refund: reg 11(5).

18 Building (Local Authority Charges) Regulations 2010, SI 2010/404, reg 11(4). However, this is subject to the rule that a local authority may disregard one hour of an officer's time in calculating the amount of the supplementary charge: reg 11(5).

19 Ie under the Building Act 1984 s 16 (see PARA 33).

20 Building (Local Authority Charges) Regulations 2010, SI 2010/404, reg 11(6).

21 Building (Local Authority Charges) Regulations 2010, SI 2010/404, reg 11(7).

22 Building (Local Authority Charges) Regulations 2010, SI 2010/404, reg 12(1). A local authority must maintain a copy of any charging scheme currently in force as made by it, or as made and amended by it, and must make this available for inspection free of charge by any member of the public on request and at any reasonable time at the address which it has published in accordance with reg 12(1): see reg 12(3).

23 See the Building (Local Authority Charges) Regulations 2010, SI 2010/404, reg 12(2).

24 As to the appropriate national authority (ie the Secretary of State or, where statutory functions have been transferred in relation to Wales, the Welsh Ministers) see PARA 5.

25 In relation to a reference under the Building Act 1984 s 16(10) (see PARA 33), where the question is whether plans of proposed work are in conformity with building regulations, the fee is an amount equal to half the plan charge fixed by the charging scheme made and published by the local authority concerned, subject to a minimum of £100 and a maximum of £1,000: Building (Local Authority Charges) Regulations 2010, SI 2010/404, reg 14(1)(a). Where the question is whether the local authority is prohibited from rejecting plans of proposed work by virtue of the Building Act 1984 s 16(9), the fee is £100: Building (Local Authority Charges) Regulations 2010, SI 2010/404, reg 14(1)(b).

The fee which must accompany an application for a reference to the appropriate national authority under the Building Act 1984 s 50(2) (see PARA 83) of the question whether plans of proposed work are in conformity with building regulations is an amount equal to half the plan charge fixed by the charging scheme made and published by the local authority to which the plans certificate is or would be given, subject to a minimum of £100 and a maximum of £1,000: Building (Local Authority Charges) Regulations 2010, SI 2010/404, reg 14(2).

26 Building (Local Authority Charges) Regulations 2010, SI 2010/404, reg 14(3).

(10) Breach of Building Regulations

60. Tests for conformity with building regulations.

As from a day to be appointed, the following provisions have effect[1]. For the purpose of enabling a local authority[2] to ascertain, as regards any work or proposed work to which building regulations[3] for the enforcement of which it is responsible are applicable, whether any provision of building regulations is or would be contravened[4] by, or by anything done or proposed to be done in connection with, that work[5], the local authority has power:

(1)   to require a person by whom or on whose behalf the work was, is being or is proposed to be done to carry out such reasonable tests of or in connection with the work as may be specified in the requirement[6]; or

(2)   itself to carry out any reasonable tests of or in connection with the work, and to take any samples necessary to enable it to carry out such a test[7].

The matters with respect to which tests may be required or carried out under head (1) or head (2) above include tests of the soil or subsoil of the site of a building[8], and tests of any material, component or combination of components that has been, is being or is proposed to be used in the construction[9] of a building, and tests of any service, fitting or equipment that has been, is being or is proposed to be provided in or in connection with a building[10].

A local authority has power, for the purpose of ascertaining whether there is or has been, in the case of a building, a contravention of a continuing requirement[11] that applies in relation to that building to require the owner[12] or occupier of the building to carry out such reasonable tests as may be specified in the continuing requirement[13], or itself to carry out any such tests, and to take any samples necessary to enable it to carry out such a test[14].

The expense of carrying out any tests that a person is required to carry out[15] must be met by that person, except that the local authority, on an application made to it, may, if it thinks it reasonable to do so, direct that the expense of carrying out any such tests, or such part of that expense as may be specified in the direction, is to be met by the local authority[16]. Any question arising between a local authority and a person as to the reasonableness of:

(a)   a test specified in a requirement imposed on him by the authority[17];

(b)   a refusal by the authority to give a direction on an application made by him[18]; or

(c)   a direction given on such an application[19],

may on the application of that person be determined by a magistrates' court[20]. In a case falling within head (b) or head (c) above the court may order the expense to which the application relates to be met by the local authority to such extent as the court thinks just[21].

1   The Building Act 1984 s 33 is to be brought into force as from a day to be appointed by order made under s 134(1)(b). At the date at which this volume states the law no such day had been appointed.
2   As to the meaning of 'local authority' see PARA 1 note 12.
3   As to the meaning of 'building regulations' see PARA 7.
4   As to the meaning of 'contravention' see PARA 12 note 10.
5   Building Act 1984 s 33(1) (not yet in force: see note 1).
6   Building Act 1984 s 33(2)(a) (not yet in force: see note 1).
7   Building Act 1984 s 33(2)(b) (not yet in force: see note 1).
8   Building Act 1984 s 33(3)(a) (not yet in force: see note 1). As to the meaning of 'building' see PARA 6.
9   As to the meaning of 'construct' see PARA 9 note 3.
10   Building Act 1984 s 33(3)(b) (not yet in force: see note 1).
11   For these purposes, 'continuing requirement' means a continuing requirement imposed by building

regulations made by virtue of the Building Act 1984 s 2(1), s 2(2) or s 2A (see PARA 12): s 33(4) (amended by the Sustainable and Secure Buildings Act 2004 s 4(2)) (not yet in force: see note 1).

12 As to the meaning of 'owner' see PARA 12 note 2.
13 Building Act 1984 s 33(4)(a) (not yet in force: see note 1).
14 Building Act 1984 s 33(4)(b) (not yet in force: see note 1).
15 Ie under the Building Act 1984 s 33.
16 Building Act 1984 s 33(5) (not yet in force: see note 1).
17 Building Act 1984 s 33(6)(a) (not yet in force: see note 1).
18 Building Act 1984 s 33(6)(b) (not yet in force: see note 1).
19 Building Act 1984 s 33(6)(c) (not yet in force: see note 1).
20 Building Act 1984 s 33(6) (not yet in force: see note 1). As to the procedure on applications to a magistrates' court see s 103(1); and PARA 139. See further CRIMINAL PROCEDURE vol 27 (2015) PARA 142; MAGISTRATES vol 71 (2013) PARA 436.
21 Building Act 1984 s 33(6) (not yet in force: see note 1).

61. Contravention of building regulations.

Generally, if a person contravenes[1] any provision contained in building regulations[2], he is liable on summary conviction to a fine[3] and also to a further fine for each day on which the default continues after he is convicted[4]. Certain provisions of building regulations have been designated as ones to which this general rule does not apply[5].

An information relating to such an offence[6] may be tried by a magistrates' court if it is laid at any time within the period of two years beginning with the day on which the offence was committed, and within the period of six months beginning with the relevant date[7] (that date being the date on which evidence sufficient to justify the proceedings comes to the knowledge of the person commencing the proceedings[8]). In the case of proceedings commenced by a local authority evidence is to be regarded as sufficient to justify the proceedings if in the opinion of the proper officer or an authorised officer it is sufficient to justify the proceedings[9]. A certificate of the proper officer or, as the case may be, that authorised officer as to the date on which evidence which, in his opinion, was sufficient to justify the proceedings came to the knowledge of the person commencing the proceedings is to be conclusive evidence of that fact[10].

1 As to the meaning of 'contravene' see PARA 12 note 10.
2 As to the meaning of 'building regulations' see PARA 7.
3 The fine imposed is one not exceeding level 5 on the standard scale: Building Act 1984 s 35. As to the powers of magistrates' courts to issue fines on summary conviction see SENTENCING vol 92 (2015) PARA 176. Civil sanctions may be imposed in respect of offences under the Building Act 1984 by virtue of the powers under the Regulatory Enforcement and Sanctions Act 2008 Pt 3 (ss 36–71): see ss 36, 38(2), Sch 6; and CONSTITUTIONAL AND ADMINISTRATIVE LAW vol 20 (2014) PARA 331 et seq.
    An offence is committed when the works are completed in a way which does not comply with the relevant requirements of the regulations: *Torridge District Council v Turner* (1991) 59 BLR 31, (1991) 90 LGR 173, DC. The burden of showing non compliance with the building regulations lies initially with the local authority. However, where it is established that the work did not comply with the approved document, the burden will be on the builder to show compliance with the regulations: *Rickards and Rickards v Kerrier District Council* (1987) 151 JP 625. The offence of non compliance with the building regulations arises once and for all when the period for compliance expired: *Hertsmere Borough Council v Alan Dunn Building Contractors* [1985] Crim LR 726, 84 LGR 214, DC. A director of a company which owns a building to which structural alterations have been carried out is necessarily liable for failure to comply with the regulations: *Fuller v Nicholas* (1984) Times, 18 April.
4 Building Act 1984 s 35. The fine imposed must not exceed £50 for each day on which the default continues after conviction: see s 35. As to continuing offences see PARA 144. It appears that a person who has deposited plans and given notices as required by the regulations may commence building (otherwise than in contravention of the regulations) without waiting for approval of the plans: see *R v Tynemouth RDC* [1896] 2 QB 451, CA, although this case was decided in the

context of building byelaws. However, if such a person in so acting deviates from the deposited plans to a material extent, such action is likely to constitute an offence: see *Burton v Acton* (1887) 51 JP 566, DC; *James v Masters* [1893] 1 QB 355, DC. See also *Masters v Pontypool Local Government Board* (1878) 9 ChD 677. All these are byelaw cases, but the principle appears to stand. It has also been held, under building byelaws, that a penalty cannot be recovered if the local authority fails to give notice of disapproval of the plans within the prescribed period and the building is thereafter commenced: *Clark v Bloomfield* (1885) 1 TLR 323, DC; and see *Masters v Pontypool Local Government Board*. See also *Investors in Industry Commercial Properties Ltd v South Bedfordshire DC (Ellison & Partners (a firm), third parties)* [1986] QB 1034, [1986] 1 All ER 787, CA.

5　The following provisions of the Building Regulations 2010, SI 2010/2214, have been so designated: reg 17 (completion certificates; see PARA 29), reg 17A (certificate for building occupied before work is completed; see PARA 29), reg 25A (consideration of high-efficiency alternative systems for new building; see PARA 48, reg 27 (CO_2 emission rate calculations; see PARA 51), reg 27A (fabric energy efficiency rates; PARA 51), reg 37 (wholesome water consumption calculation; see PARA 32), reg 41 (sound insulation testing; see PARA 31), reg 42 (mechanical ventilation air flow rate testing; see PARA 31), reg 43 (pressure testing; see PARA 31), reg 44 (commissioning; see PARA 31): see reg 47 (substituted by SI 2012/3119; SI 2018/552; and SI 2018/558; amended by SI 2013/747; SI 2014/110; and SI 2014/579).). All the provisions of the Building (Approved Inspectors etc) Regulations 2010, SI 2010/2215, apart from reg 19 (local authority powers in relation to partly completed work; see PARA 82) have also been so designated: see reg 31 (amended by SI 2013/747; SI 2014/110; SI 2014/579; SI 2016/285; and SI 2016/611). The whole of the Building (Local Authority Charges) Regulations 2010, SI 2010/404, (see PARA 59) have been so designated: see reg 13.

6　The Building Act 1984 s 35A refers to an offence under s 35.

7　Building Act 1984 s 35A(1) (s 35A added by the Climate Change and Sustainable Energy Act 2006 s 13(1); and amended by the Housing and Regeneration Act 2008 s 317(1), (3)). The Building Act 1984 s 35A(1) is expressed to be effective despite anything in the Magistrates' Courts Act 1980 s 127(1) (see MAGISTRATES vol 71 (2013) PARA 526).

8　Building Act 1984 s 35A(4) (as added: see note 7).

9　Building Act 1984 s 35A(5)(a) (as added: see note 7). As to the meaning of 'local authority' see PARA 1 note 12.

10　Building Act 1984 s 35A(5)(b) (as added: see note 7).

62.　Removal or alteration of offending work.

If any work to which building regulations[1] are applicable contravenes[2] any of those regulations, the local authority[3], without prejudice to its right to take proceedings for a fine in respect of the contravention, may by notice require the owner[4] to pull down or remove the work[5], or if he so elects, to effect such alterations in it as may be necessary to make it comply with the regulations[6]. If, in a case where the local authority is, by any provision of Part I of the Building Act 1984[7], expressly required or authorised to reject plans[8], any work to which building regulations are applicable is executed:

(1)　without plans having been deposited[9];

(2)　notwithstanding the rejection of the plans[10]; or

(3)　otherwise than in accordance with any requirements subject to which the authority passed the plans[11],

the authority may by notice to the owner require him to pull down or remove the work[12], or require him either to pull down or remove the work or, if he so elects, to comply with any other requirements specified in the notice, being requirements that it might have made under the provision in question as a condition of passing plans[13].

A notice to remove or alter work contravening building regulations[14] must not be given after the expiration of 12 months from the date of the completion of the work in question[15]. If a person to whom such a notice has been given fails to comply with the notice before the expiration of 28 days, or such longer period as a magistrates' court[16] may on his application allow, the local authority may pull down or remove the work in question, or effect such alterations in it as it deems necessary, and may recover from him the expenses reasonably incurred by it in doing so[17].

A notice to remove or alter work contravening building regulations[18] must not be given, in a case where plans were deposited and the work was shown on them, on the ground that the work contravenes any building regulations or, as the case may be, does not comply with the authority's requirements under any provision of Part I of the Building Act 1984[19], if the plans were passed by the authority, or notice of their rejection was not given within the relevant period[20] from their deposit, and if the work has been executed in accordance with the plans and any requirement made by the local authority as a condition of passing the plans[21].

The provisions described above do not affect the right of a local authority, the Attorney General[22] or any other person to apply for an injunction for the removal or alteration of any work on the ground that it contravenes any regulation or any provision of the Building Act 1984[23]. However, if:

(a)   the work is one in respect of which plans were deposited[24];

(b)   the plans were passed by the local authority, or notice of their rejection was not given within the relevant period from their deposit[25]; and

(c)   the work has been executed in accordance with the plans[26],

the court on granting an injunction has power to order the local authority to pay to the owner of the work such compensation as the court thinks just, but before making any such order the court must in accordance with rules of court cause the local authority, if not a party to the proceedings, to be joined as a party to them[27].

1   As to the meaning of 'building regulations' see PARA 7.
2   As to the meaning of 'contravene' see PARA 12 note 10.
3   As to the meaning of 'local authority' see PARA 1 note 12.
4   As to the meaning of 'owner' see PARA 12 note 2.
5   Building Act 1984 s 36(1)(a).
6   Building Act 1984 s 36(1)(b). A notice under s 36 can be validly served on a person carrying out works who had not made an application for building regulation approval: *Parlett v Kerrier District Council* CO/770/96.
7   Ie any section of the Building Act 1984 Pt I (ss 1–46) (see PARA 7 et seq) other than s 16 (see PARA 33): see s 36(2).
8   As to the meaning of 'plans' see PARA 9 note 8.
9   Building Act 1984 s 36(2)(a).
10 Building Act 1984 s 36(2)(b).
11 Building Act 1984 s 36(2)(c).
12 Building Act 1984 s 36(2)(i).
13 Building Act 1984 s 36(2)(ii).
14 Ie given under the Building Act 1984 s 36(1), (2): see the text and notes 1–13.
15 Building Act 1984 s 36(4). See *R (on the application of Bello) v Lewisham London Borough Council* [2002] EWHC 1332 (Admin), [2002] EHLR 376, [2002] All ER (D) 133 (Jun) (delay between notice and enforcement did not render decision to enforce unreasonable). In any case where the Building Act 1984 s 53 (see PARA 81) applies, the reference in s 36(4) to the date of the completion of the work in question has effect, in relation to a notice under s 36(1), as if it were a reference to the date on which the initial notice ceased to be in force: s 53(5).
16 As to the procedure on applications to a magistrates' court see the Building Act 1984 s 103(1); and PARA 139. See further CRIMINAL PROCEDURE vol 27 (2015) PARA 142; MAGISTRATES vol 71 (2013) PARA 436.
17 Building Act 1984 s 36(3). The local authority must first give notice of its intention to pull down the work or make alterations and give the owner an opportunity to be heard: *Cooper v Wandsworth District Board of Works* (1863) 14 CBNS 180; *Masters v Pontypool Local Government Board* (1878) 9 ChD 677; approved and followed in *Hopkins v Smethwick Local Board of Health* (1890) 24 QBD 712, CA. See also *A-G v Hooper* [1893] 3 Ch 483; *Andrews v*

Wirral RDC [1916] 1 KB 863, CA. In *Hopkins v Smethwick Local Board of Health* above no such notice was given, although notice had been given requiring the owner to remove the buildings. A building may be pulled down in any way consistent with safety: *Jagger v Doncaster Union Rural Sanitary Authority* (1890) 54 JP 438.

18 Ie given under the Building Act 1984 s 36(1), (2): see the text and notes 1–13.
19 Ie other than the Building Act 1984 s 16: see PARA 33.
20 As to the meaning of 'relevant period' see PARA 33 note 14.
21 Building Act 1984 s 36(5).
22 As to the Attorney General see CONSTITUTIONAL AND ADMINISTRATIVE LAW vol 20 (2014) PARA 273.
23 Building Act 1984 s 36(6). See *A-G v Ashborne Recreation Ground Co* [1903] 1 Ch 101.
24 Building Act 1984 s 36(6)(a).
25 Building Act 1984 s 36(6)(b).
26 Building Act 1984 s 36(6)(c).
27 Building Act 1984 s 36(6).

63. Obtaining of report where a notice to remove or alter work contravening building regulations is given.

In a case where:

(1)   a person to whom a notice to remove or alter work contravening building regulations[1] has been given gives to the local authority[2] by whom the notice was given notice of his intention to obtain from a suitably qualified person a written report concerning work to which the notice relates[3]; and

(2)   such a report is obtained and submitted to the local authority and, as a result of its consideration of it, the local authority withdraws the notice to remove or alter work contravening building regulations[4],

the local authority may pay to the person to whom the notice was given such amount as appears to it to represent the expenses reasonably incurred by him in consequence of its having given him that notice including, in particular, his expenses in obtaining the report[5].

1   Ie a notice given under the Building Act 1984 s 36(1), (2): see PARA 62. As to the meaning of 'building regulations' see PARA 7.
2   As to the meaning of 'local authority' see PARA 1 note 12.
3   Building Act 1984 s 37(1)(a). If a person to whom such a notice has been given gives notice under s 37(1)(a), then, so far as regards the matters to which the notice relates, the reference to 28 days in s 36(3) (see PARA 62) must be construed as a reference to 70 days: s 37(2). Notice under s 37(1)(a) must be given before the expiry of the period of 28 days referred to in s 36(3), or, as the case may be, within such longer period as a court allows under s 36(3), and, where such a longer period has been so allowed before notice is given under s 37(1)(a), then s 37(2) does not apply: s 37(3).
4   Building Act 1984 s 37(1)(b).
5   Building Act 1984 s 37(1).

64. Civil liability for breach of duties imposed by building regulations.

As from a day to be appointed, the following provisions have effect[1]. Breach of a duty imposed by building regulations[2], so far as it causes damage[3], is actionable, except in so far as the regulations provide otherwise[4]. As regards such a duty, building regulations may provide for a prescribed[5] defence to be available in a claim[6] for breach of that duty[7].

These provisions do not affect the extent, if any, to which breach of a duty imposed by or arising in connection with Part I of the Building Act 1984[8] or any other enactment[9] relating to building regulations, or a duty imposed by building regulations in a case to which these provisions do not apply, is actionable[10], or prejudice a right of action that exists apart from the enactments relating to building regulations[11].

1 In so far as the Building Act 1984 s 38 enables regulations to be made, it came into force on 1 December 1984 by virtue of s 134(2). At the date at which this volume states the law, no order bringing s 38 into force for remaining purposes had been made under s 134(1).

2 As to the meaning of 'building regulations' see PARA 7.

3 For these purposes, 'damage' includes the death of, or injury to, any person, including any disease and any impairment of a person's physical or mental condition: Building Act 1984 s 38(4) (not yet in force: see note 1).

4 Building Act 1984 s 38(1)(a) (not yet in force: see note 1). The provisions of s 38(1) and any defence provided for in regulations made by of s 38(1), do not apply in the case of a breach of such a duty in connection with a building erected before the date on which s 38(1) comes into force unless the regulations imposing the duty apply to or in connection with the building by virtue of s 2(2) or s 2A (see PARA 12) or s 1(3), Sch 1 para 8 (see PARA 9): s 38(2) (amended by the Sustainable and Secure Buildings Act 2004 s 4(3)) (not yet in force: see note 1). As to the meaning of 'building' see PARA 6. As to the meaning of 'erect' see PARA 9 note 3. The defence volenti non fit injuria (see NEGLIGENCE vol 78 (2018) PARA 69 et seq) is not applicable to actions for breach of statutory duty: see *Britton v Great Western Cotton Co* (1872) LR 7 Exch 130; *Baddeley v Earl Granville* (1887) 19 QBD 423; *Davies v Thomas Owen & Co Ltd* [1919] 2 KB 39; *Wheeler v New Merton Board Mills Ltd* [1933] 2 KB 669, CA; and TORT vol 97 (2015) PARA 519.

A building owner has an overriding obligation to ensure that the building works comply with the building regulations and the local authority owes him no duty of care in passing plans: *Richardson v West Lindsey District Council* [1990] 1 All ER 296, [1990] 1 WLR 522, CA. A local authority when carrying out its building control functions owes a limited duty of care in tort which extends to owner occupiers and, in the absence of special circumstances, not even to them if they caused the building to be erected: *Peabody Donation Fund (Governors) v Sir Lindsay Parkinson & Co Ltd* [1985] AC 210, [1984] 3 All ER 529, HL; *Fry v Robert A Jackson (Builder & Contractor) Ltd* (1986) 7 Con LR 97; *Investors in Industry Commercial Properties Ltd v South Bedfordshire District Council* [1986] QB 1034, [1986] 1 All ER 787, CA; *Hambro Life Assurance plc v White Young & Partners (a firm)* (1987) 38 BLR 16, (1987) 8 Con LR 130, CA.

5 Ie prescribed by building regulations: see the Building Act 1984 s 126.

6 Ie brought by virtue of the Building Act 1984 s 38.

7 Building Act 1984 s 38(1)(b) (not yet in force: see note 1). See note 4.

8 Ie Building Act 1984 Pt I (ss 1–46): see PARA 7 et seq.

9 As to the meaning of 'enactment' see PARA 6 note 2.

10 As to breach of statutory duty generally see TORT vol 97 (2015) PARA 500 et seq. See also STATUTES AND LEGISLATIVE PROCESS vol 96 (2012) PARA 759. The general rule is that a civil action for breach of statutory duty lies if the statutory obligation was intended to be for the protection of a class of persons of whom the claimant is one: see *Solomons v R Gertzenstein Ltd* [1954] 2 QB 243, [1954] 2 All ER 625, CA; *Grant v National Coal Board* [1956] AC 649, [1956] 1 All ER 682, HL. The claim must be in respect of injury or damage of a kind against which the statute was designed to give protection (*Gorris v Scott* (1874) LR 9 Exch 125; *Grant v National Coal Board* above at 655 and 684 per Viscount Simonds), and the breach alleged must have caused or materially contributed to the injury or damage (*Bonnington Castings Ltd v Wardlaw* [1956] AC 613, [1956] 1 All ER 615, HL). The question whether the breach gives rise to a right of action depends on whether the intention of the statute considered as a whole and in the circumstances in which it was enacted was to impose a public duty only or to impose in addition a duty enforceable by an individual who has suffered damage or is otherwise aggrieved: *Phillips v Britannia Hygienic Laundry Co Ltd* [1923] 2 KB 832, CA; *Cutler v Wandsworth Stadium Ltd* [1949] AC 398, [1949] 1 All ER 544, HL; *Solomon v R Gertzenstein Ltd*. Where a criminal remedy is provided for the breach there is a strong implication that no civil action lies: *Phillips v Britannia Hygienic Laundry Co Ltd* above; *Clarke and Wife v Brims* [1947] KB 497, [1947] 1 All ER 242; *Cutler v Wandsworth Stadium Ltd* above; *Ministry of Housing and Local Government v Sharp* [1970] 2 QB 223, [1970] 1 All ER 1009, CA. Regulations made by statutory instrument have the full force and effect of a statute whether or not the statute under which they were made provides that the regulations are to have effect as if enacted in the statute (*Dale's Case, Enraght's Case* (1881) 6 QBD 376 at 398, CA, per Lord Coleridge CJ; *Kruse v Johnson* [1898] 2 QB 91 at 96, DC, per Lord Russell of Killowen; *Re Macartney, Brookhouse v Barman* (1920) 36 TLR 394), and thus the law as to civil liability for breach of statutory duty extends to regulations.

11 Building Act 1984 s 38(3). As to the general common law duty of care, which may also give rise

to liability see NEGLIGENCE vol 78 (2018) PARA 2 et seq. Where the loss is purely economic, a contractor will only be liable in tort where he has assumed a responsibility to the acquirer or user of the defective building: see *Muirhead v Industrial Tank Specialities Ltd* [1986] QB 507 at 527–528, [1985] 3 All ER 705 at 715, CA (explaining *Junior Books Ltd v Veitchi Co Ltd* [1983] 1 AC 520, [1982] 3 All ER 201, HL); and NEGLIGENCE vol 78 (2018) PARA 14. As to failure by public bodies to exercise statutory powers see NEGLIGENCE vol 78 (2018) PARA 18.

(11) Appeals in Relation to Building Regulations

65. Appeal against refusal etc to relax building regulations.

If a local authority[1] refuses an application to dispense with or relax a requirement in building regulations[2] that it has power to dispense with or relax, the applicant may by notice[3] in writing appeal to the appropriate national authority within one month from the date on which the local authority notifies the applicant of its refusal[4]. If, within a period of two months beginning with the date of an application[5], or such extended period as may at any time be agreed in writing between the applicant and the local authority[6], the local authority does not notify the applicant of its decision on the application, the right to appeal[7] to the appropriate national authority applies in relation to the application as if the local authority had refused the application and notified the applicant of its decision at the end of that period[8]. The notice of appeal must set out the grounds of appeal, and a copy of the notice of appeal must be sent to the local authority[9]. The local authority, on receiving a copy of the notice of appeal, must at once transmit to the appropriate national authority a copy of the application and a copy of all the documents furnished by the applicant for the purposes of his application[10]. The local authority must at the same time give to the appropriate national authority in writing any representations that it desires to make as regards the appeal, and must send a copy to the appellant[11]. If the appropriate national authority allows the appeal, it must give such directions for dispensing with or relaxing building regulations as may be appropriate[12].

1 As to the meaning of 'local authority' see PARA 1 note 12.
2 As to the meaning of 'building regulations' see PARA 7. As to the power of the appropriate national authority to give directions dispensing with or relaxing requirements in the building regulations see the Building Act 1984 s 8; and PARA 18. Such a direction may relate to continuing requirements (see PARA 12), and s 39 applies to any such direction: see s 2(6); and PARA 12. As to the appropriate national authority (ie the Secretary of State or, where statutory functions have been transferred in relation to Wales, the Welsh Ministers) see PARA 5.
3 As to the form, authentication and service of notices see PARAS 135–137.
4 Building Act 1984 s 39(1).
5 Building Act 1984 s 39(2)(a).
6 Building Act 1984 s 39(2)(b).
7 Ie the Building Act 1984 s 39(1): see the text to notes 1–4.
8 Building Act 1984 s 39(2).
9 Building Act 1984 s 39(3).
10 Building Act 1984 s 39(4).
11 Building Act 1984 s 39(5).
12 Building Act 1984 s 39(6).

66. Appeal against notice to remove or alter work contravening building regulations.

A person aggrieved[1] by the giving of a notice to remove or alter work contravening building regulations[2] may appeal[3] to a magistrates' court[4]. On such an appeal the court must, if it determines that the local authority[5] was entitled to give the notice, confirm the notice[6], and in any other case, give the local authority a direction to withdraw the notice[7]. Such an appeal must be brought within 28 days of the giving of the notice[8], or, in a case where the person to whom the notice was given gives to the local authority notice[9] of his intention to obtain from a suitable qualified person a written report concerning work to which the notice relates, within 70 days of the giving of the notice to remove or alter work contravening building regulations[10].

Where an appeal is brought[11] the notice to remove or alter work contravening building regulations is of no effect pending the final determination or withdrawal of the appeal[12]. If a person to whom a notice to remove or alter work contravening building regulations has been given fails to comply with the notice before the expiration of 28 days (beginning, in a case where an appeal is brought[13], on the date when the appeal is finally determined or, as the case may be, withdrawn), or such longer period as a magistrates' court may on his application allow, the local authority may pull down or remove the work in question, or effect such alterations in it as it deems necessary, and may recover from him the expenses reasonably incurred by it in doing so[14].

If, on such an appeal[15] there is produced to the court a written report from a suitably qualified person concerning work to which the notice to remove or alter work contravening building regulations relates that has been submitted to the local authority[16], the court, in making an order as to costs, may treat the expenses incurred in obtaining the report as expenses incurred for the purposes of the appeal[17].

1 As to persons aggrieved see JUDICIAL REVIEW vol 61 (2010) PARA 656.
2 Ie a notice under the Building Act 1984 s 36(1) or s 36(2): see PARA 62.
3 As to appeals generally see PARAS 139–140.
4 Building Act 1984 s 40(1) (amended by the Courts Act 2003 s 109(1), (3), Sch 8 para 279, Sch 10).
5 As to the meaning of 'local authority' see PARA 1 note 12.
6 Building Act 1984 s 40(2)(a).
7 Building Act 1984 s 40(2)(b). If, in a case where the appeal is against a notice under s 36(2) (see PARA 62), the court is satisfied that the local authority was entitled to give the notice, but in all the circumstances of the case the purpose for which was enacted the provision of the Building Act 1984 by virtue of which the notice was given has been substantially achieved, the court may give a direction under s 40(2)(b): s 40(3).
8 Building Act 1984 s 40(4)(a).
9 Ie under the Building Act 1984 s 37(1)(a): see PARA 63.
10 Building Act 1984 s 40(4)(b).
11 Ie under the Building Act 1984 s 40.
12 Building Act 1984 s 40(5)(a).
13 Ie under the Building Act 1984 s 40.
14 Building Act 1984 ss 36(3), 40(5)(b).
15 Ie under the Building Act 1984 s 40.
16 Ie under the Building Act 1984 s 37(1): see PARA 63.
17 Building Act 1984 s 40(6).

67. Appeal to the Crown Court.

Where a person is aggrieved[1] by an order, determination or other decision of a magistrates' court[2] under Part I of the Building Act 1984[3], or under Part IV[4] of that Act as it applies in relation to Part I, and is not by any other enactment[5] authorised to appeal to the Crown Court[6], he may appeal to the Crown Court[7]. This does not confer a right of appeal in a case in which each of the parties concerned might under the Building Act 1984 have required that the dispute should be determined by arbitration instead of by a magistrates' court[8].

1 As to persons aggrieved see JUDICIAL REVIEW vol 61 (2010) PARA 656.

2   See CRIMINAL PROCEDURE vol 28 (2015) PARA 665 et seq; MAGISTRATES vol 71 (2013) PARA 701 et seq.
3   Ie the Building Act 1984 Pt I (ss 1–46): see PARA 7 et seq.
4   Ie the Building Act 1984 Pt IV (ss 91–131): see PARA 70 et seq.
5   As to the meaning of 'enactment' see PARA 6 note 2.
6   See COURTS AND TRIBUNALS.
7   Building Act 1984 s 41(1).
8   Building Act 1984 s 41(2). As to arbitrations under the Building Act 1984 see PARA 36 note 16.

68.   Appeal and statement of case to the High Court in certain cases.

As from a day to be appointed, the following provisions have effect[1]. Where the appropriate national authority[2] gives a decision[3] in proceedings on certain appeals, references or applications[4], the relevant person[5] or the local authority or, as the case may be, the approved inspector[6] may appeal to the High Court against the decision on a point of law[7]. At any stage of the proceedings on such an appeal, reference or application the appropriate national authority may state a question of law arising in the course of the proceedings in the form of a special case for the decision of the High Court[8], and a decision of the High Court on a case so stated is deemed to be a judgment of the court within the meaning of the Senior Courts Act 1981[9].

In relation to such proceedings in the High Court or the Court of Appeal[10], the power to make rules of court includes power to make rules prescribing the powers of the High Court or the Court of Appeal with respect to the remitting of the matter with the opinion or direction of the court for re-hearing and determination by the appropriate national authority[11], and providing for the appropriate national authority, either generally or in such circumstances as may be prescribed by the rules, to be treated as a party to any such proceedings and to be entitled to appear and to be heard accordingly[12]. No appeal to the Court of Appeal may be brought except with the leave of the High Court or the Court of Appeal[13].

1   The Building Act 1984 s 42(1)–(3) (see the text and notes 2–9) is to be brought into force by order made under s 134(1)(b) as from a day to be appointed. At the date at which this volume states the law no such order had been made. Section 42(4)–(6) (see the text and notes 3, 10–12), in so far as it enables regulations to be made, came in to force on 1 December 1984: see s 134(1)(a), (2). At the date at which this volume states the law no order had been made bringing s 42(4)–(6) into force for the remaining purposes. Section 42(7) (see the text and notes 3–4) came into force on 1 December 1984: see s 134(2).
2   Ie the Secretary of State or, where statutory functions have been transferred in relation to Wales, the Welsh Ministers: see PARA 5.
3   For these purposes, 'decision' includes a direction, and references to the giving of a decision must be construed accordingly: Building Act 1984 s 42(6) (not yet in force: see note 1).
4   Ie on an appeal under the Building Act 1984 s 20 (use of materials unsuitable for permanent building; see PARA 35) or s 39 (refusal to relax building regulations; see PARA 65), on a reference under s 16 (passing or rejection of plans; see PARA 33) or s 50 (plans certificates; see PARA 83), or on an application for a direction under s 8 (relaxation of building regulations; see PARA 18) where the power of giving the direction is not exercisable by the local authority: s 42(1)(a)–(c) (not yet in force: see note 1). As to the meaning of 'local authority' see PARA 1 note 12.
    Until a day to be appointed by order made by the Secretary of State, s 42(1) has effect as modified by s 42(7): s 42(7)(a), (b). At the date at which this volume states the law no such day had been appointed. The power to make an order under s 42(7) is exercisable by statutory instrument, and different days may be appointed by such an order for different provisions or for different purposes: s 120(1). Note that the functions of the Secretary of State under s 42(7) are not transferred to the Welsh Ministers: see PARA 5.
5   For these purposes, the 'relevant person' means:
    (1)   as regards an appeal under the Building Act 1984 s 20 (see PARA 35) or s 39 (see PARA 65), the appellant (s 42(2)(a) (not yet in force: see note 1))

(2) as regards a reference under s 16 (see PARA 33) or s 50 (see PARA 83), the person on whose application the reference was made (s 42(2)(b) (not yet in force: see note 1));

(3) as regards such an application as is mentioned in s 42(1)(c) (see note 4), the applicant (s 42(2)(c)).

Until a day to be appointed by order made by the Secretary of State, s 42(2)(b) has effect as modified by s 42(7): s 42(7)(c). At the date at which this volume states the law no such day had been appointed. See note 4. Note that the functions of the Secretary of State under s 42(7) are not transferred to the Welsh Ministers: see PARA 5.

6 As to the meaning of 'approved inspector' see PARA 72.

7 Building Act 1984 s 42(1) (not yet in force: see note 1). As to the modification of s 42(1) see note 4.

8 Building Act 1984 s 42(3)(a) (not yet in force: see note 1).

9 Building Act 1984 s 42(3)(b) (not yet in force: see note 1). The text refers to a judgment of the court within the meaning of the Senior Courts Act 1981 s 16: see COURTS AND TRIBUNALS vol 24 (2010) PARA 693.

10 Ie brought by virtue of the Building Act 1984 s 44 (not yet in force).

11 Building Act 1984 s 42(4)(a) (not yet in force: see note 1). At the date at which this volume states the law no rules had been made under s 42(4) and none have effect by virtue of the Interpretation Act 1978 s 17(2)(b).

12 Building Act 1984 s 42(4)(b) (not yet in force: see note 1). See note 11.

13 Building Act 1984 s 42(5) (not yet in force: see note 1).

69. Procedure on appeal to Secretary of State or the Welsh Ministers.

As from a day to be appointed, the following provisions have effect[1]. On an appeal to the appropriate national authority[2] under the statutory provision relating to the use of materials unsuitable for permanent building[3] and under the statutory provision relating to appeals against a refusal to relax building regulation[4], the appropriate national authority may at its discretion afford to the appellant and the local authority[5] an opportunity of appearing before, and being heard by, a person appointed by the appropriate national authority for the purpose[6]. On determining such an appeal, the appropriate national authority must give such directions, if any, as it considers appropriate for giving effect to his determination[7]. Building regulations[8] may, in connection with such an appeal, include such supplementary provisions with respect to procedure as the appropriate national authority thinks fit[9].

1 The provisions of the Building Act 1984 s 43(1), (2) are to be brought into force by order made under s 134(1)(b) as from a day to be appointed. At the date at which this volume states the law no such day had been appointed. Section 43(3) has been brought into force in so far as it enables regulations to be made: see s 134(1)(a), (2). At the date at which this volume states the law no order bringing s 43(3) for remaining purposes had been made.

2 Ie the Secretary of State or, where statutory functions have been transferred in relation to Wales, the Welsh Ministers: see PARA 5.

3 Ie under the Building Act 1984 s 20: see PARA 35.

4 Ie under the Building Act 1984 s 39: see PARA 65.

5 As to the meaning of 'local authority' see PARA 1 note 12.

6 Building Act 1984 s 43(1) (not yet in force: see note 1).

7 Building Act 1984 s 43(2) (not yet in force: see note 1).

8 As to the meaning of 'building regulations' see PARA 7.

9 Building Act 1984 s 43(3) (not yet in force: see note 1) (which is expressed to be without prejudice to Sch 1 para 10(c) (see PARA 9)).

3. SUPERVISION

(1) Supervision by Local Authorities

70. Duties of local authorities.

It is the duty of local authorities[1] to carry the Building Act 1984 into execution in their areas, subject to[2]:

(1) the provisions of the Building Act 1984 relating to certain other authorities or persons[3];

(2) the provisions of Part I of the Public Health Act 1936[4] relating to united districts and joint boards[5];

(3) the provisions of the Local Government, Planning and Land Act 1980[6] relating to building control functions in urban development areas[7]; and

(4) the provisions of the Public Health (Control of Disease) Act 1984[8] relating to port health authorities and jurisdiction in any part of a port health district[9].

It is the function[10] of local authorities to enforce building regulations[11] in their areas[12].

As from a day to be appointed the following provisions have effect[13]. A local authority must keep in a register such information and documents[14] as may be prescribed[15] in connection with their functions, powers and duties conferred or imposed by or under the Building Act 1984[16]. Information and documents that are required to be kept in the register must be kept for the prescribed period[17] and the register must be maintained in the prescribed manner[18]. The local authority must also ensure that the register is available for inspection by members of the public during prescribed periods[19] and, in prescribed circumstances, it must provide to members of the public, on request, copies of information and documents kept in the register[20].

1 As to the meaning of 'local authority' see PARA 1 note 12.
2 Building Act 1984 s 91(1). The provisions of the Public Health Act 1936 s 333 (protection for dock and railway undertakings) apply in relation to local authorities acting under the Building Act 1984 as they apply in relation to local authorities acting under the Public Health Act 1936: Building Act 1984 s 128. As to the making of building regulations to modify or repeal the provisions of s 91 on the ground of inconsistency with other provisions see Sch 1 para 11(1); and PARA 9. As to supervision of plans and works by approved inspectors and public bodies see PARA 72 et seq.
3 Building Act 1984 s 91(1)(a).
4 Ie the Public Health Act 1936 Pt I (ss 1–13): see ENVIRONMENTAL QUALITY AND PUBLIC HEALTH vol 45 (2010) PARAS 1, 101, 106.
5 Building Act 1984 s 91(1)(b). 'Joint board' has the meaning given by the Public Health Act 1936 s 343(1) (see ENVIRONMENTAL QUALITY AND PUBLIC HEALTH vol 45 (2010) PARA 101): Building Act 1984 s 126.
6 Ie the Local Government, Planning and Land Act 1980 s 151: see PLANNING vol 83 (2018) PARA 1558.
7 Building Act 1984 s 91(1)(c).
8 Ie the Public Health (Control of Disease) Act 1984 s 1(3): see ENVIRONMENTAL QUALITY AND PUBLIC HEALTH vol 45 (2010) PARA 99.
9 Building Act 1984 s 91(1)(d). As to port health districts and authorities see ENVIRONMENTAL QUALITY AND PUBLIC HEALTH vol 45 (2010) PARA 102.
10 As to the meaning of 'functions' see PARA 3 note 19.
11 As to the meaning of 'building regulations' see PARA 7.
12 Building Act 1984 s 91(2). This provision is expressed to be subject to s 5(3) (see PARA 17), s 48(1) (see PARA 75) and s 53(2) (see PARA 81): see s 91(2) (amended by the Local Government Act 1985 s 102(2), Sch 17).

13 The Building Act 1984 s 91A was added by the Sustainable and Secure Buildings Act 2004 s 7. For the purpose of conferring power to make regulations, the Building Act 1984 s 91A came into force on 1 February 2006: see the Sustainable and Secure Buildings Act 2004 (Commencement No 1) Order 2006, SI 2006/224, art 2. At the date at which this volume states the law it had not been brought into force for remaining purposes.

14 'Documents' includes notices, certificates, orders, consents, demands and plans: Building Act 1984 s 91A(5) (as added: see note 13) (not yet in force).

15 'Prescribed' means prescribed by regulations made by the appropriate national authority under the Building Act 1984 s 91A: see s 91A(5), (8) (as added: see note 13) (not yet in force). As to the appropriate national authority (ie the Secretary of State or, where statutory functions have been transferred in relation to Wales, the Welsh Ministers) see PARA 5. Such regulations may: (1) provide for a provision to apply generally, or in a particular area; (2) make different provision for different areas and generally different provision for different circumstances or cases; and (3) include such supplemental, transitional and incidental provisions as appear to be expedient: see s 91A(6), (7) (as so added) (not yet in force).

16 Building Act 1984 s 91A(1) (as added: see note 13) (not yet in force). The information and documents that may be so prescribed include, in particular:

    (1)   documents that are given or issued to, or deposited with, a local authority in accordance with provision made by or under the Building Act 1984, or copies of such documents (s 91A(2)(a) (as so added) (not yet in force));

    (2)   copies of documents that are given, made or issued by a local authority in accordance with provision so made (s 91A(2)(b) (as so added) (not yet in force));

    (3)   information with respect to documents of the kind mentioned in head (1) or (2) (s 91A(2)(c) (as so added) (not yet in force));

    (4)   information with respect to matters to which such documents relate (s 91A(2)(d) (as so added) (not yet in force)).

17 Building Act 1984 s 91A(3) (as added: see note 13) (not yet in force).

18 Building Act 1984 s 91A(4)(a) (as added: see note 13) (not yet in force).

19 Building Act 1984 s 91A(4)(b) (as added: see note 13) (not yet in force).

20 Building Act 1984 s 91A(4)(c) (as added: see note 13) (not yet in force). The local authority may, in prescribed circumstances, charge a member of the public to whom it provides such copies a fee calculated in the prescribed manner: s 91A(4)(d) (as so added) (not yet in force).

71. Unauthorised building work.

'Unauthorised building work' means building work[1] other than work in relation to which an initial notice[2], an amendment notice[3] or a public body's notice[4] has effect, which is done without:

(1)   a building notice[5] being given to the local authority[6];

(2)   full plans of the work being deposited with the local authority[7]; or

(3)   a notice of commencement of work being given[8], where a building notice has been given or full plans[9] have been deposited[10].

Where it appears to a local authority that unauthorised building work has been carried out on or after 11 November 1985[11], the owner (referred to as the 'applicant') may apply in writing to the local authority for a regularisation certificate, and must send with his application:

(a)   a statement that the application is being made[12] in accordance with the relevant building regulation[13];

(b)   a description of the unauthorised work[14];

(c)   so far as is reasonably practicable, a plan of the unauthorised work[15]; and

(d)   so far as is reasonably practicable, a plan showing the relevant requirements (that is any additional work required to be carried out to secure that the unauthorised work complies with the requirements relating to building work in the building regulations which were applicable to that work when it was carried out)[16].

Where a local authority receives such an application, it may require the applicant to take such reasonable steps, including laying open the unauthorised work for inspection by the authority, making tests and taking samples, as the authority thinks appropriate to ascertain what work, if any, is required to secure that the relevant requirements are met[17]. When the applicant has taken any such steps required by the local authority, and having had regard to any direction given[18] dispensing with or relaxing a requirement in building regulations which applies to the unauthorised work, the local authority must notify the applicant:

(i)   of the work which in its opinion is required to comply with the relevant requirements or those requirements as dispensed with or relaxed[19];

(ii)   that it cannot determine what work is required to comply with the relevant requirements or those requirements as dispensed with or relaxed[20]; or

(iii)   that no work is required to secure compliance with the relevant requirements or those requirements as dispensed with or relaxed[21].

Where the local authority has been able to satisfy itself, after taking all reasonable steps for that purpose that the relevant requirements have been satisfied, taking account of any work carried out and any dispensation or relaxation given[22], or that no work is required to secure that the unauthorised work satisfies the relevant requirements, taking account of any such dispensation or relaxation[23], it may give a certificate to that effect (referred to as a 'regularisation certificate')[24]. A regularisation certificate is evidence, but not conclusive evidence, that the relevant requirements specified in the certificate have been complied with[25].

1   As to the meaning of 'building work' see PARA 10.
2   Ie a notice given under the Building Act 1984 s 47: see PARA 74. As to initial notices see PARA 74 et seq.
3   Ie a notice given under the Building Act 1984 s 51A: see PARA 76. As to amendment notices see PARA 76.
4   Ie a notice given under the Building Act 1984 s 54: see PARA 89. As to a public body's notice see PARA 89 et seq.
5   As to the meaning of 'building notice' see PARA 25 note 6.
6   Building Regulations 2010, SI 2010/2214, reg 18(8)(a). Where reg 18 applies, reg 12 (see PARA 25) and reg 14 (see PARA 27) do not apply, and neither the supply of plans nor the taking of any other action in accordance with reg 18 is to be treated for the purposes of the Building Act 1984 s 16 (see PARA 33) as the deposit of plans in accordance with building regulations: Building Regulations 2010, SI 2010/2214, reg 18(7).
7   Building Regulations 2010, SI 2010/2214, reg 18(8)(b).
8   Ie in accordance with the Building Regulations 2010, SI 2010/2214, reg 16(1): see PARA 28.
9   As to the meaning of 'full plans' see PARA 25 note 7.
10 Building Regulations 2010, SI 2010/2214, reg 18(8)(c).
11 Building Regulations 2010, SI 2010/2214, reg 18(1).
12 Ie in accordance with the Building Regulations 2010, SI 2010/2214, reg 18.
13 Building Regulations 2010, SI 2010/2214, reg 18(2)(a).
14 Building Regulations 2010, SI 2010/2214, reg 18(2)(b).
15 Building Regulations 2010, SI 2010/2214, reg 18(2)(c).
16 Building Regulations 2010, SI 2010/2214, reg 18(2)(d).
17 Building Regulations 2010, SI 2010/2214, reg 18(3).
18 Ie given in accordance with the Building Act 1984 s 8 (see PARA 18), s 9 (see PARA 19) and Sch 2 (see PARA 20).
19 Building Regulations 2010, SI 2010/2214, reg 18(4)(a).
20 Building Regulations 2010, SI 2010/2214, reg 18(4)(b).
21 Building Regulations 2010, SI 2010/2214, reg 18(4)(c).
22 Building Regulations 2010, SI 2010/2214, reg 18(5)(a). See note 18.
23 Building Regulations 2010, SI 2010/2214, reg 18(5)(b).
24 Building Regulations 2010, SI 2010/2214, reg 18(5).
25 Building Regulations 2010, SI 2010/2214, reg 18(6).

(2) Supervision by Approved Inspectors and Public Bodies

(i) Supervision of Plans and Works by Approved Inspectors

A.   APPROVED INSPECTORS

72.   Approved inspectors.

An approved inspector is a person who, in accordance with building regulations[1], is approved for the purposes of Part II of the Building Act 1984[2] by the appropriate national authority[3], or by a body, corporate or unincorporated, that, in accordance with the regulations, is designated by the appropriate national authority for the purpose[4]. Any such approval may limit the description of work in relation to which the person concerned is an approved inspector[5]. Any such designation may limit the cases in which and the terms on which the body designated may approve a person and, in particular, may provide that any approval given by the body is to be limited[6] as the description of work in relation to which the person concerned is an approved inspector[7]. There must be paid on an application for any such approval where the application is made to the appropriate national authority, such fee as may be prescribed[8], and where the application is made to a designated body, such fee as that body may determine[9].

Building regulations may:

(1)   contain provision prescribing the period for which, subject to any provision made by virtue of head (2) or head (3) below, any such approval continues in force[10];

(2)   contain provision precluding the giving of, or requiring the withdrawal of, any such approval as is referred to above in such circumstances as may be prescribed[11];

(3)   contain provision authorising the withdrawal of any such approval or designation as is referred to above[12];

(4)   provide for the maintenance by the appropriate national authority of a list of bodies that are for the time being designated, and provide for the maintenance by the appropriate national authority and by each designated body, of a list of persons for the time being approved by it or them[13];

(5)   make provision for the supply to local authorities[14] of copies of any list of approved inspectors maintained by virtue of head (4) above and for such copy lists to be made available for inspection[15]; and

(6)   make provision for the supply, on payment of a prescribed fee, of a certified copy of any entry in a list maintained by virtue of head (4) above or in a copy list held by a local authority by virtue of head (5) above[16].

Unless the contrary is proved, in any proceedings, whether civil or criminal, a document that appears to the court to be a certified copy of an entry either in a list maintained as mentioned in head (4) above or in a copy of such a list supplied as mentioned in head (5) above is presumed to be a true copy of an entry in the current list so maintained[17], and is evidence of the matters stated in it[18].

An approved inspector may make such charges in respect of the carrying out of such functions as may be prescribed with respect to the inspection of plans of work to which an initial notice relates, the supervision of that work and the giving of certificates and other notices[19] as may in any particular case be agreed between him and the person who intends to carry out the work[20] in question or, as the case may be, by whom that work is being or has been carried out[21].

Nothing in Part II of the Building Act 1984 prevents an approved inspector from arranging for plans[22] or work to be inspected on his behalf by another person, but such a delegation does not extend to the giving of a plans certificate[23] or a final certificate[24]; and nor does it affect any liability, whether civil or criminal, of the approved inspector which arises out of functions conferred on him by Part II of the Building Act 1984 or by building regulations[25]. However, an approved inspector is liable for negligence on the part of a person carrying out an inspection on his behalf in like manner as if it were negligence by a servant of his acting in the course of his employment[26].

1 As to the meaning of 'building regulations' see PARA 7.
2 Ie the Building Act 1984 Pt II (ss 47–58). As to supervision of works by local authorities see PARA 70. As to supervision by public bodies of their own work see PARA 88 et seq.
3 Ie the Secretary of State or, where statutory functions have been transferred in relation to Wales, the Welsh Ministers: see PARA 5.
4 Building Act 1984 s 49(1). See *Worlock v SAWS (a firm) and Rushmoor Borough Council* (1982) 22 BLR 66, CA (it was correct for the local authority to leave the interpretation of the building regulations to the good sense and experience of their building inspectors, but the final responsibility rests with the local authority itself and not with the inspector).
    If it appears to the appropriate national authority that a body might properly be designated as a body to approve inspectors it may, if the body consents, designate it for that purpose: Building (Approved Inspectors etc) Regulations 2010, SI 2010/2215, reg 3. Where the appropriate national authority has designated a body in this way, a person seeking to be an approved inspector must apply to a designated body giving particulars of his qualifications and experience in the case of a person other than a body corporate, and giving particulars of the number, qualifications and experience of the people to be employed in the discharge of its functions under the Building (Approved Inspectors etc) Regulations 2010, SI 2010/2215, in the case of a body corporate: reg 4(1). The person must answer any inquiries which that designated body makes about those matters: reg 4(1). Where there is no designated body, a person seeking to be an approved inspector must apply to the appropriate national authority giving particulars of his qualifications and experience in the case of a person other than a body corporate, and giving particulars of the number, qualifications and experience of the people to be employed in the discharge of its functions under the Building (Approved Inspectors etc) Regulations 2010, SI 2010/2215, in the case of a body corporate: reg 4(2). The person must answer any inquiries which the appropriate national authority makes about those matters: reg 4(2). The approval of an inspector or the designation of a body to approve inspectors must be given to that person or body by a notice in writing specifying any limitation on the approval or designation: reg 5. An approved inspector who gives an initial notice, an amendment notice, a plans certificate, a combined initial notice and plans certificate or a final certificate on or after 6 April 2013, to a local authority must ensure that, before or on the date of the notice or certificate, the person who approved that inspector (the Secretary of State or a body designated under reg 3 as the case may be) is in possession of a declaration of insurance in respect of the work to which the notice or certificate relates: reg 5A(1), (2) (reg 5A added in relation to England by SI 2012/3119 and in relation to Wales by SI 2012/3119; and in relation to Wales by SI 2014/58). 'Declaration of insurance' means a declaration of insurance signed by the insurer that a named scheme of insurance approved by the Secretary of State applies to the approved inspector in relation to the building work to which the notice or certificate relates: Building (Approved Inspectors etc) Regulations 2010, SI 2010/2215, reg 5A(3) (as so added).
5 Building Act 1984 s 49(2).
6 Ie limited as is mentioned in the Building Act 1984 s 49(2): see the text to note 5.
7 Building Act 1984 s 49(3).
8 Building Act 1984 s 49(4)(a). 'Prescribed' means prescribed by building regulations: see s 126.
9 Building Act 1984 s 49(4)(b).
10 Building Act 1984 s 49(5)(a). The approval of an inspector given by a designated body or by the appropriate national authority ceases to have effect at the end of a period of five years from the date on which it was given: Building (Approved Inspectors etc) Regulations 2010, SI 2010/2215, reg 6(1).
11 Building Act 1984 s 49(5)(b).

12 Building Act 1984 s 49(5)(c). The approval of an inspector may be withdrawn by a notice in writing given to the inspector by the person who approved him: Building (Approved Inspectors etc) Regulations 2010, SI 2010/2215, reg 6(2). The appropriate national authority may withdraw the designation of a designated body by giving the body notice in writing, but such withdrawal does not affect the operation of any subsisting approval given by the body, and a subsisting approval may be withdrawn by the appropriate national authority as if it had been given by it: reg 6(3). Where an approved inspector is convicted of an offence under the Building Act 1984 s 57 (false or misleading notices and certificates, etc) (see PARA 33), the person by whom the approval was given may on receipt of a certificate of the conviction forthwith withdraw the approval and no further approval may be given to an approved inspector whose approval has been withdrawn for a period of five years beginning with the date of his conviction: Building (Approved Inspectors etc) Regulations 2010, SI 2010/2215, reg 6(4).

13 Building Act 1984 s 49(5)(d). The appropriate national authority must maintain a list of bodies which are for the time being designated by it for the purpose of approving inspectors, a list of inspectors for the time being approved by it and in respect of each approved inspector listed, keep a copy of the approval certificate and the declaration of insurance referred to in reg 5A (see note 4): see the Building (Approved Inspectors etc) Regulations 2010, SI 2010/2215, reg 7(1) (amended by SI 2012/3119; and SI 2018/558; and substituted by SI 2014/58). A designated body must maintain a list of inspectors for the time being approved by it, in respect of each approved inspector listed, keep a copy of the approval certificate and the declaration of insurance referred to in reg 5A; and notify every local authority in whose area the Building (Approved Inspectors etc) Regulations 2010, SI 2010/2215, apply as soon as practicable after withdrawing approval from any inspector: reg 7(3) (as so amended and substituted). Lists maintained under reg 7 must set out any limitation placed on the approval or designation of the persons or bodies listed and must indicate the date on which each approval will expire: reg 7(4) (as so amended and substituted).

14 As to the meaning of 'local authority' see PARA 1 note 12.

15 Building Act 1984 s 49(5)(e). The appropriate national authority must supply to every local authority in whose area the Building (Approved Inspectors etc) Regulations 2010, SI 2010/2215, apply a copy of the first lists of approved inspectors and designated bodies prepared by it under reg 7, and it must notify every such local authority as soon as practicable of the withdrawal of any approval or designation and of any addition to the lists: reg 7(2) (as amended and substituted: note 13).

16 Building Act 1984 s 49(5)(f).

17 Building Act 1984 s 49(6)(a).

18 Building Act 1984 s 49(6)(b).

19 Ie the functions referred to in the Building Act 1984 s 47(1) (see PARA 74). As to the meaning of 'functions' see PARA 3 note 19.

20 A reference in the Building Act 1984 Pt II to the carrying out of work includes a reference to the making of a material change of use, as defined by and for the purposes of building regulations: s 58(2). As to the meaning of 'material change of use' see PARA 11. A builder purports to have carried out any part of the works when that part is complete, whether or not practical completion has been achieved: *Antino v Epping Forest District Council* (1991) 53 BLR 56, (1991) 155 JP 663, DC. The owner of a building who authorises a contractor to carry out building works on his behalf is a 'person carrying out building works' for the purposes of the building regulations; the meaning of that term is not restricted to the person who physically performs the work: *Blaenau Gwent Borough Council v Khan* (1993) 35 Con LR 65, DC.

21 Building Act 1984 s 49(7).

22 As to the meaning of 'plans' see PARA 9 note 8.

23 Ie a certificate under the Building Act 1984 s 50: see PARA 83.

24 Building Act 1984 s 49(8)(a). The text refers to a certificate under s 51: see PARA 84.

25 Building Act 1984 s 49(8)(b).

26 Building Act 1984 s 49(8).

73. Independence of approved inspectors.

An approved inspector must have no professional or financial interest in the work he supervises unless it is minor work[1]. 'Minor work' means:

(1)   the material alteration[2] or extension of a dwelling-house[3] which before the work is carried out[4] has two storeys[5] or less and which afterwards has no more than three storeys[6]; or

(2)   the provision, extension or material alteration of a controlled service or fitting[7] in or in connection with any building[8]; or

(3)   work consisting of the underpinning of a building[9].

A person is to be regarded as having a professional or financial interest in the work described in any notice or certificate given under the Building (Approved Inspectors etc) Regulations 2010[10] if:

(a)   he is or has been responsible for the design or construction of any of the work in any capacity[11];

(b)   he or any nominee of his is a member, officer or employee of a company or other body which has a professional or financial interest in the work[12]; or

(c)   he is a partner or is in the employment of a person who has a professional or financial interest in the work[13].

A person is to be treated as having a professional or financial interest in the work even if he has that interest only as trustee for the benefit of some other person[14], and in the case of married people or civil partners living together, the interest of one spouse or partner, if known to the other, is deemed to be also an interest of the other[15].

Involvement in the work as an approved inspector, entitlement to any fee paid for his function as an approved inspector, and potential liability to pay any sum if a claim is made under the insurance cover provided for the purposes of the Building Act 1984, are not to be regarded as constituting a professional or financial interest for these purposes[16].

1   Building (Approved Inspectors etc) Regulations 2010, SI 2010/2215, reg 9(1).
2   As to the meaning of 'material alteration' see PARA 10 note 6; definition applied by the Building (Approved Inspectors etc) Regulations 2010, SI 2010/2215, reg 2(1).
3   For these purposes, 'dwelling-house' does not include a flat or a building containing a flat (Building (Approved Inspectors etc) Regulations 2010, SI 2010/2215, reg 2(1)) and 'flat' means separate and self-contained premises constructed or adapted for use for residential purposes and forming part of a building from some other part of which it is divided horizontally (reg 2(1)). 'Building' means any permanent or temporary building but not any other kind of structure or erection, and a reference to a building includes a reference to part of a building: reg 2(1).
4   Any reference in the Building (Approved Inspectors etc) Regulations 2010, SI 2010/2215, to the carrying out of work includes a reference to the making of a material change of use: reg 2(3). As to the meaning of 'material change of use' see PARA 11; definition applied by reg 2(1).
5   For these purposes, a basement is not to be regarded as a storey: Building (Approved Inspectors etc) Regulations 2010, SI 2010/2215, reg 9(5).
6   Building (Approved Inspectors etc) Regulations 2010, SI 2010/2215, reg 9(5)(a).
7   For these purposes, 'controlled service or fitting' means a service or fitting in relation to which the Building Regulations 2010, SI 2010/2214, regs 4, 6, Sch 1 Pt G (hygiene), Pt H (drainage and waste disposal), Pt J (combustion appliances and fuel storage systems) or Pt L (conservation of fuel and power) imposes a requirement: Building (Approved Inspectors etc) Regulations 2010, SI 2010/2215, reg 2(1).
8   Building (Approved Inspectors etc) Regulations 2010, SI 2010/2215, reg 9(5)(b).
9   Building (Approved Inspectors etc) Regulations 2010, SI 2010/2215, reg 9(5)(c).
10   Ie the Building (Approved Inspectors etc) Regulations 2010, SI 2010/2215.
11   Building (Approved Inspectors etc) Regulations 2010, SI 2010/2215, reg 9(2)(a).
12   Building (Approved Inspectors etc) Regulations 2010, SI 2010/2215, reg 9(2)(b).
13   Building (Approved Inspectors etc) Regulations 2010, SI 2010/2215, reg 9(2)(c).
14   Building (Approved Inspectors etc) Regulations 2010, SI 2010/2215, reg 9(3)(a).
15   Building (Approved Inspectors etc) Regulations 2010, SI 2010/2215, reg 9(3)(b).
16   Building (Approved Inspectors etc) Regulations 2010, SI 2010/2215, reg 9(4).

B. SUPERVISION OF PLANS AND WORKS

(A) Initial Notices

74. Giving and acceptance of initial notice.

If:

(1)   a notice in the prescribed[1] form (an 'initial notice') is given jointly to a local authority[2] by a person intending to carry out work[3] and a person who is an approved inspector[4] in relation to that work[5];

(2)   the initial notice is accompanied by such plans[6] of the work as may be prescribed[7];

(3)   the initial notice is accompanied by such evidence as may be prescribed that an approved scheme applies, or the prescribed insurance cover has been or will be provided, in relation to the work[8]; and

(4)   the initial notice is accepted by the local authority[9],

then, so long as the initial notice continues in force[10], the approved inspector by whom the notice was given must undertake such functions[11] as may be prescribed with respect to the inspection of plans of the work to which the notice relates, the supervision of that work and the giving and receiving of certificates and other notices[12].

A local authority to whom an initial notice is given may not reject the notice[13] except on prescribed grounds[14], but must reject the notice if any of those prescribed grounds exists[15]. In a case where the work to which an initial notice relates is work of such a description that, if plans of it had been deposited with the local authority, the authority could, under any enactment[16], have imposed requirements as a condition of passing the plans[17], the local authority may impose the like requirements as a condition of accepting the initial notice[18]. Unless, within the prescribed period[19], the local authority to whom an initial notice is given gives notice of rejection, specifying the ground or grounds in question, to each of the persons by whom the initial notice was given, the authority is conclusively presumed to have accepted the initial notice and to have done so without imposing any such requirements[20].

A person aggrieved[21] by the local authority's rejection of an initial notice may appeal to a magistrates' court[22]. On such an appeal the court must, if it determines that the notice was properly rejected, confirm the rejection[23], and in any other case, give a direction to the local authority to accept the notice[24]. Where a person is aggrieved by such a determination, confirmation, direction or other decision of a magistrates' court, he may appeal to the Crown Court[25].

The appropriate national authority[26] may approve for these purposes[27] any scheme that appears to him to secure the provision of adequate insurance cover in relation to any work to which an initial notice relates and is work to which the scheme applies[28]. Building regulations may prescribe for these purposes the insurance cover that is to be provided in relation to any work to which an initial notice relates and is not work to which an approved scheme applies and may, in particular, prescribe the form and content of policies of insurance[29].

1   Ie prescribed by building regulations: see the Building Act 1984 s 126. An initial notice may be incorporated in a combined form together with a plans certificate, and references in s 47 to an initial notice or a plans certificate include a reference to the combined form: see s 50(4); and PARA 83. The local authority is required to keep a register of initial notices which is open to public inspection: see s 56; and PARA 98.

For the prescribed form of a notice which is not combined with a plans certificate see the Building (Approved Inspectors etc) Regulations 2010, SI 2010/2215, reg 10(1)(a), Sch 1 Form 1 (Sch 1 Forms 1, 4 substituted SI 2015/767; and SI 2018/558); and for the prescribed form of a notice which is combined with a plans certificate see the Building (Approved Inspectors etc) Regulations 2010, SI 2010/2215, reg 10(1)(b), Sch 1 Form 4. An initial notice must be accompanied by the plans and documents described in the relevant form prescribed by the Building (Approved Inspectors etc) Regulations 2010, SI 2010/2215, reg 10(1): reg 10(2). Where any regulation requires the use of a numbered form in Sch 1, a form substantially to the like effect may be used: reg 2(2). Any reference in the Building (Approved Inspectors etc) Regulations 2010, SI 2010/2215, to an initial notice, whether or not combined with a plans certificate, is in an appropriate case to be construed as a reference to that initial notice as amended by an amendment notice which has been accepted by a local authority: reg 2(4). As to amendment notices see PARA 76.

   The form prescribed for an initial notice may be such as to require either or both of the persons by whom the notice is to be given to furnish information relevant for the purposes of the Public Health Act 1936 Pt II (ss 33–90) or Pt IV (ss 124–141) or any provision of building regulations and the approved inspector by whom the notice is to be given to enter into undertakings with respect to his performance of any of the functions referred to in the Building Act 1984 s 47(1) (see the text and notes 2–12) (s 47(5)(b)).

   The provisions in the Public Health Act 1936 relating to building regulations were repealed by the Building Act 1984 s 133(2), Sch 7. As to the meaning of 'building regulations' see PARA 7.

2   As to the meaning of 'local authority' see PARA 1 note 12.

3   As to references to the carrying out of work see PARA 72 note 20. Subject to certain exceptions, the Building Act 1984 s 47 does not permit an initial notice to be submitted after the works have substantially commenced: see *Butler & Young Ltd v Bedford Borough Council* [2003] EWHC 1289 (Admin), [2003] All ER (D) 274 (May).

4   As to the meaning of 'approved inspector' see PARA 72. An approved inspector may make charges in respect of matters referred to in the Building Act 1984 s 47(1): see s 49(7); and PARA 72.

5   Building Act 1984 ss 47(1)(a), 58(1).

6   As to the meaning of 'plans' see PARA 9 note 8.

7   Building Act 1984 s 47(1)(b). See note 4.

8   Building Act 1984 s 47(1)(c).

9   Building Act 1984 s 47(1)(d).

10 Where an initial notice has continued in force for some period the local authority is entitled to require information to be furnished to it: see the Building Act 1984 s 56(5); and PARA 98. An initial notice: (1) comes into force when it is accepted by the local authority, either by notice given within the prescribed period to each of the persons by whom it was given or by virtue of s 47(3) (see the text and notes 19–20); and (2) subject to s 51(3) (see PARA 84) continues in force until it is cancelled by a notice under s 52 (see PARA 79), or the occurrence of, or the expiry of a prescribed period of time beginning on the date of, such event as may be prescribed: s 47(4). Building regulations may empower a local authority to extend (whether before or after its expiry) any such period of time as is referred to in head (2) above: s 47(4). As to the effect of an initial notice ceasing to be in force by virtue of s 47(4)(b)(i) or s 47(4)(b)(ii) see s 53; and PARA 81. As to events causing an initial notice to cease to be in force see PARA 80.

11 As to the meaning of 'functions' see PARA 3 note 19. An approved inspector by whom an initial notice has been given must, so long as the notice continues in force, take such steps, which may include the making of tests of building work and the taking of samples of material, as are reasonable to enable him to be satisfied within the limits of professional skill and care that the Building Regulations 2010, SI 2010/2214, reg 4 (requirements relating to building work) (see PARA 10), reg 6 (requirements relating to material change of use) (see PARA 11), reg 7 (materials and workmanship) (see PARA 10), reg 22 (requirements relating to a change to energy status) (see PARA 45), reg 23 (requirements relating to thermal elements) (see PARA 45), reg 25A (consideration of high-efficiency alternative systems for new buildings (see PARA 46), reg 26 (CO_2 emission rates for new buildings) (see PARA 46), reg 26A (fabric energy efficiency rates (see PARA 46, reg 28 (consequential improvements to energy performance) (see PARA 45), reg 36 (water efficiency of new dwellings) (see PARA 53), reg 38 (fire safety information) (see PARA 56), reg 39 (information about ventilation) (see PARA 10) and reg 40 (information about use of fuel and power) (see PARA 10), and in relation to Wales, reg 37A (provision of automatic fire suppression systems) (see PARA 58) are complied with, and that the requirements of reg 20 (self-certification schemes) (see PARA 10) and the Energy Performance of Buildings (England and Wales) Regulations 2012, SI 2012/3118, reg 7A (energy performance certificates on construction) (PARA 48, are complied with: Building (Approved Inspectors etc) Regulations 2010, SI 2010/2215, reg 8(1) (amended by SI 2012/3119, SI 2013/747; SI 2013/2730; SI 2014/110; SI 2014/579; SI 2016/285;

and SI 2016/611). In relation to Wales band in a case where any requirement of the Building Regulations 2010, SI 2010/2214, Sch 1 Pt L (requirement as to the conservation of fuel and power) (see PARA 10) is to be complied with by the insertion of insulating material into the cavity in a wall after that wall has been constructed, the approved inspector need not supervise the insertion of the insulating material but must state in the final certificate whether or not at the date of that certificate the material has been inserted: Building (Approved Inspectors etc) Regulations 2010, SI 2010/2215, reg 8(2) (revoked in relation to England by SI 2014/579; added in relation to Wales by SI 2018/558). As to the meaning of 'building work' see PARA 10; definition applied by reg 2(1). As to final certificates see PARA 84.

12 Building Act 1984 s 47(1) (amended by the Sustainable and Secure Buildings Act 2004 s 8(2); and SI 1996/1905). As to the form of certificates and notices see PARA 135. As to their service see PARA 137.
       As to supervision of works by local authorities see PARA 70. As to supervision by public bodies of their own work see PARA 88 et seq.
13 A person aggrieved by the rejection of an initial notice may appeal to a magistrates' court: see the Building Act 1984 s 55(1)(a): see the text to note 22.
14 As to the grounds which have been prescribed see the Building (Approved Inspectors etc) Regulations 2010, SI 2010/2215, reg 10(3), Sch 2.
15 Building Act 1984 s 47(2)(a), (b).
16 As to the meaning of 'enactment' see PARA 6 note 2.
17 As to the power of a local authority to impose conditions on passing plans under building regulations see the Building Act 1984 s 16(2)–(4); and PARA 33.
18 Building Act 1984 s 47(2).
19 The period within which a local authority may give notice of rejection of an initial notice is five days beginning with the day on which the notice is given: Building (Approved Inspectors etc) Regulations 2010, SI 2010/2215, reg 10(4). 'Day' means any period of 24 hours commencing at midnight and excludes any Saturday, Sunday, Bank holiday or public holiday: reg 2(1).
20 Building Act 1984 s 47(3). The requirements referred to in the text are those mentioned in s 47(2): see the text and notes 16–18.
21 As to persons aggrieved see JUDICIAL REVIEW vol 61 (2010) PARA 656.
22 Building Act 1984 s 55(1) (amended by the Courts Act 2003 s 109(1), (3), Sch 8 para 280, Sch 10). As to appeals generally see PARAS 139–140. See further CRIMINAL PROCEDURE vol 28 (2015) PARA 665 et seq; MAGISTRATES vol 71 (2013) PARA 697 et seq.
23 Building Act 1984 s 55(2)(a).
24 Building Act 1984 s 55(2)(b).
25 Building Act 1984 s 55(3).
26 Ie the Secretary of State or, where statutory functions have been transferred in relation to Wales, the Welsh Ministers: see PARA 5.
27 Ie for the purposes of the Building Act 1984 s 47.
28 Building Act 1984 s 47(6) (amended by SI 1996/1905).
29 Building Act 1984 s 47(7) (amended by SI 1996/1905).

75. Effect of initial notice.

So long as an initial notice continues in force[1], the function[2] of enforcing building regulations[3] that is conferred on a local authority[4] is not exercisable in relation to the work to which the notice relates, and accordingly a local authority may not give a notice to remove or alter work contravening building regulations[5] in relation to that work[6], and it may not institute proceedings[7] for a contravention[8] of building regulations that arises out of the carrying out of that work[9].

In relation to the removal or alteration of work contravening building regulations[10] and in relation to securing payment of the expenses of the execution of street works in private streets adjacent to new buildings under the advance payments code[11], special provision is made with respect to the effect of initial notices[12]. The giving of an initial notice accompanied by such plans as may be prescribed to accompany the initial notice[13] is to be treated as the deposit of plans[14], and plans accompanying an initial notice are to be treated as the deposited plans[15]. Acceptance or rejection of an initial notice is to be treated as the passing or, as the case may be, the rejection of plans[16], and the cancellation of an initial notice[17] is to be treated as a declaration[18] that the deposit of plans is of no effect[19].

1   As to initial notices (including their duration) see PARA 74.
2   As to the meaning of 'functions' see PARA 3 note 19.
3   As to the meaning of 'building regulations' see PARA 7.
4   Ie by the Building Act 1984 s 91(2): see PARA 70. As to the meaning of 'local authority' see PARA 1 note 12.
5   Ie under the Building Act 1984 s 36(1): see PARA 62.
6   Building Act 1984 s 48(1)(a) (amended by SI 1996/1905).
7   Ie under the Building Act 1984 s 35: see PARA 61.
8   As to the meaning of 'contravention' see PARA 12 note 10.
9   Building Act 1984 s 48(1)(b) (amended by SI 1996/1905). As to references to the carrying out of work see PARA 72 note 20.
10 Ie under the Building Act 1984 s 36(2) (see PARA 62), s 36(5) (see PARA 62) in so far as it relates to a notice under s 36(2) and to non-compliance with any such requirement as is referred to in s 36(2), and s 36(6) (see PARA 62) in so far as it relates to a contravention of the Building Act 1984: s 48(3)(a)–(c).
11 Ie under the Highways Act 1980 ss 219–225 (see HIGHWAYS, STREETS AND BRIDGES vol 55 (2012) PARA 180 et seq): Building Act 1984 s 48(3)(e).
12 See the Building Act 1984 s 48(2).
13 Ie such plans as are referred to in the Building Act 1984 s 47(1)(b) (see PARA 74). As to the meaning of 'plans' see PARA 9 note 8.
14 Building Act 1984 s 48(2)(a).
15 Building Act 1984 s 48(2)(b).
16 Building Act 1984 s 48(2)(c).
17 Ie under the Building Act 1984 s 52(2): see PARA 79.
18 Ie under the Building Act 1984 s 32: see PARA 42.
19 Building Act 1984 s 48(2)(d).

76. Variation of work to which initial notice relates.

Where it is proposed that the work to which an initial notice[1] relates should be varied[2], if:

(1)   a notice in the prescribed[3] form (an 'amendment notice')[4] is given to the local authority[5] by whom the initial notice was accepted, and is jointly given by the approved inspector[6] who gave the initial notice[7] and by the person shown in the amendment notice as the person intending to carry out the relevant work[8];

(2)   the amendment notice is accompanied by such plans[9] of the proposed variation as may be prescribed[10];

(3)   the amendment notice is accompanied by such evidence as may be prescribed that a scheme approved for the purposes of the giving and acceptance of an initial notice[11] applies, or the insurance cover prescribed for those purposes has been, or will be provided, in relation to the relevant work[12]; and

(4)   the amendment notice is accepted by the local authority giving notice of acceptance within the prescribed period to each of the persons by whom the amendment notice was given, or is deemed[13] to have been accepted by the local authority[14],

the work to which the initial notice relates must be treated as varied as proposed in the amendment notice[15]. A local authority to whom an amendment notice is given may not reject the notice except on prescribed grounds[16], but must reject the notice if any of the prescribed grounds exists[17].

Where the relevant work is of such a description that, if plans of it had been deposited with the local authority, the authority could, under any enactment[18], have imposed requirements as a condition of passing the plans, the local authority may impose the like requirements as a condition of accepting the amendment notice[19]. Unless, within the prescribed period, the local authority to whom an amendment notice is given gives notice of rejection[20], specifying the ground or grounds in question, to each of the persons by whom the notice was given, the authority is conclusively presumed to have accepted it and to have done so without imposing any such requirements[21].

A person aggrieved[22] by the local authority's rejection of an amendment notice may appeal to a magistrates' court[23]. On such an appeal the court must if it determines that the notice was properly rejected confirm the rejection[24], and in any other case, give a direction to the local authority to accept the notice[25]. Where a person is aggrieved by such a determination, confirmation, direction or other decision of a magistrates' court, he may appeal to the Crown Court[26].

1 As to initial notices see PARA 74.
2 Building Act 1984 s 51A(1) (s 51A added by SI 1996/1905).
3 Ie prescribed by building regulations: see the Building Act 1984 s 126.
4 The form prescribed for an amendment notice may be such as to require: (1) either or both of the persons by whom the notice is to be given to furnish information relevant for the purposes of the Public Health Act 1936 Pt II (ss 33–90) or Pt IV (ss 124–141) (see ENVIRONMENTAL QUALITY AND PUBLIC HEALTH) or any provision of building regulations; and (2) the approved inspector by whom the notice is to be given to enter into undertakings with respect to his performance of any of the functions referred to in the Building Act 1984 s 47(1) (see PARA 74): ss 47(5), 51A(6) (as added: see note 2). The provisions in the Public Health Act 1936 relating to building regulations were repealed by the Building Act 1984 s 133(2), Sch 7. For the prescribed form of an amendment notice see the Building (Approved Inspectors etc) Regulations 2010, SI 2010/2215, reg 11(1), Sch 1 Form 2 (substituted by SI 2015/767; and SI 2018/558).
5 As to the meaning of 'local authority' see PARA 1 note 12.
6 As to the meaning of 'approved inspector' see PARA 72.
7 As to references to an initial notice given by an approved inspector see PARA 83 note 11.
8 Building Act 1984 s 51A(2)(a) (as added: see note 2), s 58(1) (amended by SI 1996/1905). For these purposes, references to the relevant work are to the work to which the initial notice, as proposed to be varied, relates: Building Act 1984 s 51A(7) (as so added).
9 As to the meaning of 'plans' see PARA 9 note 8.
10 Building Act 1984 s 51A(2)(b) (as added: see note 2). An amendment notice must be accompanied by the plans and documents described in the Building (Approved Inspectors etc) Regulations 2010, SI 2010/2215, Sch 1 Form 2: reg 11(2).
11 Ie for the purposes of the Building Act 1984 s 47: see PARA 74.
12 Building Act 1984 s 51A(2)(c) (as added: see note 2).
13 Ie by virtue of the Building Act 1984 s 51A(5): see the text to notes 20–21.
14 Building Act 1984 s 51A(2)(d) (as added: see note 2).
15 Building Act 1984 s 51A(2) (as added: see note 2).
16 Building Act 1984 s 51A(3)(a) (as added: see note 2). The prescribed grounds are set out in the Building (Approved Inspectors etc) Regulations 2010, SI 2010/2215, reg 11(3), Sch 2 paras 1–11 (amended by SI 2012/3119; SI 2014/58; SI 2015/767; and SI 2018/558).
17 Building Act 1984 s 51A(3)(b) (as added: see note 2).
18 As to the meaning of 'enactment' see PARA 6 note 2.
19 Building Act 1984 s 51A(4) (as added: see note 2).
20 The period within which a local authority may give notice of rejection of an amendment notice is five days beginning with the day on which the notice is given: Building (Approved Inspectors etc) Regulations 2010, SI 2010/2215, reg 11(4).
21 Building Act 1984 s 51A(5) (as added: see note 2). The requirements referred to in the text are those mentioned in s 51A(4): see the text and notes 18–19. Section 47(5) (form prescribed for an initial notice) (see PARA 74) applies in relation to the form prescribed for an amendment notice as it applies in relation to the form prescribed for an initial notice: s 51A(6) (as so added).
22 As to persons aggrieved see JUDICIAL REVIEW vol 61 (2010) PARA 656.
23 Building Act 1984 s 55(1) (amended by SI 1996/1905). As to appeals generally see PARAS 139–140. See further CRIMINAL PROCEDURE vol 28 (2015) PARA 665 et seq; MAGISTRATES vol 71 (2013) PARA 697 et seq.

24 Building Act 1984 s 55(2)(a).
25 Building Act 1984 s 55(2)(b).
26 Building Act 1984 s 55(3).

77. Effect of amendment notice.

In relation to the removal or alteration of work contravening building regulations[1] and in relation to securing payment of the expenses of the execution of street works in private streets adjacent to new buildings under the advance payments code[2], special provision is made with respect to the effect of amendment notices[3]. The giving of an amendment notice accompanied by the prescribed plans of the proposed variation[4] is to be treated as the deposit of plans[5], and the acceptance or rejection of an amendment notice is to be treated as the passing, or, as the case may be, the rejection of plans[6]. Where an initial notice[7] is varied by an amendment notice, the deposited plans are to be treated as including the plans accompanying the amendment notice[8], and as excluding such of the plans previously treated as the deposited plans as are superseded by the plans accompanying the amendment notice[9]. Where an initial notice has been varied by an amendment notice, the cancellation of the initial notice[10] is to be treated as a declaration[11] that the deposit of plans constituted by the giving of the amendment notice is of no effect[12].

1 Ie under the Building Act 1984 s 36(2) (see PARA 62), s 36(5) (see PARA 62) in so far as it relates to a notice under s 36(2) and to non-compliance with any such requirement as is referred to in s 36(2), and s 36(6) (see PARA 62) in so far as it relates to a contravention of the Building Act 1984: s 48(3)(a)–(c). As to the meaning of 'building regulations' see PARA 7.
2 Ie under the Highways Act 1980 ss 219–225 (see HIGHWAYS, STREETS AND BRIDGES vol 55 (2012) PARA 180 et seq): Building Act 1984 s 48(3)(e).
3 See the Building Act 1984 ss 48(3), 51B(1) (s 51B added by SI 1996/1905). As to amendment notices see PARA 76.
4 Ie such plans as are referred to in the Building Act 1984 s 51A(2)(b) (see PARA 76). As to the meaning of 'plans' see PARA 9 note 8.
5 Building Act 1984 s 51B(1)(a) (as added: see note 3).
6 Building Act 1984 s 51B(1)(b) (as added: see note 3).
7 As to initial notices see PARA 74.
8 Building Act 1984 s 51B(1)(c)(i) (as added: see note 3).
9 Building Act 1984 s 51B(1)(c)(ii) (as added: see note 3).
10 Ie under the Building Act 1984 s 52(5): see PARA 79.
11 Ie under the Building Act 1984 s 32: see PARA 42.
12 Building Act 1984 s 51B(1)(d) (as added: see note 3).

78. Change of person intending to carry out work.

Where it is proposed that the work to which an initial notice[1] relates should be carried out by a different person[2], if the approved inspector[3] who gave the initial notice[4], and the person who now proposes to carry out the work to which the initial notice relates, jointly give written notice of the proposal to the local authority[5] by whom the initial notice was accepted, the initial notice is to be treated as showing as the person intending to carry out the work to which it relates the person mentioned in the notice[6].

1 As to initial notices see PARA 74.
2 Building Act 1984 s 51C(1) (s 51C added by SI 1996/1905).
3 As to the meaning of 'approved inspector' see PARA 72.
4 As to references to an initial notice given by an approved inspector see PARA 83 note 11.
5 As to the meaning of 'local authority' see PARA 1 note 12.
6 Building Act 1984 s 51C(2) (as added: see note 2).

(B)   Cessation of Effect of Initial Notice

79.   Cancellation of initial notice.

If, at a time when an initial notice[1] is in force, the approved inspector[2]:

(1)   becomes or expects to become unable to carry out, or to continue to carry out, his functions[3] with respect to any of the work to which the initial notice relates[4];

(2)   is of the opinion that any of the work is being so carried out that he is unable adequately to carry out his functions with respect to it[5]; or

(3)   is of the opinion that there is a contravention[6] of any provision of building regulations[7] with respect to any of that work, and: (a) the approved inspector has, in accordance with building regulations, given notice of the contravention to the person carrying out the work[8] or intending to carry out the work[9]; and (b) within the prescribed[10] period the prescribed steps are not taken by the person who, in accordance with building regulations, is required to take them[11],

the approved inspector must cancel the initial notice by notice in the prescribed form given to the local authority[12] concerned and to the person carrying out or intending to carry out the work[13].

If, at a time when an initial notice is in force, it appears to the person carrying out or intending to carry out the work to which the notice relates that the approved inspector is no longer willing or able to carry out his functions with respect to any of that work, he must cancel the initial notice by notice in the prescribed form given to the local authority concerned and, if it is practicable to do so, to the approved inspector[14]. If a person fails without reasonable excuse to give to a local authority such a notice[15], he is liable on summary conviction to a fine[16].

If, at a time when an initial notice is in force, it appears to the local authority by whom the initial notice was accepted that the work to which the initial notice relates has not been commenced within the period of three years beginning on the date on which the initial notice was accepted, the authority may cancel the initial notice by notice in the prescribed form[17] given to the approved inspector by whom the initial notice was given[18], and to the person shown in the initial notice as the person intending to carry out the work[19].

Such notices[20] have the effect of cancelling the initial notice to which they relate with effect from the day on which the notice is given[21].

1   As to initial notices see PARA 74.
2   As to the meaning of 'approved inspector' see PARA 72.
3   As to the meaning of 'functions' see PARA 3 note 19. As to the functions of approved inspectors see PARA 72.
4   Building Act 1984 s 52(1)(a) (amended by SI 1996/1905).
5   Building Act 1984 s 52(1)(b).
6   As to the meaning of 'contravention' see PARA 12 note 10.
7   As to the meaning of 'building regulations' see PARA 7.
8   As to the meaning of 'carrying out of work' see PARA 72 note 20.
9   Building Act 1984 s 52(1)(c), (2)(a) (amended by the Sustainable and Secure Buildings Act 2004 s 8(3)). Where an approved inspector is of the opinion that any of the work described in an initial notice which has been carried out contravenes any provision of building regulations, he may give notice in writing to the person carrying out the work specifying: (1) the requirement of building regulations which in his opinion has not been complied with; and (2) the location of the work which contravenes that requirement: Building (Approved Inspectors etc) Regulations 2010, SI 2010/2215, reg 18(1). A notice of contravention given in accordance with reg 18(1) must inform the person carrying out the work that if within the prescribed period he has neither pulled down nor removed the work nor effected such alterations in it as may be necessary to make it comply

with building regulations, the approved inspector will cancel the initial notice: reg 18(2). The period within which the person carrying out the work is to remedy the contravention as described in reg 18(2) is three months beginning with the day on which the notice is given: reg 18(3). As to initial notices see PARA 74 et seq. As to the meaning of 'day' see PARA 74 note 19.

10 Ie prescribed by building regulations: see the Building Act 1984 s 126.

11 Building Act 1984 s 52(1)(c), (2)(b) (amended by the Sustainable and Secure Buildings Act 2004 s 8(3)).

12 As to the meaning of 'local authority' see PARA 1 note 12.

13 Building Act 1984 s 52(1). For the form of notice to be given by an approved inspector to cancel an initial notice in accordance with the Building Act 1984 s 52(1) in circumstances referred to in s 52(2) (see head (2)(a) and head (2)(b) in the text) see the Building (Approved Inspectors etc) Regulations 2010, SI 2010/2215, reg 18(4), Sch 1 Form 6 (substituted by SI 2015/767; and SI 2018/558). Where notice of a contravention has been given under the Building Act 1984 s 52(2) and no further initial notice relating to the work has been accepted, that notice must specify the contravention: Building (Approved Inspectors etc) Regulations 2010, SI 2010/2215, reg 18(4).

The owner of a building who authorises a contractor to carry out building works on his behalf is a 'person carrying out building works' for the purposes of the building regulations; the meaning of that term is not restricted to the person who physically performs the work: *Blaenau Gwent Borough Council v Khan* (1993) 35 Con LR 65, DC.

14 Building Act 1984 s 52(3) (amended by SI 1996/1905). For the form of notice to be given by a person carrying out or intending to carry out work to cancel an initial notice in accordance with the Building Act 1984 s 52(3) see the Building (Approved Inspectors etc) Regulations 2010, SI 2010/2215, reg 18(5), Sch 1 Form 7 (substituted by SI 2015/767; and SI 2018/558).

15 Ie the notice required by the Building Act 1984 s 52(3): see the text to note 14.

16 Building Act 1984 s 52(4). The fine imposed is one not exceeding level 5 on the standard scale: s 52(4). As to the standard scale see SENTENCING vol 92 (2015) PARA 176. Civil sanctions may be imposed in respect of offences under the Building Act 1984 by virtue of the powers under the Regulatory Enforcement and Sanctions Act 2008 Pt 3 (ss 36–71): see ss 36, 38(2), Sch 6; and CONSTITUTIONAL AND ADMINISTRATIVE LAW vol 20 (2014) PARA 331 et seq.

17 For the form of notice to be given by the local authority to cancel an initial notice in accordance with the Building Act 1984 s 52(5) (see the text to notes 18–19) see the Building (Approved Inspectors etc) Regulations 2010, SI 2010/2215, reg 18(6), Sch 1 Form 8.

18 Building Act 1984 s 52(5)(a).

19 Building Act 1984 s 52(5)(b).

20 Ie notices under the Building Act 1984 s 52(1) (see the text to notes 1–13), s 52(3) (see the text and note 14), s 52(5) (see the text to notes 17–19): see s 52(6).

21 Building Act 1984 s 52(6).

80. Events causing initial notice to cease to be in force.

Where a final certificate[1] given in respect of work described in an initial notice[2] is rejected, the initial notice ceases to be in force in relation to the work described in the final certificate on the expiry of a period of four weeks beginning with the date on which notice of rejection is given[3].

Where work described in an initial notice includes the erection, extension or material alteration[4] of a building[5], and the building or, as the case may be, the extension or any part of the building which has been materially altered is occupied[6], and no final certificate is given[7], the initial notice ceases to be in force in relation to the building, extension or part of a building which is occupied:

(1)   if the building is a relevant building[8] (except where it contains only flats and common parts for those flats) on the expiry of a period of four weeks beginning with the date of occupation[9]; and

(2)   in any other case, on the expiry of a period of eight weeks beginning with the date of occupation[10].

Where work described in an initial notice involves a material change of use[11] of a building, and no final certificate is given, and that change of use takes place, the initial notice ceases to be in force in relation to that change of use on the expiry of a period of eight weeks beginning with the date on which the change of use takes place[12].

In any other case where no final certificate is given, an initial notice ceases to be in force on the expiry of a period of eight weeks beginning with the date on which the work described in the initial notice is substantially completed[13].

A local authority may extend any period referred to above either before or after its expiry[14].

1   As to final certificates see PARA 84.
2   As to initial notices see PARA 74 et seq.
3   Building (Approved Inspectors etc) Regulations 2010, SI 2010/2215, reg 17(1).
4   As to the meaning of 'material alteration' see PARA 10 note 6; definition applied by the Building (Approved Inspectors etc) Regulations 2010, SI 2010/2215, reg 2(1).
5   As to the meaning of 'building' see PARA 73 note 3.
6   Building (Approved Inspectors etc) Regulations 2010, SI 2010/2215, reg 17(2)(a). An initial notice will not cease to be in force by virtue of reg 17(2) because part of a building or extension is occupied if a final certificate has been accepted in respect of that part: reg 17(6).
7   Building (Approved Inspectors etc) Regulations 2010, SI 2010/2215, reg 17(2)(b). See note 6.
8   A 'relevant building' is a building or any part of it to which the Regulatory Reform (Fire Safety) Order 2005, SI 2005/1541, applies, or will apply after the completion of building work: Building (Approved Inspectors etc) Regulations 2010, SI 2010/2215, reg 12(6)(a).
9   Building (Approved Inspectors etc) Regulations 2010, SI 2010/2215, reg 17(3)(a). An initial notice will not cease to be in force by virtue of reg 17(3) because part of a building or extension is occupied if a final certificate has been accepted in respect of that part: reg 17(6).
10 Building (Approved Inspectors etc) Regulations 2010, SI 2010/2215, reg 17(3)(b). See note 9.
11 As to the meaning of 'material change of use' see PARA 11; definition applied by the Building (Approved Inspectors etc) Regulations 2010, SI 2010/2215, reg 2(1).
12 Building (Approved Inspectors etc) Regulations 2010, SI 2010/2215, reg 17(4).
13 Building (Approved Inspectors etc) Regulations 2010, SI 2010/2215, reg 17(5).
14 Building (Approved Inspectors etc) Regulations 2010, SI 2010/2215, reg 17(7).

81. Effect of initial notice ceasing to be in force.

Where an initial notice[1] ceases[2] to be in force[3], building regulations[4] may provide that, if:

(1)   a plans certificate[5] was given before the day on which the initial notice ceased to be in force[6];

(2)   that certificate was accepted by the local authority[7], before, on or after that day[8]; and

(3)   before that day, that acceptance was not rescinded by a notice[9],

then, with respect to the work specified in the certificate, such of the functions of enforcing building regulations[10] of a local authority[11] as may be prescribed[12] are not exercisable or are exercisable only in prescribed circumstances[13].

If, before the day on which the initial notice ceased to be in force, a final certificate[14] was given in respect of part of the work to which the initial notice relates, and was accepted by the local authority (before, on or after that day), then, despite the fact that the initial notice has ceased to be in force, a local authority's functions in relation to enforcing building regulations are not exercisable in relation to that part of the work[15].

For the purpose of enabling the local authority to perform its functions in relation to enforcing building regulations in relation to any part of the work not specified in a plans certificate or final certificate, as the case may be, building regulations may require the local authority to be provided with plans that relate not only to that part but also to the part to which the certificate in question relates[16].

The fact that an initial notice has ceased to be in force does not affect the right to give a new initial notice relating to any of the work to which the original notice related and in respect of which no final certificate has been given and accepted[17].

1   As to initial notices see PARA 74 et seq.
2   Ie by virtue of the Building Act 1984 s 47(4)(b)(i) or s 47(4)(b)(ii): see PARA 74.
3   Building Act 1984 s 53(1). In any case where s 53 applies, the reference in s 36(4) (period within which a notice under s 36 may be given) (see PARA 62) to the date of the completion of the work in question has effect, in relation to a notice under s 36(1) (notice to pull down or alter work which contravenes building regulations) (see PARA 62), as if it were a reference to the date on which the initial notice ceased to be in force: s 53(5).
4   As to the meaning of 'building regulations' see PARA 7.
5   As to the meaning of 'plans certificate' see PARA 83. As to the meaning of 'plans' see PARA 9 note 8.
6   Building Act 1984 s 53(2)(a).
7   As to the meaning of 'local authority' see PARA 1 note 12.
8   Building Act 1984 s 53(2)(b).
9   Building Act 1984 s 53(2)(c). The text refers to a notice under s 50(8): see PARA 83.
10 As to the meaning of 'functions' see PARA 3 note 19.
11 Ie referred to in the Building Act 1984 s 48(1): see PARA 75.
12 Ie prescribed by building regulations: see the Building Act 1984 s 126.
13 Building Act 1984 s 53(2). As to local authority powers in relation to partly completed work see PARA 82.
    Subject to any provision of building regulations made by virtue of s 53(2), if, before the initial notice ceased to be in force, an offence under s 35 (penalty for contravention of building regulations) (see PARA 61) was committed with respect to any of the work to which that notice relates, proceedings for that offence may be commenced by the local authority at any time within six months beginning with the day on which the functions of the local authority referred to in s 48(1) (see PARA 75) became exercisable with respect to the provision of building regulations to which the offence relates: s 53(6). This is without prejudice to any ability which, after that function has become exercisable, the local authority may have under s 35A (see PARA 61) to commence proceedings for the offence after the end of that period of six months: s 53(6A) (added by the Climate Change and Sustainable Energy Act 2006 s 13(2)).
14 As to final certificates see PARA 84.
15 See the Building Act 1984 ss 51(3), 53(3) (amended by SI 1996/1905).
16 Building Act 1984 s 53(4) (which is expressed to be notwithstanding anything in s 53(2), (3) (see the text and notes 4–15)).
17 Building Act 1984 s 53(7) (amended by SI 1996/1905). However, where a plans certificate has been given in respect of any of that work, the conditions in the Building Act 1984 s 53(2)(a)–(c) (see heads (1)–(3) in the text) are fulfilled with respect to that certificate, and such a new initial notice is given and accepted, s 50(1) (giving of plans certificate) (see PARA 83) does not apply in relation to so much of the work to which the new initial notice relates as is work specified in the plans certificate: see s 53(7).

82. Local authority powers in relation to partly completed work.

Where:

(1)   any part of the work described in an initial notice[1] has been carried out[2]

(2)   the initial notice has ceased to be in force[3], or has been cancelled[4] by notice[5]; and

(3)   no other initial notice relating to that part of the work has been accepted[6],

the owner must[7]:

(a)   on being given reasonable notice by the local authority, provide it with:

(i)   sufficient plans of the work carried out, in respect of which no final certificate[8] has been given, to show whether any part of that work would, if carried out in accordance with the plans, contravene any provision of the Building Regulations 2010[9]; and

(ii)   where a plans certificate[10] was given and not rejected in respect of any such part of the work, a copy of the plans to which it relates[11]; and

(b)   comply with any notice in writing from the local authority requiring him within a reasonable time to cut into, lay open or pull down so much of the work as prevents the local authority from ascertaining whether any work in relation to which there is no final certificate contravenes any requirement in the Building Regulations 2010[12].

Where heads (1) to (3) above apply and work in relation to a building[13] has been begun but not completed, a person who intends to carry out further work in relation to the partly completed work must give the local authority sufficient plans to show that the intended work will not contravene any requirement in the Building Regulations 2010[14], including such plans of any part of the work already carried out as may be necessary to show that the intended work can be carried out without contravening any such requirement[15].

1   As to initial notices see PARA 74 et seq.
2   Building (Approved Inspectors etc) Regulations 2010, SI 2010/2215, reg 19(1)(a). As to references to the carrying out of work see PARA 73 note 4.
3   Ie by reason of the Building (Approved Inspectors etc) Regulations 2010, SI 2010/2215, reg 17: see PARA 80.
4   Ie under the Building Act 1984 s 52: see PARA 79.
5   Building (Approved Inspectors etc) Regulations 2010, SI 2010/2215, reg 19(1)(b).
6   Building (Approved Inspectors etc) Regulations 2010, SI 2010/2215, reg 19(1)(c).
7   As to the penalty for contravention of the Building (Approved Inspectors etc) Regulations 2010, SI 2010/2215, reg 19 see PARA 61.
8   As to final certificates see PARA 84.
9   Building (Approved Inspectors etc) Regulations 2010, SI 2010/2215, reg 19(2)(a)(i). The text refers to the Building Regulations 2010, SI 2010/2214.
10 As to plans certificates see PARA 83.
11 Building (Approved Inspectors etc) Regulations 2010, SI 2010/2215, reg 19(2)(a)(ii).
12 Building (Approved Inspectors etc) Regulations 2010, SI 2010/2215, reg 19(2)(b). See note 9.
13 As to the meaning of 'building' see PARA 73 note 3.
14 See note 9.
15 Building (Approved Inspectors etc) Regulations 2010, SI 2010/2215, reg 19(3). Plans given to a local authority in accordance with reg 19(3) are not to be regarded as plans deposited in accordance with building regulations: reg 19(4).

(C)   Plans Certificates

83.   Plans certificates.

Where an approved inspector[1]:

(1)   has inspected plans[2] of the work to which an initial notice[3] given by him[4] relates[5];

(2)   is satisfied that the plans neither are defective nor show that work carried out[6] in accordance with them would contravene[7] any provision of building regulations[8]; and

(3)   has complied with any prescribed[9] requirements as to consultation or otherwise[10],

he must, if requested to do so by the person intending to carry out the work, give a certificate in the prescribed form[11] (referred to as a 'plans certificate') to the local authority[12] and to that person[13]. If any question arises between an approved inspector and a person who proposes to carry out any work whether plans of the work are in conformity with building regulations, that person may refer the question to the appropriate national authority[14] for determination[15]. Such an application for a reference must be accompanied by such fee as may be prescribed[16]. A plans certificate may relate either to the whole or to part only of the work to which the initial notice concerned relates[17], and does not have effect unless it is accepted by the local authority to whom it is given[18].

A local authority to whom a plans certificate is given may not reject the certificate except on prescribed grounds[19], but must reject the certificate if any of the prescribed grounds exists[20]. Unless, within the prescribed period, the local authority to whom a plans certificate is given gives notice of rejection[21], specifying the ground or grounds in question, to the approved inspector by whom the certificate was given, and the other person to whom the approved inspector gave the certificate, the authority is conclusively presumed to have accepted the certificate[22].

A person aggrieved[23] by the local authority's rejection of a plans certificate may appeal to a magistrates' court[24]. On such an appeal the court must if it determines that the notice was properly rejected confirm the rejection[25], and in any other case, give a direction to the local authority to accept the notice[26]. Where a person is aggrieved by such a determination, confirmation, direction or other decision of a magistrates' court, he may appeal to the Crown Court[27].

If it appears to a local authority by whom a plans certificate has been accepted that the work to which the certificate relates has not been commenced within the period of three years beginning on the date on which the certificate was accepted, the authority may rescind its acceptance of the certificate by notice, specifying the ground or grounds in question, given to the approved inspector by whom the certificate was given[28], and to the person shown in the initial notice concerned as the person intending to carry out the work[29].

If an initial notice ceases to be in force[30] and the conditions[31] as to plans certificate given, accepted and not rescinded are satisfied, the local authority may not give a notice[32] for the removal or alteration of work which contravenes building regulations, or institute proceedings[33] for a contravention of building regulations in relation to any work described in the certificate which has been carried out in accordance with the plans to which the certificate relates[34].

1   As to the meaning of 'approved inspector' see PARA 72.
2   As to the meaning of 'plans' see PARA 9 note 8.
3   As to initial notices see PARA 74 et seq.
4   A reference in the Building Act 1984 Pt II (ss 47–58) to an initial notice given by an approved inspector is a reference to a notice given by him jointly with another person as mentioned in s 47(1)(a) (see PARA 74): s 58(3).
5   Building Act 1984 s 50(1)(a) (amended by SI 1996/1905).
6   As to references to the carrying out of work see PARA 72 note 20.
7   As to the meaning of 'contravene' see PARA 12 note 10.
8   Building Act 1984 s 50(1)(b). As to the meaning of 'building regulations' see PARA 7.
9   Ie prescribed by building regulations: see the Building Act 1984 s 126.
10 Building Act 1984 s 50(1)(c). As to the prescribed requirements as to consultation see PARAS 85–86.
11 Building regulations may authorise the giving of an initial notice combined with a certificate under the Building Act 1984 s 50(1), and may prescribe a single form for such a combined notice and certificate: s 50(4). Where such a prescribed form is used a reference in Pt II to an initial notice or to a plans certificate includes a reference to that form: s 50(4)(a). However, should the form cease to be in force as an initial notice by virtue of s 47(4) (see PARA 74), nothing in s 47(4) affects the continuing validity of the form as a plans certificate: s 50(4)(b). For the prescribed form of a plans certificate which is not combined with an initial notice see the Building (Approved Inspectors etc) Regulations 2010, SI 2010/2215, reg 14(1)(a), Sch 1 Form 3 (Sch 1 Forms 3, 4 substituted by SI 2015/767; and SI 2018/558); and for the prescribed form of a plans certificate which is

combined with an initial notice see the Building (Approved Inspectors etc) Regulations 2010, SI 2010/2215, reg 14(1)(b), Sch 1 Form 4 (as so substituted).

12 As to the meaning of 'local authority' see PARA 1 note 12.

13 Building Act 1984 ss 50(1), 58(1). The approved inspector may not delegate his power to give a certificate under s 50: see s 49(8)(a); and PARA 72. See *Butler & Young Ltd v Bedford Borough Council* [2003] EWHC 1289 (Admin), [2003] All ER (D) 274 (May) (where a valid initial notice had not been served, the local authority was entitled to refuse to issue a plans certificate).

14 Ie the Secretary of State or, where statutory functions have been transferred in relation to Wales, the Welsh Ministers: see PARA 5.

15 Building Act 1984 s 50(2).

16 Building Act 1984 s 50(3).

17 Building Act 1984 s 50(5)(a) (amended by SI 1996/1905).

18 Building Act 1984 s 50(5)(b). A local authority must keep a register of plans certificates which must be available for public inspection: see PARA 98.

19 Building Act 1984 s 50(6)(a). As to the grounds which have been prescribed see the Building (Approved Inspectors etc) Regulations 2010, SI 2010/2215, reg 14(2), (3), Schs 2, 3 (amended by SI 2012/3119; SI 2014/58; SI 2015/767; and SI 2018/558).

20 Building Act 1984 s 50(6)(b).

21 The period within which a local authority may give notice of rejection of a plans certificate, whether or not combined with an initial notice, is five days beginning on the day on which the certificate is given: Building (Approved Inspectors etc) Regulations 2010, SI 2010/2215, reg 14(4).

22 Building Act 1984 s 50(7).

23 As to persons aggrieved see JUDICIAL REVIEW vol 61 (2010) PARA 656.

24 Building Act 1984 s 55(1). As to appeals generally see PARAS 139–140. See further CRIMINAL PROCEDURE vol 28 (2015) PARA 665 et seq; MAGISTRATES vol 71 (2013) PARA 697 et seq.

25 Building Act 1984 s 55(2)(a).

26 Building Act 1984 s 55(2)(b).

27 Building Act 1984 s 55(3).

28 Building Act 1984 s 50(8)(a).

29 Building Act 1984 s 50(8)(b).

30 Ie as described in the Building Act 1984 s 47(4)(b) (cancellation etc of initial notice): see PARA 74.

31 Ie in the Building Act 1984 s 53(2): see PARA 81.

32 Ie under the Building Act 1984 s 36(1): see PARA 62.

33 Ie under the Building Act 1984 s 35: see PARA 61.

34 Building (Approved Inspectors etc) Regulations 2010, SI 2010/2215, reg 15.

(D) Final Certificates

84. Final certificates.

Where an approved inspector[1] is satisfied that any work to which an initial notice[2] given by him[3] relates has been completed, he must give to the local authority[4] by whom the initial notice was accepted such certificate with respect to the completion of the work and the discharge of his functions[5] as may be prescribed[6] (a 'final certificate')[7]. A final certificate may relate either to the whole or to part only of the work to which the initial notice concerned relates[8], and does not have effect unless it is accepted by the local authority to whom it is given[9]. A local authority to whom a final certificate is given may not reject the certificate except on prescribed grounds[10], but must reject the certificate if any of the prescribed grounds exists[11]. Unless, within the prescribed period, the local authority to whom a final certificate is given gives notice of rejection[12], specifying the ground or grounds in question, to the approved inspector by whom the certificate was given, and the other person to whom the approved inspector gave the certificate, the authority is conclusively presumed to have accepted the certificate[13].

A person aggrieved[14] by the local authority's rejection of a final certificate may appeal to a magistrates' court[15]. On such an appeal the court must if it determines that the notice was properly rejected confirm the rejection[16], and in any other case, give a direction to the local authority to accept the notice[17]. Where a person is aggrieved by such a determination, confirmation, direction or other decision of a magistrates' court, he may appeal to the Crown Court[18].

Where a final certificate has been given with respect to any of the work to which an initial notice relates, and has been accepted by the local authority concerned, the initial notice ceases to apply to that work[19].

1   As to the meaning of 'approved inspector' see PARA 72.
2   As to initial notices see PARA 74 et seq.
3   A reference in the Building Act 1984 Pt II (ss 47–58) to an initial notice given by an approved inspector is a reference to a notice given by him jointly with another person as mentioned in s 47(1)(a) (see PARA 74): s 58(3).
4   As to the meaning of 'local authority' see PARA 1 note 12.
5   As to the meaning of 'functions' see PARA 3 note 19.
6   Ie prescribed by building regulations: see the Building Act 1984 s 126.
7   Building Act 1984 s 51(1) (substituted by SI 1996/1905), Building Act 1984 s 58(1). For the prescribed form of a final certificate see the Building (Approved Inspectors etc) Regulations 2010, SI 2010/2215, reg 16(1), Sch 1 Form 5 (substituted by SI 2015/767; and SI 2018/558).
8   Building Act 1984 ss 50(5)(a), 51(2) (s 50(5)(a) amended by SI 1996/1905).
9   Building Act 1984 ss 50(5)(b), 51(2). A local authority must keep a register of final certificates which is available for public inspection: see PARA 98.
10 Building Act 1984 ss 50(6)(a), 51(2). As to the grounds which have been prescribed see the Building (Approved Inspectors etc) Regulations 2010, SI 2010/2215, reg 16(1), Sch 4 (Sch 4 amended by SI 2012/3119; SI 2014/58; SI 2015/767; and SI 2018/558).
11 Building Act 1984 ss 50(6)(b), 51(2).
12 The period within which a local authority may give notice of rejection of a final certificate is ten days beginning with the day on which the certificate is given: Building (Approved Inspectors etc) Regulations 2010, SI 2010/2215, reg 16(2). A final certificate given by an approved inspector to a local authority in accordance with Building (Approved Inspectors etc) Regulations 2010, SI 2010/2215 is evidence (but not conclusive evidence) that the requirements specified in the certificate have been complied with: reg 16(3) (added in relation to England by SI 2012/3119; and in relation to Wales by SI 2013/747).
13 Building Act 1984 ss 50(7), 51(2).
14 As to persons aggrieved see JUDICIAL REVIEW vol 61 (2010) PARA 656.
15 Building Act 1984 s 55(1). As to appeals generally see PARAS 139–140. See further CRIMINAL PROCEDURE vol 28 (2015) PARA 665 et seq; MAGISTRATES vol 71 (2013) PARA 697 et seq.
16 Building Act 1984 s 55(2)(a).
17 Building Act 1984 s 55(2)(b).
18 Building Act 1984 s 55(3).
19 Building Act 1984 s 51(3) (amended by SI 1996/1905). However, the provision which prohibits a local authority from exercising its functions of enforcing building regulations where an initial notice is in force (ie the Building Act 1984 s 48(1) (see PARA 75)) continues by virtue of s 51(3) to apply in relation to that work as if the initial notice continued in force in relation to it: s 51(3).

(E)   Consultation

85. Approved inspector's consultation with the fire and rescue authority.
Where an initial notice[1] is to be given or has been given in relation to the erection, extension or material alteration[2] of a relevant building[3] or in relation to building work in connection with a relevant change of use[4] of a building and requirements as to fire safety are imposed[5] in relation to the work[6], the approved inspector must consult the fire and rescue authority[7]:

(1)   before or as soon as practicable after giving an initial notice in relation to the work[8];

(2)   before or as soon as practicable after giving a relevant amendment notice[9] in relation to the work[10];

(3)   before giving a plans certificate[11], whether or not combined with an initial notice[12]; and

(4)   before giving a final certificate[13].

Where an approved inspector is required to consult the fire and rescue authority in this way, he must give to the fire and rescue authority:

(a)   in a case where he is consulting it in connection with an initial notice or an amendment notice, sufficient plans to show whether the work would, if carried out in accordance with those plans, comply with the applicable requirements[14] as to fire safety[15]; and

(b)   in a case where he is consulting it in connection with the giving of a plans certificate, a copy of the plans in relation to which he intends to give the certificate[16].

Where an approved inspector is required to consult the fire and rescue authority he must have regard to any views it expresses[17], and he must not give a plans certificate or a final certificate until 15 days[18] have elapsed from the date on which he consulted it, unless it has expressed its views to him before the expiry of that period[19].

Where a local enactment would, if plans were deposited in accordance with building regulations, require the local authority to consult the fire and rescue authority before or during the carrying out of any work, the approved inspector must consult the fire and rescue authority in a manner similar to that required by the enactment[20].

1   As to initial notices see PARA 74 et seq.
2   As to the meaning of 'material alteration' see PARA 10 note 6; definition applied by the Building (Approved Inspectors etc) Regulations 2010, SI 2010/2215, reg 2(1).
3   A 'relevant building' is a building or any part of it to which the Regulatory Reform (Fire Safety) Order 2005, SI 2005/1541, applies, or will apply after the completion of building work: Building (Approved Inspectors etc) Regulations 2010, SI 2010/2215, reg 12(6)(a).
4   For these purposes, 'relevant change of use' is a material change of use where, after the change of use takes place, the Regulatory Reform (Fire Safety) Order 2005, SI 2005/1541, will apply, or continue to apply, to the building or any part of it: Building (Approved Inspectors etc) Regulations 2010, SI 2010/2215, reg 12(6)(b). As to the meaning of 'material change of use' see PARA 11; definition applied by reg 2(1).
5   Ie by the Building Regulations 2010, SI 2010/2214, Sch 1 Pt B: see PARA 10.
6   Building (Approved Inspectors etc) Regulations 2010, SI 2010/2215, reg 12(1).
7   As to the meaning of 'fire and rescue authority' see PARA 55 note 11; definition applied by the Building (Approved Inspectors etc) Regulations 2010, SI 2010/2215, reg 2(1).
8   Building (Approved Inspectors etc) Regulations 2010, SI 2010/2215, reg 12(2)(a).
9   For these purposes, a 'relevant amendment notice' is an amendment notice where any of the work specified in the initial notice, as varied by the amendment notice, being work which could not have been carried out under the original notice ('additional work'), concerns the erection, extension or material alteration of a relevant building or is building work in connection with a relevant change of use of a building and the Building Regulations 2010, SI 2010/2214, Sch 1 Pt imposes requirements in relation to the additional work: Building (Approved Inspectors etc) Regulations 2010, SI 2010/2215, reg 12(6)(c). As to references to the carrying out of work see PARA 73 note 4. As to amendment notices see PARA 76.
10 Building (Approved Inspectors etc) Regulations 2010, SI 2010/2215, reg 12(2)(b).
11 As to plans certificates see PARA 83.
12 Building (Approved Inspectors etc) Regulations 2010, SI 2010/2215, reg 12(2)(c).
13 Building (Approved Inspectors etc) Regulations 2010, SI 2010/2215, reg 12(2)(d). As to final certificates see PARA 84.
14 Ie of the requirements of the Building Regulations 2010, SI 2010/2214, Sch 1 Pt B: see PARA 10.
15 Building (Approved Inspectors etc) Regulations 2010, SI 2010/2215, reg 12(3)(a).
16 Building (Approved Inspectors etc) Regulations 2010, SI 2010/2215, reg 12(3)(b).
17 Building (Approved Inspectors etc) Regulations 2010, SI 2010/2215, reg 12(4)(a).
18 As to the meaning of 'day' see PARA 74 note 19.
19 Building (Approved Inspectors etc) Regulations 2010, SI 2010/2215, reg 12(4)(b).
20 Building (Approved Inspectors etc) Regulations 2010, SI 2010/2215, reg 12(5).

86. Approved inspector's consultation with the sewerage undertaker.

Where an initial notice[1] or amendment notice[2] is to be given or has been given in respect of work in relation to which requirements are imposed[3] relating to building over sewers[4], the approved inspector must consult the sewerage undertaker:

(1) before or as soon as practicable after giving an initial notice in relation to the work[5];

(2) before or as soon as practicable after giving an amendment notice in relation to the work[6];

(3) before giving a plans certificate[7], whether or not combined with an initial notice[8]; and

(4) before giving a final certificate[9].

Where an approved inspector is required to consult the sewerage undertaker in this way, he must give to the sewerage undertaker:

(a) in a case where he is consulting it in connection with an initial notice or an amendment notice, sufficient plans to show whether the work would, if carried out[10] in accordance with those plans, comply with the applicable requirements[11] of the provision relating to building over sewers[12]; and

(b) in a case where he is consulting it in connection with the giving of a plans certificate, a copy of the plans in relation to which he intends to give the certificate[13].

Where an approved inspector is required[14] to consult the sewerage undertaker he must have regard to any views it expresses[15], and he must not give a plans certificate or a final certificate until 15 days[16] have elapsed from the date on which he consulted it, unless it has expressed its views to him before the expiry of that period[17].

1 As to initial notices see PARA 74 et seq.
2 As to amendment notices see PARA 76.
3 Ie the requirements imposed by the Building Regulations 2010, SI 2010/2214, Sch 1 para H4: see PARA 10.
4 Building (Approved Inspectors etc) Regulations 2010, SI 2010/2215, reg 13(1).
5 Building (Approved Inspectors etc) Regulations 2010, SI 2010/2215, reg 13(2)(a).
6 Building (Approved Inspectors etc) Regulations 2010, SI 2010/2215, reg 13(2)(b).
7 As to plans certificates see PARA 83.
8 Building (Approved Inspectors etc) Regulations 2010, SI 2010/2215, reg 13(2)(c).
9 Building (Approved Inspectors etc) Regulations 2010, SI 2010/2215, reg 13(2)(d). As to final certificates see PARA 84.
10 As to references to the carrying out of work see PARA 73 note 4.
11 Ie the requirements of the Building Regulations 2010, SI 2010/2214, Sch 1 para H4: see PARA 10.
12 Building (Approved Inspectors etc) Regulations 2010, SI 2010/2215, reg 13(3)(a).
13 Building (Approved Inspectors etc) Regulations 2010, SI 2010/2215, reg 13(3)(b).
14 Ie by the Building (Approved Inspectors etc) Regulations 2010, SI 2010/2215, reg 13(2): see the text and notes 5–9.
15 Building (Approved Inspectors etc) Regulations 2010, SI 2010/2215, reg 13(4)(a).
16 As to the meaning of 'day' see PARA 74 note 19.
17 Building (Approved Inspectors etc) Regulations 2010, SI 2010/2215, reg 13(4)(b).

(F) Testing and Assessment

87. Testing and assessment where an initial notice is in force.

Building regulations relating to testing and assessment[1] apply with modifications in relation to building work[2] which is the subject of an initial notice[3]. The regulations which are modified are those which deal with:

(1)   self-certification schemes[4];

(2)   consideration of high-efficiency alternative systems for new buildings[5];

(3) CO_2 emission rate calculations[6];

(4)   fabric energy efficiency rate calculations[7];

(5)   wholesome water consumption calculation[8];

(6)   sound insulation testing[9];

(7)   mechanical ventilation air flow rate testing[10];

(8)   pressure testing[11];

(9)   commissioning[12].

(10)   in relation to England, third party certification schemes[13];

(11)   energy performance certificates on construction[14].

In such cases references to the local authority[15] are replaced with references to the approved inspector[16]. The modifications relate principally to the calculation of time periods within which the required certificates and notices must be given to the approved inspector[17]. The provisions are set out elsewhere in this title[18].

1   See the text and notes 4–11.

2   As to the meaning of 'building work' see PARA 10; definition applied by the Building (Approved Inspectors etc) Regulations 2010, SI 2010/2215, reg 2(1).

3   See the Building (Approved Inspectors etc) Regulations 2010, SI 2010/2215, reg 20. As to initial notices see PARA 74 et seq.

4   See the Building Regulations 2010, SI 2010/2214, reg 20; and PARA 10.

5   See the Building Regulations 2010, SI 2010/2214, reg 25A; and PARA 46.

6   See the Building Regulations 2010, SI 2010/2214, reg 27; and PARA 46.

7   See the Building Regulations 2010, SI 2010/2214, reg 27A; and PARA 46.

8   See the Building Regulations 2010, SI 2010/2214, reg 37; and PARA 32.

9   See the Building Regulations 2010, SI 2010/2214, reg 41; and PARA 31.

10   See the Building Regulations 2010, SI 2010/2214, reg 42; and PARA 31.

11   See the Building Regulations 2010, SI 2010/2214, reg 43; and PARA 31.

12   See the Building Regulations 2010, SI 2010/2214, reg 44; and PARA 31.

13   See the Building Regulations 2010, SI 2010/2214, reg 20A; and PARA 10.

14   See the Energy Performance of Buildings (England and Wales) Regulations 2012, SI 2012/3118, reg 7A; and PARA 10.

15   As to the meaning of 'local authority' see PARA 1 note 12.

16   Building (Approved Inspectors etc) Regulations 2010, SI 2010/2215, reg 20(1) (substituted by SI 2012/3119 and SI 2013/747; amended by SI 2013/1959; SI 2014/110; SI 2014/579; SI 2016/285, SI 2016/611; and SI 2018/558). As to approved inspectors see PARA 72.

17   The notice relating to CO_2 emission rate calculations required by the Building Regulations 2010, SI 2010/2214, reg 27 must be given to the approved inspector not later than five days after the work has been completed or, if earlier, the date on which in accordance with the Building (Approved Inspectors etc) Regulations 2010, SI 2010/2215, reg 17 (see PARA 80) the initial notice ceases to be in force: see reg 20(2); and PARA 46.

     The notice relating to fabric energy efficiency rate calculations required by the Building Regulations 2010, SI 2010/2214, reg 27A must be given to the approved inspector not later than five days after the work has been completed or, if earlier, the date on which in accordance with the Building (Approved Inspectors etc) Regulations 2010, SI 2010/2215, reg 17 (see PARA 80) the initial notice ceases to be in force: see reg 20(2A); and PARA 46.

     The notice relating to wholesome water consumption calculations required by the Building Regulations 2010, SI 2010/2214, reg 37 must be given to the approved inspector not later than five days after the work has been completed, or, if earlier, the date on which, in accordance with the Building (Approved Inspectors etc) Regulations 2010, SI 2010/2215, reg 17, the initial notice ceases to be in force: see reg 20(4); and PARA 32.

     The results of sound insulation testing required by the Building Regulations 2010, SI 2010/2214, reg 41 must be given to the approved inspector not later than five days after completion of the work to which the initial notice relates: see reg 20(5); and PARA 31.

     The notice confirming that the fixed building services have been commissioned in accordance with the approved procedure (as required by the Building Regulations 2010, SI 2010/2214, reg 44) must be given to the approved inspector: (1) not later than five days after completion of the work to which the initial notice relates; or (2) where reg 17 applies, not later than the date on which the initial notice ceases to be in force or, if earlier, the end of the period referred to head (1); or (3) where the Building Regulations 2010, SI 2010/2214, reg 20 applies by virtue of the Building (Approved Inspectors etc) Regulations 2010, SI 2010/2215, reg 20, not later than the date on which the notice or certificate required by that regulation must be given: see reg 20(6); and PARA 31.

The energy performance certificate and notice must be given not later than five days (as required by the Energy Performance of Buildings (England and Wales) Regulations 2012, SI 2012/3118, reg 7A(3) after the building work has been completed or, if earlier, the date in which in accordance with the Building (Approved Inspectors etc) Regulations 2010, SI 2010/2215, reg 17 (see PARA 80), the initial notice ceases to be in force: see reg 20(7) added in relation to England by SI 2016/285; and in relation to Wales by SI 2016/285; and SI 2016/611).

18 See notes 4–11.

(ii) Supervision by Public Bodies of Their Own Work

A.   APPROVAL OF PUBLIC BODIES

88. Approval of public bodies.
If it appears to the appropriate national authority[1] that:
(1)   public bodies of a certain description should be enabled to supervise[2] their own work[3]; or
(2)   that a public body should be approved for the purpose of supervising its own work[4],
the appropriate national authority must approve that description of body or, as the case may be, that body in writing and take such steps as appear appropriate to inform those local authorities and public bodies which will be affected by the giving of the approval[5]. The appropriate national authority may withdraw the approval by a notice in writing given to any public body affected, and must take such steps as appear appropriate to inform local authorities of such withdrawal[6].

1   Ie the Secretary of State or, where statutory functions have been transferred in relation to Wales, the Welsh Ministers: see PARA 5.
2   Ie under the Building Act 1984 s 54: see PARA 89. As to supervision of works by local authorities see PARA 70. As to supervision of plans and works by approved inspectors see PARA 72 et seq.
3   Building (Approved Inspectors etc) Regulations 2010, SI 2010/2215, reg 21(1)(a).
4   Building (Approved Inspectors etc) Regulations 2010, SI 2010/2215, reg 21(1)(b).
5   Building (Approved Inspectors etc) Regulations 2010, SI 2010/2215, reg 21(1).
6   Building (Approved Inspectors etc) Regulations 2010, SI 2010/2215, reg 21(2).

B.   SUPERVISION OF PLANS AND WORKS

(A)   Public Body's Notice

89. Giving and acceptance of public body's notice.
Where a public body[1]:
(1)   intends to carry out in relation to a building[2] belonging to it work[3] to which the substantive requirements[4] of building regulations apply[5];
(2)   considers that the work can be adequately supervised by its own servants or agents[6]; and
(3)   gives to the local authority[7] in whose district the work is to be carried out notice in the prescribed[8] form (referred to as a 'public body's notice') together with such plans[9] of the work as may be prescribed[10],
then the following principles apply.
A public body's notice is of no effect unless it is accepted by the local authority to whom it is given, and that local authority may not reject the notice except on

prescribed grounds[11], but must reject the notice if any of the prescribed grounds exists[12]. In a case where the work to which the public body's notice relates is work of such a description that, if plans of it had been deposited with the local authority, the authority could, under an enactment, have imposed requirements as a condition of passing the plans[13], the local authority may impose the like requirements as a condition of accepting the public body's notice[14]. Unless, within the prescribed period[15], the local authority to whom a public body's notice is given gives notice of rejection, specifying the ground or grounds in question, the authority is conclusively presumed to have accepted the public body's notice and to have done so without imposing any such requirements[16].

A public body's notice comes into force when it is accepted by the local authority, either by notice given within the prescribed period to the public body by which it was given or by virtue of[17] the local authority not giving a notice of rejection within the prescribed period, and continues[18] in force until the occurrence of, or the expiry of a prescribed period of time beginning on the date of such event as may be prescribed[19].

A person aggrieved[20] by the local authority's rejection of a public body's notice may appeal to a magistrates' court[21]. On such an appeal the court must, if it determines that the notice was properly rejected, confirm the rejection[22], and in any other case, give a direction to the local authority to accept the notice[23]. Where a person is aggrieved by such a determination, confirmation, direction or other decision of a magistrates' court, he may appeal to the Crown Court[24].

1   References in the Building Act 1984 Pt II (ss 47–58) (see PARA 74 et seq) to a public body are references to a body, corporate or unincorporated, that acts under an enactment for public purposes and not for its own profit and is, or is of a description that is, approved by the appropriate national authority in accordance with building regulations: see ss 54(1), 58(1). As to the meaning of 'enactment' see PARA 6 note 2. As to the appropriate national authority (ie the Secretary of State or, where statutory functions have been transferred in relation to Wales, the Welsh Ministers) see PARA 5. As to the approval of public bodies see PARA 88.

2   As to the meaning of 'building' see PARA 6.

3   As to references to the carrying out of work see PARA 72 note 20.

4   As to the meaning of 'substantive requirements' see PARA 14 note 4.

5   Building Act 1984 s 54(1)(a).

6   Building Act 1984 s 54(1)(b). As to supervision of works by local authorities see PARA 70. As to supervision of plans and works by approved inspectors see PARA 72 et seq.

7   As to the meaning of 'local authority' see PARA 1 note 12.

8   Ie prescribed by building regulations: see the Building Act 1984 s 126. A public body's notice may be incorporated into a combined form together with a public body's plans certificate, and references in s 54 to a public body's notice include a reference to the combined form: see Sch 4 para 2(2)(a); and PARA 93. The local authority is required to keep a register of initial notices which is available for public inspection: see PARA 98.

    For the prescribed form of a public body's notice which is not combined with a public body's plans certificate see the Building (Approved Inspectors etc) Regulations 2010, SI 2010/2215, reg 22(1)(a), Sch 1 Form 9 (Sch 1 Forms 9, 11 substituted by SI 2015/767; and SI 2018/558). For the prescribed form of a public body's notice which is combined with a public body's plans certificate see reg 22(1)(b), Sch 1 Form 11 (as so substituted). As to a public body's plans certificate see PARA 93.

    The form prescribed for a public body's notice may be such as to require the public body by whom it is to be given: (1) to furnish information relevant for the purposes of the Building Act 1984, the Public Health Act 1936 Pt II (ss 33–90) or Pt IV (ss 124–141) of or any provision of building regulations; and (2) to enter into undertakings with respect to consultation and other matters: Building Act 1984 s 54(5). The provisions in the Public Health Act 1936 relating to building regulations were repealed by the Building Act 1984 s 133(2), Sch 7.

9   As to the meaning of 'plans' see PARA 9 note 8. A public body's notice must be accompanied by the plans and documents described in the relevant form prescribed by the Building (Approved Inspectors etc) Regulations 2010, SI 2010/2215, reg 22(1) (see note 8): reg 22(2).

10 Building Act 1984 ss 54(1)(c), 58(1).
11 Building Act 1984 s 54(2)(a). As to the prescribed grounds on which a local authority must reject a public body's notice see the Building (Approved Inspectors etc) Regulations 2010, SI 2010/2215, reg 22(3), Sch 5 (Sch 5 amended by SI 2015/767; and SI 2018/558).
12 Building Act 1984 s 54(2)(b).
13 As to the power of a local authority to impose conditions on passing plans see PARA 33.
14 Building Act 1984 s 54(2).
15 The period within which a local authority may give notice of rejection of a public body's notice is ten days beginning with the day on which the notice is given: Building (Approved Inspectors etc) Regulations 2010, SI 2010/2215, reg 22(4).
16 Building Act 1984 s 54(3). The requirements referred to in the text are those mentioned in s 54(2): see the text and notes 13–14.
17 Ie by virtue of the Building Act 1984 s 54(3): see the text and notes 15–16.
18 Ie subject to the Building Act 1984 Sch 4 para 3(3): see PARA 94.
19 Building Act 1984 s 54(6), Sch 4 para 1(1). Building regulations may empower a local authority to extend, whether before or after its expiry, any such period of time as is referred to in Sch 4 para 1(1): Sch 4 para 1(2). As to events causing a public body's notice to cease to be in force see PARA 91.
20 As to persons aggrieved see JUDICIAL REVIEW vol 61 (2010) PARA 656.
21 Building Act 1984 s 55(1). As to appeals generally see PARAS 139–140. See further CRIMINAL PROCEDURE vol 28 (2015) PARA 665 et seq; MAGISTRATES vol 71 (2013) PARA 697 et seq.
22 Building Act 1984 s 55(2)(a).
23 Building Act 1984 s 55(2)(b).
24 Building Act 1984 s 55(3).

90. Effect of public body's notice.

So long as a public body's notice[1] continues in force, the function[2] of enforcing building regulations[3] that is conferred on a local authority[4] is not exercisable in relation to the work to which the notice relates, and accordingly a local authority may not give a notice to remove or alter work contravening building regulations[5] in relation to that work[6], and a local authority may not institute proceedings[7] for a contravention[8] of building regulations that arises out of the carrying out of that work[9].

In relation to the removal or alteration of work contravening building regulations[10] and in relation to securing payment of the expenses of the execution of street works in private streets adjacent to new buildings under the advance payments code[11], special provision is made with respect to the effect of a public body's notice[12]. The giving of a public body's notice accompanied by such plans as may be prescribed to accompany the public body's notice[13] is to be treated as the deposit of plans[14], and plans accompanying a public body's notice are to be treated as the deposited plans[15]. Acceptance or rejection of a public body's notice is to be treated as the passing or, as the case may be, the rejection of plans[16].

1 As to the meaning of 'public body's notice' see PARA 89.
2 As to the meaning of 'functions' see PARA 3 note 19.
3 As to the meaning of 'building regulations' see PARA 7.
4 Ie by the Building Act 1984 s 91(2) (see PARA 70). As to the meaning of 'local authority' see PARA 1 note 12.
5 Ie under the Building Act 1984 s 36(1): see PARA 62.
6 Building Act 1984 ss 48(1)(a), 54(4) (s 48(1)(a) amended by SI 1996/1905).
7 Ie under the Building Act 1984 s 35: see PARA 61.
8 As to the meaning of 'contravention' see PARA 12 note 10.
9 Building Act 1984 ss 48(1)(b), 54(4) (s 48(1)(b) amended by SI 1996/1905). As to references to the carrying out of work see PARA 72 note 20.
10 Ie under the Building Act 1984 s 36(2) (see PARA 62), s 36(5) (see PARA 62) in so far as it relates to a notice under s 36(2) and to non-compliance with any such requirement as is referred to in s 36(2), and s 36(6) (see PARA 62) in so far as it relates to a contravention of the Building Act 1984: ss 48(3)(a)–(c), 54(4).

11 Ie under the Highways Act 1980 ss 219–225 (see HIGHWAYS, STREETS AND BRIDGES vol 55 (2012) PARA 180 et seq): Building Act 1984 ss 48(3)(e), 54(4).
12 See the Building Act 1984 ss 48, 54.
13 Ie such plans as are referred to in the Building Act 1984 s 54(1)(c): see PARA 89. As to the meaning of 'plans' see PARA 9 note 8.
14 Building Act 1984 ss 48(2)(a), 54(4).
15 Building Act 1984 ss 48(2)(b), 54(4).
16 Building Act 1984 ss 48(2)(c), 54(4).

(B) Cessation of Effect of Public Body's Notice

91. Events causing initial notice to cease to be in force.

Where a public body's final certificate[1] given in respect of work described in a public body's notice[2] is rejected, the public body's notice ceases to be in force in relation to the work described in the public body's final certificate on the expiry of a period of four weeks beginning with the date on which notice of rejection is given[3].

Where work described in a public body's notice includes the erection, extension or material alteration[4] of a building[5], and the building or, as the case may be, the extension or any part of the building which has been materially altered is occupied[6], and no public body's final certificate is given[7], the public body's notice ceases to be in force in relation to the building, extension or part of a building which is occupied:

(1)   if the building is a relevant building[8] (except where it contains only flats and common parts for those flats) on the expiry of a period of four weeks beginning with the date of occupation[9]; and

(2)   in any other case, on the expiry of a period of eight weeks beginning with the date of occupation[10].

Where work described in a public body's notice involves a material change of use[11] of a building, and no public body's final certificate is given, and that change of use takes place, the public body's notice ceases to be in force in relation to that change of use on the expiry of a period of eight weeks beginning with the date on which the change of use takes place[12].

In any other case where no public body's final certificate is given, a public body's notice ceases to be in force on the expiry of a period of eight weeks beginning with the date on which the work described in the public body's notice is substantially completed[13].

A local authority may extend any period referred to above either before or after its expiry[14].

1   As to a public body's final certificate see PARA 94.
2   As to the giving of a public body's notice see PARA 89.
3   Building (Approved Inspectors etc) Regulations 2010, SI 2010/2215, regs 17(1), 28.
4   As to the meaning of 'material alteration' see PARA 10 note 6; definition applied by the Building (Approved Inspectors etc) Regulations 2010, SI 2010/2215, reg 2(1).
5   As to the meaning of 'building' see PARA 73 note 3.
6   Building (Approved Inspectors etc) Regulations 2010, SI 2010/2215, regs 17(2)(a), 28. A public body's notice will not cease to be in force by virtue of regs 17(2), 28 because part of a building or extension is occupied if a final certificate has been accepted in respect of that part: regs 17(6), 28.
7   Building (Approved Inspectors etc) Regulations 2010, SI 2010/2215, regs 17(2)(b), 28. See note 6.
8   A 'relevant building' is a building or any part of it to which the Regulatory Reform (Fire Safety) Order 2005, SI 2005/1541, applies, or will apply after the completion of building work: Building (Approved Inspectors etc) Regulations 2010, SI 2010/2215, reg 12(6)(a).

9   Building (Approved Inspectors etc) Regulations 2010, SI 2010/2215, regs 17(3)(a), 28. A public body's notice will not cease to be in force by virtue of reg 17(3) because part of a building or extension is occupied if a public body's final certificate has been accepted in respect of that part: regs 17(6), 28.

10 Building (Approved Inspectors etc) Regulations 2010, SI 2010/2215, regs 17(3)(b), 28. See note 6.

11 As to the meaning of 'material change of use' see PARA 11; definition applied by the Building (Approved Inspectors etc) Regulations 2010, SI 2010/2215, reg 2(1).

12 Building (Approved Inspectors etc) Regulations 2010, SI 2010/2215, regs 17(4), 28.

13 Building (Approved Inspectors etc) Regulations 2010, SI 2010/2215, regs 17(5), 28.

14 Building (Approved Inspectors etc) Regulations 2010, SI 2010/2215, regs 17(7), 28.

92. Effects of public body's notice ceasing to be in force.

Where a public body's notice[1] ceases[2] to be in force[3], building regulations[4] may provide that if:

(1)   a public body's plans certificate[5] was given before the day on which the public body's notice ceased to be in force[6]; and

(2)   that certificate was accepted by the local authority[7], before, on or after that day[8]; and

(3)   before that day, that acceptance was not rescinded by a notice[9],

then, with respect to the work specified in the certificate, such of the functions[10] of a local authority[11] as may be prescribed[12] for these purposes either are not exercisable or are exercisable only in prescribed circumstances[13].

If, before the day on which the public body's notice ceased to be in force, a public body's final certificate[14] was given in respect of part of the work specified in the notice and that certificate was accepted by the local authority (before, on or after that day), then, despite the fact that the public body's notice has ceased to be in force, a local authority's functions in relation to enforcing building regulations are not exercisable in relation to that part of the work[15].

For the purpose of enabling the local authority to perform its functions in relation to the enforcement of building regulations[16] in relation to any part of the work not specified in a public body's plans certificate or final certificate, as the case may be, building regulations may require the local authority to be provided with plans[17] that relate not only to that part but also to the part to which the certificate in question relates[18].

1   As to the meaning of 'public body's notice' see PARA 89.

2   Ie by virtue of the Building Act 1984 s 54(6), Sch 4 para 1(1): see PARA 89.

3   Building Act 1984 Sch 4 para 4(1). In any case where Sch 4 para 4 applies, the reference in s 36(4) (period within which a notice under s 36 may be given) (see PARA 62) to the date of the completion of the work in question has effect, in relation to a notice under s 36(1) (notice to pull down or alter work which contravenes building regulations) (see PARA 62), as if it were a reference to the date on which the public body's notice ceased to be in force: Sch 4 para 4(5).

4   As to the meaning of 'building regulations' see PARA 7.

5   As to the meaning of 'public body's plans certificate' see PARA 93.

6   Building Act 1984 Sch 4 para 4(2)(a).

7   As to the meaning of 'local authority' see PARA 1 note 12.

8   Building Act 1984 Sch 4 para 4(2)(b).

9   Building Act 1984 Sch 4 para 4(2)(c). The text refers to a notice under Sch 4 para 2(6): see PARA 93.

10 As to the meaning of 'functions' see PARA 3 note 19.

11 Ie referred to in the Building Act 1984 s 48(1) (see PARA 75). Any reference in Sch 4 para 4(1)–(6) to s 48(1) is a reference to s 48 (see PARA 75) as applied by s 54(2) (see PARA 89): Sch 4 para 4(7).

12 Ie prescribed by building regulations: see Building Act 1984 s 126.

13 Building Act 1984 Sch 4 para 4(2). Subject to any provision of building regulations made by virtue of Sch 4 para 4(2), if, before the public body's notice ceased to be in force, an offence under s 35

(penalty for contravention of building regulations) (see PARA 61) was committed with respect to any of the work specified in that notice, summary proceedings for that offence may be commenced by the local authority at any time within six months beginning with the day on which the functions of the local authority referred to in s 48(1) (see PARA 75) became exercisable with respect to the provision of building regulations to which the offence relates: Sch 4 para 4(6). See note 11.

14 As to the meaning of 'public body's final certificate' see PARA 94.

15 See the Building Act 1984 Sch 4 paras 3(3), 4(3).

16 Ie referred to in Building Act 1984 s 48(1): see PARA 75. See note 11.

17 As to the meaning of 'plans' see PARA 9 note 8.

18 Building Act 1984 Sch 4 para 4(4) (which is expressed to be notwithstanding anything in Sch 4 para 4(2), (3) (see the text and notes 4–15)).

(C)   *Public Body's Plans Certificate*

93.   Public body's plans certificate.

Where a public body[1]:

(1)   is satisfied that plans[2] of the work specified in a public body's notice[3] given by it have been inspected by a servant or agent of the body who is competent to assess the plans[4];

(2)   in the light of that inspection is satisfied that the plans neither are defective nor show that work carried out[5] in accordance with them would contravene[6] any provision of building regulations[7]; and

(3)   has complied with any prescribed[8] requirements as to consultation or otherwise[9],

the body may give to the local authority[10] a certificate in the prescribed form ('public body's plans certificate')[11]. A public body's plans certificate may relate either to the whole or to part only of the work specified in the public body's notice concerned[12], and does not have effect unless it is accepted by the local authority to whom it is given[13].

A local authority to whom a public body's plans certificate is given may not reject the certificate except on prescribed grounds[14], but must reject the certificate if any of the prescribed grounds exists[15]. Unless, within the prescribed period, the local authority to whom a public body's plans certificate is given gives notice of rejection[16], specifying the ground or grounds in question, to the public body by which the certificate was given, the authority is conclusively presumed to have accepted the certificate[17].

A person aggrieved[18] by the local authority's rejection of a public body's plans certificate may appeal to a magistrates' court[19]. On such an appeal the court must if it determines that the notice was properly rejected confirm the rejection[20], and in any other case, give a direction to the local authority to accept the notice[21]. Where a person is aggrieved by such a determination, confirmation, direction or other decision of a magistrates' court, he may appeal to the Crown Court[22].

If it appears to a local authority by whom a public body's plans certificate has been accepted that the work to which the certificate relates has not been commenced within the period of three years beginning on the date on which the certificate was accepted, the authority may rescind its acceptance of the certificate by notice, specifying the ground or grounds in question, given to the public body[23].

If a public body's notice ceases to be in force[24] and the conditions[25] as to a public body's plans certificate being accepted and not rescinded are satisfied, the local authority may not give a notice[26] for the removal or alteration of work which contravenes building regulations, or institute proceedings[27] for a contravention of building regulations, in relation to any work which is described in the certificate and is carried out in accordance with the plans to which the certificate relates[28].

1   As to the meaning of 'public body' see PARA 89.
2   As to the meaning of 'plans' see PARA 9 note 8.
3   As to the meaning of 'public body's notice' see PARA 89.
4   Building Act 1984 s 54(6), Sch 4 para 2(1)(a).
5   As to references to the carrying out of work see PARA 72 note 20.
6   As to the meaning of 'contravene' see PARA 12 note 10.
7   Building Act 1984 Sch 4 para 2(1)(b). As to the meaning of 'building regulations' see PARA 7.
8   Ie prescribed by building regulations: see the Building Act 1984 s 126.
9   Building Act 1984 Sch 4 para 2(1)(c). As to the prescribed requirements as to consultation see PARAS 95–97.
10   As to the meaning of 'local authority' see PARA 1 note 12.
11   Building Act 1984 s 58(1), Sch 4 para 2(1). Building regulations may authorise the giving of a public body's notice combined with a public body's plans certificate, and may prescribe a single form for such a combined notice and certificate: Sch 4 para 2(2). Where such a prescribed form is used a reference in Sch 4 or in any other provision of Pt II (ss 47–58) (see PARA 74 et seq) to a public body's notice or to a public body's plans certificate includes a reference to that form: Sch 4 para 2(2)(a). However, should the form cease to be in force as a public body's notice by virtue of Sch 4 para 1(1) (see PARA 89), nothing in Sch 4 para 1(1) affects the continuing validity of the form as a public body's plans certificate: Sch 4 para 2(2)(b). For the prescribed form of a public body's plans certificate which is not combined with a public body's notice see the Building (Approved Inspectors etc) Regulations 2010, SI 2010/2215, reg 25(1)(a), Sch 1 Form 10 (Sch 1 Forms 10, 11 substituted by SI 2015/767; and amended by SI 2018/558). For the prescribed form of a public body's plans certificate which is combined with a public body's notice see reg 25(1)(b), Sch 1 Form 11 (as so substituted).
12   Building Act 1984 Sch 4 para 2(3)(a).
13   Building Act 1984 Sch 4 para 2(3)(b).
14   Building Act 1984 Sch 4 para 2(4)(a). As to the grounds on which a local authority must reject a public body's plans certificate see the Building (Approved Inspectors etc) Regulations 2010, SI 2010/2215, reg 25(2), Sch 6 (Schs 5, 6 amended s by SI 2015/767; and SI 2018/558). As to the grounds on which a local authority must reject a public body's plans certificate combined with a public body's notice see the Building (Approved Inspectors etc) Regulations 2010, SI 2010/2215, reg 25(2), Sch 5, Sch 6 (as so amended).
15   Building Act 1984 Sch 4 para 2(4)(b).
16   The period within which a local authority may give notice of rejection of a public body's plans certificate or combined notice and certificate is ten days beginning on the day on which the certificate is given: Building (Approved Inspectors etc) Regulations 2010, SI 2010/2215, reg 25(4).
17   Building Act 1984 Sch 4 para 2(5).
18   As to persons aggrieved see JUDICIAL REVIEW vol 61 (2010) PARA 656.
19   Building Act 1984 s 55(1). As to appeals generally see PARAS 139–140. See further CRIMINAL PROCEDURE vol 28 (2015) PARA 665 et seq; MAGISTRATES vol 71 (2013) PARA 697 et seq.
20   Building Act 1984 s 55(2)(a).
21   Building Act 1984 s 55(2)(b).
22   Building Act 1984 s 55(3).
23   Building Act 1984 Sch 4 para 2(6).
24   As to events causing a public body's notice to cease to be in force see PARA 91.
25   Ie the conditions in the Building Act 1984 Sch 4 para 4(2).
26   Ie under the Building Act 1984 s 36(1): see PARA 62.
27   Ie under Building Act 1984 s 35: see PARA 61.
28   Building (Approved Inspectors etc) Regulations 2010, SI 2010/2215, reg 26.

(D)   Public Body's Final Certificate

94. Public body's final certificate.

Where a public body[1] is satisfied that any work specified in a public body's notice[2] given by it has been completed, the body may give to the local authority[3] such certificate with respect to the completion of the work and compliance with building regulations[4] as may be prescribed[5] (a 'public body's final certificate')[6]. A public body's final certificate may relate either to the whole or to part only of the work specified in the public body's notice concerned[7], and does not have effect unless it is accepted by the local authority to whom it is given[8]. A local authority to whom a public body's final certificate is given may not reject the certificate except on prescribed grounds[9], but must reject the certificate if any of the prescribed grounds exists[10]. Unless, within the prescribed period, the local authority to whom a public body's final certificate is given gives notice of rejection[11], specifying the ground or grounds in question, to the public body by which the certificate was given, the authority is conclusively presumed to have accepted the certificate[12].

A person aggrieved[13] by the local authority's rejection of a public body's final certificate may appeal to a magistrates' court[14]. On such an appeal the court must if it determines that the notice was properly rejected confirm the rejection[15], and in any other case, give a direction to the local authority to accept the notice[16]. Where a person is aggrieved by such a determination, confirmation, direction or other decision of a magistrates' court, he may appeal to the Crown Court[17].

Where a public body's final certificate has been given with respect to any of the work specified in a public body's notice and that certificate has been accepted by the local authority concerned, the public body's notice ceases to apply to that work[18].

1 As to the meaning of 'public body' see PARA 89.
2 As to the meaning of 'public body's notice' see PARA 89.
3 As to the meaning of 'local authority' see PARA 1 note 12.
4 As to the meaning of 'building regulations' see PARA 7.
5 Ie prescribed by building regulations: see the Building Act 1984 s 126.
6 Building Act 1984 ss 54(6), 58(1), Sch 4 para 3(1). For the prescribed form of a public body's final certificate see the Building (Approved Inspectors etc) Regulations 2010, SI 2010/2215, reg 27(1), Sch 1 Form 12 (Sch 1 Form 12 substituted by SI 2015/767; and SI 2018/558).
7 Building Act 1984 Sch 4 paras 2(3)(a), 3(2).
8 Building Act 1984 Sch 4 paras 2(3)(b), 3(2).
9 Building Act 1984 paras 2(4)(a), 3(2). As to the prescribed grounds on which a local authority must reject a public body's final certificate see the Building (Approved Inspectors etc) Regulations 2010, SI 2010/2215, reg 27(1), Sch 7 (amended by SI 2015/767; and SI 2018/558).
10 Building Act 1984 Sch 4 paras 2(4)(b), 3(2).
11 The period within which a local authority may give notice of rejection of a public body's final certificate is ten days beginning with the day on which the certificate is given: Building (Approved Inspectors etc) Regulations 2010, SI 2010/2215, reg 27(2).
12 Building Act 1984 Sch 4 paras 2(5), 3(2).
13 As to persons aggrieved see JUDICIAL REVIEW vol 61 (2010) PARA 656.
14 Building Act 1984 s 55(1). As to appeals generally see PARAS 139–140. See further CRIMINAL PROCEDURE vol 28 (2015) PARA 665 et seq; MAGISTRATES vol 71 (2013) PARA 697 et seq.
15 Building Act 1984 s 55(2)(a).
16 Building Act 1984 s 55(2)(b).
17 Building Act 1984 s 55(3).
18 Building Act 1984 Sch 4 para 3(3). However, the provision which prohibits a local authority from exercising its functions of enforcing building regulations where a public body's notice is in force (ie s 48(1) (see PARA 75), as applied by s 54(4) (see PARA 90)) continues by virtue of Sch 4 para 3(3) to apply in relation to that work as if the public body's notice continued in force in relation to it: Sch 4 para 3(3).

(E) Consultation

95. Requirements as to consultation.

Building regulations[1] may make provision for requiring, in such circumstances as may be prescribed[2], a public body[3] that has given a public body's notice[4] to consult any prescribed person before taking any prescribed step in connection with any work specified in the notice[5].

1 As to the meaning of 'building regulations' see PARA 7.
2 Ie prescribed by building regulations: see the Building Act 1984 s 126. As to a public body's consultation with the fire and rescue authority see PARA 96. As to a public body's consultation with the sewerage undertaker see PARA 97.
3 As to the meaning of 'public body' see PARA 89.
4 As to the meaning of 'public body's notice' see PARA 89.
5 Building Act 1984 Sch 4 para 5.

96. Public body's consultation with the fire and rescue authority.

Where a public body's notice[1] is to be given or has been given in relation to the erection, extension or material alteration[2] of a relevant building[3] or in relation to building work in connection with a relevant change of use[4] of a building and requirements as to fire safety are imposed[5] in relation to the work[6], the public body must consult the fire and rescue authority[7]:

(1) before or as soon as practicable after giving a public body's notice in relation to the work[8];

(2) before or as soon as practicable after giving a relevant amendment notice[9] in relation to the work[10];

(3) before giving a public body's plans certificate[11], whether or not combined with a public body's notice[12]; and

(4) before giving a public body's final certificate[13].

Where a public body is required to consult the fire and rescue authority in this way, it must give to the fire and rescue authority:

(a) in a case where the public body is consulting the fire and rescue authority in connection with a public body's notice, sufficient plans to show whether the work would, if carried out in accordance with those plans, comply with the applicable requirements[14] as to fire safety[15]; and

(b) in a case where the public body is consulting the fire and rescue authority in connection with the giving of a public body's plans certificate, a copy of the plans in relation to which it intends to give the certificate[16].

Where a public body is required to consult the fire and rescue authority it must have regard to any views it expresses[17], and the public body must not give a public body's plans certificate or a public body's final certificate until 15 days[18] have elapsed from the date on which it consulted it, unless it has expressed its views to the public body before the expiry of that period[19].

Where a local enactment would, if plans were deposited in accordance with building regulations, require the local authority to consult the fire and rescue authority before or during the carrying out of any work, the public body must consult the fire and rescue authority in a manner similar to that required by the enactment[20].

1 As to the giving of a public body's notice see PARA 89.
2 As to the meaning of 'material alteration' see PARA 10 note 6; definition applied by the Building (Approved Inspectors etc) Regulations 2010, SI 2010/2215, reg 2(1).
3 A 'relevant building' is a building or any part of it to which the Regulatory Reform (Fire Safety) Order 2005, SI 2005/1541, applies, or will apply after the completion of building work: Building (Approved Inspectors etc) Regulations 2010, SI 2010/2215, regs 12(6)(a), 23.
4 For these purposes, 'relevant change of use' is a material change of use where, after the change of use takes place, the Regulatory Reform (Fire Safety) Order 2005, SI 2005/1541, will apply, or continue to apply, to the building or any part of it: Building (Approved Inspectors etc) Regulations

2010, SI 2010/2215, regs 12(6)(b), 23. As to the meaning of 'material change of use' see PARA 11; definition applied by reg 2(1).

5   Ie by the Building Regulations 2010, SI 2010/2214, Sch 1 Pt B: see PARA 10.
6   Building (Approved Inspectors etc) Regulations 2010, SI 2010/2215, regs 12(1), 23.
7   As to fire and rescue authorities see FIRE AND RESCUE SERVICES vol 51 (2013) PARA 17.
8   Building (Approved Inspectors etc) Regulations 2010, SI 2010/2215, regs 12(2)(a), 23.
9   For these purposes, a 'relevant amendment notice' is an amendment notice where any of the work specified in the initial notice, as varied by the amendment notice, being work which could not have been carried out under the original notice ('additional work'), concerns the erection, extension or material alteration of a relevant building or is building work in connection with a relevant change of use of a building and the Building Regulations 2010, SI 2010/2214, Sch 1 Pt imposes requirements in relation to the additional work: Building (Approved Inspectors etc) Regulations 2010, SI 2010/2215, regs 12(6)(c), 23. As to references to the carrying out of work see PARA 73 note 4. As to amendment notices see PARA 76.
10 Building (Approved Inspectors etc) Regulations 2010, SI 2010/2215, regs 12(2)(b), 23.
11 As to a public body's plans certificate see PARA 93.
12 Building (Approved Inspectors etc) Regulations 2010, SI 2010/2215, regs 12(2)(c), 23.
13 Building (Approved Inspectors etc) Regulations 2010, SI 2010/2215, regs 12(2)(d), 23. As to a public body's final certificate see PARA 94.
14 Ie of the requirements of the Building Regulations 2010, SI 2010/2214, Sch 1 Pt B: see PARA 10.
15 Building (Approved Inspectors etc) Regulations 2010, SI 2010/2215, regs 12(3)(a), 23.
16 Building (Approved Inspectors etc) Regulations 2010, SI 2010/2215, regs 12(3)(b), 23.
17 Building (Approved Inspectors etc) Regulations 2010, SI 2010/2215, regs 12(4)(a), 23.
18 As to the meaning of 'day' see PARA 74 note 19.
19 Building (Approved Inspectors etc) Regulations 2010, SI 2010/2215, regs 12(4)(b), 23.
20 Building (Approved Inspectors etc) Regulations 2010, SI 2010/2215, regs 12(5), 23.

97. Public body's consultation with the sewerage undertaker.

Where a public body's notice[1] is to be given or has been given in respect of work in relation to which requirements are imposed[2] relating to building over sewers[3], the public body must consult the sewerage undertaker:

(1)   before or as soon as practicable after giving a public body's notice in relation to the work[4];

(2)   before giving a public body's plans certificate[5], whether or not combined with a public body's notice[6]; and

(3)   before giving a public body's final certificate[7].

Where a public body is required to consult the sewerage undertaker in this way, it must give to the sewerage undertaker:

(a)   in a case where it is consulting it in connection with a public body's notice, sufficient plans to show whether the work would, if carried out[8] in accordance with those plans, comply with the applicable requirements[9] of the provision relating to building over sewers[10]; and

(b)   in a case where it is consulting it in connection with the giving of a public body's plans certificate, a copy of the plans in relation to which it intends to give the certificate[11].

Where a public body is required[12] to consult the sewerage undertaker it must have regard to any views the sewerage undertaker expresses[13], and it must not give a public body's plans certificate or a public body's final certificate until 15 days[14] have elapsed from the date on which it consulted the sewerage undertaker, unless the sewerage undertaker has expressed its views to the public body before the expiry of that period[15].

1   As to the giving of a public body's notice see PARA 89.
2   Ie the requirements imposed by the Building Regulations 2010, SI 2010/2214, Sch 1 para H4: see PARA 10.
3   Building (Approved Inspectors etc) Regulations 2010, SI 2010/2215, regs 13(1), 24.
4   Building (Approved Inspectors etc) Regulations 2010, SI 2010/2215, regs 13(2)(a), 24.

5 As to a public body's plans certificate see PARA 93.
6 Building (Approved Inspectors etc) Regulations 2010, SI 2010/2215, regs 13(2)(c), 24.
7 Building (Approved Inspectors etc) Regulations 2010, SI 2010/2215, regs 13(2)(d), 24. As to a public body's final certificate see PARA 94.
8 As to references to the carrying out of work see PARA 73 note 4.
9 Ie the requirements of the Building Regulations 2010, SI 2010/2214, Sch 1 para H4: see PARA 10.
10 Building (Approved Inspectors etc) Regulations 2010, SI 2010/2215, regs 13(3)(a), 24.
11 Building (Approved Inspectors etc) Regulations 2010, SI 2010/2215, regs 13(3)(b), 24.
12 Ie by the Building (Approved Inspectors etc) Regulations 2010, SI 2010/2215, reg 13(2): see the text and notes 4–7.
13 Building (Approved Inspectors etc) Regulations 2010, SI 2010/2215, regs 13(4)(a), 24.
14 As to the meaning of 'day' see PARA 74 note 19.
15 Building (Approved Inspectors etc) Regulations 2010, SI 2010/2215, regs 13(4)(b), 24.

(iii) Recording and Furnishing of Information

98. Recording and furnishing of information.

Every local authority[1] must keep, in such manner as may be prescribed[2], a register containing such information as may be prescribed with respect to initial notices[3], amendment notices[4], notices indicating a change in the person intending to carry out the work[5], public bodies' notices[6] and certificates[7] given to it, including information, where applicable, as to whether such notices or certificates have been accepted or rejected[8]. The information that may be so prescribed with respect to an initial notice or amendment notice includes information about the insurance cover provided with respect to the work to which the notice relates[9]. Every such register must be available for inspection by the public at all reasonable hours[10].

Where an initial notice or a public body's notice has continued in force for any period, the local authority by whom it was accepted may require the approved inspector[11] or public body[12] by whom it was given to furnish it with any information that:

(1)   it would have obtained itself if, during that period, its function[13] of enforcing building regulations[14] had continued to be exercisable in relation to the work to which the notice relates[15]; and

(2)   it requires for the purpose of performing its duty[16] in relation to reports and returns[17].

1 As to the meaning of 'local authority' see PARA 1 note 12.
2 Ie prescribed by building regulations: see the Building Act 1984 s 126.
3 As to initial notices see PARA 74.
4 As to amendment notices see PARA 76.
5 Ie notices under the Building Act 1984 s 51C: see PARA 78.
6 As to public body's notices see PARA 89.
7 The reference in the Building Act 1984 s 56(1) to certificates is a reference to plans certificates, final certificates, public bodies' plans certificates and public bodies' final certificates: s 56(3) (prospectively repealed). As from a day to be appointed, s 56(1)–(4) is repealed by the Sustainable and Secure Buildings Act 2004 s 11(2), Schedule. At the date at which this volume states the law no such day had been appointed. As to the registers to be kept by a local authority see the Building Act 1984 s 91A; and PARA 70. As to the meaning of 'plans certificate' see PARA 83. As to final certificates see PARA 84. As to the meaning of 'public body's plans certificate' see PARA 93. As to the meaning of 'public body's final certificate' see PARA 94.
8 Building Act 1984 s 56(1) (amended by SI 1996/1905) (prospectively repealed: see note 7).
     The register which local authorities must keep under the Building Act 1984 s 56 must contain information as to:

(1) the description of the work to which the notice or certificate relates and of the location of the work (Building (Approved Inspectors etc) Regulations 2010, SI 2010/2215, reg 30(2)(a));

(2) the name and address of any person who signed the notice or certificate (reg 30(2)(b));

(3) the date on which the notice or certificate was accepted or was presumed to have been accepted (reg 30(2)(d)),

with respect to:

(a) initial notices, amendment notices, notices under the Building Act 1984 s 51C or public bodies' notices currently in force (Building (Approved Inspectors etc) Regulations 2010, SI 2010/2215, reg 30(1)(a)); and

(b) plans certificates, final certificates, public bodies' plans certificates, public bodies' final certificates and certificates given under the Building Act 1984 s 16(9) (see PARA 33), which have been accepted or are presumed to have been accepted (reg 30(1)(b), (3)).

The information prescribed in heads (1)–(4) above must be entered in the register as soon as practicable and in any event within 14 days of the occurrence to which it relates: reg 30(5). A register must include an index for enabling a person to trace any entry in the register by reference to the address of the land to which the notice or certificate relates: reg 30(4).

9 Building Act 1984 s 56(2) (amended by SI 1996/1905) (prospectively repealed: see note 7).

10 Building Act 1984 s 56(4) (prospectively repealed: see note 7).

11 As to the meaning of 'approved inspector' see PARA 72.

12 As to the meaning of 'public body' see PARA 89.

13 As to the meaning of 'functions' see PARA 3 note 19.

14 As to the meaning of 'building regulations' see PARA 7.

15 Building Act 1984 s 56(5)(a) (amended by SI 1996/1905).

16 Ie under the Local Government Act 1972 s 230 (see LOCAL GOVERNMENT vol 69 (2018) PARA 601). The Local Government Act 1972 s 230 has effect as if during that period that function had continued to be so exercisable: see the Building Act 1984 s 56(5).

17 Building Act 1984 s 56(5)(b).

(iv) Offences

99. Offences in relation to falsifying notices and certificates.

A person is guilty of an offence if he gives a notice or certificate that purports to comply with the provisions relating to the supervision of building work otherwise than by local authorities[1], and that contains a statement that he knows to be false or misleading in a material particular[2]. He is also guilty of an offence if he recklessly gives a notice or certificate that purports to comply with those requirements, and that contains a statement that is false or misleading in a material particular[3].

Where an approved inspector[4] is convicted of such an offence, the court by or before whom he is convicted must, within one month of the date of conviction, forward a certificate of the conviction to the person by whom the approval was given[5].

1 Ie the requirements of the Building Act 1984 Pt II (ss 47–58) (see PARA 74 et seq), s 16(9) (see PARA 33) or building regulations falling within Sch 1 para 4A(1)(a) or Sch 1 para 4A(b) (see PARA 9).

2 Building Act 1984 s 57(1)(a) (amended by the Sustainable and Secure Buildings Act 2004 s 8(4)). A person guilty of such an offence is liable on summary conviction to a fine not exceeding the statutory maximum or imprisonment for a term not exceeding six months or both, and on conviction on indictment to a fine or imprisonment for a term not exceeding two years or both: Building Act 1984 s 57(2). As to the powers of magistrates' courts to issue fines on summary conviction see SENTENCING vol 92 (2015) PARA 176. Civil sanctions may be imposed in respect of offences under the Building Act 1984 by virtue of the powers under the Regulatory Enforcement and Sanctions Act 2008 Pt 3 (ss 36–71): see ss 36, 38(2), Sch 6; and CONSTITUTIONAL AND ADMINISTRATIVE LAW vol 20 (2014) PARA 331 et seq.

3 Building Act 1984 s 57(1)(b). As to the penalty for this offence see note 2.

4   As to the meaning of 'approved inspector' see PARA 72.
5   Building Act 1984 s 57(3).

4. SPECIFIC BUILDING REQUIREMENTS

(1) Drainage

100. Drainage of building.

If it appears to a local authority[1] that in the case of a building:

(1)   satisfactory provision has not been, and ought to be, made for drainage[2];

(2)   a cesspool[3], private sewer[4], drain[5], soil pipe, rain water pipe, spout, sink or other necessary appliance provided for the building is insufficient or, in the case of a private sewer or drain communicating directly or indirectly with a public sewer[6], is so defective as to admit subsoil water[7];

(3)   a cesspool or other such work or appliance mentioned in head (2) above provided for the building is in such a condition as to be prejudicial to health[8] or a nuisance[9]; or

(4)   a cesspool, private sewer or drain formerly used for the drainage of the building, but no longer used for it, is prejudicial to health or a nuisance[10],

the local authority must by notice[11] require the owner[12] of the building[13] to make satisfactory provision for the drainage of the building, or, as the case may be, require either the owner or the occupier of the building to do such work as may be necessary for renewing, repairing or cleansing the existing cesspool, sewer[14], drain, pipe, spout, sink or other appliance, or for filling up, removing or otherwise rendering innocuous the disused cesspool, sewer or drain[15].

This duty, so far as it empowers a local authority to take action in the cases mentioned in head (1) and head (2) above, does not apply in relation to a building belonging to statutory undertakers[16], the Civil Aviation Authority or a person who holds a licence under the provisions relating to air traffic services[17] and held or used by such a body or person for the purposes of that body's or that person's undertaking, unless it is[18]:

(a)   a house[19]; or

(b)   a building used as offices or showrooms and not forming part of a railway station[20].

1 As to the meaning of 'local authority' see PARA 1 note 12.
2 Building Act 1984 s 59(1)(a) (amended by SI 2001/3335). For these purposes, 'drainage' includes the conveyance, by means of a sink and any other necessary appliance, of refuse water and the conveyance of rainwater from roofs: Building Act 1984 s 59(6) (added by SI 2001/3335; and renumbered by SI 2002/440).
    As to the making of building regulations to modify or repeal the provisions of the Building Act 1984 s 59 on the ground of inconsistency with other provisions see s 1(3), Sch 1 para 11(1); and PARA 9. The provisions of s 59 do not apply to the Inner Temple or the Middle Temple: see s 88(1), Sch 3 para 6; and PARA 3.
3 As to the meaning of 'cesspool' see PARA 9 note 52.
4 As to the meaning of 'private sewer' see PARA 37 note 6.
5 As to the meaning of 'drain' see PARA 36 note 6.
6 For these purposes, 'public sewer' has the same meaning as in the Water Industry Act 1991 s 219(1) (see WATER AND WATERWAYS vol 100 (2018) PARA 506): Building Act 1984 s 126 (definition substituted by the Water Act 1989 s 190(1), (3), Sch 25 para 70(4), Sch 27 Pt I; and amended by the Water Consolidation (Consequential Provisions) Act 1991 s 2(1), Sch 1 para 39(1), (6)).
7 Building Act 1984 s 59(1)(b).
8 'Prejudicial to health' means injurious, or likely to cause injury, to health: Building Act 1984 s 126.
9 Building Act 1984 s 59(1)(c). As to nuisance generally see NUISANCE.

10 Building Act 1984 s 59(1)(d).

11 The provisions of the Building Act 1984 s 99 (content and enforcement of notice requiring works) (see PARA 126) and s 102 (appeal against notice requiring works) (see PARA 138) apply in relation to a notice given under s 59(1): s 59(2).

12 As to the meaning of 'owner' see PARA 12 note 2.

13 The local authority may agree to do the work (*Hall v Batley Corpn* (1877) 47 LJQB 148), but may be liable to the owner or occupier of the premises for defective work (*Hall v Batley Corpn* above; *Duke of Devonshire v St Mary, Islington, Vestry* (1895) 59 JP 745).

14 As to the meaning of 'sewer' see PARA 36 note 7.

15 Building Act 1984 s 59(1). A local authority which had substituted a new sewer for an old one was not empowered to require an owner or occupier to make a new drain connecting with the new sewer: *St Marylebone Vestry v Viret* (1865) 19 CBNS 424; *St Martin-in-the-Fields Vestry v Ward* [1897] 1 QB 40, CA. See also *Austin v St Mary, Lambeth, Vestry* (1858) 27 LJ Ch 677 (power to prescribe make of pipe); *Lorden v Westminster Corpn* (1909) 73 JP 126, DC (power to order additional vent pipe) (both cases being decided under local legislation relating to London). In *R v Paddington Vestry* (1891) 55 JP 52, it was held that action under a similar former London provision was obligatory upon the authority. An owner or occupier who, in compliance with such a notice, remedied a defective pipe which afterwards proved to be a sewer vested in the local authority, could recover the expenses from the authority: *Andrew v St Olave's Board of Works* [1898] 1 QB 775, DC. The position is now doubtful, as sewers vest in the sewerage undertaker. If an occupier of a house so remedies a defect which it is the duty of an owner to remedy, he may recover the expenses from the owner: *Gebhardt v Saunders* [1892] 2 QB 452, DC.

The provisions of the Building Act 1984 s 21(4), (5), (6) (provision of drainage) (see PARA 36) apply in relation to a drain that a local authority requires to be constructed under s 59 as they apply in relation to such a proposed drain as is mentioned in s 21 (see PARA 36): s 59(3).

16 As to the meaning of 'statutory undertakers' see PARA 16 note 10.

17 Ie under the Transport Act 2000 Pt I Ch I (ss 1–40).

18 Building Act 1984 s 59(4) (amended by the Airports Act 1986 s 83(5), Sch 6 Pt I; and SI 2001/4050). For these purposes, the undertaking of a person who holds a licence under the Transport Act 2000 Pt I Ch I is taken to be the person's undertaking as licence holder: Building Act 1984 s 59(5) (added by SI 2001/4050). As from a day to be appointed, the Building Act 1984 s 59(4), (5) is repealed by the Sustainable and Secure Buildings Act 2004 s 5, 11(2), Schedule. At the date at which this volume states the law no such day had been appointed.

19 Building Act 1984 s 59(4)(a) (amended by the Airports Act 1986 Sch 6 Pt I) (prospectively repealed: see note 18). As to the meaning of 'house' see PARA 16 note 10.

20 Building Act 1984 s 59(4)(b) (amended by the Airports Act 1986 Sch 6 Pt I; and SI 2011/2491) (prospectively repealed: see note 18).

101. Use and ventilation of soil pipes.

A pipe for conveying rain water from a roof must not be used for the purpose of conveying the soil or drainage from a sanitary convenience[1]. The soil pipe from a water closet[2] must be properly ventilated[3]. A pipe for conveying surface water[4] from premises[5] must not be permitted to act as a ventilating shaft to a drain[6] or sewer[7] conveying foul water[8]. If it appears to the local authority[9] that there is on any premises a contravention[10] of this statutory requirement[11], it may by notice[12] require the owner[13] or the occupier of those premises to execute such work as may be necessary to remedy the matter[14].

1 Building Act 1984 s 60(1). 'Sanitary convenience' means closet or urinal: s 126. 'Closet' includes privy: s 126.

As the making of building regulations to modify or repeal the provisions of s 60 on the ground of inconsistency with other provisions see s 1(3), Sch 1 para 11(1); and PARA 9. The provisions of s 60 do not apply to the Inner Temple or the Middle Temple: see s 88(1), Sch 3 para 6; and PARA 3.

2 'Water closet' means a closet that has a separate fixed receptacle connected to a drainage system and separate provision for flushing from a supply of clean water either by the operation of mechanism or by automatic action: Building Act 1984 s 126.

3 Building Act 1984 s 60(2).

4 'Surface water' includes water from roofs: Building Act 1984 s 126.

5 As to the meaning of 'premises' see PARA 12 note 2.

6   As to the meaning of 'drain' see PARA 36 note 6.
7   As to the meaning of 'sewer' see PARA 36 note 7.
8   Building Act 1984 s 60(3).
9   As to the meaning of 'local authority' see PARA 1 note 12.
10 As to the meaning of 'contravention' see PARA 12 note 10.
11 Ie the provisions of the Building Act 1984 s 60.
12 The provisions of the Building Act 1984 s 99 (content and enforcement of notice requiring works) (see PARA 126) and s 102 (appeal against notice requiring works) (see PARA 138) apply in relation to a notice given under s 60(4): s 60(5).
13 As to the meaning of 'owner' see PARA 12 note 2.
14 Building Act 1984 s 60(4) (amended by the Water Act 1989 ss 69, 190(3), Sch 8 para 7, Sch 27 Pt I).

102. Repair etc of drain.

No person must:

(1)   except in case of emergency, repair, reconstruct or alter the course of an underground drain[1] that communicates with a sewer[2], or with a cesspool[3] or other receptacle for drainage[4]; or

(2)   where in a case of emergency any such works have been executed without notice, cover over the drain or sewer[5],

without giving to the local authority[6] at least 24 hours' notice[7] of his intention to do so[8]. While any such work is being executed, all persons concerned must permit the proper officer[9], or any other authorised officer[10], of the local authority to have free access to the work[11]. A person who fails to comply with this is liable on summary conviction to a fine[12].

The provisions described above do not apply to so much of a drain or sewer constructed by, or belonging to, a railway company as runs under, across or along its railway[13], or so much of a drain or sewer constructed by, or belonging to, dock undertakers as is situated in or on land of the undertakers that is held or used by them for the purposes of their undertaking[14].

1   As to the meaning of 'drain' see PARA 36 note 6.
2   As to the meaning of 'sewer' see PARA 36 note 7.
3   As to the meaning of 'cesspool' see PARA 9 note 52.
4   Building Act 1984 s 61(1)(a). As to the making of building regulations to modify or repeal the provisions of s 61 on the ground of inconsistency with other provisions see s 1(3), Sch 1 para 11(1); and PARA 9.
      The provisions of s 61 do not apply to the Inner Temple or the Middle Temple: see s 88(1), Sch 3 para 6; and PARA 3.
5   Building Act 1984 s 61(1)(b).
6   As to the meaning of 'local authority' see PARA 1 note 12.
7   As to the form, authentication and service of such a notice see PARAS 135–137.
8   Building Act 1984 s 61(1).
9   'Proper officer', in relation to a purpose and to a local authority, means an officer appointed for that purpose by that authority: Building Act 1984 s 126. 'Officer' includes servant: s 126.
10 'Authorised officer', in relation to a local authority, means: (1) an officer of the local authority authorised by it in writing, either generally or specially, to act in matters of a specified kind or in a specified matter; or (2) by virtue of his appointment and for the purpose of matters within his province, a proper officer of the local authority: Building Act 1984 s 126 (definition amended by the Local Government Act 1985 s 102(2), Sch 17).
11 Building Act 1984 s 61(2).
12 Building Act 1984 s 61(3).
      The fine imposed is one not exceeding level 3 on the standard scale: s 61(3). As to the powers of magistrates' courts to issue fines on summary see SENTENCING vol 92 (2015) PARA 176.
      Civil sanctions may be imposed in respect of offences under the Building Act 1984 by virtue of the powers under the Regulatory Enforcement and Sanctions Act 2008 Pt 3 (ss 36–71): see ss 36, 38(2), Sch 6; and CONSTITUTIONAL AND ADMINISTRATIVE LAW vol 20 (2014) PARA 331 et seq.

13 Building Act 1984 s 61(4)(a).
14 Building Act 1984 s 61(4)(b).

103. Disconnection of drain.
Where a person:

(1) reconstructs in the same or a new position a drain[1] that communicates with a sewer[2] or another drain[3];

(2) executes any works to such a drain so as permanently to discontinue its use[4]; or

(3) executes any works on premises[5] served by such a drain so as permanently to discontinue its use[6],

he must cause any drains or parts of drains thereby becoming disused or unnecessary to be disconnected and sealed at such points as the local authority[7] may reasonably require[8]. A person who knowingly fails so to comply[9] is liable on summary conviction to a fine[10] and also to a further fine for each day on which the default continues after he is convicted[11]. Any question as to the reasonableness of a requirement of a local authority must be determined by a magistrates' court[12], and the court may vary the requirement as it thinks fit[13].

No one may be so required to carry out any work in land outside the premises served by the drain if he has no right to carry out that work, but[14] the person undertaking the reconstruction of the drain or the execution of the works may break open any street[15] for the purpose of complying with such a requirement[16]. Before a person complies with such a requirement, he must give at least 48 hours' notice[17] to the local authority, and a person who fails to do so is liable on summary conviction to a fine[18].

The provisions described above do not apply in relation to anything done in the course of the demolition of a building, or of part of a building, being a demolition as respects which the local authority has power[19] to serve a notice on the person undertaking the demolition[20].

1 As to the meaning of 'drain' see PARA 36 note 6.
2 As to the meaning of 'sewer' see PARA 36 note 7.
3 Building Act 1984 s 62(1)(a). As to the making of building regulations to modify or repeal the provisions of s 62 on the ground of inconsistency with other provisions see s 1(3), Sch 1 para 11(1); and PARA 9.
4 Building Act 1984 s 62(1)(b).
5 As to the meaning of 'premises' see PARA 12 note 2.
6 Building Act 1984 s 62(1)(c).
7 As to the meaning of 'local authority' see PARA 1 note 12.
8 Building Act 1984 s 62(1).
9 Ie fails to comply with the Building Act 1984 s 62(1): see the text and notes 1–8.
10 Ie not exceeding level 1 on the standard scale: see the Building Act 1984 s 62(5). AAs to the powers of magistrates' courts to issue fines on summary conviction see SENTENCING vol 92 (2015) PARA 176. Civil sanctions may be imposed in respect of offences under the Building Act 1984 by virtue of the powers under the Regulatory Enforcement and Sanctions Act 2008 Pt 3 (ss 36–71): see ss 36, 38(2), Sch 6; and CONSTITUTIONAL AND ADMINISTRATIVE LAW vol 20 (2014) PARA 331 et seq.
11 Building Act 1984 s 62(5). The fine imposed must not exceed £1 for each day on which the default continues after conviction: see s 62(5). As to continuing offences see PARA 144.
12 As to the procedure on applications to a magistrates' court see the Building Act 1984 s 103(1); and PARA 139. See further CRIMINAL PROCEDURE vol 27 (2015) PARA 142; MAGISTRATES vol 71 (2013) PARA 436.
13 Building Act 1984 s 62(2).
14 Ie subject to the Building Act 1984 s 101 (breaking open of streets): see PARA 128.
15 'Street' includes a highway, including a highway over a bridge, and a road, lane, footway, square, court, alley or passage, whether a thoroughfare or not: Building Act 1984 s 126.

16 Building Act 1984 s 62(3).
17 As to the form, authentication and service of such a notice see PARAS 135–137.
18 Building Act 1984 s 62(4). The fine imposed is one not exceeding level 1 on the standard scale: s 62(4).
19 Ie under the Building Act 1984 s 81 : see PARA 118.
20 Building Act 1984 s 62(6).

104.   Improper construction or repair of water closet or drain.

If a water closet[1], drain[2] or soil pipe is so constructed or repaired as to be prejudicial to health[3] or a nuisance[4], the person who undertook or executed the construction or repair is liable on summary conviction to a fine[5], unless he shows that the prejudice to health or nuisance could not have been avoided by the exercise of reasonable care[6].

A person charged with such an offence (the 'original defendant') is entitled, upon information duly laid by him and on giving to the prosecutor not less than three clear days' notice of his intention, to have any other person, being his agent or servant, to whose act or default he alleges that the offence was due brought before the court at the time appointed for the hearing of the charge[7]. If, after the commission of the offence has been proved, the original defendant proves that the offence was due to the act or default of that other person, that other person may be convicted of the offence[8], and if the original defendant further proves that he used all due diligence to secure that the water closet, drain or soil pipe in question was so constructed or repaired as not to be prejudicial to health or a nuisance, he must be acquitted of the offence[9]. Where the original defendant seeks to avail[10] himself of this entitlement, the prosecutor as well as the person whom the original defendant charges with the offence has the right to cross-examine the original defendant, if he gives evidence, and any witness called by him in support of his pleas, and to call rebutting evidence[11], and the court may make such order as it thinks fit for the payment of costs by any party to the proceedings to any other party to them[12].

1   As to the meaning of 'water closet' see PARA 101 note 2. For the purposes of the Building Act 1984 s 63 in its application to Greater London, a reference to a water closet includes a reference to a urinal: s 63(4).
2   As to the meaning of 'drain' see PARA 36 note 6.
3   As to the meaning of 'prejudicial to health' see PARA 100 note 8.
4   As to nuisance generally see NUISANCE.
5   Ie a fine not exceeding level 1 on the standard scale: Building Act 1984 s 63(1).As to the powers of magistrates' courts to issue fines on summary conviction see SENTENCING vol 92 (2015) PARA 176. Civil sanctions may be imposed in respect of offences under the Building Act 1984 by virtue of the powers under the Regulatory Enforcement and Sanctions Act 2008 Pt 3 (ss 36–71): see ss 36, 38(2), Sch 6; and CONSTITUTIONAL AND ADMINISTRATIVE LAW vol 20 (2014) PARA 331 et seq.
6   Building Act 1984 s 63(1). As to the making of building regulations to modify or repeal the provisions of s 63 on the ground of inconsistency with other provisions see s 1(3), Sch 1 para 11(1); and PARA 9.
7   Building Act 1984 s 63(2).
8   Building Act 1984 s 63(2)(a).
9   Building Act 1984 s 63(2)(b).
10   Ie seeks to avail himself of the Building Act 1984 s 63(2): see the text to notes 7–9.
11   Building Act 1984 s 63(3)(a).
12   Building Act 1984 s 63(3)(b).

(2) Sanitary Conveniences

105. Provision of closets in buildings.

If it appears to a local authority[1] that:

(1)   a building is without sufficient closet[2] accommodation[3];

(2)   a part of a building, being a part that is occupied as a separate dwelling, is without sufficient closet accommodation[4]; or

(3)   any closets provided for or in connection with a building are in such a state as to be prejudicial to health[5] or a nuisance[6] and cannot without reconstruction be put into a satisfactory condition[7],

the authority must, by notice[8] to the owner[9] of the building, require him to provide the building with such closets or additional closets, or such substituted closets, being in each case either water closets[10] or earth closets[11], as may be necessary[12]. Unless a sufficient water supply and sewer[13] are available[14], the authority may not require the provision of a water closet except in substitution for an existing water closet[15].

Among the grounds on which an appeal may be brought[16] against such a notice is that:

(a)   the need for the works to be executed under the notice would not, in whole or in part, arise but for the occupation of part of the building as a separate dwelling, and the occupation of that part as a separate dwelling is a matter in respect of which the appellant has a cause of action[17]; and

(b)   the person against whom the appellant has a cause of action ought to contribute towards the expenses of executing the works[18].

Where the grounds on which an appeal[19] is brought include the ground specified in head (a) or head (b) above, the appellant must serve a copy of his notice of appeal on the person or persons referred to in that ground of appeal[20], and on the hearing of the appeal the court may make such order as it thinks fit with respect to the contribution to be made by any such person towards the cost of the works[21], or the proportion in which any expenses that may be recoverable by the local authority are to be borne by the appellant and any such other person[22].

The provisions described above do not apply to a factory[23], a building that is used as a workplace[24], or premises[25] to which the Offices, Shops and Railway Premises Act 1963[26] applies[27].

1   As to the meaning of 'local authority' see PARA 1 note 12.
2   As to the meaning of 'closet' see PARA 101 note 1.
3   Building Act 1984 s 64(1)(a). As to the making of building regulations to modify or repeal the provisions of s 64 on the ground of inconsistency with other provisions see s 1(3), Sch 1 para 11(1); and PARA 9.
4   Building Act 1984 s 64(1)(b).
5   As to the meaning of 'prejudicial to health' see PARA 100 note 8.
6   As to nuisance generally see NUISANCE.
7   Building Act 1984 s 64(1)(c).
8   The provisions of the Building Act 1984 s 99 (content and enforcement of notice requiring works) (see PARA 126), and s 102 (appeal against notice requiring works) (see PARA 138) apply in relation to a notice given under s 64(1): s 64(3). As to the form, authentication and service of such notices see PARAS 135–137.
9   As to the meaning of 'owner' see PARA 12 note 2.
10   As to the meaning of 'water closet' see PARA 101 note 2.

11 'Earth-closet' means a closet having a movable receptacle for the reception of faecal matter and its deodorisation by the use of earth, ashes or chemicals, or by other methods: Building Act 1984 s 126.

12 Building Act 1984 s 64(1).

13 As to the meaning of 'sewer' see PARA 36 note 7.

14 For these purposes, a building or proposed building:

    (1)   is not deemed to have a sufficient water supply available unless: (a) it has a sufficient supply of water laid on (Building Act 1984 s 125(2)(a)(i)); or (b) such a supply can be laid on to it from a point within 100 feet of the site of the building or proposed building, and the intervening land is land through which the owner of the building or proposed building is, or will be, entitled to lay a communication pipe (s 125(2)(a)(ii)); and

    (2)   is not deemed to have a sewer available unless: (a) there is within 100 feet of the site of the building or proposed building, and at a level that makes it reasonably practicable to construct a drain to communicate with it, a public sewer or other sewer that the owner of the building or proposed building is, or will be, entitled to use (s 125(2)(b)(i)); and (b) the intervening land is land through which he is entitled to construct a drain (s 125(2)(b)(ii)).

As to the meaning of 'drain' see PARA 36 note 6. As to the meaning of 'public sewer' see PARA 100 note 6. The limit of 100 feet does not apply, for the purposes of the Building Act 1984 s 125(2), if the local authority undertakes to bear so much of the expenses reasonably incurred in constructing, and maintaining and repairing, a drain to communicate with a sewer, or in laying, and maintaining and repairing, a pipe for the purpose of obtaining a supply of water, as the case may be, as is attributable to the fact that the distance of the sewer, or of the point from which a supply of water can be laid on, exceeds 100 feet: s 125(3).

15 Building Act 1984 s 64(2).

16 Ie under the Building Act 1984 s 102: see PARA 138.

17 Building Act 1984 s 64(4)(a).

18 Building Act 1984 s 64(4)(b).

19 Ie under the Building Act 1984 s 102: see PARA 138.

20 Building Act 1984 s 64(5)(a).

21 Building Act 1984 s 64(5)(b)(i).

22 Building Act 1984 s 64(5)(b)(ii).

23 Building Act 1984 s 64(6)(a). For these purposes, 'factory' has the same meaning as in the Factories Act 1961 s 175 (see HEALTH AND SAFETY AT WORK vol 52 (2014) PARA 306): Building Act 1984 s 126.

24 Building Act 1984 s 64(6)(b). 'Workplace' does not include a factory, but otherwise it includes any place in which persons are employed otherwise than in domestic service: s 126.

25 As to the meaning of 'premises' see PARA 12 note 2.

26 See HEALTH AND SAFETY AT WORK vol 52 (2014) PARA 306.

27 Building Act 1984 s 64(6)(c).

106. Provision of sanitary conveniences in workplace.

A building that is used as a workplace[1] must be provided with:

    (1)   sufficient and satisfactory accommodation in the way of sanitary conveniences[2], regard being had to the number of persons employed in, or in attendance at, the building[3]; and

    (2)   where persons of both sexes are employed or in attendance, sufficient and satisfactory separate accommodation for persons of each sex, unless the local authority[4] is satisfied that in the circumstances of the particular case the provision of such separate accommodation is unnecessary[5].

If it appears to the local authority that head (1) and head (2) above are not complied with in the case of any building, it must by notice[6] require the owner[7] or the occupier of the building to make such alterations in the existing conveniences, and to provide such additional conveniences, as may be necessary[8].

The provisions described above do not apply to premises[9] to which the Offices, Shops and Railway Premises Act 1963[10] applies[11].

1　As to the meaning of 'building' see PARA 6. As to the meaning of 'workplace' see PARA 105 note 24.

2 As to the meaning of 'sanitary convenience' see PARA 101 note 1.
3 Building Act 1984 s 65(1)(a). As to the making of building regulations to modify or repeal the provisions of s 65 on the ground of inconsistency with other provisions see s 1(3), Sch 1 para 11(1); and PARA 9.
4 As to the meaning of 'local authority' see PARA 1 note 12.
5 Building Act 1984 s 65(1)(b).
6 The provisions of the Building Act 1984 s 99 (content and enforcement of notice requiring works) (see PARA 126), and s 102 (appeal against notice requiring works) (see PARA 138) apply in relation to a notice given under s 65(2): s 65(3). As to the form, authentication and service of such notices see PARAS 135–137.
7 As to the meaning of 'owner' see PARA 12 note 2.
8 Building Act 1984 s 65(2).
9 As to the meaning of 'premises' see PARA 12 note 2.
10 See HEALTH AND SAFETY AT WORK vol 52 (2014) PARA 306.
11 Building Act 1984 s 65(4).

107. Replacement of earth closets etc.

If a building has a sufficient water supply and sewer[1] available[2], the local authority[3] may by notice[4] to the owner[5] of the building require that any closets[6], other than water closets[7], provided for, or in connection with, the building must be replaced by water closets, notwithstanding that the closets are not insufficient in number and are not prejudicial to health[8] or a nuisance[9]. Such a notice must require the owner to execute the necessary works, or require that the authority itself must be allowed to execute them, and must state the effect of head (1) and head (2) below[10]. Where the local authority gives such a notice:

  (1)   if it requires the owner to execute the works, the owner is entitled to recover from it one-half of the expenses reasonably incurred by him in the execution of the works[11]; and

  (2)   if it requires that it must be allowed to execute the works, it is entitled to recover from the owner one-half of the expenses reasonably incurred by it in the execution of the works[12].

Where the owner of a building proposes to provide it with a water closet in substitution for a closet of any other type, the local authority may, if it thinks fit, agree to pay him a part, not exceeding one-half, of the expenses reasonably incurred in effecting the replacement, notwithstanding that such a notice has not been given by it[13].

1 As to the meaning of 'sewer' see PARA 36 note 7.
2 As to the sufficiency of the water supply and the availability of a sewer for the purposes of the Building Act 1984 s 66(1) see s 125(2), (3); and PARA 105 note 14.
3 As to the meaning of 'local authority' see PARA 1 note 12.
4 The provisions of the Building Act 1984 s 99 (content and enforcement of notice requiring works) (see PARA 126), and s 102 (appeal against notice requiring works) (see PARA 138) apply in relation to a notice given under s 66(1), subject to the modifications that no appeal lies on the ground that the works are unnecessary, and any reference in s 99 to the expenses reasonably incurred in executing works is a reference to one-half of those expenses: s 66(5). As to the form, authentication and service of such notices see PARAS 135–137.
5 As to the meaning of 'owner' see PARA 12 note 2.
6 As to the meaning of 'closet' see PARA 101 note 1.
7 As to the meaning of 'water closet' see PARA 101 note 2.
8 As to the meaning of 'prejudicial to health' see PARA 100 note 8.
9 Building Act 1984 s 66(1). As to the making of building regulations to modify or repeal the provisions of s 66 on the ground of inconsistency with other provisions see s 1(3), Sch 1 para 11(1); and PARA 9. As to nuisance generally see NUISANCE.
10 Building Act 1984 s 66(2).
11 Building Act 1984 s 66(3)(a).

12 Building Act 1984 s 66(3)(b).
13 Building Act 1984 s 66(4).

108.   Loan of temporary sanitary conveniences.

A local authority[1] may, at the request of the occupier of any premises[2] connected with a cesspool[3], sewer[4] or drain[5] on which any work of maintenance, improvement or repair that necessitates the disconnection of the sanitary conveniences[6] provided for or in connection with the premises is to be carried out by a local authority, or by the owner[7] or occupier of the premises[8], supply on loan temporary sanitary conveniences in substitution for any sanitary conveniences so disconnected[9].

The local authority may make reasonable charges for supplying, removing and cleansing any temporary sanitary conveniences so lent for more than seven days[10]. No charge may be made for the use of the temporary sanitary conveniences for the first seven days[11], or in a case where the work is made necessary by a defect in a public sewer[12]. No charge may be made where the work is made necessary by a defect in a cesspool, private sewer[13] or drain in respect of which the local authority has served a notice[14], but, if the temporary sanitary conveniences are provided for a period of more than seven days, the reasonable expenses of supplying, removing and cleansing them are recoverable from the owner of the premises (but not any charge for the use of them for the first seven days)[15]. In proceedings to recover expenses[16] where the work is made necessary by such a defect in a cesspool, private sewer or drain, the court may:

   (1)   inquire whether the expenses ought to be borne wholly or in part by some person other than the defendant in the proceedings[17]; and

   (2)   make such order concerning the expenses or their apportionment as appears to the court to be just[18],

but the court cannot order the expenses or any part of them to be borne by any person other than the defendant in the proceedings unless the court is satisfied that that other person has had notice of the proceedings and an opportunity of being heard[19].

1   As to the meaning of 'local authority' see PARA 1 note 12.
2   As to the meaning of 'premises' see PARA 12 note 2.
3   As to the meaning of 'cesspool' see PARA 9 note 52.
4   As to the meaning of 'sewer' see PARA 36 note 7.
5   As to the meaning of 'drain' see PARA 36 note 6.
6   As to the meaning of 'sanitary convenience' see PARA 101 note 1.
7   As to the meaning of 'owner' see PARA 12 note 2.
8   Ie in pursuance of the Building Act 1984 s 59: see PARA 100.
9   Building Act 1984 s 67(1). As to the making of building regulations to modify or repeal the provisions of s 67 on the ground of inconsistency with other provisions see s 1(3), Sch 1 para 11(1); and PARA 9.
10 Building Act 1984 s 67(2).
11 Building Act 1984 s 67(3)(a).
12 Building Act 1984 s 67(3)(b) (amended by the Water Act 1989 s 190(3), Sch 27 Pt I). As to the meaning of 'public sewer' see PARA 100 note 6.
13 As to the meaning of 'private sewer' see PARA 37 note 6.
14 Ie under the Building Act 1984 s 59: see PARA 100.
15 Building Act 1984 s 67(4) (amended by the Water Act 1989 Sch 27 Pt I).
16 Ie under the Building Act 1984 s 67(4): see the text and notes 13–15.
17 Building Act 1984 s 67(5)(a).
18 Building Act 1984 s 67(5)(b).
19 Building Act 1984 s 67(5).

109. Erection of public conveniences.

No person may erect[1] a public sanitary convenience[2] in, or so as to be accessible from, a street[3] without the consent[4] of the local authority[5], which may give its consent upon such terms as to the use of the convenience or its removal at any time, if required by it, as it thinks fit[6]. A person aggrieved[7] by the refusal of a local authority to give such a consent, or by any terms imposed by it, may appeal to a magistrates' court[8]. The local authority may by notice[9] require the owner[10] of a sanitary convenience:

(1)   that has been erected without such consent being given[11], or that the authority is, by virtue of the terms of a consent so given, entitled to require to be removed, to remove it[12]; or

(2)   that opens on a street, and is so placed or constructed as to be a nuisance[13] or offensive to public decency, to remove it or permanently close it[14].

1   For the purposes of the Building Act 1984 Pt III (ss 59–90) (see PARA 100 et seq), each of the following operations is deemed to be the erection of a building:
    (1)   the re-erection of a building or part of a building when an outer wall of that building or, as the case may be, that part of a building has been pulled down, or burnt down, to within 10 feet of the surface of the ground adjoining the lowest storey of the building or of that part of the building (s 123(2)(a));
    (2)   the re-erection of a frame building or part of a frame building when that building or part of a building has been so far pulled down, or burnt down, as to leave only the framework of the lowest storey of the building or of that part of the building (s 123(2)(b));
    (3)   the roofing over of an open space between walls or buildings (s 123(2)(c)),
    and 'erect' is to be construed accordingly: s 123(2).
2   As to the meaning of 'sanitary convenience' see PARA 101 note 1.
3   As to the meaning of 'street' see PARA 103 note 15.
4   As to the form, authentication and service of a consent by a local authority see PARAS 135–137.
5   As to the meaning of 'local authority' see PARA 1 note 12. For these purposes, a reference to a local authority, in relation to a street that is a highway for which the local authority is not the highway authority, is a reference to the highway authority: Building Act 1984 s 68(6). 'Highway authority' means, in the case of a highway repairable by the inhabitants at large, the council in whom the highway is vested: s 126. As to highway authorities see HIGHWAYS, STREETS AND BRIDGES vol 55 (2012) PARA 52 et seq.
6   Building Act 1984 s 68(1). A person who contravenes s 68(1) is liable on summary conviction to a fine not exceeding level 1 on the standard scale (as to which see SENTENCING vol 92 (2015) PARA 176), without prejudice to the right of the authority under s 68(4) (see the text and notes 9–14) to require the convenience to be removed: s 68(2). Civil sanctions may be imposed in respect of offences under the Building Act 1984 by virtue of the powers under the Regulatory Enforcement and Sanctions Act 2008 Pt 3 (ss 36–71): see ss 36, 38(2), Sch 6; and CONSTITUTIONAL AND ADMINISTRATIVE LAW vol 20 (2014) PARA 331 et seq.
    The Building Act 1984 s 68(1) does not apply to a sanitary convenience erected by a railway company within its railway station or its yard or approaches, or erected by dock undertakers in or on land that belongs to them and is held or used by them for the purposes of their undertaking: s 68(7). As to the meaning of 'contravene' see PARA 12 note 10.
    The provisions of s 68 do not affect the powers of: (1) a county council under the Public Health Act 1936 s 87 (see ENVIRONMENTAL QUALITY AND PUBLIC HEALTH vol 46 (2010) PARA 996); (2) the appropriate national authority under the Highways Act 1980 s 112 (see HIGHWAYS, STREETS AND BRIDGES vol 55 (2012) PARA 737); or (3) a county council under s 114(1) (see HIGHWAYS, STREETS AND BRIDGES vol 55 (2012) PARA 577): Building Act 1984 s 68(8) (amended by the Local Government Act 1985 s 102(2), Sch 17). As to the appropriate national authority (ie the Secretary of State or, where statutory functions have been transferred in relation to Wales, the Welsh Ministers) see PARA 5.
    As to the making of building regulations to modify or repeal the provisions of the Building Act 1984 s 68 on the ground of inconsistency with other provisions see s 1(3), Sch 1 para 11(1); and PARA 9.
7   As to persons aggrieved see JUDICIAL REVIEW vol 61 (2010) PARA 656.

8   Building Act 1984 s 68(3). As to appeals generally see PARAS 139–140. See further CRIMINAL PROCEDURE vol 28 (2015) PARA 665 et seq; MAGISTRATES vol 71 (2013) PARA 697 et seq.
9   The provisions of the Building Act 1984 s 99 (content and enforcement of notice requiring works) (see PARA 126), and s 102 (appeal against notice requiring works) (see PARA 138) apply in relation to a notice given under s 68(4): s 68(5). As to the form, authentication and service of such notices see PARAS 135–137.
10 As to the meaning of 'owner' see PARA 12 note 2.
11 Ie in contravention of the Building Act 1984 s 68(1): see the text to notes 1–6.
12 Building Act 1984 s 68(4)(a).
13 As to nuisance generally see NUISANCE.
14 Building Act 1984 s 68(4)(b).

(3) Buildings

110.   Provision for the disabled in premises open to the public.

Any person undertaking the provision of any building or premises to which the public are to be admitted, whether on payment or otherwise, must, in the means of access both to and within the building or premises and in the parking facilities and sanitary conveniences to be available (if any), make provision, in so far as it is in the circumstances both practicable and reasonable, for the needs of members of the public visiting the building or premises who are disabled[1]. This provision does not apply to any building or premises intended for purposes of specified universities or institutions which provide higher education or further education[2] or specified office premises, shop premises, railway premises or factories[3].

1   Chronically Sick and Disabled Persons Act 1970 s 4(1). As to provisions relating to access for disabled persons under the Chronically Sick and Disabled Persons Act 1970 to ensure see DISCRIMINATION vol 33 (2017) PARA 214
2   Ie any building or premises intended for purposes mentioned in the Chronically Sick and Disabled Persons Act 1970 s 8(2). These purposes are:
   (1)   universities, university colleges and colleges, schools and halls of universities (Chronically Sick and Disabled Persons s 8(2)(a));
   (2)   institutions within the higher education sector within the meaning of the Further and Higher Education Act 1992 s 91(5) (Chronically Sick and Disabled Persons s 8(2)(aa) (substituted by the Further and Higher Education Act 1992 Sch 8 para 72));
   (3)   schools and institutions which provide higher education or further education (or both) and are maintained or assisted by local authorities (Chronically Sick and Disabled Persons s 8(2)(b) (substituted by the Education Reform Act 1988 Sch 12 para 69; and amended by SI 2010/1158));
   (4)   institutions within the further education sector within the meaning of the Further and Higher Education Act 1992 s 91(3) (Chronically Sick and Disabled Persons s 8(2)(ba) (added by the Further and Higher Education Act 1992 Sch 8 para 72));
   (5)   educational establishments within the meaning of the Education (Scotland) Act 1980 s 135(1) (Chronically Sick and Disabled Persons s 8(2)(c) (substituted by the Further and Higher Education (Scotland) Act 1992 Sch 9 para 3)).
   and expressions used in head (3) above and in the Education Act 1996 have the same meanings as in the Education Act 1996: s 8(2) (amended by the Education Act 1996 Sch 37 para 19).
3   Chronically Sick and Disabled Persons Act 1970 s 4(2) (amended by the Chronically Sick and Disabled Persons (Amendment) Act 1976 s 1). The text refers to any building or premises intended for purposes mentioned in the Chronically Sick and Disabled Persons Act 1970 s 8A(2). The premises referred to here are office premises, shop premises and railway premises to which the Offices, Shops and Railway Premises Act 1963 applies, premises which are deemed to be such premises for the purposes of the Offices, Shops and Railway Premises Act 1963 and factories as defined by the Factories Act 1961 s 175, being (in each case) premises in which persons are employed to work: s 8A(2) added by the Chronically Sick and Disabled Persons (Amendment) Act 1976 s 2).

111. Provision of food storage accommodation in house.

If it appears to a local authority[1] that a house[2], or part of a building that is occupied as a separate dwelling, is without sufficient and suitable accommodation for the storage of food, the local authority may by notice[3] require the owner[4] of the house or building to provide the house or building with sufficient and suitable accommodation for that purpose[5]. Among the grounds on which an appeal may be brought[6] against such a notice are:

(1)   that it is not reasonably practicable to comply with the notice[7];

(2)   that:

    (a)   the need for the works to be executed under the notice would not, in whole or in part, arise but for the occupation of part of the building as a separate dwelling, and that the occupation of that part as a separate dwelling is a matter in respect of which the appellant has a cause of action[8]; and

    (b)   the person against whom the appellant has a cause of action ought to contribute towards the expenses of executing the works[9].

Where the grounds on which such an appeal is brought include the ground specified in head (2)(b) above:

(i)   the appellant must serve a copy of his notice of appeal on the person or persons referred to in that ground of appeal[10]; and

(ii)   on the hearing of the appeal the court may make such order as it thinks fit with respect to the contribution to be made by any such person towards the cost of the works[11], or the proportion in which any expenses that may be recoverable by the local authority are to be borne by the appellant and any such other person[12].

1   As to the meaning of 'local authority' see PARA 1 note 12.
2   As to the meaning of 'house' see PARA 16 note 10.
3   The provisions of the Building Act 1984 s 99 (content and enforcement of notice requiring works) (see PARA 126), and s 102 (appeal against notice requiring works) (see PARA 138) apply in relation to a notice given under s 70(1): s 70(2). As to the form, authentication and service of such notices see PARAS 135–137.
4   As to the meaning of 'owner' see PARA 12 note 2.
5   Building Act 1984 s 70(1). As to the making of building regulations to modify or repeal the provisions of s 70 on the ground of inconsistency with other provisions see s 1(3), Sch 1 para 11(1); and PARA 9.
6   Ie under the Building Act 1984 s 102: see PARA 138.
7   Building Act 1984 s 70(3)(a).
8   Building Act 1984 s 70(3)(b)(i).
9   Building Act 1984 s 70(3)(b)(ii).
10   Building Act 1984 s 70(4)(a).
11   Building Act 1984 s 70(4)(b)(i).
12   Building Act 1984 s 70(4)(b)(ii).

112. Raising of chimney.

Where, after 3 October 1961[1]:

(1)   a person erects[2] or raises a building (the 'taller building') to a greater height than an adjoining building[3]; and

(2)   any chimneys or flues of an adjoining building are in a party wall between the two buildings or are six feet or less from the nearest part of the taller building[4],

the local authority[5] may by notice[6]:

(a)   require that person, within such time as may be specified in the notice, to build up those chimneys and flues, if it is reasonably practicable so to do, so that their top will be of the same height as the top of the chimneys of the taller building or the top of the taller building, whichever is the higher[7]; and

(b)   require the owner[8] or occupier of the adjoining building to allow the first mentioned person to enter on that building and carry out such work as may be necessary to comply with the notice served on him[9],

except that, if the owner or occupier, within 14 days from the date of service of the notice on him, serves on the first mentioned person and on the local authority a notice (a 'counter-notice') that he elects to carry out the work himself, the owner or occupier must comply with the notice served under head (a) above instead of the first mentioned person and may recover the expenses reasonably incurred in so doing from that person[10]. A person on whom a notice is served under head (a) or head (b) above may appeal to a magistrates' court[11].

If:

(i)   a person on whom a notice is served under head (a) above fails to comply with the notice, except in a case where the owner or occupier of an adjoining building has refused to allow entry on that building, or has refused to allow the carrying out of any such work as may be necessary to comply with the notice, or has served a counter-notice[12]; or

(ii)   a person on whom a notice is served under head (b) above fails to comply with the notice or, having served a counter-notice, fails to comply with the notice served under head (a) above[13],

he is liable on summary conviction to a fine[14], and the local authority may itself carry out such work as may be necessary to comply with the notice served[15], and recover the expenses reasonably incurred in doing so from the person on whom that notice was served[16].

1   Ie the date of commencement of the relevant provisions of the Public Health Act 1961. The relevant provisions of the Public Health Act 1961 have been repealed by the Building Act 1984 s 133(2), Sch 7.
2   As to the meaning of 'erect' see PARA 109 note 1.
3   Building Act 1984 s 73(1)(a). The provisions of s 73 do not apply to inner London: see s 88(1), Sch 3 para 5; and PARA 3. As to the making of building regulations to modify or repeal the provisions of s 73 on the ground of inconsistency with other provisions see s 1(3), Sch 1 para 11(1); and PARA 9.
4   Building Act 1984 s 73(1)(b).
5   As to the meaning of 'local authority' see PARA 1 note 12.
6   As to the form, authentication and service of such notices see PARAS 135–137.
7   Building Act 1984 s 73(1)(i).
8   As to the meaning of 'owner' see PARA 12 note 2.
9   Building Act 1984 s 73(1)(ii).
10 Building Act 1984 s 73(1).
11 Building Act 1984 s 73(2). As to appeals generally see PARAS 139–140. See further CRIMINAL PROCEDURE vol 28 (2015) PARA 665 et seq; MAGISTRATES vol 71 (2013) PARA 697 et seq.
12 Building Act 1984 s 73(3)(a).
13 Building Act 1984 s 73(3)(b).
14 Ie a fine not exceeding level 1 on the standard scale: Building Act 1984 s 73(3). As to the powers of magistrates' courts to issue fines on summary conviction see SENTENCING vol 92 (2015) PARA 176. Civil sanctions may be imposed in respect of offences under the Building Act 1984 by virtue of the powers under the Regulatory Enforcement and Sanctions Act 2008 Pt 3 (ss 36–71): see ss 36, 38(2), Sch 6; and CONSTITUTIONAL AND ADMINISTRATIVE LAW vol 20 (2014) PARA 331 et seq.
15 Ie under the Building Act 1984 s 73(1): see the text and notes 1–10.
16 Building Act 1984 s 73(3).

113. Cellars and rooms below subsoil water level.

No person may without the consent[1] of the local authority construct a cellar or room in, or as part of, a house, shop, inn, hotel or office if the floor level of the cellar or room is lower than the ordinary level of the subsoil water on, under or adjacent to the site of the house, shop, inn, hotel or office[2]. This does not apply to the construction of a cellar or room in connection with a shop, inn, hotel or office that forms part of a railway station[3].

If a person who constructs a cellar or room acts in contravention of the requirement to obtain consent[4], or of any condition attached to such a consent he is liable on summary conviction to a fine[5], and the local authority may by notice[6] require him either to alter the cellar or room so that its construction will no longer contravene that requirement or condition or, if he so elects, to fill it in or otherwise make it unusable[7].

If the owner for the time being of the house, shop, inn, hotel or office causes or permits a cellar or room forming part of it to be used in a manner that he knows to be in contravention of a condition attached to such a consent, he is liable on summary conviction to a fine[8].

1   As to the form, authentication and service of such consents see PARAS 135–137. A consent under the Building Act 1984 s 74 may be given subject to such conditions as to the construction or use of the premises as may be specified in it, and conditions specified in such a consent are binding on successive owners of the house, shop, inn, hotel or office: s 75(1). As to the meaning of 'house' see PARA 16 note 10. As to the meaning of 'premises' see PARA 12 note 2. As to the meaning of 'owner' see PARA 12 note 2.

   If a local authority: (1) refuses an application for such a consent; or (2) attaches any conditions to such a consent, the person applying for the consent may appeal to a magistrates' court against the refusal or, as the case may be, against any of the conditions, and if a magistrates' court allows an appeal against a refusal to grant a consent it may direct the local authority to give its consent subject to such conditions, if any, as appears to the court to be appropriate: s 75(2). As to the meaning of 'local authority' see PARA 1 note 12. As to appeals generally see PARAS 139–140.

   An application may be made at any time to the local authority for the variation or withdrawal of a condition attached to such a consent, and, if the local authority refuses the application, the applicant may appeal to a magistrates' court: s 75(3).

   Sections 74 and 75 do not apply to inner London: see s 88(1), Sch 3 para 5; and PARA 3. As to the making of building regulations to modify or repeal the provisions of ss 74, 75 on the ground of inconsistency with other provisions see s 1(3), Sch 1 para 11(1); and PARA 9.
2   Building Act 1984 s 74(1).
3   Building Act 1984 s 74(2) (amended by the Licensing Act 2003 ss 198(1), 199, Sch 6 paras 90, 92, Sch 7).
4   Ie in contravention of the Building Act 1984 s 74(1) (see the text to notes 1–2). As to the meaning of 'contravention' see PARA 12 note 10.
5   Building Act 1984 s 74(3)(a). The fine imposed is one not exceeding level 1 on the standard scale: s 74(3)(a). As to the powers of magistrates' courts to issue fines on summary conviction see SENTENCING vol 92 (2015) PARA 176. Civil sanctions may be imposed in respect of offences under the Building Act 1984 by virtue of the powers under the Regulatory Enforcement and Sanctions Act 2008 Pt 3 (ss 36–71): see ss 36, 38(2), Sch 6; and CONSTITUTIONAL AND ADMINISTRATIVE LAW vol 20 (2014) PARA 331 et seq.
6   The provisions of the Building Act 1984 s 99 (content and enforcement of notice requiring works) (see PARA 126), and s 102 (appeal against notice requiring works) (see PARA 138) apply in relation to a notice given under s 74(3), subject to the following modifications:
    (1)   s 99(1) requires the notice to indicate the nature of the works of alteration and that of the works for making the cellar or room unusable (s 74(4)(a)); and
    (2)   s 99(2) authorises the local authority to execute, subject to s 99(2), at its election either the works of alteration or the works for making the cellar or room unusable (s 74(4)(b)).

   As to the meaning of 'modifications' see PARA 3 note 21. As to the form, authentication and service of such notices see PARAS 135–137.
7   Building Act 1984 s 74(3)(b).

8 Building Act 1984 s 74(5). The fine imposed is one not exceeding level 1 on the standard scale: s 74(5). See note 5.

(4) Defective and Dangerous Premises

114. Defective premises.

If it appears to a local authority[1] that:

(1)   any premises[2] are in such a state (a 'defective state') as to be prejudicial to health[3] or a nuisance[4]; and

(2)   unreasonable delay in remedying the defective state would be occasioned by following the procedure prescribed[5] for abatement notices[6],

the local authority may serve on the person on whom it would have been appropriate to serve such an abatement notice a notice[7] stating that the local authority intends to remedy the defective state and specifying the defects that it intends to remedy[8].

The local authority may, after the expiration of nine days after service of such a notice, execute such works as may be necessary to remedy the defective state, and recover the expenses reasonably incurred in so doing from the person on whom the notice was served[9]. If, within seven days after service of such a notice, the person on whom the notice was served serves a counter-notice[10] that he intends to remedy the defects specified in the first mentioned notice, the local authority must take no action in pursuance of the first mentioned notice unless the person who served the counter-notice fails within what seems to the local authority a reasonable time to begin to execute works to remedy the said defects[11], or having begun to execute such works fails to make such progress towards their completion as seems to the local authority reasonable[12].

In proceedings to recover such expenses[13], the court:

(a)   must inquire whether the local authority was justified in concluding that the premises were in a defective state, or that unreasonable delay in remedying the defective state would have been occasioned by following the prescribed procedure[14]; and

(b)   if the defendant proves that he served such a counter-notice, must inquire whether the defendant failed to begin the works to remedy the defects within a reasonable time, or failed to make reasonable progress towards their completion[15],

and if the court determines that the local authority was not justified in either of the conclusions mentioned in head (a) above[16], or there was no failure under head (b) above[17],

the local authority cannot recover the expenses or any part of them[18]. In such proceedings to recover expenses, the court may inquire whether the said expenses ought to be borne wholly or in part by some person other than the defendant in the proceedings[19], and make such order concerning the expenses or their apportionment as appears to the court to be just[20], but the court cannot order the expenses or any part of them to be borne by a person other than the defendant in the proceedings unless the court is satisfied that that other person has had due notice of the proceedings and an opportunity of being heard[21].

1   As to the meaning of 'local authority' see PARA 1 note 12.
2   As to the meaning of 'premises' see PARA 12 note 2.
3   As to the meaning of 'prejudicial to health' see PARA 100 note 8.

4   Building Act 1984 s 76(1)(a). As to nuisance generally see NUISANCE. As to the making of building
    regulations to modify or repeal the provisions of s 76 on the ground of inconsistency with other
    provisions see s 1(3), Sch 1 para 11(1); and PARA 9.
5   Ie prescribed by the Environmental Protection Act 1990 s 80: see NUISANCE vol 78 (2018)
    PARA 200 et seq.
6   Building Act 1984 s 76(1)(b) (amended by the Environmental Protection Act 1990 s 162(1), Sch 15
    para 24).
7   As to the form of the notice see PARA 135, and as to its authentication see PARA 136.
8   Building Act 1984 s 76(1), (7) (amended by the Housing (Consequential Provisions) Act 1985 s 4,
    Sch 2 para 58(2)). A local authority must not serve a notice under the Building Act 1984 s 76(1),
    or proceed with the execution of works in accordance with a notice so served, if the execution of
    the works would, to its knowledge, be in contravention of a building preservation order under the
    Town and Country Planning Act 1947 s 29 (repealed): Building Act 1984 s 76(6). The Town and
    Country Planning Act 1947 s 29 was repealed and was not re-enacted in the Town and Country
    Planning Act 1971 (repealed). Buildings which were subject to building preservation orders on 1
    January 1969 are now deemed to be listed buildings: see the Planning (Listed Buildings and
    Conservation Areas) Act 1990 s 1(6), Sch 1 para 1; and PLANNING vol 83 (2018) PARA 1186.
9   Building Act 1984 s 76(2).
10 As to the form of counter-notice see PARA 135, and as to the service of a counter-notice see PARA
    137.
11 Building Act 1984 s 76(3)(a).
12 Building Act 1984 s 76(3)(b).
13 Ie under the Building Act 1984 s 76(2): see the text to note 9.
14 Building Act 1984 s 76(4)(a) (amended by the Environmental Protection Act 1990 Sch 15 para 24).
    The text refers to the procedure prescribed by the Environmental Protection Act 1990 s 80: see
    NUISANCE vol 78 (2018) PARA 200 et seq.
15 Building Act 1984 s 76(4)(b).
16 Building Act 1984 s 76(4)(i).
17 Building Act 1984 s 76(4)(ii).
18 Building Act 1984 s 76(4).
19 Building Act 1984 s 76(5)(a).
20 Building Act 1984 s 76(5)(b).
21 Building Act 1984 s 76(5).

115. Dangerous buildings.

If it appears to a local authority[1] that a building or structure, or part of a
building or structure, is in such a condition, or is used to carry such loads, as to
be dangerous, the authority may apply to a magistrates' court[2], and the court may:

(1)   where danger arises from the condition of the building or structure,
        make an order requiring the owner[3] of it to execute such work as may
        be necessary to obviate the danger[4], or, if he so elects, to demolish the
        building or structure, or any dangerous part of it, and remove any
        rubbish[5] resulting from the demolition[6]; or

(2)   where danger arises from overloading of the building or structure, make
        an order restricting its use until a magistrates' court, being satisfied that
        any necessary works have been executed, withdraws or modifies the
        restriction[7].

If the person on whom an order is made under head (1) above fails to comply
with the order within the time specified, the local authority may execute the order
in such manner as it thinks fit, and recover the expenses[8] reasonably incurred by
it in doing so from the person in default, and, without prejudice to the right of the
authority to exercise those powers, the person is liable on summary conviction to
a fine[9].

If it appears to a local authority that a building or structure, or part of a
building or structure, is in such a state, or is used to carry such loads, as to be
dangerous, and immediate action should be taken to remove the danger, it may
take such steps as may be necessary for that purpose[10]. Before exercising its

powers, the local authority must, if it is reasonably practicable to do so, give notice[11] of its intention to the owner and occupier of the building, or of the premises[12] on which the structure is situated[13]. The local authority may recover from the owner the expenses reasonably incurred[14] by it in taking such emergency measures[15]. In proceedings to recover such expenses, the court must inquire whether the local authority might reasonably have proceeded[16] instead by applying to a magistrates' court for an order such as is mentioned in head (1) or head (2) above, and, if the court determines that the local authority might reasonably have so proceeded instead, the local authority may not recover the expenses or any part of them[17]. In proceedings to recover such expenses, the court may inquire whether the expenses ought to be borne wholly or in part by some person other than the defendant in the proceedings, and make such order concerning the expenses or their apportionment as appears to the court to be just, but the court must not order the expenses or any part of them to be borne by any person other than the defendant in the proceedings unless it is satisfied that that other person has had due notice of the proceedings and an opportunity of being heard[18].

Where in consequence of the exercise of the power to take emergency measures in relation to dangerous buildings[19] the owner or occupier of any premises sustains damage, but the provisions with respect to compensation for damage[20] do not apply because the owner or occupier has been in default:

(a)   the owner or occupier may apply to a magistrates' court to determine whether the local authority was justified in so exercising its powers so as to occasion the damage sustained[21]; and

(b)   if the court determines that the local authority was not so justified, the owner or occupier is entitled to compensation, and the provisions with respect to compensation for damage[22]

apply in relation to any dispute as regards compensation so arising[23].

1   As to the meaning of 'local authority' see PARA 1 note 12.
2   As to the procedure on applications to a magistrates' court see PARA 139. See further MAGISTRATES; CRIMINAL PROCEDURE vol 27 (2015) PARA 142.
3   As to the meaning of 'owner' see PARA 12 note 2.
4   Building Act 1984 s 77(1)(a)(i). The provisions of s 77 and s 78 do not apply to inner London: see s 88(1), Sch 3 para 5; and PARA 3. Section 77 has effect subject to the provisions of the Planning (Listed Buildings and Conservation Areas) Act 1990 relating to listed buildings, buildings subject to building preservation notices and buildings in conservation areas: Building Act 1984 s 77(3) (added by the Housing and Planning Act 1986 s 40(f), Sch 9 Pt I para 6(2); and amended by the Planning (Consequential Provisions) Act 1990 s 4, Sch 2 para 67(3)). See further PLANNING vol 83 (2018) PARA 1165 et seq.
    As to the making of building regulations to modify or repeal the provisions of the Building Act 1984 s 77 and s 78 on the ground of inconsistency with other provisions see s 1(3), Sch 1 para 11(1); and PARA 9.
5   'Rubbish' does not include machinery, at least if its condition is not altered by the demolition: *McVittie v Bolton Corpn* [1945] KB 281, [1945] 1 All ER 379, CA.
6   Building Act 1984 s 77(1)(a)(ii).
7   Building Act 1984 s 77(1)(b).
8   These expenses are chargeable against income as between a tenant for life of leaseholds and a remainderman (*Re Copland's Settlement, Johns v Carden* [1900] 1 Ch 326: see SETTLEMENTS vol 91 (2012) PARA 862), and are outgoings for the purpose of a contract of sale (*Tubbs v Wynne* [1897] 1 QB 74: see CONVEYANCING vol 23 (2016) PARA 190). With regard to the liability as between vendor and purchaser of leaseholds see *Re Highett and Bird's Contract* [1903] 1 Ch 287, CA; and as regards the liability of a tenant under a covenant to repair see *Lister v Lane and Nesham* [1893] 2 QB 212, CA; and LANDLORD AND TENANT vol 62 (2016) PARA 329 et seq.
9   Building Act 1984 s 77(2). The fine imposed is one not exceeding level 1 on the standard scale: s 77(2). As to the powers of magistrates' courts to issue fines on summary conviction see

SENTENCING vol 92 (2015) PARA 176. Civil sanctions may be imposed in respect of offences under the Building Act 1984 by virtue of the powers under the Regulatory Enforcement and Sanctions Act 2008 Pt 3 (ss 36–71): see ss 36, 38(2), Sch 6; and CONSTITUTIONAL AND ADMINISTRATIVE LAW vol 20 (2014) PARA 331 et seq.

10 Building Act 1984 s 78(1). The proper officer of a local authority may, as an officer of the local authority, exercise the powers conferred on the local authority by s 78(1): s 78(8). As to the meaning of 'proper officer' see PARA 102 note 9. Section 78 does not apply to premises forming part of a mine or quarry within the meaning of the Mines and Quarries Act 1954 (see MINES, MINERALS AND QUARRIES vol 76 (2013) PARA 3): Building Act 1984 s 78(9). The provisions of the Mines and Quarries Act 1954 relating to quarries have been replaced by the Quarries Regulations 1999, SI 1999/2024: see MINES, MINERALS AND QUARRIES vol 76 (2013) PARA 4.

11 As to the form, authentication and service of notices see PARAS 135–137.

12 As to the meaning of 'premises' see PARA 12 note 2.

13 Building Act 1984 s 78(2).

14 Ie expenses incurred under the Building Act 1984 s 78.

15 Building Act 1984 s 78(3). However, so far as expenses incurred by the local authority under s 78 consist of expenses of fencing off the building or structure, or arranging for it to be watched, the expenses are not recoverable in respect of any period after the danger has been removed by other steps under s 78 (s 78(4)(a)), or after an order made under s 77(1) (see the text to notes 1–7) for the purpose of its removal has been complied with or has been executed as mentioned in s 77(2) (see the text to notes 8–9) (s 78(4)(b)).

16 Ie under the Building Act 1984 s 77(1): see the text to notes 1–7.

17 Building Act 1984 s 78(5).

18 Building Act 1984 s 78(6).

19 Ie the exercise of the powers conferred by the Building Act 1984 s 78.

20 Ie under the Building Act 1984 s 106(1): see PARA 129.

21 Building Act 1984 s 78(7)(a).

22 Ie under the Building Act 1984 s 106(2), (3): see PARA 129.

23 Building Act 1984 s 78(7)(b).

116. Building detrimental to amenities.

If it appears to a local authority[1] that a building or structure is by reason of its ruinous or dilapidated condition seriously detrimental to the amenities of the neighbourhood, the local authority may by notice[2] require the owner[3] of it to execute such works of repair or restoration, or if he so elects, to take such steps for demolishing the building or structure, or any part of it, and removing any rubbish or other material resulting from or exposed by the demolition, as may be necessary in the interests of amenity[4]. If it appears to a local authority that rubbish or other material resulting from, or exposed by, the demolition or collapse of a building or structure is lying on the site or on any adjoining land[5], and by reason of it the site or land is in such a condition as to be seriously detrimental to the amenities of the neighbourhood[6], the local authority may by notice[7] require the owner of the site or land to take steps for removing the rubbish or material as may be necessary in the interests of amenity[8].

1 As to the meaning of 'local authority' see PARA 1 note 12.

2 The provisions of the Building Act 1984 s 99 (content and enforcement of notice requiring works) (see PARA 126), and s 102 (appeal against notice requiring works) (see PARA 138) apply in relation to a notice given under s 79(1), (2), subject to the following modifications: (1) s 99(1) requires the notice to indicate the nature of the works of repair or restoration and that of the works of demolition and removal of rubbish or material; and (2) s 99(2) authorises the local authority to execute at its election either the works of repair or restoration or the works of demolition and removal of rubbish or material: s 79(3). As to the form, authentication and service of such notices see PARAS 135–137.

3 As to the meaning of 'owner' see PARA 12 note 2.

4 Building Act 1984 s 79(1). Section 79 does not apply to inner London (see s 88(1); Sch 3 para 5; and PARA 3) or to an advertisement as defined in the Town and Country Planning Act 1990 s

336(1) (see PLANNING vol 82 (2018) PARA 699) (Building Act 1984 s 79(4) (amended by the Planning (Consequential Provisions) Act 1990 s 4, Sch 2 para 67(4)(a))). The provisions of the Building Act 1984 s 79 have effect subject to the provisions of the Planning (Listed Buildings and Conservation Areas) Act 1990 relating to listed buildings, buildings subject to building preservation notices and buildings in conservation areas (see PLANNING vol 83 (2018) PARA 1165 et seq): Building Act 1984 s 79(5) (added by the Housing and Planning Act 1986 s 40, Sch 9 para 6(2); and amended by the Planning (Consequential Provisions) Act 1990 s 4, Sch 2 para 67(4)(b)).

    As to the making of building regulations to modify or repeal the provisions of the Building Act 1984 s 79 on the ground of inconsistency with other provisions see s 1(3), Sch 1 para 11(1); and PARA 9.

5 Building Act 1984 s 79(2)(a).
6 Building Act 1984 s 79(2)(b).
7 See note 2.
8 Building Act 1984 s 79(2). See *Liverpool City Council v Derwent Holdings Ltd* [2008] EWHC 679 (Admin), [2008] All ER (D) 204 (Mar) (building debris left on site for over two years was not seriously detrimental to the amenity of the neighbourhood).

117. Notice to local authority of intended demolition.

The provisions described below apply in relation to any demolition of the whole or part of a building except:

(1)   a demolition in pursuance of a demolition order or obstructive building order made under Part IX of the Housing Act 1985[1]; and

(2)   a demolition:

    (a)   of an internal part of a building, where the building is occupied and it is intended that it should continue to be occupied[2];

    (b)   of a building that has a cubic content, as ascertained by external measurement, of not more than 1750 cubic feet, or, where a greenhouse, conservatory, shed or prefabricated garage forms part of a larger building, of that greenhouse, conservatory, shed or prefabricated garage[3]; or

    (c)   without prejudice to head (2)(b) above, of an agricultural building[4], unless it is contiguous to another building that is not itself an agricultural building or a building of a kind mentioned in head (2)(b) above[5].

No person may begin a demolition for which such provision is made unless he has given the local authority[6] notice of his intention to do so, and either the local authority has given a notice[7] concerning demolition to him[8], or the relevant period[9] has expired[10]. Such a notice must specify the building to which it relates and the works of demolition intended to be carried out, and it is the duty of a person giving such a notice to a local authority to send or give a copy of it to certain persons[11]. A person who contravenes[12] these requirements in relation to such a notice is liable on summary conviction to a fine[13].

1 Building Act 1984 s 80(1)(a) (amended by the Housing (Consequential Provisions) Act 1985 s 4, Sch 2 para 58(3); and the Housing and Planning Act 1986 s 24(1)(j), Sch 5 Pt I para 11). The text refers to the Housing Act 1985 Pt IX (ss 265–323): see HOUSING vol 56 (2017) PARA 620 et seq.

    The Building Act 1984 s 80 does not apply to inner London: see s 88(1), Sch 3 para 5; and PARA 3.

    As to the making of building regulations to modify or repeal the provisions of s 80 on the ground of inconsistency with other provisions see s 1(3), Sch 1 para 11(1); and PARA 9.

2 Building Act 1984 s 80(1)(b)(i).
3 Building Act 1984 s 80(1)(b)(ii).
4 For these purposes, 'agricultural building' has the same meaning as in any of the provisions of the Local Government Finance Act 1988 Sch 5 paras 3–7 (see LOCAL GOVERNMENT FINANCE vol 70 (2018) PARA 118 et seq); definition applied by the Building Act 1984 s 80(1)(b)(iii) (amended by SI 1990/1285).
5 Building Act 1984 s 80(1)(b)(iii).

6 As to the meaning of 'local authority' see PARA 1 note 12.

7 As to the form and service of such notices see PARAS 135, 137. As to the authentication of local authority notices see PARA 136.

8 Ie under the Building Act 1984 s 81: see PARA 118.

9 As to the meaning of 'relevant period' see PARA 118 note 26.

10 Building Act 1984 s 80(2).

11 Building Act 1984 s 80(3). The persons to whom a copy must be given are: (1) the occupier of any building adjacent to the building (s 80(3)(a)); (2) any public gas supplier (as defined in the Gas Act 1986 Pt I (ss 4AA–48) (see ENERGY AND CLIMATE CHANGE vol 42 (2011) PARA 266)) in whose authorised area (as so defined) the building is situated (Building Act 1984 s 80(3)(b) (substituted by the Gas Act 1986 s 67(1), Sch 7 para 30)); and (3) the public electricity supplier (as defined in the Electricity Act 1989 Pt I (ss 3A–64) (see ENERGY AND CLIMATE CHANGE vol 43 (2011) PARA 539)) in whose authorised area (as so defined) the building is situated and any other person authorised by a licence under the Electricity Act 1989 Pt I to supply electricity to the building (Building Act 1984 s 80(3)(c) (substituted by the Electricity Act 1989 s 112(1), Sch 16 para 31)). The reference in the Building Act 1984 s 80(3)(b) to any public gas supplier as defined in the Gas Act 1986 Pt I has effect as if it were a reference to a gas transporter as defined in the Gas Act 1986 Pt I: see the Gas Act 1995 s 16(1), Sch 4 para 2(2)(i); Utilities Act 2000 s 76(7). As to gas transporters see ENERGY AND CLIMATE CHANGE vol 43 (2011) PARA 297 et seq. The reference in the Building Act 1984 s 80(3)(c) to the public electricity supplier as defined in the Electricity Act 1989 Pt I has effect as a reference to an electricity supplier, electricity distributor or both an electricity supplier and an electricity distributor according to the nature of the activities carried on by the persons to whom it referred before that time: see the Utilities Act 2000 s 31(1). As to electricity suppliers and electricity providers see ENERGY AND CLIMATE CHANGE vol 43 (2011) PARA 505 et seq.

12 Ie a person who contravenes the Building Act 1984 s 80(2) (see the text and notes 6–10) As to the meaning of 'contravene' see PARA 12 note 10.

13 Building Act 1984 s 80(4). The fine imposed is one not exceeding level 4 on the standard scale: s 80(4). As to the standard scale see SENTENCING vol 92 (2015) PARA 176. Civil sanctions may be imposed in respect of offences under the Building Act 1984 by virtue of the powers under the Regulatory Enforcement and Sanctions Act 2008 Pt 3 (ss 36–71): see ss 36, 38(2), Sch 6; and CONSTITUTIONAL AND ADMINISTRATIVE LAW vol 20 (2014) PARA 331 et seq.

118. Local authority's power to serve notice about demolition.

A local authority[1] may give a notice about a demolition[2] which may require the person to whom it is given[3]:

(1) to shore up any building adjacent to the building to which the notice relates[4];

(2) to weatherproof any surfaces of an adjacent building that are exposed by the demolition[5];

(3) to repair and make good any damage to an adjacent building caused by the demolition or by the negligent act or omission of any person engaged in it[6];

(4) to remove material or rubbish resulting from the demolition and clearance of the site[7];

(5) to disconnect and seal, at such points as the local authority may reasonably require, any sewer[8] or drain[9] in or under the building[10];

(6) to remove any such sewer or drain, and seal any sewer or drain with which the sewer or drain to be removed is connected[11];

(7) to make good to the satisfaction of the local authority the surface of the ground disturbed by anything done under head (5) or head (6) above[12];

(8) to make arrangements with the relevant statutory undertakers[13] for the disconnection of the supply of gas, electricity and water to the building[14];

(9)   to make such arrangements with regard to the burning of structures or materials on the site as may be reasonably required by the fire and rescue authority[15]; and

(10)   to take such steps relating to the conditions subject to which the demolition is to be undertaken, and the condition in which the site is to be left on completion of the demolition, as the local authority may consider reasonably necessary for the protection of the public and the preservation of public amenity[16],

to any of the following persons:

(a)   a person on whom a demolition order or obstructive building order has been served under Part IX of the Housing Act 1985[17];

(b)   a person who appears to it not to be intending to comply with an order[18] made with regard to a dangerous building or a notice[19] given with regard to dilapidated buildings and neglected sites[20]; and

(c)   a person who appears to it to have begun or to be intending to begin a demolition[21].

Where a person has given a notice[22] to a local authority of an intended demolition[23], or the local authority has served a demolition order or obstructive building order on a person under Part IX of the Housing Act 1985[24], a local authority's notice about a demolition[25] may only be given to the person in question within the relevant period[26]. It is the duty of the local authority to send or give a copy of such a local authority's notice about a demolition to the owner[27] and occupier of any building adjacent to the building to which the notice relates[28].

1   As to the meaning of 'local authority' see PARA 1 note 12.
2   Ie a notice under the Building Act 1984 s 81(1): see the text and note 3. The provisions of s 99 (content and enforcement of notice requiring works) (see PARA 126), and s 102 (appeal against notice requiring works) (see PARA 138) apply in relation to a notice given under s 81(1): ss 82(6), 83(1). Among the grounds on which an appeal may be brought under s 102 against such a notice are: (1) in the case of a notice requiring an adjacent building to be shored up, that the owner of the building is not entitled to the support of that building by the building that is being demolished, and ought to pay, or contribute towards, the expenses of shoring it up (s 83(2)(a)); (2) in the case of a notice requiring any surfaces of an adjacent building to be weatherproofed, that the owner of the adjacent building ought to pay, or contribute towards, the expenses of weatherproofing those surfaces (s 83(2)(b)). Where the grounds on which an appeal under s 102 is brought include a ground specified in s 83(2): (a) the appellant must serve a copy of his notice of appeal on the person or persons referred to in that ground of appeal (s 83(3)(a)); and (b) on the hearing of the appeal the court may make such order as it thinks fit in respect of the payment of, or contribution towards, the cost of the works by any such person, or as to how any expenses that may be recoverable by the local authority are to be borne between the appellant and any such person (s 83(3)(b)). As to the meaning of 'owner' see PARA 12 note 2. As to the form, authentication and service of such notices see PARAS 135–137.
    A notice under s 81 is necessary before a person who has given notice of his intention to undertake a demolition may begin: see s 80(2); and PARA 117. Where a local authority has power to serve a notice under s 81 on a person undertaking a demolition, s 62 (see PARA 103) (disconnecting drains) does not apply: see s 62(6); and PARA 103.
    Nothing contained in a notice under s 81 prejudices or affects the operation of any of the relevant statutory provisions, as defined in the Health and Safety at Work etc Act 1974 s 53(1) (see HEALTH AND SAFETY AT WORK vol 52 (2014) PARA 302); or the relevant provisions and accordingly, if a requirement of such a notice is inconsistent with a requirement imposed by or under the Health and Safety at Work etc Act 1974, the latter requirement prevails: Building Act 1984 s 81(2) (amended by SI 2014/469). For these purposes, 'relevant provisions' means the relevant statutory provisions (within the meaning the Energy Act 2013 Pt 3) other than the provisions of the Nuclear Safeguards Act 2000 and any provision of nuclear regulations identified in accordance with the Energy Act 2013 s 74(9) as being made for the nuclear safeguards purposes: Building Act 1984 s 81(2A) (added by SI 2014/469).
3   Building Act 1984 ss 81(1), 82(1).

4   Building Act 1984 s 82(1)(a). Sections 81, 82, 83 do not apply to inner London: see s 88(1); Sch 3
    para 5; and PARA 3.
        As to the making of building regulations to modify or repeal the provisions of ss 81, 82, 83 on
    the ground of inconsistency with other provisions see s 1(3), Sch 1 para 11(1); and PARA 9.
5   Building Act 1984 s 82(1)(b).
6   Building Act 1984 s 82(1)(c). No one may be required under s 82(1)(c), (e), (f) (see heads (3), (5)
    and (6) in the text) to carry out any work in land outside the premises on which the works of
    demolition are being carried out if he has no right to carry out that work, but, subject to s 101
    (breaking open of streets) (see PARA 128), the person undertaking the demolition, or the local
    authority acting in his default, may break open any street for the purpose of complying with any
    such requirement: s 82(2). As to the meaning of 'premises' see PARA 12 note 2. As to the meaning
    of 'street' see PARA 103 note 15.
7   Building Act 1984 s 82(1)(d).
8   As to the meaning of 'sewer' see PARA 36 note 7.
9   As to the meaning of 'drain' see PARA 36 note 6.
10 Building Act 1984 s 82(1)(e). See note 6. Before a person complies with a requirement under s
    82(1)(e), (f), (g) (see heads (5), (6) and (7) in the text), he must give to the local authority at least
    48 hours' notice, in the case of a requirement under head (5) or head (6) in the text, or at least 24
    hours' notice, in the case of a requirement under head (7) in the text, and a person who fails to
    comply with s 82(3) is liable on summary conviction to a fine not exceeding level 2 on the standard
    scale: s 82(3). As to the powers of magistrates' courts to issue fines on summary conviction see
    SENTENCING vol 92 (2015) PARA 176. Civil sanctions may be imposed in respect of offences
    under the Building Act 1984 by virtue of the powers under the Regulatory Enforcement and
    Sanctions Act 2008 Pt 3 (ss 36–71): see ss 36, 38(2), Sch 6; and CONSTITUTIONAL AND
    ADMINISTRATIVE LAW vol 20 (2014) PARA 331 et seq.
11 Building Act 1984 s 82(1)(f). See notes 6, 10.
12 Building Act 1984 s 82(1)(g). See note 10.
13 As to the meaning of 'statutory undertakers' see PARA 16 note 10. The provisions of the Building
    Act 1984 s 82 do not authorise interference with apparatus or works of statutory undertakers
    authorised by an enactment to carry on an undertaking for the supply of electricity, or gas or with
    apparatus or works of a water undertaker or sewerage undertaker: s 82(4) (amended by the Water
    Act 1989 s 190, Sch 25 para 70(2)(a)). As to the meaning of 'enactment' see PARA 6 note 2. The
    reference in the Building Act 1984 s 82(4) to a person authorised by an enactment to carry on an
    undertaking for the supply of electricity is to be construed as a reference to a holder of a licence
    under the Electricity Act 1989 s 6 (see ENERGY AND CLIMATE CHANGE vol 43 (2011) PARA 539):
    see s 112(1), Sch 16 para 1(7). The reference in the Building Act 1984 s 82(4) to a person
    authorised by an enactment to carry on an undertaking for the supply of gas is to be construed as
    a reference to a gas transporter: see the Gas Act 1995 s 16(1), Sch 4 para 2(8); Utilities Act 2000
    s 76(7). As to gas transporters see ENERGY AND CLIMATE CHANGE vol 43 (2011) PARA 297 et
    seq.
        Without prejudice to the generality of the Building Act 1984 s 82(4), s 82 does not exempt a
    person from:
    (1)   the obligation to obtain any consent required under the Water Industry Act 1991 s 174
          (see WATER AND WATERWAYS vol 101 (2018) PARA 752) or the Water Resources Act
          1991 s 176 (see WATER AND WATERWAYS vol 101 (2018) PARAS 712, 715)
          (interference with water supplies or with waterworks) (Building Act 1984 s 82(5)(a)
          (amended by the Water Act 1989 Sch 25 para 70(2)(b); and the Water Consolidation
          (Consequential Provisions) Act 1991 s 2(1), Sch 1 para 39(1), (4)));
    (2)   criminal liability under any enactment relating to the supply of gas or electricity
          (Building Act 1984 s 82(5)(b)); or
    (3)   the requirements of regulations relating to public safety under the Gas Act 1972 s 31
          (repealed: see now as to safety regulations the Gas Act 1986 s 18; and ENERGY AND
          CLIMATE CHANGE vol 43 (2011) PARA 350) (Building Act 1984 s 82(5)(c)).
14 Building Act 1984 s 82(1)(h). If a notice under s 81 contains such a requirement as is specified in
    s 82(1)(h), it is the duty of the local authority to send or give a copy of it to the statutory
    undertakers concerned: s 81(6)(a).
15 Building Act 1984 s 82(1)(i) (substituted by SI 2005/1541). As to the meaning of 'fire and rescue
    authority' see PARA 55 note 11. If a notice under the Building Act 1984 s 81 contains such a
    requirement as is specified in s 82(1)(i), it is the duty of the local authority to send or give a copy
    of it to the fire and rescue authority, if it is not itself the fire and rescue authority: s 81(6)(b)
    (substituted by SI 2005/1541).

16 Building Act 1984 s 82(1)(j).
17 Building Act 1984 s 81(1)(a) (amended by the Housing (Consequential Provisions) Act 1985 s 4, Sch 2 para 58(1), (3); and the Housing and Planning Act 1986 s 24(1)(j), Sch 5 Pt I para 11(1)). The text refers to the Housing Act 1985 Pt IX (ss 264–323): see HOUSING vol 56 (2017) PARA 620 et seq.
18 Ie an order under the Building Act 1984 s 77: see PARA 115.
19 Ie a notice under the Building Act 1984 s 79: see PARA 116.
20 Building Act 1984 s 81(1)(b).
21 Building Act 1984 s 81(1)(c). The text refers to a demolition to which s 80 (see PARA 117) otherwise applies: see s 81(1)(c).
22 Ie under the Building Act 1984 s 80: see PARA 117.
23 Building Act 1984 s 81(3)(a).
24 Building Act 1984 s 81(3)(b) (amended by the Housing (Consequential Provisions) Act 1985 Sch 2 para 58(1), (3); and the Housing and Planning Act 1986 Sch 5 Pt I para 11(1)).
25 Ie under the Building Act 1984 s 81.
26 For the purposes of the Building Act 1984 ss 80, 81, the 'relevant period' means:
    (1)   in a case such as is mentioned in s 81(3)(a) (see the text to notes 22–23), six weeks from the giving of the notice under s 80 (see PARA 117), or such longer period as the person who gave that notice may in writing allow (s 81(4)(a)); and
    (2)   in a case such as is mentioned in s 81(3)(b) (see the text to note 24), seven days after the local authority served a copy of the demolition order or obstructive building order in accordance with the Housing Act 1985 Pt IX, or such longer period as the person on whom the copy was served may in writing allow (Building Act 1984 s 81(4)(b) (amended by the Housing (Consequential Provisions) Act 1985 Sch 2 para 58(1), (3); and the Housing and Planning Act 1986 Sch 5 Pt I para 11(1))).
27 As to the meaning of 'owner' see PARA 12 note 2.
28 Building Act 1984 s 81(5).

(5) Yards, Passages and Courtyards

119. Paving and drainage of yards and passages.

If a court or yard appurtenant to, or a passage giving access to[1], houses[2] and industrial and commercial buildings is not so formed, flagged, asphalted or paved, or is not provided with such works on, above or below its surface, as to allow of the satisfactory drainage of its surface or subsoil to a proper outfall, the local authority[3] may by notice[4] require any person who is the owner[5] of any of the buildings to execute all such works as may be necessary to remedy the defect[6]. This applies in relation to any court, yard or passage that is used in common by the occupiers of two or more houses, or a house and a commercial or industrial building, but is not a highway maintainable at the public expense[7].

1   This does not include a path in the owner's garden leading from his front gate to the door of his house: *Denton UDC v Bursted Properties Ltd* [1955] 1 All ER 273, sub nom *Bursted Properties Ltd v Denton UDC* [1955] 1 WLR 82, DC.
2   As to the meaning of 'house' see PARA 16 note 10.
3   As to the meaning of 'local authority' see PARA 1 note 12.
4   The provisions of the Building Act 1984 s 99 (content and enforcement of notice requiring works) (see PARA 126), and s 102 (appeal against notice requiring works) (see PARA 138) apply in relation to a notice given under s 84(1): s 84(2). As to the form, authentication and service of such notices see PARAS 135–137.
5   As to the meaning of 'owner' see PARA 12 note 2.
6   Building Act 1984 s 84(1), (3). As from a day to be appointed, s 84(1) is amended as follows. If a court or yard appurtenant to, or a passage giving access to, houses and industrial and commercial buildings is not so formed, flagged, asphalted or paved, or is not provided with such works on, above or below its surface, as to allow of the satisfactory drainage of its surface or subsoil (having regard both to the need to remove water from the court, yard or passage and also to the need to dispose of it satisfactorily in the course of or after its removal), the local authority may by notice require any person who is the owner of any of the buildings to execute all such works as may be

necessary to remedy the defect: s 84(1) (prospectively amended by the Flood and Water Management Act 2010 s 32, Sch 3 para 26(4)). At the date at which this volume states the law no such day had been appointed for this amendment to take effect.

As to the making of building regulations to modify or repeal the provisions of the Building Act 1984 s 84 on the ground of inconsistency with other provisions see s 1(3), Sch 1 para 11(1); and PARA 9.

7 Building Act 1984 s 84(4). As to highways maintainable at the public expense see HIGHWAYS, STREETS AND BRIDGES vol 55 (2012) PARA 250 et seq.

120. Maintenance of entrances to courtyards.

Except with the consent[1] of the local authority[2] an entrance to a court or yard on which two or more houses[3] front or abut must not be closed, narrowed, reduced in height or otherwise altered so as to impede the free circulation of air through the entrance[4], and no permanent structure may be erected so as to impede the free circulation of air through such an entrance[5]. A local authority in giving such a consent may impose such conditions as it thinks fit with respect to the provision of other openings or means of access, or other means for securing free circulation of air throughout the court or yard[6].

A person aggrieved[7] by the refusal of a local authority to give such a consent, or by a condition imposed by it, may appeal to a magistrates' court[8]. A person who contravenes[9] the provisions described above is liable on summary conviction to a fine[10] and also to a further fine for each day on which the offence continues after he is convicted[11].

1 As to the form, authentication and the giving of a consent see PARAS 135–137.
2 As to the meaning of 'local authority' see PARA 1 note 12.
3 As to the meaning of 'house' see PARA 16 note 10.
4 Building Act 1984 s 85(1)(a). Section 85 does not apply to inner London: see s 88(1), Sch 3 para 5; and PARA 3. As to the making of building regulations to modify or repeal the provisions of s 85 on the ground of inconsistency with other provisions see s 1(3), Sch 1 para 11(1); and PARA 9.
5 Building Act 1984 s 85(1)(b). See note 4.
6 Building Act 1984 s 85(2). See note 4.
7 As to persons aggrieved see JUDICIAL REVIEW vol 61 (2010) PARA 656.
8 Building Act 1984 s 85(3). See note 4. As to appeals generally see PARAS 139–140. See further MAGISTRATES; CRIMINAL PROCEDURE.
9 As to the meaning of 'contravene' see PARA 12 note 10.
10 Ie a fine not exceeding level 1 on the standard scale: Building Act 1984 s 85(4). As to the powers of magistrates' courts to issue fines on summary conviction see SENTENCING vol 92 (2015) PARA 176. Civil sanctions may be imposed in respect of offences under the Building Act 1984 by virtue of the powers under the Regulatory Enforcement and Sanctions Act 2008 Pt 3 (ss 36–71): see ss 36, 38(2), Sch 6; and CONSTITUTIONAL AND ADMINISTRATIVE LAW vol 20 (2014) PARA 331 et seq.
11 Building Act 1984 s 85(4). See note 4. The fine imposed must not exceed £2 for each day on which the default continues after conviction: see s 85(4). As to continuing offences see PARA 144.

(6) Appeals to Crown Court

121. Appeal to Crown Court.

Appeals in respect of certain matters lie to the Crown Court. Where a person is aggrieved[1] by an order, determination or other decision of a magistrates' court[2] under Part III of the Building Act 1984[3], or under Part IV of that Act[4] as it applies in relation to Part III, and is not by any other enactment[5] authorised to appeal to the Crown Court, he may appeal to the Crown Court[6]. However, this does not confer a right of appeal in a case in which each of the parties concerned might under the Building Act 1984 have required that the dispute should be determined by arbitration instead of by a magistrates' court[7].

1   As to persons aggrieved see JUDICIAL REVIEW vol 61 (2010) PARA 656.
2   See MAGISTRATES; CRIMINAL PROCEDURE vol 28 (2015) PARA 665 et seq.
3   Ie the Building Act 1984 Pt III (ss 59–90): see PARA 100 et seq.
4   Ie the Building Act 1984 Pt IV (ss 91–131): see PARA 70 et seq.
5   As to the meaning of 'enactment' see PARA 6 note 2.
6   Building Act 1984 s 86(1).
     As to the making of building regulations to modify or repeal the provisions of s 86 on the ground of inconsistency with other provisions see s 1(3), Sch 1 para 11(1); and PARA 9.
7   Building Act 1984 s 86(2). As to arbitrations under the Building Act 1984 see PARA 36 note 16. As to arbitration generally see ARBITRATION.

(7) Crown Property

122. Application of Part III of the Building Act 1984 to Crown property.
Provision is made in relation to the application of Part III of the Building Act 1984[1] to any house[2], building[3] or other premises[4] being property belonging to Her Majesty in right of the Crown or of the Duchy of Lancaster, or belonging to the Duchy of Cornwall, or belonging to a government department, or held in trust for Her Majesty for purposes of a government department[5]. In relation to any such property, the appropriate authority[6] may agree with the council of the county[7], or the local authority[8] of the district[9], in which the property is situated that any particular provisions of Part III of the Building Act 1984, and of Part IV of that Act[10] so far as it relates to Part III, apply to the property, and, while the agreement is in force, those provisions apply to that property accordingly, subject to the terms of the agreement[11]. Any such agreement may contain such consequential and incidental provisions (including, with the approval of the Treasury, provisions of a financial character) as appear to the appropriate authority to be necessary or equitable[12].

1   Ie the Building Act 1984 Pt III (ss 59–90): see PARA 100 et seq.
2   As to the meaning of 'house' see PARA 16 note 10.
3   As to the meaning of 'building' see PARA 6.
4   As to the meaning of 'premises' see PARA 12 note 2.
5   Building Act 1984 s 87(1).
     As to the making of building regulations to modify or repeal the provisions of s 87 on the ground of inconsistency with other provisions see s 1(3), Sch 1 para 11(1); and PARA 9.
6   For these purposes, the 'appropriate authority' means, in the case of property belonging to:
    (1)   Her Majesty in right of the Crown, the Crown Estate Commissioners or other government department having the management of the property (Building Act 1984 s 87(4)(a));
    (2)   Her Majesty in right of the Duchy of Lancaster, the Chancellor of the Duchy (s 87(4)(b));
    (3)   the Duchy of Cornwall, such person as the Duke of Cornwall, or the possessor for the time being of the Duchy of Cornwall, appoints (s 87(4)(c)); and
    (4)   a government department or held in trust for Her Majesty for purposes of a government department, that department (s 87(4)(d)),
     and, if a question arises as to what authority is the appropriate authority in relation to any property, that question must be referred to the Treasury, whose decision is final: s 87(4). As to the Treasury see CONSTITUTIONAL AND ADMINISTRATIVE LAW vol 20 (2014) PARA 262 et seq.
7   Building Act 1984 s 87(2)(a).
8   As to the meaning of 'local authority' see PARA 1 note 12.
9   Ie the Building Act 1984 Pt IV (ss 91–131): see PARA 70 et seq.
10   Building Act 1984 s 87(2)(b).

11 Building Act 1984 s 87(2). Section 87(2) applies in relation to property in Wales as if in s 87(2)(a)
   (see the text to note 7) the reference to a county included a reference to a county borough, and as
   if s 87(2)(b) (see the text to notes 8–10) were omitted: s 87(2A) (added by the Local Government
   (Wales) Act 1994 s 22(3), Sch 9 para 15(2)). As to areas and authorities in Wales see LOCAL
   GOVERNMENT vol 69 (2018) PARA36 et seq.
12 Building Act 1984 s 87(3).

5. ADMINISTRATIVE MATTERS UNDER THE BUILDING ACT 1984

(1) Entry on Premises and Execution of Works

123. Power to enter premises.

An authorised officer[1] of a local authority[2], on producing, if so required, some duly authenticated document[3] showing his authority, has a right to enter any premises[4] at all reasonable hours:

(1)   for the purpose of ascertaining whether there is, or has been, on or in connection with the premises, a contravention[5] of the Building Act 1984, or of any building regulations[6], that it is the duty of the local authority to enforce[7];

(2)   for the purpose of ascertaining whether or not circumstances exist that would authorise or require the local authority to take any action, or execute any work, under that Act or under building regulations[8];

(3)   for the purpose of taking any action, or executing any work, authorised or required by that Act, or by building regulations, or by an order made under the Act, to be taken, or executed, by the local authority[9]; or

(4)   generally for the purpose of the performance by the local authority of its functions[10] under that Act or under building regulations[11].

Admission to premises, other than a factory[12] or workplace[13], must not be demanded as of right unless 24 hours' notice of the intended entry has been given to the occupier[14]. If it is shown to the satisfaction of a justice of the peace[15] on sworn information in writing that:

(a)   admission to any premises has been refused or refusal is apprehended, or the premises are unoccupied, or the occupier is temporarily absent, or the case is one of urgency, or an application for admission would defeat the object of the entry[16]; and

(b)   there is reasonable ground for entry into the premises for any of the purposes mentioned in head (1) above[17],

the justice may by warrant under his hand authorise the local authority by any authorised officer to enter the premises, if need be by force[18]. A warrant must not be issued unless the justice is satisfied that:

(i)   notice of the intention to apply for a warrant has been given to the occupier[19];

(ii)   the premises are unoccupied, or the occupier is temporarily absent, or the case is one of urgency, or the giving of the notice would defeat the object of the entry[20].

A warrant continues in force until the purpose for which the entry is necessary has been satisfied[21].

An authorised officer entering premises[22] may take with him such other persons as may be necessary, and on leaving unoccupied premises that he has entered by virtue of a warrant he must leave them as effectually secured against trespassers as he found them[23]. A person who is admitted into a factory or workplace[24] and discloses to another person information obtained by him in the factory or workplace with regard to a manufacturing process or trade secret, is liable on summary conviction to a fine[25] or to imprisonment[26], unless the disclosure was made in the performance of his duty[27].

1 As to the meaning of 'authorised officer' see PARA 102 note 10. In relation to the Inner Temple and the Middle Temple, a reference in a provision of the Building Act 1984 Pt IV (ss 91–131) to the proper officer or an officer or authorised officer of a local authority is a reference to an officer authorised by the Sub-Treasurer or the Under Treasurer, as the case may be, to act for the purposes of that provision: s 127. As to the meaning of 'proper officer' see PARA 102 note 9.

2 As to the meaning of 'local authority' see PARA 1 note 12.

3 As to the authentication of documents see PARA 136.

4 As to the meaning of 'premises' see PARA 12 note 2.

5 As to the meaning of 'contravention' see PARA 12 note 10.

6 As to the meaning of 'building regulations' see PARA 7.

7 Building Act 1984 s 95(1)(a). As to the making of building regulations to modify or repeal the provisions of ss 95, 96 on the ground of inconsistency with other provisions see s 1(3), Sch 1 para 11(1); and PARA 9.

8 Building Act 1984 s 95(1)(b).

9 Building Act 1984 s 95(1)(c).

10 As to the meaning of 'functions' see PARA 3 note 19.

11 Building Act 1984 s 95(1)(d).

12 'Factory' has the meaning given by the Factories Act 1961 s 175 (see HEALTH AND SAFETY AT WORK vol 52 (2014) PARA 306): Building Act 1984 s 126.

13 As to the meaning of 'workplace' see PARA 105 note 24.

14 Building Act 1984 s 95(2).

15 As to justices of the peace see generally MAGISTRATES.

16 Building Act 1984 s 95(3)(a).

17 Building Act 1984 s 95(3)(b).

18 Building Act 1984 s 95(3).

19 Building Act 1984 s 95(4)(a).

20 Building Act 1984 s 95(4)(b).

21 Building Act 1984 s 96(2).

22 Ie by virtue of the Building Act 1984 s 95 or of a warrant issued under that section: see the text and notes 1–20.

23 Building Act 1984 s 96(1).

24 Ie in compliance with the Building Act 1984 s 95 or a warrant issued under that section: see the text and notes 1–20.

25 Ie a fine not exceeding level 3 on the standard scale: Building Act 1984 s 96(3). As to the powers of magistrates' courts to issue fines on summary conviction see SENTENCING vol 92 (2015) PARA 176. Civil sanctions may be imposed in respect of offences under the Building Act 1984 by virtue of the powers under the Regulatory Enforcement and Sanctions Act 2008 Pt 3 (ss 36–71): see ss 36, 38(2), Sch 6; and CONSTITUTIONAL AND ADMINISTRATIVE LAW vol 20 (2014) PARA 331 et seq.

26 Ie for a term not exceeding three months: Building Act 1984 s 96(3). As from a day to be appointed s 96(3) is amended and the reference to imprisonment is repealed by the Criminal Justice Act 2003 s 332, Sch 37 Pt 9. At the date at which this volume states the law no such day had been appointed.

27 Building Act 1984 s 96(3).

124. Power to execute work.

A local authority[1] may, by agreement with the owner[2] or occupier of any premises[3], itself execute at his expense any work that it has under the Building Act 1984 required him to execute, or any work in connection with the construction, laying, alteration or repair of a sewer[4] or drain[5] that the owner or occupier is entitled to execute, and for that purpose it has all the rights that he would have[6].

1 As to the meaning of 'local authority' see PARA 1 note 12.

2 As to the meaning of 'owner' see PARA 12 note 2.

3 As to the meaning of 'premises' see PARA 12 note 2.

4 As to the meaning of 'sewer' see PARA 36 note 7.

5 As to the meaning of 'drain' see PARA 36 note 6.

6   Building Act 1984 s 97. As to the making of building regulations to modify or repeal the provisions
    of s 97 on the ground of inconsistency with other provisions see s 1(3), Sch 1 para 11(1); and PARA
    9.

125.   Power to require occupier to permit work.

If, on a complaint made by the owner[1] of premises[2], it appears to a magistrates'
court[3] that the occupier of those premises is preventing the owner from executing
any work that he is by or under the Building Act 1984 required to execute, the
court may order the occupier to permit the execution of the work[4].

1   As to the meaning of 'owner' see PARA 12 note 2.
2   As to the meaning of 'premises' see PARA 12 note 2.
3   See MAGISTRATES; CRIMINAL PROCEDURE.
4   Building Act 1984 s 98. As to the making of building regulations to modify or repeal the provisions
    of s 98 on the ground of inconsistency with other provisions see s 1(3), Sch 1 para 11(1); and PARA
    9.

126.   Content and enforcement of notice requiring works.

Certain notices under the Building Act 1984[1] must indicate the nature of the
works to be executed and state the time within which they are to be executed[2].
Subject to any right of appeal[3], if the person required by such a notice to execute
works fails to execute them within the time limited by the notice the local
authority[4] may itself execute the works and recover from that person the expenses
reasonably incurred by it in doing so[5], and without prejudice to that power, he is
liable on summary conviction to a fine[6] and to a further fine for each day on which
the default continues after he is convicted[7].

1   Ie a notice in relation to which it is declared by any provision of the Building Act 1984 that s 99
    applies: see s 99(1). Section 99 is expressly applied by s 2(5) (see PARA 12), s 59(2) (see PARA 100),
    s 60(5) (see PARA 101), s 64(3) (see PARA 105), s 65(3) (see PARA 106), s 66(5) (see PARA 107),
    s 68(5) (see PARA 109), s 70(2) (see PARA 111), s 72(2) (see PARA 57), s 74(4) (see PARA 113), s
    79(3) (see PARA 116), s 82(6) (see PARA 118), s 84(2) (see PARA 119).
2   Building Act 1984 s 99(1). Section 99 has effect subject to any modification specified in the
    provision under which the notice is given: s 99(3). As to the meaning of 'modifications' see PARA
    3 note 21. As to the making of building regulations to modify or repeal the provisions of s 99 on
    the ground of inconsistency with other provisions see s 1(3), Sch 1 para 11(1); and PARA 9.
3   Ie conferred by the Building Act 1984 s 102: see PARA 138.
4   As to the meaning of 'local authority' see PARA 1 note 12.
5   Building Act 1984 s 99(2)(a). See also note 2.
6   Ie a fine not exceeding level 4 on the standard scale: Building Act 1984 s 99(2)(b). As to the powers
    of magistrates' courts to issue fines on summary conviction see SENTENCING vol 92 (2015)
    PARA 176. Civil sanctions may be imposed in respect of offences under the Building Act 1984 by
    virtue of the powers under the Regulatory Enforcement and Sanctions Act 2008 Pt 3 (ss 36–71):
    see ss 36, 38(2), Sch 6; and CONSTITUTIONAL AND ADMINISTRATIVE LAW vol 20 (2014)
    PARA 331 et seq.
7   Building Act 1984 s 99(2)(b). The fine imposed must not exceed £2 for each day on which the
    default continues after conviction: see s 99(2)(b). See also note 2. As to continuing offences see
    PARA 144.

127.   Sale of materials.

A local authority[1] may sell any materials that:

(1)   have been removed by it from any premises[2], including a street[3], when
        executing works under the Building Act 1984 or otherwise carrying the
        Act into effect[4]; and

(2)   are not before the expiration of three days from the date of their
        removal claimed by the owner[5] and taken away by him[6].

Where a local authority sells such materials, it must pay the proceeds to the person to whom the materials belonged, after deducting the amount of any expenses recoverable by it from him[7]. This power does not apply to refuse removed by a local authority[8].

1   As to the meaning of 'local authority' see PARA 1 note 12.
2   As to the meaning of 'premises' see PARA 12 note 2.
3   As to the meaning of 'street' see PARA 103 note 15.
4   Building Act 1984 s 100(1)(a). As to the making of building regulations to modify or repeal the provisions of s 100 on the ground of inconsistency with other provisions see s 1(3), Sch 1 para 11(1); and PARA 9.
5   As to the meaning of 'owner' see PARA 12 note 2.
6   Building Act 1984 s 100(1)(b).
7   Building Act 1984 s 100(2).
8   Building Act 1984 s 100(3).

128.   Breaking open of streets.

Where, under the Building Act 1984, local authorities[1] have power to construct, lay or maintain sewers[2], drains[3] or pipes, the provisions relating to the power to lay pipes in streets under the Water Industry Act 1991[4] apply, with the necessary modifications[5], as they apply for the purpose of conferring power on a water undertaker[6] or sewerage undertaker[7] to lay a relevant pipe[8]. Those provisions also apply so far as necessary for the purposes of any power to lay or maintain a sewer or drain which is conferred by the Building Act 1984 on a person other than a local authority[9].

1   As to the meaning of 'local authority' see PARA 1 note 12.
2   As to the meaning of 'sewer' see PARA 36 note 7.
3   As to the meaning of 'drain' see PARA 36 note 6.
4   Ie the Water Industry Act 1991 s 158: see WATER AND WATERWAYS vol 101 (2018) PARA 728.
5   As to the meaning of 'modifications' see PARA 3 note 21.
6   As to water undertakers see WATER AND WATERWAYS vol 100 (2018) PARA 505 et seq.
7   As to sewerage undertakers see ENVIRONMENTAL QUALITY AND PUBLIC HEALTH vol 46 (2010) PARA 999 et seq.
8   Building Act 1984 s 101(1) (amended by the Water Act 1989 s 190, Sch 25 para 70; and the Water Consolidation (Consequential Provisions) Act 1991 s 2, Sch 1 para 39(1), (5)). 'Relevant pipe' refers to a relevant pipe within the meaning of the Water Industry Act 1991 s 158(7) (see WATER AND WATERWAYS vol 101 (2018) PARA 728): see the Building Act 1984 s 101(1) (as so amended).
    As to the making of building regulations to modify or repeal the provisions of s 101 on the ground of inconsistency with other provisions see the Building Act 1984 s 1(3), Sch 1 para 11(1); and PARA 9.
9   Building Act 1984 s 101(2) (substituted by the Water Act 1989 s 190, Sch 25 para 70; and amended by the Water Consolidation (Consequential Provisions) Act 1991 s 2, Sch 1 para 39(5)).

(2)   Compensation and Recovery

129.   Compensation for damage.

A local authority[1] must make full compensation to a person who has sustained damage by reason of the exercise by the authority, in relation to a matter as to which he has not himself been in default, of any of its powers under the Building Act 1984[2]. Any dispute as to the fact of damage, or as to the amount of compensation, must be determined by arbitration[3]. However, if the compensation claimed does not exceed £50, all questions as to the fact of damage, liability to pay compensation and the amount of compensation may on the application of either party be determined by, and any compensation awarded may be recovered before, a magistrates' court[4].

1   As to the meaning of 'local authority' see PARA 1 note 12.
2   Building Act 1984 s 106(1). 'Default' under the Building Act 1984 s 106(1) does not refer solely to default under the Act itself: see *Hastings BC v Manolete Partners plc* [2016] UKSC 50, [2016] 1 WLR 3059, [2016] All ER (D) 142 (Jul) (local authority liable to pay compensation for loss incurred by occupier of premises on pier after used emergency powers to close pier as danger to public following freeholder's failure to make repairs).As to the making of building regulations to modify or repeal the provisions of s 106 on the ground of inconsistency with other provisions see s 1(3), Sch 1 para 11(1); and PARA 9.
3   Building Act 1984 s 106(2). As to arbitrations under the Building Act 1984 see PARA 36 note 16.
4   Building Act 1984 s 106(3). As to the procedure on application to a magistrates' court see PARA 139. See further MAGISTRATES; CRIMINAL PROCEDURE vol 27 (2015) PARA 142.

130.   Recovery of expenses.

Where a local authority[1] has incurred expenses for whose repayment the owner[2] of the premises[3] in respect of which the expenses were incurred is liable, either under the Building Act 1984 or by agreement with the authority, those expenses, together with interest from the date of service of a demand for the expenses[4], may be recovered by the authority:

(1)   from the person who is the owner of the premises at the date on which the works are completed[5]; or

(2)   if he has ceased to be the owner of the premises before the date on which a demand for the expenses is served, either from him or from the person who is the owner at the date on which the demand is served[6].

As from the date of the completion of the works, the expenses and interest accrued due on it are, until recovered, a charge[7] on the premises and on all estates and interests in them[8].

A sum that a local authority is entitled to recover under the Building Act 1984, and with respect to whose recovery provision is not made by any other provision of the Act, may be recovered as a simple contract debt in any court of competent jurisdiction[9].

A local authority may by order declare any expenses recoverable by it[10] to be payable with interest[11] by instalments within a period not exceeding 30 years, until the whole amount is paid[12]. Such an order may be made at any time with respect to an unpaid balance of expenses and accrued interest, but the period for repayment must not in any case extend beyond 30 years from the service of the first demand for the expenses[13]. Any such instalments and interest, or any part of it, may be recovered from the owner or occupier for the time being of the premises in respect of which the expenses were incurred, and, if recovered from the occupier, may be deducted by him from the rent of the premises[14]. However, an occupier is not required to pay at any one time a sum in excess of the amount that was due from him on account of rent at[15], or has become due from him on account of rent since[16], the date on which he received a demand from the local authority together with a notice requiring him not to pay rent to his landlord without deducting the demanded sum[17].

1   As to the meaning of 'local authority' see PARA 1 note 12.
2   As to the meaning of 'owner' see PARA 12 note 2.
3   As to the meaning of 'premises' see PARA 12 note 2.
4   The rate of interest chargeable under the Building Act 1984 s 107(1) is such reasonable rate as the authority may determined: s 107(3). As to the making of building regulations to modify or repeal the provisions of ss 107, 108 on the ground of inconsistency with other provisions see s 1(3), Sch 1

para 11(1); and PARA 9.

5   Building Act 1984 s 107(1)(a).
6   Building Act 1984 s 107(1)(b).
7   For the purposes of enforcing such a charge, a local authority has all the same powers and remedies under the Law of Property Act 1925 and otherwise as if it was mortgagee by deed having power of sale and lease, of accepting surrenders of leases and of appointing a receiver: Building Act 1984 s 107(2).
8   Building Act 1984 s 107(1). Nothing in the Building Act 1984 about the recovery of expenses from owners of premises affects the Local Land Charges Act 1975 (see REAL PROPERTY AND REGISTRATION vol 87 (2017) PARA 641 et seq): Building Act 1984 s 129.
9   Building Act 1984 s 107(4). Where a person has been given a notice in relation to which s 102 (see PARA 138) applies, and the local authority takes proceedings against him for the recovery of expenses that it is entitled to recover from him, it is not open to him to raise any question that he could have raised on an appeal under s 102: s 107(5).
10 Ie under the Building Act 1984 s 107(1): see the text and notes 1–8.
11 The rate of interest chargeable under the Building Act 1984 s 108(1) is such reasonable rate as the authority may determine: s 108(4).
12 Building Act 1984 s 108(1).
13 Building Act 1984 s 108(2).
14 Building Act 1984 s 108(3).
15 Building Act 1984 s 108(3)(a).
16 Building Act 1984 s 108(3)(b).
17 Building Act 1984 s 108(3).

131. Liability of agent or trustee.

Where a local authority[1] claims to recover expenses under the Building Act 1984 from a person as being the owner[2] of the premises[3] in respect of which the expenses were incurred, and that person proves that:

(1)   he is receiving the rent of those premises merely as agent or trustee for some other person[4]; and

(2)   he has not, and since the date of the service[5] on him of a demand for payment has not had, in his hands on behalf of that other person sufficient money to discharge the whole demand of the authority[6],

his liability is limited to the total amount of the money that he has or has had in his hands[7]. However, a local authority which is, or would be, so debarred from recovering the whole of any such expenses from an agent or trustee may recover the whole or any unpaid balance of it from the person on whose behalf the agent or trustee receives the rent[8].

1   As to the meaning of 'local authority' see PARA 1 note 12.
2   As to the meaning of 'owner' see PARA 12 note 2. As to the recovery of expenses see PARA 130.
3   As to the meaning of 'premises' see PARA 12 note 2.
4   Building Act 1984 s 110(a).
5   As to the service of documents see PARA 137.
6   Building Act 1984 s 110(b).
7   Building Act 1984 s 110. As to the making of building regulations to modify or repeal the provisions of s 110 on the ground of inconsistency with other provisions see s 1(3), Sch 1 para 11(1); and PARA 9.
8   Building Act 1984 s 110.

(3) Protection from Liability

132. Protection of members of authorities etc.

Nothing done, and no contract entered into by a local authority[1], port health authority[2] or joint board[3], and nothing done by a member or officer[4] of, or person acting under the direction of, such an authority or board, subjects it or him personally to any action, liability, claim or demand whatsoever, if it is done or entered into bona fide for the purpose of executing the Building Act 1984[5]. Any expense incurred by such an authority, board, member, officer or other person acting bona fide for the such purposes must be borne and repaid out of the fund or rate applicable by the authority or board for the general purposes of the Act[6].

1   As to the meaning of 'local authority' see PARA 1 note 12.
2   As to port health districts and authorities see ENVIRONMENTAL QUALITY AND PUBLIC HEALTH vol 45 (2010) PARA 102.
3   'Joint board' has the meaning given by the Public Health Act 1936 s 343(1) (see ENVIRONMENTAL QUALITY AND PUBLIC HEALTH vol 45 (2010) PARA 101): Building Act 1984 s 126.
4   As to the meaning of 'officer' see PARA 102 note 9. As to references to an officer in relation to the Inner Temple and the Middle Temple see PARA 123 note 1.
5   Building Act 1984 s 115(1). As to the making of building regulations to modify or repeal the provisions of s 115 on the ground of inconsistency with other provisions see s 1(3), Sch 1 para 11(1); and PARA 9.
6   Building Act 1984 s 115(2). See note 5.

(4) Default Powers

133.   Default powers.

If the appropriate national authority[1] is satisfied that a local authority[2] or joint board[3] has failed to discharge its functions[4] under the Building Act 1984 in a case in which it ought to have discharged them, the appropriate national authority may make an order declaring it to be in default and directing it for the purposes of removing the default to discharge such of its functions, in such manner and within such time or times, as may be specified in the order[5]. If a local authority or joint board with respect to whom such an order has been made fails to comply with a requirement of the order within the time limited by the order for compliance with that requirement, the appropriate national authority, in lieu of enforcing a mandatory order[6] or otherwise, may make an order transferring to itself such of the functions of the body in default as may be specified in the order[7].

Where the appropriate national authority has transferred functions to itself by order, any expenses incurred in discharging those functions must be paid in the first instance out of moneys provided by Parliament, but the amount of those expenses as certified by the appropriate national authority must be paid to it by the body in default on demand, and is recoverable by the appropriate national authority from it as a debt due to the Crown, and that body has the like power of raising the money required as it has of raising money for defraying expenses incurred directly by it[8]. The payment of such expenses is, to such extent as may be sanctioned by the appropriate national authority, a purpose for which a local authority or joint board may borrow money in accordance with the statutory provisions relating to borrowing by such an authority or board[9].

Where the appropriate national authority has made an order transferring to itself such of the functions of the body in default as may be specified in the order[10], it may at any time by a subsequent order vary or revoke that order, but without prejudice to the validity of anything previously done[11]. Where an order is revoked, the appropriate national authority may, either by the revoking order or by a subsequent order, make such provision as appears to be desirable with respect to the transfer, vesting and discharge of any property or liabilities acquired or incurred by it in discharging functions to which the revoked order related[12].

1   Ie the Secretary of State or, where statutory functions have been transferred in relation to Wales,

the Welsh Ministers: see PARA 5.
2   As to the meaning of 'local authority' see PARA 1 note 12.
3   'Joint board' has the meaning given by the Public Health Act 1936 s 343(1) (see ENVIRONMENTAL
    QUALITY AND PUBLIC HEALTH vol 45 (2010) PARA 101): Building Act 1984 s 126.
4   As to the meaning of 'functions' see PARA 3 note 19.
5   Building Act 1984 s 116(1). As to the making of building regulations to modify or repeal the
    provisions of ss 116, 117, 118 on the ground of inconsistency with other provisions see s 1(3),
    Sch 1 para 11(1); and PARA 9.
6   As to mandatory orders see JUDICIAL REVIEW vol 61 (2010) PARA 703.
7   Building Act 1984 s 116(2).
8   Building Act 1984 s 117(1).
9   Building Act 1984 s 117(2).
10 Ie an order under the Building Act 1984 s 116(2): see the text and notes 6–7.
11 Building Act 1984 s 118(1).
12 Building Act 1984 s 118(2).

(5) Local Inquiries

134. Local inquiries.

The appropriate national authority[1] may cause a local inquiry to be held in a case where it is authorised by a provision of the Building Act 1984 to determine a difference, to make an order, to give a consent or approval or otherwise to act under such a provision[2].

1   Ie the Secretary of State or, where statutory functions have been transferred in relation to Wales,
    the Welsh Ministers: see PARA 5.
2   Building Act 1984 s 119. As to the making of building regulations to modify or repeal the
    provisions of s 119 on the ground of inconsistency with other provisions see s 1(3), Sch 1 para
    11(1); and PARA 9.

(6) Documentation

135. Form of documents.

All notices, orders, consents, demands and other documents authorised or required by or under the Building Act 1984 to be given, made or issued by a local authority[1], and notices and applications authorised or required by or under that Act to be given or made to, or to any officer[2] of, a local authority, must be in writing[3].

The appropriate national authority[4] may, by regulations made by statutory instrument, prescribe the form of any notice, advertisement, certificate or other document to be used for any of the purposes of the Act, and if forms are prescribed those forms or forms to the like effect may be used in all cases to which those forms are applicable[5].

1   As to the meaning of 'local authority' see PARA 1 note 12.
2   As to the meaning of 'officer' see PARA 102 note 9. As to references to an authorised officer in
    relation to the Inner Temple and the Middle Temple see PARA 123 note 1. As to the meaning of
    'authorised officer' see PARA 102 note 10.
3   Building Act 1984 s 92(1). As to the making of building regulations to modify or repeal the
    provisions of s 92 on the ground of inconsistency with other provisions see s 1(3), Sch 1 para 11(1);
    and PARA 9.
4   Ie the Secretary of State or, where statutory functions have been transferred in relation to Wales,
    the Welsh Ministers: see PARA 5.

5 Building Act 1984 s 92(2). At the date at which this volume states the law, no such forms had been prescribed.

136. Authentication of documents.

A notice, order, consent, demand or other document that a local authority[1] is authorised or required by or under the Building Act 1984 to give, make or issue may be signed on behalf of the authority:

(1)   by the proper officer[2] of the authority[3], as respects documents relating to matters within his province[4]; or

(2)   by an officer[5] of the authority authorised by it in writing to sign documents of the particular kind or, as the case may be, the particular document[6].

A document purporting to bear the signature[7] of an officer expressed to hold an office by virtue of which he is empowered to sign such a document[8], or expressed to be authorised by the local authority to sign such a document or the particular document[9], is deemed, for the purposes of the Building Act 1984 and of any building regulations[10] and orders made under it, to have been duly given, made or issued by authority of the local authority, until the contrary is proved[11].

1 As to the meaning of 'local authority' see PARA 1 note 12.

2 As to the meaning of 'proper officer' see PARA 102 note 9. As to references to a proper officer in relation to the Inner Temple and the Middle Temple see PARA 123 note 1.

3 The Building Act 1984 s 93 also refers to the district surveyor. The office of district surveyor (whose function was to supervise the operation of the London Building Acts in inner London) no longer exists and his functions have been transferred to the inner London borough councils and the Common Council of the City of London: see the Local Government Act 1985 s 16, Sch 8 para 14(1); and the Local Government Reorganisation (Miscellaneous Provision) (No 4) Order 1986, SI 1986/452, art 3, Sch 3 Pt I. As to the Common Council of the City of London see LONDON GOVERNMENT vol 71 (2013) PARAS 34–38.

4 Building Act 1984 s 93(1)(a). The Building Act 1984 s 93 applies to documents authorised or required to be given, made, issued or served by or under the Domestic Fire Safety (Wales) Measure 2011: see s 4 (not yet in force); and PARA 58.As to the making of building regulations to modify or repeal the provisions of s 93 on the ground of inconsistency with other provisions see s 1(3), Sch 1 para 11(1); and PARA 9.

5 As to the meaning of 'officer' see PARA 102 note 9.

6 Building Act 1984 s 93(1)(b).

7 'Signature' includes a facsimile of a signature by whatever process reproduced: Building Act 1984 s 93(3).

8 Building Act 1984 s 93(2)(a).

9 Building Act 1984 s 93(2)(b).

10 As to the meaning of 'building regulations' see PARA 7.

11 Building Act 1984 s 93(2).

137. Service of documents.

A notice, order, consent, demand or other document that is authorised or required by or under the Building Act 1984 to be given to or served on a person may, in any case for which no other provision is made by the Act, be given or served either:

(1)   by delivering it to that person[1];

(2)   in the case of an officer[2] of a local authority[3], by leaving it, or sending it in a prepaid letter addressed to him, at his office[4];

(3)   in the case of any other person, by leaving it, or sending it in a prepaid letter addressed to him, at his usual or last known residence[5];

(4)   in the case of an incorporated company or body, by delivering it to its secretary or clerk at its registered or principal office, or by sending it in a prepaid letter addressed to him at that office[6];

(5)   in the case of a document to be given to or served on a person as being the owner[7] of any premises[8] by virtue of the fact that he receives the rackrent[9] of it as agent for another, or would so receive it if the premises were let at a rackrent, by leaving it, or sending it in a prepaid letter addressed to him, at his place of business[10];

(6)   in the case of a document to be given to or served on the owner or the occupier of any premises, if it is not practicable after reasonable inquiry to ascertain the name and address of the person to or on whom it should be given or served, or if the premises are unoccupied, by addressing it to the person concerned by the description of 'owner' or 'occupier' of the premises (naming them) to which it relates, and delivering it to some person on the premises, or, if there is no person on the premises to whom it can be delivered, by affixing it, or a copy of it, to some conspicuous part of the premises[11].

Certain documents[12] may be transmitted to the recipient by means of an electronic communication[13], which has effect as delivery of the document to the recipient if, and only if, the following conditions are met[14]. The conditions are:

(a)   that the recipient has stated a willingness to receive the document by means of an electronic communication[15];

(b)   that the statement has not been withdrawn[16]; and

(c)   that the document was transmitted to an electronic address specified by the recipient[17].

Such a statement may be limited to documents of a specified description[18], and may require a document to be in a specified electronic form[19]. A statement may be modified or withdrawn (i) in a case where the statement was made by being published, by publishing the modification or withdrawal in the same or in a similar manner[20]; and (ii) in any other case, by giving a notice to the person to whom the statement was made[21].

1   Building Act 1984 s 94(a). The Building Act 1984 ss 94, 94A apply to documents authorised or required to be given, made, issued or served by or under the Domestic Fire Safety (Wales) Measure 2011: s 4 (not yet in force). As to the making of building regulations to modify or repeal the provisions of s 94 on the ground of inconsistency with other provisions see s 1(3), Sch 1 para 11(1); and PARA 9.

2   As to the meaning of 'officer' see PARA 102 note 9. As to references to an officer in relation to the Inner Temple and the Middle Temple see PARA 123 note 1.

3   As to the meaning of 'local authority' see PARA 1 note 12.

4   Building Act 1984 s 94(b).

5   Building Act 1984 s 94(c).

6   Building Act 1984 s 94(d).

7   As to the meaning of 'owner' see PARA 12 note 2.

8   As to the meaning of 'premises' see PARA 12 note 2.

9   As to the meaning of 'rackrent' see PARA 12 note 2.

10 Building Act 1984 s 94(e).

11 Building Act 1984 s 94(f).

12 The documents are listed in the Building Act 1984 s 94A(7) (s 94A added by SI 2008/2334) as follows:

   (1)   a notice under the Building Act 1984 s 16(6) (see PARA 33), s 47 (see PARA 74), s 50(7) or s 50(8) (see PARA 83), s 51A (see PARA 76), s 51C (see PARA 78), s 52 (see PARA 79), s 54 (see PARA 89), Sch 4 para 1(1) (see PARA 89), Sch 4 para 2(5) (see PARA 93) or Sch 4 para 2(6) (see PARA 93);

   (2)   a document containing plans or evidence which accompanies a notice under s 47(1) (see PARA 74), s 51A(2) (see PARA 76) or s 54(1) (see PARA 89);

   (3)   a certificate under s 50(1) (see PARA 83), s 51(1) (see PARA 84) or Sch 4 para 2(1) (see PARA 93) or Sch 4 para 3(1) (see PARA 94);

(4)   a combined notice and certificate under s 50(4) (see PARA 83) or Sch 4 para 2(2) (see
       PARA 93).
For the purposes of the Building Regulations 2010, SI 2010/2214, the Building Act 1984 s 94A
has effect as if the following documents were documents mentioned in s 94A(7):
(a)   a building notice and any accompanying statement, description, particulars or plan
       under the Building Regulations 2010, SI 2010/2214, reg 13 (see PARA 26) (reg 48(1)(a));
(b)   full plans and any accompanying statement under reg 14 (see PARA 27) (reg 48(1)(b));
(c)   a notice under reg 16 (see PARA 28) (reg 48(1)(c));
(d)   a completion certificate under reg 17 or 17A (see PARA 29) (reg 48(1)(d) (amended by
       SI 2012/311 and SI 2013/747);
(e)   an application for a regularisation certificate under reg 18(2) (see PARA 71) (reg
       48(1)(e));
(f)   a regularisation certificate under reg 18(5) (see PARA 71) (reg 48(1)(f));
(g)   a certificate or notice under reg 20 (see PARA 10) (reg 48(1)(g));
(h)   a notice under reg 25A (see PARA 48) (reg 48(1)(ga) (added in relation to England by
       SI 2012/3119 and in relation to Wales by SI 2013/747).
(i)   a notice under the Building Regulations 2010, SI 2010/2214, reg 27(2) or reg 27(3) (see
       PARA 46) (reg 48(1)(h));
(j)   a notice under reg 37(1) (see PARA 32) (reg 48(1)(k));
(k)   results of sound insulation testing under reg 41(2)(b) (see PARA 31) (reg 48(1)(l));
(l)   a notice under reg 42(2)(b) (see PARA 31) (reg 48(1)(m));
(m)   a notice of the results of pressure testing under reg 43(2)(b) (see PARA 31) (reg 48(1)(n));
(n)   a notice under reg 44(3) (see PARA 31) (reg 48(1)(o)).
For the purposes of the Building (Approved Inspectors etc) Regulations 2010, SI 2010/2215,
the Building Act 1984 s 94A has effect as if the following documents were documents mentioned
in s 94A(7):
(i)   a notice under the Building (Approved Inspectors etc) Regulations 2010, SI 2010/2215,
       reg 18(1) (see PARA 79) (reg 32(a));
(ii)   a notice under reg 19(2)(b) (see PARA 82) (reg 32(b));
(iii) a certificate or notice under the Building Regulations 2010, SI 2010/2214, reg 20 as
       applied by the Building (Approved Inspectors etc) Regulations 2010, SI 2010/2215, reg
       20 (see head (g) above) (reg 32(c));
(iv)   a notice under the Building Regulations 2010, SI 2010/2214, reg 27(2) or (3) as applied
       by the Building (Approved Inspectors etc) Regulations 2010, SI 2010/2215, reg 20 (reg
       32(d));
(v)   a notice under the Building Regulations 2010, SI 2010/2214, reg 37(1) as applied by the
       Building (Approved Inspectors etc) Regulations 2010, SI 2010/2215, reg 20 reg 32(g));
(vi)   results of sound insulation testing under the Building Regulations 2010, SI 2010/2214,
       reg 41(2)(b) as applied by the Building (Approved Inspectors etc) Regulations 2010,
       SI 2010/2215, reg 20 (see head (g) above) (reg 32(h));
(vii) a notice under the Building Regulations 2010, SI 2010/2214, reg 42(2)(b) as applied by
       the Building (Approved Inspectors etc) Regulations 2010, SI 2010/2215, reg 20 (reg
       32(i));
(viii) a notice of the results of pressure testing under the Building Regulations 2010,
       SI 2010/2214, reg 43(2)(b) as applied by the Building (Approved Inspectors etc)
       Regulations 2010, SI 2010/2215, reg 20 (reg 32(j));
(ix)   a notice under the Building Regulations 2010, SI 2010/2214, reg 44(3) as applied by the
       Building (Approved Inspectors etc) Regulations 2010, SI 2010/2215, reg 20 (reg 32(k));
(x)   an energy performance certificate under the Energy Performance of Buildings (England
       and Wales) Regulations 2012, SI 2012/3118, reg 7A(2)(a) (see PARA 48) as applied by
       the Building (Approved Inspectors etc) Regulations 2010, SI 2010/2215, reg 20 (reg
       32(l), (m) added in relation to England by SI 2016/285; and in relation to Wales by
       SI 2016/285; and SI 2016/611));
(xi)   a notice under the Energy Performance of Buildings (England and Wales) Regulations
       2012, SI 2012/3118, reg 7A(2)(b) as applied by the Building (Approved Inspectors etc)
       Regulations 2010, SI 2010/2215, reg 20 (reg 32(m) (as so added)). See note 1.
13 Electronic service of documents may be used where the Building Act 1984 s 94 authorises the
giving or serving of a document by its delivery to a particular person (the 'recipient') and the
document is of a kind mentioned in s 94A(7) (see note 12): s 94A(1) (as added: see note 12).
'Electronic communication' means a communication transmitted (whether from one person to
another, from one device to another or from a person to a device or vice versa): (1) by means of

an electronic communications network; or (2) by other means but while in an electronic form: Electronic Communications Act 2000 s 15 (definition amended by the Communications Act 2003 s 406(1), Sch 17 para 158); Building Act 1984 s 94A(8) (as so added).
14 Building Act 1984 s 94A(2) (as added: see note 12).
15 Building Act 1984 s 94A(3)(a) (as added: see note 12).
16 Building Act 1984 s 94A(3)(b) (as added: see note 12).
17 Building Act 1984 s 94A(3)(c) (as added: see note 12). 'Electronic address' includes any number or address used for the purposes of receiving electronic communications: s 94A(8) (as so added). 'Specified' means specified in a statement made for the purposes of s 94A(3)(a) (see head (a) in the text): s 94A(8) (as so added).
18 Building Act 1984 s 94A(4) (as added: see note 12).
19 Building Act 1984 s 94A(5) (as added: see note 12).
20 Building Act 1984 s 94A(6)(a) (as added: see note 12).
21 Building Act 1984 s 94A(6)(b) (as added: see note 12).

(7) General Provisions Relating to Appeals under the Building Act 1984

138. Appeal against notice requiring works.

Where a person is given certain notices under the Building Act 1984[1], he may appeal to a magistrates' court on any of the following grounds that are appropriate in the circumstances of the particular case[2]:

(1)   that the notice or requirement is not justified by the terms of the provision under which it purports to have been given[3];

(2)   that there has been some informality, defect or error in, or in connection with, the notice[4];

(3)   that the authority has refused unreasonably to approve the execution of alternative works, or that the works required by the notice to be executed are otherwise unreasonable in character or extent, or are unnecessary[5];

(4)   that the time within which the works are to be executed is not reasonably sufficient for the purpose[6];

(5)   that the notice might lawfully have been served on the occupier of the premises[7] in question instead of on the owner[8], or on the owner instead of on the occupier, and that it would have been equitable for it to have been so served[9];

(6)   where the works are works for the common benefit of the premises in question and other premises, that some other person, being the owner or occupier of premises to be benefited, ought to contribute towards the expenses of executing any works required[10].

The appellant must, where the grounds upon which the appeal is brought include a ground specified in head (5) or head (6) above, serve a copy of his notice of appeal on each other person referred to[11]. The appellant may, in the case of any appeal, serve a copy of his notice of appeal on any other person having an estate or interest in the premises in question, and on the hearing of the appeal the court may make such order as it thinks fit with respect to[12]:

(a)   the person by whom any works are to be executed and the contribution to be made by any other person towards the cost of the works[13]; or

(b)   (b) the proportions in which any expenses that may become recoverable by the local authority[14] are to be borne by the appellant and such other person[15].

In exercising such powers, the court must have regard (i) as between an owner and an occupier, to the terms and conditions, whether contractual or statutory, of the tenancy and to the nature of the works required[16]; and (ii) in any case, to the degree of benefit to be derived by the different persons concerned[17].

1   Ie a notice in relation to which it is declared by any provision of the Building Act 1984 that s 102 applies: see s 102(1). Section 102 is expressly applied by s 2(5) (see PARA 12), s 59(2) (see PARA 100), s 60(5) (see PARA 101), s 64(3) (see PARA 105), s 65(3) (see PARA 106), s 66(5) (see PARA 107), s 68(5) (see PARA 109), s 70(2) (see PARA 111), s 72(2) (see PARA 57), s 74(4) (see PARA 113), s 79(3) (see PARA 116), s 83(1) (see PARA 118), s 84(2) (see PARA 119).
2   Building Act 1984 s 102(1). Section 102 has effect subject to any modification specified in the provision under which the notice is given: s 102(5). As to the meaning of 'modifications' see PARA 3 note 21. As to the making of building regulations to modify or repeal the provisions of s 102 on the ground of inconsistency with other provisions see s 1(3), Sch 1 para 11(1); and PARA 9.
3   Building Act 1984 s 102(1)(a).
4   Building Act 1984 s 102(1)(b). If and in so far as an appeal under s 102 is based on the ground of some informality, defect or error in or in connection with the notice, the court must dismiss the appeal, if it is satisfied that the informality, defect or error was not a material one: s 102(2).
5   Building Act 1984 s 102(1)(c).
6   Building Act 1984 s 102(1)(d).
7   As to the meaning of 'premises' see PARA 12 note 2.
8   As to the meaning of 'owner' see PARA 12 note 2.
9   Building Act 1984 s 102(1)(e).
10 Building Act 1984 s 102(1)(f).
11 Building Act 1984 s 102(3)(a).
12 Building Act 1984 s 102(3)(b).
13 Building Act 1984 s 102(3)(b)(i).
14 As to the meaning of 'local authority' see PARA 1 note 12. As to the recovery of expenses generally see PARAS 130–131.
15 Building Act 1984 s 102(3)(b)(ii).
16 Building Act 1984 s 102(4)(a).
17 Building Act 1984 s 102(4)(b).

139. Procedure on appeal or application to magistrates' court.
Where the Building Act 1984 provides for an appeal to a magistrates' court[1] against a requirement, refusal or other decision of a local authority[2], or for a matter to be determined by, or for an application in respect of a matter to be made to, a magistrates' court, the procedure must be by way of complaint for an order[3]. The time within which such an appeal may be brought is 21 days from the date on which notice of the local authority's requirement, refusal or other decision was served[4] upon the person desiring to appeal, and for these purposes the making of the complaint is deemed to be the bringing of the appeal[5]. In a case where such an appeal lies, the document notifying to the person concerned the local authority's decision in the matter must state the right of appeal to a magistrates' court and the time within which such an appeal may be brought[6].

1   See further CRIMINAL PROCEDURE vol 27 (2015) PARA 142; MAGISTRATES vol 71 (2013) PARA 436.
2   As to the meaning of 'local authority' see PARA 1 note 12.
3   Building Act 1984 s 103(1). As to the making of building regulations to modify or repeal the provisions of s 103 on the ground of inconsistency with other provisions see s 1(3), Sch 1 para 11(1); and PARA 9.
4   As to the service of documents see PARA 137.
5   Building Act 1984 s 103(2).
6   Building Act 1984 s 103(3).

140. Local authority to give effect to appeal.

Where upon an appeal under the Building Act 1984 a court varies or reverses a decision of a local authority[1], it is the duty of the local authority to give effect to the order of the court and, in particular, to grant or issue any necessary consent, certificate or other document, and to make any necessary entry in any register[2].

1 As to the meaning of 'local authority' see PARA 1 note 12.
2 Building Act 1984 s 104. As to the making of building regulations to modify or repeal the provisions of s 104 on the ground of inconsistency with other provisions see s 1(3), Sch 1 para 11(1); and PARA 9.

141. Judge not disqualified by liability to rates.

A judge of a court or a justice of the peace[1] is not disqualified from acting in cases arising under the Building Act 1984 by reason only of his being, as one of several ratepayers, or as one of any other class of persons, liable in common with the others to contribute to, or be benefited by, a rate or fund out of which expenses of a local authority[2] are to be defrayed[3].

1 As to justices of the peace see MAGISTRATES vol 71 (2013) PARA 401 et seq.
2 As to the meaning of 'local authority' see PARA 1 note 12.
3 Building Act 1984 s 105. As to the making of building regulations to modify or repeal the provisions of s 105 on the ground of inconsistency with other provisions see s 1(3), Sch 1 para 11(1); and PARA 9.

(8) Offences

142. Obstruction.

A person who wilfully obstructs a person acting in the execution of the Building Act 1984, or of building regulations[1], or of an order or warrant made or issued under the Act, is, in a case for which no other provision is made by the Act, liable on summary conviction to a fine[2].

1 As to the meaning of 'building regulations' see PARA 7.
2 Building Act 1984 s 112. The fine imposed must not exceed level 1 on the standard scale: see s 112. As to the powers of magistrates' courts to issue fines on summary conviction see SENTENCING vol 92 (2015) PARA 176. Civil sanctions may be imposed in respect of offences under the Building Act 1984 by virtue of the powers under the Regulatory Enforcement and Sanctions Act 2008 Pt 3 (ss 36–71): see ss 36, 38(2), Sch 6; and CONSTITUTIONAL AND ADMINISTRATIVE LAW vol 20 (2014) PARA 331 et seq.
    As to the making of building regulations to modify or repeal the provisions of s 112 on the ground of inconsistency with other provisions see s 1(3), Sch 1 para 11(1); and PARA 9.

143. Prosecution of offences.

Proceedings in respect of an offence created by or under the Building Act 1984 must not, without the written consent of the Attorney General[1], be taken by any person other than a party aggrieved, or a local authority[2] or a body whose function[3] it is to enforce the provision in question[4].

1 As to the Attorney General see CONSTITUTIONAL AND ADMINISTRATIVE LAW vol 20 (2014) PARA 273.
2 As to the meaning of 'local authority' see PARA 1 note 12.
3 As to the meaning of 'functions' see PARA 3 note 19.
4 Building Act 1984 s 113. As to the making of building regulations to modify or repeal the provisions of s 113 on the ground of inconsistency with other provisions see s 1(3), Sch 1 para 11(1); and PARA 9.

144. Continuing offences.

Where provision is made by or under the Building Act 1984 for the imposition of a daily penalty in respect of a continuing offence the court by which a person is convicted of the original offence may fix a reasonable period from the date of conviction for the defendant to comply with any directions given by the court[1]. Where the court has fixed such a period, the daily penalty is not recoverable in respect of any day before the period expires[2].

1 Building Act 1984 s 114.
2 Building Act 1984 s 114. As to the making of building regulations to modify or repeal the provisions of s 114 on the ground of inconsistency with other provisions see s 1(3), Sch 1 para 11(1); and PARA 9.

6. SAFETY OF CERTAIN BUILDINGS AND STRUCTURES

(1) Platforms and other Structures for Public Occasions

145. Safety of platforms and other structures for public occasions.
Whenever large numbers of persons are likely to assemble on the occasion of any show, entertainment, public procession, open air meeting or other like occasion, every roof of a building, and every platform, balcony or other structure or part of it let or used or intended to be let or used for the purpose of affording sitting or standing accommodation for a number of persons must be safely constructed or secured[1]. Any person who uses or allows to be used any roof of a building, platform, balcony or structure not so safely constructed or secured, or who neglects to comply with these provisions, is liable to a penalty[2].

1 Public Health Acts Amendment Act 1890 s 37(1). Section 37(1) refers to platforms, etc being safely constructed or secured to the satisfaction of the surveyor of the urban sanitary authority: see ss 11(3), 37(1) (s 11(3) amended by the Local Government Act 1972 s 272(1), Sch 30). Functions of sanitary authorities are now largely carried out by local authorities, and the reference to the surveyor of the urban authority, in the Public Health Acts Amendment Act 1890 s 37(1), is to be construed as a reference to the proper officer of a local authority: see the Local Government Act 1972 s 180(1), Sch 29 Pt I para 4. While a general safety certificate is in force in relation to a sports ground under the Safety of Sports Grounds Act 1975 or the Fire Safety and Safety of Places of Sport Act 1987 (see SPORTS LAW vol 96 (2012) PARA 136), the requirements of the Public Health Acts Amendment Act 1890 s 37(1) do not apply to that ground: see the Safety of Sports Grounds Act 1975 s 9(1) (see SPORTS LAW vol 96 (2012) PARA 141); and the Fire Safety and Safety of Places of Sport Act 1987 s 33(1)(a) (see SPORTS LAW vol 96 (2012) PARA 152).
2 Public Health Acts Amendment Act 1890 s 37(2). The penalty is one not exceeding level 3 on the standard scale: s 37(2) (amended by virtue of the Criminal Justice Act 1982 ss 38, 46). As to the standard scale see SENTENCING vol 92 (2015) PARA 176.

(2) Sports Grounds

146–200. Safety of sports grounds.
Under the Safety of Sports Grounds Act 1975 safety certificates are required for sports grounds which, in the opinion of the Secretary of State[1], have accommodation for more than 10,000 spectators and which have been designated by him as requiring such a certificate[2]. Safety certificates are also required under Part III of the Fire Safety and Safety of Places of Sport Act 1987, which makes provision in relation to sports grounds providing covered accommodation in certain stands for spectators, and which are not designated as sports grounds[3].

While a general safety certificate[4] is in force in relation to a sports ground the statutory provisions relating to the safety of platforms, etc erected or used on public occasions[5] and the statutory provisions relating to public health requirements as to exits and entrances to certain public and other buildings[6] do not apply to that sports ground[7].

The law relating to the safety of sports grounds is dealt with in more detail elsewhere in this work[8].

1 As to the Secretary of State see PARA 5.
2 See the Safety of Sports Grounds Act 1975 (and the various designation orders made under s 1), the Safety of Sports Grounds Regulations 1987, SI 1987/1941; and SPORTS LAW vol 96 (2012) PARAS 135–136.
3 See the Fire Safety and Safety of Places of Sport Act 1987 Pt III (ss 26–41), the Safety of Places of Sport Regulations 1988, SI 1988/1807; and SPORTS LAW vol 96 (2012) PARA 147 et seq.

4　Ie a certificate issued under the Safety of Sports Grounds Act 1975 s 1 or a certificate issued under the Fire Safety and Safety of Places of Sport Act 1987 s 26.

5　Ie the Public Health Acts Amendment Act 1890 s 37(1): see PARA 145.

6　Ie the Building Act 1984 s 24: see PARA 39.

7　See the Safety of Sports Grounds Act 1975 s 9(1)(a), (c) (amended by the Building Act 1984 s 133(1), Sch 6 para 15; and SI 2005/1541); Fire Safety and Safety of Places of Sport Act 1987 s 33(1)(a), (d) (amended by SI 2005/1541).

8　See SPORTS LAW vol 96 (2012) PARA 135 et seq.

BUILDING CONTRACTS

1. CREATION AND NATURE OF BUILDING CONTRACTS

(1) Preliminary Considerations

201. The law of contract and scope of this title.
English law does not treat a building contract as a nominate contract. A building contract is a contract by which a person (commonly called a contractor) undertakes, for consideration, to carry out works of construction (or demolition) for another person (commonly called the employer or owner)[1]. The term 'building contract' as used in this title describes not only contracts for or in connection with the construction of buildings (such as houses, extensions, offices and factories) but also contracts for major infrastructure, civil engineering works (such as roads, bridges and tunnels), dredging contracts, mechanical engineering and electrical engineering contracts and chemical engineering contracts. The term also includes contracts for complex projects such as power stations, ports, airports and underground systems. Building contracts have attributes of contracts for services and of contracts for the supply of goods and thus are contracts for work and materials[2]. As such, building contracts have many similarities with shipbuilding contracts except that the product of a building contract will be either directly or indirectly attached to land and therefore will ultimately form part of the realty.

Part II of the Housing Grants, Construction and Regeneration Act 1996[3] created a new type of contract called a 'construction contract'[4]. The terms 'building contract' and 'construction contract' are not synonymous. Whilst each 'construction contract' will also be a 'building contract', the opposite is not necessarily the case.

The law applicable to building contracts is the general law of contract (which is dealt with elsewhere in this work)[5]. This title does not reiterate the general principles of the law of contract applicable to building contracts. Furthermore, much of the supposed law or principles relating to building contracts is on analysis found to be no more than the result of the interpretation of the relevant building contract and not a rule of law. This title is therefore confined to those matters which are or may be regarded as rules of law applicable to building contracts, but it must be emphasised that virtually all such rules may be displaced by the terms of the relevant contract.

For many construction contracts an employer may have retained an architect, engineer, surveyor or some other professional person to specify and/or supervise the work to be carried out by the contractor. The roles of such people are dealt with later in this title[6].

1 In relation to the Locomotives Act 1898 s 12 (repealed) Buckley LJ defined the term 'building contract' as meaning 'a contract for the building of anything, not necessarily a house, but any other physical construction': *Carlisle RDC v Carlisle Corpn* [1909] 1 KB 471 at 483, CA. In *Gilbert-Ash (Northern) Ltd v Modern Engineering (Bristol) Ltd* [1974] AC 689 at 717, [1973] 3 All ER 195 at 215, HL, Lord Diplock stated: 'a building contract is an entire contract for the sale of goods and work and labour for a lump sum price payable by instalments as the goods are delivered and the work is done'. However, note that the definition was relevant only to the facts of that case.
2 See SALE OF GOODS AND SUPPLY OF SERVICES.
3 Ie the Housing Grants, Construction and Regeneration Act 1996 Pt II (ss 104–117): see PARAS 210–211, 352–357, 410.
4 See PARA 210.
5 See CONTRACT.
6 See PARA 424 et seq.

202. Standard forms.

In the United Kingdom there are numerous standard forms of contract for use on construction projects. Because of the proliferation of these standard forms and because they are frequently amended, this title does not provide references to standard forms of contract. However, it may be noted that for building works the Joint Contracts Tribunal ('JCT')[1] issues a series of standard form contracts for use as principal or main contracts, nominated or named sub-contracts, ordinary or domestic sub-contracts and contracts of supply, as well as a major project form, an intermediate form and a form for minor building works. Each JCT contract covers a different method of procurement which could involve placing responsibility for design and workmanship on the contractor or sub-contractor, or purely workmanship and/or the supply of services. For civil engineering projects the Infrastructure Conditions of Contract (ICC)[2] are commonly used or adapted for use by major employers. Standard form contracts produced by bodies fully representative of the interests of prospective parties are in principle unlikely to attract the contra proferentem rule[3]. The government in the past generally used its own sets of general conditions for works contracts, which encompass all aspects of building, civil engineering, mechanical and electrical engineering, as well as maintenance works[4]. However, many of these contracts, whilst available, are no longer being updated by the government who are moving towards frequent use of the New Engineering Contracts, now in their fourth edition (NEC)[5].

1   The Joint Contracts Tribunal is not a judicial or statutory body but a consultative group comprising the following (or representatives of the following): the British Property Federation; the Contractors' Legal Group; the Local Government Association; the National Specialist Contractors Council; the Royal Institute of British Architects; the Royal Institution of Chartered Surveyors; and the Scottish Building Contracts Committee. The forms are available from the Royal Institute of British Architects and the Royal Institution of Chartered Surveyors. Copyright is vested in Joint Contracts Tribunal Limited.
2   The Infrastructure Conditions of Contract (ICC) is a standard suite of conditions of contract for infrastructure contracts jointly sponsored by the Association of Consultancy and Engineering (ACE) and the Civil Engineering Contractors Association (CECA). The ICC contracts were published in 2011 and replace the ICE Conditions of Contract. There are separate versions of the ICC Conditions of Contract for different types of contract (for example, a Measurement Version, a Design and Construct Version).
       The Institution of Mechanical Engineers and the Institution of Engineering and Technology (formerly the Institution of Electrical Engineers) publish various forms of contracts suitable for mechanical and electrical engineering works. The Institution of Chemical Engineers publishes a form of contract for use on chemical and process plant work which is widely used. Many major employers base their own forms of contract on the standard form appropriate to their industry.
3   See *Tersons Ltd v Stevenage Development Corpn* [1963] 2 Lloyd's Rep 333 at 368, CA, per Pearson LJ. As to the contra proferentem rule see CONTRACT vol 22 (2012) PARA 363.
4   See the Government General Conditions for Works Contracts, known as the GC/Works suite of contracts. The conditions demonstrate that it is not necessary to have separate conditions for building and for civil engineering work. The GC/Works suite of contracts is published by The Stationery Office (TSO).
5   NEC was first published in 1993 as the New Engineering Contract. It is a suite of construction contracts intended to promote partnering and collaboration between the contractor and employer. It was developed as a reaction to other more traditional forms of construction contract which have been portrayed by some as adversarial. The fourth edition was published in 2016.

203. The Secretary of State and the Welsh Ministers.

Certain statutory functions[1] relating to the law pertaining to building contracts are exercisable by the Secretary of State[2] (in relation to England) and the Welsh Ministers (in relation to Wales)[3]. The functions exercisable by the Welsh Ministers are those functions originally transferred to the National Assembly for Wales[4] by Order in Council and subsequently transferred to the Welsh Ministers[5]. Further statutory functions may be transferred to the Welsh Ministers by Order in Council[6], or may be conferred on the Welsh Ministers by enactments made after the establishment of the Welsh Assembly Government (now renamed the Welsh Government)[7].

1   Eg the power to make regulations.
2   In any enactment, 'Secretary of State' means one of Her Majesty's principal secretaries of state: see the Interpretation Act 1978 s 5, Sch 1. As to the office of Secretary of State see CONSTITUTIONAL AND ADMINISTRATIVE LAW vol 20 (2014) PARA 153 et seq.
3   Many statutory functions which were formerly exercised by the Secretary of State, so far as exercisable in relation to Wales, are now almost exclusively the responsibility of the Welsh Ministers following the establishment of the Welsh Assembly Government (now renamed the Welsh Government or Llywodraeth Cymru: see the Wales Act 2014 s 4(1)) under the Government of Wales Act 2006. As to the Welsh Ministers and the Welsh Government see Pt 2 (ss 45–92); and CONSTITUTIONAL AND ADMINISTRATIVE LAW vol 20 (2014) PARA 373 et seq. Legislation enacted following the establishment of the Welsh Government which confers functions on the Secretary of State and the Welsh Ministers often refers to those bodies collectively as 'the appropriate national authority'.
4   The statutory functions under the Defective Premises Act 1972 (see PARAS 275–277), the Local Government Act 1988 (see PARA 225), and the Housing Grants, Construction and Regeneration Act 1996 (see PARAS 351–358, 407 et seq) were originally transferred to the National Assembly for Wales by Order in Council under the Government of Wales Act 1998 s 22 (now repealed) (see the National Assembly for Wales (Transfer of Functions) Order 1999, SI 1999/672, Sch 1).
5   Ie by the operation of the Government of Wales Act 2006 Sch 11 paras 26, 30 (see CONSTITUTIONAL AND ADMINISTRATIVE LAW vol 20 (2014) PARA 380), which provide that instruments transferring functions to the National Assembly for Wales under the Government of Wales Act 1998 s 22 (repealed) continue to have effect following the transfer of the Assembly's executive functions to the Welsh Ministers as conferring those functions on those Ministers.
6   Ie by Order in Council under the Government of Wales Act 2006 s 58 (see CONSTITUTIONAL AND ADMINISTRATIVE LAW vol 20 (2014) PARA 380). At the date at which this volume states the law no functions relating to the law of building contracts had been transferred to the Welsh Ministers by Order in Council under s 58.
    For provisions as to the exercise of transferred functions see the Government of Wales Act 2006 Sch 3, Sch 11 paras 33–35; and CONSTITUTIONAL AND ADMINISTRATIVE LAW vol 20 (2014) para 380.
7   See note 3.

(2) Parties and Types of Contract

(i) Parties

204. Architects and engineers.

In large contracts, the employer will usually[1] require the services of a professionally qualified person to design[2] the work, to prepare the contract documents and to ensure compliance with the requirements of planning[3] and building regulations[4]. Usually the person chosen to design a building or building works will be a professionally qualified architect (or a firm or company of architects) and the person engaged to design civil and other types of engineering works will be a chartered or other qualified engineer and a member of an institution such as the Institution of Civil Engineers, the Institution of Structural Engineers, the Institution of Mechanical Engineers or the Institution of Engineering and Technology[5] (or a firm or company with such engineers).

The architect or engineer may also be required to inspect or supervise the construction of the works periodically. It is common for the building or engineering contract to give the architect or engineer express authority to act as the employer's agent[6]. Further, contracts for works of construction commonly give the architect or the engineer certain functions such as to determine disputes which may arise in the course of the contract, to issue certificates, to express opinions, or to make determinations, for example stating the amount due to the contractor. In the discharge of these functions, the architect or engineer acts as the agent of the employer and must act fairly[7]; he owes a duty to the employer but not necessarily to the contractor in so doing[8]. Although an architect or engineer may be given considerable powers by the building contract and may be required to carry out important functions under it he is not a party to it. Any duties that the architect may owe to the employer will derive from the architect's appointment by the employer. Any duties that the architect may owe to the contractor will derive from particular circumstances[9] and not from the fact of appointment under the contract[10]. Where more than one consultant is engaged the contract and appointments should make clear their respective authorities and functions[11].

1   Where the contractor has produced the design of the works, the contract between him and the employer is sometimes called a 'package-deal' or 'design and build' or 'turnkey' contract: see PARA 209.
2   Generally design connotes what the contractor is required to complete, not how he is to do it; this will depend, however, on the contract documents in any particular case: see *Thorn v London Corpn* (1876) 1 App Cas 120, HL (where the method of realising the design was set out in the contract documents). As to contract documents see PARA 214.
3   See PARA 301; and PLANNING.
4   See BUILDING vol 6 (2018) PARA 1 et seq.
5   There are a large number of professional bodies. As to the qualifications and professional conduct of architects and engineers in general see PARA 424 et seq. As to the nature of the Institution of Civil Engineers see *Institution of Civil Engineers v IRC* [1932] 1 KB 149, CA. As to the Institution of Civil Engineers see PARA 424.
6   As to the rights and duties arising between the architect or engineer and the employer see PARA 458 et seq. As to the relationship between agent and principal see generally AGENCY vol 1 (2017) PARA 72 et seq.
7   *Sutcliffe v Thackrah* [1974] AC 727, [1974] 1 All ER 859, HL; *Pacific Associates Inc v Baxter* [1990] 1 QB 993, [1989] 2 All ER 159, CA.
8   *Hosier & Dickinson Ltd v P & M Kaye Ltd* [1971] 1 All ER 301 at 305, [1970] 1 WLR 1611 at 1616, CA, per Lord Denning MR (affd sub nom *P & M Kaye Ltd v Hosier & Dickinson Ltd* [1972] 1 All ER 121, [1972] 1 WLR 146, HL); *Sutcliffe v Thackrah* [1974] AC 727, [1974] 1 All ER 859, HL; *Pacific Associates Inc v Baxter* [1990] 1 QB 993, [1989] 2 All ER 159, CA.
9   See eg *Townsends (Builders) Ltd v Cinema News and Property Management Ltd (David A Wilkie & Partners, third party)* [1959] 1 All ER 7, [1959] 1 WLR 119, 20 BLR 118, CA. See also PARA 471.
10 *Pacific Associates Inc v Baxter* [1990] 1 QB 993, [1989] 2 All ER 159, CA.
11 Eg that all instructions to the contractor are issued by the architect or lead consultant only and not by anyone else, or that instructions are not given directly to the contractor's sub-contractors by any consultant.

205. Surveyors and quantity surveyors.

There are many aspects to surveying, such as estate management, building surveying, quantity surveying, land surveying and town and country planning[1]. A surveyor is often employed to survey a building on behalf of a prospective purchaser. Building surveyors are commonly engaged to supervise work but unless they are undertaking a multi-disciplinary role within a project that includes design input, they rarely carry out design. When they do they are to be equated to architects and engineers. The branch of the profession most closely concerned with the letting and execution of contracts for major works of construction is that of quantity surveyor[2]. The quantity surveyor is normally engaged by the employer and his duties derive from the terms of his appointment. The complexity of major construction works is such that it is now considered necessary to calculate the amount of excavation, sub-structure and super-structure work and all other work and operations required to complete them in order to enable a contractor to submit a tender. Where such calculation is commissioned in order to obtain tenders it is a function of the quantity surveyor to make and set out the results of the calculations derived from the architect's drawings and specifications[3]. The quantity surveyor will now generally be required to value the work executed during the progress of the contract, and some standard forms even refer to the role of quantity surveyor and his duties in relation to the building contract. These will include, for example, advising the architect or engineer on the amount of interim or final certificates[4]. Where the contractor has a claim for payment under the provisions of a contract, the quantity surveyor may be required to ascertain the sum due, but he is not normally given the power to determine whether or not a sum so ascertained is due to the contractor[5]. A valuation by a quantity surveyor will not fetter the jurisdiction of a certifier. The growth of the tasks of a quantity surveyor has led to the use of the description 'construction cost consultant'. Although a quantity surveyor may have duties under the building contract he is not a party to it. Any duties that the quantity surveyor may owe to the employer will derive from the quantity surveyor's appointment by the employer. Sizeable contractors will employ quantity surveyors to safeguard their interests during the performance of a building contract, hence the description 'contractor's quantity surveyor'.

1   As to surveyors generally see PARA 488 et seq.
2   The term 'quantity surveyor' has been judicially construed as meaning a person 'whose business consists in taking out in detail the measurements and quantities, from plans prepared by an architect, for the purpose of enabling the builders to calculate the amounts for which they would execute the plans': *Taylor v Hall* (1870) IR 4 CL 467 at 476 per Morris J. Today a quantity surveyor may be as much concerned with post-contract as with pre-contract services. As to the rights and duties of the quantity surveyor see PARA 516 et seq.
3   The quantity surveyor may also be responsible for compiling the specification. The description of specialist work such as mechanical and electrical work or heating and ventilation services may be carried out by the relevant consultant engineer's representatives.
4   It is for the architect to determine whether work has been properly executed and not the quantity surveyor: see *Sutcliffe v Chippendale and Edmondson (a firm)* (1971) 18 BLR 149 at 165–166 per Judge Stabb QC.
5   Even where he is empowered to agree amounts with the contractor he will not have authority to waive requirements as to liability: *John Laing Construction Ltd v County and District Properties Ltd* (1983) 23 BLR 1. See also *Rosehaugh Stanhope Properties (Broadgate Phase 6) plc and Rosehaugh Stanhope (Phase 7) plc v Redpath Dorman Long Ltd* (1990) 50 BLR 69 (construction manager's authority).

206.   Supervising and superintending officers and project managers.
The term 'supervising officer' describes a person who is not entitled to be called an architect[1], but is enabled to discharge the functions given to an architect under standard forms of contract. 'Superintending officer' is the term used by the government in some of its contracts (but not the NEC contracts). It is frequently abbreviated to 'SO' and refers to the government's supervisor of the construction works. Project managers are often appointed today. In NEC contracts the employer appoints both a project manager and a supervisor who have different responsibilities. When project managers are appointed by employers they usually take over a co-ordinating or organisational role formerly exercised by the architect, but the ambit of their responsibilities and the nature of their relationship with the other professionals engaged will depend upon the terms of their

appointment[2]. They should be distinguished from project managers employed by contractors to manage building contracts formerly and traditionally known as 'agents' or 'foremen'.

1   As to restrictions on the use of the title of 'architect' see PARA 427. As to the unlawful use of the title of 'architect' see PARA 429.
2   Where a project manager who, under the terms of engagement, owes a duty of ensuring that any required insurance is in place, but does not have the expertise to advise his employer as to the adequacy of the proposed insurance arrangements, he ought either to obtain independent expert advice or inform the employer that independent expert advice is required: *Pozzolanic Lytag Ltd v Bryan Hobson Associates* [1999] BLR 267, (1998) 63 Con LR 81.

207.   The resident engineer and the clerk of works.

The person named in the contract as the engineer or the architect may not be required by the employer to give constant attention to the day-to-day supervision of the works[1]. A resident engineer or clerk of works may be appointed for this purpose and may also be authorised by the employer to exercise delegated powers of the engineer or architect[2]. On engineering contracts the resident engineer may be appointed from the staff of the consulting engineer or may be appointed and paid by the employer and in this event the resident engineer, even though working under the control of the engineer, will be the servant of the employer[3]. On building contracts, the clerk of works is employed to observe the progress of the work on behalf of the employer. While the clerk of works will assist the architect in the supervision of the work, the architect cannot generally delegate his responsibility for important matters to the clerk of works[4].

1   As to the degree of supervision ordinarily expected of an architect see *East Ham Corpn v Bernard Sunley & Sons Ltd* [1966] AC 406 at 443, [1965] 3 All ER 619 at 636, HL, per Lord Upjohn; *Sutcliffe v Chippendale and Edmondson (a firm)* (1971) 18 BLR 149 at 162, 165 per Judge Stabb QC; *Trustees of London Hospital v TP Bennett & Son* (1987) 13 ConLR 22, sub nom *Gray (Special Trustees of the London Hospital) v TP Bennett & Son (a firm)* (1987) 43 BLR 63 at 82 per Sir William Stabb QC; *Corfield v Grant* (1992) 59 BLR 102 at 119–120 per Judge Bowsher QC; and for that of an engineer see *Oldschool v Gleeson (Constructors) Ltd* (1976) 4 BLR 103 at 123 per Judge Stabb QC; *Kensington and Chelsea and Westminster Health Authority v Wettern Composites Ltd* (1984) 31 BLR 57 at 82 per Judge Smout QC; *Department of National Heritage v Steensen Varming Mulcahy* (1998) 60 Con LR 33 at 98–99 per Judge Bowsher QC.
2   See eg *Ministry of Defence v Scott Wilson Kirkpatrick & Partners* [2000] BLR 20, CA. But see *A-G v Briggs* (1855) 1 Jur NS 1084 (where it was held that the resident engineer's approval of plans required to be approved by the principal engineer was unauthorised). Cf *Re De Morgan Snell & Co and Rio de Janeiro Flour Mills and Granaries Ltd* (1892) 8 TLR 292, CA (where the resident engineer was held to be in a position analogous to that of the engineer).
3   *Morren v Swinton and Pendlebury Borough Council* [1965] 2 All ER 349, [1965] 1 WLR 576, DC.
4   *Saunders and Collard v Broadstairs Local Board* (1890) 2 Hudson's BC (4th Edn) 164, DC; *Leicester Guardians v Trollope* (1911) 75 JP 197. On complex work more than one resident engineer or clerk of works may be employed, eg where specialist work requires specialist inspection or supervision.

208.   Sub-contractors and suppliers.

A sub-contractor is one who agrees with the contractor to carry out part of the works of construction or works required for it (such as where services are provided). A supplier is also a sub-contractor to the contractor, but the term commonly refers to one who supplies to the contractor but does not erect or install, goods or materials (such as prefabricated parts) necessary for the completion of the works[1].

In the interest of retaining control over the cost and quality of the works, the employer may require the contractor to employ particular sub-contractors or suppliers, or that the person selected by the contractor be approved by the employer[2]. The employer may have powers under the main contract to direct that the contractor enter into a sub-contract or contract of supply on terms agreed between the employer and the sub-contractor. In the latter circumstances the sub-contractor or supplier is sometimes called a 'nominated' sub-contractor or supplier[3] or a 'named' sub-contractor[4]. Whilst 'nomination' still exists its use is less common nowadays.

A labour only sub-contractor is one who supplies workmen to the contractor to work under the contractor's direction; a labour only sub-contractor does not undertake responsibility for any particular part of the works[5].

In certain circumstances, the contractor may be under a statutory duty[6] to deduct from payments due to a sub-contractor. The sum so deducted must be remitted by the contractor to the Commissioners for Her Majesty's Revenue and Customs as tax payable by the sub-contractor[7].

1   The term 'builders' merchant' is commonly used to denote the supplier.
2   See *Leedsford Ltd v Bradford City Council* (1956) 24 BLR 45, CA.
3   See PARAS 238–239.
4   Under the JCT forms of building contract, nominated sub-contractors are replaced by named sub-contractors, being sub-contractors who are specifically identified in the contract documents and with whom the contractor is required to sub-contract upon a standard form of named contract. As to JCT standard forms of contract see PARA 202.
5   See PARA 251.
6   See the special tax provisions which apply to sub-contractors in the construction industry in the Finance Act 2004 Pt 3 Ch 3 (ss 57–77); the Income Tax (Construction Industry Scheme) Regulations 2005, SI 2005/2045; PARA 252; and INCOME TAXATION vol 58 (2014) PARA 993 et seq.
7   See the Finance Act 2004 s 61; the Income Tax (Construction Industry Scheme) Regulations 2005, SI 2005/2045, reg 7; and INCOME TAXATION vol 58 (2014) PARA 1001.

(ii) Types of Contract

209. Types of contract.
It is sometimes convenient to label building contracts either by reference to the manner by which the contractor's remuneration is arrived at or by reference to the nature of the contractor's obligations. Many modern contracts are hybrid and only the simplest warrant such descriptions, and then only because the contract does not itself provide for the consequences.

A 'lump sum' contract is one under which the contractor will receive on completion of the whole works payment of a single sum. If the contractor fails to complete the works he will not have earned the payment due[1]. An employer cannot, however, refuse to pay the lump sum because the work is incomplete by reason only of minor defects. He is liable to pay the full price but subject to an abatement on account of the defects. What constitutes minor defects depends on the facts[2].

An 'entire' contract is one where complete performance by a party is a condition precedent to the liability of the other party[3]. Whether a contract is an entire one is a matter of construction[4]. A lump sum contract is not necessarily an entire contract[5]. A contract for payment by instalments is not an entire contract but the principles applicable to entire contracts may also apply to contractor's rights to an instalment, for example the contractor's right to be paid retention money[6]. Clear words are required to bring an entire contract into existence[7].

A 'measure and value' contract is one in which the amount payable to the contractor is on completion determined by measuring the work done and valuing it in accordance with the contract rates and prices set out in a bill of quantities or schedule of rates[8]. This type of contract is used where the general nature of the work to be executed is clear but its extent is not.

A 'cost plus' contract is one in which the contractor is to be paid the costs actually expended plus an amount (fixed or calculated as a percentage on the cost) for profit and such costs as are not vouched for. These contracts are sometimes also called 'prime cost' or 'fixed fee' contracts. They are akin also to contracts in which the contractor is paid on a 'time and materials' basis or 'for dayworks'.

A 'term' contract is one under which the contractor undertakes for a term (for example, a year) to carry out such work as may be required of him by the employer. Payment will generally be made by the application of an agreed schedule of rates for the work called for. Examples would be an annual contract for the maintenance of roads within part of a county[9] or contracts in relation to local authority owned housing.

The trend in the United Kingdom has been for most of the work on large building projects to be sub-contracted by the contractor so that the only personnel directly employed are the management and supervisory staff. Such arrangements have been formalised with the now fairly common use of a 'management contract' under which the contractor undertakes only to manage the project and employs as sub-contractors designated persons in respect of whom his liability may be limited. The management contractor is normally paid the prime cost of the works plus a fee[10].

'Design and build' or 'turnkey' contracts (colloquially, 'package deal' contracts) are contracts under which the contractor undertakes to design the whole or part of the works in accordance with the employer's requirements, to carry out such works and to hand them over completed to meet such requirements[11].

Part II of the Housing Grants, Construction and Regeneration Act 1996[12] created a type of contract called a 'construction contract', and introduced certain statutory rights and entitlements for parties to such contracts in relation to payment and adjudication[13].

1   *Cutter v Powell* (1795) 6 Term Rep 320; *Munro v Butt* (1858) 8 E & B 738.
2   See PARA 262.
3   See *Holland Hannen & Cubitts (Northern) Ltd v Welsh Health Technical Services Organisation* (1981) 18 BLR 80 at 122 per Judge Newey QC, citing *Hoenig v Isaacs* [1952] 2 All ER 176 at 180–181, CA, per Denning LJ.
4   See *Tern Construction Group (in administrative receivership) v RBS Garages Ltd* (1992) 34 Con LR 137 (where the JCT standard form of contract was held not to be an entire contract). As to JCT standard forms of contract see PARA 202.
5   *Holland Hannen & Cubitts (Northern) Ltd v Welsh Health Technical Services Organisation* (1981) 18 BLR 80.
6   *Hoenig v Isaacs* [1952] 2 All ER 176 at 180–181, CA, per Denning LJ. As to retention money see PARA 346.
7   *Appleby v Myers* (1867) LR 2 CP 651.
8   In *AE Farr Ltd v Ministry of Transport* (1965) 5 BLR 94 the ICE conditions of contract were treated as a measure and value form of contract (see now ICC Conditions of Contract; and PARA 202). See eg *Arcos Industries Pty Ltd v Electricity Commission* (1973) 12 BLR 65, NSW CA (where a schedule of rates contract was used).
9   See also *Kelly Pipelines Ltd v British Gas plc* (1989) 48 BLR 126.
10   The JCT publishes a standard form of management contract, with related standard works contract conditions.
11   'Turnkey contract' was defined in *High Mark (M) Sdn Bhd Ltd v Patco Malaysian Sdn Bhd* (1984) 28 BLR 129, Malaysian HC, although in *Cable (1956) Ltd v Hutcherson Ltd* (1969) 43 ALJR 321 at 324, Aust HC, it was held not to be a term of art. For an example in which this type of contract

was considered see *Viking Grain Storage Ltd v TH White Installations Ltd* (1985) 33 BLR 103. The JCT publishes a modified version of its standard main form intended for use where the contractor's design is used.

12 Ie the Housing Grants, Construction and Regeneration Act 1996 Pt II (ss 104–117).

13 As to the meaning of 'construction contract' see PARA 210. As to the rights in relation to payment see PARAS 351–358. As to the right to refer disputes to adjudication see the Housing Grants, Construction and Regeneration Act 1996 s 108; and PARA 407 et seq.

210. Meanings of 'construction contract' and 'construction operations'.

Part II of the Housing Grants, Construction and Regeneration Act 1996[1] created a new type of contract called a 'construction contract' and introduced statutory rights and entitlements for parties to such contracts. The statutory provisions have two primary purposes. First, to provide that every construction contract must include a mechanism for determining what payments become due, and when and the circumstances in which payment may be withheld[2]. Secondly, to provide a right to a party to a construction contract to refer any disputes arising under the contract for adjudication[3]. The appropriate national authority[4] has power by regulations to make a scheme for construction contracts, which contains provisions about the matters referred to in Part II of the Act[5]. Where a construction contract does not comply with the requirements of certain provisions of Part II[6], the relevant provisions of the scheme have effect. Where any provisions of the scheme so apply in default of contractual provision agreed[7] by the parties, they have effect as implied terms of the contract concerned[8].

'Construction contract' means an agreement with a person for any of the following[9]:

(1)   the carrying out of construction operations[10];

(2)   arranging for the carrying out of construction operations by others, whether under sub-contract to him or otherwise[11];

(3)   providing his own labour, or the labour of others, for the carrying out of construction operations[12].

A construction contract includes an agreement to do architectural, design, or surveying work, or to provide advice on building, engineering, interior or exterior decoration or on the laying-out of landscape, in relation to construction operations[13], but does not include a contract of employment or any other contract described as being excluded from the operation of Part II of the Housing Grants, Construction and Regeneration Act 1996[14].

Since 2013, a collateral warranty may now be a construction contract for the purposes of Part II of the Housing Grants, Construction and Regeneration Act 1996[15]. Therefore the payment and adjudication provisions of Part II of the Housing Grants, Construction and Regeneration Act 1996 may apply to these documents in circumstances where it could be clearly interpreted as being a contract for the 'carrying out of construction operations'[16].

'Construction operations' means, subject to the exceptions stated below, operations of any of the following descriptions[17]:

(a)   construction, alteration, repair, maintenance, extension, demolition or dismantling of buildings, or structures forming, or to form, part of the land (whether permanent or not)[18];

(b)   construction, alteration, repair, maintenance, extension, demolition or dismantling of any works forming, or to form, part of the land, including walls, roadworks, power-lines, electronic communications apparatus, aircraft runways, docks and harbours, railways, inland waterways, pipe-lines, reservoirs, water-mains, wells, sewers, industrial plant and installations for purposes of land drainage, coast protection or defence[19];

(c)   installation in any building or structure of fittings forming part of the land, including systems of heating, lighting, air-conditioning, ventilation, power supply, drainage, sanitation, water supply or fire protection, or security or communications systems[20];

(d)   external or internal cleaning of buildings and structures, so far as carried out in the course of their construction, alteration, repair, extension or restoration[21];

(e)   operations which form an integral part of, or are preparatory to, or are for rendering complete, such operations as are described in heads (a) to (d) above, including site clearance, earth-moving, excavation, tunnelling and boring, laying of foundations, erection, maintenance or dismantling of scaffolding, site restoration, landscaping and the provision of roadways and other access works[22];

(f)   painting or decorating the internal or external surfaces of any building or structure[23].

The following operations are not construction operations[24]:

(i)   drilling for, or extraction of, oil or natural gas[25];

(ii)   extraction (whether by underground or surface working) of minerals; tunnelling or boring, or construction of underground works, for this purpose[26];

(iii)   assembly, installation or demolition of plant or machinery, or erection or demolition of steelwork for the purposes of supporting or providing access to plant or machinery, on a site where the primary activity is[27]: (A) nuclear processing, power generation, or water or effluent treatment[28]; or (B) the production, transmission, processing or bulk storage (other than warehousing) of chemicals, pharmaceuticals, oil, gas, steel or food and drink[29];

(iv)   manufacture or delivery to site of:

    (A)   building or engineering components or equipment[30];

    (B)   materials, plant or machinery[31]; or

    (C)   components for systems of heating, lighting, air-conditioning, ventilation, power supply, drainage, sanitation, water supply or fire protection, or for security or communications systems[32] except under a contract which also provides for their installation[33];

(v)   the making, installation and repair of artistic works, being sculptures, murals and other works which are wholly artistic in nature[34].

1   Ie the Housing Grants, Construction and Regeneration Act 1996 Pt II (ss 104–117). As to the application of Pt II see PARA 211.

2   See PARAS 351–358.

3   See PARA 407 et seq.

4   Ie the Secretary of State or, where statutory functions have been transferred in relation to Wales, the Welsh Ministers: see PARA 203.

5   See the Housing Grants, Construction and Regeneration Act 1996 s 114(1), (3). Before making any such regulations the appropriate national authority must consult such persons as it thinks fit: s 114(2). As to the regulations made under s 114 in relation to England and Wales see the Scheme for Construction Contracts (England and Wales) Regulations 1998, SI 1998/649; and PARAS 358, 411–416.

Orders, regulations and directions under the Housing Grants, Construction and Regeneration Act 1996 may make different provision for different cases or descriptions of case, including different provision for different areas (s 146(1)), and may contain incidental, supplementary or transitional provisions and savings (see s 146(2)).

6 Ie the Housing Grants, Construction and Regeneration Act 1996 s 108 (see PARA 410), s 108A (see PARA 422), s 109 (see PARA 352), s 110 (see PARA 353), s 110A (see PARA 354), s 110B (see PARA 354), s 111 (see PARA 355) and s 113 (see PARA 357).

7 As to the application of the Housing Grants, Construction and Regeneration Act 1996 Pt II see PARA 211.

8 Housing Grants, Construction and Regeneration Act 1996 s 114(4).

9 Housing Grants, Construction and Regeneration Act 1996 s 104(1). The appropriate national authority may by order add to, amend or repeal any of the provisions of s 104(1), (2), (3). As to the agreements which are construction contracts for the purposes of Pt II or are to be taken or not to be taken as included in references to such contracts: s 104(4). At the date at which this volume states the law no such orders had been made. See note 5.

10 Housing Grants, Construction and Regeneration Act 1996 s 104(1)(a). Whether the relevant works were 'construction operations' or fell within the exclusion provisions had to be looked at broadly and was a question of fact and degree: see *North Midland Construction plc v AE & E Lentjes UK Ltd* [2009] EWHC 1371 (TCC), 126 Con LR 213, [2009] BLR 574; *Cleveland Bridge (UK) Ltd v Whessoe-Volker Stevin Joint Venture* [2010] EWHC 1076 (TCC), 130 Con LR 159, [2010] BLR 415.

11 Housing Grants, Construction and Regeneration Act 1996 s 104(1)(b). As to sub-contracting see PARA 236 et seq.

12 Housing Grants, Construction and Regeneration Act 1996 s 104(1)(c).

13 Housing Grants, Construction and Regeneration Act 1996 s 104(2). See note 9.

14 Housing Grants, Construction and Regeneration Act 1996 s 104(3). See note 9. The reference to a contract of employment in the text is a reference to a contract of employment within the meaning of the Employment Rights Act 1996 (see EMPLOYMENT vol 39 (2014) PARA 2): Housing Grants, Construction and Regeneration Act 1996 s 104(3). See *Melville Dundas Ltd v Hotel Corporation of Edinburgh Ltd* [2006] BLR 474, [2006] CSOH 136 (settlement agreement arising out of a construction contract was not itself a construction contract); *Captiva Estates Ltd v Rybarn Ltd (in administration)* [2005] EWHC 2744 (TCC), [2006] BLR 66 (a 'development agreement' being an agreement which provides for the grant or disposal of a relevant interest in the land on which take place the principal construction operations to which the contract relates, was not a construction contract). See also PARA 211 note 7.

15 See *Parkwood Leisure Ltd v Laing O'Rourke Wales and West Ltd* [2013] EWHC 2665 (TCC), [2013] 3 EGLR 6, [2013] All ER (D) 221 (Aug).

16 See *Parkwood Leisure Ltd v Laing O'Rourke Wales and West Ltd* [2013] EWHC 2665 (TCC) at [27], [29], [2013] 3 EGLR 6, [2013] All ER (D) 221 (Aug) per Akenhead J.

17 Housing Grants, Construction and Regeneration Act 1996 s 105(1). The appropriate national authority may by order add to, amend or repeal any of the provisions of s 105(1) or s 105(2) as to the operations and work to be treated as construction operations for the purposes of Pt II: s 105(3). At the date at which this volume states the law no such orders had been made. See note 5. As to the meaning of 'construction operations' see *Palmers Ltd v ABB Power Construction Ltd* (1999) 68 Con LR 52, [1999] BLR 426 (scaffolding may be 'construction operations' even though, since it was scaffolding provided in connection with the assembly of a boiler, it fell within the exclusion under the Housing Grants, Construction and Regeneration Act 1996 s 105(2)(c)(i) (see head (iii)(A) in the text)); *Nottingham Community Housing Association Ltd v Powerminster Ltd* (2000) 75 Con LR 65, [2000] BLR 759 (maintenance and repair of domestic gas appliances are 'construction operations'); *ABB Zantingh Ltd v Zedal Building Services Ltd* (2000) 77 Con LR 32, [2001] BLR 66 (construction of generators may be 'construction operations' even though power generation is excluded under the Housing Grants, Construction and Regeneration Act 1996 s 105(2)(c)(i)); *Mitsui Babcock Energy Services v Foster Wheeler Energia OY* 2001 SLT 1158, Ct of Sess (construction of boilers for operation by separate enterprise supplying steam to petrochemical company was not construction operation by virtue of exclusion under the Housing Grants, Construction and Regeneration Act 1996 s 105(2)(c)(ii) (see head (iii)(B) in the text)); *Gibson Lea Retail Interiors Ltd v Makro Self Service Wholesalers Ltd* [2001] BLR 407, [2001] All ER (D) 333 (Jul) (installation of shop fittings was not 'construction operations'); *Burgess (Homer) Ltd v Chirax (Annan) Ltd* (1999) 71 Con LR 245, [2000] BLR 124, Ct of Sess (installation of pipework fell within the scope of the Housing Grants, Construction and Regeneration Act 1996 s 105(2)(c)(ii) and was not a construction operation).

18 Housing Grants, Construction and Regeneration Act 1996 s 105(1)(a).

19 Housing Grants, Construction and Regeneration Act 1996 s 105(1)(b) (amended by the Communications Act 2003 s 406(1), Sch 17 para 137).
20 Housing Grants, Construction and Regeneration Act 1996 s 105(1)(c).
21 Housing Grants, Construction and Regeneration Act 1996 s 105(1)(d).
22 Housing Grants, Construction and Regeneration Act 1996 s 105(1)(e).
23 Housing Grants, Construction and Regeneration Act 1996 s 105(1)(f).
24 Housing Grants, Construction and Regeneration Act 1996 s 105(2). See note 17.
25 Housing Grants, Construction and Regeneration Act 1996 s 105(2)(a).
26 Housing Grants, Construction and Regeneration Act 1996 s 105(2)(b).
27 Housing Grants, Construction and Regeneration Act 1996 s 105(2)(c).
28 Housing Grants, Construction and Regeneration Act 1996 s 105(2)(c)(i). See, however, *Palmers Ltd v ABB Power Construction Ltd* (1999) 68 Con LR 52, [1999] BLR 426; *ABB Zantingh Ltd v Zedal Building Services Ltd* (2000) 77 Con LR 32, [2001] BLR 661; *North Midland Construction plc v AE & E Lentjes UK Ltd* [2009] EWHC 1371 (TCC), 126 Con LR 213, [2009] BLR 574; and note 17.
29 Housing Grants, Construction and Regeneration Act 1996 s 105(2)(c)(ii). See *Burgess (Homer) Ltd v Chirax (Annan) Ltd* (1999) 71 Con LR 245, [2000] BLR 124, Ct of Sess; *Mitsui Babcock Energy Services v Foster Wheeler Energia OY* 2001 SLT 1158, Ct of Sess; and note 17.
30 Housing Grants, Construction and Regeneration Act 1996 s 105(2)(d)(i).
31 Housing Grants, Construction and Regeneration Act 1996 s 105(2)(d)(ii).
32 Housing Grants, Construction and Regeneration Act 1996 s 105(2)(d)(iii).
33 Housing Grants, Construction and Regeneration Act 1996 s 105(2)(d).
34 Housing Grants, Construction and Regeneration Act 1996 s 105(2)(e).

211. Application of Part II of the Housing Grants, Construction and Regeneration Act 1996.

Where an agreement relates to construction operations and other matters, Part II of the Housing Grants, Construction and Regeneration Act 1996[1] applies to it only so far as it relates to construction operations[2]. It applies only to construction contracts which are entered into after 1 May 1998[3], and relate to the carrying out of construction operations in England, Wales or Scotland[4]. Part II applies whether or not the law of England and Wales or Scotland is otherwise the applicable law in relation to the contract[5].

Part II of the Act does not apply to a construction contract with a residential occupier[6].The Secretary of State may by order provide that any or all of the provisions of Part II, so far as extending to England and Wales, do not apply to any description of construction contract relating to the carrying out of construction operations, not being operations in Wales, which is specified in the order, and the Welsh Ministers may by order provide that any or all of the provisions of Part II so far as extending to England and Wales, do not apply to any description of construction contract relating to the carrying out of construction operations in Wales which is specified in the order[7].

Part II of the Act applies to a construction contract entered into by or on behalf of the Crown otherwise than by or on behalf of Her Majesty in her private capacity[8], and applies to a construction contract entered into on behalf of the Duchy of Cornwall notwithstanding any Crown interest[9]. Where a construction contract is entered into by or on behalf of Her Majesty in right of the Duchy of Lancaster, Her Majesty is represented, for the purposes of any adjudication or other proceedings arising out of the contract by virtue of Part II, by the Chancellor of the Duchy or such person as he may appoint[10]. Where a construction contract is entered into on behalf of the Duchy of Cornwall, the Duke of Cornwall or the possessor for the time being of the Duchy is represented, for the purposes of any adjudication or other proceedings arising out of the contract by virtue of Part II, by such person as he may appoint[11].

1 Ie the Housing Grants, Construction and Regeneration Act 1996 Pt II (ss 104–117).

2   Housing Grants, Construction and Regeneration Act 1996 s 104(5). An agreement relates to construction operations so far as it makes provision of any kind within s 104(1) or s 104(2) (see PARA 210): s 104(5). As to the meaning of 'construction operations' see PARA 210.

3   Ie the commencement date of the Housing Grants, Construction and Regeneration Act 1996 Pt II for these purposes: see the Housing Grants, Construction and Regeneration Act 1996 (England and Wales) (Commencement No 4) Order 1998, SI 1998/650. The Housing Grants, Construction and Regeneration Act 1996 ss 104, 105, 106, 108, 114, so far as conferring the power to consult, to make orders, regulations or determinations, to give directions, guidance, approvals or consents, to specify matters, or to impose conditions, were brought into force on 11 September 1996 by the Housing Grants, Construction and Regeneration Act 1996 (Commencement No 1) Order 1996, SI 1996/2352.

4   Housing Grants, Construction and Regeneration Act 1996 s 104(6). 'England' means, subject to any alteration of boundaries under the Local Government Act 1972 Pt IV (ss 53–78), the area consisting of the counties established by s 1 (see LOCAL GOVERNMENT vol 69 (2018) PARAS 5, 38, 41), Greater London and the Isles of Scilly: Interpretation Act 1978 s 5, Sch 1. 'Wales' means the combined area of the counties which were created by the Local Government Act 1972 s 20 (see LOCAL GOVERNMENT vol 69 (2018) PARAS 5, 51, 63), but subject to any alteration made under s 73 (consequential alteration of boundary following alteration of watercourse) (see LOCAL GOVERNMENT vol 69 (2018) PARA 116): Interpretation Act 1978 Sch 1 (definition substituted by the Local Government (Wales) Act 1994 s 1(3), Sch 2 para 9). As to Greater London see LONDON GOVERNMENT vol 71 (2013) PARA 14.

5   Housing Grants, Construction and Regeneration Act 1996 s 104(7).

6   Housing Grants, Construction and Regeneration Act 1996 s 106(1)(a). A construction contract with a residential occupier means a construction contract which principally relates to operations on a dwelling which one of the parties to the contract occupies, or intends to occupy, as his residence: Housing Grants, Construction and Regeneration Act 1996 s 106(2). For these purposes, 'dwelling' means a dwelling-house or a flat; 'dwelling-house' does not include a building containing a flat; and 'flat' means separate and self-contained premises constructed or adapted for use for residential purposes and forming part of a building from some other part of which the premises are divided horizontally: s 106(2). The appropriate national authority (ie the Secretary of State or, where statutory functions have been transferred in relation to Wales, the Welsh Ministers: see PARA 203) may by order amend s 106(2): s 106(3), (4). At the date at which this volume states the law no such order had been made. As to the making of orders under s 106(4) see PARA 210 note 5. 'Occupation' is an ongoing process and cannot be tested by reference to a single snapshot in time: *Westfields Construction Ltd v Lewis* [2013] EWHC 376 (TCC), [2013] 1 WLR 3377, [2013] All ER (D) 328 (Feb).

7   Housing Grants, Construction and Regeneration Act 1996 s 106A(1), (2) (s 106A added by the Local Democracy, Economic Development and Construction Act 2009 s 138). In exercise of these powers, the Construction Contracts (Wales) Exclusion Order 2011, SI 2011/1713 and the Construction Contracts (England) Exclusion Order 2011, SI 2011/2332 have been made, which both provide that a construction contract is excluded from the operation of the Housing Grants, Construction and Regeneration Act 1996 s 110(1A) (see PARA 353) if it is a contract pursuant to which a party to a relevant contract has sub-contracted to a third party some or all of its obligations under that contract to carry out, or arrange that others carry out, construction operations (private finance initiative sub-contracts) (see art 3).

   Prior to the repeal of the Housing Grants, Construction and Regeneration Act 1996 s 106(1)(b) by the Local Democracy, Economic Development and Construction Act 2009 s 138, in exercise of the power in the Housing Grants, Construction and Regeneration Act 1996 s 106(1)(b) to exclude certain types of construction contracts from the operation of Pt II by order of the appropriate national authority, the Construction Contracts (England and Wales) Exclusion Order 1998, SI 1998/648, had been made, and provided that the following were excluded agreements: agreements made under specified statutory provisions dealing with highway works, planning obligations, sewage works and externally financed NHS Trust agreements (see art 3); externally financed development agreement entered into by an NHS foundation trust (see art 3A (added by SI 2004/696)); agreements entered into by specified public bodies under the private finance initiative (or a project applying similar principles) (see art 4 (amended by SI 2005/757; SI 2013/1466)); agreements which primarily relate to the financing of works (see art 5); and development agreements, which contain provision for the disposal of an interest in land (see art 6). As to savings following the amendments made by the Local Democracy, Economic Development and Construction Act 2009 see s 149(3).

8   Housing Grants, Construction and Regeneration Act 1996 s 117(1).

9   Housing Grants, Construction and Regeneration Act 1996 s 117(2).

10 Housing Grants, Construction and Regeneration Act 1996 s 117(3).
11 Housing Grants, Construction and Regeneration Act 1996 s 117(4).

212. Collateral contracts and warranties.

In the ordinary course of business pre-contract statements[1] may be made which may be enforceable, for example, as collateral contracts or warranties[2]. In the construction industry it is common for special contracts or warranties[3] to be made or given to enable a person to pursue a remedy otherwise than through a contractual chain of responsibility because it may not be practicable or possible to do so. For example, nominated sub-contractors are generally required to give undertakings to the employer as to design where a main contractor is or may not be liable for that design[4]. Similarly, because a lessee may have no claim in respect of defects in a new building, those primarily responsible for its construction may give undertakings in the nature of indemnities directly to the lessee (usually by deed). The stipulations in such contracts or warranties may be treated as if they had been contained in a building contract[5].

1 Post-contract statements may also be made: see *Independent Broadcasting Authority v EMI Electronics Ltd and BICC Construction Ltd* (1980) 14 BLR 1, HL.
2 See eg *Miller v Cannon Hill Estates Ltd* [1931] 2 KB 113, DC; *Birch v Paramount Estates (Liverpool) Ltd* (1956) 167 Estates Gazette 396, CA; *Shanklin Pier Co Ltd v Detel Products Ltd* [1951] 2 KB 854, [1951] 2 All ER 471; *Wells (Merstham) Ltd v Buckland Sand and Silica Co Ltd* [1965] 2 QB 170, [1964] 1 All ER 41; *George Fischer Holdings Ltd v Multi Design Consultants Ltd* (1998) 61 Con LR 85, [1998] All ER (D) 134; *Liberty Mercian v Cuddy Civil Engineering Ltd* [2013] EWHC 2688 (TCC), [2014] 1 All ER (Comm) 761. As to collateral warranties or contracts see CONTRACT vol 22 (2012) PARA 332.
3 Standard forms have been published by, for example, the Joint Contracts Tribunal. As to standard forms of contract see PARA 202.
4 As to the influence of the possibility of obtaining such a contract see *Greater Nottingham Co-Operative Society Ltd v Cementation Piling and Foundations Ltd* [1989] QB 71, [1988] 2 All ER 971, 41 BLR 43, CA. As to sub-contracting generally see PARA 238 et seq.
5 An employer can confer an enforceable benefit upon a lessee in his building contract with the contractor: see the Contracts (Rights of Third Parties) Act 1999; and CONTRACT.

213. International contracts.

It is occasionally necessary to determine the law applicable to a building contract where it is not expressly selected. The selection of a law governing building contracts will be determined by the rules relating to the choice of the applicable law or proper law of the contract[1]. If the law has to be inferred then the law of the country where the building works are to be carried out will normally be the proper law unless there are circumstances which will impute to the parties an intention that some other law will apply[2].

1 See CONFLICT OF LAWS vol 19 (2011) PARA 628 et seq.
2 Thus, where works were to be carried out in Scotland by a Scottish builder but for English building owners under a contract in the English standard form, the proper law was held to be English law: *James Miller and Partners Ltd v Whitworth Street Estates (Manchester) Ltd* [1970] AC 583, [1970] 1 All ER 796, HL. Yet where work was to be carried out in Iraq by a Northern Irish sub-contractor for an English contractor under a main contract for an Iraqi employer which was governed by Iraqi law, it was held that the proper law of the sub-contract was Iraqi law because the sub-contract had to operate in conjunction with the main contract, even though the sub-contract was in the standard form intended for use with the United Kingdom ICE Conditions (now ICC Conditions of Contract: see PARA 202): *JMJ Contractors Ltd v Marples Ridgway Ltd* (1985) 31 BLR 100. Note, however, that these cases were decided before the Convention on the Law Applicable to Contractual Obligations (Rome, 19 June 1980) had force of law in the United Kingdom. The Convention is set out in the Contracts (Applicable Law) Act 1990 s 2, Sch 1: see CONFLICT OF LAWS vol 19 (2011) PARA 628 et seq.

(iii) Contract Documents

214. Contract documents generally.

A building contract may comprise the following documents[1]:
(1)   the agreement itself[2];
(2)   the conditions[3];
(3)   the drawings[4];
(4)   the specification[5];
(5)   a bill or bills of quantities[6];
(6)   schedules of rates or prices for the valuation of the works[7];
(7)   a programme or method statement[8] for the order or manner in which the works may or will be carried out[9].

If the building contract does not itself prescribe a method for reconciling conflicting provisions of the various contract documents then the provisions drawn up for or most relevant to the project may be preferred[10].

1   Standard forms will usually define the documents which form part of the contract. A document may be incorporated by reference provided that there is evidence of the parties' intention to incorporate: *Moore v Shawcross* [1954] JPL 431, [1954] CLY 342. See also *Aqua Design and Play International Ltd (t/a Aqua Design) v Kier Regional Ltd (t/a French Kier Anglia)* [2002] EWCA Civ 797, 82 Con LR 107, [2003] BLR 111. As to standard forms for building contracts see PARA 202.

2   This may also be constituted by the contractor's tender, quotation or estimate (frequently in the form sent out with the invitation to tender) and some letter or other document of acceptance.

3   Sometimes there are two or more sets of conditions, for example general and special or particulars or supplementary.

4   These will have been prepared by or for the employer (sometimes by the tenderer or contractor) and will generally have been used to prepare the tender. The architect may issue 'working' drawings after the contract is concluded. As to the position where such drawings contain details outside the contemplation of the contract see PARA 272.

5   This is prepared similarly to the drawings (see note 4) and frequently split into elements or sections referable to parts of works or the relevant trades. It may comprise preliminary or general clauses as well as particular clauses.

6   This document itemises the work described in the drawings and specification. It will be split into sections or elements frequently in accordance with the rules or recommendations of standard methods of measurement (there are separate methods for building works and civil engineering works). As to the effect of the omission of work from the bills see eg *C Bryant & Son Ltd v Birmingham Hospital Saturday Fund* [1938] 1 All ER 503; and *AE Farr Ltd v Ministry of Transport* (1965) 5 BLR 94, HL.

7   This document is used especially where the rates and prices in the bill of quantities may not be applicable to variations and some scheme of valuation on a time and materials basis is needed (commonly called 'dayworks').

8   See eg *Yorkshire Water Authority v Sir Alfred McAlpine & Son (Northern) Ltd* (1985) 32 BLR 114; *Holland Dredging (UK) Ltd v Dredging & Construction Co Ltd* (1987) 14 Con LR 30, 37 BLR 1, CA.

9   This is not always incorporated as it can subject the parties to obligations which may be incapable of fulfilment.

10 See eg *Gleeson (MJ) (Contractors) Ltd v Hillingdon London Borough Council* (1970) 215 Estates Gazette 165.

(3) Agreement, Consideration and Factors Vitiating Agreement

(i) Tenders and Estimates

215. Tenders.

Where the contractor agrees to carry out work without more but in the expectation of payment, the employer must pay a reasonable sum in respect of the work done[1]. To obtain a fixed price for the work, an employer will often seek estimates or tenders from contractors. Choice of name is immaterial; there is no custom that a document headed 'quotation' or 'estimate' or even 'budget price' should not be treated as an offer[2].

The conduct of contractor and employer at the tender stage is restricted by domestic and European Union legislation against protectionism and unfair competition, mainly in relation to public works above a specified value[3].

1 See eg *Whittle v Frankland* (1862) 2 B & S 49; *Re Walton-on-the-Naze UDC and Moran* (1905) 2 Hudson's BC (4th Edn) 376; *Ramsden and Carr v J Chessum & Sons and Ward* (1913) 110 LT 274, HL.
2 *Croshaw v Pritchard and Renwick* (1899) 16 TLR 45.
3 See PARA 223 et seq.

216. Invitation to tender.

Letters asking contractors to tender for work are invitations to treat[1]; it is generally unnecessary for the building owner or employer to state that he does not bind himself to accept the lowest tender[2]. Where such a letter states that the lowest tender will be accepted[3] or where the parties have negotiated on that basis[4], the letter may amount to an offer[5]. An invitation to tender may be revoked at any time, and a tender may be withdrawn at any time before acceptance on giving notice to the employer[6]. A tender will also lapse if it is not accepted within a reasonable time[7].

If a tender is rejected, a contractor will generally be unable to claim the costs of preparing the tender from the building owner[8]. Where a contractor performs services beyond those necessary for the submission of his tender in the reasonable expectation of payment, the contractor may recover on a quantum meruit basis[9].

1 For the distinction between offers and invitations to treat see CONTRACT vol 22 (2012) PARA 234 et seq.
2 *Spencer v Harding* (1870) LR 5 CP 561. See, however, in relation to public works contracts PARA 223 et seq.
3 Cf *Spencer v Harding* (1870) LR 5 CP 561 at 563 per Willes J; *Harvela Investments Ltd v Royal Trust Co of Canada (CI) Ltd* [1986] AC 207, [1985] 2 All ER 966, HL.
4 See *Pauling v Pontifex* (1852) 20 LTOS 126.
5 It must be capable of amounting to an offer: see *Gibson v Manchester City Council* [1979] 1 All ER 972, [1979] 1 WLR 294, HL. Further, failure to consider a tender may amount to a breach of contract: *Blackpool and Fylde Aero Club Ltd v Blackpool Borough Council* [1990] 3 All ER 25, [1990] 1 WLR 1195, CA. See also *Harmon CFEN Façades (UK) Ltd v The Corporate Officer of the House of Commons* [1999] All ER (D) 1178, (1999) 67 Con LR 1 at 168–169 per Judge Lloyd QC (which concerned invitations to tender in relation to contracts subject to the Public Works Contracts Regulations 1991, SI 1991/2680 (revoked; see now the Public Contracts Regulations 2015, SI 2015/102; PARA 224; and CONSTITUTIONAL AND ADMINISTRATIVE LAW vol 20 (2014) PARA 528A)).
   A tender may be rejected by reason of disqualifying factors personal to the tenderer: see *Fairclough Building Ltd v Port Talbot Borough Council* (1992) 62 BLR 82, CA (where a director of the tenderer was married to the council's principal architect).
6 *Bristol, Cardiff & Swansea Aerated Bread Co v Maggs* (1890) 44 ChD 616; *Byrne & Co v Leon Van Tienhoven & Co* (1880) 5 CPD 344; and CONTRACT vol 22 (2012) PARA 245.

7 *Murray v Rennie and Angus* (1897) 24 R 965, Ct of Sess. What is a reasonable time is a question of fact; in *Metropolitan Asylums Board of Managers v Kingham & Sons* (1890) 6 TLR 217 at 218, Fry LJ said that reasonable time can never extend after the time at which the contract was to commence, although Fry LJ's dictum is doubted (see *Bedford Insurance Co Ltd v Instituto de Resseguros do Brasil* [1985] QB 966 at 987, [1984] 3 All ER 766 at 776, where Parker J says 'in so holding I am conscious that I differ from that judgment of Fry LJ in *Metropolitan Asylums Board Managers v Kingdom & Sons* (1889) 6 LR 217 at 218, where he said: " . . . if ratification is to bind, it must be made within a reasonable time after acceptance by an unauthorised person. That reasonable time can never extend after the time at which the contract is to committee". However, no authority was cited in support on this very wide statement and I know of no principle to sustain it. A further point was faintly raised by counsel for the defendants, namely that the ratification was subject to an unfulfilled condition. As to this, I say only that I reject the submission as being the unproven.').

8 See *Harris v Nickerson* (1873) LR 8 QB 286; and AUCTION vol 4 (2011) PARA 41. In *Marston Construction Co Ltd v Kigass* (1989) 46 BLR 109, the costs of tendering were awarded on the basis of an implied request (sed dubitante). If the invitation to the contractor was made fraudulently and without any intention of accepting the tender in any event, the costs of tendering may be recoverable as damages for deceit: *Richardson v Silvester* (1873) LR 9 QB 34, DC.

9 *Sinclair v Logan* 1961 SLT 10, Sh Ct; *William Lacey (Hounslow) Ltd v Davis* [1957] 2 All ER 712, [1957] 1 WLR 932; *British Steel Corpn v Cleveland Bridge and Engineering Co Ltd* [1984] 1 All ER 504, 24 BLR 94 per Robert Goff J; and see *Sabemo Ltd v North Sydney Municipal Council* [1977] 2 NSWLR 880, NSW SC. See also *Regalian Properties plc v London Docklands Development Corpn* [1995] 1 All ER 1005, [1995] 1 WLR 212 (contractor cannot recover costs of preparation for contract where tender accepted subject to contract). As to quantum meruit see RESTITUTION vol 88 (2012) PARAS 407, 513 et seq.

217. Unfair competition.

At common law, an agreement made by deed between two or more persons that one should not tender or should tender at an excessive price is valid and enforceable[1]. Such an agreement is not unlawful so as to give rise to a claim for conspiracy[2]. However, agreements between undertakings which may affect trade within the United Kingdom and have as their object or effect the prevention, restriction or distortion of competition within the United Kingdom are prohibited and void[3]. Similar principles apply to agreements between undertakings which may affect trade between member states of the European Union (EU)[4].

Many contractors subscribe for membership of trade associations. Stipulations in the rules of the association that members should press a proposed employer to accept standard conditions or should charge for work at particular rates, may amount to a breach of United Kingdom or EU competition law[5].

Collusive practices not embodied in any formal or informal agreement between tenderers, or between employers inviting tenders, may also be unlawful. As well as agreements between undertakings, decisions by associations of undertakings or concerted practices which may affect trade within the United Kingdom, and have as their object or effect the prevention, restriction or distortion of competition within the United Kingdom, are prohibited and void[6]. Similar provisions apply to agreements between undertakings which may affect trade between EU member states[7]. A tenderer or employer in a dominant position in the market[8] will be restricted from abusing that position at the tender stage as at other stages if trade within the United Kingdom, or between EU member states, is affected[9].

1 *Jones v North* (1875) LR 19 Eq 426; *Re Electrical Installations at Exeter Hospital Agreement* [1971] 1 All ER 347, [1970] 1 WLR 1391.

2 *Mogul Steamship Co Ltd v McGregor Gow & Co* [1892] AC 25, HL; *Sorrell v Smith* [1925] AC 700, HL; *Crofter Hand-Woven Harris Tweed Co Ltd v Veitch* [1942] AC 435, [1942] 1 All ER 142, HL.

3 See the Competition Act 1998 s 2(1), (4); and COMPETITION vol 18 (2009) PARA 116. Certain agreements are excluded (see COMPETITION vol 18 (2009) PARAS 117–120), and provision is also

made for exemption from the prohibition (see COMPETITION vol 18 (2009) PARAS 121–124). Investigations may be conducted if it is suspected that the prohibition has been infringed: see COMPETITION vol 18 (2009) PARA 129 et seq. As to enforcement see COMPETITION vol 18 (2009) PARA 135 et seq. 'United Kingdom' means Great Britain and Northern Ireland: Interpretation Act 1978 s 5, Sch 1. 'Great Britain' means England, Scotland and Wales: Union with Scotland Act 1706 preamble art I; Interpretation Act 1978 s 22(1), Sch 2 para 5(a). Neither the Isle of Man nor the Channel Islands are within the United Kingdom: See further CONSTITUTIONAL AND ADMINISTRATIVE LAW vol 20 (2014) PARA 3. As to the meanings of 'England' and 'Wales' see PARA 211 note 4.

4   See the Treaty on the Functioning of the European Union (Rome, 25 March 1957; TS 1 (1973); Cmnd 5179) ('TFEU') art 101; and COMPETITION vol 18 (2009) PARA 61 et seq. This treaty was formerly entitled 'the Treaty Establishing the European Community'. In 1999 its articles were renumbered by the Treaty of Amsterdam (ie the Treaty of Amsterdam Amending the Treaty on European Union, the Treaties Establishing the European Communities and Related Acts (Amsterdam, 2 October 1997, ECS 14 (1997); Cm 3780)): see *Treaty Citation (No 2) (Note)* [1999] All ER (EC) 646, ECJ. In 2007 it was renamed and renumbered by the Treaty of Lisbon (ie the Treaty of Lisbon Amending the Treaty Establishing the European Union and the Treaty Establishing the European Community (Lisbon, 13 December 2007, ECS 13 (2007); Cm 7294)). See EUROPEAN UNION vol 47A (2014)PARA 6 .
    The Treaty on the Functioning of the European Union art 101 may be inapplicable in the case of certain agreements, decisions and practices: see art 101(3); and COMPETITION vol 18 (2009) PARAS 66–67. See also EC Commission Notice of December 1997 concerning Agreements of Minor Importance (OJ C372, 9.12.97, p 13), which states that 'only those agreements are prohibited which have an appreciable impact on market conditions'; and COMPETITION vol 18 (2009) PARA 64. Undertakings may be investigated by the European Commission (see COMPETITION vol 18 (2009) PARA 90) and sanctions and penalties imposed in relation to any infringement (see COMPETITION vol 18 (2009) PARA 107 et seq).

5   See the Competition Act 1998 s 2(1); TFEU art 101; and COMPETITION vol 18 (2009) PARAS 61, 116 et seq. Cf *Re Birmingham Association of Building Trades Employers' Agreement* [1963] 2 All ER 361, [1963] 1 WLR 484 (decided under the Restrictive Trade Practices Act 1976 (repealed)).

6   See note 3.

7   See note 4.

8   Elements of the construction or engineering industries may constitute a market in themselves.

9   See the Competition Act 1998 s 18; the TFEU art 102; and COMPETITION vol 18 (2009) PARAS 68 et seq, 125 et seq.
    There are some cases excluded from the prohibition under the Competition Act 1998 s 18: see COMPETITION vol 18 (2009) PARA 126 et seq. Investigations may be conducted if it is suspected that the prohibition has been infringed: see COMPETITION vol 18 (2009) PARA 129 et seq. As to enforcement see COMPETITION vol 18 (2009) PARA 135 et seq.
    In relation to the Treaty on the Functioning of the European Union art 102, undertakings may be investigated by the European Commission (see COMPETITION vol 18 (2009) PARA 90) and sanctions and penalties imposed in relation to any infringement (see COMPETITION vol 18 (2009) PARA 107 et seq).

218.   Acceptance of a tender.

The unconditional acceptance of a tender gives rise to a contract[1]. An acceptance is effective when communicated to the tenderer[2]. Where the parties are otherwise agreed on the terms of the contract but acceptance is made subject to a condition that a formal document should be executed, it is a question of construction whether such a condition is a condition precedent which prevents a concluded contract from arising[3]. The use of the term 'subject to contract' is a strong indication that no enforceable obligation was intended to arise before the execution of a formal document[4]; but a statement in the acceptance that a formal contract is being prepared may not prevent a binding contract arising[5].

Where the acceptance of a tender is qualified by the introduction of a new term, a counter offer has been made to the tenderer which will require acceptance if a contract is to be concluded[6]. Such an acceptance can be made by conduct and a contractor who starts work, or an employer who permits work to be started, after the receipt of a counter offer and without objection to the terms of the counter offer will be taken to have accepted those terms by conduct[7]. There is no concluded contract where the parties stipulate that certain matters be left for further agreement[8]. Where at the date the work is begun the parties have not reached full agreement on all the terms of the contract, on their arriving at full agreement the resultant contract will, unless otherwise agreed, normally have effect retrospectively to the date on which the work was begun[9]. Acceptance of a tender must be unambiguous[10].

1   *Wimshurst v Deeley* (1845) 2 CB 253; *Thorn v Public Works Comrs* (1863) 32 Beav 490; *Tancred, Arrol & Co v Steel Co of Scotland Ltd* (1890) 15 App Cas 125, HL; *Nicolene Ltd v Simmonds* [1953] 1 QB 543, [1953] 1 All ER 822, CA. Where, however, the invitation to tender is for such goods as may be ordered from time to time (a standing offer), although the acceptance of the offer binds the tenderer, the other party is not liable until an order is placed: see *Great Northern Rly Co v Witham* (1873) LR 9 CP 16; *A-G v Stewards & Co Ltd* (1901) 18 TLR 131, HL. As to offer and acceptance see CONTRACT vol 22 (2012) PARAS 233–276.

2   *Willcocks and Barnes v Paignton Co-operative Society Ltd* (1930) 74 Sol Jo 247. See also CONTRACT vol 22 (2012) PARA 260. Special rules may apply where an acceptance is made by post, e-mail, telex or fax: see eg *Entores Ltd v Miles Far East Corpn* [1955] 2 QB 327, [1955] 2 All ER 493, CA; *Holwell Securities Ltd v Hughes* [1974] 1 All ER 161, [1974] 1 WLR 155, CA; *Brinkibon Ltd v Stahag Stahl und Stahlwarenhandelsgesellschaft mbH* [1983] 2 AC 34, [1982] 1 All ER 293, HL; and CONTRACT vol 22 (2012) PARA 277 et seq.

3   See eg *Rossiter v Miller* (1878) 3 App Cas 1124, HL; *Filby v Hounsell* [1896] 2 Ch 737; *Branca v Cobarro* [1947] KB 854, [1947] 2 All ER 101, CA; *Pagnan SpA v Feed Products Ltd* [1987] 2 Lloyd's Rep 601, CA; *Metal Scrap Trade Corpn v Kate Shipping Co Ltd, The Gladys (No 2)* [1994] 2 Lloyd's Rep 402. See also CONTRACT vol 22 (2012) PARAS 270–271.

4   *Rossdale v Denny* [1921] 1 Ch 57, CA, especially per Lord Sterndale MR at 66; but see *Law v Jones* [1974] Ch 112, [1973] 2 All ER 437, CA; *Alpenstow Ltd v Regalian Properties plc* [1985] 2 All ER 545, [1985] 1 WLR 721; *Galliard Homes Ltd v J Jarvis & Sons plc* (1999) 71 Con LR 219, [1999] All ER (D) 1266, sub nom *Jarvis Interiors Ltd v Galliard Homes Ltd* [2000] BLR 33, CA; cf *Fraser Williams v Prudential Holborn Ltd* (1993) 64 BLR 1, CA. As to conditional agreements see CONTRACT vol 22 (2012) PARA 271.

5   *Lewis v Brass* (1877) 3 QBD 667, CA; and cf the ICE form of tender, which provides that unless and until a formal agreement is prepared and executed, the tender, together with written acceptance of it, constitutes a binding contract between the parties. As to standard forms see PARA 202. See also CONTRACT vol 22 (2012) PARA 270.

6   *Hyde v Wrench* (1840) 3 Beav 334; *Trollope and Colls Ltd and Holland, Hannen and Cubitts Ltd v Atomic Power Constructions Ltd* [1962] 3 All ER 1035, [1963] 1 WLR 333; *Butler Machine Tool Co Ltd v Ex-Cell-O-Corpn (England) Ltd* [1979] 1 All ER 965, [1979] 1 WLR 401, CA. As to counter-offers see CONTRACT vol 22 (2012) PARA 264.

7   *A Davies & Co (Shopfitters) Ltd v William Old Ltd* (1969) 113 Sol Jo 262, 67 LGR 395; *Sauter Automation v HC Goodman (Mechanical Services)* (1986) 34 BLR 81; *G Percy Trentham v Archital Luxfer Ltd* [1993] 1 Lloyd's Rep 25, (1992) 63 BLR 44, CA; and see CONTRACT vol 22 (2012) PARA 265.

8   *May and Butcher v R* [1934] 2 KB 17n, HL. See also *Tiverton Estates Ltd v Wearwell Ltd* [1975] Ch 146, [1974] 1 All ER 209, CA; *Munton v GLC* [1976] 2 All ER 815, [1976] 1 WLR 649, CA; cf *Foley v Classique Coaches Ltd* [1934] 2 KB 1, CA. See also *Haden Young Ltd v Laing O'Rourke Midlands Ltd* [2008] EWHC 1016 (TCC), [2008] All ER (D) 49 (Jun). As to incomplete agreements see CONTRACT vol 22 (2012) PARA 268.

9   *Trollope and Colls Ltd and Holland, Hannen and Cubitts Ltd v Atomic Power Constructions Ltd* [1962] 3 All ER 1035, [1963] 1 WLR 333.

10 *Peter Lind & Co Ltd v Mersey Docks and Harbour Board* [1972] 2 Lloyd's Rep 234 (two tenders submitted; acceptance of 'your tender' led to no contract).

219.   Rights and obligations created by tendering.

If the contractor carries out work, such as preparing designs, schedules or estimates, as part of the tendering process in the reasonable belief either that he will be paid for these services or that the contract will be placed with him, he is entitled to reasonable remuneration for that work on a quantum meruit basis[1]. Equally, the contractor is entitled to remuneration where the employer makes use of the contractor's input into his tender or causes him to carry out work beyond that reasonably necessary in the circumstances[2].

An employer is not usually bound to keep the tender period open for the advertised period, to open and consider every valid tender or to accept any, or the lowest tender. Equally, a contractor may withdraw his tender prior to its acceptance even if it is stated to be irrevocable since there is no general obligation to negotiate in good faith[3]. However, any irrevocable commitment by either the employer or the tenderer that is supported by consideration may not be withdrawn[4].

1 As to quantum meruit see RESTITUTION vol 88 (2012) PARAS 407, 513 et seq.
2 *William Lacey (Hounslow) Ltd v Davis* [1957] 2 All ER 712, [1957] 1 WLR 932; *British Steel Corpn v Cleveland Bridge and Engineering Co Ltd* [1984] 1 All ER 504, 24 BLR 94; *Sabemo Ltd v North Sydney Municipal Council* [1977] 2 NSWLR 880, NSW SC; *Marston Construction Co Ltd v Kigass* (1989) 46 BLR 109. See also *Regalian Properties v London Docklands Development Corpn* [1995] 1 All ER 1005, [1995] 1 WLR 212 (contractor cannot recover costs of preparation for contract where tender accepted subject to contract). For valuation on a quantum meruit basis see eg *Serck Controls Ltd v Drake & Scull Engineering Ltd* (2000) 73 Con LR 100.
3 *Walford v Miles* [1992] 2 AC 128, [1992] 1 All ER 453, HL. See *Interfoto Picture Library Ltd v Stiletto Visual Programmes Ltd* [1989] QB 433 at 439, [1988] 1 All ER 348 at 352–353, CA, per Bingham LJ.
4 *Percival Ltd v LCC Asylums and Mental Deficiency Committee* (1918) 87 LJKB 677; *Blackpool and Fylde Aero Club Ltd v Blackpool Borough Council* [1990] 3 All ER 25, [1990] 1 WLR 1195, CA. In *Northern Construction Co Ltd v Gloge Heating and Plumbing Ltd* [1986] 2 WWR 649, 27 DLR (4th) 265, Alta CA, a sub-contractor was held to his tender, despite its purported withdrawal; the court relied on the custom of the Canadian industry that such tenders are irrevocable. See also *R v Ron Engineering and Construction Eastern Ltd* (1981) 119 DLR (3rd) 267, Can SC.

220. Letters of intent.

A letter of intent is a communication expressing an intention to enter into a contract in the future. A letter of intent may be appropriate when the price is either agreed or there is a clear mechanism in place for it to be agreed, the contract terms are, or are very likely to be, agreed and there are good reasons to start work in advance of the finalisation of all the contract documents[1].

The effect of such a communication depends upon the objective meaning of the words used[2]. The various possibilities are: (1) it may have no binding effect[3]; (2) it may take effect as an executory ancillary contract entitling the recipient to costs consequently incurred if the intended contract does not materialise; or (3) it may affect a contractual offer to the effect that if the recipient undertakes the proposed action, he will be remunerated either reasonably or by the terms he states[4]. Finally, the recipient might be entitled to reasonable remuneration where he acts to the benefit of the sender pursuant to the communication[5].

1 *Cunningham v Collett* [2006] EWHC 1771 (TCC), 113 Con LR 142.
2 *British Steel Corpn v Cleveland Bridge and Engineering Co Ltd* [1984] 1 All ER 504, (1981) 24 BLR 94.
3 As was the finding in *British Steel Corpn v Cleveland Bridge and Engineering Co Ltd* [1984] 1 All ER 504, (1981) 24 BLR 94, where, however, the contractor recovered on a quantum meruit basis.
4 *Turriff Construction Ltd v Regalia Knitting Mills Ltd* (1971) 9 BLR 20; *Edwin Hill & Partners v Leakcliffe Properties Ltd* (1984) 29 BLR 43. See also *Monk Construction Ltd v Norwich Union Life Assurance Society* (1992) 62 BLR 107, CA; *Drake & Scull Engineering Ltd v Higgs & Hill Northern Ltd* (1995) 11 Const LJ 214; *Gallard Homes Ltd v J Jarvis & Sons plc* (1999) 71 Con LR 219, sub nom *Jarvis Interiors Ltd v Galliard Homes Ltd* [2000] BLR 33, CA.

5   *Wilson Smithett & Cape (Sugar) Ltd v Bangladesh Sugar and Food Industries Corpn* [1986] 1 Lloyd's Rep 378. See also *ERDC Group Ltd v Brunel University* [2006] EWHC 687 (TCC), 109 Con LR 114, [2006] BLR 255.

221. Failure to finalise contract and estoppel.

If a contractor carries out work in circumstances in which no contract has been concluded, he may, but will not necessarily, be entitled to remuneration on a quantum meruit basis[1]. The rates or basis of remuneration that would have been included in the contract had it been concluded will be taken into account in determining that reasonable remuneration[2]. If both parties have proceeded on the basis that a binding contract has been entered into that governs their relationship, both parties may be estopped by convention from subsequently denying that there was a contract governing their relationship[3].

1   As to quantum meruit see RESTITUTION vol 88 (2012) PARAS 407, 513 et seq. See also PARA 219.
2   See eg *Trollope and Colls Ltd and Holland and Hannen and Cubitts Ltd v Atomic Power Constructions Ltd* [1962] 3 All ER 1035, [1963] 1 WLR 333; *Gilbert & Partners (a firm) v Knight* [1968] 2 All ER 248, 4 BLR 9, CA; *Peter Lind & Co Ltd v Mersey Docks and Harbour Board* [1972] 2 Lloyd's Rep 234.
3   *Amalgamated Investment and Property Co Ltd (in liquidation) v Texas Commerce International Bank Ltd* [1982] QB 84, [1981] 3 All ER 577, CA; *Whittal Builders Co Ltd v Chester-le-Street District Council* (1987) 40 BLR 82; *Mitsui Babcock Energy Ltd v John Brown Engineering Ltd* (1996) 51 Con LR 129; cf *Russell Bros (Paddington) Ltd v John Lelliott Management Ltd* (1991) 11 Const LJ 377. See also *Stent Foundations v Carillion Construction* (2001) 78 Con LR 188, [2000] All ER (D) 984; *Tesco Stores Ltd v Costain Construction Ltd* [2003] EWHC 1487 (TCC), [2003] All ER (D) 394 (Jul); *Haden Young Ltd v Laing O'Rourke Midlands Ltd* [2008] EWHC 1016 (TCC), [2008] All ER (D) 49 (Jun). As to estoppel generally see ESTOPPEL vol 47 (2014) PARA 301 et seq.

(ii) Consideration

222. Necessity for consideration.

Except in the case of a contract made by deed, consideration is necessary to support a contract[1]. In a building contract context the consideration given by the employer is the amount paid or the promise to make payment, and by the contractor in executing the works or promising to do so. A promise for additional payment for work included in the contract or a promise to carry out other existing contractual obligations such as those concerned with the time for completion is given without consideration[2], unless it provides the other party with a genuine practical benefit[3], or there is uncertainty whether or not an item of work falls within the original contract[4]. An agreement to pay existing liabilities by instalments may not be good consideration[5].

Any other variation of the terms of the contract will generally be unenforceable unless supported by fresh consideration[6]. A mere promise by a builder to perform work without any mention of price needs to be supported by some consideration in order to become binding on him[7], but, if he is employed to do the work, that is sufficient consideration as it implies an agreement to pay reasonable remuneration for the work done and the materials supplied[8].

If the consideration for the contract is illegal, the contract is not enforceable[9].

1   See CONTRACT vol 22 (2012) PARA 308 et seq.
2   *Sharpe v San Paulo Rly Co* (1873) LR 8 Ch App 597 at 608 per James LJ; *Harris v Watson* (1791) Peake 72; *Stilk v Myrick* (1809) 2 Camp 317; *Atlas Express Ltd v Kafco (Importers and Distributors) Ltd* [1989] QB 833, [1989] 1 All ER 641. This includes promises given under

'economic duress': *Atlas Express Ltd v Kafco (Importers and Distributors) Ltd* above; *Williams v Roffey Bros & Nicholls (Contractors) Ltd* [1991] 1 QB 1, [1990] 1 All ER 512, CA (where no such duress was found); and see *B & S Contracts and Design Ltd v Victor Green Publications Ltd* [1984] ICR 419, CA; and CONTRACT vol 22 (2012) PARA 293.

3   *Williams v Roffey Bros & Nicholls (Contractors) Ltd* [1991] 1 QB 1, [1990] 1 All ER 512, CA.
4   *Williams v O'Keefe* [1910] AC 186 at 191, PC; *Simon Container Machinery Ltd v Emba Machinery AB* [1998] 2 Lloyd's Rep 429.
5   *Re Selectmove Ltd* [1995] 2 All ER 531, [1995] 1 WLR 474, CA.
6   See PARAS 272, 343 et seq; and CONTRACT vol 22 (2012) PARA 308 et seq.
7   *Ramsden and Carr v Chessum & Sons and Ward* (1913) 110 LT 274, HL.
8   See eg *Whittle v Frankland* (1862) 2 B & S 49. See also the cases in PARAS 215, 350.
9   *Windhill Local Board of Health v Vint* (1890) 45 ChD 351, CA; *Taylor v Bhail* (1995) 50 Con LR 70, CA; but if the contract is unenforceable only in law a builder may recover in restitution: *Pavey & Matthews Pty Ltd v Paul* (1987) 162 CLR 221, (1987) 6 Const LJ 59, Aust HC; *Rover International Ltd v Cannon Film Sales Ltd (No 3)* [1989] 3 All ER 423, [1989] 1 WLR 912, CA; and see RESTITUTION vol 88 (2012) PARA 516.

(iii) Public Works Contracts

223. General principles of EU law applicable to tenders to public bodies.

Invitations to tender from public bodies are subject to the provisions of the Treaty on the Functioning of the European Union[1] concerning free movement of goods and services[2]. Conditions attached to invitations to tender which restrict the free movement of goods, have equivalent effect to such a restriction, or discriminate on the grounds of nationality are in breach of the Treaty and will be struck down if proceedings are brought by the EC Commission against the member state concerned. Thus provisions requiring compliance of tender materials and tenderers with national standards may have equivalent effect to a restriction[3]. The mere fact that a particular contract is exempted from the specific provisions relating to public works contracts[4] does not absolve the member state from observing the general provisions of the Treaty[5].

1   Ie the Treaty on the Functioning of the European Union (Rome, 25 March 1957; TS 1 (1973); Cmnd 5179) ('TFEU'). The Treaty has been renamed and its provisions renumbered: see PARA 217 note 4.
2   As to the free movement of goods see TFEU Pt 3 Title II (arts 28–37); and CUSTOMS AND EXCISE vol 30 (2012) PARA 3; EUROPEAN UNION vol 47A (2014) PARA 301. As to the free movement of persons, services and capital see TFEU Pt 3 Title IV (arts 45–66); and EUROPEAN UNION vol 47A (2014) PARAS 302–304.
3   Case 45/87 *Commission v Ireland* [1989] 1 CMLR 225, 44 BLR 1, ECJ. Similarly, laws providing that nationalised entities should be preferred to private entities have been held to be contrary to Community law: Case 3/88 *EC Commission v Italy* [1989] ECR 4035, [1991] 2 CMLR 115, ECJ. See also Case C-456/08 *EC Commission v Ireland* [2010] 2 CMLR 1138, [2010] All ER (D) 205 (Jan), ECJ.
4   See EEC Council Directive 93/37 (OJ L199, 9.8.93, p 54) concerning the co-ordination of procedures for the award of public works contracts: and PARA 224.
5   Case 45/87 *EC Commission v Ireland* [1989] 1 CMLR 225, 44 BLR 1, ECJ. See also Case C-59/00 *Vestergaard v Spottrup Boligselkab* [2001] ECRI-9505, [2002] 2 CMLR 1112, ECJ (clause in tender document providing that specified Danish make of product was to be used constituted infringement of the EC Treaty (as it was then known)).

224. Public works contracts.

Contracts with government departments and certain other authorities, and the tendering procedures relating to any such contracts, are, with specified exceptions, subject to European Union directives on the co-ordination of procedures for the advertisement and award of public works, public supply and public services contracts[1]. These directives have been implemented by regulations in the United Kingdom and are dealt with elsewhere in this work[2].

1   See European Parliament and Council Regulation (EU) 2014/24 (OJ L94, 28.3.2014, p 65) on public procurement (amended by Commission Delegated Regulation (EU) 2015/2170 (OJ L307, 25.11.2015, p 5); Commission Delegated Regulation (EU) 2017/2365 (OJ L337, 19.12.2017, p 19)). See also EC Council Directive 2006/97 (OJ L363, 20.12.2006, p 107); EC Commission Regulation 213/2008 (OJ L74, 15.3.2008, p 1); European Parliament and Council Directive 2009/81 (OJ L216, 20.8.2009, p 76) (amended by Commission Regulation (EU) 1251/2011 (OJ L319, 2.12.2011, p 43); Commission Regulation (EU) 1336/2013 (OJ L335, 14.12.2013, p 17); Commission Regulation (EU) 2015/2340 (OJ L330, 16.12.2015, p 14); Commission Regulation (EU) 2015/2341 (OJ L330, 16.12.2015, p 16); Commission Regulation (EU) 2015/2342 (OJ L330, 16.12.2015, p 18)); European Parliament and Council Regulation 596/2009 (OJ L188, 18.7.2009, p 14); EC Commission Regulation 1177/2009 (OJ L314, 1.12.2009, p 64).
    Provision has also been made in relation to co-ordinating the procurement procedures of entities operating in the water, energy, transport and postal services sectors: see European Parliament and Council Regulation (EU) 2014/25 (OJ L94, 28.3.2014, p 243) on procurement by entities operating in the water, energy, transport and postal services sectors (amended by Commission Delegated Regulation (EU) 2015/2171 (OJ L307, 25.11.2015, p 7); Commission Delegated Regulation (EU) 2017/2364 (OJ L337, 19.12.2017, p 17)); EC Council Directive 2006/97 (OJ L 363, 20.12.2006, p 107); EC Commission Regulation 213/2008 (OJ L 74, 15.3.2008, p 1); European Parliament and Council Directive 2009/81 (OJ L 216, 20.8.2009, p 76) (amended by Commission Regulation (EU) 1251/2011 (OJ L319, 2.12.2011, p 43); Commission Regulation (EU) 1336/2013 (OJ L335, 14.12.2013, p 17); Commission Regulation (EU) 2015/2340 (OJ L330, 16.12.2015, p 14); Commission Regulation (EU) 2015/2341 (OJ L330, 16.12.2015, p 16); Commission Regulation (EU) 2015/2342 (OJ L330, 16.12.2015, p 18); European Parliament and Council Regulation 596/2009 (OJ L 188, 18.7.2009, p 14); EC Commission Regulation 1177/2009 (OJ L 314, 1.12.2009, p 64)), which have been implemented in the United Kingdom by the Utilities Contracts Regulations 2016, SI 2016/274 (see ENERGY AND CLIMATE CHANGE, POSTAL SERVICES, WATER AND WATERWAYS); and the Defence and Security Public Contracts Regulations 2011, SI 2011/1848 (see CONSTITUTIONAL AND ADMINISTRATIVE LAW vol 20 (2014) PARA 528A). As to public procurement see further CONSTITUTIONAL AND ADMINISTRATIVE LAW vol 20 (2014) PARA 528 et seq.
    See also European Parliament and Council Directive (EU) 2014/23 (OJ L94, 28.3.2014, p 1) on the award of concession contracts (member states must bring into force the laws, regulations and administrative provisions necessary to comply with Directive 2014/23 by 18 April 2016: art 51(1)) (corrected in OJ L114, 5.5.2015, p 24; and amended by Commission Delegated Regulation (EU) 2017/2366 (OJ L337, 19.12.2017, p 21); Commission Delegated Regulation (EU) 2015/2172 (OJ L307, 25.11.2015, p 9) (implemented in the UK by virtue of the Concession Contracts Regulations 2016, SI 2016/273 (see CONSTITUTIONAL AND ADMINISTRATIVE LAW vol 20 (2014) PARA 528A) which came into force on 18 April 2016); European Parliament and Council Directive (EU) 2014/55 (OJ L133, 6.5.2014, p 1) on electronic invoicing in public procurement (member states must adopt, publish and apply the laws, regulations and administrative provisions necessary to comply with Directive 2014/55 by 27 November 2018: art 11(1)).
    See also Council Directive (EEC) 89/665 (OJ L 395, 30.12.1989, p 33–35) on the coordination of the laws, regulations and administrative provisions relating to the application of review procedures to the award of public supply and public works contracts (amended by Council Directive (EEC) 92/50 (OJ L 209, 24.7.1992, p 1–24, corrected in OJ L63, 10.3.2016, p 44; and amended by European Parliament and Council Regulation (EU) 2014/24 (OJ L94, 28.3.2014, p 65)); and European Parliament and Council Directive (EC) 2007/66 (OJ L 335, 20.12.2007, p 31–46), which requires member states to provide effective remedies at a national level for breaches of regulations relating to procurement.
2   See the Public Contracts Regulations 2015, SI 2015/102; the Defence and Security Public Contracts Regulations 2011, SI 2011/1848; and CONSTITUTIONAL AND ADMINISTRATIVE LAW vol 20 (2014) PARA 528A.

225. Exclusion of non-commercial considerations; 'best value' requirements.

Local and certain other public authorities[1] must exercise their functions in relation to public works and public supply contracts[2] without reference to non-commercial matters[3]. The duty arises whenever the authority exercises one of the following functions[4]:

(1)   including persons in or excluding⁵ persons from approved lists of contractors⁶ or lists of persons who may be invited to tender⁷;

(2)   accepting or refusing the submission of tenders⁸;

(3)   selecting the person with whom to enter into the contract⁹;

(4)   giving or withholding approval for, or selecting or nominating, sub-contractors¹⁰; and

(5)   terminating contracts¹¹.

For these purposes non-commercial matters relate to¹²: (a) the terms of employment of the contractor's workforce¹³; (b) the composition of the workforce and opportunities afforded to it¹⁴; (c) whether the contractor uses self-employed labour¹⁵; (d) the contractor's involvement with irrelevant fields of government policy¹⁶; (e) conduct relating to industrial disputes¹⁷; (f) the country or territory of origin of supplies to the contractor, or the location of the contractor's business interests in any country or territory¹⁸; (g) political, industrial, or sectarian affiliations or interests of the contractor and its directors, partners or employees¹⁹; (h) financial support or the withholding of it by the contractor for any institution to or from which the authority gives or withholds support²⁰; and (i) the use or non-use of certain services provided by the authority under building legislation²¹. The appropriate national authority²² may add to the list by order made by statutory instrument²³. The matters listed in the Local Government Act 1988 are described in broad terms and if necessary a purposive construction will be given to the descriptions to give effect to the statute²⁴. Corresponding matters referable to associated bodies, suppliers and customers, and sub-contractors are to be treated as matters referable to the contractor for these purposes²⁵.

Local and certain other authorities also have imposed upon them a duty to comply with 'best value' requirements, having regard to a combination of economy, efficiency and effectiveness, and they must make arrangements to secure continuous improvements in the way in which their functions are exercised²⁶.

1   As to the public authorities see the Local Government Act 1988 s 17(2), Sch 2; and LOCAL GOVERNMENT vol 69 (2018) PARA 557.
2   Ie contracts for the supply of goods or materials, for the supply of services or for the execution of works: see the Local Government Act 1988 s 17(3); and LOCAL GOVERNMENT vol 69 (2018) PARA 557.
3   See the Local Government Act 1988 s 17(1). Any potential or former potential contractor or body representing contractors may bring proceedings for judicial review of a decision breaching the duty of exercising functions without reference to non-commercial matters: see s 19(7)(a). Failure to comply with the duty under s 17(1) is actionable by any person who in consequence suffers loss or damage: see s 19(7)(b). The damages recoverable are limited to expenditure reasonably incurred in submitting the tender: see s 19(8). See further LOCAL GOVERNMENT vol 69 (2018) PARA 557.
4   Where a public authority exercises a function regulated by the Local Government Act 1988 s 17, it is the duty of the authority, in relation to certain decisions it makes, to notify that person of the decision, and that person may require the authority to furnish him with a written statement of the reasons for the decision: see s 20; and LOCAL GOVERNMENT vol 69 (2018) PARA 560.
5   This includes removing persons from a list: see the Local Government Act 1988 s 17(8).
6   'Contractor', except in relation to a subsisting contract, means a 'potential contractor', ie: (1) in relation to functions as respects an approved list, any person who is or seeks to be included in the list; and (2) in relation to functions as respects a proposed public supply or works contract, any person who is or seeks to be included in the group of persons from whom tenders are invited or who seeks to submit a tender for or enter into the proposed contract, as the case may be: Local Government Act 1988 s 17(8).
7   See the Local Government Act 1988 s 17(4)(a), (b)(i); and LOCAL GOVERNMENT vol 69 (2018) PARA 558.
8   See the Local Government Act 1988 s 17(4)(b)(ii); and LOCAL GOVERNMENT vol 69 (2018) PARA 558.

9   See the Local Government Act 1988 s 17(4)(b)(iii); and LOCAL GOVERNMENT vol 69 (2018) PARA 558.

10 See the Local Government Act 1988 s 17(4)(b)(iv), (c)(i); and LOCAL GOVERNMENT vol 69 (2018) PARA 558.

11 See the Local Government Act 1988 s 17(4)(c)(ii); and LOCAL GOVERNMENT vol 69 (2018) PARA 558.

12 The non-commercial matters specified in the Local Government Act 1988 s 17(5) include matters which have occurred in the past as well as those subsisting when the function is to be exercised: s 17(6).

13 See the Local Government Act 1988 s 17(5)(a); and LOCAL GOVERNMENT vol 69 (2018) PARA 559.

14 See the Local Government Act 1988 s 17(5)(a); and LOCAL GOVERNMENT vol 69 (2018) PARA 559.

15 See the Local Government Act 1988 s 17(5)(b); and LOCAL GOVERNMENT vol 69 (2018) PARA 559.

16 See the Local Government Act 1988 s 17(5)(c); and LOCAL GOVERNMENT vol 69 (2018) PARA 559.

17 See the Local Government Act 1988 s 17(5)(d); and LOCAL GOVERNMENT vol 69 (2018) PARA 559.

18 See the Local Government Act 1988 s 17(5)(e); and LOCAL GOVERNMENT vol 69 (2018) PARA 559.

19 See the Local Government Act 1988 s 17(5)(f); and LOCAL GOVERNMENT vol 69 (2018) PARA 559.

20 See the Local Government Act 1988 s 17(5)(g); and LOCAL GOVERNMENT vol 69 (2018) PARA 559.

21 See the Local Government Act 1988 s 17(5)(h); and LOCAL GOVERNMENT vol 69 (2018) PARA 559.

22 Ie the Secretary of State or, where statutory functions have been transferred in relation to Wales, the Welsh Ministers: see PARA 203.

23 See the Local Government Act 1988 s 19(1); and LOCAL GOVERNMENT vol 69 (2018) PARA 559.

24 *R v Islington London Borough Council, ex p Building Employers' Federation* [1989] IRLR 382, 45 BLR 45 (where the Local Government Act 1988 s 17(5)(a) was considered).

25 See the Local Government Act 1988 s 17(7); and LOCAL GOVERNMENT vol 69 (2018) PARA 559.

26 See LOCAL GOVERNMENT vol 69 (2018) PARA 779 et seq.

(iv) Factors Vitiating Agreement

226. Secret commissions.
Where the contractor has agreed to pay a commission to any agent of the employer in order to secure the acceptance of a tender, the employer may rescind the contract[1] and may sue the agent for any commission received and for damages[2]. He may also sue the contractor for damages[3].

The employer may dismiss an architect who agrees to accept a secret commission from a contractor and can refuse to pay the architect's fees[4]. It is a breach of his terms of engagement for an architect or surveyor to have any financial relationship with the contractor unknown to the employer and such breach, unless waived, releases the employer from his liability to the architect or surveyor[5].

Such a commission arrangement would also affect the ability of the architect or the surveyor to act fairly in its capacity as agent for the employer and impartially as between the employer and the contractor particularly in relation to their duties under any building contract[6].

1 *Alexander v Webber* [1922] 1 KB 642; *Panama and South Pacific Telegraph Co v India Rubber, Gutta Percha and Telegraph Works Co* (1875) 10 Ch App 515 at 526 per James LJ; *Logicrose v Southend United Football Club Ltd* [1988] 1 WLR 1256, 132 Sol Jo 1591.

2 *Salford Corpn v Lever* [1891] 1 QB 168, CA; cf *Arab Monetary Fund v Hashim* [1993] 1 Lloyd's
   Rep 543 (revsd on another point [1996] 1 Lloyd's Rep 589, CA); and see AGENCY vol 1 (2017)
   PARAS 94–95, 140.
3 *Salford Corpn v Lever* [1891] 1 QB 168, CA; *Mahesan S/O Thambiah v Malaysia Government
   Officers' Co-operative Housing Society Ltd* [1979] AC 374, [1978] 2 All ER 405, PC.
4 *Tahrland v Rodier* (1866) 16 LCR 473 (Que); *Temperley v Blackpool Manufacturing Co Ltd*
   (1907) 71 JP Jo 341.
5 *Thornton Hall & Partners v Wembley Electrical Appliances Ltd* [1947] 2 All ER 630, CA.
6 *Sutcliffe v Thackrah* [1974] AC 727, [1974] 1 All ER 859, HL; *Pacific Associates Inc v Baxter*
   [1990] 1 QB 993, [1989] 2 All ER 159, CA. See also *AMEC Civil Engineering Ltd v Secretary of
   State for Transport* [2005] EWCA Civ 291 at [44] et seq, [2005] 1 WLR 2339 at 2354 per May
   LJ; *Scheldebouw BV v St James Homes (Grosvenor Dock) Ltd* [2006] EWHC 89 (TCC), 105
   ConLR 90, [2006] BLR 113.

227. Misrepresentation.

A misrepresentation is a false statement of fact and is fraudulent if made
recklessly or with intention to deceive[1]. A contractor induced to enter a contract
by a fraudulent misrepresentation may either rescind the contract or claim
damages or both[2]. A contractor induced to enter a contract by reason of an
innocent misrepresentation may also rescind the contract or claim damages, but
the court has discretion to award damages in lieu of rescission[3]. Generally, the
measure of damages payable under the Misrepresentation Act 1967 is the sum of
money which will place the representee in the position he would have been in if
the representation had not been made[4].

It is a defence to a claim for damages for innocent misrepresentation to show
that the defendant had reasonable grounds for believing the statement to be true
and that such belief continued until the date of the contract[5]. A contractor who
continues to act upon a contract after discovering that a statement was false loses
his right to rescind by reason of his affirmation of the contract[6] and he will only
be entitled to the price agreed under that contract[7]. A clause limiting liability for
misrepresentation in business to business contracts will only have effect in so far
as it satisfies the requirement[8] of reasonableness[9].

In business to consumer contracts the general rule is that contract terms and
notices are required to be fair[10]. The employer does not impliedly warrant that
statements in bills of quantities are accurate; statements in bills of quantities are
not representations that the work there described is sufficient for the completion
of the contract[11].

1 See *Derry v Peek* (1889) 14 App Cas 337, HL; and MISREPRESENTATION vol 76 (2013)
   PARA 754 et seq.
2 *Moss & Co Ltd v Swansea Corpn* (1910) 74 JP 351 (rescission); *S Pearson & Son Ltd v Dublin
   Corpn* [1907] AC 351, HL (it is immaterial that the statement was made by the employer's agent).
   See also AGENCY vol 1 (2017) PARAS 136, 153. As to the personal liability of a company officer
   on a fraudulent misrepresentation made by him in his capacity as such see *Thomas Saunders
   Partnership v Harvey* (1989) 30 Con LR 103. As to the rescission of contracts see CONTRACT vol
   22 (2012) PARA 553 et seq. As to damages for breach of contract see DAMAGES vol 29 (2014)
   PARA 499 et seq.
3 See the Misrepresentation Act 1967 s 2(2); and MISREPRESENTATION vol 76 (2013) PARA 832.
   See also *Thomas Witter Ltd v TBP Industries Ltd* [1996] 2 All ER 573; *William Sindall plc v
   Cambridgeshire County Council* [1994] 3 All ER 932, [1994] 1 WLR 1016, CA; *Floods of
   Queensbury Ltd v Shand Construction Ltd* [2000] BLR 81.
4 See *Gran Gelato Ltd v Richcliff (Group) Ltd* [1992] Ch 560 at 574, [1992] 1 All ER 865 at 876
   per Sir Donald Nicholls VC.
      The measure of damages for misrepresentation under the Misrepresentation Act 1967 s 2(1) is
   the same as that which applies to an action for fraudulent misrepresentation at common law: see
   Royscot Trust Ltd v Rogerson [1991] 2 QB 297, [1991] 3 All ER 294, CA; and DAMAGES vol 29

(2014) PARA 546; MISREPRESENTATION vol 76 (2013) PARAS 800, 810. The correctness of this decision was left open by the House of Lords: see *Smith New Court Securities Ltd v Citibank NA* [1997] AC 254 at 282–283, sub nom *Smith New Court (Securities) Ltd v Scrimgeour Vickers (Asset Management) Ltd* [1996] 4 All ER 769 at 792, HL, per Lord Steyn.
   The measure of damages in lieu of rescission for innocent misrepresentation under the Misrepresentation Act 1967 s 2(2) is the difference in value between what the representee was misled into thinking he was contracting for and the value of what he in fact received: see *William Sindall plc v Cambridgeshire County Council* [1994] 3 All ER 932, [1994] 1 WLR 1016, CA; and DAMAGES vol 29 (2014) PARA 547; MISREPRESENTATION vol 76 (2013) PARA 832.

5 See the Misrepresentation Act 1967 s 2(1); and MISREPRESENTATION vol 76 (2013) PARA 800. See also *Walker v Boyle* [1982] 1 All ER 634, [1982] 1 WLR 495; *Garden Neptune Shipping Ltd v Occidental Worldwide Investment Corpn* [1990] 1 Lloyd's Rep 330, CA.

6 *Ormes v Beadel* (1860) 2 De GF & J 333. See also *Long v Lloyd* [1958] 2 All ER 402, [1958] 1 WLR 753, CA. See further CONTRACT.

7 *Selway v Fogg* (1839) 5 M & W 83; *Glasgow and South Western Rly Co v Boyd and Forrest* [1915] AC 526, HL.

8 Ie under the Unfair Contract Terms Act 1977 s 11(1) for business to business contracts: see CONTRACT vol 22 (2012) PARA 419.

9 See the Misrepresentation Act 1967 s 3; and MISREPRESENTATION vol 76 (2013) PARAS 802, 826. See also *S Pearson & Son Ltd v Dublin Corpn* [1907] AC 351, HL.

10 See the Consumer Rights Act 2015 Pt 2 (ss 61–76); and CONSUMER PROTECTION vol 21 (2016) PARAS 391–402. Note that in business to consumer contracts, the Consumer Rights Act 2015 sets out in Pt 1 Ch 2 (ss 3–32) (goods) (see CONSUMER PROTECTION vol 21 (2016) PARA 329 et seq) and Ch 4 (ss 48–57) (services) (see CONSUMER PROTECTION vol 21 (2016) PARA 363) terms in consumer contracts which purport to exclude or restrict the trader's liability under listed headings and which if included in a consumer contract will make the contract non-binding on the consumer.

11 *Sherren v Harrison* (1860) 2 Hudson's BC (4th Edn) 5; *Scrivener v Pask* (1886) LR 1 CP 715; *Re Ford & Co and Bemrose & Sons Ltd* (1902) 2 Hudson's BC (10th Edn) 513, CA, per Collins MR; *Kimberley v Dick* (1871) LR 13 Eq 1.

(4) Special Parties and Formalities

(i) Special Parties

228. Local authorities.

Local authorities must make standing orders in relation to contracts for the supply of goods or materials or for the execution of works[1], and they may make standing orders in respect of any other contract to be made by them or on their behalf[2]. The contractor is not required to inquire whether the standing orders applicable to his contract have been complied with, and despite non-compliance with such orders contracts otherwise valid will have full force and effect[3]. A contract entered into by a committee of the local authority may be ratified[4] even though the power to enter contracts had not been delegated to the committee[5]. A contractor may rely on a contract or variation of the terms of a contract agreed by an officer of a local authority having ostensible authority to contract on its behalf[6].

1 See the Local Government Act 1972 s 135(2); and LOCAL GOVERNMENT vol 69 (2018) PARA 554. As to public works contracts awarded by local authorities see PARA 224. As to contracts of local authorities see AGENCY vol 1 (2017) PARA 23; LOCAL GOVERNMENT vol 69 (2018) PARA 554 et seq. As to standard forms see PARA 202.

2 See the Local Government Act 1972 s 135(1); and LOCAL GOVERNMENT vol 69 (2018) PARA 554. As to the general power of the local authority to make, vary or revoke standings orders with respect to proceedings and business see LOCAL GOVERNMENT vol 69 (2018) PARA 697.

3   See the Local Government Act 1972 s 135(4); and LOCAL GOVERNMENT vol 69 (2018)
    PARA 554. But see *North West Leicestershire District Council v East Midlands Housing
    Association Ltd* [1981] 3 All ER 364, [1981] 1 WLR 1396, CA.
4   *Kidderminster Corpn v Hardwick* (1873) LR 9 Exch 13.
5   Any delegation should be made in pursuance of the Local Government Act 1972 ss 101, 102: see
    LOCAL GOVERNMENT vol 69 (2018) PARA 399 et seq.
6   *Carlton Contractors Ltd v Bexley Corpn* (1962) 60 LGR 331; *A Roberts & Co Ltd v
    Leicestershire County Council* [1961] Ch 555, [1961] 2 All ER 245. Cf *North West Leicestershire
    District Council v East Midlands Housing Association Ltd* [1981] 3 All ER 364, [1981] 1 WLR
    1396, CA (council clerk had no ostensible authority).

229. Companies, corporations and partnerships.

A contract may be executed by a company:

(1)   by the affixing of its common seal[1]; or
(2)   by being signed, on behalf of the company, by: (a) two authorised
       signatories[2]; or (b) a director of the company in the presence of a witness
       who attests the signature[3].

The validity of an act done by a company is not to be called into question on
the ground of lack of capacity by reason of anything in the company's
constitution[4]. Where a person deals with a company in good faith, the power of
the directors to bind the company, or authorise others to do so, is deemed to be
free of any limitation under the company's constitution[5].

Contracts made by or on behalf of a corporation which if made by private
persons would be required to be in writing, or which would be valid although
made by parol only, may be similarly made on behalf of a corporation by any
person acting under its express or implied authority[6]. The capacity of a
corporation to contract depends on the terms of the Act under which it was
incorporated or on its charter[7].

When either party is a member of a partnership, the partnership will be liable
under the contract if the contracting partner was acting within the scope of his
authority[8].

1   See the Companies Act 2006 s 44(1)(a); and COMPANIES vol 14 (2016) PARA 287.
2   See the Companies Act 2006 s 44(1)(b), (2)(a); and COMPANIES vol 14 (2016) PARA 287. The
    following are 'authorised signatories' for these purposes: (1) every director of the company; and (2)
    in the case of a private company with a secretary or a public company, the secretary (or any joint
    secretary) of the company: s 44(3).
3   See the Companies Act 2006 s 44(1)(b), (2)(b); and COMPANIES vol 14 (2016) PARA 287.
4   See the Companies Act 2006 s 39(1); and COMPANIES vol 14 (2016) PARA 264.
5   See the Companies Act 2006 s 40(1); and COMPANIES vol 14 (2016) PARA 262.
6   See the Corporate Bodies' Contracts Act 1960 s 1(1); and CORPORATIONS vol 24 (2010)
    PARA 474. A corporation may continue to make its contracts under seal if it so wishes: see s 1(4);
    and CORPORATIONS vol 24 (2010) PARA 474.
7   See CORPORATIONS vol 24 (2010) PARA 329 et seq.
8   See the Partnership Act 1890 ss 5–8; and PARTNERSHIP vol 79 (2014) PARAS 39, 40, 47, 52.

230. The Crown and government departments.

The Crown is bound by a contract made by a proper agent acting within the
scope of his authority but not otherwise. A Crown agent who enters into a
contract beyond the scope of his authority is not liable for breach of warranty of
authority[1]. Actions against the Crown are instituted against the appropriate
government department[2]. Contracts entered into by government departments are
subject to control under European Union law unless exempted from it[3].

1   *Dunn v Macdonald* [1897] 1 QB 401; affd [1897] 1 QB 555, CA; and see further AGENCY vol 1

(2017) PARA 161; and CONSTITUTIONAL AND ADMINISTRATIVE LAW vol 20 (2014) PARAS 197, 644.

2   A list of departments is published from time to time by the Minister for the Civil Service in accordance with the Crown Proceedings Act 1947 s 17 (see CROWN AND CROWN PROCEEDINGS vol 29 (2014) PARA 100).

3   See PARAS 223–224.

(ii) Formalities

231. Where writing is required.

Contracts for works of construction are almost invariably in writing[1]. Where the contract involves the sale or other disposition of an interest in land, the contract must be in writing[2] and must be signed by or on behalf of each party to the contract[3]. The employer may require sureties for the due performance of the contract by the contractor[4] and any such contract of surety must be in writing[5].

1   It is, however, not essential for such a contract to be in writing, and the amendments to the Housing Grants, Construction and Regeneration Act 1996 by virtue of the repeal of s 107 pursuant to the Local Democracy, Economic Development and Construction Act 2009 s 139 makes it clear a 'construction contract' need not be in writing to receive the protection of the statute. However, where it is not in writing, the question whether or not a contract has actually been entered into will be determined by a consideration of all the facts upon which the contract is said to be based: *Allen v Yoxall* (1844) 1 Car & Kir 315. See also *Smith v Neale* (1857) 2 CBNS 67; *Russell v Trickett* (1865) 13 LT 280. See also CONTRACT vol 22 (2012) PARA 222 et seq; DEEDS AND OTHER INSTRUMENTS vol 32 (2012) PARA 201 et seq.

2   See the Law of Property (Miscellaneous Provisions) Act 1989 s 2; and CONVEYANCING vol 23 (2016) PARA 27 et seq. Where the contract for the sale of land is varied the formalities also apply to the variation: see *McCausland v Duncan Lawrie Ltd* [1996] 4 All ER 995, [1997] 1 WLR 38, CA; and CONVEYANCING vol 23 (2016) PARA 34.

3   See the Law of Property (Miscellaneous Provisions) Act 1989; *Firstpost Homes Ltd v Johnson* [1995] 4 All ER 355, [1995] 1 WLR 1567, CA; and CONVEYANCING vol 23 (2016) PARA 27 et seq.

4   As to sureties generally see PARA 383 et seq.

5   See the Statute of Frauds (1677) s 4; and FINANCIAL INSTRUMENTS AND TRANSACTIONS vol 49 (2015) PARA 677. See also *Elpis Maritime Co Ltd v Marti Chartering Co Inc* [1992] 1 AC 21, [1991] 3 All ER 758, HL; and FINANCIAL INSTRUMENTS AND TRANSACTIONS vol 49 (2015) PARA 689 et seq. But a contract of indemnity does not have to be in writing: *Lakeman v Mountstephen* (1874) LR 7 HL 17.

(iii) The Ascertainment and Meaning of Terms

232. Whether a question of law or of fact.

Where the contract has been reduced to writing, its interpretation is a question of law for the court to decide[1]. Evidence of an oral term which would add to or vary the written instrument will generally be inadmissible[2]. However, where the meaning of a term depends on a particular custom, evidence is admissible to prove the custom[3]. Oral evidence is also admissible to establish the meaning of a technical term[4]. There is a presumption that a written contract is intended to contain all the agreed terms, but the presumption is rebuttable[5] and it is possible for the contract to be partly oral and partly in writing. Where the contract was made orally, the ascertainment of its terms is a question of fact[6].

1   As to the construction of written contracts generally see CONTRACT vol 22 (2012) PARA 357 et seq; DEEDS AND OTHER INSTRUMENTS vol 32 (2012) PARA 364 et seq. When a concluded written contract has been entered into, extrinsic evidence of, for example, preliminary negotiations, subsequent conduct or intent are normally inadmissible as an aid to the construction

of the contract: see CONTRACT vol 22 (2012) PARAS 221, 288; DEEDS AND OTHER INSTRUMENTS vol 32 (2012) PARA 385 et seq. Restricted evidence of the factual background to and surrounding circumstances of a contract will be admissible: see *Prenn v Simmonds* [1971] 3 All ER 237, [1971] 1 WLR 1381, HL; *Reardon Smith Line Ltd v Hansen-Tangen, Hansen-Tangen v Sanko Steamship Co* [1976] 3 All ER 570, [1976] 1 WLR 989, HL; *Investors' Compensation Scheme Ltd v West Bromwich Building Society* [1998] 1 All ER 98, [1998] 1 WLR 896, HL; *Chartbrook Ltd v Persimmon Homes Ltd* [2009] UKHL 38, [2009] AC 1101, [2009] 4 All ER 677; and DEEDS AND OTHER INSTRUMENTS vol 32 (2012) PARAS 364, 398. See also *Matthew Hall Ortech Ltd v Tarmac Roadstone Ltd* (1997) 87 BLR 96 (where the guidance notes to a standard form were admissible as part of the surrounding circumstances).

2   See DEEDS AND OTHER INSTRUMENTS vol 32 (2012) PARA 365 et seq.

3   *North v Bassett* [1892] 1 QB 333; and see CUSTOM AND USAGE vol 32 (2012) PARA 69. See also *Tony Cox (Dismantlers) Ltd v Jim 5 Ltd* (1996) 13 Const LJ 209 (custom in the construction industry that prices quoted were exclusive of VAT); cf *Lancaster v Bird* (1998) 73 Con LR 22, (1999) Times, 9 March, CA (no implied term that prices generally are exclusive of VAT).

4   *Symonds v Lloyd* (1859) 6 CBNS 691; *Myers v Sarl* (1860) 3 E & E 306; *Bank of New Zealand v Simpson* [1900] AC 182, PC. See also DEEDS AND OTHER INSTRUMENTS vol 32 (2012) PARA 402 et seq.

5   See eg *Allan v Pink* (1838) 4 M & W 140.

6   *Smith v Hughes* (1871) LR 6 QB 597; and see CONTRACT vol 22 (2012) PARA 233 et seq.

233. Implied terms.

In a building contract there are four principal ways in which a term will be implied:

(1)   implication by statute[1];

(2)   implication to make the contract work[2];

(3)   implication of 'usual terms'[3]; or

(4)   implication by custom[4].

Implied terms are dealt with in more detail elsewhere in this work[5].

1   Terms may be implied into building contracts by virtue of, for example, the Housing Grants, Construction and Regeneration Act 1996 Pt II (ss 104–117), the Supply of Goods and Services Act 1982 Pt II (ss 12–16), the Consumer Rights Act 2015 Pt 1 Ch 2 (ss 3–22), Ch 4 (ss 48–57), and the Late Payment of Commercial Debts (Interest) Act 1998 s 1. As to implication by law see CONTRACT vol 22 (2012) PARA 366.

   Under the Housing Grants, Construction and Regeneration Act 1996 Pt II, where a building contract is also a construction contract within the meaning of that Act (see PARA 210), it must contain certain provisions in relation to the right to refer disputes to adjudication and as to matters concerning payment, and where it does not contain such provisions, the relevant provisions of the scheme for construction contracts apply by default: see PARAS 210–211, 351–358, 407 et seq. Where any provisions of the scheme so apply, they have effect as implied terms of the contract concerned: see s 114(4).

   A building contract is a contract for the supply of a service, and as such the Supply of Goods and Services Act 1982 Pt II applies to building contracts, and implies that a supplier acting in the course of business will carry out the service with reasonable care and skill (see s 13), and, subject to certain qualifications, that the supplier will carry out the service within a reasonable time (see s 14) and that the supplier will be paid a reasonable charge (see s 15). See SALE OF GOODS AND SUPPLY OF SERVICES vol 91 (2012) PARAS 330–332.

   In relation to a contract to which the Late Payment of Commercial Debts (Interest) Act 1998 applies, it is an implied term that any qualifying debt created by the contract carries simple interest subject to and in accordance with the Late Payment of Commercial Debts (Interest) Act 1998 Pt I (ss 1–6): see s 1; PARA 348; and SALE OF GOODS AND SUPPLY OF SERVICES vol 91 (2012) PARA 218 et seq.

2   Where the parties have drawn up a detailed contract it may be necessary to imply a term to make it work and give efficacy to the contract: see eg *The Moorcock* (1889) 14 PD 64, CA; *Reigate v Union Manufacturing Co (Ramsbottom) Ltd* [1918] 1 KB 592, 118 LT 479, CA; *Luxor (Eastbourne) Ltd v Cooper* [1941] AC 108, [1941] 1 All ER 33, HL; *Trollope & Colls Ltd v North West Metropolitan Regional Hospital Board* [1973] 2 All ER 260, [1973] 1 WLR 601, HL; *Liverpool City Council v Irwin* [1977] AC 239, [1976] 2 All ER 39, HL; *BP Refinery (Westernport) Pty Ltd v Hastings Shire Council* (1977) 180 CLR 266, 52 ALJR 20, PC; *Tai Hing*

Cotton Mill Ltd v Liu Chong Hing Bank Ltd [1986] AC 80, [1985] 2 All ER 947, PC; *Dominion Corporate Trustees Ltd v Capmark Bank Europe plc* [2010] EWHC 1605 (Ch), 13 ITELR 154; *Cassa di Risparmio della Repubblica di San Marino SpA v Barclays Bank Ltd* [2011] EWHC 484 (Comm), [2011] NLJR 437. See also CONTRACT vol 22 (2012) PARA 376.

3   If a contract deals expressly with a matter, no term dealing with the same matter will be implied: *Jones v St John's College, Oxford* (1870) LR 6 QB 115; *Lynch v Thorne* [1956] 1 All ER 744, [1956] 1 WLR 303, CA; *Multiplex Constructions (UK) Ltd v Cleveland Bridge UK Ltd* [2006] EWHC 1341 (TCC), 107 Con LR 1, [2006] All ER (D) 167 (Jun). Where, however, its terms do not deal with certain matters or where there is no express written contract particular terms are usually implied.

So far as the employer is concerned it is implied that all necessary co-operation will be afforded to bring about completion of the contract: *Mackay v Dick* (1881) 6 App Cas 251, HL; Compagnie *Noga D'Importation et D'Exportation SA v Abacha (Noga No 3)* [2001] Lexis Citation 1780, [2001] All ER (D) 339 (Oct); *Luxor (Eastbourne) Ltd v Cooper* [1941] AC 108, [1941] 1 All ER 33, HL; *Merton London Borough Council v Stanley Hugh Leach Ltd* (1985) 32 BLR 51, (1985) 2 Const LJ 189. The corollary to this is that the employer will not prevent the contractor from performing the contract: *William Cory & Son Ltd v City of London Corpn* [1951] 2 KB 476, [1951] 2 All ER 85, CA. Examples of the implied terms referred to include:

(1)   giving possession of the site to the contractor (*Freeman & Son v Hensler* (1900) 2 Hudson's BC (10th Edn) 319, (1900) 64 JP 260, CA; *Hounslow London Borough Council v Twickenham Garden Developments* [1971] Ch 233, [1970] 3 All ER 326);

(2)   appointing an architect to supervise the work (see *Hunt v Bishop* (1853) 8 Exch 675);

(3)   requiring the employer to ensure the certifier performs his duties properly (save where the contract contains an arbitration clause making such an implied term unnecessary), not to interfere with the proper performance of his duties and not act so as to disqualify the certifier (*Frederick Leyland & Co Ltd v Compania Panamena Europea Navegacion Ltda* (1943) 76 Ll L Rep 113, CA; *Perini Corpn v Commonwealth of Australia* (1969) 12 BLR 82; *Minster Trust Ltd v Traps Tractors Ltd* [1954] 3 All ER 136, [1954] 1 WLR 963; *Lubenham Fidelities and Investments Co Ltd v South Pembrokeshire DC* (1986) 33 BLR 39, CA);

(4)   implied obligation to supply instructions, nominations, information, plans and details as required at reasonable times (*Roberts v Bury Improvement Comrs* (1870) LR 5 CP 310; *McAlpine v Lanarkshire and Ayrshire Rly Co* (1889) 17 R 113, Ct of Sess; *Wells v Army and Navy Co-operative Society* (1902) 86 LT 764; *Neodox Ltd v Swinton and Pendlebury Borough Council* (1958) 5 BLR 34; *Holland & Hannen Cubitts (Northern) Ltd v Welsh Health Technical Services Organisation* (1981) 18 BLR 80);

(5)   not to interfere in the supply of goods necessary for the completion of the contract (*Acrow (Automation) Ltd v Rex Chainbelt Inc* [1971] 3 All ER 1175, [1971] 1 WLR 1676, CA);

(6)   not to interfere with or impede the completion of work by the contractor by the completion date set in a contract (*Percy Bilton Ltd v Greater London Council* [1982] 2 All ER 623, [1982] 1 WLR 794).

So far as the contractor is concerned he is obliged to execute the work with all proper skill and care or in a good and workmanlike manner: see *Duncan v Blundell* (1820) 3 Stark 6; *Charnock v Liverpool Corpn* [1968] 3 All ER 473, [1968] 1 WLR 1498, CA; *Young & Marten Ltd v McManus Childs Ltd* [1969] 1 AC 454, [1968] 2 All ER 1169, HL. If he is to supply materials then, unless there is an operative exclusion, he impliedly warrants that the materials are reasonably fit for their intended use and are of good quality: *Young & Marten Ltd v McManus Childs Ltd* above; *Gloucestershire County Council v Richardson (t/a WJ Richardson & Son)* [1969] 1 AC 480, [1968] 2 All ER 1181, HL; *Rotherham Metropolitan Borough Council v Frank Haslam Milan & Co Ltd* (1996) 78 BLR 1, (1996) 59 Con LR 33, CA.

4   A term may be implied from custom and usage. Such terms may be proved by parol evidence, but the custom must be reasonable and must not contradict the contract: see *Robinson v Thompson* (1890) 89 LT Jo 137, DC; *North v Bassett* [1892] 1 QB 333; *Knox and Robb v Scottish Garden Suburb Co Ltd* 1913 SC 872, Ct of Sess (authority of architect); *Produce Brokers Co Ltd v Olympia Oil and Cake Co Ltd* [1916] 1 AC 314, HL; and see CONTRACT vol 22 (2012) PARA 365; CUSTOM AND USAGE vol 32 (2012) PARA 50 et seq; DEEDS AND OTHER INSTRUMENTS vol 32 (2012) PARAS 381, 403. Whether there is such a custom is a question of fact and whether the custom is reasonable is a question of law for the court to decide: see *Gwyther v Gaze* (1875) 2 Hudson's BC (10th Edn) 196; *Ebdy v McGowan* (1870) 2 Hudson's BC (10th Edn) 189; *Thorn v London Corpn* (1876) 1 App Cas 120 at 132, HL, per Lord Chelmsford; *Croshaw*

v Pritchard and Renwick (1899) 16 TLR 45; and CUSTOM AND USAGE vol 32 (2012) PARA 1 et seq.

5   See CONTRACT vol 22 (2012) PARA 364 et seq.

234. Explanation of words and phrases.

Certain words and phrases occurring in building contracts have been construed judicially for the purposes of the particular contracts in which they occur. These are set out below, but it must be borne in mind that the meanings given to them are not necessarily applicable in all cases as the interpretation of each contract must depend upon the construction of its particular terms.

'Abut' and 'abutting' denote physical contact[1].

An act of God is such an operation of the forces of nature as reasonable foresight and ability could not foresee or reasonably provide against[2].

The degree of proximity denoted by the term 'adjacent' is a question of circumstances[3].

'Adjoining' does not necessarily imply absolute contiguity[4].

To 'afford access' means that there must be a physical means of access and at the relevant time the contractor must have the opportunity to enter by means of that access[5].

'Approval' means, it would seem, in general approval with full knowledge, or at all events approval with the opportunity of full knowledge[6].

An 'approved plan', referring to a plan approved by a local authority, means one lawfully approved, and not one which, though approved by the authority, is illegal[7].

In the context of a clause prohibiting assignment, 'any sum which is or may become due or payable' means a claim which can be expressed simply as a present or future claim for a fixed amount due under the contract and excludes claims for damages or for sums which fall to be assessed under or in accordance with the terms of the contract[8].

'Arise out of, under or in connection with the contract or the works' includes a claim for damages under the Misrepresentation Act 1967[9].

'As far as possible' means as far as possible consistently with reasonable trade requirements[10].

'Brick-built' means brick-built in the ordinary sense, and does not include a house built partly of brick and partly of timber, with some parts of the exterior composed of lath and plaster, and without party walls[11].

A building in its popular sense is a structure with walls and roof[12]. The following constructions have been judicially held to be included in the term 'building' as contained in various statutes, byelaws and deeds: an addition to an existing building[13]; a bay or bow window[14]; a church[15]; a place with four walls, a roof and a door used for keeping manure[16]; a trellis 12 feet high[17]; a high wall[18]; a structure of wood 16 feet by 13 feet not let into the ground, but merely laid upon timbers upon the surface, and intended to be permanently used as a shop[19]; a reservoir[20]; a viaduct[21]; a glasshouse[22]; a van fixed on foundations in the ground[23]; a tunnel[24]; a summerhouse[25]; a shed on a wharf[26]; an unfinished structure[27]; a roof inclosure[28]; a greenhouse[29]; a glass showcase in front of a photographer's house[30]; a temporary wooden platform[31]. The following have been held not to be included in the term 'building': a conservatory erected at the side of and leaning against a house[32]; a hoarding[33]; hustings for an election[34]; a timber stack[35]; a boundary wall[36]; a screen to prevent newly-erected houses acquiring a right to light[37]; the entire undertaking of a canal company[38]; a dwarf wall[39]; a separate set of chambers in one building[40]; a wall for a covered way[41]; a temporary brick kiln[42]; a temporary brick structure for storing tools[43]; a portable theatre constructed of wood[44].

Lands used for 'building purposes' within the meaning of the Lands Clauses Consolidation Act 1845[45], are lands actually laid out for that purpose[46].

'Bungalow' means primarily a one-storey building[47]; a building of which the walls, with the exception of any gables, are no higher than the ground floor, and of which the roof starts at a point substantially not higher than the top of the wall of the ground floor, regardless of the manner in which the space left in the roof is used[48].

'Bursting of tanks or pipes' in a JCT form means the rupture of the tank or pipe from within, typically caused by the exertion of forces, such as expansion or pressure, from within the vessel or pipe itself[49].

'Completion' means 'practical completion'[50]. 'Completion', as regards third parties, means completion in fact, and not completion to the satisfaction of the architect or otherwise ascertained in some manner prescribed by the contract[51].

'Consequential loss' means loss and damage which does not directly and naturally result from a defendant's breach of contract[52].

The term 'contingency sums' has no specific legal meaning[53].

'Continuity of work' involves the contractor having on site and using effectively such labour, materials and equipment as are needed in order to complete the works in a reasonable time[54].

'Day-work' is work which under the terms of the contract is to be paid for by time and materials, and not by measurement.

'Direct loss and/or expense' in JCT forms means that which arises naturally and in the ordinary course of things[55].

As respects a dwelling house[56], the term 'dwelling' implies a building used or capable of being used as a residence by one or more families, and provided with all necessary parts and appliances, such as floors, windows, staircases[57].

Where a house is pulled down leaving a wall of an adjoining house thereby exposed, the exposed wall forms an 'external part' of the house which is left standing[58].

'Flood' in a JCT form means an invasion of property by a large volume of water caused by a rapid accumulation or sudden release of water from an external source, usually, but not necessarily, confined to the result of a natural phenomenon such as a storm, tempest or downpour[59].

The meaning of the term 'front main wall' depends on all the circumstances of the case; the building must be looked at as a whole, and no particular portion must be selected to determine it[60].

The term 'house' is similar in meaning to the term 'dwelling house'[61]. In the interpretation of various instruments and statutes the term 'house' has been held to include the following[62]: a collection of buildings used for one purpose[63]; a building containing several residential flats[64]; each of two tenements, the one on the ground floor and the other on the first floor of the same building, there being no intercommunication between them, and each having a separate front door[65]; a mews building with the ground floors occupied by garages and the upper floors used as dwelling places[66]; a shop with living rooms over it[67]; a tenement[68]; an aeroplane hangar[69]; a chapel with vestry and rooms for caretaker attached[70]; everything that would pass under the grant or devise of house[71]; a building belonging to trustees of a religious association and used for purposes of religious service in the daytime, and at night as a shelter for homeless and destitute poor[72].

On the other hand, a building intended for a dwelling house, but never completed[73] and used as a store for straw and agricultural implements, is not a house[74].

'In due time' in a JCT form means 'in a reasonable time' and not 'in time to avoid delay'[75].

'Maintain' has a double meaning, namely to maintain in exactly the same state as it was found, or by making improvements without any alteration of purpose[76].

'Minerals' comprise all substances lying in the strata of the land which are commonly worked for profit and have a value independent of the surface[77], unless there is something in the context or in the nature of the transaction which gives rise to a more limited interpretation[78], and the words must be construed in the vernacular of the mining world, commercial world and landowners at the time of the execution of the instrument[79]. In the interpretation of various instruments and statutes the term 'minerals' has been held to include the following: stones dug from quarries[80]; all fossil bodies[81]; granite[82]; brine[83]; gravel[84]; freestone[85].

'Necessary' includes what is proper[86].

'Or other approved' does not give a contractor a right to have a reasonable alteration accepted[87].

The term 'plastering' does not include 'gauging', that is mixing plaster of Paris[88].

'Possession of like site' means in a JCT form possession of the whole site[89].

'Practical completion' in JCT forms means completion of all the work that has to be constructed other than items de minimis and latent defects[90].

'Premises', although applied to buildings, in legal language means the subject or thing previously expressed[91].

The term 'prime cost sum' or 'p c' is used in building and engineering contracts to indicate that a sum has been provided in the contract to enable the contractor to cover work or services to be provided by a nominated sub-contractor[92] or goods to be obtained from a nominated supplier[93]. The sum provided is only an estimate of the actual cost of the work, the true value of which will be calculated by the architect and paid by the employer to the contractor. The contractor can only deduct and keep for himself the value of a sub-contractor's or supplier's discount if this is expressly provided for in the main contract, whether the deduction is to be made as a trade discount or as a discount for payment in cash[94].

'Probationary drawings' means drawings to be approved by or on behalf of the employer[95].

A 'provisional sum' will be inserted in a bill of quantities to cover certain items of work in building or engineering contracts which cannot be accurately defined, detailed or valued at the time when the tendering documents are issued by the employer. In such cases the contractor will be paid the true value of the item after it has been calculated by the architect.

'Rate of wages' in a rise and fall clause includes holiday money credited to the employee weekly[96].

'Rebuild' means to rebuild the whole of a house or building, and not merely partially to replace old work by new[97].

In the phrase 'regularly and diligently', the word 'regularly' imports a requirement to 'attend for work on a regular daily basis with sufficient in the way of men, materials and plant to have the physical capacity to progress the works substantially in accordance with the contractual obligations. What in particular the word 'diligently' contributes to the concept is the need to apply that physical capacity industriously and efficiently towards that same end. Taken together the obligation upon the contractor is essentially to proceed continuously, industriously and efficiently with appropriate physical resources so as to progress the works steadily towards completion substantially in accordance with the contractual requirements as to time, sequence and quality of work'[98].

The term 'repair' may mean either patching or renewing, according to circumstances[99]. Under the Landlord and Tenant Act 1954, 'repairs' includes any work of maintenance, decoration or restoration and references to repairing, to keeping or yielding up in repair and to 'state of repair' must be construed accordingly[100].

The expression 'several works' means 'the whole works,' and, for the purpose of calculating the period of maintenance, not each separate section of them[101].

A 'specification' is a detailed description of building, engineering, and other works executed or proposed to be executed[102].

A 'structure' includes anything to which the term 'built' can applied[103].

Parol evidence may be admitted to show that by the usage of the building trade 'weekly accounts' means accounts of day-work only, and does not extend to extra work which is capable of being measured[104].

'Works for the erection of a building' includes demolition and clearance work as preparation for erecting a building[105].

1   See *Roberts v Karr* (1809) 1 Taunt 495; *R v Strand Board of Works* (1863) 4 B & S 526; *Lightbound v Higher Bebington Local Board* (1885) 16 QBD 577, CA; *Barnett v Covell* (1903) 90 LT 29; *R (on prosecution of Lewisham Borough Council) v South Eastern Rly Co* (1910) 74 JP 137, CA.

2   *Baldwin's Ltd v Halifax Corpn* (1916) 85 LJKB 1769 at 1774 per Atkin J.

3   *Wellington Corpn v Lower Hutt Corpn* [1904] AC 773, PC; *Re Ecclesiastical Comrs for England's Conveyance* [1936] Ch 430 at 440–441 per Luxmoore J.

4   A piece of land separated from a churchyard by a public highway 20 feet broad is adjoining to an existing churchyard within the meaning of the Consecration of Churchyards Act 1867 s 1: *Re Baroness Bateman and Parker's Contract* [1899] 1 Ch 599. See also *Harrison v Good* (1871) LR 11 Eq 338; *Lightbound v Higher Bebington Local Board* (1885) 16 QBD 577, CA; *Haynes v King* [1893] 3 Ch 439; *Vale & Sons v Moorgate Street and Broad Street Buildings Ltd and Albert Baker & Co Ltd* (1899) 80 LT 487; *Ind Coope & Co Ltd v Hamblin* (1900) 84 LT 168, CA; *Cave v Horsell* [1912] 3 KB 533, CA; *Derby Motor Cab Co v Crompton and Evans Union Bank* (1913) 29 TLR 673; *Foster v Lyons & Co* [1927] 1 Ch 219; *Cobstone Investments Ltd v Maxim* [1985] QB 140 at 151, [1984] 2 All ER 635 at 642–643, CA, per Wood J. In *R v Hodges* (1829) Mood & M 341 and *White v Harrow* (1902) 86 LT 4, 50 WR 259, CA, the word was held to connote physical contact. Cf *Southwark Revenue Officer v R Hoe & Co Ltd* (1930) 143 LT 544. As to 'adjoining owners' and 'adjoining occupiers' see also the London Building Act 1930 s 5. As to the London Building Acts see BUILDING vol 6 (2018) PARA 1 et seq.

5   *LRE Engineering Services Ltd v Otto Simon Carves Ltd* (1981) 24 BLR 127.

6   See *Davis v Leicester Corpn* [1894] 2 Ch 208. As to the meaning of 'or other approval' see *Leedsford Ltd v Bradford City Council* (1956) 24 BLR 45, CA. As to architect's or employer's approval of works see PARA 290 et seq.

7   *Yabbicom v King* [1899] 1 QB 444, DC; *Re McIntosh and Pontypridd Improvements Co, Re Pontypridd (Mill Street and Rhondda Road) Improvements Act 1890* (1891) 61 LJQB 164, DC. As to approval unreasonably withheld see *Railways Comr v Avrom Investments Pty Ltd* [1959] 2 All ER 63, [1959] 1 WLR 389, PC. See also PARAS 224 et seq, 228.

8   *Flood v Shand Construction Ltd* (1996) 81 BLR 31, (1996) 54 Con LR 125, CA.

9   *Strachan & Henshaw Ltd v Stein Industries (UK) Ltd* (1997) 87 BLR 52, CA. As to damages under the Misrepresentation Act 1967 see DAMAGES vol 29 (2014) PARA 546 et seq; MISREPRESENTATION vol 76 (2013) PARAS 800, 810.

10   Where furnaces were to be constructed so as to consume 'as far as possible' the smoke arising from them, it was held that 'as far as possible' meant 'as far as possible consistently with carrying on the trade in an ordinary manner and with a careful use and management of a properly constructed furnace': *Cooper v Woolley* (1867) LR 2 Exch 88 at 91 per Kelly CB.

11   *Powell v Doubble* (1832) cited in Sugden's Vendors and Purchasers (14th Edn) 29.

12 'One may say of this or that structure: 'this or that is not a building'; but no general definition can be given, and our lexicographers do not attempt it. Without, therefore, presuming to do what others have failed to do, I may venture to suggest, that, by 'a building' is usually understood a structure of considerable size, and intended to be permanent, or at least to endure for a considerable time': *Stevens v Gourley* (1859) 7 CBNS 99 at 112 per Byles J. See also *Leicester Corpn v Brown* (1892) 62 LJMC 22, DC.

13 *R v Gregory* (1833) 5 B & Ad 555 at 563 per Parke J.

14 *Western v MacDermott* (1866) 2 Ch App 72; *Lord Manners v Johnson* (1875) 1 ChD 673.

15 *Folkestone Corpn v Woodward* (1872) LR 15 Eq 159; *R v Hickman* (1784) 1 Leach 318.

16 *Morish (or Norrish) v Harris* (1865) LR 1 CP 155.

17 *Wood v Cooper* [1894] 3 Ch 671.

18 *Child v Douglas* (1854) 5 De GM & G 739; *Morish (or Norrish) v Harris* (1865) LR 1 CP 155; *Bowes v Law* (1870) LR 9 Eq 636.

19 *Stevens v Gourley* (1859) 7 CBNS 99.

20 *Moran & Son Ltd v Marsland* [1909] 1 KB 744, DC; and cf *Carlisle RDC v Carlisle Corpn* [1909] 1 KB 471, CA.

21 *Lloyd v London, Chatham and Dover Rly Co* (1865) 2 De GJ & Sm 568.

22 *Smith v Richmond* [1899] AC 448, HL.

23 *James v Tudor* (1912) 77 JP 130.

24 *Schweder v Worthing Gas Light and Coke Co* [1912] 1 Ch 83.

25 *R v Norris* (1804) Russ & Ry 69.

26 *R v Rice* (1859) Bell CC 87.

27 *R v Worrall* (1836) 7 C & P 516; *R v Manning and Rogers* (1871) LR 1 CCR 338.

28 *Clark v St Pancras Vestry* (1869) 34 JP 181.

29 *Clifford v Holt* [1899] 1 Ch 698; but see *Haigh v Waterman* (1867) 16 LT 375.

30 *Leicester Corpn v Brown* (1892) 62 LJMC 22.

31 *Aylward v Matthews* [1905] 1 KB 343, CA.

32 *Hibbert v Acton Local Board* (1889) 5 TLR 274, CA.

33 *Slaughter v Sunderland Corpn* (1891) 60 LJMC 91; *Foster v Fraser* [1893] 3 Ch 158. A hoarding, however, has been held to be 'a building or erection': *Pocock v Gilham* (1883) Cab & El 104; and cf *Nussey v Provincial Bill Posting Co and Eddison* [1909] 1 Ch 734, CA, and *Stevens v Willing & Co Ltd* [1929] WN 53 (where for the purpose of a restrictive covenant which used the word 'building' in a wide sense, a permanent advertisement hoarding was held to be a building).

34 *Allen v Ayre* (1823) 1 LJOSKB 204.

35 *Harris v De Pinna* (1886) 33 ChD 238, CA.

36 *Ellis v Plumstead Board of Works* (1893) 68 LT 291; *Urban Housing Co Ltd v Oxford City Council* [1940] Ch 70, [1939] 4 All ER 211, CA.

37 *Paddington Corpn v A-G* [1906] AC 1, HL.

38 *Regent's Canal and Dock Co v LCC* [1912] 1 Ch 583.

39 *Lavy v LCC* [1895] 2 QB 577, CA.

40 *Moir v Williams* [1892] 1 QB 264, CA.

41 *St Botolph, Aldersgate Without (Vicar) v St Botolph, Aldersgate Without (Parishioners)* [1900] P 69.

42 *Fielding v Rhyl Improvement Comrs* (1878) 3 CPD 272.

43 *Fielding v Rhyl Improvement Comrs* (1878) 3 CPD 272; *Gardiner v Walsh* [1936] 3 All ER 870.

44 *Newell v Ormskirk UDC* (1907) 71 JP 119.

45 See the Lands Clauses Consolidation Act 1845 s 128; and COMPULSORY ACQUISITION OF LAND vol 18 (2009) PARA 904.

46 *Coventry v London, Brighton and South Coast Rly Co* (1867) LR 5 Eq 104 at 109 per Lord Romilly MR; and see *Charlton v Gibson* (1844) 1 Car & Kir 541; *London and South Western Rly Co v Blackmore* (1870) LR 4 HL 610. In the Law of Property Act 1925 s 205(1)(iii), and the Settled Land Act 1925 s 117(1)(i), the term 'building purposes' includes the erecting and improving of, and the adding to, and the repairing of buildings.

47 *Clothier v Snell* (1966) 198 Estates Gazette 27.

48 *Ward v Paterson* [1929] 2 Ch 396.

49 *Computer & Systems Engineering plc v John Lelliott (Ilford) Ltd* (1990) 54 BLR 1 at 10, CA, per Beldam LJ. As to JCT standard forms of contract see PARA 202.

50 *Emson Eastern Ltd v EME Developments Ltd* (1991) (1991) 26 ConLR 57, 55 BLR 114; although there only in the context of a special clause of the JCT form (sed quaere in this instance) it would normally be so construed. As to practical completion see the text and note 90.

51 *Lewis v Hoare* (1881) 44 LT 66, CA.

52 *British Sugar plc v NEI Power Projects Ltd* (1997) 87 BLR 42, CA. See also *Millar's Machinery Co Ltd v David Way & Son* (1935) 40 Com Cas 204, CA; *Wraight Ltd v PH & T (Holdings) Ltd* (1968) 13 BLR 26; *Croudace Construction Ltd v Cawoods Concrete Products Ltd* [1978] 2 Lloyd's Rep 55, 8 BLR 20, CA; *Caledonia North Sea Ltd v British Telecommunications plc* [2002] UKHL 4, [2002] 1 All ER (Comm) 321, [2002] 1 Lloyd's Rep 553.

53 *Mander Raikes and Marshall v Severn Trent Water Authority* (1980) 16 BLR 34 at 45 per Parker J, who there describes the various ways in which that phrase and similar phrases may be used.

54 *Franks & Collingwood (a firm) v Gates* (1983) 1 Con LR 21 at 25 per Judge Newey QC.

55 *FG Minter Ltd v Welsh Health Technical Services Organisation* (1980) 13 BLR 1, CA; and see *Rees & Kirby Ltd v Swansea City Council* (1985) 30 BLR 1, (1985) 5 Con LR 34, CA. The duty to 'ascertain' loss and/or expense under the JCT standard form precludes the making of general assessments and means 'to find out for certain': *Alfred McAlpine Homes North Ltd v Property and Land Contractors Ltd* (1995) 76 BLR 59. As to JCT standard forms of contract see PARA 202.

56 See also the definition of 'house' in the text to notes 61–74.

57 *Williams v Fitzmaurice* (1858) 3 H & N 844. A shed may be part of a dwelling house for some purposes: see *Ashworth v Heyworth* (1869) LR 4 QB 316; *McHole v Davies* (1875) 1 QBD 59 at 61 per Cockburn CJ. A building physically capable of being used as a human habitation but prevented either by common law or statute from being put to such use cannot be termed a house: *Wright v Ingle* (1885) 16 QBD 379, CA. In the London Building Act 1930 s 5, 'dwelling house' is defined as 'a building used or constructed or adapted to be used wholly or principally for human habitation'. As to the London Building Acts see BUILDING vol 6 (2018) PARA 1.

58 *Green v Eales* (1841) 2 QB 225. As to party walls see BOUNDARIES vol 4 (2011) PARA 364 et seq.

59 *Computer & Systems Engineering plc v John Lelliott (Ilford) Ltd* (1990) 54 BLR 1 at 10, CA, per Beldam LJ.

60 *A-G v Edwards* [1891] 1 Ch 194; *Ravensthorpe Local Board v Hinchliffe* (1889) 24 QBD 168, DC; and *Leyton Local Board v Causton* (1893) 9 TLR 180, all decided under the Public Health (Buildings in Streets) Act 1888 s 3 (repealed).

61 A permanent building in which the tenant or the owner and his family dwell or live: *Chapman v Royal Bank of Scotland* (1881) 7 QBD 136 at 140 per Huddleston B.

62 See further 2 Stroud's Judicial Dictionary (6th Edn) 1172–1173.

63 *Richards v Swansea Improvement and Tramways Co* (1878) 9 ChD 425, CA (under the Lands Clauses Consolidation Act 1845 s 92). See COMPULSORY ACQUISITION OF LAND vol 18 (2009) PARA 625 et seq.

64 *Kimber v Admans* [1900] 1 Ch 412, CA, under a covenant not to erect more than a certain number of houses; but see *Rogers v Hosegood* [1900] 2 Ch 388, CA.

65 *Ilford Park Estates Ltd v Jacobs* [1903] 2 Ch 522, under a covenant not to erect more than one house on a site.

66 *Re Butler, Camberwell (Wingfield Mews) No 2 Clearance Order 1936* [1939] 1 KB 570, [1939] 1 All ER 590, CA, decided under the Housing Act 1936 s 25 (repealed; see now the Housing Act 1985 s 289). See further HOUSING vol 56 (2017) PARA 631 et seq.

67 *Re Bainbridge, South Shields (D'Arcy Street) Compulsory Purchase Order 1937* [1939] 1 KB 500, [1939] 1 All ER 419.

68 *Quiltotex Co Ltd v Minister of Housing and Local Government* [1966] 1 QB 704, [1965] 2 All ER 913.

69 *B Aerodrome Ltd v Dell* [1917] 2 KB 380, DC.

70 *Caiger v St Mary, Islington, Vestry* (1881) 50 LJMC 59; and see *Wright v Ingle* (1885) 16 QBD 379, CA.

71 *King v Wycombe Rly Co* (1860) 28 Beav 104; *Governors of St Thomas' Hospital v Charing Cross Rly Co* (1861) 1 John & H 400; *Hewson v South Western Rly Co* (1860) 2 LT 369; *Fergusson v London, Brighton and South Coast Rly Co* (1863) 3 De GJ & Sm 653; *Pulling v London, Chatham and Dover Rly Co* (1864) 3 De GJ & Sm 661; *Steele v Midland Rly Co* (1866) 1 Ch App 275; *Low v Staines Reservoirs Joint Committee* (1900) 64 JP 212, CA; all cases decided under the Lands Clauses Consolidation Act 1845 s 92. See COMPULSORY ACQUISITION OF LAND vol 18 (2009) PARA 625 et seq.

72 *R v Mead, ex p Gates* (1895) 64 LJMC 169, DC; and cf *R v Slade* (1896) 65 LJMC 108, DC.

73 *HE Green & Sons v Minister of Health* [1946] KB 608 at 612 per Henn-Collins J.

74 *Elsmore v St Briavells Inhabitants* (1828) 8 B & C 461, under the repealed statute 9 Geo 1 c 22 (1722) s 7. See *R v Edgell and Smith* (1867) 32 JP 168; *R v Manning* (1871) LR 1 CCR 338.

75 *Percy Bilton Ltd v Greater London Council* [1982] 2 All ER 623, [1982] 1 WLR 794, 20 BLR 1, HL.

76 'It is very difficult to define what works of maintenance are. It is a very large term, and useful or reasonable ameliorations are not excluded by it ... You may maintain by keeping in the same state, or you may maintain by keeping in the same state and improving the state, always bearing in mind that it must be maintenance as distinguished from alteration of purpose': *Sevenoaks, Maidstone and Tunbridge Rly Co v London, Chatham and Dover Rly Co* (1879) 11 ChD 625 at 634–635 per Jessel MR; and cf *A-G v Great Northern Rly Co* [1916] 2 AC 356, HL. In covenants in leases, to 'maintain' means to keep in substantially the same condition as at the date of the demise: *Lister v Lane and Nesham* [1893] 2 QB 212, CA.

77 *Midland Rly Co v Checkley* (1867) LR 4 Eq 19 at 25 per Lord Romilly MR; *Midland Rly Co v Haunchwood Brick and Tile Co* (1882) 20 ChD 552; *Tucker v Linger* (1883) 8 App Cas 508, HL; *Glasgow Corpn v Farie* (1888) 13 App Cas 657, HL; *Earl of Jersey v Neath Poor Law Union Guardians* (1889) 22 QBD 555, CA; *Ruabon Brick and Terra Cotta Co v Great Western Rly Co* [1893] 1 Ch 427, CA; *Midland Rly Co and Kettering, Thrapston, and Huntingdon Rly Co v Robinson* (1889) 15 App Cas 19, HL; *Re Todd, Birleston & Co and North Eastern Rly Co* [1903] 1 KB 603, CA; *North British Rly Co v Turners Ltd* (1904) 6 F 900, Ct of Sess. See also MINES, MINERALS AND QUARRIES vol 76 (2013) PARAS 10–11.

78 *Hext v Gill* (1872) 7 Ch App 699 at 719 per Sir WM James LJ.

79 *Waring v Foden* [1932] 1 Ch 276, CA.

80 *Micklethwait v Winter* (1851) 6 Exch 644.

81 *Wainman v Earl of Rosse* (1848) 2 Exch 800.

82 *A-G v Welsh Granite Co* (1887) 35 WR 617, CA.

83 *A-G v Salt Union Ltd* [1917] 2 KB 488.

84 *Scott v Midland Rly Co* [1901] 1 QB 317, DC. Cf *Waring v Foden* [1932] 1 Ch 276, CA (where gravel was not included).

85 *Bell v Wilson* (1866) 1 Ch App 303.

86 *Lytton v Great Northern Rly Co* (1856) 2 K & J 394; *Sanderson v Cockermouth and Workington Rly Co* (1849) 11 Beav 497 at 500 per Lord Langdale; affd (1850) 2 H & Tw 327, where an agreement for accommodation works provided for 'such roads, etc as may be necessary', and it was held that this meant such roads, etc as may be necessary and proper for convenient communication between the severed portions of the land.

87 *Leedsford Ltd v Bradford City Council* (1956) 24 BLR 45, CA.

88 *Wallis v Robinson* (1862) 3 F & F 307 at 309 per Martin B.

89 *Whittal Builders Ltd v Chester-le-Street District Council* (1987) 40 BLR 82. See also *Rapid Building Group Ltd v Ealing Family Housing Association Ltd* (1984) 29 BLR 5, CA.

90 *Westminster City Council v J Jarvis & Sons Ltd* [1970] 1 All ER 943 at 948–949, [1970] 1 WLR 637 at 646–647, HL, per Viscount Dilhorne; *HW Nevill (Sunblest) Ltd v William Press & Son Ltd* (1981) 20 BLR 78 at 87 per Judge Newey QC; *Emson Eastern Ltd (in receivership) v EME Developments Ltd* (1991) 55 BLR 114, (1991) 26 Con LR 57.

91 *Beacon Life and Fire Assurance Co v Gibb* (1862) 1 Moo PCCNS 73; *Metropolitan Water Board v Paine* [1907] 1 KB 285. See further 3 Words and Phrases (3rd Edn) 413 et seq.

92 *North West Metropolitan Regional Hospital Board v TA Bickerton & Son Ltd* [1970] 1 All ER 1039 at 1042, [1970] 1 WLR 607 at 610, HL, per Lord Reid. As to the nomination and renomination of sub-contractors see PARA 239.

93 As to the nomination and designation of suppliers see PARA 279.

94 As to 'cost plus' and 'prime cost' contracts see generally PARA 209.

95 *Moffatt v Dickson* (1853) 13 CB 543.

96 *LCC v Henry Boot & Sons Ltd* [1959] 3 All ER 636, [1959] 1 WLR 1069, HL.

97 *London City v Nash* (1747) 3 Atk 512; *A-G v Hatch* [1893] 3 Ch 36 at 45, CA, per Lindley LJ. See also the cases on the meaning of the words 'rebuilding of the principal mansion house' in the Settled Land Act 1925 s 83, Sch 3 Pt I para (xxv) (see SETTLEMENTS vol 91 (2012) PARA 717); *Re De Teissier's Trusts* [1893] 1 Ch 153 and *Re Dunham Massey Settled Estates* (1906) 22 TLR 595, DC (structural alterations); *Re Lord Gerard's Settled Estate* [1893] 3 Ch 252, CA (architectural improvements); *Re Walker's Settled Estate* [1894] 1 Ch 189 and *Re Wright's Settled Estates* (1900) 83 LT 159 (partial reconstruction); *Re Windham's Settled Estate* [1912] 2 Ch 75 (addition of new wings); *Re Legh's Settled Estate* [1902] 2 Ch 274 (dry rot). As to land improvement generally see AGRICULTURAL LAND AND ALLOTMENTS vol 1 (2017) PARA 597 et seq; SETTLEMENTS vol 91 (2012) PARAS 695, 710 et seq.

98 *West Faulkner Associates v Newham London Borough Council* (1994) 42 Con LR 144 at 154, (1994) 71 BLR 1 at 14, CA, per Brown LJ.

99 *Inglis v John Buttery & Co* (1878) 3 App Cas 552 at 373, HL, per Lord O'Hagan; *Greg v Planque* [1936] 1 KB 669 at 677, CA, per Slesser LJ. 'Repair' in the Landlord and Tenant Act 1927 s 18(1) includes 'reinstatement': *Cunliffe v Goodman* [1950] 1 KB 267, [1949] 2 All ER 946; revsd on another point [1950] 2 KB 237, [1950] 1 All ER 720, CA.

100 Landlord and Tenant Act 1954 s 69(1). As to covenants to repair see LANDLORD AND TENANT vol 62 (2016) PARA 329 et seq.

101 *Cunliffe v Hampton Wick Local Board* (1893) 9 TLR 378, DC.

102 See *National Coal Board v William Neill & Son (St Helens) Ltd* [1985] QB 300, [1984] 1 All ER 555 (work required to be completed 'in the manner set out in the specification, if any, and to the reasonable satisfaction of the engineer'; both stipulations had to be satisfied).

103 See *Lavy v LCC* [1895] 2 QB 577, CA; *Mills and Rockleys Ltd v Leicester Corpn* as reported in [1946] 1 All ER 424 at 427, DC, per Lord Goddard CJ; *Engineering Industry Training Board v Foster Wheeler John Brown Boilers Ltd* [1970] 2 All ER 616, [1970] 1 WLR 881, CA (boiler may be a structure) (applied in *Daniel Contractors Ltd v Construction Industry Training Board* [2007] EWHC 2848 (Admin), [2007] All ER (D) 52 (Dec)); *British Transport Docks' Board v Williams* [1970] 1 All ER 1135, [1970] 1 WLR 652, DC (crane not a structure).

104 *Myers v Sarl* (1860) 3 E & E 306.

105 *Marks and Spencer Ltd v LCC* [1952] Ch 549, [1952] 1 All ER 1150, CA; affd sub nom *LCC v Marks and Spencer Ltd* [1953] AC 535, [1953] 1 All ER 1095, HL.

(5) Discharge and Waiver

235. Rescission and modification.

The same principles apply to the rescission and modification of contracts for works of construction as apply to other contracts[1]. An agreement to rescind a contract or to modify its terms will normally be of no effect in the absence of fresh consideration[2]. If one party simply undertakes not to dishonour one of its existing contractual obligations that in itself will not be enforceable without good consideration, but a practical benefit to the other party flowing from that affirmation of existing obligations will be good consideration for these purposes[3]. In a contract for work and materials where the employer has reason to doubt whether the contractor will complete his work, if the employer agrees to pay him further amounts and the contractor simply affirms his existing obligations, the contractor gives good consideration as long as the employer thereby receives a benefit or avoids a disadvantage. It is not necessary that the contractor should suffer a detriment[4]. It is a question of construction whether a subsequent agreement is intended to modify or to replace the original agreement or to be incorporated in it[5], but clear evidence will be required before a court will find that a second agreement was intended to rescind the whole of the original contract[6].

1 See CONTRACT. For variations to the works, building contracts have special provisions and fresh consideration may not be necessary: see PARA 272.

2 As to consideration generally see PARA 222; and CONTRACT vol 22 (2012) PARA 308 et seq.

3 *Stilk v Myrick* (1809) 2 Camp 317, as affirmed and limited by *Williams v Roffey Bros and Nicholls (Contractors) Ltd* [1991] 1 QB 1, [1990] 1 All ER 512, 48 BLR 69, CA. See also CONTRACT vol 22 (2012) PARA 326. Where the whole contract is rescinded by mutual agreement and parts of either party's obligations have not been performed, consideration exists.

4 *Williams v Roffey Bros and Nicholls (Contractors) Ltd* [1991] 1 QB 1, [1990] 1 All ER 512, 48 BLR 69, CA.

5 *Macintosh v Midland Counties Rly Co* (1845) 14 M & W 548.

6 *Munro v Butt* (1858) 8 E & B 738, DC.

236. Estoppel and waiver.

The term 'waiver' is used in a number of situations[1]:

(1)   where there has been a new agreement or an accord and satisfaction which releases one party from its original obligations[2];

(2)   where there has been a repudiatory breach of contract and the innocent party affirms the contract[3];

(3)   where there are circumstances from which one party can be said to have 'accepted' defective or incomplete performance by the other party[4];

(4)   where one party promises to forego its strict contractual rights, producing a temporary suspension of those rights which may later result in an estoppel.

Where one party has promised to forego his strict contractual rights and the other party relies on that promise to his detriment, the promisor cannot go back to the original position without giving notice[5]. Where a course of dealing is inconsistent with the strict enforcement of the terms of the contract, such dealings may raise an implication that those terms inconsistent with the parties' behaviour have been waived by the party who would have benefited by them[6]. Where a course of dealing assumes one set of facts to be true, one or other party may be estopped from contradicting that assumption[7].

Where an employer fails to pay a contractor in full and offers part payment in full satisfaction, while refusing to offer full payment, the contractor does not waive his right to sue for the balance of the money by accepting that part payment. This will be so even though the transaction in which part payment was accepted has given the contractor the real benefit of relief from financial difficulties and is therefore supported by consideration[8].

Where one party has used economic duress to compel the other to waive its rights the agreement to waive may be voidable under general principles of contract[9].

1   As to waiver see CONTRACT vol 22 (2012) PARA 587 et seq.

2   See PARA 235. As to accord and satisfaction see CONTRACT vol 22 (2012) PARA 605 et seq.

3   As to the exercise of a power to determine see PARA 312 et seq. As to affirmation see CONTRACT vol 22 (2012) PARAS 573–574.

4   See PARA 237.

5   *Hughes v Metropolitan Rly Co* (1877) 2 App Cas 439, HL; *Central London Property Trust Ltd v High Trees House Ltd* [1947] KB 130, [1956] 1 All ER 256; *Tool Manufacturing Co Ltd v Tungsten Electric Co Ltd* [1955] 2 All ER 657, [1955] 1 WLR 761, HL; *Rees & Kirby Ltd v Swansea City Council* (1985) 30 BLR 1, (1985) 5 Con LR 34, CA. See also CONTRACT vol 22 (2012) PARA 592 et seq; ESTOPPEL vol 47 (2014) PARA 388.

6   *Munro v Butt* (1858) 8 E & B 738, DC; *Whitaker v Dunn* (1887) 3 TLR 602, DC; *Amalgamated Investment & Property Co Ltd (in liquidation) v Texas Commerce International Bank Ltd* [1982] QB 84 at 121–122, [1981] 3 All ER 577 at 584, CA, per Lord Denning MR, discussed in *Hiscox v Outhwaite* [1992] 1 AC 562 at 574, [1991] 3 All ER 124 at 134, CA, per Lord Donaldson, and at 583 and 142 per Leggatt LJ (affd [1992] 1 AC 562, [1991] 3 All ER 641, HL).

7   *Amalgamated Investment & Property Co Ltd (in liquidation) v Texas Commerce International Bank Ltd* [1982] QB 84, [1981] 3 All ER 577, CA.

8   *D & C Builders Ltd v Rees* [1966] 2 QB 617, [1965] 3 All ER 837, CA; *Foakes v Beer* (1884) 9 App Cas 605, HL; *Pinnel's Case* (1602) 5 Co Rep 117a.

9   See *B & S Contracts and Design Ltd v Victor Green Publications Ltd* [1984] ICR 419, CA. See also *North Ocean Shipping Co Ltd v Hyundai Construction Co Ltd, The Atlantic Baron* [1979] QB 705, [1978] 3 All ER 1170; *CTN Cash and Carry Ltd v Gallaher Ltd* [1994] 4 All ER 714, CA (as discussed in *Marsden v Barclays Bank plc* [2016] EWHC 1601 (QB), [2016] 2 Lloyd's Rep 420, [2016] All ER (D) 29 (Jul)); *Huyton SA v Peter Cramer GmbH & Co* [1999] 1 Lloyd's Rep 620; *Carillion Construction Ltd v Felix (UK) Ltd* (2000) 74 ConLR 144, [2000] Lexis Citation 4033, [2000] All ER (D) 1696; and *Cantor Index Ltd v Shortall* [2002] All ER (D) 161 (Nov). As to economic duress see CONTRACT vol 22 (2012) PARA 293.

237.   Acceptance of defective or incomplete performance by contractor or employer.

The employer waives defective work, and the contractor waives late or incomplete payment, where the ingredients of an estoppel, accord and satisfaction, or new agreement are present, and the party in breach of its original obligations can rely on the principles previously mentioned[1].

Generally neither the employer nor his architect owes a duty to the contractor to condemn defective work promptly[2] and acceptance will not be implied from the fact that the employer had knowledge of the defects at the time the work was done[3]. The employer does not accept defective work merely by moving into occupation and making use of the building or other structure constructed under the contract[4]. Furthermore, the fact that the employer has made interim payments[5] or paid the contractor in full does not mean that he has accepted defective work[6]. In all these circumstances, an employer has been able to maintain a claim in respect of the defective work[7].

On the other hand, where approval of some third party is deemed conclusive under the terms of the contract, and his approval has been given, the employer has no right of action for defects in the work approved[8].

1 See PARAS 235–236; and CONTRACT vol 22 (2012) PARA 587 et seq.
2 *East Ham Corpn v Bernard Sunley & Sons Ltd* [1966] AC 406, [1965] 3 All ER 619, HL; *AMF International Ltd v Magnet Bowling Ltd* [1968] 2 All ER 789 at 809, [1968] 1 WLR 1028 at 1053 per Mocatta J.
3 *Whitaker v Dunn* (1887) 3 TLR 602, DC, per Lord Coleridge CJ.
4 *Whitaker v Dunn* (1887) 3 TLR 602, DC; *Sumpter v Hedges* [1898] 1 QB 673 at 674–675, CA, per Smith LJ; *Forman & Co Pty Ltd v The Liddlesdale* [1900] AC 190 at 204, PC; *Munro v Butt* (1858) 8 E & B 738 at 752 per Lord Campbell CJ.
5 *Cooper v Uttoxeter Burial Board* (1864) 11 LT 565.
6 *Rigge v Burbidge* (1846) 15 LJEx 309; *Davis v Hedges* (1871) LR 6 QB 687 at 690 per Hannen J.
7 See eg *Multiplex Constructions (UK) Ltd v Cleveland Bridge UK Ltd* [2006] EWHC 1341 (TCC), 107 Con LR 1, [2006] All ER (D) 167 (Jun) (claimant entitled to abatement in respect of partially completed steelwork of a national stadium that was under construction; the difference in value between the steelwork in its actual condition and the steelwork as it ought to be was the cost of remedial works).
8 *Goodyear v Weymouth and Melcombe Regis Corpn* (1865) 35 LJCP 12; *Laidlaw v Hastings Pier Co* (1874) 2 Hudson's BC (10th Edn) 428, 554, 636, 642; *Crown Estate Comrs v John Mowlem & Co Ltd* (1994) 70 BLR 1, (1994) 40 Con LR 36, CA; *Matthew Hall Ortech Ltd v Tarmac Roadstone Ltd* (1997) 87 BLR 96.

(6) Sub-contracting and Vicarious Performance

(i) Sub-contracting

238.   Types of sub-contracting.

Sub-contracting by main contractors in building and engineering contracts takes four principal forms:

(1)   conventional sub-contracting, known as domestic sub-contracting, in which the employer has no relationship with the sub-contractor, and the obligations of the parties to the main contract are unaffected by the method by which the main contractor has chosen to perform his obligations;

(2)   nominated sub-contracting in which the employer instructs the main contractor to employ a particular sub-contractor[1];

(3)   named sub-contracting in which sub-contractors are named in the contract documents and whom the contractor is obliged to engage[2]; and

(4)   works or trade sub-contractors engaged by a management contractor[3].

1   Nominated sub-contracting is not commonly used nowadays: see PARA 239.

2   See the JCT intermediate form of building contract and the related standard form of named sub-contract. The arrangement is similar to nomination. Under the JCT intermediate form of building contract, nominated sub-contractors are replaced by named sub-contractors, being sub-contractors who are specifically identified in the contract documents and with whom the contractor is required to sub-contract upon a standard form of named contract. As to JCT standard forms of contract see PARA 202.

3   See the JCT standard form of management contract and the related standard form of works contract conditions.

239. Nomination and renomination.

Nomination provisions oblige the contractor to perform part of the works by sub-contracting to a particular named person[1]. The extent to which this alters all the contractor's other obligations in relation to that part of the work will always depend on the construction of the terms relating to nomination, of the contract as a whole and all relevant surrounding circumstances. If through insolvency or some other cause the nominated sub-contractor cannot perform, some nomination provisions oblige the contractor to seek a renomination by the employer rather than perform the work himself or immediately relet it[2]. Such inflexibility in practice causes delay and expense[3]. For these reasons, among others, nomination is not commonly used today.

1   These are to be distinguished from a requirement to obtain work, goods or services from a source specified in the contract or chosen by the contractor but approved by or on behalf of the employer: see *Leedsford Ltd v Bradford City Council* (1956) 24 BLR 45, CA.

2   *North West Metropolitan Regional Hospital Board v TA Bickerton & Son Ltd* [1970] 1 All ER 1039, [1970] 1 WLR 607, HL.

3   As to the risk of delay caused by the withdrawal of a nominated sub-contractor and the financial consequences of such renomination under a JCT contract see *Percy Bilton Ltd v Greater London Council* [1982] 2 All ER 623, [1982] 1 WLR 794, 20 BLR 1, HL; *Fairclough Building Ltd v Rhuddlan Borough Council* (1985) 30 BLR 26, (1985) 2 Const LJ 55, CA; *Fairweather & Co Ltd v Wandsworth London Borough Council* (1987) 39 BLR 106. As to JCT standard forms of contract see PARA 202.

240. Prohibitions on sub-contracting.

In general a contractor is entitled to arrange for vicarious performance of a building contract wherever it is a matter of indifference to an employer whether the work is done by the immediate party or by someone on his behalf. However, he has no such entitlement in the following circumstances: (1) where there is an express stipulation against sub-contracting; (2) where an intention of the parties not to permit vicarious performance can be implied from the circumstances[1], as where a contractor is employed because of a particular qualification in respect of skill[2], financial position or the possession of special plant adapted for the work[3]; (3) where the work is of a special nature[4], such as the construction of a lighthouse[5], and where the performance required from the contractor is personal[6], or possibly where the works require techniques special to the contractor.

1   *Robson v Drummond* (1831) 2 B & Ad 303; *Knight v Burgess* (1864) 33 LJCh 727. The contract and its circumstances must be considered as a whole: *Davies v Collins* [1945] 1 All ER 247, CA (where the construction of a clause limiting the contractor's liability was held to exclude the right to sub-contract the performance of the work). As to the assignment of rights and obligations see PARA 253 et seq.

2   *Southway Group Ltd v Wolff* (1991) 57 BLR 33, 28 Con LR 109, CA.

3 *Knight v Burgess* (1864) 33 LJCh 727; *British Waggon Co v Lea and Co* (1880) 5 QBD 149 at 153 per Cockburn CJ (as explained in *Nokes v Doncaster Amalgamated Collieries Ltd* [1940] AC 1014 at 1019, HL, per Viscount Simon LC and followed in *Whiteley Ltd v Hilt* [1918] 2 KB 808); *Cooper v Micklefield Coal and Lime Co Ltd* (1912) 107 LT 457; *Kollerich & Cie SA v State Trading Corpn of India* [1980] 2 Lloyd's Rep 32, CA.

4 *Johnson v Raylton, Dixon & Co* (1881) 7 QBD 438, CA.

5 *Anon* (prior to 1839), cited in *Wentworth v Cock* (1839) 10 Ad & El 42 at 45.

6 *Southway Group Ltd v Wolff* (1991) 57 BLR 33, 28 Con LR 109, CA.

241. Relationship between main contractor and sub-contractor.

By sub-letting part of the work, the main contractor impliedly contracts with the sub-contractor that he will not by any act or default of his own prevent the sub-contractor from performing his share of the work. Thus if, in consequence of the default of the main contractor, the employer forfeits the main contract and ousts the sub-contractor, the sub-contractor will, subject to the sub-contract terms, have a claim for damages against the main contractor[1]. The sub-contract may include a term under which the sub-contract will automatically terminate if the main contract is terminated, in which case the procedures for ascertaining what is due under the sub-contract upon termination will be followed.

The sub-contractor, on his part, is liable to the main contractor for defective work, as the relation between them is similar to that of employer and contractor[2]. Thus where the sub-contractor is in breach of either an express or an implied term of the sub-contract and this has caused injury to a third party, the sub-contractor will be liable in contract to the contractor even if both have been held liable to the third party in tort[3]. The sub-contractor's liability in contract may include damages and costs that the contractor has had to pay to the third party[4] including the employer[5].

1 See *McBrian v Shanley* (1874) 24 CP 28 (Can).

2 As to the effect of a stipulation limiting the responsibility of the sub-contractor to the replacement of faulty work supplied by him see *Prince of Wales Dry Dock Co (Swansea) Ltd v Fownes Forge and Engineering Co Ltd* (1904) 90 LT 527, CA (where it was held that a sub-contractor denying that his work was faulty was liable to the main contractor for the costs of a counterclaim successfully raised by the employer for defects in such work). A sub-contractor may also have an implied contractual duty to warn the main contractor when it knows, or ought to know, that the works are obviously dangerous: *Plant Construction plc v Clive Adams Associates* [2000] BLR 137, (1999) 69 ConLR 106, sub nom *Plant Construction Ltd v JMH Construction Services Ltd* (2000) 2 TCLR 513, CA (as considered in *Goldswain v Beltec Ltd* [2015] EWHC 556 (TCC), [2015] BLR 300, [2015] All ER (D) 101 (Mar). Cf *Aurum Investments Ltd v Avonforce Ltd (in liquidation) and Knapp Hicks & Partners and Advanced Underpinning Ltd (Pt 20 defendants)* (2001) 3 TCLR 461, [2000] All ER (D) 2148 (no implied contractual duty to warn of the possible way in which work might be carried out).

3 *Sims v Foster-Wheeler Ltd* [1966] 2 All ER 313, [1966] 1 WLR 769, 6 BLR 39, CA, following *Mowbray v Merryweather* [1895] 2 QB 640, CA (and applied in *Driver v William Willett (Contractors) Ltd* [1969]1 All ER 665). In *Sims v Foster-Wheeler Ltd*, the main contractors recovered from the sub-contractor an apportioned part of the damages awarded against them, under the Fatal Accidents Acts, to a widow whose husband was killed when staging on which he was working collapsed, the collapse being caused by the negligent work of a sub-sub-contractor. The main contractor had been found partly to blame for breach of statutory duty. The sub-contractor was found to be in breach of an implied warranty to the main contractor that the staging was fit for its purpose. See also *AMF International v Magnet Bowling Ltd* [1968] 2 All ER 789, [1968] 1 WLR 1028. The terms of a sub-contract can expressly exclude any liability implied by law as to quality or fitness for purpose of the works carried out by them: *Southern Water Authority v Carey* [1985] 2 All ER 1077, sub nom *Southern Water Authority v Lewis and Duvivier (No 2)* 27 BLR 116. See also *Genesis Housing Association Ltd v Liberty Syndicate Management Ltd* [2013] EWCA Civ 1173, [2013] BLR 565, [2013] All ER (D) 51 (Oct).

4 See eg *Caister Group Developments Ltd v Paul Rackham Construction Ltd* (1973) 226 Estates Gazette 809.

5 As to liability for damages generally see DAMAGES. See, in particular, the rule in *Hadley v*

Baxendale (1854) 9 Exch 341; and DAMAGES vol 29 (2014) PARA 532 et seq. The second limb of the rule will be relevant, when, as is often the case, the sub-contractor has specific knowledge of the losses the contractor will suffer upon breach by the sub-contractor.

242. Indemnity by sub-contractor.

In many sub-contracts the sub-contractor is required to indemnify the contractor against losses which the contractor may suffer and which arise out of the sub-contract work[1]. An indemnity clause in the sub-contract has to be construed separately from any indemnity provisions in the main contract. The sub-contractor can be required to indemnify the contractor for loss caused partly or wholly by the fault of the contractor, but only if: (1) this is expressly stated in the indemnity clause; or (2) the meaning of the words in the indemnity clause is wide enough to provide for loss caused by negligence and no loss arising without fault could reasonably be covered by the clause[2].

1   The main contractor's cause of action against a sub-contractor accrues on the date the loss was established: *County and District Properties Ltd v C Jenner & Son Ltd* [1976] 2 Lloyd's Rep 728, 3 BLR 38. See also *Laing Management Ltd v Aegon Insurance Co (UK) Ltd* (1997) 86 BLR 70 (unequivocal and clearly communicated affirmation of main contract required to prevent contractor recovering losses from sub-contractor).

2   *Smith v South Wales Switchgear Co Ltd* [1978] 1 All ER 18, [1978] 1 WLR 165, HL. As to contracts of indemnity see FINANCIAL INSTRUMENTS AND TRANSACTIONS vol 49 (2015) PARA 880 et seq. See also, in relation to building contracts, *Walters v Whessoe Ltd and Shell Refining Co Ltd* [1968] 2 All ER 816n, 6 BLR 23, CA; *AMF International Ltd v Magnet Bowling Ltd* [1968] 2 All ER 789, [1968] 1 WLR 1028; *Sonat Offshore SA v Amerada Hess Development Ltd* [1988] 1 Lloyd's Rep 145, 39 BLR 1, CA. See also *Greenwich Millennium Village Ltd v Essex Services Group plc* [2014] EWCA Civ 960, [2014] 1 WLR 3517, [2014] All ER (D) 73 (Aug).

243. How far terms of the main contract are binding on sub-contractor.

Where, in breach of contract, the sub-contractor delays the completion of the sub-contract works having known at the date of contracting that under the contract between the employer and the main contractor the main contractor is liable to liquidated damages or forfeiture for delay, the liability of the sub-contractor to the contractor for delay is increased[1]. The main contractor will then be entitled to recover from the sub-contractor the damages he has had to pay owing to the delay caused by the sub-contractor, or profit he would have made on a contract rescinded from that cause, together with the cost of work thrown away[2].

Such knowledge of the terms of the main contract is, however, not sufficient to prove that the sub-contractor agreed with the main contractor to be bound by the terms of the contract. Thus if the sub-contractor properly completes his part of the work, his right to payment will not depend upon the certificate of the architect, notwithstanding that it is a condition precedent to payment to the main contractor[3].

Where the sub-contractor expressly contracts to be bound by the terms of the main contract, provisions as to retention money will be applied to him proportionally in the ratio that his contract bears to the whole contract[4]. A sub-contractor who voluntarily and in the absence of any request from the contractor or employer undertakes extra work or uses better materials than those stipulated for has no claim against either for more than the contract price[5].

1   *Hadley v Baxendale* (1854) 9 Exch 341; *Victoria Laundry (Windsor) Ltd v Newman Industries Ltd* [1949] 2 KB 528, [1949] 1 All ER 997, CA (applied in *Parsons (H) (Livestock) Ltd v Uttley Ingham & Co Ltd* [1978] QB 791, [1978] 1 All ER 525, [1977] 3 WLR 990; *The Heron II, Koufos*

v Czarnikow Ltd [1969] 1 AC 350, [1967] 3 All ER 686, HL. Since a liability to pay liquidated damages is not a natural consequence of delay, the sub-contractor without knowledge will be liable for such damages as he should have contemplated as a serious possibility, or not unlikely, resulting from his breach. See further DAMAGES.

2   *Hydraulic Engineering Co Ltd v McHaffie* (1878) 4 QBD 670, CA. If the main contractor compromises the employer's claim arising from the sub-contractor's breach, the amount paid in settlement is admissible prima facie evidence of the amount of loss and damage caused by the sub-contractor, although liability would still need to be established: see eg *Biggin & Co Ltd v Permanite Ltd* [1951] 2 KB 314, [1951] 2 All ER 191, CA; *Siemens Building Technology FE Ltd v Supershield Ltd* [2009] EWHC 927 (TCC), [2009] 2 All ER (Comm) 900, 124 ConLR 158.

3   *Lewis v Hoare* (1881) 44 LT 66, HL. However, the sub-contract often provides that the payment of the sub-contractor for any work only becomes due when the contractor receives the certificate which values that work: see eg *Dunlop & Ranken Ltd v Hendall Steel Structures Ltd* [1957] 3 All ER 344, [1957] 1 WLR 1102. See also *Southern Water Authority v Carey* [1985] 2 All ER 1077, sub nom *Southern Water Authority v Lewis and Duvivier (No 2)* 27 BLR 116. See also PARA 244.

     Some sub-contracts provide that the sub-contractor's right to payment does not arise until the main contractor has been paid the sum due by the employer. However, where such a sub-contract is construction contract under the Housing Grants, Construction and Regeneration Act 1996 (see PARA 210), a provision making payment under a construction contract conditional on the payer receiving payment from a third person is ineffective, unless that third person, or any other person payment by whom is under the contract (directly or indirectly) a condition of payment by that third person, is insolvent (see s 113(1); and PARA 357).

4   *Geary, Walker & Co Ltd v Lawrence & Son* (1906) 2 Hudson's BC (10th Edn) 768, CA.
5   *Ashwell and Nesbit Ltd v Allen & Co* (1912) 2 Hudson's BC (10th Edn) 410.

244. Incorporation of terms of main contract by agreement.

An agreement by a sub-contractor to carry out work in accordance with the terms of the main contract does not necessarily incorporate all the relevant terms of the main contract into the sub-contract[1]. Thus when a sub-contract expressly incorporated some of the terms of the main contract but not the term empowering the employer to require the contractor to dismiss a sub-contractor, it was held that the term could not be implied in the sub-contract so as to put an end to the contract between the contractor and the sub-contractor on the exercise by the employer of his power, although the sub-contractor had knowledge of the terms of the main contract when he entered into the sub-contract[2].

Provisions in the main contract, which are not applicable as between the contractor and sub-contractor, will not be incorporated by implication in the sub-contract[3]. Although ultimately a question of the construction of the relevant contractual material, a clause in the principal contract referring disputes between the employer and contractor to arbitration will not necessarily be incorporated so as to refer disputes between the contractor and the sub-contractor to arbitration[4]. But where the terms of the main contract are expressly incorporated in the sub-contract, the provision as to arbitration will apply[5].

1   *Aughton Ltd (formerly Aughton Group Ltd) v MF Kent Services Ltd* (1991) 57 BLR 1, 31 ConLR 60, CA; *Lexair Ltd (in administrative receivership) v Edgar W Taylor Ltd* (1993) 65 BLR 87.
2   *Chandler Bros Ltd v Boswell* [1936] 3 All ER 179, CA. As to implied terms generally see CONTRACT vol 22 (2012) PARA 364 et seq.
3   *Brightside Kilpatrick Engineering Services v Mitchell Construction (1973) Ltd* [1975] 2 Lloyd's Rep 493, 1 BLR 64, CA.
4   *Goodwins, Jardine & Co v Brand* (1905) 7 F 995, Ct of Sess; *Aughton Ltd (formerly Aughton Group Ltd) v MF Kent Services Ltd* (1991) 57 BLR 1, CA; *Giffen (Electrical Contractors) Ltd v Drake & Scull Engineering Ltd* (1993) 37 Con LR 84, CA; *Lexair Ltd (in administrative receivership) v Edgar W Taylor Ltd* (1993) 65 BLR 87; *Extrudakerb (Maltby Engineering) Ltd v Whitemountain Quarries Ltd* [1996] NI 567. See also *Roche Products Ltd v Freeman Process Systems Ltd; Black Country Development Corporation v Kier Construction Ltd* (1996) 80 BLR 102; *Secretary of State for Foreign and Commonwealth Affairs v Percy Thomas Partnership (a*

firm) (1998) 65 Con LR 11. All of these cases concern the incorporation of arbitration clauses. It must be shown that the parties had a clear intention to incorporate the arbitration clause particularly when the clause is not specific to the subject contract. As to arbitration clauses see PARA 398 et seq.

5   *Modern Building Wales Ltd v Limmer & Trinidad Co Ltd* [1975] 2 All ER 549, [1975] 1 WLR 1281, CA.

245. Relationship between employer and sub-contractor: no privity of contract.

There is no privity of contract between the employer and the sub-contractor[1] or between the architect and the sub-contractor[2], although the employer or his architect may rarely nominate the sub-contractor under the provisions of the main contract. The employer may, however, secure a direct warranty from a sub-contractor[3]. When a nominated sub-contractor subsequently repudiates his contract with the main contractor, there is an implied term of the main contract that the employer or his architect will nominate a replacement[4]. If the sub-contractor is ordered directly by the employer to do work, the employer must pay him for it[5]. If the sub-contractor claims against the employer for work done as extra to the main contract, he must show that the work does not form part of the main contract, but is a distinct contract with the employer to do the work for which the claim is made[6]. However, it is possible for an employer and sub-contractor to make a collateral contract if the employer warrants that the sub-contractor will be paid (sometimes referred to as a collateral warranty which contains step-in rights in favour of the employer)[7], or the sub-contractor gives a warranty in consideration of the letting of the sub-contract to him[8]. Acceptance by the employer of work done by a sub-contractor will in no way bring about an implication that the employer has made any contract with the sub-contractor[9]. A sub-contractor has no lien upon the money payable under a building contract to the contractor by the employer for the price of goods supplied by the sub-contractor the property in which has passed to the contractor[10]. Conversely, the employer may acquire no property in materials supplied by a sub-contractor even if he has paid the main contractor for them if, by the terms of the sub-contract, property has not passed to the main contractor[11]. Where the sub-contractor is liable to compensate the contractor for inferior work or defects in the work supplied by him, and the contractor is under a similar liability to the employer, the employer can take an assignment of the contractor's right to compensation and proceed against the sub-contractor[12].

1   *Hampton v Glamorgan County Council* [1917] AC 13, HL; *Vigers Sons & Co Ltd v Swindell* [1939] 3 All ER 590; *Leslie & Co Ltd v Managers of Metropolitan Asylums District* (1901) 68 JP 86, CA. In certain circumstances, a person who is not a party to a contract may in his own right enforce a term of such a contract: see the Contracts (Rights of Third Parties) Act 1999; and CONTRACT. As to privity of contract see CONTRACT vol 22 (2012) PARA 327 et seq.

2   *Davies & Co (Shopfitters) Ltd v William Old Ltd* (1969) 67 LGR 395.

3   See eg *Greater Nottingham Co-operative Society Ltd v Cementation Piling and Foundations Ltd* [1989] QB 71, [1988] 2 All ER 971, 41 BLR 43, CA, where the effect of such a warranty was to restrict the sub-contractor's liability for negligence causing economic loss.

4   *North West Metropolitan Regional Hospital Board v TA Bickerton & Sons Ltd* [1970] 1 All ER 1039, [1970] 1 WLR 607, HL (if the contractor himself completes the sub-contractor's work he is entitled to remuneration on a quantum meruit and is not restricted to the prime cost sum in the bill of quantities).

5   *Wallis v Robinson* (1862) 3 F & F 307; and see *Bramah v Lord Abingdon* (1810) 15 East 66 cited in *Paterson v Gandesequi* (1812) 15 East 62 at 66 per Lord Ellenborough (as distinguished in *Mahoney v Kekule (or Rukull)* (1854) 23 LJCP 54.

6   *Eccles v Southern* (1861) 3 F & F 142. As to variations and extras see PARA 272.

7   By so doing an employer may enter a contract of guarantee or indemnity with the sub-contractor but note that in many warranties, the right to step-in must be exercised prior to any obligation to pay being crystallised and step-in is not generally mandatory (see *Wiltshier Construction (South) Limited v Parkers Developments Limited* [1996] Lexis Citation 2496, 13 Const LJ 129).

8   *Brown v Sheen and Richmond Car Sales Ltd* [1950] 1 All ER 1102; *Shanklin Pier Co v Detel Products Ltd* [1951] 2 KB 854, [1951] 2 All ER 471; *Wells (Merstham) Ltd v Buckland Sand and Silica Co Ltd* [1965] 2 QB 170, [1964] 1 All ER 41. As to collateral contracts see CONTRACT vol 22 (2012) PARA 332.

9   *Bramah v Lord Abingdon* (1810) 15 East 66 cited in *Paterson v Gandesequi* (1812) 15 East 62 at 66 per Lord Ellenborough. The sub-contractor needs to establish the nature of the transaction which led to the work being carried out.

10   *Pritchett and Gold and Electrical Power Storage Co v Currie* [1916] 2 Ch 515, CA (in which the earlier case of *Bellamy v Davey* [1891] 3 Ch 540 was doubted and distinguished). In the later case the lien was claimed upon money paid into court by the employer in an action brought by the sub-contractor for money due under the main contract. As to lien generally see LIEN. As to when property in goods sold passes to the purchaser see SALE OF GOODS AND SUPPLY OF SERVICES vol 91 (2012) PARA 138 et seq.

11   *Dawber Williamson Roofing Ltd v Humberside County Council* (1979) 14 BLR 70; cf *Archivent Sales and Developments Ltd v Strathclyde Regional Council* (1984) 27 BLR 98, 1985 SLT 154, Ct of Sess.

12   *Constant v Kincaid & Co* (1902) 4 F 901, Ct of Sess. As to obligations as to workmanship and materials see PARA 274.

246. Duty of care of sub-contractor.

Whether a sub-contractor owes a duty of care to an employer is determined by reference to the general law of negligence[1]. To establish a claim in negligence the employer would also have to establish the other essential ingredients of the tort[2]. Economic loss, absent a relevant contractual duty, is not recoverable in tort unless there exists a special relationship of proximity imposing on the tortfeasor a duty of care to safeguard the claimant from economic loss[3], save where it is consequential upon physical damage in respect of which a duty of care is owed[4].

The scope of any duty may be circumscribed by a contractual matrix which places certain risks on the employer, to the extent of exempting the sub-contractor from liability, even though there is no privity between the two[5].

The employer owes the sub-contractor the common duty of care[6] in any case where he remains an occupier[7].

1   See PARA 363; and NEGLIGENCE.

2   Ie: (1) that the sub-contractor had fallen below the required standard of care; (2) causation; and (3) foreseeability of the type of damage claimed: see further NEGLIGENCE. An employer would need to establish an assumption of responsibility by the sub-contractor and reliance by the employer: *Henderson v Merrett Syndicates Ltd* [1995] 2 AC 145, [1994] 3 All ER 506, HL (applied in *James-Bowen v Metropolitan Police Commissioner* [2016] EWCA Civ 1217, [2016] All ER (D) 10 (Dec));*White v Jones* [1995] 2 AC 207, [1995] 1 All ER 691, HL (applied in *Sebry v Companies House* [2015] EWHC 115 (QB), [2015] 4 All ER 681, [2016] 1 WLR 2499). Whether a duty of care will be imposed will depend upon proximity, foreseeability of damage and whether it is fair, just and reasonable to impose the duty contended for: see *Sutherland Shire Council v Heyman* (1985) 60 ALR 1, Aust HC; *Caparo Industries plc v Dickman* [1990] 2 AC 605, [1990] 1 All ER 568, HL; *Murphy v Brentwood District Council* [1991] 1 AC 398, [1990] 2 All ER 908, HL; *Marc Rich & Co AG v Bishop Rock Marine Co Ltd* [1996] AC 211, sub nom *Marc Rich & Co AG v Bishop Rock Marine Co Ltd, The Nicholas H* [1995] 3 All ER 307, HL; *R (on the application of A) v Secretary for the Home Department; R (on the application of Kanidagli) v Secretary of State for the Home Department* [2004] EWHC 1585 (Admin), [2004] NLJR 1141, [2004] All ER (D) 91 (Jul); and see NEGLIGENCE vol 78 (2018) PARA 4.

3   *Murphy v Brentwood District Council* [1991] 1 AC 398 at 475, [1990] 2 All ER 908 at 925, HL, per Lord Bridge of Harwich. 'There may, of course, be situations where, even in the absence of contract, there is a special relationship of proximity between builder and building owner which is

sufficiently akin to contract to introduce the element of reliance so that the scope of the duty of care owed by the builder to the owner is wide enough to embrace purely economic loss': *Murphy v Brentwood District Council* at 481 and 930 per Lord Bridge of Harwich. As to pure economic loss see NEGLIGENCE vol 78 (2018) PARA 12.

4   See *SCM (United Kingdom) Ltd v WJ Whittal & Son Ltd* [1971] 1 QB 337; [1970] 3 All ER 245, CA; *Spartan Steel and Alloys Ltd v Martin & Co (Contractors) Ltd* [1973] QB 27; [1972] 3 All ER 557, CA; *Londonwaste Ltd v Amec Civil Engineering Ltd* (1997) 83 BLR 136, (1997) 53 Con LR 66.

5   *Norwich City Council v Harvey* [1989] 1 All ER 1180, [1989] 1 WLR 828, CA (applied in *John F Hunt Demolition Ltd v ASME Engineering Ltd* [2007] EWHC 1507 (TCC), [2008] 1 All ER 180, [2008] 1 All ER (Comm) 473);*Greater Nottingham Co-operative Society Ltd v Cementation Piling and Foundations Ltd* [1989] QB 71, [1988] 2 All ER 971, 41 BLR 43, CA (sub-contractor's liability in negligence causing economic loss effectively excluded by the existence of a direct warranty between the sub-contractor and the employer); *Southern Water Authority v Carey* [1985] 2 All ER 1077, sub nom *Southern Water Authority v Lewis and Duvivier (No 2)* 27 BLR 116. See also *How Engineering Services Ltd v Southern Insulation (Medway) Ltd* [2010] EWHC 1878 (TCC), [2010] BLR 537, [2010] All ER (D) 256 (Jul) (a case where, on the facts, the sub-contractor owed the main contractor a duty of care in tort concurrent with its contractual duty to carry out the works with reasonable care and skill).

6   See the Occupiers' Liability Act 1957 s 2(1); and NEGLIGENCE vol 78 (2018) PARA 29 et seq. The 'common duty of care' is the duty of an occupier to take such care as is in all the circumstances reasonable to see that a visitor is reasonably safe in using the premises for the purposes for which he is invited by the occupier to be there: see s 2(2); and NEGLIGENCE vol 78 (2018) PARA 32. It is provided by s 2(4)(b) that if the damage is caused by a danger due to the faulty execution of any work of construction, maintenance or repair by an independent contractor employed by the occupier, the occupier is not to be treated without more as answerable for the danger if in all the circumstances he had acted reasonably in entrusting the work to an independent contractor and had taken such steps (if any) as he reasonably ought in order to satisfy himself that the contractor was competent and that the work had been properly done: see NEGLIGENCE vol 78 (2018) PARA 35. See *AMF International Ltd v Magnet Bowling Ltd* [1968] 2 All ER 789, [1968] 1 WLR 1028, where the employer was unable to avail himself of the Occupiers' Liability Act 1957 s 2(4) when the property of one direct contractor was damaged by the failure of another independent contractor to take proper precautions against flooding and this failure had not been detected by the employer's architect.

7   *Wheat v E Lacon & Co Ltd* [1966] AC 552, [1966] 1 All ER 582, HL. Cases where 'occupier' has been construed in relation to building works are *Savory v Holland, Hannen and Cubitts (Southern) Ltd* [1964] 3 All ER 18, [1964] 1 WLR 1158, CA (applied in *Makepeace v Evans Brothers (Reading)* [2001] ICR 241, [2000] BLR 737); *Fisher v CHT Ltd (No 2)* [1966] 2 QB 475, [1966] 1 All ER 88, CA; *Kearney v Eric Waller Ltd* [1967] 1 QB 29, [1965] 3 All ER 352; *AMF International Ltd v Magnet Bowling Ltd* [1968] 2 All ER 789, [1968] 1 WLR 1028; *Bunker v Charles Brand & Son Ltd* [1969] 2 QB 480, [1969] 2 All ER 59 (doubted and not followed in *Baron v B French Ltd* [1971] 3 All ER 1111). See further NEGLIGENCE vol 78 (2018) PARA 29 et seq.

247.   Limitations on employer's right to pay sub-contractor.

In general, the employer cannot discharge his liability to the contractor by paying the sub-contractor. In case of the bankruptcy of the contractor, the architect cannot deduct a payment made to a sub-contractor for work and materials supplied by him from the balance certified as due to the main contractor, but may be compelled to certify payment to the main contractor without such deduction[1]. A wide provision that in the event of the main contractor unduly delaying proper payment to the sub-contractors the employer may pay them himself, has been held to justify the employer in paying the sub-contractors when the contractor has unduly delayed proper payment to the sub-contractors by presenting his petition in bankruptcy. Such a provision is useful and justifiable in circumstances other than insolvency[2], but even a provision of such general effect may not discharge the employer's liability to the contractor's trustee in bankruptcy, since in the context of bankruptcy and insolvency the court will refuse to give effect to it[3].

A condition in a contract which enables a building owner to pay someone other than the contractor must be strictly construed[4]. If the contract authorises payment either to the contractor or alternatively directly to the sub-contractors appointed by the architect, the building owner may elect which right to exercise. If he elects to pay the contractor amounts including sums owing for work done by the sub-contractors, he may not in the case of future payments be permitted to pay the sub-contractors direct and deduct such payments from sums owing to the contractor if it turns out that the contractor has not paid over to the sub-contractors the amount owed to them[5]. This, however, will depend upon the construction of the contract terms[6].

1   *Re Holt, ex p Gray* (1888) 58 LJQB 5, DC.
2   See the JCT standard form of contract which permits direct payment subject to detailed conditions but expressly states that such a clause ceases to have effect upon the contractor's insolvency. As to JCT standard forms of contract see PARA 202.
3   *Re Wilkinson, ex p Fowler* [1905] 2 KB 713 and *Re Tout and Finch Ltd* [1954] 1 All ER 127, [1954] 1 WLR 178, support the efficacy of such clauses; however, in *British Eagle International Airlines Ltd v Compagnie Nationale Air France* [1975] 2 All ER 390, [1975] 1 WLR 758, HL, it was held that clauses which contracted out of the *pari passu* principle of the insolvency legislation were contrary to public policy and would be overridden by the general rules of the liquidation, even if the clauses were agreed for good business reasons and with no intention to circumvent the insolvency legislation. See also *Mayhew v King* [2010] EWHC 1121 (Ch), [2010] 2 BCLC 440; *Folgate London Market Ltd v Chaucer Insurance plc* [2011] EWCA Civ 328, [2012] 1 BCLC 550, [2011] All ER (D) 24 (Apr) applying *British Eagle International Airlines Ltd v Compagnie Nationale Air France* [1975] 2 All ER 390, [1975] 1 WLR 758, HL. See also *B Mullan & Sons (Contractors) Ltd v Ross* (1996) 86 BLR 1, (1996) 54 Con LR 163, NI CA (which distinguished *Re Wilkinson, ex p Fowler* and *Re Tout and Finch Ltd* above, and followed *British Eagle International Airlines Ltd v Compagnie Nationale Air France* above). See also *Re Right Time Construction Co Ltd* (1990) 52 BLR 117, HK CA.
4   *JA Milestone & Sons Ltd v Yates Castle Brewery Ltd* [1938] 2 All ER 439 at 443 per Singleton J.
5   *British Steamship Investment Trust Ltd v Foundation Co Ltd* (15 December 1930, unreported) per Maugham J, cited in *Milestone & Sons Ltd v Yates Castle Brewery Ltd* [1938] 2 All ER 439 at 442–443.
6   See *Hobbs v Turner* (1902) 18 TLR 235, CA, where under the main contract either the employer or the contractor could make payment to a sub-contractor and it was held that a sub-contractor could look to the employer for payment rather than to the contractor since his instructions had come from the architect and the architect had certified payment against the employer.

248.   When employer liable to sub-contractor.

There may be communications or dealings between the employer and the sub-contractor which amount to a contract, express or implied, on the part of the employer to pay the sub-contractor[1]. If there is a promise by the employer to pay or see that the sub-contractor is paid, the question arises whether the promise is collateral to the contract between the contractor and the sub-contractor, and given by way of guarantee, in which case it must be in writing[2], or whether it is a direct promise to pay, in which case an oral promise is sufficient[3].

If the employer promises to pay the sub-contractor 'out of the money' that he has to pay to the main contractor, that is a direct promise, and not a guarantee to be liable for the main contractor's debt[4].

Where it appears that the main contractor was acting as the agent of the employer in contracting with the sub-contractor, the employer will be liable to the latter. The burden of proof lies on the sub-contractor to show that the employer, and not the main contractor, was the real principal, and he may call evidence to show that the employer personally gave orders to do work and supply materials for the same building to third parties as corroboration of his evidence that the employer gave him personal orders to do the work[5]; but the employer can prove that on the accounts between the principal contractor and the sub-contractor nothing is due to the latter[6].

The allowance in a lump sum contract[7] of a provisional sum does not raise any presumption that the employer and not the contractor is responsible as principal for the payment of the person who supplies the goods to which the prime cost item refers[8]. Where it appears from the terms of a written contract that the main contractor or other alleged agent contracted personally, extrinsic evidence is not admissible to show that it was intended that he should not be liable[9].

1   *Smith v Rudhall* (1862) 3 F & F 143.
2   See PARA 231; and FINANCIAL INSTRUMENTS AND TRANSACTIONS vol 49 (2015) PARA 677 et
    seq.
3   See CONTRACT vol 22 (2012) PARA 220.
4   *Dixon v Hatfield* (1825) 2 Bing 439; *Andrews v Smith* (1835) 2 Cr M & R 627; *Stevenson's
    Trustee v Campbell & Sons* (1896) 23 R 711, Ct of Sess.
5   *Woodward v Buchanan* (1870) LR 5 QB 285; and see AGENCY vol 1 (2017) PARA 122 et seq.
6   *Gerish v Chartier* (1845) 1 CB 13.
7   As to lump sum contracts see PARA 209.
8   *Hampton v Glamorgan County Council* [1917] AC 13, HL, in which the contrary view expressed
    by Channell J in *Crittall Manufacturing Co v LCC and March* (1910) 75 JP 203, and followed in
    Young & Co Ltd v White (1911) 76 JP 14, was negatived with the case being considered in
    Macdonald v Costello [2011] EWCA Civ 930, [2012] QB 244, [2012] 1 All ER (Comm) 357, and
    being distinguished from *Hobbs v Turner* (1902) 18 TLR 235. As to the meanings of 'prime cost'
    and 'provisional sums' see PARA 234.
9   *Sika Contracts Ltd v BL Gill & Closeglen Properties Ltd* (1978) 9 BLR 11. As to the admissibility
    of extrinsic evidence as an aid to construction see PARA 232; and CONTRACT vol 22 (2012)
    PARAS 221, 288; DEEDS AND OTHER INSTRUMENTS vol 32 (2012) PARA 385 et seq.

249.   Relationship between sub-contractors.

There is no contractual relationship between two or more sub-contractors of the same main contractor, whether the sub-contractors are nominated or not[1]. However, two sub-contractors can be held jointly liable in tort for injuries suffered by a third party even if the third party is an employee of one of the sub-contractors[2]. Similarly a sub-contractor liable in respect of any damage suffered by another can claim contribution from another sub-contractor who is liable in respect of the same damage if both are or could be held to be tortfeasors, or if they are both liable in contract, or for breach of trust, or otherwise[3].

1   As to nominated sub-contracting see PARAS 238–239.
2   *McArdle v Andmac Roofing Co* [1967] 1 All ER 583, [1967] 1 WLR 356, CA.
3   See the Civil Liability (Contribution) Act 1978 ss 1, 6(1); and TORT vol 97 (2015) PARA 450.

250.   Effect of sub-contracting on main contractor's obligations to perform.

In general a main contractor who sublets part of the works with the tacit consent of the employer does not thereby alter his obligations to the employer. The contractor will be liable for defects in or delay in carrying out such work in the same way and to the same extent as if he had performed it himself[1] unless the terms of the main contract or the surrounding circumstances show otherwise.

However, where the employer has instructed the main contractor to perform by subletting part of his work to a particular sub-contractor, the main contractor's obligation to the employer in respect of defects or non performance may be simply to use his rights under the sub-contract to compel proper performance from the sub-contractor, or compensation for non performance. He may have no obligation to undertake the works himself or remedy defects in them[2]. Terms in the main contract giving the employer control over the nomination of sub-contractors and the terms of the sub-contract may exclude or reduce the contractor's obligations in respect of workmanship and materials[3].

1   *British Waggon Co and Parkgate Waggon Co v Lea Co* (1880) 5 QBD 149 (followed in *Whiteley Ltd v Hilt* [1918] 2 KB 808. See also *Nokes v Doncaster Amalgamated Collieries Ltd* [1940] AC 1014, [1940] 3 All ER 549, HL, where *British Waggon Co v Lea* was explained by reference to the distinction between vicarious performance and assignment.

2   *North West Metropolitan Regional Hospital Board v TA Bickerton & Son Ltd* [1970] 1 All ER 1039, [1970] 1 WLR 607, HL. Although the main contractor may be liable for the acts and omissions of a nominated sub-contractor he will not ordinarily be liable for the consequences of delayed nomination or renomination (as to which see PARA 239).

3   *Young and Marten Ltd v McManus Childs Ltd* [1969] 1 AC 454, [1968] 2 All ER 1169, HL; *Gloucestershire County Council v Richardson* [1969] 1 AC 480, [1968] 2 All ER 1181, HL; *Parsons (H) (Livestock) Ltd v Uttley Ingham & Co Ltd* [1978] QB 791, [1978] 1 All ER 525. Ultimately, it is a question of construction of the terms of each contract concerned whether and, if so, to what extent, the liability of the main contractor is affected by the nomination procedure.

251.   Labour only sub-contracting.

The common law distinguishes between the status of an employee employed under a 'contract of service', and the status of a self-employed person offering services to customers under a 'contract for services'. The contractual and other duties owed to the employee are more numerous and onerous. Statutory provisions relating to taxation, health and safety, and employment protection adopt the distinction and incorporate it[1]. The distinction is therefore fundamental to all rights and liabilities relating to labour, but it is complicated in the construction industry by the existence of sub-contractors whose only function is to provide labour.

No simple test exists to classify employment contracts. The nature of the relationship should be judged by weighing the terms of the contract which point one way or the other[2]. Considerations supported by authority are: whether the alleged employee is under the control of the employer when carrying out his duty[3], whether the individual is in business on his own[4], ownership of tools or plant and the risk of loss and gain[5]. The label put on the contract by the parties, and the intentions of the parties, should be considered but cannot be conclusive[6]. Whether or not a person is an employee or self-employed is a mixed question of law and fact, possibly involving consideration of each term of the contract, and the decision of a court at first instance will not be overturned unless there was no evidence for its conclusion[7].

The labour only sub-contractor has the same statutory and common law duties to his employees as any other employer. Therefore, for purposes other than taxation, once the proper employer has been identified the fact that he may be a labour only sub-contractor does not of itself alter the nature of his rights and obligations. However, an employer who employs small firms of sub-contractors for building work may assume a duty to provide proper supervision towards the sub-contractors' employees[8].

1   See EMPLOYMENT vol 39 (2014) PARA 1; HEALTH AND SAFETY AT WORK; INCOME TAXATION.

2   *Mersey Docks and Harbour Board v Coggins & Griffith (Liverpool) Ltd* [1947] AC 1, [1946] 1 All ER 345, HL. For the tests as to whether a person is a sub-contractor or employee see *Ferguson v John Dawson & Partners (Contractors) Ltd* [1976] 3 All ER 817, [1976] 1 WLR 1213, CA; *Calder v H Kitson Vickers & Sons (Engineers) Ltd* [1988] ICR 232, CA.

3   *Ready Mixed Concrete (South East) Ltd v Minister of Pensions and National Insurance* [1968] 2 QB 497, [1968] 1 All ER 433.

4   *Market Investigations Ltd v Minister of Social Security* [1969] 2 QB 173, [1968] 3 All ER 732 (as followed in *Lewis v Revenue and Customs Comrs* [2006] STC (SCD) 253; and applied in *Lee Ting Sang v Chung Chi-Keung* [1990] 2 AC 374, [1990] 2 WLR 1173).

5   *Mersey Docks and Harbour Board v Coggins & Griffith (Liverpool) Ltd* [1947] AC 1, [1946] 1
    All ER 345, HL.
6   *Massey v Crown Life Insurance Co* [1978] 2 All ER 576, [1978] 1 WLR 676, CA; *Warner
    Holidays Ltd v Secretary of State for Social Services* [1983] ICR 440.
7   *Global Plant Ltd v Secretary of State for Social Services* [1972] 1 QB 139, [1971] 3 All ER 385;
    O'Kelly v Trusthouse Forte plc [1984] QB 90, [1983] 3 All ER 456, CA. See also *Byrne Bros
    (Formwork) Ltd v Baird* [2002] ICR 667, [2002] IRLR 96, EAT; *Haggerty v St Ives Plymouth Ltd*
    [2008] All ER (D) 317 (May).
8   *McArdle v Andmac Roofing Co* [1967] 1 All ER 583, [1967] 1 WLR 356, CA.

252. Tax provisions applicable to contractors and sub-contractors.

Special tax provisions apply to sub-contractors in the construction industry[1],
and this regime is known as the Construction Industry Scheme.

Where a contractor makes a payment to a sub-contractor under a contract,
other than a contract of employment, relating to construction operations, the
contractor must deduct and pay a percentage of the payment on account of tax[2].
If, however, the Commissioners for Her Majesty's Revenue and Customs are
satisfied that the appropriate documentation has been provided, the
sub-contractor will be registered for gross payment[3].

1   See the Finance Act 2004 Pt 3 Ch 3 (ss 57–77); the Income Tax (Construction Industry Scheme)
    Regulations 2005, SI 2005/2045; and INCOME TAXATION vol 58 (2014) PARA 992 et seq.
2   See the Finance Act 2004 s 61; and INCOME TAXATION vol 58 (2014) PARA 998.
3   See the Finance Act 2004 ss 63–68; the Income Tax (Construction Industry Scheme) Regulations
    2005, SI 2005/2045, regs 25–37; and INCOME TAXATION vol 58 (2014) PARA 1009 et seq.

(ii) Assignment of Rights and Obligations

253. Assignment of rights in general.

The same considerations apply to the assignment of rights under building and
engineering contracts as to the assignment of rights in general[1]. Thus to create a
legal assignment notice in writing of the assignment must be given to the debtor,
or other person liable to make the payment, in order to entitle the assignee to
bring a claim for the money or the debt, and the rights of the assignee are subject
to all equities having a priority over the rights of the assignor[2].

Most building and engineering contracts contain express clauses dealing with
assignment, for example clauses which forbid the assignment of rights under the
contract without consent, and clauses which expressly permit the assignment of
warranties or 'guarantees' in certain circumstances. Such clauses will be effective
to modify or exclude the rights of the parties under the general rules set out
below[3].

1   For a detailed treatment of the legal and equitable assignment of rights see CHOSES IN ACTION.
    As to assignment of the benefit or the burden of a contract see further CONTRACT vol 22 (2012)
    PARAS 335–336. As to the assignment of arbitration clauses see PARA 402.
2   See the Law of Property Act 1925 s 136; and CHOSES IN ACTION vol 13 (2017) PARA 72 et seq.
3   See eg *Helstan Securities Ltd v Hertfordshire County Council* [1978] 3 All ER 262, 76 LGR 735;
    Linden Gardens Trust Ltd v Lenesta Sludge Disposals Ltd [1994] 1 AC 85, [1993] 3 All ER 417,
    HL; *Darlington Borough Council v Wiltshier Northern Ltd* [1995] 3 All ER 895, [1995] 1 WLR
    68, CA; *Norglen Ltd (in liquidation) v Reeds Rains Prudential Ltd* [1999] 2 AC 1, [1998] 1 All
    ER 218, HL; *Alfred McAlpine Construction Ltd v Panatown Ltd* [2001] 1 AC 518, sub nom
    Panatown Ltd v Alfred McAlpine Construction Ltd [2000] 4 All ER 97, [2000] All ER (D) 1078,
    HL; *Bovis Lend Lease Ltd v RD Fire Protection Ltd, Huthco Ltd v Bovis Lend Lease Ltd* [2003]
    EWHC 939 (TCC), 89 ConLR 169, [2003] All ER (D) 35 (May); *Offer-Hoar v Larkstore Ltd*

(Technotrade Ltd Pt 20 defendant) [2006] EWCA Civ 1079, [2006] 1 WLR 2926, [2007] 1 All ER (Comm) 104; *Hall v Van der Heiden* [2010] EWHC 586 (TCC), [2010] All ER (D) 79 (Nov); *Co-operative Group Ltd v Birse Developments Ltd* [2014] EWHC 530 (TCC), 153 ConLR 103, [2014] BLR 359; and PARA 254 et seq.

254. Assignment of benefit by the contractor.

The contractor can assign his beneficial rights under the contract and these rights include the right to receive payment of money due or to become due whether by instalments or otherwise[1], the right to payment of instalments of the agreed price on the production of certificates from the architect and the right to any 'retention money held by the employer[2]. When a contract prohibits assignment, an assignment of the benefit of that contract is of no effect and therefore unenforceable against the debtor, although it may create rights as between assignor and assignee[3]. Such a prohibition may also prevent the assignment of the fruits of performance such as accrued rights of action or debts[4].

1   *Re Toward, ex p Moss* (1884) 14 QBD 310, DC; *Hughes v Pump House Hotel Co* [1902] 2 KB 190, CA (applied in *Bexhill UK Ltd v Razzaq* [2012] EWCA Civ 1376, [2012] All ER (D) 257 (Oct)); *G and T Earle Ltd v Hemsworth RDC* (1928) 44 TLR 758, CA; *Re Warren, Wheeler v Trustee in Bankruptcy* [1938] Ch 725, [1938] 2 All ER 331, DC. As to assignment of the benefit or the burden of a contract see further CONTRACT vol 22 (2012) PARAS 335–336.
2   *Drew & Co v Josolyne* (1887) 18 QBD 590, CA; *G and T Earle Ltd v Hemsworth RDC* (1928) 44 TLR 758, CA; *Re Tout and Finch Ltd* [1954] 1 All ER 127, [1954] 1 WLR 178. As to instalment payments see PARA 345. As to retention money see PARA 346.
3   *Helstan Securities Ltd v Hertfordshire County Council* [1978] 3 All ER 262; *Linden Gardens Trust Ltd v Lenesta Sludge Disposals Ltd* [1994] 1 AC 85, [1993] 3 All ER 417, HL.
4   *Linden Gardens Trust Ltd v Lenesta Sludge Disposals Ltd* [1994] 1 AC 85, [1993] 3 All ER 417, HL. 'The question in each case must turn on the terms of the contract in question': *Linden Gardens Trust Ltd v Lenesta Sludge Disposals Ltd* above at 105 and 429 per Lord Browne-Wilkinson. A prohibition on the assignment of accrued rights of action under a JCT standard form is not void as being contrary to public policy: see *Linden Gardens Trust Ltd v Lenesta Sludge Disposals Ltd*. As to JCT standard forms of contract see PARA 202. If a contract contains a general prohibition against assignment but permits the assignment of any sum due or to become due under it, claims for damages falling to be assessed in accordance with the terms of the contract are non-assignable, though there may be an assignment once liability and the amount of damages have been established: *Flood v Shand Construction Ltd* (1996) 81 BLR 31, (1996) 54 Con LR 125, CA. See also *Herkules Piling Ltd v Tilbury Construction Ltd* (1992) 61 BLR 107, (1992) 32 Con LR 112 (non-assignability of right to arbitration even though sums payable under the contract assignable). See also *Alfred McAlpine Construction Ltd v Panatown Ltd* [2001] 1 AC 518, sub nom *Panatown Ltd v Alfred McAlpine Construction Ltd* [2001] 1 AC 518, [2000] 4 All ER 97, [2000] 3 WLR 946, HL.

255. Effect of forfeiture.

Where the contract is properly determined[1] by the employer, either because of repudiation by the contractor or by virtue of the proper exercise by the employer of a determination clause in the contract, the contract is never completed and no right to further payment ever accrues to the contractor. There is therefore nothing on which an assignment of the right to money yet to become due can operate[2]. However, the determination clause may provide that the contractor be paid any balance left after the deduction of the employer's damages and expenses. An assignment by the contractor of money to become due to him would cover such a sum[3].

1   As to the determination of a building contract see PARA 312 et seq.
2   *McMahon Ltd v O'Neill* (1915) 49 ILT 129.
3   Subject, of course, to any contractual prohibition against assignment: see PARA 254. Whether, upon a determination, the assignee has a claim against the assignor will depend upon the terms of the assignment: see *Humphreys v Jones* (1850) 20 LJ Ex 88. As to assignment of the benefit or the burden of a contract see further CONTRACT vol 22 (2012) PARAS 335–336.

256. Assignment of burden of contract by the contractor.

The contractor cannot assign the burden of his contract without the assent of the employer. In fact any assignment of a burden is actually called a 'novation' because to transfer a burden to another party needs the consent of all three parties; the original two contracting parties and the third party being the transferee[1].

Where the contract would otherwise not be assignable, if the employer acquiesces in the assignment and accepts the services of the assignee, he will be estopped from raising any objection on the ground that the contract ought to have been carried out by the original contractor, and this will be so even where there is no formal assignment, substituted contract or sub-contract[2].

If the consideration for the assignment as between assignor and assignee is the payment of money to the assignor on completion, then, if the assignee prevents the completion of the contract or enters into a substituted contract so that the event on which the money may have become payable never happens, the assignor will have no claim for the money[3]; but he may have a claim in damages against the assignee.

1   *Tolhurst v Associated Portland Cement Manufacturers (1900) Ltd* [1902] 2 KB 660 at 668, CA, per Collins MR; affd [1903] AC 414, HL (where the House of Lords upheld the assignment on the grounds that it dealt with the benefit and not the burden of the contract). As to assignment of the benefit or the burden of a contract see further CONTRACT vol 22 (2012) PARAS 335–336. See also *Commercial Bank of Tasmania v Jones* [1893] AC 313, 57 JP 644; *Chatsworth Investments Ltd v Cussins (Contractors) Ltd* [1969] 1 All ER 143, [1969] 1 WLR 1. As to the effect of novation see PARA 259.
2   *Falle v Le Sueur and Le Huguel* (1859) 12 Moo PCC 501. As to estoppel see PARA 236; and ESTOPPEL vol 47 (2014) PARA 301 et seq.
3   *Humphreys v Jones* (1850) 5 Exch 952.

257. Assignment by employer of burden.

An employer can assign the benefits and burdens of a contract, as between himself and his assignee, but cannot by such an assignment relieve himself of his obligations to the contractor. The contractor may, however, be a party to the assignment, in which case the assignment operates not only as an assignment between the employer and the assignee, but also as a new contract between the assignee and the contractor, involving novation[1].

The employer cannot get rid of his liability to pay the price to the contractor by assignment without the consent of the latter. The contractor cannot be compelled to carry out a building contract with all its onerous conditions and then have to rely for payment on a person with whom he never contracted and who may be a man of straw[2].

If on an assignment by the employer the contractor refuses to go on with the works, and is then induced to do so by a promise by the assignee to pay him, the performance of the works would be a sufficient consideration to support the promise, and the contractor would have a right of action against the assignee, at all events for all work done subsequently to the promise[3].

1   As to assignment of a contract see *Linden Gardens Trust Ltd v Lenesta Sludge Disposals Ltd* [1994] 1 AC 85, [1993] 3 All ER 417, HL. As to the effect of novation see PARA 259. As to assignment of the benefit or the burden of a contract see further CONTRACT vol 22 (2012) PARAS 335–336.
2   *Robson v Drummond* (1831) 2 B & Ad 303 at 307 per Lord Tenterden CJ.
3   *Scotson v Pegg* (1861) 6 H & N 295; *New Zealand Shipping Co Ltd v AM Satterthwaite & Co Ltd* [1975] AC 154, [1974] 1 All ER 1015, PC.

258.   Assignment by employer of benefit.

Two types of benefit may be assigned by the employer under a building contract. First, he may assign the right to call on the contractor to carry out or complete the works. Such an assignment is invalid if the contractor's obligations depend to any extent on the particular requirements of the employer[1], as may frequently be the case in contracts to build on a particular site, or in contracts which provide a mechanism for varying the scope of the works in accordance with those requirements. The benefit of such obligations is incapable of assignment. In practice, assignment of the right to obtain performance of the works by the contractor is often made subject to the contractor's consent by an express provision in the contract[2].

Second, the employer may after completion or partial completion assign the benefit of warranties in respect of the works made by the contractor, unless those warranties are of a kind incapable of assignment by reason of the principles set out above. Such assignments may for example transfer to a new owner of a building the protection of warranties made to the vendor when the building was built or repaired. Where a contract contains a general clause of the usual kind forbidding assignment of the employer's rights, another clause often permits assignment of a particular warranty. Such an assignment is valid and enforceable against the contractor if the warranty is of a kind capable of assignment. If the warranty includes an assignable obligation on the contractor to return to rectify defects, then the assignee can enforce that promise by action if necessary, and no special difficulties arise. If the warranty is simply a promise that at the time of building the work was not defective, then the assignee may only be able to recover in respect of loss actually suffered by the assignor, or in respect of loss which would have been suffered by the assignor if the assignor still owned both the building and the benefit of the warranty[3].

1   *Tolhurst v Associated Portland Cement Manufacturers (1900) Ltd* [1903] AC 414, HL; *Kemp v Baerselman* [1906] 2 KB 604, CA.
2   See *Linden Gardens Trust Ltd v Lenesta Sludge Disposals Ltd* [1994] 1 AC 85, [1993] 3 All ER 417, HL, where a restriction against assignment without written consent was confirmed as prohibiting the assignment of the benefit of the contract both as to the right to future performance and the right to accrued benefits under the contract (although, in this case, it was held that the assignor was entitled to recover substantial damages on the basis that the parties were to be treated as having entered into the contract on the footing that the assignor would be entitled to enforce contractual rights for the benefit of those who suffered from defects in performance but who, under the terms of the contract, could not acquire any right to hold the contractor liable for breach); applied in *Offer-Hoar v Larkstore Ltd (Technotrade Ltd, Pt 20 defendant)* [2006] EWCA Civ 1079, [2007] 1 All ER (Comm) 104, sub nom *Technotrade Ltd v Larkstore Ltd* [2006] 1 WLR 2926 (assignee could recover no more damages than the assignor could have recovered if there had been no assignment). See also *Darlington Borough Council v Wiltshier Northern Ltd* [1995] 3 All ER 895, [1995] 1 WLR 68, CA; and *Alfred McAlpine Construction Ltd v Panatown Ltd* [2001] 1 AC 518, sub nom *Panatown Ltd v Alfred McAlpine Construction Ltd* [2000] 4 All ER 97, HL; *Co-operative Group (CWS) Ltd v Stansell Ltd* [2006] EWCA Civ 538, [2006] 1 WLR 1704, [2006] 2 BCLC 599.
3   *Linden Gardens Trust Ltd v Lenesta Sludge Disposals Ltd* [1994] 1 AC 85, [1993] 3 All ER 417, HL; *Dawson v Great Northern and City Rly Co* [1905] 1 KB 260, CA.

(iii)   Novation and New Agreement

259.   Effect of novation.

The introduction of a new party into a contract, either by substitution or by addition, is termed novation[1]. When a new party is substituted for the original party, the original party is, to an extent depending on the terms of the new contract, released from further performance of the original contract, and the new party will take the benefit of any period of limitation that has accrued to the advantage of the original party[2]. Where a new contractor is substituted for the original one and takes over the work on the terms of the original contract, he will be bound by stipulations therein relating to deduction of liquidated damages[3]. If a contractor consents to the employer assigning the burden of the contract (that is, the liability to make payment under it), there is effectively a novation so that the original employer will be released from his obligations and the new employer will take his place[4]. When the original parties enter into a new contract, only those stipulations of the old contract which would necessarily apply will be implied into the new contract; any special terms from the old contract can only be included in the new contract by express incorporation[5].

1   For a full explanation of novation see CONTRACT vol 22 (2012) PARA 598 et seq.
2   *Commercial Bank of Tasmania v Jones* [1893] AC 313, 57 JP 644; *Chatsworth Investments Ltd v Cussins (Contractors) Ltd* [1969] 1 All ER 143, [1969] 1 WLR 1, CA. As to limitation periods generally see LIMITATION PERIODS.
3   *Re Yeadon Waterworks Co and Wright* (1895) 72 LT 538.
4   See CONTRACT vol 22 (2012) PARA 598 et seq.
5   Eg terms providing for liquidated damages (*Kemp v Rose* (1858) 1 Giff 258 at 266); or terms giving remedies on forfeiture (*Hunt v South Eastern Rly Co* (1875) 45 LJQB 87, HL).

2. PERFORMANCE OF THE CONTRACT

(1) Duty to Complete the Works

(i) In General

260. Duty to complete.
Most contracts provide that the contractor is to carry out and complete the works described in the contract. Even where it is not so stated then, if the extent of the work is defined, a duty to complete the work is implied, the contractor having a correlative right to complete the work. Without a right to omit part of the work contracted for the employer cannot, without breaking the terms of the contract, carry out any part of the contract works himself[1] or, it seems, exercise a power to omit to have the work carried out by another[2].

1 As to the employer's power to vary the contract by omitting part of the works see PARA 272. As to the duty to carry out work see also PARA 300.
2 *Simplex Floor Furnishing Appliance Co v Duranceau* [1941] 4 DLR 260 (Can); *Carr v JA Berriman Pty Ltd* (1953) 27 ALJ 273, Aust HC; *Main Roads Comr v Reed Stuart Pty Ltd* (1974) 48 ALJR 461, (1974) 12 BLR 55, Aust HC; *Amec Building Ltd v Cadmus Investment Co Ltd* (1996) 51 Con LR 105, (1996) 13 Const LJ 50.

261. Extent of the obligation.
The obligation to complete includes an obligation to provide anything which is indispensably necessary to complete the work[1]. This may include work not mentioned in the contract[2], work inaccurately described in the drawings, specification or bill of quantities[3], work required to overcome unforeseen problems in the ground[4] or in the method of working[5] and work required to obtain the satisfaction of the architect where that is a contractual criterion[6]. Whether the contractor is responsible for the design of the building or engineering works depends on the terms of the contract. Where the contractor has undertaken that the works will be fit for a particular purpose[7], there is no completion if the work is useless and the employer is not bound to pay for a building which is not fit for its purpose[8]. Where the contractor merely undertakes to carry out work in accordance with drawings or bills of quantities or a specification, he must complete the work as shown in those documents and it is immaterial that the completed work may be unsuitable for its purpose[9]. However, there is no implied warranty on behalf of the employer that the design as shown on the drawings or in the specification is practicable[10]. Accordingly, the contractor cannot excuse a failure to complete on the ground that the employer refused to make an additional payment for work necessary to realise the design[11], nor can the contractor claim additional payment, in the absence of a variation order[12], for work necessary to achieve completion[13].

1 *Williams v Fitzmaurice* (1858) 3 H & N 844; *Sharpe v San Paulo Rly* (1873) 8 Ch App 597.
2 See *Williams v Fitzmaurice* (1858) 3 H & N 844.
3 *Williams v Fitzmaurice* (1858) 3 H & N 844; *Sharpe v San Paulo Rly* (1873) 8 Ch App 597.
4 *Bottoms v York Corpn* (1892) 2 Hudson's BC (10th Edn) 270, CA.
5 *Thorn v London Corpn* (1876) 1 App Cas 120, HL; *Canterbury Pipe Lines Ltd v Christchurch Drainage Board* (1979) 16 BLR 76, NZ CA. See also *Amec Civil Engineering Ltd v Secretary of State for Transport* [2005] EWCA Civ 291, [2005] 1 WLR 2339, 101 Con LR 26.
6 *Neodox v Swinton and Pendlebury Borough Council* (1958) 5 BLR 34; *National Coal Board v William Neill & Son (St Helens) Ltd* [1985] QB 300, [1984] 1 All ER 555, 26 BLR 81.

7 Where a dwelling house is being constructed there is an implied warranty that the building will be
   fit for human habitation: see *Jennings v Tavener* [1955] 2 All ER 769, [1955] 1 WLR 932
   (approved in *Hancock v BW Brazier (Anerley) Ltd* [1966] 2 All ER 901, [1966] 1 WLR 1317).
   Under the Defective Premises Act 1972 there is a statutory duty to carry out work for or in
   connection with the provision of a dwelling so that as regards that work the dwelling will be fit for
   habitation when completed. See also PARAS 275–277. Where the contractor expressly undertakes
   to design and construct a building or other work to an outline specification provided by the
   employer, the contract is colloquially known as a 'package deal' contract: see PARA 209. As to
   implied terms relating to suitability see also PARAS 275–277. See also *Co-operative Insurance
   Society Ltd v Henry Boot Scotland Ltd* [2002] EWHC 1270 (TCC), 84 Con LR 164, [2002] All
   ER (D) 08 (Jul), where it was held that when someone undertook on terms to complete a design
   commenced by someone else, that person agreed that the result, however much of the design work
   was done before the process of completion commenced, would have been prepared with
   reasonable skill and care.
8 *Farnsworth v Garrard* (1807) 1 Camp 38; *Denew v Daverell* (1813) 3 Camp 451; *Grounsell v
   Lamb* (1836) 1 M & W 352; *Hall v Burke* (1886) 3 TLR 165, CA. See also *Basten v Butter* (1806)
   7 East 479; *Cousins v Paddon* (1835) 5 Tyr 535. See also *MT Højgaard v EON Climate and
   Renewables UK Robin Rigg East Ltd* [2017] UKSC 59, [2018] 2 All ER 22, (2017) 173 ConLR
   1 which discusses the central question around whether a double obligation existed within
   somewhat diffuse documents: both to achieve a specific purpose for the works and to work to a
   specific design with reasonable skill and care. On the facts of that particular case the Supreme
   Court held that the stricter obligation of fitness for purpose trumped any duty to exercise
   reasonable skill and care against facts where reasonable skill and care had been used but fitness for
   purpose was not achieved.
9 Cf *Ollivant v Bayley* (1843) 5 QB 288; *Chanter v Hopkins* (1838) 4 M & W 399. See also *Aldi
   Stores Ltd v Holmes Building plc* [2002] All ER (D) 453 (Mar) (reversed on other grounds [2003]
   EWCA Civ 1882, [2003] All ER (D) 19 (Dec)), which considered whether the building contractor
   in the case could add the structural advisor to the proceedings by means of a CPR Pt 20, which was
   allowed on appeal. The contractor must however meet any with implied terms relating to
   workmanship and materials: see PARA 274. Cf *MT Højgaard v EON Climate and Renewables UK
   Robin Rigg East Ltd* [2017] UKSC 59, [2018] 2 All ER 22, (2017) 173 ConLR 1.
10 *Thorn v London Corpn* (1876) 1 App Cas 120, HL; *Jackson v Eastbourne Local Board* (1886) 2
   Hudson's BC (10th Edn) 270, 356, HL.
11 *Bottoms v York Corpn* (1892) 2 Hudson's BC (10th Edn) 270, CA; *McDonald v Workington
   Corpn* (1893) 9 TLR 230, CA; *Jackson v Eastbourne Local Board* (1886) 2 Hudson's BC (10th
   Edn) 270, 356, HL.
12 See PARA 272. This will not operate to extricate a contractor from a difficulty for which he is
   liable: see *Simplex Concrete Piles Ltd v St Pancras Borough Council* (1958) 14 BLR 80;
   distinguished in *Howard de Walden Estates Ltd v Costain Management Design Ltd* (1991) 55
   BLR 124.
13 *Re Nuttall and Lynton and Barnstaple Rly Co's Arbitration* (1899) 2 Hudson's BC (10th Edn)
   271, 82 LT 17, CA; *CJ Pearce & Co Ltd v Hereford Corpn* (1968) 66 LGR 647; and see PARA
   272.

262. Effect of substantial completion.

Where a contract, which does not fall within the definition of a construction
contract under the Housing Grants, Construction and Regeneration Act 1996[1] or
which is for work of less than 45 days' duration[2], provides for a specific sum to
be paid on completion of specified work, the courts lean against a construction of
the contract which would deprive the contractor of any payment at all simply
because there are some defects or omissions[3]. In the absence of a very clear
stipulation that entire completion is a condition precedent to the contractor's right
to payment, the contractor can claim the contract price if he can show that he has
substantially completed the contract[4]. In such a case, the contractor can recover
the price subject to the deduction of the reasonable cost of completing the
defective or unfinished work[5]. However, no deduction may be made from the price
unless the omission resulted from a breach of contract by the contractor[6].

Whether or not the contractor has substantially completed the work is a question of fact in each case[7].

1 As to construction contracts generally see PARA 210. As to the meaning of 'construction contract' see PARA 210.

2 The Housing Grants, Construction and Regeneration Act 1996 provides for a statutory entitlement to payment by instalments, stage payments or other periodic payments in construction contracts where the duration of the work is to be more than 45 days: see s 109(1); and PARA 352. In default of agreement between the parties, the scheme for construction contracts will determine the amount of, and dates for, payment: see s 109(3); and PARA 352. As to payment provisions under the scheme for construction contracts see PARA 358.

3 *Hoenig v Isaac* [1952] 2 All ER 176 at 182, CA, per Denning LJ.

4 *Hoenig v Isaacs* [1952] 2 All ER 176, CA; *H Dakin & Co Ltd v Lee* [1916] 1 KB 566, CA; cf *Appleby v Myers* (1867) LR 2 CP 651; *Sumpter v Hedges* [1898] 1 QB 673, CA (applied in *ISG Construction Ltd v Seevic College* [2014] EWHC 4007 (TCC), [2015] 2 All ER (Comm) 545, [2015] BLR 233);*Forman & Co Pty Ltd v The Liddesdale* [1900] AC 190, PC; *Eshelby v Federated European Bank Ltd* [1932] 1 KB 254, DC; affd [1932] 1 KB 423, CA. As to entire contracts see PARA 209.

5 *Broom v Davis* (1794) 7 East 480n; *Thornton v Place* (1832) 1 Mood & R 218 (applied in *Multiplex Constructions (UK) Ltd v Cleveland Bridge UK Ltd* [2006] EWHC 1341 (TCC), 107 ConLR 1, [2006] All ER (D) 167 (Jun)); *Cutler v Close* (1832) 5 C & P 337; *H Dakin & Co Ltd v Lee* [1916] 1 KB 566, CA. For the applicability of these principles to the professional's right to payment of fees see *Hutchinson v Harris* (1978) 10 BLR 19, CA; *Turner Page Music Ltd v Torres Design Associates Ltd* [1997] CILL 1263, [1997] Lexis Citation 2290, CA.

6 *SWI Ltd v P&I Data Services Ltd* [2007] EWCA Civ 663, [2007] BLR 430, [2007] All ER (D) 42 (Jul).

7 See the cases cited in notes 3–5; and *Kiely & Sons Ltd v Medcraft* (1965) 109 Sol Jo 829, CA; *Ibmac Ltd v Marshall (Homes) Ltd* (1968) 208 Estates Gazette 851, CA; *Bolton v Mahadeva* [1972] 2 All ER 1322, [1972] 1 WLR 1009, CA; *Technistudy Ltd v Kelland* [1976] 1 WLR 1042 at 1045, CA, per Lord Denning MR.

(ii) Time for Completion

263. When time is of the essence of the contract.

The expression 'time is of the essence' means that a breach of the condition as to time for performance will entitle the innocent party to treat the breach as a repudiation of the contract, without regard to the magnitude of the breach[1], and normally, to claim damages for loss of bargain[2]. Exceptionally, however, the completion of the work by a specified date may be a condition precedent to the contractor's right to be paid[3]. Ordinarily time is not of the essence in building contracts. Time may be provided to be of the essence of the contract by the express agreement of the parties or by necessary implication[4]. Such an implication may be excluded by construction of other provisions of the contract: time is normally not of the essence where a sum is payable for each week that the work remains incomplete after the date fixed for completion[5], nor when the parties contemplate a postponement of completion[6]. Time cannot be of the essence if a date is not specified or capable of precise determination by the parties[7].

1 See CONTRACT vol 22 (2012) PARA 499 et seq; and *United Scientific Holdings Ltd v Burnley Borough Council* [1978] AC 904, [1977] 2 All ER 62, HL; *Lombard North Central plc v Butterworth* [1987] QB 527, [1987] 1 All ER 267, CA.

2 *Peak Construction (Liverpool) Ltd v McKinney Foundations Ltd* (1970) 1 BLR 111 at 120, CA, per Salmon LJ; *Bunge Corpn v Tradax SA* [1981] 2 All ER 513, [1981] 1 WLR 711, HL. See also *Gold Group Properties Ltd v BDW Trading Ltd (formerly known as Barratt Homes Ltd)* [2010] EWHC 1632 (TCC), [2010] All ER (D) 18 (Jul) (developer in repudiatory breach of a development agreement by failing to start the works by the due date and failing to proceed with due diligence).

3   *Maryon v Carter* (1830) 4 C & P 295; *Munro v Butt* (1858) 8 E & B 738. However, see now the Housing Grants, Construction and Regeneration Act 1996 which provides for a statutory entitlement to payment by instalments, stage payments or other periodic payments in construction contracts where the duration of the work is to be more than 45 days and where the contract is a 'construction contract' (see PARA 210) within the meaning of that Act: see s 109(1); and PARA 352.
4   See CONTRACT vol 22 (2012) PARA 503.
5   *Lamprell v Billericay Union* (1849) 3 Exch 283 at 303 per Rolfe B; *Lombard North Central plc v Butterworth* [1987] QB 527, [1987] 1 All ER 267, CA.
6   *Webb v Hughes* (1870) LR 10 Eq 281; *Hartley v Hymans* [1920] 3 KB 475; *Lock v Bell* [1931] 1 Ch 35. See also *Lowther v Heaver* (1889) 41 ChD 248 at 268, CA, per Lindley LJ; but cf *Peak Construction (Liverpool) Ltd v McKinney Foundations Ltd* (1970) 69 LGR 1, (1970) 1 BLR 111, CA, per Salmon LJ.
7   *British and Commonwealth Holdings plc v Quadrex Holdings Inc* [1989] QB 842 at 857, [1989] 3 All ER 492 at 504, CA, per Sir Nicholas Browne-Wilkinson.

264. When time is not of the essence.

Where time is not of the essence of the contract, but a time for completion is specified, the employer will be entitled to damages upon the contractor's default[1]. Where there is no completion date specified, the contractor must complete the work within a reasonable time[2]. In either of the above situations, or when time has ceased to be of the essence by waiver or agreement, then, a reasonable time for performance having elapsed, the employer can serve a notice requiring completion by a certain date and dismiss the contractor on a failure to complete by the fixed date[3]. If, by reason of the breach of contract or by reason of extra work ordered by him, the employer prevents the contractor from completing the work by the date fixed or materially abridges the period for execution of work, then unless the contract clearly provides to the contrary, the employer can only insist on completion within a reasonable time[4]. The onus of proof that delay has been caused by some act or default of the employer is on the contractor[5]. Some building contracts provide for determination in specific circumstances of delay.

1   *Lucas v Godwin* (1837) 3 Bing NC 737 (applied in *Dakin (H) & Co Ltd v Lee* [1916] 1 KB 566); cf *Tidey v Mollett* (1864) 16 CBNS 298. See also *Cleveland Bridge UK Ltd v Severfield – Rowen Structures Ltd* [2012] EWHC 3652 (TCC), [2012] All ER (D) 239 (Dec). See generally DAMAGES.
2   *Startup v McDonald* (1843) 6 Man & G 593 at 611 per Rolfe B (applied in *Afovos Shipping Co SA v Pagnan and Lli, The Afovos* [1982] 3 All ER 18, [1982] 1 WLR 848, [1982] 1 Lloyd's Rep 562).
3   *Charles Rickards Ltd v Oppenheim* [1950] 1 KB 616, [1950] 1 All ER 420, CA (applied in *Shawton Engineering Ltd v DGP International Ltd; DGP International Ltd v Limit (No 3) Ltd* [2005] EWCA Civ 1359, [2006] BLR 1, [2005] All ER (D) 241 (Nov); *Al Nasr Co for Coke & Chemicals v Fairdeal Supplies Ltd* [2013] EWHC 3131 (Comm), [2013] All ER (D) 173 (Oct); *United Scientific Holdings Ltd v Burnley Borough Council* [1978] AC 904, [1977] 2 All ER 62, HL. As to the giving of notice generally see *British and Commonwealth Holdings plc v Quadrex Holdings Inc* [1989] QB 842, [1989] 3 All ER 492, CA; *Behzadi v Shaftesbury Hotels Ltd* [1992] Ch 1, [1991] 2 All ER 477, CA. The service of such a notice will not cancel a time breach already committed: *Raineri v Miles* [1981] AC 1050, [1980] 2 All ER 145, HL.
4   See note 3; and *British and Commonwealth Holdings plc v Quadrex Holdings Inc* [1989] QB 842, [1989] 3 All ER 492, CA.
5   *Morts Dock and Engineering Co Ltd v Wadey* (1905) 22 TLR 61, PC.

265. Degree of completion necessary.

Modern standard forms of contract[1] for works of construction require the architect or engineer (or employer's agent as commonly called in design and build procurement) to certify that the works have been practically or substantially completed, and the contractor's obligation to complete the works by a specified date is in such cases usually discharged if the works are practically completed by the contract date[2]. If, owing to latent defects, substantial remedial work is necessary after the contractor has left the site, the contract is nevertheless completed at the date the contractor left the site[3].

1 As to standard forms of contract see PARA 202.
2 As to the degree of completion otherwise see PARA 209 text and notes 1–7; and the cases cited in note 3.
3 See *Westminster City Council v Jarvis & Sons Ltd* [1970] 1 All ER 943 at 949, [1970] 1 WLR 637 at 647, HL, per Viscount Dilhorne; and see *HW Nevill (Sunblest) Ltd v William Press & Son Ltd* (1981) 20 BLR 78 at 87 per Judge Newey QC; *Emson Eastern Ltd v EME Developments Ltd* (1991) 55 BLR 114, (1991) 26 Con LR 57.

266. Time at large.

Time is said to be 'at large'[1] in situations such as the following[2]:

(1)   where a building contractor is prevented from completing by the time specified in the contract by an act of the employer or an act for which the employer is responsible under the contract (such as a breach of contract or ordering additional or varied work[3]);

(2)   where a building contract contains provisions enabling the time for completion to be extended and thus to preserve the right to damages for failure to complete on time[4], notwithstanding the occurrence of an act of prevention, and either: (a) the act of prevention which occurs is not one which enables time to be extended; or (b) the machinery for extending time has not been operated properly (or cannot be saved by, for example, the operation of an arbitration clause) or cannot be operated at all because the architect or engineer has not been appointed or re-appointed to determine the amount of the extension of time[5].

In situations such as these the contractor's obligation to complete by the contract date or within the contract period (or extended date or period) is discharged but nevertheless an obligation to complete within a reasonable time or within a reasonable period remains. In cases where the contract contains a power to extend time there is likely to be no practical difference in the result as the expiration of a reasonable time or period will be equivalent to the time or period that would have been granted by extension (unless events also occur which would not have entitled the contractor to an extension of time but are to be taken into account in determining a reasonable time or period for completion[6]). Where, however, the right to recover liquidated damages is dependent upon a failure to complete by the contract completion date or extended date that right will fall with the discharge of the contractor's obligation so to do[7]. However, the contractor will be liable to pay unliquidated damages for failure to complete within the reasonable time or period, and a right to recover unliquidated damages will continue to subsist in circumstances where a breach of a contractual completion date or extended date, or an inability to complete within a reasonable time or period occurs and liquidated damages are not mentioned in the contract. But note if liquidated damages are set at zero or nil, this has the effect of providing a negative figure for liquidated damages and excludes any right to claim general damages for failure to complete in a reasonable time[8]

1 *Holme v Guppy* (1838) 3 M & W 387 at 389–390 per Parke B.
2 The situations described are those which commonly arise. For cases on the subject see *Roberts v Bury Comrs* (1870) LR 5 CP 310; *Dodd v Churton* [1897] 1 QB 562, CA; *Wells v Army and Navy Co-operative Society* (1902) 86 LT 764; *Amalgamated Building Constructions Ltd v Waltham Holy Cross UDC* [1952] 2 All ER 452, 50 LGR 667, CA; *Peak Construction (Liverpool) Ltd v McKinney Foundations Ltd* (1970) 69 LGR 1, (1970) 1 BLR 111, CA; *Astilleros Canarios SA v Cape Hateras Shipping Co Inc, The Cape Hatteras* [1982] 1 Lloyd's Rep 518; *Rapid Building*

Group Ltd v Ealing Family Housing Association Ltd (1984) 29 BLR 5, CA; *S MK Cabinets v Hili Modern Electrics Pty Ltd* [1984] VR 391; *McAlpine Humberoak Ltd v McDermott International Inc* (1992) 58 BLR 1, CA; and *Perini Pacific v Greater Vancouver Sewerage and Drainage District* (1966) 57 DLR (2d) 307, BC CA.

3 It is a question of construction, however, whether the contractor may still be obliged to complete the additional varied work within the time specified.

4 See eg *Peak Construction (Liverpool) Ltd v McKinney Foundations Ltd* (1970) 69 LGR 1 at 11, (1970) 1 BLR 111 at 121, CA, per Salmon LJ.

5 The principles stated will most likely still apply even if the contractor has been guilty of delays of his own such that the due date for completion cannot be met: see *SMK Cabinets v Hili Modern Electrics Pty Ltd* [1984] VR 391, Vic SC; cf *Astilleros Canarios SA v Cape Hateras Shipping Co Inc, The Cape Hatteras* [1982] 1 Lloyd's Rep 518.

6 Cf eg *British Steel Corpn v Cleveland Bridge and Engineering Co Ltd* [1984] 1 All ER 504 at 511 per Robert Goff J.

7 See *Peak Construction (Liverpool) Ltd v McKinney Foundations Ltd* (1970) 69 LGR 1 at 11, (1970) 1 BLR 111 at 121, CA, per Salmon LJ.

8 See *Peak Construction (Liverpool) Ltd v McKinney Foundations Ltd* (1970) 69 LGR 1 at 11, (1970) 1 BLR 111 at 121, CA, per Salmon LJ; *Rapid Building Group Ltd v Ealing Family Housing Association Ltd* (1984) 29 BLR 5 at 16, CA, per Stephenson LJ, and at 19 per Lloyd LJ; *McAlpine Humberoak Ltd v McDermott International Inc* (1992) 58 BLR 1, CA. See also *Elsley v J G Collins Insurance Agencies Ltd* (1978) 83 DLR (3d) 1, Can SC; *Temloc Ltd v Errill Properties Ltd* (1987) 12 ConLR 109, 39 BLR 30. See further PARA 271.

(iii) Extension of Time and Liquidated Damages for Delay

267. Extension of time and liquidated damages.

Generally, contracts for construction works provide that in the event of the contractor's failure to complete by the date specified for completion the contractor is to pay a specified sum or that the employer may deduct a specified sum from money due to the contractor[1]. There must be a definite date from which liquidated damages are to run; if there is no specified date or if the date for completion is invalidated by an instruction to the contractor to carry out additional work[2] or by some other fault of the employer the employer's right to claim or deduct liquidated damages will be lost[3]. The parties therefore frequently give to the architect or engineer power to grant the contractor an extension of time for the completion of the works, and thus a new completion date is substituted and the right to liquidated damages remains alive[4].

Liquidated damages and extension of time clauses are construed against the party wishing to enforce them and will not embrace delays caused by a breach of contract by the employer or acts of the architect unless clear words are used[5]. If, however, the contractor has undertaken to complete the work and any additional work which may be ordered within the specified time, he is bound to do so and the existence of an extension of time clause in the contract is immaterial[6]. A contractual provision for extension of time for delay due to the employer's breach of contract or by ordering extra work will not exclude the contractor's rights to damages or additional payment[7].

1 Such provision will be unenforceable as a penalty if it stands against the principle mentioned in PARA 270. In particular such clauses are found in the standard forms of building contracts. As to standard forms of contract see PARA 202.

2 As to variations and extras see PARA 272.

3 *Legge v Harlock* (1848) 12 QB 1015; *Dodd v Churton* [1897] 1 QB 562, CA.

4 *Trollope & Colls Ltd v North West Metropolitan Regional Health Board* [1973] 2 All ER 260, [1973] 1 WLR 601, HL; *Multiplex Constructions (UK) Ltd (No 2) v Honeywell Control Systems Ltd* [2007] EWHC 447 (TCC), 111 ConLR 78, [2007] BLR 195; *Percy Bilton Ltd v GLC* [1982] 2 All ER 623, [1982] 1 WLR 794, 20 BLR 1, HL. When an agreement for the acceleration of work has been made, the dates in the provisions of an existing sectional completion agreement can be

replaced with dates corresponding to the acceleration agreement and the extension of time and liquidated damages provisions are capable of continuing to have force by reference to the new dates for completion of each section: *John Barker Construction Ltd v London Portman Hotel Ltd* (1996) 83 BLR 31.

5   *Wells v Army and Navy Co-operative Society Ltd* (1902) 86 LT 764; *Perini Pacific Ltd v Greater Vancouver Sewerage and Drainage District* (1966) 57 DLR (2d) 307, BC CA; *Peak Construction (Liverpool) Ltd v McKinney Foundations Ltd* (1970) 69 LGR 1, (1970) 1 BLR 111, CA; *North Midland Building Ltd v Cyden Homes Ltd* [2017] EWHC 2414 (TCC), [2017] All ER (D) 13 (Oct).

6   *Jones v St John's College, Oxford* (1870) LR 6 QB 115; *Tew v Newbold-on-Avon United District School Board* (1884) Cab & El 260.

7   *Roberts v Bury Improvement Comrs* (1870) LR 5 CP 310 at 327 per Kelly CB; *Miller v LCC* (1934) 151 LT 425.

268.   Exercise of a power to extend time.

The time when and the conditions under which the architect or engineer should exercise his jurisdiction to extend the date for completion will depend upon the terms of the contract. Standard forms of contract[1] require the contractor to make a written application for the grant of an extension of time[2]. Occasionally a contract may still provide that an extension of time must be granted before completion so that a later exercise of the power is invalid and liquidated damages are irrecoverable[3]. Where an extension is for the contractor's benefit it seems that the power can be exercised retrospectively[4]. If, however, the wording of the extension of time provision is sufficiently clear a retrospective extension can also be granted in respect of delays caused by the employer[5]. An extension of time may be conditional on a proper application therefor but the architect would still be expected to be aware of the reason for a delay[6]. If the contractor applies for and obtains an extension of time from the architect, he may be deemed to have waived any objection to the architect's jurisdiction[7]. The proper discharge of an architect's function in determining a fair and reasonable extension of time requires a logical and methodical analysis of the impact that the relevant matters had on the contractor's programme[8].

1   As to standard forms of contract see PARA 202.
2   *Miller v LCC* (1934) 151 LT 425.
3   *Miller v LCC* (1934) 151 LT 425; *Amalgamated Building Contractors Ltd v Waltham Holy Cross UDC* [1952] 2 All ER 452, 50 LGR 667, CA.
4   *Amalgamated Building Contractors Ltd v Waltham Holy Cross UDC* [1952] 2 All ER 452, 50 LGR 667, CA.
5   *Balfour Beatty Building Ltd v Chestermount Properties Ltd* (1993) 62 BLR 1 (construing the extension of time clause in the JCT standard form of contract). As to JCT standard forms of contract see PARA 202.
6   *Merton London Borough Council v Stanley Hugh Leach Ltd* (1985) 32 BLR 51 at 89–94 per Vinelott J. If such a provision is construed as a condition precedent it seems doubtful, if the delay has been caused by the employer's default, that although the contractor may be deprived of an extension of time, the employer could maintain a claim for liquidated damages since to do so would be to condone his own breach of contract.
7   *Sattin v Poole* (1901) 2 Hudson's BC (10th Edn) 630.
8   *John Barker Construction Ltd v London Portman Hotel Ltd* (1996) 83 BLR 31.

269.   Exercise of power to deduct liquidated damages.

The terms of the contract may provide for notice of intention to deduct liquidated damages to be given by the employer to the contractor as a condition precedent to such deduction, and the issue of a certificate of failure to complete may also be such a condition precedent[1]. If the architect fails pursuant to any terms of the contract to give a proper extension of time, the deduction of liquidated damages may be disallowed[2]. Liquidated damages clauses may provide the sole remedy for delay so that unliquidated damages cannot be claimed instead[3]. If a liquidated damages clause is void for uncertainty, unliquidated damages may still be claimed[4].

1 See *A Bell & Son (Paddington) Ltd v CBF Residential Care and Housing Association* (1989) 46 BLR 102; *JF Finnegan Ltd v Community Housing Association Ltd* (1993) 65 BLR 103, 34 Con LR 104; affd on this point (1995) 77 BLR 22, 47 Con LR 25, CA. See also *Skanska Construction UK Ltd (formerly Kvaerner Construction Ltd) v Egger (Barony) Ltd (No 2)* [2002] All ER (D) 15 (Jun), where delay in considering applications for extensions of time did not render a notice of deduction of liquidated and ascertained damages invalid.
2 *Amalgamated Building Contractors Ltd v Waltham Holy Cross UDC* [1952] 2 All ER 452, 50 LGR 667, CA.
3 *Cellulose Acetate Silk Co Ltd v Widnes Foundry (1925) Ltd* [1933] AC 20, HL. If parties to a contract enter '£nil' for liquidated damages, then there is no remedy in damages at all for delay: *Temloc Ltd v Erroll Properties Ltd* (1987) 39 BLR 30, CA; cf *Baese Pty Ltd v RA Bracken Building Pty Ltd* (1989) 52 BLR 130, NSW SC.
4 *Arnhold v A-G of Hong Kong* (1989) 47 BLR 129, HK HC; *Philips Hong Kong Ltd v A-G of Hong Kong* (1990) 50 BLR 122, HK HC; revsd on other grounds (1991) 58 BLR 112, HK CA; affd (1993) 61 BLR 41, PC. The latter case was primarily concerned with whether the relevant clause was a penalty (see PARA 270). The proposition was not contradicted but the Privy Council determined that the liquidated damages provisions under consideration were not uncertain so as to be unenforceable. See also PARA 266.

270. Penalty or liquidated damages.

Although expressed in the contract to be a liquidated damages clause, in law such a clause may amount to a penalty[1]. The question whether such provision is in the nature of liquidated damages or is unenforceable as a penalty is a question of the construction of the terms and the inherent circumstances of each contract judged at the time the contract was made[2]. The fact that it would be difficult to ascertain the loss caused to the employer by delaying completion indicates that the provision is in the nature of liquidated damages[3]. When a sum specified as payable is extravagant or totally out of proportion to the range of possible losses which might be incurred, the provision will be a penalty and unenforceable to any extent greater than the party's actual loss[4].

In 2015 the Supreme Court said the penalty rule in England was ancient but that the rule should not be abolished, and laid out a modern day application of the penalty clause rule[5]. In their Lordships' view, the law relating to penalties had become the prisoner of artificial categorisation, itself the result of unsatisfactory distinctions: between a penalty and genuine pre-estimate of loss, and between a genuine pre-estimate of loss and a deterrent. The fact that the clause was not a pre-estimate of loss did not necessarily mean that it was penal[6]. The true test was whether the impugned provision was a secondary obligation which imposed a detriment on the contract-breaker out of all proportion to any 'legitimate interest' of the innocent party in the enforcement of the primary obligation. The innocent party could have no proper interest in simply punishing the defaulter. His interest was in performance or in some appropriate alternative to performance[7]. In a negotiated contract between properly advised parties of comparable bargaining power, the strong initial presumption had to be that the parties themselves were the best judges of what was legitimate in a provision dealing with the consequences of breach[8].

Liquidated damages clauses will not be easily set aside as unenforceable since what the parties have agreed should normally be upheld[9]. A forfeiture clause may also be a penalty clause. For example, a provision, that on failure to complete on time, the contractor will forfeit the retention money is a penalty because the amount of retention money held will vary according to the amount of work done and it cannot therefore be a genuine pre-estimate of the loss likely to be caused to the employer in the event of delay[10]. If the contract provides for a variable rate but with a minimum amount, liquidated damages may not be recoverable[11].

1   The label used by the parties is not conclusive: see *Dunlop Pneumatic Tyre Co Ltd v New Garage and Motor Co Ltd* [1915] AC 79 at 86, HL, per Lord Dunedin. See also DAMAGES vol 29 (2014) PARA 549 et seq; and as to the equitable doctrine of relief against penalties see EQUITABLE JURISDICTION vol 47 (2014) PARA 220 et seq.

2   *Ranger v Great Western Rly Co* (1854) 5 HL Cas 72; *Public Works Comr v Hills* [1906] AC 368, PC; *Webster v Bosanquet* [1912] AC 394, PC; *Dunlop Pneumatic Tyre Co Ltd v New Garage and Motor Co Ltd* [1915] AC 79, HL; *Cellulose Acetate Silk Co Ltd v Widnes Foundry (1925) Ltd* [1933] AC 20, HL; *Philips Hong Kong Ltd v A-G of Hong Kong* (1993) 61 BLR 41, PC.

3   *Fletcher v Dyche* (1787) 2 Term Rep 32.

4   *Kemble v Farren* (1829) 6 Bing 141; *Re Newman, ex p Capper* (1876) 4 ChD 724, CA; cf *Cameron-Head v Cameron* 1919 SC 627, Ct of Sess; *Watts, Watts & Co Ltd v Mitsui & Co Ltd* [1917] AC 227, HL.

5   *Cavendish Square Holding BV v Talal El Makdessi; ParkingEye Ltd v Beavis* [2015] UKSC 67, [2016] 2 All ER 519, [2015] 3 WLR 1373 (as applied in *EE Ltd v Mundio Mobile Ltd* [2016] EWHC 531 (TCC), [2016] All ER (D) 155 (Mar); and *Vivienne Westwood Ltd v Conduit Street Development Ltd* [2017] EWHC 350 (Ch), [2017] EGLR 11, [2017] All ER (D) 47 (Mar)).

6   *Cavendish Square Holding BV v Talal El Makdessi; ParkingEye Ltd v Beavis* [2015] UKSC 67 at [31], [2016] 2 All ER 519, [2015] 3 WLR 1373 per Lord Neuberger and Lord Sumption.

7   *Cavendish Square Holding BV v Talal El Makdessi; ParkingEye Ltd v Beavis* [2015] UKSC 67 at [32], [2016] 2 All ER 519, [2015] 3 WLR 1373 per Lord Neuberger and Lord Sumption.

8   *Cavendish Square Holding BV v Talal El Makdessi; ParkingEye Ltd v Beavis* [2015] UKSC 67 at [35], [2016] 2 All ER 519, [2015] 3 WLR 1373 per Lord Neuberger and Lord Sumption.

9   *Philips Hong Kong Ltd v A-G of Hong Kong* (1993) 61 BLR 41, PC (it will normally be insufficient to establish that a provision is objectionably penal by simply identifying situations when the application of the provision could result in a larger sum being recovered than the actual loss suffered). See also *JF Finnegan Ltd v Community Housing Association Ltd* (1993) 65 BLR 103, (1993) 34 Con LR 104; revsd on another point (1995) 77 BLR 22, 47 Con LR 25, CA.

10   *Public Works Comr v Hills* [1906] AC 368, PC; *Jobson v Johnson* [1989] 1 All ER 621, [1989] 1 WLR 1026, CA.

11   In *Philips Hong Kong Ltd v A-G of Hong Kong* (1993) 61 BLR 41, the Privy Council held that there could conceivably be circumstances where it was so obvious, before completion of the works as a whole, that the actual loss to be sustained would be less than a specified minimum figure that to include that minimum figure in a provision for the payment of liquidated damages on a reduced sliding scale would have the effect of transforming an otherwise perfectly proper liquidated damages provision into a penalty, in so far as it prevents the liquidated damages from being reduced below that figure. On the facts it was held that neither the case under consideration, nor the facts of *Arnhold & Co Ltd v A-G of Hong Kong* (1987) 47 BLR 129, HK HC, justified such a finding.

271. Recovery of unliquidated damages.

Where the time fixed for completion in the contract has ceased to be applicable in consequence of some fault of the employer, and consequently his right to liquidated damages has gone, he can have no claim for unliquidated damages unless the builder fails to complete within a reasonable time[1].

Where a right to liquidated damages is lost, unliquidated damages may still be recoverable[2].

1   See PARA 266; and *Ford v Cotesworth* (1870) LR 5 QB 544; *Tyers v Rosedale and Ferryhill Iron Co* (1875) LR 10 Exch 195; *Rapid Building Group Ltd v Ealing Family Housing Association Ltd* (1985) 29 BLR 5 at 16, CA, per Stephenson LJ, and at 19 per Lloyd LJ. It is undecided whether time is at large in this situation: see *Dodd v Churton* [1897] 1 QB 562, CA; *Trollope & Colls Ltd v North West Metropolitan Regional Health Board* [1973] 2 All ER 260, [1973] 1 WLR 601, HL; *Percy Bilton Ltd v GLC* [1982] 2 All ER 623, [1982] 1 WLR 794, 20 BLR 1, HL.

2   See the cases cited in PARA 266 note 8. The right to liquidated damages may be lost because the relevant provision is a penalty, by reason of some fault of the employer or in consequence of a drafting error in the contract. It is an open question whether in any of these circumstances the

employer can recover as unliquidated damages a sum greater than the agreed liquidated amount. The answer may not be the same in each circumstance. As to the distinction between a penalty and liquidated damages see PARA 270.

(2) Extra Work and Variations

272. Extra work and variations.

Unless the building contract expressly provides that the contractor is obliged to comply with the requirements of the employer to change the works contracted for (whether by way of addition, alteration or omission) the contractor is not obliged to do so[1]. They must form the subject of a new contract or be a variation of the original contract[2]. If a contractor carries out unauthorised work he is not entitled to be paid in the absence of special circumstances[3]. Even where the contract does contain express provisions for the contractor to make changes, it is a matter of interpretation whether the changes fall within the power[4]. If the work falls outside the scope of the contract the employer may be liable to pay if a promise to pay can be found[5].

1 *SWI Ltd v P&I Data Services Ltd* [2007] EWCA Civ 663, [2007] BLR 430, [2007] All ER (D) 42 (Jul) (where there is a fixed price contract to perform works, the paying party is not entitled to vary the contract by reducing the work to be done, unless there is some term in the contract allowing for variations).
2 See *Holland Hannen and Cubitts (Northern) Ltd v Welsh Health Technical Services Organisation* (1981) 18 BLR 80; *Blue Circle Industries plc v Holland Dredging Co (UK) Ltd* (1987) 37 BLR 40, CA.
3 Such as conduct tantamount to fraud: *Hill v South Staffordshire Rly* (1865) 12 LT 63; *Molloy v Liebe* (1910) 102 LT 616, PC; *Brodie v Cardiff Corpn* [1919] AC 337, HL.
4 See eg *Blue Circle Industries plc v Holland Dredging Co (UK) Ltd* (1987) 37 BLR 40, CA.
5 *Russell v Viscount Sa da Bandeira* (1862) 13 CBNS 149; cf *Lusty v Finsbury Securities Ltd* (1991) 58 BLR 66, CA; *Gilbert & Partners (a firm) v Knight* [1968] 2 All ER 248, CA.

(3) Obligations as to Design, Workmanship and Materials

(i) In General

273. Obligations as to design.

The building contract may provide for the allocation of responsibility for the design of the works, which commonly means the determination of what is necessary to meet the requirements of the building owner or the person for whom the building is intended to be occupied (for example, the house owner). An obligation as to design is frequently no more than the obligation to complete so that the works are fit for their purpose[1]. This may entail not only preparing the proposed design of the works but also making changes to it as may be necessary if the works proceed or after completion so that the works are fit for their purpose[2]. Where the contract is silent, design obligations are a matter of implication although, unless a contrary intention appears, the person responsible for building works will be treated as the designer since reliance will have been placed upon that person[3].

The contractor may be liable to the employer for a defective design produced by a third party[4].

1 See PARAS 204, 446.

2 As to variations and extras see PARAS 272, 453 et seq.
3 See PARA 274.
4 See *Independent Broadcasting Authority v EMI Electronics Ltd and BICC Construction Ltd* (1980) 14 BLR 1, HL; *Lindenberg v Canning* (1992) 62 BLR 147, (1992) 29 Con LR 71.

274. Obligations as to workmanship and materials.

The drawings and the specification or bill of quantities will normally specify the quality and type of materials to be used, the workmanship to be employed and sometimes also the method of work to be adopted. They may also specify the purpose or purposes for which the completed works are to be fit. The contractor may thereby come under an express obligation to furnish or be responsible for the design of the works. Such a specification is sometimes called a 'performance specification', particularly for mechanical, electrical or other engineering works or services but also for building works generally.

Building contracts made after 4 July 1983 are subject to the Supply of Goods and Services Act 1982[1], which regulates obligations as to the quality and fitness of building work and services. Building contracts may similarly be subject to the provisions of the Consumer Protection Act 1987[2]. In respect of the fitness and quality of materials, the terms which at common law will be implied in a building contract[3], that is a contract for work and materials, correspond to the terms implied in the case of a sale of goods[4]. Three warranties will be implied: (1) that the materials used in the works and the completed works themselves will be reasonably fit for the purpose for which they are required[5]; (2) that the materials used will be of good quality[6]; and (3) that the work will be carried out in a good and workmanlike manner[7].

Where a contractor undertakes to erect and sell a dwelling or to complete and sell a dwelling in the course of erection, it is an implied term that the dwelling will be fit for its purpose, that is for human habitation[8]. Where the contract is for the completion of a dwelling, the implied term may embrace defects existing at the date of the contract[9]. The implication of a warranty of fitness may be excluded where the employer has ordered particular materials under a trade name[10], and will be excluded where the express terms of the contract are inconsistent with such an implication[11], or where the circumstances are such that the employer has not relied on the skill and judgment of the contractor[12]. The partial reliance on the skill of the contractor may be sufficient for the implication of a warranty of fitness[13].

At common law the contractor's obligations in respect of fitness, quality and workmanship will not generally merge in a subsequent conveyance of the dwelling[14] and a claim for breach of such implied terms can therefore be maintained after conveyance.

A warranty of fitness is implied in every contract unless it is displaced by the express terms or other relevant circumstances[15]. The reason for this presumption is the practical convenience of having a chain of contractual liability from the employer to the main contractor and from the main contractor to the sub-contractor[16], but it may be displaced by the selection of materials obtainable only from a particular source under a contract by which the contractor is not entitled to an indemnity[17] or where the work or materials are to be provided by a sub-contractor or supplier nominated by the employer[18] or where there is no reliance[19].

1 For a full account of the Supply of Goods and Services Act 1982 see SALE OF GOODS AND SUPPLY OF SERVICES. See in particular ss 13, 14, 16; and SALE OF GOODS AND SUPPLY OF SERVICES vol 91 (2012) PARA 330 et seq. Note the Supply of Goods and Services Act 1982 only

applies to business to business transactions following the coming into force of the Consumer Rights Acts 2015 on 1 October 2015 which replaces a number of laws as far as business to consumer transactions are concerned including the Sale of Goods Act 1979 and the Supply of Goods and Services Act 1982 and parts of the Unfair Contracts Terms Act 1977 and the revocation of the Unfair Terms in Consumer Contracts Regulations 1999.

2   See PARA 294; and CONSUMER PROTECTION.

3   Also in a licence: see *Wettern Electric Ltd v Welsh Development Agency* [1983] QB 796, [1983] 2 All ER 629.

4   *Young and Marten Ltd v McManus Childs Ltd* [1969] 1 AC 454, [1968] 2 All ER 1169, HL; *Independent Broadcasting Authority v EMI Electronics Ltd and BICC Construction Ltd* (1980) 14 BLR 1, HL. See generally SALE OF GOODS AND SUPPLY OF SERVICES.

5   *Test Valley Borough Council v GLC* (1979) 13 BLR 63, CA; *Viking Grain Storage Ltd v TH White Installations Ltd* (1985) 33 BLR 103. See also *Francis v Cockrell* (1870) LR 5 QB 501. See also *Rotherham Metropolitan Borough Council v Frank Haslam Milan & Co Ltd* (1996) 78 BLR 1, 59 Con LR 33, CA.

6   *Young and Marten Ltd v McManus Childs Ltd* [1969] 1 AC 454, [1968] 2 All ER 1169, HL. If the materials are merchantable in the sense that they are saleable and capable of being used for one or more purposes, even though unsuitable for the precise application contemplated by the contractor, there will be no breach of the implied warranty of quality: see *Henry Kendall & Sons (a firm) v William Lillico & Sons Ltd; Holland Colombo Trading Society Ltd v Grimsdale & Sons Ltd* [1969] 2 AC 31, [1968] 2 All ER 444, HL; *BS Brown & Son Ltd v Craiks Ltd* [1970] 1 All ER 823, [1970] 1 WLR 752, HL; *M/S Aswan Engineering Establishment Co v Lupdine Ltd* [1987] 1 All ER 135, [1987] 1 WLR 1, CA; *Rotherham Metropolitan Borough Council v Frank Haslam Milan & Co Ltd* (1996) 78 BLR 1, (1996) 12 Const LJ 333, CA; *KG Bominflot Bunkergesellschaft fur Mineraloele mbH & Co v Petroplus Marketing AG* [2010] EWCA Civ 1145, [2011] 2 All ER (Comm) 522, [2011] 1 Lloyd's Rep 442.

7   *Hancock v BW Brazier (Anerley) Ltd* [1966] 2 All ER 901 at 903, [1966] 1 WLR 1317 at 1332, CA, per Lord Denning MR. As to workmanship see *Duncan v Blundell* (1820) 3 Stark 6; *Pearce v Tucker* (1862) 3 F & F 136; *Billyack v Leyland Construction Co Ltd* [1968] 1 All ER 783, [1968] 1 WLR 471 (applied in *National Coal Board v William Neill & Son (St Helens) Ltd* [1985] QB 300, [1984] 1 All ER 555, [1984] 3 WLR 1135).

8   *Lawrence v Cassel* [1930] 2 KB 83, CA; *Miller v Cannon Hill Estates Ltd* [1931] 2 KB 113; *Jennings v Tavener* [1955] 2 All ER 769, [1955] 1 WLR 932; and see *Test Valley Borough Council v GLC* (1979) 13 BLR 63, CA.

9   *Perry v Sharon Development Co Ltd* [1937] 4 All ER 390 at 395, CA, per Romer LJ; *Hancock v BW Brazier (Anerley) Ltd* [1966] 2 All ER 1 at 7, [1966] 1 WLR 1317 at 1325 per Diplock LJ; affd [1966] 2 All ER 901, [1966] 1 WLR 1317, CA.

10 *Young and Marten Ltd v McManus Childs Ltd* [1969] 1 AC 454 at 469, [1968] 2 All ER 1169 at 1174, HL, per Lord Pearce; cf, however, Lord Upjohn at 474, 1177.

11 *Lynch v Thorne* [1956] 1 All ER 744, [1956] 1 WLR 303, CA. See also *Hancock v BW Brazier (Anerley) Ltd* [1966] 2 All ER 901 at 904, [1966] 1 WLR 1317 at 1333, CA, per Lord Denning MR; and see *King v Victor Parsons & Co* [1972] 2 All ER 625, [1972] 1 WLR 801; affd [1973] 1 All ER 206, [1973] 1 WLR 29, CA.

12 *Duncan v Blundell* (1820) 3 Stark 6 at 7 per Bayley J; *Bower v Chapel-en-le-Frith RDC* (1910) 75 JP 122; *GH Myers & Co v Brent Cross Service Co* [1934] 1 KB 46 at 55 per du Parcq J; *Stewart v Reavell's Garage* [1952] 2 QB 545 at 550, [1952] 1 All ER 1191 at 1193 per Sellers J. The illustration given by du Parcq J in *Myers v Brent Cross Service Co* above at 55 was disapproved in *Young and Marten Ltd v McManus Childs Ltd* [1969] 1 AC 454, [1968] 2 All ER 1169, HL, but the statement of principle was approved. In *Rotherham Metropolitan Borough Council v Frank Haslam Milan & Co Ltd* (1996) 78 BLR 1, 59 Con LR 33, CA, whether the employer had relied upon the skill and judgment of the contractor was regarded as the critical question.

13 *Cammell Laird & Co Ltd v Manganese Bronze and Brass Co Ltd* [1934] AC 402, HL. See further the Sale of Goods Act 1979 s 14(3); the Supply of Goods and Services Act 1982 s 4; and SALE OF GOODS AND SUPPLY OF SERVICES vol 91 (2012) PARAS 81 et seq, 87 et seq. See also note 1.

14 *Hancock v BW Brazier (Anerley) Ltd* [1966] 2 All ER 901 at 904, [1966] 1 WLR 1317 at 1333, CA, per Lord Denning MR; affg [1966] 2 All ER 1 at 5–6, [1966] 1 WLR 1317 at 1324 per Diplock LJ. For the statutory provisions see PARAS 275–277.

15 *Young and Marten Ltd v McManus Childs Ltd* [1969] 1 AC 454, [1968] 2 All ER 1169, HL. For the circumstances to be taken into account see *Rotherham Metropolitan Borough Council v Frank Haslam Milan & Co Ltd* (1996) 78 BLR 1, 59 Con LR 33, CA. See *MT Højgaard A/S v E.ON*

Climate & Renewables UK Robin Rigg East Ltd [2017] UKSC 59, [2017] All ER (D) 19 (Aug) (contractor liable for works which were not fit for purpose despite having met all other contractual obligations).

16 *Independent Broadcasting Authority v EMI Electronics Ltd and BICC Construction Ltd* (1980) 14 BLR 1 at 44, HL, per Lord Fraser of Tullybelton, citing *Young and Marten Ltd v McManus Childs Ltd* [1969] 1 AC 454, [1968] 2 All ER 1169, HL.

17 *Gloucestershire County Council v Richardson* [1969] 1 AC 480, [1968] 2 All ER 1181, HL.

18 See PARA 238 et seq.

19 *University of Warwick v Sir Robert McAlpine* (1988) 42 BLR 1; sed quaere whether on the facts there was not such reliance.

275. Duty to build dwellings fit for habitation.

Under the Defective Premises Act 1972[1], a person who takes on work for or in connection with the provision of a dwelling, whether the dwelling is provided by the erection or by the conversion or enlargement of a building[2], owes a duty to ensure that the work he takes on is done in a workmanlike or, as the case may be, professional manner, with proper materials and so that as regards that work the dwelling, when completed, will be fit for human habitation[3]. The duty includes both misfeasance and non-feasance[4], and is owed by all persons taking on such work, including the building owner himself[5] and those who carry out the work voluntarily[6], and by any person who in the course of a business, which includes the provision of or arranging for the provision of dwellings or installations in dwellings, arranges for such work to be carried out[7]. The duty is owed to the first owner of the dwelling and to any person who subsequently acquires a legal or equitable interest in it[8]. Any cause of action in respect of a breach of that duty is deemed for the purposes of the provisions relating to the limitation of actions[9] to have accrued at the time when the dwelling was completed unless any further work is done by the same person to rectify his earlier work, when the cause of action in respect of that further work is deemed to have accrued on its completion[10].

Where a person takes on any such work for another on terms that he is to do it in accordance with the instructions given by or on behalf of that other[11], then provided that he has done the work properly and in accordance with those instructions he will be treated as having discharged his duty under the Act, unless he owes a duty to warn of any defects in the instructions and has failed to discharge that duty[12].

This duty is additional to any duty otherwise owed[13] and cannot be excluded or restricted[14].

1 See NEGLIGENCE vol 78 (2018) PARA 41 et seq. As to the effect of the Defective Premises Act 1972 on the existing law see *D & F Estates v Church Comrs for England* [1989] AC 177 at 193 et seq, [1988] 2 All ER 992 at 996 et seq, HL, per Lord Bridge of Harwich; *Murphy v Brentwood District Council* [1991] 1 AC 398, [1990] 2 All ER 908, HL. It does not cover work taken on before 1 January 1974: see the Defective Premises Act 1972 s 7(2); *Alexander v Mercouris* [1979] 3 All ER 305, [1979] 1 WLR 1270, CA; *Rimmer v Liverpool City Council* [1985] QB 1 at 7, [1984] 1 All ER 930 at 933, CA, per Stephenson LJ.

2 The Defective Premises Act 1972 does not include repair works to an existing dwelling: *Jacobs v Morton and Partners* (1994) 72 BLR 92.

3 See the Defective Premises Act 1972 s 1(1). A claimant must prove that the defect alleged makes the dwelling unfit for habitation: *Thompson v Clive Alexander & Partners (a firm)* (1992) 59 BLR 81. The duty owed by a building contractor to see that work is done in such a manner that the dwelling is fit for habitation when complete, applies only to new building: *Jenson v Faux* [2011] EWCA Civ 423, [2011] 1 WLR 3038, [2011] All ER (D) 128 (Apr).

4 *Andrews v Schooling* [1991] 3 All ER 723, [1991] 1 WLR 783, 53 BLR 68, CA.

5 The owner of a dwelling does not 'take on work' merely by giving instructions to others for work to be done: *Mirza v Bhandal* [1999] All ER (D) 435.

6 *Alexander v Mercouris* [1979] 3 All ER 305, [1979] 1 WLR 1270, CA.

7   See the Defective Premises Act 1972 s 1(4). The use of the word 'dwellings' in the plural in s 1(4) does not exclude a one-off activity for the business in question, ie it is not necessary for the business to provide more than one dwelling. Section 1(4) will also apply to each member of a partnership when the definition is satisfied as regards the partnership itself: *Mirza v Bhandal* [1999] All ER (D) 435.

   For the purposes of the Defective Premises Act 1972 s 1, the 'dwelling' is the individual apartment as described in the lease together with, possibly, those parts of the building to which the occupiers of a particular apartment have in practice exclusive access for living, such as their balconies: *Rendlesham Estates plc v Barr Ltd* [2014] EWHC 3968 (TCC), [2015] 1 WLR 3663, [2015] BLR 37.

8   See the Defective Premises Act 1972 s 1(1). As to cases excluded from these provisions see PARA 276.

9   Ie the Limitation Act 1980: see LIMITATION PERIODS.

10 See the Defective Premises Act 1972 s 1(5); Interpretation Act 1978 s 17(2)(a).

11 A person is not to be treated as having given instructions for the doing of work merely because he has agreed to the work being done in a specified manner, with specified materials or to a specified design: Defective Premises Act 1972 s 1(3).

12 See the Defective Premises Act 1972 s 1(2).

13 See the Defective Premises Act 1972 s 6(2).

14 See the Defective Premises Act 1972 s 6(3).

276. Excluded cases.

No claim for a breach of the duty to provide dwellings fit for human habitation[1] may be brought by any person who has or who acquires an interest in a dwelling provided or sold or let for habitation under an approved scheme[2], provided that it is stated in a document of an approved type[3] that the requirements as to design or construction imposed by or under the scheme have been, or appear to have been, substantially complied with[4].

Where an interest in a dwelling is compulsorily acquired[5] no claim may be brought by the acquiring authority for breach of the duty and if any work for or in connection with the provision of the dwelling was done, otherwise than in the course of business, by the person in occupation of the dwelling at the time of the compulsory acquisition, the acquiring authority and not that person is to be treated as the person who took on the work and accordingly as owing that duty[6].

1   See PARA 275.

2   An approved scheme must be approved by the appropriate national authority (see the Defective Premises Act 1972 s 2(3)), and it must confer, by virtue of agreements entered into with persons having or acquiring an interest in the dwellings to which the scheme applies, rights on such persons in respect of defects in the state of the dwellings (s 2(2)(b)). The appropriate national authority is the Secretary of State or, where statutory functions have been transferred in relation to Wales, the Welsh Ministers: see PARA 203. The power of the appropriate national authority to approve a scheme or document is exercisable by order, but approval of requirements as to construction or design imposed under the scheme does not have to be by order (see s 2(3)). The appropriate national authority may approve a document or scheme with or without limiting the duration of his approval and it may by order revoke or vary a previous order or, if an approval has been given otherwise than by order, it may revoke or vary it without making an order: see s 2(4), (6). At the date at which this volume states the law no order has been in force since 31 March 1979 as the House Building Standards (Approved Scheme etc) Order 1973, SI 1973/1843, the House Building Standards (Approved Scheme etc) Order 1975, SI 1975/1402, and the House Building Standards (Approved Scheme etc) Order 1977, SI 1977/642, were then superseded by the House Building Standards (Approved Scheme etc) Order 1979, SI 1979/381, which did not take effect.

3   A scheme may consist of any number of documents and any number of agreements or other transactions between any number of persons: Defective Premises Act 1972 s 2(2)(a). The production of a document purporting to be a copy of an approval given by the appropriate national authority otherwise than by order (see note 2) and certified to be a true copy of the approval is conclusive evidence of that approval without proof of the handwriting or official position of the person purporting to sign the certificate: s 2(5).

4   See the Defective Premises Act 1972 s 2(1).

5   See generally COMPULSORY ACQUISITION OF LAND.
6   Defective Premises Act 1972 s 2(7).

277. Continuing duty of care on disposal of premises.

Where work of construction, repair, maintenance or demolition or any other work is done on or in relation to premises[1], the duty of care owed, because of the doing of that work, to persons who might reasonably be expected to be affected by defects in the premises created by the doing of the work is not abated by the subsequent disposal[2] of the premises by the person who owed the duty[3].

This does not apply to certain transactions[4] occurring before 1 January 1974[5].

1   The term 'premises' is not defined in the Defective Premises Act 1972; but see PARA 234.
2   'Disposal', in relation to premises, includes a letting, and an assignment or surrender of a tenancy, of the premises and the creation by contract of any other right to occupy the premises, and 'dispose' is to be construed accordingly: Defective Premises Act 1972 s 6(1). 'Tenancy' means: (1) a tenancy created either immediately or derivatively out of the freehold, whether by a lease or underlease, by an agreement for a lease or underlease or by a tenancy agreement, but not including a mortgage term or any interest arising in favour of a mortgagor by his attorning tenant to his mortgagee; or (2) a tenancy at will or on sufferance; or (3) a tenancy, whether or not constituting a tenancy at common law, created by or in pursuance of any enactment, and cognate expressions must be construed accordingly: s 6(1).
3   Defective Premises Act 1972 s 3(1). Contracting out of this provision is prohibited: s 6(3).
4   Defective Premises Act 1972 s 3(2). The transactions concerned are: (1) where the premises are let and the relevant tenancy of the premises commenced, or the relevant tenancy agreement was entered into, before 1 January 1974 (s 3(2)(a)); (2) where the premises are otherwise disposed of, when the disposal of the premises was completed, or a contract for their disposal was entered into, before that date (s 3(2)(b)); or (3) in either case, where the relevant transaction disposing of the premises is entered into in pursuance of an enforceable option by which the consideration for the disposal was fixed before that date (s 3(2)(c)).
5   Ie the date on which the Defective Premises Act 1972 came into force: s 7(2). See *Alexander v Mercouris* [1979] 3 All ER 305, [1979] 1 WLR 1270, CA.

278. Building regulation.

Unless the contract[1] expressly provides to the contrary the contractor will, as part of the obligation to complete the works, be obliged to complete them so they meet the requirements of the provisions relating to building regulation[2].

1   As to the creation and nature of building contracts see PARA 201 et seq. As to contractual terms generally see CONTRACT vol 22 (2012) PARAS 352–423.
2   As to building regulation see BUILDING vol 6 (2018) PARA 1 et seq.

(ii) Materials and Nominations

279. Nominated and designated suppliers.

Employers often wish to ensure that goods used in the works are supplied by a particular supplier. They may do so by way of a formal nomination of a supplier by a mechanism prescribed in the main contract, or they may simply specify the name of a supplier in the Contract Bills. Nomination under a standard form[1] may have the result that the contractor's obligation in relation to items supplied by the nominated supplier is limited and may be confined to taking steps required by the contract to secure timely performance by the supplier. He may be under no obligation to obtain the goods from an alternative source if the supplier should wholly fail, unless and until the employer nominates another supplier[2]. The specification of suppliers may not affect the main contractor's primary liability to supply the goods specified, although it may affect warranties in respect of the goods[3].

1 As to standard forms of contract see PARA 202.
2 *North West Metropolitan Regional Hospital Board v TA Bickerton & Sons Ltd* [1970] 1 All ER 1039, [1970] 1 WLR 607, HL; *Fairclough Building Ltd v Rhuddlan Borough Council* (1985) 30 BLR 26, CA.
3 *Gloucestershire County Council v Richardson* [1969] 1 AC 480, [1968] 2 All ER 1181, HL. See PARAS 280–281. Where the contract provides for a particular supplier or any other approved supplier, the contractor must obtain the agreement of the employer before substituting an alternative supplier: *Leedsford Ltd v Bradford City Council* (1956) 24 BLR 45, CA.

280. Warranties of fitness.

Where the employer instructs the contractor to obtain specified materials from a particular manufacturer or supplier, whether by formal nomination or by simple designation, the employer may not rely on the skill and judgment of the contractor in selecting such materials. Accordingly the implied term of the main contract as to suitability may not extend to materials supplied by a nominated supplier[1]. Where such materials are defective only by reason of being unfit for their purpose, and where the employer did not seek and rely on the main contractor's skill and judgment in respect of them, the employer will generally have no remedy in the absence of an express warranty given to him by the supplier[2]. In some cases, the supplier may be liable to the employer on a collateral contract[3]. There are forms of warranty for use in conjunction with standard form building contracts[4].

1 *Young and Marten Ltd v McManus Childs Ltd* [1969] 1 AC 454 at 468, [1968] 2 All ER 1169 at 1173, HL, per Lord Reid, at 475, 1178 per Lord Upjohn, and at 479, 1180 per Lord Wilberforce; *Rotherham Metropolitan Borough Council v Frank Haslam Milan* (1996) 78 BLR 1, 59 Con LR 33, CA. See further the Sale of Goods Act 1979 s 14(3); and SALE OF GOODS AND SUPPLY OF SERVICES vol 91 (2012) PARAS 81–82.
2 *Comyn Ching & Co Ltd v Oriental Tube Co Ltd* (1981) 17 BLR 47 at 81, CA, per Robert Goff LJ. See *Independent Broadcasting Authority v EMI Electronics Ltd and BICC Construction Ltd* (1980) 14 BLR 1, HL; and *University of Warwick v Sir Robert McAlpine* (1988) 42 BLR 1.
3 *Shanklin Pier Ltd v Detel Products Ltd* [1951] 2 KB 854, [1951] 2 All ER 471; *Wells (Merstham) Ltd v Buckland Sand and Silica Co Ltd* [1965] 2 QB 170, [1964] 1 All ER 41; cf *British Steel plc v Celtic Process Control Ltd* (1991) 28 ConLR 70; *George Fischer Holding Ltd v Multi Design Consultants Ltd* (1998) 61 Con LR 85, [1995] All ER (D) 134.
4 For an illustration see *Greater Nottingham Co-operative Society Ltd v Cementation Piling and Foundations Ltd* [1989] QB 71, [1988] 2 All ER 971, 41 BLR 43, CA. As to standard forms of contract see PARA 202.

281. Warranties of quality.

Generally the implied term of the main contract that the materials used should be of good quality will apply where materials are supplied by a nominated supplier. Where the contract provides that the contractor may reasonably object to the nomination of a sub-contractor but gives no similar right in respect of the nomination of suppliers, the implied warranty of quality may be excluded from the main contract in respect of materials supplied by a nominated supplier[1]. Where the nominated supplier contracts on terms which limit his liability for defects of quality, the implied warranty of quality may to a like extent be excluded from the main contract[2].

1 *Gloucestershire County Council v Richardson* [1969] 1 AC 480 at 496, [1968] 2 All ER 1181 at 1185, HL, per Lord Pearce, at 503, 1190 per Lord Upjohn, at 507, 1192 per Lord Wilberforce; cf per Lord Pearson, at 511, 1195.
2 *Gloucestershire County Council v Richardson* [1969] 1 AC 480 at 496, [1968] 2 All ER 1181 at 1186, HL, per Lord Pearce, at 503, 1190 per Lord Upjohn, at 507, 1192 per Lord Wilberforce; cf per Lord Pearson at 511, 1195. As to the exclusion of implied terms and conditions see the Sale

of Goods Act 1979 s 55(1); and SALE OF GOODS AND SUPPLY OF SERVICES vol 91 (2012) PARA 98. For breach of the implied warranty of quality see *Rotherham Metropolitan Borough Council v Frank Haslam Milan* (1996) 78 BLR 1, 59 Con LR 33, CA; and PARA 274.

282. Vesting of materials: fixed materials in the absence of an express term.
Once materials are fixed as part of the permanent works, the maxim *quicquid plantatur solo, solo cedit* applies and the property in fixed materials passes to the owner of the land[1]. A contractor has no lien on fixed materials and can only sue the employer for sums due under the contract[2]. A contractor has no right to materials which although once fixed are subsequently severed[3].

Once materials are so fixed that their separate identity has been subsumed into that of the new product, then no separate title to them remains[4].

1   Whatever is fixed to the soil belongs to the soil: *Elwes v Maw* (1802) 3 East 38; *Appleby v Myers* (1867) LR 2 CP 651. This doctrine applies equally to goods subject to retention of title clauses: see *Borden (UK) Ltd Scottish Timber Products Ltd* [1981] Ch 25, [1979] 3 All ER 961, CA. A contractor may, however, remove and substitute fixed materials without leave for the purpose of carrying out remedial work: see *Appleby v Myers* above at 659 per Blackburn J.
2   *Sims v London Necropolis Co* (1885) 1 TLR 584, DC. As to lien see PARA 288; and LIEN.
3   *Lyde v Russell* (1830) 1 B & Ad 394 (a case of landlord and tenant).
4   *Borden (UK) Ltd v Scottish Timber Products Ltd* [1981] Ch 25, [1979] 3 All ER 961, CA.

283. Unfixed materials and plant in the absence of an express term.
When the property in unfixed materials passes to the employer depends upon the intention of the parties, but generally it will remain in the contractor until the materials are fixed[1]. Where the materials are subject to a contract of sale, the delivery of such materials to the site will appropriate them to the contract and pass the property to the person ordering the materials[2]. The mere fact that it would be difficult to remove the materials from the site is not sufficient to show that the property in them has passed[3]. Where the contract provides that the employer shall pay for unfixed materials delivered to the site, on the certificate of an architect to the effect that they have in fact been delivered, the property in such materials may be intended to pass to the employer on the issue of the certificate or on payment[4].

Equipment and plant, although not forming part of the permanent works, may in the course of construction become temporarily fixed. Whether the property in such plant and equipment passes to the employer depends on the intention of the parties, but generally the property will remain vested in the contractor[5]. The passing of property in unfixed materials in the above circumstances is, however, defeasible if the contractor fails to fulfil his obligations and the employer consequently rescinds the contract[6]. Note whether property in fixed or unfixed materials passes to the employer, risk of damage to and/or loss of the materials may remain with the contractor who retains the responsibilty of insuring against those risks if the contract so prescribes.

1   *Tripp v Armitage* (1839) 4 M & W 687; *Appleby v Myers* (1867) LR 2 CP 651.
2   See eg *Pritchett and Gold and Electrical Power Storage Co Ltd v Currie* [1916] 2 Ch 515, CA. See generally SALE OF GOODS AND SUPPLY OF SERVICES vol 91 (2012) PARA 127.
3   *Bellamy v Davey* [1891] 3 Ch 540.
4   *Banbury and Cheltenham Direct Rly Co v Daniel* (1884) 54 LJCh 265 (distinguishing *Tripp v Armitage* (1839) 4 M & W 687); cf, however, *Beeston v Marriott* (1864) 8 LT 690; and *W Hanson (Harrow) Ltd v Rapid Civil Engineering Ltd and Usborne Developments Ltd* (1987) 11 ConLR 119, 38 BLR 106. In the latter case it was held that inclusion in an interim certificate indicated only that in the opinion of the architect an advance in respect of those goods should in fairness be made to the contractor. The question depends on the construction of the particular contract.

5   See *Wood v Hewett* (1846) 15 LJQB 247; *Lancaster v Eve* (1859) 28 LJCP 235 (not building cases); *Partington Advertising Co v Willing & Co Ltd* (1896) 12 TLR 176. If the property in such plant has passed to the employer it does so as security for the contractor's performance and it is implicit that when and if completion is achieved it revests in the contractor and can be removed: *Hart v Porthgain Harbour Co Ltd* [1903] 1 Ch 690.
6   *McDougall v Aeromarine of Emsworth Ltd* [1958] 3 All ER 431, [1958] 1 WLR 1126.

284.   Express vesting clauses.

Contracts for construction projects often provide that the property in unfixed materials and even materials not yet on site shall automatically vest in the employer on the happening of a specified event[1]. When the property is intended to pass is a question of construction; it is a question of fact whether that stage has been reached[2]. A vesting clause will not pass the property in unfixed materials unless clearly worded[3]. A vesting clause will not be affected by another clause giving the employer the right to take possession of and use unfixed materials[4]. A clause in terms that unfixed materials are 'to be considered' or 'to be deemed' the property of the employer may not bring about an absolute transfer of property[5]. A clause in terms that unfixed materials are 'to become' the property of the employer will normally transfer the property[6].

An express term that the property in the materials is to remain in the contractor until payment is ineffective once the materials have been fixed[7].

Vesting clauses do not constitute bills of sale[8].

1   The purpose of vesting clauses is to secure to the employer the due performance of the contract: see *Hart v Porthgain Harbour Co Ltd* [1903] 1 Ch 690 at 696 per Farwell J. A vesting clause should be distinguished from forfeiture clauses under which the employer may have power to determine the contract and seize and use materials.
2   *Bennett and White (Calgary) Ltd v Municipal District of Sugar City (No 5)* [1951] AC 786, PC; *Seath v Moore* (1886) 11 App Cas 350 at 370, HL, per Lord Blackburn; *Byford v Russell* [1907] 2 KB 522; *Garrett v Salisbury and Dorset Rly Co* (1866) LR 2 Eq 358.
3   *Baker v Gray* (1856) 17 CB 462 at 479 per Jervis CJ.
4   *Brown v Bateman* (1867) LR 2 CP 272 (considered in *Alstom Power Ltd v SOMI Impianti SRL* [2012] EWHC 2644 (TCC), 145 ConLR 17, [2012] All ER (D) 74 (Oct)).
5   *Re Winter, ex p Bolland* (1878) 8 ChD 225; *Re Keen and Keen, ex p Collins* [1902] 1 KB 555 (considered in *Alstom Power Ltd v SOMI Impianti SRL* [2012] EWHC 2644 (TCC), 145 ConLR 17, [2012] All ER (D) 74 (Oct)); *Bennett and White (Calgary) Ltd v Municipal District of Sugar City (No 5)* [1951] AC 786 at 813–814, PC; *Re Cosslett (Contractors) Ltd* [1998] Ch 495, [1997] 4 All ER 115, CA (applied in *Alstom Power Ltd v SOMI Impianti SRL* [2012] EWHC 2644 (TCC), 145 ConLR 17, [2012] All ER (D) 74 (Oct)); cf *Brown v Bateman* (1867) LR 2 CP 272; *Re Weibking, ex p Ward* [1902] 1 KB 713; *Hart v Porthgain Harbour Co Ltd* [1903] 1 Ch 690.
6   See *Reeves v Barlow* (1884) 12 QBD 436, CA; *Bennett and White (Calgary) Ltd v Municipal District of Sugar City (No 5)* [1951] AC 786, PC; but cf *Beeston v Marriot* (1864) 8 LT 690.
7   *Re Yorkshire Joinery Co Ltd* (1967) 111 Sol Jo 701.
8   Because a true vesting clause causes ownership to pass, not merely an equitable claim: *Brown v Bateman* (1867) LR 2 CP 272; *Reeves v Barlow* (1884) 12 QBD 436, CA. It follows that a poorly drafted vesting clause may fail to pass full ownership and may be subject to the Bills of Sale Acts. See *Great Eastern Rly Co v Lord's Trustee* [1909] AC 109, HL; and FINANCIAL INSTRUMENTS AND TRANSACTIONS vol 49 (2015) PARAS 416, 430, 434.

285.   Effects of transfer of property.

Notwithstanding the transfer of property to the employer by a vesting clause, the contractor retains the right to use unfixed materials for the construction of the works[1]. If on the completion of the works there are surplus materials or if materials are removed as not being in accordance with the contract, the property in them will revest in the contractor[2]. After the passing of property, materials cannot be taken in execution of a judgment obtained against the contractor[3]. Although the vesting clause may be insufficiently clear to pass property in the contractor's plant to the employer, a clause entitling the employer to use the plant to complete the works and then sell it to defray the additional costs incurred in completing the works does not create an equitable charge over the plant[4].

1   See *Appleby v Myers* (1867) LR 2 CP 651 at 659 per Blackburn J; *Bennett and White (Calgary) Ltd v Municipal District of Sugar City (No 5)* [1951] AC 786, PC.
2   *Hart v Porthgain Harbour Co Ltd* [1903] 1 Ch 690.
3   *Brown v Bateman* (1867) LR 2 CP 272; *Blake v Izard* (1867) 16 WR 108; *Reeves v Barlow* (1884) 12 QBD 436 at 442, CA, per Bowen LJ; cf *Byford v Russell* [1907] 2 KB 522.
4   *Re Cosslett (Contractors) Ltd* [1998] Ch 495, [1997] 4 All ER 115, CA (on the facts the power of sale was a floating charge which was void as against the liquidator for want of registration); approved in *Smith (Administrator of Cosslett (Contractors) Ltd) v Bridgend County Borough Council* [2001] UKHL 58, [2002] 1 AC 336, [2002] 1 All ER 292.

286. Effect of earlier express retention of title clauses.

Under modern conditions a contractor may himself not have acquired title to materials at the time those materials are brought to site or fixed on site, because he gained possession of them under a contract containing a *Romalpa* clause or other retention of title clause[1]. Such clauses are common in contracts for the supply of building materials.

Where title has remained in the seller in this way, the original seller may take the benefit of his retention of title clause and deprive an employer or main contractor or sub-contractor of materials already paid for[2].

A building contract usually results in the extinction of the original title to the materials as they are incorporated into the land, and no retention of title clauses as between employer and main contractor appear in any of the standard forms[3]. An express term that the property in the materials is to remain in the contractor until payment is ineffective once the materials have been fixed[4].

Where the contract containing the retention of title clause is one for sale of goods only, the Sale of Goods Act 1979 operates to protect third parties if the original seller has consented to the buyer obtaining possession and the buyer subsequently disposes of them to a third party receiving them in good faith and without notice of the seller's rights[5]. Therefore, in a building contract, an employer acting in good faith and without notice obtains good title against the original seller if the goods are transferred to him under the building contract with the original buyer[6].

Where materials are mingled in a product by manufacture and lose their separate identity, title in them is extinguished and, although the new product can in theory be subject to a charge, that charge is unlikely to be effective against a third party[7]. In a building contract the fixing of goods or the preparation of goods for fixing are likely so to extinguish the original title.

On its true construction, the retention of title clause may confer no right to the proceeds of a resale[8], and may contemplate that a valid sale might be made before the buyer has obtained title[9]. In those circumstances the seller will have no remedy against third parties who buy the goods. But where a part of the goods originally sold under the contract containing the retention of title clause remains unfixed, unsold, or otherwise available for repossession by the seller, the mere fact that the seller contemplated resale or consumption by the buyer before payment of the full price does not make the seller's retention of title clause ineffective unless and until resale or consumption takes place[10].

1   Ie a clause expressly reserving to the seller the title in goods sold and delivered, until payment, as in *Aluminium Industrie Vaassen BV v Romalpa Aluminium Ltd* [1976] 2 All ER 552, [1976] 1 WLR 676, CA. As to retention of title clauses generally see SALE OF GOODS AND SUPPLY OF SERVICES vol 91 (2012) PARA 108.

2   *Dawber Williamson Roofing Ltd v Humberside County Council* (1979) 14 BLR 70, where roofing slates were delivered by the plaintiff sub-contractors for fixing, and their value included in a certificate under the main contract. The defendant employer paid the certificate; the main contractor failed to pay the plaintiff. The employer determined the main contract by reason of the main contractor's liquidation. The plaintiff sued the employer for damages and return of the slates, relying on its retention of title clause. It was held that title in the slates which had never vested in the main contractor could not pass to the defendant employer title in the slates. See also *W Hanson (Harrow) Ltd v Rapid Civil Engineering Ltd and Usborne Developments Ltd* (1987) 38 BLR 106.

3   As to the standard forms of building contracts see PARA 202.

4   *Re Yorkshire Joinery Co Ltd* (1967) 111 Sol Jo 701; *Borden (UK) Ltd v Scottish Timber Products Ltd* [1981] Ch 25, [1979] 3 All ER 961, CA; cf *Hendy Lennox (Industrial Engines) Ltd v Grahame Puttick Ltd* [1984] 2 All ER 152, [1984] 1 WLR 485. See also the cases on *quicquid plantatur solo, solo cedit*, cited in PARA 282 note 1.

5   See the Sale of Goods Act 1979 s 25(1); and SALE OF GOODS AND SUPPLY OF SERVICES vol 91 (2012) PARA 156.

6   *Archivent v Strathclyde Regional Council* (1985) 27 BLR 98, Ct of Sess. The correct ground on which this case should be distinguished from *Dawber Williamson Roofing Ltd v Humberside County Council* (1979) 14 BLR 70 (in which no attempt was made by the defendant employer to rely on the Sale of Goods Act 1979 s 25(1)) has not been made clear by subsequent authority, although several material distinctions exist.

7   *Borden (UK) Ltd v Scottish Timber Products Ltd* [1981] Ch 25, [1979] 3 All ER 961, CA. See also the cases on *quicquid plantatur solo, solo cedit*, cited in PARA 282.

8   Eg it may make no provision for the goods to be kept separate: *Re Andrabell Ltd* [1984] 3 All ER 407. See *Sauter Automation v HC Goodman (Mechanical Services) Ltd (in liquidation)* (1986) 34 BLR 81.

9   *Clough Mill Ltd v Martin* [1984] 3 All ER 982, [1985] 1 WLR 111, CA.

10 *Clough Mill Ltd v Martin* [1984] 3 All ER 982, [1985] 1 WLR 111, CA.

287. Property in existing materials.

Where the works comprise the replacement of parts of an existing structure, the property in the old materials will not pass to the contractor in the absence of a term in the contract to that effect. If the contractor has agreed to allow in his price for the value of old materials but fails to do so, the employer is entitled to set off such value against the contract price.

Under a building lease, the lessee is entitled to the materials dug out for the purpose of laying the foundations contemplated by the agreement[1]. In the absence of express agreement, items of value such as money or antiquities found in the sub-soil are the property of the person in possession of the land[2]. If there is a reservation in respect of minerals, in general everything that can be dug out of the land for the purpose of profit will belong to the grantor subject to the terms and conditions of the reservation[3].

1   *Robinson v Milne* (1884) 53 LJCh 1070 (the lessee will not be entitled to materials resulting from overexcavation). If the builder is in possession of land as a licensee under a building agreement entitling him to a lease on completion of the works, he may not take away excavated materials save as required for building purposes: *Pedley v Cooper* (1892) 36 Sol Jo 729.

2   *South Staffordshire Water Co v Sharman* [1896] 2 QB 44; *London Corpn v Appleyard* [1963] 2 All ER 834, [1963] 1 WLR 982.

3   *Hext v Gill* (1872) 7 Ch App 699; *Waring v Foden, Waring v Booth Crushed Gravel Co Ltd* [1932] 1 Ch 276, CA; *Coleman v Ibstock Brick Ltd* [2007] All ER (D) 499 (Mar).

288. Extent of lien in building and engineering contracts.

A lien is a right to keep the property of another pending the discharge of a debt. When the right to retain such property is limited to debts outstanding from a particular transaction, it is known as a particular lien; if it is not so limited it is a general lien[1]. Liens arise by operation of law.

A lien might arise in favour of the contractor where unfixed materials are in his possession after the property in them has passed to the employer. Otherwise it seems that a true lien cannot arise in building or engineering contracts since both ownership and possession will be in one party or the other. The contractor's right, where the contract so provides, to withhold materials, the property in which has not passed, until the employer has paid for them is sometimes described as a lien[2]. Further, where the contract gives the employer rights less than ownership over unfixed materials or where the employer has advanced money on the security of unfixed materials, the employer is sometimes said to have a 'lien' over such materials even though they remain in the possession of the contractor[3]. When the property passes, the employer's contractual rights against unfixed materials will merge with his ownership[4].

1 See generally LIEN.
2 *Bellamy v Davey* [1891] 3 Ch 540; doubted in *Pritchett and Gold and Electrical Power Storage Co Ltd v Currie* [1916] 2 Ch 515, CA.
3 *Re Waugh, ex p Dickin* (1876) 4 ChD 524 (where the employer had taken possession of materials and was held entitled to detain them against the trustee of the contractor); *Banbury and Cheltenham Direct Rly Co v Daniel* (1884) 54 LJCh 265.
4 *Hawthorn v Newcastle-upon-Tyne and North Shields Rly Co* (1840) 3 QB 734n.

289. Effect of contractor's bankruptcy.

Where by the contract the employer is given a 'lien'[1] on the unfixed materials coupled with a power to seize and use them on the bankruptcy of the contractor, the employer is not protected against the contractor's trustee in bankruptcy[2]. He is protected, however, if the 'lien' on the materials has been given from the very commencement of the contract, as then the 'lien' has vested in the employer prior to the bankruptcy[3]. If it is stipulated that the 'lien' is only to arise on the happening of any other event, such as neglect to proceed with the works, and the contractor becomes bankrupt, and the event also happens, the employer can seize the materials on the happening of the event, as the deemed date of the transaction is that of the contract, so that the transaction is protected. But if an execution under a judgment against the contractor is levied on the materials before the event happens, such as a notice of failure to proceed with the works, it is no longer competent for the building owner to acquire a 'lien' by subsequently giving notice[4].

1 See PARA 288; and LIEN.
2 *Re Harrison, ex p Jay* (1880) 14 ChD 19, CA. A lien is, however, ordinarily effective against a receiver of a company: *George Barker (Transport) Ltd v Eynon* [1974] 1 All ER 900, [1974] 1 WLR 462, CA.
3 *Re Waugh, ex p Dickin* (1876) 4 ChD 524; *Re Harrison, ex p Jay* (1880) 14 ChD 19 at 26, CA, per Cotton LJ; both decided under the Bankruptcy Act 1869 (repealed).
4 *Byford v Russell* [1907] 2 KB 522.

(4) Approval, Defects and Defective Materials

(i) Approval

290. Approval.

The contract may provide that the employer's architect or other person must approve or be satisfied with the performance of the contract by the contractor. In such cases it is a matter of construction whether the contractor's obligation is to meet the requirements of the contract and also obtain the requisite approval or satisfaction or whether one or the other is paramount[1].

1   *Billyack v Leyland Construction Co Ltd* [1968] 1 All ER 783, [1968] 1 WLR 471; *National Coal Board v William Neill & Son (St Helens) Ltd* [1985] QB 300, [1984] 1 All ER 555, (1983) 26 BLR 81; *Crown Estates Comrs v John Mowlem & Co* (1994) 70 BLR 1, CA. As to certification of satisfaction see PARA 322 et seq.

291.   Implication of reasonableness.

Where the contract provides that the work is to be carried out to the satisfaction or approval of the employer himself, the courts will generally imply that such satisfaction or approval is not to be unreasonably withheld[1], but where it appears from the tenor of the agreement that one party is entitled to withhold approval or satisfaction without reasonable grounds, such an implication will be precluded[2]. Whether an employer has reasonable grounds for withholding approval will depend on the circumstances of the case. Sometimes the contract provides for work to be done to the satisfaction of the employer or the architect. It will be implied that neither could unreasonably refuse to express satisfaction[3].

1   *Dallman v King* (1837) 4 Bing NC 105, DC; *Parsons v Sexton* (1847) 4 CB 899; *Smith v Sadler* (1880) 6 VLR 5; *Docker v Hyams* [1969] 3 All ER 808, [1969] 1 WLR 1060, CA.
2   *Stadhard v Lee* (1863) 3 B & S 364, (1863) 32 LJQB 75; and see *Viscount Tredegar v Harwood* [1929] AC 72, HL (this case concerned a landlord's refusal to approve a tenant's choice of an insurance company, but the principle seems to be the same); *Minster Trust Ltd v Traps Tractors* [1954] 3 All ER 136, [1954] 1 WLR 963; cf *Renard Constructions (ME) Pty Ltd v Minister for Public Works* (1992) 26 NSWLR 234, 33 Con LR 72, NSW CA.
3   See PARAS 290, 326. See *Parsons v Sexton* (1847) 4 CB 899; *Andrews v Belfield* (1857) 2 CBNS 779. As to approval by certificate see PARA 322 et seq.

292.   Matters of taste.

Aesthetic considerations will often arise in the execution of building work. Where a contractor agrees to carry out work to the aesthetic satisfaction of the employer, there can be no implication that the employer would not unreasonably withhold his approval of the work, for in such circumstances approval is not susceptible of objective ascertainment. The employer must, however, act honestly; he cannot avoid paying the contractor by capriciously withholding approval[1].

1   *Andrews v Belfield* (1857) 2 CBNS 779; *James Shoolbred & Co v Wyndham and Albery* (1908) Times, 1 December. See also *Docker v Hyams* [1969] 3 All ER 808, [1969] 1 WLR 1060, CA, where cases concerning the provision of ships and goods to the purchaser's approval are considered.

(ii)   Defects and Defective Materials

293.   Defects.

A defect commonly means that some of the work or materials does not conform with the requirements of the contract, and thus the contractor is in breach of contract in that respect. However, not every failure to execute the works in accordance with the contract prior to completion is a breach resulting in a breach of contract[1]. A contractor may also be under an obligation to warn the building owner or his professional agent of any defect or any deficiencies in the plans or specifications which might result in a defect during the works[2], or even after completion[3]. Under some building contracts the contractor may be under an express obligation to put right defects, and failure to afford the contractor the opportunity may constitute a failure to mitigate the claimant's damage[4].

1   See *Lintest Builders v Roberts* (1978) 10 BLR 120 (affd (1980) 13 BLR 39, CA); *Surrey Heath Borough Council v Lovell Construction Ltd and Haden Young Ltd* (1988) 42 BLR 25 at 34 per Judge Fox-Andrews QC; *Guinness plc v CMD Property Developments Ltd* (1995) 76 BLR 40.
2   *Brunswick Construction Ltd v Nowlan* (1974) 49 DLR (3d) 93, (1974) 21 BLR 27; *Equitable Debenture Assets Corpn Ltd v William Moss Group Ltd* (1984) 2 Con LR 1, (1984) 1 Const LJ 131; *Victoria University of Manchester v Hugh Wilson* (1984) 2 Con LR 43, (1984) 1 Const LJ 162; *University Court of the University of Glasgow v William Whitfield and John Laing (Construction) Ltd* (1988) 42 BLR 66; *Oxford University Press v John Stedman Design Group* (1990) 34 Con LR 1; *Lindenberg v Canning* (1992) 62 BLR 147, (1992) 29 Con LR 71; *Plant Construction plc v Clive Adams Associates* [2000] BLR 137, sub nom *Plant Construction plc v Clive Adams Associates (No 2)* 69 Con LR 106, CA.
3   See *Stag Line Ltd v Tyne Shiprepair Group Ltd, The Zinnia* [1984] 2 Lloyd's Rep 211.
4   In such circumstances the employer will not be able to recover more than the amount which it should have cost the contractor himself to remedy the defects: *Pearce and High Ltd v Baxter* [1999] BLR 101, 66 Con LR 110, CA. As to the duty to mitigate damage see *Hutchinson v Harris* (1978) 10 BLR 19, CA; and DAMAGES vol 29 (2014) PARA 378 et seq.

294.   Civil liability for damage caused by defective products.

The Consumer Protection Act 1987 imposes liability for defective products on producers and suppliers. For the purposes of that Act, building and engineering contractors are suppliers of products, but in general will not be producers of products[1].

A contractor is a supplier of goods within the meaning of the Consumer Protection Act 1987 if he performs any contract for work and materials to furnish the goods[2]. So in building contracts to supply and fix items, the contractor is a supplier of those items. The Consumer Protection Act 1987 makes special provision to define the extent of supply in building contracts generally. Execution of a building contract is a supply of goods within the meaning of the Act in so far as, but only in so far as, it involves the provision of any goods by incorporation into the works[3]. Supply of goods by sale of an interest in land is specifically excluded from the Act[4]. So a builder who repairs or completes a dwelling which is then sold is a supplier of the goods incorporated during the course of his repair or completion work. A builder who builds a complete dwelling is a supplier of all the individual products incorporated in that dwelling. A developer who sells a dwelling he has not built or repaired supplies none of the products in that dwelling[5].

As a supplier the builder or developer is liable for damage caused by a defect in the product only if he fails to comply with the relevant provisions of the Consumer Protection Act 1987[6]. On the request of the person who suffered the damage to identify one or all of those primarily liable under the Act[7], he must either identify the person who supplied the product to him, or comply with a request to identify one or more of several specified persons associated with the manufacture and production of the product[8]. The request must be made within a reasonable period after the damage occurred, and at a time when it is not reasonably practicable for the person making the request to identify all of those primarily liable[9]. If the supplier fails to comply with the request or identify his supplier, he will remain liable even if the person suffering the damage subsequently discovers by other means the identity of other potential defendants, since liability is joint and several[10].

1   'Suppliers of products' are defined for the purposes of the Consumer Protection Act 1987 in s 46. Those primarily liable under Pt I (ss 1–9) as producers, or as importers into the European Union, or as persons holding themselves out as producers, are defined in ss 1(2), 2(2). The Consumer

Protection Act 1987 was passed to give effect to EC Council Directive 85/374 (OJ L210, 7.8.85, p 29) on the approximation of the laws, regulations and administrative provisions of the member states concerning liability for defective products, which may be used in the interpretation of the Consumer Protection Act 1987 and is appended to it: see s 1(1), (2). See further CONSUMER PROTECTION vol 21 (2016) PARA 412 et seq.

2   See the Consumer Protection Act 1987 s 46(1)(c); and CONSUMER PROTECTION vol 21 (2016) PARA 417.
3   See the Consumer Protection Act 1987 s 46(3); and CONSUMER PROTECTION vol 21 (2016) PARA 417.
4   See the Consumer Protection Act 1987 s 46(4); and CONSUMER PROTECTION vol 21 (2016) PARA 417.
5   See the Consumer Protection Act 1987 s 1(3); and CONSUMER PROTECTION vol 21 (2016) PARA 415.
6   Ie complies with the Consumer Protection Act 1987 s 2(3): see CONSUMER PROTECTION vol 21 (2016) PARA 415.
7   Ie under the Consumer Protection Act 1987 s 2(1), (2): see CONSUMER PROTECTION vol 21 (2016) PARA 415.
8   See the Consumer Protection Act 1987 ss 1(2), 2(3); and CONSUMER PROTECTION vol 21 (2016) PARA 415.
9   See the Consumer Protection Act 1987 s 2(3)(b); and CONSUMER PROTECTION vol 21 (2016) PARA 415.
10 See the Consumer Protection Act 1987 s 2(3)(c), (5); and CONSUMER PROTECTION vol 21 (2016) PARA 415.

295. Nature and extent of product liability.

Product liability is strict in that fault on the part of the defendant is not a necessary element of liability, and the claimant has only to prove supply or production of the product by the defendant, a defect, actionable damage, and causation. However, the Consumer Protection Act 1987 provides six specific defences to liability[1].

A defect exists in a product for the purposes of product liability if the safety of the product is not such as persons are entitled to expect. 'Safety' for these purposes includes safety with respect to property and with respect to other products comprised in that product[2]. All circumstances must be taken into account in judging what degree of safety persons generally are entitled to expect, but certain relevant considerations are explicitly set out in the Consumer Protection Act 1987[3]. In particular, what might reasonably be expected to be done with or in relation to the product must be considered[4].

The types of damage for which proceedings may be brought under the Consumer Protection Act 1987 include personal injury, death, and damage to personal property to the value of more than £275[5]. There is no liability under the Act for damage to property not ordinarily intended for private use, occupation, or consumption, or for damage to property not so used, occupied, or consumed by the person suffering damage[6]. There is no liability under the Act for damage to the defective product itself[7]. Liability for damage recoverable under the Act cannot be excluded by any notice or contract term[8].

The statutory provisions relating to contributory negligence are specifically applied to product liability under the Consumer Protection Act 1987[9]. Specific provision has been made as to the applicable limitation period for a claim for damages in relation to product liability under that Act[10].

1   See the Consumer Protection Act 1987 s 4; and CONSUMER PROTECTION vol 21 (2016) PARA 418. The defences are:
    (1)   that the defect is attributable to compliance with any requirement imposed by or under any enactment or with any EU obligation (s 4(1)(a) (amended by SI 2011/1043);

(2)   that the person proceeded against did not at any time supply the product to another (Consumer Protection Act 1987 s 4(1)(b));

(3)   that the only supply by the defendant was not in the course of the defendant's business and the defendant is not a producer or importer (see s 4(1)(c));

(4)   that the defect did not exist in the product at the time the producer or importer last supplied it (ss 4(1)(d), (2), 2(2));

(5)   that at the time the producer or importer last supplied it the state of scientific knowledge was not such that the producer or importer might reasonably have been expected to discover the defect (see s 4(1)(e), (2));

(6)   that the defect was wholly attributable to the design of a subsequent product in which the product was comprised, or to directions to the producer of the product by the producer of the subsequent product in which the product was comprised (see s 4(1)(f)).

Contributory negligence may also afford a partial or complete defence: see s 6(4). See further CONSUMER PROTECTION vol 21 (2016) PARA 415.

2   See the Consumer Protection Act 1987 s 3(1); and CONSUMER PROTECTION vol 21 (2016) PARA 416.

3   See the Consumer Protection Act 1987 s 3(2). Particular considerations are set out in s 3(2)(a)–(c): see CONSUMER PROTECTION vol 21 (2016) PARA 416.

4   See the Consumer Protection Act 1987 s 3(2)(b); and CONSUMER PROTECTION vol 21 (2016) PARA 416.

5   See the Consumer Protection Act 1987 s 5(1), (4); and CONSUMER PROTECTION vol 21 (2016) PARA 419.

6   See the Consumer Protection Act 1987 s 5(3); and CONSUMER PROTECTION vol 21 (2016) PARA 419.

7   See the Consumer Protection Act 1987 ss 5(2), 6; and CONSUMER PROTECTION vol 21 (2016) PARAS 415, 419.

8   See the Consumer Protection Act 1987 s 7; and CONSUMER PROTECTION vol 21 (2016) PARA 420.

9   See the Consumer Protection Act 1987 s 6(4); and CONSUMER PROTECTION vol 21 (2016) PARA 415.

10   See the Limitation Act 1980 s 11A ; the Consumer Protection Act 1987 s 6(6), Sch 1 ; and CONSUMER PROTECTION vol 21 (2016) PARA 415.

296.   Criminal liability for defective consumer goods and unsuitable new construction products.

Provisions imposing criminal liability[1] for unsafe goods affect building and engineering contractors engaged on works which will be used for private use and enjoyment. The general principle that no producer may place a product on the market unless the product is a safe product applies to products used in the construction industry[2]. A distributor[3] must act with due care in order to help ensure compliance with the applicable safety requirements and in particular he:

(1)   must not expose or possess for supply or offer or agree to supply, or supply, a product to any person which he knows or should have presumed, on the basis of the information in his possession and as a professional, is a dangerous product[4]; and

(2)   must, within the limits of his activities, participate in monitoring the safety of a product placed on the market, in particular by: (a) passing on information on the risks posed by the product; (b) keeping the documentation necessary for tracing the origin of the product; (c) producing the documentation necessary for tracing the origin of the product, and cooperating in action taken by a producer or an enforcement authority to avoid the risks[5].

It is an offence to contravene these provisions[6], but it is a defence for that person to show that he took all reasonable steps and exercised all due diligence to avoid committing the offence[7].

Provision is also made in relation to the implementation of European legislation[8] which lays down harmonised conditions for the marketing of construction products, including prescribing criminal penalties for the supply of new construction products without the necessary characteristics and creating powers of enforcement[9].

1 See the General Product Safety Regulations 2005, SI 2005/1803, reg 20; and CONSUMER PROTECTION vol 21 (2016) PARA 603 et seq.
2 See the General Product Safety Regulations 2005, SI 2005/1803, reg 5(1); and CONSUMER PROTECTION vol 21 (2016) PARA 603. 'Producer' means:
    (1)   the manufacturer of a product, when he is established in a member state and any other person presenting himself as the manufacturer by affixing to the product his name, trade mark or other distinctive mark, or the person who reconditions the product;
    (2)   when the manufacturer is not established in a member state (a) if he has a representative established in a member state, the representative; (b) in any other case, the importer of the product from a state that is not a member state into a member state;
    (3)   other professionals in the supply chain, in so far as their activities may affect the safety properties of a product: reg 2.
    'Safe product' means a product which, under normal or reasonably foreseeable conditions of use including duration and, where applicable, putting into service, installation and maintenance requirements, does not present any risk or only the minimum risks compatible with the product's use, considered to be acceptable and consistent with a high level of protection for the safety and health of persons: reg 2. See further CONSUMER PROTECTION vol 21 (2016) PARA 603.
3 'Distributor' means a professional in the supply chain whose activity does not affect the safety properties of a product: General Product Safety Regulations 2005, SI 2005/1803, reg 2.
4 See the General Product Safety Regulations 2005, SI 2005/1803, reg 8(1)(a); and CONSUMER PROTECTION vol 21 (2016) PARA 609.
5 See the General Product Safety Regulations 2005, SI 2005/1803, reg 8(1)(b), (2); and CONSUMER PROTECTION vol 21 (2016) PARA 609.
6 See the General Product Safety Regulations 2005, SI 2005/1803, reg 20.
7 See the General Product Safety Regulations 2005, SI 2005/1803, reg 29; and CONSUMER PROTECTION vol 21 (2016) PARA 603.
8 Ie European Parliament and Council Regulation (EU) 305/2011 (OJ L88, 4.4.2011, p 5).
9 See the Construction Products Regulations 2013, SI 2013/1387; and CONSUMER PROTECTION vol 21 (2016) PARA 482.

(5) Obligations of the Employer

297. Duties towards contractor.

An employer under a building contract will normally be subject to the usual implied obligations as to co-operation[1]. Thus, if instructions, drawings, etc are to be supplied, the employer must provide them within a reasonable time[2]. What is a reasonable time will depend on the circumstances. If drawings and plans are not supplied, then the contractor should apply for them[3]. The fact that the contractor has applied to the employer for the issue of plans and drawings is material to the question whether the drawings were supplied at a reasonable time[4]. Where the employer fails to provide drawings, the contractor is entitled to damages and, if appropriate, an extension of time for the completion of the works[5].

1 *Mackay v Dick* (1881) 6 App Cas 251, HL; *Merton London Borough Council v Stanley Hugh Leach Ltd* (1985) 32 BLR 51.
2 *Neodox v Swinton and Pendlebury Borough Council* (1958) 5 BLR 34; *SJ and MM Price Ltd v Milner* (1968) 206 Estates Gazette 313; *Holland Hannen and Cubitts (Northern) Ltd v Welsh Health Technical Services Organisation* (1981) 18 BLR 80. See also *Royal Brompton Hospital National Health Trust v Hammond* [2000] BLR 75 (engineers had duty to provide co-ordination drawings to contractor so as to ensure employer complied with its duty to provide corresponding information).

3 *Stevens v Taylor* (1860) 2 F & F 419.
4 *Neodox v Swinton and Pendlebury Borough Council* (1958) 5 BLR 34. Although, within limits, it is for the contractor to decide when working drawings and details are required: *Wells v Army & Navy Co-operative Society* (1902) 86 LT 764 (the contractor cannot unilaterally determine what is a reasonable time; his stated requirements are a material factor but not determinative). See also *Glenlion Construction Ltd v Guinness Trust* (1987) 39 BLR 89 (no implied term that the employer should enable the contractor to finish earlier than the contractual completion date).
5 *Re Trollope & Sons and Colls Ltd and Singer* (1913) 1 Hudson's BC (4th Edn) 849. In the absence of an extension of time clause, delay in giving working drawings will invalidate the date for completion and any right to liquidated damages for delay. As to extension of time and liquidated damages see PARA 267 et seq.

298. Appointment of architect or engineer.

Where the contract provides that work is to be done under the superintendence of the employer's architect or engineer, and no architect or engineer is named in the contract, the appointment of an architect or engineer is a condition precedent to the contractor's obligation to carry out the work[1].

If the original architect dies or becomes incapable the employer is under a duty to the contractor to appoint another, presumably within a reasonable time. It is normally also an implied term of the contract that the architect will discharge the functions for which he has been appointed[2], and if he does not do so another must be appointed[3]. The absence of a person to perform the functions of the architect affords the employer no defence to a claim for an amount which the architect ought to have certified[4].

In many contracts for large works, the employer may also be entitled to appoint a clerk of works[5] or other supervisor; but unless the contract gives the clerk of works powers and duties in relation to the contractor, it is submitted that the failure of the employer to appoint a clerk of works is immaterial.

1 *Coombe v Greene* (1843) 11 M & W 480; *Hunt v Bishop* (1853) 8 Exch 675. Some contracts provide that if the architect should cease to act, the employer should appoint another. In such a case, the failure of the employer to appoint a second architect within a reasonable time would be a breach entitling the contractor to refuse further performance. As to the employment of architects and engineers see PARA 446 et seq.
2 *Frederick Leyland & Co Ltd v Compania Panamena Europea Navigacion Limitada* (1943) 76 Ll L Rep 113, CA (affd sub nom *Panamena Europea Navigacion (Compania Limitada) v Frederick Leyland & Co Ltd (J Russell & Co)* [1947] AC 428, HL); *Perini Corpn v Commonwealth of Australia* (1969) 12 BLR 82, [1969] 2 NSWLR 530, NSW SC. Such a term may not be implied if the contract contains a relevant arbitration clause: *Lubenham Fidelities and Investments Co Ltd v South Pembrokeshire District Council* (1986) 33 BLR 39, (1986) Con LR 85, CA.
3 *Merton London Borough Council v Stanley Hugh Leach Ltd* (1985) 32 BLR 51; *Kellett v Stockport Corpn* (1906) 70 JP 154.
4 *Croudace v Lambeth London Borough Council* (1986) 33 BLR 20, CA.
5 As to the clerk of works see PARA 207.

299. Duty to provide the site.

The employer must give the contractor possession of the site on the agreed date or, if no date is specified, within a reasonable time[1]. The provision of the site is a condition precedent to the contractor's obligation to carry out the work[2]. If, however, the contractor starts work at a later date than that agreed, because of delay on the part of the employer, he is deemed to have waived his right to treat the occupation of the site as a condition precedent or to have affirmed the contract; he is then confined to a remedy in damages[3]. Where delay in giving possession of the site is caused by the wrongful interference of a third party with the access to the site, the contractor may have no remedy against the employer[4].

Generally the contractor's right to the possession of the site amounts to a licence and not to an interest in land[5]. During the progress of the work, such licence may be irrevocable[6]. An interim injunction will not necessarily be granted to expel the contractor from the site where the employer seeks to revoke the licence and there is a bona fide dispute as to whether the employer is entitled under the contract to expel the contractor[7].

The employer gives no implied undertaking that the site is suitable for the execution of the works[8]. Nor does the employer warrant that the site complies with health and safety requirements[9].

1   *Freeman & Son v Hensler* (1900) 64 JP 260, CA; *R v Walter Cabott Construction Ltd* (1975) 69 DLR (3d) 542, (1975) 21 BLR 42, Can CA.
2   *Arterial Drainage Co v Rathangan River Drainage Board* (1880) 6 LR Ir 513.
3   *Roberts v Bury Improvement Comr* (1870) LR 5 CP 310, ExCh. See generally DAMAGES.
4   *Porter v Tottenham UDC* [1915] 1 KB 776, CA; *LRE Engineering Services Ltd v Otto Simon Carves Ltd* (1981) 24 BLR 127; but see *Rapid Building Group Ltd v Ealing Family Housing Association Ltd* (1984) 29 BLR 5, CA (employer in breach of JCT contract where two people and a dog were squatting in a car on the site).
5   See also PARA 317.
6   *Hounslow London Borough Council v Twickenham Garden Developments Ltd* [1971] Ch 233, [1970] 3 All ER 326; cf *Porter v Hannah Building Pty Ltd* [1969] VR 673, Vic SC; and *Surrey Heath Borough Council v Lovell Construction Ltd* (1988) 42 BLR 25 at 51. As to the revocation of a contractor's licence to occupy the site see PARA 317.
7   *Hounslow London Borough Council v Twickenham Garden Developments Ltd* [1971] Ch 233, [1970] 3 All ER 326. However, the result of this decision would now be inconsistent with a proper application of the principles in *American Cyanamid Co v Ethicion Ltd* [1975] AC 396, [1975] 1 All ER 504, HL. It has also been criticised: see eg (1971) 87 LQR 309; *Mayfield Holdings Ltd v Moana Reef Ltd* [1973] 1 NZLR 309; *Graham H Roberts Pty Ltd v Maurbeth Investments Pty Ltd* [1974] 1 NSWLR 93, NSW SC. See also *Surrey Heath Borough Council v Lovell Construction Ltd* (1988) 42 BLR 25; *A-G of Hong Kong v Ko Hon Mau* (1988) 44 BLR 144, HK CA; *Tara Civil Engineering v Moorfield Developments Ltd* (1989) 46 BLR 72.
8   *Appleby v Myers* (1867) LR 2 CP 651; *Bottoms v York Corpn* (1892) 2 Hudson's BC (10th Edn) 270, CA.
9   *Allridge (Builders) Ltd v Grand Actual Ltd* (1996) 55 Con LR 91 at 122 per Mr Recorder David Blunt QC.

300.   Duty to carry out work and supply materials at the right time.

Part of a proposed building may be excluded from the contract and the employer may choose to carry out that work himself or by other contractors, or it may be a term of the contract that the employer should supply the contractor with materials. In such circumstances it will, in general, be an implied term of the contract that neither the employer nor his direct contractors or suppliers will hinder the contractor in the performance of the contract nor prevent its completion[1]. However, where, with the consent of the contractor, an employer arranged for the supply of materials which the contractor was bound to supply and it was agreed that the price of the materials would be deducted from the contract price, the employer was held not liable when the materials were delivered late[2].

1   *MacIntosh v Midland Counties Rly Co* (1845) 14 M & W 548; *Yates v Law* (1866) 25 UCR 562, Ont CA; *Lawson v Wallasey Local Board* (1882) 11 QBD 229, DC; affd (1883) 48 LT 507, CA. The implied term might, it is submitted, be excluded where the contract provides that the contractor should co-ordinate his work with that of other contractors. In circumstances where the materials supplier has no direct contract with the contractor, interference by the employer in the supply of goods necessary for the contract will be a breach of the implied term: *Acrow (Automation) Ltd v Rex Chainbelt Inc* [1971] 3 All ER 1175 at 1178–1179, [1971] 1 WLR 1676 at 1680, CA, per Lord Denning MR.

As to the duty to complete see PARA 260. As to the employer's power to vary the contract by omitting part of the works see PARA 272.

2 WH *Gaze & Sons Ltd v Port Talbot Corpn* (1929) 93 JP 89. See also *Simplex Concrete Piles Ltd v St Pancras Borough Council* (1958) 14 BLR 80.

(6) Building and Environmental Controls

(i) Building Control

301. Planning permission and the building regulations.

Where the work which is to be carried out under a building contract involves development within the meaning of the Town and Country Planning Act 1990[1], it is unlawful to begin the work without first obtaining planning permission[2]. Second, it is necessary to submit the plans and drawings to the local authority so that the authority can approve them as complying with the provisions relating to building regulation[3]. If work is carried out without such permission, the relevant authority may require the work to be taken down[4]. It is usual for building contracts expressly to provide that the contractor should comply with such statutory obligations, but even without such a term a court might find the contractor, who does not satisfy himself that the requirements of any statute affecting the work have been complied with, to be in breach of an implied term that the work is to be carried out in a good and workmanlike manner[5].

1 'Development' is defined as involving the carrying out of building, engineering, mining or other operations in, on, over or under land or the making of any material change in the use of any buildings or other land: see the Town and Country Planning Act 1990 s 55(1); and PLANNING vol 81 (2018) PARA 333. The demolition of houses does not constitute development within the meaning of s 55(1): *Cambridge City Council v Secretary of State for the Environment* (1992) 90 LGR 275, [1992] 1 EGLR 201, CA. In some cases no application need be made: see generally PLANNING vol 81 (2018) PARA 355.
2 See the Town and Country Planning Act 1990 s 57(1). An offence is committed at a later stage when an enforcement notice or stop notice is not complied with: see PLANNING vol 82 (2018)PARAS 875, 885.
3 As to building regulation see BUILDING vol 6 (2018) PARA 1 et seq. The Building Act 1984 s 38 creates civil liability for breach of building regulations in that, subject to the provisions of s 38, breach by a builder of a duty imposed by the building regulations is, so far as it causes damage, actionable unless the regulations provide otherwise: see BUILDING vol 6 (2018) PARA 64.
4 See the Town and Country Planning Act 1990 s 172; and PLANNING vol 82 (2018) PARA 868 et seq. Work may also be subject to a stop notice: see s 183; and PLANNING vol 82 (2018) PARA 880 et seq.
5 See PARA 274. Carrying out work in breach of the building regulations may also amount to an offence: see the Building Act 1984 s 35; and BUILDING vol 6 (2018) PARA 61.

302. Where consent or approval is not given.

The planning authority may refuse permission for the execution of the work described in the contract. Whether in that event the employer is in breach of contract and liable to the contractor in damages depends on the construction of the contract[1]. If the employer has expressly or impliedly undertaken to obtain the permission and that undertaking is absolute, the employer is liable if permission is not obtained[2]. In most cases, however, the contract will be conditional on permission being granted and if it is not forthcoming, both parties will be discharged[3].

Where plans are not approved for the purposes of the provisions relating to building regulation[4] the position may be different where the employer has power to vary the work described in the contract[5]. It will usually be possible to obtain approval by exercising that power and altering the work.

1 *Smith v Harwich Corpn* (1857) 2 CBNS 651; *Re Northumberland Avenue Hotel Co, Fox and Braithwaite's Claim* (1887) 56 LT 883, CA; *Bywaters & Sons v Curnick & Co* (1906) 2 Hudson's BC (4th Edn) 393, CA; *Ellis-Don Ltd v Parking Authority of Toronto* (1978) 28 BLR 98, Ont SC.

2 Cf *Brauer & Co (Great Britain) Ltd v James Clark (Brush Materials) Ltd* [1952] 2 All ER 497, [1952] 2 Lloyd's Rep 147, CA (which relates to export licences). Cf *Agroexport State Enterprise for Foreign Trade v Cie Européene de Céréales* [1974] 1 Lloyd's Rep 499; *Pagnan SpA v Tradax Ocean Transportation SA* [1987] 3 All ER 565, [1987] 2 Lloyd's Rep 342, CA.

3 Cf *Lehmann v McArthur* (1868) 3 Ch App 496, where a contract to assign a lease was discharged on the failure of the lessee, after taking reasonable steps, to obtain the landlord's consent; but see *Day v Singleton* [1899] 2 Ch 320, CA.

4 As to building regulation see BUILDING vol 6 (2018) PARA 1 et seq.

5 For the power to vary the contract see PARA 272.

(ii) Environmental Control

303. Nuisance.

A claim for private nuisance is only maintainable by a person having an interest in the land affected by the alleged nuisance[1]. In relation to building and engineering work, nuisance consists of acts or omissions generally connected with the use or occupation of land which causes damage to another person in connection with that other person's use of land or interference with the enjoyment of land or of some other rights connected with the land. It also consists of acts or omissions which have been designated or treated by statute as nuisances. Building operations may give rise to liability in nuisance in many ways. Particular examples are: noise from building works and vibration from, for example, pile driving, the creation of dust and constant heavy traffic to and from the site[2].

The demolition of a building resulting in exposure of a neighbouring building to the elements is not a nuisance[3] unless the building is subject to an entitlement to support or maintenance[4]. Equally, the lowering of the water table by dewatering is not a nuisance[5]. However, a landowner may be liable in nuisance if, by mere omission, his neighbour's rights of support are adversely affected[6].

The ordinary use of residential premises could not constitute a nuisance unless the use was unusual or unreasonable having regard to the purpose for which the premises were constructed[7].

1 *Hunter v Canary Wharf Ltd* [1997] AC 655, [1997] 2 All ER 426, HL (applied in *Raymond v Young* [2015] EWCA Civ 456, [2015] HLR 805, [2015] All ER (D) 160 (May)). In relation to claims for private nuisance in connection with building works, 'actionability at common law depends on showing that the building works were conducted without reasonable consideration for the neighbours': *Wildtree Hotels Ltd v Harrow London Borough Council* [2001] 2 AC 1 at 13, [2000] 3 All ER 289 at 300, HL, per Lord Hoffmann. As to nuisance generally see NUISANCE.

2 See further NUISANCE vol 78 (2018) PARA 124; and *Harrison v Southwark & Vauxhall Water Co* [1891] 2 Ch 409; *Andreae v Selfridge & Co Ltd* [1938] Ch 1, CA; *Ellison v Ministry of Defence* (1996) 81 BLR 101; *Hiscox Syndicates Ltd v The Pinnacle Ltd* [2008] EWHC 145 (Ch), [2008] All ER (D) 193 (Jan); *Northumbrian Water Ltd v Sir Robert McAlpine Ltd* [2014] EWCA Civ 685, 154 ConLR 26, [2014] All ER (D) 157 (May).

3 *Phipps v Pears* [1965] 1 QB 76, [1964] 2 All ER 35, CA.

4 *Marchant v Capital and Counties Property Co Ltd* [1983] 2 EGLR 156, 267 Estates Gazette 843, CA; *Bradburn v Lindsay* [1983] 2 All ER 408.

5 *Langbrook Properties Ltd v Surrey County Council* [1969] 3 All ER 1424, [1970] 1 WLR 161; *Chetwynd v Tunmore* [2016] EWHC 156 (QB), [2017] QB 188, [2016] 3 WLR 1159. For further examples of activities which have or have not been held to be nuisances, and for defences see NUISANCE vol 78 (2018) PARAS 101 et seq, 192 et seq.

6   *Holbeck Hall Hotel Ltd v Scarborough Borough Council* [2000] QB 836, [2000] 2 All ER 705, [2000] BLR 109, CA.
7   *Baxter v Camden London Borough Council (No 2)* [2001] QB 1 at 12, sub nom *Baxter v Camden London Borough Council* [1999] 1 All ER 237 at 244, CA, per Tuckey LJ; affd sub nom *Southwark London Borough Council v Tanner* [2001] 1 AC 1, sub nom *Southwark London Borough Council v Mills* [1999] 4 All ER 449, HL.

304. Noise.

A local authority exercises special control over noise in respect of: (1) the erection, construction, alteration, repair or maintenance of buildings, structures or roads; (2) breaking up, opening or boring under any road or adjacent land in connection with the construction, inspection, maintenance or removal of works; (3) demolition and dredging works; and (4) whether or not also comprised in heads (1) to (3) above, any work of engineering construction[1]. In such situations the authority may serve a notice imposing requirements as to the way the works are to be carried out[2].

The fact that such a notice has been served prescribing the hours during which noisy work can be done does not affect the common law rights of neighbouring owners who may, in appropriate cases, obtain interim injunctions restraining work in more restrictive terms than those contained in the notice[3]. If a person contravenes any requirement of such a notice, he is guilty of an offence[4] and may be made the subject of an injunction if criminal proceedings are wholly inadequate[5]. Statutory nuisances, occurring on a construction site, including nuisances caused by noise, dust and effluence, can be made the subject of a complaint to a magistrates' court by a local authority[6] or by persons aggrieved[7] by the nuisance[8].

1   Control of Pollution Act 1974 s 60(1); and see ENVIRONMENTAL QUALITY AND PUBLIC HEALTH vol 46 (2010) PARA 835. See also the Environmental Protection Act 1990; and ENVIRONMENTAL QUALITY AND PUBLIC HEALTH; NUISANCE; PLANNING.
2   See the Control of Pollution Act 1974 s 60(2); and ENVIRONMENTAL QUALITY AND PUBLIC HEALTH vol 46 (2010) PARA 835. The notice must be served on the person carrying out the work, it is not sufficient that the notice came to the attention of that person: *AMEC Building Ltd v Camden London Borough Council* (1996) 55 Con LR 82. As to the content of these notices, appeals against these notices, prior consent to provisions relating to the control of noise and appeals as to prior consent see ENVIRONMENTAL QUALITY AND PUBLIC HEALTH vol 46 (2010) PARA 825 et seq.
3   *Lloyds Bank plc v Guardian Assurance plc and Trollope and Colls Ltd* (1986) 35 BLR 34, CA; *City of London Corpn v Bovis Construction Ltd* [1992] 3 All ER 697, (1988) 49 BLR 1, CA.
4   See the Control of Pollution Act 1974 s 60(8); and ENVIRONMENTAL QUALITY AND PUBLIC HEALTH vol 46 (2010) PARA 835. As to the penalties see ENVIRONMENTAL QUALITY AND PUBLIC HEALTH vol 46 (2010) PARA 822. A notice only applies to works being carried out or to be carried out at the date of the notice. A fresh notice is required for works on the same site under a separate, later contract: *Walter Lilly & Co Ltd v Westminster City Council* (1994) CILL 937, DC.
5   *City of London Corpn v Bovis Construction Ltd* [1992] 3 All ER 697, (1988) 49 BLR 1, CA.
6   See the Environmental Protection Act 1990 s 80; and ENVIRONMENTAL QUALITY AND PUBLIC HEALTH vol 46 (2010) PARA 822.
7   As to persons aggrieved see JUDICIAL REVIEW vol 61 (2010) PARA 656.
8   See the Environmental Protection Act 1990 s 82; and NUISANCE vol 78 (2018) PARA 210 et seq.

305. Trespass.

An unlawful entry by one person on land in the possession of another is a trespass for which a claim may be brought[1]. On building sites, tower cranes are frequently used and the oversailing of the jib over neighbouring property is a trespass since the ownership of land includes ownership of the air up to the sky[2].

Thus, an adjoining owner can compel a contractor to desist from oversailing his air space and the contractor cannot resist an injunction by reliance upon the balance of convenience[3]. Any licence granted to allow oversailing will be personal to the adjoining owner and will not bind subsequent purchasers unless it is granted in the form of an easement and is registered[4]. The working of minerals below the surface of another's land amounts to a trespass[5]. Damages together with or in lieu of an injunction may be awarded against the trespasser, even without proof of damage[6].

1 See TORT vol 97 (2015) PARA 563 et seq.
2 *Kenyon v Hart* (1865) 6 B & S 249; *Wandsworth Board of Works v United Telephone Co* (1884) 13 QBD 904, CA; *Gifford v Dent* [1926] WN 336; *Kelsen v Imperial Tobacco Co (of Great Britain and Ireland) Ltd* [1957] 2 QB 334, [1957] 2All ER 343. See also *Baron Bernstein of Leigh v Skyviews and General Ltd* [1978] QB 479, [1977] 2 All ER 902. As to the maxim *cujus est solum, ejus est usque ad coelum et ad inferos* see BOUNDARIES vol 4 (2011) PARA 302.
3 *Graham v KD Morris and Sons Property Ltd* [1974] Qd R 1, Qld SC; *Anchor Brewhouse Development Ltd v Berkley House Docklands Developments Ltd* (1987) 38 BLR 82; *London and Manchester Assurance Co Ltd v O and H Construction Ltd* [1989] 2 EGLR 185. See, however, *Woollerton and Wilson Ltd v Richard Costain Ltd* [1970] 1 All ER 483, [1970] 1 WLR 411 (disapproved in *Jaggard v Sawyer* [1995] 2 All ER 189, [1995] 1 WLR 269), where the injunction was granted but suspended for a period that allowed the defendant a reasonable period of time to complete the work requiring the use of the tower crane. Absent special circumstances, it is doubtful whether such suspension is correct: see *Anchor Brewhouse Developments Ltd v Berkley House (Docklands Developments) Ltd* (1987) 38 BLR 82.
4 See REAL PROPERTY AND REGISTRATION vol 87 (2017) PARA 731 et seq.
5 *Smith v Lloyd* (1854) 9 Exch 562 at 574 per Parke B.
6 *Patel v WH Smith (Eziot) Ltd* [1987] 2 All ER 569, [1987] 1 WLR 853, CA. See generally DAMAGES; TORT vol 97 (2015) PARAS 591–592.

306. Other heads of liability.

The carrying out of works of construction may involve the employer in liability to adjoining landowners, in nuisance[1] or under the rule in *Rylands v Fletcher*[2]. A local authority is empowered by statute to serve a notice[3] specifying the way in which building works are to be carried out, so as to minimise inconvenience to those in the locality. An occupier is absolutely liable for the maintenance of any part of a building which projects over the highway[4]; and if in the course of carrying out building operations in or near a street an accident occurs which gives rise to the risk of serious bodily injury[5] to a passer-by, the owner of the land or building on which the building operation is being carried out may be guilty of an offence and liable on summary conviction to a fine[6]. Except possibly in some cases of nuisance[7], it is not a defence to these causes of action that the damage was caused by an independent contractor unless the negligence of the independent contractor was collateral to the purpose for which he was employed[8]. The performance of a statutory duty cannot be delegated by the employer to the contractor[9].

1 See eg *Andreae v Selfridge & Co Ltd* [1938] Ch 1, [1937] 3 All ER 255, CA; *Spicer v Smee* [1946] 1 All ER 489; *Brybrook Barn Centre Ltd v Kent County Council* [2001] BLR 55, CA; *Northumbrian Water Ltd v Sir Robert McAlpine Ltd* [2014] EWCA Civ 685, 154 ConLR 26, [2014] All ER (D) 157 (May); PARAS 303–304; and NUISANCE vol 78 (2018) PARAS 124 et seq, 164 et seq
2 See eg *Hoare & Co v McAlpine* [1923] 1 Ch 167; *Rylands v Fletcher* (1868) LR 3 HL 330. As to the rule in *Rylands v Fletcher* see NUISANCE vol 78 (2018) PARA 148.
3 See the Control of Pollution Act 1974 s 60; and ENVIRONMENTAL QUALITY AND PUBLIC HEALTH vol 46 (2010) PARA 835. See, in relation to noise, PARA 304. As to penalties in relation to contravention of such a notice see generally ENVIRONMENTAL QUALITY AND PUBLIC HEALTH vol 46 (2010) PARA 822.

4   *Tarry v Ashton* (1876) 1 QBD 314; and see NEGLIGENCE vol 78 (2018) PARA 61.
5   Or would have given rise to such a risk but for the fact that the highway authority or local authority took steps to ensure that if an accident occurred it would not give rise to the risk of serious bodily injury: see the Highways Act 1980 s 168(1)(b); and HIGHWAYS, STREETS AND BRIDGES vol 55 (2012) PARA 375.
6   See the Highways Act 1980 s 168(1); and HIGHWAYS, STREETS AND BRIDGES vol 55 (2012) PARA 375. Additional sanctions may be imposed under the Regulatory Enforcement and Sanctions Act 2008 Pt 3 (ss 36–71): see s 37(2), Sch 6. See further CONSTITUTIONAL AND ADMINISTRATIVE LAW vol 20 (2014) PARA 331 et seq. As to defences see the Highways Act 1980 s 168(3); and HIGHWAYS, STREETS AND BRIDGES vol 55 (2012) PARA 375.
7   *Bower v Peate* (1876) 1 QBD 321 at 326–327 per Cockburn CJ.
8   *Padbury v Holliday and Greenwood Ltd* (1912) 28 TLR 494, CA. Cf *Holliday v National Telephone Co* [1899] 2 QB 392, CA.
9   *Gray v Pullen* (1864) 5 B & S 970. As to delegation of the performance of a statutory duty see further TORT vol 97 (2015) PARA 511.

(7) Non-completion, Termination and Insolvency

(i) Illegality

307. Types of illegality.

Contracts may be illegal either as formed or as performed[1]. A contract to perform an act, which is at the time of the contract illegal, is void[2]. In such a case, the employer cannot seek to recover payments made under the illegal contract[3], nor can the contractor claim the contract price[4]. Thus a contractor cannot claim the value of work carried out in excess of that permitted by a licence[5], but if the employer expressly undertakes that he will obtain the necessary licence and the contractor reasonably relies on the employer to do so, the contractor will have a claim for breach of a collateral warranty should it prove that the employer has failed to obtain the appropriate licence[6]. A building or engineering contract may be illegal by reason of a failure to comply with a statute or it may be prohibited by statute[7]. Thus it is generally illegal to build on a disused burial ground[8]; and, where a statute required a construction not to be built of wood, a contract to build in such material was unenforceable[9].

Where, however, the illegality lies only in the method of performing the contract, the contractor will not lose his right of action on the contract unless from the outset he intended to perform it in an illegal manner[10]. In some contracts it is an express term that the contractor will comply with any relevant statute, statutory regulation and byelaw. If the employer suffers loss as a result of the contractor's failure to perform the contract in accordance with such statute or regulation the contractor will be liable to the employer in damages. So too where the illegality lies in the method of execution chosen by the contractor there will be no fundamental illegality[11]. A contract may not itself be illegal but it may be tainted with illegality by reason of its connection with some other illegal transaction. If the illegality is merely incidental to the primary purpose of the transaction it will be enforced but if the claim is founded directly upon the illegality it is likely to fail[12].

1   See generally CONTRACT vol 22 (2012) PARA 427 et seq.
2   *Bartlett v Vinor* (1692) Carth 251 at 252 per Holt CJ. As to illegal contracts see CONTRACT vol 22 (2012) PARA 452 et seq.

3 See *Kearley v Thomson* (1890) 24 QBD 742 at 745–746, CA, per Fry LJ; *A Smith & Son (Bognor Regis) Ltd v Walker* [1952] 2 QB 319 at 328, [1952] 1 All ER 1008 at 1012, CA, per Denning LJ. See also *Patel v Mirza* [2016] UKSC 42, [2017] AC 467, [2017] 1 All ER 191.

4 *Stevens v Gourley* (1859) 7 CBNS 99 (contract to build in wood when the use of such material was prohibited); *Barton v Piggott* (1874) LR 10 QB 86; *Taylor v Bhail* (1995) 50 Con LR 70, CA.

5 *Brightman & Co Ltd v Tate* [1919] 1 KB 463; *Bostel Bros Ltd v Hurlock* [1949] 1 KB 74, [1948] 2 All ER 312, CA; *Dennis & Co Ltd v Munn* [1949] 2 KB 327, [1949] 1 All ER 616, CA; *Woolfe v Wexler* [1951] 2 KB 154, [1951] 1 All ER 635, CA; *A Smith & Son (Bognor Regis) Ltd v Walker* [1952] 2 QB 319, [1952] 1 All ER 1008, CA; *Brewer Street Investments Ltd v Barclays Woollen Co Ltd* [1954] 1 QB 428, [1953] 2 All ER 1330, CA; *Frank W Clifford Ltd v Garth* [1956] 2 All ER 323, [1956] 1 WLR 570, CA; *Phoenix General Insurance Co of Greece SA v Halvanon Insurance Co Ltd* [1988] QB 216, [1987] 2 All ER 152, CA; *Mohamed v Alaga & Co* [1998] 2 All ER 720.

6 *Strongman (1945) Ltd v Sincock* [1955] 2 QB 525, [1955] 3 All ER 90, CA.

7 When statutory control of building work was operative, it was illegal to carry out building work without first obtaining the appropriate licence (eg under the Building Control Act 1966 (repealed)).

8 *Gibbons v Chambers* (1885) 1 TLR 530; *Re Trustees of St Saviour's Rectory and Oyler* (1886) 31 ChD 412; *Re Ponsford and Newport District School Board* [1894] 1 Ch 454, CA; *Re Jewison's Will Trusts; Till v Market Weighton Parish Council* [1962] Ch 414, [1961] 3 All ER 1022, [1961] 3 WLR 1290. As to when buildings may be erected on a disused burial ground see CREMATION AND BURIAL vol 24 (2010) PARA 1326.

9 *Stevens v Gourley* (1859) 7 CBNS 99.

10 *St John Shipping Corpn v Joseph Bank Ltd* [1957] 1 QB 267, [1956] 3 All ER 683; and see *Townsends (Builders) Ltd v Cinema News and Property Management Ltd* [1959] 1 All ER 7, [1959] 1 WLR 119, 20 BLR 118, CA, where it was held that work done in contravention of byelaws was not illegal work if the local authority was prepared to allow it to remain on the employer's undertaking to carry out further work to cure the defects. See also *Shaw v Groom* [1970] 2 QB 504, [1970] 1 All ER 702, CA; *SA Ancien Maison Marcel Bauche v Woodhouse Drake and Carey (Sugar) Ltd* [1982] 2 Lloyd's Rep 516; *Phoenix General Insurance Co of Greece v Halvanon Insurance Co Ltd* [1988] QB 216, [1987] 2 All ER 152, CA.

11 *Townsends (Builders) Ltd v Cinema News and Property Management Ltd* [1959] 1 All ER 7, [1959] 1 WLR 119, 20 BLR 118, CA.

12 *Thackwell v Barclays Bank plc* [1986] 1 All ER 676; *Saunders v Edwards* [1987] 2 All ER 651 at 666, [1987] 1 WLR 1116 at 1134, CA, per Bingham LJ; *Euro-Diam Ltd v Bathurst* [1990] 1 QB 1, [1987] 2 All ER 113, CA; *Tinsley v Milligan* [1994] 1 AC 340, [1993] 3 All ER 65, HL (disapproved in *Patel v Mirza* [2016] UKSC 42, [2017] AC 467, [2017] 1 All ER 191).

308. Supervening illegality.

Where, during the course of the works, it becomes illegal to perform the contract at all, the contract will be frustrated and both parties will be discharged[1]. However, the contract will not necessarily be frustrated where the illegality affects only one of the contractor's obligations or the time at which the contract is to be performed[2]. If the execution of the works is rendered illegal for a period of time longer than any delay contemplated by the parties at the time of the contract, the contract will be frustrated[3]. If an ancillary or subsidiary part of a contract is illegal, it may be possible to sever the illegal part and enforce the lawful remainder. The court will consider the substance of the transaction concerned to determine whether the contract is divisible[4].

1 See PARA 310. As to frustration generally see CONTRACT vol 22 (2012) PARA 468 et seq. As to supervening illegality see CONTRACT vol 22 (2012) PARA 473.

2 See eg *Cricklewood Property and Investment Trust Ltd v Leighton's Investment Trust Ltd* [1945] AC 221, [1945] 1 All ER 252, HL.

3 *Metropolitan Water Board v Dick, Kerr & Co Ltd* [1918] AC 119, HL. See also *Codelfa Construction Pty Ltd v State Rail Authority of New South Wales* (1982) 149 CLR 337, Aust HC.

4 *Carney v Herbert* [1985] AC 301, [1985] 1 All ER 438, PC; *Harbour Assurance Co (UK) Ltd v Kansa General International Insurance Co Ltd* [1993] QB 701, [1993] 3 All ER 897, CA; *Taylor v Bhail* (1995) 50 Con LR 70, CA.

(ii) Impossibility of Performance

309. Impossibility.

Factors existing at the time of the contract may make its performance wholly or partly impossible[1]. It may prove impossible to construct the works at all or to do so by the proposed method of construction. Where it is impossible to carry out the works at all, it is a question of construction whether the parties intended that the contract should in such circumstances cease to bind them[2]. If the contractor has expressly or impliedly undertaken to complete the contract, he will be liable in damages in the event of his failing to do so, notwithstanding that the completion of the works may have proved impossible[3].

If the method of constructing the works proves impossible, the contractor must adopt another method. The contractor is not entitled to abandon the contract because the employer refuses to make additional payment in respect of additional expense incurred by the contractor in adopting a more effective and expensive method[4]. Further, the employer does not warrant that his architect's design is practicable and he is not liable to the contractor should the design prove impracticable[5].

1   As to impossibility of performance see CONTRACT vol 22 (2012) PARA 468 et seq. Impossibility of performance may lead to frustration of the contract: see PARA 310.
2   A contract will not be construed as an undertaking to perform an impossibility if any other reasonable construction is possible: *Lord Clifford v Watts* (1870) LR 5 CP 577 at 585 per Willes J. The contract may expressly provide that the contractor must construct and complete the works save in so far as it is legally or physically impossible to do so: see eg the ICC conditions of contract. As to standard forms of contract see PARA 202.
3   *Jones v St John's College Oxford* (1870) LR 6 QB 115 at 127 per Hannen J; *Taylor v Caldwell* (1863) 3 B & S 826 at 833 per Blackburn J.
4   See PARA 261. See also *Jackson v Eastbourne Local Board* (1886) 2 Hudson's BC (10th Edn) 270, 356, HL; *Bottoms v York Corpn* (1892) 2 Hudson's BC (10th Edn) 270, CA; *McDonald v Workington Corpn* (1893) 9 TLR 230, CA.
5   *Thorn v London Corpn* (1876) 1 App Cas 120, HL; *Tharsis Sulphur and Copper Co v M'Elroy & Sons* (1878) 3 App Cas 1040, HL.

310. Frustration.

Where the execution of the works is rendered impossible by the occurrence of an event which was not foreseen at the time of the contract, the contract may be frustrated[1]. Frustration occurs whenever the law recognises that without the default of either party a contractual obligation has become incapable of being performed because the circumstances in which performance is called for would render it a thing radically different from that which was undertaken by the contract[2]. A contractor cannot disregard the contract and claim on a quantum meruit basis merely because, by reason of a shortage of labour, the execution of the works took much longer and was more expensive than anticipated[3]. Where the contract is for work in or to an existing building, the destruction of that building before the start or during the progress of work may frustrate the contract[4]. On the other hand, it is generally the contractor who takes the risk of the accidental destruction of the works themselves[5] and in such a case the contractor will not be discharged. Most contracts for building or engineering work entitle the contractor to an extension of time for completion if events occur which might, if prolonged, frustrate the contract. Since it is essential to the operation of the doctrine of frustration that the parties have not made an express provision in respect of the alleged frustrating event[6], it seems that in those cases the contract will not be frustrated[7].

Neither the employer nor the contractor can rely on an event which they themselves caused as frustrating the contract[8].

1 As to frustration generally and as to the effects of frustration on building contracts where the Law Reform (Frustrated Contracts) Act 1943 applies see CONTRACT vol 22 (2012) PARA 468 et seq.
2 *Davis Contractors Ltd v Fareham UDC* [1956] AC 696 at 729, [1956] 2 All ER 145 at 160, HL, per Lord Radcliffe. Various factors must be considered, including: the terms of the contract, the parties' knowledge, expectations, assumptions and contemplations (in particular as to risk, as at the time of contract), the nature of the supervening event, and the parties' calculations as to the possibilities of future performance in the new circumstances: see *Edwinton Commercial Corpn v Tsavliris Russ (Worldwide Salvage and Towage) Ltd, The Sea Angel* [2007] EWCA Civ 547, [2007] 2 All ER (Comm) 634, [2007] 2 Lloyd's Rep 517; and CONTRACT vol 22 (2012) PARA 469.
3 *Davis Contractors Ltd v Fareham UDC* [1956] AC 696, [1956] 2 All ER 145, HL; disapproving *Bush v Whitehaven Port and Town Trustees* (1888) 52 JP 392, CA; and see *Sir Lindsay Parkinson & Co Ltd v Works and Public Buildings Comrs* [1949] 2 KB 632, [1950] 1 All ER 208, CA.
4 *Wong Lai Ying v Chinachem Investment Co Ltd* (1979) 13 BLR 81, PC (works destroyed by a landslip); *Taylor v Caldwell* (1863) 3 B & S 826; *Appleby v Myers* (1867) LR 2 CP 651; and see *J Lauritzen AS v Wijsmuller BV, The Super Servant Two* [1989] 1 Lloyd's Rep 148 (affd [1990] 1 Lloyd's Rep 1, CA).
5 *Appleby v Myers* (1867) LR 2 CP 651; *Brecknock and Abergavenny Canal Navigation Co v Pritchard* (1796) 6 Term Rep 750. It is for this reason that the contractor is required by most contracts to insure the works.
6 *The Eugenia* [1964] 2 QB 226 at 239, [1964] 1 All ER 161 at 166, CA, per Lord Denning MR.
7 Ultimately, however, the question is one of construction and the fact that the contract makes some express provision as to a particular event does not mean that in no circumstances can the contract be frustrated by that event: see *Metropolitan Water Board v Dick, Kerr & Co Ltd* [1918] AC 119, HL; and *Bank Line Ltd v Capel* [1919] AC 435 at 456, HL, per Lord Sumner; *Sir Lindsay Parkinson & Co Ltd v Works and Public Buildings Comrs* [1949] 2 KB 632 at 665, CA, per Asquith LJ; *The Eugenia* [1964] 2 QB 226 at 239, CA, per Lord Denning MR; *Joseph Constantine Steamship Line Ltd v Imperial Smelting Ltd, The Kingswood* [1942] AC 154, [1941] 2 All ER 165, HL.
8 *Mertens v Home Freeholds Co* [1921] 2 KB 526, CA.

311. Excuses for non-performance not amounting to frustration.

Liability in contract is strict and an unforeseen event short of frustration will not normally excuse a failure to perform a contract. Where the contractor's costs greatly increased because of inflation but the contract did not enable all the increase to be recovered, there was no frustration[1]. In the absence of an express provision entitling the contractor to an extension of time, bad weather will not excuse late completion[2]. Again, in the absence of an express provision, a strike causing a failure to complete by a fixed day is immaterial[3]. But where the contractor's obligation is to complete within a reasonable time, delay caused by a strike is a factor to be considered in determining what is a reasonable date for completion[4]. Where the contract provides that the contractor is not to be liable in the event of force majeure[5], the events contemplated by the expression 'force majeure' depend upon the construction of the contract[6].

1 *Wates Ltd v GLC* (1983) 25 BLR 1 at 35, CA, where Stephenson LJ said 'inflation increased not at a trot or a canter, but at a gallop'. As to frustration see PARA 310; and CONTRACT vol 22 (2012) PARA 468 et seq.
2 *Maryon v Carter* (1830) 4 C & P 295; *Matsoukis v Priestman & Co* [1915] 1 KB 681. As to extensions of time for completion see PARA 267. See also *Electric Power Equipment Ltd v RCA Victor Co Ltd* (1963) 41 DLR (2d) 727, BC SC. However, extreme weather conditions may amount to an act of God which, whilst not ordinarily excusing a breach of contract, may, on a proper construction of the parties' contract, bring the contract to an end: *Baily v de Crespigny* (1869) LR 4 QB 180 at 185 per Hannen J.
3 *Budgett & Co v Binnington & Co* [1891] 1 QB 35, CA.
4 *Hick v Raymond and Reid* [1893] AC 22, HL; see also *H Fairweather & Co Ltd v Wandsworth London Borough Council* (1987) 39 BLR 106 at 118–119 per Judge Fox-Andrews QC.

5   As to force majeure see CONTRACT vol 22 (2012) PARA 477; and the definition in *Lebeaupin v R Crispin & Co* [1920] 2 KB 714 at 718 per McCardie J; but note that many of the events there mentioned are the subject of express provisions in most standard form contracts and the term will then have a narrower meaning. See also *Sonat Offshore SA v Amerada Hess Development Ltd* (1987) 39 BLR 1, CA.
6   *Matsoukis v Priestman & Co* [1915] 1 KB 681.

(iii) Termination

A.   POWER TO DETERMINE

312.   Right to terminate contract.
In building contracts a clear distinction usually needs to be made between:
(1)   the contractual rights and powers which derive from the occurrence of events which entitle one party to terminate the employment of the contractor under the contract[1]; and
(2)   the common law rights and powers which entitle the party to treat himself as released from his acceptance of a repudiatory breach of contract by the other party[2].
The latter form part of the general law of contract and are not considered in detail here[3]. This part of this title is concerned with the former.

In practice the relevant event may be both a repudiation and one which entitles a party to exercise a contractual right of determination. However, the facts necessary to entitle a party to determine the other party's employment under the contract may not amount to conduct which is repudiatory[4]. Unless the contract expressly so provides, common law rights and remedies are not to be regarded as excluding the operation of contractual rights and remedies[5].

Acceptance of a repudiatory breach releases both parties from the further performance of their obligations under the contract and will prevent the exercise thereafter of a contractual right of determination. Similarly the exercise of a contractual right of determination will not be regarded as itself being an acceptance of repudiation[6].

The innocent party should therefore, if possible, make it clear that one course is being adopted without prejudice to his other rights should the former course be held to be invalid[7]. But if the former course were the contractual right of determination then the innocent party might be treated as having repudiated the contract.

1   Frequently the events would not otherwise justify the discharge of the contract. But a contractual provision may be unenforceable as a penalty: *Ranger v Great Western Rly Co* (1854) 5 HL Cas 72; *Public Works Comr v Hills* [1906] AC 368, PC; *Gilbert-Ash (Northern) Ltd v Modern Engineering (Bristol) Ltd* [1974] AC 689 at 698, [1973] 3 All ER 195 at 199, HL, per Lord Reid, at 704, 204 per Lord Morris, and at 711, 210 per Viscount Dilhorne; *Jobson v Johnson* [1989] 1 All ER 621 at 633–634, [1989] 1 WLR 1026 at 1041, CA, per Nicholls J.
2   See CONTRACT vol 22 (2012) PARA 565 et seq.
3   See generally CONTRACT.
4   *Laing Management Ltd and Morrison-Knudson Ltd v Aegon Insurance Co (UK) Ltd* (1997) 86 BLR 70, (1997) 55 Con LR 1.
5   *Gilbert-Ash (Northern) Ltd v Modern Engineering (Bristol) Ltd* [1974] AC 689, [1973] 3 All ER 195, HL; *Architectural Installation Services Ltd v James Gibbons (Windows) Ltd* (1989) 46 BLR 91 at 100 per Judge Bowsher QC; *Lockland Builders Ltd v John Kim Rickwood* (1995) 77 BLR 38, (1995) 46 Con LR 92, CA.

6   *ER Dyer Ltd v Simon Build/ER Peter Lind Partnership* (1982) 23 BLR 23 at 33 per Nolan J (but the contract there expressly provided that the exercise of the contractual right would not avoid or release the contractor from any of its obligations or liabilities under the contract, etc); *Mvita Construction Co Ltd v Tanzania Harbours Authority* (1988) 46 BLR 19 at 33, Tanz CA, per Nyalali CJ (dealing with a contract in similar terms).

7   See *Architectural Installation Services Ltd v James Gibbons (Windows) Ltd* (1989) 46 BLR 91 at 100 per Judge Bowsher QC.

313. Express powers of determination or forfeiture generally.

Building contracts frequently give a party (be it employer, contractor or sub-contractor) power to determine the contract or the contractor's employment or to 'forfeit' the contract on the happening of some event or on some default by the contractor. Such provisions used commonly to be called 'forfeiture clauses' (and the description is still prevalent in engineering and international contracts) but the term more widely used particularly in standard form contracts is 'determination clause'. Determination clauses are inserted for two principal reasons: first, a party (especially the employer) will be able to determine the contractor's employment (but not the contract) in the event of a breach which might not amount to a repudiation[1], and secondly, to secure to the employer more extensive rights than he would have if he accepted a repudiatory breach by the contractor[2].

The power to determine may be limited by the contract to arise:

(1)   where the contractor is in default in:
   (a)   failing to commence the work[3];
   (b)   failing to proceed regularly with the work for a fixed period[4];
   (c)   failing to proceed to the satisfaction of the employer or the architect[5];
   (d)   failing to proceed with such dispatch as will in the opinion of the architect enable the works to be completed by the time stipulated[6];
   (e)   failing to continue with the work[7];
   (f)   failing to proceed in the manner required by the architect[8], or not complying with his orders and directions[9];
   (g)   failing to perform the work as specified[10], or not observing some stipulation of the contract[11], or being guilty of any default[12];
   (h)   not completing as stipulated[13], or by the time agreed[14], or not completing under the direction and to the satisfaction of the surveyor[15];
   (i)   leaving the works in an unfinished state[16];
   (j)   failing, after proper notice, to rectify defective work[17];
   (k)   removing materials from the site[18];
   (l)   not maintaining the works[19];
   (m)   sub-contracting without prior consent[20];
   (n)   failing to proceed regularly and diligently[21];
(2)   where the employer is in default by:
   (a)   failing to pay the amount certified[22];
   (b)   withholding[23], interfering with or obstructing the issue of a certificate[24];
   (c)   having the work suspended[25];
   (d)   failing to provide drawings[26].

In addition a power to determine is often given if the other party should go bankrupt or go into liquidation[27].

1   As to what amounts to a repudiation see PARA 312.
2   See PARA 316 et seq. The rights of the employer over the contractor's plant and materials, in particular, are more extensive than those arising from the acceptance of a repudiatory breach. See also *Re Cosslett (Contractors) Ltd* [1997] 4 All ER 115, sub nom *Cosslett v Mid-Glamorgan County Council* (1997) 85 BLR 1, CA.
3   *Mohan and Homes v Dundalk, Newry and Greenore Rly Co* (1880) 6 LR Ir 477.
4   See *Re Walker, ex p Barter, ex p Black* (1881) 26 ChD 510, CA. Consider *Ampurius Nu Homes Holdings Ltd v Telford Homes (Creekside) Ltd* [2013] EWCA Civ 577, [2013] 4 All ER 377 which looked at whether a failure to commence works in circumstances where works could and did commence later amounted to repudiatory breach (the court held that recommencement before the injured party purported to terminate was a relevant factor and repudiatory breach had not occurred: had the contract contained contractual rights to terminate if a set of circumstances had existed it may have afforded the claimant a right to terminate on the basis the breach had already occurred, causing loss, and it may have been less relevant that the breach was later remedied as the damage would already have been done).
5   See *Davis v Swansea Corpn* (1853) 8 Exch 808 (followed in *Wilkinson v Lowndes* (1860) 24 JP 487); *Stadhard v Lee* (1863) 3 B & S 364.
6   See *Brown v Bateman* (1867) LR 2 CP 272 at 275; *Roberts v Bury Improvement Comrs* (1870) LR 5 CP 310; *Arterial Drainage Co Ltd v Rathangan River Drainage Board* (1880) 6 LR Ir 513; *Cork Corpn v Rooney* (1881) 7 LR Ir 191.
7   See *Rouch v Great Western Rly Co* (1841) 1 QB 51 at 52.
8   See *Walker v London and North Western Rly Co* (1876) 1 CPD 518.
9   See *Hunt v South Eastern Rly Co* (1875) 45 LJQB 87 at 88, HL.
10   *Mohan and Homes v Dundalk, Newry and Greenore Rly Co* (1880) 6 LR Ir 477.
11   See *Stevens v Taylor* (1860) 2 F & F 419.
12   See *Garrett v Salisbury and Dorset Junction Rly Co* (1866) LR 2 Eq 358.
13   See *Baker v Gray* (1856) 17 CB 462.
14   See *Tooth v Hallett* (1869) 4 Ch App 242; *Marsden v Sambell* (1880) 28 WR 952 at 953.
15   See *Hunt v Bishop* (1853) 8 Exch 675.
16   See *Re Garrud, ex p Newitt* (1881) 16 ChD 522, CA (disapproved in *Perpetual Trustee Co Ltd v BNY Corporate Trustee Services Ltd*; *Butters v BBC Worldwide Ltd* [2009] EWCA Civ 1160, [2010] Ch 347, [2010] 3 WLR 87 but on other grounds).
17   See *Arterial Drainage Co v Rathangan River Drainage Board* (1880) 6 LR Ir 513.
18   See *Marsden v Sambell* (1880) 28 WR 952.
19   See *Walker v London and North Western Rly Co* (1876) 1 CPD 518.
20   *Thomas Feather & Co (Bradford) Ltd v Keighley Corpn* (1953) 52 LGR 30.
21   *JM Hill & Sons Ltd v Camden London Borough Council* (1980) 18 BLR 31, CA. See also *West Faulkner Associates v Newham London Borough Council* (1994) 71 BLR 1, CA.
22   *Lubenham Fidelities and Investments Co Ltd v South Pembrokeshire District Council* (1986) 33 BLR 39, CA. See also *Reinwood Ltd v L Brown & Sons Ltd (No 2)* [2008] EWCA Civ 1090, 121 Con LR 1, [2009] BLR 37 (failure to pay value added tax according to contractor's provisional assessment).
23   *Smith v Howden Union Rural Sanitary Authority and Fowler* (1890) 2 Hudson's BC (4th Edn) 156, DC.
24   *RB Burden Ltd v Swansea Corpn* [1957] 3 All ER 243 at 253, [1957] 1 WLR 1167 at 1180, HL, per Lord Tucker.
25   *John Jarvis Ltd v Rockdale Housing Association Ltd* (1986) 36 BLR 48, CA.
26   *Roberts v Bury Improvement Comrs* (1870) LR 5 CP 310.
27   See PARA 321.

314. Means of ascertaining whether the power to determine has arisen.
In general the contract will specify the means of ascertaining the event giving rise to a power to determine the contractor's employment. Modern standard form contracts generally give to the architect or the engineer power to decide when the employer may be able to determine the contract or the employment of the contractor[1]. Where the decisions of the architect are not subject to review[2], then the contractor can only impugn such a decision on the grounds that the architect has not exercised an independent judgment[3] on the issue or is in some way

disqualified from making the decision[4]. But in the absence of such provision, the occurrence of the event will be determined by adjudication[5], arbitration[6] or by litigation[7]. Where the contract provides that the employer himself is to decide whether the contractual power to determine the contractor's employment has arisen, the employer must act reasonably, but the terms of the contract may make it clear that the decision of the employer is to be final[8].

1   As to standard forms of contract see PARA 202.
2   Cf *Loke Hong Kee Pte Ltd v United Overseas Land Ltd* (1982) 23 BLR 35, PC.
3   See *Scott v Liverpool Corpn* (1858) 3 De G & J 334; *Pawley v Turnbull* (1861) 3 Giff 70; *Hickman & Co v Roberts* [1913] AC 229, HL.
4   See PARAS 333–335.
5   As to adjudication see PARAS 407–422.
6   *Garrett v Salisbury and Dorset Junction Rly Co* (1866) LR 2 Eq 358. See also *Central Provident Fund Board v Ho Bock Kee* (1981) 17 BLR 21, Sing CA. As to arbitration see PARAS 398–406.
7   *Northampton Gas Light Co v Parnell* (1855) 15 CB 630 at 648–649 per Jervis CJ; *Roberts v Bury Improvement Comrs* (1870) LR 5 CP 310 at 326–327 per Kelly CB. As to litigation see PARAS 391–397.
8   See *Stadhard v Lee* (1863) 32 LJQB 75 at 78 per Cockburn CJ; and *Central Provident Fund Board v Ho Bock Kee* (1981) 17 BLR 21, Sing CA. An employer is obliged to act honestly, fairly and reasonably in all its judgments, decisions and certificates: *Balfour Beatty Civil Engineering Ltd v Docklands Light Railway Ltd* (1996) 78 BLR 42, (1996) 49 Con LR 1, CA. Whilst the decision in *Balfour Beatty Civil Engineering Ltd v Docklands Light Railway Ltd* above was overruled by the House of Lords in *Beaufort Developments (NI) Ltd v Gilbert Ash NI Ltd* [1999] 1 AC 266, (1998) 88 BLR 1, the principle stated remains unaffected.

315.   Exercise of a power to determine.

The contract will usually state how a power to determine the contract, or to determine the contractor's employment under it, is to be exercised. In the absence of any such requirement, no formality is necessary provided there is some act which is sufficient to inform the other party that the power has been exercised[1], for such a power must be exercised in an unequivocal and unambiguous manner[2]. The contract may provide that the power arises on a failure by the contractor to comply with a notice previously served on him. If the employer or the architect required the contractor to do some particular act, then the first notice should specify that act[3], but if such a first or warning notice complains of general neglect in the execution of the work, the notice is not bad in form by reason of its failure to specify every default[4].

A clause giving the employer power to determine the contract for dilatory progress may remain exercisable after the stipulated date for completion has passed[5], but where the power to determine for dilatory progress, on the proper construction of the contract, is related to the progress required to complete on the stipulated date, such power must be exercised before the stipulated date has passed[6]. An ordinary commercial businessman should, however, be able to see that there is a sensible connection between the two notices both in content and time[7]. Where a contractor's right to determine must not be exercised 'unreasonably or vexatiously' the test to be applied is that of a reasonable contractor in the circumstances of the case[8]. Where the contract does not provide for the time between the two notices the second should be given within a reasonable time[9]. Formal defects may not vitiate a notice if there is no prejudice[10].

1   *Drew & Co v Josolyne* (1887) 18 QBD 590 at 597, CA, per Bowen LJ; *JM Hill & Sons Ltd v Camden London Borough Council* (1980) 18 BLR 31 at 43, CA, per Lawton LJ, and at 46–47 per Ormrod LJ.
2   *Roberts v Davey* (1833) 4 B & Ad 664. In *Marsden v Sambell* (1880) 43 LT 120 it was held that the sending of an agent to 'keep an eye' on the contractor and to prevent him from removing materials contrary to the contract was not enough to amount to an election to determine.

3   *Pauling v Dover Corpn* (1855) 10 Exch 753.
4   *Pauling v Dover Corpn* (1855) 10 Exch 753.
5   *Joshua Henshaw & Son v Rochdale Corpn* [1944] KB 381, [1944] 1 All ER 413, CA.
6   *Walker v London and North Western Rly Co* (1876) 1 CPD 518.
7   *Architectural Installation Services Ltd v James Gibbons (Windows) Ltd* (1989) 46 BLR 91 at 98 per Judge Bowsher QC.
8   *John Jarvis Ltd v Rockdale Housing Association* (1986) 36 BLR 48 at 68, CA, per Bingham LJ (a notice is unreasonable only if no reasonable contractor would have issued a notice of determination in the circumstances).
9   See *Mvita Construction Co Ltd v Tanzania Harbours Authority* (1988) 46 BLR 19, Tanz CA.
10   *Goodwin & Son v Fawcett* (1965) 195 EG 27; *JM Hill & Sons Ltd v Camden London Borough Council* (1980) 18 BLR 31 at 47, CA, per Ormrod LJ; but cf *Central Provident Fund Board v Ho Bock Kee* (1981) 17 BLR 21, Sing CA; *Eriksson v Whalley* [1971] 1 NSWLR 397, NSW SC.

B.   EFFECTS OF TERMINATION

316. Effects of the exercise of an express power to determine.
The principal effect of the exercise of a power to determine is that the rights of a party in default are suspended (for example until the works have been completed by the employer) and superseded by a new contractual code. Thus the contractor may have no further rights to payment until the employer has completed the work left outstanding[1] and may have to permit his materials, plant and equipment to be used by the employer for the purposes of completing the works[2]. An employer in default may have to pay the contractor whatever is due and to compensate him for the losses caused by the determination.

Where there is a dispute about the validity of determination and the dispute is to be decided by an arbitrator, the court will treat the notice of termination as provisionally valid[3]. An injunction will not normally be granted to restrain a forfeiture as this would be tantamount to ordering specific performance[4].

1   See eg *Davies v Swansea Corpn* (1853) 8 Exch 808.
2   See PARA 319.
3   *A-G of Hong Kong v Ko Hon Mau* (1988) 44 BLR 144, HK CA; *Tara Civil Engineering Ltd v Moorfield Developments Ltd* (1989) 46 BLR 72. As to arbitration see PARAS 398–406.
4   *Munro v Wivenhoe and Brightlingsea Rly Co* (1865) 12 LT 655; but cf *Foster and Dicksee v Hastings Corpn* (1903) 87 LT 736. See also *Scandinavian Trading Tanker Co AB v Flota Petrolera Ecuatoriana* [1983] 2 AC 694, [1983] 2 All ER 763, HL; *Sport International Bussum BV v Inter-Footwear Ltd* [1984] 2 All ER 321, [1984] 1 WLR 776, HL; *BICC plc v Burndy Corpn* [1985] Ch 232, [1985] 1 All ER 417, CA; *Firma C-Trade SA v Newcastle Protection and Indemnity Association* [1991] 2 AC 1, [1990] 2 All ER 705, HL; *Transag Haulage Ltd v Leyland DAF Finance plc* [1994] 2 BCLC 88, [1994] BCC 356. As to the remedy of specific performance see generally SPECIFIC PERFORMANCE vol 95 (2017) PARA 501 et seq.

317. Revocation of contractor's licence to occupy site.
Usually the contractor's licence to occupy the site is revoked either expressly or by necessary implication[1], since it is of course granted only to enable the works under the contract to be carried out. If an employer purports to revoke the licence by wrongly relying on a power to determine the contract, the licence subsists and may be protected by the courts against the employer's wish to re-enter to complete the works[2].

1   *Joshua Henshaw & Sons v Rochdale Corpn* [1944] KB 381, [1944] 1 All ER 413, CA.
2   *Hounslow London Borough Council v Twickenham Garden Developments Ltd* [1971] Ch 233, [1970] 3 All ER 326; cf *Mayfield Holdings Ltd v Moana Reef Ltd* [1973] 1 NZLR 309; *Graham H Roberts Pty Ltd v Maurbeth Investments Pty Ltd* [1974] 1 NSWLR 93, NSW Equity Div. As to remedy by way of injunction see CIVIL PROCEDURE vol 12 (2015) PARA 1098 et seq.

318. Where the property in materials and plant remains in the contractor.

In relation to a determination otherwise than for insolvency[1], and where the employer is given no rights over the contractor's materials, the contractor has a reasonable time in which to remove them and his plant from the site[2]. The employer may have the right to seize and use materials and plant. In such a case, the property in materials will vest in the owner of land if and when the materials are incorporated in the permanent work[3], but the property in plant will not pass[4]. It is a breach of contract giving rise to a claim for damages for the contractor after determination to remove materials which the employer is entitled to use[5].

A provision vesting the contractor's property absolutely in the employer may be unenforceable as being a penalty[6]. Generally such a provision will be intended to operate by way of security for the completion of the works and will not be construed as a penalty[7].

1   This paragraph and PARA 319 assume that neither party is insolvent. For the position where there is insolvency see PARA 321.
2   Where a licence is revoked, the licensee will have a right analogous to that stated in the text: *Mellor v Watkins* (1874) LR 9 QB 400.
3   See PARA 279 et seq.
4   *Re Winter, ex p Bolland* (1878) 8 ChD 225.
5   *Hawthorn v Newcastle-upon-Tyne and North Shields Rly Co* (1840) 3 QB 734n; *Re Winter, ex p Bolland* (1878) 8 ChD 225. See also *Poulton v Wilson* (1858) 1 F & F 403.
6   *Ranger v Great Western Rly Co* (1854) 5 HL Cas 72; *Marshall v MacIntosh* (1898) 78 LT 750.
7   *Ranger v Great Western Rly Co* (1854) 5 HL Cas 72 at 108–109 per Lord Cranworth.

319. Position of the employer completing after termination.

Unless the contract otherwise provides, an employer who completes the work with the use of the contractor's materials and plant must account for them to the contractor[1]. The duty of the employer is, however, less strict than that imposed on a mortgagee in possession[2]. The contract may provide for the costs to the employer in completing the work to be set off against the sum that would have been payable to the contractor and for the balance to be payable by one party to the other as the case may be. The employer is not entitled to vary the work, as shown in the specification or on the drawings, at the expense of the contractor[3], but the employer ought, in principle, to be entitled to a full allowance for any extra costs caused by the delay and disruption consequent upon the contractor's default[4].

1   *Ranger v Great Western Rly Co* (1854) 5 HL Cas 72. The contract may require the contractor to assign the benefit of any sub-contract to the employer. Since the employer cannot require a sub-contractor to complete his work, a right to require an assignment from the contractor is of value; in the absence of such a power, the employer would have to negotiate fresh terms with specialist sub-contractors. However, many sub-contracts render this right nugatory as they provide that the sub-contractor's employment will automatically determine upon the termination, forfeiture or repudiation of the contract or the contractor's employment under it.
2   *Fulton v Dornwell* (1885) 4 NZLR 207, NZ SC. As to mortgagees in possession see MORTGAGE vol 77 (2016) PARA 193.
3   *Dillon v Jack* (1903) 23 NZLR 547 at 549 per Stout CJ.
4   *Dunkirk Colliery Co v Lever* (1878) 9 ChD 20 at 25, CA, per James LJ.

320. Remedies for wrongful termination.

A wrongful termination does not ipso facto amount to a repudiation of the contract[1]. But if, after a wrongful termination, the employer ousts the contractor from the site or otherwise shows an intention not to be bound by the contract, the contractor may, in such a case, claim the value of the work done and claim, in addition, damages, the measure of which is normally the loss of profit on the incomplete balance[2]. The value of the work done will be assessed on the basis of any instalment payments which have become due under the contract[3] together with payment at contractual rates or prices for work executed but not included in the instalments[4]. In the absence of contractual provisions for calculating the value of the work done a reasonable sum will be assessed and payable as a contractual entitlement. The employer will be entitled to an abatement of the sum otherwise due if the work done is defective[5]. There is conflicting authority as to whether instead of pursuing a claim on the basis outlined above a contractor can simply claim a reasonable sum for work and labour on a quantum meruit basis[6]. However, it is more likely that there is no such option open to the contractor[7].

1 Sub-contracts commonly provide, however, that they shall determine if the contractor's employment under the main contract is determined for any reason. In such cases a right to assignment of the benefit of further performance of the sub-contract if reserved in the main contract is of no value. See also *ER Dyer Ltd v Simon Build/Peter Lind Partnership* (1982) 23 BLR 23, in which it was held that a contractual determination under a main contract was not the determination provided by the sub-contract (which was read as referring to a repudiation of the main contract).

2 See generally DAMAGES.

3 These remain payable: see *Bank of Boston Connecticut v European Grain and Shipping Ltd* [1989] AC 1056, [1989] 1 All ER 545, HL.

4 *Felton v Wharrie* (1906) 2 Hudson's BC (10th Edn) 344, 613, 709, CA.

5 *Slater v CA Duquemin Ltd* (1992) 29 Con LR 24.

6 As to quantum meruit see RESTITUTION vol 88 (2012) PARAS 407, 513 et seq.

7 *Ranger v Great Western Railway Co* (1854) 5 HL Cas 72, HL; *Johnson v Agnew* [1980] AC 367, [1979] 1 All ER 883, HL; *Bank of Boston Connecticut v European Grain and Shipping Ltd* [1989] AC 1056 at 1098, [1989] 1 All ER 545 at 549, HL, per Lord Brandon of Oakbrook. Cases to the contrary include: *Planché v Colburn* (1831) 5 C & P 58; *Prickett v Badger* (1856) 1 CBNS 296; *Appleby v Myers* (1867) LR 2 CP 651; *Luxor (Eastbourne) v Cooper* [1941] AC 108, [1941] 1 All ER 33; *Lusty v Finsbury Securities Ltd* (1991) 58 BLR 66, CA.

(iv) Insolvency

321. Insolvency.

The insolvency of individual[1] or corporate[2] employers, contractors or professionals involved in a construction project is governed by the Insolvency Act 1986. Determination[3] or forfeiture[4], vesting and direct payment clauses[5] in building contracts give rise to particular insolvency considerations.

Most building contracts purport to give the employer, or in the case of a main contract, the sub-contractor, certain rights to determine the employment of the contractor or to determine (or formerly to forfeit) the contract in the event of the insolvency of the main contractor[6]. These provisions are enforceable against the trustee in bankruptcy or liquidator if the contract is a personal contract[7] since the licence given to the contractor to enter upon the site is not included in the definition of property given in the Insolvency Act 1986[8].

A provision providing for the forfeiture of any property of the contractor is void against the trustee in bankruptcy or the liquidator[9]. However, if the property has already vested in the employer or if the employer has a lien upon it, a provision allowing the employer to seize it is valid[10]. The same is true of a provision that creates an equitable charge over, or an assignment of, the plant or materials[11]. Such clauses do not create interests registrable as a bill of sale[12]. A provision providing for the forfeiture of any property of the contractor is also valid if it is stated to operate in the event of some cause other than insolvency, such as delay, albeit that that event has been caused by insolvency[13].

Most building contracts also purport to allow an employer to make direct payments to sub-contractors in the event of non-payment by the contractor. The operation of such clauses after the insolvency of the contractor has been held to be valid[14] but these decisions are of doubtful validity since they infringe the pari passu rule[15].

An employer can recover set-off money[16] owed to the contractor under the immediate or other contracts[17], by virtue of the mutual dealings provisions[18]. The right applies to retention money but not so as to defeat the claim of a secured creditor[19].

1   As to individual insolvency see BANKRUPTCY AND INDIVIDUAL INSOLVENCY.
2   As to corporate insolvency see COMPANY AND PARTNERSHIP INSOLVENCY.
3   See the text and notes 6–8; and PARA 312 et seq.
4   See the text and notes 9–13.
5   See the text and notes 14–19.
6   The same principles apply, mutatis mutandis, as between the main contractor and sub-contractors.
7   *Re Walker, ex p Gould* (1884) 13 QBD 454. See also, for the comparable position of the architect, PARA 485.
8   See the Insolvency Act 1986 s 436; and BANKRUPTCY AND INDIVIDUAL INSOLVENCY vol 5 (2013) PARA 412.
9   See the Insolvency Act 1986 ss 127, 284 (relating to bankruptcy and liquidation respectively); and BANKRUPTCY AND INDIVIDUAL INSOLVENCY vol 5 (2013) PARA 213; COMPANY AND PARTNERSHIP INSOLVENCY vol 17 (2017) PARA 596. See *Re Harrison, ex p Jay* (1850) 14 ChD 19, CA; *Re Walker, ex p Barter, ex p Black* (1884) 26 ChD 510, CA.
10 *Crowfoot v London Dock Co* (1834) 2 Cr & M 637; *Hawthorn v Newcastle-upon-Tyne and North Shields Rly Co* (1840) 3 QB 734n; *Brown v Bateman* (1867) LR 2 CP 272; *Re Waugh, ex p Dickin* (1876) 4 ChD 524; *Re Walker, ex p Barter, ex p Black* (1884) 26 ChD 510, CA; *Byford v Russell* [1907] 2 KB 522.
11 *Re Waugh, ex p Dickin* (1876) 4 ChD 524.
12 *Brown v Bateman* (1807) LR 2 CP 272; *Blake v Izard* (1867) 16 WR 108; *Reeves v Barlow* (1884) 12 QBD 436, CA. But see *Re Cosslett (Contractors) Ltd* [1997] 4 All ER 115, sub nom *Cosslett v Mid-Glamorgan County Council* (1997) 85 BLR 1, CA.
13 *Hart v Porthgain Harbour Co Ltd* [1903] 1 Ch 690.
14 *Re Holt, ex p Gray* (1888) 58 LJQB 5; *Re Wilkinson, ex p Fowler* [1905] 2 KB 713; *Re Tout and Finch Ltd* [1954] 1 All ER 127, [1954] 1 WLR 178.
15 See *British Eagle International Airlines Ltd v Cie Nationale Air France* [1975] 2 All ER 390, [1975] 1 WLR 758, HL. The cases referred to in note 14 were not cited in this case, but they were not followed in *Administrator, Natal v Magill, Grant & Nell (Pty) Ltd (in liquidation)* 1969 (1) SA 660, SA SC (App Div) (but note the different provisions of South African law); *A-G v McMillan & Lockwood Ltd* [1991] 1 NZLR 53, NZ CA; *Joo Yee Construction (Pte) Ltd v Diethelm Industries (Pte) Ltd* [1990] 2 MLJ 66; *Re Right Time Construction Co Ltd* [1990] 2 HKLR 223, 52 BLR 117, HK CA; and *B Mullan & Sons Contractors Ltd v John Ross and Malcolm London* (1996) 86 BLR 1, NI CA (a direct payment provision offended against the pari passu principle). This decision is likely to be followed in England and Wales. See contra *Re CG Monkhouse Properties Ltd* (1968) 69 SRNSW 429, NSW CA; *Gericeuich Contracting Pty Ltd v Sabemo (WA) Pty Ltd* (1984) 9 ACLR 452.
16 This includes damages: *Peat v Jones & Co* (1881) 8 QBD 147, CA.
17 *Re Asphaltic Wood Pavement Co, Lee and Chapman's Case* (1885) 30 ChD 216, CA.
18 See the Insolvency Act 1986 ss 323, 411; and BANKRUPTCY AND INDIVIDUAL INSOLVENCY vol 5 (2013) PARA 561. For the operation of those provisions see *National Westminster Bank Ltd v Halesowen Presswork and Assemblies Ltd* [1972] AC 785, [1972] 1 All ER 641, HL; and for building contracts see *Willment Bros Ltd v North West Thames Regional Health Authority* (1984) 26 BLR 51, CA; *Farley v Housing and Commercial Developments Ltd* (1984) 26 BLR 66.
19 *MacJordan Construction v Brookmount Erostin* (1991) 56 BLR 1, CA. An employer cannot use retention money due to the sub-contractor by way of set-off on the insolvency of the contractor: *PC Harrington Contractors Ltd v Co-partnership Development Ltd* (1998) 88 BLR 44, CA. As to retention money see further PARA 346.

3. CERTIFICATION AND REMUNERATION

(1) Certification

(i) In General

322. Classes of certificate.

In contracts for works of construction, it is common for the parties to confer on an architect, engineer or some other third party a power to issue certificates. The principal purpose of a certificate is to secure payment to the contractor of sums properly due to him under the contract or to express approval of work that has been done. The function of an interim certificate is to provide for payment generally on account to the contractor and the function of a final certificate will normally be to state the final balance due or to express the architect's satisfaction with the completed works[1] or both. Modern contracts often require a number of certificates to be given. Thus the architect or engineer may be required to certify the date on which the works were practically complete[2], because on practical completion the employer will cease to be entitled to liquidated damages[3] for delay and in some contracts the contractor will be entitled to the release of part of the retention money[4]. Further, the architect or engineer may be required to give a certificate when the contractor has finished making defects good and the works are finally complete, for again the final release of retention money may be conditional on such a certificate[5]. Certificates may also be issued to confirm circumstances exist where the works have not been completed which will then trigger other processes such as the right of the employer to claim contractual delay damages from the contractor for delay, or alternatively to grant an extension of time to the completion date under a contract which allows the contractor to avoid payment of contractual delay damages[6].

1   For the construction of a contract empowering the certifier to give certificates that the work has been satisfactorily carried out see *Panamena Europea Navigacion (Compania Limitada) v Frederick Leyland & Co Ltd (J Russell & Co)* [1947] AC 428, HL; *Crown Estate Comrs v John Mowlem & Co Ltd* (1994) 70 BLR 1, (1994) 40 Con LR 36, CA. See also *Scheldebouw BV v St James Homes (Grosvenor Dock) Ltd* [2006] EWHC 89 (TCC), 105 ConLR 90, [2006] BLR 113. As to interim certificates see PARAS 327–329; and as to final certificates see PARAS 330–331.
2   As to practical completion see PARA 265.
3   See PARA 267 et seq.
4   As to retention money see PARA 346.
5   As to the effect of making a certificate a condition precedent to payment see PARA 326.
6   *Reinwood Ltd v L Brown & Sons Ltd* [2008] UKHL 12, [2008] 2 All ER 885, [2008] 1 WLR 696.

323. Form of certificate.

Generally each contract will provide for the form of certificates required under it but, subject to an express provision to the contrary, a certificate need not be in writing[1]. Whether the document or statement relied on constitutes a certificate for the purposes of the contract is a question of construction[2]. In practice, however, certificates in modern building and engineering contracts are invariably required to be in writing.

If the contract requires only that the architect should certify his satisfaction with the works, it is not necessary that the certificate should state a balance due and, if an amount is stated, neither party is bound by it[3]. Similarly, a statement by the certifier approving the contractor's account may be taken as an expression of satisfaction[4].

1　*Coker v Young* (1860) 2 F & F 98 at 101 per Hill J; *Roberts v Watkins* (1863) 14 CBNS 592; *Elmes v Burgh Market Co* (1891) 2 Hudson's BC (4th Edn) 170. A direction in the contract that the certificate should be 'delivered' does not imply that the certificate should be in writing: *Oates v Bromell* (1704) 1 Salk 75.

2　*Coleman v Gittins* (1884) 1 TLR 8; *Minster Trust Ltd v Traps Tractors Ltd* [1954] 3 All ER 136, [1954] 1 WLR 963; and see *Token Construction Co Ltd v Charlton Estates Ltd* (1973) 1 BLR 50, CA. Whether a document constitutes a certificate may be decided by reference to the surrounding circumstances: see *Merton London Borough Council v Lowe* (1981) 18 BLR 130, CA, where it was held that the document was a certificate after reference to the accompanying letter which stated that it was enclosing the final certificate. Minor errors will not invalidate a certificate if no one is misled: *Emson Contractors Ltd v Protea Estates Ltd* (1987) 39 BLR 126, (1987) 13 Con LR 41.

3　*Pashby v Birmingham Corpn* (1856) 18 CB 2.

4　*Harman v Scott* (1874) 2 CA 407, NZ CA; *Clarke v Murray* (1885) 11 VLR 817, Vic CA; but cf *Morgan v Birnie* (1833) 9 Bing 672. See also *Goodman v Layborn* (1881) Roscoe's BC (4th Edn) 162.

324.　Status of a certificate.

A certificate is not akin to the award of an arbitrator[1]. Thus it is unnecessary that an agreement to be bound by certificates should be in writing[2]. Even a stipulation that the certifier is to act as 'exclusive judge' does not make a certificate an award[3]. A certificate is binding only between the parties; accordingly, as between the employer or contractor and a stranger to the contract, whether the contract works are complete is a question of fact and will not depend on the issue of a certificate[4]. The employer may claim damages for negligent supervision from the architect notwithstanding a certificate expressing satisfaction with the works[5].

1　*Northampton Gas Light Co v Parnell* (1855) 15 CB 630.

2　*Northampton Gas Light Co v Parnell* (1855) 15 CB 630 at 646–648 per Jervis CJ. See also *Reed v Van der Vorm* (1985) 35 BLR 136.

3　*Northampton Gas Light Co v Parnell* (1855) 15 CB 630; *Kennedy Ltd v Barrow-in-Furness Corpn* (1909) 2 Hudson's BC (4th Edn) 411, CA.

4　*Lewis v Hoare* (1881) 44 LT 66, HL.

5　*Sutcliffe v Thackrah* [1974] AC 727, [1974] 1 All ER 859, HL.

325.　Position of certifier.

An architect or engineer exercising jurisdiction to certify under a contract must act impartially and independently[1]. In addition he will owe a duty to the employer to carry out the certification procedure with reasonable skill and care and will be liable to him for any loss caused by his negligence[2]. However, he is unlikely to be liable for loss caused to the contractor[3].

Once the jurisdiction has been conferred on the certifier, in the absence of an express provision in the contract, it cannot be revoked[4], but if a second architect is properly appointed to succeed the original architect, the successor will become the certifier[5].

The certifier must exercise his jurisdiction in accordance with the terms of the contract[6]. Thus where the contract calls for the certificate of two architects, the certificate of one of them is not sufficient[7].

1　*Sutcliffe v Thackrah* [1974] AC 727, [1974] 1 All ER 859, HL; cf *Beaufort Developments (NI) Ltd v Gilbert-Ash NI Ltd* [1999] 1 AC 266 at 276, [1998] 2 All ER 778 at 786, HL, per Lord Hoffmann. See also *Scheldebouw BV v St James Homes (Grosvenor Dock) Ltd* [2006] EWHC 89 (TCC), 105 ConLR 90, [2006] BLR 113.

2　*Sutcliffe v Thackrah* [1974] AC 727, [1974] 1 All ER 859, HL (overruling *Chambers v Goldthorpe* [1901] 1 KB 624, CA, where it was held that the certifier was acting in a judicial or quasi-judicial role and could not be liable for loss caused by negligent certification). The architect may be able to claim immunity by agreement: *Sutcliffe v Thackrah* above; and see PARAS 457, 459. As to the position of arbitrators see PARA 403.

3   *Pacific Associates Inc v Baxter* [1990] 1 QB 993, [1989] 2 All ER 159, (1988) 44 BLR 33, CA, where the court found that taking into account all the circumstances including the terms of the building contract and the relationship between the parties, the engineers were not under a duty to prevent the contractor suffering economic loss. The situation may possibly be different if the building contract does not contain an arbitration clause: see *Pacific Associates Inc v Baxter* at 1024, 180–181, 68–69 per Purchas LJ, at 1028–1029, 184, 74–75 per Ralph Gibson LJ, and at 1037, 190, 83 per Russell LJ. See also *Edgeworth Construction Ltd v ND Lea & Associates Ltd* (1993) 66 BLR 56, Can SC, where it was held that an engineer might in principle be liable to a contractor for negligent misrepresentation in relation to errors in tender drawings. See *Spandeck Engineering (S) Pte Ltd v Defence Science & Technology Agency* [2007] SGCA 37, [2008] 4 LRC 61, 114 ConLR 166, Sing CA; *Galliford Try Infrastructure Ltd v Mott Macdonald* [2008] EWHC 1570 (TCC), 120 ConLR 1, [2008] All ER (D) 254 (Jul).

4   *Mills v Bayley* (1863) 2 H & C 36. See also *Murray v Cohen* (1888) 9 NSW Eq 124.

5   *Kellett v Stockport Corpn* (1906) 70 JP 154; cf *Wangler v Swift* 90 NY 38 (NY CA, 1882).

6   See PARA 338.

7   *Lamprell v Billericay Union* (1849) 18 LJEx 282.

326. Whether a certificate is a condition precedent.

All types of certificate may be expressly made a condition precedent to payment. Where a certificate is a condition precedent[1], even though the works are complete the contractor cannot recover the contract price in the absence of a certificate[2], unless the certifier is disqualified[3], or the case is one in which the need for a certificate can be dispensed with[4]. Whether a certificate is a condition precedent to payment is a question of construction[5]. Where the architect or engineer exercises skill and judgment in making the certificate, the courts have leaned towards the view that a certificate is a condition precedent to the contractor's entitlement to payment[6]. The contractor may, however, have an immediate right to adjudication[7], arbitration[8] or litigation[9] to seek to obtain or alter a certificate. He may also be entitled to suspend performance for non-payment[10].

1   Such a condition will not necessarily be imported into a new contract substituted for one (containing such a stipulation) which has been abandoned: *Hunt v South Eastern Rly Co* (1875) 45 LJQB 87, HL.

2   *Lewis v Hoare* (1881) 44 LT 66, HL; *Eaglesham v McMaster* [1920] 2 KB 169.

3   See PARAS 333–335.

4   See PARAS 336–338. However, the contract may allow the contractor to refer the matter to arbitration for the grant of a certificate or to alter the contents of an existing one: *Lubenham Fidelities and Investments Co Ltd v South Pembrokeshire District Council* (1986) 33 BLR 39, CA.

5   For a useful illustration see *Crestar Ltd v Carr* (1987) 37 BLR 113, CA. See also *Costain Building & Engineering Ltd v Scottish Rugby Union plc* (1993) 69 BLR 80, Ct of Sess.

6   *Glenn v Leith* (1853) 1 CLR 569; *Grafton v Eastern Counties Rly Co* (1853) 8 Exch 699; *Westwood v Secretary of State for India in Council* (1863) 7 LT 736; *Dunaberg and Witepsk Rly Co Ltd v Hopkins, Gilkes & Co Ltd* (1877) 36 LT 733; *Wallace v Brandon and Byshottles UDC* (1903) 2 Hudson's BC (4th Edn) 362, CA. See also *Howden & Co v Powell Duffryn Steam Coal Co* 1912 SC 920, Ct of Sess.

7   See the Housing Grants, Construction and Regeneration Act 1996 s 108; and PARA 410. As to adjudication see PARA 407 et seq.

8   See PARA 339. As to arbitration see PARA 398 et seq.

9   See PARAS 339–340. As to litigation see PARA 391 et seq.

10   See the Housing Grants, Construction and Regeneration Act 1996 s 112; and PARA 356.

327. Interim certificates.

The purpose of interim certificates is to provide for payments on account, for example by reference to the value of the works or by stage payments of fixed or variable sums[1]. Most contracts expressly provide that sums paid on interim certificates will be subject to adjustment on the issuing of the final certificate but interim payments have always been regarded as subject to such adjustment[2]. An interim certificate will not be taken as an approval of the work[3]. In general, an interim certificate creates a debt in favour of the contractor which the employer must pay at once[4] subject to any right to set-off. Moreover, the employer may not withhold payment under a construction contract unless he has given an effective withholding notice[5]. Where, however, in contracts other than construction contracts, the contract provides that payment shall not legally be due until completion but that advances may be made against certificates, the contractor has no right of action before completion[6].

Where the contract provides that no reference of any dispute to arbitration may be made until the completion of the works, the amount certified by way of interim certificate cannot be challenged by arbitration before completion. Often a dispute as to withholding an interim certificate is excepted from such a provision so that such a dispute can be submitted to arbitration at once, but a dispute relating to the valuation of work included in an interim certificate does not amount to a dispute over the withholding of an interim certificate[7].

However, the contractor under a construction contract generally has an immediate remedy for under-valuation by adjudication, which remedy he may pursue at any time[8].

1 A party to a construction contract is, subject to limited exceptions, entitled to payment by instalments, stage payments or other periodic payments: see the Housing Grants, Construction and Regeneration Act 1996 s 109; and PARA 352. As to the meaning of 'construction contract' for the purposes of the Housing Grants, Construction and Regeneration Act 1996 see PARA 210. As to construction contracts see PARAS 210–211, 352–357, 407 et seq.

2 *Lamprell v Billericay Union* (1849) 3 Exch 283 at 305 per Rolfe B; *Tharsis Sulphur and Copper Co v M'Elroy & Sons* (1878) 3 App Cas 1040 at 1048–1049, HL, per Lord Hatherley LC.

3 *Tripp v Armitage* (1839) 4 M & W 687; *Cooper v Uttoxeter Burial Board* (1864) 11 LT 565; *Richardson v Mahon* (1879) 4 LR Ir 486; *Beaufort Developments (NI) Ltd v Gilbert-Ash NI Ltd* [1999] 1 AC 266 at 276, [1998] 2 All ER 778 at 786, HL, per Lord Hoffmann.

4 *Pickering v Ilfracombe Rly Co* (1868) LR 3 CP 235. See also PARA 329.

5 See the Housing Grants, Construction and Regeneration Act 1996 s 111; and PARA 355. See also *Rupert Morgan Building Services (LLC) Ltd v Jervis* [2003] EWCA Civ 1563, [2004] 1 All ER 529, [2004] 1 WLR 1867 (the interim certificate might be wrong, but in the absence of a withholding notice, the Housing Grants, Construction and Regeneration Act 1996 s 111(1) operated to prevent the client withholding the sum due); applied in applied in *Kilker Projects Ltd v Purton* [2016] EWHC 2616 (TCC), [2017] Bus LR 418, [2016] All ER (D) 130 (Oct); and *Adam Architecture Ltd v Halsbury Homes Ltd* [2017] EWCA Civ 1735, 175 ConLR 1, [2017] All ER (D) 91 (Nov). See also *Melville Dundas Ltd v George Wimpey UK Ltd* [2007] UKHL 18, [2007] 3 All ER 889, [2007] 1 WLR 1136.

6 *Tharsis Sulphur and Copper Co v M'Elroy & Sons* (1878) 3 App Cas 1040 at 1048–1049, HL. See also *Henry Boot Construction Ltd v Alstom Combined Cycles Ltd* [2005] EWCA Civ 814, [2005] 3 All ER 932, [2005] 1 WLR 3850 (certificates were a condition precedent to the claimant's entitlement to payment).

7 *AE Farr Ltd v Ministry of Transport* [1960] 3 All ER 88, [1960] 1 WLR 956.

8 See the Housing Grants, Construction and Regeneration Act 1996 s 108; and PARA 410. See also *Herschel Engineering Ltd v Breen Property Ltd* [2000] BLR 272, [2000] TCLR 473; and PARA 410.

328. Ascertaining the amount of an interim certificate.

It depends upon the terms of the contract whether the certifier is to take into account not only the value of work done but also the value of the contractor's materials and plant[1]. The certifier may be required, or be given discretion, to include the value of materials intended for incorporation in the works not yet brought onto the site. Where the architect or engineer is required to value work done, it is submitted that 'value' means the proportion that the work done bears to the value of the contract as a whole; the cost to the contractor is irrelevant[2]. The architect may have power to include in an interim certificate an amount in respect of work carried out by a nominated sub-contractor[3].

1 See eg *Pickering v Ilfracombe Rly Co* (1868) LR 3 CP 235; and see *Tripp v Armitage* (1839) 4 M & W 687.
2 See *FR Absalom Ltd v Great Western (London) Garden Village Society Ltd* [1933] AC 592, HL.
3 As to the nomination of sub-contractors see PARA 239.

329. Payment of interim certificate.

The express or implied terms of the contract will determine the time when the employer is to make payment on an interim certificate. If a construction contract[1] fails to make adequate express provision as to the time for payment, the relevant provisions of the scheme for construction contracts apply[2]. In most cases, an unliquidated cross-claim for defective work or delay arising out of the performance of the contract will provide an employer with a defence by way of set-off to a claim by a contractor[3]. However, if a contract clearly and unequivocally purports to exclude or restrict the right of set-off the courts will give effect to such a provision[4]. In such a case the employer can only deduct sums permitted by the contract. It is now established, however, that the employer can raise unliquidated damages for delay or defective work as a defence to a claim brought on interim certificates by way of set-off[5] or abatement[6]. However, under a construction contract the employer's defence of set-off or abatement is subject to the service of an effective notice of intention to withhold payment[7].

1 Ie a 'construction contract' as defined in the Housing Grants, Construction and Regeneration Act 1996: see PARA 210.
2 See the Housing Grants, Construction and Regeneration Act 1996 s 110(3); and PARA 353. As to payment provisions under the scheme for construction contracts see PARA 358.
3 *Hanak v Green* [1958] 2 QB 9, [1958] 2 All ER 141, CA. As to set-off see PARA 379; and CIVIL PROCEDURE vol 11 (2015) PARA 382 et seq.
4 *Gilbert-Ash (Northern) Ltd v Modern Engineering (Bristol) Ltd* [1974] AC 689, [1973] 3 All ER 195, HL.
5 *Frederick Mark Ltd v Schild* [1972] 1 Lloyd's Rep 9, 1 BLR 34, CA; *GKN Foundations Ltd v Wandsworth London Borough Council* [1972] 1 Lloyd's Rep 528, 1 BLR 40, CA; and *Gilbert-Ash (Northern) Ltd v Modern Engineering (Bristol) Ltd* [1974] AC 689, [1973] 3 All ER 195, HL (overruling *Dawnays Ltd v FG Minter Ltd* [1971] 2 All ER 1389, [1971] 1 WLR 1205, CA). See PARA 379.
6 *Gilbert-Ash (Northern) Ltd v Modern Engineering (Bristol) Ltd* [1974] AC 689, [1973] 3 All ER 195, HL; *Acsim (Southern) v Dancon Danish Contracting and Development Co Ltd* (1989) 47 BLR 55, CA. See PARA 379.
7 See the Housing Grants, Construction and Regeneration Act 1996 s 111 (see PARA 355). See also *Northern Developments (Cumbria) Ltd v J & J Nichol* [2000] BLR 158; *VHE Construction plc v RBSTB Trust Co Ltd* [2000] BLR 187, 70 Con LR 51; *Beck Interiors Ltd v Classic Decorative Finishing Ltd* [2012] EWHC 1956 (TCC), [2012] NLJR 999, [2012] All ER (D) 152 (Jul).

330. Function of final certificates.

The effect of a final certificate will depend on the terms of the contract[1]. The contract may provide that the final certificate must: (1) state the amount finally due to the parties; (2) express the architect's satisfaction with the works; (3) release to the contractor the retention money[2]; or (4) contain any combination of these provisions. Thus where the architect has no power to certify the final balance due, a statement of the final balance due in a final certificate will not bind the parties[3] and in such a case the final balance must be ascertained by litigation[4], arbitration[5] or adjudication[6]. An architect or engineer will be functus officio after the issue of the final certificate[7], unless he has other functions to perform[8] under the contract.

1 See the cases cited in PARA 323 note 2.
2 As to retention money see PARA 346.
3 *Pashby v Birmingham Corpn* (1856) 18 CB 2.
4 As to litigation see PARA 391 et seq.
5 As to arbitration see PARA 398 et seq.
6 As to adjudication see PARA 407 et seq.
7 See *H Fairweather Ltd v Asden Securities Ltd* (1979) 12 BLR 40.
8 Eg resolving disputes in civil engineering contracts.

331. Effect of a final certificate.

Except where the architect is disqualified from certifying[1] or where the certificate may otherwise be dispensed with[2], the final certificate will be binding and, depending on the terms of the contract, may also be conclusive, otherwise than where there is fraud. Thus, where a final certificate states an amount as due to the contractor which includes sums in respect of additional work which is not ordered in writing, the employer cannot resist payment in respect of the additional work[3].

The binding effect of a final certificate may, subject to the express terms of the contract, be open to review by the court, adjudicator or arbitrator in proceedings[4]. Whether (and, if so, upon what matters) a final certificate is conclusive is a question of the construction of the particular terms of the contract[5]. The contract may provide that the final certificate will not become conclusive until the expiration of a specified period from issue. It may also provide that the certificate may be prevented from becoming conclusive by either side taking prescribed steps[6].

Even where the arbitrator or court has the power to review certificates in general, the final certificate may be expressly rendered conclusive in some respects. Where a contractor has agreed to take proceedings in the courts, he is not estopped or precluded from relying on the conclusive effect of the final certificate issued on a date subsequent to the start of the proceedings. But a final certificate may be conclusive that the works have been properly completed only when the matter is judged at the date of the certificate[7].

Where the certificate has been given within the jurisdiction conferred on the architect or engineer, and in the absence of fraud or collusion, it cannot be attacked on the grounds that the certifier was mistaken or that the certificate is unreasonable[8]. If the certificate is based on erroneous reports by an agent of the employer, and not on the fraud of the contractor, it is conclusive against the employer[9]. In the context of payments and pay less notices[10], the Courts have held that the issue of a final certificate, as opposed to an interim certificate, for payment still requires a pay less notice be given in due time for the employer to have the right to withhold sums due, including where the final certificate is issued after a termination of the contract. But the final certificate will not, in such circumstances, be conclusive evidence of the amounts due between the parties[11].

1 See PARAS 333–335.
2 See PARA 336 et seq.
3 *Goodyear v Weymouth and Melcombe Regis Corpn* (1865) 35 LJCP 12; *Connor v Belfast Water Comrs* (1871) IR 5 CL 55; *Laidlaw v Hastings Pier Co* (1874) 2 Hudson's BC (10th Edn) 428, 554, 636, 642.
4 See PARAS 339–340.

5 *East Ham Corpn v Bernard Sunley & Sons Ltd* [1966] AC 406, sub nom *East Ham Borough Council v Bernard Sunley & Sons Ltd* [1965] 3 All ER 619, HL; *P & M Kaye Ltd v Hosier & Dickinson Ltd* [1972] 1 All ER 121, [1972] 1 WLR 146, HL; *Crestar Ltd v Carr* (1987) 37 BLR 113, (1987) 131 Sol Jo 1154, CA; *Colbart Ltd v Kumar* (1992) 59 BLR 89; *Crown Estate Comrs v John Mowlem & Co Ltd* (1994) 70 BLR 1, (1994) 40 Con LR 36, CA; *Matthew Hall Ortech Ltd v Tarmac Roadstone Ltd* (1997) 87 BLR 96.

6 Contracts often contain provisions which enable either party to avoid the conclusive effect of the final certificate by commencing arbitration proceedings within a specified period. However, if proceedings are not brought within this period, the court will not grant an extension of time so as to relieve the conclusive effect of the certificate: *Crown Estate Comrs v John Mowlem & Co Ltd* (1994) 70 BLR 1, (1994) 40 Con LR 36, CA; overruling *McLaughlin & Harvey plc v P & O Developments Ltd* (1991) 55 BLR 101. As to the power of the court to extend the time for beginning arbitral proceedings see the Arbitration Act 1996 s 12; and ARBITRATION vol 2 (2017) PARA 521.

7 *P & M Kaye Ltd v Hosier and Dickinson Ltd* [1972] 1 All ER 121, [1972] 1 WLR 146, HL; *HW Nevill (Sunblest) Ltd v William Press & Son Ltd* (1981) 20 BLR 78.

8 *Goodyear v Weymouth and Melcombe Regis Corpn* (1865) 35 LJCP 12; *Harvey v Lawrence* (1867) 15 LT 571; *Sharpe v San Paulo Rly Co* (1873) 8 Ch App 597; *Laidlaw v Hastings Pier Co* (1874) 2 Hudson's BC (10th Edn) 428, 554, 636, 642; *Lord Bateman v Thompson* (1875) 2 Hudson's BC (10th Edn) 383, 428, CA; *Campbell v Edwards* [1976] 1 All ER 785, [1976] 1 WLR 403, CA; *Lubenham Fidelities and Investments Co Ltd v South Pembrokeshire District Council* (1986) 33 BLR 39; *Jones v Sherwood Computer Services plc* [1992] 2 All ER 170, [1992] 1 WLR 277, CA; *Dixons Group plc v Murray-Oboynski* (1997) 86 BLR 16.

9 *Ayr Road Trustees v Adams* (1883) 11 R 326, Ct of Sess. Similarly, an incorrect report from an agent of the certifier will not invalidate the certificate: *Clemence v Clarke* (1879) 2 Hudson's BC (10th Edn) 443, 466, CA.

10 Ie under the Housing Grants, Construction and Regeneration Act 1996 s 111: see PARA 355.

11 *Adam Architecture Ltd v Halsbury Homes Ltd* [2017] EWCA Civ 1735, 175 ConLR 1, [2017] All ER (D) 91 (Nov) (employer was ordered to pay the value of the final certificate in the absence of a pay less notice being served. Jacob LJ (at [50]) discussed what happens where a final certificate includes items not done or charged for twice and the time for serving a pay less notice has passed. An obvious concern would arise if the section in the Act had the effect of not only requiring the client to pay for such items, but was conclusive). See also *Harding (trading as M.J. Harding Contractors) v Paice* [2015] EWCA Civ 1231, [2016] 2 All ER 819, [2016] 1 WLR 4068, which makes it clear that whilst the employer may have to make the payment, the employer was also entitled to proceed to adjudication in order to determine the correct value of the contractor's claims and the employer's counterclaims and the final certificate in such cases will not be conclusive as to monies due, simply because the Act is not complied with and payment in full has to be made.

(ii) Recovery without or in Disregard of Certificates

332. Ultra vires certificates.

The certificates of architects and engineers are only conclusive as to matters entrusted to them, and if the certificate is ultra vires as to any matter it is to that extent not conclusive[1]. Thus, it may be conclusive as to quantity and not as to liability, or vice versa[2].

Again, if there is no power in the contract to vary the work to be done, a valid certificate cannot be given for work done at variance with the contract, even though the variation was made on the instructions of the architect, and is of equivalent value to that which should have been done[3].

If the power to certify only arises on the happening of a certain event (such as the builder making default) the ascertainment of the event must precede the exercise of the power. Where no method of ascertaining the happening of the event is prescribed in the contract, the question, in case of dispute, must be left to the court, adjudication or arbitration[4]. If the architect has power to ascertain whether the event has happened, he must have actually determined that question before his power to certify arises.

1   *Lawson v Wallasey Local Board* (1882) 11 QBD 229, DC (affd (1883) 48 LT 507, CA); *Brunsdon v Staines Local Board* (1884) Cab & El 272.
2   Cf *Northampton Gas Light Co v Parnell* (1855) 15 CB 630.
3   *Ashwell and Nesbit Ltd v Allen & Co* (1912) 2 Hudson's BC (10th Edn) 410, CA.
4   *Northampton Gas Light Co v Parnell* (1855) 15 CB 630. As to the determination of disputes see PARA 391 et seq.

333. Disqualification generally.

A court or arbitrator can disregard an existing certificate or dispense with the need for a certificate if the certifier is disqualified from certifying. The certifier must act impartially[1] and independently and will be disqualified if he fails to do so[2]. He should not give an opportunity to be heard to one party which he does not give to another[3]. The certifier may be disqualified by reason of some interest which was unknown to one of the parties at the time of the contract[4] or on the ground of fraud or collusion between the certifier and one of the parties[5]. Collusion between employer and certifier may also amount to an interference by the employer enabling the contractor to recover without a certificate[6]. Even where there is no fraud or bad faith a certifier may be disqualified if he is so influenced by one or other of the parties that he loses his independence[7].

1   *Sutcliffe v Thackrah* [1974] AC 727, [1974] 1 All ER 859, HL; *Beaufort Developments (NI) Ltd v Gilbert-Ash NI Ltd* [1999] 1 AC 266 at 276, [1998] 2 All ER 778 at 786, HL, per Lord Hoffmann.
2   *Hickman & Co v Roberts* [1913] AC 229, HL.
3   *Page v Llandaff and Dinas Powis RDC* (1901) 2 Hudson's BC (4th Edn) 316; *Re Fuerst Bros & Co Ltd and Stephenson* [1951] 1 Lloyd's Rep 429; and see *Armstrong v South London Tramways Co Ltd* (1890) 7 TLR 123, CA; *Eaglesham v McMaster* [1920] 2 KB 169. Such conduct by the certifier might also be contrary to the Human Rights Act 1998 (see RIGHTS AND FREEDOMS vol 88A (2018) PARA 45 et seq), but cf the position of an adjudicator, as to which see *Austin Hall Building Ltd v Buckland Securities Ltd* [2001] BLR 272, 80 Con LR 115.
4   See PARA 334.
5   *Kimberley v Dick* (1871) LR 13 Eq 1; *Wakefield and Barnsley Banking Co v Normanton Local Board* (1881) 44 LT 697, CA.
6   The border line between collusion and interference is very fine: see PARA 337.
7   *Hickman & Co v Roberts* [1913] AC 229, HL.

334. Disqualification for interest.

Where a certifier has a sufficient interest in the outcome of his decision to create a likelihood of bias he will be disqualified from exercising the jurisdiction[1]. Where objection to a certificate under a contract is taken on the ground of interest, it must be shown that the interest was not known to the complaining party at the time the contract was made[2]. A contractor will be presumed to have known: (1) that the certifier is an agent, and in some cases an employee, of the employer[3]; (2) that the certifier may have given the employer estimates in respect of the cost of the works and therefore has an interest in seeing that such estimates are not exceeded; (3) that an architect or engineer often advises the employer on the contract which gives such architect or engineer jurisdiction to certify; (4) that an architect or engineer has an interest in keeping down the cost of extras; (5) that, in his capacity as agent, the certifier will have frequent communication with both employer and contractor.

Where the employer is a company, the fact that the certifier is a shareholder may not give rise to disqualification[4]. If the architect or engineer has given the employer a clear undertaking that the cost of the works will not exceed a stated amount, such architect or engineer will be disqualified from certifying[5]. It is material that the certifier is related to or in the debt of one of the parties; such facts ought to be disclosed and if they are not disclosed the certifier may be disqualified[6].

1 *Dimes v Proprietors of Grand Junction Canal Co* (1852) 3 HL Cas 759 (it is immaterial that the certifier did not allow his interest to affect his judgment). But a suspicion of bias will not of itself disqualify an arbitrator named in a reference: *Bright v River Plate Construction Co* [1900] 2 Ch 835.
2 *Ranger v Great Western Rly Co* (1854) 5 HL Cas 72; *Matthew v Ollerton* (1693) 4 Mod Rep 226.
3 *Pickthall v Merthyr Tydvil Local Board* (1886) 2 TLR 805; *Jackson v Barry Rly Co* [1893] 1 Ch 238, CA; *Eckersley v Mersey Docks and Harbour Board* [1894] 2 QB 667, CA; *Ives and Barker v Willans* [1894] 2 Ch 478, CA; *Beaufort Developments (NI) Ltd v Gilbert-Ash NI Ltd* [1999] 1 AC 266 at 276, [1998] 2 All ER 778 at 786, HL, per Lord Hoffmann.
4 *Ranger v Great Western Rly Co* (1854) 5 HL Cas 72; but cf *Sellar v Highland Rly Co* 1919 SC (HL) 19.
5 *Kemp v Rose* (1858) 1 Giff 258; *Kimberley v Dick* (1871) LR 13 Eq 1.
6 *Ludlam v Wilson* (1901) 2 OLR 549, Ont CA.

335. Disqualification for fraud or collusion.

Neither the employer nor the contractor will be bound by a certificate given as a result of collusion between the certifier and one of the parties. In such a case, the certifier is disqualified[1]. It is immaterial whether the fraudulent or collusive conduct took place before or after the contract was made[2]. Where the contractor alleges that the works are complete and that the architect has withheld a certificate in collusion with the employer, he has a good cause of action notwithstanding the absence of the certificate[3]. Further, a contractor may sue where he alleges that the engineer has fraudulently certified less than what is due to him[4].

1 *Batterbury v Vyse* (1863) 32 LJEx 177.
2 *Panama and South Pacific Telegraph Co v India Rubber, Gutta Percha and Telegraph Works Co* (1875) 10 Ch App 515.
3 *Batterbury v Vyse* (1863) 32 LJEx 177. Refusal to certify is not of itself proof of fraud: *Stevenson v Watson* (1879) 4 CPD 148 (distinguishing *Sutcliffe v Thackrah* [1974] AC 727, [1974] 1 All ER 859, [1974] 2 WLR 295).
4 *Waring v Manchester, Sheffield and Lincolnshire Rly Co* (1849) 18 LJCh 450. As to the position of a quantity surveyor fraudulently making out quantities short see *Priestly v Stone* (1888) 4 TLR 730, CA.

336. Dispensing with or disregarding certificates generally.

Whether or not there is an existing certificate, either party may sue if the certifier is disqualified[1]. The contractor can claim payment if the employer has interfered with the exercise of the certifier's jurisdiction or prevented the issue of a certificate, and both parties may take action if the certifier has exceeded or abused his jurisdiction under the contract[2]. A contractor cannot be restrained by injunction from bringing a claim for payment even though a certificate which is a condition precedent to payment[3] has not been granted[4]. The requirement of a certificate as a condition precedent to payment may also, of course, be waived by the employer.

1 See PARA 333.
2 See PARA 338.
3 See PARA 326.
4 *Baron de Worms v Mellier* (1873) LR 16 Eq 554.

337. Interference or prevention by the employer.

If the employer interferes with or prevents the issue of a certificate, the contractor can recover the sums due and the employer cannot rely on the absence of a certificate[1]. Alternatively, in such a case the contractor can recover the sums due to him as damages for breach of an implied term that the employer should not interfere with or prevent the exercise of the certifier's jurisdiction[2] or of an implied term that the employer should act honestly, fairly and reasonably[3]. An express instruction by the employer that the architect should not issue a further certificate will amount to interference if the architect is in any way influenced by it[4]. There is interference if the employer directs the certifier to value the works in a manner not sanctioned by the contract[5]. A failure to replace an architect who has retired, become incapacitated or died may amount to prevention, allowing the contractor to recover without a certificate[6].

1 *Hotham v East India Co* (1787) 1 Term Rep 638 at 645 per Ashurst J; *Bliss v Smith* (1865) 34 Beav 508; *Mackay v Dick* (1881) 6 App Cas 251, HL; *Brunsden v Beresford* (1883) Cab & El 125; *McDonald v Workington Corpn* (1893) 9 TLR 230, CA. In *Smith v Peters* (1875) LR 20 Eq 511 the court granted an order of mandamus directing the employer to permit the certifier to enter the site to make a valuation. See also *Sudbrook Trading Estate Ltd v Eggleton* [1983] 1 AC 444, [1982] 3 All ER 1, [1982] 3 WLR 315.

2 *McIntosh v Great Western Rly Co* (1850) 19 LJCh 374; *Smith v Howden Union RSA and Fowler* (1890) 2 Hudson's BC (10th Edn) 461, 709, 711; *John Mowlem & Co plc v Eagle Star Insurance Co Ltd* (1992) 62 BLR 126, (1992) 33 Con LR 131.

3 *Balfour Beatty Civil Engineering Ltd v Docklands Light Railway Ltd* (1996) 78 BLR 42, (1996) 49 Con LR 1, CA; but see discussion of this case in *Beaufort Developments (NI) Ltd v Gilbert-Ash NI Ltd* [1999] 1 AC 266 at 281–282, [1998] 2 All ER 778 at 790–791, HL, per Lord Hoffmann.

4 *Hickman & Co v Roberts* [1913] AC 229, HL.

5 *Page v Llandaff and Dinas Powis RDC* (1901) 2 Hudson's BC (4th Edn) 316. In *Watts v McLeay* (1911) 19 WLR 916 (Alta) the architect consulted the employer's solicitors and this was held to amount to interference by the employer.

6 *Croudace Ltd v Lambeth London Borough Council* (1986) 33 BLR 20, (1986) 6 Con LR 70, CA.

338. Abuse or excess of jurisdiction by certifier.

A certifier must act impartially[1]. It is possible for a certificate to be attacked on the ground that the certifier did not give the parties an equal opportunity of being heard[2]. While the certifier can use the assistance of others in deciding whether or not he can issue a certificate, the decision must be his own and not that of an assistant[3].

The certifier abuses his powers if he persistently refuses to certify[4] or if he expressly refuses to come to a decision on a matter over which he has jurisdiction by virtue of the contract[5], and in these circumstances the contractor can recover without a certificate. It seems that the contractor may recover where, in refusing a certificate, a certifier has not conducted himself with impartiality[6]. Again the certifier must act within his jurisdiction and in coming to a decision cannot have regard to matters which are not referred to him by the contract[7].

Where the parties have expressly agreed to be bound by the determination of a certifier acting as an independent expert then, in the absence of collusion or fraud, the certificate can only be challenged on the ground of mistake if there is evidence that the certifier has exceeded his jurisdiction and departed from his instructions in a material respect[8].

1 *Pawley v Turnbull* (1861) 3 Giff 70; and see *Smith v Howden Union RSA and Fowler* (1890) 2 Hudson's BC (10th Edn) 461, 709, 711; *Sutcliffe v Thackrah* [1974] AC 727, [1974] 1 All ER 859, HL. See also *Scheldebouw BV v St James Homes (Grosvenor Dock) Ltd* [2006] EWHC 89 (TCC), [2006] BLR 113 105 Con LR 90.

2 *Page v Llandaff and Dinas Powis RDC* (1901) 2 Hudson's BC (4th Edn) 316; *Re Fuerst Bros & Co Ltd and Stephenson* [1951] 1 Lloyd's Rep 429. The extent to which the audi alteram partem rule applies to certifiers is not clear, but see *Hounslow London Borough Council v Twickenham Garden Developments Ltd* [1971] Ch 233, [1970] 3 All ER 326. As to the right to a fair trial

(including the right to a fair and public hearing within a reasonable time by an independent and impartial tribunal) under the Convention for the Protection of Human Rights and Fundamental Freedoms (1950) (Rome, 4 November 1950; TS 71 (1953); Cmd 8969) art 6 (set out in the Human Rights Act 1998) see RIGHTS AND FREEDOMS vol 88A (2018) PARA 45 et seq.

3   *Ess v Truscott* (1837) 2 M & W 385; *A-G v Briggs* (1855) 1 Jur NS 1084.
4   *Kellett v New Mills UDC* (1900) 2 Hudson's BC (4th Edn) 298.
5   *Watts v McLeay* (1911) 19 WLR 916, Alta; *Neale v Richardson* [1938] 1 All ER 753, CA.
6   *Pawley v Turnbull* (1861) 3 Giff 70.
7   *Panamena Europea Navigacion (Compania Limitada) v Frederick Leyland & Co Ltd (J Russell & Co)* [1947] AC 428, HL.
8   *Campbell v Edwards* [1976] 1 All ER 785, [1976] 1 WLR 403, CA; *Jones v Sherwood Computer Services plc* [1992] 2 All ER 170, [1992] 1 WLR 277, CA; *Dixons v Murray-Oboynski* (1997) 86 BLR 16.

339.   Effect of proceedings.

Where a certificate is withheld, the contractor or the employer may have a remedy by way of adjudication, arbitration or court proceedings[1]. In relation to construction contracts[2], an adjudicator is empowered by statute to decide the rights and obligations of the parties, albeit temporarily, notwithstanding the presence or absence of certificates[3]. Subject to the express terms of the contract, the court and the arbitrator may also have such powers[4]. In none of these proceedings is a certificate a condition precedent to a decision, award or judgment that a sum of money is to be paid by one party to the other[5].

1   As to dispute resolution see PARA 391 et seq.
2   Ie a 'construction contract' as defined in the Housing Grants, Construction and Regeneration Act 1996: see PARA 210.
3   See the Housing Grants, Construction and Regeneration Act 1996 s 108; and PARA 410. As to adjudication generally see PARA 407 et seq.
4   As to the powers of an arbitrator and the court see PARA 340.
5   *Brodie v Cardiff Corpn* [1919] AC 337, HL; *Neale v Richardson* [1938] 1 All ER 753, 82 Sol Jo 331, CA; *Prestige & Co Ltd v Brettell* [1938] 4 All ER 346, 82 Sol Jo 929, CA; *Beaufort Developments (NI) Ltd v Gilbert-Ash NI Ltd* [1999] 1 AC 266, [1998] 2 All ER 778, HL; *R and C Electrical Engineers Ltd v Shaylor Construction Ltd* [2012] EWHC 1254 (TCC), (2012) 142 ConLR 129.

340.   Powers of the arbitrator and the court.

Where a contract contains an arbitration clause in sufficiently wide terms, the decisions of the certifier may be reviewed by the arbitrator[1]. The extent of the arbitrator's powers will depend on the wording of the arbitration clause. However, the arbitrator is commonly given an express power to open up, review or revise the decisions of the certifier.

In certain cases, despite an arbitration clause, on the proper construction of the contract some decisions of the certifier will not be subject to review[2]. Thus where matters left by the contract to the decision or determination of the engineer were excepted from the arbitration clause it was held that an engineer's certificate of completion and satisfaction was binding[3].

The court has an inherent power to open up, review and revise any certificate, opinion, decision, requirement or notice of a certifier and to determine matters in dispute as if they had not been given unless the contract in question makes clear by express words that such powers are to be exercised by the arbitrator only[4].

The powers of the arbitrator and of the courts summarised in this paragraph would, it is thought, extend to the review both of the certifier's decision to withhold a certificate and to the contents of any certificate that had been given.

These powers do not, however, extend to the review of certificates which are provided by the contract to be final and conclusive[5].

1 As to arbitration see PARA 398 et seq; and ARBITRATION.
2 *Scott v Liverpool Corpn* (1858) 28 LJCh 230; *Clemence v Clarke* (1879) 2 Hudson's BC (10th Edn) 443, 466, CA; and see also *Eaglesham v McMaster* [1920] 2 KB 169.
3 *Re Meadows and Kenworthy* (1897) 2 Hudson's BC (10th Edn) 443, HL; *Ata Ul Haq v City Council of Nairobi* (1962) 28 BLR 76, PC.
4 *Beaufort Developments (NI) Ltd v Gilbert-Ash NI Ltd* [1999] 1 AC 266, [1998] 2 All ER 778, HL; overruling *Northern Regional Health Authority v Derek Crouch Construction Co Ltd* [1984] QB 644, [1984] 2 All ER 175, CA. Prior to this decision of the House of Lords, it was thought that the court could review the certifier's decision only if the parties so agreed pursuant to the Senior Courts Act 1981 s 43A (see COURTS AND TRIBUNALS vol 24 (2010) PARA 701) or the arbitration or certification machinery had broken down (see eg *John Barker Construction Ltd v London Portman Hotel Ltd* (1996) 83 BLR 31). The Senior Courts Act 1981 was previously known as the Supreme Court Act 1981 and was renamed by the Constitutional Reform Act 2005 s 59(5), Sch 11 Pt 1 as from 1 October 2009: see the Constitutional Reform Act 2005 (Commencement No 11) Order 2009, SI 2009/1604: and COURTS AND TRIBUNALS vol 24 (2010) PARA 687.
5 See PARA 331.

(2) Remuneration

(i) Amounts Payable

341. Price fixed by the contract.
There are two ways in which the price may be fixed by the contract. First, the contractor may have undertaken to execute specified work for a specified sum, in which case a claim by him for the lump sum price or an agreed instalment is a liquidated demand and he can apply for summary judgment[1]. Secondly, where the extent of the work is at the time of the contract uncertain, the contract may provide that the price be ascertained by measuring the work done against items in a bill of quantities or in a schedule of rates[2]; in such a case the contractor can recover the price when the measurement has been certified[3].

In both cases, the employer can only avoid paying the contract price by showing that the contract was frustrated[4] or that it was void ab initio or that by reason of the number of variations the identity of the original contract has been lost[5]. In the vary rare cases where these arguments succeed, the contractor will be entitled to recover on a quantum meruit basis[6].

1 Where the price is payable by instalments summary judgment may be obtained in respect of each instalment: *Workman, Clark & Co Ltd v Lloyd Brazileño* [1908] 1 KB 968, CA. As to the different forms of building contract see PARA 209.
2 See *Jamieson v M'Innes* (1887) 15 R 17, Ct of Sess; *Wilkie v Hamilton Lodging House Co* (1902) 4 F 951, Ct of Sess.
3 See *Whitaker v Dunn* (1887) 3 TLR 602; see also *Stephenson v Weir* (1879) 4 LR Ir 369; *Meade v Mouillott* (1879) 4 LR Ir 207.
4 See PARA 310. A quantum meruit claim (see RESTITUTION vol 88 (2012) PARA 513 et seq) will only lie in respect of work done after the date of frustration; the Law Reform (Frustrated Contracts) Act 1943 (see CONTRACT vol 22 (2012) PARA 484 et seq) will apply to work done before the date of frustration.
5 See eg *Sir Lindsay Parkinson & Co Ltd v Works and Public Buildings Comrs* [1949] 2 KB 632, [1950] 1 All ER 208, CA; cf *McAlpine Humberoak Ltd v McDermott International Inc* (1992) 58 BLR 1, (1992) 28 Con LR 76, CA. Providing there was an instruction to do work and an acceptance of that instruction, there was a contract and the law would imply into it an obligation to pay a reasonable sum for that work: *ACT Construction Ltd v E Clarke & Son (Coaches) Ltd* [2002] EWCA Civ 972, 85 Con LR 1, [2002] All ER (D) 241 (Jul).

6   In *Morrison-Knudsen Co Inc v British Columbia Hydro and Power Authority* (1978) 85 DLR (3d)
    186, BC CA, there is an instructive discussion of the question (where it was held that the contractor
    was not entitled to a quantum meruit).

342.   Adjustments where the price is fixed by the contract.

In the modern standard form contracts[1], there may be adjustments to the
contract price by reason of express terms of the contract. These terms are of three
types: (1) clauses (known as 'fluctuation clauses') entitling the contractor to be
reimbursed for any increase in the cost of taxes, labour or materials or giving the
employer the benefit of any decrease in such costs[2]; (2) clauses requiring an
adjustment to the contract price in the event of variations[3]; (3) clauses by virtue
of which a contractor may claim other increases in the contract price[4]. In some
cases the subject matter of claim permitted by the contract may overlap with
circumstances which amount prima facie to a breach by the employer and in such
a case the right of the contractor to claim additional payment under the contract
is generally additional to and not in substitution of his right to claim damages for
breach[5]. The terms of the contract will often make a notice in writing a condition
precedent to a claim by the contractor; it is a question of construction whether the
contractor can recover under the contract in the absence of a notice which
complies with the terms of the contract[6].

Extra work may be required by the employer outside the contract if it is carried
out after completion of the original contract work[7] or it is not within the scope of
the variation clause[8]. The employer will generally be liable to pay a reasonable
price for such work carried out at his request[9].

1   As to standard forms of contract see PARA 202.
2   See *William Sindall Ltd v North West Thames Regional Health Authority* [1977] ICR 294, 4 BLR
    151, HL (a fluctuation clause relating to the cost of labour did not apply to a bonus incentive
    scheme operated by the contractors).
3   As to the valuation of variations see PARA 343. As to variations generally see PARA 272.
4   Many contracts include provisions for the recovery of loss and expense caused to the contractor
    by events outside his control.
5   See *Blackford & Sons (Calne) Ltd v Borough of Christchurch* (1962) 60 LGR 214, [1962] 1
    Lloyd's Rep 349; *Merton London Borough Council v Stanley Hugh Leach Ltd* (1985) 32 BLR 51;
    Architectural Installation Services Ltd v James Gibbons (Windows) Ltd (1989) 46 BLR 91;
    Fairclough Building Ltd v Vale of Belvoir (1990) 56 BLR 74.
6   *Blackford & Sons (Calne) Ltd v Borough of Christchurch* (1962) 60 LGR 214, [1962] 1 Lloyd's
    Rep 349 (a case on ICE conditions of contract: see now ICC Conditions of Contract; and PARA
    202); *Tersons Ltd v Stevenage Development Corpn* [1965] 1 QB 37, [1963] 3 All ER 863, CA;
    Merton London Borough Council v Stanley Hugh Leach Ltd (1985) 32 BLR 51. See also *WW
    Gear Construction Ltd v McGee Group Ltd* [2010] EWHC 1460 (TCC), 131 Con LR 63, [2010]
    All ER (D) 224 (Jun) (notice under clause 4.21 of the JCT Trade Contract Terms (2002 Edn), with
    amendments, was a condition precedent to the recovery of loss and expense under that clause).
7   *Russell v Sa da Bandeira* (1862) 13 CBNS 149.
8   *Costain Civil Engineering Ltd v Zanen Dredging and Contracting Co Ltd* (1996) 85 BLR 77.
9   *Russell v Sa da Bandeira* (1862) 13 CBNS 149; *Astilleros Canarios SA v Cape Hatteras Shipping
    Co Inc* [1982] 1 Lloyd's Rep 518.

(ii) Valuing Variations

343.   Express provision.

The architect or engineer may be given power to value additional or omitted
work and to add the sum arrived at to, or deduct it from, the contract sum.
Generally the contract will provide that additional work of similar character to,
and executed under similar conditions as, the contract work should be valued at
the rates and prices contained in the bills of quantities or schedule of rates[1]. Where

there is no appropriate rate in the bills of quantities or schedule of rates, the architect or engineer may have power to adjust the rates provided or to fix a rate, but where it is impossible to measure the varied work the contractor may be entitled to be paid on daywork rates. The decision of the architect or engineer as to the valuation of variations may be final but such decision is likely to be capable of review in adjudication or court proceedings or (subject to the extent of the powers conferred on the arbitrator) in arbitration[2].

1 See eg *Henry Boot Construction Ltd v Alstom Combined Cycles Ltd* [2000] BLR 247, 69 Con LR 27, CA. See also *BHC Ltd v Galliford Try Infrastructure Ltd* [2018] EWHC 368 (TCC), [2018] All ER (D) 01 (Mar).
2 See PARAS 272, 339–340. As to dispute resolution see PARA 391 et seq.

344. No express provision.

Where there is an express provision in the contract for variations to the contract work but no machinery for ascertaining the value, the parties will be bound by any agreement as to the price of such works, and in default of agreement the employer must pay a reasonable sum[1].

Where there is no express provision in the contract the contractor will be entitled to claim payment for the variations if he can establish a new contract or a promise to pay for the varied works by showing that the employer, or the architect as agent of the employer acting within the scope of his authority[2], ordered or accepted the works or allowed them to proceed in circumstances where the contractor is led to believe that he will be paid for them. Where the work has been ordered or accepted by the architect acting outside his authority the contractor will still be entitled to be paid if the employer subsequently ratifies the architect's orders[3].

Where an order or approval in writing is a condition precedent to payment the contractor will not be able to recover where the condition has not been complied with[4] unless he can show that there was an implied promise by the employer to pay for the variations[5] or he can show that the varied works were not covered by the contract[6].

1 As to the circumstances in which, to value a variation, the rates contained in the bill of quantities must be used, or such rates may be discarded in favour of a 'fair valuation' see *Henry Boot Construction Ltd v Alstom Combined Cycles Ltd* [2000] BLR 247, 69 Con LR 27, CA.
2 *R v Peto* (1826) 1 Y & J 37; *Cooper v Langdon* (1841) 9 M & W 60; *Forrest v Scottish County Investment Co* 1916 SC (HL) 28; *Ashwell and Nesbit Ltd v Allen & Co* (1912) 2 Hudson's BC (10th Edn) 410, CA.
3 See AGENCY vol 1 (2017) PARA 58 et seq.
4 *Kirk v Bromley Union Guardians* (1848) 12 Jur 85; *Ranger v Great Western Rly Co* (1854) 5 HL Cas 72; *Taverner & Co Ltd v Glamorgan County Council* (1941) 57 TLR 243. The architect has no authority to waive the requirements for written orders: *Kirk v Bromley Union Guardians*.
5 *Molloy v Liebe* (1910) 102 LT 616, PC; *Taverner & Co Ltd v Glamorgan County Council* (1940) 57 TLR 243.
6 See PARA 261.

(iii) Method of Payment

345. Instalment payments.

Most building or engineering contracts expressly entitle the contractor to be paid instalments of the contract sum.

A contractor under a construction contract[1] is entitled to payment by instalments, stage payments or other periodic payments for any work under the contract unless it is specified in the contract that the duration is to be less than 45 days, or it is agreed between the parties that the duration of the work is estimated to be less than 45 days[2]. The parties are free to agree the amounts of the payments and the intervals at which, or circumstances in which, they become due[3]. In the absence of such agreement, the relevant provisions of the scheme for construction contracts will apply[4].

In the majority of contracts, payments on account are made to the contractor by way of interim certificates[5]. Sometimes the contract will provide that a specified part of the contract price will be paid when the works reach a particular stage, for instance second floor level[6].

Where there is no express or statutory provision for payments on account and where the contract is not entire in the sense that the completion of the whole is a condition precedent to payment[7], there may be an implied term that the employer will pay the contractor a reasonable sum on account from time to time as the work progresses[8].

An instalment which falls due after termination resulting in a repudiatory breach is not payable[9].

1   Ie a 'construction contract' as defined in the Housing Grants, Construction and Regeneration Act 1996: see PARA 210.
2   See the Housing Grants, Construction and Regeneration Act 1996 s 109(1); and PARA 352.
3   See the Housing Grants, Construction and Regeneration Act 1996 s 109(2); and PARA 352.
4   See the Housing Grants, Construction and Regeneration Act 1996 s 109(3); and PARA 352. As to payment provisions under the scheme for construction contracts see the Scheme for Construction Contracts (England and Wales) Regulations 1998, SI 1998/649; and PARA 358.
5   See PARAS 327–329.
6   *Terry v Duntze* (1795) 2 Hy Bl 389; *Needler v Guest* (1647) Aleyn 9.
7   See PARA 209.
8   *Roberts v Havelock* (1832) 3 B & Ad 404; *The Tergeste* [1903] P 26 at 34 per Phillimore J.
9   *Multiplex Constructions (UK) Ltd v Cleveland Bridge UK Ltd* [2008] EWHC 2280 (TCC), [2008] All ER (D) 04 (Oct). Cf *Adam Architecture Ltd v Halsbury Homes Ltd* [2017] EWCA Civ 1735, [2017] All ER (D) 91 (Nov) which is distinguished as there was no acceptance of a repudiatory breach in that case.

346. Retention money.

The contract may provide that the employer is entitled to deduct from sums due to the contractor by way of interim payment, a specified percentage as 'retention' money. The retention money is retained by the employer as security for the due performance of the contract by the contractor and as a fund to be drawn upon either to complete the work or to rectify defects should the contractor fail to do so. Some contracts provide for the employer's interest in the retention to be fiduciary as trustee[1] although the employer may be allowed recourse to it in respect of debts due to him arising out of the contract. On the completion of the work, in the absence of some other express provision[2], the employer must account for retention money.

1   The court may grant the contractor an injunction requiring the employer to pay the sums into a separate account (see *Rayack Construction Ltd v Lampeter Meat Co Ltd* (1979) 12 BLR 30; *Henry Boot Building Ltd v Croydon Hotel and Leisure Co Ltd* (1985) 36 BLR 41, CA; *Wates Construction (London) Ltd v Franthom Property Ltd* (1991) 53 BLR 23, CA; but cf *Herbert Construction (UK) Ltd v Atlantic Estates plc* (1993) 70 BLR 46, [1993] CILL 858, CA; *PC Harrington Contractors Ltd v Co-Partnership Developments Ltd* (1998) 88 BLR 44, CA) and if a separate fund is created the retention money will form the subject of a trust and so be protected if the employer goes into liquidation. However, an injunction will not be granted after liquidation and the contractor will be an unsecured creditor: see *Re Jartray Developments Ltd* (1982) 22 BLR 134; *MacJordan Construction v Brookmount Erostin* (1991) 56 BLR 1, CA.
2   Eg that some or all of the retention money will not be paid out until the end of a defects or maintenance period: see PARA 322.

347. Bonus payments.

The contract may provide that the contractor is to be entitled to an addition to the contract sum in the event of his completing the works before the stipulated date[1]. The contractor will be entitled to claim the bonus if he completes before the date stated in the bonus clause, but if he is prevented from earning the bonus by some act on the part of the employer he can claim damages but the measure of such damages may not be the amount of the bonus[2]. Liability to pay liquidated damages for late completion does not imply a right to an equivalent or any amount as a bonus for early completion; an employer may not want early completion[3]. Delay caused by a nominated sub-contractor does not amount to prevention by the employer[4].

1 *Ranger v Great Western Rly Co* (1854) 5 HL Cas 72 at 78; *Mackintosh v Midland Counties Rly Co* (1845) 14 M & W 548.
2 *Bywaters & Sons v Curnick & Co* (1906) 2 Hudson's BC (10th Edn) 578, CA; cf *Mackintosh v Midland Counties Rly Co* (1845) 14 M & W 548 at 558 per Alderson B. See also *John Barker Construction Ltd v London Portman Hotel Ltd* (1996) 83 BLR 31, 50 ConLR 43.
3 Eg a developer who has not sold or let the building.
4 *Leslie & Co Ltd v Managers of Metropolitan Asylums District* (1901) 68 JP 86, CA. As to nominated sub-contractors see PARA 239.

348. Interest.

Generally the contractor will not be entitled to interest on any sums due to him unless there is an express or implied term in the contract to this effect[1]. The Late Payment of Commercial Debts (Interest) Act 1998 provides that it is an implied term of any contract to which that Act applies[2] that any 'qualifying debt created by the contract'[3] carries simple interest at a rate prescribed by Order[4]. The Late Payment of Commercial Debts (Interest) Act 1998 applies to contracts for the supply of goods or services where the purchaser and the supplier are each acting in the course of a business, other than an excepted contract[5].

Where the contractor takes legal action to recover sums due to him or to claim damages, a court of record[6] or an arbitrator[7] may award interest at the rate it thinks fit. In the absence of the exercise of this discretion interest is not payable on a claim in debt unless there is an express or implied agreement or mercantile usage[8]. Where the claim is for breach of contract, interest can be recovered as special damages[9] and not otherwise[10]. There is no mercantile usage whereby interest is payable on a debt due under a building contract[11].

1 Where the contract contains provisions for the payment of loss and expense the cost of financing the additional expenditure incurred as a result of the events giving rise to the entitlement to loss and expense may be recovered: see *FG Minter Ltd v Welsh Health Technical Services Organisation* (1980) 13 BLR 1, CA; *Rees and Kirby Ltd v Swansea City Council* (1985) 30 BLR 1, CA.
2 As to the contracts to which the Late Payment of Commercial Debts (Interest) Act 1998 applies see s 2; and SALE OF GOODS AND SUPPLY OF SERVICES vol 91 (2012) PARA 219.
3 See the Late Payment of Commercial Debts (Interest) Act 1998 s 1; and SALE OF GOODS AND SUPPLY OF SERVICES vol 91 (2012) PARA 218 et seq.
4 See the Late Payment of Commercial Debts (Interest) Act 1998 s 6; and SALE OF GOODS AND SUPPLY OF SERVICES vol 91 (2012) PARA 228. The rate of statutory interest so prescribed is currently 8% over the official dealing rate of the Bank of England per annum: see the Late Payment of Commercial Debts (Rate of Interest) (No 3) Order 2002, SI 2002/1675, art 4.
5 See the Late Payment of Commercial Debts (Interest) Act 1998 s 2; and SALE OF GOODS AND SUPPLY OF SERVICES vol 91 (2012) PARA 219.
6 See the Senior Courts Act 1981 s 35A. See also *Food Corpn of India v Marastro Cia Naviera SA, The Trade Fortitude* [1986] 3 All ER 500, [1987] 1 WLR 134, CA. As to courts of record see COURTS AND TRIBUNALS vol 24 (2010) PARA 618.
7 *Chandris v Isbrandtsen-Moller Co* [1951] 1 KB 240 at 262–263, [1950] 2 All ER 618 at 623, CA,

per Tucker LJ; and see the Arbitration Act 1996 s 49; and ARBITRATION vol 2 (2017) PARA 560. Note that the arbitrator is empowered to award compound as well as simple interest.

8 *London, Chatham and Dover Rly Co v South Eastern Rly Co* [1892] 1 Ch 120; affd [1893] AC 429, HL.

9 *President of India v La Pintada Cia Navegacion SA* [1985] AC 104, [1984] 2 All ER 773, HL; *President of India v Lips Maritime Corpn* [1988] AC 395, [1987] 3 All ER 110, HL. Interest must be pleaded and proved: *Hutchinson v Harris* (1978) 10 BLR 19 at 42, CA, per Stephenson LJ.

10 *London, Chatham and Dover Rly Co v South Eastern Rly Co* [1892] 1 Ch 120 at 140, CA, per Lindley LJ; *Barclay v Harris and Cross* (1915) 85 LJKB 115.

11 But see note 1.

349. Appropriation of payments.

There is a general rule of law that, in the absence of any appropriation by the employer at the time of payment, the contractor is at liberty to appropriate a general payment on account to any debt he pleases[1]. However, when a payment has once been appropriated the appropriation cannot be varied subsequently without the consent of the debtor[2]. It is especially important, in the case of building and engineering contracts, to remember that the appropriation must be to a debt[3]. A contractor, therefore, cannot get over the non-fulfilment of a condition precedent to his right to payment by purporting to appropriate a payment for extras not properly ordered in accordance with the contract[4]. Accordingly, when the contractor constructs additional works which are not ordered in a manner prescribed by the contract, or which have not been certified for by the architect when such certificate is a condition precedent to payment, no debt in respect of this additional work has been incurred by the employer, and the contractor cannot alter the position of the employer by purporting to appropriate a payment to this claim[5]. Where a contractor performs work, part of which is unlawful by reason of its being in excess of the work licensed, he cannot appropriate payments made generally on account of work done to the unlawful work, payment for which is unrecoverable[6], so as to enable him to obtain sums in addition to those owing for the lawful work[7].

1 *Thompson v Hudson* (1871) 6 Ch App 320; *Devaynes v Noble, Clayton's Case* (1816) 1 Mer 572; *Cory Bros & Co Ltd v Turkish SS Mecca (Owners), The Mecca* [1897] AC 286, HL; and cf *Deeley v Lloyds Bank Ltd* [1912] AC 756, HL. See CONTRACT vol 22 (2012) PARA 525 et seq.

2 *Mahomed Jan v Ganga Bishun Singh* (1911) LR 38 Ind App 80, PC.

3 *Lamprell v Billericay Union* (1849) 3 Exch 283 at 307 per Rolfe B.

4 A creditor receiving money on account is not authorised to apply it towards the satisfaction of any claim which does not rest on some legal or equitable demand against the debtor: *Lamprell v Billericay Union* (1849) 3 Exch 283 at 307 per Rolfe B.

5 *Lamprell v Billericay Union* (1849) 3 Exch 283.

6 *Dennis & Co Ltd v Munn* [1949] 2 KB 327, [1949] 1 All ER 616, CA.

7 *A Smith & Son (Bognor Regis) Ltd v Walker* [1952] 2 QB 319, [1952] 1 All ER 1008, CA.

350. Where price is not fixed by the contract.

In business to business contracts, where the work is carried out in the reasonable expectation of payment but either there is no contract governing that work[1] or the contract does not specify the price to be paid[2] the contractor is entitled to be paid on a quantum meruit basis[3]. In addition the contractor may possibly be entitled to be paid on a quantum meruit basis where the employer has repudiated the contract[4], but there is conflicting authority on this point and it is more likely that the contractor has no such entitlement[5]. An ascertainment of a reasonable price for the work is a question of fact depending on all the circumstances. A reasonable price includes payment for the skill, supervision and services of the contractor as well as for the materials and labour supplied[6]. A contract to pay the market price has been held to mean payment of the market price ascertained at the date of the contract[7]. Where the bills of quantities or schedule of rates failed to give an item for necessary work, the contractor may be able to claim a reasonable price in respect of that work, if there is no express contractual term to cover such a situation[8].

The contractor may also have a restitutionary remedy entitling him to payment of the value of a benefit conferred on the employer where it would be inequitable for the employer to retain this benefit[9]. For consumer contracts the total price of the goods or services inclusive of taxes, or where the nature of the goods or services is such that the price cannot reasonably be calculated in advance, the manner in which the price is to be calculated must be provided to the consumer before the contract is entered into[10].

1   This includes situations where the original contract was void (see eg *Craven-Ellis v Canons Ltd* [1936] 2 KB 403, [1936] 2 All ER 1066, CA; and *Rover International Ltd v Cannon Film Sales Ltd (No 3)* [1989] 3 All ER 423, [1989] 1 WLR 912, CA); unenforceable (*Pavey & Matthews Pty Ltd v Paul* (1987) 162 CLR 221, Aust HC); frustrated (see PARA 310: a quantum meruit claim (see RESTITUTION vol 88 (2012) PARA 513 et seq) will only lie in respect of work done after the date of frustration; the Law Reform (Frustrated Contracts) Act 1943 (see CONTRACT vol 22 (2012) PARA 484 et seq) will apply to work done before the date of frustration); where the circumstances of the contract have changed so that the contract becomes inapplicable to all or part of the works (see eg *British Movietonews Ltd v London and District Cinemas Ltd* [1952] AC 166, [1952] 2 All ER 617, HL); or the scope of the work has increased greatly (see eg *Sir Lindsay Parkinson & Co Ltd v Works and Public Buildings Comrs* [1949] 2 KB 632, [1950] 1 All ER 208, CA; but note that this is a case on very special facts; and cf *McAlpine Humberoak Ltd v McDermott International Inc* (1992) 58 BLR 1, (1992) 28 Con LR 76, CA); where negotiation of terms had broken down (see *Trollope & Colls Ltd and Holland & Hannen and Cubitts Ltd (t/a Nuclear Civil Constructors (a firm)) v Atomic Power Constructions Ltd* [1962] 3 All ER 1035, [1963] 1 WLR 333; *Peter Lind & Co Ltd v Mersey Docks and Harbour Board* [1972] 2 Lloyd's Rep 234; and *British Steel Corpn v Cleveland Bridge and Engineering Co Ltd* [1984] 1 All ER 504, 24 BLR 94; but cf *Regalian Properties plc v London Docklands Development Corpn* [1995] 1 All ER 1005, [1995] 1 WLR 212); or where the work is not within the scope of the variation clause (see *Costain Civil Engineering Ltd v Zanen Dredging and Contracting Co Ltd* (1996) 85 BLR 77).

2   *Moffat v Laurie* (1855) 15 CB 583; and see the Supply of Goods and Services Act 1982 s 15 (see SALE OF GOODS AND SUPPLY OF SERVICES vol 91 (2012) PARA 332).

3   Whether payment will be deferred until the completion of the contract or paid in instalments (see PARA 345) will in such a case depend upon the construction of the contract: *Roberts v Havelock* (1832) 3 B & Ad 404. See *ERDC Group Ltd v Brunel University* [2006] EWHC 687 (TCC), 109 Con LR 114, [2006] BLR 255 (where it was held that a reasonable price did not become unreasonable simply because the authority in the letter of appointment had expired. The amount due was recoverable on a quantum meruit basis, assessed primarily by reference to the rates and prices applicable to the earlier work, but subject to a reduction to reflect the delay and the sub-standard work). For descriptions of the different types of contract used in relation to building and engineering works see PARAS 202, 209. As to quantum meruit see RESTITUTION vol 88 (2012) PARA 513 et seq.

4   *Lodder v Slowey* [1904] AC 442, PC; *ERDC Construction Ltd v HM Love & Co* (1994) 70 BLR 67, Ct of Sess.

5   See PARA 320.

6   *Grafton v Armitage* (1845) 2 CB 336; *British Steel Corpn v Cleveland Bridge and Engineering Co Ltd* [1984] 1 All ER 504, 24 BLR 94. A claim for work and labour only does not cover materials which should be specifically claimed: see *Heath v Freeland* (1836) 1 M & W 543; *Cotterill v Apsey* (1815) 6 Taunt 322.

7   *Mallock v Hodghton* (1849) 12 D 215, Ct of Sess.

8   *Re Walton-on-the-Naze UDC and Moran* (1905) 2 Hudson's BC (4th Edn) 376.

9   *Craven-Ellis v Canons Ltd* [1936] 2 KB 403, [1936] 2 All ER 1066, CA; *William Lacey (Hounslow) Ltd v Davis* [1957] 2 All ER 712, [1957] 1 WLR 932; *British Steel Corpn v Cleveland Bridge and Engineering Co Ltd* [1984] 1 All ER 504, 24 BLR 94; *Pavey & Matthews Pty Ltd v Paul* (1987) 162 CLR 221, Aust HC. Cf *Morrison-Knudsen Co Inc v British Columbia Hydro and Power Authority* (1978) 85 DLR (3d) 186, BC CA; *Regalian Properties plc v London Docklands Development Corpn* [1995] 1 All ER 1005, [1995] 1 WLR 212.

10 See the Consumer Contracts (Information, Cancellation and Additional Charges) Regulations
   2013, SI 2013/3134, regs 9-13; and CONSUMER PROTECTION vol 21 (2016) PARA 307 et seq.

(iv) Payment Provisions in Construction Contracts

A. INTRODUCTION

351. Operation of the Housing Grants, Construction and Regeneration Act 1996 and the scheme.

Part II of the Housing Grants, Construction and Regeneration Act 1996[1]
introduced statutory requirements in relation to payment provisions in
construction contracts[2]. Construction contracts must comply with those statutory
requirements, and where the contract does not so comply, the payment provisions
of the scheme for construction contracts apply instead[3].

1 Ie the Housing Grants, Construction and Regeneration Act 1996 Pt II (ss 104–117). As to the
  application of Pt II see PARA 211.
2 See the Housing Grants, Construction and Regeneration Act 1996 ss 109–113; and PARAS
  352–357. The text refers to a 'construction contract' as defined in the Housing Grants,
  Construction and Regeneration Act 1996: see PARA 210.
3 The scheme is contained in the Scheme for Construction Contracts (England and Wales)
  Regulations 1998, SI 1998/649, regs 2–4, Schedule: see PARAS 358, 410 et seq. As to the payment
  provisions of the scheme for construction contracts see PARA 358. As to the power to make the
  scheme for construction contracts see PARA 210.

B. REQUIREMENTS UNDER THE HOUSING GRANTS, CONSTRUCTION AND REGENERATION ACT 1996

352. Entitlement to stage payments.

A party to a construction contract[1] is entitled to payment by instalments, stage
payments or other periodic payments for any work under the contract unless it is
specified in the contract that the duration of the work is to be less than 45 days[2],
or it is agreed between the parties that the duration of the work is estimated to be
less than 45 days[3]. The parties are free to agree the amounts of the payments and
the intervals at which, or circumstances in which, they become due[4]. In the
absence of such agreement, the relevant provisions of the scheme for construction
contracts apply[5].

1 Ie a 'construction contract' as defined in the Housing Grants, Construction and Regeneration Act
  1996: see PARA 210.
2 For the purposes of reckoning periods of time for the Housing Grants, Construction and
  Regeneration Act 1996 Pt II (ss 104–117), where an act is required to be done within a specified
  period after or from a specified date, the period begins immediately after that date (s 116(1), (2));
  and where the period would include Christmas Day, Good Friday or a day which under the
  Banking and Financial Dealings Act 1971 (see TIME vol 97 (2015) PARA 321) is a bank holiday
  in England and Wales or, as the case may be, in Scotland, that day is also excluded (Housing
  Grants, Construction and Regeneration Act 1996 s 116(3)). As to reckoning periods of time
  generally see TIME.
3 Housing Grants, Construction and Regeneration Act 1996 s 109(1). For these purposes, references
  to a payment provided for by the contract include a payment by virtue of s 109: s 109(4) (amended
  by the Local Democracy, Economic Development and Construction Act 2009 s 143(1)).
4 Housing Grants, Construction and Regeneration Act 1996 s 109(2).
5 Housing Grants, Construction and Regeneration Act 1996 s 109(3). As to the payment provisions
  of the scheme for construction contracts see PARA 358. As to the power to make the scheme for
  construction contracts see PARA 210.

353. Dates for payment.

Every construction contract[1] must: (1) provide an adequate mechanism for determining what payments become due under the contract, and when they become due[2]; and (2) provide for a final date for payment in relation to any sum which becomes due[3]. The parties are free to agree how long the period is to be between the date on which a sum becomes due and the final date for payment[4].

If or to the extent that a contract does not contain such provisions as described above, the relevant provisions of the scheme for construction contracts apply[5].

1   Ie a 'construction contract' as defined in the Housing Grants, Construction and Regeneration Act 1996: see PARA 210.
2   Housing Grants, Construction and Regeneration Act 1996 s 110(1)(a).
      The requirement in s 110(1)(a) to provide an adequate mechanism for determining what payments become due under the contract, or when, is not satisfied where a construction contract makes payment conditional on: (1) the performance of obligations under another contract; or (2) a decision by any person as to whether obligations under another contract have been performed: s 110(1A) (s 110(1A)-(1D) added by the Local Democracy, Economic Development and Construction Act 2009 s 142). These references to obligations do not include obligations to make payments (but see the Housing Grants, Construction and Regeneration Act 1996 s 113; and PARA 357): s 110(1B) (as so added). Section 110(1A) does not apply where: (a) the construction contract is an agreement between the parties for the carrying out of construction operations by another person, whether under sub-contract or otherwise; and (b) the obligations referred to in that provision are obligations on that other person to carry out those operations: s 110(1C) (as so added). The requirement in s 110(1)(a) to provide an adequate mechanism for determining when payments become due under the contract is not satisfied where a construction contract provides for the date on which a payment becomes due to be determined by reference to the giving to the person to whom the payment is due of a notice which relates to what payments are due under the contract: s 110(1D) (as so added). A construction contract is excluded from the operation of s 110(1A) if it is a contract pursuant to which a party to a relevant contract has sub-contracted to a third party some or all of its obligations under that contract to carry out, or arrange that others carry out, construction operations: Construction Contracts (England) Exclusion Order 2011, SI 2011/2332, art 3; Construction Contracts (Wales) Exclusion Order 2011, SI 2011/1713, art 3.
3   Housing Grants, Construction and Regeneration Act 1996 s 110(1)(b).
4   Housing Grants, Construction and Regeneration Act 1996 s 110(1).
5   Housing Grants, Construction and Regeneration Act 1996 s 110(3) (amended by the Local Democracy, Economic Development and Construction Act 2009 ss 143(2), 146(1), Sch 7). As to the payment provisions of the scheme for construction contracts see PARA 358. As to the power to make the scheme for construction contracts see PARA 210.

354. Payment notices.

A construction contract[1] must, in relation to every payment provided for by the contract[2], require: (1) the payer or a specified person[3] to give a notice[4] to the payee[5] not later than five days after the payment due date[6]; or (2) the payee to give a notice[7] to the payer or a specified person not later than five days after the payment due date[8].

A notice given by the payer as referred to in head (1) above must specify the sum that the payer considers to be or to have been due at the payment due date in respect of the payment, and the basis on which that sum is calculated[9]. A notice given by a specified person as referred to in head (1) above must specify the sum that the payer or the specified person considers to be or to have been due at the payment due date in respect of the payment, and the basis on which that sum is calculated[10]. Similarly, a notice referred to in head (2) above must specify the sum that the payee considers to be or to have been due at the payment due date in respect of the payment[11], and the basis on which that sum is calculated[12].

If or to the extent that a contract does not comply with these requirements, the relevant provisions of the scheme for construction contracts apply[13].

Where, in relation to any payment provided for by a construction contract the contract requires the payer or a specified person to give the payee a notice as mentioned in head (1) above[14] not later than five days after the payment due date, but notice is not given as so required, then the following provisions apply[15]. The payee may give to the payer a notice as mentioned in head (2) above[16] at any time after the date on which the original notice[17] was required by the contract to be given[18]. Where the payee gives such a notice[19], the final date for payment of the sum specified in the notice is postponed[20]. However, if (a) the contract permits or requires the payee, before the date on which the notice referred to in head (1) above is required by the contract to be given, to notify the payer or a specified person of the sum that the payee considers will become due on the payment due date in respect of the payment, and the basis on which that sum is calculated; and (b) the payee gives such notification in accordance with the contract, then that notification is to be regarded as a notice complying with head (2) above[21] (and the payee may not give another such notice)[22].

1   Ie a 'construction contract' as defined in the Housing Grants, Construction and Regeneration Act 1996: see PARA 210.
2   References to a payment provided for by the contract include a payment by virtue of the Housing Grants, Construction and Regeneration Act 1996 s 109: see PARA 352 note 3.
3   'Payer' means the person from whom the payment is due: Housing Grants, Construction and Regeneration Act 1996 s 110A(6) (ss 110A, 110B added by the Local Democracy, Economic Development and Construction Act 2009 s 143(3)). 'Specified person' means a person specified in or determined in accordance with the provisions of the contract: Housing Grants, Construction and Regeneration Act 1996 s 110A(6) (as so added).
4   Ie a notice complying with the Housing Grants, Construction and Regeneration Act 1996 s 110A(2): see the text and notes 9–10.
5   'Payee' means the person to whom the payment is due: Housing Grants, Construction and Regeneration Act 1996 s 110A(6) (as added: see note 3).
6   Housing Grants, Construction and Regeneration Act 1996 s 110A(1)(a) (as added: see note 3). 'Payment due date' means the date provided for by the contract as the date on which the payment is due: s 110A(6) (as so added).
7   Ie a notice complying with the Housing Grants, Construction and Regeneration Act 1996 s 110A(3): see the text and notes 11–12.
8   Housing Grants, Construction and Regeneration Act 1996 s 110A(1)(b) (as added: see note 3).
9   Housing Grants, Construction and Regeneration Act 1996 s 110A(2)(a) (as added: see note 3). For these purposes, it is immaterial that the sum referred to in s 110A(2)(a) may be zero: s 110A(4) (as so added).
10   Housing Grants, Construction and Regeneration Act 1996 s 110A(2)(b) (as added: see note 3). For these purposes, it is immaterial that the sum referred to in s 110A(2)(b) may be zero: s 110A(4) (as so added).
11   Housing Grants, Construction and Regeneration Act 1996 s 110A(3)(a) (as added: see note 3). For these purposes, it is immaterial that the sum referred to in s 110A(3)(a) may be zero: s 110A(4) (as so added).
12   Housing Grants, Construction and Regeneration Act 1996 s 110A(3)(b) (as added: see note 3).
13   Housing Grants, Construction and Regeneration Act 1996 s 110A(5) (as added: see note 3). As to the payment provisions of the scheme for construction contracts see PARA 358. As to the power to make the scheme for construction contracts see PARA 210.
14   Ie a notice complying with the Housing Grants, Construction and Regeneration Act 1996 s 110A(2): see the text and notes 9–10.
15   Housing Grants, Construction and Regeneration Act 1996 s 110B(1) (as added: see note 3).
16   Ie a notice complying with the Housing Grants, Construction and Regeneration Act 1996 s 110A(3): see the text and notes 11–12.
17   Ie the notice required by the Housing Grants, Construction and Regeneration Act 1996 s 110A(2) as mentioned in s 110B(1).
18   Housing Grants, Construction and Regeneration Act 1996 s 110B(2) (as added: see note 3).
19   Ie where, pursuant to the Housing Grants, Construction and Regeneration Act 1996 s 110B(2), the payee gives a notice complying with s 110A(3).

20 Housing Grants, Construction and Regeneration Act 1996 s 110B(3) (as added: see note 3). The reference in the text to the postponement of the final date for payment is a reference to the final date for payment being postponed by the same number of days as the number of days after the date referred to in the Housing Grants, Construction and Regeneration Act 1996 s 110B(2) that the notice was given: s 110B(3) (as so added).

21 Ie a notice complying with the Housing Grants, Construction and Regeneration Act 1996 s 110A(3) given pursuant to s 110B(2).

22 Housing Grants, Construction and Regeneration Act 1996 s 110B(4) (as added: see note 3). The reference in the text to the payee not giving another notice is a reference to the payee not giving another such notice pursuant to s 110B(2): s 110B(4) (as so added).

355. Requirement to pay notified sum.

Where a payment is provided for by a construction contract[1], the payer[2] must pay the notified sum[3] (to the extent not already paid) on or before the final date for payment[4]. The payer or a specified person[5] may in accordance with these provisions give to the payee[6] a notice[7] of the payer's intention to pay less than the notified sum[8]. Such a notice must specify the sum that the payer considers to be due on the date the notice is served, and the basis on which that sum is calculated[9]

These provisions do not apply in relation to a payment provided for by a construction contract where the contract provides that, if the payee becomes insolvent the payer need not pay any sum due in respect of the payment, and the payee has become insolvent after the prescribed period[10].

1 Ie a 'construction contract' as defined in the Housing Grants, Construction and Regeneration Act 1996: see PARA 210. References to a payment provided for by the contract include a payment by virtue of s 109: see PARA 352 note 3.

2 As to the meaning of 'payer' see PARA 354 note 3.

3 For these purposes, the 'notified sum' in relation to any payment provided for by a construction contract means:

(1) in a case where a notice complying with the Housing Grants, Construction and Regeneration Act 1996 s 110A(2) (see PARA 354) has been given pursuant to and in accordance with a requirement of the contract, the amount specified in that notice (s 111(2)(a) (s 111 substituted by the Local Democracy, Economic Development and Construction Act 2009 s 144(1));

(2) in a case where a notice complying with the Housing Grants, Construction and Regeneration Act 1996 s 110A(3) (see PARA 354) has been given pursuant to and in accordance with a requirement of the contract, the amount specified in that notice (s 111(2)(b) (as so substituted));

(3) in a case where a notice complying with s 110A(3) has been given pursuant to and in accordance with s 110B(2) (see PARA 354), the amount specified in that notice (s 111(2)(c) (as so substituted)).

4 Housing Grants, Construction and Regeneration Act 1996 s 111(1) (as substituted: see note 3). See *Adam Architecture Ltd v Halsbury Homes Ltd* [2017] EWCA Civ 1735, [2017] All ER (D) 91 (Nov); *Kersfield Development (Bridge Road) Ltd v Bray and Slaughter Ltd* [2017] EWHC 15 (TCC), 170 ConLR 40; *Kilker Projects Ltd v Purton (trading as Richwood Interiors)* [2016] EWHC 2616 (TCC), [2017] Bus LR 418, [2016] All ER (D) 130 (Oct); *Harding (trading as MJ Harding Contractors) v Paice* [2015] EWCA Civ 1231, [2016] 2 All ER 819, [2016] 2 All ER (Comm) 656.

In the absence of an effective notice the right to deduct money by way of set-off is excluded: *VHE Construction plc v RBSTB Trust Co Ltd* [2000] BLR 187, 70 Con LR 51. However, 'the absence of a timeous notice to withhold payment does not relieve the party making the claim of the ordinary burden of showing that he is entitled under the contract to receive the payment he claims': *SL Timber Systems Ltd v Carillion Construction Ltd* [2001] BLR 516 at 524, Ct of Sess, per Lord Macfadyen.

A provision that a party to a construction contract cannot, unless he has given notice of intention to do so, withhold payment after the final date for payment of a sum due under the contract, does not apply to a lawful ground for withholding payment when it has not been possible for notice to have been given within the statutory time frame: *Melville Dundas Ltd (in receivership) v George Wimpey UK Ltd* [2007] UKHL 18, [2007] 3 All ER 889, [2007] BLR 257; applied in *Pierce Design International Ltd v Johnston* [2007] EWHC 1691 (TCC), (2007) 115 Con LR 110,

[2007] BLR 381. See also *Windglass Windows Ltd v Capital Skyline Construction Ltd* [2009] EWHC 2022 (TCC), (2009) 126 Con LR 118 (withholding notices ineffective as grounds not stated). See also *Rupert Morgan Building Services (LCC) v Jervis* [2003] EWCA Civ 1563, [2004] 1 All ER 529, [2004] 1 WLR 1867. The Housing Grants, Construction and Regeneration Act 1996 s 111 is intended to apply only to the withholding of payments in respect of which the contract provides a final date of payment; it does not apply to payments due in consequence of an adjudicator's decision: *Construction Centre Group Ltd v Highland Council* 2003 SLT 623, IH.

5   As to the meaning of 'specified person' see PARA 354 note 3.

6   As to the meaning of 'payee' see PARA 354 note 5.

7   As to the service of notices for the purposes of the Housing Grants, Construction and Regeneration Act 1996 Pt II (ss 104–117) see s 115. See also *Rhode v Markham-David* [2007] EWHC 1408 (TCC), [2007] All ER (D) 326 (Jul) (sending documents by special delivery to last known residence did not constitute delivery by post where recipient did not sign for documents and documents returned to post office).

8   Housing Grants, Construction and Regeneration Act 1996 s 111(3) (as substituted: see note 3). This notification requirement applies to both interim and final applications for payment: *Adam Architecture Ltd v Halsbury Homes Ltd* [2017] EWCA Civ 1735, [2017] All ER (D) 91 (Nov). Such a notice must be given not later than the prescribed period before the final date for payment, and in a case referred to in s 111(2)(b) or s 111(2)(c) (see note 3), may not be given before the notice by reference to which the notified sum is determined: s 111(5) (as so substituted). Where such a notice is given, s 111(1) applies only in respect of the sum that the payer considers to be due on the date the notice is served: s 111(4)(a), (6) (as so substituted). For these purposes, 'prescribed period' means such period as the parties may agree, or in the absence of such agreement, the period provided by the scheme for construction contracts: s 111(7) (as so substituted). As to the payment provisions of the scheme for construction contracts see PARA 358. As to the power to make the scheme for construction contracts see PARA 210.

    Where in respect of a payment:

    (1)   a notice complying with s 110A(2) (see PARA 354) has been given pursuant to and in accordance with a requirement of the contract (and no notice under s 111(3) is given); or

    (2)   notice under s 111(3) is given in accordance with s 111,
           but on the matter being referred to adjudication the adjudicator decides that more than the sum specified in the notice should be paid (s 111(8) (as so substituted), then, the decision of the adjudicator is to be construed as requiring payment of the additional amount not later than seven days from the date of the decision, or the date which apart from the notice would have been the final date for payment, whichever is the later (s 111(9) (as so substituted)). As to the right to refer disputes to adjudication see PARA 407 et seq. Nothing in the Housing Grants, Construction and Regeneration Act 1996 s 111 entitles a court to refuse to grant a stay under the Arbitration Act 1996 s 9 (see ARBITRATION vol 2 (2017) PARA 522) if it would otherwise be granted: *Collins (Contractors) Ltd v Baltic Quay Management (1994) Ltd* [2004] EWCA Civ 1757, [2005] BLR 63, (2004) 99 Con LR 1. As to the reckoning of periods of time see PARA 352 note 2.

9   Housing Grants, Construction and Regeneration Act 1996 s 111(4) (as substituted: see note 3). It is immaterial for these purposes that the sum referred to in s 111(3) may be zero: s 111(4) (as so substituted).

10 Housing Grants, Construction and Regeneration Act 1996 s 111(10) (as substituted: see note 3). The prescribed period referred to in the text is the prescribed period referred to in s 111(5)(a) (see note 8): s 111(10) (as so substituted). Section 113(2)—(5) (see PARA 357) applies for the purposes of s 111(10) it applies for the purposes of s 113: s 111(11) (as so substituted).

356. Right to suspend performance for non-payment.

Where the requirement to pay a notified sum due under a construction contract[1] on or before the final date for payment[2] applies in relation to any sum but is not complied with, the person to whom the sum is due has the right, without prejudice to any other right or remedy, to suspend performance of any or all of his obligations under the contract to the party by whom payment ought to have been made (the 'party in default')[3]. The right may not be exercised without first giving to the party in default at least seven days' notice of intention[4] to suspend performance, stating the ground or grounds on which it is intended to suspend performance[5]. The right to suspend performance ceases when the party in default makes payment in full of the required[6] sum[7].

Where such a right is exercised, the party in default is liable to pay to the party exercising the right a reasonable amount in respect of costs and expenses reasonably incurred by that party as a result of the exercise of the right[8]. Any period during which performance is suspended in pursuance of, or in consequence of the exercise of, the right so conferred is to be disregarded in computing for the purposes of any contractual time limit the time taken, by the party exercising the right or by a third party, to complete any work directly or indirectly affected by the exercise of the right[9]. Where the contractual time limit is set by reference to a date rather than a period, the date is to be adjusted accordingly[10].

1 Ie a 'construction contract' as defined in the Housing Grants, Construction and Regeneration Act 1996: see PARA 210.
2 Ie the requirement in the Housing Grants, Construction and Regeneration Act 1996 s 111(1): see PARA 355.
3 Housing Grants, Construction and Regeneration Act 1996 s 112(1) (amended by the Local Democracy, Economic Development and Construction Act 2009 ss 144, 145).
4 References in the Housing Grants, Construction and Regeneration Act 1996 Pt II (ss 104–117) to a notice or other document include any form of communication in writing and references to service are to be construed accordingly: s 115(6). As to the service of notices and documents see s 115. As to the reckoning of periods of time see PARA 352 note 2.
5 Housing Grants, Construction and Regeneration Act 1996 s 112(2).
6 Ie the sum referred to in the Housing Grants, Construction and Regeneration Act 1996 s 112(1).
7 Housing Grants, Construction and Regeneration Act 1996 s 112(3) (amended by the Local Democracy, Economic Development and Construction Act 2009 s 144).
8 Housing Grants, Construction and Regeneration Act 1996 s 112(3A) (added by the Local Democracy, Economic Development and Construction Act 2009 s 145).
9 Housing Grants, Construction and Regeneration Act 1996 s 112(4) (amended by the Local Democracy, Economic Development and Construction Act 2009 s 145).
10 Housing Grants, Construction and Regeneration Act 1996 s 112(4).

357. Prohibition of conditional payment provisions.

A provision making payment under a construction contract[1] conditional on the payer receiving payment from a third person is ineffective, unless that third person, or any other person payment by whom is under the contract, directly or indirectly, a condition of payment by that third person, is insolvent[2]. Where a provision is rendered ineffective in this way, the parties are free to agree other terms for payment, and in the absence of such agreement, the relevant provisions of the scheme for construction contracts apply[3].

1 Ie a 'construction contract' as defined in the Housing Grants, Construction and Regeneration Act 1996: see PARA 210. References to a payment under the contract include a payment by virtue of s 109 (see PARA 352): s 109(4).
    For these purposes a company becomes insolvent: (1) when it enters administration within the meaning of the Insolvency Act 1986 Schedule B1; (2) on the appointment of an administrative receiver or a receiver or manager of its property under Pt III Ch I (ss 28–49), or the appointment of a receiver under Pt III Ch II (ss 50–71); (3) on the passing of a resolution for voluntary winding-up without a declaration of solvency under s 89; or (4) on the making of a winding-up order under Pt IV (ss 73–219) or Pt V (ss 220–229): Housing Grants, Construction and Regeneration Act 1996 s 113(2) (amended by SI 2003/2096). For these purposes, a partnership becomes insolvent on the making of a winding-up order against it under any provision of the Insolvency Act 1986 as applied by an order under s 420 or when sequestration is awarded on the estate of the partnership under the Bankruptcy (Scotland) Act 2016 s 22 or the partnership grants a trust deed for its creditors: Housing Grants, Construction and Regeneration Act 1996 s 113(3) (amended by SI 2016/1034). For these purposes, an individual becomes insolvent on the making of a bankruptcy order against him under the Insolvency Act 1986 Pt IX (ss 263H–371) or on the sequestration of his estate under the Bankruptcy (Scotland) Act 2016 or when he grants a trust deed for his creditors: Housing Grants, Construction and Regeneration Act 1996 s 113(4)

(amended by SI 2016/1034). As to company insolvency and partnership insolvency see COMPANY AND PARTNERSHIP INSOLVENCY. As to individual insolvency see BANKRUPTCY AND INDIVIDUAL INSOLVENCY. A company, partnership or individual is also to be treated as insolvent on the occurrence of any event corresponding to those specified in the Housing Grants, Construction and Regeneration Act 1996 s 113(2), (3) or (4) under the law of Northern Ireland or of a country outside the United Kingdom: s 113(5). As to the meaning of 'United Kingdom' see PARA 217 note 3.

2   Housing Grants, Construction and Regeneration Act 1996 s 113(1). See *William Hare Ltd v Shepherd Construction Ltd* [2010] EWCA Civ 283, [2010] BLR 358, 130 Con LR 1.

3   Housing Grants, Construction and Regeneration Act 1996 s 113(6). As to the payment provisions of the scheme for construction contracts see PARA 358. As to the power to make the scheme for construction contracts see PARA 210.

C.   REQUIREMENTS UNDER THE SCHEME FOR CONSTRUCTION CONTRACTS

358. Payment provisions under the scheme for construction contracts.
Where a construction contract[1] does not comply with the requirements of the payment provisions under the Housing Grants, Construction and Regeneration Act 1996[2], the relevant provisions of the scheme have effect[3].

Where the parties to a relevant construction contract[4] fail to agree: (1) the amount of any instalment or stage or periodic payment for any work under the contract[5]; or (2) the intervals at which, or circumstances in which, such payments become due under that contract[6]; or (3) both the amount of any instalment or stage or periodic payment and the intervals at which or circumstances in which such payments become due[7], then the relevant provisions of the scheme for construction contracts[8] apply[9].

The scheme provides that the amount of any payment by way of instalments or stage or periodic payments in respect of a relevant period[10] is the difference between:

(a)   the aggregate of the following amounts:
    (i)   an amount equal to the value of any work[11] performed in accordance with the relevant construction contract during the period from the commencement of the contract to the end of the relevant period (excluding any amount calculated in accordance with head (ii) below)[12];
    (ii)   where the contract provides for payment for materials, an amount equal to the value of any materials manufactured on site or brought onto site for the purposes of the works during the period from the commencement of the contract to the end of the relevant period[13]; and
    (iii)   any other amount or sum which the contract specifies is payable during or in respect of the period from the commencement of the contract to the end of the relevant period[14]; and
(b)   the aggregate of any sums which have been paid or are due for payment by way of instalments, stage or periodic payments during the period from the commencement of the contract to the end of the relevant period[15].

An amount calculated in this way must not exceed the difference between the contract price and the aggregate of the instalments or stage or periodic payments which have become due[16].

Where the parties to a construction contract fail to provide an adequate mechanism for determining either what payments become due under the contract, or when they become due for payment, or both, the relevant provisions[17] of the scheme apply[18]. The scheme provides that any payment by way of instalments or stage or periodic payments in respect of a relevant period is due on whichever of the following dates occurs later: (A) the expiry of seven days following the relevant period; or (B) the making of a claim by the payee[19]. The final payment payable under a relevant construction contract, namely the payment of an amount equal to the difference, if any, between the contract price, and the aggregate of any instalment or stage or periodic payments which have become due under the contract, is due on the expiry of 30 days following completion of the work or the making of a claim by the payee, whichever is the later[20]. Payment of the contract price under a construction contract (not being a relevant construction contract) is due on the expiry of 30 days following the completion of the work or the making of a claim by the payee, whichever is the later[21]. Any other payment under a construction contract is due on the expiry of seven days following the completion of the work to which the payment relates or the making of a claim by the payee, whichever is the later[22]. Where the parties to a construction contract fail to provide a final date for payment in relation to any sum which becomes due under a construction contract, the final date for the making of any payment of a kind mentioned above[23] is 17 days from the date that payment becomes due[24].

Where the parties to a construction contract fail, in relation to a payment provided for by the contract[25], to provide for the giving of a notice[26], then the payer must, not later than five days after the payment due date, give a notice to the payee specifying the sum that the payer considers to be due or to have been due at the payment due date and the basis on which that sum is calculated[27].

Where, in relation to a notice of intention to pay less than the notified sum[28] the parties fail to agree the prescribed period[29] that notice must be given not later than seven days before the final date for payment determined either in accordance with the construction contract[30].

The scheme also makes provision in relation to relevant construction contracts and any other construction contracts for the situation where a provision making payment under a construction contract conditional on the payer receiving payment from a third person is ineffective[31], and the parties have not agreed other terms for payment[32].

1   Ie a 'construction contract' as defined in the Housing Grants, Construction and Regeneration Act 1996: see PARA 210.
2   Ie the Housing Grants, Construction and Regeneration Act 1996 s 108 (see PARA 410), s 109 (see PARA 352), s 110 (see PARA 353), s 110A (see PARA 354), s 111 (see PARA 355) and s 113 (see PARA 357).
3   The scheme for construction contracts is made by regulations made by the appropriate authority in exercise of the power in the Housing Grants, Construction and Regeneration Act 1996 s 114. See the Scheme for Construction Contracts (England and Wales) Regulations 1998, SI 1998/649. Where any provisions of the scheme for construction contracts apply by virtue of the Housing Grants, Construction and Regeneration Act 1996 Pt II (ss 104–117) in default of contractual provision agreed by the parties, they have effect as implied terms of the contract concerned: s 114(4).
4   'Relevant construction contract' means any construction contract other than one: (1) which specifies that the duration of the work is to be less than 45 days; or (2) in respect of which the parties agree that the duration of the work is estimated to be less than 45 days: Scheme for Construction Contracts (England and Wales) Regulations 1998, SI 1998/649, Schedule Pt II para 12. 'Work' means any of the work or services mentioned in the Housing Grants, Construction and Regeneration Act 1996 s 104 (see PARA 210): Scheme for Construction Contracts (England and Wales) Regulations 1998, SI 1998/649, Schedule Pt II para 12.
5   Scheme for Construction Contracts (England and Wales) Regulations 1998, SI 1998/649, Schedule Pt II para 1(a).
6   Scheme for Construction Contracts (England and Wales) Regulations 1998, SI 1998/649, Schedule Pt II para 1(b).

7   Scheme for Construction Contracts (England and Wales) Regulations 1998, SI 1998/649, Schedule Pt II para 1(c).
8   Ie the Scheme for Construction Contracts (England and Wales) Regulations 1998, SI 1998/649, Schedule Pt II paras 2–4: see the text and notes 10–16.
9   Scheme for Construction Contracts (England and Wales) Regulations 1998, SI 1998/649, Schedule Pt II para 1.
10 'Relevant period' means a period which is specified in, or is calculated by reference to the construction contract or where no such period is so specified or is so calculable, a period of 28 days: Scheme for Construction Contracts (England and Wales) Regulations 1998, SI 1998/649, Schedule Pt II para 12.
11 'Value of work' means an amount determined in accordance with the construction contract under which the work is performed or where the contract contains no such provision, the cost of any work performed in accordance with that contract together with an amount equal to any overhead or profit included in the contract price: Scheme for Construction Contracts (England and Wales) Regulations 1998, SI 1998/649, Schedule Pt II para 12. 'Contract price' means the entire sum payable under the construction contract in respect of the work: Schedule Pt II para 12.
12 Scheme for Construction Contracts (England and Wales) Regulations 1998, SI 1998/649, Schedule Pt II para 2(1), (2)(a).
13 Scheme for Construction Contracts (England and Wales) Regulations 1998, SI 1998/649, Schedule Pt II para 2(1), (2)(b).
14 Scheme for Construction Contracts (England and Wales) Regulations 1998, SI 1998/649, Schedule Pt II para 2(1), (2)(c).
15 Scheme for Construction Contracts (England and Wales) Regulations 1998, SI 1998/649, Schedule Pt II para 2(1), (3).
16 Scheme for Construction Contracts (England and Wales) Regulations 1998, SI 1998/649, Schedule Pt II para 2(4).
17 Ie the Scheme for Construction Contracts (England and Wales) Regulations 1998, SI 1998/649, Schedule Pt II paras 4–7: see the text and notes 19–22.
18 Scheme for Construction Contracts (England and Wales) Regulations 1998, SI 1998/649, Schedule Pt II para 3.
19 Scheme for Construction Contracts (England and Wales) Regulations 1998, SI 1998/649, Schedule Pt II para 4. 'Claim by the payee' means a written notice given by the party carrying out work under a construction contract to the other party specifying the amount of any payment or payments which he considers to be due and the basis on which it is, or they are calculated: Schedule Pt II para 12.
20 Scheme for Construction Contracts (England and Wales) Regulations 1998, SI 1998/649, Schedule Pt II para 5 (amended by SI 2011/2333 (England); SI 2011/1715 (Wales)).
21 Scheme for Construction Contracts (England and Wales) Regulations 1998, SI 1998/649, Schedule Pt II para 6.
22 Scheme for Construction Contracts (England and Wales) Regulations 1998, SI 1998/649, Schedule Pt II para 7.
23 Ie a payment of the kind mentioned in the Scheme for Construction Contracts (England and Wales) Regulations 1998, SI 1998/649, Schedule Pt II paras 2, 5, 6 or 7: see the text and notes 10–16, 20–22.
24 Scheme for Construction Contracts (England and Wales) Regulations 1998, SI 1998/649, Schedule Pt II para 8.
25 A payment provided for by the contract includes any payment of the kind mentioned in the Scheme for Construction Contracts (England and Wales) Regulations 1998, SI 1998/649, Schedule Pt II paras 2, 5, 6 or 7 (see the text and notes 10–16, 20–22): Schedule Pt II para 9(2) (Pt II para 9 substituted by SI 2011/2333 (England); SI 2011/1715 (Wales)).
26 Ie the giving of a notice pursuant to the Housing Grants, Construction and Regeneration Act 1996 s 110A(1): see PARA 354.
27 Scheme for Construction Contracts (England and Wales) Regulations 1998, SI 1998/649, Schedule Pt II para 9(1)-(3)(as substituted: see note 25). For these purposes, it is immaterial that the sum referred to may be zero: Schedule Pt II 9(4).
28 Ie given in accordance with the Housing Grants, Construction and Regeneration Act 1996 s 111(3): see PARA 355.
29 Ie the period as provided for in the Housing Grants, Construction and Regeneration Act 1996 s 111(5): see PARA 355.

30 Scheme for Construction Contracts (England and Wales) Regulations 1998, SI 1998/649, Schedule Pt II para 10 (Pt II para 10 substituted by SI 2011/2333 (England); SI 2011/1715 (Wales)). Where no such provision is made in the contract, the final date for payment is determined in accordance with Schedule Pt II para 8 (see the text and notes 23–24): Scheme for Construction Contracts (England and Wales) Regulations 1998, SI 1998/649, Schedule Pt II para 10 (as so substituted).

31 Ie as mentioned in the Housing Grants, Construction and Regeneration Act 1996 s 113: see PARA 357.

32 Scheme for Construction Contracts (England and Wales) Regulations 1998, SI 1998/649, Schedule Pt II para 11. The scheme provides that Schedule Pt II paras 2, 4, 5, 7, 8, 9, 10 apply in the case of a relevant construction contract, and Schedule Pt II paras 6, 7, 8, 9, 10 apply in the case of any other construction contract: Schedule Pt II para 11.

(v) Value Added Tax

359. In general.
The full application of value added tax to supplies under building contracts is outside the scope of this title[1], and a summary of the position only is provided here[2]. Within the construction industry payment of value added tax by contractors, sub-contractors and sub-sub-contractors on goods and services used by those persons during the course of the project can be reclaimed as part of the 'inputs' during the relevant accounting period[3]. However, not all goods and services are subject to tax or are standard rated.

Once a contractor issues an invoice for value added tax he becomes liable to account to the Commissioners for Her Majesty's Revenue and Customs[4] for that tax[5]. The tax point in relation to zero-rated supplies[6] is when payment is received, not when an invoice is issued.

1 As to value added tax generally see VALUE ADDED TAX.
2 See PARA 360 et seq.
3 See the Value Added Tax Act 1994 ss 24, 25; and VALUE ADDED TAX vol 99 (2012) PARAS 274–275.
4 As to the Commissioners for Her Majesty's Revenue and Customs see INCOME TAXATION vol 58 (2014) PARA 33 et seq.
5 Any delay in the invoice being paid will result in cash flow difficulties owing to this early accounting of money that the contractor has not yet received. Delay in cash flow can be avoided by the contractor if when submitting invoices to the architect for certification he ensures that a value added tax invoice is not issued. This is done by marking the invoice with the words 'This is not a VAT invoice', or a similar formula.
6 As to zero-rated supplies see VALUE ADDED TAX vol 99 (2012) PARA 220 et seq.

360. Domestic buildings and zero rating.
Some categories of goods and services in the construction industry are either 'zero-rated'[1] for or 'exempt' from value added tax. The following items are zero-rated[2]:

(1)   the grant of a freehold or lease for a term certain exceeding 21 years[3] of, or the supply of services[4] or building materials[5] in the course of construction of: (a) domestic buildings or dwellings; (b) buildings to be used for certain communal residential purposes; or (c) buildings to be used by charities for non-business purposes[6];

(2)   the first grant by a person substantially reconstructing a protected building, of a major interest in, or in any part of, the building or its site[7].

1 As to zero-rated supplies see VALUE ADDED TAX vol 99 (2012) PARA 220 et seq.
2 See the Value Added Tax Act 1994 s 30, s 96(1), Sch 8 Pt II group 5; and VALUE ADDED TAX vol 99 (2012) PARA 225.
3 See the definition of 'major interest' in the Value Added Tax Act 1994 s 96(1). 'Grant' includes an

assignment or surrender: see Sch 8 Pt II group 5; and VALUE ADDED TAX vol 99 (2012) PARA 225.

4   The services of an architect, surveyor or any person acting as consultant or in a supervisory capacity are excluded: see the Value Added Tax Act 1994 Sch 8 Pt II group 5 item 2; and VALUE ADDED TAX vol 99 (2012) PARA 225.

5   In relation to the supply of materials, the supplier must be a person making a supply of services as described in the Value Added Tax Act 1994 Sch 8 Pt II group 5 item 2 or Sch 8 Pt II group 5 item 3 in relation to a building within head (1) or head (2) in the text: see Sch 8 Pt II group 5 item 4; and VALUE ADDED TAX vol 99 (2012) PARA 225.

6   See the Value Added Tax Act 1994 Sch 8 Pt II group 5; and VALUE ADDED TAX vol 99 (2012) PARA 225.

7   See the Value Added Tax Act 1994 Sch 8 Pt II group 6; and VALUE ADDED TAX vol 99 (2012) PARA 232.

361.   Commercial buildings and standard rating.

The freehold sales of 'new' commercial buildings are standard rated[1]. The general rule is that a building is 'new' if it was completed less than three years before the sale[2]. A building completed before 1 April 1989 may still be 'new' but only if it was not fully occupied before that date and the relevant sale is the first such sale taking place after that date[3]. The freehold sale of 'old' commercial buildings is exempt from value added tax[4]. All grants of leases and assignments of leases of commercial property are exempt from value added tax[5] but the surrender of leases is standard rated[6].

1   The Value Added Tax Act 1994 s 31, Sch 9 provides for supplies which are exempt from value added tax. In relation to land and buildings see Sch 9 Pt II group 1; and VALUE ADDED TAX vol 99 (2012) PARA 187.

2   See the Value Added Tax Act 1994 Sch 9 Pt II group 1 note (4); and VALUE ADDED TAX vol 99 (2012) PARA 187.

3   See the Value Added Tax Act 1994 Sch 9 Pt II group 1 notes (5), (6); and VALUE ADDED TAX vol 99 (2012) PARA 187.

4   Value Added Tax Act 1994 Sch 9 Pt II group 1 item 1(a) refers only to incomplete or new buildings. A building is complete when an architect issues a certificate of practical completion (see PARAS 262, 322) or it is first fully occupied, whichever happens first: see Sch 9 Pt II group 1 note (2); and VALUE ADDED TAX vol 99 (2012) PARA 187.

5   Ie they are not excluded from the exemption provided by the Value Added Tax Act 1994 Sch 9 Pt II group 1.

6   See the Value Added Tax Act 1994 Sch 9 Pt II group 1 note (1); and VALUE ADDED TAX vol 99 (2012) PARA 187.

362.   The option to tax land.

A person may opt to tax any land[1]. If a person exercises that option and a grant is made in relation to the land by the person exercising that option or by a relevant associate[2] at any time when the option to tax it has effect, then the grant does not fall within the exemption for land[3].

There are exclusions from the effect of the option to tax land. An option to tax has no effect in relation to a grant: (1) in relation to buildings designed, adapted and intended for use as dwellings or solely for a relevant residential purpose[4]; (2) in relation to buildings to be converted for use as a dwelling or solely for a relevant residential purpose[5]; (3) in relation to buildings intended for use solely for a relevant charitable purpose (but not as an office)[6]; (4) in relation to a pitch for a residential caravan[7]; (5) in relation to facilities for the mooring of a residential houseboat[8]; (6) made to a relevant housing association which certifies that the land is to be used for the construction of a buildings intended for use as dwellings or solely for a relevant residential purpose[9]; (7) made to an individual if the land is to be used for the construction of a building intended for use by the individual as a dwelling, and the construction is not carried out in the course or furtherance of a business carried on by the individual[10].

A supply is not, as a result of an option to tax, a taxable supply if the grant giving rise to the supply was made by a person (the 'grantor') who was a developer of the land, and the exempt land test is met[11]. The exempt land test is met if, at the time when the grant was made, the grantor or a development financier intended or expected that the land would become exempt land (whether immediately or eventually and whether or not as a result of the grant), or would continue, for a period at least, to be exempt land[12].

1 See the Value Added Tax Act 1994 s 51, Sch 10 Pt I para 1; and VALUE ADDED TAX vol 99 (2012) PARA 188 et seq. As to the scope of the option see Sch 10 Pt I para 18; and VALUE ADDED TAX vol 99 (2012) PARA 203. An option to tax has effect from the start of the day on which it is exercised, or from the start of any later day specified in the option: see Sch 10 Pt I para 19; and VALUE ADDED TAX vol 99 (2012) PARA 188. The option only has effect if notification is given to Her Majesty's Commissioners for Revenue and Customs within the allowed time, together with such information as they may require: see Sch 10 Pt I para 20; and VALUE ADDED TAX vol 99 (2012) PARA 189. There is a 'cooling off' period, during which the option may be revoked: see Sch 10 Pt I para 23; and VALUE ADDED TAX vol 99 (2012) PARA 205. Further provisions for the revocation of the option are provided for in the Value Added Tax Act 1994 Sch 10 Pt I para 24 (lapse of six years since having a relevant interest), Sch 10 Pt I para 25 (lapse of more than 20 years since option had effect) and Sch 10 Pt I para 26: see VALUE ADDED TAX vol 99 (2012) PARA 205. As to elections to opt to tax land subsequently acquired see Sch 10 Pt I paras 21, 22; and VALUE ADDED TAX vol 99 (2012) PARA 204.

2 As to the meaning of 'relevant associate' see the Value Added Tax Act 1994 Sch 10 Pt I paras 3, 4; and VALUE ADDED TAX vol 99 (2012) PARA 188.

3 See the Value Added Tax Act 1994 Sch 10 Pt I para 2; and VALUE ADDED TAX vol 99 (2012) PARA 187 et seq. As to the exemption for land see Schedule 9 Group 1; PARA 361; and VALUE ADDED TAX vol 99 (2012) PARA 187.

4 See the Value Added Tax Act 1994 Sch 10 Pt I para 5; and VALUE ADDED TAX vol 99 (2012) PARA 192.

5 See the Value Added Tax Act 1994 Sch 10 Pt I para 6; and VALUE ADDED TAX vol 99 (2012) PARA 193.

6 See the Value Added Tax Act 1994 Sch 10 Pt I para 7; and VALUE ADDED TAX vol 99 (2012) PARA 194.

7 See the Value Added Tax Act 1994 Sch 10 Pt I para 8; and VALUE ADDED TAX vol 99 (2012) PARA 195.

8 See the Value Added Tax Act 1994 Sch 10 Pt I para 9; and VALUE ADDED TAX vol 99 (2012) PARA 195.

9 See the Value Added Tax Act 1994 Sch 10 Pt I para 10; and VALUE ADDED TAX vol 99 (2012) PARA 196.

10 See the Value Added Tax Act 1994 Sch 10 Pt I para 11; and VALUE ADDED TAX vol 99 (2012) PARA 197.

11 See the Value Added Tax Act 1994 Sch 10 Pt I para 12; and VALUE ADDED TAX vol 99 (2012) PARA 199.

12 See the Value Added Tax Act 1994 Sch 10 Pt I paras 12–14; and VALUE ADDED TAX vol 99 (2012) PARA 199 et seq. Land is exempt land if, at any time before the end of the relevant adjustment period as respects that land a relevant person (ie the grantor, a person connected with the grantor, a development financier, or a person connected with a development financier) is in occupation of the land, and that occupation is not wholly, or substantially wholly, for eligible purposes: see Sch 10 Pt I paras 15, 15A; and VALUE ADDED TAX vol 99 (2012) PARA 202. As to what qualifies as eligible purposes see Sch 10 Pt I para 16; and VALUE ADDED TAX vol 99 (2012) PARA 202.

4. LIABILITIES AND REMEDIES

(1) Negligence and other Liabilities

(i) Liability to Third Parties

363. Negligence.
Ordinary principles of negligence apply where a person is injured or property damaged as a result of construction works[1]. The contractor owes a duty of care to provide a safe means of access to the site[2]. He also owes a duty to all lawful users of the property to carry out the work with proper care[3]. This duty is owed even where the contractor is also the vendor or lessor[4] and is not abated by the subsequent disposal of the property[5].

Generally there will be no liability for economic loss unless there is a special relationship of reliance or assumption of responsibility which gives rise to a duty not to cause such loss[6] or the economic loss is consequent on physical damage[7].

A tortious duty of care may be excluded[8] or limited[9] by the existence of a contractual relationship between the two parties or between one of the parties and a third party[10]. However, where the contract is for professional services the duty of care in tort will exist alongside the duties imposed by the contract[11]. Such a parallel duty of care in tort may, it seems, exist even in relation to the provision of non-professional services[12].

An employer is not vicariously liable for the negligence of an independent contractor[13].

Where a party suffers damage which is caused partly as a result of his own fault and partly as a result of another's failure to take reasonable care and skill the court or arbitrator may reduce the amount of damages awarded to the extent it is thought just and reasonable[14].

Where two or more parties are responsible for causing the same damage one party may recover a contribution from the other parties[15]. The court will make an assessment of the amount of contribution it finds is just and equitable having regard to the extent of the person's responsibility for the damage in question[16]. A contractual time limitation clause in a warranty between a contractor and a beneficiary which prevented the beneficiary from issuing proceedings against the contractor for damage will not, without clear words, extinguish the underlying cause of action or prevent another defendant from bringing a contribution claim against the contractor[17]. Nor will a time bar defence raised in the main proceedings in defence of a claim, which is then subsequently settled, prevent the defendant from recovering a contribution from a third party who shares the damage caused[18].

1 Liability to third parties is outside the scope of this title, and this paragraph therefore only outlines some aspects. For further consideration of negligence and liability to third parties see NEGLIGENCE.
2 *AC Billings & Sons Ltd v Riden* [1958] AC 240, [1957] 3 All ER 1, HL.
3 *Gallagher v N McDowell Ltd* [1961] NI 26, CA; *Sharpe v ET Sweeting & Son Ltd* [1963] 2 All ER 455, [1963] 1 WLR 665.
4 *Dutton v Bognor Regis UDC* [1972] 1 QB 373 at 393–394, sub nom *Dutton v Bognor Regis United Building Co Ltd* [1972] 1 All ER 462 at 471–472, CA, per Lord Denning MR, and at 401–402, and 478–479 per Sachs LJ (overruled on another point in *Murphy v Brentwood District Council* [1991] 1 AC 398, [1990] 2 All ER 908, HL). See also the Defective Premises Act 1972 s 3; and PARA 277.
5 See the Defective Premises Act 1972 s 3; and PARA 277.

6   For circumstances in which such a duty arises see eg *Hedley Byrne & Co Ltd v Heller & Partners*
    [1964] AC 465, [1963] 2 All ER 575, HL; *Simaan General Contracting Co v Pilkington Glass Ltd
    (No 2)* [1988] QB 758, [1988] 1 All ER 791, CA; *D & F Estates Ltd v Church Comrs for England*
    [1989] AC 177, [1988] 2 All ER 992, HL; *Greater Nottingham Co-operative Society Ltd v
    Cementation Piling and Foundations Ltd* [1989] QB 71, [1988] 2 All ER 971, 41 BLR 43, CA;
    Caparo Industries plc v Dickman [1990] 2 AC 605, [1990] 1 All ER 568, HL; *Murphy v
    Brentwood District Council* [1991] 1 AC 398, [1990] 2 All ER 908, HL; *Department of the
    Environment v Thomas Bates and Son Ltd* [1991] 1 AC 499, [1990] 2 All ER 943, HL; *James
    McNaughton Paper Group Ltd v Hicks Anderson & Co* [1991] 2 QB 113, [1991] 1 All ER 134,
    CA; *Preston v Torfaen Borough Council* (1993) 65 BLR 1, (1993) 36 Con LR 48, CA; *Edgeworth
    Construction Ltd v ND Lea & Associates Ltd* (1993) 66 BLR 56, Can SC; *Henderson v Merrett
    Syndicates* [1995] 2 AC 145, [1994] 3 All ER 506, HL; *Spring v Guardian Assurance plc* [1995]
    2 AC 296, [1994] 3 All ER 129, HL; *Marc Rich & Co AG v Bishop Rock Marine Co Ltd* [1996]
    AC 211, sub nom *Marc Rich & Co AG v Bishop Rock Marine Co Ltd, The Nicholas H* [1995]
    3 All ER 307, HL; *Williams v Natural Life Ltd* [1998] 2 All ER 577, [1998] 1 WLR 830, HL;
    Riyad Bank v Ahli United Bank (UK) plc [2006] EWCA Civ 780, [2006] 2 All ER (Comm) 777,
    [2006] 2 Lloyd's Rep 292; *Customs and Excise Comrs v Barclays Bank plc* [2006] UKHL 28,
    [2007] 1 AC 181, [2006] 4 All ER 256. See further NEGLIGENCE vol 78 (2018) PARA 12.
       Physical damage caused to a building by negligent construction of that building is pure
    economic loss: *Murphy v Brentwood District Council* above; *Department of the Environment v
    Thomas Bates and Son Ltd.* However, physical damage to one part of a building caused by the
    negligent design or construction of another part of the same building may exceptionally be
    recoverable by virtue of the 'complex structure' exception identified in *Murphy v Brentwood
    District Council* above: see the dictum of Lord Keith of Kinkel at 470 and 922, of Lord Bridge of
    Harwich at 476–479 and 926–928, of Lord Oliver of Aylmerton at 484–485 and 932–933, and of
    Lord Jauncey of Tullichettle at 497 and 942; *Jacobs v Morton and Partners* (1994) 72 BLR 92; cf
    Tesco Stores Ltd v Norman Hitchcox Partnership Ltd (1997) 56 Con LR 42 at 168 per Judge
    Lewis QC; *Bellefield Computer Services Ltd v E Turner & Sons Ltd* [2000] BLR 97, CA (applied
    in *Holding and Management (Solitaire) Ltd v Ideal Homes North West Ltd* [2004] EWHC 2408
    (TCC), 96 ConLR 114, [2004] All ER (D) 29 (Oct)). See also *Payne v John Setchell Ltd* [2002]
    BLR 489, [2001] All (D) 203 (Mar) (no duty of care owed by designer where loss suffered was pure
    economic loss); and *Precis (521) plc v William M Mercer Ltd* [2005] EWCA Civ 114, (2005)
    Times, 24 January, [2005] All ER (D) 206 (Feb) (valuers did not assume responsibility to third
    party investors in relation to preparation of valuation report on company's pension fund). As to
    pure economic loss see further NEGLIGENCE vol 78 (2018) PARA 12.
7   *SCM (United Kingdom) Ltd v WJ Whittall & Son Ltd* [1971] 1 QB 337, [1970] 3 All ER 245, CA;
    Spartan Steel and Alloys Ltd v Martin & Co (Contractors) Ltd [1973] QB 27, [1972] 3 All ER 557,
    CA; *Muirhead v Industrial Tank Specialists Ltd* [1986] QB 507, [1985] 3 All ER 705, CA;
    Londonwaste Ltd v Amec Civil Engineering Ltd (1997) 83 BLR 136, (1997) 53 Con LR 66. See
    also *Pearson Education Ltd v Charter Partnership Ltd* [2007] EWCA Civ 130, [2007] 2 EGLR 89,
    [2007] BLR 324.
8   See *Tai Hing Cotton Mill Ltd v Liu Chong Hing Bank Ltd* [1986] AC 80, [1985] 2 All ER 947,
    PC; *Greater Nottingham Co-operative Society Ltd v Cementation Piling and Foundations Ltd*
    [1989] QB 71, [1988] 2 All ER 971, 41 BLR 43, CA; *Scally v Southern Health and Social Services
    Board* [1992] 1 AC 294, [1991] 4 All ER 563, HL.
9   *William Hill Organisation Ltd v Bernard Sunley & Sons Ltd* (1982) 22 BLR 1, CA. See also
    Robinson v P E Jones (Contractors) Ltd [2011] EWCA Civ 9, [2012] QB 44, [2011] 3 WLR 815.
10 *Southern Water Authority v Carey* [1985] 2 All ER 1077, sub nom *Southern Water Authority v
    Lewis and Duvivier* (1984) 27 BLR 116; *Pacific Associates Inc v Baxter* [1990] 1 QB 993, [1989]
    2 All ER 159, CA; *Norwich City Council v Harvey* [1989] 1 All ER 1180, [1989] 1 WLR 828,
    CA; cf *National Trust for Places of Historic Interest or Natural Beauty v Haden Young Ltd* (1994)
    72 BLR 1, CA; *British Telecommunications plc v James Thomson & Sons (Engineers) Ltd* [1999]
    2 All ER 241, [1999] 1 WLR 9, HL. See also *Smith v Eric S Bush (a firm)* [1990] 1 AC 831, [1989]
    2 All ER 514, HL.
11 *Esso Petroleum Co Ltd v Mardon* [1976] QB 801, [1976] 2 All ER 5, CA (disapproving *Bagot v
    Stevens, Scanlan & Co* [1966] 1 QB 197, [1964] 3 All ER 577); *Batty v Metropolitan Property
    Realisations Ltd* [1978] QB 554, [1978] 2 All ER 445, CA; *Midland Bank Trust Co Ltd v Hett,
    Stubbs and Kemp* [1979] Ch 384, [1978] 3 All ER 571; *Pirelli General Cable Works Ltd v Oscar
    Faber & Partners* [1983] 2 AC 1, [1983] 1 All ER 65, HL; *Richard Roberts Holdings Ltd v
    Douglas Smith Stimson Partnership* (1988) 46 BLR 50; *Lancashire and Cheshire Association of
    Baptist Churches Inc v Howard & Seddon Partnership (a firm)* [1993] 3 All ER 467, 65 BLR 21;

Henderson v Merrett Syndicates [1995] 2 AC 145, [1994] 3 All ER 506, HL; *Holt v Payne Skillington and De Groot Collis* (1995) 77 BLR 51, (1995) 49 Con LR 99, CA; *Robinson v P E Jones (Contractors) Ltd* [2011] EWCA Civ 9, [2012] QB 44, [2011] 3 WLR 815.

12 See *Barclays Bank plc v Fairclough Building Ltd (No 2)* (1995) 76 BLR 1, (1995) 44 Con LR 35.

13 See *Sharpe v ET Sweeting & Son Ltd* [1963] 2 All ER 455, [1963] 1 WLR 665; *D & F Estates Ltd v Church Comrs for England* [1989] AC 177, [1988] 2 All ER 992, HL; *Department of the Environment v Thomas Bates & Son Ltd* [1991] 1 AC 499, [1990] 2 All ER 943, HL; *Rowe v Herman* [1997] 1 WLR 1390, 58 Con LR 33, CA; and TORT vol 97 (2015) PARAS 797, 799.

14 See the Law Reform (Contributory Negligence) Act 1945 s 1; and NEGLIGENCE vol 78 (2018) PARA 75 et seq. See *Barclays Bank plc v Fairclough Building Ltd* [1995] QB 214, [1995] 1 All ER 289, CA; *Platform Home Loans Ltd v Oyston Shipways Ltd* [2000] 2 AC 190, [1999] 1 All ER 833, HL.

15 See the Civil Liability (Contribution) Act 1978 s 1; and TORT vol 97 (2015) PARA 450. The Civil Liability (Contribution) Act 1978 applies to any damage whatever the basis of the liability. See generally TORT vol 97 (2015) PARA 449 et seq. See also *Friends' Provident Life Office v Hillier Parker May & Rowden (a firm)* [1997] QB 85, [1995] 4 All ER 260, CA; *Birse Construction Ltd v Haiste Ltd* [1996] 2 All ER 1, [1996] 1 WLR 675, CA; *J Sainsbury plc v Broadway Malyan* (1998) 61 Con LR 31; *Jameson v Central Electricity Generating Board* [1998] QB 323, [1997] 4 All ER 38, CA (overruled on another point [2000] 1 AC 455, [1999] 1 All ER 193); *Royal Brompton Hospital NHS Trust v Hammond (Taylor Woodrow Construction (Holdings) Ltd, Pt 20 defendant)* [2002] UKHL 14, [2002] 2 All ER 801, [2002] 1 WLR 1397; *Rahman v Arearose Ltd* [2001] QB 351, [2000] 3 WLR 1184, CA; *Hawkins & Harrison (a firm) v Tyler* [2001] Lloyd's Rep PN 1, [2000] All ER (D) 968, CA; *Eastgate Group Ltd v Lindsey Morden Group Inc* [2001] EWCA Civ 1446, [2001] 2 All ER (Comm) 1050, [2002] 1 WLR 642, [2002] Lloyd's Rep PN 11; *BICC Ltd v Cumbria Industrials Ltd* [2001] EWCA Civ 1621, [2002] Lloyd's Rep PN 526, sub nom *BICC Ltd v Parkman Consulting Engineers (a firm)* [2002] BLR 64, CA.

16 See the Civil Liability (Contribution) Act 1978 s 2; and TORT vol 97 (2015) PARA 453. The contribution may amount to an indemnity: see s 2(2); PARAS 388–389; and TORT vol 97 (2015) PARA 453. See also *Saipern SpA and Conoco (UK) Ltd v Dredging VO$_2$ BV and Geosite Surveys Ltd, The Volvox Hollandia (No 2)* [1993] 2 Lloyd's Rep 315.

17 See *Bloomberg LP v Sandberg* [2015] EWHC 2858 (TCC), 162 ConLR 260, [2016] BLR 72 where court found that the particular wording in a time limitation clause in a collateral warranty prevented the right to bring proceedings but did not extinguish the right on which the claim in respect of the damage was based; therefore the parties to such warranty could not 'contract out' of the Civil Liability (Contribution) Act 1978 which had been put in place to benefit other third parties, those parties not being privy to the collateral warranty.

18 *WH Newson Holding Ltd v IMI plc* [2016] EWCA Civ 773, [2017] Ch 27, [2016] 3 WLR 1595 discussed the meaning of the Civil Liability (Contribution) Act 1978 s 1(4) and held that, provided the defendant can show he would have been liable for the damage assuming that the factual basis of the claim against him could be established, he does not have to investigate whether any collateral defence, including a time bar defence, would have succeeded thus avoiding liability in the first place (which might have the effect of preventing the contribution claim). The Court of Appeal considered the case of *Arab Monetary Fund v Hashim* [1993] 1 Lloyd's Rep 543 and decided it had been wrong in that case to suggest that the proviso in the Civil Liability (Contribution) Act 1978 s 1(4) does permit an investigation as to whether the collateral defence would have succeeded.

364. Liability as occupier.

The contractor may be in occupation of the site for the purposes of the Occupiers' Liability Act 1957[1] and, if he is, he will owe lawful visitors a duty to see that the premises are safe for the purpose of their visit[2] but, in discharging this duty, the contractor may rely on the visitor guarding against special risks ordinarily incident in the exercise of his calling[3]. A contractor who does not control the works is not in occupation of them[4]. During the execution of the works, an employer who retains control of the premises will be liable as an occupier to third parties[5]. Where damage is caused to a visitor by a danger arising from faulty execution of any work of construction, maintenance or repair, the employer will have a defence if he acted reasonably in entrusting the work to an independent contractor and took steps to satisfy himself that the contractor was competent and that the work had been properly done[6].

Where the occupier is or should be aware that a trespasser may be in the vicinity of a danger on the site and it is a risk against which, in all the circumstances, the occupier should offer protection, he owes the trespasser a duty to see that he does not suffer death or personal injury by reason of that danger[7].

1 See NEGLIGENCE vol 78 (2018) PARA 29 et seq.
2 *Fisher v CHT Ltd (No 2)* [1966] 2 QB 475, [1966] 1 All ER 88, CA; *Savory v Holland Hannen and Cubitts (Southern) Ltd* [1964] 3 All ER 18, [1964] 1 WLR 1158, CA; *Makepeace v Evans Brothers (Reading)* [2001] ICR 241, [2000] BLR 737, [2000] All ER (D) 720; and see *AMF International Ltd v Magnet Bowling Ltd* [1968] 2 All ER 789, [1968] 1 WLR 1028 (damage to the property of an invitee).
3 See the Occupiers' Liability Act 1957 s 2(3)(b); and NEGLIGENCE vol 78 (2018) PARA 32. See also *Roles v Nathan* [1963] 2 All ER 908 at 912–914, [1963] 1 WLR 1117 at 1123–1125, CA, per Lord Denning MR.
4 *Kearney v Eric Waller Ltd* [1967] 1 QB 29, [1965] 3 All ER 352.
5 *Wheat v E Lacon & Co Ltd* [1966] AC 552, [1966] 1 All ER 582, HL; *Fisher v CHT Ltd (No 2)* [1966] 2 QB 475, [1966] 1 All ER 88, CA; *AMF International Ltd v Magnet Bowling Ltd* [1968] 2 All ER 789, [1968] 1 WLR 1028.
6 See the Occupiers' Liability Act 1957 s 2(4)(b); and NEGLIGENCE vol 78 (2018) PARA 35. The burden of proof of this allegation is on the occupier: *Christmas v Blue Star Line Ltd and Harland and Wolff Ltd* [1961] 1 Lloyd's Rep 94.
7 See the Occupiers' Liability Act 1984 s 1; and NEGLIGENCE vol 78 (2018) PARA 40. See also *Ratcliff v McConnell* [1999] 1 WLR 670, 143 Sol Jo LB 53, CA.

365. Defective premises.

A person who takes on work in the provision of a dwelling, including the conversion of an existing building, is under a duty imposed by the Defective Premises Act 1972 to ensure that as regards that work the dwelling will be fit for habitation when completed. This is in addition to any duty otherwise owed[1].

1 See the Defective Premises Act 1972 ss 1(1), 6(2). See further PARAS 275–277; and NEGLIGENCE vol 78 (2018) PARAS 43–44. As to exclusions from the duty see PARA 276.

366. Nuisance, trespass etc.

In addition to the liability in negligence of an owner or occupier of a building[1], further liabilities may be imposed in respect of nuisance, noise or trespass occurring during the carrying out of building or engineering works, or arising out of the effect of such works on adjoining land or highways[2].

1 See PARAS 275–277, 363–365; and NEGLIGENCE vol 78 (2018) PARA 29 et seq.
2 See PARA 303 et seq; and NUISANCE vol 78 (2018) PARA 101 et seq; TORT vol 97 (2015) PARA 563 et seq.

(ii) Duty of Care to Employees

367. General duty.

An employer of workmen owes his employees a general duty to provide competent staff[1], adequate materials[2], a proper system of work and effective supervision[3]. Many of these duties are further provided for by statute and regulations[4]. The duty cannot be delegated by entrusting its observance to a competent independent contractor[5], but an employer who employs small firms of sub-contractors for building work may assume a duty to provide proper supervision towards the sub-contractors' employees[6].

1 See *Hudson v Ridge Manufacturing Co Ltd* [1957] 2 QB 348, [1957] 2 All ER 229; and EMPLOYMENT vol 39 (2014) PARA 33.
2 See EMPLOYMENT vol 39 (2014) PARA 33.
3 See *Wilsons and Clyde Coal Co Ltd v English* [1938] AC 57, [1937] 3 All ER 628, HL; and

4   See PARA 368; and EMPLOYMENT vol 39 (2014) PARA 32 et seq; HEALTH AND SAFETY AT
    WORK vol 52 (2014) PARA 376 et seq.
5   See *McDermid v Nash Dredging and Reclamation Co Ltd* [1987] AC 906, [1987] 2 All ER 878,
    HL.
6   *McArdle v Andmac Roofing Co* [1967] 1 All ER 583, [1967] 1 WLR 356, CA; cf *Makepeace v
    Evans Bros (Reading) (a firm)* [2000] BLR 737, [2001] ICR 241, CA.

368. Health and safety of workmen.

Every contractor and employer of workmen is under a statutory duty to comply
with regulations requiring the provision of safe means of carrying out building
operations and works of engineering construction[1]. Regulations prescribe the
duties relating to health and safety on construction sites[2], including specific rules
regarding safe places of work[3], good order and site security[4], stability of structures
(including scaffolding)[5], demolition and dismantling[6], explosives[7], excavations[8],
cofferdams and caissons[9], energy distribution installations[10], prevention of
drowning[11], traffic routes[12], vehicles[13], prevention of risk from fire and flooding[14],
emergency procedures[15], emergency routes and exits[16], fire detection and
fire-fighting[17], fresh air[18], temperature and weather protection[19] and lighting[20].

Where defective equipment is supplied by an employer and his employee is
injured in consequence of that defect which is attributable, wholly or in part, to
a third party, the injury is deemed to be also attributable to the employer[21].

1   See the Factories Act 1961 s 127; the Health and Safety at Work etc Act 1974 s 15; and HEALTH
    AND SAFETY AT WORK vol 52 (2014) PARAS 306, 388, 389. Pursuant to the Health and Safety
    at Work etc Act 1974 s 15, the Construction (Design and Management) Regulations 2015,
    SI 2015/51, have been made, which revoke and replace the Construction (Health, Safety and
    Welfare) Regulations 2007, SI 2007/320: see HEALTH AND SAFETY AT WORK vol 53 (2014)
    PARA 641 et seq. Other relevant regulations include the Workplace (Health, Safety and Welfare)
    Regulations 1992, SI 1992/3004 (see HEALTH AND SAFETY AT WORK vol 52 (2014) PARA 420
    et seq); the Provision and Use of Work Equipment Regulations 1998, SI 1998/2306 (see HEALTH
    AND SAFETY AT WORK vol 52 (2014) PARA 445 et seq); the Work at Height Regulations 2005,
    SI 2005/735 (see HEALTH AND SAFETY AT WORK vol 53 (2014) PARA 546 et seq); and the Supply
    of Machinery (Safety) Regulations 2008, SI 2008/1597 (see HEALTH AND SAFETY AT WORK vol
    53 (2014) PARA 495 et seq). There are other provisions which apply to particular activities, see eg
    the Manual Handling Operations Regulations 1992, SI 1992/2793; and HEALTH AND SAFETY AT
    WORK vol 53 (2014) PARA 545.
2   See the Construction (Design and Management) Regulations 2015, SI 2015/51, Pt 4 (regs 16–35);
    and HEALTH AND SAFETY AT WORK vol 53 (2014) PARA 650 et seq.
3   See the Construction (Design and Management) Regulations 2015, SI 2015/51, reg 17; and
    HEALTH AND SAFETY AT WORK vol 53 (2014) PARA 651.
4   See the Construction (Design and Management) Regulations 2015, SI 2015/51, reg 18; and
    HEALTH AND SAFETY AT WORK vol 53 (2014) PARA 651.
5   See the Construction (Design and Management) Regulations 2015, SI 2015/51, reg 19; and
    HEALTH AND SAFETY AT WORK vol 53 (2014) PARA 652.
6   See the Construction (Design and Management) Regulations 2015, SI 2015/51, reg 20; and
    HEALTH AND SAFETY AT WORK vol 53 (2014) PARA 652.
7   See the Construction (Design and Management) Regulations 2015, SI 2015/51, reg 21; and
    HEALTH AND SAFETY AT WORK vol 53 (2014) PARA 653.
8   See the Construction (Design and Management) Regulations 2015, SI 2015/51, reg 22; and
    HEALTH AND SAFETY AT WORK vol 53 (2014) PARA 654.
9   See the Construction (Design and Management) Regulations 2015, SI 2015/51, reg 23; and
    HEALTH AND SAFETY AT WORK vol 53 (2014) PARA 655.
10 See the Construction (Design and Management) Regulations 2015, SI 2015/51, reg 25; and
    HEALTH AND SAFETY AT WORK vol 53 (2014) PARA 657.
11 See the Construction (Design and Management) Regulations 2015, SI 2015/51, reg 26; and
    HEALTH AND SAFETY AT WORK vol 53 (2014) PARA 658.

12 See the Construction (Design and Management) Regulations 2015, SI 2015/51, reg 27; and HEALTH AND SAFETY AT WORK vol 53 (2014) PARA 659.

13 See the Construction (Design and Management) Regulations 2015, SI 2015/51, reg 28; and HEALTH AND SAFETY AT WORK vol 53 (2014) PARA 660.

14 See the Construction (Design and Management) Regulations 2015, SI 2015/51, reg 29; and HEALTH AND SAFETY AT WORK vol 53 (2014) PARA 661.

15 See the Construction (Design and Management) Regulations 2015, SI 2015/51, reg 30; and HEALTH AND SAFETY AT WORK vol 53 (2014) PARA 662.

16 See the Construction (Design and Management) Regulations 2015, SI 2015/51, reg 31; and HEALTH AND SAFETY AT WORK vol 53 (2014) PARA 662.

17 See the Construction (Design and Management) Regulations 2015, SI 2015/51, reg 32; and HEALTH AND SAFETY AT WORK vol 53 (2014) PARA 661.

18 See the Construction (Design and Management) Regulations 2015, SI 2015/51, reg 33; and HEALTH AND SAFETY AT WORK vol 53 (2014) PARA 663.

19 See the Construction (Design and Management) Regulations 2015, SI 2015/51, reg 34; and HEALTH AND SAFETY AT WORK vol 53 (2014) PARA 663.

20 See the Construction (Design and Management) Regulations 2015, SI 2015/51, reg 35; and HEALTH AND SAFETY AT WORK vol 53 (2014) PARA 663.

21 See the Employer's Liability (Defective Equipment) Act 1969 s 1. See also PARA 363; and EMPLOYMENT vol 39 (2014) PARA 33. See further HEALTH AND SAFETY AT WORK vol 52 (2014) PARA 377; TORT vol 97 (2015) PARA 762.

(2) Remedies

(i) Damages for Breach or Repudiation of Contract

369. Employer's right to damages.

In general[1] an employer's claim will be for breach of the contractor's single obligation to complete the works in accordance with the contract[2]. An employer may also be able to recover damages for breaches which occur earlier than completion[3]. An employer's common law right to damages for breach of contract is not removed because of his failure to notify the contractor of defects within the time limit specified in the contract, although this failure may limit the amount of damages recoverable[4].

If the contractor wholly fails to complete the work the measure of damages is the additional cost of completing the works beyond that which would have been payable or paid to the contractor[5]. Similarly if the contractor fails to complete part of the works or purports to complete it but with defective work or materials the damage recoverable is the diminution in value, measured normally by the cost of completing or putting right the work[6].

Usually the employer will have executed the work of reinstatement and the actual costs will be known but the estimated cost may be recovered and, provided it is reasonable, will be the measure of damages. The estimated cost of work not yet executed may be recovered provided that the work is reasonable and the employer genuinely intends to execute it[7]. The cost of reinstatement will be reasonable[8] even if the work produces a better building and no allowance or deduction is generally made on account of betterment[9]. Reinstatement involves producing 'new for old'[10] and as such may inevitably lead to work of a higher standard being required, for example by the provisions relating to building regulation[11]. If, however, a claimant chooses to build to a higher standard than is strictly necessary there will be a deduction in respect of betterment[12]. It is not always necessary for the employer to prove that he has paid or will himself pay for the work[13].

Where the employer has no intention of carrying out works of completion or reinstatement[14] or the cost of such works is out of all proportion to the benefit to be obtained[15], the appropriate measure of damages is the diminution in the value of the property occasioned by the breach. This may result in some cases in a nominal award of damages[16].

1　As to the right to recover damages for breach of contract generally see CONTRACT vol 22 (2012) PARA 575; DAMAGES vol 29 (2014) PARA 499 et seq.

2　This would logically include claims both for defective work and for failure to complete on time. However, there may be separate causes of action arising from such a breach: see *Idyll v Dineman Davison and Hillman* (1985) 4 Const LJ 294, CA; *Steamship Mutual Underwriting Association Ltd v Trollope & Colls (City) Ltd* (1986) 33 BLR 77, 6 Con LR 11, CA (sed quaere).

3　See *Lintest Builders v Roberts* (1980) 13 BLR 38, CA; *Surrey Heath Borough Council v Lovell Construction Ltd* (1988) 42 BLR 25 at 34 per Judge Fox-Andrews QC (revsd on other grounds (1990) 48 BLR 108, CA); *Guinness plc v CMD Property Developments Ltd* (1995) 76 BLR 40, (1995) 46 Con LR 48; *Oval (717) Ltd v Aegon Insurance Co (UK) Ltd* (1997) 85 BLR 97, 54 Con LR 74; cf *P & M Kaye Ltd v Hosier & Dickinson Ltd* [1972] 1 All ER 121 at 138–139, [1972] 1 WLR 146 at 165, HL, per Lord Diplock.

4　See *Pearce and High Ltd v Baxter* [1999] BLR 101, 66 Con LR 110, CA.

5　*Mertens v Home Freeholds Co* [1921] 2 KB 526, CA; *Radford v De Froberville* [1978] 1 All ER 33, [1977] 1 WLR 1262 (applied in *Dean v Ainley* [1987] 3 All ER 748, [1987] 1 WLR 1729). See also *DO Ferguson & Associates v M Sohl* (1992) 62 BLR 95, CA.

　　This measure of damages is not applicable where the contract is an entire contract and substantial completion has not been achieved; in such a case the employer, in his claim for damages, must, if the contractor has not deliberately been in breach, give credit for work done: see *Hoenig v Isaacs* [1952] 2 All ER 176, CA. If, however, the contractor abandons the work or fails to complete it by his own default, the employer may recover damages equalling, or even exceeding, the amount of any instalments paid, on the basis of a total failure of consideration: *Appleby v Myers* (1867) LR 2 CP 651; *Newfoundland Government v Newfoundland Rly Co* (1888) 13 App Cas 199, PC.

6　*East Ham Corpn v Bernard Sunley & Sons Ltd* [1966] AC 406, [1965] 3 All ER 619, HL; *William Cory & Son Ltd v Wingate Investments (London Colney) Ltd* (1978) 17 BLR 104, CA; *Dodd Properties (Kent) Ltd v Canterbury City Council* [1980] 1 All ER 928, [1980] 1 WLR 433, 13 BLR 45, CA; *Darlington Borough Council v Wiltshier Northern Ltd* [1995] 3 All ER 895, [1995] 1 WLR 68, CA; *Ruxley Electronics and Construction Ltd v Forsyth* [1996] AC 344, [1995] 3 All ER 268, HL. See also *London Fire and Emergency Planning Authority v Halcrow Gilbert Associates Ltd* [2007] EWHC 2546 (TCC), [2007] All ER (D) 111 (Dec); *Birse Construction Ltd v Eastern Telegraph Co Ltd* [2004] EWHC 2512 (TCC), [2004] 47 EG 164 (CS), [2004] All ER (D) 92 (Nov). Depending on the circumstances, an employer may be entitled to employ someone other than the contractor to carry out the remedial works: *Melhuish & Saunders Ltd v Hurden* [2012] EWHC 3119 (TCC), [2012] All ER (D) 234 (Nov)

7　*Dodd Properties (Kent) Ltd v Canterbury City Council* [1980] 1 All ER 928, [1980] 1 WLR 433, 13 BLR 45, CA; *Imodco v Wimpey Major Projects Ltd* (1987) 40 BLR 1, CA; cf *Ruxley Electronics and Construction Ltd v Forsyth* [1996] AC 344, [1995] 3 All ER 268, HL; *Freeman v Niroomand* (1996) 52 Con LR 116, CA.

8　See *Axa Insurance UK plc v Cunningham Lindsey United Kingdom* [2007] EWHC 3023 (TCC), [2007] All ER (D) 290 (Dec) (objective logic must be used in establishing the reasonableness of a decision to adopt one remedial solution rather than another; recovery of the cost of remedial works relating to putting right a default or defect for which the defendant was not culpable would rarely, if ever, be justified). See also *Linklaters Business Services (formerly Hackwood Services Co) v Sir Robert McAlpine Ltd* [2010] EWHC 1145 (TCC), 130 Con LR 111, [2010] BLR 537 (decision to replace defective pipework, rather than attempt a remedial scheme, was wholly reasonable).

9　*Hollebone v Midhurst and Fenhurst Builders Ltd and Eastman and White of Midhurst Ltd* [1968] 1 Lloyd's Rep 38; *Harbutt's Plasticine Ltd v Wayne Tank and Pump Co Ltd* [1970] 1 QB 447, [1970] 1 All ER 225, CA (overruled on another point by *Photo Production Ltd v Securicor Transport Ltd* [1980] AC 827, [1980] 1 All ER 556, HL); *Barclays Bank plc v Fairclough Building Ltd (No 2)* [1995] IRLR 605, (1994) 39 Con LR 144.

10　See *Re-Source America Ltd v Platt Site Services Ltd* [2005] EWHC 2242 (TCC), 106 Con LR 15, [2005] All ER (D) 23 (Nov).

11 As to building regulation see BUILDING vol 6 (2018) PARA 1 et seq.
12 *Richard Roberts (Holdings) Ltd v Douglas Smith Stimson Partnership* (1988) 46 BLR 50 at 69 per Judge Newey QC.
13 *Jones v Stroud District Council* [1988] 1 All ER 5, [1986] 1 WLR 1141, CA; *Design 5 v Kenniston Housing Association* (1986) 34 BLR 92, 10 Con LR 123; *Darlington Borough Council v Wiltshier Northern Ltd* [1995] 3 All ER 895, [1995] 1 WLR 68, CA.
14 *Tito v Waddell (No 2)* [1977] Ch 106, [1977] 3 All ER 129; *CR Taylor (Wholesale) Ltd v Hepworths Ltd* [1977] 2 All ER 784, [1977] 1 WLR 659; *Radford v De Froberville* [1978] 1 All ER 33, [1977] 1 WLR 1262; *Ward v Cannock Chase District Council* [1986] Ch 546, [1985] 3 All ER 537; *Hussey v Eels* [1990] 2 QB 227, [1990] 1 All ER 449, CA; *Ruxley Electronics and Construction Ltd v Forsyth* [1996] AC 344, [1995] 3 All ER 268, HL.
15 *Applegate v Moss* [1971] 1 QB 406, [1971] 1 All ER 747, CA; *King v Victor Parsons & Co* [1972] 2 All ER 625, [1972] 1 WLR 801 (affd [1973] 1 All ER 206, [1973] 1 WLR 29, CA); *Dodd Properties (Kent) Ltd v Canterbury City Council* [1980] 1 All ER 928, [1980] 1 WLR 433, 13 BLR 45, CA; *Ruxley Electronics and Construction Ltd v Forsyth* [1996] AC 344, [1995] 3 All ER 268, HL.
16 *Ruxley Electronics and Construction Ltd v Forsyth* [1996] AC 344, [1995] 3 All ER 268, HL.

370. Contractor's right to damages.

Where the employer repudiates the contract and no work at all has been carried out the measure of damages will be: (1) the contract price less the costs which the contractor would have had to bear in completing the work; or (2) any sums already expended subject to the employer's showing that had the contract been performed in full the contractor would still have made a loss[1].

Where the employer repudiates the contract after the work has been partially performed, and the contractor is unable to sue under the contract for the price of the work done, the damages will generally be measured as the loss of profits on the unfinished balance, plus the value of the work done at contract rates. The employer is entitled to abatement of the contractual price if the incomplete work is defective[2]. There is some authority for the proposition that the contractor may, in the alternative, opt to claim a quantum meruit for the value of any work done[3], however it is more likely that the contractor has no such entitlement[4].

If the employer's breach is not repudiatory and does not prevent completion of the works, the damages recoverable by the contractor will be the increase in the cost of completing the works caused by reason of the breach, plus any profits that would have been made on such expenditure[5].

Where the employer's conduct causes delay or disruption, the contractor is similarly entitled to the extra cost which he would not have incurred but for the delay or disruption[6].

1 This represents the measurement of damages by the application of the ordinary principles of loss of profit and wasted expenditure: see *C and P Haulage (a firm) v Middleton* [1983] 3 All ER 94, [1983] 1 WLR 1461, CA; *CCC Films (London) Ltd v Impact Quadrant Films Ltd* [1985] QB 16, [1984] 3 All ER 298 (applied in *Grange v Quinn* [2013] EWCA Civ 24, [2013] 1 P & CR 279, [2013] All ER (D) 246 (Jan)); and DAMAGES vol 29 (2014) PARA 499 et seq.
2 *Slater v CA Duquemin Ltd* (1992) 29 Con LR 24.
3 See eg *Lodder v Slowey* [1904] AC 442, PC; *Renard Constructions (ME) Pty Ltd v Minister for Public Works* (1992) 33 Con LR 72 at 128–130, NSW CA, per Meagher JA. Quaere whether the contract price limits the amount that may be recovered on a quantum meruit basis. As to quantum meruit see RESTITUTION vol 88 (2012) PARA 513 et seq.
4 See PARA 320.
5 This is measured as loss of profit on ordinary principles: see DAMAGES. See *John F Hunt Demolition Ltd v ASME Engineering Ltd* [2007] EWHC 1507 (TCC), [2008] 1 All ER 180, [2008] BLR 115; *Siemens Building Technology FE Ltd v Supershield Ltd* [2010] EWCA Civ 7, [2010] 1 Lloyd's Rep 349, [2010] BLR 145.
6 *Lawson v Wallasey Local Board* (1883) 48 LT 507, CA. See further PARA 267.

371. Amount of damages where costs are unquantifiable.

The complexity of construction work sometimes makes it difficult to establish clearly how an undoubted actual loss was caused. A claim must nevertheless be set out with sufficient particularity and specify a discernible nexus between the wrong and its consequences[1]. Provided that such a nexus has been established, then where the full extra costs depend on a complex interaction between the consequences of various events so that it is difficult to make an accurate apportionment of the total extra costs, an individual award may be made for such primary costs as can be proved to flow from the relevant event or events and a supplementary award in respect of the remainder as a composite whole[2].

1 *Wharf Properties Ltd v Eric Cumine Associates (No 2)* (1991) 52 BLR 1 at 20–21, PC; *McAlpine Humberoak Ltd v McDermott International Inc* (1992) 58 BLR 1 at 28, (1992) 28 Con LR 76 at 100–101, CA, per Lloyd LJ; *Mid-Glamorgan County Council v J Devonald Williams* (1992) 29 Con LR 129, [1991] CILL 722; *ICI plc v Bovis Construction Ltd* (1992) 32 Con LR 90, [1992] CILL 776; *Bernhard's Rugby Landscapes Ltd v Stockley Park Consortium Ltd* (1997) 82 BLR 39; *John Holland Construction & Engineering Pty Ltd v Kvaerner RJ Brown Pty Ltd* (1996) 82 BLR 81, Vic SC; cf *British Airways Pensions Trustees Ltd v Sir Robert McAlpine & Sons Ltd* (1994) 72 BLR 26, (1994) 45 Con LR 1, CA; *Laing Management (Scotland) Ltd v John Doyle Construction Ltd* [2004] BLR 295, IH (affg *John Doyle Construction Ltd v Laing Management (Scotland) Ltd* [2002] BLR 393, 85 Con LR 98, Ct of Sess); *London Underground Ltd v Citylink Telecommunications Ltd* [2007] EWHC 1749 (TCC), [2007] 2 All ER (Comm) 694, 114 Con LR 1; *City Inn Ltd v Shepherd Constructions Ltd* [2007] CSOH 190, [2008] BLR 269, OH; *Walter Lilly & Co Ltd v Mackay* [2012] EWHC 1773 (TCC), 143 ConLR 79, [2012] All ER (D) 213 (Jul).
2 *Wharf Properties Ltd v Eric Cumine Associates (No 2)* (1991) 52 BLR 1 at 20–21, PC; explaining *J Crosby & Sons Ltd v Portland UDC* (1967) 5 BLR 121; and *Merton London Borough Council v Stanley Hugh Leach Ltd* (1985) 32 BLR 51.

(ii) Specific Relief

372. Claims under contracts.

The principal contracts for construction work now contain extensive provisions whereby amounts may be recovered under the contract in respect of events which might or might not otherwise have been breaches of contract[1]. Such amounts are generally assessed as if they were damages. It is a matter of the interpretation of each contract whether such provisions are supplementary to or in lieu of a right to recover damages[2]. However, the distinction between claims under or for breach of contract is to be carefully observed[3]. Claims under contracts are sometimes assessed by the use of conventional approaches[4] but these should not be used where the actual loss could be proved[5].

1 Sometimes referred to as 'loss or expense' claims after the language used in the JCT forms. As to JCT standard forms of contract see PARA 202.
2 See PARA 342.
3 See *McAlpine Humberoak Ltd v McDermott International Inc* (1992) 58 BLR 1, (1992) 28 Con LR 76, CA.
4 Such as the so-called 'Hudson formula' (see Hudson's Building Contracts (10th Edn) 599), applied in *Ellis-Don Ltd v Parking Authority of Toronto* (1978) 28 BLR 98, Ont SC; and *JF Finnegan Ltd v Sheffield City Council* (1988) 43 BLR 124 at 136 per Sir William Stabb QC, but without regard to its assumptions and difficulties.
5 *Tate & Lyle Food and Distribution Ltd v GLC* [1981] 3 All ER 716 at 721, [1982] 1 WLR 149 at 152 per Forbes J; revsd on other grounds [1982] 2 All ER 854, [1982] 1 WLR 971, CA; decision of CA itself revsd, sub nom *Tate & Lyle Industries Ltd v Greater London Council* [1983] 2 AC 509, [1983] 1 All ER 1159, HL. For an example of the court's approach to proof of loss see *Alfred McAlpine Homes North Ltd v Property and Land Contracts Ltd* (1995) 76 BLR 59, sub nom *Property and Land Contractors Ltd v Alfred McAlpine Homes North Ltd* (1995) 76 BLR 59, (1995) 47 Con LR 74.

373. Recovery of money.

The contractor can apply for summary judgment for any sum due to him as the price of the work he has completed so long as there is no defence to the claim. Claims for liquidated sums, such as claims for the price of a lump sum contract, or for an instalment payment when the price is payable by instalments, are all within the provisions of the Civil Procedure Rules as to obtaining summary judgment[1].

Many building contracts provide that the contractor must present the certificate of an architect or valuer to the employer as a precondition of payment. In such a case the contractor cannot generally recover any sum without a certificate[2]. In certain circumstances, however, the contractor is able to recover without a certificate[3]. Where the employer is given time within which he must honour a certificate, no claim can be made until that period has expired; although from the date when the certificate is presented there may be a debt albeit payable in the future[4].

1   See CPR Pt 24; and CIVIL PROCEDURE vol 12 (2015) PARA 549. Note, however, that where the contract contains an arbitration clause, an application for summary judgment will generally be stayed to arbitration even where there is no defence to the claim: see the Arbitration Act 1996 s 9(4); and ARBITRATION vol 2 (2017) PARA 522.

2   See *Dunlop and Ranken Ltd v Hendall Steel Structures Ltd (Pitchers Ltd, garnishees)* [1957] 3 All ER 344, [1957] 1 WLR 1102, DC. Cases where the courts have held that a certificate is a condition precedent to payment include: *Milner v Field* (1850) 5 Exch 829; *Sharpe v San Paulo Rly Co* (1873) 8 Ch App 597; *Wallace v Brandon and Byshottles UDC* (1903) 2 Hudson's BC (10th Edn) 423, CA; *Eaglesham v McMaster* [1920] 2 KB 169; *Lubenham Fidelities and Investments Co Ltd v South Pembrokeshire District Council* (1986) 33 BLR 39, (1986) 6 Con LR 85, CA. See PARA 322 et seq.

3   See PARAS 332–340.

4   *Dunlop and Ranken Ltd v Hendall Steel Structures Ltd (Pitchers Ltd, garnishees)* [1957] 3 All ER 344 at 346, [1957] 1 WLR 1102 at 1104, DC, per Lord Goddard CJ.

374. Opening up, reviewing and revising certificates.

Where a certificate has the effect of affecting the substantive rights of the parties to the building contract, for example by fixing the value of a variation[1] or determining an extension of time[2], the court has inherent jurisdiction to open up, review and revise the certificate[3] (unless it is the intention of the contract that such certificates are to be of final and conclusive effect[4]) so as to determine the rights and liabilities of the parties. In relation to construction contracts[5], an adjudicator acting under the statutory adjudication regime under the Housing Grants, Construction and Regeneration Act 1996[6] has similar jurisdiction to determine the rights and obligations of the parties. Depending upon the terms of the arbitration clause in question the arbitrator may have similar powers and will certainly have such powers if the contract expressly empowers him to open up, review and revise certificates[7].

1   See PARAS 343–344.

2   See PARA 267 et seq.

3   *Beaufort Developments (NI) Ltd v Gilbert Ash NI Ltd* [1999] 1 AC 266, [1998] 2 All ER 778, HL.

4   See PARA 331.

5   Ie a 'construction contract' as defined in the Housing Grants, Construction and Regeneration Act 1996: see PARA 210.

6   See the Housing Grants, Construction and Regeneration Act 1996 s 108; and PARA 410.

7   See PARAS 339–340.

375. Specific performance.

The court does not normally order specific performance[1] of an ordinary building or engineering contract[2]. However, there are exceptions[3], and an order for specific performance of a contract to build will be made if the following conditions are fulfilled: (1) that the building work is sufficiently defined by the contract between the parties; (2) that the claimant has a substantial interest in the performance of the contract that cannot be adequately compensated in damages; (3) that the defendant is in possession of the land on which the work is contracted to be done[4].

1 As to orders of specific performance see SPECIFIC PERFORMANCE vol 95 (2017) PARA 501 et seq.
2 This is because the court cannot supervise performance of the details of a building contract, particularly where the object or specification is not clearly defined in the contract, and because damages are an adequate remedy: see *Lucas v Commerford* (1790) 3 Bro CC 166 per Lord Thurlow LC; *Mosely v Virgin* (1796) 3 Ves 184; *South Wales Rly Co v Wythes* (1854) 5 De GM & G 880, CA; *Greenhill v Isle of Wight (Newport Junction) Rly Co* (1871) 23 LT 885; *Wilkinson v Clements* (1872) 8 Ch App 96; cf *Co-operative Insurance Society Ltd v Argyll Stores (Holdings) Ltd* [1998] AC 1, [1997] 3 All ER 297, HL; *Alfa Finance Holding AD v Quarzwerke GmbH* [2015] EWHC 243 (Ch), [2015] All ER (D) 77 (Feb).
3 *Wolverhampton Corpn v Emmons* [1901] 1 KB 515, CA. Cf *Mosely v Virgin* (1796) 3 Ves 184.
4 *Molyneux v Richard* [1906] 1 Ch 34; *Carpenters Estates Ltd v Davies* [1940] Ch 160, [1940] 1 All ER 13; *Hepburn v Leather* (1884) 50 LT 660; *Cubitt v Smith* (1864) 11 LT 298; *Price v Strange* [1978] Ch 337, [1977] 3 All ER 371, CA; *Hounslow London Borough Council v Twickenham Garden Developments Ltd* [1971] Ch 233, [1970] 3 All ER 326 per Megarry J (as to which see also PARA 299).

376. Injunction and inquiry.

Injunctions are an equitable remedy, and will be granted only if the claimant's remedies at law are inadequate[1].

An injunction is not normally granted to prevent breach of the terms of a contract. Thus, as a general rule, the court will not restrain the employer even from wrongfully exercising the power of forfeiture, as the contractor can be compensated in damages for any loss he may sustain by reason of the forfeiture[2].

The court will not force the employer to employ a person to whom he objects, whether reasonably or unreasonably, to perform the works[3]. Such relief would be analogous to specific performance[4]. In an exceptional case where there was an arbitration clause by which the validity of the determination of the engineer, on which the right to forfeit was based, might be questioned, an interim injunction pending the arbitration was granted[5].

The employer, however, on proper grounds, and on giving the usual undertaking in damages[6], may obtain an injunction restraining the contractor from proceeding with the works[7].

In a case where the employer has wrongfully exercised his power of forfeiture, there may be an inquiry as to what sums have been properly expended by the employer in completing the work since he took possession for the purpose of ascertaining the damages sustained by the contractor[8].

1 See further CIVIL PROCEDURE vol 12 (2015) PARA 1098 et seq; DAMAGES vol 29 (2014) PARA 613.
2 See PARA 317.
3 *Garrett v Banstead Downs and Epsom Downs Rly Co* (1864) 12 LT 654 per Knight Bruce LJ; and see SPECIFIC PERFORMANCE vol 95 (2017) PARA 501 et seq.
4 *Munro v Wivenhoe and Brightlingsea Rly Co* (1865) 12 LT 655 at 657 per Knight Bruce LJ.
5 *Foster and Dicksee v Hastings Corpn* (1903) 87 LT 736 (but this case might not now be decided in the same way; see PARA 299 note 7).
6 See CIVIL PROCEDURE vol 12 (2015) PARA 609.

7   *Cork Corpn v Rooney* (1881) 7 LR Ir 191. See, however, *Hounslow London Borough Council v Twickenham Garden Developments Ltd* [1971] Ch 233 at 268–270, [1970] 3 All ER 326 at 355–356, where Megarry J refused to grant an interim injunction after the employer purported to determine the building contract for failure to proceed diligently with the work and after the contractor had refused to leave the site: '. . . [B]efore granting a mandatory injunction on motion the court must feel a high degree of assurance that at the trial it will appear that the injunction was rightly granted . . . [T]he borough has established some sort of a case for having validly determined the contract [but] that case falls considerably short of any standard upon which, in my judgment, it would be safe to grant this injunction on motion'. See, however, PARA 299 note 7. See also *Regan v Paul Properties Ltd* [2006] EWCA Civ 1391, [2007] Ch 135, [2007] 4 All ER 48 (mandatory injunction requiring defendants to pull down part of a building which infringed claimant's right to light was the correct remedy).

8   See the form of inquiry directed in *Macintosh v Great Western Rly Co* (1863) 1 De GJ & Sm 443. See also PARA 320.

377. Rectification and rescission.

The same principles apply in determining whether either party to a building contract can avail himself of the remedies of rectification or rescission as apply to all contracts[1]. If the contract fails to express the common intent of the parties, for example as the result of a clerical error, the court will rectify the contract to conform to that intent[2]. A contract will also be rectified if one party enters into it believing it to contain a particular term, and the other party knows of that belief and also that the term is omitted[3]. A party cannot obtain rectification where, by his conduct, he appears to have affirmed the contract in its defective form[4].

1   See generally CONTRACT vol 22 (2012) PARA 553 et seq; MISTAKE vol 77 (2016) PARAS 48 et seq, 53 et seq.

2   For the operation of rectification in building cases see *Simpson v Metcalf* (1854) 24 LTOS 139; *Neill v Midland Rly Co* (1869) 17 WR 871; *Crane v Hegeman-Harris Co Inc* [1939] 1 All ER 662, [1971] 1 WLR 1390n; *Carlton Contractors v Bexley Corpn* (1962) 60 LGR 331; *George Wimpey UK Ltd v VIC Construction Ltd* [2005] EWCA Civ 77, 103 Con LR 67, [2005] BLR 135. See also *JIS (1974) Ltd v MCE International Nominees Ltd* [2003] EWCA Civ 721, [2003] 24 LS Gaz R 36, [2003] All ER (D) 155 (Apr) (term in lease); *Rowallan Group Ltd and Edgehill Portfolio No 1 Ltd* [2007] EWHC 32 (Ch), [2007] All ER (D) 106 (Jan); *Hawksford Trustees Jersey Ltd v Stella Global UK Ltd* [2011] EWHC 503 (Ch), [2011] All ER (D) 154 (Mar).

3   *A Roberts & Co Ltd v Leicestershire County Council* [1961] Ch 555, [1961] 2 All ER 545; *Thomas Bates & Son Ltd v Wyndham's (Lingerie) Ltd* [1981] 1 All ER 1077, [1981] 1 WLR 505,; *Traditional Structures Ltd v HW Construction Ltd* [2010] EWHC 1530 (TCC), [2010] All ER (D) 197 (Jun).

4   See *Page v Taunton UDC* (1904) Hudson's BC (7th Edn) 126; *Ewing and Lawson v Hanbury & Co* (1900) 16 TLR 140.

378. Misrepresentation.

A party to a building contract may rescind the contract for fraudulent[1], negligent or innocent misrepresentation[2]. Also, the court may award damages for negligent misrepresentation; and, in the case of a misrepresentation made otherwise than negligently, the court may award damages in lieu of rescinding the contract if it would be equitable to do so[3].

1   See PARA 227; and generally MISREPRESENTATION vol 76 (2013) PARA 754 et seq.

2   See the Misrepresentation Act 1967 s 1; and MISREPRESENTATION vol 76 (2013) PARA 701 et seq.

3   See the Misrepresentation Act 1967 s 2; and MISREPRESENTATION vol 76 (2013) PARA 832. See also *Royscot Trust Ltd v Rogerson* [1991] 2 QB 297, [1991] 3 All ER 294, CA; *Gran Gelato Ltd v Richcliff (Group) Ltd* [1992] Ch 560, [1992] 1 All ER 865; *William Sindall plc v Cambridgeshire County Council* [1994] 3 All ER 932, [1994] 1 WLR 1016, CA; *Smith New Court Securities v Citibank NA* [1997] AC 254, sub nom *Smith New Court Securities Ltd v Scrimgeour Vickers (Asset Management) Ltd* [1996] 4 All ER 769, HL; *Floods of Queensferry Ltd v Shand Construction Ltd* [2000] BLR 81; and see PARA 227.

379. Set-off.

The parties to a building contract, as with any other contract, may agree by the words of their contract to preclude a party to it from exercising his rights of set-off and counterclaim[1], but there is no general principle that an architect's certificate must be honoured in full without the right to exercise the power to set off and counterclaim or to apply for a stay of proceedings pending recourse to arbitration where there is an arbitration clause[2]. A set-off proper should be distinguished from the right to have the price abated by reason of a breach of contract which made the subject matter of the contract less[3]. There is a presumption that a building contract does not disentitle a party to the remedies that would arise by operation of law, including the rights of abatement and set-off[4], and if these remedies are to be excluded the contract must contain clear unequivocal words that such a remedy should not be available[5]. However, a party to a construction contract[6] may not withhold payment after the final date for payment of a sum due under the contract unless he has given an effective pay less notice evidencing the intention to withhold payment[7]. It is thought that such a notice must be given in cases of set-off or abatement[8]. Set-off rights can adversely affect third parties benefitting from collateral warranties in respect of construction projects if they are not expressly excluded[9].

1   See *Hanak v Green* [1958] 2 QB 9, [1958] 2 All ER 141, CA. As to set-off see generally CIVIL PROCEDURE vol 11 (2015) PARA 382 et seq.
2   *Gilbert-Ash (Northern) Ltd v Modern Engineering (Bristol) Ltd* [1974] AC 689, [1973] 3 All ER 195, HL. See PARA 329.
3   *Gilbert-Ash (Northern) Ltd v Modern Engineering (Bristol) Ltd* [1974] AC 689, [1973] 3 All ER 195, HL; *Acsim (Southern) Ltd v Dancon Danish Contracting and Development Co Ltd* (1989) 47 BLR 55, 19 Con LR 1, CA; *CA Duquemin Ltd v Raymond Slater* (1993) 65 BLR 124, 35 Con LR 147; *Mellowes Archital Ltd v Bell Projects Ltd* (1997) 87 BLR 26, 58 Con LR 22, CA.
4   *Gilbert-Ash (Northern) Ltd v Modern Engineering (Bristol) Ltd* [1974] AC 689 at 718, [1973] 3 All ER 195 at 215, HL, per Lord Diplock.
5   *Gilbert-Ash (Northern) Ltd v Modern Engineering (Bristol) Ltd* [1974] AC 689, [1973] 3 All ER 195, HL. See also *Connaught Restaurants Ltd v Indoor Leisure Ltd* [1994] 4 All ER 834, [1994] 1 WLR 501, CA.
6   Ie a 'construction contract' as defined in the Housing Grants, Construction and Regeneration Act 1996: see PARA 210.
7   See the Housing Grants, Construction and Regeneration Act 1996 s 111; and PARA 355.
8   *VHE Construction plc v RBSTB Trust Co Ltd* [2000] BLR 187, 70 Con LR 51; *Northern Developments (Cumbria) Ltd v J & J Nichol* [2000] BLR 158, [2000] All ER (D) 68.
9   *Safeway Stores Ltd v Interserve Project Services Ltd (formerly known as Tilbury Douglas Construction Ltd)* [2005] EWHC 3085 (TCC), 105 ConLR 60 where the absence of an exclusion of set-off allowed a contractor to set-off sums due to him by the employer against a claim made by the third party beneficiary of a collateral warranty under which a duty of care was owed.

(iii) Restriction and Limitation of Actions

380. Exclusion of remedies.

The ordinary rules relating to all commercial contracts apply to building contracts (unless with a consumer) in determining whether a provision has the effect of excluding or restricting the right or remedy that would otherwise be available[1]. Some building contracts do, however, limit the right of the parties to question the subject matter of certificates unless a specific step is taken at or about the time when that certificate is issued[2]. Such provisions are subject to the test of reasonableness in the Unfair Contract Terms Act 1977 for business to business contracts[3] or to what is fair in the Consumer Rights Act 2015 for consumer contracts where one contracting party deals as a consumer or on the other's written terms of business[4]. However, once a certificate has acquired conclusive effect, the court will not exercise its powers to extend time for the commencement of an arbitration[5] for the purpose of challenging such a certificate[6].

1 See generally CONTRACT. See the Consumer Rights Act 2015 Pt 2 (ss 61–76) (unfair terms); and CONSUMER PROTECTION vol 21 (2016) PARA 391 et seq. Note that in business to consumer contracts, the Consumer Rights Act 2015 sets out in Pt 1 Ch 2 (ss 3–32) (goods) (see CONSUMER PROTECTION vol 21 (2016) PARA 329 et seq) and Ch 4 (ss 48–57) (services) (see CONSUMER PROTECTION vol 21 (2016) PARA 363) terms in consumer contracts which purport to exclude or restrict the trader's liability under listed headings and which if included in a consumer contract will make the contract non-binding on the consumer.
2 See eg *P & M Kaye Ltd v Hosier & Dickinson Ltd* [1972] 1 All ER 121, [1972] 1 WLR 146; *Scottish & Newcastle plc v GD Construction (St Albans) Ltd* [2003] EWCA Civ 16, [2003] Lloyd's Rep IR 809, [2003] BLR 131.
3 *Chester Grosvenor Hotel Co Ltd v Alfred McAlpine Management Ltd* (1991) 56 BLR 115.
4 See the Unfair Contract Terms Act 1977 ss 3, 13 (see CONTRACT vol 22 (2012) PARAS 411, 421); and the Consumer Rights Act 2015 s 62 (see CONSUMER PROTECTION vol 21 (2016) PARA 392 et seq).
5 See the Arbitration Act 1996 s 12; and ARBITRATION vol 2 (2017) PARA 521.
6 *Crown Estate Comrs v John Mowlem & Co Ltd* (1994) 70 BLR 1, (1994) 40 Con LR 36, CA; overruling *McLaughlin & Harvey plc v P & O Developments Ltd* (1991) 55 BLR 101.

381. Limitation.

Any claim founded on a building contract must be brought within six years from the date on which the cause of action accrued[1], unless the contract is made by deed, in which case the period is 12 years from the date on which the cause of action arose[2]. The period of limitation does not begin to run if the right of action is based upon the fraud of or is deliberately concealed by the defendant[3]. In such cases the date from which any period of limitation is calculated is the date on which the claimant discovered the fraud or concealment or could with reasonable diligence have discovered it[4]. In building contract cases deliberate concealment has been extended to assist a claimant who has based a cause of action upon faulty foundations which were covered by the builder before the claimant or his agent could ascertain the defective work[5]. Any other wrongful act knowingly committed by the defendant without informing the claimant or his agent may amount to deliberate concealment[6], such as the concealment of improper work by the contractor from the architect, engineer and clerk of works[7]. Thus a contractor who substituted a different type of facing brick for the kind stipulated in the contract and used them though he knew they were different and in some cases substandard in quality was guilty of deliberate concealment[8]. However, for the concept of fraudulent concealment to be applied, there must be more than the covering up of bad work in the due succession of building work; the conscience of the defendant must be affected so that it was unconscionable to proceed with the work so as to cover up the defect without putting it right[9]. Where a builder deliberately conceals defective work or behaves in any other way which constitutes deliberate concealment, that conduct may be imputed to the builder's employer since the builder is for this purpose the agent of the employer[10].

In general the cause of action for defective work will arise at the time when the works as a whole are or ought to have been completed or, in the case where defective work ought to have been corrected, at a date when the work ought to have been done[11] (for example at the time when the instructions ought to have been complied with or the work attended to as maintenance work). In the case of a failure to complete on time the cause of action will arise at the date when the works ought to have been completed. In the case of a claim for payment the cause of action will arise when the price, instalment, or sum certified ought to have been paid. Normally the latest date, for example the date when the final certificate should have been issued or paid, will be the relevant date[12]. A cause of action against a designer normally accrues upon preparation of the design. A fresh cause of action may accrue if there is a subsequent requirement to review the design, for example, upon the manifestation of defects[13].

1   See the Limitation Act 1980 s 5; and LIMITATION PERIODS vol 68 (2016) PARA 956. The Latent Damage Act 1986 (see LIMITATION PERIODS vol 68 (2016) PARA 982) does not apply to claims in contract (*Iron Trade Mutual Insurance Co Ltd v JK Buckenham Ltd* [1990] 1 All ER 808, [1992] 1 Lloyd's Rep 85, [1989] 2 Lloyd's Rep 85; *Société Commerciale de Réassurance v ERAS* [1992] 2 All ER 82n, [1992] 1 Lloyd's Rep 570, CA) and is therefore not considered here. The parties may make provision for an additional contractual limitation on the ability to bring a claim, but this does not necessarily define when a cause of action accrues for the purpose of the Limitation Act 1980: see *Oxford Architects Partnership v Cheltenham Ladies College* [2007] Bus LR D25, [2007] BLR 293.

2   See the Limitation Act 1980 s 8; and LIMITATION PERIODS vol 68 (2016) PARA 953.

3   See the Limitation Act 1980 s 32; and LIMITATION PERIODS vol 68 (2016) PARA 1220.

4   See the Limitation Act 1980 s 32; LIMITATION PERIODS vol 68 (2016) PARA 1220 et seq; and *Sheldon v RHM Outhwaite (Underwriting Agencies) Ltd* [1996] AC 102, [1995] 2 All ER 558, HL; *Brocklesby v Armitage & Guest (a firm)* [2001] 1 All ER 172, [2002] 1 WLR 598, CA; *Cave v Robinson, Jarvis & Rolf (a firm)* [2002] UKHL 18, [2003] 1 AC 384, [2002] 2 All ER 641.

5   *Applegate v Moss* [1971] 1 QB 406, [1971] 1 All ER 747, CA; *King v Victor Parsons & Co* [1973] 1 All ER 206, [1973] 1 WLR 29, CA.

6   In *King v Victor Parsons & Co* [1973] 1 All ER 206, [1973] 1 WLR 29, CA, it was held that there was no fraudulent concealment if the defendant committed a wrongful act which he did not know about but ought to have known about.

7   *Gray (Special Trustees of the London Hospital) v TP Bennett & Son* (1987) 43 BLR 63, sub nom *Trustees of London Hospital v TP Bennett & Son* 13 Con LR 22. As to the clerk of works see PARA 207.

8   *Clark v Woor* [1965] 2 All ER 353, [1965] 1 WLR 650.

9   *William Hill Organisation Ltd v Bernard Sunley & Sons Ltd* (1982) 22 BLR 1, CA; *Kijowski v New Capital Properties Ltd* (1987) 15 Con LR 1; *British Steel plc v Wyvern Structures Ltd* (1996) 52 Con LR 67.

10   *Applegate v Moss* [1971] 1 QB 406, [1971] 1 All ER 747, CA; *King v Victor Parsons & Co* [1973] 1 All ER 206, [1973] 1 WLR 29, CA, where an estate agent was held liable to the purchaser of a house built to the estate agent's order on weak foundations.

11   *Bellway (South East) Ltd v Holley* (1984) 28 BLR 139, 1 Con LR 76; *Chelmsford District Council v Evers* (1983) 25 BLR 99, 4 Con LR 98.

12   See *Henry Boot Construction Ltd v Alstom Combined Cycles Ltd* [2005] EWCA Civ 814, [2005] 3 All ER 932, [2005] 1 WLR 3850 (the right to payment arose when a certificate was issued or ought to be issued, and not when the work was done (although the doing of the work was itself a condition precedent to the right to a certificate)).

13   *Oxford Architects Partnership v Cheltenham Ladies College* [2007] Bus LR D25, [2007] BLR 293.

(3) Bonds, Insurance and Indemnities

(i) Bonds and Sureties

382. Bonds.

A bond is a document made by deed whereby a third party guarantees the fulfilment by the contractor of the contract[1]. In contracts for construction work, bonds will often support payment or performance obligations[2]. Most commonly, a performance bond is given whereby the bondsman promises to pay up to the amount of the bond if the contractor fails to perform his contract. It is a matter of construction[3] whether this amounts to a default[4] or 'on demand' bond[5]. In all cases such bonds are surety contracts. Thus, unless a bond expressly allows for variations in the terms of the underlying contract, the bondsman will be discharged if there is any variation in the terms of the contract for construction work relating to the time for payment or performance by the contractor or any material variation of any other term if made without the bondsman's consent[6] or if there is a not insubstantial departure from a term of the principal contract embodied in the guarantee[7]. If an 'on demand' bond is called the court will not restrain payment unless there is prima facie evidence of fraud[8]. Liability under a default bond will only arise when the default provided for has occurred. This may require proof of the contractor's default (if not admitted)[9] and the ascertainment of what is due to the employer[10].

1 See DEEDS AND OTHER INSTRUMENTS vol 32 (2012) PARA 289 et seq. As to the enforceability of a bond see *OTV Birwelco Ltd v Technical and General Guarantee Co Ltd* [2002] EWHC 2240 (TCC), [2002] 4 All ER 668, 84 Con LR 117; and FINANCIAL INSTRUMENTS AND TRANSACTIONS vol 49 (2015) PARAS 681, 900.

2 A guarantee for the repayment of an advance payment is not a performance guarantee: *Mercers' Company v New Hampshire Insurance Co* [1992] 3 All ER 57, [1992] 2 Lloyd's Rep 365, CA.

3 See *Trafalgar House Construction (Regions) Ltd v General Surety & Guarantee Co Ltd* [1996] AC 199, [1995] 3 All ER 737, HL. See also *Marubeni Hong Kong and South China Ltd v Government of Mongolia* [2005] EWCA Civ 395, [2005] 2 All ER (Comm) 289, [2005] 1 WLR 2497.

4 For examples in use in the construction industry see *General Surety & Guarantee Co Ltd v Francis Parker* (1977) 6 BLR 16; *Tins Industrial Co v Kono Insurance* (1987) 42 BLR 110, HK CA; *Perar BV v General Surety & Guarantee Co Ltd* (1994) 66 BLR 72, (1994) 43 Con LR 110, CA; *Trafalgar House Construction (Regions) Ltd v General Surety & Guarantee Co Ltd* [1996] AC 199, [1995] 3 All ER 737, HL.

5 *Trade Indemnity Co Ltd v Workington Harbour and Dock Board* [1937] AC 1, [1936] 1 All ER 454, HL. See also *Carey Value Added SL v Grupo Urvasco SA* [2010] EWHC 1905 (Comm), 132 Con LR 15, [2010] All ER (D) 307 (Jul).

6 *Edward Owen Engineering Ltd v Barclays Bank International Ltd and Umma Bank* [1978] QB 159, [1978] 1 All ER 976, CA; *Holme v Brunskill* (1877) 3 QBD 495, CA (applied in *Topland Portfolio No. 1 Ltd v Smith News Trading Ltd* [2014] EWCA Civ 18, [2014] 1 P & CR 290, [2014] 1 EGLR 38; and *Metall Market OOO v Vitorio Shipping Co Ltd; The Lehmann Timber* [2013] EWCA Civ 650, [2014] QB 760, [2014] 2 WLR 979). A side agreement advancing payments to a contractor does not discharge the surety's liability under a bond: *Hackney Empire Ltd v Aviva Insurance UK Ltd* [2012] EWCA Civ 1716, [2012] All ER (D) 186 (Dec).

7 *National Westminster Bank plc v Riley* [1986] BCLC 268 at 275, CA, per May LJ; applied in *Mercers' Company v New Hampshire Insurance Co* [1992] 3 All ER 57n, [1992] 2 Lloyd's Rep 365, CA.

8 See eg *Themehelp Ltd v West* [1996] QB 84, [1995] 4 All ER 215, CA. As to the need for the call to conform to the precise requirements of the bond see *IE Contractors Ltd v Lloyds Bank plc and Rafidain Bank* [1990] 2 Lloyd's Rep 496, 51 BLR 1, CA.

9 *RD Harbottle (Mercantile) Ltd v National Westminster Bank Ltd* [1978] QB 146, [1977] 2 All ER 862 (applied in *Aria Inc v Credit Agricole Corporate and Investment Bank* [2014] EWHC 872 (Comm), [2014] All ER (D) 244 (Mar); *Alternative Power Solution Ltd v Central Electricity Board* [2014] UKPC 31, [2014] 4 All ER 882, [2015] 1 WLR 697; and National *Infrastructure Development Company Ltd v Banco Santander SA* [2017] EWCA Civ 27, [2018] 1 All ER (Comm) 156, [2017] All ER (D) 91 (Jan)). But see *Potton Homes Ltd v Coleman Contractors Ltd* (1984) 28 BLR 19, CA.

10 See the cases cited in notes 3–9; and *Nene Housing Society Ltd v National Westminster Bank Ltd* (1980) 16 BLR 22.

383. Sureties in general.

A building or engineering contract may provide that a contractor should give sureties for the due performance of his obligations under the contract, and where a contractor does undertake to give sureties it is a question of construction whether the provision of sureties is a condition of the contract[1]. Occasionally the employer will undertake to provide sureties to guarantee payment to the contractor[2].

The general principles governing the validity and enforcement of contracts of guarantee, the release of the sureties and the general obligations of the parties apply where a contract of guarantee is collateral to a building contract[3]. Difficulties can arise in relation to building contracts: (1) where the surety claims to be released by reason of the completion of the work[4]; (2) because of the conduct of the employer (as creditor under the guarantee)[5]; and (3) where there has been an alteration in the terms or extent of the contract[6].

1   *Roberts v Brett* (1865) 11 HL Cas 337; *State Trading Corpn Ltd of India v Golodetz Ltd* [1989] 2 Lloyd's Rep 277, CA. See also *Swartz & Son (Pty) Ltd v Wolmaransstad Town Council* 1960 (2) SA 1, SA SC.
2   See eg *Andrews v Lawrence* (1865) 19 CBNS 768; *Oastler v Pound* (1863) 7 LT 852 (where a contractor obtained guarantors for payments falling due to a sub-contractor).
3   See generally FINANCIAL INSTRUMENTS AND TRANSACTIONS vol 49 (2015) PARA 638 et seq.
4   See PARA 384.
5   See PARA 385.
6   See PARA 386.

384. Discharge of surety on completion.

Generally a contract of guarantee ends when the guaranteed obligation has been fulfilled[1]. Under many building contracts, however, the contractor's obligation to complete the work is not fulfilled until: (1) the work is complete in fact; and (2) the architect or engineer has issued a certificate[2] that the work has been completed to his satisfaction. A surety is not discharged where the works have only been substantially completed[3]. Where the contractor has in fact completed the work but the architect has not certified his satisfaction, the question whether the surety is released will depend on the construction of the contract of guarantee[4]. Where a certificate of satisfaction has been given, the surety will not be released if that certificate was obtained by the contractor improperly[5].

1   See generally FINANCIAL INSTRUMENTS AND TRANSACTIONS vol 49 (2015) PARA 638 et seq.
2   As to such certificates see PARAS 330–331.
3   *Eshelby v Federated European Bank Ltd* [1932] I KB 423, CA (where the contractor sued a guarantor of the employer, it was held that the surety's liability did not arise if the contractor could not show entire completion).
4   *Lewis v Hoare* (1881) 44 LT 66, HL.
5   *Kingston-upon-Hull Corpn v Harding* [1892] 2 QB 494, CA.

385. Discharge by conduct of the creditor.

A contract of guarantee is not a contract of the utmost good faith[1]; but where a surety guarantees the due performance of the contract by the contractor, it has been said that the surety must be made aware of anything which is abnormal in the contract between contractor and employer[2] and possibly the surety may be discharged by the non-disclosure of an unusual obligation in the building contract. A contractor's surety may also be discharged if the employer fails to comply with the terms of the contract of guarantee[3]; thus the surety will be discharged if the employer fails to insure the works[4] or to give notice of the contractor's default[5] if required by the terms of the guarantee. Further if the employer, without the consent of the surety, advances to the contractor by way of interim payment more than the contractor is entitled to, the surety will be discharged[6], unless such advances were obtained by fraud[7].

1   As to contracts of the utmost good faith (uberrimae fidei) see further CONTRACT vol 22 (2012) PARAS 212, 213, 289.
2   *Stiff v Eastbourne Local Board* (1869) 20 LT 339, CA, where the works were subject to the supervision of a third party's surveyor; and see *Hamilton v Watson* (1845) 12 Cl & Fin 109, HL.
3   *Kingston-upon Hull Corpn v Harding* [1892] 2 QB 494 at 508, CA, per Bowen LJ.

4 *Watts v Shuttleworth* (1861) 7 H & N 353.
5 *Clydebank and District Water Trustees v Fidelity and Deposit Co of Maryland* 1916 SC (HL) 69.
6 *General Steam Navigation Co v Rolt* (1858) 6 CBNS 550 at 584; and see *Warre v Calvert* (1837)
   7 Ad & El 143; *Calvert v London Dock Co* (1838) 7 LJCh 90.
7 *Kingston-upon-Hull Corpn v Harding* [1892] 2 QB 494, CA.

386. Discharge by alteration in terms or extent of the contract.

The surety will be discharged by any alteration in the terms of the building
contract made after the contract of guarantee was signed unless such alteration
was clearly not prejudicial to the surety[1]. A minor alteration made by the debtor
for his advantage is not material[2], and a surety will not be released because a
recital in a specification states erroneously that it has been signed when it is
immaterial whether or not the specification was so signed[3].

A surety may also be affected by a variation requiring the contractor to carry
out additional work or the grant of an extension of time for completion[4].
Additional work will not, however, discharge the surety where the contract whose
performance is guaranteed is drafted in terms which recognise the employer's
(usual) power to require the contractor to carry out extra work, and the
contractor's rights to extensions of time. An employer should insist on a guarantee
which binds the surety to guarantee the contractor's performance of the building
contract notwithstanding any variations which may be made under it; variations
required by the employer which are outside the scope of the contract will release
the surety from liability[5].

1 *Andrews v Lawrence* (1865) 19 CBNS 768; *Holme v Brunskill* (1877) 3 QBD 495, CA; *Hoole
   UDC v Fidelity and Deposit Co of Maryland* [1916] 2 KB 568, CA; *Provident Accident and White
   Cross Insurance Co Ltd v Dahne and White* [1937] 2 All ER 255; *Mercers' Company v New
   Hampshire Insurance Co* [1992] 3 All ER 57n, [1992] 2 Lloyd's Rep 365, CA. See also PARA 382.
2 *Andrews v Lawrence* (1865) 19 CBNS 768.
3 *Russell v Trickett* (1865) 13 LT 280.
4 *Harrison v Seymour* (1866) LR 1 CP 518; and see *Midland Motor Showrooms Ltd v Newman*
   [1929] 2 KB 256, CA.
5 See *Wren v Emmetts Contractors Pty Ltd* (1969) 43 ALJR 213, Aust HC.

(ii) Insurance and Indemnities

387. Insurance requirements.

The standard forms of contract[1] contain provisions requiring the contractor to
maintain insurance against injury to persons or property and in respect of damage
to the works until, for example, the employer regains possession[2]. Most
employers[3] are required by statute[4] to maintain a policy of insurance against
liability for bodily injury or disease sustained by their employees and arising out
of or in the course of their employment in Great Britain; there is a penalty for
failing to do so[5].

1 As to standard forms of contract see PARA 202. The ambit and interpretation of insurance
   provisions is outside the scope of this title; see generally INSURANCE. See, however, *Gold v
   Patman and Fotheringham Ltd* [1958] 2 All ER 497, [1958] 1 WLR 697, CA; *Higgs & Hill
   Building Ltd v University of London* (1983) 24 BLR 139; *Computer & Systems Engineering plc
   v John Lelliott (Ilford) Ltd* (1990) 54 BLR 1, CA; *Kruger Tissue (Industrial) Ltd v Frank Galliers
   Ltd* [2002] EWCA Civ 310, (1998) 57 Con LR 1; *Skanska Construction UK Ltd v Egger (Barony)
   Ltd* [2002] BLR 236, 83 Con LR 132.
2 As to retaking possession of the works see *English Industrial Estates Corpn v George Wimpey &
   Co Ltd* [1973] 1 Lloyd's Rep 118, 7 BLR 122, CA. See also *TFW Printers Ltd v Interserve Project
   Services Ltd* [2006] EWCA Civ 875, [2006] BLR 299, 109 Con LR 1 (obligation to insure ceased
   on practical completion of the works).
3 Certain authorities are exempted: see the Employers' Liability (Compulsory Insurance) Act 1969

s 3(1), (2); and EMPLOYMENT vol 39 (2014) PARA 43. See further the Employers' Liability (Compulsory Insurance) Regulations 1998, SI 1998/2573; and EMPLOYMENT vol 39 (2014) PARA 40 et seq.

4 See the Employers' Liability (Compulsory Insurance) Act 1969; and EMPLOYMENT vol 39 (2014) PARA 40 et seq. For the limits of this obligation see *Reid v Rush & Tompkins Group plc* [1989] 3 All ER 228, [1990] 1 WLR 212, CA.

5 As to the penalty for failure to insure see the Employers' Liability (Compulsory Insurance) Act 1969 s 5; and EMPLOYMENT vol 39 (2014) PARA 40.

388. Need for indemnity clauses.

A claim may be made against the employer for injury or damage arising by reason of the negligence or default of the contractor in carrying out the works[1]. Consequently, standard form contracts frequently contain clauses requiring the contractor to indemnify the employer against such claims as well as to insure against them[2]. Sometimes the employer will give a cross-indemnity to the contractor where the latter is liable by reason of the default of the employer.

1 See *Richardson v Buckinghamshire County Council* (1971) 69 LGR 327, (1971) 6 BLR 58, CA. Where such injury or damage arises from a sub-contractor's failure to fulfil an express duty assigned to him under a specific term of his contract of employment, a general indemnity clause will not render the sub-contractor's employer liable: *Anglian Water Services Ltd v Crawshaw Robbins & Co Ltd* [2001] BLR 173, [2001] All ER (D) 59 (Feb). See generally FINANCIAL INSTRUMENTS AND TRANSACTIONS vol 49 (2015) PARA 638 et seq.

2 As to standard forms of contract see PARA 202. As to insurance requirements see PARA 387.

389. Construction of indemnity clauses.

An indemnity clause will not permit a party to recover loss caused by his own negligence[1] unless very clear words are used[2] or unless there is no other loss which the clause could be intended to cover[3]. Liability does not arise until the loss has been incurred[4].

1 *AMF International Ltd v Magnet Bowling Ltd* [1968] 2 All ER 789 at 815, [1968] 1 WLR 1028 at 1060 per Mocatta J; *Walters v Whessoe Ltd and Shell Refining Co Ltd* [1968] 2 All ER 816n, 6 BLR 23, CA; *Alderslade v Hendon Laundry Ltd* [1945] KB 189, [1945] 1 All ER 244, CA; *Smith v South Wales Switchgear Ltd* [1978] 1 All ER 18, [1978] 1 WLR 165, HL; *City of Manchester v Fram Gerrard Ltd* (1974) 6 BLR 70. See also *Caledonia North Sea Ltd v British Telecommunications plc* [2002] UKHL 4, [2002] BLR 139. See generally FINANCIAL INSTRUMENTS AND TRANSACTIONS vol 49 (2015) PARA 638 et seq.
     An indemnity clause in the main contract must be construed separately from any indemnity clause that is contained in a sub-contract entered into by the contractor: *Richardson v Buckinghamshire County Council* (1971) 69 LGR 327, (1971) 6 BLR 58, CA.

2 See eg *AE Farr Ltd v Admiralty* [1953] 2 All ER 512, [1953] 1 WLR 965.

3 See eg *Alderslade v Hendon Laundry Ltd* [1945] KB 189, [1945] 1 All ER 244, CA; cf *EE Caledonia Ltd v Orbit Valve plc* [1995] 1 All ER 174, [1994] 1 WLR 1515, CA. See also *Tyco Fire and Integrated Solutions (UK) Ltd v Rolls-Royce Motor Cars Ltd* [2008] EWCA Civ 286, [2008] 2 All ER (Comm) 584, [2008] Lloyd's Rep IR 617 (contract not intended to give contractor liability insurance in respect of matters outside its own works).

4 *County and District Properties Ltd v C Jenner & Son Ltd* [1976] 2 Lloyd's Rep 728, 3 BLR 38; *R & H Green and Silley Weir Ltd v British Railways Board (Kavanagh, third party)* [1985] 1 All ER 237, [1985] 1 WLR 570n, 17 BLR 94.

390. National House Building Council scheme.

A large number of contracts to build new homes incorporate the provisions of the National House Building Council ('NHBC') scheme, a typical system of insurance which gives the purchaser of a new house an alternative remedy against the NHBC in case of defects, and places certain obligations upon the house builder[1].

The scheme operates by compelling all builders registered under it to offer to the house buyer standard contract documents which include a limited insurance policy, and certain undertakings to remedy defects. The scheme provides for two periods: (1) an initial period of two years after completion, during which the builder is obliged to return to remedy defects notified to him by the beneficiary of the scheme; and (2) a further period of ten years in respect of serious structural defects, during which the beneficiary has the benefit of insurance from the NHBC[2]. Further provisions provide limited insurance against bankruptcy or non-completion on the part of the house builder[3].

1   Compliance with the provisions of the scheme does not exempt a builder from compliance with the Defective Premises Act 1972 s 1 (see PARA 275). The NHBC scheme is not an approved scheme for the purposes of s 2: see further PARA 276.
2   The failure to notify the early signs of a major defect does not restrict the remedy of the homeowner: *Marchant v Caswell and Redgrave Ltd and NHBC* (1976) 240 Estates Gazette 127. See also, for cases on the operation of the scheme, *Bellway (South East) Ltd v Holley* (1984) 28 BLR 139, 1 Con LR 76; *Kijowski v New Capital Properties Ltd* (1987) 15 Con LR 1; *Harrison v Shepherd Homes Ltd* [2010] EWHC 1398 (TCC), [2010] All ER (D) 209 (Jun).
3   Counter-indemnities may be provided: see *National House Building Council v Fraser* [1983] 1 All ER 1090, 22 BLR 43.

5. DISPUTES

(1) Litigation

391. In general.

Proceedings in respect of building or engineering contracts are generally commenced in the Queen's Bench Division of the High Court (or in the county court within the applicable jurisdictional limits)[1]. Certain types of building or engineering contract claims, for example those related to the shipping or petrochemical industries (such as contracts for oil rigs or production platforms), are sometimes commenced and retained in the Commercial Court. However, all High Court claims concerning building contracts or professional negligence in the construction industry are, as a matter of general practice, now commenced as or liable to be transferred to be dealt with as, Technology and Construction Court claims ('TCC claims')[2]. The Technology and Construction Court is part of the Queen's Bench Division[3].

1   As to the jurisdiction of the courts see COURTS AND TRIBUNALS vol 24 (2010) PARA 623 et seq. As to civil procedure generally see CIVIL PROCEDURE vol 11 (2015) PARA 6 et seq.
2   See CPR 30.5(2); and CIVIL PROCEDURE vol 11 (2015) PARA 106. The Technology and Construction Court is a specialist list for the purpose of CPR 30: CPR 60.2(1). As to the meaning of 'TCC claim' see PARA 392 note 1.
3   See the Queen's Bench Guide para 1.5.3.

392. Technology and Construction Court claims.

The majority of claims relating to building or engineering contracts are begun as Technology and Construction Court claims ('TCC claims')[1]. A claim may be brought as a TCC claim if it involves issues or questions which are technically complex, or if a trial by a TCC judge is desirable[2]. Typical claims which are brought in the Technology and Construction Court include building or other construction disputes, including claims for the enforcement of the decisions of adjudicators under the Housing Grants, Construction and Regeneration Act 1996[3], engineering disputes[4], claims by and against engineers, architects, surveyors, accountants and other specialised advisers relating to the services they provide[5], claims relating to the quality of goods sold or hired, and work done, materials supplied or services rendered[6], and challenges to decisions of arbitrators in construction and engineering disputes including applications for permission to appeal and appeals[7].

There is a Pre-Action Protocol for Construction and Engineering Disputes, and its purpose is to encourage the frank and early exchange of information about the prospective claim and any defence to it; to enable parties to avoid litigation by agreeing a settlement of the claim before the commencement of proceedings; and to support the efficient management of proceedings where litigation cannot be avoided[8].

TCC claims must be issued in the High Court or in a specified County Court hearing centre[9]. Designated High Court judges, certain circuit judges, deputy circuit judges and recorders are nominated by the Lord Chief Justice (after consulting the Lord Chancellor) to deal with TCC claims[10]. A claim will be allocated to a named TCC judge who will have the primary responsibility for the case management of the claim[11] and should try the case[12]. Every claim allocated to the Technology and Construction Court will be allocated to the multi-track[13]. The provisions relating to the management of cases allocated to the multi-track[14] apply to TCC claims except where they are inconsistent with the practice direction[15] made in relation to such claims[16].

Directions will be given appropriate to the case and in conformity with the overriding objective of the Civil Procedure Rules[17]. These may involve the preparation of a schedule setting out the cases of the relevant parties[18]. Directions given by the Technology and Construction Court Judges are intended to enable a case to be tried with expedition and economy[19].

1 See CPR PD 60—*Technology and Construction Court Claims* paras 1, 2. 'TCC claim' means a claim which satisfies the requirements of CPR 60.1(3) (see the text and note 2), and which has been issued in or transferred into the specialist list for such claims: CPR 60.1(2)(a). As to the Technology and Construction Court see further COURTS AND TRIBUNALS vol 24 (2010) PARA 709; CIVIL PROCEDURE vol 11 (2015) PARA 180.

2 CPR 60.1(3). 'TCC judge' means any judge authorised to hear TCC claims: CPR 60.1(2)(c).

3 CPR PD 60—*Technology and Construction Court Claims* para 2.1(a).

4 CPR PD 60—*Technology and Construction Court Claims* para 2.1(b).

5 CPR PD 60—*Technology and Construction Court Claims* para 2.1(c).

6 CPR PD 60—*Technology and Construction Court Claims* para 2.1(f).

7 CPR PD 60—*Technology and Construction Court Claims* para 2.1(l). TCC claims are not restricted to issues arising in the building and construction industry; other examples of the types of claim which it may be appropriate to bring as TCC claims are: (1) claims by and against local authorities relating to their statutory duties concerning the development of land or the construction of buildings; (2) claims relating to the design, supply and installation of computers, computer software and related network systems; (3) claims between landlord and tenant for breach of a repairing covenant; (4) claims between neighbours, owners and occupiers of land in trespass, nuisance etc; (5) claims relating to the environment (for example, pollution cases); (6) claims arising out of fires; and (7) claims involving taking of accounts where these are complicated: see CPR PD 60—*Technology and Construction Court Claims* para 2.1. The list is not exhaustive, however, and other types of claim may be brought in the Technology and Construction Court if they demonstrate the characteristics in CPR 60.1(3) (see the text to note 2): CPR PD 60—*Technology and Construction Court Claims* para 2.2. The Technology and Construction Court Guide is available, at the date at which this volume states the law, on the government website.

8 See the Technology and Construction Court Guide Section 2.

9 See CPR PD 60—*Technology and Construction Court Claims* paras 3, 4. See also the Technology and Construction Court Guide Section 3. TCC claims designated by CPR PD 60 para 3 must be started in a designated County Court hearing centre: CPR PD 2C—*Starting Proceedings in the County Court* para 3.1(3). As to the transfer of proceedings see CPR PD 60—*Technology and Construction Court Claims* para 5. See further CIVIL PROCEDURE vol 11 (2015) PARA 180.

10 See the Senior Courts Act 1981 s 68(1)(a); and COURTS AND TRIBUNALS vol 24 (2010) PARA 709. As to the powers of Technology and Construction Court judges see PARA 393.

11 See CPR PD 60—*Technology and Construction Court Claims* para 6. Applications should normally be made to the named judge: see CPR PD 60 para 7.

12 See CPR PD 60—*Technology and Construction Court Claims* para 11. The provisions about listing questionnaires and listing in CPR Pt 29 (see CIVIL PROCEDURE vol 11 (2015) PARA 233 et seq) do not apply to Technology and Construction Court claims: CPR PD 60—*Technology and Construction Court Claims* para 10.

13 CPR 60.6.

14 Ie CPR 29: see CIVIL PROCEDURE vol 11 (2015) PARA 233 et seq.

15 Ie CPR PD 60—*Technology and Construction Court Claims* .

16 CPR 60.6(2).

17 See the Technology and Construction Court Guide Section 5. The court will normally require the parties to attend an oral hearing for the purposes of the first case management conference as there may be matters which the judge would wish to raise with the parties arising out of the answers to the case management information sheets and the parties' proposed directions: Technology and Construction Court Guide para 4.2.1. As to the provisions made in relation to case management conferences and pre-trial reviews see CPR PD 60—*Technology and Construction Court Claims* paras 8, 9; and the Technology and Construction Court Guide Sections 4, 5. As to applications after the first case management conference see the Technology and Construction Court Guide

Section 6. As to the overriding objective of the CPR see CPR 1.1; and CIVIL PROCEDURE vol 12 (2015) PARA 504 et seq.

18 This is generally known as a 'Scott Schedule' (as it was devised by George Alexander Scott, an official referee from 1920–1933).

19 See the Technology and Construction Court Guide Section 5.

393. Powers of Technology and Construction Court judges.

A Technology and Construction Court Judge has all the powers of a judge of the High Court[1]. In particular, a Technology and Construction Court Judge has power to open up, review and revise interim certificates and the like so as to determine the rights of the parties[2]. If all parties to an arbitration agreement agree a Technology and Construction Court Judge may exercise powers otherwise specific to the arbitrator[3]. A Technology and Construction Court Judge may also sit as an arbitrator[4].

1 See CPR 60.

2 See *Beaufort Developments (NI) Ltd v Gilbert Ash NI Ltd* [1999] 1 AC 266, [1998] 2 All ER 778, HL.

3 See the Senior Courts Act 1981 s 43A; and COURTS AND TRIBUNALS vol 24 (2010) PARA 701.

4 See the Arbitration Act 1996 s 93(1); and ARBITRATION vol 2 (2017) PARA 526 et seq. As to arbitration as a method of resolution in building disputes see PARA 398.

394. Preliminary issues.

Some issues between the parties may be resolved by way of a preliminary issue ('PI') hearing in advance of the main trial[1]. These might include: (1) disputes as to whether or not there was a binding contract between the parties; (2) disputes as to what documents make up or are incorporated within the contract between the parties and disputes as to the contents or relevance of any conversations relied on as having contractual status or effect; (3) disputes as to the proper construction of the contract documents or the effect of an exclusion or similar clause; (4) disputes as to the correct application of a statute or binding authority to a situation where there is little or no factual dispute; (5) disputes as to the existence and/or scope of a statutory duty; (6) disputes as to the existence and/or scope of a duty of care at common law in circumstances where there is no or little dispute about the relevant facts[2]. The court would expect that any issue proposed as a suitable PI would, if decided in a particular way, be capable of: (a) resolving the whole proceedings or a significant element of the proceedings; or (b) significantly reducing the scope, and therefore the costs, of the main trial; or (c) significantly improving the possibility of a settlement of the whole proceedings[3]. A PI hearing may be used as an adjunct to alternative dispute resolution (ADR)[4].

1 See the Technology and Construction Court Guide Section 8. The Technology and Construction Court Guide is available at the date, at which this volume states the law, on the government website.

2 Technology and Construction Court Guide para 8.3. For other possible preliminary issues see the Technology and Construction Court Guide (2nd Edn) para 8.4.

3 Technology and Construction Court Guide para 8.2.1.

4 Technology and Construction Court Guide para 8.5. As to alternative dispute resolution see PARA 423.

395. The trial.

The practical arrangements for the conduct of the trial are usually determined at the pre-trial review, which takes place four to six weeks before the date set for trial[1]. The parties should, if possible, provide the judge at the pre-trial review with an agreed list of the main issues for the forthcoming trial (including, where appropriate, a separate list of technical issues to be covered by the experts)[2]. Detailed guidance as to the conduct of the trial itself is provided in the Technology and Construction Court Guide[3].

Expert evidence is frequently needed and used in cases before the Technology and Construction Court, and such experts are often appointed at an early stage[4]. Most types of case heard in the Technology and Construction Court involve more than one expertise and some, even when the dispute is concerned with relatively small sums, involve several different experts[5]. Such disputes include those concerned with building failures and defects, delay and disruption, dilapidations and subsidence[6].

1 See the Technology and Construction Court Guide Section 14. The Technology and Construction Court Guide is available, at the date at which this volume states the law, on the government website.
2 Technology and Construction Court Guide para 14.4.1.
3 See the Technology and Construction Court Guide Section 15, which gives details regarding such issues as opening notes, trial bundles and opening speeches (see the Technology and Construction Court Guide paras 15.2, 15.10); simultaneous transcription (see the Technology and Construction Court Guide para 15.3); time limits (see the Technology and Construction Court Guide para 15.4); oral evidence (see the Technology and Construction Court Guide para 15.5); submissions (see the Technology and Construction Court Guide paras 15.6, 15.7); and views and judgments (see the Technology and Construction Court Guide paras 15.8, 15.9). As to the guidance in relation to witness statements and factual evidence for use at trial see CPR 22.1 (see CIVIL PROCEDURE vol 11 (2015) PARA 363) and Pt 32 (see CIVIL PROCEDURE vol 12 (2015) PARA 689); and the Technology and Construction Court Guide Section 12. As to disclosure see CPR Pt 31; the Technology and Construction Court Guide Section 11; and CIVIL PROCEDURE vol 12 (2015) PARA 621. See further CIVIL PROCEDURE vol 11 (2015) PARA 180.
4 See the Technology and Construction Court Guide Section 13. As to the rules relating to expert evidence see CPR Pt 35; and CIVIL PROCEDURE vol 12 (2015) PARA 890 et seq.
5 Technology and Construction Court Guide para 13.2.1.
6 Technology and Construction Court Guide para 13.2.1.

396. Appeals.

Appeals from decisions of Technology and Construction Court Judges on fact and law (subject to certain limited exceptions[1]) lie to the Court of Appeal[2].

1 See the Senior Courts Act 1981 s 18(1); and CIVIL PROCEDURE vol 12A (2015) PARA 1557.
2 As to permission to appeal see CPR 52.3; and CIVIL PROCEDURE vol 12A (2015) PARA 1517 et seq. See also *Multiplex Constructions (UK) Ltd v Honeywell Control Systems Ltd* [2007] EWHC 236 (TCC), [2007] Bus LR D13, [2007] BLR 167.

397. Litigation and arbitration.

There may be proceedings arising out of the same contract and even about the same subject matter before both the court and an arbitrator[1]. However, the court retains jurisdiction to restrain an arbitrator from deciding matters before the court[2]. A court may also have powers not available to an arbitrator[3].

1 *Lloyd v Wright* [1983] QB 1065, [1983] 2 All ER 969, CA. As to arbitration as a method of resolution in building disputes see PARA 398 et seq.
2 *Northern Regional Health Authority v Derek Crouch Construction Ltd* [1984] QB 644 at 673, [1984] 2 All ER 175 at 191, CA, per Sir John Donaldson MR; *University of Reading v Miller Construction Ltd* (1994) 75 BLR 91, [1994] CILL 1011.
3 See PARA 340; and ARBITRATION.

(2) Arbitration

398. Usual arbitration clauses.

It is very common to insert in building and engineering contracts a clause to the effect that, if a dispute arises between the contractor and the employer or his architect or engineer, it is to be referred to arbitration[1]. The scope of such a clause depends upon its wording but it is to be applied in accordance with the general law of arbitration[2] and the provisions of the Arbitration Act 1996[3].

The proceedings in the arbitration will usually be governed by the system of law of the place where the arbitration is held[4]. In particular, the provisions of the Arbitration Act 1996 apply where the 'seat of the arbitration'[5] is in England and Wales or Northern Ireland[6].

1 This part of the title deals with certain aspects of the law of arbitration only as it relates to building contracts. For a full discussion of the law see Mustill and Boyd *Commercial Arbitration* (3rd Edn, 2008). As to the law relating to arbitration see generally ARBITRATION.

2 As to the construction and scope of arbitration agreements see ARBITRATION vol 2 (2017) PARA 513 et seq. Note that claims relating to building contracts will generally be stayed in favour of arbitration under the Arbitration Act 1996 s 9(4) where there is a dispute and an applicable arbitration agreement: see eg *Collins (Contractors) Ltd v Baltic Quay Management (1994) Ltd* [2004] EWCA Civ 1757, 99 Con LR 1, [2005] BLR 63. A stay may also be ordered even if the dispute cannot immediately be referred to arbitration: *Channel Tunnel Group Ltd v Balfour Beatty Construction Ltd* [1992] QB 656, [1992] 2 All ER 609, CA; affd on different grounds [1993] AC 334, [1993] 1 All ER 664, HL.

3 For the purposes of the Arbitration Act 1996 Pt I (ss 1–84), the expression 'arbitration agreement' means, unless the context otherwise requires, a written agreement to submit present or future disputes to arbitration, whether an arbitrator is named therein or not: see s 5, 6; and ARBITRATION vol 2 (2017) PARA 513. Oral arbitration agreements are governed by the common law and are not subject to what is now the Arbitration Act 1996, which applies only to arbitration based on written agreements (see *Imperial Metal Industries (Kynoch) Ltd v Amalgamated Union of Engineering Workers (Technical, Administrative and Supervisory Section)* [1979] 1 All ER 847, [1979] ICR 23, CA).

4 *James Miller & Partners Ltd v Whitworth Street Estates (Manchester) Ltd* [1970] AC 583, [1970] 1 All ER 796, HL; *Channel Tunnel Group Ltd v Balfour Beatty Construction Ltd* [1993] AC 334, [1993] 1 All ER 664, HL; and see ARBITRATION vol 2 (2017) PARA 523. As to the lex fori principle see CONFLICT OF LAWS vol 19 (2011) PARA 313.

5 As to the meaning of 'seat of the arbitration' see the Arbitration Act 1996 s 3; and ARBITRATION vol 2 (2017) PARA 512.

6 See the Arbitration Act 1996 s 2(1); and ARBITRATION vol 2 (2017) PARA 509.

399. Application of arbitration clause.

Whether a particular dispute is within the scope of an arbitration clause depends in each particular case on the wording of the clause[1]. If the submission covers all disputes arising out of the contract, including disputes on questions of law, questions as to the true meaning and effect of the contract are thereby left to the arbitrator[2]; moreover such an arbitration clause will apply even if the contract has been repudiated by the party seeking to rely upon the arbitration clause[3]. The arbitration clause may be wide enough to enable an arbitrator to determine claims for rectification, misrepresentation or negligent misstatement[4] and even fraudulent misrepresentation[5]. An arbitrator has power to determine allegations of fraud arising out of the execution of the contract[6]. Any question as to whether a contract was in fact entered into or was void for illegality or fraud[7] may not, however, be covered by the arbitration clause[8].

Unless otherwise agreed, the arbitrator may rule on his own substantive jurisdiction as to: (1) whether there is a valid arbitration agreement; (2) whether the tribunal is properly constituted; and (3) what matters have been submitted to arbitration in accordance with the arbitration agreement[9].

1   See ARBITRATION vol 2 (2017) PARA 515.
2   *Produce Brokers Co Ltd v Olympia Oil and Cake Co Ltd* [1916] 1 AC 314 at 327, HL, per Lord Parker. See also *Government of Gibraltar v Kenney* [1956] 2 QB 410, [1956] 3 All ER 22, where a claim for a quantum meruit and an alternative claim under the Law Reform (Frustrated Contracts) Act 1943 (see CONTRACT vol 22 (2012) PARA 484 et seq) both arose out of an agreement within the scope of the arbitration clause. As to quantum meruit see RESTITUTION vol 88 (2012) PARA 513 et seq.
3   *Heyman v Darwins Ltd* [1942] AC 356, [1942] 1 All ER 337, HL.
4   *Ashville Investments Ltd v Elmer Contractors Ltd* [1989] QB 488, [1988] 2 All ER 577, CA.
5   *Government of Gibraltar v Kenney* [1956] 2 QB 410, [1956] 3 All ER 22. Where a contract includes comprehensive arbitration provisions, the circumstances in which the court may properly refuse an application to refer the matter to arbitration are strictly limited: *Strathmore Building Services v Greig* 2000 SLT 815, Ct of Sess (no referral where no arbitral dispute).
6   Formerly, under the Arbitration Act 1950 s 24(2) (now repealed), in disputes which arose involving the question of whether one party to an arbitration agreement had been guilty of fraud, the High Court had power to order that the agreement should cease to have effect, and to give leave to revoke the authority of any arbitrator appointed by the agreement, but that provision has been repealed and the court no longer has such powers.
7   See PARA 307 et seq.
8   *Heyman v Darwins Ltd* [1942] AC 356 at 371, [1942] 1 All ER 337 at 345, HL, per Lord Macmillan. Cf *Harbour Assurance Co (UK) Ltd v Kansa General International Insurance Co Ltd* [1993] QB 701, [1993] 3 All ER 897, CA, where it was held that the question of initial illegality of a contract, not directly impeaching the arbitration clause, was capable of being within the jurisdiction of an arbitrator.
9   See the Arbitration Act 1996 s 30(1). See also ss 31, 32, 66, 67; and ARBITRATION vol 2 (2017) PARA 539 et seq.

400.   Appointment of arbitrator.

In the past, it was common practice for the architect or engineer under the contract to be appointed as arbitrator[1]. Nowadays such an appointment is very unusual. Where the reference is to an independent arbitrator, an arbitration clause will generally be given a wide construction[2].

A judge of the Technology and Construction Court ('TCC') (previously an Official Referee[3]) may, if in all the circumstances he thinks fit, accept appointment as a sole arbitrator or as an umpire by or by virtue of an arbitration agreement[4]. Judges of the TCC may accept appointments as sole arbitrators or umpires pursuant to these statutory provisions[5]. A TCC judge cannot accept such an appointment unless the Lord Chief Justice has informed him that, having regard to the state of TCC business, he can be made available[6].

Following the appointment of the judge arbitrator, the rules governing the arbitration will be decided upon, and the judge arbitrator will manage the reference to arbitration in a similar way to a TCC case[7]. The judge sitting as an arbitrator will sit in a TCC court room (suitably rearranged) unless the parties and the judge arbitrator agree to some other arrangement[8].

1   Precise words were required to bring about this result. See eg *Northampton Gas Light Co v Parnell* (1855) 15 CB 630; *Tough v Dumbarton Waterworks Comrs* (1872) 11 M 236, Ct of Sess; *Lawson v Wallasey Local Board* (1883) 48 LT 507, CA.
2   *Re Hohenzollern AG für Locomotivbahn and City of London Contract Corpn Ltd, and Common Law Procedure Act 1854* (1886) 2 TLR 470, CA; *Brodie v Cardiff Corpn* [1919] AC 337, HL. In appropriate circumstances the Arbitration Act 1996 s 18 gives the Court power to appoint an arbitral tribunal: see *Chalbury McCouat International Ltd v PG Foils Ltd* [2010] EWHC 2050 (TCC), [2010] BLR 593, [2010] All ER (D) 34 (Aug). See also ARBITRATION vol 2 (2017) PARA 528.

3   The Arbitration Act 1996 s 93 refers to an 'official referee', meaning a person nominated under the
    Senior Courts Act 1981 s 68(1)(a) to deal with official referees' business: see the Arbitration Act
    1996 s 93(5) (amended by the Constitutional Reform Act 2005 s 59(5), Sch 11 para 1(2)). The
    official referees' court has been renamed the Technology and Construction Court: see COURTS
    AND TRIBUNALS vol 24 (2010) PARA 709.
4   See the Arbitration Act 1996 s 93(1); and ARBITRATION vol 2 (2017) PARA 526.
5   Technology and Construction Court Guide para 18.1.1. The Technology and Construction Court
    Guide is available at the date, at which this volume states the law, on the government website.
6   See the Arbitration Act 1996 s 93(3); and the Technology and Construction Court Guide para
    18.1.2. In exceptional cases a judge of the Technology and Construction Court may also accept an
    appointment as a member of a three-member panel of arbitrators if the Lord Chief Justice consents
    but such arbitrations cannot be under the Arbitration Act 1996 s 93 because s 93(6) modifies the
    provisions of the 1996 Act where there is a judge-arbitrator and this could not apply to arbitral
    tribunals with three arbitrators, one of whom was a judge-arbitrator: Technology and
    Construction Court Guide para 18.1.2.
7   Technology and Construction Court Guide para 18.2.1. Fees are payable to the Court Service for
    the judge arbitrator's services: see para 18.2.3.
8   Technology and Construction Court Guide para 18.2.2.

401.   Disqualification of arbitrator for bias.

An arbitrator has a general duty to act fairly and impartially as between the
parties, giving each party a reasonable opportunity of putting its case and dealing
with that of its opponent[1]. The court may remove an arbitrator where
circumstances exist that give rise to justifiable doubts as to his impartiality[2]. These
doubts may be held to exist where the arbitrator is actually biased, where he has
an interest in the outcome of the case or where there is a real possibility of bias[3].

The general law as to the disqualification of arbitrators for bias or lack of
impartiality applies equally to building contract arbitrations.

1   See the Arbitration Act 1996 s 33(1)(a); and ARBITRATION vol 2 (2017) PARA 543.
2   See the Arbitration Act 1996 s 24(1)(a); and ARBITRATION vol 2 (2017) PARA 533.
3   *R v Gough* [1993] AC 646, [1993] 2 All ER 724, HL; *Porter v Magill, Weeks v Magill* [2001]
    UKHL 67 at [103], [2002] 2 AC 357 at [103], [2002] 1 All ER 465 at [103] (restating the test in
    R v Gough as the test of 'a real possibility'). See also *Locabail (UK) Ltd v Bayfield Properties Ltd*
    [2000] QB 451, [2000] 1 All ER 65, CA; *AT & T Corpn v Saudi Cable Co* [2000] BLR 743, [2000]
    2 Lloyd's Rep 127, CA; *ASM Shipping Ltd of India v TTMI Ltd of England* [2005] EWHC 2238
    (Comm), [2006] 2 All ER (Comm) 122, [2005] All ER (D) 271 (Nov); *Norbrook Laboratories Ltd
    v Challenger* [2006] EWHC 1055 (Comm), [2006] 2 Lloyd's Rep 485, [2006] BLR 412; *Lanes
    Group plc v Galliford Try Infrastructure Ltd* [2011] EWCA Civ 1617, (2011) 141 ConLR 46;
    Sierra Fishing Company v Farran [2015] EWHC 140 (Comm), [2015] 1 All ER (Comm) 560,,
    [2015] All ER (D) 04 (Feb). As to bias of arbitrators see further ARBITRATION vol 2 (2017)
    PARAS 533, 577. As to the rule against bias see JUDICIAL REVIEW vol 61 (2010) PARA 631 et seq.

402.   When arbitration clause does not apply.

If the contract is itself assignable, the arbitration clause, being part of that
contract, is also assignable[1]; but if a contractor assigns the right to receive all the
money due or to become due under a contract, the contract otherwise remaining
in force between himself and the employer, and the contract contains an
arbitration clause, the arbitrator has no power to make an award of such money
in favour of the contractor[2].

Where the arbitration clause provided that the reference should not be opened
until after the completion of the works and the contractor determined the contract
before completion (as he had power to do under a clause in the contract) it was
held that the arbitrator had no jurisdiction[3]. Limitations on the opening of the
reference are strictly construed[4].

Where a sub-contractor agrees to be bound by the terms of a principal contract,
which contains a clause referring disputes between the employer and the

contractor to arbitration, this does not necessarily operate as a submission to arbitration of disputes between the contractor and the sub-contractor, unless the language used by the parties to the sub-contract points plainly to an intention to incorporate the arbitration clause[5] in the main contract[6].

In many building disputes the employer will wish to bring a claim against the contractor, with whom he may have an arbitration agreement, and against the architect or engineer, with whom he may not have an arbitration agreement or an agreement requiring the disputes to be referred to the same arbitrator[7]. In these circumstances, the court is nonetheless obliged to grant a stay of proceedings[8] unless the applicant has taken a step in proceedings to answer the substantive claim[9] or the court is satisfied that the arbitration agreement is null and void, inoperative or incapable of being performed[10]. Once arbitration proceedings are started, the court will not readily revoke the authority of the arbitrator[11].

Unless otherwise agreed by the parties, an arbitration agreement which forms or was intended to form part of another agreement (whether or not in writing) is not to be regarded as invalid, non-existent or ineffective because that other agreement is invalid, or did not come into existence or has become ineffective, and it for that purpose it is to be treated as a distinct agreement[12]. This principle of severability means that the invalidity or rescission of the main contract does not necessarily entail the invalidity or rescission of the arbitration agreement[13].

1 *Shayler v Woolf* [1946] Ch 320, [1946] 2 All ER 54, CA (explaining observations of Wright J in *Cottage Club Estates Ltd v Woodside Estates Co (Amersham)* [1928] 2 KB 463); *Aspell v Seymour* [1929] WN 152, CA; cf *Herkules Piling Ltd and Hercules Piling Ltd v Tilbury Construction Ltd* (1992) 61 BLR 107, (1992) 32 Con LR 112.
2 *Cottage Club Estates Ltd v Woodside Estates Co (Amersham) Ltd* [1928] 2 KB 463.
3 *Smith v Martin* [1925] 1 KB 745, CA. Note that the arbitrator has power under the Arbitration Act 1996 to rule on his own jurisdiction: see PARA 399.
4 See *AE Farr Ltd v Ministry of Transport* [1960] 3 All ER 88, [1960] 1 WLR 956, where all disputes 'except as to the withholding by the engineer of any certificate' were not to be referred until after the completion of the works. A refusal to include a particular item within any certificate by the engineer was held by Buckley J to create a dispute to which the proviso applied. See also the observations of Viscount Dilhorne in *Gilbert-Ash (Northern) Ltd v Modern Engineering (Bristol) Ltd* [1974] AC 689 at 709, [1973] 3 All ER 195 at 208, HL. See also *Anglian Water Services Ltd v Laing O'Rourke Utilities Ltd* [2010] EWHC 1529 (TCC), 131 Con LR 94, [2010] All ER (D) 252 (Jun).
5 *Giffen (Electrical Contractors) Ltd v Drake & Scull Engineering Ltd* (1993) 37 Con LR 84, CA.
6 Note that authority, both in the Court of Appeal and at first instance, provides somewhat uncertain guidance as to the evidence which will be sufficient to show an intention to incorporate an arbitration clause by reference. In some cases such an intention has been discerned, notwithstanding the absence of express words of incorporation: *Modern Building Wales Ltd v Limmer and Trinidad Co Ltd* [1975] 2 All ER 549, [1975] 1 WLR 1281, CA; *Roche Products Ltd v Freeman Process Systems Ltd* (1996) 80 BLR 102; *Secretary of State for Foreign and Commonwealth Affairs v Percy Thomas Partnership* (1998) 65 Con LR 11. In other cases, the absence of such express words has proved fatal to the incorporation: *Aughton Ltd v MF Kent Services Ltd* (1991) 57 BLR 1, (1991) 31 Con LR 60, CA; *Lexair Ltd v Edgar W Taylor Ltd* (1993) 65 BLR 87; *Co-operative Wholesale Society Ltd v Saunders & Taylor Ltd* (1994) 39 Con LR 77, (1994) 11 Const LJ 118.
7 *Sidney Kaye, Eric Firmin & Partners v Bronesky* (1973) 4 BLR 1, (1973) 226 Estates Gazette 1395, CA.
8 See the Arbitration Act 1996 s 9; *El Nasharty v J Sainsbury plc* [2007] EWHC 2618 (Comm), [2008] 1 Lloyd's Rep 360, [2007] All ER (D) 200 (Nov); and ARBITRATION vol 2 (2017) PARA 522.
9 See the Arbitration Act 1996 s 9(3); and ARBITRATION vol 2 (2017) PARA 522.
10 See the Arbitration Act 1996 s 9(4); and ARBITRATION vol 2 (2017) PARA 522.
11 For the circumstances in which the arbitrator's authority may be revoked see the Arbitration Act 1996 ss 18, 23, 24; and PARA 403. See generally ARBITRATION vol 2 (2017) PARAS 528, 532–533.

12 See the Arbitration Act 1996 s 7; and ARBITRATION vol 2 (2017) PARA 514.
13 See *Fiona Trust and Holding Corpn v Privalov* [2007] UKHL 40, [2007] 4 All ER 951, [2008] 1 Lloyd's Rep 254 (the arbitration agreement had to be treated as a 'distinct agreement' and could be void or voidable only on grounds which related directly to the arbitration agreement); and ARBITRATION vol 2 (2017) PARA 515.

403. Distinction between arbitration and certification.

Under most building contracts, the architect or engineer is required to issue certificates[1]. In the nineteenth and early twentieth centuries it was common for contracts to provide that, in the case of dispute, the architect or engineer was also to act as arbitrator[2]. Such provisions are now uncommon, if not unknown. A court would, it is thought, nowadays require very clear words to conclude that the contract was intended to confer such powers upon an architect or engineer[3].

The granting of certificates under a building contract is not an arbitration or award within the meaning of the Arbitration Act 1996[4] unless express words show that the certificates were intended to be given only after arbitration proceedings[5].

When the architect acts as certifier, his appointment is irrevocable unless the contract shows a contrary intention[6]. The authority of an arbitrator under an arbitration agreement may be revoked by the parties acting jointly, an arbitral institution in whom the parties have vested such powers or, in certain circumstances, the court[7].

1 As to certification see PARA 322 et seq.
2 See PARA 400.
3 *Beaufort Developments (NI) Ltd v Gilbert-Ash NI Ltd* [1999] 1 AC 266 at 276, [1998] 2 All ER 778 at 786, HL, per Lord Hoffmann. For examples of cases concerning the distinction between the architect's role as certifier and arbitrator see *Ranger v Great Western Rly Co* (1854) 5 HL Cas 72; *Northampton Gas Light Co v Parnell* (1855) 15 CB 630; *Collins v Collins* (1858) 26 Beav 306; *Scott v Liverpool Corpn* (1858) 28 LJCh 230; *Mills v Bayley* (1863) 2 H & C 36; *Wadsworth v Smith* (1871) LR 6 QB 332 at 337 per Blackburn J; *Tough v Dumbarton Waterworks Comrs* (1872) 11 M 236, Ct of Sess; *Lawson v Wallasey Local Board* (1883) 48 LT 507, CA; *Re Dawdy* (1885) 15 QBD 426, CA; *Re Carus-Wilson and Greene* (1886) 18 QBD 7, CA; *Re Hammond and Waterton* (1890) 62 LT 808, DC; *North British Rly Co v Wilson* 1911 SC 730, Ct of Sess; *Taylor v Yielding* (1912) 56 Sol Jo 253; *Monmouth County Council v Costelloe and Kemple Ltd* (1965) 63 LGR 429 at 434, CA, per Harman LJ; *A Cameron Ltd v John Mowlem & Co plc* (1990) 52 BLR 24, 25 ConLR 11, CA.
4 *Sutcliffe v Thrackrah* [1974] AC 727, [1974] 1 All ER 859, HL.
5 Again, it is thought that very clear words would be required to give rise to such a conclusion. Even in the nineteenth century such a construction was generally rejected: see eg *Wadsworth v Smith* (1871) LR 6 QB 332.
6 *Mills v Bayley* (1863) 2 H & C 36.
7 See the Arbitration Act 1996 ss 18, 23, 24; and ARBITRATION vol 2 (2017) PARAS 528, 532–533.

404. Effect of arbitration clause on certification.

Where a building contract contains a clause by which the determination or certificate of the architect is made final and conclusive between the parties, or is made a condition precedent to any right of the contractor to payment[1], and the contract also contains a clause by which all disputes are to be referred to arbitration, a question arises as to how far the arbitration clause affects the certificate clause[2].

Where the arbitration clause excludes certain matters in express terms and leaves them to the sole discretion of the architect, no arbitration can arise in respect of these matters except by agreement, and, in the absence of an allegation of fraud, neither the court nor the arbitrator has jurisdiction to review the determination of the architect as to those matters[3].

On the other hand, where there is no express restriction of the scope of the arbitration clause but nevertheless the wording of the contract makes it clear that the certificate or the absence of one is to be conclusive of some matter the arbitrator may not review the correctness of the certificate or the failure to issue one[4].

However, the existence of an arbitration clause in wide terms may show an intention that the certificate is not to be binding and conclusive at all. Such a certificate will have provisional validity only, unless and until reviewed by the arbitrator or court[5].

When there are two clauses giving similar jurisdiction to the architect or to the arbitrator, and the architect's certificate is made final and conclusive between the parties, the effect seems to be that when the architect has given his certificate before a dispute has actually arisen it is final and conclusive between the parties, but that if a dispute has arisen before the architect has certified, then his power of certifying is destroyed, and the jurisdiction of the arbitrator arises[6].

Where there is a dispute on an issue which has clearly been referred to the arbitrator for decision the court is likely to hold that it was also intended that the arbitrator should have the powers necessary to give effect to his decision on that issue[7].

Some contracts provide that a certificate is to have conclusive evidential effect unless specified steps (for example to commence arbitration proceedings) are commenced within a particular period of time. The court's power to extend the time within which an arbitration may be commenced[8] does not apply to such a step[9].

1   See PARAS 322 et seq, 373.
2   As to certification see PARA 322 et seq. As to the distinction between arbitration and certification see PARA 403.
3   *Sharpe v San Paulo Rly Co* (1873) 8 Ch App 597; *Lawson v Wallasey Local Board* (1883) 48 LT 507, CA.
4   *East Ham Corpn v Bernard Sunley & Sons Ltd* [1966] AC 406, [1965] 3 All ER 619, HL; cf *Loke Hong Kee Pte Ltd v United Overseas Land Ltd* (1982) 23 BLR 35, PC.
5   *Beaufort Developments (NI) Ltd v Gilbert-Ash NI Ltd* [1999] 1 AC 266, [1998] 2 All ER 778, HL.
6   *Clemence v Clarke* (1879) 2 Hudson's BC (10th Edn) 443, 466, CA; *Lloyd Bros v Milward* (1895) 2 Hudson's BC (10th Edn) 439, CA.
7   *Brodie v Cardiff Corpn* [1919] AC 337, HL; *Prestige & Co Ltd v Brettell* [1938] 4 All ER 346, CA; *Beaufort Developments (NI) Ltd v Gilbert-Ash NI Ltd* [1999] 1 AC 266, [1998] 2 All ER 778, HL.
8   See the Arbitration Act 1996 s 12; and ARBITRATION vol 2 (2017) PARA 521.
9   *Crown Estates Comrs v John Mowlem & Co* (1994) 70 BLR 1, 40 Con LR 36, CA; overruling *McLaughlin & Harvey plc v P & O Developments Ltd* (1991) 55 BLR 101. See further PARA 380.

405. Multiparty and 'name borrowing' arbitration.

Unless all relevant parties expressly agree to confer such power on the arbitrator, he has no power to order consolidation of proceedings or concurrent hearings in two arbitrations arising out of different contracts[1]. Thus some standard forms of contract[2] attempt to overcome this difference by providing for a dispute concerning a contract or sub-contract to be referred to the arbitrator appointed under another related contract. However, these attempts can be subject to procedural difficulties arising from the absence of contractual privity between three or more parties[3]. Where the dispute may in reality not concern one person, such as the contractor, but concerns only a sub-contractor and the employer, provision is sometimes made for the claimant to borrow the name of the party not involved and to prosecute the claim in its name. The efficacy of these procedures depends largely on the co-operation of all the parties[4]. For example, where a sub-contractor had obtained, as part of a compromise with the contractor, the right to conduct and control the contractor's arbitration against the employer, the sub-contractor was not bound by the contractor's defence to its claim[5]. Where in a main contract arbitration the arbitrator made an award of a sum which should have been certified as due in respect of the sub-contract works, that sum fell to be treated as a sum duly certified so that, in this respect, the award was binding in the sub-contract arbitration[6].

1   See the Arbitration Act 1996 s 35; and ARBITRATION vol 2 (2017) PARA 549. See also *Oxford Shipping Co Ltd v Nippon Yusen Kaisha* [1984] 3 All ER 835, [1984] 2 Lloyd's Rep 373.
2   As to standard forms of contracts see PARA 202.
3   For cases on the subject see *Higgs & Hill Building Ltd v Campbell Denis Ltd* [1983] Com LR 34, 28 BLR 47; *Multi-Construction (Southern) Ltd v Stent Foundations Ltd* (1988) 41 BLR 98, (1988) 14 Con LR 110; *Hyundai Engineering and Construction Co Ltd v Active Building and Civil Construction Pte Ltd* (1988) 45 BLR 62; *MJ Gleeson Group Ltd v Wyatt of Snetterton* (1994) 72 BLR 15, (1994) 11 Const LJ 59, CA; *Trafalgar House Construction (Regions) Ltd v Railtrack plc* (1995) 75 BLR 55, [1995] CILL 1056; *Lafarge Redland Aggregates Ltd v Shephard Hill Civil Engineering Ltd* [2001] 1 All ER 34, [2000] 1 WLR 1621, HL. As to privity of contract see CONTRACT vol 22 (2012) PARA 327 et seq.
4   For cases on 'name borrowing' provisions see *A Monk & Co Ltd v Devon County Council* (1978) 10 BLR 9, CA; *Lorne Stewart Ltd v William Sindall plc & North West Thames Regional Health Authority* (1986) 35 BLR 109, 11 Con LR 99; *Gordon Durham & Co Ltd v Haden Young Ltd* (1990) 52 BLR 61; *Belgravia Property Co Ltd v S & R (London) Ltd* [2001] BLR 424, 93 Con LR 59.
5   *A Monk & Co Ltd v Devon County Council* (1978) 10 BLR 9.
6   *Birse Construction Ltd (formerly Peter Birse Ltd) v Co-operative Wholesale Society Ltd (t/a CWS Engineering Group)* (1997) 84 Con LR 58, sub nom *Co-operative Wholesale Society Ltd v Birse Construction Ltd* 57 Con LR 98, 84 BLR 58, CA.

406. Arbitration claims in the Technology and Construction Court.

Arbitration claims arising out of or connected with a construction or engineering arbitration are made to the Technology and Construction Court[1] which follows the practice and procedure for arbitration claims established by Part 62 of the Civil Procedure Rules[2]. Claims which may be made in this way include:

(1)   applications under the Arbitration Act 1996[3];
(2)   claims to determine (a) whether there is a valid arbitration agreement; (b) whether an arbitration tribunal is properly constituted; or (c) what matters have been submitted to arbitration in accordance with an arbitration agreement[4];
(3)   claims to declare that an award by an arbitral tribunal is not binding on a party[5]; or
(4)   any other application affecting arbitration proceedings (whether started or not) or an arbitration[6].

Common examples of arbitration claims under the Arbitration Act 1996 are challenges to an award on grounds of jurisdiction[7], challenges to an award for serious irregularity[8] or appeals on points of law[9]. Where a party is seeking to appeal a question of law arising out of an award and the parties have not in their underlying contract agreed that such an appeal may be brought, the party seeking to appeal must apply for leave to appeal under the Arbitration Act 1996[10]. Parties to a construction contract should check whether they have agreed in the underlying contract that an appeal may be brought without leave, since some construction and engineering standard forms of contract so provide. If that is the case, the appeal may be set down for a substantive hearing without leave being sought[11].

In some arbitration claims arising out of construction and engineering arbitrations, a party will seek to appeal a question of law[12] and, at the same time, seek to challenge the award on the grounds of serious irregularity[13]. This raises questions of procedure, since material may be admissible in one application which is inadmissible on the other. In these circumstances the court will give directions as to how the applications will be dealt with before hearing or determining any application[14].

1 Technology and Construction Court Guide para 10.1.2. The Technology and Construction Court Guide is available at the date, at which this volume states the law, on the government website.
2 Technology and Construction Court Guide (2nd Edn) para 10.1.3. See CPR Pt 62; and ARBITRATION vol 2 (2017) PARA 583 et seq.
3 See CPR 62.2(1)(a). See also the text and notes 7–14.
4 See CPR 62.2(1)(b). See also *Costain Ltd v Tarmac Holdings Ltd* [2017] EWHC 319 (TCC), [2017] 2 All ER (Comm) 645, [2017] All ER (D) 44 (Mar).
5 See CPR 62.2(1)(c).
6 See CPR 62.2(1)(d).
7 Ie under the Arbitration Act 1996 s 67 (see ARBITRATION vol 2 (2017) PARA 576). See the Technology and Construction Court Guide para 10.1.1.
8 Ie under the Arbitration Act 1996 s 68 (see ARBITRATION vol 2 (2017) PARA 577). See the Technology and Construction Court Guide para 10.1.1.
9 Ie under the Arbitration Act 1996 s 69 (see ARBITRATION vol 2 (2017) PARA 578). See the Technology and Construction Court Guide para 10.1.1.
10 Ie pursuant to the Arbitration Act 1996 s 69(2), (3), (4): see the Technology and Construction Court Guide para 10.2.1.
11 Technology and Construction Court Guide para 10.3.
12 Ie under the Arbitration Act 1996 s 69: see note 9.
13 Ie under the Arbitration Act 1996 s 68: see note 8.
14 Technology and Construction Court Guide para 10.5.

(3) Adjudication under Construction Contracts

(i) Introduction

407. Statutory adjudication.

The high cost and perceived delay in the resolution of court and arbitral proceedings has led to the adoption of other means of dispute resolution in the construction industry. These include mediation, expert determination and other methods of alternative dispute resolution[1].

Part II of the Housing Grants, Construction and Regeneration Act 1996[2] introduced a statutory right of adjudication. A party to a construction contract[3] has the right to refer a dispute arising under the contract to adjudication[4], and provision must be made in the contract to comply with the statutory requirements as to the adjudication procedure[5]. Where the contract does not comply with such requirements, the adjudication provisions of the scheme for construction contracts apply[6].

The introduction of a statutory right has given rise to a substantial volume of adjudications and reported cases[7]. The statutory regime has largely superseded the procedure formerly found in some standard forms for the appointment of a person to make provisional decisions, binding until decided otherwise in arbitration or litigation[8].

It has been held that a construction dispute cannot be referred to adjudication once one of the parties involved enters liquidation[9].

1   See PARA 423.
2   Ie the Housing Grants, Construction and Regeneration Act 1996 Pt II (ss 104–117). As to the application of Pt II see PARA 211.
3   Ie a 'construction contract' as defined in the Housing Grants, Construction and Regeneration Act 1996: see PARA 210.
4   See the Housing Grants, Construction and Regeneration Act 1996 s 108(1); and PARA 410.
5   See the Housing Grants, Construction and Regeneration Act 1996 s 108(2)–(4); and PARA 410.
6   As to the adjudication provisions under the scheme for construction contracts see PARAS 411–416. As to the power to make the scheme for construction contracts see PARA 210.
7   As to the general provisions relating to adjudication arising from such cases see PARA 410 et seq.
8   See eg *A Cameron Ltd v John Mowlem & Co plc* (1990) 52 BLR 24, 25 ConLR 11, CA.
9   See *Enterprise Managed Services Ltd v Tony McFadden Utilities Ltd* [2009] EWHC 3222 (TCC), [2010] BLR 89, [2011] 1 BCLC 414 (the High Court was the appropriate forum).

408. The role of the Technology and Construction Court.
The Technology and Construction Court is ordinarily the court in which the enforcement of an adjudicator's decision[1] and any other business connected with adjudication is undertaken[2]. In addition to enforcement applications, declaratory relief is sometimes sought in the Technology and Construction Court at the outset of an adjudication in respect of matters such as the jurisdiction of the adjudicator or the validity of the adjudication[3].

1   As to enforcement of the adjudicator's decision see PARA 418 et seq.
2   Technology and Construction Court Guide para 9.1.1. The Technology and Construction Court Guide is available at the date, at which this volume states the law, on the government website.
3   Technology and Construction Court Guide paras 9.1.2, 9.4. Such matters might include: (1) disputes over the jurisdiction of an adjudicator; (2) disputes over whether there is a construction contract within the meaning of the Housing Grants, Construction and Regeneration Act 1996 (and, in older contracts, whether there was a written contract between the parties); and (3) disputes over the permissible scope of the adjudication, and, in particular, whether the matters which the claimant seeks to raise in the adjudication are the subject of a pre-existing dispute between the parties: see the Technology and Construction Court Guide para 9.4. The court may also be required to consider whether, in circumstances where a referral to adjudication was unreasonable or oppressive, a party should be restrained from taking any substantive steps in the adjudication: see *Mentmore Towers Ltd v Packman Lucas Ltd* [2010] EWHC 457 (TCC), [2010] BLR 393, [2010] All ER (D) 236 (Oct); *Jacobs UK Ltd v Skanska Construction UK Ltd* [2017] EWHC 2395, 174 ConLR 61 (TCC). See also *MW High Tech Projects UK Ltd v Haase Environmental Consulting GmbH* [2015] EWHC 152 (TCC), [2015] All ER (D) 33 (Feb) (declaratory relief to be granted sparingly by courts and never where it would be, at best, hypothetical). As to the jurisdiction of the adjudicator see PARA 417.

409. Existence and composition of disputes.
The statutory right to refer disputes to adjudication is a right to refer a dispute arising under the contract[1]. A dispute must therefore already be in existence before a valid referral can be made[2]. It is a question of fact in each case as to what is in dispute at any particular moment[3]. The dispute which may be referred to adjudication is all or part of whatever is in dispute at the moment that the referring party first intimates an adjudication reference[4]. The dispute is whatever claims, heads of claim, issues, contentions or causes of action that are then in dispute which the referring party has chosen to crystallise into an adjudication reference[5].

1   See the Housing Grants, Construction and Regeneration Act 1996 s 108(1); and PARA 410.
2   See *Fastrack Contractors Ltd v Morrison Construction Ltd* [2000] BLR 168, 75 Con LR 33.

3   *Fastrack Contractors Ltd v Morrison Construction Ltd* [2000] BLR 168, 75 Con LR 33. See also
    VGC Construction Ltd v Jackson Civil Engineering Ltd [2008] EWHC 2082 (TCC), 120 Con LR
    178, [2006] CILL 2627.
4   *Fastrack Contractors Ltd v Morrison Construction Ltd* [2000] BLR 168 at 176, 75 Con LR 33 at
    44 per Judge Thornton QC.
5   *Fastrack Contractors Ltd v Morrison Construction Ltd* [2000] BLR 168 at 176–177, 75 Con LR
    33 at 44 per Judge Thornton QC. See also *Northern Developments (Cumbria) Ltd v J & J Nichol*
    [2000] BLR 158, [2000] All ER (D) 68; *Grovedeck Ltd v Capital Demolition Ltd* [2000] BLR 181,
    [2000] 2 TCLR 689; *Edmund Nuttall Ltd v RG Carter Ltd* [2002] EWHC 400 (TCC), [2002] BLR
    312, [2002] 2 TCLR 27; *Midland Expressway Ltd v Carillion Construction Ltd* [2006] EWCA Civ
    936, 107 Con LR 235. See also *St Austell Printing Co Ltd v Dawnus Construction Holdings Ltd*
    [2015] EWHC 96 (TCC), [2015] All ER (D) 167 (Jan) (dispute about sums due had crystallised
    long before notice of adjudication). See *AMD Environmental Ltd v Cumberland Construction Co
    Ltd* [2016] EWHC 285 (TCC), [2017] 1 All ER (Comm) 823, [2016] All ER (D) 169 (Feb) for a
    discussion on crystallisation of a dispute.

(ii) Requirements under the Housing Grants, Construction and Regeneration Act 1996

410. The right to refer a dispute.
A party to a construction contract[1] has the right to refer a dispute[2] arising
under the contract for adjudication[3]. The contract must include provision in
writing so as to[4]:

(1)   enable a party to give notice at any time of his intention to refer a
      dispute to adjudication[5];
(2)   provide a timetable with the object of securing the appointment of the
      adjudicator and referral of the dispute to him within seven days of such
      notice[6];
(3)   require the adjudicator to reach a decision within 28 days of referral or
      such longer period as is agreed by the parties after the dispute has been
      referred[7];
(4)   allow the adjudicator to extend the period of 28 days by up to 14 days,
      with the consent of the party by whom the dispute was referred[8];
(5)   impose a duty on the adjudicator to act impartially[9]; and
(6)   enable the adjudicator to take the initiative in ascertaining the facts and
      the law[10].

The contract must provide in writing that the decision of the adjudicator is
binding until the dispute is finally determined either by legal proceedings, or by
arbitration (if the contract provides for arbitration or the parties otherwise agree
to arbitration) or by agreement[11]. The parties may agree to accept the decision of
the adjudicator as finally determining the dispute[12]. The contract must also
provide in writing that the adjudicator is not liable for anything done or omitted
in the discharge or purported discharge of his functions as adjudicator unless the
act or omission is in bad faith, and that any employee or agent of the adjudicator
is similarly protected from liability[13].

If the contract does not comply with such requirements[14], the adjudication
provisions of the scheme for construction contracts apply[15].

1   Ie a 'construction contract' as defined in the Housing Grants, Construction and Regeneration Act
    1996: see PARA 210.
2   For these purposes, 'dispute' includes any difference: Housing Grants, Construction and
    Regeneration Act 1996 s 108(1). See also PARA 409.
3   Housing Grants, Construction and Regeneration Act 1996 s 108(1). However, s 108 is irrelevant
    where there is a binding agreement making compulsory the reference of disputes to adjudication
    in the first instance: *DGT Steel and Cladding Ltd v Cubbitt Building and Interiors Ltd* [2007]

EWHC 1584 (TCC), [2008] Bus LR 132, [2007] BLR 371. See also *Domsalla (t/a Domsalla Building Services) v Dyason* [2007] EWHC 1174 (TCC), [2007] BLR 348, (2007) 112 Con LR 95 (adjudication involving residential occupier came within the Housing Grants, Construction and Regeneration Act 1996 s 108).

4 Housing Grants, Construction and Regeneration Act 1996 s 108(2) (amended by the Local Democracy, Economic Development and Construction Act 2009 s 139(2)(a)).

5 Housing Grants, Construction and Regeneration Act 1996 s 108(2)(a). A notice to refer a dispute to adjudication may be given at any time: *John Mowlem & Co plc v Hydra-Tight Ltd* [2000] CILL 1649. There is no time limit for referring a dispute to adjudication: *Connex South Eastern Ltd v MJ Building Services Group plc* [2005] EWCA Civ 193, [2005] 2 All ER 870, [2005] BLR 201 (adjudication brought 18 months after contract repudiated not abuse of process). Such notice may therefore be given after determination of the contract (*A & D Maintenance and Construction Ltd v Pagehurst Construction Services Ltd* (1999) 16 Const LJ 199, [2000] CILL 1518) or subsequent to the issue of court proceedings in respect of the same dispute (*Herschel Engineering Ltd v Breen Property Ltd* [2000] BLR 272, 70 Con LR 1 (cf *Cygnet Healthcare plc v Higgins City Ltd* (2000) 16 Const LJ 394; and *Trustees of the Marc Gilbard 2009 Settlement Trust v OD Developments and Projects Ltd* [2015] EWHC 70 (TCC), 159 ConLR 150, [2015] All ER (D) 194 (Jan)). See also *A Straume (UK) Ltd v Bradlor Developments Ltd* [2000] 2 TCLR 409, [2000] CILL 1520; *NAP Anglia Ltd v Sun-Land Development Co Ltd* [2011] EWHC 2846 (TCC), [2012] BLR 110, [2011] All ER (D) 172 (Nov). The requirement relating to service of the referral notice has to be operated in a sensible and businesslike way: *Cubitt Building and Interiors Ltd v Fleetglade Ltd* [2006] EWHC 3413 (TCC), (2006) 110 Con LR 36, [2007] All ER (D) 268 (Jan).

6 Housing Grants, Construction and Regeneration Act 1996 s 108(2)(b). As to the reckoning of periods of time see PARA 352 note 2. See *William Verry Ltd v North West London Communal Mikvah* [2004] EWHC 1300 (TCC), 96 Con LR 96, [2004] BLR 308; *Cubitt Building and Interiors Ltd v Fleetglade Ltd* [2006] EWHC 3413, 110 ConLR 36, [2007] All ER (D) 268 (Jan).

7 Housing Grants, Construction and Regeneration Act 1996 s 108(2)(c). See *Barnes & Elliot Ltd v Taylor Woodrow Property Management Ltd* [2003] EWHC 3100 (TCC), [2004] BLR 111, [2004] All ER (D) 142 (Apr) (adjudicator reaching decision and communicating it to parties within specified time period; written decision sent to parties one day outside specified time period; adjudication enforceable).

8 Housing Grants, Construction and Regeneration Act 1996 s 108(2)(d).

9 Housing Grants, Construction and Regeneration Act 1996 s 108(2)(e).

10 Housing Grants, Construction and Regeneration Act 1996 s 108(2)(f).

11 Housing Grants, Construction and Regeneration Act 1996 s 108(3) (amended by the Local Democracy, Economic Development and Construction Act 2009 s 139(2)(b)). See *JT Mackley & Co Ltd v Gosport Marina Ltd* [2002] EWHC 1315 (TCC), [2002] BLR 367, [2002] All ER (D) 39 (Jul). The enforcement of an adjudicator's award is not subject to the terms of the contract: *Levolux AT Ltd v Ferson Contractors Ltd* [2003] EWCA Civ 11, [2003] 1 All ER (Comm) 385, (2003) 86 Con LR 98. See *Trustees of the Harbours of Peterhead v Lilley Construction Ltd* 2003 SLT 731, OH (term in contract enabling parties to refer same dispute to arbitration in addition to adjudication). See also *SG South v King's Head Cirencester LLP* [2009] EWHC 2645 (TCC), [2010] BLR 47, [2009] All ER (D) 120 (Nov).

The contract must include provision in writing permitting the adjudicator to correct his decision so as to remove a clerical or typographical error arising by accident or omission: Housing Grants, Construction and Regeneration Act 1996 s 108(3A) (added by the Local Democracy, Economic Development and Construction Act 2009 s 140).

12 Housing Grants, Construction and Regeneration Act 1996 s 108(3). See also *Khurana v Webster Construction Ltd* [2015] EWHC 758 (TCC), [2016] 1 All ER (Comm) 466, 159 ConLR 208, where the parties agreed to adjudicate under the scheme for construction contracts save that the adjudicator's decision, through very clear language and by agreement between the parties, was held to be permanently binding, thus excluding any right to bring matters before the court.

13 Housing Grants, Construction and Regeneration Act 1996 s 108(4) (amended by the Local Democracy, Economic Development and Construction Act 2009 s 139(2)(b)).

14 Ie the requirements of the Housing Grants, Construction and Regeneration Act 1996 s 108(1)–(4): see the text and notes 1–13.

15 Housing Grants, Construction and Regeneration Act 1996 s 108(5). See *Pegram Shopfitters Ltd v Tally Weijl (UK) Ltd* [2003] EWCA 1750, [2004] 1 All ER 818, [2004] 1 WLR 2082; and *Dacy Building Services Ltd v IDM Properties LLP* [2016] EWHC 3007 (TCC), 170 ConLR 176, [2016] All ER (D) 18 (Dec) (adjudicator and judge wrong to proceed on premise that contract existed when defendant had claimed in the alternative that no contract had been formed).

The scheme is contained in the Scheme for Construction Contracts (England and Wales)

Regulations 1998, SI 1998/649 (see PARAS 358, 411–416). As to the adjudication provisions under the scheme for construction contracts see PARAS 411–416. As to the power to make the scheme for construction contracts see PARA 210. For England and Wales, the scheme may apply the provisions of the Arbitration Act 1996 (see ARBITRATION) with such adaptations and modifications as appear to the minister making the scheme to be appropriate: Housing Grants, Construction and Regeneration Act 1996 s 108(6). As to the meanings of 'England' and 'Wales' see PARA 211 note 4.

See also *Aspect Contracts (Asbestos) Ltd v Higgins Construction plc* [2015] UKSC 38, [2015] 2 All ER (Comm) 965, [2015] 1 WLR 2961 (term implied into statutory scheme that party who had made payment in accordance with adjudicator's decision remained entitled to dispute decision and repayment if successful).

(iii) Requirements under the Scheme for Construction Contracts

411. Adjudication provisions under the scheme for construction contracts.
Where a construction contract[1] does not comply with the requirements of the adjudication procedure under the Housing Grants, Construction and Regeneration Act 1996[2], the adjudication provisions of the scheme for construction contracts apply[3].

1 Ie a 'construction contract' as defined in the Housing Grants, Construction and Regeneration Act 1996: see PARA 210.
2 Ie the Housing Grants, Construction and Regeneration Act 1996 s 108: see PARA 410.
3 See the Housing Grants, Construction and Regeneration Act 1996 s 108(5); and PARA 410. The scheme is contained in the Scheme for Construction Contracts (England and Wales) Regulations 1998, SI 1998/649, reg 2, Schedule Pt I: see PARAS 412–416. As to the power to make the scheme for construction contracts see PARA 210.

412. Notice of intention to seek adjudication.
Any party to a construction contract[1] (the 'referring party') may give written notice ('notice of adjudication') at any time of his intention to refer any dispute arising under the contract, to adjudication[2], and such notice must be given to every other party to the contract[3]. The notice of adjudication must set out briefly:
(1) the nature and a brief description of the dispute and of the parties involved[4];
(2) details of where and when the dispute has arisen[5];
(3) the nature of the redress which is sought[6]; and
(4) the names and addresses of the parties to the contract, including, where appropriate, the addresses which the parties have specified for the giving of notices[7].

1 Ie a 'construction contract' as defined in the Housing Grants, Construction and Regeneration Act 1996: see PARA 210.
2 Scheme for Construction Contracts (England and Wales) Regulations 1998, SI 1998/649, reg 2, Schedule Pt I para 1(1) (amended by SI 2011/1715 (Wales); SI 2011/2333 (England)). As to the application of the scheme for construction contracts see PARA 411. See also *Camden London Borough Council v Makers UK Ltd* [2009] EWHC 605 (TCC), 124 ConLR 32, [2009] All ER (D) 301 (Mar) where the council had obtained judgment in default of defence against Makers who were insolvent, but Makers started a separate adjudication of its own. The court held in that case it was not appropriate to impose any condition restraining Makers from starting an adjudication, which was a statutory right, and that adjudication could be started at any time despite the fact Makers was insolvent and would not be able to repay any money that was paid to it if it was successful in the adjudication.
3 Scheme for Construction Contracts (England and Wales) Regulations 1998, SI 1998/649, Schedule Pt I para 1(2).
4 Scheme for Construction Contracts (England and Wales) Regulations 1998, SI 1998/649, Schedule Pt I para 1(3)(a).

5 Scheme for Construction Contracts (England and Wales) Regulations 1998, SI 1998/649, Schedule Pt I para 1(3)(b).
6 Scheme for Construction Contracts (England and Wales) Regulations 1998, SI 1998/649, Schedule Pt I para 1(3)(c).
7 Scheme for Construction Contracts (England and Wales) Regulations 1998, SI 1998/649, Schedule Pt I para 1(3)(d). The requirements for a notice of adjudication as set out in Schedule Pt I para 1 are merely directory; it would be contrary to the purpose of the adjudication scheme to construe it in a legalistic manner: *Williams (t/a Sanclair Construction) v Noor (t/a India Kitchen)* [2007] All ER (D) 51 (Dec) (failure to name claimant was not fatal to notice).

413.   Selection and appointment of adjudicator.

Following the giving of a notice of adjudication[1] and subject to any agreement between the parties to the dispute as to who is to act as adjudicator:

(1) the referring party[2] must request[3] the person, if any, specified in the contract to act as adjudicator[4]; or

(2) if no person is named in the contract or the person named has already indicated that he is unwilling or unable to act, and the contract provides for a specified nominating body to select a person, the referring party must request the nominating body named in the contract to select a person to act as adjudicator[5]; or

(3) where neither head (1) nor head (2) above applies, or where the person specified in the contract to act as adjudicator has already indicated that he is unwilling or unable to act and head (2) does not apply, the referring party must request an adjudicator nominating body[6] to select a person to act as adjudicator[7].

A person so requested to act as adjudicator must indicate whether or not he is willing to act within two days of receiving the request[8]. The nominating body[9] or the adjudicator nominating body[10] must communicate the selection of an adjudicator to the referring party within five days of receiving a request to do so[11]. Where the nominating body or the adjudicator nominating body fails to comply, the referring party may agree with the other party to the dispute to request a specified person to act as adjudicator or request any other adjudicator nominating body to select a person to act as adjudicator[12]. The person so requested to act as adjudicator must indicate whether or not he is willing to act within two days of receiving the request[13].

Where an adjudicator who is named in the contract indicates to the parties that he is unable or unwilling to act, or where he fails to respond to a request to act as adjudicator[14], the referring party may[15]: (a) request another person, if any, specified in the contract to act as adjudicator[16]; or (b) request the nominating body, if any, referred to in the contract to select a person to act as adjudicator[17]; or (c) request any other adjudicator nominating body to select a person to act as adjudicator[18]. The person so requested to act must indicate whether or not he is willing to act within two days of receiving the request[19].

Where an adjudicator has been selected[20], the referring party must, not later than seven days from the date of the notice of adjudication, refer the dispute in writing (by way of 'referral notice') to the adjudicator[21]. A referral notice must be accompanied by copies of, or relevant extracts from, the construction contract[22] and such other documents as the referring party intends to rely upon[23]. The referring party must, at the same time as he sends to the adjudicator such documents[24], send copies of those documents to every other party to the dispute[25].Upon receipt of the referral notice, the adjudicator must inform every party to the dispute of the date that it was received[26].

Any person requested or selected to act as adjudicator[27] must be a natural person acting in his personal capacity[28]. A person requested or selected to act as an adjudicator must not be an employee of any of the parties to the dispute and must declare any interest, financial or otherwise, in any matter relating to the dispute[29].

The adjudicator may, with the consent of all the parties to those disputes, adjudicate at the same time on more than one dispute under the same contract[30], and may also, with the consent of all the parties to those disputes, adjudicate at the same time on related disputes under different contracts, whether or not one or more of those parties is a party to those disputes[31].

Where any party to the dispute objects to the appointment of a particular person as adjudicator, that objection does not invalidate the adjudicator's appointment nor any decision[32] he may reach[33].

1   As to giving of a notice of adjudication under the scheme for construction contracts see PARA 412.
2   As to the 'referring party' see PARA 412.
3   The request referred to in the Scheme for Construction Contracts (England and Wales) Regulations 1998, SI 1998/649, reg 2, Schedule Pt I paras 2, 5, 6 must be accompanied by a copy of the notice of adjudication: Schedule Pt I para 3. As to the application of the scheme for construction contracts see PARA 411.
4   Scheme for Construction Contracts (England and Wales) Regulations 1998, SI 1998/649, Schedule Pt I para 2(1)(a).
5   Scheme for Construction Contracts (England and Wales) Regulations 1998, SI 1998/649, Schedule Pt I para 2(1)(b).
6   For the purposes of the Scheme for Construction Contracts (England and Wales) Regulations 1998, SI 1998/649, Schedule Pt I paras 2, 5, 6, an 'adjudicator nominating body' means a body (not being a natural person and not being a party to the dispute) which holds itself out publicly as a body which will select an adjudicator when requested to do so by a referring party: Schedule Pt I para 2(3). See *Makers UK Ltd v Camden London Borough Council* [2008] EWHC 1836 (TCC), [2008] BLR 470, (2008) 120 Con LR 161 (nominating body not in breach of its own rules in listening to and acting on representations made to it as to attributes or name of the person to be appointed).
7   Scheme for Construction Contracts (England and Wales) Regulations 1998, SI 1998/649, Schedule Pt I para 2(1)(c).
8   Scheme for Construction Contracts (England and Wales) Regulations 1998, SI 1998/649, Schedule Pt I para 2(2).
9   Ie the nominating body referred to in the Scheme for Construction Contracts (England and Wales) Regulations 1998, SI 1998/649, Schedule Pt I paras 2(1)(b), 6(1)(b): see the text and notes 5, 17.
10 Ie the adjudicator nominating body referred to in the Scheme for Construction Contracts (England and Wales) Regulations 1998, SI 1998/649, Schedule Pt I paras 2(1)(c), 5(2)(b) and 6(1)(c).
11 Scheme for Construction Contracts (England and Wales) Regulations 1998, SI 1998/649, Schedule Pt I para 5(1). See note 3.
12 Scheme for Construction Contracts (England and Wales) Regulations 1998, SI 1998/649, Schedule Pt I para 5(2). See note 3.
13 Scheme for Construction Contracts (England and Wales) Regulations 1998, SI 1998/649, Schedule Pt I para 5(3). See note 3.
14 Ie respond in accordance with the Scheme for Construction Contracts (England and Wales) Regulations 1998, SI 1998/649, Schedule Pt I para 2(2): see the text and note 8.
15 Scheme for Construction Contracts (England and Wales) Regulations 1998, SI 1998/649, Schedule Pt I para 6(1). See note 3.
16 Scheme for Construction Contracts (England and Wales) Regulations 1998, SI 1998/649, Schedule Pt I para 6(1)(a). See note 3.
17 Scheme for Construction Contracts (England and Wales) Regulations 1998, SI 1998/649, Schedule Pt I para 6(1)(b). See note 3.
18 Scheme for Construction Contracts (England and Wales) Regulations 1998, SI 1998/649, Schedule Pt I para 6(1)(c). See note 3.
19 Scheme for Construction Contracts (England and Wales) Regulations 1998, SI 1998/649, Schedule Pt I para 6(2). See note 3.
20 Ie in accordance with the Scheme for Construction Contracts (England and Wales) Regulations 1998, SI 1998/649, Schedule Pt I paras 2, 5 and 6.

21 Scheme for Construction Contracts (England and Wales) Regulations 1998, SI 1998/649, Schedule Pt I para 7(1).
22 Ie a 'construction contract' as defined in the Housing Grants, Construction and Regeneration Act 1996: see PARA 210.
23 Scheme for Construction Contracts (England and Wales) Regulations 1998, SI 1998/649, Schedule Pt I para 7(2).
24 Ie documents referred to in the Scheme for Construction Contracts (England and Wales) Regulations 1998, SI 1998/649, Schedule Pt I para 7(1), (2): see the text and notes 20–23.
25 Scheme for Construction Contracts (England and Wales) Regulations 1998, SI 1998/649, Schedule Pt I para 7(3).
26 Scheme for Construction Contracts (England and Wales) Regulations 1998, SI 1998/649, Schedule Pt I para 7(4) (added by SI 2011/1715 (Wales), SI 2011/2333 (England)).
27 See note 20.
28 Scheme for Construction Contracts (England and Wales) Regulations 1998, SI 1998/649, Schedule Pt I para 4.
29 Scheme for Construction Contracts (England and Wales) Regulations 1998, SI 1998/649, Schedule Pt I para 4.
30 Scheme for Construction Contracts (England and Wales) Regulations 1998, SI 1998/649, Schedule Pt I para 8(1). All the parties in Schedule Pt I para 8(1), (2) may agree to extend the period within which the adjudicator may reach a decision in relation to all or any of these disputes: Schedule Pt I para 8(3). Where an adjudicator ceases to act because a dispute is to be adjudicated on by another person in terms of Schedule Pt I para 8, that adjudicator's fees and expenses are to be determined in accordance with Schedule Pt I para 25 (see PARA 416): Schedule Pt I para 8(4).
31 Scheme for Construction Contracts (England and Wales) Regulations 1998, SI 1998/649, Schedule Pt I para 8(2). See note 30.
32 Ie a decision reached in accordance with the Scheme for Construction Contracts (England and Wales) Regulations 1998, SI 1998/649, Schedule Pt I para 20: see PARA 416.
33 Scheme for Construction Contracts (England and Wales) Regulations 1998, SI 1998/649, Schedule Pt I para 10.

414. Resignation or revocation of appointment of adjudicator.
An adjudicator may resign at any time on giving notice in writing to the parties to the dispute[1], and where an adjudicator so ceases to act, the referring party[2] may serve a fresh notice of adjudication[3], and must request an adjudicator to act in accordance with the procedure under the scheme for construction contracts[4]. If requested by the new adjudicator and in so far as it is reasonably practicable, the parties must supply him with copies of all documents which they had made available to the previous adjudicator[5].

An adjudicator must resign where the dispute is the same or substantially the same as one which has previously been referred to adjudication, and a decision has been taken in that adjudication[6]. Where an adjudicator resigns in such circumstances, or where a dispute varies significantly from the dispute referred to him in the referral notice[7] and for that reason he is not competent to decide it, the adjudicator is entitled to the payment of such reasonable amount as he may determine by way of fees and expenses reasonably incurred by him[8].

The parties to a dispute may at any time agree to revoke the appointment of the adjudicator[9]. The adjudicator is entitled to the payment of such reasonable amount as he may determine by way of fees and expenses incurred by him[10]. Where the revocation of the appointment of the adjudicator is due to the default or misconduct of the adjudicator, the parties are not liable to pay the adjudicator's fees and expenses[11].

1 Scheme for Construction Contracts (England and Wales) Regulations 1998, SI 1998/649, reg 2, Schedule Pt I para 9(1). As to the application of the scheme for construction contracts see PARA 411.
2 As to the 'referring party' see PARA 412.
3 Ie under the Scheme for Construction Contracts (England and Wales) Regulations 1998, SI 1998/649, Schedule Pt I para 1: see PARA 412.

4 Scheme for Construction Contracts (England and Wales) Regulations 1998, SI 1998/649, Schedule Pt I para 9(3)(a). The procedure is set out in Schedule Pt I paras 2–7: see PARA 413.
5 Scheme for Construction Contracts (England and Wales) Regulations 1998, SI 1998/649, Schedule Pt I para 9(3)(b).
6 Scheme for Construction Contracts (England and Wales) Regulations 1998, SI 1998/649, Schedule Pt I para 9(2). 'Decision' means a decision in relation to the dispute presently being referred to adjudication: *Harding t/a MJ Harding Contractors v Paice* [2015] EWCA Civ 1231, [2016] 1 WLR 4068, [2015] All ER (D) 11 (Dec).
7 As to the referral notice see PARA 413.
8 Scheme for Construction Contracts (England and Wales) Regulations 1998, SI 1998/649, Schedule Pt I para 9(4). Subject to any contractual provision pursuant to the Housing Grants, Construction and Regeneration Act 1996 s 108A(2) (see PARA 422), the adjudicator may determine how the payment is to be apportioned and the parties are jointly and severally liable for any sum which remains outstanding following the making of any such determination: Scheme for Construction Contracts (England and Wales) Regulations 1998, SI 1998/649, Schedule Pt I para 9(4) (amended by SI 2011/1715 (Wales); SI 2011/2333 (England)).
9 Scheme for Construction Contracts (England and Wales) Regulations 1998, SI 1998/649, Schedule Pt I para 11(1).
10 Scheme for Construction Contracts (England and Wales) Regulations 1998, SI 1998/649, Schedule Pt I para 11(1). Subject to any contractual provision pursuant to the Housing Grants, Construction and Regeneration Act 1996 s 108A(2) (see PARA 422), the adjudicator may determine how the payment is to be apportioned and the parties are jointly and severally liable for any sum which remains outstanding following the making of any such determination: Scheme for Construction Contracts (England and Wales) Regulations 1998, SI 1998/649, Schedule Pt I para 11(1) (amended by SI 2011/1715 (Wales); SI 2011/2333 (England)).
11 Scheme for Construction Contracts (England and Wales) Regulations 1998, SI 1998/649, Schedule Pt I para 11(2).

415. Powers of the adjudicator.

The adjudicator must act impartially in carrying out his duties and must do so in accordance with any relevant terms of the contract and must reach his decision in accordance with the applicable law in relation to the contract[1]. He must also avoid incurring unnecessary expense[2].

The adjudicator may take the initiative in ascertaining the facts and the law necessary to determine the dispute, and must decide on the procedure to be followed in the adjudication[3]. In particular he may:

(1)   request any party to the contract to supply him with such documents as he may reasonably require including, if he so directs, any written statement from any party to the contract supporting or supplementing the referral notice[4] and certain[5] other documents[6];

(2)   decide the language or languages to be used in the adjudication and whether a translation of any document is to be provided and if so by whom[7];

(3)   meet and question any of the parties to the contract and their representatives[8];

(4)   subject to obtaining any necessary consent from a third party or parties, make such site visits and inspections as he considers appropriate, whether accompanied by the parties or not[9];

(5)   subject to obtaining any necessary consent from a third party or parties, carry out any tests or experiments[10];

(6)   obtain and consider such representations and submissions as he requires, and, provided he has notified the parties of his intention, appoint experts, assessors or legal advisers[11];

(7)   give directions as to the timetable for the adjudication, any deadlines, or limits as to the length of written documents or oral representations to be complied with[12]; and

(8)   issue other directions relating to the conduct of the adjudication[13].

The parties must comply with any request or direction of the adjudicator in relation to the adjudication[14]. If, without showing sufficient cause, a party fails to comply with any request, direction or timetable of the adjudicator made in accordance with his powers, or fails to produce any document or written statement requested by the adjudicator, or in any other way fails to comply with a requirement under these provisions relating to the adjudication, the adjudicator may[15]: (a) continue the adjudication in the absence of that party or of the document or written statement requested[16]; (b) draw such inferences from that failure to comply as the circumstances may, in the adjudicator's opinion, justify[17]; and (c) make a decision on the basis of the information before him attaching such weight as he thinks fit to any evidence submitted to him outside any period he may have requested or directed[18].

The adjudicator must consider any relevant information submitted to him by any of the parties to the dispute and must make available to them any information to be taken into account in reaching his decision[19]. The adjudicator and any party to the dispute must not disclose to any other person any information or document provided to him in connection with the adjudication which the party supplying it has indicated is to be treated as confidential, except to the extent that it is necessary for the purposes of, or in connection with, the adjudication[20].

Subject to any agreement between the parties to the contrary, any party to the dispute may be assisted by, or represented by, such advisers or representatives, whether legally qualified or not, as he considers appropriate[21]. However, where the adjudicator is considering oral evidence or representations, a party to the dispute may not be represented by more than one person, unless the adjudicator gives directions to the contrary[22].

1   Scheme for Construction Contracts (England and Wales) Regulations 1998, SI 1998/649, reg 2, Schedule Pt I para 12(a). As to the application of the scheme for construction contracts see PARA 411.
2   Scheme for Construction Contracts (England and Wales) Regulations 1998, SI 1998/649, Schedule Pt I para 12(b).
3   Scheme for Construction Contracts (England and Wales) Regulations 1998, SI 1998/649, Schedule Pt I para 13.
4   As to the referral notice see PARA 413.
5   Ie documents given under the Scheme for Construction Contracts (England and Wales) Regulations 1998, SI 1998/649, Schedule Pt I para 7(2): see PARA 413.
6   Scheme for Construction Contracts (England and Wales) Regulations 1998, SI 1998/649, Schedule Pt I para 13(a).
7   Scheme for Construction Contracts (England and Wales) Regulations 1998, SI 1998/649, Schedule Pt I para 13(b).
8   Scheme for Construction Contracts (England and Wales) Regulations 1998, SI 1998/649, Schedule Pt I para 13(c).
9   Scheme for Construction Contracts (England and Wales) Regulations 1998, SI 1998/649, Schedule Pt I para 13(d).
10 Scheme for Construction Contracts (England and Wales) Regulations 1998, SI 1998/649, Schedule Pt I para 13(e).
11 Scheme for Construction Contracts (England and Wales) Regulations 1998, SI 1998/649, Schedule Pt I para 13(f).
12 Scheme for Construction Contracts (England and Wales) Regulations 1998, SI 1998/649, Schedule Pt I para 13(g).
13 Scheme for Construction Contracts (England and Wales) Regulations 1998, SI 1998/649, Schedule Pt I para 13(h).
14 Scheme for Construction Contracts (England and Wales) Regulations 1998, SI 1998/649, Schedule Pt I para 14.
15 Scheme for Construction Contracts (England and Wales) Regulations 1998, SI 1998/649, Schedule Pt I para 15.

16 Scheme for Construction Contracts (England and Wales) Regulations 1998, SI 1998/649, Schedule Pt I para 15(a).
17 Scheme for Construction Contracts (England and Wales) Regulations 1998, SI 1998/649, Schedule Pt I para 15(b) (amended by SI 2011/1715 (Wales); SI 2011/2333 (England)).
18 Scheme for Construction Contracts (England and Wales) Regulations 1998, SI 1998/649, Schedule Pt I para 15(c).
19 Scheme for Construction Contracts (England and Wales) Regulations 1998, SI 1998/649, Schedule Pt I para 17.
20 Scheme for Construction Contracts (England and Wales) Regulations 1998, SI 1998/649, Schedule Pt I para 18.
21 Scheme for Construction Contracts (England and Wales) Regulations 1998, SI 1998/649, Schedule Pt I para 16(1).
22 Scheme for Construction Contracts (England and Wales) Regulations 1998, SI 1998/649, Schedule Pt I para 16(2).

416. Adjudicator's decision.

The adjudicator must decide the matters in dispute[1]. He may take into account any other matters which the parties to the dispute agree should be within the scope of the adjudication or which are matters under the contract which he considers are necessarily connected with the dispute[2]. In particular, he may:

(1)   open up, revise and review any decision taken or any certificate given by any person referred to in the contract unless the contract states that the decision or certificate is final and conclusive[3];

(2)   decide that any of the parties to the dispute is liable to make a payment under the contract (whether in sterling or some other currency) and when[4] that payment is due and the final date for payment[5];

(3)   having regard to any term of the contract relating to the payment of interest decide the circumstances in which, and the rates at which, and the periods for which, simple or compound rates of interest must be paid[6].

The adjudicator must reach his decision not later than: (a) 28 days after receipt of the referral notice[7]; or (b) 42 days after receipt of the referral notice if the referring party so consents[8]; or (c) such period exceeding 28 days after receipt of the referral notice as the parties to the dispute may, after the giving of that notice, agree[9]. Where the adjudicator fails, for any reason, to reach a decision: (i) any of the parties to the dispute may serve a fresh notice of intention to seek adjudication[10] and must request an adjudicator to act in accordance with the relevant provisions[11] of the scheme for construction contracts[12]; and (ii) if requested by the new adjudicator and in so far as it is reasonably practicable, the parties must supply him with copies of all documents which they had made available to the previous adjudicator[13].

As soon as possible after he has reached a decision, the adjudicator must deliver a copy of that decision to each of the parties to the contract[14]. If requested by one of the parties to the dispute, the adjudicator must provide reasons for his decision[15].

The decision of the adjudicator is binding on the parties, and they must comply with it until the dispute is finally determined by legal proceedings, or by arbitration[16] (if the contract provides for arbitration or the parties otherwise agree to arbitration) or by agreement between the parties[17].

In the absence of any directions by the adjudicator relating to the time for performance of his decision, the parties are required to comply with any decision of the adjudicator immediately on delivery of the decision to the parties[18].

The adjudicator is entitled to the payment of such reasonable amount as he may determine by way of fees and expenses reasonably incurred by him[19].

The adjudicator is not liable for anything done or omitted in the discharge or purported discharge of his functions as adjudicator unless the act or omission is in bad faith, and any employee or agent of the adjudicator is similarly protected from liability[20].

1   Scheme for Construction Contracts (England and Wales) Regulations 1998, SI 1998/649, reg 2, Schedule Pt I para 20. As to the application of the scheme for construction contracts see PARA 411.

2   Scheme for Construction Contracts (England and Wales) Regulations 1998, SI 1998/649, Schedule Pt I para 20.

3   Scheme for Construction Contracts (England and Wales) Regulations 1998, SI 1998/649, Schedule Pt I para 20(a).

4   Ie subject to the Housing Grants, Construction and Regeneration Act 1996 s 111(9): see PARA 355.

5   Scheme for Construction Contracts (England and Wales) Regulations 1998, SI 1998/649, Schedule Pt I para 20(b) (amended by SI 2011/1715 (Wales); SI 2011/2333 (England)).

6   Scheme for Construction Contracts (England and Wales) Regulations 1998, SI 1998/649, Schedule Pt I para 20(c).

7   Scheme for Construction Contracts (England and Wales) Regulations 1998, SI 1998/649, Schedule Pt I para 19(1)(a) (amended by SI 2011/1715 (Wales); SI 2011/2333 (England)). The reference to the referral notice in the text is a reference to the notice mentioned in the Scheme for Construction Contracts (England and Wales) Regulations 1998, SI 1998/649, Schedule Pt I para 7(1) (see PARA 413): Schedule Pt I para 19(1)(a) (as so amended).

8   Scheme for Construction Contracts (England and Wales) Regulations 1998, SI 1998/649, Schedule Pt I para 19(1)(b) (amended by SI 2011/1715 (Wales); SI 2011/2333 (England)). As to the 'referring party' see PARA 412.

9   Scheme for Construction Contracts (England and Wales) Regulations 1998, SI 1998/649, Schedule Pt I para 19(1)(c) (amended by SI 2011/1715 (Wales); SI 2011/2333 (England)). See *AC Yule & Son Ltd v Speedwell Roofing & Cladding Ltd* [2007] EWHC 1360 (TCC), [2007] BLR 499, [2007] All ER (D) 100 (Jul) (party acquiesced to extension of time by failing to challenge adjudicator's intention to provide decision at later date). Cf *Lee v Chartered Properties (Building) Ltd* [2010] EWHC 1540 (TCC), [2010] BLR 500, [2010] All ER (D) 112 (Jul) (adjudicator's decision unenforceable as he failed to deliver a copy to the parties within the applicable time limit).

10 Ie under the Scheme for Construction Contracts (England and Wales) Regulations 1998, SI 1998/649, Schedule Pt I para 1: see PARA 412.

11 Ie the Scheme for Construction Contracts (England and Wales) Regulations 1998, SI 1998/649, Schedule Pt I paras 2–7: see PARA 413.

12 Scheme for Construction Contracts (England and Wales) Regulations 1998, SI 1998/649, Schedule Pt I para 19(2)(a).

13 Scheme for Construction Contracts (England and Wales) Regulations 1998, SI 1998/649, Schedule Pt I para 19(2)(b).

14 Scheme for Construction Contracts (England and Wales) Regulations 1998, SI 1998/649, Schedule Pt I para 19(3). See *Lee v Chartered Properties (Building) Ltd* [2010] EWHC 1540 (TCC), [2010] BLR 500, [2010] All ER (D) 112 (Jul).

15 Scheme for Construction Contracts (England and Wales) Regulations 1998, SI 1998/649, Schedule Pt I para 22.

16 As to arbitration see PARA 398 et seq.

17 Scheme for Construction Contracts (England and Wales) Regulations 1998, SI 1998/649, Schedule Pt I para 23(2). Unlike the determination made in typical arbitration proceedings, an adjudicator's decision is not final and binding, and neither his nomination nor his decision gives rise to an estoppel preventing a party from referring a dispute to the court or to arbitration: *Herschel Engineering Ltd v Breen Property Ltd* [2000] BLR 272, 70 Con LR 1 (distinguished from *Trustees of the Marc Gilbard 2009 Settlement Trust v OD Developments and Projects Ltd* [2015] EWHC 70 (TCC), 159 ConLR 150, [2015] All ER (D) 194 (Jan)).

18 Scheme for Construction Contracts (England and Wales) Regulations 1998, SI 1998/649, Schedule Pt I para 21.

19 Scheme for Construction Contracts (England and Wales) Regulations 1998, SI 1998/649, Schedule Pt I para 25. Subject to any contractual provision pursuant to the Housing Grants, Construction and Regeneration Act 1996 s 108A(2) (see PARA 422), the adjudicator may determine how the payment is to be apportioned and the parties are jointly and severally liable for any sum which remains outstanding following the making of any such determination: Scheme for Construction

Contracts (England and Wales) Regulations 1998, SI 1998/649, Schedule Pt I para 25 (amended by SI 2011/1715 (Wales); SI 2011/2333 (England)).

An adjudicator who fails to produce an enforceable decision determining the matters in dispute is not entitled to his fees: *PC Harrington Contractors Ltd v Systech International Ltd* [2012] EWCA Civ 1371, [2013] 2 All ER 69.

20 Scheme for Construction Contracts (England and Wales) Regulations 1998, SI 1998/649, Schedule Pt I para 26.

(iv) Enforcement of Adjudicator's Decision

417. Jurisdiction of adjudicator.

It is open to a defendant in enforcement proceedings to challenge the decision of an adjudicator on the grounds that he was not empowered by the Housing Grants, Construction and Regeneration Act 1996 to make the decision[1]. For example, a decision purportedly made under the statutory provisions relating to the binding nature of an adjudicator's decision[2] by an adjudicator in respect of a contract which is not a construction contract[3] at all, or which is a construction contract entered into before Part II of the Housing Grants, Construction and Regeneration Act 1996[4] came into force[5], is not a decision within the meaning of that Act[6] and is, therefore, not binding on the parties[7].

An adjudicator has jurisdiction over a broad dispute where a narrower dispute has already been adjudicated, but must take care not to override the first decision[8]. A contract avoided on the grounds of duress renders any adjudication provisions void and an adjudicator would therefore have no jurisdiction[9].

Where parties invite the adjudicator to decide the question of jurisdiction they will be bound by his decision[10], but they will not be so bound if they participate in the adjudication expressly without prejudice to a jurisdictional objection[11]. Participation in an adjudication without objection may estop a party from arguing subsequently that the adjudicator lacked jurisdiction[12].

If an adjudicator's decision properly addresses more than one dispute, a successful jurisdictional challenge or allegation that there had been non-compliance with the rules of natural justice in relation to that part of the decision which deals with one such dispute or difference will not undermine the validity and enforceability of that part of the decision that deals with others, subject to the proviso that, if the decision, as drafted, is simply not severable in practice, or if the breach of the rules of natural justice is so severe or all-pervading that the remainder of the decision is tainted, it will not be enforced[13].

Disputes over the jurisdiction of an adjudicator are dealt with in the Technology and Construction Court[14]. It can sometimes be appropriate to seek a declaration as to jurisdiction at the outset of an adjudication, rather than both parties incurring considerable costs in the adjudication itself, only for the jurisdiction point to emerge again at the enforcement hearing[15].

1 *Project Consultancy Group v Trustees of Gray Trust* [1999] BLR 377 at 380 per Dyson J. See, for example, *Edmund Nuttall Ltd v RG Carter Ltd* [2002] EWHC 400 (TCC), [2002] BLR 312, 82 Con LR 24; *Carillion Construction Ltd v Smith* [2011] EWHC 2910 (TCC), (2012) 141 ConLR 117, [2011] All ER (D) 121 (Dec); *Wales and West Utilities Ltd v PPS Pipeline Systems GmbH* [2014] EWHC 54 (TCC), [2014] All ER (D) 215 (Jan). As to enforcement of the decision see PARA 418 et seq.

2 Ie under the Housing Grants, Construction and Regeneration Act 1996 s 108(3): see PARA 410.

3 Ie a 'construction contract' as defined in the Housing Grants, Construction and Regeneration Act 1996: see PARA 210. See *Cleveland Bridge (UK) Ltd v Whessoe-Volker Stevin Joint Venture* [2010] EWHC 1076 (TCC), [2010] BLR 415, 130 Con LR 159 (an adjudicator's decision was unenforceable where part of the dispute concerned 'construction operations' and was therefore within the adjudicator's jurisdiction, but part fell within the exception in the Housing Grants,

Construction and Regeneration Act 1996 s 105(2)). See also *Severfield (UK) Ltd v Duro Felguera UK Ltd* [2015] EWHC 3352 (TCC), 163 ConLR 235, [2015] All ER (D) 256 (Nov); *Equitix ESI CHP (Wrexham) Ltd v Bester Generacion UK Ltd* [2018] EWHC 177 (TCC), [2018] All ER (D) 57 (Feb).

4 Ie the Housing Grants, Construction and Regeneration Act 1996 Pt II (ss 104–117).

5 The Housing Grants, Construction and Regeneration Act 1996 ss 104, 105, 106, 108, 114, so far as conferring the power to consult, to make orders, regulations or determinations, to give directions, guidance, approvals or consents, to specify matters, or to impose conditions, were brought into force on 11 September 1996 (see the Housing Grants, Construction and Regeneration Act 1996 (Commencement No 1) Order 1996, SI 1996/2352) and were brought into force for all remaining purposes on 1 May 1998 (see the Housing Grants, Construction and Regeneration Act 1996 (England and Wales) (Commencement No 4) Order 1998, SI 1998/650).

6 Ie within the meaning of the Housing Grants, Construction and Regeneration Act 1996 s 108(3): see PARA 410.

7 *Project Consultancy Group v Trustees of Gray Trust* [1999] BLR 377 at 380 per Dyson J.

8 *Balfour Beatty Engineering Services (HY) Ltd v Shepherd Construction Ltd* [2009] EWHC 2218 (TCC), (2009) 127 Con LR 110, [2009] All ER (D) 125 (Oct) (applied in *Allied P & L Ltd v Paradigm Housing Group Ltd* [2009] EWHC 2890 (TCC), [2010] BLR 59, [2009] All ER (D) 240 (Nov)).

9 *Capital Structures plc v Time & Tide Construction Ltd* [2006] BLR 226, [2006] All ER (D) 98 (Mar); applying *Heyman v Darwins Ltd* [1942] AC 356, [1942] 1 All ER 337, HL.

10 *Whiteways Contractors (Sussex) Ltd v Impresa Castelli Construction UK Ltd* (2000) 75 Con LR 92, 16 Const LJ 453 (doubted in *Harris Calnan Construction Co Ltd v Ridgewood (Kensington) Ltd* [2007] EWHC 2738 (TCC), [2008] Bus LR 636, [2007] EWHC 2738 (TCC)). See also *Homer Burgess Ltd v Chirex (Aman) Ltd* [2000] BLR 124, 71 Con LR 245, Ct of Sess, where it was held that although the adjudicator must address the question of whether a particular dispute arose under a construction contract as a preliminary issue, since a decision of the adjudicator is binding only when it relates to matters of dispute arising under the construction contract, his decision as to whether a particular dispute, or aspect of a dispute, fell within his jurisdiction was not a decision which is binding on the parties. An adjudicator has no jurisdiction to determine whether he has jurisdiction except in limited circumstances: *Ecovision Systems Ltd v Vinci Construction UK Ltd* [2015] EWHC 587 (TCC), [2015] All ER (D) 160 (Mar).

11 See *Project Consultancy Group v Trustees of the Gray Trust* [1999] BLR 377; cf *Nordot Engineering Services plc v Siemens plc* [2001] CILL 1778; *Allied P & L Ltd v Paradigm Housing Group Ltd* [2009] EWHC 2890 (TCC), [2010] BLR 59, [2009] All ER (D) 240 (Nov); *Pilon Ltd v Breyer Group plc* [2010] EWHC 837 (TCC), 130 Con LR 90, [2010] BLR 452; *Aedifice Partnership Ltd v Shah* [2010] EWHC 2106 (TCC), 132 Con LR 100, [2010] All ER (D) 65 (Aug); *ZVI Construction Co LLC v University of Notre Dame (USA) in England* [2016] EWHC 1924 (TCC), 167 ConLR 237, [2016] All ER (D) 68 (Sep).

12 *Maymac Environmental Services Ltd v Faraday Building Services Ltd* (2000) 75 Con LR 101, [2000] CILL 1685.

13 *Cantillon Ltd v Urvasco Ltd* [2008] EWHC 282 (TCC), 117 Con LR 1, [2008] BLR 250, (adjudicator's jurisdiction extended to addressing consequences of defendant's defence). See also *Brim Construction Ltd v A2M Developments Ltd* [2013] EWHC 3262 (TCC), [2013] All ER (D) 317 (Oct). It is wrong in principle to suggest that a dispute has not arisen until every last particular of every last element of the claim has been provided: *AMD Environmental Ltd v Cumberland Construction Co Ltd* [2016] EWHC 285 (TCC), [2016] All ER (D) 169 (Feb).

14 Technology and Construction Court Guide para 9.4. The Technology and Construction Court Guide is available at the date, at which this volume states the law, on the government website.

15 Technology and Construction Court Guide para 9.4.1. As to enforcement of the adjudicator's decision see PARAS 416, 418 et seq.

418. Enforcement.

The courts will generally enforce any decision made by an adjudicator within his jurisdiction[1]. The scheme for construction contracts[2] makes provision in relation to the enforcement of the adjudicator's decision[3], but apart from that, the usual remedy for failure to pay in accordance with such a decision is to issue proceedings claiming the sum due, followed by an application for summary judgment[4].

The court has held that the following matters do not constitute valid grounds for refusing summary judgment or granting a stay of execution:

(1)   the existence of a possible substantial counterclaim[5];
(2)   the alleged impecuniosity of the party which is referring the dispute to adjudication[6];
(3)   an erroneous decision by the adjudicator acting within his jurisdiction[7];
(4)   a defence based upon an alleged breach of the right to a fair trial under the Convention for the Protection of Human Rights and Fundamental Freedoms (1950)[8].

However, summary enforcement has been refused or a stay of execution has been granted where:

(a)   the issues raised could not be resolved by summary process since the defendant had a real prospect of showing that the adjudicator lacked jurisdiction to make his decision, and was questioning whether the contract had ever been concluded[9];
(b)   the party referring the matter to adjudication is in liquidation at the date of the application for summary judgment so that the provisions relating to mutual credits and set-off[10] apply, and all claims and cross claims should be resolved in the liquidation[11];
(c)   the adjudicator has proceeded in breach of the rules of natural justice[12].
(d)   the evidence demonstrated a real risk that the judgment would go unsatisfied by reason of the claimant organising its financial affairs with the purpose of dissipating or disposing of the adjudication sum so that it would not be available to be repaid[13].

1   As to the jurisdiction of the adjudicator see PARA 417. As to the Technology and Construction Court's role in enforcement see PARA 421. The enforcement of an adjudicator's award is not subject to the terms of the contract: *Levolux AT Ltd v Ferson Contractors Ltd* [2003] EWCA Civ 11, [2003] 1 All ER (Comm) 385, (2003) 86 Con LR 98.
2   Ie a 'construction contract' as defined in the Housing Grants, Construction and Regeneration Act 1996: see PARA 210.
3   See PARA 416.
4   See *Macob Civil Engineering Ltd v Morrison Construction Ltd* [1999] BLR 93 at 100, [1999] CILL 1470 at 1472 per Dyson J. See also *Outwing Construction Ltd v H Randell* [1999] BLR 156, 64 Con LR 59; *David McLean Housing Contractors Ltd v Swansea Housing Association Ltd* [2002] BLR 125, [2001] All ER (D) 519 (Jul). See also *CIB Properties Ltd v Birse Construction* [2005] EWHC 2365 (TCC), [2005] 1 WLR 2252, [2005] BLR 173; *Redworth Construction Ltd v Brookdale Healthcare Ltd* [2006] EWHC 1994 (TCC), [2006] BLR 366, 110 Con LR 77; *Balfour Beatty Construction Northern Ltd v Modus Corovest (Blackpool) Ltd* [2008] EWHC 3029 (TCC), [2008] All ER (D) 157 (Dec); *Hart v Smith* [2009] EWHC 2223 (TCC), [2009] NLJR 1296, [2009] All ER (D) 29 (Sep); *Ritchie Brothers (PWC) Ltd v David Philp (Commercials) Ltd* [2005] CSIH 32, [2005] BLR 384, 2005 SC 384 (adjudicator's jurisdiction ceased on expiry of time limit); *Workspace Management Ltd v YJL London Ltd* [2009] EWHC 2017 (TCC), [2009] BLR 497, [2009] All ER (D) 119 (Aug) (unjust to allow employer to enforce payment in respect of court costs without taking into account cross-claim based on adjudicator's decision regarding interim certificate); *Squibb Group Ltd v Vertase FLI Ltd* [2012] EWHC 1958 (TCC), [2013] BLR 11, [2012] All ER (D) 151 (Jul); *Dawnus Construction Holdings Ltd v Marsh Life Ltd* [2017] EWHC 1066 (TCC), [2017] All ER (D) 87 (May).
5   *A & D Maintenance & Construction Ltd v Pagehurst Construction Services Ltd* (1999) 16 Const LJ 199, [1999] CILL 1518.
6   *Absolute Rentals Ltd v Gencor Enterprises Ltd* [2000] CILL 1637; cf *Rainford House td v Cadogan Ltd* [2001] BLR 416, [2001] All ER (D) 144 (Feb).
7   As to mistakes by an adjudicator see PARA 419.
8   Ie the Convention for the Protection of Human Rights and Fundamental Freedoms (Rome, 4 November 1950; TS 71 (1953); Cmd 8969) art 6: see PARA 420; and RIGHTS AND FREEDOMS vol 88A (2018) PARA 307 et seq. As to the jurisdiction of the adjudicator see PARA 417.
9   See *Project Consultancy Group v Trustees of the Gray Trust* [1999] BLR 377, 65 Con LR 146.

10 Ie under the Insolvency (England and Wales) Rules 2016, SI 2016/1024, r 14.25 (see COMPANY
   AND PARTNERSHIP INSOLVENCY vol 17 (2017)PARA 683. See also *Enterprise Managed Services
   Ltd v Tony McFadden Utilities Ltd* [2009] EWHC 3222 (TCC), [2010] BLR 89, [2010] All ER (D)
   126 (Apr).
11 See *Bouygues (UK) Ltd v Dahl-Jensen (UK) Ltd* [2000] BLR 522, [2001] 1 All ER (Comm) 1041,
   73 Con LR 135, CA. Where a party is subject to a company voluntary arrangement, it is important
   to consider whether the arrangement is in any way due to failure of the other party to pay sums
   awarded: *Mead General Building Ltd v Dartmoor Properties Ltd* [2009] EWHC 200 (TCC),
   [2009] BLR 225, [2009] All ER (D) 224 (Mar) (company voluntary arrangement direct result of
   defendant's failure to pay).
12 See PARA 420. As to natural justice generally see JUDICIAL REVIEW vol 61 (2010) PARA 629 et
   seq.
13 *Gosvenor London Ltd v Aygun Aluminium UK Ltd* [2018] EWHC 227 (TCC), [2018] All ER (D)
   17 (Apr).

419. Mistakes by the adjudicator.

Where the adjudicator's award contains an error, the award stands and is
enforceable[1] as long as the adjudicator made the error while acting within his
jurisdiction[2]. If the adjudicator decided a dispute that was referred to him, but his
decision was mistaken, then his decision is a valid and binding decision even if the
mistake was of fundamental importance[3].

The adjudicator may on his own initiative or on the application of a party
correct his decision so as to remove a clerical or typographical error arising by
accident or omission[4]. Any correction of a decision must be made within five days
of the delivery of the decision to the parties[5], and as soon as possible after so
correcting a decision, the adjudicator must deliver a copy of the corrected decision
to each of the parties to the contract[6]. Any correction of a decision forms part of
the decision[7].

1 As to the enforcement of the adjudicator's decisions see PARAS 416, 418.
2 *Bouygues (UK) Ltd v Dahl-Jensen (UK) Ltd* [2000] BLR 522, [2001] 1 All ER (Comm) 1041, CA;
   Shimizu Europe Ltd v Automajor Ltd [2002] BLR 113, 18 Const LJ 259. See also *Macob Civil
   Engineering Ltd v Morrison Construction Ltd* [1999] BLR 93, [1999] CILL 1470; *C & B Scene
   Concept Design Ltd v Isobars Ltd* [2002] EWCA Civ 46, [2002] BLR 93, 82 Con LR 154; *Ritchie
   Bros (PWC) Ltd v David Philp (Commercials) Ltd* [2005] CSIH 32, [2005] BLR 384, 2005 SLT
   341 (adjudicator's jurisdiction ceased on expiry of time limit). As to the jurisdiction of the
   adjudicator see PARA 417.
3 *Bouygues (UK) Ltd v Dahl-Jensen (UK) Ltd* [2000] BLR 49 at 54, (1999) 70 Con LR 41 at 48 per
   Dyson J; affd [2001] 1 All ER (Comm) 1041, [2000] BLR 522, CA. Where an adjudicator
   misconstrues a statutory provision and consequently makes a decision outside the scope of his
   jurisdiction it is subject to review by the courts and has no temporary binding effect: *Homer
   Burgess Ltd v Chirex (Annan) Ltd* [2000] BLR 124, 2000 SLT 277, Ct of Sess; *Ballast plc v Burrell
   Co (Construction Management) Ltd* [2001] BLR 529, 2001 SLT 1039, Ct of Sess.
4 Scheme for Construction Contracts (England and Wales) Regulations 1998, SI 1998/649, Schedule
   Pt I para 22A(1) (Schedule Pt I para 22A added by SI 2011/1715 (Wales); SI 2011/2333 (England)).
      Before the addition of the Scheme for Construction Contracts (England and Wales)
   Regulations 1998, SI 1998/649, Schedule Pt I para 22A, since neither the adjudication provisions
   of the Housing Grants, Construction and Regeneration Act 1996 (see PARA 410) nor the scheme
   for construction contracts (see PARA 411 et seq) addressed the question of whether a decision, once
   taken, could be amended, in the absence of a specific agreement by the parties to the contrary, a
   term was to be implied into the agreement for adjudication giving the adjudicator the power to
   correct an error arising from an accidental slip or omission in the decision, provided that it was
   done within a reasonable time and without prejudicing the other party: *Bloor Construction (UK)
   Ltd v Bowmer & Kirkland (London) Ltd* [2000] BLR 314. See also *Rok Building Ltd v Celtic
   Composting* [2010] EWHC 66 (TCC), 130 Con LR 74, [2010] All ER (D) 107 (Feb) (the
   adjudicator did not have the right of correction so as to wholly reconsider and re-draft substantive
   parts of his decision).
5 Scheme for Construction Contracts (England and Wales) Regulations 1998, SI 1998/649, Schedule
   Pt I para 22A(2) (as added: see note 4).

6   Scheme for Construction Contracts (England and Wales) Regulations 1998, SI 1998/649, Schedule Pt I para 22A(3) (as added: see note 4).
7   Scheme for Construction Contracts (England and Wales) Regulations 1998, SI 1998/649, Schedule Pt I para 22A(4) (as added: see note 4).

420. Human rights and natural justice.

It has been held that a party resisting summary enforcement is not able to rely on the right to a fair trial[1] under the Convention for the Protection of Human Rights and Fundamental Freedoms (1950)[2]. The right to a fair trial does not apply to an adjudicator's award or adjudication proceedings because they do not involve a final determination[3].

However, an adjudicator is obliged to act impartially[4] and in accordance with the rules of natural justice or as fairly as the limitations imposed by Parliament permit[5]. The court has declined to enforce decisions reached in breach of the rules of natural justice[6], and refused to enforce decisions vitiated by actual or perceived bias[7], failure by the adjudicator to consult one party on important submissions made by the other[8] or participation by the adjudicator in an earlier unsuccessful mediation[9]. However, if an adjudicator declines to consider evidence which, on his analysis of the facts or the law, is irrelevant, that is neither a breach of the rules of natural justice, nor a failure to consider relevant material[10].

1   Ie the Convention for the Protection of Human Rights and Fundamental Freedoms (Rome, 4 November 1950; TS 71 (1953); Cmd 8969) art 6: see RIGHTS AND FREEDOMS vol 88A (2018) PARA 307 et seq.
2   See *Elanay Contracts Ltd v The Vestry* [2001] BLR 33; *Austin Hall Building Ltd v Buckland Securities Ltd* [2001] BLR 272, 80 Con LR 115. Although the Human Rights Act 1998 s 6(1) (see RIGHTS AND FREEDOMS vol 88A (2018) PARA 54) provides that it is unlawful for a public authority to act in a way which is incompatible with a right under the Convention for the Protection of Human Rights and Fundamental Freedoms (1950), an adjudicator under the Housing Grants, Construction and Regeneration Act 1996 is not a public authority for those purposes, and is therefore not bound by it: *Austin Hall Building Ltd v Buckland Securities Ltd* [2001] BLR 272, 80 Con LR 115.
3   See *Elanay Contracts Ltd v The Vestry* [2001] BLR 33.
4   See the Housing Grants, Construction and Regeneration Act 1996 s 108(2)(e); and PARA 410.
5   *Glencot Development and Design Co v Ben Barrett & Son (Contractors) Ltd* [2001] BLR 207 at 218, 80 Con LR 14 at 31 per Judge Lloyd QC; *Discain Project Services Ltd v Opecprime Development Ltd* [2001] BLR 285, 80 Con LR 95. See also *Balfour Beatty Construction Ltd v Lambeth London Borough Council* [2002] BLR 288, 84 Con LR 1; and also *Balfour Beatty Engineering Services (HY) Ltd v Shepherd Construction Ltd* [2009] EWHC 2218 (TCC), 127 Con LR 110, [2009] All ER (D) 125 (Oct) (adverse inference against a party resulting from non-disclosure of documents not a breach of natural justice).
6   See *Discain Project Services Ltd v Opecprime Development Ltd* [2001] BLR 285, 80 Con LR 95. As to disregarding evidence see *Quietfield Ltd v Vascroft Contractors Ltd* [2006] EWHC 174 (TCC), 109 Con LR 29, [2006] All ER (D) 17 (Feb) (affd [2006] EWCA Civ 1737, [2007] BLR 67, 114 Con LR 81) (adjudicator ought to have considered the defendant's entitlement to an extension of time, and, accordingly, the award would not be enforced). See, however, *Kier Regional Ltd (t/a Wallis) v City & General (Holborn)* [2006] EWHC 848 (TCC), [2006] BLR 315, [2006] All ER (D) 64 (Mar); and the text to note 10. In an adjudication a failure to give reasons or to give adequate reasons was not a breach of natural justice: see *Multiplex Constructions (UK) Ltd v West India Quay Development Co (Eastern) Ltd* [2006] EWHC 1569 (TCC), 111 Con LR 33. See also *Balfour Beatty Engineering Services (HY) Ltd v Shepherd Construction Ltd* [2009] EWHC 2218 (TCC), 127 ConLR 110, [2009] NLJR 1475. If an adjudicator places a deliberate, material and erroneous restriction on his jurisdiction (eg by failing to consider the defence to the claim) this amounts to a breach of natural justice: see *Pilon Ltd v Breyer Group plc* [2010] EWHC 837 (TCC), 130 Con LR 90, [2010] BLR 452.
7   See *Discain Project Services Ltd v Opecprime Development Ltd* [2001] BLR 285, 80 Con LR 95; *Woods Hardwick Ltd v Chiltern Air-Conditioning Ltd* [2001] BLR 23. Cf *Fileturn Ltd v Royal Garden Hotel Ltd* [2010] EWHC 1736 (TCC), 131 Con LR 118, [2010] BLR 512.

8   See *Discain Project Services Ltd v Opecprime Development Ltd* [2001] BLR 285, 80 Con LR 95;
    Glencot Development and Design Co Ltd v Ben Barrett & Son (Contractors) Ltd [2001] BLR 207,
    80 Con LR 14.
9   See *Glencot Development and Design Co Ltd v Ben Barrett & Son (Contractors) Ltd* [2001] BLR
    207, 80 Con LR 14.
10 *Kier Regional Ltd (t/a Wallis) v City & General (Holborn)* [2006] EWHC 848 (TCC), [2006] BLR
    315, [2006] All ER (D) 64 (Mar) (the decision by the adjudicator to disregard the evidence was not
    a failure to consider relevant material and was therefore not a breach of justice; decision not
    rendered unenforceable).

421. Enforcement proceedings.

Proceedings for the enforcement of an adjudicator's decision are taken in the
Technology and Construction Court[1]. Enforcement proceedings normally seek a
monetary judgment so that proceedings under Part 7 of the Civil Procedure Rules
are usually appropriate[2]. However, if the enforcement proceedings are known to
raise a question which is unlikely to involve a substantial dispute of fact and no
monetary judgment is sought, CPR Part 8 proceedings may be used instead[3]. It is
intended that enforcement applications before the Technology and Construction
Court are dealt with promptly[4].

1   See the Technology and Construction Court Guide para 9.1. The Technology and Construction
    Court Guide is available at the date, at which this volume states the law, on the government
    website.
2   See the Technology and Construction Court Guide para 9.2.1. As to CPR Pt 7 see CIVIL
    PROCEDURE vol 11 (2015) PARA 139 et seq. See note 3.
3   See the Technology and Construction Court Guide para 9.2. As to CPR Pt 8 see CIVIL
    PROCEDURE vol 11 (2015) PARA 150 et seq. It sometimes happens that one party to an
    adjudication commences enforcement proceedings, whilst the other commences proceedings under
    Pt 8, in order to challenge the validity of the adjudicator's award. This duplication of effort is
    unnecessary and it involves the parties in extra costs so there should be discussions between the
    parties in order to agree the appropriate venue and also to agree who is to be the claimant and who
    is to be the defendant. All the issues raised by each party can and should be raised in a single action:
    Technology and Construction Court Guide para 9.4.3.
4   Technology and Construction Court Guide para 9.2. As to the detailed procedure to be followed
    in enforcement proceedings see the Technology and Construction Court Guide paras 9.2, 9.3.

(v) Costs, Fees and Expenses

422. Costs and adjudicator's fees and expenses.

Whether an adjudicator has jurisdiction to determine liability for the costs of
the parties to the adjudication depends upon the proper construction of any
relevant contractual terms or applicable adjudication rules[1]. There is no power in
the scheme for construction contracts[2] for the adjudicator to award costs between
the parties, and, in general, the adjudicator has no jurisdiction to award such
costs, but it has been held that he may be given such jurisdiction by an implied
agreement between the parties[3].

The adjudicator may not impose a lien on his decision or reasons and refuse to
deliver it pending the payment of his fees[4].

Any contractual provision made between the parties to a construction contract
which concerns the allocation as between those parties of costs relating to the
adjudication of a dispute arising under the construction contract is ineffective
unless: (1) it is made in writing, is contained in the construction contract and
confers power on the adjudicator to allocate his fees and expenses as between the

parties[5]; or (2) it is made in writing after the giving of notice of intention to refer the dispute to adjudication[6].

1   See *Bridgeway Construction Ltd v Tolent Construction Ltd* [2000] CILL 1662. See also *Cubitt Building and Interiors Ltd v Fleetglade Ltd* [2006] EWHC 3413 (TCC), 110 Con LR 36, [2007] All ER (D) 268 (Jan) (applied in *Costain Ltd v Tarmac Holdings Ltd* [2017] EWHC 319 (TCC)), [2017] 2 All ER (Comm) 645, 1 Lloyd's Rep 331).

2   Ie a 'construction contract' as defined in the Housing Grants, Construction and Regeneration Act 1996: see PARA 210. The scheme is contained in the Scheme for Construction Contracts (England and Wales) Regulations 1998, SI 1998/649: see PARAS 358, 411–416.

3   *Northern Developments (Cumbria) Ltd v J & J Nichol* [2000] BLR 158, [2000] All ER (D) 68; cf *John Cothliff Ltd v Allen Build (North West) Ltd* [1999] CILL 1530. See also *John Roberts Architects Ltd v Parkcare Homes (No 2) Ltd* [2006] EWCA Civ 64, [2006] BLR 106, 105 Con LR 36; *Yuanda (UK) Co Ltd v WW Gear Construction Ltd* [2010] EWHC 720 (TCC), [2011] 1 All ER (Comm) 550; *Clark Electrical Ltd v JMD Developments (UK) Ltd* [2012] EWHC 2627 (TCC), [2012] BLR 546, [2012] All ER (D) 181 (Sep) (no ad hoc agreement amounting to submission to jurisdiction of adjudicator); *TSG Building Services plc v South Anglia Housing Ltd* [2013] EWHC 1151 (TCC), [2013] BLR 484, [2013] All ER (D) 102 (May). As to liability for costs see generally CIVIL PROCEDURE vol 12A (2015) PARA 1680 et seq.

4   *Mott MacDonald Ltd v London & Regional Properties Ltd* [2007] EWHC 1055 (TCC), 113 Con LR 33, [2007] All ER (D) 431 (May) (making it a condition of his appointment that his fees would first have to be paid by the referring party might indicate a lack of impartiality).

5   Housing Grants, Construction and Regeneration Act 1996 s 108A(1) (added by the Local Democracy, Economic Development and Construction Act 2009 s 141).

6   Housing Grants, Construction and Regeneration Act 1996 s 108A(2) (as added: see note 5).

(4) Alternative Dispute Resolution

423.   The role of the Technology and Construction Court in ADR.

Alternative dispute resolution ('ADR') includes any voluntary process through which the parties attempt to resolve their dispute[1]. In most cases, ADR takes the form of inter-party negotiations or a mediation conducted by a neutral mediator. Alternative forms of ADR include early neutral evaluation either by a judge or some other neutral person who receives a concise presentation from each party and then provides his or her own evaluation of the case[2]. Although the Technology and Construction Court is an appropriate forum for the resolution of all construction and engineering disputes, the use of ADR can lead to a significant saving of costs and may result in a settlement which is satisfactory to all parties[3]. ADR may be appropriate before the proceedings have begun or at any subsequent stage[4].

The Technology and Construction Court will encourage the parties to use ADR and will, whenever appropriate, facilitate the use of such a procedure[5]. In an appropriate case, the court may indicate the type of ADR that it considers suitable, but the decision in this regard must be made by the parties. In most cases, the appropriate ADR procedure will be mediation, but the court will not ordinarily recommend any individual or body to act as mediator or to perform any other ADR procedure[6].

At the end of the trial, there may be costs arguments on the basis that one or more parties unreasonably refused to take part in ADR. The court will determine such issues having regard to all the circumstances of the particular case[7]. It has been held that the factors which might be relevant to the question whether a party had unreasonably refused ADR include (but are not limited to): (1) the true nature of the dispute; (2) the merits of the case; (3) the extent to which other settlement methods had been attempted; (4) whether the costs of the ADR would be disproportionately high; (5) whether any delay in setting up and attending the ADR would have been prejudicial; and (6) whether the ADR had a reasonable prospect of success[8].

1   See the Technology and Construction Court Guide para 7.1.1. The Technology and Construction Court Guide is available at the date, at which this volume states the law, on the government website.
2   See the Technology and Construction Court Guide para 7.1.1.
3   See the Technology and Construction Court Guide para 7.1.2.
4   See the Technology and Construction Court Guide para 7.2.1. However the later ADR takes place, the more the costs which will have been incurred, often unnecessarily. The timing of ADR needs careful consideration: Technology and Construction Court Guide para 7.2.1.
5   See the Technology and Construction Court Guide para 7.1.1.
6   See the Technology and Construction Court Guide paras 7.3.1, 7.3.3.
7   See the Technology and Construction Court Guide para 7.4.1.
8   *Halsey v Milton Keynes General NHS Trust* [2004] EWCA Civ 576, [2004] 4 All ER 920, [2004] 1 WLR 3002.

6. ARCHITECTS AND ENGINEERS

(1) The Professions

(i) In General

424. The professions engaged in building and civil engineering work.
The professional people who may be engaged in building contract work include architects, engineers[1], surveyors and quantity surveyors[2]. Of these, only architects are regulated by statute. An architect[3], who must be registered in the register of architects[4], is one who possesses, with due regard to aesthetic as well as practical considerations, adequate skill and knowledge to enable him to: (1) originate; (2) design and plan; (3) arrange for and supervise the erection of such building or other works calling for skill in design and planning as he might, in the course of his business, reasonably be asked to carry out or in respect of which he offers his services as a specialist[5]. Architects profess in varying degrees to have the knowledge necessary to estimate the probable cost of works to be done and the value of works executed[6], but this knowledge is usually within the province of quantity surveyors. Naval architects are persons who have corresponding qualifications with regard to the construction of ships.

In building and engineering contracts, the term 'engineer' or 'consulting engineer'[7] usually means either a civil engineer or a structural engineer[8]. Whilst no prescribed educational or professional qualifications are necessary in order to practise and be known as an engineer, a chartered civil engineer must be a member of the Institution of Civil Engineers[9]. An engineer who does not belong to a professional body will usually hold himself out as having professional experience and skill in some particular type of engineering works, for example bridges, roads, or docks.

The Provision of Service Regulations 2009 set out the duties of service providers[10] and competent authorities[11] in relation to such service providers[12].

1 As to the general functions of architects and engineers see PARA 204. As to resident engineers see PARA 207.

2 As to surveyors and quantity surveyors see PARAS 205, 488 et seq. On some large contracts, the employer may, in addition, engage a project manager to co-ordinate the work of, and liaise with, the professional team. The duties and liabilities of a project manager will depend upon the terms of his engagement. See *Chesham Properties Ltd v Bucknall Austin Project Management Services Ltd* (1996) 82 BLR 92, (1996) 53 Con LR 1; *Pozzolanic Lytag Ltd v Bryan Hobson Associates* [1999] BLR 267, 63 Con LR 81. As to project managers see PARA 206.

3 The Architects Act 1997 deals with the registration and qualification of architects, but the word 'architect' itself is not defined in the Act. The Act consolidates and replaces a number of enactments relating to architects, namely the Architects (Registration) Act 1931, the Architects (Registration) Act 1934, the Architects Registration Act 1938, and the Architects Registration (Amendment) Act 1969. The Architects Act 1997, except for s 28 (short title, commencement and extent) came into force on 21 July 1997: Architects Act 1997 (Commencement) Order 1997, SI 1997/1672, art 2. The substitution of the Architects Act 1997 for the provisions repealed or revoked by that Act does not affect the continuity of the law: s 27, Sch 2, para 1. Anything done, or having effect as if done (including the making of rules) under or for the purposes of any provision repealed or revoked by the Architects Act 1997, has effect as if done under or for the purposes of any corresponding provision of that Act: Sch 2 para 2. Any reference, express or implied, in that Act or any other enactment, or in any instrument or document, to a provision of that Act is, so far as the context permits, to be read as, according to the context, being or including in relation to times, circumstances and purposes before that Act came into force a reference to the corresponding provision repealed or revoked by that Act: Sch 2 para 3. Any reference, express or implied, in any enactment, or in any instrument or document, to a provision repealed or revoked by the Architects

Act 1997 is, so far as the context permits, to be read as, according to the context, being or including in relation to times, circumstances and purposes after that Act came into force a reference to the corresponding provision of that Act: Sch 2 para 4(1). In particular, where a power conferred by an Act is expressed to be exercisable in relation to enactments contained in an Act passed before or in the same session as the Act conferring the power, the power is also exercisable in relation to provisions of the Architects Act 1997 which reproduces such enactments: Sch 2 para 4(2). Schedule 2 paras 1–4 have effect in place of the Interpretation Act 1978 s 17(2), but are without prejudice to any other provision of that Act: Architects Act 1997 Sch 2 para 5. Transitional provisions relating to the transition from the Housing Grants, Construction and Regeneration Act 1996 Pt III (repealed) to the Architects Act 1997 are contained in Sch 2 paras 6–19.

4   As to the register of architects see PARA 435. As to restrictions on the use of the title of 'architect' see PARA 427.

5   This is the test laid down by the tribunal set up by the Architects Registration Act 1938 s 2 (repealed), and not disapproved in *R v Architects' Registration Tribunal, ex p Jagger* [1945] 2 All ER 131.

6   As to the liability of the architect for want of competent professional skill see PARA 458.

7   'One whose profession is the designing and constructing of works of public utility, such as bridges, roads, canals, railways, harbours, drainage works, gas and water works, etc': Oxford English Dictionary (2nd Edn, 1989). See also the entry relating to 'civil engineer' in the Dictionary of Architecture.

8   Structural engineers have a particular knowledge of modern building materials and of stresses and loadings involved in structures. Other engineers involved in building and engineering contracts include mechanical engineers and electrical engineers.

9   Founded in 1818 and incorporated by royal charter in 1828. See also *Institution of Civil Engineers v IRC* [1932] 1 KB 149, CA; and PARA 425.

10 'Service' means any self-employed economic activity normally provided for remuneration: Provision of Services Regulations 2009, SI 2009/2999, regs 2, 4. As to the services to which the regulations do not apply see reg 2. 'Provider', in relation to a service, means a person who provides, or offers to provide, the service: reg 4.

11 For these purposes, 'competent authority' means a body or authority having supervisory or regulatory functions in the United Kingdom in relation to service activities (and includes in particular a professional body, professional association or other professional organisation, that regulates access to, or the exercise of, a service activity: Provision of Services Regulations 2009, SI 2009/2999, reg 3.

12 See the Provision of Services Regulations 2009, SI 2009/2999, regs 7–11 (service providers to make information available), reg 12 (complaints), regs 13–20 (competent authorities' duties in relation to authorisation schemes), regs 21–22 (requirements which are prohibited or subject to evaluation), regs 23–28 (duties of competent authorities in relation to providers of services provided from another member state), regs 29–30 (recipients of services), regs 31–35 (other duties of competent authorities in relation to providers and recipients), regs 36–37 (provision of information by competent authorities), regs 38 (duty to provide an electronic assistance facility), regs 39–44 (administrative co-operation between EEA states), regs 45–49 (supplementary and miscellaneous provisions).

The regulations implement the European Parliament and Council Directive (EC) 2006/123 (OJ L376, 27.12.2006, p 36) on services in the internal market.

425.   Right to practise in the European Union.

Professions connected with building and engineering are subject to European Union principles and directives relating to freedom of establishment and free movement of workers. A competent authority[1] must not, for any reasons related to professional qualifications, restrict an applicant who moves to the United Kingdom to provide professional services[2]. The competent United Kingdom authority may, however, require, from such an applicant, evidence of professional experience, and completion of an adaptation period or of an aptitude test[3].

Regulations set out the duties of competent authorities in relation to providers of services provided from other member states[4].

1   The competent authorities in the United Kingdom for the regulated professions listed in the European Communities (Recognition of Professional Qualifications) Regulations 2015, SI 2015/2059, are set out in reg 4(1)–(3), Sch 1. The competent authority in another relevant European State in relation to: (1) any document, certificate, attestation of competence, diploma or

qualification; (2) any period of professional experience; or (3) any application, action or decision, is the authority, body or person who under laws, regulations or administrative provisions is authorised in that State to issue, award or recognise the document or information concerned or (as the case may be) to certify the period of professional experience, to receive the application or to take the action or decision: reg 4(5). See also reg 5 (functions of competent authorities).

2　European Communities (Recognition of Professional Qualifications) Regulations 2015, SI 2015/2059, reg 12. The European Communities (Recognition of Professional Qualifications) Regulations 2015, SI 2015/2059, implement in part Council Directive (EC) 2005/36 (OJ L255, 30.9.2005, p 22) on the recognition of professional qualifications. The following professional associations and organisations connected with building and engineering are among those explicitly included in a non-exhaustive list of professional bodies subject to the regulations set out in the European Communities (Recognition of Professional Qualifications) Regulations 2015, SI 2015/2059, Sch 1: the Royal Institution of Chartered Surveyors, the Chartered Institute of Building, the Engineering Council UK, the Institution of Structural Engineers, the Institution of Civil Engineers, the Institution of Engineering and Technology, the Institution of Gas Engineers and Managers, the Institution of Mechanical Engineers, and the Chartered Institution of Building Services Engineers. Absence from the list does not imply that a profession or activity is exempt from the regulations. As to registration as an architect see PARA 431 et seq.

3　See the European Communities (Recognition of Professional Qualifications) Regulations 2015, SI 2015/2059, reg 9. As to the requirements in relation to aptitude tests and adaptation periods see regs 30–34.

4　See the Provision of Services Regulations 2009, SI 2009/2999, regs 23–28 (duties of competent authorities in relation to providers of services provided from another EEA state), regs 39–44 (administrative co-operation between EEA states); and PARA 424. As to the meaning of 'competent authority' in this context see PARA 424 note 11. As to the meanings of 'service' and 'provider' see PARA 424 note 10.

426.　Unfair competition.

Architects and consulting engineers[1] are no longer excluded[2] from the scope of Chapter I of Part I of the Competition Act 1998[3], which prohibits agreements between undertakings which may affect trade within the United Kingdom and have as their object or effect the prevention, restriction or distortion of competition within the United Kingdom[4].

1　See PARA 424.
2　The Competition Act 1998 s 3(1)(d) and Sch 4 were repealed by the Enterprise Act 2002 ss 207, 278(2), Sch 26 as from 1 April 2003: see the Enterprise Act 2002 (Commencement No 2, Transitional and Transitory Provisions) Order 2003, SI 2003/766.
3　Ie the Competition Act 1998 Pt I Ch I (ss 1–16): see COMPETITION vol 18 (2009) PARA 116 et seq.
4　See the Competition Act 1998 s 2(1), (4); and COMPETITION vol 18 (2009) PARA 116.

427.　Restrictions on use of title of 'architect'.

A person must not practise or carry on any business[1] under any name, style or title containing the word 'architect'[2] unless he is a person registered in Part 1 of the register of architects[3] maintained by the Architects Registration Board[4]. A person is not, for the purposes of this restriction, to be treated as not practising by reason only of his being in the employment of another person[5].

The prohibition of the use of the word 'architect' does not affect the use of the designation 'naval architect', 'landscape architect' or 'golfcourse architect'[6], or the validity of any building contract in customary form[7].

The statutory restriction[8] does not prevent a person registered in Part 2 of the register[9] using the title recorded for the person in that part, or any other title that could have been recorded for the person in that part[10].

1　For these purposes, 'business' includes any undertaking which is carried on for gain or reward or in the course of which services are provided otherwise than free of charge: Architects Act 1997 s 20(7).

2 See *Jacobowitz v Wicker* [1956] Crim LR 697, DC (use of the letters 'Dip Inc Arch' was not an offence); *Jones v Hellard* (1998) Independent, 19 March, DC (use of 'FRIBA' by a person no longer a registered architect offering his services as an arbitrator was an offence).
3 As to the register of architects see PARA 435. As to registration in Part 1 of the register see PARAS 436–437.
4 Architects Act 1997 s 20(1) (amended by SI 2008/1331). As to the Architects Registration Board see PARA 431 et seq. See also *R v Breeze* [1973] 2 All ER 1141, [1973] 1 WLR 994, CA, where it was held that a man falsely describing himself as an architect was in breach of the Trade Descriptions Act 1968 s 14(1)(a)(i) (now repealed), but that it was not necessary to decide whether or not s 14 extended to work of a professional character since the defendant lacked the necessary professional qualifications. See also *Jones, ex p Architects Registration Board v R Baden Hellard* (1999) 14 Const LJ 299, where it was held that the words 'produce' or 'business' should not be limited to practise as an architect or the business of architecture but that, even if they were so limited, they would cover practise as an arbitrator in a building dispute.
5 Architects Act 1997 s 20(6).
6 Architects Act 1997 s 20(2).
7 Architects Act 1997 s 20(8). For the use of the title 'architect' by companies, partnerships, etc see PARA 428.
8 Ie the restriction contained in the Architects Act 1997 s 20(1): see the text and note 4.
9 As to the register of architects see PARA 435. As to registration in Part 2 of the register see PARAS 438–439.
10 Architects Act 1997 s 20(5) (substituted by SI 2008/1331).

428. Body corporate, firm or partnership as registered architect.

A body corporate, firm or partnership may carry on business under a name, style or title containing the word 'architect' if the business so far as it relates to architecture is under the control and management of a person registered in Part 1 of the register[1] who does not act at the same time in a similar capacity for any other body corporate, firm or partnership, and if in every premises where such business is carried on it is carried on by or under the supervision of a person registered in Part 1 of the register[2]. Where a partnership has been formed by a group of architects, the liabilities of the partnership and the rights and liabilities of the partners amongst themselves are governed by the general law relating to partnership[3].

There is no maximum limit on the number of members in a partnership or limited partnership, company or association[4].

1 As to the register of architects see PARA 435. As to registration in Part 1 of the register see PARAS 436–437.
2 Architects Act 1997 s 20(3) (amended by SI 2008/1331). The Architects Registration Board may by rules provide that the Architects Act 1997 s 20(3) does not apply in relation to a body corporate, firm or partnership unless it has provided to the Board such information necessary for determining whether s 20(3) applies as may be prescribed: s 20(4). Such rules are not made by statutory instrument and are not recorded in this work. Since members of the Royal Institute of British Architects are no longer prohibited by their Code of Professional Conduct from being directors of public or private companies, architectural services are commonly provided by companies, whose liability is limited. As to the Architects Registration Board see PARA 431 et seq.
3 See generally PARTNERSHIP. As to the right to partnership documents and drawings see PARA 486.
4 See the Regulatory Reform (Removal of 20 Member Limit in Partnerships etc) Order 2002, SI 2002/3203; and PARTNERSHIP vol 79 (2014) PARA 4.

429. Unlawful use of title of 'architect'.

An unregistered person[1] practising or carrying on business under any name, style or title containing the word 'architect' is liable, on summary conviction, to a fine[2].

A person will not, however, be guilty of an offence by reason of the contravention on any particular date of the restrictions on the use of the title 'architect' if the contravention is occasioned by:

(1)   the fact that an application on his part for registration under the Architects Act 1997 had not been granted and notice of the decision not to grant the application had not been duly served under that Act before that date[3]; or

(2)   the removal of his name from the register of architects in circumstances in which notice is required to be served on him and:

    (a)   the notice had not been duly served before that date[4];

    (b)   the time for bringing an appeal against the removal had not expired at that date[5]; or

    (c)   such an appeal had been duly brought but had not been determined before that date[6].

1   As to the meaning of 'registered person' see PARA 435 note 5. 'Person' includes a body of persons corporate or unincorporate: Interpretation Act 1978 s 5, Sch 1. As to the register of architects see PARA 435.

2   See the Architects Act 1997 s 20(1) (see PARA 427), s 21(1). The fine imposed must not exceed level 4 on the standard scale: s 21(1). As to the powers of the magistrates' courts to issue fines on summary conviction see SENTENCING vol 92 (2015) PARA 176.

    A magistrates' court must not try an information for an offence under the Architects Act 1997 s 21(1) unless the information was laid within two years from the time when the offence was committed: see the Magistrates' Courts Act 1980 s 127(1); Architects Act 1997 s 21(4)(a).

3   Architects Act 1997 s 21(2). As to applications for registration in Part 1 of the register see PARA 436. As to the duty to give notice of a refusal of an application for registration see PARA 437.

4   Architects Act 1997 s 21(3)(a). As to the duty to give notice of removal see PARA 444.

5   Architects Act 1997 s 21(3)(b). As to the bringing of appeals see PARA 445.

6   Architects Act 1997 s 21(3)(c).

430. The Design Council Cabe.

In 1999 the Commission for Architecture and the Built Environment ('CABE') replaced the Royal Fine Art Commission which had been established in 1924[1] to influence the quality of public design and architecture[2].

In 2011 the CABE was merged with the Design Council and a subsidiary organisation was formed, the Design Council Cabe[3]. The Design Council Cabe provides independent and expert design consultation to professionals in the built environment[4].

1   The Royal Fine Art Commission was established by royal warrant on 29 May 1924.

2   The former Commission for Architecture and the Built Environment was dissolved and replaced by a statutory corporation with same name on 1 January 2006: see the Clean Neighbourhoods and Environment Act 2005 ss 87, 91; Clean Neighbourhoods and Environment Act 2005 (Commencement No 3) Order 2005, SI 2005/3439.

3   The CABE was dissolved and its property, rights and liabilities transferred to the Secretary of State on 21 January 2012: see the Commission for Architecture and the Built Environment (Dissolution) Order 2012, SI 2012/147; the Clean Neighbourhoods and Environment Act 2005 ss 90–93. As to the Design Council see NATIONAL CULTURAL HERITAGE vol 77 (2016) PARA 960

4   See the Design Council website.

(ii) Architects' Registration

A. THE ARCHITECTS REGISTRATION BOARD

431. Functions and powers of the Architects Registration Board.

The Architects Registration Board[1] is a body corporate[2] and the independent regulator for the architects' profession in the United Kingdom[3]. The Board is responsible for appointing a Registrar of Architects to maintain the register of architects[4]. In relation to professional conduct, the Board is responsible for maintaining a Professional Conduct Committee[5] and devising a code of conduct[6]. The Board has power to establish other committees to discharge any of its functions[7].

The Board may make rules governing its meetings and procedure[8]. It has a common seal which is authenticated in the prescribed[9] manner, and any document purporting to be sealed with the seal authenticated in that manner is receivable as evidence of the particulars stated in it[10].

1   The Architects Registration Board was formerly known as the Architects' Registration Council of the United Kingdom and was established by the Architects (Registration) Act 1931 s 3, Sch 1 (repealed). The Architects' Registration Council was renamed as the Architects Registration Board by the Housing Grants, Construction and Regeneration Act 1996 s 118(1) (repealed). For the transitional provisions in relation to the Board see the Architects Act 1997 s 27, Sch 2.

     Provisions relating to the constitution of the Board are set out in Sch 1. As to the election and appointment of members of the Board, including the election of the chairman see Sch 1 paras 1–3, 7, 8 (Sch 1 paras 2, 3, 6 amended by SI 2008/1331). Specific provision is made regulating the term of office (see the Architects Act 1997 Sch 1 paras 4, 5 (amended by SI 2014/4)) and the filling of casual vacancies among members (see Sch 1 para 6). The Board has power to appoint staff to carry out such duties as it directs: see Sch 1 para 11.

2   Architects Act 1997 s 1.

3   The Board is designated as the competent authority in the United Kingdom for the purposes of the European Parliament and Council Directive (EC) 2005/36 (OJ L255, 30.9.2005, p 22) on the recognition of professional qualifications ('the Directive') so far as relating to architects: see the Architects Act 1997 s 1A; and PARA 433.

4   See PARA 435.

5   See PARA 442.

6   See PARA 441.

7   See the Architects Act 1997 Sch 1 paras 18–21. As to the payment of fees and allowances to the Board and its committees see Sch 1 para 23.

8   Architects Act 1997 Sch 1 para 10. Such rules are not made by statutory instrument and are not recorded in this work. As to the provisions relating to quorum see Sch 1 para 9. The Board, the Professional Conduct Committee and any committee established by the Board may exercise its functions even though there is a vacancy among its members, and no Board or committee proceedings are invalidated by any defect in the election or appointment of a member: Sch 1 para 22.

9   Ie prescribed by rules made by the Board: see the Architects Act 1997 s 25; and note 8.

10 Architects Act 1997 Sch 1 para 12.

432. Power of the Architects Registration Board to make rules.

The Architects Registration Board[1] may make rules[2] generally for carrying out or facilitating the purposes of the Architects Act 1997[3]. The Board must, before making any such rules, publish a draft of them and give those to whom the rules would be applicable an opportunity of making representations to the Board[4]. The Registrar of Architects[5] must on payment of the prescribed[6] charges supply a copy of any rules so made and of any forms prescribed by such rules to any person applying for them[7].

1   As to the functions and powers of the Architects Registration Board see PARA 431.

2 The power to make such rules is not exercisable by statutory instrument and such rules are not recorded in this work.
3 Architects Act 1997 s 23(1).
4 Architects Act 1997 s 23(2).
5 As to the Registrar of Architects see PARA 435.
6 Ie prescribed by rules made by the Board: see the Architects Act 1997 s 25; and note 2.
7 Architects Act 1997 s 23(3).

433. Administrative co-operation and recognition of professional qualifications.

The Architects Registration Board[1] is designated as the competent authority in the United Kingdom[2] for the purposes of the European Parliament and Council Directive on the recognition of professional qualifications ('the Directive')[3] so far as relating to architects[4]. As a competent authority, the Board is able to: (1) issue, or receive, evidence of qualifications or other information or documents; or (2) receive applications, and take the decisions, referred to in the Directive, in connection with the profession of architect[5].

Accordingly, the Board must carry out in the United Kingdom (in particular) the mutual-recognition functions[6] so far as relating to architects[7] and, in its capacity as competent authority for the purposes of the Directive, must work in close collaboration with competent authorities of other relevant European States[8], and it must also provide assistance to competent authorities of other relevant European States in accordance with and in order to facilitate the application of the Directive[9]. In particular, the Board must exchange professional-regulation information[10] about:

(1)　registered persons who are Directive-rights nationals[11]; or
(2)　Directive-rights nationals who have made an application for registration in the register,

with competent authorities of other relevant European States[12].

If in any case the Board receives professional-regulation information from a competent authority of another relevant European State, the Board is responsible for investigating and establishing the position in the case[13], and must also pass on its conclusions in the case to a competent authority in each relevant European State in which the person concerned is established as an architect or (without being established) is providing services as an architect[14].

The Board may make inquiries of registered persons[15] where it considers it necessary to do so for the purposes of enabling it to discharge certain of these duties[16]. Where a registered person receives such inquiries, the person must reply using their best endeavours to assist the Board[17].

Where a competent authority of a relevant European State other than the United Kingdom requests information relevant to the legality of a person's establishment and his good conduct, as well as the absence of any disciplinary or criminal sanctions of a professional nature in respect of a registered architect who is established in the United Kingdom and who wishes to provide services in that relevant European State, the Board must provide that information[18]. The Registrar may make inquiries of registered persons where the Registrar considers it necessary to do so for the purposes of enabling the Board to discharge this duty[19], and where a registered person receives such inquiries the person must reply using their best endeavours to assist the Registrar[20].

The Board must ensure the exchange with other competent authorities of all information necessary for service complaints to be correctly pursued[21].

1 As to the functions and powers of the Architects Registration Board see PARA 431.

2   As to the meaning of 'United Kingdom' see PARA 217 note 3.
3   Ie the European Parliament and Council Directive (EC) 2005/36 (OJ L255, 30.9.2005, p 22) on
    the recognition of professional qualifications ('the Directive'): see the Architects Act 1997 s 25.
    Any reference to the Directive includes (without prejudice to the operation of the Interpretation
    Act 1978 s 20A) a reference to the Directive as extended by the EEA Agreement (see the
    amendments made to that Agreement by Decision of the EEA Joint Committee No 142/2007 on
    26 October 2007), and any reference to an Annex to the Directive is, except where the reference
    to the Directive is to the Directive as extended by the EEA Agreement, a reference to the Annex as
    amended from time to time: Architects Act 1997 s 25 (definition substituted by SI 2008/1331).
4   Architects Act 1997 s 1A(1) (s 1A added by SI 2008/1331). However, this designation does not
    extend to the awarding of degrees, diplomas or other qualifications in architecture: Architects Act
    1997 s 1A(2) (as so added).
5   'Competent authority' means any authority or body designated by a relevant European State for
    the purposes of the Directive as competent to:
       (1)   issue, or receive, evidence of qualifications or other information or documents; or
       (2)   receive applications, and take the decisions, referred to in the Directive,
    in connection with the profession of architect: Architects Act 1997 s 25 (definition substituted
    by SI 2008/1331).
6   For these purposes, 'mutual-recognition functions' means the functions specified in the Directive
    that a Member State, in giving effect to the Directive, must or may cause to become functions of
    the State's competent authorities: Architects Act 1997 s 1A(5) (as added: see note 4).
7   Architects Act 1997 s 1A(3) (as added: see note 4). However, the carrying-out of the following
    functions in the United Kingdom is not entrusted to the Board: (1) the function of awarding
    degrees, diplomas or other qualifications in architecture (s 1A(4)(a) (as so added)); (2) any other
    mutual-recognition functions the carrying out of which, so far as relating to architects, is entrusted
    to the Board or any other person by or under any enactment other than s 1A (s 1A(4)(b) (as so
    added)).
8   Architects Act 1997 s 22B(1)(a) (s 22B added by SI 2008/1331). 'Relevant European State' means
    an EEA State or Switzerland: Architects Act 1997 s 25 (definition added by SI 2008/1331;
    amended by SI 2014/4).
9   Architects Act 1997 s 22B(1)(b) (as added: see note 8). The Board may make inquiries of registered
    persons where the Board considers it necessary to do so for the purposes of enabling it to discharge
    its duties under s 22B(1)(b): s 22B(5) (as so added).
10 'Professional-regulation information' means information regarding:
       (1)   disciplinary action taken,
       (2)   criminal sanctions imposed; or
       (3)   any other serious, specific circumstances,
    where the action is, or the sanctions or circumstances are, likely to have consequences for the
    pursuit of the profession of architect by a person: Architects Act 1997 s 22B(3) (as added: see note
    8).
11 'Directive-rights national' means:
       (1)   a national of a relevant European State other than the United Kingdom;
       (2)   a national of the United Kingdom who is seeking access to, or is pursuing, the profession
             of architect by virtue of an enforceable EU right; or
       (3)   a person who is not a national of a relevant European State but who is, by virtue of an
             enforceable EU right, entitled to be treated, for the purposes of access to and pursuit of
             the profession of architect, no less favourably than a national of a relevant European
             State,
    but does not include a person who, by virtue of Article 2 of Protocol No 3 (Channel Islands
    and Isle of Man) to the Treaty of Accession, is not to benefit from EU provisions relating to the free
    movement of persons and services: Architects Act 1997 s 25 (definition added by SI 2008/1331;
    amended by SI 2011/1043). As to the meaning of 'United Kingdom' see PARA 217 note 3.
12 Architects Act 1997 s 22B(2) (as added: see note 8).
13 Architects Act 1997 s 22B(4)(a) (as added: see note 8). The Board may make inquiries of registered
    persons where the Board considers it necessary to do so for the purposes of enabling it to discharge
    its duties under s 22B(4)(a): s 22B(5) (as so added).
14 Architects Act 1997 s 22B(4)(b) (as added: see note 8).
15 'Registered person' means a person whose name is in the register: Architects Act 1997 s 25.
16 Ie its duties under the Architects Act 1997 s 22B(1)(b) (see the text and note 9) and s 22B(4)(a) (see
    the text and note 13).

17 Architects Act 1997 s 22B(6) (as added: see note 8). The power to make inquiries of registered persons under s 22B(5) is not to be taken to prejudice any other power to make inquiries of registered persons: s 22B(7) (as so added).

18 Ie in accordance with the provisions of Art 56 of the Directive: Architects Act 1997 s 5D(1), (2) (s 5D added by SI 2008/1331).

19 Architects Act 1997 s 5D(3) (as added: see note 18). The power to make inquiries under s 5D(3) is not to be taken to prejudice any other power to make inquiries of registered persons: s 5D(5) (as so added). As to the Registrar of Architects see PARA 435.

20 Architects Act 1997 s 5D(4) (as added: see note 18).

21 Architects Act 1997 s 5E(2) (s 5E added by SI 2008/1331). 'Service complaint' means a complaint by a recipient of services made against a person in respect of services provided, by that person as an architect on a temporary and occasional basis (see PARA 438), in any relevant European State other than the relevant European State where that person is lawfully established as an architect: Architects Act 1997 s 5E(1) (as so added). Where the Registrar knows the outcome of a service complaint but it appears to the Registrar that the person who made the complaint does not or may not know the outcome, the Registrar must inform the person of the outcome of the complaint: s 5E(3) (as so added).

434. Duty not to disclose information.

The Architects Registration Board[1], the Registrar of Architects[2], and persons acting on behalf of either of them, are prohibited from disclosing information[3] if:

(1)   the information is received in the course of the carrying-out of functions of the Board or the Registrar[4];

(2)   the functions are functions under the European Parliament and Council Directive on the recognition of professional qualifications ('the Directive')[5] or under any enactment giving effect to the Directive[6]; and

(3)   the information is provided by a competent authority[7] of another relevant European State[8], or relates to an application made by a Directive-rights national[9] for registration in the register of architects[10].

This prohibition on disclosure of information, however, does not apply to disclosure which is to the Secretary of State, or which is necessary in order to facilitate the carrying-out of functions of the Board, or of functions of the Registrar, under the Architects Act 1997 or any other enactment[11].

The Board and the Registrar must, so far as it is within their power to do so, ensure the confidentiality of information which, in the course of the carrying-out of their functions under the Directive or under any enactment giving effect to the Directive, is disclosed by or on behalf of the Board or the Registrar to a competent authority of another relevant European State[12].

1 As to the Architects Registration Board see PARA 431.

2 As to the Registrar of Architects see PARA 435.

3 Architects Act 1997 s 22C(1) (s 22C added by SI 2008/1331).

4 Architects Act 1997 s 22C(2)(a) (as added: see note 3).

5 Ie the European Parliament and Council Directive (EC) 2005/36 (OJ L255, 30.9.2005, p 22) on the recognition of professional qualifications. See also PARA 433 note 3.

6 Architects Act 1997 s 22C(2)(b) (as added: see note 3).

7 As to the meaning of 'competent authority' see PARA 433 note 5.

8 As to the meaning of 'relevant European State' see PARA 433 note 8.

9 As to the meaning of 'Directive-rights national' see PARA 433 note 11.

10 Architects Act 1997 s 22C(2)(c) (as added: see note 3).

11 Architects Act 1997 s 22C(3) (as added: see note 3). As to the functions of the Board see PARA 431. As to the functions of the Registrar see PARA 435.

12 Architects Act 1997 s 22C(4), (5) (as added: see note 3).

(A)   Introduction

435.   The register of architects and the Registrar.

The Architects Registration Board[1] must appoint a person to be known as the Registrar of Architects[2], and the period for which, and the terms on which, the Registrar is appointed are decided by the Board[3]. The Registrar has the functions provided by or by virtue of the Architects Act 1997 and any other functions which the Board directs[4].

The Registrar must maintain the register of architects, in which there must be entered the name of every person entitled to be registered[5]. The register consists of two parts (known as Part 1 and Part 2[6]) and there are different criteria for eligibility to be registered in each part[7].

The register must show the regular business address of each registered person[8]. The Registrar must make any necessary alterations to the register and, in particular, must remove from the register the name of any registered person who has died or has applied in the prescribed[9] manner requesting the removal of his name[10].

The Board must publish the current version of the register annually and a copy of the most recently published version must be provided to any person who requests one on payment of a reasonable charge decided by the Board[11]. A copy of the register purporting to be published by the Board is evidence of any matter mentioned in it[12]. A certificate purporting to be signed by the Registrar which states that a person: (1) is registered[13]; (2) is not registered[14]; (3) was registered on a specified date or during a specified period[15]; (4) was not registered on a specified date or during a specified period[16]; or (5) has never been registered[17], is evidence of any matter stated[18].

1   As to the Architects Registration Board see PARA 431.
2   Architects Act 1997 s 2(1).
3   Architects Act 1997 s 2(2). The Board may, in addition to paying to the Registrar a salary or fees, pay pensions to or in respect of him, or make contributions to the payment of such pensions, and pay him allowances, expenses and gratuities: s 2(4).
4   Architects Act 1997 s 2(3). Where functions of a competent authority under the European Parliament and Council Directive (EC) 2005/36 (OJ L255, 30.9.2005, p 22) on the recognition of professional qualifications ('the Directive') are exercised by the Registrar, he exercises them on behalf of the Board: Architects Act 1997 s 2(3A) (added by SI 2008/1331). See also PARA 433 note 3. As to the meaning of 'competent authority' see PARA 433 note 5.
5   Architects Act 1997 s 3(1). For these purposes, 'registered person' means a person whose name is in the register of architects: s 25. As to the entitlement to be registered see PARA 436 et seq.
6   Architects Act 1997 s 3(1A) (added by SI 2008/1331).
7   As to registration in Part 1 of the register see PARA 436, and as to registration in Part 2 of the register see PARA 438.
8   Architects Act 1997 s 3(2). As to removal from the register following failure to notify a change of address see PARA 437.
9   Ie prescribed by rules made by the Board: see the Architects Act 1997 s 25. Such rules are not made by statutory instrument and are not recorded in this work.
10   Architects Act 1997 s 3(3).
11   Architects Act 1997 s 3(4).
12   Architects Act 1997 s 3(5).
13   Architects Act 1997 s 3(6)(a).
14   Architects Act 1997 s 3(6)(b).
15   Architects Act 1997 s 3(6)(c).
16   Architects Act 1997 s 3(6)(d).
17   Architects Act 1997 s 3(6)(e).
18   Architects Act 1997 s 3(6).

(B)   Part 1 of the register

436.   Registration in Part 1 of the register.

A person who has applied to the Registrar of Architects[1] in the prescribed[2] manner for registration in Part 1 of the register of architects is entitled to be registered if:

(1)   he holds such qualifications and has gained such practical experience as may be prescribed[3]; or

(2)   he has a standard of competence which, in the opinion of the Architects Registration Board[4], is equivalent to that demonstrated by satisfying head (1)[5].

The Board may require a person who applies for registration on the ground that he satisfies head (2) to pass a prescribed examination in architecture[6].

A Directive-rights national[7] is to be treated as having achieved a standard of competence equivalent to that demonstrated by satisfying head (1) if:

(a)   he produces requisite evidence[8] which provides access to the profession of architect in the relevant European State[9] in which that evidence was issued[10];

(b)   he produces to the Registrar a certificate, awarded by a relevant European state other than the United Kingdom, that attests that he is authorised[11] to use the title of architect by reason of being especially distinguished by quality of work in the field of architecture[12]; or

(c)   he is a person to whom certain provisions of the European Union (Recognition of Professional Qualifications) Regulations 2015[13] apply and who is permitted by those regulations to pursue the profession of architect in the United Kingdom (having, in particular, successfully passed any aptitude test that may be required)[14].

Where a person applies for registration in pursuance of these provisions and, in doing so, relies on head (a), (b) or (c), the Registrar may, for the purposes of deciding whether the person is entitled to be registered, demand certain documents[15]. In the event of justified doubts as to whether the person is entitled to be registered[16], the Registrar may require from the competent authorities[17] of a relevant European State confirmation of the authenticity of the attestations and evidence of formal qualifications awarded in that other relevant European State, as well as confirmation of the fact that the person fulfils the minimum training conditions[18]. In case of justified doubt as to whether the person is entitled to be registered, where evidence of formal qualifications has been issued by a competent authority in a relevant European State and includes evidence as to training received in whole or in part in an establishment legally established in the territory of another relevant European state, the Registrar is entitled to verify with the competent authority in the relevant European State of origin of the award whether:

(i)   the training course at the establishment which gave the training has been formally certified by the educational establishment based in the relevant European State of origin of the award[19];

(ii)   the evidence of formal qualifications issued is the same as that which would have been awarded if the course had been followed entirely in the relevant European State of origin of the award[20]; and

(iii)   the evidence of formal qualifications confers the same professional rights in the territory of the relevant European State of origin of the award[21].

Where a person has duly applied for registration[22] if the Registrar is satisfied that the person is entitled to be registered[23], he must enter his name in Part 1 of the register[24], but if the Registrar is not so satisfied, he must refer the application to the Board[25]. The Registrar must not consider an application for registration[26] in any case in which it is inappropriate for him to do so (for instance because he is in any way connected with the applicant) but in such a case he must refer the application to the Board[27]. Where a person's application is referred to the Board[28], the Board must direct the Registrar to enter the person's name in Part 1 of the register if it is satisfied that he is entitled to be registered[29].

A person may appeal to the High Court if he is aggrieved by refusal of his application for registration in Part 1 of the register[30].

A person who is registered in Part 1 of the register[31] in reliance on head (a), (b) or (c)[32], when using his academic title or any abbreviation of it may express the title or abbreviation in the language, or one of the languages, of the relevant European State in which the body conferring the title is located[31]. He must also follow the title or abbreviation with the name and location of the body conferring the title[33].

1 As to the Registrar of Architects see PARA 435.
2 Ie prescribed by rules made by the Architects Registration Board (see note 3): see the Architects Act 1997 s 25.
3 Architects Act 1997 s 4(1)(a) (amended by SI 2008/1331). Before prescribing qualifications or practical experience for the purposes of the Architects Act 1997 s 4(1)(a) the Architects Registration Board (see note 4) must consult the bodies representative of architects which are incorporated by royal charter and such other professional and educational bodies as it thinks appropriate: s 4(3).
4 As to the Architects Registration Board see PARA 431 et seq.
5 Architects Act 1997 s 4(1)(b).
6 Architects Act 1997 s 4(2). Before prescribing any examination for the purposes of s 4(2), the Board must consult the bodies representative of architects which are incorporated by royal charter and such other professional and educational bodies as it thinks appropriate: s 4(3). The Board may require a candidate for any examination under s 4(2) to pay a fee of a prescribed amount: s 6(2).
7 As to the meaning of 'Directive-rights national' see PARA 433 note 11.
8 See the Architects Act 1997 s 4A(1) (s 4A added by SI 2008/1331; amended by SI 2016/1088).
9 As to the meaning of 'relevant European State' see PARA 433 note 8.
10 Architects Act 1997 s 4(2A)(a) (s 4(2A) added by SI 2008/1331; s 4(2A)(a) amended by SI 2011/2008). Evidence is to be treated as issued in a relevant European State if it is issued in a country (or former country) whose territory at any time consisted of, or included, the whole or part of the territory of that State: Architects Act 1997 s 4(7) (added by SI 2008/1331).
     Where a Directive-rights national applies to be registered in Part 1 of the register and, in doing so, relies on the Architects Act 1997 s 4(2A), the Board must: (1) acknowledge receipt of the application within one month of receipt; and (2) inform the applicant of any missing document required for the purposes of the application: s 6(3B) (added by SI 2008/1331).
11 Ie that attests that Art 48(2) of the European Parliament and Council Directive (EC) 2005/36 (OJ L255, 30.9.2005, p 22) on the recognition of professional qualifications ('the Directive') applies to him.
12 Architects Act 1997 s 4(2A)(b) (as added: see note 10).
13 Ie the European Communities (Recognition of Professional Qualifications) Regulations 2015, SI 2015/2059: see note 14.
14 Architects Act 1997 s 4(2A)(c) (as added (see note 10); and amended by SI 2016/1088). For these purposes the applicant must demonstrate that he is a person:
     (1)   whose case falls within the European Union (Recognition of Professional Qualifications) Regulations 2015, SI 2015/2059, reg 3(8)(a), (b), (c) or (e) (see the Architects Act 1997 s 4(2A)(c)(i) (as so added and amended));
     (2)   to whom the European Union (Recognition of Professional Qualifications) Regulations 2015, SI 2015/2059, regs 27–34 apply by reason of operation of reg 3(5) (see the Architects Act 1997 s 4(2A)(c)(ii) (as so added and amended)); and
     (3)   who is permitted to pursue the profession of architect in the United Kingdom by virtue of the European Union (Recognition of Professional Qualifications) Regulations 2015,

SI 2015/2059, Pt 3 (having, in particular, successfully passed any aptitude test that he may be required to undertake pursuant to that Part) (see the Architects Act 1997 s 4(2A)(c)(iii) (as so added and amended)).

The Board may require an applicant for registration in Part 1 of the register to pay a fee for taking an aptitude test which the applicant is required by the Board to take under the European Union (Recognition of Professional Qualifications) Regulations 2015, SI 2015/2059, reg 32: see the Architects Act 1997 s 6(2A) (added by SI 2008/1331; amended by SI 2016/1088).

15 The Registrar may demand any documents within Annex VII to the Directive and may, where the demand relates to a document within point 1(d), (e) or (f) of that Annex, treat the demand as unsatisfied if the document submitted to the Registrar in response to the demand is more than three months old when submitted: Architects Act 1997 s 4A(2)(a) (as added: see note 8).
16 Ie in pursuance of the Architects Act 1997 s 4.
17 As to the meaning of 'competent authority' see PARA 433 note 5.
18 Architects Act 1997 s 4A(2)(b) (as added: see note 8). The minimum training conditions referred to in the text are those set out in Art 46 of the Directive (including training which is, under Art 22(a), to be treated as meeting those conditions): see the Architects Act 1997 s 4A(2)(b).
19 Architects Act 1997 s 4A(2)(c)(i) (as added: see note 8).
20 Architects Act 1997 s 4A(2)(c)(ii) (as added: see note 8).
21 Architects Act 1997 s 4A(2)(c)(iii) (as added: see note 8).
22 Ie in pursuance of the Architects Act 1997 s 4.
23 Ie in pursuance of the Architects Act 1997 s 4.
24 Architects Act 1997 s 4(4)(a) (amended by SI 2008/1331).
25 Architects Act 1997 s 4(4)(b).
26 Ie in pursuance of the Architects Act 1997 s 4.
27 Architects Act 1997 s 4(5).
28 Ie under the Architects Act 1997 s 4(4) (see the text and notes 24–25) or s 4(5) (see the text and note 27).
29 Architects Act 1997 s 4(6) (amended by SI 2008/1331).
30 See the Architects Act 1997 s 22; and PARA 445.
31 Ie in pursuance of the Architects Act 1997 s 4.
32 Architects Act 1997 s 4A(3) (as added: see note 8).
31 Architects Act 1997 s 4A(4)(a) (as added: see note 8).
33 Architects Act 1997 s 4A(4)(b) (as added: see note 8).

437. Fees and continuation of registration in Part 1 of the register.

The Architect's Registration Board[1] may require an applicant for registration in Part 1 of the register of architects[2] to pay a fee of a prescribed amount[3]. The Board may prescribe the information and evidence to be provided to the Registrar of Architects[4] in connection with applications for registration in Part 1 of the register[5].

Where a person requests the Board to issue a certificate of architectural education confirming that the person's training as an architect:

(1)   meets the minimum training conditions[6];

(2)   gives that person entitlement[7] to be registered in Part 1 of the register; or

(3)   includes prescribed or equivalent qualifications,

the Board may issue such a certificate to that person if the training does meet those conditions, gives that entitlement or includes those qualifications[8]. The Board may require a person making such a request to pay a fee of a prescribed amount[9].

The Registrar must deal expeditiously with all applications for registration[10]. He must serve on an applicant for registration in Part 1 of the register written notice of the decision on his application[11]. A person may appeal to the High Court if he is aggrieved by the failure of the Registrar to comply with this requirement[12]. Notice of a refusal in the case of an application by a Directive-rights national[13] must state reasons for the refusal[14].

The Board may require a registered person to pay a retention fee of a prescribed amount if he wishes his name to be retained in Part 1 of the register in any calendar year after that in which it was entered[15]. Where, after the Registrar has sent a registered person who is liable to pay a retention fee a written demand for the payment of the fee, the person fails to pay the fee within the prescribed period, the Registrar may remove the person's name from Part 1 of the register[16]. Where a person whose name has been so removed from Part 1 of the register pays the retention fee, together with any further prescribed fee, before the end of the calendar year for which the retention fee is payable or such longer period as the Board may allow: (a) his name will be re-entered in Part 1 of the register, without his having to make[17] an application[18]; and (b) if the Board so directs, it is to be treated as having been re-entered on the date on which it was removed[19].

Where the Registrar serves notice in writing on a registered person asking if he has changed his regular business address, if no answer is received within six months from the sending of the notice, the Registrar must serve further written notice on him, and if no answer is received within three months from the sending of the further notice, the Registrar may remove his name from Part 1 of the register[20].

Where the Board is not satisfied that a person who: (i) applies[21] for registration[22]; (ii) wishes his name to be retained or re-entered[23] in Part 1 of the register after the payment of a retention fee[24]; or (iii) applies for his name to be re-entered in Part 1 of the register[25] after it has been removed following an erasure order[26], has gained such recent practical experience as the Board may prescribe, his name must not be entered or re-entered in Part 1 of the register, or must be removed from it, unless he satisfies the Board of his competence to practise[27]. A person may appeal to the High Court if he is aggrieved by his name not being re-entered in, or his name being removed from, Part 1 of the register by virtue of these provisions[28].

1   As to the Architects Registration Board see PARA 431 et seq.
2   As to the register of architects see PARA 435. As to registration in Part 1 of the register see PARA 436.
3   Architects Act 1997 s 6(1) (amended by SI 2008/1331). Fees may also be charged for examinations and aptitude tests: see the Architects Act 1997 s 6(2), (2A); and PARA 436 notes 6, 14. 'Prescribed' means prescribed by rules made by the Board: see s 25. Such rules are not made by statutory instrument and are not recorded in this work.
4   As to the Registrar of Architects see PARA 435.
5   Architects Act 1997 s 6(3) (amended by SI 2008/1331). The reference in the Architects Act 1997 s 6(3) to an application for registration in Part 1 of the register does not include an application for registration in that Part made by a Directive-rights national who, in making the application, relies on the Architects Act 1997 4(2A) (see PARA 436): s 6(3A) (added by SI 2008/1331).
6   Ie the minimum training conditions in Art 46 of the European Parliament and Council Directive (EC) 2005/36 (OJ L255, 30.9.2005, p 22) on the recognition of professional qualifications ('the Directive'). See also PARA 433 note 3.
7   Ie under the Architects Act 1997 s 4: see PARA 436.
8   Architects Act 1997 s 6A(1) (s 6A added by SI 2008/1331).
9   Architects Act 1997 s 6A(2) (as added: see note 8). As to the prescription of fees see note 3.
10   Architects Act 1997 s 6(3C) (added by SI 2008/1331). As to applications for registration in Part 1 of the register see PARA 436.
11   Architects Act 1997 s 6(4) (substituted by SI 2002/2842; amended by SI 2008/1331). The written notice must be served (in the case of an application by a person who in making the application: (1) relies on the Architects Act 1997 s 4(1)(a) (see PARA 436) without also relying on s 4(2A) (see PARA 436); or (2) relies on s 4(2A)) within three months beginning with the date on which the application is made: s 6(4A)(a) (s 6(4A) added by SI 2002/2842; and substituted by SI 2008/1331). In any other case, it must be served within six months beginning with the date on which the application is made: Architects Act 1997 s 6(4A)(b) (as so added).

12 See the Architects Act 1997 s 22; and PARA 445.

13 Ie an application by a person who in making the application relies on the Architects Act 1997 s 4(2A): see PARA 436. As to the meaning of 'Directive-rights national' see PARA 433 note 11.

14 Architects Act 1997 s 6(4B) (added by SI 2002/2842; and amended by SI 2008/1331).

15 Architects Act 1997 s 8(1) (amended by SI 2008/1331).

16 Architects Act 1997 s 8(2) (amended by SI 2008/1331).

17 Ie under the Architects Act 1997 s 4: see PARA 436.

18 Architects Act 1997 s 8(3)(a) (amended by SI 2008/1331).

19 Architects Act 1997 s 8(3)(b).

20 Architects Act 1997 s 11 (amended by SI 2008/1331). The notice must be sent by post as a registered letter: Architects Act 1997 s 24(2).

21 Ie in pursuance of the Architects Act 1997 s 4: see PARA 436.

22 Architects Act 1997 s 9(1)(a) (amended by SI 2008/1331).

23 Ie under the Architects Act 1997 s 8: see the text to notes 15–19.

24 Architects Act 1997 s 9(1)(b) (amended by SI 2008/1331). Where the Board decides that the name of a person to whom the Architects Act 1997 s 9(1)(b) applies is to be removed from, or not to be re-entered in, Part 1 of the register, the Registrar must serve written notice of the decision on him within the prescribed period after the date of the decision: s 9(2) (amended by SI 2008/1331). The notice must be sent by post as a registered letter: s 24(2).

25 Ie under the Architects Act 1997 s 18: see PARA 444.

26 Architects Act 1997 s 9(1)(c) (amended by SI 2008/1331).

27 Architects Act 1997 s 9(1) (amended by SI 2008/1331).

28 See the Architects Act 1997 s 22; and PARA 445.

(C) Part 2 of the Register

438. Registration in Part 2 of the register.

Persons lawfully established as an architect in a relevant European State[1] and wishing to provide services in the United Kingdom[2] on a temporary and occasional basis may apply to be registered in Part 2 of the register of architects[3].

A visiting practitioner[4] who proposes to provide occasional services[5] for the first time is entitled to be registered in Part 2 of the register if the practitioner sends or produces to the Registrar of Architects[6] the required declaration[7], and the other required documents[8]. The Registrar may refuse to give effect to this entitlement if, even though there is at least one other State[9] in which the visiting practitioner is lawfully established as an architect, and is not prohibited (even temporarily) from practising as an architect, there is also at least one other State where a disqualifying decision[10] is in force in respect of the practitioner[11].

Where a person seeks registration in Part 2 of the register, re-registration in that Part or continuation of registration in that Part[12], the Registrar may ask the competent authorities of the relevant European State where that person is established as an architect, for each provision of services, to provide information relevant to the legality of that person's establishment and his good conduct, as well as the absence of any disciplinary or criminal sanctions of a professional nature[13].

Where a person is registered in Part 2 of the register, the Registrar must record the person's professional title against the person's name in that Part of the register[14]. If the person satisfies the Registrar that the person would be entitled to be registered in Part 1 of the register were the person to apply to be registered in that Part[15], the professional title to be recorded for the person is 'architect'[16]. In any other case the professional title to be recorded for the person is to be as it is in the relevant European State in which the person is established as an architect[17].

If a person is entitled to be registered in Part 2 of the register and his professional title falls to be recorded in that Part of the register as just described[18], then before that person provides any services as an architect in the United Kingdom to another person, he must give the intended recipient of his services specified information in writing[19].

1   As to the meaning of 'relevant European State' see PARA 433 note 8.

2   As to the meaning of 'United Kingdom' see PARA 217 note 3.

3   Architects Act 1997 s 5A(1), Sch 1A para 1 (s 5A and Sch 1A both added by SI 2008/1331). There is no charge for registration in Part 2 of the register: Architects Act 1997 s 5A(2) (as so added). As to the register see PARA 435. As to the entitlement to be registered in respect of the provision of occasional services after the first year of registration see PARA 439.

4   'Visiting practitioner' means a person to whom the Architects Act 1997 Sch 1A applies (being a Directive-rights national who is lawfully established as an architect in a relevant European State other than the United Kingdom): Sch 1A paras 1, 2(1) (as added: see note 3). As to the meaning of 'Directive-rights national' see PARA 433 note 11.

5   A reference to the provision of occasional services is a reference to the provision in the United Kingdom, on a temporary and occasional basis, of services as an architect: Architects Act 1997 Sch 1A para 2(1) (as added: see note 3). Where it falls to be assessed whether the provision of services is on a temporary and occasional basis, the temporary and occasional nature of the provision of the services is to be assessed case by case, in particular in relation to its duration, its frequency, its regularity and its continuity: Sch 1A para 2(2), (3) (as so added).

6   As to the Registrar of Architects see PARA 435.

7   The 'required declaration' is a written declaration that: (1) states the practitioner's wish to provide occasional services; and (2) contains details of the insurance cover, or other means of personal or collective protection, that the practitioner has with regard to professional liability: Architects Act 1997 Sch 1A para 3(3) (as added: see note 3). Such a declaration may be supplied by any means: Sch 1A para 3(5) (as so added).

8   Architects Act 1997 Sch 1A para 3(1) (as added: see note 3). The 'other required documents' are:

    (1)   if the practitioner is a national of a relevant European State, proof of nationality (Sch 1A para 3(4)(a) (as so added));

    (2)   if the practitioner is not a national of a relevant European State, proof of the Community right by virtue of which the practitioner is a Directive-rights national (Sch 1A para 3(4)(b) (as so added));

    (3)   evidence certifying successful completion of any professional training undertaken by the practitioner that is relevant to practise as an architect (Sch 1A para 3(4)(c) (as so added));

    (4)   evidence of any actual and lawful pursuit of the profession of architect undertaken by the practitioner in any relevant European State (Sch 1A para 3(4)(d) (as so added));

    (5)   a certificate (or certificates) issued by a competent authority in the practitioner's home State confirming: (a) that the practitioner is lawfully established as an architect in that State; and (b) that the practitioner is not prohibited (whether on a permanent or temporary basis) from practising as an architect there (Sch 1A para 3(4)(e) (as so added)).

9   For these purposes, 'other State' means a relevant European State other than the United Kingdom: Architects Act 1997 Sch 1A para 3(2) (as added: see note 3).

10   'Disqualifying decision', in relation to any person, means a decision which (1) is made by a competent authority of a relevant European State other than the United Kingdom; and (2) has the effect in that State that the person is no longer lawfully established as an architect there or that the person is prohibited (even temporarily) from practising as an architect there: Architects Act 1997 s 25 (definition substituted by SI 2008/1331). As to the meaning of 'competent authority' see PARA 433 note 5.

11   Architects Act 1997 Sch 1A para 3(2) (as added: see note 3).

12   As to re-registration and continuation of registration see PARA 439.

13   Architects Act 1997 s 5D(1) (s 5D added by SI 2008/1331). As to administrative co-operation between competent authorities see PARA 433.

14   Architects Act 1997 s 5B(1) (s 5B added by SI 2008/1331).

15   As to registration in Part 1 of the register see PARA 436.

16   Architects Act 1997 s 5B(2) (as added: see note 14).

17 Architects Act 1997 s 5B(3)(a) (as added: see note 14). That title is to be recorded in the official language, or one of the official languages, of that State: s 5B(3)(b) (as so added). If the title that is to be recorded in accordance with s 5B(3)(a), (b) is 'architect' or is confusingly similar to 'architect', the title to be recorded for the person is to be that title followed by the name of that State in brackets: s 5B(3)(c) (as so added).

18 Ie in accordance with the Architects Act 1997 s 5B(3): see the text and note 17.

19 Architects Act 1997 s 5C(1) (s 5C added by SI 2008/1331). Before the person provides any services as an architect in the United Kingdom he must supply the following information in writing (see the Architects Act 1997 s 5C(2) (as so added)):

    (1)   if the person is registered in a commercial register or similar public register, the register in which he is registered, his registration number, or equivalent means of identification contained in that register (s 5C(2)(a) (as so added));

    (2)   if the activity is subject to authorisation in the relevant European State in which the person is established, the name and address of the competent supervisory authority (s 5C(2)(b) (as so added));

    (3)   any professional association or similar body with which the person is registered (s 5C(2)(c) (as so added));

    (4)   the person's professional title or, where no such title exists, his formal qualification and the State in which it was awarded (s 5C(2)(d) (as so added));

    (5)   if the person performs an activity which is subject to VAT, the VAT identification number (s 5C(2)(e) (as so added)); and

    (6)   details of any insurance cover or other means of personal or collective protection with regard to professional liability which the person has (s 5C(2)(f) (as so added)).

439. Renewal and duration of registration in Part 2 of the register.

Where a visiting practitioner[1] wishes to provide occasional services[2] after the first year of registration in Part 2 of the register of architects[3], the practitioner may apply for renewal of registration[4]. Where the Registrar of Architects[5] receives the required renewal documents[6] from a visiting practitioner who is entitled to be registered in Part 2 of the register[7], the visiting practitioner continues to be entitled to be registered in Part 2 of the register[8] and the Registrar must give effect to the entitlement[9]. Where the Registrar receives the required renewal documents from a visiting practitioner who is not entitled to be registered in Part 2 of the register, but who has been previously entitled to be registered in that Part[10], then the visiting practitioner is once again entitled to be registered in Part 2 of the register[11], and the Registrar must give effect to the entitlement[12].

Unless an entitlement to be registered in Part 2 of the register[13] is continued (or further continued)[14], the entitlement ceases at the end of the year that begins with the day after the day on which the Registrar received the documents whose receipt gave rise to the entitlement[15]. However, where an entitlement to be registered is continued (or further continued), the entitlement is extended so as to cease at the end of the year that begins with the day after the relevant day[16].

An entitlement to be registered in Part 2 of the register ceases if:

    (1)   the visiting practitioner concerned becomes established in the United Kingdom as an architect[17]; or

    (2)   it becomes the case that the practitioner is not lawfully established as an architect in any of the other States[18], or the practitioner is prohibited (on a permanent or temporary basis) from practising as an architect in each other State in which the practitioner is lawfully established as an architect[19].

The Registrar has power to remove the name of any person registered in Part 2 of the register[20] where a person's entitlement to be registered in Part 2 of the register ceases[21]. Where a visiting practitioner is lawfully established as an architect in a relevant European State other than the United Kingdom and is not prohibited (whether on a permanent or temporary basis) from practising as an architect there, and a disqualifying decision[22] is made against the practitioner in a different relevant European State that is not the United Kingdom, the Registrar may remove the person's name from Part 2 of the register[23]. These provisions[24] do not prejudice the application of any other provisions of the Architects Act 1997 under which a person's name may be removed from Part 2 of the register[25].

A visiting practitioner who is entitled to be registered in Part 2 of the register, but who is not registered in that Part, is to be treated as registered in that Part[26].

Where the Registrar receives documents from a person and it appears to the Registrar:

(a) that the documents were sent or produced to the Registrar for the purpose of establishing that the person is entitled to be registered, to continue to be registered or once again to be registered in Part 2 of the register, but

(b) that the person is not so entitled,

the Registrar must, as soon as may be reasonably practicable after the Registrar comes to be of that view, serve on the person written notice that the Registrar is of that view[27].

1 As to the meaning of 'visiting practitioner' see PARA 438 note 4.
2 As to occasional services see PARA 438 note 5.
3 As to the register of architects see PARA 435. As to registration in Part 2 of the register see PARA 438.
4 See the text and notes 5–12. There is no charge for registration in Part 2 of the register: see the Architects Act 1997 s 5A(2); and PARA 438.
5 As to the Registrar of Architects see PARA 435.
6 The 'required renewal documents' are a renewal declaration and each evidence of change document (if any): Architects Act 1997 Sch 1A para 4(6) (Sch 1A added by SI 2008/1331). 'Renewal declaration', in relation to a visiting practitioner, means a written declaration that states the practitioner's wish to provide occasional services in a further year and also contains details of the insurance cover, or other means of personal or collective protection, that the practitioner has with regard to professional liability: Architects Act 1997 Sch 1A para 4(7) (as so added). A renewal declaration may be supplied by any means: Sch 1A para 4(9) (as so added).
   Where a document:
   (1) is, in relation to a visiting practitioner, one of the other required documents for the purposes of Sch 1A para 3(1) (see PARA 438) (Sch 1A para 4(8)(a) (as so added)); and
   (2) substantiates a matter as respects which there has been a material change since the practitioner last (whether under Sch 1A para 3 or Sch 1A para 4) supplied the then current version of the document to the Registrar (Sch 1A para 4(8)(b) (as so added)),
   the version of the document current when the practitioner supplies a renewal declaration to the Registrar is an 'evidence of change' document.
7 Architects Act 1997 Sch 1A para 4(1) (as added: see note 6).
8 Architects Act 1997 Sch 1A para 4(2) (as added: see note 6).
9 Architects Act 1997 Sch 1A para 4(5) (as added: see note 6).
10 Architects Act 1997 Sch 1A para 4(3) (as added: see note 6).
11 Architects Act 1997 Sch 1A para 4(4) (as added: see note 6).
12 Architects Act 1997 Sch 1A para 4(5) (as added: see note 6).
13 Ie an entitlement under the Architects Act 1997 Sch 1A para 3 (see PARA 438) or Sch 1A para 4(4) (see the text and notes 10–12).
14 Ie by the Architects Act 1997 Sch 1A para 4(2) (see the text and notes 5–8).
15 Architects Act 1997 Sch 1A para 5(1) (as added: see note 6).
16 Architects Act 1997 Sch 1A para 5(2) (as added: see note 6). If the day on which the Registrar receives the documents whose receipt gives rise to the continuation (or further continuation) is an anniversary of the start day, the 'relevant day' means the day on which the Registrar receives those documents: Sch 1A para 5(3)(a) (as so added). Otherwise, the 'relevant day' means the anniversary of the start day that is the first such anniversary to occur after the Registrar receives the documents whose receipt gives rise to the continuation (or further continuation): Sch 1A para 5(3)(b) (as so added). The 'start day', in relation to an entitlement to be registered under Sch 1A para 3 or Sch 1A para 4(4), means the day on which the Registrar receives the documents whose receipt gives rise to the entitlement: Sch 1A para 5(4) (as so added).
17 Architects Act 1997 Sch 1A para 5(5)(a) (as added: see note 6). As to the meaning of 'United

Kingdom' see PARA 217 note 3.

18 For these purposes, 'other State' means a relevant European State other than the United Kingdom: Architects Act 1997 Sch 1A para 5(5) (as added: see note 6).

19 Architects Act 1997 Sch 1A para 5(5)(b) (as added: see note 6).

20 Architects Act 1997 Sch 1A para 7(3) (as added: see note 6).

21 Ie by reason of the operation of provisions of the Architects Act 1997 Sch 1A: see Sch 1A para 7(1) (as added: see note 6).

22 As to the meaning of 'disqualifying decision' see PARA 438 note 10.

23 Architects Act 1997 Sch 1A para 7(2) (as added: see note 6).

24 Ie the Architects Act 1997 Sch 1A paras 3–7: see the text and notes above.

25 Architects Act 1997 Sch 1A para 8 (as added: see note 6).

26 Architects Act 1997 Sch 1A para 6 (as added: see note 6).

27 Architects Act 1997 Sch 1A para 9 (as added: see note 6).

(D)   False Representation

440. Penalty for obtaining registration by false representation.

A person commits an offence if he intentionally:

(1)   becomes or attempts to become registered under the Architects Act 1997[1]; or

(2)   makes or produces (or causes to be made or produced) to the Architects Registration Board[2] or the Registrar of Architects[3] anywhere in or outside the United Kingdom[4] any false or fraudulent representation or declaration (whether oral or written)[5].

1 Architects Act 1997 s 7(1)(a) (s 7(1) substituted by SI 2008/1331).

2 As to the Architects Registration Board see PARA 431 et seq.

3 As to the Registrar of Architects see PARA 435.

4 As to the meaning of 'United Kingdom' see PARA 217 note 3.

5 Architects Act 1997 s 7(1)(b), (1A) (s 7(1A) added by SI 2008/1331). A person guilty of an offence under the Architects Act 1997 s 7 is liable on summary conviction to a fine not exceeding level 3 on the standard scale: s 7(2). As to the powers of the magistrates' courts to issue fines on summary conviction see SENTENCING vol 92 (2015) PARA 176.

C.   PROFESSIONAL CONDUCT

441. Code of conduct.

The Architects Registration Board[1] is under a duty to issue a code laying down standards of professional conduct and practice expected of registered persons[2]. The Board must keep the code under review and vary its provisions whenever it considers it appropriate to do so[3]. Before issuing or varying the code, the Board must: (1) consult such professional bodies and such other persons with an interest in architecture as it considers appropriate[4]; and (2) publish in such a manner as it considers appropriate notice that it proposes to issue or vary the code, stating where copies of the proposals can be obtained[5]. The Board must provide a copy of the code to any person who requests one on payment of a reasonable charge decided by the Board, and may provide a copy free of charge whenever it considers it appropriate[6].

Failure by a registered person to comply with the provisions of the code is not to be taken of itself to constitute unacceptable professional conduct[7] or serious professional incompetence on his part[8], but must be taken into account in any proceedings[9], for unacceptable professional conduct or serious professional incompetence, against him[10].

1 As to the Architects Registration Board see PARA 431.

2 Architects Act 1997 s 13(1). As to the meaning of 'registered person' see PARA 435 note 5. The Board may not establish committees to discharge its functions under s 13(1), (2) or s 13(3): see

Sch 1 para 18; and PARA 431.
3   Architects Act 1997 s 13(2). See note 2.
4   Architects Act 1997 s 13(3)(a). See note 2.
5   Architects Act 1997 s 13(3)(b). See note 2.
6   Architects Act 1997 s 13(5).
7   As to the meaning of 'unacceptable professional conduct' see PARA 443.
8   Architects Act 1997 s 13(4)(a).
9   Ie proceedings under the Architects Act 1997 s 14: see PARA 443.
10 Architects Act 1997 s 13(4)(b). As to the Professional Conduct Committee see PARA 442.

442. Professional Conduct Committee.

The Architects Registration Board[1] maintains a Professional Conduct Committee[2] which deals with allegations of unacceptable professional conduct and serious professional negligence[3] and makes disciplinary orders[4].

The Architects Act 1997 contains provisions detailing the constitution of the committee[5]. The committee may exercise its functions even though there is a vacancy among its members[6]. No proceedings of the Committee are invalidated by any defect in the election or appointment of a member[7].

1   As to the Architects Registration Board see PARA 431.
2   See the Architects Act 1997 s 1(2), (4), Sch 1 Pt II.
3   See the Architects Act 1997 s 14; and PARA 443.
4   See the Architects Act 1997 s 15; and PARA 443. The committee sets the standard to be applied by fellow practitioners and unless in a given case it is unreasonable to conclude that that standard has been set properly the court should not interfere: see *Vranicki v Architects Registration Board* [2007] EWHC 506 (Admin), [2007] All ER (D) 288 (Mar). See also *Woodman-Smith v Architects Registration Board* [2014] EWHC 3639 (Admin), [2014] All ER (D) 139 (Nov).
5   Provisions relating to the constitution of the Professional Conduct Committee are set out in Sch 1 para 13 (substituted by SI 2004/655; and amended by SI 2008/1331). As to the election and casting vote of the chairman see the Architects Act 1997 Sch 1 paras 14, 16. Specific provision is made regarding the quorum: see Sch 1 para 15 (amended by SI 2004/655; SI 2008/1331). The Board may make rules governing the selection and term of office of members of the Committee, including casual vacancies: see the Architects Act 1997 Sch 1 para 17. Such rules are not made by statutory instrument and are not recorded in this work.
6   Architects Act 1997 Sch 1 para 22(1).
7   Architects Act 1997 Sch 1 para 22(2).

443. Professional misconduct, incompetence and disciplinary orders.

Where an allegation is made that a registered person[1] is guilty of unacceptable professional conduct, that is, conduct which falls short of the standard required of a registered person, or serious professional incompetence, or it appears to the Registrar of Architects[2] that a registered person may be so guilty, the case must be investigated by persons appointed in accordance with rules made by the Architects Registration Board[3]. Where those persons find that a registered person has a case to answer, they must report their finding to the Professional Conduct Committee[4]. Where the Committee receives such a report in relation to a registered person, it must consider whether he is guilty of unacceptable professional conduct or serious professional incompetence[5]. Before considering whether a registered person is guilty of unacceptable professional conduct or serious professional incompetence, the Committee must serve[6] written notice on the person outlining the case against him and give him the opportunity to appear before the Committee to argue his case[7]. If the Committee is satisfied, after considering the case, that the registered person is guilty of unacceptable professional conduct or serious professional incompetence, it may make a disciplinary order[8], namely: (1) a reprimand[9]; (2) a penalty order[10]; (3) a suspension order[11]; or (4) an erasure order[12].

The Committee may also make a disciplinary order where a registered person has been convicted of a criminal offence other than an offence which has no material relevance to his fitness to practise as an architect[13].

Where the committee makes such an order, the Registrar must serve written notice of the order on him as soon as is reasonably practicable[14]. At appropriate intervals and in such manner as it considers appropriate, the Committee must publish: (a) the names of persons whom it has found guilty of unacceptable professional conduct or serious professional incompetence or in relation to whom it has made a disciplinary order as a result of a person being convicted of a criminal offence other than an offence which has no material relevance to his fitness to practise as an architect[15]; and (b) in the case of each person a description of the conduct, incompetence or offence concerned and the nature of any order made[16]. Where, after considering the case of a registered person, the Committee is not satisfied that he is guilty of unacceptable professional conduct or serious professional incompetence, it must, if he so requests, publish a statement of that fact in such manner as it considers appropriate[17].

Any person aggrieved by the making of a disciplinary order in relation to him may appeal to the High Court[18].

1   As to the meaning of 'registered person' see PARA 435 note 5.
2   As to the Registrar of Architects see PARA 435.
3   Architects Act 1997 s 14(1). Such rules are not made by statutory instrument and are not recorded in this work. If the Board does not make rules for the appointment of persons to investigate whether registered persons have been guilty of unacceptable professional conduct or serious professional incompetence, the Professional Conduct Committee must consider such questions without any prior investigation: s 14(7). As to the Architects Registration Board see PARA 431. As to the Professional Conduct Committee see PARA 442.
4   Architects Act 1997 s 14(2).
5   Architects Act 1997 s 14(3). See *Vranicki v Architects Registration Board* [2007] EWHC 506 (Admin), [2007] All ER (D) 288 (Mar) (serious professional incompetence established).
6   The notice must be sent by post as a registered letter: Architects Act 1997 s 24(2).
7   Architects Act 1997 s 14(4). At any such hearing the registered person is entitled to be legally represented: s 14(5). The Board may make rules as to the procedure to be followed by the Professional Conduct Committee in any proceedings under s 14: s 14(6). Such rules are not made by statutory instrument and are not recorded in this work.
8   Architects Act 1997 s 15(1)(a).
9   Architects Act 1997 s 15(2)(a).
10 Architects Act 1997 s 15(2)(b). Where a penalty order is made the registered person must pay the Board the sum specified in the order: s 16(1). A penalty order may not specify a sum exceeding the amount which, at the relevant time, is the amount specified as level 4 on the standard scale of fines for summary offences: s 16(2). As to the powers of the magistrates' courts to issue fines on summary conviction see SENTENCING vol 92 (2015) PARA 176. The 'relevant time' means: (1) in a case within s 15(1)(a) (see the text to note 8), the time of the conduct or incompetence of which the registered person is found guilty; and (2) in a case within s 15(1)(b) (see the text to note 13), the time when he committed the criminal offence of which he has been convicted: s 16(2). The order must specify the period within which the sum specified in it is to be paid: s 16(3). If the person does not pay the sum specified in the order within the period so specified, the Committee may make a suspension order or an erasure order in relation to him: s 16(4). As to suspension and erasure orders see PARA 444. The Board must pay into the Consolidated Fund any sum paid under a penalty order: s 16(5). As to the Consolidated Fund see CONSTITUTIONAL AND ADMINISTRATIVE LAW vol 20 (2014) PARA 480 et seq.
11 Architects Act 1997 s 15(2)(c).
12 Architects Act 1997 s 15(2)(d).
13 Architects Act 1997 s 15(1)(b). This includes disobedience to a byelaw: *Mellor v Denham* (1880) 5 QBD 467, CA.
14 Architects Act 1997 s 15(3). The notice must be sent by post as a registered letter: s 24(2).
15 Architects Act 1997 s 15(4)(a). The text refers to a disciplinary order being made under s 15(1)(b): see the text to note 13.

16 Architects Act 1997 s 15(4)(b).
17 Architects Act 1997 s 15(5).
18 See the Architects Act 1997 s 22; and PARA 445.

444. Removal of names from register.

The Registrar of Architects[1] will remove the name of a registered person[2] from the register of architects[3] where a suspension order[4] or an erasure order[5] is made by the Professional Conduct Committee[6] in relation to such person[7].

Where a suspension order is made, the Registrar must re-enter the name of the registered person in the register at the end of such period not exceeding two years as is specified in the order[8].

Where an erasure order is made, the name of the registered person must not be re-entered in the register unless the Architects Registration Board[9] so directs[10]. No application may be made for the name of a person in relation to whom an erasure order has been made to be re-entered in the register:

(1)   before the end of the period of two years beginning with the date of the erasure order or such longer period specified in the erasure order as the Committee considers appropriate in a particular case[11]; or

(2)   where he has made a previous application for his name to be re-entered in the register, before the end of the prescribed[12] period beginning with the date of the decision of the Board on that application[13].

The Registrar must serve[14] on a person who applies for his name to be re-entered in the register written notice of the decision on his application within the prescribed period after the date of the decision[15]. The Board may require a person whose name is re-entered in the register to pay a fee of a prescribed amount[16].

The Board may order the Registrar to remove a person's name from Part 1 of the register[17] if:

(a)   the person is a Directive-rights national whose entry in Part 1 of the register was made in reliance on the statutory provision which specifies the evidence required to demonstrate the relevant standard of competence[18];

(b)   at the time when the person's name was entered in Part 1 of the register, there was a disqualifying decision in force in respect of the person in a relevant European State other than the United Kingdom[19];

(c)   at that time the Board was unaware of that fact[20]; and

(d)   the Board is satisfied that the person was at that time and is still subject to that disqualifying decision[21].

The Registrar has power to remove the name of any person registered in Part 2 of the register[22] where the person's entitlement to be registered in Part 2 of the register ceases[23]. He may also remove the person's name from Part 2 of the register where the person is a visiting practitioner[24] lawfully established as an architect in a relevant European State other than the United Kingdom and is not prohibited (whether on a permanent or temporary basis) from practising as an architect there, and a disqualifying decision is made against the practitioner in a different relevant European State that is not the United Kingdom[25].

Any person aggrieved by the Board so ordering the Registrar to remove his name from the register may appeal to the High Court[26].

1   As to the Registrar of Architects see PARA 435.
2   As to the meaning of 'registered person' see PARA 435 note 5.
3   As to the register of architects see PARA 435.
4   See the Architects Act 1997 s 15(2)(c); and PARA 443.

5 See the Architects Act 1997 s 15(2)(d); and PARA 443.
6 As to the Professional Conduct Committee see PARA 442.
7 See the Architects Act 1997 ss 17, 18(1). As to the right of appeal against such an order see PARAS
   443, 445.
8 Architects Act 1997 s 17.
9 As to the Architects Registration Board see PARA 431.
10 Architects Act 1997 s 18(1).
11 Architects Act 1997 s 18(2)(a).
12 Ie prescribed by rules made by the Board: see the Architects Act 1997 s 25. Such rules are not made
   by statutory instrument and are not recorded in this work.
13 Architects Act 1997 s 18(2)(b).
14 As to the service of notices and documents see further PARA 437.
15 Architects Act 1997 s 18(3).
16 Architects Act 1997 s 18(4).
17 As to entry in Part 1 of the register see PARA 436.
18 Ie the person relied on the Architects Act 1997 s 4(2A) (see PARA 436) in making the application
   that led to the person's name being entered in Part 1 of the register: s 10(1)(a) (substituted by
   SI 2008/1331). As to the meaning of 'Directive-rights national' see PARA 433 note 11.
19 Architects Act 1997 s 10(1)(aa) (added by SI 2008/1331). As to the meaning of 'disqualifying
   decision' see PARA 438 note 10. As to the meaning of 'relevant European State' see PARA 433 note
   8. As to the meaning of 'United Kingdom' see PARA 217 note 3.
20 Architects Act 1997 s 10(1)(b).
21 Architects Act 1997 s 10(1)(c). Where the Board orders the Registrar to remove a person's name
   from the register under s 10, the Registrar must serve written notice of the removal on him as soon
   as reasonably practicable: s 10(2). The notice must be sent by post as a registered letter: s 24(2).
22 As to registration in Part 2 of the register see PARA 438.
23 See the Architects Act 1997 Sch 1A para 7(1), (3); and PARA 439.
24 As to the meaning of 'visiting practitioner' see PARA 438 note 4.
25 See the Architects Act 1997 Sch 1A para 7(2), (3); and PARA 439.
26 See the Architects Act 1997 s 22; and PARA 445.

D. APPEALS

445. Appeals under the Architects Act 1997.
A person may appeal to the High Court if he is aggrieved[1] by:
(1)   refusal of his application for registration in Part 1 of the register of
       architects[2];
(2)   failure of the Registrar of Architects[3] to serve on an applicant for
       registration in Part 1 of the register written notice of the decision on his
       application[4];
(3)   his name not being re-entered in, or his name being removed from, Part
       1 of the register (by virtue of the statutory provision[5] relating to
       competence to practise[6]);
(4)   the Architects Registration Board's[7] ordering (under the statutory
       provision relating to disqualification in a relevant European State[8]) that
       the Registrar remove his name from Part 1 of the register[9]; or
(5)   the making of a disciplinary order in relation to him[10].
The High Court sits as a court of appeal and may review the decision of the
Board[11].
If a person claims to be entitled to be registered in Part 2 of the register[12] but
the person's name is not entered in that Part, the person may appeal to the County
Court[13].
On an appeal the court concerned may make any order which appears
appropriate, and no appeal lies from any decision of a court on such an appeal[14].

1 See CPR PD 52D—*Statutory appeals and appeals subject to special provision* para 19.1(a). See also
   CIVIL PROCEDURE vol 12A (2015) PARA 1551.

2   Architects Act 1997 s 22(1)(a) (s 22 substituted by SI 2008/1331). As to the register see PARA 435.
    As to registration in Part 1 of the register see PARA 436.
       An appeal under the Architects Act 1997 s 22(1)(a) must generally be made not later than three
    months after the date on which notice of the decision or order concerned is served on the person:
    s 22(2) (as so substituted). However, where an appeal under s 22(1)(a) is made by a person who
    relied on s 4(2A) (see PARA 436) in applying for registration in pursuance of that section, the
    appeal must be made not later than four months after the date on which notice of the refusal is
    served on the person: s 22(3) (as so substituted).
3   As to the Registrar of Architects see PARA 435.
4   Ie failure of the Registrar to comply with the Architects Act 1997 s 6(4) (see PARA 437): s 22(1)(b)
    (as substituted: see note 2). The time limits for making an appeal under s 22(1)(b) are:
       (1)   where the appeal is made by a person who relied on s 4(2A) (see PARA 436) in applying
               for registration in pursuance of that section, within seven months; and
       (2)   where the appeal is made by a person who, in applying for registration in pursuance of
               s 4, relied on s 4(1)(a) (see PARA 436) without also relying on s 4(2A), within six months,
       beginning with the date on which the person's application for registration is made: s 22(4) (as
    so substituted). In any other case (ie where s 22(4) does not apply) an appeal under s 22(1)(b) must
    be made within nine months beginning with the date on which the person's application for
    registration is made: s 22(5).
5   Ie by virtue of the Architects Act 1997 s 9 (see PARA 437).
6   Architects Act 1997 s 22(1)(c) (as substituted: see note 2). An appeal under s 22(1)(c) must be made
    not later than three months after the date on which notice of the decision or order concerned is
    served on the person: s 22(2) (as so substituted).
7   As to the Architects Registration Board see PARA 431.
8   Ie under the Architects Act 1997 s 10 (see PARA 444).
9   Architects Act 1997 s 22(1)(d) (as substituted: see note 2). An appeal under s 22(1)(d) must be
    made not later than three months after the date on which notice of the decision or order concerned
    is served on the person: s 22(2) (as so substituted).
10 Architects Act 1997 s 22(1)(e) (as substituted: see note 2). As to disciplinary orders see PARA 443.
    An appeal under s 22(1)(e) must be made not later than three months after the date on which notice
    of the decision or order concerned is served on the person: s 22(2) (as so substituted).
11 See *Hughes v Architects' Registration Council of the United Kingdom* [1957] 2 QB 550, [1957] 2
    All ER 436; *Woodman-Smith v Architects Registration Board* [2014] EWHC 3639 (Admin),
    [2014] All ER (D) 139 (Nov); *Williams v Architect's Registration Board* [2016] EWHC 1904
    (Admin).
12 As to registration in Part 2 of the register see PARA 438.
13 Architects Act 1997 s 22(6) (as substituted (see note 2); as amended by the Crime and Courts Act
    2013 Sch 9 para 61).
14 Architects Act 1997 s 22(7) (as substituted: see note 2).

(2) Employment of Architects and Engineers

(i) The Contract and its Duration

446. Employment of architect or engineer.

Where the architect or engineer is employed to design and supervise a building
or works, the contract is often informal, but frequently the standard conditions of
engagement will be incorporated in the contract[1]. Where drawings and plans[2] are
submitted in a competition the published conditions of the competition, coupled
with the acceptance by the architect, may constitute a written contract to employ
the successful competitor[3].

Under Part II of the Housing Grants, Construction and Regeneration Act
1996[4], the definition of a construction contract[5] includes an agreement to do
architectural, design or surveying work, or to provide advice on building,
engineering, interior or external decoration or on the laying-out of landscape in

relation to construction operations[6]. Where the engagement of an architect falls within this definition, the provisions of the Housing Grants, Construction and Regeneration Act 1996 relating to the rights and entitlements for the parties to such a contract as to adjudication and payment provisions will apply[7].

Many government departments, local authorities and large companies employ their own architects and the architect in such cases will enter into a contract of employment[8].

1   See eg *Sidney Kaye, Eric Firmin & Partners (a firm) v Bronesky* (1973) 226 Estates Gazette 1395, (1973) 4 BLR 1 at 7, CA, per Lawton LJ; but cf *Edwin Hill & Partners v Leakcliffe Properties Ltd* (1984) 29 BLR 43. As to standard conditions see PARA 202.

2   As to drawings and plans see PARA 463.

3   See eg the litigation resulting from a competition held in 1939: *Adams Holder & Pearson v Trent Regional Health Authority* (1989) 47 BLR 34, CA.

4   Ie the Housing Grants, Construction and Regeneration Act 1996 Pt II (ss 104–117).

5   See PARA 210.

6   Housing Grants, Construction and Regeneration Act 1996 s 104(2).

7   See the Housing Grants, Construction and Regeneration Act 1996 ss 108–113; and PARAS 352–357, 410. See further PARA 210.

8   See *AMF International Ltd v Magnet Bowling Ltd* [1968] 2 All ER 789, [1968] 1 WLR 1028, for a consequence of having a salaried architect. In that case the employer was held liable to a third party under the Occupiers' Liability Act 1957 and was unable to rely on the defence provided by s 2(4)(b) (see NEGLIGENCE vol 78 (2018) PARA 35), namely that the damage was caused by the fault of an independent contractor, in circumstances where that defence would have been available had the work been supervised entirely by an independent architect.

447. Extent of power to delegate.

The employment of an architect or engineer being usually a personal contract, he cannot delegate his duties entirely[1], but he need not individually go into every matter in detail[2], and may make use of the skill and labour of others in the performance of his duties[3]. The ordinary course of business would make it unreasonable and impossible for the architect or engineer to be constantly on the site, supervising the construction of every part of the works, and taking upon himself the functions of a clerk of works (or a project manager as sometimes called)[4]. The architect or engineer, however, is responsible for the acts and defaults of the subordinates to whom he entrusts the supervision of details[5]. The architect is not entitled to rely implicitly on the judgment of the clerk of works, and, although a clerk of works may be appointed by the employer, the architect may in certain circumstances be liable to his employer for the negligence of the clerk of works[6]. The modern practice is that the clerk of works is the eyes and ears of the architect[7], though not necessarily the mouth.

1   *Ranger v Great Western Rly Co* (1854) 5 HL Cas 72 at 117 per Lord Brougham. See also *Moresk Cleaners Ltd v Hicks* [1966] 2 Lloyd's Rep 338, 4 BLR 50. Cf *Merton London Borough Council v Lowe* (1981) 18 BLR 130, CA; and CONTRACT vol 22 (2012) PARAS 327–349.

2   *Clemence v Clarke* (1879) 2 Hudson's BC (4th Edn) 54, CA.

3   *Kirkwood v Morrison* (1877) 5 R 79, Ct of Sess; and see *British Waggon Co and Parkgate Waggon Co v Lea & Co* (1880) 5 QBD 149.

4   See *East Ham Corpn v Bernard Sunley & Sons Ltd* [1966] AC 406, [1965] 3 All ER 619, HL. For a practical illustration see *Sutcliffe v Chippendale and Edmondson (a firm)* (1971) 18 BLR 149 (and for engineers see *Oldschool v Gleeson (Construction) Ltd* (1976) 4 BLR 103). Standard conditions of engagement generally provide that the architect is not to be responsible for work done by consultants or specialist contractors, sub-contractors or suppliers nor for the contractor's operational methods: see eg the standard form of agreement for the appointment of an architect which includes an express acknowledgement on the part of the client that it accepts the architect does not warrant the competence, performance, work, services, solvency or products of any other person including subcontractors, contractors and suppliers and consultants engaged on the works.

As to standard forms of contract see PARA 202. See also *Investors in Industry Commercial Properties Ltd v South Bedfordshire District Council* [1986] QB 1034, [1986] 1 All ER 787, (1985) 32 BLR 1, CA. As to the clerk of works see PARA 207.

5   *Moneypenny v Hartland* (1824) 1 C & P 352 at 354 per Abbott CJ; *Leicester Guardians v Trollope* (1911) 75 JP 197. See PARA 467.
6   *Leicester Guardians v Trollope* (1911) 75 JP 197.
7   *Kensington and Chelsea and Westminster Area Health Authority v Wettern Composites Ltd* (1985) 31 BLR 57 at 85 per Smout J. See also *Gray (Special Trustees of the London Hospital) v TP Bennett & Son (a firm)* (1987) 43 BLR 63 at 85 per Sir William Stabb QC.

448.   Effect of death or disability.

The contract of employment of an architect or engineer is a personal one, and consequently there is an implied condition that the contract will only continue so long as the person employed remains alive, and in sufficiently good health to perform his part of the contract[1]. For this reason the death, insanity, or continued disablement by illness of the architect dissolves the contract of employment[2], and thereafter neither party (nor, in case of death, the representatives of the deceased) can bring a claim for breach of contract save in respect of a right of action which accrued before the dissolution[3].

In case of temporary illness, the omission to perform the services contracted to be supplied would not entitle the employer to rescind the contract except where constant personal supervision had been stipulated for[4].

If the contract has relation to the personal conduct of the employer, his death or retirement puts an end to the contract, but it is not so if the contract has no such relation[5].

1   This paragraph does not apply to a limited company unless it was the alter ego of the architect or engineer: see generally COMPANIES vol 14 (2016) PARA 116. As to the death or incapacity of a party to a contract see CONTRACT vol 22 (2012) PARA 474.
2   *Stubbs v Holywell Rly Co* (1867) LR 2 Exch 311. See also *Boast v Firth* (1868) LR 4 CP 1 (apprentice); *Robinson v Davison* (1871) LR 6 Exch 269 (concert singer); *Grove v Johnston* (1889) 24 LR Ir 352 (rate collector).
3   See CONTRACT vol 22 (2012) PARA 474.
4   *Cuckson v Stones* (1858) 1 E & E 248. See also *Poussard v Spiers* (1876) 1 QBD 410. As to the payment of architects and engineers in case of death, etc during the course of their employment see *Stubbs v Holywell Rly Co* (1867) LR 2 Exch 311; and PARAS 484–485.
5   *Phillips v Alhambra Palace Co* [1901] 1 KB 59 at 63, DC, per Lord Alverstone CJ. See also *Farrow v Wilson* (1869) LR 4 CP 744; *Graves v Cohen* (1929) 46 TLR 121.

449.   Termination of duties.

In the absence of a contractual right to terminate[1], the employment of an architect or engineer in the capacity of agent of the building owner or employer may not be determined prior to completion[2]. In general, the only remedy of an architect who has been dismissed without good cause is a claim for damages[3], as the court will not normally decree specific performance of the contract of employment, because it will not generally compel persons against their will to maintain continuous personal and confidential relations. The court will not order specific performance in a contract of employment where a case is not exceptional[4]. Similarly, the court will not grant an injunction restraining the building owner from employing another architect[5].

1   See eg *Du Bosky & Partners v Shearwater Property Holdings plc* (1991) 54 BLR 71. See also the standard form of agreement for the appointment of an architect. As to standard forms of contract see PARA 202.
2   *Thomas v Hammersmith Borough Council* [1938] 3 All ER 203, CA; *Edwin Hill & Partners v Leakcliffe Properties Ltd* (1984) 29 BLR 43 at 68 per Hutchison J.
3   *Hickey v Browne* (1842) 4 ILR 277.

4 *Page One Records Ltd v Britton* [1967] 3 All ER 822, [1968] 1 WLR 157; cf *Hill v CA Parsons & Co Ltd* [1972] Ch 305, [1971] 3 All ER 1345, CA (commented upon in *Chappell v Times Newspapers Ltd* [1975] 2 All ER 233, [1975] 1 WLR 482, [1975] IRLR 90 (CA) where the court held that *Hill v CA Parsons & Co Ltd* was unusual, if not unique in that both the employer and the men had complete confidence in one another in that case: in *Chappell v Times Newspapers Ltd*, if an injunction was granted preventing the employer from terminating the contracts of employment, no one could have any confidence that the employment would continue peaceably, therefore specific performance was inappropriate). See also *Ashworth v Royal National Theatre* [2014] EWHC 1176 (QB), [2014] 4 All ER 238, [2014] IRLR 526, where the court refused specific performance in a 'standard case' where on a traditional analysis a loss of confidence was the primary block to the type of relief sort and would clearly interfere with the employer's freedoms (in this case, artistic freedoms). See SPECIFIC PERFORMANCE vol 95 (2017) PARA 508.

5 *Denmark Productions Ltd v Boscobel Productions Ltd* [1969] 1 QB 699, [1968] 3 All ER 513, CA. As to injunctions see CIVIL PROCEDURE vol 12 (2015) PARA 1098 et seq. As to the appointment of a second architect see PARA 298.

450. Liability of employer to suppliers and sub-contractors.

In general, an architect has no implied authority[1] to contract on behalf of the employer. In the absence of express authority any such purported contract is not binding upon the employer unless he with full knowledge of the facts ratifies the architect's actions[2].

However, the question of the liability of the building owner to builders' merchants employed to carry out work contemplated by provisional sums[3] has in the past occasioned litigation. This arose generally from three causes: (1) because the builders' merchant declined to take orders from the builder or preferred to take them from the architect, and the architect, without consulting his employer, gave orders to the merchant direct; or (2) because ambiguous provisions were inserted in the contract; or (3) because of conditions empowering the architect to direct payment of these sums due to the merchant[4]. It has been held that where an architect had this power, and he certified a sum as due to a merchant and deducted it from money due to the contractor, the building owner under the particular circumstances of the case was liable to pay the merchant[5].

A clause[6] is sometimes inserted in the building contract, for the protection of the merchant, to the effect that, if the contractor fails to pay the supplier, the architect is to have power to authorise direct payment by the building owner to the supplier. Such a power, if exercised for a contractual reason other than insolvency, is not annulled by the contractor's insolvency, and, if the architect acts on it, the supplier may be entitled to be paid in priority to the claim of the contractor's liquidator[7].

1 As to the architect's authority see PARAS 451–452.
2 *Vigers, Sons & Co Ltd v Swindell* [1939] 3 All ER 590.
3 As to the meaning of 'provisional sums' see PARA 234.
4 As to payment direct see PARA 247.
5 *Hobbs v Turner* (1902) 18 TLR 235, CA.
6 Such a clause has not traditionally been regarded as creating a contractual relationship between building owner and supplier but such a provision may now give the supplier direct rights against the employer pursuant to the Contracts (Rights of Third Parties) Act 1999 (see CONTRACT vol 22 (2012) PARA 341 et seq).
7 *Re Wilkinson, ex p Fowler* [1905] 2 KB 713; *Re Tout and Finch Ltd* [1954] 1 All ER 127, [1954] 1 WLR 178; but cf *British Eagle International Airlines Ltd v Compagnie Nationale Air France* [1975] 2 All ER 390, [1975] 1 WLR 758, HL; *B Mullan & Sons Contractors Ltd v Ross and London* (1996) 86 BLR 1, 54 Con LR 163, NI CA. See PARAS 247–248.

(ii) Authority as Agent

451. Extent of authority as agent.

The objects for which an architect or engineer is employed comprise the preparation of drawings and plans for the buildings or works in contemplation, and also the supervision of their construction, and he generally is the agent of the building owner or employer in both these respects[1], although his authority in dealing with the contractor may be limited by the terms of the building contract[2].

With regard to drawings and plans, although the architect is the agent of the building owner, he has no implied authority to warrant that they are correct, or that the work can be carried out in accordance with them, or that temporary constructional works, in the case of engineering contracts, are practicable[3].

If, however, the architect makes representations as to the accuracy of plans, or as to the quantities of work to be done, or other matters within the scope of his authority, and does so fraudulently, and with the intention that they should be acted on, and they have actually been acted on to the prejudice of the contractor, then independently of the architect's own liability, the employer may be liable in respect of them[4], and may not be able to escape liability by relying on a clause in the contract purporting to throw the onus of inquiry as to such matters on the contractor[5]. The employer will also be liable for any actionable misrepresentation similarly made by the architect on these matters[6]. The authority of the architect as agent does not empower him without the knowledge or consent of his employer to make promises that conditions contained in it will be varied or waived[7]. If there are omissions in the plans, drawings, or specifications, the architect has no implied authority to order as extras such things omitted as are necessary to complete the contract[8], or, where the scheme is impracticable, to order as an extra work which is necessary to enable the works to be constructed[9].

In most cases an architect has to supply detailed or working drawings during the progress of the work. This duty, however, is only to be exercised for the purpose of amplifying the work described generally in the contract plans and drawings as to be done. The architect has no authority thereby to bind the employer by authorising the contractor to deviate from the plans[10], but he may, of course, have authority to do so if he also has power to vary the works.

1   *R v Peto* (1826) 1 Y & J 37 at 54 per Alexander CB; *Wallis v Robinson* (1862) 3 F & F 307; *Kimberley v Dick* (1871) LR 13 Eq 1.
2   See generally AGENCY vol 1 (2017) PARA 29 et seq.
3   *Thorn v London Corpn* (1876) 1 App Cas 120, HL.
4   But not if the architect acted outside his authority: *Armagas Ltd v Mundogas SA, The Ocean Frost* [1986] AC 717, [1986] 2 All ER 385, HL; cf *First Energy (UK) Ltd v Hungarian International Bank Ltd* [1993] 2 Lloyd's Rep 194, [1993] BCLC 1409, CA.
5   *S Pearson & Son Ltd v Dublin Corpn* [1907] AC 351, HL; explained in *Anglo-Scottish Beet Sugar Corpn Ltd v Spalding UDC* [1937] 2 KB 607, [1937] 3 All ER 335; and see PARAS 227, 378.
6   See the Misrepresentation Act 1967 ss 1, 2; and PARAS 227, 378.
7   *Sharpe v San Paulo Rly Co* (1873) 8 Ch App 597.
8   *Sharpe v San Paulo Rly Co* (1873) 8 Ch App 597.
9   *Tharsis Sulphur and Copper Co v M'Elroy & Sons* (1878) 3 App Cas 1040, HL. As to extra work and variations generally see PARA 272.
10   *R v Peto* (1826) 1 Y & J 37 at 54 per Alexander CB; *Cooper v Langdon* (1841) 9 M & W 60. See also PARA 297.

452. Authority of architect usually implied.

The contract between the employer and the contractor will usually contain provisions which define, limit or extend the authority of the architect, and this authority will not be construed so as to confer powers not necessary for the effectual exercise of the powers expressly granted[1].

Where the architect's engagement is not on standard or otherwise clear terms, his authority may not be clearly defined. Thus, where an architect is merely instructed to prepare plans, his employment is not that of an agent, and he therefore has no implied authority to obtain tenders or to negotiate for advances[2]. However, where he has authority to obtain tenders, and if the tenders he obtains are not accepted by the building owner, it would seem that the architect is entitled to get others within the time limited, or, if time is not limited, within a reasonable time[3]. An authority to obtain tenders does not imply an authority to enter into a contract with a builder or contractor, even when the tender is within the price the employer is prepared to pay[4]. However, where the architect is in the salaried employment of the employer, he will have ostensible authority to enter into a contract with the builder[5]. If he does not disclose that he is acting as an agent he will be personally liable if he accepts the tender[6].

The architect may in the absence of express authority have implied authority to employ a quantity surveyor to prepare quantities of the contemplated building or works to be used by tenderers[7]. Therefore the employer will be liable to the quantity surveyor for his fees[8]. However, an employer may expressly limit the authority of the architect to employ a quantity surveyor[9].

In the case of engineering contracts, there is no practice as to the employment of quantity surveyors for the taking out of quantities for tenders. Many engineers take out their own quantities, and the same implied authority to employ a quantity surveyor may not exist.

If the architect or engineer has by the contract to certify the sums due to the contractor, he has implied authority to measure variations for that purpose[10].

It often occurs that when tenders are obtained the lowest of them is found to be higher than the sum which the employer is willing to expend on the construction of the required works. The architect or the quantity surveyor[11] has then been employed to reduce the scheme or the quantities so as to make the design less costly, and to bring the expense within the amount which the employer is willing to lay out. This is sometimes 'value engineering', which is a phrase that means reducing the cost of a scheme through changes in the method and type of construction, or specification, without making major reductions in scope[12]. It is doubtful whether an architect has any implied authority to employ a quantity surveyor to do this work. In any case, such an authority cannot be implied if the employer limited the authority of the architect to designing a work at a limited cost, for if the architect has disregarded his instructions by designing a building the cost of which exceeds the amount to which he was limited, he cannot charge his employer with the expense of rectifying his own mistake[13]. Even in such a case, however, the employer might ratify the employment by acquiescence[14].

1 *Sharpe v San Paulo Rly Co* (1873) 8 Ch App 597; *Lawson v Wallasey Local Board* (1883) 48 LT 507, CA; *Frederick Betts Ltd v Pickfords Ltd* [1906] 2 Ch 87.
2 Cf *Spratt v Dornford* (1862) 2 Hudson's BC (3rd Edn) 7. As to tenders see PARA 215 et seq.
3 See *Tetley v Shand* (1871) 25 LT 658; *Imperial Ottoman Bank v Cowan, Cowan v Imperial Ottoman Bank* (1873) 29 LT 52; *Borrowman Phillips & Co v Free and Hollis* (1878) 4 QBD 500, CA.
4 On the analogy of an estate agent see *Hamer v Sharp* (1874) LR 19 Eq 108. See AGENCY vol 1 (2017) PARA 41. See also *A Vigers Sons & Co Ltd v Swindell* [1939] 3 All ER 590.
5 *Carlton Contractors Ltd v Bexley Corpn* (1962) 60 LGR 331.
6 *Sika Contracts v Gill* (1978) 9 BLR 11.

7   See *Taylor v Hall* (1870) IR 4 CL 467 at 479 per Monahan CJ; *Young v Smith* (1879) 2 Hudson's
     BC (4th Edn) 70; *North v Bassett* [1892] 1 QB 333, DC. However see also *Antisell v Doyle* (1899)
     2 IR 275; *Knox and Robb v Scottish Garden Suburb Co Ltd* 1913 SC 872, Ct of Sess. As to
     quantity surveyors see PARA 516 et seq.
8   *Moon v Witney Union Guardians* (1837) 3 Bing NC 814; *Waghorn v Wimbledon Local Board*
     (1877) 2 Hudson's BC (4th Edn) 52. See also *Gwyther v Gaze* (1875) 2 Hudson's BC (4th Edn)
     34; *Bayley v Wilkins* (1849) 7 CB 886.
9   *Richardson v Beale* (1867) Times, 29 June. See also *Young v Smith* (1879) 2 Hudson's BC (4th
     Edn) 70; affd (1880) 2 Hudson's BC (4th Edn) 75, CA.
10   *Beattie v Gilroy* (1882) 10 R 226, Ct of Sess.
11   See PARA 516.
12   *Riva Properties Ltd and Others v Foster + Partners Ltd* [2017] EWHC 2574 (TCC) at [111], 175
     CONLR 45, [2017] All ER (D) 113 (Oct).
13   *Evans v Carte* (1881) 2 Hudson's BC (10th Edn) 116, DC; and see *Nye Saunders and Partners (a
     firm) v Alan E Bristow* (1987) 37 BLR 92, (1987) Times, 27 April CA; cf *Copthorne Hotel
     (Newcastle) Ltd v Arup Associates* (1996) 58 Con LR 105, CA.
14   *Evans v Carte* (1881) 2 Hudson's BC (4th Edn) 78 at 80, DC, per Lord Coleridge CJ.

453.   Varying the contract.

The architect or engineer has no general authority to vary, waive, or dispense
with any conditions contained in the contract or to vary the works without
express authority to do so[1]. Where he is authorised by the contract to give
directions as to the manner in which the work is to be carried out, he may give
only such directions as fall within the contract, and may not vary the scope of the
proposed works[2], nor allow the substitution of entirely different materials for
those specified in the contract[3].

1   *R v Peto* (1826) 1 Y & J 37; *Cooper v Langdon* (1841) 9 M & W 60; *Sharpe v San Paulo Rly Co*
     (1873) 8 Ch App 597. As to extra work and variations generally see PARA 272.
2   See the cases referred to in note 1; and *Ramsay & Son v Brand* (1898) 25 R 1212, Ct of Sess; *Bell
     v Bridlington Corpn* (1908) 72 JP 453.
3   *Steel v Young* 1907 SC 360, Ct of Sess; *Forrest v Scottish County Investment Co Ltd* 1916 SC (HL)
     28.

454.   Ordering of extras.

Unless there is express provision in the contract the architect may not certify
work as an extra, or certify for materials as having been supplied, when in fact the
work has not been done, or the materials supplied; nor has he any implied
authority to order as extras items omitted from the contract which are necessary
to complete the works or items necessary to convert an impracticable scheme into
a viable one[1]. The architect or engineer cannot waive or dispense with a condition
that extras must be ordered in writing, or any similar condition[2]. If, however, the
architect has power by a final and conclusive certificate to adjust the amount
payable by the employer to the contractor, the employer must pay the amount
certified for if the certificate is honestly given, although the certificate may include
work not done or not done properly, or materials not supplied, or extras not
executed, or work which, under the terms of the contract, has been insufficiently
authorised, or extras not ordered in the manner prescribed by the contract[3].

1   In the same way as shipowners are not liable on bills of lading for goods which have not been
     shipped: *Grant v Norway* (1851) 10 CB 665. See also *Sharpe v San Paulo Rly Co* (1873) 8 Ch
     App 597; *Tharsis Sulphur and Copper Co v M'Elroy & Son's* (1878) 3 App Cas 1040, HL.
2   As to extra work and variations generally see PARA 272.
3   *Goodyear v Weymouth and Melcombe Regis Corpn* (1865) 35 LJCP 12; *Connor v Belfast Water
     Comrs* (1871) IR 5 CL 55; *Laidlaw v Hastings Pier Co* (1874) 2 Hudson's BC (10th Edn) 428,
     554, 636, 642; *Lapthorne v St Aubyn* (1885) Cab & El 486; *Colbart Ltd v H Kumar* (1992) 59
     BLR 89, (1992) 28 Con LR 58; *Crown Estate Comrs v John Mowlem & Co Ltd* (1994) 70 BLR

1, (1994) 40 Con LR 36, CA. As to final certificates see PARAS 330–331. As to the employer's
remedies against the architect or engineer see PARA 469.

455. Measuring variations.

If the architect or engineer is designated as the person to perform the work of
measuring up variations, whether it be included or not in the work for which his
remuneration is fixed, he cannot have authority from his employer to employ a
quantity surveyor[1] to do the work and charge his employer. If, however, the
building contract merely directs that the value of the variations is to be ascertained
in some manner, without saying by whom, the architect has implied authority, at
all events in any large matter, to employ a quantity surveyor to measure up[2].
Where a quantity surveyor is employed by the architect to vindicate the
correctness of his certificate, which has been questioned by the building owner, a
customary authority to employ a quantity surveyor cannot be implied in such a
case[3]. Modern forms of building contract make express provision for these
matters[4].

1   As to quantity surveyors see PARA 516 et seq.
2   *Birdseye v Dover Harbour Board Comrs* (1881) 2 Hudson's BC (10th Edn) 117 (where evidence
    was given of a custom that in any large matter the architect was entitled to call in a quantity
    surveyor, to be paid by the employer, and the jury found in favour of the custom); *Beattie v Gilroy*
    (1882) 10 R 226, Ct of Sess.
3   *Plimsaul v Lord Kilmorey* (1884) 1 TLR 48.
4   As to standard conditions see PARA 202. As to valuing variations see PARAS 343–344.

(iii) Functions as a Certifier

456. Dual function of architect or engineer.

The architect or engineer may often act in two capacities in respect of the same
matter. For example, he may first be acting as the agent of the building owner, and
in that capacity have to decide whether work or materials are acceptable to his
client, the employer, and then as certifier have to decide whether the work or
materials do or do not comply with the contractual standards, whether payment
should be made, or the value of the relevant work or materials, and when acting
in this capacity he must act fairly and impartially between the parties[1]. However,
the contractor who has agreed, by entering into the contract, that the architect or
engineer should discharge duties in these two capacities, cannot claim that the
architect or engineer must be in the position of an independent arbitrator who has
no other duty which involves acting in the interests of one of the parties; and by
so acting the architect or engineer is not guilty of collusion or bad faith[2].

1   *Page v Llandaff and Dinas Powis RDC* (1901) 2 Hudson's BC (8th Edn) 239; *Sutcliffe v Thackrah*
    [1974] AC 727, [1974] 1 All ER 859, HL; cf *Beaufort Developments (NI) Ltd v Gilbert-Ash NI
    Ltd* [1999] 1 AC 266 at 276, [1998] 2 All ER 778 at 786, HL, per Lord Hoffmann. As to the duties
    as a certifier see PARA 457.
2   *Panamena Europea Navigacion (Compania Limitada) v Frederick Leyland & Co Ltd (J Russell &
    Co)* [1947] AC 428, HL. See also *John Holland Construction and Engineering Ltd v Majorca
    Products* (2000) 16 Const LJ 114, Vic SC.

457. Duties as a certifier.

In most building contracts the architect has to perform a number of duties as
a certifier as well as acting on behalf of the employer. His duties as certifier are
different from that of an arbitrator[1].

The most obvious example of the architect's acting as a certifier is when he
issues a certificate which records the value of the work executed[2]. The architect is

also acting as a certifier when he has to value variations[3] or grant an extension of time[4] or certify the date by which the work should have been completed[5].

Whilst acting as a certifier the architect must act fairly[6]. When he is certifying, the architect is acting in an independent capacity, but it is an administrative rather than a judicial capacity[7]. There is no necessity for the architect to hear the views of both sides before he reaches his decision[8]. Whilst acting as a certifier, the architect is liable to his employer for negligence[9]. An employer has independent, concurrent and unlimited causes of action arising out of erroneous certification against both the architect and the contractor[10] unless, in the case of the contractor, the certificate in question is, upon a true construction of the contract, intended to be final and conclusive[11].

1 See PARA 403.
2 See PARA 322 et seq.
3 See PARA 455.
4 See PARA 267 et seq.
5 See PARA 263 et seq.
6 *Sutcliffe v Thackrah* [1974] AC 727, [1974] 1 All ER 859, HL.
7 *Re Carus-Wilson and Greene* (1886) 18 QBD 7, CA. See *Chambers v Goldthorpe* [1901] 1 QB 624, CA; *Kennedy Ltd v Barrow-in-Furness Corpn* (1909) 2 Hudson's BC (10th Edn) 829, CA; *Minster Trust Ltd v Traps Tractors Ltd* [1954] 3 All ER 136, [1954] 1 WLR 963.
8 *Hounslow London Borough Council v Twickenham Garden Developments Ltd* [1971] Ch 233, [1970] 3 All ER 326 (applied in *Scheldebouw BV v St James Homes (Grosvenor Dock) Ltd* [2006] EWHC 89 (TCC), 105 ConLR 90, [2006] BLR 113). As to the right to a fair trial (including the right to a fair and public hearing within a reasonable time by an independent and impartial tribunal) under the Convention for the Protection of Human Rights and Fundamental Freedoms (1950) (Rome, 4 November 1950; TS 71 (1953); Cmd 8969) art 6 (set out in the Human Rights Act 1998 s 1(3), Sch 1) see RIGHTS AND FREEDOMS vol 88A (2018) PARA 307 et seq.
9 *Sutcliffe v Thackrah* [1974] AC 727, [1974] 1 All ER 859, HL; and see PARA 459. But probably not to the contractor: see *Pacific Associates Inc v Baxter* [1990] 1 QB 993, [1989] 2 All ER 159, CA; *John Holland Construction and Engineering Ltd v Majorca Products* (2000) 16 Const LJ 114, Vic SC. As to what constitutes negligence in certifying see *Sutcliffe v Chippendale and Edmondson (a firm)* (1971) 18 BLR 149. As to the liability of the architect or engineer to the contractor see PARAS 471–475.
10 *Wessex Regional Health Authority v HLM Design Ltd* (1995) 71 BLR 32.
11 *Colbart Ltd v H Kumar* (1992) 59 BLR 89, (1992) 28 Con LR 58; *Crown Estate Comrs v John Mowlem & Co Ltd* (1994) 70 BLR 1, 40 Con LR 36, CA. As to final certificates see PARAS 330–331.

(iv) Duties of Care and Skill

458. Liability for want of skill.

The relationship between the architect or engineer and his client is primarily contractual. Thus, the duties to be performed by the architect or engineer will principally depend upon the express or implied terms of the contract in question. However, it is clear that professionals generally owe a parallel duty and undertake a concurrent liability in tort[1]. Moreover, certain duties are customarily performed by competent experienced architects and engineers[2].

The test of whether the architect or engineer is in breach of his duty is whether he did or did not exercise the skill and care to be expected of an ordinary architect or engineer exercising and professing to have that skill[3]. Although in general the duty of an architect or engineer is only to exercise reasonable skill and care, a higher duty may exceptionally be imposed, for example if the circumstances show that it was the common intention of the parties that the architect or engineer design a building which would be fit for its purpose[4]. It is evidence of ignorance and lack of skill that the architect or engineer has acted contrary to the established practices that are universally recognised by members of the profession[5]. It is not sufficient to establish a breach of duty to show that another architect or engineer of greater experience and ability might have used a greater degree of skill or care[6].

When an architect or engineer is employed upon works which involve the use of some new invention of which he has no knowledge and with which he has not professed any acquaintance, his failure may not make him liable for want of skill[7]. Where the directions of the employer are capable of more than one meaning and the architect or engineer honestly and carefully, but erroneously, adopts the one which his employer did not intend, he will not be liable[8].

When an architect or engineer is engaged to provide services during the construction period a continuing duty to review the original design may arise. Such a duty will not arise unless there is good reason to carry out a review and whether there is good reason is to be determined objectively and by reference to the standard set by what a reasonably competent architect would do in the circumstances[9]. An architect will also have a duty to consider and find out key constraints of a project such as its budget and must also inform the client if they know the client is under a misconception about how the budget could be achieved[10].

1 *Henderson v Merrett Syndicates Ltd* [1995] 2 AC 145, [1994] 3 All ER 506, HL. See also *Lancashire and Cheshire Association of Baptist Churches Inc v Howard & Seddon Partnership (a firm)* [1993] 3 All ER 467, 65 BLR 21; *Wessex Regional Health Authority v HLM Design* (1994) 71 BLR 32, 10 Const LJ 165. The existence of this concurrent liability may have important consequences in relation to limitation of actions: see PARA 381; and LIMITATION PERIODS.

2 See further PARAS 460–468.

3 See the dicta of McNair J in *Bolam v Friern Hospital Management Committee* [1957] 2 All ER 118 at 121, [1957] 1 WLR 582 at 586, which has been generally approved; *Hawkins (George) v Chrysler (UK) Ltd and Byrne Associates* (1986) 38 BLR 36, CA (also dealing with *Greaves & Co (Contractors) Ltd v Baynham Meikle & Partners* [1975] 3 All ER 99, [1975] 1 WLR 1095, CA); and see *Nye Saunders and Partners (a firm) v AE Bristow* (1987) 37 BLR 92, CA; *Eckersley v Binnie & Partners* (1988) 18 Con LR 1 at 80, CA, per Bingham LJ; *JD Williams & Co Ltd v Michael Hyde & Associates* [2000] Lloyd's Rep 823, [2001] BLR 99, CA. See also *ConocoPhillips Petroleum Company UK Ltd v Snamprogetti Ltd* [2003] All ER (D) 134 (Oct).

4 See *Greaves & Co (Contractors) Ltd v Baynham Meikle and Partners* [1975] 3 All ER 99, [1975] 1 WLR 1095, CA; cf *Hawkins (George) v Chrysler (UK) Ltd and Byrne Associates* (1986) 38 BLR 36, CA.

5 *Greaves & Co (Contractors) Ltd v Baynham Meikle & Partners* [1975] 3 All ER 99, [1975] 1 WLR 1095, CA; *Hawkins (George) v Chrysler (UK) Ltd and Byrne Associates* (1986) 38 BLR 36, CA; *Gloucestershire Health Authority v MA Torpy & Partners Ltd* (1997) 55 Con LR 124.

6 See *Slater v Baker* (1767) 2 Wils 359. In *Worboys v Acme Investment Ltd* (1969) 210 Estates Gazette 335, (1969) 4 BLR 133, CA, an architect was held not to be negligent in omitting downstairs lavatories in houses then valued at £8,000, in the absence of professional evidence that he had failed to exercise due care.

7 *Wimpey Construction UK Ltd v Poole* [1984] 2 Lloyd's Rep 499, (1984) 27 BLR 58; *Merton London Borough Council v Lowe* (1981) 18 BLR 130, CA.

8 *Bulmer v Gilman* (1842) 4 Man & G 108; *Ireland v Livingstone* (1872) LR 5 HL 395; *Cotton v Wallis* [1955] 3 All ER 373, [1955] 1 WLR 1168, CA.

9 *Oxford Architects Partnership v Cheltenham Ladies College* [2007] BLR 293. If a duty to review arises, breach of such duty would give rise to a fresh cause of action.

10 *Riva Properties Limited and Others v Foster + Partners Limited* [2017] EWHC 2574, 175 ConLR 45, [2017] All ER (D) 113 (Oct).

459. Duty of care as regards negligence.

In addition to his liability to the client, an architect or engineer is in general also liable to anybody else who is sufficiently proximate and who suffers loss or damage by reason of his negligence[1]. Thus, a negligent architect or engineer would be liable for physical injury to a third party's person or property[2] but would not, in the absence of special circumstances, be liable for economic loss[3] suffered by such a third party. A defective design will also give rise to liability, even where the design's construction had been undertaken by a sub-contractor[4].

1   See generally NEGLIGENCE. As to liability under the Defective Premises Act 1972 see PARAS 275–277. As to failure to comply with building control see PARA 301 et seq. See also *Clay v AJ Crump & Sons Ltd* [1964] 1 QB 533, [1963] 3 All ER 687, CA (liability for injury to labourer); *Eckersley v Binnie & Partners* (1988) 18 Con LR 1, CA (engineers liable to visitors); cf *Oldschool v Gleeson (Construction) Ltd* (1976) 4 BLR 103. An engineer has a duty of care in relation to observed dangers which relate to work outside his immediate contractual responsibility: *Hart Investments v Fidler* [2007] EWHC 1058 (TCC), 112 ConLR 33, [2007] BLR 526. As to liability to the contractor see PARAS 471–475.

2   See eg *Baxall Securities Ltd v Sheard Walshaw Partnership (a firm)* [2001] BLR 36, (2000) 74 Con LR 116; revsd on the facts [2002] EWCA Civ 09, [2002] BLR 100, 83 Con LR 164.

3   For examples of cases where architects were not held to be liable for economic loss see *Lancashire and Cheshire Association of Baptist Churches Inc v Howard & Seddon Partnership (a firm)* [1993] 3 All ER 467, 65 BLR 21; *Machin v Adams* (1997) 84 BLR 79, CA. See also PARA 363; and NEGLIGENCE vol 78 (2018) PARA 42.

4   *Baxall Securities Ltd v Sheard Walshaw Partnership (a firm)* [2001] BLR 36, (2000) 74 Con LR 116; revsd on the facts [2002] EWCA Civ 09, [2002] BLR 100, 83 Con LR 164.

460. Compliance with statutes, byelaws and other legal requirements.

It is part of the duty of an architect or engineer to ascertain and to comply with the requirements of all relevant public and local statutes and with all subsidiary legislation[1], such as byelaws and the building regulations[2], made under them[3]. Ignorance or disregard of the legal requirements as to buildings may result not only in a fine on the employer, but also in an order for the whole or part of the building to be pulled down[4], and the architect or engineer would be liable to his employer for the loss so incurred[5].

The knowledge of the law which an architect or engineer is expected to have is not a minute and accurate knowledge, but a knowledge of the general rules of law applicable to the exercise of his profession[6]. The architect or engineer should, however, have a general knowledge of the law as applied to the more important clauses, at least, of standard forms of building contract[7].

Failure on the part of the architect or engineer to submit plans to the proper authorities, or to give the notices required by law, may involve the employer in penalties, and even if the contractor has undertaken to give all the necessary notices, it would seem that it is still the duty of the architect or engineer in supervising the work to see that the contractor does so, at any rate in so far as the notices are building notices, or on the contractor's default to do so himself or inform his employer. Where a judicial decision has altered what was previously supposed to be the law affecting a particular profession, it seems to be the duty of persons practising that profession to acquaint themselves within a reasonable time with the effect of such a decision and to act accordingly in the exercise of their profession[8]. If the employer, however, knowingly instructs the architect to design a building which will contravene the law, the architect will incur no liability to the employer; but on the other hand, it would seem that he would not be able to recover any fees for supervision because a contract to build in contravention of statute is illegal[9].

1   *BL Holdings Ltd v Robert J Wood & Partners* (1978) 10 BLR 48, 122 Sol Jo 525; revsd on other grounds (1979) 12 BLR 1, 123 Sol Jo 570, CA.

2   As to the building regulations see BUILDING vol 6 (2018) PARA 7 et seq.

3   As to the requirements contained in statutes, regulations and byelaws see eg PARAS 275 et seq, 301–302, 387 et seq. See also *BL Holdings Ltd v Robert J Wood & Partners* (1978) 10 BLR 48, 122 Sol Jo 525; revsd on other grounds (1979) 12 BLR 1, 123 Sol Jo 570, CA.

4 See *Hopkins v Smethwick Local Board* (1890) 59 LJQB 250, CA.
5 On the principle of *Hadley v Baxendale* (1854) 9 Exch 341 at 354 per Alderson B see DAMAGES vol 29 (2014) PARA 532 et seq. See also *Townsends (Builders) Ltd v Cinema News and Property Management Ltd (David A Wilkie & Partners, third party)* [1959] 1 All ER 7, [1959] 1 WLR 119, 20 BLR 118, CA.
6 *Jenkins v Betham* (1855) 15 CB 168 at 189 per Jervis CJ.
7 *West Faulkner Associates v Newham London Borough Council* (1994) 71 BLR 1 at 15–16, CA, per Simon Brown LJ.
8 See *Lee v Walker* (1872) LR 7 CP 121.
9 *Young v Buckles* [1952] 1 KB 220, [1952] 1 All ER 354, CA (architect's fees attributable to work within amount licensed under Defence Regulations held recoverable where the total cost of works exceeded that amount and were to that extent illegal). See also *Stevens v Gourley* (1859) 7 CBNS 99 (contravention of the Metropolitan Building Act 1855, since repealed).

461. Interference with private rights.

As regards private rights, the architect or engineer should inquire from his employer as to the existence of any easements or restrictions affecting the site, and must in the preparation of his design avoid infringing them[1]. The employer owes a duty to his neighbours not to infringe their rights, and cannot so delegate the execution of building operations to a contractor as to relieve himself from that obligation[2].

The architect or engineer may render himself liable to an adjoining owner by preparing plans and supervising work which necessitates a trespass on the adjoining owner's land[3].

1 *Kellett v York Corpn* (1894) 10 TLR 662 at 663; *Armitage v Palmer* (1960) 175 Estates Gazette 315, CA. See also REAL PROPERTY AND REGISTRATION vol 87 (2017) PARA 731 et seq.
2 *Bower v Peate* (1876) 1 QBD 321; *Hughes v Percival* (1883) 8 App Cas 443, HL; *Jolliffe v Woodhouse* (1894) 10 TLR 553, CA. See further NEGLIGENCE vol 78 (2018) PARA 39.
3 *Monks v Dillon* (1882) 12 LR Ir 321. As to trespass see TORT vol 97 (2015) PARA 563 et seq.

462. Failure to examine site, foundations, etc.

If an architect or engineer fails to exercise reasonable care in the examination of the site on which the works are to be constructed, and does not ascertain the circumstances affecting it, such as the nature of the soil and strata, the existence and condition of buildings, whether there are rights of way or of light and air, or other easements affecting it, and consequently his designs are defective or impracticable, he may be liable to the employer for any loss thereby occasioned to him[1]; and the fact that the builder or contractor is liable to the employer under a contract to construct the works, notwithstanding the defective designs, will not necessarily exonerate the architect or engineer, the employer having a double remedy and being entitled to bring a claim against either the architect (or engineer) or the builder, or against them both[2].

1 *Moneypenny v Hartland* (1826) 2 C & P 378; *Columbus Co v Clowes* [1903] 1 KB 244; *EH Cardy & Son Ltd v Taylor and Paul Roberts and Associates* (1994) 38 Con LR 79. In *Moss v Heckingbottom* (1958) 172 Estates Gazette 207, Barry J assessed damages for an architect's negligent survey of property which failed to reveal substantial defects, by calculating the difference between the purchase price and the actual value of the property with the defects that should have been discovered at the date of the purchase. See also *Rayment v HG Needham & Son* (1953) 163 Estates Gazette 4; affd (1954) 163 Estates Gazette 542, CA (dry rot).
2 *Brown v Laurie* (1854) 5 LCR 65 (Que); *Hutchinson v Harris* (1978) 10 BLR 19, CA; *Townsend v Stone Toms & Partners (a firm)* (1984) 27 BLR 26, CA; *Merton London Borough Council v Lowe* (1981) 18 BLR 130, CA; *Hudson and another v Elmbridge Borough Council and others* [1991] 4 All ER 55, [1991] 1 WLR 880, (1990) Times, 29 November; *Wessex Regional Health Authority v HLM Design Ltd* (1995) 71 BLR 32; and see PARA 260 et seq.

463. Drawings and specifications.

A breach of duty by an architect or engineer in respect of drawings and specifications may arise either through the drawings or specifications being defective or incomplete, or through their not being supplied to the contractor either in proper time or at all[1].

The design of a building or of works may be defective or incomplete, for example: (1) as not being in accordance with the art and science of architecture, or as being opposed to sound principles of building or engineering[2]; (2) as not being in accordance with the instructions of the employer; (3) as contravening statutes and byelaws[3]; (4) as disregarding restrictions imposed on the use of the land, either by public or by private rights[4]; (5) as involving the specification of unsuitable materials[5]; and (6) as failing to achieve the necessary degree of lettable space on redevelopment of a building[6].

The mere approval of the plans and specifications by the employer will not exonerate the architect or engineer from liability when the design of the works is structurally defective or does not carry out the instructions of the employer, even though the employer has been told by the architect or engineer to examine them[7], unless the client is an experienced developer[8].

1 Failure to specify design requirements to a sub-contractor, resulting in the use of an inadequate design, will give rise to liability: *Baxall Securities Ltd v Sheard Walshaw Partnership (a firm)* [2001] BLR 36, (2000) 74 Con LR 116; revsd on the facts [2002] EWCA Civ 09, [2002] BLR 100, 83 Con LR 164.
2 For example in that the design is not 'buildable' (see *Equitable Debenture Assets Corp Ltd v William Moss Group Ltd* (1984) 2 Con LR 1) or is over-designed (see *London Underground Ltd v Kenchington Ford plc* (1998) 63 Con LR 1, [1998] All ER (D) 555).
3 See *Townsends (Builders) Ltd v Cinema News and Property Management Ltd* [1959] 1 All ER 7, [1959] 1 WLR 119, 20 BLR 118, CA. See also PARA 460.
4 As to private rights see PARA 461.
5 See *Sealand of the Pacific v Robert C McHaffie Ltd* (1974) 51 DLR (3d) 702, British Columbia CA; *Richard Roberts Holdings Ltd v Douglas Smith Stimson Partnership* (1988) 46 BLR 50, 6 Const LJ 71.
6 See *Gable House Estates Ltd v The Halpern Partnership* (1995) 48 Con LR 1.
7 *Smith v Barton* (1866) 15 LT 294 (valuer). See also *Rayment v HG Needham & Son* (1953) 163 Estates Gazette 4; affd (1954) 163 Estates Gazette 542, CA, where an architect was held not liable for failing to provide sufficient ventilation in a cellar to prevent the spread of dry rot.
8 *Worboys v Acme Investments Ltd* (1969) 210 Estates Gazette 335, (1969) 4 BLR 133, CA.

464. Failure or delay in supplying drawings, etc.

The design duties of the architect or engineer do not end when the work starts. There is a continuing duty to check that the design will work in practice and to correct any errors that may emerge[1]. The architect or engineer is also usually subject to a duty to supply further necessary information to the contractor.

Where, by reason of a failure or delay in the supplying of drawings or details, the contractor becomes entitled to rescind the contract altogether, or is released from his obligation to complete the works within the specified time, or is entitled to claim against the employer[2], the architect or engineer may become liable to his employer for the loss incurred by him[3], and part of such loss may be the loss of the rent or profit which would have been derived from the building or the loss of interest on his money[4].

1 *Brickfield Properties Ltd v Newton* [1971] 3 All ER 328, [1971] 1 WLR 862, CA; *Merton London Borough Council v Lowe* (1981) 18 BLR 130, CA; *Chelmsford District Council v Evers* (1983) 25 BLR 99, 4 Con LR 98; *Oxford Architects Partnership v Cheltenham Ladies College* [2007] BLR 293.
2 See eg *Royal Brompton Hospital National Health Trust v Hammond* [2000] BLR 75, sub nom *Royal Brompton Hospital National Health Trust (No 4)* (1999) 69 Con LR 170.

3   This is on the principle of *Hadley v Baxendale* (1854) 9 Exch 341 at 354 per Alderson B. See also PARA 469; and DAMAGES vol 29 (2014) PARA 532 et seq.

4   See *The Marpessa* [1906] P 95, CA (affd sub nom *Mersey Docks and Harbour Board v Marpessa (Owners)* [1907] AC 241, HL); *Victoria Laundry (Windsor) Ltd v Newman Industries Ltd* [1949] 2 KB 528, [1949] 1 All ER 997, CA.

465. Duty as to estimates and quantities.

Where the architect or engineer is required to give an estimate of the cost of proposed work, the estimate should be careful[1] and give appropriate warnings as to inflation[2]. However, the fact that the eventual cost exceeds the estimate is not of itself sufficient to establish a breach of duty[3]. Contrast the position where the estimate is required to be given by the architect, and the position where the budget is provided by the client and there is an expectation that the architect will use skill and care to design a scheme within the constraints of the client's budget. Where he fails to do so he can be found to be in breach of the duty of care owed[4].

If the architect himself takes out the quantities, and does so negligently or unskilfully so as to make them greater than they should be, thus increasing the price, he will be in breach of duty and therefore liable to his employer[5] if the terms of the contract between builder and building owner are such that the excess cannot be taken into account and deducted from the money due to the builder.

1   *Moneypenny v Hartland* (1826) 2 C & P 378.

2   *Nye Saunders and Partners (a firm) v Alan E Bristow* (1987) 37 BLR 92, CA.

3   *Copthorne Hotel (Newcastle) Ltd v Arup Associates* (1996) 58 Con LR 105, 12 Const LJ 402.

4   See *Riva Properties Limited and Others v Foster + Partners Limited* [2017] EWHC 2574, 175 CONLR 45, [2017] All ER (D) 113 (Oct).

5   See *M'Connell v Kilgallen* (1878) 2 LR Ir 119 at 121. As to a quantity surveyor's liability under similar circumstances see PARA 517.

466. Duty when recommending the acceptance of a tender.

An architect or engineer does not warrant the solvency or capability of a builder or contractor whose tender is accepted, but he is bound to give his employer the benefit of any information he may have in respect to such solvency or capability, and not to allow his employer to enter blindly into a contract with a person whom he has any reason to suspect of being unreliable[1]. And it would seem that, in some circumstances, he might be liable for not making reasonable inquiries[2].

1   *Pratt v George J Hill Associates* (1987) 37 BLR 145, CA.

2   See *Heys v Tindall* (1861) 1 B & S 296; *Mutual Life and Citizens Assurance Co Ltd v Evatt* [1971] AC 793, [1971] 1 All ER 150, PC (applied in *Esso Petroleum Co Ltd v Mardon* [1975] QB 819, [1975] 1 All ER 203), [1975] 2 WLR 147; *Partridge v Morris* [1995] CILL 1095; and NEGLIGENCE vol 78 (2018) PARA 13. As to tenders see PARA 215 et seq.

467. Duty as to supervision and administration.

Although an architect or engineer is not expected to be constantly on the site and to supervise every detail, it is not sufficient for him to pay occasional visits and to get any defects which he may happen to notice set right; his duty is to give such an amount of supervision as will enable him to give an honest certificate whether or not the work has been done in accordance with the contract[1]. Moreover, although his supervision may be partially, as to matters of detail, entrusted to subordinates such as clerks of works or inspectors, the architect or engineer cannot exonerate himself by saying that the negligence was theirs[2].

Depending upon the express terms of the relevant engagements, the duties of an architect or engineer may include a duty to advise or warn the employer of deficiencies in his own performance or that of other members of the professional team[3].

The failure of the architect or engineer to discover at the time that the work done or materials supplied are not up to the standard of the contract may involve the employer in loss, where the employer's rights against the contractor are limited to having such defects made good as were ascertainable at some particular time[4] or where a final certificate has been issued and has become conclusive[5] or where the contractor is insolvent. The loss to the employer, due to the architect's or engineer's negligence in such a case, may be the difference between the amount for which the builder or contractor is actually liable and the whole cost of the repairs, or the whole expense of rectifying the defects[6].

An architect or engineer is obliged in administering a contract to deploy sufficient knowledge of those principles of law relevant to his professional practice in order reasonably to protect his client from damage and loss[7]. Thus an architect has been held liable in damages for failing to give notice under a building contract in relation to a contractor who did not proceed regularly and diligently[8].

1   *East Ham Corpn v Bernard Sunley & Sons Ltd* [1966] AC 406 at 443, [1965] 3 All ER 619 at 636, HL, per Lord Upjohn; and see *Florida Hotels Pty Ltd v Mayo* (1965) 113 CLR 588, Aust HC; *Sutcliffe v Chippendale and Edmondson (a firm)* (1971) 18 BLR 149; *Gray (Special Trustees of the London Hospital) v TP Bennett & Son* (1987) 43 BLR 63, sub nom *Trustees of London Hospital v TP Bennett & Son* 13 Con LR 22; *Corfield v Grant* (1992) 59 BLR 102, sub nom *Grant v Corfield* (1992) 29 Con LR 58n. See also *Consarc Design Ltd v Hutch Investments Ltd* (2002) 84 ConLR 36, [2002] All ER (D) 236 (Feb) (inspection was a lesser responsibility than supervision; an architect did not guarantee that his inspection would reveal or prevent all defective work); *McGlinn v Waltham Contractors Ltd* [2007] EWHC 149 (TCC), [2008] Bus LR 233, [2007] All ER (D) 272 (Feb) (the frequency and duration of inspections should be tailored to the nature of the works going on at site from time to time). For older cases on this point see *Jameson v Simon* (1899) 1 F 1211, Ct of Sess; *Leicester Guardians v Trollope* (1911) 75 JP 197. As to certificates see PARA 322 et seq.
2   *Armstrong v Jones* (1869) 2 Hudson's BC (4th Edn) 6; *Leicester Guardians v Trollope* (1911) 75 JP 197. In *Cotton v Wallis* [1955] 3 All ER 373, [1955] 1 WLR 1168, CA, the court thought that the low price of a building was a material factor in determining whether an architect should have passed work as having been done to his reasonable satisfaction. See also *McGlinn v Waltham Contractors Ltd* [2007] EWHC 149 (TCC), [2008] Bus LR 233, [2007] All ER (D) 272 (Feb). As to the clerk of works see PARA 207.
3   *Chesham Properties Ltd v Bucknall Austin Project Management Services Ltd* (1996) 82 BLR 92, (1996) 53 Con LR 22. If an engineer notices that the state of works outside his immediate responsibility is causing immediate danger, he is under a duty to take measures to obviate that danger: see *Hart Investments v Fidler* [2007] EWHC 1058 (TCC), 112 ConLR 33, [2007] BLR 526. Cf *Goldswain and another v Beltec Ltd (t/a BCS Consulting) and another* [2015] EWHC 556 (TCC), 159 ConLR 46, [2015] All ER (D) 101 (Mar), where the retainer between an engineer and its employer had been properly discharged and the retainer did not include any supervision or inspection role, therefore there was no breach of a duty to warn the employer about any deficiencies in the contractor's work.
4   *Re Trent and Humber Co, ex p Cambrian Steam Packet Co* (1868) LR 6 Eq 396. See, however, *East Ham Corpn v Bernard Sunley & Sons Ltd* [1966] AC 406 at 443, [1965] 3 All ER 619 at 636, HL, per Lord Upjohn, and at 449, 639 per Lord Pearson.
5   See *Crown Estate Comrs v John Mowlem & Co Ltd* (1994) 70 BLR 1, (1994) 40 Con LR 36, CA.
6   See further PARA 369 et seq.
7   *West Faulkner Associates v Newham London Borough Council* (1994) 71 BLR 1 at 15, (1994) 11 Const LJ 157 at 162, CA, per Simon Brown LJ.
8   *West Faulkner Associates v Newham London Borough Council* (1994) 71 BLR 1, (1994) 11 Const LJ 157, CA.

468.   Duty as regards certificates and measurements.

When issuing certificates or carrying out measurements or valuations the architect or engineer is liable to the employer for any negligent measurement or valuation of work done[1]. In performing the function of certifier, the architect or engineer is not immune from suit[2]. An employer has independent, concurrent and unlimited causes of action for over-certification against both the contractor and the architect or engineer[3]. If, for example, the architect or engineer should negligently or unskilfully overestimate the amount of an interim certificate[4], the employer might, in the event of the builder or contractor becoming bankrupt, have to complete the work at his own expense, and so lose the amount by which the builder has been overpaid[5].

1 *Saunders and Collard v Broadstairs Local Board* (1890) 2 Hudson's BC (4th Edn) 164, DC; and see NEGLIGENCE vol 78 (2018) PARAS 13, 20 et seq. See also *Hunt v Optima (Cambridge) Ltd* [2014] EWCA Civ 714, [2015] 1 WLR 1346, [2014] All ER (D) 70 (Aug).
2 *Sutcliffe v Thackrah* [1974] AC 727, [1974] 1 All ER 859, HL.
3 *Wessex Regional Health Authority v HLM Design Ltd* (1995) 71 BLR 32.
4 As to interim certificates see PARA 327 et seq.
5 In *Irving v Morrison* (1877) 27 CP 242, Ont CA, an architect was held to be liable to his employer for the amount of the loss so occasioned. See also *Sutcliffe v Chippendale and Edmondson (a firm)* (1971) 18 BLR 149; and cf *Wisbech RDC v Ward* [1928] 2 KB 1, CA.

(v) Liabilities

A. LIABILITY TO THE EMPLOYER

469. Rights of employer on default of architect or engineer.

If the architect or engineer is dismissed for failing to act with due care in his duties of design or supervision, he will forfeit either wholly or in part his right to remuneration, as a person who holds himself out as skilled in any art cannot recover for services which are useless, and which by the ordinary exercise of reasonable skill he ought to have known would be useless for the object in respect of which he was employed[1]. In addition to this, if the negligence or want of skill of the architect or engineer has occasioned loss to his employer, he will be liable to the latter in damages[2]. These are not limited to the amount of the remuneration which under the agreement the architect or engineer was to receive, but are measured by the actual loss occasioned to the employer[3]. The employer can set up such a claim for damages as a defence to a claim by the architect or engineer for his fees, as well as by way of counterclaim or in a separate claim for damages[4].

1 *Moneypenny v Hartland* (1826) 2 C & P 378. As to an architect's or engineer's duty of care see PARA 458 et seq. See also AGENCY vol 1 (2017) PARA 79 et seq.
2 *Gordon v Millar* (1839) 1 D 832, Ct of Sess; *Armstrong v Jones* (1869) 2 Hudson's BC (4th Edn) 6; *Ellisen v Lawrie* (1878) Times, 19 February; *Rogers v James* (1891) 56 JP 277, CA; *Leicester Guardians v Trollope* (1911) 75 JP 197. See also *West Faulkner Associates v Newham London Borough Council* (1994) 71 BLR 1, CA (architect's liability in damages for failing to give notice to contractors who did not proceed regularly and diligently). The liability will, in principle, be both in contract and in tort: see PARA 458. See generally DAMAGES.
3 *Saunders and Collard v Broadstairs Local Board* (1890) 2 Hudson's BC (4th Edn) 164. Where an architect, who has no direct part in the decision-making process, fails to warn his employer about matters falling within his brief, he is liable only for the foreseeable consequences of his failure to warn his employer: *HOK Sport Ltd v Aintree Racecourse Co Ltd* [2002] EWHC 3094 (TCC), [2003] BLR 155, 86 Con LR 165. See also *South Australia Asset Management Corp v York Montague Ltd* [1997] AC 191, [1996] 3 All ER 365, [1996] 3 WLR 87, HL, discussing losses and their calculation: a valuer was under a duty to take reasonable care to provide information on which a lender would decide on a course of action, and where he had negligently overvalued property on which the lender had secured a mortgage advance, he was not responsible for all the consequences of that course of action; he was responsible only for the foreseeable consequences of the information being wrong. However the case went on to say a duty of care which imposed upon the informant responsibility for losses which would have occurred even if the information given

had been correct was not fair and reasonable as between the parties. The correct approach to the assessment of damages was therefore to ascertain what element of the loss suffered as a result of the transaction going ahead was attributable to the inaccuracy of the information by comparing the valuation negligently provided and the correct property value at the time of the valuation, ie the figure which a reasonable valuer, using the information available at the relevant time, would have put forward as the amount which the property was most likely to fetch if sold on the open market. The valuer would not be liable for the amount of the lender's loss attributable to the fall in the property market. *South Australia Asset Management Corp v York Montague Ltd* was considered in *Hughes-Holland v BPE Solicitors* [2017] UKSC 21, [2017] 3 All ER 969, [2017] 2 WLR 1029. The court distinguished between 'information' and 'advice' cases and the impact each has on the measure of damages where loss is caused. Information is where the professional provides only 'a limited part of the material on which his client will rely in deciding whether to enter into a prospective transaction, but the process of identifying the other relevant considerations and the overall assessment of the commercial merits of the transaction are exclusively matters for the client (or possibly his other advisers)' (see at [41] per Lord Sumption). In such cases the professional's legal responsibility and duty does not extend to the decision to enter into the transaction. They are liable only for the 'financial consequences of [that information] being wrong' (see at [41]). The professional does not, effectively, underwrite the whole transaction. In advice cases, on the other hand, 'if the adviser has a duty to protect his client (so far as due care can do it) against the full range of risks associated with a potential transaction, the client will not have retained responsibility for any of them. The adviser's responsibility extends to the decision. If the adviser has negligently assessed risk A, the result is that the overall riskiness of the transaction has been understated. If the client would not have entered into the transaction on a careful assessment of its overall merits, the fact that the loss may have resulted from risks B, C or D should not matter' (see at [40] per Lord Sumption). If the professional sets the agenda, decides what factors are relevant and advises in relation to those factors, then they can be liable for the full losses caused by the transaction.

4   *Davis v Hedges* (1871) LR 6 QB 687; *Mondel v Steel* (1841) 8 M & W 858; *Armstrong v Jones* (1869) 2 Hudson's BC (4th Edn) 6; *Saunders and Collard v Broadstairs Local Board* (1890) 2 Hudson's BC (4th Edn) 164; *Rogers v James* (1891) 56 JP 277, 2 Hudson's BC (4th Edn) 172, CA; *A Martin French v Kingswood Hill Ltd* [1961] 1 QB 96, [1960] 2 All ER 251, CA. But not both as a defence and as a counterclaim: *Hutchinson v Harris* (1978) 10 BLR 19, CA. See CIVIL PROCEDURE vol 11 (2015) PARA 338.

470.   Liability for fraud and secret commissions.

Any fraudulent or dishonest act on the part of an architect or engineer in relation to his employment will render him liable to his employer, who may rescind the contract and, if he has suffered loss, claim damages[1]. In particular such liability will arise if the architect or engineer receives a secret commission from the builder[2] and whether such act results in loss to the employer or not it justifies the dismissal of the architect or engineer, who must pay over any money so received to the employer, for an agent cannot retain secret profits made at his principal's expense[3]. Nor will the courts listen to any evidence of custom or usage of agents to take such secret commissions[4]. Any such payments received by the architect from the builder, if made without the knowledge of the employer, are a breach of the right of the employer to demand the faithful services of the architect or engineer to the exclusion of any arrangement with persons whose work he has to supervise[5].

It is an offence to offer, promise or give a financial or other advantage to another person: (1) intending the advantage to induce a person to perform improperly a relevant function or activity, or to reward a person for the improper performance of such a function or activity; or (2) knowing or believing that the acceptance of the advantage would itself constitute the improper performance of a relevant function or activity[6].

1   See generally MISREPRESENTATION vol 76 (2013) PARAS 788 et seq, 811 et seq. See also DAMAGES.

2 *Temperley v Blackrod Manufacturing Co Ltd* (1907) 71 JP Jo 341. See also PARA 226. For a case concerning the distinction between secret commission and failure to obtain permission see *Hurstanger Ltd v Wilson* [2007] EWCA Civ 299, [2007] 4 All ER 1118, [2007] 1 WLR 2351 (consumer credit case).
3 *Rogers v James* (1891) 56 JP 277, CA; *Arab Monetary Fund v Hashim* [1993] 1 Lloyd's Rep 543; and see AGENCY vol 1 (2017) PARA 92 et seq.
4 *Bulfield v Fournier* (1894) 11 TLR 62 per Lord Russell of Killowen CJ. See, however, *Holden v Webber* (1860) 29 Beav 117. As to custom and usage see generally CUSTOM AND USAGE.
5 See *Harrington v Victoria Graving Dock Co* (1878) 3 QBD 549.
6 See the Bribery Act 2010 s 1; and CRIMINAL LAW vol 25 (2016) PARA 369.

B. LIABILITY TO THE CONTRACTOR

471. Liability of architect or engineer to the contractor.

As there is no contractual relationship between the architect or engineer and the contractor the only liability that can be incurred towards the contractor is in tort. In situations recognised by law a liability might arise in negligence[1], negligent misstatement[2], negligent misrepresentation[3] and other torts[4]. It appears, however, that an architect or engineer will not generally be liable to the contractor for economic loss caused by the performance of the certifying function[5]. When the architect or engineer is acting as agent for the employer he can incur no personal liability provided that he acts honestly and within the scope of his employment[6].

If an architect or engineer exceeds his authority in ordering additional works of the contractor for which the contractor could claim no remuneration under his contract with the employer, he may incur liabilities towards the contractor for breach of warranty of authority[7], but as such unauthorised acts would not normally bind his employer, it would seem that he could not incur any liability towards his employer[8] in respect of them. If the architect or engineer has apparent or ostensible authority to order additional work, the contractor can claim payment for the work and the architect or engineer would incur a liability to the employer, unless it is apparent from the contract that such work was unauthorised[9]. Moreover the architect or engineer will not be liable to pay a contractor[10] or supplier[11] himself, unless he has specifically undertaken personal liability[12].

1 See PARA 363; and NEGLIGENCE.
2 See *J Jarvis & Sons Ltd v Castle Wharf Developments Ltd* [2001] EWCA Civ 19, [2001] Lloyd's Rep PN 328, (2001) Times, 28 February, CA; cf *South Nation River Conservation Authority v Auto Concrete Curb Ltd* (1993) 11 Const LJ 155, Can SC. See MISREPRESENTATION vol 76 (2013) PARAS 761–763; NEGLIGENCE vol 78 (2018) PARA 13;
3 See *Edgeworth Construction Ltd v ND Lea & Associates Ltd* (1993) 66 BLR 56, Can SC. See MISREPRESENTATION vol 76 (2013) PARAS 761–763.
4 *John Mowlem & Co plc v Eagle Star Insurance Co Ltd* (1992) 62 BLR 126, (1992) 33 Con LR 131. See TORT.
5 *Pacific Associates Inc v Baxter* [1990] 1 QB 993, [1989] 2 All ER 159, CA (considered in *Galliford Try Infrastructure Ltd v Mott MacDonald* [2008] EWHC 1570 (TCC), 120 ConLR 1, [2008] All ER (D) 254 (Jul), which although not about certification, discusses whether there is a breach of a duty of care leading to economic losses based on a contractor's reliance on information and documents provided to it by an engineer during a tender process); *John Holland Construction and Engineering Ltd v Majorca Products* (2000) 16 Const LJ 114, Vic SC.
6 See *Ambrose v Dunmow Union* (1846) 9 Beav 508 at 515; *Robertson v Fleming* (1861) 4 Macq 167 at 184, HL; *Stevenson v Watson* (1879) 4 CPD 148. As to his liability to his employer see PARA 469.
7 See AGENCY vol 1 (2017) PARAS 161–162; and *Randell v Trimen* (1856) 18 CB 786; *Collen v Wright* (1857) 8 E & B 647; *Yonge v Toynbee* [1910] 1 KB 215, CA. Cf *Howard v Sheward* (1866) LR 2 CP 148.
8 See PARAS 272, 454.

9 *Halbot v Lens* [1901] 1 Ch 344. Any fraudulent assertion of authority would be actionable on grounds of deceit or misrepresentation: *Ludbrook v Barrett* (1877) 46 LJQB 798; *Stevenson v Watson* (1879) 4 CPD 148; see PARA 474.
10 See *Chidley v Norris* (1862) 3 F & F 228; and AGENCY vol 1 (2017) PARA 157.
11 *Beigtheil and Young v Stewart* (1900) 16 TLR 177. Where the supplier has received an order from the architect it is a question of fact whether the architect is personally liable: see *A Vigers & Sons Ltd v Swindell* [1939] 3 All ER 590.
12 *Sika Contracts v Gill* (1978) 9 BLR 11.

472. No warranty that plans are practicable.

An architect or engineer does not warrant to the builder or contractor the practicability of the plans, drawings and specifications prepared by him, or of the temporary means of construction indicated in the specification. It is the duty of the contractor to investigate these matters for himself, and it has been held that any usage or custom[1] for him to rely on the drawings or specifications will not assist him[2]. If he does not inquire into the matter he runs the risk of not being able to carry out the work, and must take the consequences[3].

1 See generally CUSTOM AND USAGE.
2 *Thorn v London Corpn* (1876) 1 App Cas 120, HL. See also PARAS 309, 451.
3 *Bottoms v York Corpn* (1892) 2 Hudson's BC (10th Edn) 270, CA. See also *Jackson v Eastbourne Local Board* (1886) 2 Hudson's BC (10th Edn) 270, 356, HL.

473. Accuracy of bills of quantities.

The architect or engineer does not normally warrant the correctness of the bills of quantities[1] supplied to the persons who propose to tender, whether they have been prepared by an independent quantity surveyor or by the architect or engineer himself[2].

The liability for inaccurate quantities prepared by the architect or engineer rests on the same principle as where they are prepared by an independent quantity surveyor. If the architect or engineer is employed by the contractor, he may of course be liable to him for negligence in their preparation[3]. In a case where the architect had been employed by the building owner to prepare the quantities, and the amount of his charges was to be added to the amount of the tender, the payment by the builder of those charges did not impose any more liability on the architect than it did in the case of an independent quantity surveyor[4].

If, however, the architect or engineer expressly makes himself responsible to the builder or contractor for the accuracy of the quantities[5], or if a duty of care were to be imposed on the architect or engineer towards the contractor by virtue of the particular circumstances of the case[6], he will be liable to compensate him if the quantities are not reasonably accurate.

1 See PARA 451.
2 *Sherren v Harrison* (1860) 2 Hudson's BC (10th Edn) 511; *Scrivener v Pask* (1866) LR 1 CP 715. See also PARA 468.
3 See *Priestley v Stone* (1888) 4 TLR 730, CA.
4 *Young v Blake* (1887) 2 Hudson's BC (4th Edn) 110.
5 *Bolt v Thomas* (1859) 2 Hudson's BC (4th Edn) 3.
6 *Hedley Byrne & Co Ltd v Heller & Partners Ltd* [1964] AC 465, [1963] 2 All ER 575, HL; *Henderson v Merrett Syndicates* [1995] 2 AC 145, [1994] 3 All ER 506, HL. See generally PARA 472. For examples of cases where claims of this kind have been advanced against an architect or engineer see *South Nation River Conservation Authority v Auto Concrete Curb Ltd* (1993) 11 Const LJ 155, Can SC; *Edgeworth Construction Ltd v ND Lea & Associates Ltd* (1993) 66 BLR 56, Can SC; *J Jarvis & Sons Ltd v Castle Wharf Developments Ltd* [2001] EWCA Civ 19, [2001] NPC 15, CA. As to fraud see *S Pearson & Son Ltd v Dublin Corpn* [1907] AC 351, HL; and PARA 474.

474. Liability for fraud.

An architect or engineer will be liable to the contractor if he acts fraudulently to the contractor's detriment, whether in preparing drawings[1] or in refusing to certify or in certifying dishonestly and whether in collusion with his employer or not[2]. He will similarly be liable if fraudulently he falsely asserts that he has authority to order additional work[3].

The architect cannot excuse himself from liability for fraud by alleging that he merely acted as the agent of his employer, for all persons directly concerned in the commission of a fraud are to be treated as principals, and a contract of agency cannot impose any obligation on the agent to commit a fraud[4].

The mere fact of an architect refusing to certify or to ascertain the amount owing[5] is no proof of fraud, nor is the fact that measurements made by him for the purpose of valuation are inaccurate, or made on a wrong principle.

1 *S Pearson & Son Ltd v Dublin Corpn* [1907] AC 351, HL.
2 *Waring v Manchester, Sheffield and Lincolnshire Rly Co* (1850) 2 H & Tw 239; *Macintosh v Great Western Rly Co* (1850) 19 LJCh 374; *Padley v Lincoln Waterworks Co* (1850) 2 Mac & G 68; *Scott v Liverpool Corpn* (1858) 3 De G & J 334; *Goodyear v Weymouth and Melcombe Regis Corpn* (1865) 35 LJCP 12 at 17; *Ludbrook v Barrett* (1877) 46 LJQB 798; *Re De Morgan, Snell & Co and Rio de Janeiro Flour Mills and Granaries Ltd* (1892) 8 TLR 292 at 293, CA. As to certificates see PARA 322 et seq.
3 *Ludbrook v Barrett* (1877) 46 LJQB 798; *Stevenson v Watson* (1879) 4 CPD 148.
4 *Cullen v Thomson's Trustees and Kerr* (1862) 4 Macq 424 at 432, HL.
5 *Stevenson v Watson* (1879) 4 CPD 148; *Le Lievre v Gould* [1893] 1 QB 491, CA.

475. Measure of damages.

The measure of damages in case of breach of warranty of authority seems to be the amount that will indemnify the contractor and put him in the same position as if the act of the architect or engineer had been within his authority[1]. Thus the contractor would be entitled to recover the amount that would have been recoverable from the alleged principal and the costs[2] which he has had to pay in the course of any litigation caused by the breach of warranty of authority[3]. If the warranty is fraudulent, the architect will be open to a claim for deceit[4].

1 *Richardson v Williamson* (1871) LR 6 QB 276 at 279 per Blackburn J; *Re National Coffee Palace Co, ex p Panmure* (1883) 24 ChD 367, CA; *Heskell v Continental Express Ltd* [1950] 1 All ER 1033 at 1043 per Devlin J; *Doyle v Olby (Ironmongers) Ltd* [1969] 2 QB 158, [1969] 2 All ER 119, CA.
2 These costs will be those assessed costs which the contractor has paid to the principal and to his own solicitor: see *Hughes v Graeme* (1864) 33 LJ QB 335. As to costs see generally CIVIL PROCEDURE vol 12A (2015) PARA 1680 et seq.
3 *Randell v Trimen* (1856) 18 CB 786; *Collen v Wright* (1857) 8 E & B 647; *Simons v Patchett* (1857) 7 E & B 568; *Meek v Wendt* [1889] WN 14, CA; *Yonge v Toynbee* [1910] 1 KB 215, CA; *Irving v Burns* 1915 SC 260. See further AGENCY vol 1 (2017) PARAS 161–162.
4 As to deceit see *Derry v Peek* (1889) 14 App Cas 337, HL; *Doyle v Olby (Ironmongers) Ltd* [1969] 2 QB 158, [1969] 2 All ER 119, CA; *Smith Kline & French Laboratories Ltd v Long* [1988] 3 All ER 887, [1989] 1 WLR 1, CA; and MISREPRESENTATION vol 76 (2013) PARA 788 et seq.

(vi) Remuneration of Architect or Engineer

A. IN GENERAL

476. Person liable to pay.

An architect or engineer is ordinarily employed by the building owner, and has to look to him for payment[1].

Where the building contract gives power to vary the works specified, and provides that additions or omissions due to such variations are to be measured by the architect so as to ascertain the amount to be added to or deducted from the contract price, the building owner may be liable to pay the architect for this service, if it falls outside the architect's original engagement and the building owner is aware that it is an additional service[2].

1   *Locke v Morter* (1885) 2 TLR 121. In certain circumstances, the architect or engineer may have rights against others by reason of the Contracts (Rights of Third Parties) Act 1999: see CONTRACT vol 22 (2012) PARA 341 et seq. As to payment provisions where the contract is a 'construction contract' within the meaning of the Housing Grants, Construction and Regeneration Act 1996 see PARAS 351–358.

2   *Gilbert & Partners (a firm) v Knight* [1968] 2 All ER 248, 4 BLR 9, CA; *Lusty v Finsbury Securities Ltd* (1991) 58 BLR 66, CA.

477.   Express or implied contract.

If the employer has entered into an express contract, whether oral or in writing, with the architect or engineer, the remuneration of the latter will necessarily be governed by the terms of that contract. If the architect or engineer enters into an express contract for a lump sum with the employer, he cannot charge an additional fee for extra work undertaken within the scope of that engagement by him unless the express contract is discharged and a new contract made[1].

Where no express contract has been entered into as to the terms of the employment of an architect or engineer, the right to remuneration rests on a contract to pay what is reasonable, implied by requesting and accepting the services[2] or by inducing the architect by fraud to perform them without intending to pay for them[3].

Where the agreement is that the employer is to decide how much the remuneration is to be, the architect or engineer need not accept the amount fixed by the employer, but is entitled to a reasonable remuneration such as the employer ought to have fixed[4].

If the contract does not specifically provide for payment, evidence is admissible to show that the parties intended the services to be gratuitous, or that payment was only to be made in the discretion of the employer[5] but note the statutory right to a reasonable price in consumer contracts[6].

1   *Gilbert & Partners (a firm) v Knight* [1968] 2 All ER 248, 4 BLR 9, CA, applying the principle stated by Lord Dunedin in *The Olanda* [1919] 2 KB 728n at 730, HL. See also *Adams Holden & Pearson v Trent Regional Health Authority* (1989) 47 BLR 34, CA; and *Lusty v Finsbury Securities Ltd* (1991) 58 BLR 66, CA.

2   *Manson v Baillie* (1855) 2 Macq 80, HL; *Moffatt v Laurie* (1855) 15 CB 583 at 593; *Landless v Wilson* (1880) 8 R 289, Ct of Sess. See also *Marston Construction Co Ltd v Kigass Ltd* (1989) 15 ConLR 116, 46 BLR 109; *Lusty v Finsbury Securities Ltd* (1991) 58 BLR 66, CA. As to restitutionary claims for work done in expectation of contract see eg *Vedatech Corpn v Crystal Decisions* [2002] EWHC 818 (Ch), [2002] All ER (D) 318 (May); and RESTITUTION vol 88 (2012) PARA 525.

3   *Rumsey v North Eastern Rly Co* (1863) 32 LJCP 244.

4   *Bryant v Flight* (1839) 5 M & W 114; *Bird v McGahey* (1849) 2 Car & Kir 707.

5   *Taylor v Brewer* (1813) 1 M & S 290.

6   For business to consumer contracts where the contract is to supply a service and does not expressly fix a price or other consideration and does not say how it is to be fixed there is an implied term that the consumer must pay a reasonable price for the service and no more: see the Consumer Rights Act 2015 s 51(1), (2); and CONSUMER PROTECTION vol 21 (2016) PARA 366. What is reasonable is a question of fact: see s 51(3).

478. Remuneration for speculative work.

Where studies or designs are submitted merely for approval or speculatively, no claim for remuneration arises unless the work is approved or used[1], and similarly in the case of plans or drawings submitted in competition, subject of course to the published terms of the competition[2].

Such 'probationary drawings'[3] are in the nature of a tender, that is a mere proposal or offer to do work, and without acceptance there is no mutuality on which an implied contract to pay for them can be based.

If the plans or drawings submitted for approval are used for any purpose, they must be paid for[4].

1 *Moffatt v Dickson* (1853) 13 CB 543; *Moffatt v Laurie* (1855) 15 CB 583; *Du Bosky & Partners v Shearwater Property Holdings plc* (1991) 54 BLR 71.
2 See *Ward v Lowndes* (1859) 1 E & E 940 at 941. On a true construction of the competition conditions it may become clear that work done in the hope of winning the competition is not work for which the winning entrant is entitled to payment in the event of his appointment as architect for a building project becoming ineffective due to cancellation of the project. If the design is not used, there is no reason why the winner should be in a better position than the losers merely by reason of an appointment being made which was ineffective: see *Jepson (HN) & Partners (a firm) v Severn Trent Water Authority* (1982) 20 BLR 53, CA.
3 See *Moffatt v Dickson* (1853) 13 CB 543.
4 *Landless v Wilson* (1880) 8 R 289, Ct of Sess. As to the copyright in plans see PARA 486.

479. Procuring of tenders.

If the architect or engineer is authorised to obtain tenders, he is entitled, unless it is otherwise agreed, to payment of any expenses reasonably or necessarily incurred in connection therewith[1].

If the architect or engineer is instructed to prepare plans for a building or for works to cost approximately a certain sum and all the tenders sent in are considerably in excess of the sum mentioned, the employer may be entitled to repudiate the employment and refuse to pay him[2], on the ground that there was a condition that the works should be capable of being constructed for the sum, or approximately the sum, estimated[3] and that the buildings as designed could not be carried out for that sum or anything near it[4]. The building owner may counterclaim damages for any cost overrun[5] incurred subject to proof of negligence[6].

1 See *Bayley v Wilkins* (1849) 7 CB 886.
2 *Burr v Ridout* (1893) Times, 22 February.
3 *Nye and Saunders & Partners v Bristow* (1987) 37 BLR 92, CA.
4 *Nelson v Spooner* (1861) 2 F & F 613 at 618. In that case Cockburn CJ left the following questions to the jury: (1) whether it was an express condition that the works should be capable of being executed for the estimated sum; if not, then (2) whether there was an implied condition that the work should be capable of being done for a sum reasonably near to the estimated sum; if so, then (3) whether the estimate was reasonably sufficient; and (4) as to a claim for work and labour on the plans, etc, whether the labour was bestowed or not under the special contract. See also *Riva Properties Limited & Ors v Foster + Partners Limited* [2017] EWHC 2574, 175 CONLR 45, [2017] All ER (D) 113 (Oct).
5 *Kidd v Mississauga Hydro-Electric Commission* (1979) 97 DLR (3d) 535, Ont HC; the claim in that case was negligent misrepresentation. As to counterclaims see generally CIVIL PROCEDURE vol 11 (2015) PARA 382 et seq.
6 But see *Copthorne Hotel (Newcastle) Ltd v Arup Associates* (1996) 58 Con LR 105 (negligence could not be established simply by contrasting the estimate with the strikingly different actual cost). As to negligence see generally NEGLIGENCE.

480. When the remuneration is payable.

The contract will generally make provision for payment by instalments[1]. If the engagement of the architect or engineer is a construction contract[2], he will be entitled to payment by instalments save in very limited circumstances[3].

If the contract is one to perform an entire work, such as to prepare plans, drawings and the specification for a fixed sum, or for a percentage of the whole cost of the work, then (unless there is express, implied or statutory provision for periodic payments) the right to payment does not arise until the whole work has been done[4]. Any instalment constitutes a debt due and payable, for which the architect can sue as and when it becomes due[5].

In respect of instalments stipulated in a construction contract under the Housing Grants, Construction and Regeneration Act 1996, the instalment schedule may provide certainty on when instalments become due by reference to set dates for payment, which will exclude further payments beyond those dates despite the fact that work may continue to be carried out after the last date specified[6].

1   This is almost invariably the case if standard forms are used, but the right to payment may only arise on entire completion of the relevant stage. See eg *Workman, Clark & Co Ltd v Lloyd Brazileño* [1908] 1 KB 968, CA (which contains facts found to be covered by the Housing Grants, Construction and Regeneration Act 1996 relating to payment in construction contracts where there is a right to payments by instalments (or on completion of stages because a stage payment can be an 'instalment' under the Act) and a right to suspend for non-payment). See also the text and note 5.
2   See the Housing Grants, Construction and Regeneration Act 1996 s 104(2); and PARAS 210, 446.
3   See the Housing Grants, Construction and Regeneration Act 1996 s 109; and PARAS 352, 345.
4   See *Johnson v Gandy* (1855) 26 LTOS 72. As to entire contracts see PARA 209. Where the contract is not an entire contract, the historical position has been that a person is entitled to payment from time to time in the absence of express or implied agreement otherwise: see *Appleby v Myers* (1867) LR 2 CP 651 at 660 per Blackburn J. See also PARA 232 et seq.
5   Cf *Workman, Clark & Co Ltd v Lloyd Brazileño* [1908] 1 KB 968, CA. Cf *Sidney Kaye, Eric Firmin & Partners (a firm) v Bronesky* (1973) 226 Estates Gazette 1395, (1973) 4 BLR 1, CA, per Lawton LJ; and PARA 482. See also the Housing Grants, Construction and Regeneration Act 1996 s 110 (dates for payment); and PARA 353.
6   See *Balfour Beatty Regional Construction Ltd v Grove Developments Ltd* [2016] EWCA Civ 990, [2017] 1 All ER (Comm) 729, [2017] 1 WLR 1893.

481. Amount payable.

Where an express agreement has been made as to the amount of the remuneration to be paid to an architect or engineer, he must be paid accordingly[1]. Where, however, no agreement has been made, the architect or engineer is entitled to reasonable remuneration. The amount of such reasonable remuneration is a question of fact[2].

1   *Gilbert & Partners (a firm) v Knight* [1968] 2 All ER 248, 4 BLR 9, CA; *Lusty v Finsbury Securities Ltd* (1991) 58 BLR 66, CA.
2   *Bryant v Flight* (1839) 5 M & W 114; *Bird v M'Gahey* (1849) 2 Car & Kir 707.

482. Professional scale of charges.

While there is no standard basis for the calculation of fees and the price is generally a matter for negotiation, in the case of architects the professional charge for designing and supervising the construction of buildings is often based on a percentage of the total cost of the works. Professional institutes used to publish recommended fee scales expressed as a percentage of construction costs for a range of different building types[1]. However, legislation aimed at preventing anti-competitive behaviour[2] forced the institutes to abolish these fee scales, leaving fee negotiation to market forces. Rates are not incorporated into the standard form of agreement for the appointment of an architect for this reason[3]. Instead fees in practice are calculated by reference to various methods including fixed lump sums, time charges, percentage of construction cost or target based fees (for example based on successful planning being achieved). However, it is right to take into consideration the practice adopted by a large proportion of the profession[4].

1   The Royal Institute of British Architects (RIBA) used to cite an independent survey of fees which recorded that the fees for providing a full service for new private houses were generally between 8% and 12% of the construction cost, fees for extension projects and renovation work could be a larger percentage of the building cost and fees for preparing designs and submitting planning applications were to be between 3% and 5% of the construction cost.
2   See the Competition Act 1998 s 2 (known as the Chapter 1 prohibition); and COMPETITION vol 18 (2009) PARA 116 et seq. The Chapter I prohibition did not apply in any case in which it is excluded by or as a result of professional rules, but this has been repealed by the Enterprise Act 2002 ss 207, 278(2), Sch 26 as from 1 April 2003 (see the Enterprise Act 2002 (Commencement No 2, Transitional and Transitory Provisions) Order 2003, SI 2003/766).
3   As to standard forms of contract see PARA 202.
4   *Whipham v Everitt* (1900) Roscoe's BC (4th Edn) 171 at 172 per Kennedy J. See more recent cases involving percentage fees and their continued use such as *Munkenbeck & Marshall v Regent Health and Fitness Club Ltd (No 2)* (1997) 59 ConLR 145; *KKA Ltd v MacDonald Hotels Ltd* [2008] CSOH 108.

483.   Scale of payment for other work.

Architects, engineers, and surveyors are often employed to perform work other than that of designing and supervising the construction of buildings and works, such as measuring, valuing, surveying, qualifying as witnesses and attending in court and before arbitrators, settling the accounts of builders and tradesmen. For work of this nature they are entitled, in the absence of any express agreement, to reasonable remuneration[1]. What is reasonable is a question of fact in each case depending upon the facts.

1   *Debenham v King's College, Cambridge* (1884) 1 TLR 170. As to payment under express and implied contracts see PARA 477. See also PARA 502.

D.   DEATH AND BANKRUPTCY

484.   Death of architect or engineer.

The contract to employ an architect or engineer, being a personal one, is dissolved by the death or incapacity of the person employed[1], and is rendered void for the future, but it is not thereby rescinded ab initio.

Where the architect or engineer is entitled to payment by instalments at particular times[2], and dies during the progress of the work, his personal representative will be entitled to recover any instalments due at the time of his death[3]. Unless the contract is an entire contract with no express, implied or statutory provision for periodic payments[4] it would seem that the personal representative of the deceased architect or engineer can recover the value of the work done by him and by which the employer has benefited[5].

Any payments made by the employer on account during the progress of the work would not seem to be recoverable by him in case of the disablement of the architect by act of God, as the consideration would not have completely failed[6].

1   See PARA 448; and generally CONTRACT.

2   See PARA 480.

3   *Stubbs v Holywell Rly Co* (1867) LR 2 Exch 311.

4   See PARA 480.

5   This was admitted on the part of the defendant company in *Stubbs v Holywell Rly Co* (1867) LR 2 Exch 311.

6   See *Cuckson v Stones* (1858) 1 E & E 248. As to failure of consideration see RESTITUTION vol 88 (2012) PARA 487. As to consideration generally see CONTRACT vol 22 (2012) PARA 308 et seq.

485. Insolvency of the architect or engineer.

On the architect's or engineer's becoming insolvent[1] all money owing to him becomes the property of his trustee in bankruptcy, to whom pass also the bankrupt's rights of action for breach of contract and wrongful dismissal[2]. If, however, the trustee does not intervene, the bankrupt can himself sue for work done after the bankruptcy[3].

If the architect or engineer is employed on the terms of being paid a salary, his remuneration does not vest in the trustee in bankruptcy, unless an order is made by the court[4], appropriating part of the bankrupt's salary or income for the benefit of his creditors[5].

1   This paragraph refers only to personal insolvency, which is regulated by the Insolvency Act 1986 Pts IX–XI (ss 264–385): see BANKRUPTCY AND INDIVIDUAL INSOLVENCY vol 5 (2013) PARA 1 et seq. Where the architect or engineer is a body corporate then the rules relating to corporate insolvency apply: see COMPANY AND PARTNERSHIP INSOLVENCY vol 16 (2017) PARA 1 et seq.

2   *Jameson & Co v Brick and Stone Co Ltd* (1878) 4 QBD 208; *Emden v Carte* (1881) 17 ChD 768, CA; *Bailey v Thurston & Co Ltd* [1903] 1 KB 137, CA; *Re Clayton, Collins v Clayton and Reade* [1940] Ch 539, [1940] 2 All ER 233. See also BANKRUPTCY AND INDIVIDUAL INSOLVENCY vol 5 (2013) PARAS 431, 447 et seq.

3   *Jameson & Co v Brick and Stone Co Ltd* (1878) 4 QBD 208.

4   See the Insolvency Act 1986 s 310; and BANKRUPTCY AND INDIVIDUAL INSOLVENCY vol 5 (2013) PARA 462. See also *Re Tennant's Application* [1956] 2 All ER 753, [1956] 1 WLR 874, CA; following *Re Landau, ex p Trustee* [1934] Ch 549, CA.

5   *Re Brindle, ex p Brindle* (1887) 4 Morr 104; *Re Shine, ex p Shine* [1892] 1 QB 522, CA.

(vii) Plans

486. Property in plans.

Plans and drawings prepared by architects and engineers on behalf of a client are, in the absence of special agreement, the property of the person who pays for them[1]. However, documents prepared in order to assist the architect or engineer to carry out his duties remain his property as they are not brought into existence on behalf of the client[2]. In the absence of any special agreement, the architect or engineer owns the copyright in the plans and in the design embodied in the owner's building[3]. Thus if an extension to an existing building is commissioned from another architect in the same style as the original there will be a breach of the copyright of the design of that building owned by the original architect[4]. When an architect or engineer prepares plans for a reasonable fee, there is an implied licence that he will allow them to be used for all purposes connected with the erection of buildings on the site to which they relate[5]. There is no such licence when he has only received nominal remuneration[6]. Where there is a breach of the architect's copyright in his plans and an injunction is inappropriate, damages are at large and are to be assessed by considering what remuneration would be due to the architect if the building owner had applied for his licence to use the plans[7].

Where two or more architects or engineers are practising as a partnership, the property of any documents is in the partnership and one partner cannot secretly copy any of those documents for his own purposes, because he would be in breach of the duty of good faith owed by one partner to another[8].

1   *Leicestershire County Council v Michael Faraday & Partners Ltd* [1941] 2 KB 205, [1941] 2 All ER 483, CA; *Beresford v Driver* (1851) 14 Beav 387; *Ebdy v M'Gowan* (1870) 2 Hudson's BC (10th Edn) 189; *Gibbon v Pease* [1905] 1 KB 810, CA.
2   *Leicestershire County Council v Michael Faraday & Partners Ltd* [1941] 2 KB 205 at 206, [1941] 2 All ER 483 at 487, CA, per MacKinnon LJ.
3   *Blair v Osborne and Tomkins* [1971] 2 QB 78, [1971] 1 All ER 468, CA; *Stovin-Bradford v Volpoint Properties Ltd* [1971] Ch 1007, [1971] 3 All ER 570, CA. As to the subsistence, ownership and duration of copyright see the Copyright, Designs and Patents Act 1988 ss 1, 2, 4, 11, 12; and COPYRIGHT vol 23 (2016) PARAS 551–552, 569, 601, 577 et seq.
4   *Meikle v Maufe* [1941] 3 All ER 144. See also *Toner v Kean Construction (Scotland) Ltd* [2009] CSOH 105, 2009 SLT 1038, 2010 SCLR 64.
5   *Blair v Osborne and Tomkins* [1971] 2 QB 78, [1971] 1 All ER 468, CA. See also *Hunter v Fitzroy Robinson & Partners* (1978) 10 BLR 84 (no injunction as damages adequate remedy).
6   *Stovin-Bradford v Volpoint Properties Ltd* [1971] Ch 1007, [1971] 3 All ER 570, CA.
7   *Chabot v Davies* [1936] 3 All ER 221; *Meikle v Maufe* [1941] 3 All ER 144; *Blair v Osborne and Tomkins* [1971] 2 QB 78, [1971] 1 All ER 468, CA; *Stovin-Bradford v Volpoint Properties Ltd* [1971] Ch 1007, [1971] 3 All ER 570, CA. See also the Copyright, Designs and Patents Act 1988 ss 96, 97 (see COPYRIGHT vol 23 (2016) PARAS 829, 832, 842); and *Cala Homes (South) Ltd v Alfred McAlpine Homes East Ltd* [1995] FSR 818.
8   *Floydd v Cheney* [1970] Ch 602, [1970] 1 All ER 446; and see PARA 428. As to the duty of good faith owed by one partner to another see PARTNERSHIP vol 79 (2014) PARA 105.

487.   Lien on plans, etc.

The architect has a lien on the plans and drawings prepared by him, and need not deliver them up until he is paid[1], and may bring a claim for his fees although he still retains the plans. Even if he demands more than a reasonable fee for the plans, and that is refused, he is not precluded from bringing a claim for his charges and recovering reasonable remuneration[2]. The employer may seek to recover such plans and drawings in proceedings and the court has power to order that he pay the amount claimed into court pending the outcome of the proceedings and that, if he does so, the plans and drawings should be given up to him[3].

1   *Hughes v Lenny* (1839) 5 M & W 183. As to liens see generally LIEN vol 68 (2016) PARA 845. After an architect has been paid, there is an implied licence that his plans may be used for the purposes for which they were prepared: *Blair v Osborne and Tomkins* [1971] 2 QB 78, [1971] 1 All ER 468, CA.
2   *Hughes v Lenny* (1839) 5 M & W 183.
3   See CPR 25.1(1)(m); and CIVIL PROCEDURE vol 12 (2015) PARA 566. See also *Segbedzi v Glah* [1989] NLJR 1303, CA.

7. VALUERS AND SURVEYORS

(1) Introduction

488. Meanings of 'valuer', 'appraiser' and 'surveyor'.

The terms 'valuer' and 'appraiser' have similar meanings[1]. An appraiser is generally taken to be a person appointed and sworn to estimate the value of property[2], while a valuer is a person who estimates or assesses values; that is, in the present context, a person who estimates or assesses the worth or value of, or who fixes a price for, property [3]. However, while definitions of 'valuer' and 'valuation' commonly place the main emphasis on value or worth in a material sense, an 'appraiser' may also be a person who estimates the amount, quality or excellence of property[4].

The term 'surveyor' usually describes a person whose business it is to inspect and examine land, houses or other property and to calculate and report upon its actual or prospective value or productiveness for certain purposes, although surveyors also perform other functions.

This part of the title covers the law relating to valuers and surveyors generally, including their statutory functions[5], their legal relationships with clients[6] and third parties[7] and the extent of their liability[8]. It also deals specifically with the employment of quantity surveyors[9]. Quantity surveyors are employed by the architect[10] or his agent in most sizeable building contracts and engineering works. They prepare cost estimates and plans, audit projects, manage construction costs and administer building contracts.

1 The term 'appraiser' was the more commonly used in statutes passed before the beginning of the twentieth century: see eg the Distress for Rent Act 1689 s 1 (repealed); the Appraisers Licences Act 1806 (repealed); and the Law of Distress Amendment Act 1888 s 5 (repealed).
2 An appraiser is not necessarily required to be sworn before he acts, notwithstanding that statute may require him to be sworn in particular cases.
3 'The term 'valuer' (with a capital 'V' at any rate) is used nowadays to denote a member of a recognised profession comprised of persons possessed of skill and experience in assessing the market price of property, particularly real property': *Sudbrook Trading Estate Ltd v Eggleton* [1983] 1 AC 444 at 477, [1982] 3 All ER 1 at 5, HL, per Lord Diplock. As to valuations for statutory purposes see PARAS 493–497; and as to contractual valuations see PARAS 498–500.
4 As to appraisement as opposed to valuation see *Pappa v Rose* (1872) LR 7 CP 525, ExCh (broker required to decide whether raisins delivered were of 'fair average quality' as specified in contract of sale). As to the appraisement of arrested ships see SHIPPING AND MARITIME LAW vol 93 (2017) PARAS 177.
5 See PARA 493 et seq.
6 See PARAS 501–503.
7 See PARAS 504–505.
8 See PARAS 506–515.
9 See PARA 516 et seq.
10 As to architects see PARA 424 et seq.

489. Professional bodies.

There is no general statutory regulation of, or restriction upon qualification and practice as, a valuer or surveyor[1], but most valuers and surveyors are members of one or more of a number of professional organisations, in particular the Royal Institution of Chartered Surveyors[2]. Members of the Central

Association of Agricultural Valuers[3] and of the Institute of Revenues, Rating and Valuation are frequently concerned with valuations of land for specific purposes[4].

1 Certain inspections or valuations must be carried out by members of the Royal Institution of Chartered Surveyors (see note 2) or persons satisfying other prescribed requirements: see eg the Charities Act 2011 s 119 (see CHARITIES vol 8 (2015) PARA 401). Certain instruments relating to farm business tenancies may be prepared by a member or fellow of that body, or by a fellow of the Central Association of Agricultural Valuers ('CAAV'): see the Legal Services Act 2007 ss 13, 19, Sch 3 para 3(5), (6); and LEGAL PROFESSIONS vol 65 (2015) PARA 360.
2 The Royal Institution of Chartered Surveyors ('RICS'), which was founded in 1868 and incorporated by Royal Charter in 1881, adopted its present title in 1947. It was established to advance the profession of surveyor and the interests of its members. The RICS merged with the Incorporated Society of Valuers and Auctioneers in 2000. The RICS publishes valuation guidance and standards (known as 'the Red Book'). The manual lays down mandatory standards of professional practice for RICS members: see *RICS Valuation— Global Standards* (2017) and *RICS Valuation— Professional Standards UK* (January 2014, revised April 2015). All chartered surveyors are expected to comply with regulations governing their conduct: see *Rules of Conduct for Firms* (2007) and *Rules of Conduct for Members* (2007). See also *Royal Institution of Chartered Surveyors v Shepherd* (1947) 149 Estates Gazette 370.
3 See note 1.
4 The Institute of Revenues, Rating and Valuation ('IRRV'), like the RICS, requires its members to comply with the Red Book (see note 2).

490. Right to practise in the European Union.
Professions connected with valuing and surveying are subject to European Union principles and directives relating to freedom of establishment and free movement of workers[1].

1 See Council Directive (EC) 2005/36 (OJ L255, 30.9.2005, p 22) on the recognition of professional qualifications, which is implemented in part by the European Communities (Recognition of Professional Qualifications) Regulations 2015, SI 2015/2059. See further PARA 425. The Royal Institution of Chartered Surveyors ('RICS') is among those professional associations and organisations explicitly included in a non-exhaustive list of professional bodies subject to the regulations set out in Sch 1: see PARA 425 note 2.

491. Unfair competition.
Surveyors are no longer excluded[1] from the scope of Chapter I of Part I of the Competition Act 1998[2], which prohibits agreements between undertakings which may affect trade within the United Kingdom and have as their object or effect the prevention, restriction or distortion of competition within the United Kingdom[3].

1 The Competition Act 1998 s 3(1)(d) and Sch 4 were repealed by the Enterprise Act 2002 ss 207, 278(2), Sch 26 as from 1 April 2003: see the Enterprise Act 2002 (Commencement No 2, Transitional and Transitory Provisions) Order 2003, SI 2003/766.
2 Ie the Competition Act 1998 Pt I Ch I (ss 1–16): see COMPETITION vol 18 (2009) PARA 116 et seq.
3 See the Competition Act 1998 s 2(1), (4); and COMPETITION vol 18 (2009) PARA 116.

492. The Valuation Office Agency.
The Valuation Office Agency ('VOA') is an executive agency sponsored by Her Majesty's Revenue and Customs[1], and was created in 1991 through the merger of the valuation office organisations for England and Wales and for Scotland[2].The VOA exists to provide a range of estate surveying and valuation services to government departments and to other clients in the public sector.

Most of the work of the office consists in helping local authorities to administer the rating and council tax systems[3], and it undertakes valuations of land and buildings on behalf of the Her Majesty's Revenue and Customs[4].

An officer of the VOA has power to enter upon land in order to survey it or estimate its value in connection with claims for the compulsory acquisition of that land or any other land or with claims for compensation arising under various statutes[5].

1 See INCOME TAXATION vol 58 (2014) PARA 33 et seq.
2 These organisations had been established in 1910 as part of the Inland Revenue to undertake valuation work in connection with land value duties which were imposed by the Finance Act 1910 and have since been abolished.
3 Ie by compiling and keeping up to date lists of assessments on which liability to council tax or non-domestic rates is based: see PARA 494.
4 Such valuations are carried out mainly, though not exclusively, for the purposes of capital gains tax and inheritance tax: see generally CAPITAL GAINS TAXATION; INHERITANCE TAXATION.
5 See eg NATIONAL CULTURAL HERITAGE vol 77 (2016) PARA 1061; OPEN SPACES AND COUNTRYSIDE vol 78 (2018) PARA 453; PLANNING vol 81 (2018) PARA 13; PLANNING vol 83 (2018) PARA 1433.

(2) Statutory and Contractual Valuations

(i) Valuation for Statutory Purposes

493. Compulsory acquisition.
If a person served with a notice to treat[1] by an authority possessing powers of compulsory acquisition[2] does not agree with the authority as to the amount of compensation to be paid for his interest in the land or for any damage sustained by him by reason of the execution of the works, the question of the disputed compensation must be referred to the Upper Tribunal[3]. If a person claims compensation in respect of any land which has been taken for, or injuriously affected by, the execution of works, any dispute as to the compensation must likewise be referred to the Upper Tribunal[4].

If a person whose land is to be compulsorily acquired is prevented from treating by absence from the United Kingdom[5], or if he cannot be found after diligent inquiry has been made, the amount of compensation must normally be determined by an able practical surveyor selected from the members of the Upper Tribunal and must be paid into court[6]. If land is to be compulsorily acquired from a person under any disability or incapacity, compensation must not be less than an amount determined by the valuation of two able practical surveyors, one appointed by each party, except where compensation has been determined under compulsory powers[7].

Where an authority acquiring land under compulsory powers wishes to enter and use the land before the purchase price or compensation has been fixed, it may do so by paying into court the value of the land as determined by an able practical surveyor[8]. Such a surveyor must examine the premises properly to form a fair judgment of their value[9] but, if he does so in good faith and in pursuance of his duty, the fact that the sum is inadequate or that he valued without sufficient knowledge of the relevant facts does not entitle the owner to an injunction restraining the purchaser from taking possession of the land pending a proper valuation[10].

1 As to the notice to treat see COMPULSORY ACQUISITION OF LAND vol 18 (2009) PARA 616 et seq.
2 As to such authorities see generally COMPULSORY ACQUISITION OF LAND vol 18 (2009) PARA 519 et seq.

3 See COMPULSORY ACQUISITION OF LAND vol 18 (2009) PARA 718. As to the Upper Tribunal see COMPULSORY ACQUISITION OF LAND vol 18 (2009) PARA 720; and COURTS AND TRIBUNALS vol 24 (2010) PARA 883 et seq.

4 See COMPULSORY ACQUISITION OF LAND vol 18 (2009) PARA 718 (reference of dispute), PARA 877 et seq (assessment of compensation).

5 As to the meaning of 'United Kingdom' see PARA 217 note 3.

6 See COMPULSORY ACQUISITION OF LAND vol 18 (2009) PARA 718.

7 See COMPULSORY ACQUISITION OF LAND vol 18 (2009) PARA 554.

8 See COMPULSORY ACQUISITION OF LAND vol 18 (2009) PARA 639 et seq.

9 *Cotter v Metropolitan Rly Co* as reported in (1864) 10 LT 777, where it was held that it was insufficient for the valuer to conclude that all houses in a street were of the same value because their exteriors were identical.

10 *River Roden Co Ltd v Barking Town UDC* (1902) 18 TLR 542; affd 18 TLR 608, CA. Cf *Cotter v Metropolitan Rly Co* as reported in (1864) 10 LT 777, where an injunction was granted because the surveyor had never entered the buildings which he purported to have valued.

494. Rating and council tax.

Valuation officers appointed by the Her Majesty's Revenue and Customs[1] are responsible for compiling and maintaining valuation lists of non-domestic property for the purposes of rating[2] and for dealing with proposals for alterations to such lists[3]. Listing officers appointed by Her Majesty's Revenue and Customs[4] have similar responsibilities in relation to the valuation of dwellings for the purposes of council tax[5].

1 Commissioners for Her Majesty's Revenue and Customs must appoint a valuation officer for each billing authority and the central valuation officer: Local Government Finance Act 1988 s 61(1) (amended by the Local Government Finance Act 1992 ss 117(1), 118(1), Sch 13 para 69). The remuneration of, and any expenses incurred by, valuation officers in carrying out their functions in relation to non-domestic rating (including the remuneration and expenses of persons, whether or not in the service of the Crown, employed to assist them) must be paid out of money provided by Parliament: Local Government Finance Act 1988 s 61(2). See further LOCAL GOVERNMENT FINANCE vol 70 (2018) PARA 54.

2 See the Local Government Finance Act 1988 s 41; and LOCAL GOVERNMENT FINANCE vol 70 (2018) PARA 191.

3 See the Local Government Finance Act 1988 s 55(2); the Non-Domestic Rating (Alteration of Lists and Appeals) (England) Regulations 2009, SI 2009/2268; the Valuation Tribunal for England (Council Tax and Rating Appeals) (Procedure) Regulations 2009, SI 2009/2269; the Non-Domestic Rating (Alteration of Lists and Appeals) (Wales) Regulations 2005, SI 2005/758; the Valuation Tribunal for Wales Regulations 2010, SI 2010/713; and LOCAL GOVERNMENT FINANCE vol 70 (2018) PARA 199.

4 Commissioners for Her Majesty's Revenue and Customs must appoint a listing officer for each billing authority: Local Government Finance Act 1992 s 20(1). The remuneration of, and any expenses incurred by, listing officers in carrying out their functions in relation to council tax (including the remuneration and expenses of persons, whether or not in the service of the Crown, to assist them) must be paid out of money provided by Parliament: see s 20(2), (3). See further LOCAL GOVERNMENT FINANCE vol 70 (2018) PARA 347.

5 See the Local Government Finance Act 1992 Pt I Ch II (ss 20–29); the Council Tax (Alteration of Lists and Appeals) (England) Regulations 2009, SI 2009/2270; the Council Tax (Alteration of Lists and Appeals) Regulations 1993, SI 1993/290 (which still apply in relation to Wales); and LOCAL GOVERNMENT FINANCE vol 70 (2018) PARA 409 et seq.

495. Companies and other corporate bodies.

A public company must not allot shares as fully or partly paid up for a consideration other than cash unless the consideration has been independently valued and a report as to its value made to the company within the preceding six months[1]. Before a building society advances money on the security of land, a written report on the value of the land and any factors likely materially to affect its value must be obtained from a person who is competent to value and who is not disqualified from making such a report[2]. Periodic actuarial valuations are required as a means of investigating the financial condition of certain authorised societies[3] and registered societies which are not friendly societies[4].

1 See the Companies Act 2006 s 593(1); and COMPANIES vol 15A (2016) PARA 1309 et seq.
2 See the Building Societies Act 1986 ss 6A, 6B; and FINANCIAL INSTITUTIONS vol 48 (2015) PARAS 480–481.
3 See FINANCIAL INSTITUTIONS vol 48 (2015) PARA 676 et seq.
4 See the Friendly Societies Act 1974 s 41 (repealed in relation to friendly societies by the Friendly Societies Act 1992 s 95); and FINANCIAL INSTITUTIONS vol 48 (2015) PARA 675.

496. Enforcement by taking control of goods.

The common law right to distrain for arrears of rent was abolished, with effect from 6 April 2014, by the Tribunals, Courts and Enforcement Act 2007[1], which introduced new statutory provisions for enforcement by taking control of goods (the 'TCG procedure')[2].

A landlord under a lease of commercial premises may use the TCG procedure to recover from the tenant rent payable under the lease[3]. This power is referred to as CRAR (commercial rent arrears recovery)[4].

Using the TCG procedure to recover a sum means taking control of goods and selling them to recover that sum in accordance with the relevant statutory provisions and any regulations made thereunder[5]. As part of the procedure, an enforcement agent[6] must make or obtain a valuation of the controlled goods in accordance with regulations and give the debtor, and separately any co-owner, an opportunity to obtain an independent valuation of the goods[7].

Where the enforcement agent makes the required valuation: (1) the valuation must be in writing, signed by the enforcement agent, and set out the required details; and (2) the enforcement agent must provide a copy of the written valuation, once made, to the debtor and any co-owner[8]. Where the enforcement agent obtains the valuation, the enforcement agent must: (i) only instruct a qualified, independent valuer; (ii) instruct the valuer to make a written valuation and, where appropriate, to value each item of goods separately; and (iii) provide a copy of the written valuation, once made by the valuer, to the debtor and any co-owner[9].

1 See the Tribunals, Courts and Enforcement Act 2007 s 71; the Tribunals, Courts and Enforcement Act 2007 (Commencement No 11) Order 2014, SI 2014/768, art 2(1); and LANDLORD AND TENANT vol 62 (2016) PARA 282.
2 See the Tribunals, Courts and Enforcement Act 2007 ss 62–90, Sch 12; and CIVIL PROCEDURE vol 12A (2015) PARA 1334 et seq. The TCG procedure is available where an enactment, writ or warrant confers power to use the procedure: see the Tribunals, Courts and Enforcement Act 2007 s 62(1); and CIVIL PROCEDURE vol 12A (2015) PARA 1334.
3 See the Tribunals, Courts and Enforcement Act 2007 s 72(1); and LANDLORD AND TENANT vol 62 (2016) PARA 283 et seq.
4 See the Tribunals, Courts and Enforcement Act 2007 s 72(2); and LANDLORD AND TENANT vol 62 (2016) PARA 283.
5 See the Tribunals, Courts and Enforcement Act 2007 Sch 12 para 1; and CIVIL PROCEDURE vol 12A (2015) PARA 1334.
6 In the Tribunals, Courts and Enforcement Act 2007 Sch 12, 'enforcement agent', means an individual authorised by s 63(2) to act as an enforcement agent: see Sch 12 para 2(1); and CIVIL PROCEDURE vol 12A (2015) PARA 1334.
7 See the Tribunals, Courts and Enforcement Act 2007 Sch 12 para 36(1)(a); and CIVIL PROCEDURE vol 12A (2015) PARA 1353. In exercise of the powers conferred by Sch 12 para 36, inter alia, the Lord Chancellor has made the Taking Control of Goods Regulations 2013, SI 2013/1894.

8 See the Taking Control of Goods Regulations 2013, SI 2013/1894, reg 35(2); and CIVIL
   PROCEDURE vol 12A (2015) PARA 1353.
9 See the Taking Control of Goods Regulations 2013, SI 2013/1894, reg 35(3); and CIVIL
   PROCEDURE vol 12A (2015) PARA 1353.

497. Executors and trustees.

If a personal representative proposes to exercise his statutory power of appropriation[1], he may ascertain and fix the value of the respective parts of the assets and liabilities of the deceased, and for that purpose must employ a duly qualified valuer when necessary[2]. An appropriation of a mortgage at par without such an ascertainment of the value of the mortgage as a security may be a breach of trust if the mortgaged property is in fact in bad condition[3].

Trustees may employ duly qualified agents to ascertain the value of trust property, and any valuation so made in good faith is binding on all persons interested under the trust[4].

1 As to the statutory power of appropriation see WILLS AND INTESTACY vol 103 (2016)
   PARA 1153.
2 See the Administration of Estates Act 1925 s 41(3); and WILLS AND INTESTACY vol 103 (2016)
   PARA 1157.
3 See *Re Brookes, Brookes v Taylor* [1914] 1 Ch 558, where the mortgaged premises were derelict
   and practically worthless and the trustee had appropriated the mortgage at par without either
   inspecting the mortgaged premises or making any inquiry as to their actual value as a security.
4 See the Trustee Act 1925 s 22(3); and TRUSTS AND POWERS vol 98 (2013) PARA 520.

(ii) Valuation for Contractual Purposes

498. Effect of contractual provision for valuation.

An agreement under which property is to be transferred at a 'fair price' or at a 'reasonable valuation' is not void for uncertainty, and the court may decree specific performance of such an agreement and order such inquiries as may be necessary to ascertain the fair price[1].

Where parties have agreed to transfer property at a price to be fixed by a valuer or valuers appointed by the parties and the valuation machinery breaks down[2], a fundamental question of construction is whether the prescribed mode of ascertaining the price is an essential term of the contract or whether the mode of ascertainment, though indicated in the contract, is subsidiary and non-essential[3]. If the valuation machinery which has broken down is held to be subsidiary and not an essential term of the contract (or testamentary option)[4], the court may intervene and substitute other machinery to ascertain the price in order that the agreement may be carried out[5]. Even where, on a true construction, the use of the valuation machinery which has broken down is to be regarded as an essential term of the agreement[6], the court may intervene and provide substitute machinery if the agreement has already been partly performed[7], or if the valuation provision relates to a subsidiary part of a wider contract which is itself valid and enforceable[8].

1 *Gaskarth v Lord Lowther* (1805) 12 Ves 107; *Milnes v Gery* (1807) 14 Ves 400 at 407 per Grant
   MR; *Morgan v Milman* (1853) 3 De GM & G 24 at 34 per Lord Cranworth LC; *Talbot v Talbot*
   [1968] Ch 1, [1967] 2 All ER 920, CA; and see SPECIFIC PERFORMANCE vol 95 (2017)
   PARAS 545–549.
2 Such a breakdown may result from the act of one of the parties (eg where he refuses to appoint a
   valuer or denies an appointed valuer access to the property), from failure of the duly appointed
   valuers to agree on the price or on the identity of a required umpire, or from causes beyond the
   control of the parties or their valuers, such as the death of an umpire or his failure to complete the

valuation by the prescribed date. But such distinctions, being tangential to the question of whether a prescription as to the mode of valuation is an essential term, are rarely to be relied on: see *Sudbrook Trading Estate Ltd v Eggleton* [1983] 1 AC 444 at 484, [1982] 3 All ER 1 at 10, HL, per Lord Fraser of Tullybelton.

3   Under modern conditions, contractual terms providing for a particular method of assessing price will normally be regarded as subsidiary to the main purpose of the agreement, which is for sale and purchase of the property at a fair or reasonable value: *Sudbrook Trading Estate Ltd v Eggleton* [1983] 1 AC 444 at 484, [1982] 3 All ER 1 at 10, HL, per Lord Fraser of Tullybelton (applied in *Bruce v Carpenter* [2006] EWHC 3301 (Ch), [2006] All ER (D) 405 (Nov)).

4   'A testamentary option is something which potentially can become a contract on its exercise at any time by the person holding the option . . . because the person getting a property under a testamentary option gets it by exercising that option and entering into a contract in that behalf with the executors': *Talbot v Talbot* [1968] Ch 1 at 9–10, [1967] 2 All ER 920 at 921–922, CA, per Scarman LJ (testator provided for two of his children to have option of purchasing two farms at a 'reasonable valuation', but prescribed no valuation machinery and none was agreed by the beneficiaries).

5   *Sudbrook Trading Estate Ltd v Eggleton* [1983] 1 AC 444, [1982] 3 All ER 1, HL (lease gave the lessee an option to purchase the freehold at a price to be agreed by valuers appointed by the parties and the landlord refused to appoint a valuer); *Re Malpass* [1985] Ch 42, [1984] 2 All ER 313 (an option was given by will to purchase a farm at a value to be determined by the district valuer, but the district valuer declined to value the property). The alternative remedy of a mandatory injunction compelling the vendor to appoint a valuer has been held to be unsuitable because the only sanction for non-compliance would be imprisonment for contempt of court: see *Sudbrook Trading Estate Ltd v Eggleton*. However, the court probably may, in an appropriate case, order a party to do what is necessary to make the contractual machinery work, eg by appointing a valuer or seeking such an appointment from the designated professional body (*Royal Bank of Scotland plc v Jennings* (1994) 70 P&CR 459, [1995] 2 EGLR 87; disapproving *Harben Style Ltd v Rhodes Trust* [1995] 1 EGLR 118) or by allowing a duly appointed valuer to enter and carry out his valuation (*Morse v Merest* (1821) 6 Madd 26; *Smith v Peters* (1875) LR 20 Eq 511).

6   In most present-day cases a prescription as to the mode of valuation is unlikely to be construed as an essential term of the contract unless it seeks to harness special knowledge which is needed to determine the value of the property in question, such as an auditor's knowledge of a company whose shares are to be valued: see *Sudbrook Trading Estate Ltd v Eggleton* [1983] 1 AC 444 at 484, [1982] 3 All ER 1 at 10, HL, per Lord Fraser of Tullybelton. See also *Bruce v Carpenter* [2006] EWHC 3301 (Ch), [2006] All ER (D) 405 (Nov) where the court ruled that, where parties chose to select an expert, recourse to the court was virtually non-existent except in circumstances where the machinery of the expert valuation had broken down. It was fundamental that the court should respect the parties' decision in those circumstances since it was not simply a matter of saying whether the court could ignore the special knowledge of the expert but whether it could replace the parties' choice of method of valuation with a different one, namely valuation by the court. In that case the claimant had agreed to the method of valuation, namely a private valuation by one named person and that reasons would not be given; by his claim he sought a declaration that part of the process should be carried out by the court, which was the total antithesis of a private valuation. Where the court interfered in cases where an expert was appointed it did so on the principle that it was giving effect to the agreement of the parties; in the instant case the interference would be doing the exact opposite of the agreement. The claimant contended that there had been a breakdown in the process of the expert valuation and the court was entitled to interfere. The court did not agree.

7   *Sudbrook Trading Estate Ltd v Eggleton* [1983] 1 AC 444 at 484, [1982] 3 All ER 1 at 11, HL, per Lord Fraser of Tullybelton; *Gregory v Mighell* (1811) 18 Ves 328; *Dinham v Bradford* (1869) 5 Ch App 519; *Beer v Bowden* [1981] 1 All ER 1070, [1981] 1 WLR 522n, CA; cf *Bruce v Carpenter* [2006] EWHC 3301 (Ch), [2006] All ER (D) 405 (Nov).

8   *Sudbrook Trading Estate Ltd v Eggleton* [1983] 1 AC 444 at 485, [1982] 3 All ER 1 at 11, HL, per Lord Fraser of Tullybelton; *Dinham v Bradford* (1869) 5 Ch App 519; *Richardson v Smith* (1870) 5 Ch App 648; *Smith v Peters* (1875) LR 20 Eq 511.

499.   Valuer as arbitrator or independent expert.

Where a valuer[1] is appointed to settle a dispute between two parties, or to decide a matter on which they have opposing interests[2], the valuer may or may not act as an arbitrator in reaching his decision[3]. Whether or not he is so acting affects his potential liability for negligence[4] and also determines the extent to which his decision is binding upon the parties[5]. It is provided by statute that an arbitrator (unlike an ordinary valuer)[6] is not liable for anything done or omitted in the discharge or purported discharge of his functions as arbitrator, unless the act or omission is shown to have been in bad faith[7], and will thus not be liable for negligence[8]. The extent to which this statutory provision changes the existing law is doubtful, since many authorities have decided that an arbitrator already enjoys such immunity[9]. An arbitrator's decision is, however, subject to certain rights of appeal[10]. Neither a 'mutual valuer'[11] nor a 'quasi-arbitrator' is likely to enjoy an arbitrator's immunity[12], and if the primary process intended is one of valuation rather than arbitration, calling the valuer an 'umpire' will not give him immunity[13].

The question whether a given valuer has been appointed as an arbitrator[14] is determined not only by the way he is described in the agreement which appoints him[15], but by the agreement construed as a whole[16]. Thus the parties' original intent may be inferred from the appointing clause interpreted in the light of other clauses in the document[17]. Where the agreement is ambiguous or allows for different options, subsequent events may indicate which option was taken up, and, therefore, whether in the event the valuer appointed was an arbitrator[18].

A valuer who is not appointed as an arbitrator but who nevertheless claims immunity from liability for negligence must show that, in all the circumstances of the case, his functions are judicial in character[19]. That is not simply a matter of acting fairly as between the parties[20], or being required to determine a question as between opposed interests[21], and has been said to depend on the existence of a formulated dispute between two parties[22]. Where the valuer's functions are not judicial in character, a valuer by whose decision two parties agree to be bound owes a duty of care to both parties and, if negligent in reaching his decision, will be liable to the party who is disadvantaged by his negligent valuation[23]. There is no material difference in legal principle between a valuer who undertakes to provide a valuation of property and one who undertakes to determine the rent under a rent review clause[24].

1 As to the meaning of 'valuer' see PARA 488.
2 Eg the rental value of premises for the purpose of a rent review. See also *Campbell v Edwards* [1976] 1 All ER 785, [1976] 1 WLR 403, CA (surveyor appointed to determine the surrender value of a lease); *Arenson v Casson Beckman Rutley & Co* [1977] AC 405, [1975] 3 All ER 901, HL (auditors instructed to value shares in a private company pursuant to an agreement for their sale at the price so determined).
3 See *Sutcliffe v Thackrah* [1974] AC 727 at 745, [1974] 1 All ER 859 at 870, HL, per Lord Morris of Borth-y-Gest and at 735 and 862 per Lord Reid. 'The position of a valuer is very different from an arbitrator. If a valuer is negligent in making a valuation he may be sued by the party – vendor or purchaser – who is injured by his wrong valuation. But an arbitrator is different. In my opinion he cannot be sued by either party to the dispute': *Campbell v Edwards* [1976] 1 All ER 785 at 788, [1976] 1 WLR 403 at 408, CA, per Lord Denning MR. As arbitrators see generally ARBITRATION. It has been argued that such an arbitrator, being appointed by one or more of the parties to the eventual dispute, does not exercise 'judicial functions' analogous to those of a judge or statutory arbitrator, whose appointment is in no way governed by parties to individual disputes which eventually come before him: see *Arenson v Casson Beckman Rutley & Co* [1977] AC 405 at 431–432, [1975] 3 All ER 901 at 918–919, HL, per Lord Kilbrandon (uncle gave shares to nephew (his employee); shares to be sold back to uncle if employment terminated at value determined by company's auditors; employment terminated and valuation and sale took place; subsequent valuation when company 'went public' disclosed apparent negligence in original (low) valuation; nephew sued uncle; held that auditor was liable if he made valuation negligently unless he could show that a formulated dispute between at least two parties had been submitted to him to resolve in such a manner that he was called upon to exercise a judicial function and the parties had agreed to accept his decision).
4 See the text and notes 6–9.

5 See PARA 500.

6 As to a valuer's negligence see PARAS 504, 507 et seq.

7 See the Arbitration Act 1996 s 29(1). This immunity applies to an employee or agent of an arbitrator as it applies to the arbitrator himself: see s 29(2). The provisions of Pt I (ss 1–84) apply only where the arbitration agreement is in writing, and any other agreement between the parties as to any matter is effective for the purposes of Pt I only if in writing: s 5(1). See further ARBITRATION vol 2 (2017) PARAS 513, 537.

8 It has been doubted whether it is right to allow immunity to attach to arbitrators as a class when that class includes arbitrators whose role is primarily to use their professional expertise as a mutual valuer might do (see *Arenson v Casson Beckman Rutley & Co* [1977] AC 405 at 442, [1975] 3 All ER 901 at 927, HL, per Lord Fraser of Tullybelton); and it has been questioned whether a valuer appointed as arbitrator under the Arbitration Acts who has a purely investigatory role, and who performs no function even remotely resembling the judicial function save that he finally decides a dispute or difference that has arisen between the parties, should enjoy a judicial immunity which so-called 'quasi-arbitrators' do not, albeit that the question has yet to be determined conclusively (see *Arenson v Casson Beckman Rutley & Co* at 440 and 925 per Lord Salmon).

9 See eg *Turner v Goulden* (1873) LR 9 CP 57, and this view was supported obiter by a majority of the House of Lords in *Sutcliffe v Thackrah* [1974] AC 727, [1974] 1 All ER 859, HL. See also *Campbell v Edwards* [1976] 1 All ER 785 at 788, [1976] 1 WLR 403 at 408, CA, per Lord Denning MR; but see note 8. The Supply of Goods and Services Act 1982 s 13, which implies a duty of reasonable care and skill into a contract for the supply of a service, does not apply to services rendered by an arbitrator: see the Supply of Services (Exclusion of Implied Terms) Order 1985, SI 1985/1, arts 1, 2; and SALE OF GOODS AND SUPPLY OF SERVICES vol 91 (2012) PARA 36. The Consumer Rights Act 2015 Pt 1 Ch 4 (ss 48–57) (see CONSUMER PROTECTION vol 21 (2016) PARA 363) applies to all service sectors except where they are expressly excluded from one or all of its provisions. Those provisions do not cover contracts of employment or apprenticeships (see s 48(2)) and, where there is legislation that gives more detailed provision about rights or duties of particular services, that legislation will take precedence over Chapter 4 (see s 53(2)). It appears that the Arbitration Act 1996 s 29 which says an arbitrator is not liable for anything done or omitted in the discharge or purported discharge of his functions as arbitrator unless the act or omission is shown to have been in bad faith will take precedence over the duty of skill and care under the Consumer Rights Act 2015.

10 As to the remission or setting aside of an arbitrator's award see ARBITRATION vol 2 (2017) PARA 576 et seq.

11 See *Arenson v Casson Beckman Rutley & Co* [1977] AC 405 at 441, [1975] 3 All ER 901 at 927, HL, per Lord Fraser of Tullybelton.

12 'Quasi-arbitrator' and 'quasi-judicial functions' have been invoked but never defined. They cannot mean more than in much the same position as an arbitrator or judge': *Sutcliffe v Thackrah* [1974] AC 727 at 758, [1974] 1 All ER 859 at 882, HL, per Lord Salmon. 'There may be circumstances in which what is in effect an arbitration is not one that is within the provisions of the Arbitration Act. The expression quasi-arbitrator should only be used in that connection': *Sutcliffe v Thackrah* at 752–753 and 876–877 per Lord Morris of Borth-y-Gest. See also, as to several possible meanings of 'quasi-arbitrator', *Arenson v Casson Beckman Rutley & Co* [1977] AC 405 at 422–423, [1975] 3 All ER 901 at 910–911, HL, per Lord Simon of Glaisdale. The expression appears subsequently to have acquired no settled meaning.

13 '. . . The mere word 'umpire' is quite neutral, and does not cast any real light on the matter in dispute': *Safeway Food Stores Ltd v Banderway Ltd* [1983] 2 EGLR 116 at 118 per Goulding J.

14 The parties may arrange for the agent of one party to become an arbitrator as between them should a certain event occur, but this must be a definite arrangement: see *Sutcliffe v Thackrah* [1974] AC 727 at 745, [1974] 1 All ER 859 at 870, HL, obiter, per Lord Morris of Borth-y-Gest.

15 'You cannot make a valuer an arbitrator by calling him so or vice versa': *Taylor v Yielding* (1912) 56 Sol Jo 253 per Neville J.

16 *Taylor v Yielding* (1912) 56 Sol Jo 253 (agreement that value of shares would be determined by two valuers appointed by the parties or by an umpire appointed by the valuers was an agreement to arbitrate as to value and not a mere agreement to have a valuation); and see *Sutcliffe v Thackrah* [1974] AC 727, [1974] 1 All ER 859, HL; *Arenson v Casson Beckman Rutley & Co* [1977] AC 405, [1975] 3 All ER 901, HL.

17 See *Langham House Developments Ltd v Brompton Securities Ltd* [1980] 2 EGLR 117 (clause in lease concerning rent drafted so as to suggest intended valuation by nominated surveyor compared with adjacent clause concerning insurance which 'reeks of arbitration'; different intent inferred from obvious contrast); *Safeway Food Stores Ltd v Banderway Ltd* [1983] 2 EGLR 116 (meanings of contrasting clauses illuminated by comparison).

18 *North Eastern Co-operative Society Ltd v Newcastle-upon-Tyne City Council* [1987] 1 EGLR 142 (contrasting clauses in lease; 'independent surveyor or arbitrator' prescribed and instructed was not, in the event, an arbitrator, owing to circumstances of his appointment).
19 See *Sutcliffe v Thackrah* [1974] AC 727 at 738, [1974] 1 All ER 859 at 865, HL, per Lord Reid.
20 See *Sutcliffe v Thackrah* [1974] AC 727, [1974] 1 All ER 859, HL, especially at 745 and 870 per Lord Morris of Borth-y-Gest; *Arenson v Casson Beckman Rutley & Co* [1977] AC 405, [1975] 3 All ER 901, HL. See also *Palacath Ltd v Flanagan* [1985] 2 All ER 161, [1985] 1 EGLR 86 (surveyor determining rent under a rent review clause not acting as an arbitrator since he had been appointed as an expert and was entitled to rely on his own judgment and opinion and to reach a decision unfettered by the submissions of the parties).
21 *Arenson v Casson Beckman Rutley & Co* [1977] AC 405, [1975] 3 All ER 901, HL.
22 'The main difference between [a mutual valuer and an arbitrator] is that the latter, like the judge, has to decide a dispute that has already arisen, and he usually has rival contentions before him, while the mutual valuer is called in before a dispute has arisen, in order to avoid it': *Arenson v Casson Beckman Rutley & Co* [1977] AC 405 at 441, [1975] 3 All ER 901 at 927, HL, per Lord Fraser of Tullybelton. 'In my view the essential prerequisite for [a valuer] to claim immunity is that, by the time the matter is submitted to him for decision, there should be a formulated dispute between at least two parties which his decision is required to resolve': *Arenson v Casson Beckman Rutley & Co* at 424 and 912 per Lord Simon of Glaisdale.
23 *Zubaida v Hargreaves* [1995] 1 EGLR 127 at 128, CA, per Hoffmann LJ (rent review; held on facts that RICS-appointed surveyor had not been negligent). See also *Campbell v Edwards* [1976] 1 All ER 785 at 788, [1976] 1 WLR 403 at 408, CA, per Lord Denning MR (rent review; agreed surveyor appointed to determine value of lease; report was 'non-speaking' report and had been prepared honestly and in good faith; held that landlord was bound by valuation). The existence of the independent expert's duty of care was also recognised in *Belvedere Motors Ltd v King* [1981] 2 EGLR 131; *Wallshire Ltd v Aarons* [1989] 1 EGLR 147; *Lewisham Investment Partnership Ltd v Morgan* [1997] 2 EGLR 150; *Currys Group plc v Martin* [1999] 3 EGLR 165, although in each case it was held on the facts that the valuer had not been negligent.
24 *Currys Group plc v Martin* [1999] 3 EGLR 165.

500. Judicial review of valuation.

Where a valuer[1] acts as an arbitrator in making a valuation[2], an appeal from his valuation lies to the court[3] on a point of law[4].

Where a valuer acts as an independent expert in making a valuation[5], the extent to which his valuation is subject to review by the court depends upon the construction of the agreement under which he is appointed to act[6]. If, on its true construction, that agreement expressly or by implication confers upon the valuer the exclusive remit to determine a question, and provides for the parties to be bound by his determination, then the valuation is not open to review by the court if the valuer acted honestly and in good faith[7].

If the parties have agreed that the expert's decision should be final and conclusive, it remains so even where it is a 'speaking' valuation whose reasoning contains errors of law[8]. A 'non-speaking' valuation clearly cannot err in its reasoning if it contains no reasoning at all, and the relevant question is not whether defective reasoning can be found in a report that happens to be unusually voluble, but whether it is possible to say from all the evidence which is properly before the court what the valuer has done and why he has done it[9]. A valuation made by an independent expert may, however, be set aside where the agreement so provides[10], where the appointment of the expert is invalid[11], where there is fraud or collusion between the valuer and one of the parties[12], or where the expert has gone outside his remit by answering a different question from that which was remitted to him[13] or has failed to comply with any conditions imposed by the agreement[14].

1 As to the meaning of 'valuer' see PARA 488.
2 See PARA 499.
3 Ie to the High Court or the County Court under the Arbitration Act 1996 ss 69, 105: see ARBITRATION vol 2 (2017) PARAS 551, 578.

4   See the Arbitration Act 1996 s 69(7); and ARBITRATION vol 2 (2017) PARA 578. As to judicial review see generally JUDICIAL REVIEW vol 61 (2010) PARA 601 et seq; CIVIL PROCEDURE vol 11 (2015) PARA 185.

5   See PARA 499.

6   The court has jurisdiction in advance of a valuation by an independent expert to determine a question as to the limits of the expert's remit or the conditions governing his valuation, but it will normally decline to do so where the question is merely hypothetical: *British Shipbuilders v VSEL Consortium plc* [1997] 1 Lloyd's Rep 106 per Lightman J. See also *Norwich Union Life Insurance Society v P & O Property Holdings Ltd* [1993] 1 EGLR 164, CA; *Mercury Communications Ltd v Director General of Telecommunications* [1996] 1 All ER 575, [1996] 1 WLR 48, HL (contract between BT and Mercury provided for issue between them to be determined by Director General of Telecommunications; held that his actions could lead to disputes falling outside the realm of public law, and whether his determination could be challenged depended, inter alia, on terms of his remit in the contract).

7   *Campbell v Edwards* [1976] 1 All ER 785, [1976] 1 WLR 403, CA; *Baber v Kenwood Manufacturing Co* [1978] 1 Lloyd's Rep 175, CA; *Belchier v Reynolds* (1754) 3 Keny 87 at 91 per Strange MR.

8   *Jones v Sherwood Computer Services plc* [1992] 2 All ER 170, [1992] 1 WLR 277, CA (disapproving *Burgess v Purchase & Sons (Farms) Ltd* [1983] Ch 216, [1983] 2 All ER 4). 'If [the expert] has answered the right question in the wrong way, his decision will be binding. If he has answered the wrong question, his decision will be a nullity': *Nikko Hotels (UK) Ltd v MEPC plc* [1991] 2 EGLR 103 at 108 per Knox J. See also *Pontsarn Investments Ltd v Kansallis-Osake-Pankki* [1992] 1 EGLR 148; *British Shipbuilders v VSEL Consortium plc* [1997] 1 Lloyd's Rep 106 (and see the discussion of the principles set out in this case in *National Grid Co plc v M25 Group Ltd* [1998] 2 EGLR 85 (on appeal [1999] 1 EGLR 65, CA, where the appeal was allowed but the discussion was held to be a useful summary)). Earlier cases, which suggested that valuation could be impugned on the ground of mistake, now appear supportable only on the ground that the agreements under consideration did not confer exclusive jurisdiction on the valuers: see *Collier v Mason* (1858) 25 Beav 200 at 204 per Romilly MR; *Johnston v Chestergate Hat Manufacturing Co Ltd* [1915] 2 Ch 338; *Dean v Prince* [1954] Ch 409, [1954] 1 All ER 749, CA.

9   *Jones v Sherwood Computer Services plc* [1992] 2 All ER 170 at 177, [1992] 1 WLR 277 at 284, CA, per Dillon LJ; applied in *Dixons Group plc v Jan Andrew Murray-Oboynski* (1997) 86 BLR 16 (where there is no evidence of the basis of determination to be applied by the valuer, it cannot be shown that he has failed to follow instructions). In the case of a non-speaking valuation, a court should not, other than in wholly exceptional circumstances, permit attempts to argue by inference that the reasoning of the valuer must have been wrong: *Morgan Sindall plc v Sawston Farms (Cambs) Ltd* [1999] 1 EGLR 90, CA. See also *Doughty Hanson & Co v Roe* [2007] EWHC 2212 (Ch), [2008] 1 BCLC 404, [2007] All ER (D) 56 (Oct).

10   *British Shipbuilders v VSEL Consortium plc* [1997] 1 Lloyd's Rep 106.

11   Eg because it is made out of time: see *Darlington Borough Council v Waring & Gillow (Holdings) Ltd* [1988] 2 EGLR 159.

12   *Campbell v Edwards* [1976] 1 All ER 785 at 788, [1976] 1 WLR 403 at 407, CA, per Lord Denning MR.

13   Ie such as would occur if an independent expert appointed to value shares in a company valued the wrong number of shares or valued shares in the wrong company: *Jones v Sherwood Computer Services plc* [1992] 2 All ER 170 at 179, [1992] 1 WLR 277 at 287, CA, per Dillon LJ. See also *Macro v Thompson (No 2)* [1997] 1 BCLC 626, [1996] BCC 707, CA.

14   *Nikko Hotels (UK) Ltd v MEPC plc* [1991] 2 EGLR 103 at 108 per Knox J; *Pontsarn Investments Ltd v Kansallis-Osake-Pankki* [1992] 1 EGLR 148; *British Shipbuilders v VSEL Consortium plc* [1997] 1 Lloyd's Rep 106 (and see the discussion of the principles set out in this case in *National Grid Co plc v M25 Group Ltd* [1998] 2 EGLR 85 (on appeal [1999] 1 EGLR 65, CA, where the appeal was allowed but the discussion was held to be a useful summary)).

(3) Valuer and Client

501. Basis of relationship.

The engagement or instruction of a valuer is normally a matter of contract between the valuer and the client[1]. Where the client engages a firm of valuers, the contract is made with the firm and not with the individual who may carry out the valuation[2], and the firm is responsible to the client for the due performance of its contractual obligations by its employees and probably for the performance of a person other than an employee to whom it delegates the task of valuation[3].The relationship which is created between the valuer and the person who appoints him is not merely one of agent and principal, but of professional person and client[4], and documents which a valuer brings into existence in order to carry out the service which he is engaged to perform are therefore the property of the valuer and not of the client[5].

1 Such a contract is one for the supply of a service and is governed by the Supply of Goods and Services Act 1982 Pt II (ss 12–16) (in relation to non-consumer contracts) (see SALE OF GOODS AND SUPPLY OF SERVICES vol 91 (2012) PARA 36) or the Consumer Rights Act 2015 Pt I (ss 48–57) (in relation to consumer contracts) (see CONSUMER PROTECTION vol 21 (2016) PARA 336). See also generally CONTRACT.

2 The individual valuer may nevertheless be liable to the client in tort for negligence: see *Smith v Eric S Bush, Harris v Wyre Forest District Council* [1990] 1 AC 831 at 866, [1989] 2 All ER 514 at 537, HL, per Lord Griffiths; *Merrett v Babb* [2001] EWCA Civ 214, [2001] QB 1174, [2001] BLR 483. See generally PARAS 504–505.

3 *Luxmoore-May v Messenger May Baverstock (a firm)* [1990] 1 All ER 1067, [1990] 1 WLR 1009, CA (auctioneers).

4 *Leicestershire County Council v Michael Faraday & Partners Ltd* [1941] 2 KB 205, [1941] 2 All ER 483, CA.

5 *Leicestershire County Council v Michael Faraday & Partners Ltd* [1941] 2 KB 205, [1941] 2 All ER 483, CA; *London School Board v Northcroft* (1889) 2 Hudson's BC (4th Edn) 147.

502. Remuneration of valuer.

A valuer is entitled to charge the client for his professional services, in accordance with the contract under which he is engaged[1]. It was formerly common practice for valuers to charge by reference to a scale of fees published by the Royal Institution of Chartered Surveyors[2], but that institution has now abolished scale fees. Similarly, where an authority acquires land compulsorily, or by agreement when the parties know that it could be acquired compulsorily[3], the surveyors' fees incurred by the former owner were traditionally calculated according to Ryde's Scale [4], although more recently surveyors have tended to charge fees on an hourly basis[5]. Expenditure such as the fees paid by the owner to a valuer or surveyor properly incurred in preparing the owner's claim for compensation and negotiating its settlement should be included in any compensation awarded against the acquiring authority[6]. Whether fees have been properly incurred for this purpose is a question of fact[7].

If the valuer and client do not expressly agree about how much the valuer is to be paid, or as to how that amount is to be determined, a term will be implied into the contract between them that the client will pay a reasonable charge[7]. What is a reasonable charge is a question of fact[8].

A valuer is not entitled to be paid for services which have been performed negligently, and are therefore useless to the client[9]. Payment made for such services may be reclaimed[10].

1 Where services are rendered in connection with litigation, an agreement under which fees are payable on a contingency basis is unenforceable on grounds of public policy, although this does not apply to fees payable to a surveyor for securing a reduction in the rateable value of a client's property, not least because a local valuation court is not a court of law: *Pickering (t/a City Agents) v Sogex Services (UK) Ltd* [1982] 1 EGLR 42, 20 BLR 66. Nor does this stricture apply to fees for obtaining planning permission, as, even if such an arrangement is in breach of the rules of the profession, such a breach is not necessarily contrary to law: *Picton Jones & Co v Arcadia Developments Ltd* [1989] 1 EGLR 43. This remains the case even if such services may require the surveyor to appear before a valuation tribunal or a public planning inquiry. The Courts and Legal

Services Act 1990 s 58, which allows a solicitor to enter into a conditional fee agreement in certain limited circumstances, has not changed public policy because of its narrow scope: see *Aratra Potato Co Ltd v Taylor Joynson Garrett (a firm)* [1995] 4 All ER 695 at 707 per Garland J. See further LEGAL PROFESSIONS vol 66 (2015) PARA 724.

2   As to the Royal Institution of Chartered Surveyors see PARA 489.

3   As to valuations and surveys carried out in connection with the compulsory acquisition of land see PARA 493.

4   Ryde's Scale (1996) was formerly published by the Royal Institution of Chartered Surveyors ('RICS'). The Office of the Deputy Prime Minister (now the Ministry of Housing, Communities and Local Government) announced the abandonment of Ryde's Scale on 18 July 2002.

5   This approach has been confirmed in a number of decisions including *Matthews v Environment Agency* [2002] 3 EGLR 168; *Newman v Cambridgeshire County Council* [2011] UKUT 56 (LC); *Poole v South West Water Ltd* [2011] UKUT 84 (LC). See also COMPULSORY ACQUISITION OF LAND vol 18 (2009) PARA 746

6   See *LCC v Tobin* [1959] 1 All ER 649, [1959] 1 WLR 354, CA; *Johns v Edmonton Corpn* (1958) 9 P & CR 366 at 370, Lands Tribunal.

7   *Beckett v Birmingham Corpn* (1956) 6 P & CR 352 at 354. Surveyors' fees may be included in the compensation recoverable by a landowner from an acquiring authority on the withdrawal of a notice to treat: *Duke of Grafton v Secretary of State for Air* (1956) 6 P & CR 374, CA; *Merediths Ltd v LCC* (1957) 9 P & CR 128, Lands Tribunal. As to the measure of compensation on compulsory acquisition, and as to the recovery of such compensation, see COMPULSORY ACQUISITION OF LAND vol 18 (2009)PARA 715 et seq.

7   See the Supply of Goods and Services Act 1982 s 15(1) (in relation to non-consumer contracts); and SALE OF GOODS AND SUPPLY OF SERVICES vol 91 (2012) PARA 332. See also the Consumer Rights Act 2015 s 51 (in relation to consumer contracts); and CONSUMER PROTECTION vol 21 (2016) PARA 366.

8   Supply of Goods and Services Act 1982 s 15(2); Consumer Rights Act 2015 s 51(3). See note 7. Where a surveyor appears as an expert witness on a client's behalf, a reasonable fee will normally be based upon the surveyor's time and trouble and not upon the value of the property concerned: *Upsdell v Stewart* (1793) Peake 255; *Debenham v King's College, Cambridge* (1884) 1 TLR 170; *Drew v Josolyne* (1888) 4 TLR 717; *Faraday v Tamworth Union* (1916) 86 LJ Ch 436. However, a surveyor may be entitled by a binding custom to a fee assessed on some other basis: *Wilkie v Scottish Aviation Ltd* 1956 SC 198 at 205, Ct of Sess obiter per Lord Clyde.

9   *Moneypenny v Hartland* (1824) 1 C & P 352; *Whitty v Lord Dillon* (1860) 2 F & F 67; *Sincock v Bangs (Reading)* (1952) 160 Estates Gazette 134; *Hill v Debenham Tewson and Chinnocks* (1958) 171 Estates Gazette 835; *Buckland v Watts* (1968) 208 Estates Gazette 969, CA. Where the services, albeit negligently performed, nevertheless retain some value to the client, he cannot refuse to pay for them: see *Hutchinson v Harris* (1978) 10 BLR 19, CA.

10 *Chong v Scott Collins & Co* (1954) 164 Estates Gazette 662; *Hoadley v Edwards* [2001] EGCS 46, [2001] All ER (D) 335 (Mar).

503.   Valuer's liability to client.

A valuer will be liable to his client for breach of contract if he fails to carry out any service which he has expressly undertaken to perform[1], or if he breaches an express term of the contract under which he is engaged[2]. In addition, a valuer other than one acting as an arbitrator[3] will be liable for breach of an implied term of his contract[4] if he does not carry out the agreed service with reasonable care and skill[5], or if he does not carry out that service within a reasonable time[6].

A valuer who fails to exhibit the requisite standard of professional skill and care may alternatively be liable to the client in negligence[7].

1   See *Moss v Heckingbottom* (1958) 172 Estates Gazette 207.

2   See generally CONTRACT.

3   As to acting as an arbitrator see PARA 499.

4   A person who holds himself out as a valuer impliedly represents that he has the necessary skill, knowledge and competence so to act: *Jenkins v Betham* (1855) 15 CB 168; *Harmer v Cornelius* (1858) 5 CBNS 236.

5   See the Supply of Goods and Services Act 1982 s 13 (in relation to non-consumer contracts); and SALE OF GOODS AND SUPPLY OF SERVICES vol 91 (2012) PARA 330 et seq. See also the

Consumer Rights Act 2015 s 49 (in relation to consumer contracts); and CONSUMER PROTECTION vol 21 (2016) PARA 363. As to what amounts to reasonable care and skill see PARAS 507–509.

6 See the Supply of Goods and Services Act 1982 s 14(1) (in relation to non-consumer contracts); and SALE OF GOODS AND SUPPLY OF SERVICES vol 91 (2012) PARA 331. This applies only where the contract does not itself fix either the time for performance or the means by which that time is to be determined: see s 14(1). What is a reasonable time is a question of fact: s 14(2). See also the Consumer Rights Act 2015 s 52 (in relation to consumer contracts); CONSUMER PROTECTION vol 21 (2016) PARA 365

7 *Henderson v Merrett Syndicates Ltd* [1995] 2 AC 145, [1994] 3 All ER 506, HL; *Arenson v Casson Beckman Rutley & Co* [1977] AC 405 at 430, [1975] 3 All ER 901 at 917, HL, per Lord Kilbrandon and at 434 and 920 per Lord Salmon; *Smith v Eric S Bush, Harris v Wyre Forest District Council* [1990] 1 AC 831 at 870, [1989] 2 All ER 514 at 540, HL, per Lord Jauncey of Tullichettle; *South Australia Asset Management Corpn v York Montague Ltd* [1997] AC 191 at 211, [1996] 3 All ER 365 at 370, HL, per Lord Hoffmann. This may benefit the client in terms of the limitation period applicable to his claim: see PARA 515. As to professional negligence see NEGLIGENCE vol 78 (2018) PARA 22.

(4) Valuer and Third Parties

504. Basis of valuer's liability to third parties.

Where a valuer[1] knows[2] that his report will be shown to a third party who will act in reliance on it, he owes a duty of care in tort to that party[3], provided that there is a sufficiently proximate relationship between them[4]. A duty of care may also be owed by a valuer who ought to know, though he does not actually know, that a third party is likely to rely on his report[5], even if the third party is not actually shown the report[6], and at least where there is a high degree of probability of such reliance[7]. A valuer does not, however, owe a duty of care to a third party of whose likely reliance he neither knows nor ought to know[8], and a surveyor employed in relation to one property is not liable to the eventual purchaser of an adjacent property[9]. In terms of recoverability of losses, there is a distinction between what is 'advice' on the overall merits of a transaction on which the third party may rely and 'information' where the third party has simply relied on given information which is then factored into the third party's own assessment of whether to proceed with a transaction. In the former category, it is likely that all losses flowing from entering into the transaction will be recoverable in the event of negligence whereas in the latter category it is only the loss attributable to the incorrect information which can be recovered[10].

1 Ie other than one acting as an arbitrator: see PARA 499. As to the meaning of 'valuer' see PARA 488.

2 Such knowledge may be actual or inferential: *Caparo Industries plc v Dickman* [1990] 2 AC 605 at 638, [1990] 1 All ER 568 at 589, HL, per Lord Oliver of Aylmerton.

3 It is not necessary for the valuer to know the identity of the particular third party, so long as he is aware of him as a member of an identifiable class, such as prospective purchaser (*Shankie-Williams v Heavey* [1986] 2 EGLR 139, CA) or prospective mortgagee (*Corisand Investments Ltd v Druce & Co* [1978] 2 EGLR 86; *Assured Advances Ltd v Ashbee & Co* [1994] EGCS 169).

4 *Cann v Willson* (1888) 39 ChD 39, overruled by *Le Lievre v Gould* [1893] 1 QB 491, CA, but specifically approved in *Hedley Byrne & Co Ltd v Heller & Partners Ltd* [1964] AC 465, [1963] 2 All ER 575, HL; *Smith v Eric S Bush, Harris v Wyre Forest District Council* [1990] 1 AC 831 at 865, [1989] 2 All ER 514 at 536, HL, per Lord Griffiths. A sufficiently proximate relationship has been held to exist between a prospective purchaser and a surveyor engaged by the vendor (*Shankie-Williams v Heavey* [1986] 2 EGLR 139, CA; *Bourne v McEvoy Timber Preservation* [1976] 1 EGLR 100) and between a mortgagee, and the mortgagee's insurers, and a valuer engaged by a prospective borrower (*Banque Bruxelles Lambert SA v Eagle Star Insurance Co Ltd* [1995]

2 All ER 769 per Phillips J; revsd in part on other grounds [1995] QB 375, [1995] 2 All ER 769, CA; and see *South Australia Asset Management Corpn v York Montague Ltd* [1997] AC 191, [1996] 3 All ER 365, HL). It also appears that a surveyor advising a mortgagee on the exercise of a power of sale, following repossession of the mortgaged property, owes a duty of care to the mortgagor to see that the property is not sold at an undervalue: *Cuckmere Brick Co Ltd v Mutual Finance Ltd* [1971] Ch 949, [1971] 2 All ER 633, CA. See also *Raja v Austin Gray (a firm)* [2002] EWCA Civ 1965, [2003] 1 EGLR 91, [2002] All ER (D) 317 (Dec) (revsg *Raja v Austin Gray (a firm)* [2002] EWHC 1607 (QB), [2002] 3 EGLR 61, [2002] All ER (D) 509 (Jul)), where it was held that any duty of care owed by the valuers to the mortgagor would have been limited by the scope of their instructions from the receiver, and in the instant case there was not a relationship of sufficient proximity between them. Cf *Huish v Ellis* [1995] NPC 3. However, a marine surveyor employed by a vessel's classification society owes no duty of care to the owner of cargo carried on the vessel: *Marc Rich & Co v Bishop Rock Marine Co Ltd* [1996] AC 211, [1995] 3 All ER 307, HL.

5   See *Bourne v McEvoy Timber Preservation* [1976] 1 EGLR 100; *UCB Bank plc v Dundas & Wilson* 1989 SLT 243, Ct of Sess; *Wolverhampton Ltd v Herring Son & Daw plc* [1996] EGCS 137 (letter from seller who had instructed the valuer agreed that the plaintiff, the prospective buyer, could rely on valuation as if the plaintiff were a person on whose instruction it had been made).

6   *Smith v Eric S Bush, Harris v Wyre Forest District Council* [1990] 1 AC 831, [1989] 2 All ER 514, HL; *Beaumont v Humberts (a firm)* [1990] 2 EGLR 166, [1990] 49 EG 46, CA.

7   'The necessary proximity arises from the surveyor's knowledge that the overwhelming probability is that the purchaser will rely on his valuation – the evidence was that the surveyors knew that approximately 90% of purchasers did so – and the fact that the surveyor only obtains the work because the purchaser is willing to pay his fee . . . I would certainly wish to stress that, in cases where the advice has not been given for the specific purpose of the recipient acting on it, it should only be in cases where the adviser knows that there is a high degree of probability that some other identifiable person will act on the advice that a duty of care should be imposed': *Smith v Eric S Bush, Harris v Wyre Forest District Council* [1990] 1 AC 831 at 865, [1989] 2 All ER 514 at 536, HL, per Lord Griffiths.

8   *Le Lievre v Gould* [1893] 1 QB 491, CA, revsd on other grounds in *Hedley Byrne & Co Ltd v Heller & Partners Ltd* [1964] AC 465, [1963] 2 All ER 575, HL. See also *Beaumont v Humberts* [1990] 2 EGLR 166, CA.

9   *Shankie-Williams v Heavey* [1986] 2 EGLR 139, CA (adjacent flat).

10 *Hughes-Holland v BPE Solicitors and another* [2017] UKSC 21, [2017] 3 All ER 969, [2017] 2 WLR 1029.

505. Valuation for mortgage purposes.

A valuer who reports on a property for a prospective mortgagee, knowing that a prospective purchaser is likely to rely on his report when deciding whether or not to buy the property, owes a duty of care to that purchaser[1]. The purchaser may rely on a valuer's report which is shown to him, and on a report which is not shown to him where it is reasonable for him to assume from the offer of a loan on mortgage that the property has been valued at no less than the amount of the loan[2]. Where, however, the existing owner of a property wishes to raise money on the security of a property (such as by a remortgage or further advance) a valuer who makes a report to the prospective mortgagee cannot be liable to the owner for a negligent over-valuation, since the owner does not suffer a loss merely by receiving the requested loan[3].

A mortgagee will be vicariously liable to the purchaser for the negligence of a valuer who is the mortgagee's employee[4], but will not be so liable for the negligence of an independent valuer whom the purchaser has engaged[5] unless the mortgagee is in breach of the duty which he owes to the purchaser to take reasonable care to engage a reasonably competent valuer[6], or he has adopted the valuer's report as his own[7].

1   *Smith v Eric S Bush, Harris v Wyre Forest District Council* [1990] 1 AC 831, [1989] 2 All ER 514, HL, approving *Yianni v Edwin Evans & Sons* [1982] QB 438, [1981] 3 All ER 592. A valuer has been held to be more likely to know of the purchaser's reliance where the property valued is

comparatively cheap (*Smith v Eric S Bush, Harris v Wyre Forest District Council* above at 872 and 541 per Lord Jauncey of Tullichettle), but such reliance may be implied in relation to more expensive properties where the evidence and circumstances warrant (*Beaumont v Humberts* [1990] 2 EGLR 166, CA (reinstatement value of house bought for £110,000 in 1984)), or to the purchaser of a small shop (*Qureshi v Liassides* (22 April 1994, unreported); revsd on another point (22 March 1996, unreported), CA). See also *Merrett v Babb* [2001] EWCA Civ 214, [2001] QB 1174, [2001] BLR 483 (valuer owed personal duty of care for negligent valuation report).

2 *Smith v Eric S Bush, Harris v Wyre Forest District Council* [1990] 1 AC 831, [1989] 2 All ER 514, HL; *Yianni v Edwin Evans & Sons* [1982] QB 438, [1981] 3 All ER 592. See also *Nash v Evens & Matta* [1988] 1 EGLR 130 at 132 per Ewbank J (rusted wall-tie in late nineteenth century cavity-walled house only revealed by structural survey two years later; house, owing to age, appearance and absence of cracks, had previously been imagined to have solid walls).

3 *Saddington v Colleys Professional Services* [1999] Lloyd's Rep PN 140, CA.

4 *Smith v Eric S Bush, Harris v Wyre Forest District Council* [1990] 1 AC 831, [1989] 2 All ER 514, HL; *Beaton v Nationwide Building Society* [1991] 2 EGLR 145.

5 *Smith v Eric S Bush, Harris v Wyre Forest District Council* [1990] 1 AC 831 at 865, [1989] 2 All ER 514 at 536, HL, per Lord Griffiths. See also *Halifax Building Society v Edell* [1992] Ch 436 at 454 per Morritt J.

6 *Smith v Eric S Bush, Harris v Wyre Forest District Council* [1990] 1 AC 831 at 865, [1989] 2 All ER 514 at 536, HL, per Lord Griffiths. See also *Ward v McMaster* [1985] IR 29, Irish HC (careless valuation by valuer for the local authority which lent part of purchase price; house unsafe and recommended to be demolished).

7 See *Beresforde v Chesterfield Borough Council* [1989] 2 EGLR 149, CA.

(5) Extent of Valuer's Liability

(i) Liability for Fraudulent Valuation

506. Fraudulent valuation.

A valuer who makes a valuation which is fraudulent, namely one which he knows to be false or which he makes recklessly without regard to whether it is true or false, with the intention that it should be acted upon, is liable to an action of deceit by any person who was intended to act upon that valuation and who acts upon it to his detriment[1]. A disclaimer attached to such a valuation will not be effective to exclude or restrict the valuer's liability for fraud[2]. Nor can the defence of contributory negligence be used in an action for deceit, even by one whose liability is purely vicarious and who is not personally guilty of fraud[3].

Special provisions apply in relation to the limitation period where a claim against a valuer is based on fraud[4].

1 See *Derry v Peek* (1889) 14 App Cas 337, HL; and MISREPRESENTATION vol 76 (2013) PARA 754 et seq. As to deceit generally see MISREPRESENTATION vol 76 (2013) PARA 788 et seq.

2 See *S Pearson & Son Ltd v Dublin Corpn* [1907] AC 351, HL; and *Commercial Banking Co of Sydney Ltd v RH Brown & Co* [1972] 2 Lloyd's Rep 360, Aust HC.

3 *Alliance & Leicester Building Society v Edgestop Ltd* [1994] 2 All ER 38, [1993] 1 WLR 1462; *Nationwide Building Society v Thimbleby & Co* [1999] Lloyd's Rep PN 359, [1999] All ER (D) 211; *Standard Chartered Bank v Pakistan National Shipping Coron (No 4)* [2001] QB 167, sub nom *Standard Chartered Bank v Pakistan National Shipping Corpn (No 2)* [2000] 2 Lloyd's Rep 511, CA.

4 See PARA 515.

(ii) Professional Standards

507. In general.

The standard which a valuer or surveyor is required to achieve is that of the ordinary skilled person exercising the same skill as himself[1]. He is not liable for a mere error of judgment, unless the error was one that no reasonably well-informed and competent member of the profession could have made[2]. The required standard will normally be the same whether a claim is made in contract or tort[3], and whether it is made by a client or a third party[4].

Whether or not a valuer has exercised the required standard of skill and care is a question of fact[5] on which expert witnesses may be called to give evidence[6]. This question is to be answered in the light of knowledge which is current in the profession at the time of the valuation or survey, with care being taken to guard against hindsight[7]. A valuer will thus be adjudged negligent if he fails to take reasonable steps to keep his professional knowledge up to date[8]. However, failure to comply with guidance notes issued by the relevant professional bodies does not necessarily constitute negligence[9].

1　See *Bolam v Friern Hospital Management Committee* [1957] 2 All ER 118 at 121, [1957] 1 WLR 582 at 586 per McNair J (applied in *TW (a child suing by his Father and Litigation Friend LF AXX) v Royal Bolton Hospital NHS Foundation Trust* [2017] EWHC 3139 (QB), [2017] All ER (D) 23 (Dec); and *Haywood v University Hospitals of North Midlands NHS Trust* [2017] EWHC 335 (QB), [2017] All ER (D) 178 (Feb)). The standard will not be lower because a defendant has no professional qualifications (*Freeman v Marshall & Co* (1966) 200 Estates Gazette 777); nor because he lacks relevant experience (*Kenney v Hall, Pain & Foster* [1976] 2 EGLR 29; *Baxter v FW Gapp & Co Ltd* [1938] 4 All ER 457 at 459 per Goddard LJ; *Whalley v Roberts and Roberts* [1990] 1 EGLR 164, [1990] 06 EG 104).

2　*Saif Ali v Sydney Mitchell & Co (a firm)* [1980] AC 198 at 220, [1978] 3 All ER 1033 at 1043, HL, per Lord Diplock; *Banque Bruxelles Lambert SA v Eagle Star Insurance Co Ltd* [1995] 2 All ER 769 at 821 per Phillips J (on appeal [1995] QB 375, [1995] 2 All ER 769, CA); *Moy v Pettman Smith (a firm)* [2005] UKHL 7, 1 All ER 903, [2005] 1 WLR 581; *Middle Level Commissioners v Atkins Ltd* [2012] EWHC 2884 (TCC), [2012] All ER (D) 260 (Oct); and see *South Australia Asset Management Corpn v York Montague Ltd* [1997] AC 191, [1996] 3 All ER 365, HL; and *Hughes-Holland v BPE Solicitors* [2017] UKSC 21, [2017] 3 All ER 969, [2017] 2 WLR 1029.

3　However, the contract under which the valuer is engaged may limit the service which is to be provided, and to which the standard of skill and care will therefore apply: see *Predeth v Castle Phillips Finance Co Ltd* [1986] 2 EGLR 144, 279 Estates Gazette 1355, CA (surveyor asked for a 'crash sale valuation' held to be under no duty to provide an open market valuation as well); *Sutcliffe v Sayer* [1987] 1 EGLR 155, 281 Estates Gazette 1452, CA (estate agent asked to advise potential purchaser on asking price held to be under no duty to warn that defects might render property difficult to resell); *Tenenbaum v Garrod* [1988] 2 EGLR 178, [1988] 35 EG 77, CA. Cf *McIntyre v Herring Son & Daw* [1988] 1 EGLR 231. As to the possibility of excluding or restricting liability by contract see PARA 514.

4　The standard will not be lower merely because the valuer does not charge a fee for the service which he carries out (*Kenney v Hall, Pain & Foster* [1976] 2 EGLR 29 at 33 per Goff J) nor because he charges a standard fee, and therefore one which may be low for the work required in valuing some properties (*Roberts v J Hampson & Co* [1989] 2 All ER 504 at 510, [1990] 1 WLR 94 at 101 per Ian Kennedy J).

5　This issue will not as a general rule be suitable to be resolved on an application for summary judgment: *European Partners In Capital (EPIC) Holdings BV v Goddard & Smith* [1992] 2 EGLR 155 at 157, CA, per Scott LJ.

6　As to the power of the court to appoint an expert see *Abbey National Mortgages plc v Key Surveyors Nationwide Ltd* [1996] 3 All ER 184, [1996] 2 EGLR 99, CA.

7　*Private Bank & Trust Co Ltd v S (UK) Ltd* [1993] 1 EGLR 144 at 146 per Rice J. See also *Hill v Debenham, Tewson and Chinnocks* (1958) 171 Estates Gazette 835.

8　See *Hooberman v Salter Rex* (1984) 1 Con LR 63, [1985] 1 EGLR 144; *Peach v Iain G Chalmers & Co* [1992] 2 EGLR 135, Ct of Sess; *Weedon v Hindwood, Clarke & Esplin* [1975] 1 EGLR 82; *Corisand Investments Ltd v Druce & Co* [1978] 2 EGLR 86.

9   *PK Finans International (UK) Ltd v Andrew Downs & Co Ltd* [1992] 1 EGLR 172 at 174 per Sir
    Michael Ogden QC. Members of the Royal Institution of Chartered Surveyors and the Institute of
    Revenues, Rating and Valuation follow the guidance contained in the *RICS Valuation— Global
    Standards* (2017) and the *RICS Valuation— Professional Standards UK* (January 2014, revised
    April 2015); see PARA 489.

508. Valuer's standard of care and skill.

A person who holds himself out or purports to act as a valuer represents himself as having the skill and knowledge which a reasonably competent member of his profession or calling would have[1], and it is his duty to take reasonable care to give a reliable and informed opinion on the open market value of the land in question at the date of valuation[2]. In the absence of special instructions it is not a valuer's duty to advise on future movements in property prices, whether nationally or locally; his concern is with current value only[3].

Valuation is not an exact science[4], but rather a matter of opinion on which competent valuers may reach different conclusions[5]. A valuer is accordingly not guilty of negligence merely because another valuer produces a different answer[6], nor because his valuation turns out to be wrong[7]. However, a valuation which falls outside a permissible margin of error[8] brings into question the valuer's competence and the care with which he carried out his task[9].

A valuer is not negligent merely because he adopts a method of valuation which is not the best[10], provided that it is one which is accepted by a responsible body of opinion among valuers[11]. A valuer will, however, be negligent if he gives an open market valuation without considering the implications of a recent sale of the property, unless he has been specifically instructed to disregard it[12].

1   *Jenkins v Betham* (1855) 15 CB 168; *Harmer v Cornelius* (1858) 5 CBNS 236. The knowledge
    which a competent valuer may be expected to possess includes an understanding of the general
    legal rules governing particular types of valuation (*Jenkins v Betham* (1855) 15 CB 168; *Weedon
    v Hindwood, Clarke & Esplin* [1975] 1 EGLR 82) and an awareness of the state of the property
    market in general, and, while he is not expected to foresee a general collapse in property prices, his
    valuation must not contain a substantial speculative element (*Corisand Investments Ltd v Druce
    & Co* [1978] 2 EGLR 86 at 92 per Gibson J; *Private Bank & Trust Co Ltd v S (UK) Ltd* (1993)
    67 P&CR 166, [1993] 1 EGLR 144). A valuer is normally expected to be familiar with property
    values in the relevant locality: *Baxter v FW Gapp & Co Ltd* [1938] 4 All ER 457 at 459 per
    Goddard LJ; *Singer & Friedlander Ltd v John D Wood & Co* [1977] 2 EGLR 84 per Watkins J;
    Capita Alternative Fund Services (Guernsey) Ltd v Drivers Jonas [2011] EWHC 2336 (Comm),
    139 ConLR 125, [2011] NLJR 1335 (reversed on different grounds on appeal [2012] EWCA Civ
    1417, [2013] 1 EGLR 119, [2012] All ER (D) 109 (Nov)); cf *Abbey National Mortgages plc v Key
    Surveyors Nationwide Ltd* [1996] 3 All ER 184 at 190–191, CA, per Sir Thomas Bingham MR.
    See also *Currys Group plc v Martin* [1999] 3 EGLR 165.
2   *Banque Bruxelles Lambert SA v Eagle Star Insurance Co Ltd* [1995] QB 375 at 403–404, [1995]
    2 All ER 769 at 840, CA, per Sir Thomas Bingham MR (but see *South Australia Asset Management
    Corpn v York Montague Ltd* [1997] AC 191, [1996] 3 All ER 365, HL; and *Hughes-Holland v
    BPE Solicitors* [2017] UKSC 21, [2017] 3 All ER 969, [2017] 2 WLR 1029). Where it is
    particularly difficult to arrive at a reliable conclusion as to value (for instance because of a lack of
    suitable comparable evidence), a valuer may be negligent if he fails to warn the client of this:
    Merivale Moore plc v Strutt & Parker [1999] 2 EGLR 171, CA (applied in *Barclays Bank plc v
    RBS & V Ltd* [2016] EWHC 2948 (QB), [2016] All ER (D) 183 (Nov); *Paratus AMC Ltd v
    Countrywide Surveyors Ltd* [2011] EWHC 3307 (Ch), [2012] NLJR 95, [2012] All ER (D) 32
    (Jan); *Goldstein v Levy Gee (a firm)*[2003] EWHC 1574 (Ch), [2003] 34 LS Gaz R 32, (2003)
    Times). See also *Montlake (as trustees of Wasps Football Club) v Lambert Smith Hampton Group
    Ltd* [2004] EWHC 938 (Comm), [2004] 3 EGLR 149 (valuation failed to take into consideration
    the fact that planning permission had been granted in respect of sports ground). Although there is
    a presumption that those who provide professional services normally do no more than undertake
    to exercise the degree of care and skill to be expected of a competent professional in the relevant
    field, there is nothing to prevent them from assuming an unqualified obligation in relation to
    particular aspects of their work: see *Platform Holdings Ltd v Bank of Scotland plc* [2008] EWCA
    Civ 930, [2009] QB 426, [2009] 2 All ER 344.

3 *Banque Bruxelles Lambert SA v Eagle Star Insurance Co Ltd* [1995] QB 375 at 404, [1995] 2 All
   ER 769 at 840, CA, per Sir Thomas Bingham MR (but see *South Australia Asset Management
   Corpn v York Montague Ltd* [1997] AC 191, [1996] 3 All ER 365, HL; and *Hughes-Holland v
   BPE Solicitors* [2017] UKSC 21, [2017] 3 All ER 969, [2017] 2 WLR 1029)). However, where a
   belief among buyers and sellers as to future market movements has an effect on current prices, his
   valuation should reflect this: *Banque Bruxelles Lambert SA v Eagle Star Insurance Co Ltd*. In
   advising trustees as to property on the security of which it is proposed to invest trust funds, a
   valuer must advise as to the amount which it is safe to advance on that property, as well as its
   actual value: *Shaw v Cates* [1909] 1 Ch 389 at 398; *Re Solomon, Nore v Meyer* [1912] 1 Ch 261
   at 274.
4 *Zubaida v Hargreaves* [1995] 1 EGLR 127 at 128, CA, per Hoffmann LJ; *Craneheath Securities
   Ltd v York Montague Ltd* [1996] 1 EGLR 130 at 132, CA, per Balcombe LJ.
5 *Singer & Friedlander Ltd v John D Wood & Co* [1977] 2 EGLR 84 at 85 per Watkins J; *Banque
   Bruxelles Lambert SA v Eagle Star Insurance Co Ltd* [1995] 2 All ER 769 at 789 per Phillips J (on
   appeal [1995] QB 375, [1995] 2 All ER 769, CA; and see *South Australia Asset Management
   Corpn v York Montague Ltd* [1997] AC 191, [1996] 3 All ER 365, HL).
6 *Zubaida v Hargreaves* [1995] 1 EGLR 127 at 128, CA, per Hoffmann LJ; *Campbell v Edwards*
   [1976] 1 All ER 785 at 789, [1976] 1 WLR 403 at 408, CA, per Geoffrey Lane LJ.
7 *Baxter v FW Gapp & Co Ltd* [1938] 4 All ER 457 at 459 per Goddard LJ.
8 This is normally 10% either side of a notional 'right' figure, but can be extended to 15% either
   way, or a little more, in exceptional circumstances: *Singer & Friedlander Ltd v John D Wood &
   Co* [1977] 2 EGLR 84 at 85 per Watkins J; and see *K/S Lincoln v CB Richard Ellis Hotels Ltd (No
   2)* [2010] EWHC 1156 (TCC), [2010] NLJR 905, [2010] All ER (D) 138 (Jun). See also *Banque
   Bruxelles Lambert SA v Eagle Star Insurance Co Ltd* [1995] 2 All ER 769 at 789 per Phillips J
   (20% 'bracket') (on appeal [1995] QB 375, [1995] 2 All ER 769; and see *South Australia Asset
   Management Corpn v York Montague Ltd* [1997] AC 191, [1996] 3 All ER 365, HL); *Nykredit
   Mortgage Bank plc v Edward Erdman Group Ltd* [1996] 1 EGLR 119 at 120, CA, per Staughton
   LJ. It has been held that for a standard residential property, the margin of error could be as low
   as plus or minus 5%: see *K/S Lincoln v CB Richard Ellis Hotels Ltd (No 2)* above.
9 *Singer & Friedlander Ltd v John D Wood & Co* [1977] 2 EGLR 84 at 85 per Watkins J. The effect
   of this is to place the onus on the defendant to prove that he exercised an appropriate degree of
   skill and care in carrying out the valuation: *Legal & General Mortgage Services Ltd v HPC
   Professional Services* [1997] PNLR 567 at 574 per Judge Langan QC, approved in *Merivale Moore
   plc v Strutt & Parker* [1999] 2 EGLR 171 at 176, CA, per Buxton LJ); *Lloyds TSB Bank plc v
   Edward Symmons & Partners* [2003] EWHC 346 (TCC), [2003] EGLR 95, [2003] 13 LS Gaz R
   31. Conversely, a claimant cannot recover merely because there have been errors at some stages of
   a valuation, unless the final valuation can also be shown to be wrong: *Craneheath Securities Ltd
   v York Montague Ltd* [1996] 1 EGLR 130 at 132, CA, per Balcombe LJ; *South Australia Asset
   Management Corpn v York Montague Ltd* [1997] AC 191 at 223, [1996] 3 All ER 365 at 381, HL,
   per Lord Hoffmann; and *Hughes-Holland v BPE Solicitors* [2017] UKSC 21, [2017] 3 All ER 969,
   [2017] 2 WLR 1029. See also *Arab Bank plc v John D Wood Commercial Ltd* [2000] 1 WLR 857,
   [2000] Lloyd's Rep PN 173, CA; *Goldstein v Levy Gee (a firm)* [2003] EWHC 1574 (Ch), (2003)
   Times, 16 July, [2003] All ER (D) 12 (Jul). Whilst a valuer might be in breach of duty because he
   fell below the standard of a reasonable valuer in his methodology, he would not be liable in
   negligence if it could be shown that, notwithstanding the error, the valuation figure that he
   produced was within a reasonable bracket: see *K/S Lincoln v CB Richard Ellis Hotels Ltd (No 2)*
   [2010] EWHC 1156 (TCC), [2010] NLJR 905, [2010] All ER (D) 138 (Jun).
10 *Love v Mack* (1905) 92 LT 345 at 349–350 per Kekewich J.
11 *Singer & Friedlander Ltd v John D Wood & Co* [1977] 2 EGLR 84 at 87–88 per Watkins J. As
   to valuation methods adopted for different types of property see *Singer & Friedlander Ltd v John
   D Wood & Co* (development sites); *Mount Banking Corpn Ltd v Brian Cooper & Co* [1992] 2
   EGLR 142; *Nykredit Mortgage Bank plc v Edward Erdman Group Ltd* [1996] 1 EGLR 119, CA
   (residual valuations of development projects); *Corisand Investments Ltd v Druce & Co* [1978] 2
   EGLR 86 (hotels); *Craneheath Securities Ltd v York Montague Ltd* [1994] 1 EGLR 159, CA
   (restaurants); *Beaumont v Humberts* [1990] 2 EGLR 166, CA (insurance); *McIntyre v Herring Son
   & Daw* [1988] 1 EGLR 231 (rating); *Zubaida v Hargreaves* [1995] 1 EGLR 127, CA (rent
   reviews); and *Merivale Moore plc v Strutt & Parker* [1999] 2 EGLR 171, CA.
12 *Banque Bruxelles Lambert SA v Eagle Star Insurance Co Ltd* [1995] 2 All ER 769 at 789–791 per
   Phillips J (on appeal [1995] QB 375, [1995] 2 All ER 769, CA; and see *South Australia Asset
   Management Corpn v York Montague Ltd* [1997] AC 191, [1996] 3 All ER 365, HL);
   Hughes-Holland v BPE Solicitors [2017] UKSC 21, [2017] 3 All ER 969, [2017] 2 WLR 1029.

509. Surveyor's standard of care and skill.

A surveyor's duty is to survey the property to the standard of a reasonably competent surveyor exercising due skill, care and diligence and possessing the necessary knowledge and experience[1]. The extent to which this requires the use of special equipment is a question of fact[2].

In the absence of contrary agreement, a surveyor is normally expected to inspect all parts of the property which are visible[3], but not to uncover or open up those parts which are not visible[4]. However, a surveyor whose inspection reveals grounds for suspecting the existence of defects must take reasonable steps to follow the trail of suspicion[5].

1 *Kerridge v James Abbott & Partners* [1992] 2 EGLR 162. The extent and depth of inspection which is expected will depend on the type of survey to be carried out, although a surveyor must show the same level of expertise even when carrying out a limited inspection: *Cross v David Martin & Mortimer* [1989] 1 EGLR 154 at 155 per Phillips J. As to the limited inspection which is required in carrying out a mortgage valuation see *Roberts v J Hampson & Co* [1989] 2 All ER 504, [1990] 1 WLR 94; *Lloyd v Butler* [1990] 2 EGLR 155 at 160 per Henry J.
2 See eg *Fryer v Bunney* [1982] 2 EGLR 130 (surveyor negligent for failure to make sufficient use of a damp meter); *Eley v King & Chasemore* [1989] 1 EGLR 181, CA (surveyor not negligent for inspecting roof from ground level, rather than obtaining a long ladder); *Hacker v Thomas Deal & Co* [1991] 2 EGLR 161 (surveyor not negligent in failing to use torch and mirror to check behind cupboards for damp; RICS guidelines specifically stated that use of mirror was a matter of individual preference).
3 See *Hill v Debenham, Tewson & Chinnocks* (1958) 171 Estates Gazette 835; *Stewart v HA Brechin & Co* 1959 SC 306, Ct of Sess.
4 *Roberts v J Hampson & Co* [1989] 2 All ER 504 at 510, [1990] 1 WLR 94 at 101 per Ian Kennedy J.
5 *Roberts v J Hampson & Co* [1989] 2 All ER 504, [1990] 1 WLR 94; *Lloyd v Butler* [1990] 2 EGLR 155; *Sneesby v Goldings* (1994) 45 Con LR 11, [1995] 2 EGLR 102, CA. Such reasonable steps may not require the surveyor 'to follow up every trail to discover whether there is trouble or the extent of any such trouble. But where such an inspection can reasonably show a potential trouble or risk of potential trouble . . . it is necessary . . . to alert the purchaser to that risk': *Lloyd v Butler* [1990] 2 EGLR 155 at 161 per Henry J.

(iii) Damages

510. Damages for negligent valuation; in general.

In order to recover damages[1] in respect of a negligent valuation, a claimant must establish that he has suffered loss or damage which the valuer's negligence caused or to which it contributed[2]. In normal circumstances, proof of the necessary causal link will require evidence that the claimant acted in reliance on information provided by the valuer[3]. Where such reliance is established, the damages awarded for a negligent valuation are such as would fairly and reasonably be considered as resulting[4] from the failure of the valuer to report as he should have done, had he used due care[5]. In particular, the damages should not impose upon the valuer responsibility for losses which would have occurred even if the valuation had been correct[6].

Damages awarded in cases of negligent valuation will not extend to any part of the claimant's loss which the claimant ought reasonably to have avoided[7]. Damages may also be reduced where the claimant's loss is offset by benefit he has received[8].

Subject to rules of court, in proceedings (whenever instituted) before the High Court for the recovery of a debt or damages there may be included in any sum for which judgment is given simple interest, at such rate as the court thinks fit or as rules of court may provide, on all or any part of the debt or damages in respect of which judgment is given, or payment is made before judgment, for all or any part of the period between the date when the cause of action arose and: (1) in the case of any sum paid before judgment, the date of the payment; and (2) in the case of the sum for which judgment is given, the date of the judgment[9]. Where damages are awarded against a negligent valuer, the court will normally exercise its statutory discretion to order that the damages are to bear simple interest[10].

1   Ie other than nominal damages, which may be awarded in a claim for breach of contract whether or not the breach has caused any loss: see further DAMAGES vol 29 (2014) PARAS 319–320.

2   *Thomas Miller & Co v Richard Saunders & Partners* [1989] 1 EGLR 267 at 272 per Rougier J (tenant's surveyor who negligently failed to put forward relevant evidence at a rent review arbitration was held not liable for his client's losses, since the court was satisfied that the evidence in question would not have altered the arbitrator's decision).

3   See *Rona v Pearce* (1953) 162 Estates Gazette 380; *Shankie-Williams v Heavey* [1986] 2 EGLR 139, CA (actions against surveyors failed for lack of such evidence). However, it is not necessary for the claimant to have relied exclusively upon information from the defendant, provided that it played a real and substantial part in inducing him to act as he did: *Kenney v Hall, Pain & Foster* [1976] 2 EGLR 29 at 35 per Goff J; *HIT Finance Ltd v Lewis & Tucker Ltd* [1993] 2 EGLR 231 at 234 per Wright J; *Caparo Industries plc v Dickman* [1990] 2 AC 605, [1990] 1 All ER 568, HL; *Banque Bruxelles Lambert SA v Eagle Star Insurance Co Ltd* [1995] 2 All ER 769 at 794 per Phillips J (on appeal [1995] QB 375, [1995] 2 All ER 769, CA); and see *South Australia Asset Management Corpn v York Montague Ltd* [1997] AC 191, [1996] 3 All ER 365, HL; *Hughes-Holland v BPE Solicitors* [2017] UKSC 21, [2017] 3 All ER 969, [2017] 2 WLR 1029. See also PARA 469 note 3. A purchaser who has agreed to pay more for property than the value placed on it by his surveyor may nevertheless be held to have relied upon the surveyor's report: *Oswald v Countrywide Surveyors Ltd* [1996] 2 EGLR 104, 50 Con LR 1, CA; and see PARA 511 note 7. In order to establish a valuer's liability, where the property valued was not identical to the property secured, the court must ask whether the purpose for which the claimant used the valuation was a purpose which the valuer would reasonably have contemplated: *Western Trust and Savings Ltd v Strutt & Parker* [1998] 3 EGLR 89, CA. See also *Cavendish Funding Ltd v Henry Spencer & Sons Ltd* [1998] 1 EGLR 104, CA (lender who based lending decision on higher of two independent valuations had sufficiently relied on that valuation to hold valuer liable).

4   As to what losses may be said to have resulted from such failure see *Banque Bruxelles Lambert SA v Eagle Star Insurance Co Ltd* [1995] QB 375 at 405–431, [1995] 2 All ER 769 at 841–864, CA, per Sir Thomas Bingham MR; but cf *South Australia Asset Management Corpn v York Montague Ltd* [1997] AC 191 at 212–218, [1996] 3 All ER 365 at 371–376, HL, per Lord Hoffmann; *Hughes-Holland v BPE Solicitors* [2017] UKSC 21, [2017] 3 All ER 969, [2017] 2 WLR 1029; and see PARA 512.

5   *Philips v Ward* [1956] 1 All ER 874 at 878, [1956] 1 WLR 471 at 475, CA, per Morris LJ. As to the kind of losses which a valuer might reasonably be expected to foresee, and which are therefore not too remote a consequence of his negligence, see *Morgan v Perry* (1973) 229 Estates Gazette 1737; *Banque Bruxelles Lambert SA v Eagle Star Insurance Co Ltd* [1995] QB 375 at 405, [1995] 2 All ER 769 at 840, CA, per Sir Thomas Bingham MR (but see *South Australia Asset Management Corpn v York Montague Ltd* [1997] AC 191, [1996] 3 All ER 365, HL; and note 4); *Drinnan v CW Ingram & Sons* 1967 SLT 205; *Allen v Ellis & Co* [1990] 1 EGLR 170 (survey report failed to mention roof in poor condition; it leaked; owner investigated and fell through; valuer liable for owner's injuries). As to the correct measure of damages for negligent advice on the value of property for insurance purposes see *Beaumont v Humberts* [1990] 2 EGLR 166, CA.

6   *South Australia Asset Management Corpn v York Montague Ltd* [1997] AC 191 at 214, [1996] 3 All ER 365 at 371, HL, per Lord Hoffmann (a duty of care which imposed such responsibility would not be fair and reasonable and could not therefore be justified either as an implied term of a contract or as a tortious duty). As to earlier law see *Banque Bruxelles Lambert SA v Eagle Star Insurance Co Ltd* [1995] QB 375, [1995] 2 All ER 769, CA. However, a different result might be justified if the valuer were engaged, not merely to provide information, but to advise on the suitability of a proposed transaction, as he would then be responsible not merely for all the foreseeable consequences of the information being wrong, but for all the foreseeable loss which is a consequence of that course of action having been taken: *South Australia Asset Management Corpn v York Montague Ltd* above at 214–215 and 372–373 per Lord Hoffmann. See also *Hughes-Holland v BPE Solicitors* [2017] UKSC 21, [2017] 3 All ER 969, [2017] 2 WLR 1029.

7   As to the doctrine of mitigation of damage see DAMAGES vol 29 (2014) PARA 378 et seq. As to

the operation of this principle in the context of negligent valuations see PARAS 511 note 11, 513 note 3.

8 Eg, a mortgage lender who claims damages from a negligent valuer must bring into account the amount realised by a sale of the mortgaged property, and also any repayments made by the borrower prior to default: see PARA 512. However, the principle of 'res inter alios acta' means that a claimant need not bring into account the proceeds of an insurance policy: *Banque Bruxelles Lambert SA v Eagle Star Insurance Co Ltd* [1995] 2 All ER 769 per Phillips J (on appeal [1995] QB 375, [1995] 2 All ER 769, CA; and see *South Australia Asset Management Corpn v York Montague Ltd* [1997] AC 191, [1996] 3 All ER 365, HL; *Hughes-Holland v BPE Solicitors* [2017] UKSC 21, [2017] 3 All ER 969, [2017] 2 WLR 1029). Nor need he bring into account a discretionary statutory grant given by a local authority to enable the claimant to repair defective property. 'I am clearly of the view that the sum does not fall to be deducted. Firstly, because it is irrelevant to a claim where the difference in value is the measure of damage and, secondly, because, to use legal shorthand, it is a collateral benefit which does not have to be taken into account': *Treml v Ernest W Gibson and Partners* [1984] 2 EGLR 162 at 164 per Popplewell J. See also *Gardner v Marsh & Parsons (a firm)* [1997] 3 All ER 871, [1997] 1 WLR 489, CA; and PARA 511 note 5.

9 Senior Courts Act 1981 s 35A(1) (added by the Administration of Justice Act 1982 s 15(1), Sch 1 Pt 1). As to the Senior Courts Act 1981 see PARA 340 note 4. Thus the court's discretion extends to both the rate of interest awarded and the period over which it is to be calculated.

10 The court has refused to interfere with a trial judge's decision to apply the rate of interest laid down under the Judgments Act 1838 for interest on judgment debts, even where it considers that it would have been preferable to apply a rate of interest reflecting the cost or value of money over the relevant period: *Watts v Morrow* [1991] 4 All ER 937 at 960, [1991] 1 WLR 1421 at 1446, CA, per Bingham LJ (applied in *Persimmon Homes (South Coast) Ltd v Hall Aggregates (South Coast) Ltd* [2012] EWHC 2429 (TCC), [2012] All ER (D) 295 (Oct)).

511. Measure of damages in claim by purchaser or vendor.

The proper measure of damages is the difference between what the property would have been worth[1] had it been in the condition in which the valuer represented it[2] and its actual value[3], which should have been reported to the party who relied on the valuer's report[4]. This remains the case even where the purchaser, acting reasonably to cut his losses, sells the property for more than he paid before the valuer admits liability or is found liable[5]. If, despite the negligent valuation, the purchaser paid no more than the property was worth in its actual condition, only nominal damages will be awarded[6]. If the purchaser chose to pay more than the property would have been worth had it been in the condition in which the valuer represented it, the valuer or surveyor is not liable for that excess[7]. Damages are assessed according to the difference in 'as represented' and 'actual' values which obtained when the purchaser became legally committed to the purchase, and the damages bear interest from that date until the date of judgment[8].

The purchaser is not entitled to recover the cost of repairing defects which the valuer or surveyor has negligently overlooked[9], although the cost of such repairs may be relevant evidence when assessing what the property is actually worth in its defective condition[10].

If the purchaser decides to dispose of the defective property, he will also be entitled to recover damages in relation to certain incidental losses, such as legal fees and other costs, occasioned by both the purchase and the resale[11]. If he decides to retain the property and rectify its defects, he will probably be entitled to recover in respect of reasonable incidental expenses, such as fees incurred in investigating the defects and the cost of alternative accommodation while repairs are being carried out[12], but damages are not recoverable for the cost of the repair work itself[13].

The damages recoverable from a negligent surveyor or valuer by the purchaser of a dwelling may include a sum for physical inconvenience and discomfort[14] caused by the breach of duty and for mental suffering directly related to that inconvenience and discomfort[15]. That sum will reflect the amount and duration of the discomfort[16], but it should in any event be modest and not excessive[17].

Where a vendor sells property at an undervalue in reliance on advice negligently given to him by a valuer, the vendor may recover the difference between the market value of the property and the price for which he sold it[18].

1   This, in most cases, is the price paid, at least where no point is taken that the claimant chose to pay above market value: see *Watts v Morrow* [1991] 4 All ER 937 at 945, [1991] 1 WLR 1421 at 1430, CA, per Ralph Gibson LJ; *Shepherd Homes Ltd v Encia Remediation Ltd* [2007] EWHC 1710 (TCC), [2007] All ER (D) 334 (Jul); and *Persimmon Homes (South Coast) Ltd v Hall Aggregates (South Coast)* [2012] EWHC 2429 (TCC), [2012] All ER (D) 295 (Oct) (discussing the rate of interest which should reflect the rate at which the claimant would have had to borrow money).

2   The claimant's damages will be reduced if in fact he bought it for less than this figure, as he will have suffered a correspondingly smaller loss, and if he bought it for so much less that he turns out to have paid no more than the property's actual value, he will get nominal damages only: see the text and notes 5–8.

3   This figure should be that which the court considers it most likely that a reasonable valuer, using the information available at the relevant date, would have put forward as the amount which the property was most likely to fetch if sold on the open market; it is not the highest possible valuation which would not have been negligent: *South Australia Asset Management Corpn v York Montague Ltd* [1997] AC 191 at 221–222, [1996] 3 All ER 365 at 379, HL, per Lord Hoffmann.

4   See *Philips v Ward* [1956] 1 All ER 874 at 876, [1956] 1 WLR 471 at 473, CA, per Denning LJ; *Ford v White & Co* [1964] 2 All ER 755 at 758–761, [1964] 1 WLR 885 at 888–892 per Pennycuick J (plaintiffs bought house and vacant plot, with building restriction against the plot, at actual value; solicitor negligently failed to tell plaintiffs of restriction; held that plaintiffs had suffered no loss as the difference between the price paid and the property's actual value was nil; they were therefore in the same position as if the defendants had fulfilled their duty and so were not entitled to damages; the plaintiffs' claim in the case arose in contract, and not in tort, and agreement between the parties as to the measure of damage in the event of the court so deciding precluded an award of nominal damages); *Perry v Sidney Phillips & Son (a firm)* [1982] 3 All ER 705, [1982] 1 WLR 1297, CA; *Watts v Morrow* [1991] 4 All ER 937 at 945–954, [1991] 1 WLR 1421 at 1429–1439, CA, per Ralph Gibson LJ. See also *Gardner v Marsh & Parsons (a firm)* [1997] 3 All ER 871, [1997] 1 WLR 489, CA; *Smith v Peter North & Partners* [2001] EWCA Civ 1553, [2002] 1 P & CR 480, 82 Con LR 126. See also *Capita Alternative Fund Services (Guernsey) Ltd v Drivers Jonas* [2012] EWCA Civ 1417, [2012] All ER (D) 109 (Nov) (tax considerations had been integral to the claimant's investment therefore, it would, in principle, wrong to ignore them when assessing the damages recoverable by them). See also *Hughes-Holland v BPE Solicitors* [2017] UKSC 21, [2017] 3 All ER 969, [2017] 2 WLR 1029 (distinguishing between advice and information); and the commentary at PARA 504.

5   *Perry v Sidney Phillips & Son (a firm)* [1982] 3 All ER 705, [1982] 1 WLR 1297, CA (house, though defective, was sold unrepaired for more than the plaintiff paid for it); and see the text and note 8. See also *Gardner v Marsh & Parsons (a firm)* [1997] 3 All ER 871, [1997] 1 WLR 489, CA (applied in *Needler Financial Services Ltd v Taber* [2002] 3 All ER 501, [2002] Lloyd's Rep PN 32).

6   *Upstone v GDW Carnegie & Co* 1978 SLT (Sh Ct) 4. See also *Smith v Peter North & Partners* [2001] EWCA Civ 1553, [2002] 1 P & CR 480, 82 Con LR 126.

7   *Hardy v Wamsley-Lewis* (1967) 203 Estates Gazette 1039; but see *Oswald v Countrywide Surveyors Ltd* [1996] 2 EGLR 104, 50 Con LR 1, CA (plaintiffs paid £225,000 for property valued at £215,000; surveyor advised caution on woodworm but failed to notice death watch beetle; plaintiffs said they would have paid £165,000 for the property in its actual condition; on appeal held that it was open for the judge to decide as a matter of fact that the price paid by the plaintiffs was the best evidence of its market value in the condition in which the surveyor represented it, and that one could have regard to the cost of repairs in calculating its actual market value; allowance was made for betterment resulting from repairs).

8   *Perry v Sidney Phillips & Son* [1982] 3 All ER 705, [1982] 1 WLR 1297, CA; and see PARA 510.

9   *Philips v Ward* [1956] 1 All ER 874, [1956] 1 WLR 471, CA; *Perry v Sidney Phillips & Son* [1982] 3 All ER 705, [1982] 1 WLR 1297, CA; *Watts v Morrow* [1991] 4 All ER 937, [1991] 1 WLR 1421, CA; *Smith v Peter North & Partners* [2001] EWCA Civ 1553, [2002] 1 P & CR 480, 82 Con LR 126. See also *Patel v Hooper & Jackson (a firm)* [1999] 1 All ER 992, [1999] 1 WLR 1792, CA.

10 *Steward v Rapley* [1989] 1 EGLR 159, CA. As to the position where a purchaser of a lease subsequently discovers that it contains terms to his disadvantage about which he was not warned see *Simple Simon Catering Ltd v Binstock Miller & Co* (1973) 228 Estates Gazette 527 at 529, CA, per Lord Denning MR.

11 *Philips v Ward* [1956] 1 All ER 874 at 879, [1956] 1 WLR 471 at 478, CA, per Romer LJ; *Watts v Morrow* [1991] 4 All ER 937 at 950, [1991] 1 WLR 1421 at 1435, CA, per Ralph Gibson LJ and at 959 and 1445 per Bingham LJ; *Heatley v William H Brown Ltd* [1992] 1 EGLR 289 at 296 per Peter Bowsher J, QC. A purchaser who decides to sell the defective property may also be entitled to recover costs incurred through renting alternative accommodation: *Patel v Hooper & Jackson (a firm)* [1999] 1 All ER 992, [1999] 1 WLR 1792, CA.

12 See eg *Morgan v Perry* (1973) 229 Estates Gazette 1737; *Treml v Ernest W Gibson and Partners* [1984] 2 EGLR 162; *Cross v David Martin & Mortimer* [1989] 1 EGLR 154 at 159 per Phillips J.

13 See note 9.

14 'If the cause of the inconvenience or discomfort is a sensory (sight, touch, hearing, smell etc) experience, damages can, subject to the remoteness rule, be recovered': *Farley v Skinner* [2001] UKHL 49 at [85], [2002] 2 AC 732 at [85], [2001] 4 All ER 801 at [85] per Lord Scott of Foscote (damages awarded for aircraft noise).

15 *Perry v Sidney Phillips & Son* [1982] 3 All ER 705, [1982] 1 WLR 1297, CA (inconvenience, distress and discomfort); *Watts v Morrow* [1991] 4 All ER 937, [1991] 1 WLR 1421, CA (damages awarded for distress caused by physical consequences of breach but not for mental distress not caused by physical discomfort or inconvenience resulting from the breach); *Ezekiel v McDade* [1995] 2 EGLR 107 at 110, CA, per Nourse LJ. Damages may be awarded for discomfort foreseeably suffered during the period when defects in the property are repaired even though the cost of repairs is not itself recoverable: *Watts v Morrow* [1991] 4 All ER 937 at 960, [1991] 1 WLR 1421 at 1445, CA, per Bingham LJ. In the absence of such physical discomfort a surveyor or valuer is not normally liable for distress, frustration, anxiety, displeasure, vexation, tension or aggravation suffered by the purchaser: *Perry v Sidney Phillips & Son* [1982] 3 All ER 705 at 712, [1982] 1 WLR 1297 at 1307, CA, per Kerr LJ; *Watts v Morrow* above at 956–957, 959 and 1442, 1445 per Bingham LJ. However, damages may be awarded for such consequences where a major object of a contract for a survey is the provision of pleasure, relaxation or peace of mind: *Farley v Skinner* [2001] UKHL 49, [2002] 2 AC 732, [2001] 4 All ER 801 (surveyor held negligent for breach of specific undertaking to investigate possibility of aircraft noise affecting property).

16 *Watts v Morrow* [1991] 4 All ER 937 at 958, [1991] 1 WLR 1421 at 1443, CA, per Ralph Gibson LJ. A purchaser may be precluded by the doctrine of mitigation from recovering damages for discomfort suffered after the time when he ought reasonably to have repaired defects in the property: *Cross v David Martin & Mortimer* [1989] 1 EGLR 154 at 159 per Phillips J. However, where the defendant persists in denying liability, a purchaser does not act unreasonably in failing to carry out repairs which he lacks the means to pay for: *Perry v Sidney Phillips & Son* [1982] 3 All ER 705, [1982] 1 WLR 1297, CA, distinguishing *Liesbosch, Dredger (Owners) v SS Edison (Owners)* [1933] AC 449, HL.

17 *Perry v Sidney Phillips & Son* [1982] 3 All ER 705 at 709, [1982] 1 WLR 1297 at 1303, CA, per Lord Denning MR. Awards under this head have, however, been reduced on appeal: see *Watts v Morrow* [1991] 4 All ER 937, [1991] 1 WLR 1421, CA; *Ezekiel v McDade* [1995] 2 EGLR 107, CA.

18 *Weedon v Hindwood, Clarke & Esplin* [1975] 1 EGLR 82 (valuer negligently agreed too low a figure with the district valuer for the compulsory acquisition of his client's property); *Kenney v Hall, Pain & Foster* [1976] 2 EGLR 29 (valuer negligently over-estimated potential sale price of property; intending vendor relied on over-estimation when taking on other financial commitments; valuer liable for losses arising out of those commitments); *Montlake (as trustees of Wasps Football Club) v Lambert Smith Hampton Group Ltd* [2004] EWHC 938 (Comm), [2004] 3 EGLR 149 (valuation failed to take into consideration the fact that planning permission had been granted in respect of sports ground).

512. Measure of damages in claim by mortgage lender.

Where a valuer negligently values a property and a lender consequently agrees to advance money on the security of that property, the lender will not be able to recover damages greater than the amount by which the property has been overvalued because, in the absence of fraud, the valuer is responsible only for the foreseeable consequences of the valuation being wrong, and not for all the consequences of the loan having been made[1]. Where the lender would not have lent if he had known the property's actual value, and suffers losses because the value of the property falls after the mortgage has been taken out, he cannot recover for those losses if they exceed the amount of the overvaluation[2].

Generally, the basic measure of damages recoverable by the lender in a case where, had the valuation been accurate, he would not have lent at all will consist of the entire amount which has been lent[3], together with all costs reasonably incurred in repossessing and reselling the mortgaged property[4], less whatever is recovered on the resale and any repayments of capital or interest made by the borrower[5]. The basic measure of damages recoverable by the lender in a case where, had the valuation been accurate, he would have lent a smaller amount will consist of the difference between what has been lent and lost and the smaller amount which would have been lent and lost if the valuer had provided an accurate valuation of the property, less any repayments of capital or interest made by the borrower[6].

In addition to these capital sums, the lender is entitled to damages to compensate him for the interest which he could have earned on the money had it not been locked up in the mortgage loan[7], although such damages will not reflect the high contractual rate provided for in the actual mortgage unless the lender can show that, had he not lent to the borrower in question, the money would in fact have earned interest[8] at a comparable rate on another loan[8]. A lender is not, however, entitled to damages based on the cost of repairing the property[9].

1   *South Australia Asset Management Corpn v York Montague Ltd* [1997] AC 191, [1996] 3 All ER 365, HL. However, where a valuer is engaged not merely to provide information, but to advise a lender as to whether or not a loan should be made, the valuer's responsibility for negligent advice will extend to all the foreseeable loss which is a consequence of the loan being made, including that which results from a subsequent fall in the value of the property: *South Australia Asset Management Corpn v York Montague Ltd* at 214–215 and 372 per Lord Hoffmann. See also *Western Trust and Savings Ltd v Strutt & Parker* [1998] 3 EGLR 89, CA (see PARA 510 note 3).
2   *South Australia Asset Management Corpn v York Montague Ltd* [1997] AC 191, [1996] 3 All ER 365, HL, per Lord Hoffmann (overruling *Banque Bruxelles Lambert SA v Eagle Star Insurance Co Ltd* [1995] QB 375, [1995] 2 All ER 769, CA). '[A negligent valuer] is not liable for consequences which would have arisen even if the advice had been correct . . . because they are the consequences of risks the lender would have taken upon himself if the valuation advice had been sound. [Note: this case concerned a fall in the property market and that was not part of the liability of the valuer when establishing quantum of loss]. As such they are not within the scope of the duty owed to the lender by the valuer': *Nykredit Mortgage Bank plc v Edward Erdman Group Ltd (No 2)* [1998] 1 All ER 305 at 309, [1997] 1 WLR 1627 at 1631, HL, per Lord Nicholls of Birkenhead (applied in *Preferred Mortgages Ltd v Bradford and Bingley Estate Agencies Ltd* [2002] EWCA Civ 336, [2002] All ER (D) 122 (Mar)).
3   *Baxter v FW Gapp & Co Ltd* [1938] 4 All ER 457; affd [1939] 2 KB 271, [1939] 2 All ER 752, CA. Damages should not be assessed at the date of breach and should not reflect the difference between the amount of the loan and the value of the lender's rights under the mortgage: *South Australia Asset Management Corpn v York Montague Ltd* [1997] AC 191, [1996] 3 All ER 365, HL.
4   *Baxter v FW Gapp & Co Ltd* [1938] 4 All ER 457; affd [1939] 2 KB 271, [1939] 2 All ER 752, CA; *Swingcastle Ltd v Alastair Gibson* [1991] 2 AC 223, [1991] 2 All ER 353, HL.
5   *London and South of England Building Society v Stone* [1983] 3 All ER 105, [1983] 1 WLR 1242, CA. See also *Banque Bruxelles Lambert SA v Eagle Star Insurance Co Ltd* [1995] 2 All ER 769 at 818 per Phillips J (on appeal [1995] QB 375, [1995] 2 All ER 769, CA; and see *South Australia Asset Management Corpn v York Montague Ltd* [1997] AC 191, [1996] 3 All ER 365, HL). It has been held that the lender will not be required to give credit for sums which could have been, but which have not been, received (either from sale of the property or by taking action against the borrower on his personal covenant to pay) unless the lender is guilty of failing to take reasonable steps to mitigate his loss: *London and South of England Building Society v Stone* above (personal covenant not enforced in order to protect commercial reputation), overruling *Eagle Star Insurance Co Ltd v Gale and Power* (1955) 166 Estates Gazette 37; *Nyckeln Finance Co Ltd v Stumpbrook Continuation Ltd* [1994] 2 EGLR 143 (failure to accept an offer for the property). However, it is

not clear how far this principle is affected by the view expressed by Lord Nicholls of Birkenhead that the lender must bring into account the value of the borrower's covenant to repay: see *Nykredit Mortgage Bank plc v Edward Erdman Group Ltd (No 2)* [1998] 1 All ER 305 at 309, [1997] 1 WLR 1627 at 1631, HL.

6 *Corisand Investments Ltd v Druce & Co* [1978] 2 EGLR 86. In this situation the lender will not be entitled to recover the costs of repossessing and reselling the mortgaged property, since these would have been incurred in any event: *Corisand Investments Ltd v Druce & Co* at 101 per Gibson J.

7 *Swingcastle Ltd v Alastair Gibson* [1991] 2 AC 223, [1991] 2 All ER 353, HL (overruling on this point *Baxter v FW Gapp & Co Ltd* [1938] 4 All ER 457; affd [1939] 2 KB 271, [1939] 2 All ER 752, CA).

8 As to the appropriate rate of interest to be adopted in assessing damages see *Swingcastle Ltd v Alastair Gibson* [1991] 2 AC 223, [1991] 2 All ER 353, HL; *Corisand Investments Ltd v Druce & Co* [1978] 2 EGLR 86; *HIT Finance Ltd v Lewis & Tucker Ltd* [1993] 2 EGLR 231; *Banque Bruxelles Lambert SA v Eagle Star Insurance Co Ltd* [1995] QB 375, [1995] 2 All ER 769, CA (but see *South Australia Asset Management Corpn v York Montague Ltd* [1997] AC 191, [1996] 3 All ER 365, HL). The date on which the lender's cause of action arises, and from which interest on damages may be awarded under the Senior Courts Act 1981 s 35A(1) is the date on which the lender actually suffers the loss attributable to the valuer's breach of duty; this will vary according to the facts of the case: *Nykredit Mortgage Bank plc v Edward Erdman Group Ltd (No 2)* [1998] 1 All ER 305, [1997] 1 WLR 1627, HL.

9 *London and South of England Building Society v Stone* [1983] 3 All ER 105, [1983] 1 WLR 1242, CA.

513. Reduction of damages for contributory negligence.

Where a person who claims damages in respect of an inaccurate valuation is contributorily negligent, the damages recoverable may be reduced to such extent as the court thinks just and equitable[1]. A person may be contributorily negligent for this purpose where it is unreasonable for him to place reliance on the valuation in question[2]. In addition, a person who relies on a negligent valuation in deciding to enter into a transaction may be contributorily negligent if his decision to enter into that transaction is unreasonable on other grounds[3].

1 See the Law Reform (Contributory Negligence) Act 1945 s 1(1). The Law Reform (Contributory Negligence) Act 1945 applies to claims in tort for negligence, and also to claims for breach of a contractual duty of care (which is the same as a duty which would arise in tort irrespective of any contract): *Forsikringsaktieselskapet Vesta v Butcher* [1989] AC 852, [1988] 2 All ER 43, CA. However, it does not apply to a claim for breach of a contractual provision which does not depend on negligence by the defendant (*Barclays Bank plc v Fairclough Building Ltd* [1995] QB 214, [1995] 1 All ER 289, CA) or to an action in deceit arising out of a fraudulent valuation (*Alliance & Leicester Building Society v Edgestop Ltd* [1994] 2 All ER 38, [1993] 1 WLR 1462). See also *Nationwide Building Society v Thimbleby & Co* [1999] Lloyd's Rep PN 359; *Standard Chartered Bank v Pakistan National Shipping Corpn (No 4)* [2001] QB 167, sub nom *Standard Chartered Bank v Pakistan National Shipping Corpn (No 2)* [2000] 2 Lloyd's Rep 511, CA. As to contributory negligence see NEGLIGENCE vol 78 (2018) PARA 75 et seq. See also *Trebor Bassett Holdings Ltd v ADT Fire and Security plc* [2011] EWHC 1936 (TCC) at [540], [2011] BLR 661, [2011] All ER (D) 295 (Jul) per Coulson J, where the court held that whilst a defendant asserting a break in the chain of causation had to discharge the evidential burden of proving such a break on the balance of probabilities, the legal burden of proof would rest on the claimants to demonstrate that the defendant's breach of contract had caused their loss.

The percentage reduction for contributory negligence should be applied to the lender's basic loss before any reduction for the loss exceeding the extent of the overvaluation is made: *Platform Home Loans Ltd v Oyston Shipways Ltd* [2000] 2 AC 190, [1999] 1 All ER 833, HL.

2 *Banque Bruxelles Lambert SA v Eagle Star Insurance Co Ltd* [1995] 2 All ER 769 per Phillips J (on appeal [1995] QB 375, [1995] 2 All ER 769, CA; and see *South Australia Asset Management Corpn v York Montague Ltd* [1997] AC 191, [1996] 3 All ER 365, HL); *Nyckeln Finance Co Ltd v Stumpbrook Continuation Ltd* [1994] 2 EGLR 143 (the damages awarded against a negligent valuer were reduced on proof that the plaintiff mortgage lender was aware of a substantial discrepancy between the valuation on which reliance was placed and the price at which the subject property had just been sold on the open market); *Cavendish Funding Ltd v Henry Spencer & Sons Ltd* [1998] 1 EGLR 104, CA (lender who based lending decision on higher of two independent

valuations held contributorily negligent in failing to investigate discrepancy between the valuations). See also *PK Finans International (UK) Ltd v Andrew Downs & Co Ltd* [1992] 1 EGLR 172 (had the plaintiff lenders succeeded in establishing negligence against the defendant valuers, the court would have in any event held the plaintiffs responsible for 80% of their losses). As to the difficulty in establishing that a house purchaser has acted unreasonably in relying on a valuation or survey see *Yianni v Edwin Evans & Sons* [1982] QB 438, [1981] 3 All ER 592; *Davies v Parry* (1988) 20 HLR 452, [1988] 1 EGLR 147; *Allen v Ellis & Co* [1990] 1 EGLR 170 at 172 per Garland J.

3   Eg where a mortgage lender has substantial reason for doubting the honesty or financial stability of the proposed borrower (see *HIT Finance Ltd v Lewis & Tucker Ltd* [1993] 2 EGLR 231 at 235 obiter per Wright J; *United Bank of Kuwait plc v Prudential Property Services Ltd* [1995] EGCS 190, CA; *Kendall Wilson Securities Ltd v Barraclough* [1986] 1 NZLR 576, NZ CA); or where the amount lent represents an unreasonably high proportion of the estimated value of the property (*Platform Home Loans Ltd v Oyston Shipways Ltd* [1996] 2 EGLR 110; affd [2000] 2 AC 190, [1999] 1 All ER 833, HL).

(iv) Limitations on Liability

514. Exclusion or restriction of liability.

In principle, a valuer may: (1) exclude or restrict his liability for negligently causing financial loss to his client by means of an appropriate term in the contract under which he is engaged[1]; and (2) exclude or restrict his liability for negligently causing financial loss to a third party by means of an appropriate notice or disclaimer[2].

In consumer contracts excluding liability for negligence is barred under the Consumer Rights Act 2015[3] where a breach of any obligation to take reasonable care or exercise reasonable skill in the performance of a contract arises from an express or implied term of the contract, or where there is a common law duty to take reasonable care or exercise reasonable skill. It is immaterial whether a breach of duty or obligation was inadvertent or intentional, or whether liability for it arises directly or vicariously. So if the purpose of an obligation to provide a valuation is to enable the recipient to decide whether to proceed with a purchase of property, an exclusion of liability for negligent valuation is arguably non-binding as the specific purpose of the obligation is reliance on the findings and the recipient acting on it. In addition. there is a common law duty on a valuer, who owes a duty of care to the intending purchasers/mortgagors[4].

In non-consumer contracts, the exclusion or restriction of liability must be reasonable in the circumstances[5], since a disclaimer of liability by or on behalf of a valuer is a notice which purports to exclude liability for negligence within the meaning of the Unfair Contract Terms Act 1977[6]

Consumer contracts are subject to the provisions of the Consumer Rights Act 2015, which provide, inter alia, that an unfair term of a contract between a trader and a consumer is not binding on the consumer[7]. Where a term of a consumer contract, or a consumer notice, purports to exclude or restrict a trader's liability for negligence, a person is not taken to have voluntarily accepted any risk merely because the person agreed to or knew about the term or notice[8].

1   As to exclusion clauses generally see CONTRACT vol 22 (2012) PARA 388 et seq.
2   *Hedley Byrne & Co Ltd v Heller & Partners Ltd* [1964] AC 465, [1963] 2 All ER 575, HL; *Hadden v City of Glasgow District Council* 1986 SLT 557, Ct of Sess; *Bank of Scotland v Fuller Peiser* 2002 SLT 574, Ct of Sess. To be effective, such a notice must be brought to the attention of the third party before he acts in reliance on the valuation: *Martin v Bell-Ingram* 1986 SLT 575, Ct of Sess.
3   See the Consumer Rights Act 2015 s 65; and CONSUMER PROTECTION vol 21 (2016) PARA 397.

4   See *Freemont (Denbigh) Ltd v Knight Frank LLP* [2014] EWHC 3347 (Ch), [2014] All ER (D) 165
    (Oct) where the extent of the common law duty of care owed by a valuer is discussed (at [22] et
    seq per Stephen Smith QC) and refers to *Smith v Eric Bush, Harris v Wyre Forest District Council*
    [1990] 1 AC 831, [1989] 2 All ER 514, [1989] 2 WLR 790. The case summarises the common law
    duty of care owed by a valuer as follows (at [34] per Stephen Smith QC):
    (1)   that a duty of care in tort is likely to be owed to the person for whom the report was
          prepared (even though a contractual duty of care may also be owed to the same party);
    (2)   that the duty of care in tort is likely to be limited to the purposes for which the report
          was prepared;
    (3)   that a duty of care in tort may also be owed by a valuer valuing premises for mortgage
          purposes (at least if they are modestly valued residential premises), to the purchaser of
          those premises, if (a) the valuer knows that his report is likely to be shown to the
          purchaser, and (b) the purchaser intends to use the premises for his own residential
          purposes, not to let them, and (c) the valuer knows that his report is likely to be relied
          upon by the purchaser for the purpose of deciding whether to purchase the premises; but
    (4)   that a duty of care in tort is unlikely to be owed by a valuer instructed to produce a
          report for a lender for security purposes, to an investor who relies on the report for other
          purposes.
5   See the Unfair Contract Terms Act 1977 s 2; and CONTRACT vol 22 (2012) PARA 410. The Unfair
    Contract Terms Act 1977 s 2 no longer applies to a term in a consumer contract or a notice to the
    extent that it is a consumer notice: s 2(4). In the case of a contract term, it must be shown that the
    term was a fair and reasonable one to have been included, having regard to the circumstances
    which were, or ought reasonably to have been, known to or in the contemplation of the parties
    when the contract was made: s 11(1). In relation to a notice not having contractual effect, the
    requirement of reasonableness under the Unfair Contract Terms Act 1977 is that it should be fair
    and reasonable to allow reliance on it, having regard to all the circumstances obtaining when the
    liability arose or, but for the notice, would have arisen: s 11(3). In either case, it is for those
    claiming that a contract term or notice satisfies the requirement of reasonableness to show that it
    does: s 11(5).
6   See the Unfair Contract Terms Act 1977 s 2(2); and CONTRACT vol 22 (2012) PARA 410. Such a
    disclaimer is therefore ineffective by reason of s 2(2) unless it satisfies the test of reasonableness
    provided by s 11(3): see the text and note 5. See also *Stevenson v Nationwide Building Society*
    [1984] 2 EGLR 165 at 170 per Wilmers J, QC (the purchaser of a relatively substantial commercial
    property was an estate agent who was familiar with disclaimers; held that it was reasonable for the
    mortgage valuer to disclaim liability for negligence); *Omega Trust Co Ltd v Wright Son & Pepper*
    (1996) 75 P&CR 57, [1997] 1 EGLR 120, CA.
7   See the Consumer Rights Act 2015 s 62(3); and CONSUMER PROTECTION vol 21 (2016)
    PARA 391 et seq.
8   See the Consumer Rights Act 2015 s 65; and CONSUMER PROTECTION vol 21 (2016) PARA 397.

515.   Limitation periods applicable to claim against valuer.

A claim against a valuer for breach of contract may not be brought after the
expiration of six years from the date on which the cause of action accrued[1], that
is, the date on which the breach of contract occurred[2]. A claim against a valuer
which is founded on tort[3] may not be brought after the expiration of six years
from the date on which the cause of action accrued[4], that is, the date on which the
claimant suffered loss or damage[5].

A special time limit applies to any action for damages for negligence[6] where
certain facts are not known to the claimant, or any person in whom the cause of
action was previously vested[7], at the date on which the cause of action accrues[8].
In such circumstances the claim must be brought either within six years of the date
on which the cause of action accrued[9] or, if this period would expire later, within
three years of the date on which the claimant or any person in whom the cause of
action was vested before him first had both the necessary knowledge[10] and the
right to bring the claim[11]. However, such a claim may not be brought after the
expiration of 15 years from the occurrence of the act or omission which is alleged
to constitute negligence[12].

Subject to certain exceptions[13], where, in the case of any action for which a period of limitation is prescribed by the Limitation Act 1980[14], either (1) the claim is based upon the fraud of the defendant[15]; or (2) any fact relevant to the claimant's right of action has been deliberately concealed[16] from him by the defendant; or (3) the claim is for relief from the consequences of a mistake, the period of limitation will not begin to run until the claimant has discovered the fraud, concealment or mistake (as the case may be) or could with reasonable diligence have discovered it[17]. For these purposes, deliberate commission of a breach of duty in circumstances in which it is unlikely to be discovered for some time amounts to deliberate concealment of the facts involved in that breach of duty[18].

1   Limitation Act 1980 s 5. As to limitation periods see further LIMITATION PERIODS vol 68 (2016) PARA 952.
2   If the contract in question is made by deed, the limitation period is 12 years: see the Limitation Act 1980 s 8; and LIMITATION PERIODS vol 68 (2016) PARA 975.
3   As to the special time limit applicable to actions in tort for negligence where certain facts relevant to the cause of action are not known at the date of accrual see the text and notes 6–12.
4   Limitation Act 1980 s 2. As to when the limitation period will begin where fraud is concealed see *Sheldon v RHM Outhwaite (Underwriting Agencies) Ltd* [1996] AC 102, [1995] 2 All ER 558, HL (applied in *Ezekiel v Lehrer* [2002] EWCA Civ 16, [2002] Lloyd's Rep PN 260, [2002] All ER (D) 267 (Jan)); *Westlake v Bracknell District Council* (1987) 19 HLR 375, [1987] 1 EGLR 161 (valuer deliberately concealed the fact that his earlier inspection of a property had been negligently carried out); and the text and notes 13–18.
5   Identification of relevant loss or damage is a question of fact: *Kitney v Jones Lang Wootton* [1988] 1 EGLR 145; *Whitley (FG) & Sons Co Ltd v Thomas Bickerton* [1993] 1 EGLR 139. A purchaser or tenant who relies on a negligent valuation or survey generally suffers loss for this purpose on entering into a binding contract to acquire the property: *Secretary of State for the Environment v Essex, Goodman & Suggitt* [1986] 2 All ER 69, [1985] 2 EGLR 168; *Spencer-Ward v Humberts* [1995] 1 EGLR 123, CA; *Byrne v Hall Pain & Foster (a firm)* [1999] 2 All ER 400, [1999] 1 WLR 1849, CA. Where a mortgagee would not have lent money but for a negligent over-valuation of the mortgaged property, the mortgagee's loss is suffered at the moment when the amount outstanding on the mortgage (including accrued interest) first exceeds the value of the lender's rights: *First National Commercial Bank plc v Humberts* [1995] 2 All ER 673, [1995] 1 EGLR 142, CA; *Nykredit Mortgage Bank plc v Edward Erdman Group Ltd (No 2)* [1998] 1 All ER 305, [1997] 1 WLR 1627, HL (applied in *Tiuta International Ltd (in liquidation) v De Villiers Surveyors Ltd* [2017] UKSC 77, [2018] 2 All ER 203, [2017] 1 WLR 4627).
6   Ie an action in tort: *Iron Trades Mutual Insurance Co Ltd v JK Buckenham Ltd* [1990] 1 All ER 808, [1989] 2 Lloyd's Rep 85; *Société Commerciale de Réassurance v ERAS (International) Ltd, Re ERAS EIL appeals* [1992] 2 All ER 82n, [1992] 1 Lloyd's Rep 570, CA.
7   See the Limitation Act 1980 s 14A(5); and LIMITATION PERIODS vol 68 (2016) PARA 982.
8   See the Limitation Act 1980 s 14A; and LIMITATION PERIODS vol 68 (2016) PARA 982. As to the knowledge which is relevant for this purpose see s 14A(6)–(10); note 10; and LIMITATION PERIODS vol 68 (2016) PARA 982.
9   See the text and notes 4–5.
10   For these purposes, a person's knowledge includes knowledge which he might reasonably have been expected to acquire: (1) from facts observable or ascertainable by him; or (2) from facts ascertainable by him with the help of appropriate expert advice which it is reasonable for him to seek; but a person is not to be taken by virtue of the Limitation Act 1980 s 14A(10) to have knowledge of a fact ascertainable only with the help of expert advice so long as he has taken all reasonable steps to obtain (and, where appropriate, to act on) that advice: s 14A(10) (added by the Latent Damage Act 1986 s 1); see LIMITATION PERIODS vol 68 (2016) PARA 982. As to the degree of knowledge required to 'trigger' the three-year period see *Spencer-Ward v Humberts* [1995] 1 EGLR 123, CA. It is irrelevant that the claimants do not know the identity of the negligent valuer when a simple inquiry would have revealed it: *Heathcote v David Marks & Co* [1996] 1 EGLR 123. A negligent valuation or survey gives rise to a single cause of action, and the claimant's knowledge of one defect which has been negligently overlooked therefore causes the three-year period to run in respect of all defects, including those which are discovered subsequently: *Hamlin v Edwin Evans* [1996] 2 EGLR 106, CA. See also *Mortgage Corpn v Lambert & Co* [2000] Lloyd's Rep PN 624, [2000] BLR 265, CA.

11 See the Limitation Act 1980 s 14A(3)–(5); and LIMITATION PERIODS vol 68 (2016) PARA 982.

12 See the Limitation Act 1980 s 14B; and LIMITATION PERIODS vol 68 (2016) PARA 982.

13 Ie the Limitation Act 1980 s 32(3), (4A) (time limits in relation to defective products and fatal accidents): see LIMITATION PERIODS vol 68 (2016) PARAS 1220, 1222.

14 As to the limitation periods prescribed by the Limitation Act 1980 generally see LIMITATION PERIODS.

15 References in the Limitation Act 1980 s 32(1) to the defendant include references to the defendant's agent and to any person through whom the defendant claims and his agent: see s 32(1).

16 Deliberate concealment of facts relevant to a cause of action will postpone the running of time until the concealment is or should be discovered, regardless of whether it is concealed when the cause of action accrues or afterwards: *Sheldon v RHM Outhwaite (Underwriting Agencies) Ltd* [1996] AC 102, [1995] 2 All ER 558, HL. See also *Ezekiel v Lehrer* [2002] EWCA Civ 16, [2002] Lloyd's Rep PN 260, [2002] All ER (D) 267 (Jan)).

17 Limitation Act 1980 s 32(1) (amended by the Consumer Protection Act 1987 s 6, Sch 1 para 5).

18 Limitation Act 1980 s 32(2). See *Cave v Robinson Jarvis & Rolf (a firm)* [2002] UKHL 18, [2003] 1 AC 384, [2002] 2 All ER 641. Nothing in the Limitation Act 1980 s 32 enables any action: (1) to recover, or recover the value of, any property; or (2) to enforce any charge against, or set aside any transaction affecting, any property, to be brought against the purchaser of the property or any person claiming through him in any case where the property has been purchased for valuable consideration by an innocent third party since the fraud or concealment or (as the case may be) the transaction in which the mistake was made took place: s 32(3). A purchaser is an innocent third party for the purposes of s 32: (a) in the case of fraud or concealment of any fact relevant to the claimant's right of action, if he was not a party to the fraud or (as the case may be) to the concealment of that fact and did not at the time of the purchase know or have reason to believe that the fraud or concealment had taken place; and (b) in the case of mistake, if he did not at the time of the purchase know or have reason to believe that the mistake had been made: s 32(4).

(6) Employment of Quantity Surveyors

516. Relationship between quantity surveyor and employer.

The employer, or the architect as his agent, employs a quantity surveyor and is liable for his fees[1]. The quantity surveyor owes a duty of care to the employer to perform his work skilfully[2].

1 For the authority of the architect to employ a quantity surveyor see PARA 452. Where a quantity surveyor became, with the knowledge of his employer and during the time of his employment, the managing director of the contractors engaged on the same contract, by continuing his employment the employer was held to have waived the surveyor's breach of duty and to be liable for his fees: *Thornton Hall & Partners v Wembley Electrical Appliances Ltd* [1947] 2 All ER 630, 150 EG 344, CA.

In the 19th century the building contractor either employed and paid for the quantity surveyor or paid the quantity surveyor out of money certified to him and paid by the employer: see *Young v Smith* (1879) 2 Hudson's BC (4th Edn) 70 (affd (1880) 2 Hudson's BC (4th Edn) 75, CA); *Locke v Morter* (1885) 2 TLR 121; *North v Bassett* [1892] 1 QB 333. In the latter case the contractor did not enter into any contractual relationship with the quantity surveyor (*Young v Blake* (1887) 2 Hudson's BC (10th Edn) 163, 513; *Priestley v Stone* (1888) 4 TLR 730, CA. See also *Scrivener v Pask* (1866) LR 1 CP 715) and the quantity surveyor owed the contractor no duty of care (see *Stevenson v Watson* (1879) 4 CPD 148, and *Ludbrook v Barrett* (1877) 46 LJQB 798). These arrangements would nowadays be exceptional other than in certain types of project or construction management contracts.

2 *Moneypenny v Hartland* (1826) 2 C & P 378.

517. Liability of quantity surveyor.

The quantity surveyor is usually employed to prepare bills of quantities[1], to measure and value the works for the purposes of payment[2], and to perform other duties. His authority may be defined by the contract[3]. He must prepare the bills of quantities and make his measurements and valuations skilfully, though he will not be liable if he makes a few arithmetical errors in carrying out a large number of intricate calculations[4].

The quantity surveyor is not liable to the contractor for any representations contained in the bills of quantities, unless such representations are made fraudulently[5], but he may be liable in tort if he is negligent[6].

If the quantity surveyor fraudulently either for his own purposes, or in collusion with the employer, takes out the quantities short, he is liable to the contractor in the first case alone, and in the second jointly with the employer[7].

If one or more persons intending to tender for a contract employ a quantity surveyor to estimate the quantities, the quantity surveyor is liable to him or them, on ordinary principles, if he is negligent.

In the absence of a special relationship it is not thought that a quantity surveyor retained by a prospective employer owes a duty of care to point out to a tenderer mistakes in his tender[8].

If the contractor requires a quantity surveyor to measure variations he will be liable for his fees[9], but usually the architect will instruct the quantity surveyor to do this.

Quantity surveyors in more recent times have begun to take on responsibilities for contractual supervision and administration more traditionally performed by architects or engineers. They are obliged to perform these functions also with reasonable skill and care[10] and if acting as certifier with responsibility of having to decide whether the work or materials do or do not comply with the contractual standards, whether payment should be made, or what the value of the relevant work or materials may be, when acting in this capacity they must act fairly and impartially between the parties[11].

1   As to bills of quantities see PARA 214.
2   See eg *Sutcliffe v Chippendale and Edmondson (a firm)* (1971) 18 BLR 149 at 165 per Judge Stabb QC.
3   See eg *John Laing Construction Ltd v County and District Properties Ltd* (1982) 23 BLR 1.
4   *London School Board v Northcroft* (1889) 2 Hudson's BC (10th Edn) 174, 192.
5   *Priestley v Stone* (1888) 4 TLR 730, CA.
6   *Hedley Byrne & Co Ltd v Heller & Partners* [1964] AC 465, [1963] 2 All ER 575, HL; *Henderson v Merrett Syndicates* [1995] 2 AC 145, [1994] 3 All ER 506, HL; *South Nation River Conservation Authority v Auto Concrete Curb Ltd* (1993) 11 Const LJ 155, Can SC; *Edgeworth Construction Ltd v ND Lea & Associates Ltd* (1993) 66 BLR 56, Can SC; *J Jarvis & Sons Ltd v Castle Wharf Developments Ltd* [2001] EWCA Civ 19, [2001] NPC 15. See generally PARA 363; and NEGLIGENCE vol 78 (2018) PARAS 13, 22.
7   *Priestley v Stone* (1888) 4 TLR 730, CA. See also PARA 471.
8   See *Dutton v Louth Corpn* (1955) 116 Estates Gazette 128, CA.
9   *Beattie v Gilroy* (1882) 10 R 226, Ct of Sess; *Plimsaul v Lord Kilmorey* (1884) 1 TLR 48.
10   *George Fischer Holding Ltd v Multi Design Consultants Ltd* (1998) 61 ConLR 85.
11   As to the duties as a certifier see PARA 457.

518.   Remuneration of quantity surveyor and printing charges.

The amount which a quantity surveyor is entitled to claim, in the absence of any express contract fixing his remuneration, is a reasonable reward for the work and labour expended by him. The fact that a licence may not be obtainable to enable all the work to be carried out should not affect the surveyor's remuneration[1].

Quantity surveyors usually charge a percentage on the contract price, but there is no custom binding on the persons employing them to pay on such a basis [2] or will agree a fixed fee to perform the services.

If the quantity surveyor charges for printing his quantities, he may retain any cash discount[3] but not a trade discount.

1 *Debney v Enoch & Co (General Merchants) Ltd* (1953) 162 Estates Gazette 204. As to planning permission see PARAS 301–302.
2 *Gwyther v Gaze* (1875) 2 Hudson's BC (10th Edn) 196. See also PARAS 482–483.
3 *London School Board v Northcroft* (1889) 2 Hudson's BC (10th Edn) 174, 192.

INDEX

Building

References are to paragraph numbers; superior figures refer to notes

References are to paragraph numbers; superior figures refer to notes

References are to paragraph numbers; superior figures refer to notes

SUPERVISION OF BUILDING
  WORK—*continued*
 public bodies—*continued*
  plans certificates of 93

Building Contracts

References are to paragraph numbers; superior figures refer to notes

References are to paragraph numbers; superior figures refer to notes

CONSTRUCTION
  CONTRACT—*continued*
  adjudication under—*continued*
    disputes—*continued*
      right to refer 410
      human rights 420
      natural justice 420
      notice of intention to seek 412
      scheme, provisions of 411
      statutory adjudication 407
      Technology and Construction Court,
        role of 408
    adjudicator—
      appointment of 413
      decision of—
        enforcement 418
        enforcement proceedings 421
        generally 416
      fees and expenses of 422
      jurisdiction of 417
      mistakes by 419
      powers of 415
      resignation of 414
      revocation of appointment of 414
      selection of 413
    alternative dispute resolution 423
  construction operations: meaning 210
  Housing Grants, Construction and
    Regeneration Act 1996,
    application of 211
  insurance, provisions requiring 387
  parties to—
    architect. *See* ARCHITECT
    clerk of works 207
    engineer. *See* ENGINEER
    project manager 206
    quantity surveyor. *See* QUANTITY
      SURVEYOR
    resident engineer 207
    sub-contractor. *See*
      SUB-CONTRACTOR
    superintending officer 206
    supervising officer 206
    supplier. *See* SUPPLIER
    surveyor. *See* SURVEYOR
  payment—
    conditional payment provisions,
      prohibition of 357
    dates for 353
    failure to pay, suspension of
      performance for 356
    notices 354
    notified sum, requirement to
      pay 355

CONSTRUCTION
  CONTRACT—*continued*
  payment—*continued*
    statutory scheme for—
      operation of 351
      provisions under 358
      stage payments, entitlement
        to 352
    standard forms 202
CONTRACTOR
  duty of care to employees—
    general duty 367
    health and safety of workers 368
  insolvency of 321
CORPORATION
  contract executed by 229
CROWN
  contract, as bound by 230
DAMAGES
  breach or repudiation of contract,
    for—
    contractor's right to damages 370
    costs are unquantifiable, amount
      where 371
    employer's right to damages 369
    money, recovery of 373
DEFECTIVE PREMISES
  third parties, liability to 365
DEFECTIVE PRODUCTS
  civil liability for damage caused
    by 294
  criminal liability for 296
  defect: meaning 293
  nature and extent of product
    liability 295
  unsuitable new construction products,
    liability for 296
EMPLOYER
  duty of care to employees—
    general duty 367
    health and safety of workers 368
ENGINEER
  meaning 424
  agent, authority as—
    contract, variation of 453
    extent of 451
    extras, ordering of 454
    measuring variations 455
  appointment of 298
  care and skill, duties of—
    acceptance of tender, as to
      recommending 466
    certificates and measurements, as
      to 468

References are to paragraph numbers; superior figures refer to notes

References are to paragraph numbers; superior figures refer to notes

References are to paragraph numbers; superior figures refer to notes